CADOGAN

Dana Facaros & Michael Pauls

Italy

W9-BGO-355

Cadogan Guides
West End House, 11 Hills Place, London W1R 1AH

The Globe Pequot Press
6 Business Park Road, PO Box 833, Old Saybrook,
Connecticut 06475–0833

Copyright © Dana Facaros and Michael Pauls 1994, 1999
Illustrations © Horatio Monteverde 1994

Book and cover design by Animage
Cover photographs: front: Corbis/Dennis Marsico
                      back: The Travel Library/Philip Enticknap

Maps © Cadogan Guides, drawn by Map Creation Ltd

Editorial Director: Vicki Ingle
Series Editor: Linda McQueen

Editing: Catherine Charles
Updating: Ros Belford, Jon Eldan, Joseph Fullman, Nicky Swallow,
          Kicca Tommasi
Proofreading: Susannah Wight
Indexing: Judith Wardman
Production: Book Production Services

A catalogue record for this book is available from the British Library

ISBN 1-86011-900-X

Printed in Finland by Werner Söderström Corporation

All rights reserved. No part of this publication may
be reproduced, stored in a retrieval system, or
transmitted, in any form or by any means, electronic or mechanical, including photocopying and
recording, or by any information storage and
retrieval system except as may be expressly
permitted by the UK 1988 Copyright Design &
Patents Act and the USA 1976 Copyright Act or in
writing from the publisher. Requests for permission should be addressed to Cadogan Guides, West
End House, 11 Hills Place, London W1R 1AH.

The author and publishers have made
every effort to ensure the accuracy of
the information in the book at the
time of going to press. However, they
cannot accept any responsibility for
any loss, injury or inconvenience
resulting from the use of information
contained in this guide.

About the Authors

Dana Facaros and Michael Pauls are professional travel writers. To research this book, they spent three years based in a small Umbrian village, where they suffered massive overdoses of art, food and wine, and enjoyed every minute of it. And they reckon they could now whip 98 per cent of the world's non-Italian population in Italian Trivial Pursuit (except for the sport questions). Though now acclaimed as the authorities on Italy for travellers, Dana and Michael have pretty much covered it completely; they regret there isn't more of it. They now live in Ireland.

Acknowledgements

For the first edition, we would like to thank the Italian National Tourist Office, and all the local and municipal tourist boards who so kindly answered our questions that had answers and loaded us down with enough information to write several more volumes about Italy. Also, we would like to extend our warmest gratitude to Michael Davidson and Brian Walsh, whose unfailing good humour helped us through the darkest corners of Italy; to Mario, Fiorella, Alessandra and Sara who never minded having a couple of extra children in their happy home; to Anna and Tito Illuminati, who guided us through the intricacies of life in Rosciano and always let us use their phone; to Bruce Johnston, for his innumerable suggestions and his Deux Chevaux; to longtime residents Clare Pedrick, Anne and Santino, for their invaluable insights into the Italian miasma; to Carolyn Steiner and Chris Malumphy, who crossed the Atlantic to cheer us up; and especially to Rachel Fielding and Janey Dalrymple.

For this edition, a big thank you to the updaters—Ros, Jon, Joe (who in turn would like to thank Joanne Taborn, Grahame Foreman and Amy Goldberger), Nicky and Kicca—for their hard work; and to Linda and Nico who watched Lily and fed her lots of ice-cream; and especially *mille mille grazie* to Catherine, who took the hefty project of editing this monster on her slender shoulders, and made it come out right.

Extract from Petrarch and corresponding English translation on p.78 from *Some Love Songs of Petrarch*, translated and annotated and with a biographical introduction by William Dudley Foulke LL.D (OUP CAT 1920, OUP 1915), included by permission of Oxford University Press.

Please help us keep this guide up to date

We have done our best to ensure that the information in this guide is correct at the time of going to press. But places and facilities are constantly changing, and standards and prices in hotels and restaurants fluctuate. We would be delighted to receive any comments concerning existing entries or omissions. Significant contributions will be acknowledged in the next edition, and authors of the best letters will receive a copy of the Cadogan Guide of their choice.

Contents

Art and Architecture: A Bare Outline   61–6

Keeping Up Appearances   67–72

Italian Culture   73–8

Piemonte and Valle d'Aosta   79–128

Liguria   129–70

Maps

To Rachel Fielding, with love

the publisher who contributed more than tongue can tell to making this series distinctive.

Although our own relationship with Rachel started off on a rather shaky note, in a furious argument around her kitchen table over the proper use of commas, we soon learned to appreciate the true Rachel, her graciousness and kindness, her insights and wisdom and wacky sense of humour even when she was being bossy.

She was legendary for coming up with oddball nuggets of information, often just as the book was going to press: 'Did you put in that little bakery in Asturias? Did you put in that bit about the true identity of Manet's portrait of so and so?' The editors (not to mention the authors) often wanted to wring her pretty little neck.

We dedicate this book to her, with all the best wishes in the world for her future, although we can't help but envy the lucky bums who will have the pleasure of working with her from now on.

Introduction

Italy dangles from the centre of western Europe like a Christmas stocking, stuffed to the brim with marvels, some as soaring and grand as a Verdi opera or Brunelleschi's dome over Florence Cathedral, some as weird and unexpected as the pagan tombs buried underneath St Peter's in Rome, or Galileo's erect middle finger, carefully, significantly preserved in a reliquary in Florence's science museum. Even first-time visitors, with eyes and brains spinning, soon become uneasily aware that for every Italian cliché, every Mount Vesuvius, St Mark's Basilica and Leonardo's *Last Supper*, Italy has a hundred other natural wonders and artistic showpieces that any other nation would die for. Someone once tried to count up all the works of art, and concluded that there was at least one per inhabitant, no less. This national patrimony is echoed by even the most ephemeral arts, whether cranked out by the fashion and design workshops or simmered in the kitchen: for every Italian dish or wine you've been craving to try on its home turf, expect a hundred other delights you've never heard of before.

Even the common, everyday Italy that co-exists next to the overflow of museums, art cities, ruins and rivieras is an extravagant, daunting place to digest, and as the headlines over the past few years confirm (the Mafia trials, the Tangentopoli bribery scandals), it is a country that operates on rules entirely unlike those in force back home, full of contradictions and paradoxes, depths and shallows. As an Umbrian friend of ours told us, you cry twice in Italy: when you first arrive and when you have to leave. In the meantime, pack your intellect, gird your senses and watch out, not only for pickpockets but for a country that might just pick your heart.

NOTE: *This book covers only the Italian mainland—and it's long enough at that. We have tried to say a little bit about the islands close to the mainland, however, and which ferries will take you there. As part of our Italy series, we publish a separate guide to Sicily (see p.924).*

A Little Geography

This is not a complex subject; there are tall mountains, and there are not-so-tall mountains. From the Alps down through the Apennines, the Italians are often at a loss to find enough level ground to plant a football field. In all Italy, you'll find only three substantial flatlands: the broad valley of the Po, separating the Alps and Apennines, offering forgettable scenery but Italy's richest farmlands and a score of her most interesting cities; the coastal plain that includes the Maremma of southern Tuscany and Lazio; and the thoroughly flat *tavoliere* stretching across Puglia. Most of the really impressive mountains are in the Alps (Mont Blanc, the Matterhorn and the fantastical Dolomites) but the tallest completely within Italy is the Gran Sasso d'Italia (the 'Big Rock of Italy'), centre of a mighty patch of snow-clad peaks in the northwestern Abruzzo.

Not counting the islands, there are about 260,000 square km of Italy, roughly the size of the island of Britain (Americans can think of it as a New York, a Pennsylvania and most of a New Jersey). Even with some 55 million Italians, busily tending the world's 5th or 6th most opulent economy, the country rarely seems too crowded. Some large patches of urban sprawl exist— in the Po Valley, for example, or around the Bay of Naples—but the Italians enjoy each other's company, and generally live in tightly packed cities, hill towns and villages, with plenty of good green countryside in between. It is about 1,000 km, as the crow flies, from Mont Blanc to the furthest corner of Puglia, the 'heel' of the Italian boot (1,400 km if you're driving), and the long peninsula is in most places 150–250 km across.

There are very few easy routes over the Apennines between the Adriatic and the Tyrrhenian; now as in ancient times the main highways parallel the coast or converge on Rome from all points. The long coastline is unevenly blessed; at one extreme there is the delicious Amalfi Coast, the Riviera, the Gargano in Puglia and a few isolated lovely expanses (Calabria's Tyrrhenian Coast, Monte Cónero near Ancona, near Terracina and Gaeta in Lazio, the cliffs by Trieste). Most of the rest is surprisingly dull—much of Tuscany and Lazio, and the greater part of the Adriatic and Ionian coasts.

Some Features of the Landscape

In the north: the beautiful, jagged Dolomites, made of coral of eons past; the 'seven seas', a string of lagoons from Venice to Ravenna along the Adriatic; the caves and underground streams of the karst topography around Trieste and the Friuli; the Italian Lakes, formed by Alpine rivers that can't reach the sea, large enough to form Mediterranean micro-climates on the edge of the Alps; the Ligurian Alps, blocking off the Italian Riviera from the rest of the continent and giving it the mildest winter weather north of Calabria.

In the centre: the Apennines flanked by rolling hills in Tuscany, Umbria and the Marche; in Umbria and Lazio, a string of lakes, mostly of volcanic origin, of which the largest is Lake Trasimeno; the Gran Sasso and Monte Terminillo, the tallest of the Apennines.

In the south: the volcanic playground of coastal Campania, full of extinct volcanoes, dangerous volcanoes, baby volcanoes and bubbling pits; the exotic Gargano Peninsula in Puglia, which geologically has nothing to do with the rest of Italy; and the rough, mountainous toe of Calabria, enclosing a green Alpine plateau called the Sila. Southern Italy is hot and dry, and wanton deforestation in the late 19th century has turned many of its mountain regions into barren wastelands. It is a bit wetter on the coastal plains—enough for most of them to have been malarial wastelands until the Allied occupation forces bathed them in DDT at the end of the Second World War.

As for trees, some very striking ones decorate the landscape, including the beautiful parasol pine, tall erect Lombardy poplars and cypresses, all of which make Italy Italy. Old forests have large numbers of oaks, beeches and evergreens, and palms can be seen around the deep south and in Liguria. Koala bears would thrive in Calabria if anyone wanted to introduce them; a century ago the government planted millions of eucalyptus trees to dry out the wet ground where the malaria mosquitoes lived. However, Italian hunters blast anything that moves, and so wildlife is kept to a minimum. Even in country districts it's rare to hear many birds singing. Up in the mountains there are still plenty of boar, foxes and such. The famous Abruzzo bears still hang on in the Abruzzo National Park, and in the Alps mountain chamois and wolves are still occasionally seen. If you're out in the woods, especially in late spring and summer, watch out for vipers. The late spring is also the best time for wild flowers, of course; they are at their best in the Alps and the mountainous regions in the south.

A Guide to the Guide: Italian Regions, Italian Art

To the geographical features mentioned above, add a preposterous amount of history, tradition and language, and you have the political map of Italy, which only acquired its present divisions in the 1960s. There are now 21 amazingly diverse regions with various degrees of political autonomy, two of which are Sicily and Sardinia, while the rest are described in this book from north to south according to regional boundaries, except where from a visitor's viewpoint it made more sense to combine parts of one region with another. This is a brief Guide to the Guide, in the order they are presented in this book.

Northern Italy

This is the wealthiest third of the republic, the most industrial, expensive and dramatically scenic, the land of Alps and lakes. Beginning in the northwestern corner, you have **Piemonte** (Piedmont), the birthplace of modern Italy. At the 'mountains' feet', as the name implies, green Piemonte encompasses both excellent ski slopes in its western Alpine arc and table-flat rice paddies to the east. Car-manufacturing Turin is the region's capital, a rather unexpected and quirky Baroque city that some people love and others hate. Southern Piemonte, around Asti and Alba, produces Barolo, Asti Spumanti and vinous delights. The proximity of France scents the Piemontese kitchen; white truffles are the speciality in the autumn.

The northwest's most spectacular scenery, however, is contained in the small, autonomous, bilingual (French and Italian) region of the **Valle d'Aosta**. The Aosta valleys are one of Italy's great holiday playgrounds, with Courmayeur, Breuil-Cervinia and other stunning resorts on the south slopes of Mont Blanc (Monte Bianco) and the Matterhorn (Cervino), near legendary passes like the Great St Bernard, and in lovely Gran Paradiso National Park. Aosta, the handsome capital, is nicknamed the 'Rome of the Alps' for its extensive ruins.

Over the lush Maritime Alps lies Italy's smallest region, **Liguria**, a rugged rainbow of a coast better known as the Italian Riviera. In the centre lies Genoa, Italy's greatest seaport, while on either side shimmer famous resorts like San Remo, Alassio, Rapallo, Portofino, Portovenere and the magnificent Cinque Terre. The climate is especially mild; palms, olives, flowers and vines grow in profusion. The seafood and the dishes with *pesto* are reason enough to linger.

East of Piemonte lies the large and dynamic region of **Lombardy**. First is a section on Milan, adopted city of Leonardo da Vinci, feverish centre of fashion and finance, home of one of Europe's greatest cathedrals and opera houses, and a vision of the new Italy. This is followed by the three jewels of Lombardy's Po plain: medieval, scholarly Pavia, curley-cue violin-making Cremona, and Renaissance Mantua, product of the exquisite Gonzaga dukes.

Northern Lombardy, and a piece of eastern Piemonte and western Veneto, form the **Italian Lakes**, that fabled district beloved of poets since Roman times. From west to east you'll find charming little Lake Orta; Lake Maggiore with the Borromean Islands and the world-famous resort of Stresa; zig-zagging Lake Lugano, which Italy shares with Switzerland; and romantic Lake Como, forked in the middle with villas at Bellagio, Cernobbio, Tremezzo and Menaggio. North of Como extends the great Alpine valley, the Valtellina, splendid but scarcely known outside Italy. To the south of the Valtellina are more lakes—sweet Iseo and tiny Idro—and two fascinating art cities: Bergamo and Brescia. Westernmost is dramatic Lake Garda, the 'Riviera of the Dolomites', its shores dotted with lovely villages: Sirmione, Gardone, Limone and more, and Italy's biggest theme park, Gardaland.

The next three regions to the east, for centuries influenced or governed by the Most Serene Republic, are collectively known as **Venetia**. The main attraction of the **Veneto** is of course Venice itself, which only becomes more remarkable the more you learn about it; but there are other lovely cities as well—St Anthony's (and Giotto's) Padua; Palladio's Vicenza; and lovely Verona, of rose-coloured marble, the Scaligers, Valpolicella and Romeo and Juliet. Magnificent white villas dot the lush landscapes of the Euganean Hills and foothills of the Dolomites; to the south lie the haunting flatlands of the Po Delta.

Rising up in northern Venetia, the strange and fabulous peaks of the **Dolomites** are the most beautiful mountains in the world. The eastern half, still part of the Veneto, includes Cortina d'Ampezzo, site of the 1956 Winter Olympics, while the western mountains are in the confines of the large autonomous region of Trentino-Alto Adige. Trento, the capital of Trentino, is a fine old town associated with the 16th-century Counter-Reformation council; nearby are the rugged Brenta Dolomites, valleys of apple orchards, castles and vineyards. Bilingual Alto Adige, on the Austrian border, prefers to be known as Süd Tirol—an intriguing mix of strudel and pasta, fairytale castles and resorts, vineyards and spas. Bolzano is its capital, Merano its most celebrated watering hole. Much of the western portion of Alto Adige is occupied by Stelvio National Park, Italy's largest, where glaciers permit year-round skiing.

East lies the third region of Venetia, **Friuli-Venezia Giulia**, a rich ethnic mix wedged in the corner between Austria and Slovenia, with the neoclassical seaport of Trieste as its capital, a city now regaining some of its lustre of old with the opening of eastern Europe. The region has popular resorts on the coast like Grado and Lignano, intriguing towns like Ùdine and Cividale, more Alps in the north, and more wine than you can shake a stick at in between.

In between North and Central Italy, **Emilia-Romagna** nearly crosses the entire peninsula, occupying the Po plain and the northern Apennines. Home of Italy's finest cuisine, it also has delicious cities: the arty medieval university town of Bologna; elegant Parma, city of cheese and ham; Modena, of Ferrari, Lambrusco and balsamic vinegar; Busseto, the home of Verdi; Ferrara, fief of the great Renaissance patrons, the Este; Faenza, city of faence ware; and

Ravenna, with its unique and utterly luminous mosaics from the Dark Ages. Here, too, the string of Adriatic resorts begins—with Rimini, biggest and brashest of them all, yet secreting a Renaissance pearl in its heart. Just a short ride from Rimini, up in the mountains you'll find San Marino, the world's smallest and oldest republic, where tourists are more than welcome.

Central Italy

Here, for many, lies the archetypical Italy: those rolling hills, faded ochre farmhouses and villas, the cypresses, the olive groves, the hill towns, the pines of Rome. It was the birthplace of two momentous chapters in Western history—the Roman Empire and the Renaissance.

The first chapter begins where Emilia-Romagna left off, in one of the lesser-known corners of Central Italy, the **Marche** (Marches), although landscapes resemble those of Tuscany. Here are two exceptional cities: Urbino, built around Duke Federico's perfect Renaissance palace; and lovely, medieval Ascoli Piceno. In between are a score of pleasant, seldom-visited hill towns, a major pilgrimage target—Loreto—and a string of modest resorts, on either side of the salty old port city of Ancona.

South of the Marche are two even less familiar regions, **Abruzzo and Molise**. Abruzzo, containing the loftiest peaks in the Apennines, is Rome's winter and summer mountain playground; the National Park of the Abruzzi is the home of the Abruzzo bear and other fauna. The coast is fairly nondescript, lined with family resorts; inland there's a fascinating collection of unspoiled medieval villages and churches. With the highest villages in the Apennines, Molise is a small rather poor region tucked in south of Abruzzo, utterly obscure, quiet and artlessly unprepared for mass tourism.

Back on the western or Tyrrhenian Coast, **Tuscany** probably needs no introduction. There's more to it, however, than just the charmed trio of sublime art cities: Florence, Siena and Pisa. Lucca, Pistoia, Prato and Arezzo have also accumulated more than their share of notable art and architecture, and the rolling, civilized landscape will take you to beautiful hill towns in every direction: San Gimignano, with its medieval 'skyscrapers', brooding Etruscan Volterra, Cortona, Montepulciano and dozens more.

Landlocked, vaguely other-worldly **Umbria** is in many ways a more rustic version of Tuscany, spangled with historic hill towns like Perugia, the capital and cultural centre; Orvieto with its famous cathedral; Spoleto, synonymous with Italy's most important arts festival; medieval Gubbio; and Assisi, the city of St Francis, as well as a dozen others, set in lovely emerald valleys and hills.

Lazio, ancient *Latium*, includes Rome and a good deal more; despite being right at the centre of things Lazio's attractions are not well known. Northern Lazio was the homeland of the Etruscans, containing fascinating archaeological sites such as those at Tarquinia and Cerveteri. There's plenty to see in Viterbo and Anagni, two places that contributed much to the history of the Popes in the Middle Ages, extraordinary Renaissance villas and gardens (as at Caprarola, Tivoli and Bomarzo), major Roman ruins at Ostia Antica and Tivoli—not to mention Rome itself—and a pretty stretch of coast between Cape Circeo and Formia.

Southern Italy

The four regions of Italy's *Mezzogiorno* often seem an entirely different country from the green and tidy north. Not many visitors ever make it further south than **Campania**, where Naples and its famous bay make up the south's prime attraction—including Pompeii,

Vesuvius, Capri, Sorrento, the infernal volcanic Phlegraean Fields, dozens of Roman ruins and much more. The wonderful Amalfi Drive between Sorrento and Salerno covers the most spectacular bit of coastline in Italy, passing the truly unique towns of Positano, Amalfi and Ravello. Naples itself, famous for pizza and animated *Italianità*, is the best antidote out to the de-caffeinated control-freak Europe being forged in Brussels, as well as the south's great art capital. The rest of Campania includes venerable and interesting towns like Salerno, Caserta, Capua and Benevento; the well-preserved Greek temples at Paestum; and the pleasant, unspoiled Cilento Coast.

Lovers of fine Italian art and cuisine will not find them in **Calabria and the Basilicata**, once the most backward corners of the nation and now struggling gamely to catch up. The west coast from Maratea to Reggio di Calabria, the 'Calabrian Riviera', offers some clean beaches and beautiful scenery (especially around Maratea and Cape Vaticano), and the heavily forested mountain plateau west of Cosenza, the Sila, attracts hikers and nature-lovers. Of the once-mighty Greek cities of the Ionian Coast, there's little left but the great museum at Reggio and some scanty ruins at Metaponto. The bare, eroded hills of the inland Basilicata are not particularly inviting, unless you want to see the famous *sassi* (cave-dwellers' quarters) of Matera.

Puglia (Apulia) for many will be the real find in the south. The flat corn fields of the *tavoliere* cover most of the region, but the rugged limestone Gargano Peninsula offers scenery unique in Italy, along with growing but still enjoyable resorts like Vieste. Puglia did quite well in the Middle Ages, seen in the fine Romanesque cathedrals, including that of Bari, the south's prosperous second city and the burial place of Santa Claus. The *tavoliere* also grows robust wines; on it Emperor Frederick II built his mysterious Castel del Monte. Tàranto, founded by the ancient Greeks, has a museum full of Greek vases, great seafood and a wonderful maritime atmosphere. You won't see anything in Italy like the *trulli*, the whitewashed houses with conical stone roofs that turn the areas around Alberobello into a fairytale landscape; further south on Italy's 'heel', on the Salentine Peninsula, you can visit Baroque Lecce, the south's most beautiful city.

Travel

By Air

From the UK and Ireland

Flying is obviously the quickest and most painless way of getting to Italy from the UK. There are direct flights to over 20 destinations from over half a dozen British airports. Rome, Milan, Pisa and Venice have the greatest choice of year-round services, though there are plenty of regular flights to the business cities of Genoa and Bologna too; coastal or island resort destinations may be much more seasonal. Florence and Turin have more limited air links with Britain, but are well connected by rail to Pisa, Milan, etc. Scheduled services are, in the main, more expensive than charters although there are a couple of low-cost airlines whose scheduled flight prices can compete with the very lowest charter fares (*see* below).

major carriers

Alitalia: London, ✆ (020) 7602 7111; Dublin, ✆ (01) 844 6035.
British Airways: ✆ (0345) 222 111.
Air UK: ✆ (0345) 666 777.
Meridiana: ✆ (020) 7839 2222.
Sabena: ✆ (020) 8780 1444.
Lufthansa: ✆ (0345) 737 747.
Aer Lingus: Dublin, ✆ (01) 705 3333; or Belfast, (0645) 737 747.

Return fares vary greatly, depending on the season. The best-value deals are usually **Apex** or **SuperApex** fares, for which you must book seven days ahead, and stay a Saturday night in Italy—no alterations or refunds are possible without high penalties. Return scheduled fares range typically from around £200 off-season; midsummer fares will probably be well over £250. Full fares on the major carriers, especially to some of the more unfashionable destinations such as Turin, can be as high as £500. There are cheaper fares on offer (around £180), but these often have restrictions and involve flying via another European destination.

low-cost carriers

Go: ✆ (0845) 605 4321, a branch of British Airways, operates flights between London Stansted and Bologna (7 times a week), Venice (7 times a week), Rome (14 times a week) and Milan (21 times a week).
Ryanair: ✆ (0541) 569 569, offer flights from Stansted to Treviso, Pisa and Rimini.

charter flights

Many inexpensive charter flights are available to popular Italian destinations in summer, though you are unlikely to find the sort of rock-bottom bargains as, say, to Spain. You may find cheaper fares by combing the small ads in the travel pages, or from a specialist agent (use a reputable ABTA-registered one), which offer good student and youth rates too. The main problems with cheaper flights tend to be inconvenient or unreliable flight schedules, and booking restrictions. Take good travel insurance, however cheap your ticket is.

discount agencies and youth fares

Italy Sky Shuttle, 227 Shepherd's Bush Rd, London W6 7AS, ✆ (020) 8748 1333.
Italflights, 125 High Holborn, London WC1V 6QA, ✆ (020) 7405 6771.
Italy Sky Bus, 37 Harley Street, London W1N 1DB, ✆ (020) 7631 3444.

Trailfinders, 215 Kensington High Street, London W8, ✆ (020) 7937 5400.
Budget Travel, 134 Lower Baggot Street, Dublin 2, ✆ (01) 661 1866.
Untied Travel, Stillorgan Bowl, Stillorgan, Dublin, ✆ (01) 288 4346/7.

Besides saving 25 per cent on regular flights, young people under 26 have the choice of flying on special discount charters.

Campus Travel, 52 Grosvenor Gardens, SW1, ✆ (020) 7730 3402, with branches at most
    UK universities; *www.campustravel.co.uk*
STA, 74 and 86 Old Brompton Rd, London SW7, ✆ (020) 7937 9921, and other branches.
USIT, Aston Quay, Dublin 2, ✆ (01) 679 8833, and other branches in Ireland.

From Mainland Europe

Air travel between Italy and other parts of Europe can be expensive, especially for short hops. Some airlines (**Alitalia, Qantas, Air France**, etc.) offer excellent rates on the European stages of intercontinental flights, and Italy is an important touchdown for many long-haul services to the Middle or Far East. Amsterdam, Paris and Athens are good centres to find cheap flights.

From the USA and Canada

The main Italian air gateways for direct flights from North America are Rome and Milan, though, if you're doing a grand tour, check fares to other European destinations (Paris or Amsterdam, for example) which may well be cheaper.

Alitalia: (USA) ✆ (800) 223 5730; (Canada) ✆ (800) 563 5954.
British Airways: ✆ (800) 247 9297.
Delta: ✆ (800) 241 414.
Air Canada: ✆ (800) 555 1212.
KLM: ✆ (800) 361 5330, operate from Toronto and Montreal.

It may be worth catching a cheap flight to London (New York–London fares are always very competitive) and then flying on from there. Prices are rather more from Canada, so you may prefer to fly from the States.

charters, discounts and special deals

For discounted flights, try the small ads in newspaper travel pages (e.g. *New York Times*, *Chicago Tribune*, *Toronto Globe & Mail*). Numerous travel clubs and agencies also specialize in discount fares, but may require an annual membership fee.

discount agencies and youth fares

Airhitch, 2472 Broadway, Suite 200, New York, NY 10025, ✆ (212) 864 2000.
Council Travel, 205 E 42nd Street, New York, NY 10017, ✆ (800) 743 1823. Major
    specialists in student and charter flights; branches all over the USA.
Last Minute Travel Club, 132 Brookline Avenue, Boston, MA 02215, ✆ (800) 527 8646.
Now Voyager, 74 Varick St, Suite 307, New York, NY 10013, ✆ (212) 431 1616, for courier
    flights.
Board Courier Services, ✆ (514) 633 0740, for courier flights from Canada.
STA, 48 East 11th Street, New York, NY 10003, ✆ (212) 627 3111, or freephone ✆ (800)
    777 0112.

Travel Cuts 187 College Street, Toronto, Ontario M5T 1P7, ℗ (416) 979 2406. Canada's largest student travel specialists; branches in most provinces.

By Rail

From the UK and Europe

A train journey from London to Rome used to be something of a nightmare involving ferries and station changes and taking the best part of 24 hours. This experience can still be repeated, should you so desire it, and will cost you around £160 second-class return plus an extra £14 for a couchette. There is, however, following the opening of the Channel Tunnel and the construction of new fast rail networks throughout Europe, an alternative. Take a Eurostar to Paris and a high-speed Eurocity train to Italy and your journey could be reduced by as much as 12 hours. Unfortunately the price will increase to around £500. Train travel, at whatever speed, has its benefits—the opportunity it gives travellers to watch the changing scenery, to acclimatize themselves to new surroundings and take time to prepare for their arrival in a new country—but in an age of low-cost airlines, it is not much of an economy.

Rail Europe Travel Centre, (UK) 179 Piccadilly, London W1, ℗ (0990) 300 003; (USA) 226–230 Westchester Ave, White Plains, NY 10604, ℗ (914) 682 2999, or ℗ (800) 438 7245.

Eurostar, EPS House, Waterloo Station, London SE1, ℗ (0345) 881 881.

International Rail Centre, London Victoria Station, adjacent to Platform 2.

Eurotrain, 52 Grosvenor Gardens, London SW1, ℗ (020) 7730 8518.

Wasteels Travel, (UK) adjacent Platform 2, London Victoria Station, ℗ (020) 7834 7066; (USA) 5728 Major Boulevard, Suite 308, Orlando, FL 32819.

CIT, (UK) Marco Polo House, 3–5 Lansdowne Rd, Croydon, Surrey, ℗ (0891) 71551 (50p a minute), ℗ (020) 8681 1712; (USA) 15 West 44th Street, 10th Floor, New York, NY 10036, ℗ (800) 248 7245, ℗ (888) FAX CIT; (Canada) 1450 City Councillors St, Suite 750, Montreal H3A 2E6, ℗ (514) 845 4310.

The **Orient Express** deserves a special mention: it whirls you from London through Paris, Zurich, Innsbruck and Verona to Venice in a cocoon of traditional twenties and thirties glamour, with beautifully restored Pullman/wagon-lits. It's fiendishly expensive—and quite unforgettable for a once-in-a-lifetime treat. Current prices (including meals) are about £1095 per person (London–Venice one-way). Several operators offer packages including smart Venice hotels and return flights home. Contact **Venice-Simplon Orient Express**, Suite 200, Hudson's Place, Victoria Station, London SW1, ℗ (020) 7928 6000 for more information.

Interail (UK) or **Eurail** passes (USA/Canada) give unlimited travel for under-26s throughout Europe for one or two months. Various other cheap youth fares (BIJ tickets etc.) are also available; organize these before you leave home.

If you are just planning to see Italy, inclusive rail passes may not be worthwhile. Fares on FS (*Ferrovie dello Stato*), the Italian State Railway, are among the lowest (km for km) in Europe. A month's full Interail pass costs £249, though you can now buy cheaper zonal passes covering three or four countries only. If you intend travelling extensively by train, one of the special Italian tourist passes may be a better bet (*see* 'Getting Around').

A convenient pocket-sized **timetable** detailing all the main and secondary Italian railway lines is now available in the UK, costing £6 (plus 50p postage). Contact **Accommodation Line Ltd**, 11–12 Hanover Square, London W1; **Y Knot Travel**, Morley House, 1st Floor, 314–320 Regent Street, London W1; or **Italwings**, Travel & Accommodation, 87 Brewer Street, London W1. If you wait until you arrive in Italy, however, you can pick up the Italian timetable (in two volumes) at any station for about L4,500 each.

By Road

by bus and coach

Eurolines, London Victoria Coach Station, ✆ (0990) 808 080, are booked in the UK through National Express (return ticket London–Rome £130; single £90). Within Italy you can obtain more information on long-distance bus services from any CIT office (*see* above).

by car

Italy is the best part of 24 hours' driving time from the UK, even if you stick to fast toll roads. Calais–Florence via Nancy, Lucerne and Lugano is about 1042km. The most scenic and hassle-free route is via the Alps but, if you take a route through Switzerland, expect to pay for the privilege (around £14 or 30SFr for motorway use). In winter the passes may be closed and you will have to stick to those expensive tunnels (one-way tolls range from about L37,000 for a small car). You can avoid some of the driving by putting your car on the train. **Express Sleeper Cars** run to Milan from Paris or Boulogne (infrequently in winter). The **Italian Auto Club** (ACI), ✆ 06 44 77, offers reasonably priced breakdown assistance.

To bring a GB-registered car into Italy, you need a **vehicle registration document**, **full driving licence**, and **insurance papers** (these must be carried at all times when driving). Non-EU citizens should preferably have an **international driving licence** which has an Italian translation incorporated. Your vehicle should display a nationality plate indicating its country of registration. Before travelling, check everything is in perfect order. Minor infringements like worn tyres or burnt-out sidelights can cost you dear in any country. A **red triangular hazard sign** is obligatory; also recommended are a spare set of bulbs, a first-aid kit and a fire extinguisher. Spare parts for non-Italian cars can be difficult to find, especially Japanese models. Before crossing the border, fill her up; *benzina* is very expensive in Italy.

For more information on driving in Italy, contact the **AA**, ✆ (0990) 500 600, or **RAC**, ✆ (0800) 550 550 in the UK, and **AAA**, ✆ (407) 444 4000, in the USA.

Entry Formalities

Passports and Visas

EU nationals with a valid passport can enter and stay in Italy as long as they like. Citizens of the USA, Canada, Australia and New Zealand need only a valid passport to stay up to three months in Italy, unless they get a visa in advance from an Italian embassy or consulate.

UK, 38 Eaton Place, London SW1X, ✆ (020) 7235 9371; 32 Melville Street, Edinburgh EH3 7HA, ✆ (0131) 226 3631; 2111 Piccadilly, Manchester, ✆ (0161) 236 3024.

Ireland, 63–65 Northumberland Road, Dublin, ✆ (01) 660 1744; 7 Richmond Park, Stranmillis, Belfast BT9 5EF, ✆ (01232) 668 854.

USA, 690 Park Avenue, New York, NY, ✆ (212) 737 9100; 12400 Wilshire Blvd, Suite 300, Los Angeles, CA, ✆ (213) 820 0622.

Canada, 136 Beverley Street, Toronto, ✆ (416) 977 1566.

Australia, Level 45, The Gateway Building, Macquarie Place, Circular Quay, Sydney 2000, NSW, ✆ (02) 2478 442.

New Zealand, 34 Grant Rd, Thorndon, Wellington, ✆ (04) 7473 5339.

France, 47 rue de Varennes, 73343 Paris, ✆ 01 45 44 38 90.

Germany, Karl Finkelnburgstrasse 49–51, 5300 Bonn 2, ✆ (0228) 82 00 60.

Netherlands, Herengracht 609, 1017 CE Amsterdam, ✆ (3120) 624 0043.

By law you should register with the police within eight days of your arrival in Italy. In practice this is done automatically for most visitors when they check in at their first hotel.

Customs

EU nationals over the age of 17 can now import a limitless amount of goods for personal use. Non-EU nationals have to pass through the Italian Customs which are usually benign. How the frontier police manage to recruit such ugly, mean-looking characters to hold the sub-machine guns and dogs from such a good-looking population is a mystery, but they'll let you be if you don't look suspicious and haven't brought along more than 200 cigarettes or 100 cigars, or not more than a litre of hard drink or three bottles of wine, a couple of cameras, a movie camera, 10 rolls of film for each, a tape-recorder, radio, record-player, one canoe less than 5.5m, sports equipment for personal use, and one TV (though you'll have to pay for a licence for it at Customs). You can take the same items listed above home with you without hassle—except of course your British pet. USA citizens may return with $400 worth of merchandise—keep your receipts.

Pets must always be accompanied by a bilingual Certificate of Health from your local Veterinary Inspector.

Currency

There are no limits to how much money you bring into Italy: legally you may not export more than L20,000,000 in Italian banknotes, a sum unlikely to trouble many of us, though officials rarely check.

Special-interest Holidays

A selection of specialist companies are listed below. Not all of them are necessarily ABTA-bonded; we recommend you check before booking.

in the UK

Abercrombie & Kent, Sloane Square House, Holbein Place, London SW1W 8NS ✆ (020) 7730 9600; city breaks, country retreats and island-hopping cruises.

Alternative Travel, 69–71 Banbury Road, Oxford OX2 6PE, ✆ (01865) 310399; walking and cycling tours.

Arblaster & Clarke, 104 Church Road, Steep, Petersfield, Hants GU32 2PD, ✆ (01730) 893 344; wine tours, truffle hunts.

Blair Travel for the Arts, 117 Regent's Park Rd, London NW1 8UR, ✆ (020) 7483 4466; opera.

British Museum Tours, 46 Bloomsbury Street, London WC1B 3QQ, ✆ (020) 7323 8895; guest lecturers, art and architecture.

Brompton Travel, Brompton House, 64 Richmond Road, Kingston-upon-Thames, Surrey KT2 5EH, ✆ (020) 8549 3334; tailor-made and opera.

Citalia, Marco Polo House, 3–5 Lansdowne Road, Croydon CR9 1LL, ✆ (020) 8686 5533; opera.

Cox & Kings, 4th Floor, Garden House, 10 Green Court Place, London SW1P 1PH, ✆ (020) 7873 5002; short breaks, escorted tours, gastronomic tours.

Gordon Overland, 76 Croft Road, Carlisle, Cumbria CA3 9AG, ✆ (01228) 526 795; annual month-long painting holidays.

Italia 2000, 8 Timperley Way, Up Hatherley, Cheltenham, Gloucestershire GL51 5RH, ✆ (01242) 234 215; golf.

Italiatour, 205 Holland Park Avenue, London W11 4XB, ✆ (020) 7371 1114; 4–5 Dawson St, Dublin 2, ✆ (01) 671 7821; football tickets, equestrian, cooking classes, agriturism.

JMB, Rushwick, Worcester WR2 5SN, ✆ (01905) 425 628; opera.

Kirker, 3 New Concordia Wharf, Mill Street, London SE1 2BB, ✆ (020) 7231 3333; city breaks, tailor-made tours and trips to the Verona Opera.

Magic of Italy, 227 Shepherd's Bush Road, London W6 7AS, ✆ (020) 8748 7575.

Owners Abroad Travel, 2nd Floor, Astral Towers, Betts Way, Crawley, West Sussex, ✆ (01293) 554 455.

Martin Randall Travel, 10 Barley Mow Passage, Chiswick, London W4 4PH, ✆ (020) 8742 3355; cultural tours with expert guides: art and architecture, wines, gardens.

Ramblers, Box 43, Welwyn Garden City, Hertfordshire AL8 6PQ, ✆ (01707) 331 133; walking tours.

Special Tours, 81a Elizabeth St, London SW1W 9PG, ✆ (020) 7730 2297; escorted cultural tours: art, architecture, gardens.

Swan Hellenic, 77 New Oxford Street, London WC1, ✆ (020) 7800 2200; cruises.

Tasting Italy, 97 Bravington Road, London W9 3AA, ✆ (020) 7229 7020; cookery courses.

The Travel Club of Upminster, Station Road, Upminster, Essex RM14 2TT, ✆ (01708) 225 000; painting holidays, garden tours.

Travelsphere, Compass House, Rockingham Road, Market Harborough, Leicestershire LE16 7QD, ✆ (01858) 464 818; coach tours.

Venice Simplon-Orient Express, Suite 200, Hudson's Place, Victoria Station, London SW1V 1JL, ✆ (020) 7928 6000; luxury rail tours.

Wallace Arnold, Gelderd Road, Leeds LS12 6DH, ✆ (01132) 310 739; coach tours.

in the USA/Canada

American Express Vacations, 300 Pinnacle Way, Norcross, GA 30093, ✆ (800) 241 1700; prepacked or tailor-made tours.

Archaeological Tours Inc., Suite 904271, Adison Avenue, New York, NY 1116, ✆ (212) 986 3054; tours of Etruscan sites in Tuscany and Umbria.

Bike Riders, PO Box 130254, Boston, MA 02113, ✆ (617) 723 2354, 🖷 (617) 723 2355; cycling tours.

CIT Tours, 342 Madison Ave, Suite 3207, New York, NY 10173, ✆ (212) 697 2100; general and skiing.

Connaissance & Cie, 790 Madison Ave, New York, NY 10021, ✆ (212) 472 5772; wine.

Dailey-Thorp Travel, 330 West 58th Street, New York, NY 10019, ✆ (212) 307 1555; music/opera.

Esplanade Tours, 581 Boyston Street, Boston, MA 02116, ✆ (617) 266 7465; art and architecture.

Italiatour, 666 5th Avenue, New York, NY 10103, ✆ (212) 765 2183; fly-drive.

Maupintour, 1515 St Andrew's Drive, Lawrence, Kansas 66047, ✆ (913) 843 1211.

Olson Travelworld, 970 West 190th Street, Suite 425, Torrance, California 90502, ✆ (310) 354 2600.

Travel Concepts, 62 Commonwealth Ave, Suite 3, Boston, MA 02116, ✆ (617) 266 8450; wine/food.

Getting Around

Italy has an excellent network of airports, railways, highways and byways and you'll find getting around fairly easy—until one union or another takes it into its head to go on strike (to be fair they rarely do it during the high holiday season). There's plenty of talk about passing a law to regulate strikes, but it won't happen soon if ever. Instead, learn to recognize the word in Italian: *sciopero* (SHO-per-o), and do as the Romans do—quiver with resignation. There's always a day or two's notice, and strikes usually last only a day, just long enough to throw a spanner in the works if you have to catch a plane. Keep your ears open and watch for notices posted in the stations.

By Air

Air traffic within Italy is intense, with up to ten flights a day on popular routes. Domestic flights are handled by Alitalia, ATI (its internal arm) or Avianova. Air travel makes most sense when hopping between north and south. Shorter journeys are often just as quick (and usually much less expensive) by train or even bus, if you take travelling to the airport and check-in times into account.

Mainland cities with airports include Ancona, Bari, Bergamo, Bologna, Brindisi, Florence, Genoa, Lamezia Terme (near Catanzaro), Milan, Naples, Parma, Pisa, Reggio Calabria, Turin, Trieste, Venice and Verona, all of which have direct flights to and from Rome.

Domestic flight costs are comparable to those in other European countries, and a complex system of discounts is available. Each airport has a bus terminal in the city; ask about schedules as you purchase your ticket to avoid hefty taxi fares. Baggage allowances vary between airlines. Tickets can be bought at CIT offices and other large travel agencies.

FS national train information: © 1478 888 088 (*open 7am–9pm*); *www.fs-on-line.com*

Italy's national railway, the **FS** (*Ferrovie dello Stato*) is well run, inexpensive and often a plea-sure to ride. There are also several private rail lines that may not accept Interail or Eurail passes. On the FS, some of the trains are sleek and high-tech, but much of the rolling stock hasn't been changed for fifty years. Possible FS unpleasantnesses you may encounter, besides a strike, are delays, crowding (especially at weekends and in the summer), and crime on overnight trains, where someone rifles your bags while you sleep. Reserve a seat in advance (*fare una prenotazione*): the fee is small and can save you hours standing in some train corridor. On the more expensive trains, and for sleepers and couchettes on overnight trains, **reservations** are mandatory. Check when you purchase your ticket that the date is correct; tickets are only valid the day they're purchased unless you specify otherwise. At sleepy rural train stations without information boards, the imminent presence of a train is signalled by a platform bell.

It is easier to buy **tickets** at a travel agent in one of the city centres. Fares are strictly deter-mined by the kilometres travelled. The system is computerized and runs smoothly, at least until you try to get a reimbursement for an unused ticket (usually not worth the trouble). Be sure you ask which platform (*binario*) your train arrives at; the big permanent boards in the stations are not always correct. Always remember to stamp your ticket (*convalidare*) in the not-very-obvious yellow machines at the head of the platform before boarding the train. Failure to do so could result in a fine. If you get on a train without a ticket you can buy one from the conductor, with an added 20 per cent penalty. You can also pay a conductor to move up to first class or get a couchette, if there are places available.

There is a fairly straightforward **hierarchy of trains**. At the bottom of the pyramid is the humble, sometimes excruciatingly slow, *Locale* (euphemistically known sometimes as an *Accelerato*) which often stops even where there's no station in sight. When you're checking the schedules, beware of what may look like the first train to your destination—if it's a *Locale*, it will be the last to arrive. A *Diretto* stops far less, an *Expresso* just at the main towns. *Intercity* trains whoosh between the big cities and rarely deign to stop. *Eurocity* trains link Italian cities with major European centres. Both of these services require a supplement—some 30% more than a regular fare.

Above these are the *ETR 500 pendolino* trains, similar to the French TGV, which can travel at up to 186mph. Reservations are free, but must be made at least five hours before the trip, and on some trains there are only first-class coaches. The super-swish, super-fast (Florence–Rome in 1½ hours) *Eurostars* make very few stops, have both first and second class carriages, and carry a supplement which includes an obligatory seat reservation. Trains serving the most important routes have names such as the *Vesuvio* (Milan, Bologna, Florence, Rome, Naples), the *Adriatico* (Milan, Rimini, Pesaro, Ancona, Pescara, Foggia, Bari), or the *Colosseo/Ambrosiano* (Milan, Bologna, Florence, Rome).

The FS offers several **passes**. The 'Flexi Card' (marketed as a 'Freedom Pass' in the UK) allows unlimited travel for either four days within a month (L206,000), 8 days within a month (L287,000), 12 days within a month (L368,000) plus seat reservations and supplements on

Eurostars. The *Kilometrico* allows 3000kms of travel, made on a maximum of 20 journeys, and is valid for two months (2nd Class L206,000, 1st Class 338,000); one advantage is that it can be used by up to five people at the same time—however, supplements are payable on *Intercity* trains. Other discounts are available for day returns, families, senior citizens and the under-26s.

Refreshments on routes of any great distance are provided by bar cars or trolleys; you can usually get sandwiches and coffee from vendors along the tracks at intermediary stops. Station bars often have a good variety of take-away travellers' fare; consider at least investing in a plastic bottle of mineral water, since there's no drinking water on the trains.

Besides trains and bars, Italy's stations offer other **facilities**. Most have a *deposito*, where you can leave your bags for hours or days for a small fee. The larger ones have porters (who charge L1500–2000 per piece) and some even have luggage trolleys; major stations have an *albergo diurno* ('day hotel', where you can take a shower, get a shave and have a haircut, etc.), information offices, currency exchanges open at weekends (not at the most advantageous rates, however), hotel-finding and reservation services, kiosks with foreign papers, restaurants, etc. You can also arrange to have a rental car awaiting you at your destination—Avis, Hertz and Maggiore are the firms most widespread in Italy.

Beyond that, some words need to be said about riding the rails on the most serendipitous national line in Europe. The FS may have its strikes and delays, its petty crime and bureaucratic inconveniences, but when you catch it on its better side it will treat you to a dose of the real Italy before you even reach your destination. If there's a choice, try for one of the older cars, depressingly grey outside but fitted with comfortably upholstered seats, Art Deco lamps and old pictures of the towns and villages of the country. The washrooms are invariably clean and pleasant. Best of all, the FS is relatively reliable, and even if there has been some delay you'll have an amenable station full of clocks to wait in; some of the station bars have astonishingly good food (some do not), but at any of them you may accept a well-brewed cappuccino and look blasé until the train comes in. Try to avoid travel on Friday evenings, when the major lines out of the big cities are packed.

By Coach and Bus

Inter-city coach travel is sometimes quicker than train travel, but also a bit more expensive. The Italians aren't dumb; you will find regular coach connections only where there is no train to offer competition. Coaches almost always depart from the vicinity of the train station, and tickets usually need to be purchased before you get on. In many regions they are the only means of public transport and well used, with frequent schedules. If you can't get a ticket before the coach leaves, get on anyway and pretend you can't speak a word of Italian; the worst that can happen is that someone will make you pay for a ticket.

City buses are the traveller's friend. Most cities (at least in the north) label routes well; all charge flat fees for rides within the city limits and immediate suburbs (c. L1500). Bus tickets must always be purchased before you get on, either at a tobacconist's, a newspaper kiosk, in bars, or from ticket machines near the main stops. Once you get on, you must 'obliterate' your ticket in the machines in the front or back of the bus; controllers stage random checks to make sure you've punched your ticket. Fines for cheaters are about L50,000, and the odds are about 12 to 1 against a check, so many passengers take a chance. If you're good-hearted, you'll buy a ticket and help some overburdened municipal transit line meet its annual deficit.

The advantages of driving in Italy generally outweigh the disadvantages, but, before you bring your own car or hire one, consider the kind of holiday you're planning. For a tour of Italy's great art cities, you'd be better off not driving at all: parking is impossible, traffic impossible, deciphering one-way streets, signals and signs impossible. In Naples, don't even think about it. But for touring the countryside a car gives immeasurable freedom.

Third-party **insurance** is a minimum requirement in Italy (and you should be a lot more than minimally insured, as many of the locals have none whatever!). Obtain a Green Card from your insurer, which gives proof that you are fully covered. Also get hold of a **European Accident Statement** form, which may simplify things if you are unlucky enough to have an accident. Always insist on a full translation of any statement you are asked to sign. Breakdown assistance insurance is obviously a sensible investment.

Petrol (*benzina*, unleaded is *benzina senza piombo*, and diesel *gasolio*) is still very expensive in Italy (around L1800 per litre). Many petrol stations close for lunch in the afternoon, and few stay open late at night, though you may find a 'self-service' where you feed a machine nice smooth L10,000 notes. Motorway (*autostrada*) tolls are quite high (the journey from Milan to Rome on the A1 will cost you around L60,000). Rest stops and petrol stations along the motorways stay open 24 hours.

Italians are famously anarchic behind a wheel. The only way to beat the locals is to join them by adopting an assertive and constantly alert driving style. Bear in mind the maxim that he/she who hesitates is lost (especially at traffic lights, where the danger is less great of crashing into someone at the front than being rammed from behind). All drivers from boy racers to elderly nuns seem to tempt providence by overtaking at the most dangerous bends, and no matter how fast you are hammering along the *autostrada*, plenty will whizz past at apparently supersonic rates. North Americans used to leisurely speeds and gentler road manners may find the Italian interpretation of the highway code especially stressful. Speed limits (generally ignored) are officially 130kph on motorways, 110kph on main highways, 90kph on secondary roads, and 50kph in built-up areas. Speeding fines may be as much as L500,000, or L100,000 for jumping a red light (a popular Italian sport).

If you are undeterred, you may actually enjoy driving in Italy, at least away from the congested tourist centres. Signposting is generally good, and roads are well maintained. Some are feats of engineering that the Romans themselves would have admired—bravura projects suspended on cliffs, crossing valleys on vast stilts and winding up hairpins.

Buy a good road map (the Italian Touring Club series is excellent). The **Automobile Club of Italy** (ACI) is a good friend to the foreign motorist. Besides having bushels of useful information and tips, they can be reached from anywhere by dialling ✆ **116**—also use this number to find the nearest service station. If you need major repairs, the ACI can make sure the prices charged are according to their guidelines.

Hiring a Car

Hiring a car (*autonoleggio*) is simple but not particularly cheap. Remember to take into account that some hire companies require a deposit amounting to the estimated cost of the hire. The minimum age limit is usually 25 (sometimes 23) and the driver must have held their licence for over a year. Most major rental companies have offices in airports or main stations, though it may be worthwhile checking prices of local firms. If you need a car for longer than three weeks, leasing may be a more economic alternative. The National Tourist Office has a list of firms in Italy that hire caravans (trailers) or camper vans. Non-residents are not allowed to buy cars in Italy.

It is probably easiest to arrange your car hire with a domestic firm before you depart and, in particular, to check-out fly-drive discounts.

Avis, (UK) ✆ (020) 8848 8733; (USA) ✆ (800) 331 1084.

Hertz, (UK) ✆ (0990) 996 699; (Ireland), ✆ (01) 660 2255; (USA), ✆ (800) 654 3001; (Canada) ✆ (800) 263 0600.

Eurodollar, ✆ (01895) 233 300.

Car Rental Direct, (UK) ✆ (020) 7625 7766.

hitch-hiking

It is illegal to hitch on the *autostrade*, though you may pick up a lift near one of the toll booths. Don't hitch from the city centres, head for suburban exit routes. For the best chances of getting a lift, travel light, look respectable and take your shades off. Hold a sign indicating your destination if you can. Risks for women are lower in northern Italy than in the more macho south, but it is not advisable to hitch alone. Two or more men may encounter some reluctance. On major roads, heading out of town, you may sometimes see some scantily clad women, usually of African origin, standing or sitting on stools on the edges of corn fields trying to attract your attention. These are not hitch-hikers, although you may still pick them up.

By Motorcycle or Bicycle

Mopeds, vespas and scooters are the vehicles of choice for a great many Italians. You will see them everywhere. In the traffic-congested towns this is a ubiquity born of necessity; when driving space is limited, two wheels are always better than one. Despite the obvious dangers, there are clear benefits to moped-riding in Italy. For one thing it is cheaper than car hire and can prove an excellent way of covering a town's sites in a limited space of time. Furthermore, because Italy is such a scooter-friendly place, car drivers are more conditioned to their presence and so are less likely to hurtle in to them when taking corners. Nonetheless, you should only consider hiring a moped if you have ridden one before (Italy's hills and alarming traffic are no place to learn) and, despite local examples, you should always wear a helmet. Also, be warned that some travel insurance policies exclude claims resulting from scooter or motorbike accidents.

You can hire a bicycle in most Italian towns. Alternatively, if you bring your own bike, check the airlines' policy on transporting them. Bikes can be transported by train in Italy, either with you or within a couple of days—apply at the baggage office (*ufficio bagagli*).

Practical A–Z

Children

Children are the royalty of Italy, pampered, often obscenely spoiled, probably more fashionably dressed than you are, and never allowed to get dirty. Surprisingly, most of them somehow manage to be well-mannered little charmers. If you're bringing your own *bambini* to Italy, they'll receive a warm welcome everywhere.

Many hotels offer advantageous rates for children and most of the larger cities have permanent **Luna Parks**, or funfairs. Rome's version in the EUR is huge and charmingly old-fashioned (a great trade-off for a day in the Vatican Museums).

Apart from endless quantities of pizza, spaghetti and ice cream, children love the **Bomarzo Monster Park** in northern Lazio (a collection of huge, weird 16th-century follies); the Disneyesque amusement parks of **Edenlandia** near Naples and **Gardaland** on Lake Garda; **Minitalia** between Bergamo and Milan (a relief model of Italy studded with replica monuments); **Pinocchio Park** in Collodi, near Pisa; the fairy-tale playground of **Città della Domenica** in Perugia; and the whole city of **Venice**.

If a **circus** visits town, you're in for a treat: it will either be a sparkling showcase of daredevil skill or a poignant, family-run version of Fellini's *La Strada*. Try to catch one or two of Italy's more vivacious **festivals** or **carnivals**—famous ones are in Venice and Viareggio.

Climate and When to Go

'*O Sole Mio*' notwithstanding, all of Italy isn't always sunny; it rains just as much in Rome every year as in London, and Turin's climate in the winter is said to be about the same as that of Copenhagen. **Summer** comes on dry and hot in the south and humid and hot in much of the northern lowlands and inland hills; the Alps and high Apennines stay fairly cool, while the coasts are often refreshed by breezes, except for Venice, which tends to swelter.

You can probably get by without an umbrella, but take a light jacket for cool evenings. For average touring, August is probably the worst month to stump through Italy. Transport facilities are jammed to capacity, prices are at their highest, and Rome, Milan, Florence, Venice and the other large cities are abandoned to hordes of tourists while the locals take to the beach. In Milan especially so many restaurants close down that you could starve, and the few staff left behind to man the galleys are sullen captives.

Spring and **autumn** are perhaps the loveliest times to go; spring for the infinity of wildflowers in Italy's countryside, autumn for the colour of the trees in the hills and the vineyards. The weather is mild, places aren't crowded, and you won't need your umbrella too much, at least until November.

From December to March the happiest visitors are probably those on skis in the Alps or Apennines or opera buffs in La Scala, San Carlo or La Fenice, but it's the best time to go if you want the art and museums to yourself. Beware though, it can rain and rain, and mountain valleys can lie for days under banks of fog and mist. The Italian Riviera enjoys the mildest **winter** climate on the peninsula.

Average Temperatures in °C (°F)

	January	April	July	October
Bari	8.4 (46)	13.9 (57)	24.5 (76)	18.2 (64)
Florence	5.6 (42)	13.3 (55)	25.0 (77)	15.8 (60)
Genoa	8.4 (46)	14.5 (58)	24.6 (76)	18.1 (64)
Milan	1.9 (35)	13.2 (55)	24.8 (77)	13.7 (56)
Cortina	2.3 (28)	5.2 (41)	15.8 (60)	7.6 (44)
Naples	8.7 (47)	14.3 (58)	24.8 (77)	14.5 (58)
Rome	7.4 (44)	14.4 (58)	25.7 (79)	17.7 (63)
Venice	3.8 (38)	12.6 (54)	23.6 (74)	15.1 (59)
Lake Garda	4.0 (39)	13.2 (55)	24.5 (76)	14.7 (58)

Average Monthly Rainfall in Millimetres (inches)

	January	April	July	October
Bari	39 (2)	35 (1)	19 (1)	111 (4)
Florence	61 (3)	74 (3)	23 (1)	96 (4)
Genoa	109 (4)	82 (3)	35 (2)	135 (5)
Milan	62 (3)	82 (3)	47 (2)	75 (3)
Cortina	51 (2)	138 (5)	148 (6)	119 (4)
Naples	87 (3)	55 (2)	14 (1)	102 (4)
Rome	74 (3)	62 (3)	06 (3)	123 (5)
Venice	58 (2)	77 (3)	37 (1)	66 (3)
Lake Garda	31 (1)	62 (3)	72 (3)	89 (3)

The Rome rainfall in July is the official average. *That* you can believe if you like.

Crime

There is a fair amount of petty crime in Italy—purse-snatchings, pickpocketing, minor thievery of the white collar kind (always check your change) and car break-ins and theft—but violent crime is rare. Nearly all mishaps can be avoided with adequate precautions. Scooter-borne purse-snatchers can be foiled if you stay on the inside of the pavement and keep a firm hold on your property (sling your bag-strap across your body, not dangling from one shoulder); pickpockets strike in crowded buses or trams and gatherings; don't carry too much cash, and split it so you won't lose the lot at once. In cities and popular tourist sites, beware groups of scruffy-looking women or children with placards, apparently begging for money. They use distraction techniques to perfection. The smallest and most innocent-looking child is generally the most skilful pickpocket.

If you are targeted, the best technique is to grab sharply hold of any vulnerable possessions or pockets and shout furiously. (Italian passers-by or plain-clothes police will often come to your assistance if they realize what is happening.) Be extra careful in train stations, don't leave valuables in hotel rooms, and always park your car in garages, guarded lots or on well-lit streets, with portable temptations well out of sight. Purchasing small quantities of soft drugs for personal consumption is technically legal in Italy, though what constitutes a small quantity is unspecified, and if the police don't like you to begin with, it will probably be enough to get you into big trouble.

Political terrorism, once the scourge of Italy, has declined greatly in recent years, mainly thanks to special quasi-military squads of black-uniformed national police, the *Carabinieri*. Local matters are usually in the hands of the *Polizia Urbana*; the nattily dressed *Vigili Urbani* concern themselves with directing traffic, and handing out parking fines. If you need to summon any of them, dial ✆ **113**.

Disabled Travellers

Italy has been relatively slow off the mark in its provision for disabled visitors. Cobblestones, uneven or non-existent pavements, the appalling traffic conditions, crowded public transport and endless flights of steps in many public places are all disincentives. Progress is gradually being made, however. A national support organization in your own country may well have specific information on facilities in Italy, or will at least be able to provide general advice.

The Italian tourist office, or CIT (travel agency) can also advise on hotels, museums with ramps and so on. If you book rail travel through CIT, you can request assistance. Once in Italy, you can ring the disabled cooperative, ✆ 167 179 179, for advice on accommodation and travel.

Royal Association for Disability & Rehabilitation (RADAR), 25 Mortimer St, London W1N 8AB, ✆ (020) 7637 5400, sell a guide, *Holidays & Travel Abroad: A Guide for Disabled People* (£3.50).

Society for the Advancement of Travel for the Handicapped (SATH), 347 Fifth Avenue, Suite 610, New York, NY 10016, ✆ (212) 447 7284.

Mobility International, 228 Borough High Street, London SE1, ✆ (020) 7403 5688; or PO Box 3551, Eugene, OR 97403, USA, ✆ (503) 343 1284.

Australian Council for the Rehabilitation of the Disabled (ACROD), 55 Charles Street, Ryde, New South Wales, ✆ (02) 9809 4488.

Embassies and Consulates

Bari, (UK) Via Dalmazia 127, ✆ 080 554 3668.

Florence, (UK) Lungarno Corsini 2, ✆ 055 284 133; (USA) Lungarno Vespucci 38, ✆ 055 239 8276.

Milan, (Australia) Via Borgagna 2, ✆ 02 7601 1330; (Canada) Via Vittorio Pisani 19, ✆ 02 669 7451; (UK) Via San Paulo 7, ✆ 02 723 001; (USA) Largo Donegani 1, ✆ 02 2900 1841.

Naples, (UK) Via Crispi 122, ✆ 081 663 511; (USA) Piazza Repubblica 2, ✆ 081 583 8111.

Rome, (Australia) Via Alessandria 215, ✆ 06 852 721; (Canada) Via Zara 30, ✆ 06 440 3028; (Ireland) Largo Nazareno 3, ✆ 06 678 2541; (New Zealand) Via Zara 28, ✆ 06 440 2928; (UK) Via XX Settembre 80/a, ✆ 06 482 5441; (USA) Via V. Veneto 119/a, ✆ 06 46741.

Festivals

Every 50 years the Catholic Church celebrates a Holy Year (*Giubileo*) and thousands of pilgrims descend on Italy's holiest sights. The next Holy Year coincides with the Year 2000, and Italy is gearing itself up for the hordes of pilgrims who will arrive throughout the year to join in the special events and festivities organized in every corner of the country.

There are literally thousands of other festivals answering to every description in Italy. Every *comune* has at least one or two honouring patron saints, at which the presiding Madonna is paraded through the streets decked in fairy lights and gaudy flowers. Shrovetide and Holy Week are great focuses of activity. *Carnival*, after being suppressed and ignored for decades, has been revived in many places, displaying the gorgeous music and pageantry of the *Commedia dell'Arte* with Harlequin and his motley crew. In Venice, the handmade carnival masks now constitute a new art form and make popular souvenirs.

Holy Week celebrations take on a dirgelike Spanish flavour in the south, when robed and hooded penitents haul melodramatic floats through the streets. Meanwhile in Rome the Supreme Pontiff himself officiates at the Easter ceremonies. Other festivals are more earthily pagan, celebrating the land and the harvest in giant phallic towers. Some are purely secular affairs sponsored by political parties (especially the Communists and Socialists), where everyone goes to meet friends.

There are great costume pageants dating back to the Middle Ages or Renaissance like the Sienese *Palio* (a bareback horserace), an endless round of carnivals, music festivals, opera seasons and antique fairs. Relaxed village *festas* can be just as enjoyable as (or more so than) the big national crowd-pullers. Outsiders are nearly always welcome. Whatever the occasion, eating is a primary pastime at all Italian jamborees, and all kinds of regional specialities are prepared. Check at the local tourist office for precise dates, which alter from year to year, and often slide into the nearest weekend.

Jan–July	Opera and ballet at La Scala, **Milan.**
Jan 5–6	Child-oriented Epiphany celebrations throughout Italy, honoured the good stocking filling witch La Befana; Three Kings Procession, **Milan.**
Late Jan	Festival of Italian Popular Song, **San Remo.**
30–31 Jan	Sant'Orso handicrafts fair, **Aosta.**
Feb–March	Shrovetide Carnivals all over Italy, especially in **Venice** (boat procession); **Viareggio**; Sa Sartiglia (medieval tournament masquerade).

March	Fashion collections, **Milan**.
	Sant'Ambrogio carnival, **Milan**.
March–April	Holy Week and Easter celebrations: processions **Tàranto**, **Bari**, **Brindisi**; Scoppio del Carro (Explosion of the Cart), **Florence**; Good Friday procession led by the Pope, **Rome**; concerts at San Maurizio church in Monastero Maggiore, **Milan**.
End April	Ortafiori flower festival, **Orta San Giulio**.
May	Feast of San Nicola, **Bari**.
	Festival of Snakes, **Cocullo** (Abruzzo).
	Palio del Carroccio, **Legnano** (Milan), celebrating defeat of Barbarossa by the Lombard League in 1176 (medieval parade and horse-race).
	Feast of San Gennaro (first of three such occasions when the faithful assemble in **Naples** cathedral to await the miraculous liquefaction of a phial of the saint's blood).
	Corsa dei Ceri (Race of the Candles), **Gubbio** (Umbria)—(huge wooden shrines are raced uphill to the basilica).
	Palio della Balestra (Crossbow Palio), **Gubbio**—medieval contest with antique weapons.
	Vogolonga, **Venice** (the 'long row' from San Marco to Burano).
May–June	Maggio Musicale Fiorentino, **Florence**.
June	Historical Regatta of the Four Ancient Maritime Republics (boat race between the rival sea-towns of **Pisa**, **Venice**, **Amalfi** and **Genoa**—location alternates).
	Gioco del Ponte (Game of the Bridge), **Pisa** (mock battle).
June 21	Infiorata, **Genzano** (Rome) and **Spello** (Umbria) (Corpus Domini celebrations with flower decorations).
	Feast of St Antonio, **Padua**.
	Gioco del Calcio, **Florence** (football in medieval costume).
	Festa dei Gigli, **Nola** (Naples) ('lily' procession—the lillies in this instance are large wooden towers).
mid-June–July	Festival of Two Worlds, **Spoleto** (Umbria) (Italy's biggest arts festival).
July	Joust of the Bear, **Pistoia**.
	Feast of the Redeemer, **Venice** (fireworks and gondola procession).
	Umbria Jazz Festival in **Perugia**.
	Archery contest, **Fivizzano** (Massa).
July and August	Palio, **Siena**—bareback horserace (held twice).
	Summer Operetta Festival, **Trieste**.
	Verona Outdoor Opera Season.

August	Joust of the Quintana, **Ascoli Piceno** (Marche).
	Bravo delle Botti, **Montepulciano** (barrel race).
	International Film Festival, **Venice**.
	Regatta, **Ventimiglia**.
	Wheat Festival, **Foglianise** (Benevento) (decorated tractors).
Aug–Sept	Settimane Musicali, **Stresa** (musical weeks).
September	Joust of the Saracen, **Arezzo** (knights in armour).
	Historic Regatta, **Venice**.
	Living Chess Game, **Maròstica** (Veneto) (even years).
	Feast of San Gennaro, **Naples**.
	Luminaria di Santa Croce, **Lucca** (torchlit procession).
	Italian Grand Prix, **Monza**.
	Neapolitan song contest, **Piedigrotta**.
October	Truffle Fair, **Alba**.
	Feast of St Francis, **Assisi**.
November	Festa della Salute, **Venice**.
December	Opera season opens throughout Italy.
	Advent and Christmas celebrations.
	Christmas Fair of the presepi, **Naples**.
	Sausage and polenta festival, **Benevento**.

Food and Drink

There are those who eat to live and those who live to eat, and then there are the Italians, for whom food has an almost religious significance, unfathomably linked with love, La Mamma, and tradition. In this singular country, where millions of otherwise sane people spend much of their waking hours worrying about their digestion, standards both at home and in the restaurants are understandably high. Few Italians are gluttons, but all are experts on what is what in the kitchen; to serve a meal that is not properly prepared and more than a little complex is tantamount to an insult.

For the visitor this national culinary obsession comes as an extra bonus to the senses—along with Italy's remarkable sights, music, and the warm sun on your back, you can enjoy some of the best tastes and smells the world can offer, prepared daily in Italy's kitchens and fermented in its countless wine cellars. Eating all'Italiana is not only delicious and wholesome, but now undeniably trendy. Foreigners flock here to learn the secrets of Italian cuisine and the even more elusive secret of how the Italians can live surrounded by such delights and still fit into their sleek Armani trousers.

Breakfast (*colazione*) in Italy is no lingering affair, but an early morning wake-up shot to the brain: a *cappuccino* (espresso with hot foamy milk, often sprinkled with chocolate—incidentally first thing in the morning is the only time of day at which any self-respecting Italian will touch the stuff), a *caffè latte* (white coffee) or a *caffè lungo* (a generous portion of espresso), accompanied by a croissant-type roll, called a *cornetto* or *briosce*, or a fancy pastry. This repast can be consumed in any bar and repeated during the morning as often as necessary. Breakfast in most Italian hotels seldom represents great value.

Lunch (*pranzo*), generally served around 1pm, is the most important meal of the day for the Italians, with a minimum of a first course (*primo piatto*—any kind of pasta dish, broth or soup, or rice dish or pizza), a second course (*secondo piatto*—a meat dish, accompanied by a *contorno* or side dish—a vegetable, salad, or potatoes usually), followed by fruit or dessert and coffee. You can, however, begin with a platter of *antipasti*—the appetizers Italians do so brilliantly, ranging from warm seafood delicacies, to raw ham (*prosciutto crudo*), salami in a hundred varieties, lovely vegetables, savoury toasts, olives, pâté and many many more. There are restaurants that specialise in *antipasti*, and they usually don't take it amiss if you decide to forget the pasta and meat and just nibble on these scrumptious hors-d'œuvres (though in the end it will probably cost more than a full meal). Most Italians accompany their meal with wine and mineral water—*acqua minerale*, with or without bubbles (*con* or *senza gas*), which supposedly aids digestion—concluding their meals with a *digestivo* liqueur.

Cena, the **evening meal**, is usually eaten around 8pm. This is much the same as *pranzo* although lighter, without the pasta; a pizza and beer, eggs or a fish dish. In restaurants, however, they offer all the courses, so if you have only a sandwich for lunch you have a full meal in the evening.

In Italy the various terms for types of **restaurants**—*ristorante*, *trattoria*, or *osteria*—have been confused. A *trattoria* or *osteria* can be just as elaborate as a restaurant, though rarely is a *ristorante* as informal as a traditional *trattoria*. Unfortunately the old habit of posting menus and prices in the windows has fallen from fashion, so it's often difficult to judge variety or prices. Invariably the least expensive eating place is the *vino e cucina*, a simple establishment serving simple cuisine for simple everyday prices. It is essential to remember that the fancier the fittings, the fancier the **bill**, though neither of these points has anything at all to do with the quality of the food. If you're uncertain, do as you would at home—look for lots of locals. When you eat out, mentally add to the bill (*conto*) the bread and cover charge (*pane e coperto*, between L2000 and L4000), and a 15% service charge. This is often included in the bill (*servizio compreso*); if not, it will say *servizio non compreso*, and you'll have to do your own arithmetic. Additional tipping is at your own discretion, but never do it in family-owned and family-run places.

People who haven't visited Italy for years and have fond memories of eating full meals for under a pound will be amazed at how much **prices** have risen; though in some respects eating out in Italy is still a bargain, especially when you figure out how much all that wine would have cost you at home. In many places you'll often find restaurants offering a *menu turistico*—full, set meals of usually meagre inspiration for L20,000–30,000. More imaginative chefs often offer a *menu degustazione*—a set-price gourmet meal that allows you to taste their daily specialities and seasonal dishes. Both of these are cheaper than if you had ordered the same food *à la carte*.

Restaurant price categories	
very expensive	over L80,000
expensive	L50,000–80,000
moderate	L30,000–50,000
cheap	below L30,000

When you leave a restaurant you will be given a receipt (*scontrino* or *ricevuto fiscale*) which according to Italian law you must take with you out of the door and carry for at least 60 metres. If you aren't given one, it means the restaurant is probably fudging on its taxes and thus offering you lower prices. There is a slim chance the tax police (*Guardia di Fianza*) may have their eye on you and the restaurant, and if you don't have a receipt they could slap you with a heavy fine.

As the pace of modern urban life militates against traditional lengthy homecooked repasts with the family, followed by a siesta, alternatives to sit-down meals have mushroomed. Many office workers now behave much as their counterparts elsewhere in Europe and consume a rapid snack at lunchtime, returning home after a busy day to throw together some pasta and salad in the evenings.

The original Italian fast food alternative, a buffet known as the 'hot table' (*tavola calda*) is becoming harder and harder to find among the international and made-in-Italy fast food franchises of various descriptions; bars often double as *panicotecas* (which make hot or cold sandwiches to order, or serve *tramezzini*, little sandwiches on plain, square white bread that are always much better than they look); outlets selling pizza by the slice (*al taglio*) are common in city centres. At any grocer's (*alimentari*) or market (*mercato*) you can buy the materials for countryside or hotel-room picnics; some will make the sandwiches for you.

What comes as a surprise to many visitors is the tremendous regional diversity at the table; often next to nothing on the menu looks familiar, disguised by a local or dialect name. Expect further mystification, as many Italian chefs have wholeheartedly embraced the concept of *nouvelle cuisine*, or rather *nuova cucina*, and are constantly inventing dishes with even more names. If your waiter fails to elucidate, the menu decoder at the back of this book may help.

In northern Italy, look for dishes prepared with butter and cream. Egg pasta and *risotto* are favourite first courses, while game dishes, liver, *bollito misto* (mixed boiled meats), *ossobuco* (veal shin cooked in tomato sauce), seafood and sausages appear as main courses. Towards the Trentino-Adige the cooking displays hearty Austrian influences, with goulash and smoked meats with rye bread. Sometimes you may find dishes served with *polenta* (a pudding or cake of yellow maize flour), a brick-heavy substance to be approached with caution.

But here, too, is Emilia-Romagna, Italy's gourmet region par excellence, the land of delicious tortellini and lasagne, Parmesan cheese, Parma ham, balsamic vinegar and a hundred other delicacies. Central Italy is the land of beans and chick peas, game, tripe, salt cod (*baccala*), *porchetta* (whole roast pork with rosemary), Florentine steaks, *saltimbocca alla romana* (veal scallops with ham and sage), and freshwater fish in interesting guises. Tuscan and Umbrian cooking uses fresh, simple, high-quality ingredients flavoured with herbs and olive oil, and the local *porcini* mushrooms or truffles.

The further south you go, the spicier and oilier things get, and the richer the puddings and cakes. Modern Romans are as adventurous at the table as their classical ancestors, and include some stomach-churning offal in their diets. But the capital is an excellent place to delve into any style of regional cooking, with dozens of restaurants from all over Italy. Southern Italy is the land of homemade pasta, wonderful vegetables and superb seafood, often fried or laced with olive oil. Naples, of course, is the birthplace of pizza, and home of rich tomato sauces. Regional specialities are often seasoned with condiments like capers, anchovies, lemon juice, oregano, olives and fennel.

Wine and Spirits

Italy is a country where everyday wine is cheaper than Coca-Cola or milk, and where nearly every family owns some vineyards or has some relatives who supply most of their daily needs—which are not great. Even though they live in one of the world's largest wine-growing countries, Italians imbibe relatively little, and usually only at meals.

If Italy has an infinite variety of regional dishes, there is an equally bewildering array of **regional wines**, many of which are rarely exported because they are best drunk young. Even wines that are well known and often-derided clichés abroad, like Chianti or Lambrusco, can be wonderful new experiences when tasted on their home turf. Unless you're dining at a restaurant with an exceptional cellar, do as the Italians do and order a carafe of the local wine (*vino locale* or *vino della casa*). You won't often be wrong.

Most Italian wines are named after the grape and the district they come from. If the label says DOC (*Denominazione di Origine Controllata*) it means that the wine comes from a specially defined area and was produced according to a certain traditional method. DOCG (*Denominazione d'Origine Controllata e Garantia*) is allegedly a more rigorous classification, indicating that the wines not only conform to DOC standards, but are tested by government-appointed inspectors. At present few wines have been granted this status, but the number is planned to increase steadily. *Classico* means that a wine comes from the oldest part of the zone of production, though is not necessarily better than a non-Classico. *Riserva, superiore* or *speciale* denotes a wine that has been aged longer and is more alcoholic; *recioto* is a wine made from the outer clusters of grapes, with a higher sugar and therefore alcohol content.

Other Italian wine words are *spumante* (sparkling), *frizzante* (pétillant), *amabile* (semi-sweet), *abbocato* (medium dry), *passito* (strong sweet wine made from raisins). *Rosso* is red, *bianco* white; between the two extremes lie *rubiato* (ruby), *rosato, chiaretto* or *cerasuolo* (rose). *Secco* is dry, *dolce* sweet, *liquoroso* fortified and sweet. *Vendemmia* means vintage, a *cantina* is a cellar, and an *enoteca* is a wine-shop or museum where you can taste and buy wines.

The regions of Piedmont, Tuscany and Veneto produce Italy's most prestigious red wines, while Friuli-Venezia Giulia and Trentino-Alto Adige are the greatest regions for white wines. King of the Tuscans is the mighty Brunello di Montalcino (DOCG), an expensive blockbuster. Pinot Grigio and the unusual Tocai make some of the best whites. But almost every other corner of Italy has its vinous virtues, be it the Lambrusco of Emilia-Romagna, the Orvieto of Umbria, the Taurasi of Campania or the Frascati of Lazio. The well-known Valpolicella, Bardolino and Soave are produced on the shores of Lake Garda. Even in the south, with much of its stronger, rougher wine shipped north for blending, you will find some wonderful varieties, such as the Sicilian Corvo (red and white).

Italy turns its grape harvest to other uses too, producing Sicilian **Marsala**, a famous fortified wine fermented in wooden casks, ranging from very dry to flavoured and sweet and **vin santo**, a sweet Tuscan speciality often served with almond biscuits. **Vermouth** is an idea from Turin made of wine flavoured with Alpine herbs and spices. Italians are fond of post-prandial brandies (to aid digestion)—**Stock** or **Vecchia Romagna** appear on the best-known Italian brandy bottles. **Grappa** is a rough, Schnapps-like spirit drunk in black coffee after a meal (a *caffè corretto*). Other drinks you'll see in any Italian bar include **Campari**, a red bitter drunk on its own or in cocktails; **Fernet Branca, Cynar** and **Averno** (popular aperitif/digestifs); and a host of liqueurs like **Strega**, the witch potion from **Benevento**, apricot-flavoured **Amaretto**, cherry **Maraschino**, aniseed **Sambuca** or herby **Millefiori**.

Spirits like whisky or gin are reasonably priced in Italy; locals rarely drink them, despite intensive advertising.

Health and Emergencies

You can insure yourself for almost any possible mishap—cancelled flights, stolen or lost baggage and health. Check any current policies you hold to see if they cover you while abroad, and under what circumstances, and judge whether you need a special **traveller's insurance** policy for the journey. Travel agencies sell them, as well as insurance companies.

Citizens of EU countries are entitled to **reciprocal health care** in Italy's National Health Service and a 90% discount on prescriptions (bring **Form E111** with you). The E111 does not cover all medical expenses (no repatriation costs, for example, and no private treatment), and it is advisable to take out separate travel insurance for full cover. Citizens of non-EU countries should check carefully that they have adequate insurance for any medical expenses, and the cost of returning home. Australia has a reciprocal health care scheme with Italy, but New Zealand, Canada and the USA do not. If you already have health insurance, a student card, or a credit card, you may be entitled to some medical cover abroad.

In an **emergency**, dial **115** for fire and **113** for an ambulance in Italy (*ambulanza*) or to find the nearest hospital (*ospedale*). Less serious problems can be treated at a *Pronto Soccorso* (casualty/first aid department) at any hospital clinic (*ambulatorio*), or at a local health unit (*Unita Sanitarial Locale*—USL). Airports and main railway stations also have **first-aid posts**. If you have to pay for any health treatment, make sure you get a receipt, so that you can make any claims for reimbursement later.

Dispensing **chemists** (*farmacia*) are generally open from 8.30am to 1pm and from 4 to 8pm. Pharmacists are trained to give advice for minor ills. Any large town will have a *farmacia* that stays open 24 hours; others take turns to stay open (the address rota is posted in the window).

No specific **vaccinations** are required or advised for citizens of most countries before visiting Italy; the main health risks are the usual travellers' woes of upset stomachs or the effects of too much sun. Take a supply of **medicaments** with you (insect repellent, anti-diarrhœal medicine, sun lotion and antiseptic cream), and any drugs you need regularly.

Most Italian doctors speak at least rudimentary English, but if you can't find one, contact your embassy or consulate for a list of English-speaking doctors. Standards of health care in the north are generally higher than in the deep south.

Living and Working in Italy

Registration and Residency

If you are planning to stay in Italy long-term without working, you should register with the police within eight days of arrival and apply for a *permesso di soggiorno* from the local **Questura** (police station)—get there early in the morning as most state offices close in the afternoon. You need a *permesso* in order to open a bank account in Italy, or buy a car. It lasts for three months, after which you will need to renew it. If you can prove you have enough money to live on, permission is usually granted, though non-whites may have a hard time. However frustrating the process of obtaining documentation in Italy, try to appear calm and remain polite, or things will only get worse. Take your passport, a supply of photographs and as much convincing ID as you can muster.

If you wish to be registered as a resident you should apply to the local **Ufficio Anagrafe** (registry office). If you are in Italy for work, your employer should help you with the red-tape, though many small businessmen prefer to take unregistered foreigners (so that they don't have to declare them and pay tax). Students attending courses at Italian universities must obtain a declaration from the Italian Consulate in their home countries before their departure, certifying their 'acceptability' for further study, and that they have adequate health insurance. A surprising number of scholarships are offered to foreign students (especially post-graduates) by the Italian Ministry of Foreign Affairs; ask your Italian embassy for details, or write to the Ministry directly (Direzione Generale per la Cooperazione Culturale Scientifica e Tecnica, Piazzale della Farnesina 1, Roma).

Maps

The maps in this guide are for orientation only and to explore in any detail it is worth investing in a good, up-to-date regional map before you arrive from any of the following bookshops:

Stanford's, 12–14 Long Acre, London WC2 9LP, ✆ (020) 7836 1321.

The Travel Bookshop, 13 Blenheim Crescent, London W11 2EE, ✆ (020) 7229 5260.

The Complete Traveller, 199 Madison Ave, New York, NY 10016, ✆ (212) 685 9007.

Excellent maps are produced by **Touring Club Italiano**, **Michelin** and **Istituto Geografico de Agostini**. They are available at all major bookshops in Italy or sometimes on news stands. Italian tourist offices are helpful and can often supply good area maps and town plans.

Money

It's a good idea to order a wad of lire from your home bank to have on hand when you arrive in Italy, the land of strikes, unforeseen delays and quirky banking hours (*see* below). Take great care how you carry it, however (don't keep it all in one place). Obtaining money is often a frustrating business involving much queueing and form-filling. The major banks and exchange bureaux licensed by the Bank of Italy give the best exchange rates for currency or traveller's cheques. Hotels, private exchanges in resorts and FS-run exchanges at railway stations usually have less advantageous rates, but are open outside normal banking hours.

Weekend exchange offices

Milan: Banca Ponti, Piazza del Duomo 19; Banca delle Comunicazioni, Stazione Centrale; American Express, Via Brera 3.

Florence: Thomas Cook, Lungarno Acciaioli 6r; American Express, Via de' Guicciardini 49r.

Rome: Banco Nazionale delle Comunicazione, Stazione Termini; Thomas Cook Piazza Barberini 21D.

Naples: CIT, Piazza Municipio 70; Ashiba, Piazza Municipio 1.

Venice: American Express, S. Moise 1471; CIT, Piazza S. Marco.

In addition there are exchange offices at most airports. Remember that Italians indicate decimals with commas and thousands with full points.

Most British banks have an arrangement with their Italian counterparts, whereby you can (for a significant commission) use your bank card to take money out of Italian ATMs (Bancomats), but check with your bank first. Bancomats also take Eurocheque cards and credit cards (as long as you know your PIN number). Banks will advance you cash on a credit card or Eurocheque with a Eurocheque card. Visa, American Express and Diner's are more widely accepted than MasterCard (Access). Large hotels, resort area restaurants, shops and car hire firms will accept plastic as well; smaller places may not.

On 1 January 1999 Italy joined the first wave of European Monetary Union, thus making the **euro** its official new currency (and the lira a denomination thereof). In the short term this is unlikely to make much of a difference to the lives of either Italians or tourists—euro notes and coins are not due to be introduced until the launch of the second stage of monetary union on 1 January 2002, and the lira will continue to be used during the three year transitional period. The only visible difference that you will notice is that prices are now usually displayed in both lire and euros.

National Holidays

Most museums, as well as banks and shops, are closed on the following national holidays.

1 January (New Year's Day)

6 January (Epiphany)

Easter Monday

25 April (Liberation Day)

1 May (Labour Day)

15 August (Assumption, also known as *Ferragosto*, the official start of the Italian holiday season)

1 November (All Saints' Day)

8 December (Immaculate Conception)

25 December (Christmas Day)

26 December (*Santo Stefano*, St Stephen's Day)

In addition to these general holidays, many towns also take their patron saint's day off.

Opening Hours and Museums

Although it varies from region to region, with the north bearing more resemblance to the rest of Europe than the Mediterranean south, most of Italy closes down at 1pm until 3 or 4pm to eat and properly digest the main meal of the day. Afternoon hours are from 4 to 7, often from 5 to 8 in the hot summer months. Bars are often the only places open during the early afternoon. Some cities (notably Milan) close down completely during August when locals flee to the hills, lakes or coast. In any case, don't be surprised if you find anywhere in Italy unexpectedly closed (or open for that matter), whatever its official stated hours.

banks:	open Mon–Fri 8.30–1 and 3–4, closed weekends and on local and national holidays (see below).
shops:	open Mon–Sat 8–1 and 3.30–7.30. Some supermarkets and department stores stay open throughout the day, and hours vary according to season and are shorter in smaller centres.

Government-run dispensers of red tape (e.g. visa departments) often stay open for quite limited periods, usually during the mornings (*Mon–Fri*). It pays to get there as soon as they open (or before) to spare your nerves in an interminable queue. Anyway, take something to read, or write your memoirs.

museums and galleries

Many of Italy's museums are magnificent, many are run with shameful neglect, and many have been closed for years for 'restoration' with slim prospects of reopening in the foreseeable future. With at least one work of art per inhabitant, Italy has a hard time financing the preservation of its national heritage; enquire at the tourist office to find out exactly what is open and what is 'temporarily' closed before setting off on a wild-goose chase.

churches

Italy's churches have always been a prime target for art thieves and as a consequence are usually locked when there isn't a sacristan or caretaker to keep an eye on things. All churches, except for the really important cathedrals and basilicas, close in the afternoon at the same hours as the shops, and the little ones tend to stay closed. Always have a pocketful of coins for the light machines in churches, or whatever work of art you came to inspect will remain clouded in ecclesiastical gloom. Don't do your visiting during services, and don't come to see paintings and statues in churches the week preceding Easter—you will probably find them covered with mourning shrouds.

In general, Sunday afternoons and Mondays are dead periods for the sightseer—you may want to make them your travelling days. Places without specified opening hours can usually be visited on request—but it is best to go before 1pm. We have listed the hours of important sights and museums, and specified which ones charge admission. Entrance charges vary widely; major sights are fairly steep (L10,000 plus), but others may be completely free. EU citizens under 18 and over 65 get free admission to state museums, at least in theory.

Packing

You simply cannot overdress in Italy; whatever grand strides Italian designers have made on the international fashion merry-go-round, most of their clothes are purchased domestically, prices be damned. Now whether or not you want to try to keep up with the natives is your own affair. It's not that the Italians are very formal; they simply like to dress up with a gorgeousness that adorns their cities just as much as those old Renaissance churches and palaces. The few places with dress codes are the major churches and basilicas (no shorts, sleeveless shirts or strappy sundresses—women should tuck a light silk scarf in a bag to throw over the shoulders), casinos, and a few posh restaurants.

Your electric appliances will work in Italy if you adapt and convert them to run on 220 AC with two round prongs on the plug.

Post Offices

post offices: *usually open Mon–Sat 8–1; in large cities 8–6 or 7.*

Dealing with *la posta italiana* has always been a risky, frustrating, time-consuming affair. It is one of the most expensive and slowest postal services in Europe. Even buying the right stamps requires dedicated research and saintly patience. One of the scandals that mesmerized Italy in recent years involved the minister of the post office, who disposed of literally tons of backlog mail by tossing it in the Tiber. When the news broke, he was replaced—the new minister, having learned his lesson, burned all the mail the post office was incapable of delivering.

Not surprisingly, fed-up Italians view the invention of the fax machine as a gift from the Madonna. From these harsh judgements, however, we must exempt the Vatican City, whose special postal service (on angelic wings?) knocks spots off the rest of the country for speed and efficiency. If you're anywhere in Rome, be sure to post your mail in the Holy See. You need to buy special Vatican stamps, which provide a tidy profit for the papal coffers.

To have your mail sent *poste restante* (general delivery), have it addressed to the central post office (*Fermo Posta*) and expect three to four weeks for it to arrive. Make sure your surname is clearly written in block capitals. To pick up your mail you must present your passport and pay a nominal charge. Stamps (*francoboli*) are available in post offices or at tobacconists (*tabacchi*, identified by their blue signs with a white T). Prices fluctuate.

You can also have money telegraphed to you through the post office; if all goes well, this can happen in a mere three days, but expect a fair proportion of it to go into commission.

Shopping

'Made in Italy' has become a byword for style and quality, especially in fashion and leather, but also in home design, ceramics, kitchenware, jewellery, lace and linens, glassware and crystal, chocolates, bells, Christmas decorations, hats, straw work, art books, engravings, handmade stationery, gold and silverware, bicycles, sports cars, woodworking, a hundred kinds of liqueurs, aperitifs, coffee machines, gastronomic specialities, and antiques (both repro-ductions, and the real thing). You'll find the best variety of goods in Milan, Rome, Florence and Venice—in other words, where the money is. Design-conscious Milan is Italy's major shopping centre and a cynosure of innovative style and fashion throughout the world.

If you are looking for antiques, be sure to demand a certificate of authenticity—reproductions can be very good. To get your antique or modern art purchases home, you will have to apply to the Export Department of the Italian Ministry of Education and pay an export tax as well; your seller should know the details. Non-EU citizens should save all receipts for Customs.

Italians don't much like department stores, but there are a few chains—the classiest is the oldest, Rinascente, while COIN stores often have good buys in almost the latest fashions. Standa and UPIM are more like Woolworths; they have good clothes selections, housewares, etc., and often contain basement supermarkets. The main attraction of Italian shopping, however, is to buy classy luxury items; for less expensive clothes and household items you can nearly always do better at home. Prices for clothes are generally very high.

cycling

About three-quarters of Italy is hilly or mountainous, so a cycling holiday is no soft option. It is best to bring your own bike (a mountain bike if possible) and spare parts; cycling is growing fast, but nowhere near as fanatically practised in Italy as, say, in France or Denmark. Facilities for hiring or repairing bikes are less widespread, but you can buy a good bike for L200–300,000. Good biking regions include Tuscany and Umbria, Puglia and the Alpine areas, where there are some good trails. Most airlines and rail companies will transport bikes quite cheaply. The spring Tour d'Italia is Italy's great annual cycling event.

fishing

You don't need a permit for sea-fishing (without an aqualung), but Italy's coastal waters, polluted and over-exploited, may disappoint. Commercial fishing has depleted stocks to such an extent that the government has begun to declare two- and three-month moratoria on all fishing to give the fish a break. Many freshwater lakes and streams are stocked, and if you're more interested in fresh fish than the sport of it, there are innumerable trout farms where you can practically pick the fish up out of the water with your hands. To fish in fresh water you need to purchase a year's membership card (currently L189,000) from the **Federazione Italiana della Pesca Sportiva**, which has an office in every province; they will inform you about local conditions and restrictions. Bait and equipment are readily available.

football

Soccer (*il calcio*) is a national obsession. For many Italians its importance far outweighs tedious issues like the state of the nation, the government of the day, or any momentous international event—not least because of the weekly chance (slim but real) of becoming an instant lira billionaire in the Lotteria Sportiva. All major cities, and most minor ones, have at least one team of some sort. The sport was actually introduced by the English, but a Renaissance game, something like a cross between football and rugby, has existed in Italy for centuries. Rivalries between Italian teams are intense, and scandals, especially involving bribery and cheating, are rife; yet crowd violence is minimal. Big-league matches are played on Sunday afternoons (*Sept–May*). For information, contact the Federazione Italiana Giuoco Calcio, Via G. Allegri 14, 00198 Rome, © 06 84911.

golf

Italians have been slower than some nationalities to appreciate the delights of biffing a small white ball into a hole in the ground, but they're catching on fast. The north is a good place to practise, particularly around Lake Como. Contact the Federazione Italiana Golf, Via Flaminia 388, 00196 Rome, © 06 323 1825, for more information.

hiking and mountaineering

These sports are becoming steadily more popular among native Italians every year. Walking in the Alps is generally practicable between May and October. Strategically placed **Alpine refuges** (*rifugi alpini*) provide shelter, but if you come in early June or October when the refuges are closed you'll need to carry camping gear. The refuges are open from the end of June to the end of September; in July and August it's wise to book a bed in advance to avoid disappointment. They vary dramatically. Many are owned by the Italian Alpine Club, while others are privately owned, primarily by ski resorts. Some are along trails, while others may be reached via cable car. All offer bed and board; nearly all now require that you bring a sleeping sheet, or buy one on the site. Prices vary mainly by altitude: the higher up and more difficult of access, the more expensive. Besides these refuges, there are the *baite* (wooden huts), *casere* (stone huts) and bivouacs (beds but no food) found along some of the higher trails: they generally have no custodians but offer shelter. For more information write to the **Italian Alpine Club** (CAI, Via Fonseca Pimental 7, 20121 Milan, ✆ 02 2614 1378, 🖷 02 2614 1395.

Some Alpine resorts have taken to offering *Settimane Verdi* (Green Weeks)—good-value accommodation and activity packages for summer visitors similar to skiers' White Weeks. Tuscany and the Apennines (Abruzzo National Park) offer less strenuous but equally enjoyable walking country.

hunting

Italy's most controversial sport pits avid enthusiasts against a growing number of environmentalists. The debate is fierce and the start of the season is marked by huge protests. Indiscriminate trapping, netting and shooting is responsible for the decimation of many migrant Mediterranean songbirds. Less controversial, at least from the conservation point of view, is duck, pigeon and wild-boar shooting.

motor racing

The homeland of Ferrari, Maserati and Alfa Romeo naturally fosters a keen interest in motor sports, proof of which can be witnessed along any Italian road, which Italians regard as practice tracks. Monza, near Milan, hosts the Italian Grand Prix every September. The Formula I track, built in 1922, is 15km out of town.

riding holidays

Riding holidays are now available in many parts of Italy, particularly in areas where *Agriturist* (*see* 'Where to Stay—Rural Self-Catering') is well represented, such as Tuscany, Umbria and Lazio, where tours staying at country estates are organized. There are riding stables in most cities and resorts. For more information contact the local Agriturist office, or the Associazione Nazionale per il Turismo Equestre, Via A. Borelli 5, 00161 Rome, ✆ 06 444 1179. Rome's International Riding Show in the Villa Borghese draws a big crowd each May. Horse-racing is staged in many large cities, but easily the most exciting race of all is Siena's bareback **Palio**, a medieval pageant arousing huge local rivalries (*see* p.632).

rowing and canoeing

The annual regatta between the four ancient maritime republics of Venice, Amalfi, Genoa and Pisa (held in turn at each city) is a splendidly colourful event. Lake Piediluco in Umbria hosts an international rowing championship. If you prefer the DIY version, try the Arno or any of Lombardy's lakes. The fast rivers of the mountain areas provide exciting white-water sport. Kayak races are held in the Dolomites. For more information contact the Federazione Italiana Canoa e Kayak, Viale Tiziano 70, 00196 Rome, ✆ 06 368 58215.

skiing and winter sports

Italy still lacks the cachet of neighbouring Switzerland or Austria among the skiing fraternity, but has caught up significantly and now has a better reputation for safety and efficiency than it once did, though erratic snow cover is always a problem. Its main resorts are obviously in the Alps, particularly the scenic Dolomites. Downhill and cross-country (*sci di fondo*) skiing are available, along with more exotic variants (for experts only) like helicopter skiing. Equipment hire is generally not too expensive, but lift passes and accommodation can push up the cost of a winter holiday. Some of the most fashionable (and expensive) resorts include **Cortina** and **Courmayeur**. The Sella Ronda links several resorts in an exhilarating day's circuit. The Marmolada glacier in Trentino-Adige and Cervinia at the foot of the Matterhorn provide year-round sources of snowy runs. Lombardy's most famous ski resort is **Bormio**, at the entrance to Italy's largest national park, which has hosted world events in recent years (glacier skiing is practised above the Stelvio pass).

Prices are highest during Christmas and New Year holidays, in February and at Easter. Most resorts offer *Settimane Bianche* (White Weeks)—off-season packages at economical rates. Other winter sports such as ice-skating and bob-sleighing are available at larger resorts.

tennis

If soccer is Italy's most popular spectator sport, tennis is probably the game most people actually play. Every *comune* has public courts for hourly hire, especially resorts. Private clubs may offer temporary membership to passing visitors, and hotel courts can often be used by non-residents for a reasonable fee. Contact local tourist offices for information. Italy's big tennis event is the Grand Prix tournament held in Rome in May.

watersports

Despite Italy's notorious coastal pollution, watersports are immensely popular, especially sailing and windsurfing. The best areas for sailing include the Ligurian Riviera and the Tuscan or Lazio coasts. Lakes Como and Garda also have well-equipped sailing and windsurfing schools. Waterskiing is possible on all the major lakes, as well as at many coastal resorts. A few areas are good for diving, e.g. Alassio (Liguria) and Capri. Boat and equipment hire is often quite expensive.

Mainland Italy is not remarkable for its **beaches**. Much of the coast is disappointingly flat and dull and many seaside resorts are plagued by that peculiarly Italian phenomenon, the concessionaire, who parks ugly lines of sunbeds and brollies all the way along the best stretches of coast, and charges all-comers handsomely for the privilege of spending some time at the seaside. During the winter you can see what happens when the beaches miss out on their manicures; many get depressingly rubbish-strewn.

The beaches in the south (Calabria, Basilicata and Puglia) are generally cleaner and less developed than those further north; those around the Bay of Naples, Rome's Lido di Ostia and the Venetian Lido are best avoided for swimming. Head for the islands for cleaner water and prettier scenery. In Lombardy, the smaller, less crowded lakes like Viverone, Varese and Mergozzo are preferable to the larger lakes for swimming. No one bats an eye at topless bathing, though nudism requires more discretion.

For further information, contact the **Italian State Tourist Office** or write to the following organizations:

Federazione Italiana Vela (Italian Sailing Federation), Via Brigata Bisagno 2/17, Genoa, Ⓣ 010 565 723.

Federazione Italiana Motonautica (Italian Motorboat Federation) and **Federazione Italiana Sci Nautico** (Italian Waterskiing Federation), Via Piranesi 44b, Milan, Ⓣ 02 761 050.

Telephones

Public telephones for international calls may be found in the offices of **Telecom Italia**, Italy's telephone company. They are the only places where you can make reverse-charge calls (*a erre*, collect calls) but be prepared for a wait, as all these calls go through the operator in Rome. Rates for long-distance calls are among the highest in Europe. Calls within Italy are cheapest after 10pm; international calls after 11pm.

Most phone booths now take either coins (L100, 200, 500 or 1000) or phone cards (*schede telefoniche*), available in L5000, L10,000 and sometimes 15,000 amounts at tobacconists and news-stands—you have to snap off the small perforated corner in order to use them. In smaller villages you can usually find *telefoni a scatti*, with a meter on it, in at least one bar (a small commission is generally charged). Try to avoid telephoning from hotels, which often add 25% to the bill.

Direct calls may be made by dialling the international prefix (for the UK 0044, Ireland 00353, USA and Canada 001, Australia 0061, New Zealand 0064). If you're calling Italy from abroad, dial 39 first. Many places have public fax machines, but the speed of transmission may make costs very high.

Time

Italy is on Central European Time, one hour ahead of Greenwich Mean Time and six hours ahead of Eastern Standard Time. From the last weekend of March to the end of September, Italian Summer Time (daylight saving time) is in effect.

Toilets

Frequent travellers have noted a steady improvement over the years in the cleanliness of Italy's public conveniences, although as ever you will only find them in places like train and bus stations and bars. Ask for the *bagno*, *toilette* or *gabinetto*; in stations and the smarter bars and cafes there are washroom attendants who expect a few hundred lire for keeping the place decent. You'll probably have to ask them for paper (*carta*). Don't confuse the Italian plurals; s*ignori* (gents), *signore* (ladies).

Tourist Offices

tourist information offices: *open 8–12.30 or 1 and 3–7, possibly longer in summer. Few open on Saturday afternoons or Sundays.*

Known as EPT, APT or AAST, information booths provide hotel lists, town plans and terse information on local sights and transport. Queues can be maddeningly long. If you're stuck, you may get more sense out of a friendly travel agency than an official tourist office. Nearly every city and province now has a web page, and you can often book your hotel direct through the Internet.

UK, 1 Princes Street, London W1R 8AY, ✆ (020) 7408 1254; **Italian Travel Centre**, Thomas Cook, 45 Berkeley Street, London W1A 1EB, ✆ (020) 7499 4000.

USA, 630 Fifth Ave, Suite 1565, New York, NY 10111, ℗ (212) 245 4822; 12400 Wilshire Blvd, Suite 550, Los Angeles, CA 90025, ℗ (310) 820 0098; 500 N. Michigan Ave, Suite 1046, Chicago, IL 60611, ℗ (312) 644 0990.

Australia, c/o Italian Embassy, 61–69 Macquarie St, Sydney 2000, NSW, ℗ (02) 9247 8442.

Canada, 1 Place Ville Marie, Suite 1914, Montréal, Quebec H3B 3M9, ℗ (514) 866 7667.

N. Zealand, c/o Italian Embassy, 36 Grant Road, Thomdon, Wellington, ℗ (04) 736 065.

Tourist and travel information may also be available from **Alitalia** (Italy's national airline) or **CIT** (Italy's state-run travel agency) offices in some countries. In the UK, contact the **Italian Travel Centre**, at Thomas Cook, 45 Berkeley Street, London W1A 1EB, ℗ (020) 7499 4000.

Where to Stay

All accommodation in Italy is classified by the Provincial Tourist Boards. Price control, however, has been deregulated since 1992. Hotels now set their own tariffs, which means that in some places prices have rocketed. After a period of rapid and erratic price fluctuation, tariffs are at last settling down again to more predictable levels under the influence of market forces. Good-value, interesting accommodation in cities can be very difficult to find. Milan has the most expensive and heavily booked hotels in Italy; check the calendar of events with the tourist office—a major trade fair or conference could put all your travel plans in jeopardy.

The quality of furnishings and facilities has generally improved in all categories in recent years. Many hotels have installed smart bathrooms and electronic gadgetry. At the top end of the market, Italy has a number of exceptionally sybaritic hotels, furnished and decorated with real panache. But you can still find plenty of older-style hotels and *pensioni*, whose eccentricities of character and architecture (in some cases undeniably charming) may frequently be at odds with modern standards of comfort or even safety.

prices

Category	Double with bath
luxury (*****)	L450–800,000
very expensive (****)	L300–450,000
expensive (***)	L200–300,000
moderate (**)	L120–200,000
cheap (*)	up to L120,000

Hotels and Guesthouses

Italian *alberghi* come in all shapes and sizes. They are rated from one to five stars, depending what facilities they offer (not their character, style or charm). The star ratings are some indication of price levels, but for tax reasons not all hotels choose to advertise themselves at the rating to which they are entitled, so you may find a modestly rated hotel just as comfortable (or more so) than a higher rated one. Conversely, you may find a hotel offers few stars in hopes of attracting budget-conscious travellers, but charges just as much as a higher-rated neighbour. *Pensioni* are generally more modest establishments, though the distinction between these and ordinary hotels is becoming rather blurred. *Locande* are traditionally an even more basic form of hostelry, but these days the term may denote somewhere fairly chic. Other inexpensive accommodation is sometimes known as *alloggi* or *affittacamere*. There are usually plenty of cheap dives around railway stations; for somewhere more salubrious, head for the historic quarters. Whatever the shortcomings of the décor, furnishings and fittings, you can usually rely at least on having clean sheets.

Price lists, by law, must be posted on the back of the door of every room, along with meal prices and any extra charges (such as air-conditioning, or even a shower in cheap places). Many hotels display two or three different rates, depending on the season. Low-season rates may be about a third lower than peak-season tariffs. Some resort hotels close down altogether for several months a year. During high season you should always book ahead to be sure of a room (a fax reservation may be less frustrating to organize than one by post, and certainly more likely to reach its destination).

If you have paid a deposit, your booking is valid under Italian law, but don't expect it to be refunded if you have to cancel. Tourist offices publish annual regional lists of hotels and pensions with current rates, but do not generally make reservations for visitors. Major city business hotels may offer significant discounts at weekends.

Main railway stations generally have accommodation booking desks; inevitably, a fee is charged. Chain hotels or motels are generally the easiest hotels to book, though not always the most interesting to stay in. Top of the list is CIGA (*Compagnia Grandi Alberghi*) with some of the most luxurious establishments in Italy, many of them grand, turn-of-the-century places that have been exquisitely restored. Venice's legendary Cipriani is one of its flagships. The French consortium *Relais et Châteaux* specializes in tastefully indulgent accommodation, often in historic buildings. At a more affordable level, one of the biggest chains in Italy is *Jolly Hotels*, always reliable if not all up to the same standard; these can generally be found near the centres of larger towns. Many motels are operated by the ACI (Italian Automobile Club) or by AGIP (the oil company) and usually located along major exit routes.

If you arrive without a reservation, begin looking or phoning round for accommodation early in the day. If possible, inspect the room (and bathroom facilities) before you book, and check the tariff carefully. Italian hoteliers may legally alter their rates twice during the year, so printed tariffs or tourist board lists (and prices quoted in this book!) may be out of date. Hoteliers who wilfully overcharge should be reported to the local tourist office. You will be asked for your passport for registration purposes.

Prices listed in this guide are for double rooms, and you can expect to pay about two-thirds the rate for single occupancy—though in high season you may be charged the full double rate in some popular beach resorts. Extra beds are usually charged at about a third more of the room rate. Rooms without private bathrooms generally charge 20–30% less, and most offer discounts for children sharing parent's rooms, or children's meals. A *camera singola* (single room) may cost anything from about L25,000 upwards. Double rooms (*camera doppia*) go from about L60,000 to L250,000 or more. If you want a double bed make sure you specify a *camera matrimoniale*.

Breakfast is usually optional in hotels, though obligatory in *pensioni*. You can usually get better value by eating breakfast in a bar or café. In high season you may be expected to take half-board in resorts if the hotel has a restaurant, and one-night stays may be refused.

There aren't many youth hostels (*alberghi* or *ostelli per la gioventù*) in Italy, but they are generally pleasant and sometimes located in historic buildings. The **Associazione Italiana Alberghi per la Gioventù** (Italian Youth Hostel Association, or AIG) is affiliated to the International Youth Hostel Federation. For a full list of hostels, contact AIG at Via Cavour 44, 00184 Roma (✆ 06 487 1152; ✆ 06 488 0492). An international membership card will enable you to stay in any of them. You can obtain these in advance from:

UK, Youth Hostels Association of England and Wales, 14 Southampton Street, London, WC2, ✆ (020) 7836 1036.

USA, American Youth Hostels Inc., Box 37613, Washington DC 20013-7613, ✆ (202) 783 6161.

Australia, Australian Youth Hostel Association, 60 Mary Street, Surry Hills, Sydney, NSW 2010, ✆ (02) 9621 1111.

Canada, Canadian Hostelling Association, 1600 James Naismith Drive, Suite 608, Gloucester, Ontario K1B 5N4, ✆ (613) 237 7884.

(Cards can usually be purchased on the spot in many hostels if you don't already have one.)

Religious institutions also run hostels; some are single sex, others will accept Catholics only. Rates are usually somewhere between L15,000 and L20,000, including breakfast. Discounts are available for senior citizens, and some family rooms are available. You generally have to check in after 5pm, and pay for your room before 9am. Hostels usually close for most of the daytime, and many operate a curfew. During the spring, noisy school parties cram hostels for field trips. In the summer, it's advisable to book ahead. Contact the hostels directly.

Villas, Flats and Chalets

If you're travelling in a group or with a family, self-catering can be the ideal way to experience Italy. The National Tourist Office has lists of agencies in the UK and USA which rent places on a weekly or fortnightly basis. The small ads in the weekend papers are crammed with suggestions, especially for Tuscany. If you have set your heart on a particular region, write to its tourist office for a list of agencies and owners, who will send brochures or particulars of their accommodation. Maid service is included in the more glamorous villas; ask whether bed linen and towels are provided. A few of the larger operators are listed below:

in the UK and Ireland

Citalia, Marco Polo House, 3–5 Lansdowne Road, Croydon CR9 1LL, ✆ (020) 8686 5533.

Eurovillas, 36 East Street, Coggeshall, Essex CO6 1SH, ✆ (01376) 561156.

Inghams, 10–18 Putney Hill, London SW15 6AX, ✆ (020) 8780 4450.

Interhome, 383 Richmond Road, Twickenham, Middx TW1 2EF, ✆ (020) 8891 1294.

International Chapters, 102 St John's Wood Terrace, London NW8 6PL, ✆ (020) 7722 9560.

Magic of Italy, 227 Shepherds Bush Road, London W6 7AS, ✆ (020) 8748 7575.

Topflight, D'Olier Chambers, D'Olier Street, Dublin 2, ✆ (01) 679 9177.

Vacanze in Italia, Manor Courtyard, Bignor, Pulborough, West Sussex RH20 1QD, ✆ (01798) 7426.

in the USA

CIT, ✆ (800) 248 8687; in New York, ✆ (212) 730 2121, who can also arrange fly-drive rental car packages.

At Home Abroad, 405 East 56th Street 6-H, New York, NY 10022-2466, ✆ (212) 421 9165, ✉ 752 1591, *athomabrod@aol.com*

CUENDET: Rentals for Italy (and Elsewhere!), ✆ (800) 726 7602 *www.rentvillas.com*

Hideaways International, 767 Islington Street, Portsmouth, NH 03801, ✆ (617) 486 8955.

Homeowners International, 1133 Broadway, New York, NY 10010, ✆ (212) 691 2361.

RAVE (Rent-a-Vacation Everywhere), 135 Meigs Street, Rochester, New York, NY 14607, ✆ (716) 246 0760.

Rural Self-catering

For a breath of rural seclusion, the gregarious Italians head for a spell on a **working farm**, in accommodation (usually self-catering) that often approximates to the French *gîte*. Often, however, the real pull of the place is a restaurant in which you can sample some home-grown produce. Outdoor activities may include riding, fishing, and so forth.

This branch of the Italian tourist industry is run by **Agriturist**. It has burgeoned in recent years, and every region now has several offices. Prices of farmhouse accommodation, compared with the over-hyped 'Tuscan villa', are still reasonable. To make the most of your rural hosts, it's as well to have a little Italian under your belt. Local tourist offices will have information on this type of accommodation in their areas; complete listings are compiled by the national organisation **Agriturist**, Corso Vittorio Emanuele 101, 00186 Rome ✆ 06 651 2342, or **Turismo Verde**, Via Mariano Fortuny 20, 00196 Rome ✆ 06 366 9931. Both publications are available in Italian bookshops.

Alpine Refuges

The Italian Alpine Club operates refuges (*rifugi*) on the main mountain trails (some accessible only by *funivie*). These may be predictably spartan, or surprisingly comfortable. Many have restaurants. For an up-to-date list, write to the Club Alpino Italiano, Via Fonseca Pimental 7, Milan, ✆ 02 2614 1378. Charges average L18,000–L25,000 per person per night, including breakfast. Most are open only from July to September, but those used by skiers are about 20% more expensive from December to April. Book ahead in August.

Camping

Life under canvas is not the fanatical craze it is in France, nor necessarily any great bargain, but there are over 2000 sites in Italy, particularly popular with holidaymaking families in August, when you can expect to find many sites at bursting point. Unofficial camping is generally frowned on and may attract a stern rebuke from the local police. Camper vans (and facilities for them) are increasingly popular. You can obtain a list of local sites from any regional tourist office. Campsite charges generally range from about L6–8000 per adult; tents and vehicles additionally cost about L7000 each. Small extra charges may also be levied for hot showers and electricity. A car-borne couple could therefore spend practically as much for a night at a well-equipped campsite as in a cheap hotel. To obtain a camping carnet and to book ahead, write to the **Centro Internazionale Prenotazioni Campeggio**, Casella Postale 23, 50041 Calenzano, Firenze, ✆ 055 882 381, 🖷 055 882 3918 (ask for their list of campsites with the booking form). The **Touring Club Italiano** (TCI) publishes a comprehensive annual guide to campsites throughout Italy which is available in bookshops for L29,500. Write to: TCI, Corso Italia 10, Milan, ✆ 02 85261/02 852 6245.

Women Travellers

Italian men, with the heritage of Casanova, Don Giovanni, and Rudolph Valentino as their birthright, are very confident in their role as Great Latin Lovers, but the old horror stories of gangs following the innocent tourist maiden and pinching her bottom are way behind the times. Italian men these days are often exquisitely polite and flirt on a much more sophisticated level, especially in the more 'Europeanised' north. Milan or Venice are easier cities for single women than Rome or Naples.

Still, women travelling alone may frequently receive hisses, wolf-whistles and unsolicited comments (complimentary or lewd, depending on your attitude) 'assistance' from local swains—usually of the balding, middle-age-crisis variety. A confident, indifferent poise is usually the best policy. Failing that, a polite 'I am waiting for my *marito*' (avoiding damaged male egos which can turn nasty), followed by a firm '*no!*' or '*Vai via!*' (Scram!) will generally solve the problem. Flashers and wandering hands on crowded buses may be an unpleasant surprise, but rarely present a serious threat (unless they're after your purse!).

Risks can be greatly reduced if you use common sense and avoid lonely streets or parks and train stations after dark. Choose hotels and restaurants within easy and safe walking distance of public transport. Travelling with a companion of either sex will buffer you considerably from such nuisances (a guardian male, of course, instantly converts you into an inviolable chattel in Italian eyes). Two women travelling together may still find they attract unwanted advances, particularly in the south. Avoid hitch-hiking alone in Italy.

History

The First Italians

Some 50,000 years ago, when the Alps were covered by an ice cap and the low level of the Mediterranean made Italy a much wider peninsula than it is now, Neanderthal man graced the Ligurian Riviera with his low-browed presence. Even that, however, is not the beginning of the story. Recently, scientists have become excited over the discovery of a new type, *Homo Aeserniensis*, the first known inhabitant of Europe, living in caves around Isernia a million years ago. Italy makes a convenient bridge from Africa to Europe, and it seems that there was a lot of traffic throughout prehistory.

Nevertheless, none of the earliest inhabitants of Italy left much in terms of art or culture, and the peninsula remained a backwater until about the 8th century BC. At that time, most of the population were lumped together as 'Italics', a number of powerful, distinct tribes with related languages.

Among them were the Samnites, who dominated much of Campania and the south, the dolmen-building Messapians in Puglia, the Piceni and Umbrii along the northern Adriatic coast, and a boiling kettle of contentious peoples in the centre: Sabines, Aequi, Volscii and Latins. The mighty walls of their cities, called *cyclopean walls*, can still be seen today around southern Lazio.

Two of Italy's most culturally sophisticated peoples lived on the islands: the Siculi of Sicily and the castle-building, bronze-working Sards of the Nuraghe culture. Both kept to themselves and interfered little with affairs on the mainland. Much of the north, the classical Cisalpine Gaul, was the stomping ground of Celtic Ligurians; at the time this area north of the Po was not really thought of as part of Italy.

750–509 BC: Greeks and Etruscans

The most interesting nations of the time, however, were two relative newcomers who contributed much towards bringing Italy out of its primitive state, the **Etruscans** and **Greeks**. With their shadowy past and as yet undeciphered language, the Etruscans are one of the puzzles of ancient history. According to their own traditions, they arrived from somewhere in western Anatolia about 900 BC—Etruscan inscriptions have been found on the Greek island of Lemnos—probably as a sort of warrior aristocracy that imposed itself on the existing populations of Tuscany and north Lazio.

By the 8th century BC they were the strongest people in Italy, grouped in a loose confederation of 12 city states called the *Dodecapolis*. At the same time the Greeks—whose trading routes had long covered Italy's southern coasts—began to look upon that 'under-developed' country as a New World for exploration and colonization. Cumae, on the Campanian coast, became the first Greek foundation in 750 BC, a convenient base for trading with the Etruscans and their newly discovered iron mines. A score of others soon followed, in Sicily and along the Ionian Sea, and soon they were rivalling the cities of Greece itself in wealth and culture. A third new factor in the Italian equation also appeared at this time, without much fanfare. The year 753 BC, according to the legends, saw the foundation of **Rome**.

Italy was ripe for civilization. In the centuries that followed, the Etruscans spread their rule and their culture over most of the north while the Italic tribes learned from Etruscans and Greeks alike. Some of them, especially the Latins and the Samnites, developed into urbanized, cultured nations in their own right. For the Greek cities, it was a golden age, as Taras (Táranto), Metapontum, Sybaris, Croton, and especially the Sicilian cities like Syracuse and Akragas grew into marble metropolises that dominated central Mediterranean trade and turned much of inland Italy into tribute-paying allies.

In the 6th century BC, they had more wealth than was probably good for them; stories are told of the merchants of Sybaris sending across the Mediterranean, offering fortunes for a cook who could produce the perfect sauce for seafood, and of the sentries of Akragas' army going on strike for softer pillows. From the first, also, these cities dissipated their energies by engaging in constant wars with each other. Some, like Sybaris, were completely destroyed, and by c.400 BC, the failure of the rest to work together sent them into a slow but irreversible economic decline.

The Etruscan story is much the same. By about 600 BC the 12 cities and their allies ruled almost all northern Italy (excluding Cisalpine Gaul), and wealth from their Tuscan mines made them a political force on a Mediterranean scale. Their decline was to be as rapid as that of Magna Graecia. Repeated defeats at the hands of the wild Gauls weakened their confederation, but the economic decline that led to Etruria's virtual evaporation in the 4th century BC is harder to account for. Rome, a border city between the Etruscans and Latins, threw out its Etruscan king and established a

Republic in 509 BC (see 'Rome': History p.718). Somehow, probably by the absorption of conquered populations, this relatively new city managed to grow to perhaps 100,000 people, ranking it with Taras and Capua, an Etruscan colony in the growing region of Campania, as the largest on the peninsula. With an economy insufficient to support so many Romans, the city could only live by a career of permanent conquest.

509–268 BC: The Rise of Rome

After the expulsion of the Etruscans, Rome spent a hundred years at war with the various cities of Etruria, while gradually subjugating the rest of the Latins and neighbouring tribes. It was successful on all fronts, and a sacking by marauding Gauls in 390 BC proved only a brief interruption in Rome's march to conquest. Southern Etruria and Latium were swallowed up by 358 BC, and Rome next turned its attention to the only power in Italy capable of competing with her on an equal basis: the Samnites.

These rugged highlanders of the southern Apennines, with their capital at Benevento, had begun to seize parts of coastal Campania. The Romans drove them out in 343–41 BC, but in the **Second Samnite War** the Samnites dealt them a severe defeat (Battle of Caudine Forks, 321 BC). In the third war, feeling themselves surrounded by Roman allies, the Samnites formed an alliance with the Northern Etruscans and Celts, leading to a general Italian commotion in which the Romans beat everybody, annexing almost all of Italy by 283 BC.

A strange interlude, delaying Rome's complete domination of Italy, came with the arrival of **Pyrrhus of Epirus**, a Greek adventurer with a large army who was invited in by the cities of Magna Graecia as a protector. From him we get the term 'Pyrrhic victories', for he outmatched the Romans in one battle after another, but was never able to follow up his advantage. After finally losing at Benevento in 275 BC, he quit and returned to Epirus, while the Romans took the deserted Greek cities one by one.

Now the conquest was complete. All along the Romans had been diabolically clever in managing their new demesne, maintaining most of the tribes and cities as nominally independent states, while planting Latin colonies everywhere (re-founded cities like Paestum, Ascoli Piceno, and Benevento were such colonies, together with new ones in the north like Florence). The great network of roads centred on Rome was extended with great speed, and a truly united Italy seemed close to becoming a reality.

268–91 BC: Empire Abroad, Disarray at Home

After all this, Rome deserved at least a shot at the Mediterranean heavyweight title. The current champ, the powerful merchant thalassocracy of Carthage, was alarmed enough at the successes of its precocious neighbour, and proved happy to oblige. Rome won the first bout, beating Carthage and her ally Syracuse in the **First Punic War** (264–41 BC), and gained Sicily, Sardinia, and Corsica. For the rematch, the **Second Punic War** (219–202 BC), Carthage sent **Hannibal** and his elephants from Spain into Italy over the Alps to bring the war into the Romans' backyard. Undeterred by the brilliant African general's victory at Cannae in 216 BC, where four legions were destroyed, the Romans hung on tenaciously even when Hannibal appeared at the gates of Rome. In Hannibal's absence, they took Spain and much of Africa, and after Scipio Africanus' victory at Zama in 202 BC, Carthage surrendered. The **Third Punic War** was a sorry affair. Rome only waited long enough for Carthage to miss a step in its treaty obligations before razing the city to the ground. The west conquered, Rome looked east. Already by 200 BC she had been interfering in Greek affairs. The disunited Greeks and successor states of Alexander's empire proved easy targets, and by 64 BC the legions were camped on the Cataracts of the Nile, in Jerusalem, and half across Asia Minor.

Nothing corrupts a state like easy conquests, and all this time things in Italy were going wrong. Taxation ceased for Roman citizens, as booty provided the state with all the revenues it needed, and tens of thousands of slaves were imported. Italy became a parasite nation. Vast amounts of cheap grain from Africa and Egypt ruined the Italian farmer, who had the choice of selling his freehold and becoming a sharecropper, joining the army, or moving to Rome as part of the burgeoning lumpen proletariat. The men who profited the most from the wars bought up tremendous amounts of land, turning Italy into a country of huge estates (*latifundia*), and becoming an aristocracy powerful enough to stifle any attempts at reform. Only Rome, of course, and a few other cities prospered. In this period many of the Greek and Etruscan towns withered. Many country districts became abandoned, and rural Italy knew constant famine and plagues, while in Rome the new rich were learning the delights of orgies, gladiatorial combats, and being carried about the streets by slaves.

Not that degeneracy and social disintegration had proceeded far enough for Italy to fail to resist. Rome, and indeed all Italy, divided into extremist factions: the reactionary 'Senatorial Party' and the radical 'Popular Party'. (The Senate and the senatorial class were not yet a nobility *per se*. A hefty fortune was all that was needed for entry. Their populist opponents included not only the poor, but most of the businessmen, and the hard-pressed middle class.) In 133 BC a remarkable reformer named **Tiberius Gracchus** was elected Tribune, but his plans for land reforms earned him assassination the following year. His brother **Gaius Gracchus** went even further when he gained the Tribunate in 123 BC, attempting to expand citizenship to most Italians; but he, too, was murdered after the Senate declared martial law that same year. By this time Rome's constitution was reduced to a travesty, and both sides realized that the only real power lay with the legions. The populists staked their hopes on **Gaius Marius**, an illiterate but good-hearted general who saved Italy from the last surprise Celtic raid in 113 BC. Marius' ascent to power proved a disappointment, and a whole new generation of populist statesmen was assassinated one by one.

91–31 BC: Sixty Years of Civil War

Italy had had enough; the year 91 saw a coordinated revolt among the southern peoples called the **Social Wars**, which was defeated by the campaigns of Marius and **Sulla** (the Senate's darling in the army), and by an offer to extend Roman citizenship to all Italians. A military coup by Sulla followed, with the backing of the Senate; it was the first time armed Roman soldiers ever actually entered Rome, a religious and constitutional taboo. However, when Sulla's army left for conquest and booty on the Black Sea, a populist counter-movement succeeded in taking power, and ruled Rome for the next three years. Sulla's triumphal return threw them out, and the haughty general unleashed a bloody reign of terror, unlike anything Italy had ever seen. An effective dictatorship was created, and all opponents either murdered or exiled (a redoubtable populist general named Quintus Sertorius still held Spain, and defeated five separate legions sent against him). Italy spiralled into anarchy, with many rural districts reverting to bandit-ridden wastelands, a setting for the remarkable revolt in 73 BC of **Spartacus**, an escaped gladiator who led a motley army of dispossessed farmers and runaway slaves—some 70,000 of them—back and forth across the south until the legions finally defeated him in 71 BC.

All this had exhausted both sides, and finally discredited senatorial rule. After Sulla's death, no one minded when the consulship and real power passed to **Pompey**, another successful general but one who cared little for politics. Like Sulla before him, Pompey soon set out for the east, where the most glory and booty were to be gained, and his departure left the stage in Rome open to 33-year-old **Julius Caesar**, a tremendously clever soldier-politician, but a good man anyhow. With his two surpassing talents, one for rhetoric and the other for attracting money, he took up the popular cause in better style than anyone had done it before. A taint of connection to the **Catiline conspiracy** of 68 BC, a revolt of adventurers, disaffected nobles, and other loose ends, proved a temporary setback, just as it advanced the fortunes of **Marcus Tullius Cicero**, the great orator, writer, and statesman who dreamed of founding a real republic with a real constitution, opposing both extreme parties and pinning his hopes on the still-surviving Italian middle class. Few people in Rome cared for such principles, however, and after Pompey returned from bashing the Pontic Kingdom and the Cilician pirates, he, Caesar, and a wealthy building contractor named Licinius Crassus sliced up the republic between them, forming the **First Triumvirate** in 59 BC.

What Caesar really wanted, of course, was a military command. Following the accepted practice, he managed to buy himself one in the north, and undertook the conquest of most of Gaul, with well-known results. When Pompey grew jealous and turned against him, Caesar led his army back into Italy, defying the Senate by 'crossing the Rubicon', the river boundary between Italy and Gaul that Roman armies were not allowed to cross without senatorial authorization. Resistance collapsed before him, and he became unchallenged master of Rome while not even holding public office. Pompey and most of the Senate fled to Greece, where Caesar caught up with them three years later. In his four years as ruler of Rome, Caesar surprised everyone, even his enemies; everything received a good dose of reform, even the calendar, and a beginning was made towards sorting out the economic mess and getting Italy back on its feet. His assassination by a clique of republican bitter-enders in 44 BC plunged Italy into civil war again, and left historians to ponder the grand question of whether Caesar

Italy: Ancient Cities

With Roman roads and a composite of major cities from 500BC-500AD

■ **CUMAE** Important Greek cities c.500BC

● CAERE Etruscan foundations

N

100 km
50 miles

Augusta Praetoria
Salassi
Segusio
Augusta Taurinorum
Comum
Cis Alpine
Mediolanum
Brixia
Cremona
Mantua
Parma
Ligures
Album Ingaunum
Luni
Pisae
Etruscans
VIA AURELIA
POPULONIA
VETULONIA
CLUSIUM
VOLCI
TARQUINIA
CAERE
Ostia
Antium
Anxur

Gauls
Tridentum
Verona
Patavium
Veneti
Aquileia
Tergeste
Bononia
Ravenna
Classe
VIA EMILIA
VIA ROMEA
Ariminium
Umbri
Fanum Fortunae
FAESULAE
ARRETIUM
VIA CASSIA
PERUSIA
Spoletium
VIA FLAMINIA
Picenti
Asculum
Sabines
VIA SALARIA
VEII
Tibur
Alba Fucens
Ortona
Rome
VIA TIBURTINA
Hernici
Sulmo
Latini
VIA CASALINA
Volscia
Ausonii
Samnites
Daunii
Sipontum

CUMAE
Puteoli
Pompeii
Cape Misenum
PITHECUSA
NEAPOLIS
SURRENTUM
Capua
Beneventum
Luceria
Venusia
Salernum
VIA APPIA
TARENTUM
Mesapians
Brentesion
Salentini
Leuca

ELEA
METAPONTUM

SYBARIS

CROTON
Bruttians
Magna Graecia

EPIZEPHRYEAN LOCRI
RHEGIUM

Siculans

SYRACUSE

47

had really intended to make himself a king and finally put the now senile republic to sleep. A **Second Triumvirate** was formed, of Caesar's adopted son Octavian, a senatorial figurehead named Lepidus, and Caesar's old friend and right-hand man, a talented, dissipated fellow named Marcus Antonius (Mark Antony), who according to one historian spent the equivalent of $3 billion (of other people's money) in his brief lifetime. While he dallied in the east with Cleopatra, Octavian was consolidating his power in Italy. The inevitable battle came in 31 BC, at Actium in Greece, and it was a complete victory for Octavian.

31 BC–AD 251: The Empire

With unchallenged authority through all the Roman lands, Octavian (soon to rename himself **Augustus**) was free to complete the reforms initiated by Caesar. He maintained the forms of the republic while accumulating enough titles and offices for himself to have constitutional justification for his absolute rule. The title he chose for public use was 'first citizen', while behind the scenes the machinery was being perfected for the deification of the Caesars (a practical policy in the eastern half of the empire, where such things were common practice), and for a stable monarchy after his death. It all worked brilliantly: peace was restored, an effective administration created, and Italy was able to recover from its time of troubles with the help of Augustus' huge programmes of public works.

For his career, and those of his successors, you may read the gossipy, shocking, and wonderfully unreliable *Lives of the Caesars* of Suetonius. All Rome tittered at the scandals of the later Julian Emperors, but reality was usually much more prosaic. **Tiberius** (AD 14–37) may have been a monster to his girlfriends and boyfriends, but he proved an intelligent and just ruler; his criminally insane successor **Caligula**, or 'Bootkin', lasted only four years (37–41) while the bureaucracy kept things going. **Claudius** (41–54) governed well and conquered southern Britain, while his stepson **Nero** (54–68) generally made a nuisance of himself in Rome but otherwise did little to disturb the system. Nevertheless, a commander in Spain (Galba) declared him unfit to be emperor and marched on Rome; Nero managed to commit suicide just before they caught him. Now the genie was out of the bottle again, as the soldiers once more realized that the real power lay with them. Another general, Otho, commander of the emperor's Praetorian Guard, toppled Galba, and soon lost out in turn to Vitellius, commander on the Rhine.

The fourth emperor of the fateful years AD 68–69 was **Vespasian**, leader of the eastern armies. He had the strongest legions and so got to keep the job; his reign (69–79) and those of his sons **Titus** (79–81) and **Domitian** (81–96), the three Flavian Emperors, were remembered as a period of prosperity. Vespasian began the Colosseum; whether intentionally or not, this incomparable new charnel house made a perfect symbol for the renewed decadence and militarization of the state.

For the moment, however, things looked rosy. After the assassination of Domitian, another bad boy but not an especially calamitous ruler, Rome had the good fortune to be ruled by a series of high-minded and intelligent military men, who carefully chose their successors in advance to avoid civil war. The so-called Antonine Emperors presided over the greatest age of prosperity the Mediterranean world ever knew; in Italy they ran a surprisingly modern state (though one still based on slave labour) that would seem familiar to us today: public libraries, water boards to maintain the aqueducts, rent control, agricultural price supports, low-cost loans for starting new businesses and many other such innovations. The first of the Antonines was **Nerva** (96–8), followed by **Trajan** (98–117) and **Hadrian** (117–38), they were both great soldiers and builders on a monumental scale, especially in Rome; after them came **Antoninus Pius** (138–61), little known only because his reign was so peaceful, and **Marcus Aurelius** (161–80), soldier, statesman, and Stoic philosopher. His choice for successor was his useless son **Commodus** (180–93) and the string of good emperors was broken.

The 2nd-century prosperity was not without its darker side. The arts were in serious decline, as if the imagination of the Greco-Roman Mediterranean was somehow failing. Education was in poor shape, and every sort of fatuous mysticism imported from the East permeated the minds of the people. Economically, this period saw the emergence of the well-known north-south split in Italy. The rural south, impoverished by the Roman Republic, now sank deeper into decline, while even the commerce of wealthy Campania began to fail, ruined by foreign competition. In the north, especially Cisalpine Gaul, a sounder, more stable economy led to the growth of new centres, Milan, Padua, Verona, and Ravenna the most prominent, beginning the economic divide that continues even today. In the balance, though, both politically and economically Italy was becoming an increasingly less significant part of the empire. Of the 2nd-century emperors, fewer came from Italy than from Spain, Illyria, or Africa.

251–475: Decline and Fall

For all it cost to maintain them, the legions were no longer the formidable military machine of Augustus' day. They were bureaucratic and a little tired, and their tactics and equipment were also falling behind those of the Persians and even some of the more clever German barbarians. The Goths were the first to demonstrate this, in 251, when they overran the Balkans, Greece, and Asia Minor. Five years later Franks and Alemanni invaded Gaul, and in 268 much of the east detached itself from the empire under the leadership of Odenathus of Palmyra. Somehow the empire recovered and prevailed, under dour soldier-emperors like **Aurelian** (270–75), who built Rome's walls, and **Diocletian** (284–305) who completely revamped the structure of the state and economy. His fiscal reforms, such as the fixing of prices and a decree that every son had to follow the trade of his father, ossified the economy and made the creeping decline of Italy and all western Europe harder to arrest. A gigantic bureaucracy was created, taxes reached new heights as people's ability to pay them declined, and society became increasingly militarized in every respect. The biggest change was the division of the empire into halves, each ruled by a co-emperor equally called 'Augustus'; Diocletian, significantly, chose the wealthier east for himself. The new western emperors usually kept their court at army headquarters in Mediolanum (Milan), and later at impregnable Ravenna on the Adriatic, and Rome itself became a marble-veneered backwater.

More than ever, the empire had become an outright military dictatorship, in a society whose waning energies were entirely devoted to supporting a bloated, all-devouring army and bureaucracy. Medieval feudalism actually had its origins in this period, as the remaining freehold farmers sold their lands and liberty to the local gentry—for protection's sake, but also to get off the tax rolls. In the cities, the high taxes and uncertain times ruined business and trade; throughout Italy and the West towns both large and small began their fatal declines. Diocletian reduced Italy to the status of a mere province, and the peninsula had little to do with imperial events thereafter. The confused politics of the 4th century are dominated by **Constantine** (306–337), who ruled both halves of the empire, defeated various other contenders (Battle of the Milvian

Bridge, outside Rome, in 312), and founded the eastern capital of Constantinople. He adroitly moved to increase his and the empire's political support by favouring Christianity. Though still a small minority in most of the empire, the Christians' strong organization and determination made them a good bet for the future. The religious revolution that followed was unexpected and remarkable. Diocletian had been the most ferocious of Christianity's persecutors; by 400, it was the turn of the pagans and Jews to be persecuted. In the next decades, as the empire's cities became Christianized, the Church itself became the most powerful and coherent instrument of the Roman élite.

The military disasters began in 406, with Visigoths, Franks, Vandals, Alans and Suevi overrunning Gaul and Spain. Italy's turn came in 408, when Western Emperor Honorius, ruling from the new capital of Ravenna, had his brilliant general Stilicho (who happened to be a Vandal) murdered. A Visigothic invasion followed, leading to Alaric's sack of Rome in 410. St Augustine, probably echoing the thoughts of most Romans, wrote that the end of the world must be near. Rome should have been so lucky; judgement was postponed long enough for **Attila the Hun** to pass through Italy in 451. Then Gaiseric the Vandal, who had set up a pirate kingdom in Africa, raided Italy and sacked Rome again in 455. So completely had things changed, it was scarcely possible to tell the Romans from the barbarians. By the 470s, the real ruler in Italy was a Gothic general named **Odoacer**, who led a half-Romanized Germanic army and probably thought of himself as the genuine heir of the Caesars. In 476 he decided to dispense with the lingering charade of the western empire. The last emperor, young, silly Romulus Augustulus, was packed off to premature retirement in Naples, and Odoacer was crowned King of Italy at Pavia.

475–1000: The Dark Ages

At the beginning, the new Gothic-Latin state showed some promise. Certainly the average man was no worse off than he had been under the last emperors; trade and cities even revived a bit. In 493, Odoacer was replaced (and murdered) by a rival Ostrogoth, **Theodoric**, nominally working on behalf of the eastern emperor at Byzantium. Theodoric proved a strong and able, though somewhat paranoid ruler; his court at Ravenna witnessed a minor rebirth of Latin letters with Cassiodorus, Symmachus, and the great Christian philosopher Boethius. Nevertheless, stability was compromised by religious quarrels between the Arian Christian Goths and the orthodox Catholic populations in the cities.

A disaster as serious as those of the 5th century began in 536, with the invasion of Italy by the Eastern Empire, part of the relentlessly expansionist policy of **Justinian**. The historical irony was profound; in the ancient homeland of the Roman Empire, Roman troops now came not as liberators, but foreign, largely Greek-speaking conquerors. His brilliant generals, Belisarius and Narses, ultimately prevailed over the Goths in a series of terrible wars that lasted until 563, but the damage to an already stricken society and economy was incalculable. Italy's total exhaustion was exposed only five years later, when the **Lombards**, a Germanic tribe that worked hard to earn the title of barbarian, overran northern Italy and parts of the south, establishing a kingdom at Pavia and separate duchies in Benevento and Spoleto. A new pattern of power appeared, with semi-independent Byzantine dukes defending many coastal areas, the Byzantine Exarchs of Ravenna controlling considerable territory on the Adriatic and in Calabria, and Lombard chiefs ruling most of the interior. The popes in Rome, occasionally allied with the Lombards against Byzantium, became a force during this period, especially after the papacy of the clever, determined **Gregory the Great** (590–604). Scion of the richest family in Italy, Gregory took political control in Rome during desperate times, and laid the foundations for the papacy's claims to temporal power.

With trade and culture at their lowest ebb, the 7th century marks the rock bottom of Italian history. The 8th showed some improvement; while most of the peninsula lay in feudal darkness, **Venice** was beginning its remarkable career as a trading city, and independent Amalfi and Naples emulated its success on the Tyrrhenian coast. The popes, along with other bishops who had taken advantage of the confused times to become temporal powers, intrigued everywhere to increase their influence; they finally cashed in with a Frankish alliance in the 750s. At the time the Lombard kings were doing well, finally conquering Ravenna (751) and considerable territories formerly under the dominion of the popes, who invited in **Charlemagne** to protect them. He eliminated the last Lombard king, Desiderius (his father-in-law, incidentally), and tucked all Italy as far south as Rome (with the exception of Venice) into his short-lived patchwork empire, sanctified by a papal coronation as the heir of the Roman Empire. A

Lombard Duchy of Benevento survived for centuries up in the mountains, and the Byzantines kept a tenuous hold on the heel and toe; the Greek villages and relics of troglodyte Greek monasticism in Calabria and Puglia date from this period. Arabs from Tunisia were beginning a gradual conquest of Sicily, and their raiders menaced all the peninsula's coasts; they sacked Rome itself in 746.

When Charlemagne's empire disintegrated following his death in 814, Italy reverted to a finely balanced anarchy. Altogether the 9th century was a bad time, with Italy caught between the Arab raiders and the endless wars of petty nobles and battling bishops in the north. The 10th century proved somewhat better—perhaps much better than the scanty chronicles of the time attest. Even in the worst times, Italy's cities never entirely disappeared. Sailing and trading overseas always lead to better technologies, new ideas and economic growth, and Italy's maritime cities had become the most advanced in Europe; even inland cities like Florence and Milan were developing a new economic importance and self-consciousness. Cities do not grow by magic in such unpromising times; even though few of them had managed to attain complete freedom of action, it is clear that even in the 900s many were looking to their own resources, defending their interests against the Church and nobles alike.

A big break for the cities, and for Italy, came in 961 with the invasion of the German **Otto the Great**, heir to the imperial pretensions of the Carolingians. He deposed the last feeble King of Italy, Berengar II of Ivrea, and was crowned Holy Roman Emperor in Rome the following year. Not that any of the Italians were happy to see him, but the strong government of Otto and his successors beat down the great nobles and allowed the growing cities to expand their power and influence. A new pattern was established; Germanic Emperors would be meddling in Italian affairs for centuries, not powerful enough to establish total control, but usually at least able to keep out important rivals.

1000–1154: The Rise of the *Comuni*

On the eve of the new millennium, most Christians were convinced that the turn of the calendar would bring with it the end of the world. If there had been economists and social scientists around, however, they would have had ample evidence to reassure everyone that things were looking up. Especially in the towns, business was very good, and the political prospects even brighter. The first mention of a truly independent comune (plural: comuni; a term used throughout this book, meaning a free city state; the best translation might be 'commonwealth') was in Milan, where in 1024 a popular assembly is recorded, deciding which side the city would take in the Imperial Wars.

Throughout this period the papacy had declined greatly in power and prestige, a political football kicked between the Emperors and the piratical Roman nobles. Beginning in the 1050s, a remarkable Tuscan monk named Hildebrand controlled papal policy, working behind the scenes to reassert the influence of the Church. When he became pope himself, in 1073, **Gregory VII** immediately set himself in conflict with the emperors over the issue of investiture—whether the church or secular powers could name church officials. The various Italian (and European) powers took sides on the issue, and 50 years of intermittent war followed, including the famous penance in the snow of Emperor Henry IV in Canossa (1077). The result was a big revival for the papacy, but more importantly the cities of Lombardy and the rest of the north used the opportunity to increase their influence, and in some cases achieve outright independence, defeating the local barons in war, razing their castles and forcing them to move inside the towns.

Southern Italy knew a different fate. The first **Normans** arrived about 1020, on pilgrimages to Monte Sant'Angelo in the Gargano. They liked the opportunities they saw for conquest, and soon younger sons of Norman feudal families were moving into the south, first as mercenaries but gradually gaining large tracts of land for themselves in exchange for their services. Usually allied to the popes, they soon controlled most of Puglia and Calabria. One of their greatest chiefs, **Roger de Hauteville**, began the conquest of Sicily from the Arabs in 1060, six years before William the Conqueror sailed for England. Roger eventually united all the south into the 'Kingdom of Sicily', and by the 1140s, under **Roger II**, this strange Norman-Arab-Italian state, with its glittering, half-oriental capital of Palermo, had become the cultural centre of the Mediterranean, as well as one of the strongest, best-organized states in Europe.

1154–1300: Guelphs and Ghibellines

While all this was happening, of course, the First Crusade (1097–1130) occupied the headlines. It was, in part, a result of the new militancy of the papacy begun by Gregory VII. For Italy, especially Pisa and Venice, the two states with plenty of boats to help ship Crusaders, the affair meant nothing but pure profit.

Trade was booming everywhere, and the accumulation of money helped the Italians to create modern Europe's first banking system. It also financed the continued independence of the comuni, which flourished everywhere, with a big enough surplus for building-projects like Pisa's cathedral complex, perhaps the biggest undertaking since the time of Trajan and Hadrian. Culture and science were flourishing, too, with a big boost from contact with the Byzantines and the Moslems of Spain and Africa. By the 12th century, far in advance of most of Europe, Italy had attained a prosperity unknown since Roman times. The classical past had never been forgotten—witness the attempt of Arnold of Brescia (1154) to recreate the Roman Republic. Similarly, free comuni in the north called their elected leaders 'consuls', and artists and architects turned ancient Roman styles into the Romanesque. Even Italian names were changing, an interesting sign of the beginnings of national consciousness; quite suddenly the public records (such as they were) show a marked shift from Germanic to classical and Biblical surnames: fewer Ugos, Othos, and Astolfos; more Giuseppes, Giovannis, Giulios, and Flavios.

Emperors and popes were still embroiled in the north. **Frederick I, Barbarossa** of the Hohenstaufen—or Swabian—dynasty, was strong enough in Germany, and he made it the cornerstone of his policy to reassert imperial power in Italy. Beginning in 1154, he crossed the Alps five times, molesting free cities that asked nothing more than the right to fight one another continually. He spread terror, utterly destroying Milan in 1161, but a united front of cities called the Lombard League defeated him in 1176. Frederick's greatest triumph in Italy came by arranging a marriage with the Normans, leaving his grandson **Frederick II** not only emperor but king of Sicily, giving him a strong power base in Italy itself.

The second Frederick's career dominated Italian politics for 30 years (1220–50). With his brilliant court, in which Italian was used for the first time (alongside Arabic and Latin), his half-Moslem army, his incredible processions of dancing girls, eunuchs, and elephants, he provided Europe with a spectacle the like of which it had never seen. Frederick founded universities (as at Naples), gave Sicily a written constitution (perhaps the world's first), and built geometrically arcane castles and towers all over the south. The popes excommunicated him at least twice. The battle of pope and emperor had become serious. All Italy divided into factions: the **Guelphs**, under the leadership of the popes, supported religious orthodoxy, the liberty of the *comuni*, and the interests of their emerging merchant class. The **Ghibellines** stood for the emperor, statist economic control, the interests of the rural nobles, and religious and intellectual tolerance. Frederick's campaigns and diplomacy in the north met with very limited success, and his death in 1250 left the outcome very much in doubt.

His son **Manfred**, not emperor but merely King of Sicily, took up the battle with better luck; Siena's defeat of Florence in 1260 gained that city and most of Tuscany for the Ghibellines. The next year, however, Pope Urban IV began an ultimately disastrous precedent by inviting in **Charles of Anjou**, a powerful, ambitious leader and brother of the King of France. As protector of the Guelphs, Charles defeated Manfred (1266) and murdered the last of the Hohenstaufens, Conradin (1268). He held unchallenged sway over Italy until 1282, when the famous revolt of the Sicilian Vespers started the party wars up again. By now, however, the terms Guelph and Ghibelline had ceased to have much meaning; men and cities changed sides as they found expedient, and the old parties began to seem like the black and white squares on a chessboard. If your neighbour and enemy were Guelph, you became for the moment Ghibelline, and if he changed so would you. (Strangely enough, black and white were respectively the Ghibelline and Guelph colours. They also had distinctive styles of architecture. When you see a castle in Italy with simple rectangular crenellations along the walls, you'll know that Guelphs built it; ornate 'swallow-tail' crenellations are Ghibelline.)

Some real changes did occur out of all this sound and fury. In 1204 Venice hit its all-time biggest jackpot when it diverted the Fourth Crusade to the sack of Constantinople, winning for itself a small empire of islands in the Adriatic and Levant. Genoa emerged as its greatest rival in 1284, when its fleet put an end to Pisa's prominence at the Battle of Meloria. And elsewhere around the peninsula, some cities were falling under the rule of military *signori* whose descendants would be styling themselves counts and dukes—the Visconti of Milan, the della Scala of Verona, the Malatesta of Rimini. Everywhere the freedom of the *comuni* was in jeopardy; after so much useless strife the temptation to submit to a strong leader often proved overwhelming. During Charles of Anjou's reign the popes extracted the price for their invitation. The Papal State, including much of central Italy, was established in 1278. But most importantly, the Italian

economy never seemed to mind the trouble. Trade and money flowed as never before; cities built new cathedrals and created themselves incredible skyscraper skylines, with the tall tower-fortresses of the now urbanized nobles. And it was, in spite of everything, a great age for culture—the era of Guelphs and Ghibellines was also the time of Dante (b. 1265) and Giotto (b. 1266).

1300–1494: Renaissance Italy

This paradoxical Italy continued into the 14th century, with a golden age of culture and an opulent economy side by side with almost continuous war and turmoil. With no serious threats from the emperors or any other foreign power, the myriad Italian states were able to menace each other without outside interference. One of the secrets to this state of affairs was that war had become a sort of game, conducted on behalf of cities by bands of paid mercenaries led by a *condottiere*, who were never allowed to enter the cities. The arrangement suited everyone. The soldiers had lovely horses and armour, and no real desire to do each other serious harm. The cities were usually free from grand ambitions; everyone was making too much money to want to wreck the system. Without heavy artillery, walled towns and castles were nearly impossible to take, making the incentives to try hard even less. Best of all, the worst schemers and troublemakers on the Italian stage were fortuitously removed from the scene. Shortly after the election of the French Pope Clement V in 1305, the papacy moved to Avignon, becoming a puppet of the French king that temporarily had little influence in Italian affairs.

By far the biggest event of the 14th century was the **Black Death** of 1347–48, in which it is estimated Italy lost one-third of its population. The shock brought a rude halt to what had been 400 years of almost continuous growth and prosperity, though its effects did not prove a permanent setback for the economy. In fact, the plague's grim joke was that it actually made life better for most of the Italians who survived; working people in the cities, no longer overcrowded, found their rents lower and their labour worth more, while in the country farmers were able to increase their profits by only tilling the best land.

It is impossible to speak of 'Italian history' in this period, with the peninsula split up into long-established, cohesive states pursuing different ends and warring against one another. Italian statesmen understood the idea of a balance of power long before political theorists invented the term, and, despite all the clatter and noise, most probably believed Italy was enjoying the best of all possible worlds. Four major states, each a European power in its own right, dominated the region's politics: first **Venice**, the oldest and most glorious, with its oligarchic but singularly effective constitution, and its exotic career of trade with the East. The Venetians waged a series of wars against arch-rival Genoa, finally exhausting her after the War of Chioggia in 1379. After that, they felt strong enough to make a major change in policy. Once serenely aloof from Italian politics, Venice now carved out a small land empire for itself, by 1428 including Verona, Padua, Vicenza, Brescia and Bergamo.

Florence, the richest city-state thanks to its banking and wool trade, also enjoyed good fortune, extending its control over most of Tuscany, and gaining a seaport with its conquest of now decadent Pisa in 1406. In 1434, **Cosimo de' Medici**, head of the largest

banking house, succeeded in establishing a de facto dictatorship. Even though the forms of the old Republic were maintained, Florence was well on its way to becoming a signorial state like its greatest rival, **Milan**. Under the Visconti, Milan had become rich and powerful, basing its success on the manufactures of the city (arms and textiles) and the bountiful, progressively managed agriculture of southern Lombardy. Its greatest glory came during the reign of **Gian Galeazzo Visconti** (1385–1402), who bought himself a ducal title from the Emperor and nearly conquered all north Italy, before his untimely death caused his plans to unravel.

In the south, the huge **Kingdom of Naples** suffered from the heritage of the Normans, who had made it the only part of Italy where north-European-style feudalism had ever taken root. When times changed, the backward rural barons who dominated the south held back its commerce and its culture. Despite promising periods such as the reign of the King of Aragon, **Alfonso the Magnanimous** (1442–58), a Renaissance prince and patron of the arts who seized Naples and added it to his domains, the south was falling far behind the rest of Italy. The other Italian states included Genoa, a nasty little oligarchy that made money but contributed nothing to the cultural life of the times; the Duchy of Savoy-Piedmont, a quiet backwater still more closely tied to France than Italy; the tiny, stalwart Republics of

Lucca and Siena; refined independent courts in Ferrara, Mantua, Modena and Rimini, surviving the rough seas of Italian politics; and finally the Papal States, anarchic while the popes were in France (until 1378), and woefully misgoverned when they came back.

And what of the Renaissance? No word has ever caused more mischief for the understanding of history and culture—as if Italy had been Sleeping Beauty, waiting for some Prince Charming of classical culture to come and awaken it from a 1000-year nap. On the contrary, Italy even in the 1200s was richer, more technologically advanced, and far more artistically creative than it had ever been in the days of the Caesars. The new art and scholarship that began in Florence in the 1400s and spread across the nation grew from a solid foundation of medieval accomplishment. The gilded, opulent Italy of the 15th century felt complacently secure in its long-established cultural and economic pre-eminence. A long spell of freedom from outside interference lulled the nation into believing that its political disunity could continue safely forever; except perhaps for the sanguinely realistic Florentine Niccolò Machiavelli, no one realized that Italy in fact was a plum waiting to be picked.

1494–1529: The Wars of Italy

The Italians brought the trouble down on themselves, when Duke Lodovico Sforza of Milan invited the French King Charles VIII to cross the Alps and assert his claim to the throne of Milan's enemy, Naples. Charles did just that, and the failure of the combined Italian states to stop him (at the inconclusive Battle of Fornovo, 1494) showed just how helpless Italy was at the hands of emerging monarchies like France or Spain. When the Spaniards saw how easy it was, they, too, marched in, and restored Naples to its Spanish king the following year (an Aragonese dynasty, cousins to Ferdinand and Isabella, had ruled Naples since 1442). Before long the German emperor and even the Swiss entered this new market for Italian real estate. The popes did as much as anyone to keep the pot boiling. Alexander VI and his son Cesare Borgia carried the war across central Italy in an attempt to found a new state for the Borgia family, and Julius II's madcap policy led him to egg on the Swiss, French and Spaniards in turn, before finally crying 'Out with the barbarians!' when it was already too late.

By 1516, with the French ruling Milan and the Spanish in control of the south, it seemed as if a settlement would be possible. The worst possible luck for Italy, however, came with the accession of the insatiable megalomaniac **Charles V** to the throne of Spain in that year; in 1519 he bought himself the crown of the Holy Roman Empire, making him the most powerful ruler in Europe since Charlemagne. Charles felt he needed Milan as a base for communications between his Spanish, German and Flemish possessions, and as soon as he had emptied Spain's treasury, driven her to revolt, and plunged Germany into civil war, he turned his attentions to Italy. The wars began anew, bloodier than anything Italy had seen for centuries, climaxing with the defeat of the French at Pavia in 1525, and the sack of Rome by an out-of-control imperial army in 1527. The French invaded once more, in 1529, and were defeated this time at Naples by the treachery of their Genoese allies. All Italy, save only Venice, was now at the mercy of Charles and the Spaniards.

1529–1600: Italy in Chains

The final treaties left Spanish viceroys in Milan and Naples, and pliant dukes and counts toeing the Spanish line almost everywhere else. Besides Venice and the very careful Republic of Lucca, the last bastions of Italian liberty were Siena and Florence, where the Medici had been thrown out and the Republic re-established. Charles' army besieged and took the city in 1530, giving it back to the Medici, who gained the title of Grand Dukes of Tuscany. They collaborated with Spain in extinguishing Siena's independence, despite a desperate resistance of seven years (1552–59), and the new Medici state assumed roughly the borders of Tuscany today.

The broader context of these events, of course, was the bitter struggles of the Reformation and Counter-Reformation. In Italy, the new religious angle made the Spaniards and the popes natural allies. One had the difficult job of breaking the spirit of a nation that, though conquered, was still wealthy, culturally sophisticated and ready to resist; the other saw an opportunity to recapture by force the hearts and minds it had lost long before. With the majority of the peninsula still nominally controlled by local rulers, and an economy that continued to be sound, both the Spanish and the popes realized that the only real threat would come not from men, but from ideas. Under the banner of combating Protestantism, they commenced a reign of terror across Italy. In the 1550s, the revived Inquisition began its manhunt for free-thinkers of every variety; the Index of Prohibited Books followed in 1559 (some works of Dante included), accompanied by public book-burnings in Rome and elsewhere. A long line of

Italian intellectuals trudged to the stake, while many more buried their convictions or left for exile in Germany or England. The job of re-educating Italy was put in the hands of the new Jesuit order; their schools and propaganda campaigns bore the popes' message deeply into the Italian mind, while their sumptuous new churches, spectacles and dramatic sermons helped redefine Catholicism.

Despite the oppression, the average Italian at first had little to complain about. Spanish domination brought peace and order to a country that had long been a madhouse of conflicting ambitions. Renaissance artists attained a virtuosity never seen before, just in time to embellish the scores of new churches, palaces and villas of the mid 16th-century building boom. The combined Christian forces had turned back the Turkish threat at Malta (1566) and Lepanto (1571), and some Italians were benefiting to a great extent from Spanish imperialism in the New World—especially the Genoese, who rented ships, floated loans and even snatched up a surprising amount of the gold and silver arriving from America.

1600–1796: The Age of Baroque

However, the first signs of decay were already apparent. Palladio's country villas for the Venetian magnates, and Michelozzo's outside Florence, are landmarks in architecture but also one of the earliest symptoms. In both cities, the old mercantile economies were failing, and the wealthy began to invest their money unproductively in land instead of risking it in business or finance. Venice, between its wars with the Turks and its loss of the spice trade when the Portuguese discovered the route to the Indies, suffered the most. By 1650 she no longer had an important role to play in European affairs, though the Venetians kept their heads and made their inevitable descent into decadence a serene and enjoyable one.

The troubles were not limited to these two cities. After 1600 nearly everything started to go wrong for the Italians. The textiles and banking of the north, long the engines of the economy, both withered in the face of foreign competition, and the old port towns (with the exceptions of Genoa and the new city of Livorno) began to look half empty as the English and Dutch muscled them out of the declining Mediterranean trade. Worst off of all was the south, under direct Spanish or papal rule. Combining incompetence and brutality with outrageously high taxes (the Spaniards' to finance foreign wars, the popes' to build up Rome), they rapidly turned the already poor south into a nightmare of anarchic depravity, haunted by legions of bandits and beggars, and controlled more tightly than ever by its violent feudal barons. To everyone's surprise, the south rose up and staged an epic rebellion. Beginning in Naples (Masaniello's Revolt, 1647), the disturbances soon spread all over the south and Sicily. For over a year peasant militias ruled some areas, and makeshift revolutionary councils defended the cities. When the Spanish finally defeated them, however, they massacred some 18,000, and tightened the screws more then ever.

Bullied, humiliated and increasingly impoverished, 17th-century Italy at least tried hard to keep up its ancient prominence in the arts and sciences. Galileo Galilei looked through telescopes, Monteverdi wrote the first operas, and hun-dreds of talented though uninspired artists cranked out pretty pictures to meet the continuing high demand. Bernini and Borromini turned Rome into the capital of Baroque—the florid, expensive coloratura style that serves as a perfect symbol for the age itself, an age of political repression and thought control where art became a political tool. Baroque's heavenly grandeur and symmetry helped to impress everyone with the majesty of Church and State. At the same time, Baroque scholars wrote books that went on for hundreds of pages without saying anything, but avoided offending the government and the Inquisition. Baroque impresarios managed the wonderful pageantry of Church holidays, state occasions and carnivals that kept the ragged crowds amused. Manners and clothing became decorously berserk, and a race for easily bought noble titles occurred that would have made a medieval Italian laugh out loud. Italy was being rocked to sleep in a Baroque cradle.

By the 18th century, there were very few painters, or scholars, or scientists. There were no more heroic revolts either. Italy in this period hardly has any history at all; with Spain's increasing decadence, the great powers decided the futures of Italy's major states, and used the minor ones as a kind of overflow tank to hold surplus princes and those dispossessed by wars elsewhere (Napoleon on Elba was the last and most

famous of these). In 1713, after the War of the Spanish Succession, the Habsburgs of **Austria** came into control of Milan and Lombardy, Mantua and the Kingdom of Naples. The House of Lorraine, related to the Austrians, won Tuscany upon the extinction of the Medici in 1737.

These new rulers improved conditions somewhat. Especially during the reigns of the Empress Maria Theresa (1740–80) and her son Joseph II (1780–92), two of the most likeable Enlightenment despots, Lombardy and the other Austrian possessions underwent serious, intelligent economic reforms—giving them the head-start over the rest of Italy that helped Milan to its industrial prominence today. Naples' hard luck continued when the Austrians transferred it to a branch of the House of Bourbon (1731); under them the southern kingdom was independent, but just as poorly governed as before. A new player in Italian affairs, and from the start an important one, was **Piedmont**, which during the War of the Austrian Succession shook loose from the tutelage of France and joined the winning side, earning a royal title in 1720 for **Vittorio Amedeo II**. The infant kingdom, with its brand-new capital of Turin, was poor and a little backward in many ways, but as the only strong and free state in Italy it would be able to play the leading role in the events of the next century, and in Italian unification.

1796–1830: Napoleon, Restoration and Reaction

Napoleon, that greatest of Italian generals, arrived in Italy in 1796 on behalf of the French revolutionary Directorate, sweeping away the Piedmontese and Austrians and setting up republics in Lombardy (the 'Cisalpine Republic'), Liguria, and Naples (the 'Parthenopean Republic'). Italy woke with a start from its Baroque slumbers, and local patriots gaily joined the French cause. In 1799, however, while Napoleon was off in Egypt, the advance through Italy by an Austro-Russian army, aided by Nelson's fleet, restored the status quo. This was often accompanied by bloody reprisals, as peasant mobs led by clerics like the 'Army of the Holy Faith' marched across the south massacring liberals and French sympathizers.

In 1800 Napoleon returned in a campaign that saw the great victory at Marengo, giving him the opportunity once more to reorganize Italian affairs. He crowned himself King of Italy; Joseph Bonaparte and later Joachim Murat ruled at Naples. Elisa Bonaparte and her husband got Tuscany. Rome was annexed to France, and the pope was carted off to Fontainebleau. Napoleonic rule lasted only until 1814, but in that time important public works were begun and laws, education and everything else reformed after the French model; immense Church properties were expropriated, and medieval relics everywhere put to rest—including the Venetian Republic, which Napoleon for some reason took a special delight in liquidating. The French, however, soon wore out their welcome. Besides hauling much of Italy's artistic heritage off to the Louvre, implementing high war taxes and conscription (some 25,000 Italians died in the invasion of Russia), and brutally repressing a number of local revolts, they systematically exploited Italy for the benefit of the Napoleonic élite and the crowds of speculators who came flocking over the Alps. When the Austrians and English came to chase all the little Napoleons out, no one was sad to see them go.

The experience, though, had given Italians a taste of the opportunities offered by the modern world, as well as a sense of national feeling that had been suppressed for centuries. The 1815 Congress of Vienna put the clock back to 1796; indeed the Habsburgs and Bourbons seemed to think they could pretend the Napoleonic upheavals never happened, and the political reaction in their territories was fierce. The only major change from the *ancien régime* was that Venice and its inland empire now belonged to Austria. (Two name changes help to confuse students of this period; Piedmont is often referred to as the 'Kingdom of Sardinia', and Naples acquired the name 'Kingdom of the Two Sicilies'.)

Almost immediately, revolutionary agitators and secret societies like the famous *Carbonari* emerged that would keep Italy convulsed in plots and intrigues. A large-scale revolt in Naples forced the reactionary King Ferdinand to grant a constitution (1821), but when Austrian troops came down to crush the rebels he revoked it. The French July Revolution of 1830 also spread to Italy, encouraged by the liberal King **Carlo Alberto** in Piedmont-Savoy, but once more the universally hated Austrians intervened.

1848–1915: The Risorgimento and United Italy

Conspirators of every colour and shape, including the legendary **Giuseppe Mazzini**, had to wait another 18 years for their next chance. Mazzini, a sincere patriot and democrat, agitated frenetically all through the years 1830–70, beginning by founding the *Young Italy*

movement. Generally followed by a small cloud of cops and spies, Mazzini started parties, issued manifestos, plotted dozens of doomed revolts, defined great theories and strategies, checked in and out of exile, and chaired meetings of eternal committees, all with little practical effect. In retrospect, his career as a revolutionary can bear a slight comparison to Marx's—though less Karl than Groucho. It was typical of the times, and the disarray and futility among republicans, radicals, and those who simply wanted a united Italy set the stage for the stumbling, divisive process of the Risorgimento.

The big change came in the revolutionary year of 1848, when risings in Palermo and Naples (in January) anticipated even those in Paris itself. Soon all Italy was in the streets. Piedmont and Tuscany won constitutions from their rulers, and the people of Milan chased out the Austrians after a month of extremely bloody fighting; at the same time the Venetian Republic was restored. Carlo Alberto, the hope of most Italians for a war of liberation, marched against the Austrians, but his two badly bungled campaigns allowed the enemy to re-establish control over the peninsula. By June 1849, only Venice, under Austrian blockade, and the recently declared Roman Republic were left. Rome, led by Mazzini, and with a small army under **Giuseppe Garibaldi**, a former sailor who had fought in the wars of independence in Latin America, beat off several attacks from foreign troops invited in by the Pope. The republic finally succumbed to a large force sent by, of all people, the republic of President Louis Napoleon (soon to declare himself Napoleon III) in France. Garibaldi's dramatic escape to safety in San Marino (he was trying to reach Venice, itself soon to surrender) gave the Risorgimento one of its great heroic myths.

Despite failure on a grand scale, at least the Italians knew they would get another chance. Unification was inevitable, but there were two irreconcilable contenders for the honour of accomplishing it. On one side, the democrats and radicals dreamed of a truly reborn, revolutionary Italy, and looked to the popular hero Garibaldi to deliver it; on the other, moderates wanted the Piedmontese to do the job, ensuring a stable future by making **Vittorio Emanuele II** King of Italy. Vittorio Emanuele's minister, the polished, clever **Count Camillo Cavour**, spent the 1850s getting Piedmont in shape for the struggle, building its economy and army, participating in the Crimean War to earn diplomatic support, and plotting with the

French for an alliance against Austria.

War came in 1859, and French armies did most of the work in conquering Lombardy. Tuscany and Emilia revolted, and Piedmont was able to annex all three. In May 1860, Garibaldi and his red-shirted 'Thousand' sailed from Genoa (Cavour almost stopped them at the last minute), landed in Sicily, and electrified Europe by repeatedly beating the Bourbon forces in a quick march across the island. The Thousand had become 20,000, and when they crossed the straits bound for Naples it was clear that the affair was reaching its climax. On 7 September, Garibaldi entered Naples, and though he proclaimed himself temporary dictator on behalf of Vittorio Emanuele, the Piedmontese were alarmed enough to occupy Umbria and the Marche. The King met Garibaldi on 27 October, near Teano, and after finding out what little regard the Piedmontese had for him, the greatest and least self-interested leader modern Italy has known went off to retirement on the island of Caprara.

Just as the French made all this possible, some more unexpected help from outside allowed the new Italy to add two missing pieces and complete its unification. When the Prussians defeated Austria in the war of 1866, Italy was able to seize the Veneto. Only Rome was left, defended by a French garrison, and when the Prussians beat France at Sedan in 1870, the Italian army marched into Rome almost without opposition.

The first decades of the Italian Kingdom were just as unimpressive as its wars of independence. A liberal constitutional monarchy was established, but the parliament almost immediately decomposed into cliques and political cartels representing various interests. Finances started in disorder and stayed that way, and corruption became widespread. Peasant revolts occurred in the south, as people felt cheated by inaction after the promises of the Risorgimento, and organized brigandage became a problem, partially instigated by the Vatican as part of an all-out attempt to discredit the new regime. The outlines of foreign policy often seemed to change monthly, though like the other European powers Italy felt it necessary to snatch up some colonies. The attempt revealed the new state's limited capabilities, with embarrassing military disasters at the hands of the Ethiopians at Dogali in 1887, and again at Adowa in 1896.

After 1900, with the rise of a strong socialist movement, strikes, riots, and police repression often occupied centre stage in Italian politics. Even so, important signs of progress, such as the big new industries in Turin and Milan, showed that at least the northern half of Italy was becoming a fully integral part of the European economy. The 15 years before the war, prosperous and contented ones for many, came to be known by the slightly derogatory term *Italietta*, the 'little Italy' of modest bourgeois happiness, an age of sweet Puccini operas, the first motorcars, blooming 'Liberty'-style architecture, and Sunday afternoons at the beach.

1915–1945: War, Fascism, and War

Italy could have stayed out of the First World War, but let the chance to do so go by for the usual reasons—a hope of gaining some new territory, especially Trieste. Also, a certain segment of the intelligentsia found the *Italietta* boring and disgraceful: irredentists of all stripes, some of the artistic futurists, and the perverse, idolized poet **Gabriele D'Annunzio**. The groups helped Italy leap blindly into the conflict in 1915, with a big promise of boundary adjustments dangled by the beleaguered Allies. Italian armies fought with their accustomed flair, masterminding an utter catastrophe at Caporetto (October 1917) that any other nation but Austria would have parleyed into a total victory. No thanks to their incompetent generals, the poorly armed and equipped Italians somehow held firm for another year, until the total exhaustion of Austria allowed them to prevail (at the battle of *Vittorio Veneto* you see so many streets named after), capturing some 600,000 prisoners in November 1918.

In return for 650,000 dead, a million casualties, severe privation on the home front, and a war debt higher than anyone could count, Italy received Trieste, Gorizia, the South Tyrol, and a few other scraps. Italians felt they had been cheated, and nationalist sentiment increased, especially when D'Annunzio led a band of freebooters to seize the half-Italian city of Fiume in September 1919, after the peace conferences had promised it to Yugoslavia. The Italian economy was in shambles, and, at least in the north, revolution was in the air; workers in Turin raised the Red Flag over the Fiat plants and organized themselves into soviets. The troubles had encouraged extremists of both right and left, and many Italians became convinced that the liberal state was finished.

Enter **Benito Mussolini**, a professional intriguer in the Mazzini tradition with bad manners and no fixed principles. Before the War he had found his real talent as editor of the Socialist Party paper *Avanti*—the best it ever had, tripling the circulation in a year. When he decided that what Italy really needed was war, he left to found a new paper, and contributed mightily to the jingoist agitation of 1915. In the post-War confusion, he found his opportunity. A little bit at a time, he developed the idea of **fascism**, at first less a philosophy than an astute use of mass propaganda and a sense for design. (The *fasci*, from which the name comes, were bundles of rods carried before ancient Roman officials, a symbol of authority. *Fascii* also referred to organized bands of rebellious peasants in 19th-century Sicily.) With a little discreet money supplied by frightened industrialists, Mussolini had no trouble in recruiting for his black-shirted gangs, who found their first success beating up Slavs in Trieste and working as a sort of private police for landowners in stoutly socialist Emilia-Romagna.

The basic principle, combining left- and right-wing extremism into something the ruling classes could live with, proved attractive to many, and a series of weak governments stood by while the fascist *squadre* cast their shadow over more and more of Italy. Mussolini's accession to power came on an improbable gamble. In the particularly anarchic month of October 1922, he announced that his followers would march on Rome. King Vittorio Emanuele III refused to sign a decree of martial law to disperse them, and there was nothing to do but offer Mussolini the post of prime minister. At first, he governed Italy with undeniable competence. Order was restored, and the economy and foreign policy were handled intelligently by non-fascist professionals. In the 1924 elections, despite the flagrant rigging and intimidation, the Fascists only won a slight majority. One politician who was not intimidated was Giacomo Matteotti, and when some of Mussolini's close associates murdered him, a major scandal erupted. Mussolini survived it, and during 1925 and 1926 the Fascists used parliamentary methods to convert Italy into a permanent fascist dictatorship.

Compared to the governments that preceded him, Mussolini looked quite impressive. Industry advanced, great public works were undertaken, with special care towards the backward south, and the Mafia took some heavy blows at the hands of a determined Sicilian prefect named Mori. The most lasting achievement was the Concordat of 1929 with the pope, founding the Vatican State and ending the Church's isolation from Italian affairs. The regime evolved a new economic philosophy, the 'corporate state', where labour and capital were supposed to live in harmony under syndicalist government control. But the longer

fascism lasted, the more unreal it seemed to be, a patchwork government of Mussolini and his ageing cronies, magnified and rendered heroic by cinematic technique—stirring rhetoric before oceanic crowds, colourful pageantry, magnificent, larger-than-life post offices and railway stations built of travertine and marble, dashing aviators and winsome gymnasts from the fascist youth groups on parade. In a way it was the Baroque all over again, and Italians tried not to think about the consequences. In the words of one of Mussolini's favourite slogans, painted on walls all over Italy, 'Whoever stops is lost'.

Mussolini couldn't stop, and the only possibility for new diversions lay with the chance of conquest and empire. His invasion of Ethiopia and his meddling in the Spanish Civil War, both in 1936, compromised Italy into a close alliance with Nazi Germany. Mussolini's confidence and rhetoric never faltered as he led an entirely unprepared nation into the biggest war ever. Once more, Italian ineptitude at warfare produced embarrassing defeats on all fronts, and only German intervention in Greece and North Africa saved Italy from being knocked out of the War as early as 1941. The Allies invaded Sicily in July 1943, and the Italians began to look for a clever way out. They seized Mussolini during a meeting of the Grand Council, packed him into an ambulance and sent him off first to Ponza, then to a little ski hotel up in the Apennines. The new government under Marshal Badoglio didn't know what to do, and confusion reigned supreme.

While British and American forces slogged northwards, in this ghetto of the European theatre, with the help of the Free French, Brazilians, Costa Ricans, Poles, Czechs, New Zealanders and Norwegians, the Germans poured in divisions to defend the peninsula. They rescued Mussolini, and set him up in a puppet state called the Italian Social Republic in the north. In September 1943, the Badoglio government signed an armistice with the Allies, too late to keep the War from dragging on another year and a half, as the Germans made good use of Italy's difficult terrain to slow the Allied advance. Meanwhile Italy finally gave itself something to be proud of, a determined, resourceful Resistance that established free zones in many areas, and harassed the Germans with sabotage and strikes. The *partigiani* caught Mussolini in April 1945, while he was trying to escape to Switzerland; after shooting him and his mistress, they hung him by his feet from the roof of a petrol station in Milan.

1945–the Present

Post-war Italian *cinema verità*—Rossellini's *Rome, Open City*, or de Sica's *Bicycle Thieves*—captures the atmosphere better than words ever could. In a period of serious hardships that older Italians still remember, the nation slowly picked itself up and returned to normal. A referendum in June 1946 made IItaly a Republic, but only by a narrow margin. The first governments fell to the new Christian Democrat Party under Alcide de Gasperi, which ran the show for decades with a preposterous band of smaller parties. The main opposition was provided by the Communists, surely one of the most remarkable parties of modern European history. With the heritage of the only important socialist philosopher since Marx, Antonio Gramsci, and the democratic and broadminded leader Enrico Berlinguer, Italian communism is unique, with its stronghold and showcase in the well-run, prosperous cities of Emilia-Romagna.

The 50s was Rome's decade, when Italian style and Italian cinema caught the imagination of the world. Gradually, slowly, a little economic miracle was happening; *Signor Rossi*, the average Italian, started buzzing around in his first classic Fiat *cinquecento*, northern industries boomed, and life cruised slowly back to normal. The south continued to lag behind, despite the sincere efforts of the government and its special planning fund, the *Cassa per il Mezzogiorno*. Though the extreme poverty and despair of the postwar years gradually disappeared, today there is still little evidence that the region is catching up with the rest of Italy. Nationally, the *Democristiani*-controlled government soon evolved a Byzantine style of politics that only an Italian could understand. Through the constantly collapsing and reforming cabinets, nothing changed; all deals were made in the back rooms and everyone, from the Pope to the Communists, had a share in the decision-making. One wouldn't call it democracy with a straight face, but for four decades it worked well enough to keep Italy on its wheels. The dark side of the arrangement was the all-pervasive corruption that the system fostered. It is fascinating to read the work of journalists only a few years ago, seeing how almost without exception they would politely sidestep the facts; Italy was run by an unprincipled political machine, whose members were raking in as much for themselves as they could grab, and everyone knew it, only it couldn't be said openly, for lack of proof. Even more sinister was the extent to which the machine would go to keep on top. The 70s,

Italy's 'years of lead', witnessed the worst of the political sleaze, along with a grim reign of terrorism, culminating in the kidnapping and murder in 1978 of an honourable Christian Democrat prime minister, Aldo Moro. All along, the attacks were attributed to 'leftist groups', though even at the time many suspected that some of the highest circles in the government and army were controlling or manipulating them, with the possible collusion of the CIA. They were indeed, and only recently has some of the truth begun to seep out. On another front, Italians woke up one morning in 1992 to find that the government had magically vacuumed 7 per cent of the money out of all their savings accounts, an 'emergency measure' to meet the nation's colossal budget deficit—a deficit caused largely by the thievery of the political class and its allies in organized crime.

Italians are a patient lot but, as everyone knows, the lid has blown off, and at the time of writing Italy is well into a very Italian sort of revolution. The business started in the judiciary, the one independent and relatively uncorrupt part of the government. In the early 90s, heroic prosecutors Giovanni Falcone and Paolo Borsellino went after the Sicilian Mafia with some success, and were spectacularly assassinated for it, causing national outrage. Meanwhile, in Milan, a small group of prosecutors and judges found a minor political kickback scandal that has led them, through years of quiet and painstaking work, to the golden string that unravelled the whole rotten tangle of Italian political depravity—what Italians call the *tangentopoli*, or 'bribe city'. For over a year, the televised hearings of Judge Antonio Di Pietro and his Operation *Mani Pulite* ('clean hands') team from Milan were the nation's favourite and most fascinating serial.

All the kingpins fell, notably Socialist leader Bettino Craxi (hiding from extradition in Tunisia). Others, especially former prime minister Giulio Andreotti, have lost their parliamentary immunity. Andreotti is currently on trial on two counts—firstly for his association with the Mafia and secondly for his involvement with the assassination of a journalist (for which he could receive live imprisonment). The two ruling parties, the Christian Democrats and the Socialists, are dead; the 1993 municipal elections, held at the height of the *tangentopoli* hearings, were nearly a sweep for the PDS, the old Communists, beating the neo-fascist MSI and the Lega, the new regional party that has grown up in the north based on a resentment of corruption—and of southern Italian migrants.

Other forces on the scene included the enigmatic Mario Segni, who led a successful drive for constitutional reform of the electoral system, and most surprising of all, Silvio Berlusconi, the television and publishing magnate (and former protégé of Craxi) whose near-monopolies were seriously threatened by a possible PDS government. Berlusconi thinks big—the only way out was to buy the government for himself. He used his big bankroll and control of television to create a new, totally synthetic party, called Forza Italia, and his pitchmen sold it to Italians the same way they sell them soap and sex every day. Meanwhile, Berlusconi managed an improbable three-way alliance with the MSI and the Lega. It all worked brilliantly. In the parliamentary elections of 1994, the first of what many Italians called their 'Second Republic', Berlusconi's rightist alliance won an impressive victory, and 'Mr Television' himself became prime minister.

In reality, it soon became apparent that government under Berlusconi only meant business as usual. The media mogul's refusal to distance himself from his communications empire while in office, and his heavy-handed attempt to cripple the *Mani Pulite* investigators, made many Italians feel the egg on their faces—they had struggled so hard to topple a malodorous old order, only to merrily vote it back into office at the first chance.

It wasn't long before Judge di Pietro resigned from the *Mani Pulite* investigations, under a cloud of phony political allegations, to be followed in turn by Berlusconi himself, who—surrounded by his own fog of allegations of scandal and bribery—was forced out of office in early 1995 when Bossi withdrew his support. The political mess that remained was such that President Scalfaro followed the medieval Italian custom of calling in a political outsider to straighten out the country and institute the reforms that the politicians were incapable of. This was a banker, Lamberto Dini, whose lack of a political past and steady head were virtues enough to keep him in office while the politicians got their house in order.

To many Italians it began to seem as if the only way out of the imbroglio created by their own fragmented political system was to anchor their country as firmly as possible in Europe. Feeling very much like a founding parent of the European Union, in the Treaty of Rome, it came as a blow when German bankers publicly stated that it was very improbable indeed that Italy would meet the economic requirements to join in the new European currency.

Dini, the finance man, started the reforms, but it was Romano Prodi and his leftish-centre Olive Tree Party, in coalition with the former communists, the Democrazia di Sinistra, who brought in the necessary political will. Prodi, like Dini, had the prime virtue of entering the national scene with clean hands, but as one of the country's biggest Europhiles, he rallied the republic to swallow the difficult financial pill that allowed it to sneak over the line and enter into the first round of the Euro in January 1999.

In late-1998, however, DS leader Massimo d'Allema judged that Prodi's stringent economic measures were too much to swallow and withdrew his support. Prodi was out and d'Allema, the current prime minister, was in. No one has ever made money out of placing bets on Italian politics, but d'Allema does have a reputation for integrity, and at the time of writing has managed to keep the ship of state on a steady course.

Meanwhile, Romano Prodi has a new job as EU Commission president after the sorry debacle at Brussels that saw the resignation of all the head honchos when confronted with evidence of gross irresponsibility and patronage. The very idea of an Italian running the big show ten years ago would have been regarded as a joke, and goes to prove how respectable Italy has become in the last few years. Whether it endures into the next millennium is another story.

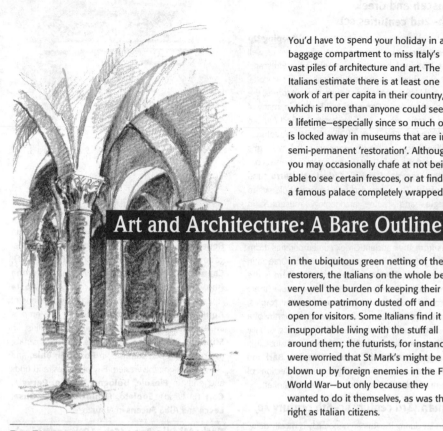

You'd have to spend your holiday in a baggage compartment to miss Italy's vast piles of architecture and art. The Italians estimate there is at least one work of art per capita in their country, which is more than anyone could see in a lifetime—especially since so much of it is locked away in museums that are in semi-permanent 'restoration'. Although you may occasionally chafe at not being able to see certain frescoes, or at finding a famous palace completely wrapped up

Art and Architecture: A Bare Outline

in the ubiquitous green netting of the restorers, the Italians on the whole bear very well the burden of keeping their awesome patrimony dusted off and open for visitors. Some Italians find it insupportable living with the stuff all around them; the futurists, for instance, were worried that St Mark's might be blown up by foreign enemies in the First World War—but only because they wanted to do it themselves, as was their right as Italian citizens.

Pre-Etruscan

To give a chronological account of the first Italian artists is an uncomfortable task. The peninsula's mountainous terrain saw many isolated developments, and many survivals of ancient cultures even during the days of the sophisticated Etruscans and Romans. Most ancient of all, however, is the palaeolithic troglodyte culture on the Riviera, credited with creating some of the first artworks in Europe—chubby images of fertility goddesses. These and other curious trappings may be seen in the Ligurian museums at **Balzi Rossi**, **Pegli** and **Finalborgo**. The most remarkable works from the Neolithic period up until the Iron Age are the thousands of graffiti rock incisions in several isolated Alpine valleys north of Lake Iseo, especially the **Val Camonica**, where these ancient outdoor masterpieces are protected in a national park. After 1000 BC Italic peoples all over the peninsula were making geometrically painted pots, weapons, tools and

bronze statuettes. The most impressive culture, however, was the tower-building, bronze-working Nuraghe civilization on **Sardinia**, of which echoes are seen in many cultures on the mainland. Among the most intriguing and beautiful artefacts to have survived are those of the Villanova culture in the archaeological museum in **Bologna**; the statues and inscriptions of the little-known Middle Adriatic culture in the museum at **Chieti** in Abruzzo, and the statue-steles of an unknown people at **Pontrémoli**, north of Viareggio; others, of the Luini culture, are in the civic museum in **La Spezia**. Dolmens and strange little temples survive in many corners of central and southern **Puglia**. If you wish to see what was going on across the Mediterranean at the same time, there's also one of the best Egyptian museums in the world in **Turin**.

Etruscan and Greek (8th–2nd centuries BC)

With the refined, art-loving Etruscans (*see* **Keeping Up Appearances**) we begin to have architecture as well as art. Not much has survived, thanks to the Etruscans' habit of building in wood and decorating with terracotta, but we do have plenty of distinctive rock-cut tombs, the best of which are at **Cerveteri** and **Tarquinia**; many of them contain exceptional frescoes that reflect Aegean Greek styles. The best of their lovely sculptures, jewellery, vases, and much more, are in the museums in **Rome** (Villa Giulia—where you can also see a reconstructed temple façade), **Chiusi**, **Volterra** and **Tarquinia**. There are also fine Etruscan holdings in **Perugia**, and in the archaeology museums in **Florence** and **Bologna**.

The Etruscans imported and copied many of their vases from their ancient Greek contemporaries, from Greece proper and the colonies of Magna Graecia in southern Italy. The Doric temple at **Paestum** is the best-surviving Greek structure on the peninsula (there are many others in Sicily); **Cumae,** west of Naples, and **Metapontum,** near Tàranto, are also worthy of a visit; of the many other excavated Greek cities, usually only foundations remain. The archaeological museums in **Reggio di Calabria, Tàranto, Naples, Bari** and the **Vatican** contain the most impressive collections of ancient Greek vases, statues, and other types of art.

Roman (3rd century BC–5th century AD)

Italian art during the Roman hegemony is mostly derivative of the Etruscan and Greek, with a special talent for mosaics, wall paintings, glasswork and portraiture; architecturally, the Romans were brilliant engineers, the inventors of concrete and grand exponents of the arch. Even today their constructions such as aqueducts, amphitheatres, bridges, baths, and the Pantheon are most impressive. Of course, **Rome** itself has no end of ancient monuments; also in the vicinity there is **Ostia Antica**, Rome's ancient port, and **Tivoli**, site of Hadrian's great villa. Rome also has a stellar set of museums filled with Roman antiquities—the National Museum (now split in two), the Vatican Museum, the Capitoline Museums and the Museum of Roman Civilization at EUR. **Naples** is the other outstanding destination for Roman art, with the ruins of ancient **Pompeii** and **Herculaneum** on its outskirts, and a spectacular museum, not only of artefacts found in the Pompeii excavations, but of statues from Rome dug up by Renaissance collectors like the Farnese.

Other impressive Roman monuments may be seen in **Benevento** (with the best triumphal arch and another good museum, full of unusual Roman-Egyptian art); **Capua** (huge amphitheatre and Mithraeum); **Verona** (the arena, gates and theatre complex); **Aosta** (theatre and gates); the museum and excavations of **Aquileia** in Friuli and **Sepino** in Molise; the temples in **Brescia** and **Assisi**; 'the villa of Catullus' in **Sirmione** on Lake Garda; villas, tunnels, canals, markets and other surprises in **Pozzuoli**, **Baia,** and elsewhere along the western Bay of Naples, and odds and ends in **Fiesole, Bologna, Trieste, Perugia, Cori** (in Lazio), **Spoleto, Rimini, Ancona, Susa, Lecce** and **Alba Fucens** in Abruzzo.

Early Middle Ages (5th–10th centuries)

After the fall of the Roman Empire, civilization's lamp flickered most brightly in **Ravenna**, where Byzantine mosaicists adorned the glittering churches of the Eastern Exarchate. Theirs was to be the prominent style in pictorial art and architecture until the 13th century.

Apart from Ravenna, there are fine mosaics and paintings in **Rome**, in churches such as Sant'Agnese, San Clemente and Santa Prassede. In Rome the Italian preference for basilican churches and octagonal baptistries began in Constantine's day, and the development of Christian art and architecture through the Dark Ages can be traced there better than anywhere else. There are also many paintings in the catacombs of Rome and **Naples**. Other good Ravenna-style mosaics may be seen in the cathedrals of **Aquileia** and Torcello in **Venice**, where the fashion lingered long enough to create St Mark's. In the vicinity of **Tàranto** there are the remains of Greek monasteries and cave paintings, and interesting early-Christian churches at **Nocera** in Campania, and in Benevento. In **Albenga,** on the Riviera, and **Novara**, you'll find unusual 5th-century baptistries with artworks.

'Lombard' art, really the work of the native population under Lombard rule, revealed an original talent in the 7th–9th centuries, especially evident in the churches of **Cividale del Friuli**, in the works in the cathedral of **Monza**, in and around **Spoleto,** and in the Abbey of San Salvatore in **Brescia**. A new style, presaging the Romanesque, may be seen in Sant'Ambrogio in **Milan**.

Romanesque (11th–12th centuries)

At this point, when an expansive society made new advances in art possible, north and south Italy went their separate ways, each contributing distinctive styles in sculpture and architecture. We also begin to learn the identities of some of their makers. The great Lombard cathedrals, masterworks of brick art and adorned with blind arcading, bas-reliefs and lofty campaniles, are best exemplified at **Modena** (by the master builder-sculptor Wiligelmo), San Michele in **Pavia**, **Cremona** Cathedral, and the Santo Stefano complex in **Bologna**. In **Verona** the cathedral and San Zeno were embellished by Guglielmo's talented student Nicolò; in **Parma** the great baptistry by Benedetto Antelami is a milestone in the synthesis of sculpture and architecture.

The rapidly accumulating wealth of **Pisa** permitted the undertaking of the cathedral—the largest building programme in Italy in a thousand years; its exotic style owed something to contacts with the Muslim world, but the inspiration for the design was completely original—in part a very conscious attempt to recapture the grandeur of the ancient world. **Florence** developed its own black and white style, exemplified in amazing buildings like the baptistry and San Miniato. Interesting variations appeared in the other Tuscan cities, each showing some Pisan stripes or Florentine rectangles.

In the south, Byzantine and Muslim influences helped create a very different tendency. **Amalfi** and **Caserta** built a Saracenic cathedral and cloister dating from this period; Amalfi's adorned with incised bronze doors from Constantinople in a style that was copied all over the south, notably at **Trani** and **Monte Sant'Angelo** in Puglia. The tradition of Byzantine painting and mosaics continued, mostly in Sicily, though there is a fine example at Sant'Angelo in Formis near **Capua**. From Muslim geometrical patterns, southern artists acquired a taste for intricate designs using enamel or marble chips in church furnishings and architectural trim—as seen in pulpits and candlesticks in the churches of **Salerno, Ravello**, and many others. The outstanding architectural advance of this period is the Pugliese Romanesque, as shown in cathedrals in almost every Puglian city (**Troia**, **Sipontum**, **Monte Sant'Angelo**, **Ruvo di Puglia**, **Trani**, **Altamura** and **Bari** have perhaps the best), a style closely related to contemporary Norman and Pisan work—it's difficult to say who should get the credit for being first. Another impressive cathedral of the southern Romanesque is that of **Anagni** in Lazio; in the same region are the two extremely unusual church façades in **Tuscània**. The Norman influence also appears in churches like the Abbazia della Trinità in **Venosa** (Basilicata) and in the wonderful mosaic pavement of **Otranto** Cathedral.

This period also saw the erection of urban skyscrapers by the nobility, family fortress-towers built when the *comuni* forced local barons to move into the towns. Larger cities once had literally hundreds of them, before the townspeople succeeded in getting them demolished. **San Gimignano** and **Ascoli Piceno** have the most surviving examples. In many cases extremely tall towers were built simply for decoration and prestige. **Bologna's** Garisendi and Asinelli Towers, along with **Pisa**'s Campanile, are the best examples of medieval Italy's occasional disdain for the horizontal.

Late-Medieval–Early-Renaissance (13th–14th centuries)

In many ways this was the most exciting and vigorous phase in Italian art history, an age of discovery when the power of the artist was almost like that of a magician. Great imaginative leaps occurred in architecture, painting and sculpture, especially in Tuscany. From Milan to Assisi a group of masons and sculptors known as the *Campionese Masters* built magnificent brick cathedrals and basilicas. Some of their buildings reflect the Gothic style of the north (most spectacularly **Milan**), while in **Como** Cathedral you can see the transition from that same Gothic to Renaissance. In **Venice** an ornate, half-oriental style called Venetian-Gothic still sets the city's palaces and public buildings apart, and influenced the exotic Basilica di Sant'Antonio in **Padua**.

This was also an era of transition in sculpture, from stiff Romanesque stylization to the more realistic, classically inspired works of the great Nicola Pisano and his son Giovanni (in the churches of **Pisa, Pistoia** and **Siena**) and his pupil Arnolfo di Cambio (**Florence**). Other outstanding works of the 14th century are Lorenzo Maitani's cathedral in **Orvieto** and the Scaliger tombs of **Verona** by the Campione masters.

Painters, especially in Rome and Siena, learned from the new spatial and expressive sculpture. Most celebrated of the masters in the dawn of the Italian Renaissance is, of course, the solemn Giotto, whose greatest works are the fresco cycles in **Padua** and **Assisi**. In the town of St Francis you can also see some excellent works by Giotto's merrier contemporaries from **Siena**. That city's artists, Duccio di Buoninsegna, Simone Martini and Pietro and Ambrogio Lorenzetti, gave Italy its most brilliant exponents of the International Gothic style—though they were also important precursors of the Renaissance. Their brightly coloured scenes, embellished with a thousand details, helped make Siena into the medieval dream-city it is today; the style carried on into the quattrocento with the courtly frescoes of the northern painter Pisanello. In **Florence**, the works of Orcagna, Gentile da Fabriano and Lorenzo Monaco continued her unique approach, laying a foundation for her launching of the Renaissance. Cathedral complexes and public buildings in the northern cities, especially at **Siena** and **Pistoia**, show a sophisticated understanding of urban design and an original treatment of the established forms. Northern European Gothic never made much headway in Italy, though French Cistercians did build fine abbey churches like those at **San Galgano** in Tuscany and **Fossanova** in Lazio, and the English-financed Sant'Andrea in **Vercelli**. The south had relatively little to contribute during this period, but **Naples** developed its own neo-Gothic architecture, and unique geometrically patterned church façades appear at **L'Aquila** and **Brindisi**.

Rome, for one of the few times in its history, achieved artistic prominence with home-grown talent. The city's architecture from this period (as seen in the campaniles of Santa Maria in Cosmedin and Santa Maria Maggiore) has largely been lost under Baroque remodellings, but the paintings and mosaics of Pietro Cavallini and his school, and the intricate, inlaid stone pavements and architectural trim of the Cosmati family and their followers, derived from the Amalfi Coast style, can be seen all over the city; both had an influence that extended far beyond Rome itself.

The Renaissance (15th–16th centuries)

The origins of this high-noon of art are very much the accomplishment of quattrocento **Florence**, where sculpture and painting embarked on a totally new way of educating the eye (*see* p.559). The idea of a supposed 'rediscovery of antiquity' has confused the understanding of the time. In general, artists broke new ground when they expanded from the traditions of medieval art; when they sought merely to copy the forms of ancient Greece and Rome, the imagination often faltered. Florentine art soon became recognized as the standard of the age, and examples can be seen everywhere in Tuscany. By 1450 Florentine artists were spreading the new style to the north, especially **Milan**, where Leonardo da Vinci and Bramante spent several years; the collections in the Brera and other galleries, the *Last Supper*, and the nearby **Certosa di Pavia** are essential works of the Renaissance. Other good museum collections are in **Rome, Parma, Turin** and **Bergamo**; the core of Bergamo is a Renaissance masterpiece. **Mantua** has important works by Alberti and Mantegna, and nearby lies the 'ideal' Renaissance town: **Sabbioneta**. Michelangelo and Bramante, among others, carried the Renaissance to **Rome**, where it thrived under the patronage of enlightened popes. Other Renaissance diversions can be seen in **Rimini**: its remarkable Malatesta Temple; and **Urbino**: the lovely palace and art collection of the archetypal Renaissance prince, Duke Federico da Montefeltro.

The most significant art in the north came out of **Venice**, which had its own distinct school led by Mantegna and Giovanni Bellini (*see* p.297); one of the best painters of the school, the fastidious Carlo Crivelli, did much of his work in the Marche (**Ascoli Piceno** and **Ancona**). Under the patronage of the Este family, Renaissance **Ferrara** produced its own school of quattrocento painters (Cosmè Tura, Ercole Roberti). In

Art and Architecture: A Bare Outline

Perugia Perugino was laying the foundations of the Umbrian school, in which Raphael and Pinturicchio earned their stripes. In **Orvieto** Cathedral, the Tuscan painter Signorelli left a *Last Judgement* that inspired Michelangelo. Piero della Francesca was the most important non-Florentine painter before Raphael; his revolutionary works are at **Urbino**, **Sansepolcro** and **Arezzo**. Southern Italy, trapped in a decline that was even more artistic than economic, hardly participated at all, though examples of the northerners' art can be seen in **Naples** (the Triumphal Arch in the Castel Nuovo).

Despite the brilliant triumphs in painting and sculpture, the story of Renaissance architecture is partially one of confusion and retreat. **Florence**, with Brunelleschi, Alberti and Michelozzo, achieved its own special mode of expression, a dignified austerity that proved difficult to transplant elsewhere. In most of Italy the rediscovery of the works of Vitruvius, representing the authority of antiquity, killed off Italians' appreciation of their own architectural heritage; with surprising speed the dazzling imaginative freedom of medieval architecture was lost forever. Some fine work still appeared, however, notably Codussi's palaces and churches in **Venice**.

High Renaissance and Mannerism (16th century)

At the beginning of the cinquecento Michelangelo, Raphael and Leonardo held court at the summit of European art. But as Italy was losing her self-confidence, and was soon to lose her liberty, artistic currents tended toward the dark and subversive. More than anyone it was Michelangelo who tipped the balance from the cool, classical Renaissance into the turgid, stormy, emotionally fraught movement labelled **Mannerism**. Among the few painters left in exhausted Florence, he had the brilliant Jacopo Pontormo and Rosso Fiorentino to help. Other painters lumped in with the Mannerists, such as Giulio Romano in Mantua and Il Sodoma around Siena, broke new ground while maintaining the discipline and intellectual rigour of the early Renaissance. Elsewhere, and especially among the fashionable Florentine painters and sculptors, art was decaying into mere interior decoration.

For **Venice** it was a golden age, with Titian, Veronese, Tintoretto, Sansovino and Palladio, whose works may be seen throughout Venetia. Another art centre of the age, **Parma**, is embellished with the Mannerist brushes of Correggio and Parmigianino. In **Cremona**, Milan, and other lucky galleries, you can see works by Arcimboldo, the cinquecento surrealist. In architecture,

attempts to recreate ancient styles and the classical orders won the day. In **Milan**, and later in **Rome**, Bramante was one of the few architects able to do anything interesting with it, while Michelangelo's great dome of St Peter's put a cap on the accomplishments of the Renaissance. Other talented architects found most of their patronage in Rome which after the 1520s became Italy's centre of artistic activity: Ligorio, Peruzzi, Vignola and the Sangallo family among them.

Baroque (17th–18th centuries)

Rome continued its artistic dominance to become the Baroque capital, where the socially irresponsible genius of artists like Bernini and Borromini was approved by the Jesuits and indulged by the tainted ducats of the popes. As an art designed to induce temporal obedience and psychical oblivion, its effects are difficult to describe, but the three great churches along Corso Vittorio Emanuele, Bernini's Piazza Navona fountains and St Peter's colonnades, are fine examples. More honest cities such as Florence and Venice chose to sit out the Baroque, though **Florence** at first approved the works of 16th-century proto-Baroque sculptors like Ammannati, Giambologna and Cellini. Not all artists fit the Baroque mould; genius could survive even in a dangerous, picaresque age, most notably in the person of Michelangelo (works in **Milan** and **Rome**), not to mention other painters such as Mattia Preti, with works in Naples and **Taverna**, in his native Calabria.

The south of Italy, with its long tradition of religious emotionalism, found the Baroque entirely to its tastes, though few towns could afford to build much. **Naples** could, and the Monastery of San Martino by Cosimo Fanzago marks the apotheosis of Neapolitan Baroque. Painting and sculpture even flourished while they were dying in northern Renaissance towns; southern art's eccentricity climaxed in the Sansevero Chapel. A very different sort of Baroque appeared in the deep south, where the studied excess seemed to strike a deep chord in the popular psyche. Much of it is in Sicily, though the Spanish-looking city of **Lecce** developed a Baroque style that lasted from the 16th to the late 18th century, consistent and beautiful enough to make as impressive an architectural ensemble as any medieval or Renaissance city in the north. **Turin**'s town plan, churches, palaces and royal hunting lodges, designed by the priest Guarini and the early 18th-century Sicilian Juvarra, are the most elegant representations of the Baroque spirit in northern Italy. This was a great age of palaces and ornate Italian gardens, most famously in **Tivoli**, Isola Bella in **Lake Maggiore**, Villa Borghese and innumerable other locations in and around **Rome**, as well as around **Padua** and **Vicenza**.

Neoclassicism and Romanticism (late 18th–19th centuries)

Baroque was a hard act to follow, and at this time Italian art and architecture almost cease to exist. Two centuries of stifling oppression had taken their toll on the national imagination, and for the first time Italy not only ceased to be a leader in art, but failed even to make significant contributions. The one bright spot was **Venice**, where Giambattista Tiepolo and son adorned the churches and palaces of the last days of the Serenissima; their works can be seen in many places in the Veneto, and **Ùdine** in Friuli. Other Venetians, such as Canaletto and Guardi, painted their famous canal scenes for Grand Tourists. In the 19th century the *Macchiaioli*, the Italian Impressionist movement led by Giovanni Fattori, was centred in **Florence**. In sculpture the neoclassical master Canova stands almost alone, a favourite in the days of Napoleon. His best works may be seen in the Villa Carlotta, on **Lake Como**, in Rome's Villa Borghese and at **Possagno**. In architecture it was the age of grand opera houses, many designed by the Bibiena family of Bologna. The Gallerias in **Milan** and **Naples** (late 19th century) and the extravagances of the Piedmontese Alessandro Antonelli (**Turin** and **Novara**) are among the most impressive public buildings, and the neoclassical royal palaces at **Caserta** and **Stra** near Venice the grandest private addresses.

20th Century

The turn-of-the-century Italian Art Nouveau—known as Liberty Style—failed to spread as widely as its counterparts in France and central Europe. There are a few good examples in **Milan**, but the best are linked with the burgeoning tourist industry: the construction of Grand Hotels, casinos and villas, especially in **Venice**, the **Lakes**, the **Riviera**, **Pésaro**, **Viareggio** and the great spas at **Merano**, **Montecatini** and **San Pellegrino**. Two art movements attracted international attention: futurism, a response to Cubism, concerned with the relevancy to the present, a movement led by Boccioni, Severini and Balla (best seen in the National Gallery of Modern Art, **Rome**, and in **Milan**); and the mysterious, metaphysical world of De Chirico; while Modigliani, Morandi and Carrà were masters of silences. Their works, among others, are displayed in the museums of **Rome, Venice** and **Milan**. Architecture in this century reached its (admittedly low) summit in the Fascist period (the **EUR** suburb in Rome, and public buildings everywhere in the south). Mussolinian architecture often makes us smile, but, as the only Italian school in the last 200 years to have achieved a consistent sense of design, it presents a challenge to all modern Italian architects—one they have so far been unable to meet.

In **Turin** and **Milan** you can see the works of the most acclaimed Italian architect of this century, Pier Luigi Nervi; good post-War buildings are very difficult to find, and the other arts have never yet risen above the level of dreary, saleable postmodernism. Much of the Italians' artistic urge has been sublimated into the shibboleth of Italian design—clothes, sports cars, suitcases, kitchen utensils, etc. At present, though business is good, Italy is generating little excitement in these fields. Europe expects more from its most artistically talented nation; after the bad centuries of shame and slumber a free and prosperous Italy may well find its own voice and its own style to help interpret the events of the day. If Italy ever does begin to speak with a single voice, whatever it has to say will be worth hearing.

Keeping Up Appearances

Bella Figura

The longer you stay in Italy, the more inscrutable it becomes. Nothing is ever quite as it seems, and you'll find yourself changing your ideas about things with disconcerting frequency. Part of the reason why is the obsession to make a good impression or appearance, *'fare una bella figura'*, one of the Italian people's most singular traits. You notice it almost immediately. Not only is every Italian an immaculately smart fashion victim (they are by far the biggest consumers of their own fashion industry), but they always seem to be modelling their spiffy threads—posing, gesturing, playing to an audience when they have one, which is nearly always because Italians rarely move about except in small herds. Their cities are their stage, the perfectly arranged *piazze* and streets designed like movie sets, with lights suspended over the middle. Long-time observers of the phenomenon have even noted that each city's women tend to dress themselves in colours that complement the local brick or stone.

The Italians' natural grace and elegance may be partly instinctive; even back in the 14th century foreigners noted their charming manners and taste for exquisite clothes. Many a painting of the Madonna served not only for piety's sake, but also to advertise Milanese silks or Venetian brocades. In the Renaissance appearance supplanted reality in a thousand ways, especially after the discovery of artificial perspective, which made artistic representations seem much more clever and interesting than the real thing. Fake, painted marble supplanted real marble, even if it cost more; Palladio built marble palaces out of stucco; *trompe l'œil* frescoes embellished a hundred churches; glorious façades on cathedrals and palaces disguise the fact that the rest is shabby, unfinished brick. Even castles were built to impress rather than keep out the enemy, in a day when battles had become brilliant bloodless games, and gorgeous Italian armour deflected few blows.

Castiglione's *The Courtier* advises that it is no use doing a brave and noble deed unless someone is watching; honour, like almost every other virtue, is something bestowed from without. After the French and Spanish burst the Italians' bubble of superiority in the 16th century, Italy's history becomes a saga of trying to do everything to keep up appearances, of nobles mending their socks in the half-light to save up for hiring a servant when visitors were expected.

Bella figura pleases the eye but irritates just about everything else. Fashionable conformity has a way of spreading from mere clothing and gestures to opinions, especially in the provinces; the Italians remain the masters of empty flattery and compliments, and will say anything to please: 'Yes, straight ahead!' they'll often reply when you need directions, hoping it will make you happy even if they've never heard of your destination. Nor does fashion slavery show any sign of abating; now that more Italians have more money than ever before, they are using it for rarely necessary fur coats, and for designer clothes for the whole family. Even little children go to bed with visions of fashion dancing in their heads; Italy is the last stand of Barbie and Ken dolls, where each little girl owns at least a dozen.

Brick Italy, Marble Italy

'Italy', begins the 1948 Constitution, 'is a Republic based on labour'—an unusual turn of phrase, but one entirely in keeping with a time when a thoroughly humbled Italy was beginning to get back on its feet after the War. The sorrows of the common man occupied the plots of post-War *cinema verità*, and artists and writers began to celebrate themes of Faith, Bread and Work as if they were in the employ of the Church's *Famiglia Cristiana* magazine. To outsiders it must have seemed that Italy was undergoing a serious change, but careful observers would have noted only another oscillation in the grandest, oldest dichotomy in Italian history. Brick Italy was once more in the driver's seat.

Brick Italy is a nation of hard work, humility and piety that knows it must be diligent and clever to wrest a comfortable living from the thin soil of this resource-poor, rocky peninsula. Marble Italy knows its citizens are perfectly capable of doing just that, just as they always have, and seeks to celebrate that diligence and cleverness by turning it into opulence, excess and foreign conquest. The two have been contending for Italy's soul ever since Roman quarrymen discovered Carrara marble during the republican era. Brick Italy's capital in former times was brilliant, republican Siena; right now it is hard-working socialist Bologna, a city with more bricks than Woolworths has nickels. Its triumphs came with the Age of the Communes, with the modest genius of the Early Renaissance, and with the hard-won successes of the last 40 years. Marble Italy reached its height in the days of Imperial Rome; its capital is (can you guess?) Rome, always and forever. After the medieval interlude, marble made its great comeback with the High Renaissance, Spaniardism and Michelangelo, the high priest of marble. The Age of Baroque belonged to it completely, as did the brief era of Mussolini. Some confirmed Marble Cities are Naples, Genoa, Turin, Pisa, Parma, Trieste, Perugia and Verona. Brick partisans include Pavia, Livorno, Lucca, Arezzo, Cremona and Mantua. Florence and Venice, the two medieval city-republics that eventually became important states on their own, are the two cities that most successfully straddle the fence. Look carefully at their old churches and palaces, and you will often find marble veneer outside, and solid brick underneath.

Keep all this in mind when you ponder the infinite subtleties of Italian history. It isn't always a perfect fit; medieval Guelphs and Ghibellines each had a little brick and a little marble in them, and the contemporary papacy changes from one to the other with every shift of the wind. Mussolini would have paved Italy over in marble if he had been able—but look at the monuments he could afford, and you'll see inexpensive travertine and brick more than anything else. For a while in the 80s, with Italy's economic successes and the glitz of Milanese fashion and design, it looked as if Marble Italy was about to make another comeback. But today, with Italy in the midst of its long and tortuous revolution, the situation is unclear. If and when a new regime emerges, will its monument to itself be a beautiful symbol of republican aspirations, like Siena's brick Palazzo Pubblico, or a florid marble pile like Rome's Altar of the Nation, the monument to Italian unification (and one of the biggest hunks of kitsch on this planet)?

Commedia dell'Arte

The first recorded mention of Arlecchino, or Harlequin, came in 1601 when the part was played by Tristano Martinelli, a celebrated actor—the year that saw the debut of *Hamlet*. Theatre as we know it was blooming all over Europe: Shakespeare and Marlowe in England, Calderón and Lope de Vega in Spain, the predecessors of Molière in France. All of these had learned their craft from late-Renaissance Italy, where the *commedia dell'arte* had created a fashion that spread across the continent. The great companies—the Gelosi, the Confidenti and the Accesi—toured the capitals, while others shared the provinces. Groups of ten or twelve actors, run as co-operatives, they could do comedies, tragedies or pastorals to their own texts, and provide music, dance, magic and juggling between acts.

The audiences liked the comedies best, with a set of masked stock characters, playing off scenes between the *magnificos* (great lords) and the *zanni* (servants), who provide the slapstick, half-improvised comic relief.

These represented every corner of Italy: Arlecchino is a Bergamese; Balanzone, the wise doctor who 'cures with Latin', from Bologna; Pulcinello, white-clad and warbling, a true Neapolitan; Meneghino, the piratical warrior, Milanese; the drunkard Rugantino, a Roman; the nervous rich merchant Pantalone, a Venetian; while the maid Colombina apparently belongs to all. To spring the plot there would be lovers (*inamorati*)—unmasked to remind us that only those in love are really alive.

Arte doesn't mean art, but a guild; these companies were made up of professional players. The term was invented in 1745 by Goldoni (who wrote one of the last plays of the genre, *Arlecchino, servitore di due padrone*); in the 1500s the companies were often known as the *commedia mercenaria*—they would hit town, set up a stage and start their show within the hour. Cultured Italians often deplored the way the 'mercenary' shows were driving out serious drama, traditionally written by scholarly amateurs in the princely courts. In the repressive climate of the day, caught between the Inquisition and the Spanish, a culture of ideas survived only in free Venice. Theatre retreated into humorous popular entertainment, but even then the Italians found a way to say what was on their minds. A new stock character appeared, the menacing but slow-witted 'Capitano', who always spoke with a Spanish accent, and Italians learned from the French how to use Arlecchino to satirize the hated emperor Charles V himself—playing on the French pronunciation of the names *harlequin* and *Charles Quint*.

Arlecchino may come from Oneta, a village north of Bergamo, but he carries a proud lineage that goes back to the ancient Greeks and Romans. From his character and appearance, theatre historians trace him back to the antique *planipedes*, comic mimes with shaven heads (everyone knew Arlecchino wore his nightcap to cover his baldness). Others note his relationship to German and Scandinavian mythological tricksters, and it has even been claimed that his patched costume is that of a Sufi dervish. No doubt he had a brilliant career all through the Middle Ages, though it was probably only in the 1500s that he took the form of the Arlecchino we know. At that time young rustics from the Bergamasque valleys would go to Venice, Milan and other cities to get work as porters (*facchini*). They all seemed to be named Johnny—*Zanni* in dialect, which became the common term for any of the clownish roles in the plays; hence our word 'zany'.

The name 'Arlecchino' seems actually to have been a French contribution. At the court of Henri III, a certain

Italian actor who played the role became a protégé of a Monsieur de Harlay, and people started calling him 'little Harlay', or Harlequin. The character developed into a stock role, the most beloved of the *commedia dell'arte* clown masks: simple-minded and easily frightened, an incorrigible prankster, a fellow as unstable as his motley dress. His foil was usually another servant, the Neapolitan Puricinella/Punchinella—Punch—more serious and sometimes boastful, but still just as much of a buffoon. Try to imagine them together on stage, and you'll get something that looks rather like Laurel and Hardy. No doubt they have always gone through the world together, and we can hope they always will.

That Etruscan Smile

Everything about them is mysterious, and that's the way they seemed to like it. Their everyday lives were wrapped up in magic and superstition, and we know only superficial details about their religion, headquartered in the *Fanum Voltumnae*, the sacred wood, around modern Viterbo, where no outsider was ever allowed. No one knows anything for sure about their origins, though they seem to have come from western Anatolia; their sudden decline and eventual complete disappearance after the 4th century BC was just as shadowy and unaccountable.

What the Etruscans did leave behind are portraits of themselves, some of the most remarkable achievements of ancient art. They weren't the most original of artists, but every style and fashion that came from Greece was adapted and given an Etruscan twist. Even more than the Greeks, they had a talent for capturing expression and character on every level, from the astute, gentlemanly *Orator* in the Florence museum, to the happy, worldly couples lounging on their stone sarcophagi, the beautiful terracotta heads of children in Rome's Villa Giulia and the grinning, rosy-cheeked grotesques that peer out from all Etruscan decoration. Usually they are smiling, a faraway smile as mysterious as anything else they have left us. Battered by dour Romans on one side and crazed Celts on the other, the Etruscans simply faded away. Or else they may have gone right into the ground, like the lost ancient people that became the fairies of Ireland. Certainly their presence is still felt in central Italy, especially in art. The Romans and the other Italic nations learned much about art from the Greeks, but when you look at their painting—at Pompeii, in Naples, or in Nero's Golden House—it will be clear that something essential, some-

thing in the soul, was their heritage from Etruria.

The thread of it has never been lost in all the centuries since. When you get to know Etruscan art, you'll see subtle reflections of it in everything that came after, from Botticelli's paintings to Mussolini's post offices. From the grotesques, revived by Raphael and now gazing out at us from the cornices of old buildings everywhere—one gets the feeling that somehow those mysterious Etruscans are still with us.

Fungus Fever

If you've brought the children, ignore their unkind scoffing. That's not spaghetti with dirt on your plate, but *spaghetti al tartufo*, with truffles, the most prized gourmet delicacy in Italy: earthy, aromatic, aphrodisiac. Admittedly truffles aren't much to look at, subterranean lumpy *funghi*, bulbous tubers that consent to sprout only in certain corners of France and Italy with the proper calcareous soils, oak trees and exposure. Per ounce these ugly lumps are the most expensive comestibles in the world. Fortunately, a little truffle goes a long way, and Italians will travel a long way to look, dreamy-eyed, at little glass jars of them displayed at truffle fairs. Two types of truffles are considered outstanding—the black, found in south-west France and, in Italy, in the Apennines; and the white, found in the Alba and Asti area of Piedmont. The white is usually the most prized, being rarer, and so more expensive. It's a creamy colour, smooth and irregularly shaped, and can vary in size from that of a walnut to something more like a football. Curiously, truffles actually have very little intrinsic taste—it's their power to impart flavour to other foods that has made them so highly valued. They are usually eaten raw, sliced very finely over virtually any dish—though most popularly with meat, fish or pasta—or used in stuffing for meat, poultry or game.

Truffles are so expensive because they are so hard to track down. An aura of mystery hangs over their birth; according to legend they are spawned by lightning bolts flicking through the oak groves. Although prices of late have led to experiments in truffle cultivation, most truffles are still brought to market by truffle-hunters with keen-nosed truffle-hounds; unlike the French, who have long used pigs, the Italians swear by their dogs, suckled on teats rubbed with truffle juice.

The truffle season is short—from October until the snows fall about Christmas. During this time daily auctions take place in Asti and Alba in the wee hours of the morning, when the secretive truffle-hunters arrive to sell the night's harvest (it's traditional to hunt at night, when truffles smell the strongest, or is it because the best ones are always on someone else's property?). A walnut-sized *tartufo* can easily sell for L100,000. However, if you are offered *tartufo* ice-cream, don't despair for the sanity of the Italian kitchen—it's made of cream and chocolate, and like French chocolate *truffes* only resembles the shape of its namesake.

Leaning Towers

It isn't always a subject the Italians like to discuss. They will be happy to sell you all the little plastic souvenirs you want of the most celebrated of the species—in Pisa— but a mention of the other dozens of listing landmarks scattered around Italy makes them uneasy. Italians, of course, think of themselves as the most skilled engineers on this planet. They built the Roman roads and aqueducts, the Pantheon and the dome of St Peter's, the biggest in the world. They invented concrete. Their endless *autostrade* zoom through mile-long tunnels and skim over deep valleys on stilts, remarkable *tours de force* of engineering that would make the Romans proud. They have built more railway tunnels, perhaps, than the rest of Europe put together. Why can't they keep their towers from drooping?

The answer may well be that they built them that way. For centuries there has been a dark undercurrent of thought on the subject that claims Pisa's tower was meant to lean. Goethe thought so, and architects who carefully measured the foundation stones came to the same conclusion. Over a hundred years ago a certain Professor Goodyear exposed the whole business as what he called 'symmetrophobia'—not a fear of the symmetrical, but a disdain for it. Italy's medieval master builders, not yet squeezed into the Renaissance strait-jacket of monumental symmetry, could still be playful—witness the parfait stripes on so many cathedrals, or the floral wallpaper print which covers Florence's.

The Italians of today do not like this explanation any better; they brusquely reject any suggestion that their ancestors could have been tempted away from the perpendicular on a whim. You can judge for yourself at Pisa—whose campanile would not look right without

the tilt—or at the Garisenda and Asinelli towers of Bologna, a pair of elephantine monstrosities that seem ready to topple any minute. None of Venice's, except for the new St Mark's, are close to being straight; Ravenna has two that are even more precarious, and other examples can be seen at Rovigo and Rome. In Naples they have tilting domes—nothing intentional, but perhaps Providence's reminder that nothing around the Bay of Naples is allowed to stand forever.

Non-leaning Towers

In most of Italy, where there are no billboards and power lines to block the view, you will see landscapes that have not essentially changed since 1500. Long ago, Italian farmers began the job of making the country into one great formal garden, planting their olives and vines in neat rows, and creating long avenues of Lombardy poplars or parasol pines. Medieval designers added cities, towns and castles in a constantly changing variety of styles, each one complementary and respectful to those that came before. The basic feature in many parts of the rugged peninsula is the *hill town*, orderly and compact, its buildings draped carefully on a peak or slope as if arranged there by the hand of a sculptor. By 1500, after a half-millennium of prosperity, the builders' work was done, and the Italian garden was perfect, cohesive and complete.

Visitors from over the Alps never ceased to be amazed; even those without an eye for beauty could be impressed by the richness and size of Italian towns, and especially by their monumental urge to the vertical. By 1150 Italians were building towers on a scale unmatched until the American cities of the 1900s. Indeed, larger Italian cities had a decidedly Manhattanish aspect with, in some cases, hundreds of tall, square defence towers creating incredible skylines—as with skyscrapers, it soon became a matter of prestige among the baronial families to try to have the tallest, and many reached over 200ft (60m). In those rough times the towers weren't just for show; city officials had to take constant complaints from neighbours about siege engines parked on the street, stray showers of boiling oil, and noisy, pitched battles keeping the children up at night. The *comuni* managed to get most of these towers pulled down by about 1350. The great bell-towers of the cathedrals and city halls survive, and even today they are usually still the tallest buildings in the city. To give some idea of how ambitiously Italy could build, here are the 10 tallest structures completed before the year 1500:

Florence (Cathedral)	110 m	(364 ft)	Bologna (Asinelli tower)	96 m	(318 ft)
Milan (Cathedral)	107 m	(351 ft)	Florence (Palazzo Vecchio)	94 m	(308 ft)
Cremona (Campanile)	113 m	(370 ft)	Modena (Ghirlandina)	84 m	(276 ft)
Siena (Palazzo Pubblico)	103 m	(338 ft)	Florence (Giotto's Campanile)	85 m	(280 ft)
Venice (Campanile)	101 m	(332 ft)	Verona (Torre dei Lamberti)	83 m	(275 ft)

Pasta

Croton and Sybaris, among other Greek cities, take the credit for introducing the Italians to their future hearts' delight. *Makaria*, a small, cylindrical form of pasta—perhaps the original *macaroni*—was eaten at funeral banquets; by 600 BC the Sybarites had invented the rolling pin and were making the equivalent of *tagliatelle* and maybe even *lasagne*.

Not yet having tomatoes, they were unable to perfect the concept at that time, but in a nation that often has trouble baking a decent loaf of bread this delicious, aesthetically stimulating and eminently practical new staple found a warm welcome everywhere. Pasta's triumphal march northwards finally slowed to a halt in the rice paddies and treacherous *polenta* morasses of Lombardy; everywhere else it remains in firm control of the country's menus.

Pasta does have its cultural ramifications. The artists of the Futurist movement wanted to declare war on spaghetti, and many of today's Italian *nouveaux riches* wouldn't be caught dead ordering pasta in a restaurant (while their counterparts in northern Europe and America wax ever more enthusiastic about it).

Do you think that pasta is all the same? Well, so do millions of Italians, though an equal number revel in the incredible variety of pasta forms and fashions; in your travels you'll find the same mixture of flour and water turned into broad *pappardelle* and narrow *linguini* ('tiny tongues'), stuffed delights like *ravioli* and *tortellini*, and regional specialities like Puglian *orecchietti* ('little ears').

Other inviting forms, among the 400 or so known shapes, include *vermicelli* ('little worms'), *lumacconi* ('slugs'), *bavette* ('dribbles'), and *strangolopreti* ('priest chokers'). But even these fail to satisfy the nation's culinary whims, and every so often one of the big pasta companies commissions a big-name fashion designer to come up with a new form.

The Pinocchio Complex

The Italians, much as they adore their *bambini*, have produced but one classic of children's literature, the story of a naughty wooden puppet who must pass through trials and tribulations before he can become a real boy—a blessing to his father in his old age.

Since the Risorgimento the Italian government has been a bit of a Pinocchio to the country that painfully carved it out of wood, admittedly half-petrified and half-rotted from the start. Each ring of the thick trunk told a dire tale of defeat and tyranny, corruption, papal misgovernment, foreign rule and betrayal. From this piece of flotsam the Italians created a new creature, a national state that sits in the class of real governments like an exasperating puppet, the bad boy of the EU, with more violations of its trade rules than any other nation. Every day its parliament is in session, its nose grows a little bit longer. With its creaky bureaucracy, unpredictable and not blessed with the soundest of judgements, it is constantly led astray—by the Mafia, power-hungry cabals of 'freemasons', Mussolinis, southern landowners, popes, Jesuits and whale-sized special interests that threaten to gobble it down whole. The parties that make up its *Commedia dell'Arte* coalitions, like flimsy wooden limbs and joints, are liable to trip up or fly off at any moment, making the poor thing collapse (something that since 1946 has occurred on the average of once every 11 months).

Just as Pinocchio is somehow able to walk without strings, so Italy functions with remarkable smoothness, and even prospers. Understandably, as Europe grows ever closer together, having a wooden-headed political system becomes rather embarrassing. Constitutional reform, with the 1993 referendum that changed the electoral system, may prove the biggest threat to this puppet's career. And, with the revelations of the last few years, Italians are beginning to interest themselves in the all-important question of who, all this time, has been pulling the strings.

Italian Culture

Cinema

After the Second World War, when Italy was at its lowest ebb, when it was financially and culturally bankrupt, when its traditional creativity in painting, architecture and music seemed to have dried up, along came a handful of Italian directors who invented a whole new language of cinema. Neorealism was a response to the fictions propagated by years of Fascism; it was also a response to the lack of movie-making equipment after the Romans, their eyes suddenly opened after a decade of deception and mindless 'White Telephone' comedies, pillaged and sacked Cinecittà in 1943. Stark, unsentimental, often shot in bleak locations and featuring non-professional actors, the genre took shape with directors like Roberto Rossellini (*Rome, Open City*, 1945), Vittorio de Sica (*Bicycle Thieves*, 1948) and Luchino Visconti (*The Earth Trembles*, 1948).

Although neorealism continued to influence Italian cinema (Rossellini's films with Ingrid Bergman, like *Europa 51* and *Stromboli*, Fellini's classic *La Strada* with Giulietta Masina and Anthony Quinn, Antonioni's *The Scream*), Italian directors began to go off in their own directions. The post-War period was the golden age of Italian cinema, when Italy's Hollywood, Cinecittà, produced scores of films every year. Like the artists of the Age of Mannerism, a new generation of individualistic (or egoistic) directors created works that needed no signature, ranging from Sergio Leone's ultra-popular kitsch westerns to the often jarring films of the Marxist poet Pasolini (*Accattone, The Decameron*). This was the period of Visconti's *The Damned*, Antonioni's *Blow Up*, Lina Wertmuller's *Seven Beauties*, De Sica's *Neapolitan Gold*, Bertolucci's *The Conformist*, and the classics of the maestro Federico Fellini—*I Vitelloni, La Dolce Vita, Juliet of the Spirits, The Clowns, Satyricon*.

In the 70s the cost of making films soared and the industry went into recession. Increasingly directors went abroad or sought out actors with international appeal to help finance their films (Bertolucci's *Last Tango in Paris* with Marlon Brando and *1900* with Donald Sutherland, the overripe Franco Zeffirelli's *Taming of the Shrew* with Taylor and Burton, Visconti's *Death in Venice*). Fellini was one of the few who managed to stay home (*Roma, Amarcord*, and later *Casanova* (although admittedly with Donald Sutherland in the lead role), *City of Women, The Ship Sails On, Orchestra Rehearsal* and *Intervista*, a film about Cinecittà itself).

Although funds for films became even scarcer in the 80s, new directors appeared to recharge Italian cinema, often with a fresh lyrical realism and sensitivity. Bright stars of the decade included Ermanno Olmi (the singularly beautiful *Tree of the Wooden Clogs* and *Cammina, Cammina*), Giuseppe Tornatore's sentimental and nostalgic *Cinema Paradiso* (1988), Paolo and Vittorio Taviani (*Padre Padrone, Night of the Shooting Stars, Kaos* and *Good Morning Babilonia*), Francesco Rosi (*Christ Stopped at Eboli, Three Brothers, Carmen* and *Cronaca d'una Morte Annunciata*), and Nanni Moretti (*La Messa è Finita*), unfortunately rarely seen outside of festivals and film clubs abroad, while Zeffirelli (*La Traviata*) and Bertolucci (*1900, The Last Emperor*) continued to represent Italy in the world's moviehouses. Comedy found new life in Mario Monticelli's hilarious *Speriamo che sia Femina* and in Bruno Bozzetto, whose animation features (especially *Allegro Non Troppo*, a satire of Disney's *Fantasia*) are a scream.

The 1990s have served up fairly thin gruel, a recession of inspiration to go with the economy. Worthy exceptions have been *Il Ladro dei Bambini* (1992) by Gianni Amelio, *Mediterraneo* (1991) by Gabriele Salvatores, about Italian soldiers marooned on a Greek island, and Nanni Moretti's travelogue to the Ionian islands, *Caro Diario* (1994). This was also the decade that Fellini spun his final reel. Although critics at home and abroad sometimes complained that he repeated himself in his last films (*Ginger and Fred* and *La Voce della Luna*, 1990), his loyal fans eagerly awaited each new instalment of his alternative hyper-Italy that exists on the other side of the looking glass. The 90s have ended in recognition on an international scale, with three Oscars for *La Vita e Bella*, Roberto Benigni's touching comedy set amidst the horrors of the holocaust.

Italian films are windows of the nation's soul, but if you don't understand Italian you may want to see them at home, where you have the advantage of subtitles. English language films in Italy rarely receive the same courtesy, however—Italians like their movies dubbed. Check listings for films labelled 'versione originale'— you're bound to find a few in Rome (*see* p.772) and Milan (*see* p.199), and often in other big cities as well. There are also Italy's film festivals (where films tend to be subtitled); the most important one is in Venice (last week of August to first week of September); also Messina (July); Verona (June); Florence (documentaries, in December); Salerno (16 and 18mm films, in September); and Trieste (science fiction, in July).

Literature

Few countries have as grand a literary tradition—even Shakespeare made extensive use of Italian stories for his plots. Besides all the great Latin authors and poets of ancient Rome, the peninsula has produced a small shelf of world classics in the Italian language; try to read a few before you come to Italy, or bring them along to read on the train. (All the books listed below are available in English translations, and may often be found in the English sections of Italian bookstores.) Once you've visited some of the settings of Dante's *Divine Comedy*, and come to know at least historically some of the inhabitants of the Inferno, Purgatorio and Paradiso, the old classic becomes even more fascinating. Dante was one of the first poets in Europe to write in the vernacular, and in doing so incorporated a good deal of topographical material from his 13th-century world.

His literary successor, Petrarch (1304–74), has been called by many 'the first modern man'; in his poetry the first buds of humanism were born, deeply thought and felt, complex, subtle and fascinating today as ever (his *Canzoniere* is widely available in English). The third literary deity in Italy's late-Medieval/early-Renaissance trinity is Boccaccio (1313–75), whose imagination, humour and realism is most apparent in his 'Human Comedy', the *Decameron*, a hundred stories 'told' by a group of young aristocrats who fled into the countryside from Florence to escape the plague of 1348.

Boccaccio's detached point of view had the effect of disenchanting Dante's ordered medieval cosmos, clearing the way for the renaissance of the secular novel.

Dante, Petrarch and Boccaccio exerted a tremendous influence over literary Europe, and in the 15th and 16th centuries a new crop of writers continued in the vanguard—Machiavelli in political thought (*The Prince*), though he also wrote two of the finest plays of the Renaissance (*Mandragola* and *Clizia*); Ariosto in the genre of knightly romance (*Orlando Furioso*, the antecedent of Spenser's *Faerie Queene*, among others); Cellini in autobiography; Vasari in art criticism and history (*The Lives of the Artists*); Castiglione in etiquette, gentlemanly arts and behaviour (*The Courtier*); Alberti in architecture and art theory (*Della Pintura*); Leonardo da Vinci in a hundred different subjects (the *Notebook*, etc.); even Michelangelo had time to write a book of sonnets, now translated into English. Other works include the writings and intriguing play (*The Candlemaker*) of the great philosopher and heretic Giordano Bruno (perhaps the only person to be excommunicated from three different churches); the risqué, scathing writings of Aretino, the 'Scourge of Princes'; the poetry and songs of Lorenzo de' Medici; and the *Commentaries* by Pope Pius II (Enea Silvio), a rare view into the life, opinions and times of one of the most accomplished Renaissance men, not to mention the only autobiography ever written by a pope.

Baroque Italy was a quieter place, dampened by the censorship of the Inquisition. The Venetians kept the flame alight: Casanova's picaresque *Life*, the tales of Carlo Gozzi, and the plays of Goldoni. Modern Italian literature has an official birthdate—the publication in 1827 of Alessandro Manzoni's *I Promessi Sposi* ('The Betrothed'), which not only spoke with sweeping humanity to the concerns of pre-Risorgimento Italy, but spoke in its language—an everyday Italian that nearly everyone could understand, no matter what their regional dialect; the novel went on to become a symbol of the aspiration of national unity. The next writer with the power to capture the turbulent emotions of his time was Gabriele D'Annunzio, whose life of daredevil, personally tailored patriotism and superman cult contrast with the lyricism of his poetry and some of his novels—still widely read in Italy. Meanwhile, and much more influentially, Pirandello, the philosophical Sicilian playwright and novelist obsessed with absurdity, changed the international vocabulary of drama before the Second World War.

The post-War era saw the appearance of neorealism in fiction as well as in cinema, and the classics, though available in English, are among the easiest books to read in Italian—Cesare Pavese's *La Luna e i Falò* (The Moon and the Bonfires), Carlo Levi's tragic *Cristo si è Fermato a Eboli* (Christ Stopped at Eboli), or Vittorini's *Conversazione in Sicilia*. Other acclaimed works of the post-War era include *The Garden of the Finzi-Contini* (about a Jewish family in Fascist Italy) by Giorgio Bassani, and another book set during the Fascist era, *That Awful Mess on Via Merulana* by Carlo Emilio Gadda; then there's the Sicilian classic that became famous around the world—*The Leopard* by Giuseppe di Lampedusa.

The late Italo Calvino, perhaps more than any other Italian writer in the past two decades, enjoyed a large international following—his *If on a Winter's Night a Traveller, Italian Folktales, Marcovaldo* and *The Baron in the Trees* were all immediately translated into English; perhaps the best of them is *Invisible Cities*, an imaginary dialogue between Marco Polo and Kublai Khan. Much maligned, Sicily continued to produce some of Italy's best literature, from the pens of Leonardo Sciascia and Gesualdo Bufalino. The current celebrity of Italian literature is of course Umberto Eco, professor of semiotics at Bologna University, whose *The Name of the Rose* kept readers all over the world at the edge of their seats over the murders of a handful of 14th-century monks in a remote Italian monastery, while magically evoking, better than many historians, all the political and ecclesiastical turmoil of the period.

Italy has inspired countless of her visitors, appearing as a setting in more novels, poems and plays than tongue can tell. There is also a long list of non-fiction classics, some of which make fascinating reading and are readily available in most bookshops: Goethe's *Italian Journey*, Ruskin's *The Stones of Venice*, D. H. Lawrence's *Etruscan Places* and *Twilight in Italy*, Hilaire Belloc's *The Path to Rome*, Norman Douglas' *Old Calabria*, James/Jan Morris' *Venice*, Mary McCarthy's *The Stones of Florence* and *Venice Observed*, and many others, including the famously over-the-top travellers' accounts of Edward Hutton and the ever-entertaining H. V. Morton. For the Italian point of view from the outside looking in, read the classic *The Italians* by the late Luigi Barzini, former correspondent for the *Corriere della Sera* in London.

Music and Opera

Italy has contributed as much to Western music as any country—and perhaps a little more. It was an Italian monk, Guido d'Arezzo, who devised the musical scale; it was a Venetian printer, Ottaviano Petrucci, who invented a method of printing music with movable type in 1501—an industry Italian printers monopolized for years (which is why we play *allegro* and not *schnell*). Italy also gave us the piano, originally the *pianoforte* because unlike the harpsichord you could play both soft and loud, and the accordion, invented in the Marche, and the violins of the Guarneri and Stradivarius of Cremona, setting a standard for the instrument that has never been equalled. But Italy is most famous as the mother of opera, in many ways the most Italian of arts.

Italian composers first came into their own in the 14th century, led by the half-legendary, blind Florentine Landini, whose *Ecco la Primavera* is one of the first Italian compositions to come down to us. Although following international trends introduced by musicians from France and the Low Countries, musicologists note from the start a special love of melody, even in the earliest Italian works, as well as a preference for vocal music over the purely instrumental.

Landini was followed by the age of the *frottolas* (secular verses accompanied by lutes), especially prominent in the court of Mantua. The frottolas were forerunners of the *madrigal*, the greatest Italian musical invention during the Renaissance. Although sung in three or six parts, the text of the madrigals was given serious consideration, and was sung to be understood; at the same time church music had become so polyphonically rich and sumptuous (most notoriously at St Mark's in Venice) that it drowned out the words of the Mass. Many melodies used were from secular and often bawdy songs, and the bishops at the Council of Trent (1545–63) seriously considered banning music from the liturgy. The day was saved by the Roman composers, led by Palestrina, whose solemn, simple but beautiful melodies set a standard for all subsequent composers.

Two contrasting strains near the end of the 16th century led to the birth of opera: the Baroque love of spectacle and the urge to make everything, at least on the surface, more beautiful, more elaborate, more showy. Musically there were the lavish Florentine *intermedii*, performed on special occasions between the acts of plays; the *intermedii* used elaborate sets and costumes, songs, choruses and dances to set a mythological scene. At the same time, in Florence, a group of humanist intellectuals who called themselves the 'Camerata' came to the conclusion from their classical studies that ancient Greek drama was not spoken, but sung, and took it upon themselves to try to recreate this pure and classical form. One of their chief theorists was Galileo's father Vincenzo, who studied Greek, Turkish and Moorish music and advocated the clear enunciation of the words, as opposed to the Venetian tendency to merge words and music as a single rich unit of sound.

One of the first results of the Camerata's debates was court musician Jacopo Peri's *L'Euridice*, performed in Florence in 1600. Peri used a kind of singing speech (recitative) to tell the story, interspersed with a few melodic songs. No one, it seems, asked for an encore; opera had to wait a few years until the Duchess of Mantua asked her court composer, Claudio Monteverdi (1567–1643), to compose something like what she had heard in Florence. Monteverdi went far beyond Peri, bringing in a large orchestra, designing elegant sets, adding dances and many more melodic songs, or

arias. His classic *L'Orfeo* (1607), still heard today, and *L'Arianna* (unfortunately lost but for fragments) were the first operatic 'hits'. He moved on to bigger audiences in Venice, which soon had 11 opera houses. After he died, Naples took over top opera honours, gaining special renown for its clear-toned *castrati*.

Other advances were developing in the more pious atmosphere of Rome, where Corelli was busily perfecting the concerto form and composing his famous *Christmas Concerto*. In Venice, Vivaldi expanded the genre by composing some four hundred concerti for whatever instruments happened to be played in the orchestra of orphaned girls where he was concert-master.

The 18th century saw the sonata form perfected by harpsichord master Domenico Scarlatti. Opera was rid of some of its Baroque excesses and a division was set between serious works and the comic *opera buffa*; Pergolesi (1710–36; his *Il Flaminio* was the basis for Stravinsky's *Pulcinella*) and Cimarosa (1749–1801) were the most sought-after composers, while the now infamous Salieri, antagonist of Mozart, charmed the court of Vienna. Italian composers held sway throughout Europe; with others, like Sammartini, who helped develop the modern symphony, they contributed more than is generally acknowledged today towards the founding of modern music.

Italy innovated less in the 19th century; at this time most of its musical energies were devoted to opera, becoming the reviving nation's clearest and most widely appreciated medium of self-expression. All of the most popular Italian operas were written in the 19th and early 20th century, most of them by the 'Big Five'— Bellini, Donizetti, Rossini, Verdi and Puccini. For Italians, Verdi (1813–1901) is supreme, the national idol even in his lifetime, whose rousing operas were practically the battle hymns of the Risorgimento. Verdi, more than anyone else, re-established Italy on the musical map; his works provided Italy's melodic answer to the ponderous turbulence of Richard Wagner. After Verdi, Puccini held the operatic stage, though not entirely singlehandedly; the later 19th century gave us a number of composers best remembered for only one opera: Leoncavallo's *Pagliacci*, Mascagni's *Cavalleria Rusticana*, Cilea's *Adriana Lecouvreur*, and many others down to obscure composers like Giordano, whose *Fedora*, famous for being the only opera with bicycles on stage, is revived frequently in his hometown of Fóggia.

Of more recent Italian and Italian-American composers, there's Ottorino Respighi (whose works were among the few 20th-century productions that the great Toscanini deigned to direct) and Gian Carlo Menotti, surely the best loved, not only for his operas but for founding the Spoleto Festival. Later there were the innovative post-War composers Luigi Nono and Luciano Berio, two respected names in contemporary academic music.

Next to all of this big-league culture, however, there survive remnants of Italy's traditional music—the pungent tunes of Italian bagpipes (*zampogna*), the ancient instrument of the Apennine shepherds, often heard in the big cities (especially in the South) at Christmas time; the lively *tarantellas* of Puglia; country accordion music, the fare of many a rural festa; and the great song tradition of the country's music capital, Naples, the cradle of everyone's favourite cornball classics, but also of many haunting, passionate melodies of tragedy and romance that are rarely heard abroad—or, to be honest, in Italy itself these days. Naples now prides itself on being the capital of Mediterranean rock 'n' roll, a spurious claim, and not too impressive even if

it's true. Listen for yourself; on the *bancarelle* in the street markets of Naples you'll have ample opportunity to audition a wide range of locally produced cassettes and see if anything catches your fancy. Italian pop music climbs to the top of its modest plateau every February at the San Remo song festival, the national run-off for the Eurovision Song Contest and just as hilariously tacky; the likes of *Volare* are nowhere to be seen.

Opera season in Italy runs roughly from November to May. Don't limit your explorations to the prestigious La Scala in Milan. The San Carlo in Naples is equally old and impressive, and La Fenice in Venice hopefully will be once more (when her restoration is complete), in cities with a longer and more intense operatic tradition; and the Teatro dell'Opera in Rome and the Teatro Comunale in Florence can both put on excellent and innovative productions. On the next rung down (in size and finances, though not necessarily in quality) are the houses in Parma, Trieste, Genoa, Bergamo, Turin, Modena, Bari and Fóggia. Summer festivals are an excellent place to hear music; check through the list of festivals on pp.23–5.

Non è questo 'l terren, ch' i' toccai pria?	*Is not this precious earth my native land?*
Non è questo il mio nido,	*And is not this the nest*
Ove nudrito fui sí dolcemente?	*From which my tender wings were taught to fly?*
Non è questa la patria in ch' io mi fido,	*And is not this the soil upon whose breast,*
Madre benigna e pia,	*Loving and soft, faithful and true and fond,*
Che copre l'un e l'altro mio parente?	*My father and my gentle mother lie?*
Per Dio, questo la mente	*'For love of God,' I cry,*
Talor vi mova; e con pietà guardate	*'Some time take thought of your humanity*
Le lagrime del popol doloroso,	*And spare your people all their tears and grief!*
Che sol da voi riposo,	*From you they seek relief*
Dopo Dio, spera: e, pur che voi mostriate	*Next after God. If in your eyes they see*
Segno, alcun di pietate,	*Some marks of sympathy,*
Vertú contra furore	*Against this mad disgrace*
Prenderà l'arme; e fia 'l combatter corto;	*They will arise, the combat will be short*
Ché l'antiquo valore	*For the stern valour of our ancient race*
Ne l' italici cor non è ancor morto.	*Is not yet dead in the Italian heart.'*
Petrarch (1304–74)	*trans. William Dudley Foulke LL D (1915)*

Piemonte and Valle d'Aosta

Piemonte (Piedmont), 'the foot of the mountains', is not only the birthplace of the modern Italian state, the source of its greatest river, the cradle of its industry, and the originator of such indispensable Italian staples as vermouth, Fiats and breadsticks, but also a beautiful region full of surprises. To the north and west tower some of the most important peaks in the Alps such as Gran Paradiso and Monviso, while the small autonomous region of Valle d'Aosta is home to such world-class heavyweights as Mont Blanc, the Matterhorn and Monte Rosa. The south is walled off from Liguria and the Mediterranean by the lush green Maritime Alps which, like the rest of Piemonte, are unspoiled, ill-equipped with the amenities of international tourism, and utterly delightful. Between the Maritime Alps and the Po are miles of rolling hills clad in the noble pinstripe patterns of some of the world's most prestigious vineyards. North of the Po the scenery changes again, flat as a railway station pizza, and criss-crossed by a complicated web of small canals that feed Europe's most important rice fields. And in the centre of the hills, plains and mountains lies the regional capital Turin, not an industrial by-product as one might suppose, but Baroque and strange.

Historically Piemonte is one of Italy's newer regions, its name not even in existence until the 13th century, when it gradually came to encompass the former Marquessates of Monferrato, Ivrea, Saluzzo and the County of Turin. The French dynasty of Savoy first got a foothold in Piemonte by marriage in the 11th century, and from the very beginning kept a much tighter reign on their realm than other Italian princes. The rise of independent *comuni*, the republics and the heady ideas of the Renaissance failed to penetrate their feudal fastness. For centuries the population didn't even consider itself Italian, and instead spoke Provençal, which still survives in many a remote valley. Yet, as unprogressive and as uninspired as Piemonte remained throughout Italy's Golden Age, it was the first region to re-surface when the peninsula went under in the 16th-century tidal wave of invasions and looting; Piemonte's French occupation, begun in 1502, ended 60 years later when Duke Emanuele Filiberto won back his lands with a series of gritty battles. From that point on the Savoys linked Piemonte's destiny with Italy, treading the troubled political waters of the day with an astute choice of alliances and cautious diplomatic manoeuvring that earned them the title of King of Sardinia in 1713, and then, in the Risorgimento, the crown of Italy herself.

There were violent riots in Turin when the first king of Italy, Vittorio Emanuele II, moved his capital to Florence, *en route* to Rome; the Piemontese rightly sensed that they had been relegated to the knick-knack shelf of history. But rather than collect dust, they began Italy's industrial revolution, building the first wool and cotton mills in the torrent-sliced

Piemonte and Valle d'Aosta

20 km
10 miles

N

SWITZERLAND

Lugano

Matterhorn
Cervino   Zermatt
Breithorn

Breuil-Cervinia
Cime Bianche   Monte Rosa
Macugnaga

Chamonix   Gt. St Bernard
Pass

St
Oyen   Valtournenche
Champoluc
Valsesia
Alagna
Omegna
Varallo

Varese
Como

L. Varese

Mont
Blanc   Entreves
Troubles   Antey-St-Andre   Chamois
Brusson   Gressoney-la-Trinite
Gressoney-St-Jean
Borgomanero

Courmayeur   Morgex   Nus   St Vincent
Gaby
A8

Pré-St-Didier
la Thuile   Aosta   Chatillon   Issime   Piedicavallo
Borgosesia
Malpensa

Chaz Dura   Tete
d'Arpy   Aymavilles   Verrès   Santuario d'Oropa
To Milan

Planavel   Villeneuve   Pila   Issogne   Pont-St-Martin
Cossato
Ticino

Little
St Bernard
Pass   Cogne   Champorcher
Biella
S228

Valsavarenche   Champorcher   Donato   Gagliànico
Novara

Rhêmes-Notre Dame   Ivrea   Magnano
A26

Gran Paradiso
Nat. Park   Noasca   Pont Canavese   A4

Val d'Isere   Ceresole Reale   Cuorgne
Vercelli

Forno Alpi Graie   Valperga

Balme   Ceres   Trino
A7

Col du
Mt Cenis   Ala di
Stura   Lanzo Torinese
Cirie

Novalesa   Venaria   Chivasso   Crei
Casale Monferrato
Valenza

Mont Cenis
Tunnel   Susa   Dora Riparia
Torino   Abbazia di
Vezzolano   Moncalvo
A21

Bardonecchia   Gravere   Avigliana   PIEMONTE   Castagnole
Castagnole
Monferrato

Chiomonte   Sacra di
San Michele   Rivoli   Chieri   Asti
Alessandria
Tortona

Exilles   Fenestrelle   Stupinigi   Montegrosso   Bosco Marengo

Oulx   Sauze d'Oulx   Vallinotto   Costigliole d'Asti   Novi
Ligure

Sestriere   Pinerolo   Carmagnola   Canelli   Nizza
Monferrato

Claviere
Montgenevre   Argentiera   Torre Péllice   Racconigi   Barbaresco   Acqui
Terme

Briançon   Bobbio Péllice   Cavour   Brà   Pollenzo   Alba   Mango
A26

Villanova   Piano del Re   Paesana   Cherasco   Grinzane
Crissolo   Revello   Saluzzo   Savigliano   La Morra

Pontechianale   Mt Viso   Manta   Barolo
Sassello

Casteldelfino   Verzuolo   Dogliani

Sampeyre   Fossano   Ceva   Milesimo   Cairo Montenotte
Varazze
Genoa

Acceglio   Dronero   Celle Ligure

Argentera   Cuneo   Mondovi   Villanova Mondovi   Albissola Marina

Pietraporzio   Borgo San Dalmazzo   Boves   Savona
Vado Ligure

Demonte   Lurisia   Frabosa
Soprana   Calizzano   Spotorno

Valdieri   Vernante   Garessio   Noli
Finale Ligure

Terme di Valdieri   Limone Piemonte   Toirano   Pietra Ligure
Loano

Palanfre   Col di Tenda   Ormea   Borghetto S. Spirito
Ceriale

Tende   Garlenda   Albenga

Monesi   Golfo di

Triora   Pontedassio   Alassio   Genova

Pigna   Baiardo   Tággia   Laigueglia
Andora

Castel Vittorio   Dolcede   Cervo

Ventimiglia   Dolceacqua   Imperia   S. Bartolomeo al Mare
Diana Marina

S. Ludovica   Arma di Tággia
San Remo

Menton   Bordighera

FRANCE

A10

valleys of Biella, the first cars in Turin, the first typewriters in Ivrea, and creating a felt-hat empire in Alessandria. Piemonte's economy has always been one of the strongest in Italy, with tourism playing only an insignificant supporting role.

But if the Italy you seek includes sensational Alpine scenery—snowy peaks and emerald valleys—and mountain resorts, either ultra-sophisticated or rustic, or somewhere in between; if it includes un-hyped medieval hill villages and castles standing like islands above rolling seas of vines; if it includes fantastic wines and regional cuisine, with a French touch; or if you have a special interest in white truffles, caves, St Bernards, trout fishing, Egyptology, Romanesque architecture, rare flowers, wildlife or kayaking, you will love Piemonte and Aosta. On the other hand, if your Italy consists of Renaissance art, lemon groves and endless sunshine, you'd better do as Hannibal did and just pass right on through.

Not to be Missed

If you're coming from the west through the Mont Blanc Tunnel, the Valle d'Aosta is worth lingering in: **Aosta** itelf is a fine Roman medieval town, **Courmayeur** and **Breuil-Cervinia** are world class resorts, there are storybook castles at **Issogne** and **Fénis**, and the lovely valleys of **Ayas** and **Cogne**. The latter leads to **Gran Paradiso National Park**, with its golden eagles, ibex and chamois and superb alpine walks.

Turin, the capital of Piemonte, may be synonymous with Fiat, but it has also inherited all the treasures of the Savoys, the last kings of Italy, and has a striking collection of Baroque churches and domes and first-class museums. Each of the surrounding valleys have their rewards, especially the **Valle di Susa** and **Valle del Chisone** to the west of Turin, offering a possible circular tour including fine medieval towns and fancy mountain resorts. Another great highlight is the famous and very beautiful wine region around **Asti** and **Alba**, dotted with castles and handsome towns. **Cuneo** is the centre for exploring the lush Maritime Alps, while **Vercelli** is king of the rice paddies.

Turin

Detroit without the degradation, the aristocratic capital of the Savoys, an elegantly planned Baroque city of arcades and squares, frequent venue of international bridge tournaments, the home of the famous shroud, of Juventus, the Red Brigades and vermouth, and reputedly the centre of black magic in the Mediterranean, Turin (Torino) makes a rather unexpected 'Gateway to Italy'. It stands on the Po, so close to its Alpine sources that this longest and most benighted of Italy's rivers is almost clean. Its cuisine is influenced by France; its winters are colder than Copenhagen's; its most renowned museum is Egyptian.

As important Italian cities go, Turin is a relative newcomer. In 1574, a time when the king of Spain held the rest of the peninsula by the bootstrap, fiesty 'iron-headed' Emanuele Filiberto of Savoy, descendant of Europe's most ancient ruling house, drove the French and Spanish troops from his territory and moved his capital from Chambéry to Turin, previously little more than a fortified Roman outpost (*Augusta Taurinorum*) and medieval university town. It was a move symbolizing the dynasty's new identity with the Italian portion of Savoy, or Piemonte, a move that was to have the greatest impact on the future. No one at the time suspected that the highly centralized duchy in this hitherto neglected corner of the peninsula would one day unite the land, and that Turin would be the first capital of the Kingdom of Italy.

It's a common cliché that the Agnelli family's Fiat Corporation is Turin's new dynasty; founded in 1899, it is not only Europe's largest car manufacturer, but one of the largest corporations in the world. While the historic centre of Turin retains its refined air of a courtly drawing room (no other Italian city looks anything like it), the glitter and sleekness of the shops are thanks mostly to Fiat money, which is also responsible for the vast suburb of Mirafiori south of Turin, built by the company to house the thousands of workers who have come up from Calabria and other points south. Paradoxically, while Turin takes credit for Italy's unification, it has suffered the consequences of that union most acutely, plagued by perhaps the worst relations and bigotry between northern and southern Italians. The latter became Italy's first and most organized proletariat: during the First World War, Gramsci, the great philosopher of the Italian Communist party, led the workers' factory councils in occupying the Fiat works in what he hoped would become an Italian Petrograd. The failure taught him that Italians required a different solution, and made him rightly fear that extremism in one form or another would be the end result.

Gramsci died in a fascist prison; fifty years after his factory councils experiment, the Red Brigades were born in the urban anonymity of Mirafiori. Their militant sympathizers and radical unionism crippled Fiat in the seventies. Since then, prosperity perhaps more than anything has exorcised most of Turin's extremist bogeys. Despite increasing European competition—and partly due to a far-sighted 'understanding' with Japanese car-makers not to intrude into each other's home markets—Fiat still supplies well over three-quarters of all the cars in Italy, through Fiat itself, or through Fiat-owned Lancia or Alfa Romeo.

Getting There

by air

Turin's **Caselle airport** is 15km north of the city; for information call ✆ 011 567 6361. Every 30 minutes an **airport bus**, run by SADEM, stops at Porta Susa Station, the main bus terminal on Corso Inghilterra and outside Porta Nuova Station. Tickets can be bought from a kiosk in the arrivals hall or at the Café Negrita on the corner of Via Sacchi and Corso Vittorio Emanuele II (opposite Porta Nuova).

by rail

Turin's massive neoclassical station, **Porta Nuova** (information, ✆ 147 888 088, *open daily 7am–9pm*), is near the centre, with connections to France and Genoa (2 hrs), Milan (1½ hrs), Aosta (2½ hrs) and Venice (5 hrs). Another station, **Porta Susa**, on the west side of town, can be a convenient getting-off point, while a third station, **Torino Ceres**, serves the regional line to Cirié, Lanzo and Ceres.

by long-distance bus

The **bus terminal** is on Corso Inghilterra, ✆ 011 433 2525, at the western end of Corso Vittorio Emanuele II, though many buses also stop near Porta Susa Station. Buses head out from here for Aosta's ski resorts as far as Chamonix and also provide year-round connections to towns in the province.

Turin is not a big city; most of its principal sites are clustered together within walking distance of each other. Otherwise, its regular grid of streets is served by old-fashioned **trams** and **buses**. The city transport office at Porta Nuova Station provides a good free city transport map (also available from tourist offices). There is also a **tourist bus** offering city tours starting from outside the tourist office in Piazza Castello (*two tours a day at 10 and 2; L12,000*). **Parking** in Turin is not as impossible as in most Italian cities, but is still very restricted in the old city centre. **Taxi** ranks are in many of the main piazzas; alternatively, call ✆ 011 5730, or ✆ 011 3399.

The main office, Piazza Castello 161, ✆ 011 535 181/✆ 011 535 901 (*open Mon–Sat 9–7.30*), operates a free room-finding service; other offices are at Porta Nuova Station, ✆ 011 531 327; Via Garibaldi 25, ✆ 011 442 3838; and Caselle Airport. For information on concerts, film times, and so on, check out the listings in *La Stampa*, or visit the InfoCulture booth, Piazza San Carlo 159, freephone ✆ 167 015 475. Ask for the Torino Culture Yearbook, translated in English.

Via Roma

Central Turin is laid out in a stately rhythm of porticoed streets and squares. Few railway stations in Italy deposit the weary traveller in a piazza as inviting as Porta Nuova's manicured **Piazza Carlo Felice**, where even the traffic intersections are covered with pots of flowers. Fashionable **Via Roma**, lined with designer clothes shops, leads from here into the heart of the city, passing through an impressive 'gateway' of twin churches, **Santa Cristina** and **San Carlo**, designed by the Sicilian Baroque genius Filippo Juvarra, court architect to the King of Sardinia in the early 18th century.

Behind the churches lies Turin's finest square, **Piazza San Carlo**, a 17th-century confection with a flamboyant centrepiece in its bronze equestrian statue of **Duke Emanuele Filiberto**, 'the Iron Head', sheathing his sword after battle, by local sculptor Carlo Marochetti (1838). This is a city of elegant cafés, and in Piazza San Carlo you can sip your cappuccino in the most celebrated of them all, the 19th-century **Caffè Torino**, a veritable palace of java with chandeliers and frescoed ceilings. Just west, the **Museo della Marionetta**, Via S. Teresa 5 (*open Tues–Fri 9–1, Sat 2–6; closed Sun and Mon; adm*) has a collection of Italian puppets from various periods. Nearby is the glass-roofed shopping arcade, **Galleria San Federico**.

The Egyptian Museum and Galleria Sabauda

These treasure troves are just off Piazza San Carlo, sharing the **Palazzo dell'Accademia delle Scienze**. This palace, designed as a Jesuit college, is the most ponderous of all the landmarks designed by the remarkable Guarino Guarini, a Theatine architect priest who came to work for Carlo Emanuele in 1668 and changed the face of Turin.

The **Museo Egizio** (*open Tues–Sat 8.30am–10pm, Sun and hols 8.30–8; adm exp*) is rated (except by the directors of the Louvre!) as the second most important in the world, after the museum in Cairo. It was begun as a collection of curios in 1628 by Carlo Emanuele I, but later Savoys took their pharaohs and mummies more seriously, especially Carlo Felice, who

Turin

N

250 metres
250 yards

CORSO CASALE

Fiume Po

LUNGO PO MACHIAVELLI

VIA NAPIONE

Giardino Zoologico

Piazza Gran Madre di Dio

Gran Madre di Dio

Ponte Vittorio Emanuele I

LUNGO PO CADORNA

Ponte Umberto I

CORSO G. LANZA

CORSO MONCALIERI

Orto Botanico

Parco del Valentino

CORSO M. D'AZEGLIO

CORSO CAIROLI

VIA VITTORIA

VIA CAVOUR

VIA MARIA VITTORIA

VIA PLANA

Piazza Vittorio Veneto

VIA MADAMA CRISTINA

VIA GIUSEPPE MAZZINI

VIA GIUSEPPE VERDI

Mole Antonelliana

S. Annunziata

VIA PO

VIA DEGLI ARTISTI

VIA SANTA GIULIA

Pza Santa Giulia

VIA C. BALBO

CORSO REGINA MARGHERITA

LUNGO DORA FIRENZE

CORSO REGINA MARGHERITA

Largo Montebello

VIA MONTEBELLO

VIA SAN MAURIZIO

VIA G. ROSSINI

CORSO S. MAURIZIO

Giardino Reale

Teatro Regio

Università

VIA PO

VIA PRINCIPE AMEDEO

VIA ACCADEMIA ALBERTINA

Piazza Carlo Emanuele II

ACCADEMIA

VIA GIOVANNI GIOLITTI

Piazza Cavour

VIA CAMILLO

Pza Bodoni

VIA CARLO ALBERTO

VIA CARLO ALBERTO

VIA MARIA VITTORIA

Pal Carignano

S. Filippo Neri

Piazza Carlo Alberto

VIA LAGRANGE

Pza Lagrange

CORSO VITTORIO EMANUELE II

VIA GOITO

VIA NIZZA

VIA SACCHI

Stazione Porta Nuova

Palazzo Reale

Armeria Reale

Teatro Romano

Piazzetta Reale

Piazza Castello

Duomo

Pza S. Giovanni

VIA XX SETTEMBRE

Museo Egizio e Gall. Sabauda

Piazza Carignano

Sta Cristina

Piazza S. Carlo

VIA ROMA

S. Carlo

VIA ROMA

VIA GRAMSCI

VIA D. ARCIVESCOVADO

Pza Paleocapa

VIA SACCHI

CORSO 11 FEBBRAIO

Porta Palatina

Piazza C. Augustino

Largo IV Marzo

S. Lorenzo

VIA BERTOLA

VIA MONTE DI PIETÀ

VIA STA TERESA

VIA ALFIERI

CORSO G. MATTEOTTI

CORSO RE. UMBERTO I

Piazza della Repubblica

VIA MILANO

VIA BARBAROUX

VIA S. FRANCESCO D'ASSISI

VIA BOTERO

Piazza Solferino

Piazza Emr. Filberto

S. Consolata

Pza d. Consolata

VIA D. BASILICA

VIA CORTE D'APPELLO

S. DOMENICO

Pza Arbarello

Giardino Cittadella

CORSO G. FERRARIS

VIA DELLA CONSOLATA

VIA C. GIULIO

VIA S. CHIARA

VIA STA CHIARA

VIA S. DOMENICO

VIA GIUSEPPE GARIBALDI

VIA STA MARIA

VIA STA MARIA

VIA JUVARRA

VIA BERTOLA

VIA CERNAIA

CORSO PALESTRO

CORSO VALDOCCO

Largo Vittorio Emanuele

CORSO G. FERRARIS

Galleria Civica d'Arte Moderna e Contemporanea

CORSO STATI UNITI

VIA V. VELA

CORSO MARGHERITA

CORSO REGINA MARGHERITA

VIA COTTOLENGO

CORSO PRINCIPE ODDONE

VIA EUGENIO

VIA STA CHIARA

VIA PR. EUGENIO

CORSO S. MARTINO

Piazza Statuto

VIA DEL CARMINE

VIA NOTA

VIA MANZONI

VIA ALLIONI

VIA GUICCIARDINI

VIA PASSALACQUA

Stazione Porta Susa

Piazza XVIII Dicembre

CORSO BOLZANO

CORSO INGHILTERRA

CORSO VINZAGLIO

CORSO G. MATTEOTTI

CORSO VITTORIO EMANUELE II

CORSO CASTELFIDARDO

85

acquired the collection of the French Consul General of Egypt and confidant of Mohammed Ali, Bernardo Drovetti (a native of Piemonte), and founded the museum in 1824—the first Egyptian museum in the world. Two major Italian expeditions this century added to the collections, and the museum played a major role in the Aswan Dam rescue digs. It was rewarded with one of the temples it had preserved—the 15th-century BC rock-cut **Temple of Ellessya**, with a relief of Thothmes III, now reconstructed in the museum—best seen in the early evening when the half-light allows the reliefs to stand out properly.

The ground floor houses an excellent collection of monumental public sculpture, notably the black granite Rameses II (13th century BC), the 15th-century BC Thothmes III, and the sarcophagus of a vizier of the 26th Dynasty, Ghemenef-Har-Bak. Upstairs, in the two main rooms, is an immense papyrus library, including copies of the *Book of the Dead* and the *Royal Papyrus*, listing all the kings of Egypt from the Sun itself down to the 17th dynasty; Turin's papyrus collection is so extensive that after Jean François Champollion cracked the Rosetta Stone he came here to complete his study of hieroglyphics. Elsewhere upstairs you can spend hours wandering through the essentials and the trivialities of ancient Egypt; there are artefacts from the Egyptians' daily lives, notably a reconstruction of the 14th-century BC **Tomb of the architect Khaiè and his wife Meriè** (18th Dynasty) that somehow managed to escape the grave robbers—even the bread and beans prepared for their afterlife remain intact. Other rooms contain mummies in various stages of deshabille, wooden models of boats and funerary processions, paintings, statuettes, jewellery, clothing and textiles

The museum is currently undergoing something of a reorganization, the first fruits of which are on display in the basement, featuring finds from the Gebelein, Assiut and Qau el Kebir sites first excavated by representatives of the museum between 1905 and 1920. There are reconstructed tombs, painted sarcophagi and dozens of beautifully preserved wooden models recovered from tombs: boats with crews and oars, kitchens and granaries, and servants performing everyday tasks as well as scale models of the dead themselves.

On the top floor, the **Galleria Sabauda** (*open Tues, Wed, Fri and Sat 9–2, Thurs 10–7, Sun 10–10; adm exp*) houses the principal collections of the House of Savoy. The Savoys liked Flemish and Dutch art just as much as Italian, which gives the Sabauda a variety most Italian galleries lack. Among the Italians are two fine Florentine works, *Tobias and the Archangel Raphael* by Antonio and Piero del Pollaiuolo, and a fine study of Botticelli's newborn *Venus*, thought to be by one of his students; other works are by Mantegna, Taddeo Gaddi, Sodoma, Tintoretto, Titian, Veronese and Bergognone. Among the Northerners are Jan Van Eyck's *St Francis*, Memling's drama-filled *Scenes from the Passion*, Van Dyck's beautiful *Children of Charles I*, popular scenes and landscapes by Jan Brueghel, *Portrait of a Doctor* by Jacobs Dirk, and Rembrandt's *Old Man Sleeping*. The French have a room to themselves, with works by Poussin, Claude and Clouet.

Across from the museum, the **Palazzo Carignano**, much more representative of Guarini's work, was begun in 1679 for the Savoy-Carignano branch of the royal family—the branch that was to produce Vittorio Emanuele II, who was born here. The palace presents two very different façades: the first, looming above Piazza Carignano, is a fine undulating Baroque concoction; the other, facing Piazza Carlo Alberti and the Biblioteca Nazionale, is dull and neoclassical. The palace is full of Italian historical fossils—the bedroom where Carlo Alberti died, Cavour's study and the chamber of the Piemontese Subalpine Parliament preserved exactly as it appeared during its final session in 1860: full of chandeliers, gilt furnishings and red plush. The Palace also hosted the first Italian Parliament, which on March 14 1861 proclaimed Vittorio Emanuele King of Italy. The themes are covered in more depth in the **Museo Nazionale del Risorgimento** (*open Tues–Sat 9–6.30, Sun 9–12.30; adm exp*), one of the more interesting of Italy's scores of Risorgimento museums.

Piazza Castello

Parallel to Via Accademia, the **Galleria Subalpina** (just right, off Via Battisti) is Turin's other shopping arcade, inspired by the Galleria Vittorio Emanuele in Milan. The Galleria Subalpina leads to the elegant Caffè Baratti & Milano, and the huge expanse of **Piazza Castello**, the main square of Turin, with the **Palazzo Madama** in the middle. Named for the two royal widows ('Madama Reale') who lived here, the palace dates back to the 15th century, though it incorporates in its structure fragments from the eastern Roman gate, the Porta Decumana, as well as the original 13th-century castle. In 1718 one of the Madamas had Juvarra give the old place a facelift—a task Juvarra responded to with a beautiful, serene façade that has little to do with the typical Baroque of his period. Unfortunately, the façade is at present covered in a mass of scaffolding and tarpaulin.

The palace houses the **Museo Civico di Arte Antica** (*closed for restoration*), with a notable collection of medieval and Renaissance sculpture and painting, and manuscripts. Among the highlights, if anyone is ever allowed in again to see them, are the illuminated 14th-century law codes of Turin, unique pieces of 15th-century glassware, copies of the *Book of Hours* of the Duc de Berry, illustrations by Jan Van Eyck, and the superb *Portrait of an Unknown Man* (1476) by Antonello da Messina.

Under the arcade flanking the north side of Piazza Castello, the **Armeria Reale** (*open Tues and Thurs 1.30–7.30, Wed, Fri, Sat and Sun 9–2; adm exp*) contains one of the finest collections of medieval and Renaissance arms, armour and guns in the world; the library upstairs contains a famous self-portrait in red ink by Leonardo da Vinci.

The Palazzo Reale and the Duomo

The dark apricot **Palazzo Reale** (*open Tues–Thurs and Sat–Sun 9–1 and 2–6, Fri 9–1 and 2–10; guided tours only; adm exp*) lies just off the Piazza Castello, behind a gate of mounted 'Dioscuri' and Turin's largest parking lot, which doesn't do much for its already bureaucratic façade. This, however, was the main residence of the princes of Savoy from 1646 until 1865, and you can take the tour to learn that they lavished a considerable amount of their subjects' taxes on chandeliers and fluffy frescoes. The cases of Chinese porcelain try hard to relieve the anomie. The Palace's **Giardino Reale** is a far more pleasant place to while away an afternoon, with the Mole Antonelliana (*see* below) rising above the horse chestnut trees like the headquarters of Ming the Merciless. The royal chapel, **San Lorenzo**, stands on the corner. Although the outside is bland—an unusual octagonal dome its only distinguishing feature—the interior by Guarini (1668–80) is an idiosyncratic Baroque fantasia.

Around the corner, just off Via XX Settembre, is Turin's plain **Duomo di San Giovanni** built by three dry 15th-century Tuscan architects. What it lacks in presence it compensates for with one of the most provocative artefacts of Christendom: the **Shroud of Turin**, brought to the city from the old Savoy capital of Chambéry in the 16th century by Emanuele Filiberto. To house the relic properly, Guarini designed the striking, black marble **Cappella della Sacra Sindone** (Chapel of the Holy Shroud), crowned by a bold oliaphonous dome-cone zig-zagging to a climax of basketweave arches full of restless energy. (*At the time of writing the chapel is closed for restoration, but much of it can be appreciated from the outside.*)

The shroud, shown only on special occasions (the ne0xt should be in the year 2000), is kept in a silver casket in an iron box in a marble coffer in the urn on the chapel altar; an exact replica, however, is displayed along with a multilingual explanation of the results of several scientific investigations, which tried to determine whether it was possible that the shroud was used at Christ's burial. Although forensic scientists and their computers have concluded that it would have been impossible to forge the unique front and back impressions of a crucified man with a wound in his side and bruises from a crown of thorns, the shroud flunked a carbon-dating test in 1989, and is now believed to date from the 12th century.

Besides the shroud, the cathedral contains in its second chapel a fine polyptych of SS. Crispin and Crispinian by Defendante Ferrari, and a copy of Leonardo da Vinci's *Last Supper*, painted when the original began to crumble. Near the cathedral's campanile are the remains of a Roman theatre, while across the piazza stands the impressive Roman gate, the **Porta Palatina**, with its two unusual 16-sided towers. On Saturday mornings the circular **Piazza della Repubblica** is the site of the 'Balôn' antique and flea market.

More of ancient Augusta Taurinorum can be found on Via XX Settembre in the **Museo delle Antichità** (*open Tues–Sat 9–1 and 2–7, Sun 2–7; adm*), and on Via Consolata, just off the Corso R. Margherita, at the **Consolata Church**. The Consolata is a regular ecclesiastical hotchpotch, with a Roman tower adjacent to its apse, an 11th-century campanile inherited from the demolished church of Sant'Andrea, and two churches, a hexagon and an oval, knitted together by Guarini.

The Mole Antonelliana

Turin's idiosyncratic landmark, the Mole Antonelliana ('Antonelli's massive bulk'), on Via Montebello, was begun in 1863 by the quirky Piemontese architect-engineer Alessandro Antonelli. Intended originally as a synagogue, the project ran out of steam until 1897, when the city completed it and declared it a monument to Italian Unity. Standing some 549ft high, the Mole is a considerable engineering feat, and manages to be harmonious and bizarre at the same time—a vaguely Greek temple façade, stacked with a colonnade, a row of windows, a majestic, sloping glass pyramid, a double-decker Greek temple, and a pinnacle crowned with a star, which the city illuminates at night. The Mole has been a lightning rod of madness—Nietzsche thought it was marvellous, then permanently went over the edge. There is a lift up to the observation terrace (282ft up) for a fine view of Turin and the Alps beyond (*closed for refurbishment; due to reopen early 2000 as the National Museum of Cinema*).

Lively, arcaded **Via Po**, two blocks from the Mole, is the main funnel from the centre down to the river; it is also the main artery of the city's student life. Although founded in the 14th century, Turin University never gained the prestige of the schools in Padua, Bologna, Naples, Salerno or Pavia. Its headquarters since 1720, the **Palazzo Università**, lies a block down from Piazza Castello on Via Po; in its courtyard there's a plaque to Erasmus, the most renowned of its alumni. Via Po widens out to form the long and bewildering **Piazza Vittorio Veneto**, half street-half parking lot, giving on to a bridge over the Po, **Ponte Vittorio Emanuele I**. Across the river stands an imitation Pantheon, the **Gran Madre di Dio** church. The **Museo Nazionale della Montagna Duca degli Abruzzi**, Via Giardino 39 (*open Tues–Fri 8.30–7.15, Sat–Mon 9–12.30 and 2.45–7.15; adm exp*), founded in 1874 by the Italian Alpine Club, is dedicated to Italy's mountains, their geography and folk traditions.

Parco del Valentino

Back along the west bank of the Po stretches Turin's largest park, Parco del Valentino, named after the 1660 **Castello del Valentino**, built by Madama Reale Maria Cristina, who felt her royal dignity required a French château. This lost château now does time as the university's School of Architecture, with the city's **Orto Botanico** (Botanical Garden) laid out beneath it, but it isn't the only castle on the block; Turin built another one, along with a mock medieval hamlet, the **Castello e Borgo Medioevale**, as part of its 1884 Exhibition. The houses are modelled on traditional styles found in Piemonte, while the castle is furnished with baronial fittings (*guided tours Tues–Sun 9–7; adm; Borgo Medioevale open Mon–Sun 9–8*). A place near the castle loans out bicycles by the day, while along the riverbank you can rent a rowing boat for a fish-eye view of Turin. At the end of Parco del Valentino are the massive buildings of the **Torino Esposizioni**, home of a famous springtime Auto Show in even-numbered years.

Museo Nazionale dell'Automobile Carlo Biscaretti di Ruffia

Three kilometres south of the Parco Valentino, is the Museo Nazionale dell'Automobile Carlo Biscaretti di Ruffia, Corso Unità d'Italia 40 (*open Tues–Sun 10–6.30; adm exp*). Founded in 1933, its present quarters are an elephantine vintage-1960s exhibition hall; highlights of the collection include the classics of the great age of Italian car design—Lancias, Maseratis, Alfa Romeos, Italicas and of course Fiats—as well as some oddities like the asymmetrical 1948 Tarf 1. Further along the Corso d'Italia is another huge exhibition hall, the **Palazzo del Lavoro**, built in 1961 by Pier Luigi Nervi.

One last museum, the **Galleria Civica d'Arte Moderna e Contemporanea**, Via Magenta 31 (*open Tues–Sun 9–7; adm exp*) is in another corner of the city, off Corso Vittorio Emanuele west of the Porta Nuova Station. It has one of Italy's best collections of modern art, with works by Klee, Chagall, Modigliani, Renoir, Picasso and others.

Basilica di Superga

Northeast along the Po, on the metropolitan fringe, a rack railway will take you up to the stately Baroque **Basilica di Superga** (*trains run April–Sept daily 9.30–12 and 3–6; Oct–Mar daily 10–12 and 3–5*). The delightful trip through the greenwood culminates with Juvarra's masterpiece, built on top of a commanding 2205ft hill to fulfil a vow made by Vittorio Amedeo II during the French siege of Superga. Two fine towers flank a magnificent drum dome, set above a deep neoclassical porch; the crypt contains the tombs of Vittorio Amedeo II and subsequent Kings of Sardinia, and the views stretch to the Alps. Another fine viewpoint, east of Turin, the **Colle della Maddalena** (2526ft) is also the site of the mile-and-a-half-long **Parco della Rimembranza**, a memorial to Turin's First World War dead, planted with some 10,000 trees and crowned by a **Victory** with her torch (1928), the largest cast bronze statue in the world, nearly 60ft tall.

Turin, with its access to Alpine herbs, invented vermouth and remains Italy's top producer: Carpano, the oldest house (1786) bottles the popular bittersweet Punt e Mes, while the competition, Martini & Rossi and Cinzano, are known for their classic dry *bianco* and the popular reddish elixir of many an Italian's Happy Hour. At **Pessione**, 19km east of Turin, the **Museo Martini di Storia dell'Enologia** (*open daily 9–12.30 and 2.30–5.30*) vividly recounts the history of wine-making, and sells some of the end products, too.

Stupinigi

Nine kilometres southwest of Turin, past the dreary suburbs of Mirafiori and the Fiat works, Stupinigi is the site of Vittorio Amedeo II's hunting lodge, the **Palazzina Mauriziana di Caccia** (*open Tues–Sun 10–7; adm exp*), built in 1730 on land belonging to the royal Mauritian Order. Designed by the great Juvarra, this magnificent, asymmetrically complex Rococo palace has a statue of a stag perched on the top, frescoes of hunting scenes by Carle Van Loo, and *trompe-l'œil* scenes of hanging game to remind the visitor of the palace's *raison d'être*. The main oval salon is especially lovely, and was used for royal wedding receptions. The Mauritians run Stupinigi as a furniture museum.

Shopping

Turin is a good shopping city, particularly for clothes, with the smartest shops located around Via Roma and Piazza Castello. Two of the best places for strolling and window shopping are the city's great *gallerie* off the Via Roma (Gallerie San Federico and Subalpina). The walls of **Pastificio Defitippis**, Via Lagrange 39, are lined with thousands of jars of pasta, sold by weight measured on an ancient pair of scales. A good buy in Turin are fine chocolates, *gianduiotti*, named after Gianduia, a comic figure associated with St John's Day; try them at **Ajiordano**, Piazza Carlo Felice 69. A few doors down is a shop selling Alessandria's famous Borsalino hats. For bargains, don't miss the Saturday morning **'Balôn' flea market** in Piazza della Repubblica.

Sports and Activities

Football is Italy's second religion, played between September and May. The vast Stadio delle Alpi, Strada Altessano 131, on the northern outskirts of town (the no.9 tram stops just outside) is home to Torino, in the Italian second division, and Juventus, the 'old lady of Turin'—reigning first division champions and one of the greatest club sides in the world. If you want to watch a game, steer clear of any match involving Juventus and Fiorentina (Florence), referred to in the Italian media as the 'derby of poison'. The rivalry started in 1990 when Roberto Baggio, Fiorentina's star player, was transferred to Juventus—an everyday sporting transaction which prompted three days of riots in Florence. However, it is generally acknowledged that the Italian league produces the highest standard of football played anywhere in the world and that no one (except perhaps AC Milan in a good year) plays it better than Juventus. (*For tickets, call © 011 65631; L45,000–L220,000.*)

Turin ✉ 10100 {style=left} ### Where to Stay {style=right}

Turin's hotels tend to be either modern, expensive and designed for business clients, or cheap and fairly seedy, with little in between. Nearly all are within easy walking distance of Porta Nuova Station.

very expensive

The ★★★★**Turin Palace**, Via Sacchi 8, © 011 562 5511, @ 011 561 2187, a traditional grand hotel across from Porta Nuova Station, has been in operation since 1872 and has the deserved reputation for being Turin's top hotel. The public rooms are sumptuous, the restaurant elegant and expensive, and the sound-proofed bedrooms luxurious.

★★★★**Villa Sassi**, Via Traforo del Pino 47, © 011 890 556, @ 011 890 095, located in the hills east of the Po in a lovely park, is the most evocative hotel in the city, converted from a 17th-century patrician villa. In its conversion it has maintained most of its original features—marble floors, Baroque fireplaces and portraits—and each room has been individually designed. The Villa also has one of Turin's finest restaurants, El Toulà (*see* below). You do need a car. *Closed Aug; minimum stay three days.* In a quiet street near the centre, the ★★★★**Grand Hotel Sitea**, Cia Carlo Alberti 35, © 011 517 0171, @ 011 548 090, has pleasantly luxurious bedrooms, and the excellent restaurant, Carignano, which serves a variety of Piemontese fare.

expensive

★★★**Victoria**, Via Nino Costa 4, © 011 561 1909, @ 011 561 1806, is furnished in a delightful hotchpotch of screens, chairs, tables and sofas, much of it Japanese, whilst the bedrooms are all determinedly singular: each is decorated in a different style including one rendered largely in leopardskin. The staff are friendly and helpful. A superb, bright and airy breakfast room overlooks the garden. Excellent value.

moderate

The ★★★**Roma & Rocca Cavour**, Piazza Carlo Felice 60, © 011 561 2772, @ 011 562 8137, is a somewhat impersonal choice. Although some of its rooms are lovely with old fashioned fittings and furnishings, others are merely adequate (although some have a balcony). They offer a special reduced rate for tourists (for one of the adequate rooms). All prices drop out of season.

cheap

★★**Sila**, Piazza Carlo Felice, © 011 544 086, has a great location and views, although the hotel itself is slightly gloomy. It is also just twenty yards from the airport-bus stop, making it a good last night stopover. **★Kariba**, Via San Frandesco d'Assisi 4, ⦰ 011 534 856, is comfortable and cheap, with double rooms for L60,000. The bedrooms are clean and welcoming (but don't have bathrooms).

Ostello Torino, Via Alby 1, ⦰ 011 660 2939, the town's youth hostel, is on the other side of the river, near the Piazza Crimea (bus no.52 from the station). It has decent rooms at L20,000 a head, bed and breakfast. *Closed 9–6.*

Eating Out

The kitchens of Piemonte are famous for their flavoursome and sophisticated specialities, combining the best of northern Italian cuisine with the traditions of Provence. *Grissini* (breadsticks) were invented in Turin, and so charmed Napoleon that he introduced them over the border. White truffles are a local obsession, and are often served grated in a *fonduta* (with melted *fontina* cheese from the Valle d'Aosta). The wintertime speciality, *bagna cauda*, a rich hot dip made with butter, olive oil, garlic, anchovies and cream, is often served with *cardi*, raw artichoke-like thistle, or roasted meats. *Bolliti misti* (mixed boiled meats) and *fricandò* (Piemontese stew) are other popular *secondi*, while the classic first course is *agnolotti*, pasta squares similar to ravioli stuffed with meat or cheese. The pastries are among the best in Italy—the *Bocca di Leone* is a sinfully rich calorific heavyweight, *torta di nocciole* a divine hazelnut torte.

very expensive

Turin's temple of fine cuisine, **Vecchia Lanterna**, Corso Re Umberto 21, ⦰ 011 537 047, is a subdued and classy turn-of-the-century restaurant where the food is an artistic achievement—specialities include gourmet delights like quail pâté, ravioli filled with duck in a truffle sauce, shellfish salad, a wide variety of stuffed trout, sea bass in the old Venetian style, all accompanied by a perfect wine list. Reserve. *Closed Sat lunch and Sun.* **Cambio**, Piazza Carignano 2, ⦰ 011 546 690, or ⦰ 011 543 760, opened in 1757 and offers a nostalgic trip back to the old royal capital, where the menu invites you every Friday 'to eat like a king' with dishes once served by the Savoys. The décor, the chandeliers, gilt mirrors, frescoes, red upholstery, and even the costume of the waiters, have all been carefully preserved—Prime Minister Cavour's favourite corner, where he could keep an eye on the Palazzo Carignano (if he were urgently needed a handkerchief would be waved from the window), is immortalized with a medallion. The old recipes have, though, been lightened to appeal to modern tastes. *Antipasto* choices include *cardi in bagna cauda*; other specialities are *agnolotti*, trout with almonds, boar, beef braised in Barolo, and *finanziera*, Cavour's favourite dish (made of veal, sweetbreads, cock's combs and porcini mushrooms, cooked in butter and wine). Top it off with home-made tarte tatin, all for a kingly bill. *Closed Sun and Aug.* Another of Turin's best, **El Toulà**, is a little way outside the city, in the **Villa Sassi** hotel (*see* above). Its menus feature garden-fresh ingredients from the estate, and there is a renowned wine cellar containing over 90,000 bottles.

expensive

Charming **Due Lampioni**, Via Carlo Alberto 45, ⦰ 011 546 721, serves a delightful array of *antipasti*, many featuring salmon, scampi and lobster. In the spring try the *gnocchi agli'asparagi*, followed by rack of lamb, or tournedos with foie gras. *Closed Sun and mid-July–mid-Aug.* **Montecarlo**, Via San Francesco da Paola 37, ✆ 011 830 815, is one of Turin's most romantic restaurants, located in the atrium of the palazzo of the notoriously well-loved Contessa di Castiglione. Under the stone arches a delectable variety of *antipasti* (marinated swordfish, a flan of peas and scampi) may be followed by carrot soup with barley and well-prepared *secondi* like baked liver, lamb or duck. Excellent desserts and wines. *Closed Sat evenings, Sun and Aug.*

moderate

Da Giuseppe, Via San Massimo 34, ✆ 011 812 2090, offers a wide array of Piemontese *antipasti* and specialities very popular with local diners. Reserve. *Closed Mon and Aug.* **L'Archimboldo**, Via Santa Chiara, ✆ 011 521 1816, is an excellent choice north of the city centre, with over a hundred sauces to accompany your pasta; the hare ravioli and homemade lemon sorbet with vodka are particularly recommended. **Deligia Ignazia**, Via Urbaro Rattazzi, ✆ 011 534 068, is a friendly family-run place packed every night with locals and serving various Piemontese specialities. **Arcadia**, Galleria Subalpina 16, ✆ 011 561 3898, is a popular lunchtime spot, with excellent *antipasti*, pasta and country-style meat dishes. *Closed Mon.*

cheap

Lullaby, Via XX Settembre 6, ✆ 011 531 024, serves delicious, filling local fare in a still-smart but unpretentious atmosphere. It's hard to spend over L20,000, and it's one of the few restaurants in Italy with no *coperto*!

Entertainment and Nightlife

There's always something to do in Turin. In November, there's a hugely popular **film festival** for new and up-and-coming directors of independent art-house movies; contact Torino Film Festival, Via Monte di Pieta 1, ✆ 011 562 3309, 📧 011 562 9796. The **Teatro Regio** in Piazza Castello was rebuilt after a fire in the 1970s and now stages ballet, symphony concerts and opera all year round; call ✆ 011 881 5241/2, or freephone ✆167 807 064. In July and August the **Punti Verdi** festival sees plays, ballets and concerts performed in Turin's parks. **Settembre Musica**, logically enough in September, is entirely devoted to classical music, featuring two concerts a day in the city's theatres and churches. On another plane entirely, **St John's Day** (24 June) is Turin's big folklore festival. If you'd like to know the future, Turin's sedate fortune-tellers and sorcerers run their operations around Porta Pila.

cafés

No visitor to Turin, hot chocolate fan or not, should pass over the city's most distinctive and seductive catering establishments—its grand 19th-century **cafés**. They're not cheap, but their chocolate, cakes, sandwiches and ice cream are usually superb, and they're very much part of the atmosphere of the city. Classic cafés include **Baratti & Milano**, in the Piazza Castello near the Galleria Subalpina, largely unchanged since 1873; the **Caffè Torino**, Piazza San Carlo 204, famed for its cocktails; and the beautifully decorated **Mulussano**, Piazza San Carlo 15.

West of Turin: the Valle di Susa

Some of the most spectacular and accessible scenery in Piemonte lies in the Upper Valleys of Susa. Skiing is the main attraction in the winter, and the resorts are especially popular among the French, who find the prices far more congenial than those on the other side of the Alps. Old villages and churches are a constant reminder that this corner of Italy sat out the Renaissance; whereas Baroque dominates in Turin, Romanesque graces the Valle di Susa.

Getting There

Trains from Turin go through the Valle di Susa to the French border at the Mont Cenis Tunnel (note that only local trains make more than a few stops *en route*) and there are frequent SADEM **bus** services from Turin to Susa, Pinerolo, Sestriere and Claviere, which also call at most of the valley villages.

Tourist Information

Avigliana: Piazza del Popolo 6, ✆ 011 932 8650; for the Valle di Susa. **Susa**: Corso Inghilterra 39, ✆ 0122 62 2 470. **Sauze d'Oulx**: Piazza Assietta 18, ✆ 0122 858 009, ✉ 0122 850 497. **Bardonecchia**: Via della Vittoria 44, ✆ 0122 99032, ✉ 0122 980 612. **Claviere**: Via Nazionale 30, ✆ 0122 878 856, ✉ 0122 878 888. **Sestriere**: Piazza G. Agnelli 11, ✆ 0122 755 444, ✉ 0122 755 171. **Pinerolo**: Viale Giolitti 7/9, ✆ 0121 794 003, ✉ 0121 794 932.

Turin to Susa

Rivoli, the first large town west of Turin, was a residence of the Savoys and preserves one of their typically Baroque, typically imposing castles. The family sold it to the municipal authorities in 1883 for the suitably regal sum of L100,000; after languishing for a century it reopened in 1984 as a **Museo dell'Arte Contemporaneo** (*open Tues–Fri 10–5, Sat–Sun 10–7, first and third Thurs of month 10–10; adm exp*). Five km west in Buttigliera Alta, the church of the 12th-century **abbey of Sant'Antonio di Ranverso** has a unique quattrocento façade, dominated by three high-pitched gables over the three doors; inside (*open Tues–Thurs, Sat and Sun 9–12 and 3–6*), fine 15th-century frescoes by Giacomo Jaquerio adorn the walls, and the altar has a polyptych by Defendante Ferrari (1531).

The next town, **Avigliana**, is a Romanesque gem, with two fine churches and a 12th-century Savoy castle clustered about the medieval Piazza di Conde Rosso. From here it's 14km up to Piemonte's most provocative church, the **Sacra di San Michele** (*open April–Sept 9–12.30 and 3–7; Oct–Mar 9–12.30 and 3–5; adm*), an abbey founded around the year 1000 on the 2018ft ridge of Monte Pichiriano, overlooking the Dora Riparia Valley and the Alps beyond.

Like all mountaintop shrines dedicated to God's archangelic *aide-de-camp*, the Sacra is a strange place, built like a seal over an ancient dragon's lair, full of mysterious, half-pagan nuances—in particular the *Porta dello Zodiaco*, a grand Romanesque archway featuring some rather alarming gargoyle-esque carvings of the zodiac. The air of spookiness is further enhanced by the sound of piped monastic chanting which filters down the stairs as you approach. Similar churches are thought to have had roles in medieval initiation rites, and it's significant that this one is located just off one of the main pilgrimage routes to Rome—the pilgrimage itself being an important rite of passage of the faith. The Sacra di San Michele, piled on a complicated mass of 90ft substructures, is reached by the covered *Scalone dei Morti*, the 154-step 'Stair of the Dead' hewn out of the rock—well named, as the climb seems designed to test your mortality. The ceiling of the mostly 12th-century church is supported by a massive, 59ft stone pillar; in the crypt are buried the early dukes and princes of the House of Savoy-Carignano. The abbey was suppressed in 1622.

Susa

The fine old town of Susa (Roman *Segusio*) may sound Persian, but actually was the seat of the Gaulish chieftain Cottius. Cottius was the kind of fraternizing Gaul that Asterix and Obelix would have liked to slap around with a menhir, one who so admired the Romans that he erected the **Arco d'Augusto** in the emperor's honour, carved with reliefs of a triumphant procession. Augustus returned the compliment by making Cottius a prefect, and naming the Cottian Alps after him. Other remains of Segusio lie above the Arco d'Augusto, including another arch, baths and the **Porta Savoia**, part of a 3rd-century aqueduct. The **Castello della Contessa Adelaide** (who gave her hand to Otho of Savoy in 1045) looms over the pretty medieval Piazza della Torre; inside, a **Museo Civico** has an archaeological collection (*open April–Sept Tues–Sun 3.30–5.30; Oct–Mar Thurs and Sun only 2.30–4.30*). In the centre of Susa, in the shadow of its own massive tower, the **Duomo di San Giusto** dates from the 11th century, and contains the prized *Triptych of Rocciamelone*, a Flemish brass portraying the Virgin, saints and donor, made in 1358; another chapel houses a polyptych by Bergognone. Note the rare 10th-century baptismal font, made of serpentine.

From Susa the Monte Cenis road leads to **Giaglione**, a tranquil hamlet spread out under the mountains; its **Cappella di Santo Stefano** has 15th-century exterior frescoes of the Virtues and Seven Deadly Sins. On 22 January, Giaglione celebrates its patron's feast day with a 'Dance of the Swordmaker'. Another medieval village near Susa, **Novalesa**, has the ruins of a Romanesque Benedictine abbey and chapels, one of which, **Sant'Eldrado**, is still in use and contains good 13th-century frescoes.

The Upper Valley

From Susa the road ascends steeply past the venerable villages of **Gravere** and **Chiomonte**, the latter also the first of the valley's important ski resorts. **Exilles**, further on, lies under a mighty fortress that long dominated the valley; illuminated at night it seems to spill over the hill like molten gold. Exilles also has a fine 11th-century parish church.

Oulx, Sauze d'Oulx and Bardonecchia, at the crossroads of several valleys near the Mont Cenis Tunnel, are fashionable winter sport centres in what the Italians like to call the Via Lattea, or 'Milky Way'. **Sauze d'Oulx**, the 'Balcony of the Alps', and its plateau **Sportinia**, surrounded by a fine natural amphitheatre, are popular ski-package destinations. They are also adored by motorcyclists, some of whom attempt to scale the **Chamberton**, apparently the highest point in Europe accessible by bike. **Bardonecchia**, a pretty village of old stone houses known as *grangia*, is an even more developed resort, with summer skiing on the Sommeiller glaciers (9843ft), and four separate ski areas with their own lifts; one, Fregiusia-Jaffereau, is for experts only. In the village, a small **Museo Civico** in Piazza Vittorio Veneto (*open April–Oct daily 10.30–12.30 and 5.30 7.30; in winter by request, © 0122 999.350*) houses local artefacts, old costumes and tools. The best views in the neighbourhood are from **Monte Colomion** (6,645ft), reached by a chairlift.

The **Mont Cenis Pass** was a favoured French route into Italy, used by conquerors from Hannibal (one of several possible routes proposed by scholars) to Charlemagne and Napoleon, who began the carriage road in 1808. The **Mont Cenis tunnel**, or Traforo del Frejus, at 12.8 kilometres, is the second-longest road tunnel in Europe, opened in 1980, though the rail tunnel was finished back in 1871. It was a bad business for Marseilles, which lost much of its importance as an eastern port, but a boon to the port of Brindisi and the rest of Europe in the increased speed in communications with that part of the world.

The Valle del Chisone

The 'Milky Way' of winter resorts sweeps around the Upper Susa Valley to **Cesana** and its ultramodern satellite **Sansicario**, lying at the junction of the road to Oulx. Besides being a ski resort, Cesana is also a good base for summer walks, as is **Claviere**, lying just below the **Monginevro Pass** (the Roman *Mons Janus*). This was the favoured pass of the Roman emperors and Napoleon (again) in his frequent comings and goings. The Roman god Janus had two faces, and his mountain does, too—Italian Claviere on one face and French Montgenèvre on the other—which nevertheless share lifts and ski passes.

Sestriere, Piemonte's most fashionable playground, was never a real village, but planned as a summer and winter resort, with tall cylindrical hotels and modern flats and hotels, as charming as university dormitories. But the mountains are the main attraction, and Sestriere boasts exceptional slopes and lifts, cross-country trails, ice tracks for winter races, a skating rink, and more; in summer you can try to shoot par at Europe's highest golf course. Above Sestriere are the old villages of **Sauze di Cesana** and **Grangesises**, with traditional wooden Alpine houses, and the tiny village and lovely wooded valley of **Argentiera**, a popular destination for cross-country skiers and hikers.

At the foot of the Valle del Chisone stands **Pinerolo**, once the capital of the Princes of Acaia, predecessors of the Savoys. Splendidly situated at the junction of two valleys, it preserves several memories of its glory days, including the 14th-century **Palazzo dei Principi d'Acaia**, the Romanesque **San Maurizio**, with the princes' tombs, the Gothic **cathedral**, and several streets of medieval houses. In the 17th century the **Fortress of Pinerolo** belonged to the French (who called it *Pignerol*) and here, between 1668 and 1678, they imprisoned the Man in the Iron Mask. Further south, between Pinerolo and Saluzzo, lies **Cavour**, birthplace of the great Prime Minister and 'architect of Italian unity'.

Pinerolo and the Waldenses

The Valle del Chisone and the Val Péllice, south of Pinerolo, are commonly known as the Valli Valdesi, or Waldensean Valleys. The Waldenses were followers of Peter Waldo of Lyon, who, like St Francis of Assisi, was the son of a wealthy merchant who renounced all his possessions to preach the gospel; unlike Francis, however, Peter Waldo criticized the corruption of the Church, and was branded a heretic instead of a saint. Condemned by a Lateran Council in 1184, his followers, many from the south of France, took refuge in Piemonte's secluded valleys. The Waldenseans joined up with Protestantism during the Swiss Reformation but were frequently persecuted, especially under Carlo Emanuele and Louis XIV of France. They briefly took refuge in Switzerland, but returned in 1698 to reconquer their mountain valleys. Vittorio Amedeo of Savoy agreed to tolerate them as his subjects, although they had to wait until 1848 to gain complete freedom of religion. Today nearly every town in Northern Italy has a small Waldensean community; Torre Péllice is their centre, with a Waldensean college and museum. It is also a base for scenic excursions up the valley to Bobbio Péllice and Villanova, which still has a flood embankment built with money sent by the Waldenses' great supporter, Oliver Cromwell.

Where to Stay and Eating Out

Susa ✉ 10059

The ★★★**Napoleon**, Via Mazzini 44, ✆ 0122 622 855, 🖷 0122 31900 (*moderate*), is the top place to stay, but don't expect unbridled luxury. The hotel is unpretentious but friendly, the rooms are equipped with the bare 3★ essentials, whilst the restaurant is affordable but uninspiring. For an excellent meal, **Del Pesce**, Via Monte Grappa 25, ✆ 0122 622 217 (*moderate*) offers good solid Piemontese cooking with a French touch, as in gnocchi Paris-style. The wine list is equally good.

Sauze d'Oulx ✉ 10050

★★★★**Capricorno**, in Le Clotes, ✆ 0122 850 273, 🖷 0122 850 273 (*expensive*) is a very intimate and quiet eight-room lodge, reached by chairlift. *Open all year; reserve well in advance.* ★★**Stella Alpina**, Via Miramonti, ✆ 0122 850 120 (*moderate*) is English-run, and is worth the slightly higher cost. *Open Dec–April and July–Sept.* ★★**Villa Daniela**, Via Monfol, ✆ 0122 850 196 (*cheap*) is small and personal, with a lovely little restaurant.

Sestriere ✉ 10058

★★★★**Grand Hotel Sestriere**, Via Assietta 1, ✆ 0122 76476, 🖷 0122 76700 (*very expensive*) is the most luxurious and elegant on the slopes, with an indoor pool, spacious rooms and a fairly good restaurant. *Open Dec–April.* The twin towers that dominate Sestriere belong to the Club Méditerranée: the ritzy one, ★★**Duchi d'Aosta**, ✆ 0122 77123, 🖷 0122 77125 (*expensive*) has comfortable if functional rooms. ★**La Torre** (same phone, *moderate*) is more simply furnished. Reserve at the Club's offices at Largo Corsica dei Servi 11, Milan, ✆ 02 704 445. *Open mid-Dec–April; full board only.* **La Baita**, Via Louset 4/a, ✆ 0122 77496 (*moderate*) is famous for its polenta, served with hare, boar or tamer dishes. *Closed Tues.* And for something completely different, try **La Tana della Volpe**, Monte Banchetta Sestiere, ✆ 0122 70169, (*moderate*), set in the mountains above the town. After a delicious meal, guests ski back to town carrying flaming torches. *Reserve.*

Bardonecchia ✉ 10052

★★★★**Des Geneys-Splendid**, Viale Einaudi 21, ✆ 0122 99001, 🖷 0122 999 295 (*moderate*) enjoys a tranquil setting in the trees and has more character than many resort hotels. *Open mid-Dec–mid-April and July–mid-Sept.* Also highly recommended, ★★★**Park Hotel Rosa Serenella**, Viale della Vittoria 37, ✆/🖷 0122 999

848 (*moderate*) has a small but attractive garden. **La Quiete**, Viale San Francesco 26, ✆ 0122 999 859, @ 0122 999 859 (*cheap*) lives up to its name—inside it is warm and cosy, log-cabin style, with good-size rooms, some with balcony. Restaurants here are fairly simple; **Tabor**, Via della Stazione 6, ✆ 0122 999 857 (*moderate*) is one place that does more than just slap out plates of mediocre pasta for the crowds.

North of Turin: the Valli di Lanzo and Ivrea

Getting There

Trains on a regional rail line head north from the Torino Ceres Station in Turin into the Valli di Lanzo, as far as Ceres, and to Cuorgné. For the valleys further north, trains run from Turin to Aosta about every two hours, stopping at Ivrea. Any destinations not on the rail line can easily be reached by SADEM **bus** services.

The Valli di Lanzo

The northern valleys are much less visited than the Valle di Susa and Valle del Chisone. The long arm of Turin's industry extends as far as Ciriè, but just beyond lies the beautiful park of **La Mandria**, once a royal hunting reserve, with a toy palace of a hunting lodge; grander digs were built in 1660 at nearby **Venaria**, with Baroque flourishes added later by Juvarra. Although now a barracks, part of it may be visited. **Lanzo Torinese** is a pretty town, and a base for excursions into the branching valleys; its most famous monument is the 1378 **Ponte del Diavolo**, spanning the River Stura. Impressive even today with its soaring single arch, like most medieval bridges the architect was none other than the devil himself.

The railway from Turin peters out at **Ceres**, a summer excursion centre at the fork of two pretty valleys. Buses from Ceres continue up the Val Grande to **Forno Alpi Graie**, the base for several good walks; another bus winds up the Valle d'Ala to the small ski resort of **Balme**, passing by way of **Ala di Stura** with a chairlift, and **Mondrone** with a lovely waterfall.

Turin to the Valle d'Aosta

A pretty glacier-carved amphitheatre, the **Canavese** is a peaceful woody region. Its capital is **Ivrea** (Roman *Eporedia*), famous for its carnivals and typewriters. It reached its peak of influence in 1002, when its Marquess Arduin was crowned King of Italy; not long after Ivrea built its **cathedral**, which, despite an unfortunate neoclassical façade, preserves its original towers by the apse and dome. Here and there you can pick out pieces from even older buildings, including Roman columns and a sarcophagus, while the interior has 12th-century frescoes and paintings in the sacristy by Defendante Ferrari. The mighty **Castle of Ivrea**, built in 1358, guards the River Dora with four lofty towers. In 1908 the Olivetti office machine company was founded in Ivrea, and continues to dominate the town's economy.

South of Ivrea is pretty lake **Candia**, guarded by a 14th-century castle and surrounded by vineyards producing Doc Erbaluce and sweet Plassito di Canluso. West of Ivrea, the N565 leads into **Gran Paradiso National Park** by way of the ancient town of **Cuorgné** (also linked separately by rail from Turin), with a cluster of fine medieval buildings, especially on Via Arduino, where King Arduin once resided. **Valperga**, just to the south, has an attractive castle and church from the 15th century; both towns are known for cottage industries producing beaten copper. From Cuorgné the road follows the River Orco, the scenery becoming increasingly splendid as it nears the waterfalls around **Noasca**. The peaks of Gran Paradiso rise up majestically around the meadows of **Ceresole Reale** at the park entrance; the 'Reale' in its name is derived from a battle in 1544, when French troops of Francis I defeated the army of Emperor Charles V. It stands on the banks of a deep blue lake among the rough and tumble snowy giants that frown down from above.

Valle d'Aosta

At French-speaking **Pont-St-Martin**, the road from Turin enters the Valle d'Aosta—one of the most spectacularly beautiful regions in Italy. Rimmed by the highest mountains in Europe—Mont Blanc (15,780ft), the Matterhorn (Cervino in Italian, 14,690ft), Monte Rosa (15,200ft) and Gran Paradiso (13,402ft), the Aosta Valleys are one of Europe's most popular summer and winter playgrounds, dotted with lakes and serenaded by rushing streams. Emerald meadows lie beneath great swathes of woodlands; hills and gorges are defended by fairy-tale castles. With Piemonte, Aosta shares one of Italy's most beautiful national parks, **Gran Paradiso**.

The Valle d'Aosta has been compared to a leaf, traversed by a main vein (the Dora Baltea valley) with a dozen smaller veins, or valleys, branching off on either side. Each valley has its own character; in most of them French or Provençal is the main language, although Italian is understood everywhere. English comes in a poor third outside the major resorts. Although the Valle d'Aosta has traditionally owed allegiance to Savoy, from the 11th to the 18th century it had its own Assembly of the three estates, a Council and body of law, the *Coutumier*. Union with Italy aggravated linguistic differences, a wound which Mussolini proceeded to rub salt in with his policy of cultural imperialism. In defiance, the Aostans played a leading role in the Resistance, and in 1945 the region was granted cultural and a certain amount of administrative autonomy. Most towns are now officially bilingual.

Skiing

The major resorts are Courmayeur, Breuil-Cervinia, St-Vincent, Brusson, Pila and Cogne, but there are many smaller, quieter and less expensive bases; write ahead for the region's ski handbook with maps of the slopes, lifts and facilities in each of Aosta's valleys. Prices on the sunny side of the Alps are, like the weather, milder than in France or Switzerland, but can be very high by Italian standards. During high season at the resorts (*Christmas–1st week Jan, 2nd week Feb–mid-March, Easter hols and July–Aug*) prices go up by about 15 per cent. If you come during the peak periods, reserve at least three months in advance. Although picking up a week's ski package (*settimana bianca*), including hotel and ski pass, from a travel agent is the easiest and least expensive way to go, families and groups of more than two may save money by writing in advance to the Aosta tourist office for their list of privately owned self-catering flats in the region (*elenco di appartamenti da affittare*).

Trains from Turin or Milan (a five-hour trip, changing at Chivasso) go through the main valley as far as Pré-St-Didier. The valleys are all served by SAVDA **buses**, though services to some of the smaller valleys are infrequent. Regular **coach** connections include Turin or Milan to Courmayeur/Chamonix; Turin–Chamonix–Geneva (two a day); Aosta–Val d'Isère–Col Iseran (one a day); Aosta–Martigny (two a day). In summer additional services include Genoa–Alessandria–Courmayeur; Courmayeur–San Remo–Rimini; and Aosta–Florence–Rome. There are regular excursion buses in summer from Aosta to Mont Blanc, Lake Geneva and the two Savoys/Annecy.

The most breathtaking way to enter Aosta is by **cable car** from Chamonix over the glaciers of Mont Blanc to Courmayeur. It's expensive (L110,000 round trip) but unforgettable, especially if you're lucky enough to catch the mountain without its frequent veil of mist. The cable car runs during the ski season and in July and August, leaving roughly every hour.

Tourist Information

Gressoney: Villa Margherita, St-Jean, © 0125 355 185, ◙ 0125 355 895.
Ayas-Champoluc: Via Varasc, © 0125 307 113, ◙ 0125 307 785.
St-Vincent: Via Roma 48, © 0166 512 239, ◙ 0166 513 149.
Breuil-Cervinia: Via J. A. Carrel 29, © 0166 949 136, ◙ 0166 949 731.

The Eastern Valleys

Pont-St-Martin and the Val du Gressoney

Besides Alpine splendour, the Valle d'Aosta is known for its picturesque castles and Roman remains that seem to mark every narrow defile and bend in the valleys. One of Italy's most remarkable Roman bridges, dating from the 1st century BC, lies just within the region, at **Pont-St-Martin**, a span later attributed to the devil. According to legend he made a pact with the village: the bridge for the first soul that wandered across, only to be cheated when St Martin sent a dog over at dawn. Pont-St-Martin itself is a fine old town, encompassed by vineyards that produce one of Aosta's finest wines.

At Pont-St-Martin two valleys meet: the main Valle d'Aosta along the River Dora, and the wide and pleasant **Val du Gressoney** (or Val de Lys), gracefully meandering up to the crystal glaciers spilling off mighty Monte Rosa. The natives of the Val du Gressoney are Walser, who speak neither French nor Italian but an obscure dialect of German, having migrated here from the Swiss Valais in the 12th century. Their valley is utterly wholesome, with a solid family feel to it: their traditional Alpine chalets, with wooden balconies bursting with pots of geraniums, are a vision as fresh as childhood and Heidi. The main resorts of the valley are **Gressoney-St-Jean**, with its **Castello Savoia**, and the loftier, trendier **Gressoney-la-Trinité**, the latter with chairlifts up Monte Rosa and ski facilities shared with the Val d'Ayas, the next valley to the west. **Issime**, on the way up from Pont-St-Martin, merits a stop for its gabled parish church, with a façade frescoed with a large 16th-century scene of sinners taking their licks in the Last Judgement as a warning to all passers-by. Issime is a small climbing centre and, like most of the valley, prefers to speak German; oddly the next village, **Gaby**, only 4km away, is an island of French Provençal.

Pont-St-Martin to Issogne

From Pont-St-Martin the main valley road continues past the **Donnaz** station, with the impressive remains of the Roman highway hewn 200 yards into the living rock, and then through the narrow **Gorge de Bard**. At the other end, the gloomy **Fortress of Bard** looms up on its promontory, over the village of the same name; in 1800 Napoleon slipped his cannons past in the dead of night, spreading the road with sacking and straw to muffle their wheels. Picturesque **Arnaz**, the next village, has a number of medieval houses and a Romanesque church built around the year 1000, adorned with 15th-century frescoes. Another old town, **Verrès**, lies at the junction of the Val d'Ayas, a crossroads defended by the massive, almost cubic, **Castello di Verrès** (*open for guided tours every half hour; Mar–Nov 9–7; Dec–Feb 9–12.30 and 2–5.30; closed Wed; adm*). Built in the 14th century by the Lord of Verrès, Ibelto di Callant, it's a stiff climb up from the town (or a quick drive). Although a treat for castle fiends, most people will find the nearby residence of the Challant lords, the **Castello di Issogne** (*open Mar–Nov daily 9–7; Dec–Feb daily 9–12.30 and 2–5.30; closed Mon; adm*), far more enchanting, with a frescoed courtyard that lacks only knights and fair ladies dallying by the fountain, in the shade of its mysterious iron pomegranate tree; the upper apartments, with their period furnishings and tapestries, are equally evocative.

Val d'Ayas

Thickly forested with pines and chestnut groves, the Val d'Ayas winds northwards with Monte Rosa on the right and the Matterhorn on the left, a walker's paradise and a good place to see traditional, massive Alpine chalets. The first *comune* of hamlets from Verrès, **Challant-St-Victor**, was the cradle of the Challant family who ran Aosta before the Savoys and their duke; their ruined castle still hangs over Villa, the main settlement. An even more impressive derelict castle stands further up the Val d'Ayas in **Graines**—an intriguing 13th-century ruin with a Romanesque chapel. You can reach it from the little resort of **Arcesaz**.

Brusson lies at the crossroads of the Val d'Ayas and the scenic road through the pine forests of the **Colle di Joux** from St-Vincent (*see* below); one of the best excursions is to walk up to the miniature mountain lakes under Punta Valfredda. From Brusson the road climbs steeply to the most important resort in the Val d'Ayas, **Champoluc**. Here, you can take the cableway and chairlift to the slopes just below **Testa Grigia** (10,875ft), one of the grandest belvederes of the Western Alps. A guide is recommended if you want to continue all the way up to the summit, an ascent rewarded with a breathtaking panorama of Mont Blanc, the Matterhorn, Gran Paradiso and Monte Rosa, towering over a sea of peaks.

St-Vincent and Châtillon

The valley widens at **St-Vincent**, the 'Riviera of the Alps', an élite, albeit slightly shabby, spa for the rich and dissipated since the 18th century, boasting more than a mild climate and waters these days, with one of Europe's largest casinos (*open all year round daily 3pm—4am; adm exp, although hotel guests usually get in for free; bring your passport*). Besides blackjack and one-armed bandits, St-Vincent offers excursions through the chestnut groves to **St Germain Castle** in **Montjovet**; or up the funicular to the **Terme di Saint Vincent**, a health spa built around a mineral spring, the **Fons Salutis**; or a cultural call at St-Vincent's frescoed Romanesque church, built over the baths of a Roman villa (*closed 12–2*). The main road continues to the Valle d'Aosta's second city, **Châtillon**, given over to industry, but where many travellers leave the train to catch a bus up the Valtournenche.

Under the Matterhorn: Valtournenche and Breuil-Cervinia

Valtournenche is Italy's picture window on the Matterhorn, its unique profile rising up majestically at the top of the valley, and visible from nearly every point. The first small resort in the Valtournenche, **Antey-St-André**, is known for its healthy, mild climate. For complete tranquillity, take the cable car from **Buisson** to the otherwise inaccessible hamlet of **Chamois**; from Chamois a chair lift continues up to the lovely green banks of Lake Lod.

Valtournenche, the valley capital, is a popular ski resort, and hometown of the renowned Matterhorn guides—memorial plaques posted around the church are a grim reminder of the dangers they face. From Valtournenche you can get a cable car up the **Cime Bianche**, or take a dramatic walk along the specially constructed galleries through the **Gouffre des Buserailles**, a narrow gorge carved out by the River Marmore above Crépin.

The valley road ends at sparkling, smart **Breuil-Cervinia**, one of Italy's most renowned ski resorts. It enjoys a uniquely grand setting—the Matterhorn to the north, the sweep of the Grandes Murailles to the west, and the Fruggen massif to the east. The resort dates from the construction of the road up in the late 1930s, and although Breuil-Cervinia may look more like a frontier boom town, the mountains are everything, with 190km of ski run, and summer skiing on the glacier at **Plateau Rosà** (11,482ft); a cablecar and lift from here can take you to the top of Piccolo Cervino (the little Matterhorn; 12,739ft), from where fantastic ski trails continue down to Zermatt in Switzerland, or along the valley to Valtournenche. The descents are so lengthy that the KL time trials for the world speed record are held here. Other winter sports at Breuil-Cervinia include ice skating, bob sledding and hockey. In the summer months it is the base for ascents of the Matterhorn for experienced climbers, a feat first achieved from this side in 1867; the route's most precipitous passages are now fitted out with ropes. Other far less demanding excursions include the easy hike from Plateau Rosà over the **Colle Superiore delle Cime Bianche**, either to emerald Lake Goillet and its view encompassing the Val d'Ayas, or to the summit of the **Breithorn** (13,684ft).

The Mian Valley: Chambave and Nus

West of Châtillon, **Chambave** lies under a crag draped with the ruins of the **Castello di Cly**; the vineyards that skirt the environs produce a rare and prized golden dessert wine called Passito di Chambave. More wine and a modest amount of tourism are the industries of **Nus**, the next town, where the Challants, the medieval Viscounts of Aosta, built their **Castello di Fénis** (*open April–Sept Wed–Mon 9–7; Oct–Mar Wed–Mon 9–12.30 and 2–5.30; adm*). More of a residence than a fortress, this is a genuine fairy-tale castle, all turrets and swallowtail crenellations. Only the ground floor is open to the public: a series of low-ceilinged rooms and alcoves filled with a random selection of medieval and modern furniture, all culminating in a beautifully preserved courtyard with wooden balconies and a 15th-century fresco of St George. From Nus you can visit two remote valleys, the **Val Clavalité**, with the striking **Tersive Pyramid** at its head, or the **Val St-Barthélemy**, with its scattered villages lost in the trees, or continue 13km to Aosta.

Verrès ✉ 11029

There's elegant dining at **Da Pierre**, Via Martorey 43, ✆ 0125 929 376 (*expensive*) where the menu varies according to season, as does the favoured spot to dine—in winter by the blazing hearth, in summer in the garden. Try the *agnolotti alla savoiarda* and venison in blueberry sauce, topped off with a warm slice of apple pie smothered in cream. *Closed Tues.*

Val d'Ayas ✉ 11020

★★★**Castor**, Via Ramey 2, ✆ 0125 307 117 (*evenings*), 🕿 0125 308 040 (*moderate*) enjoys an enchanting setting in Champoluc, with breathtaking views of Monte Rosa. It has panelled rooms with all mod cons, plenty of space and a very nice restaurant. *Open Dec–May and June–mid-Sept.* ★★★**Villa Anna Maria**, Via Croues 5, ✆ 0125 307 128, 🕿 0125 307 884 (*cheap*) is a lovely old mountain chalet, brimful of charm and simple, rustic bonhomie in a magnificent setting; the food is also delicious. *Open Oct–April and June–Sept.*

St-Vincent ✉ 11027

The ★★★★**Grand Hotel Billia**, Viale Piemonte 72, ✆ 0166 5231, 🕿 0166 523 799 (*very expensive*) is one of those elegant, terribly grand turn-of-the-century hotels, built to take advantage of St-Vincent's curative mineral springs—which it still does, although it is also a magnet for those who come to get soaked at its roulette tables as well. Amenities include an indoor pool, sauna, tennis and a large, lovely park. ★★★**Elena**, Via Biavaz, ✆ 0166 512 140, 🕿 0166 37459 (*moderate*) has large pleasantly furnished rooms with balconies and good views of the surrounding countryside. Its only drawback is its proximity to the parish church with busy bells. ★★★**Haiti**, Via E. Chanoux 15/17, ✆ 0166 512 144, 🕿 0166 512 937 (*cheap*) is the top inexpensive choice, with modern rooms with lots of space and light.

The place to celebrate a lucky streak is the elegant **Batezar da Renato**, Via Marconi 1, ✆ 0166 53164 (*very expensive*), within easy walking distance of the casino, with such delicacies as salmon mousse flavoured with wild fennel, duck with peaches, or pigeon stuffed with mushrooms, as well as a classy wine list. *Closed Wed, May and end-June–mid-July.* If your luck hasn't held out, however, try **La Rossa Bianca**, Via Chanoux 38, ✆ 0166 512 691 (*moderate*), a small friendly diner in the centre.

Breuil-Cervinia ✉ 11021

The top hotel in town is ★★★★**Cristallo**, Viale del Piolet 6, ✆ 0166 943 411, 🕿 0166 948 377 (*very expensive*), standing above the town in all its smart, modern glory. It has bold colours and styling, very comfortable rooms, an indoor swimming pool, tennis and sauna. *Closed June and Sept–Nov.* The superbly named ★★**Les Neiges d'Antan**, ✆ 0166 948 775, 🕿 0166 948 852 (*moderate*), 4km away at Perrères, is a pretty Alpine chalet in tranquil surroundings where the resort's skyscrapers are hidden from view. The restaurant is the best in the area so even if you don't stay you may want to drop by for a traditional meal of salt beef, polenta, cheeses, Valdostana wines and homemade desserts. *Open Oct–April and July–Sept.*

Aosta's setting is pure enchantment, ringed by mountains that resemble divine emanations supporting the sky on their shoulders; on clear mornings they wrap Aosta in a total, shimmering blueness, while the bright snows of their peaks merge with the clouds to form a magic circle around the city. It grew up where the roads from the Mont Blanc and St Bernard passes meet—a piece of sunny Italy at the crossroads of France and Switzerland. Although looped in by industry, army installations and dull suburbs, the city's core, with its grand Roman and medieval monuments, retains its charm. The street plan has changed little since 23 BC, when *Augusta Praetoria* was built after the conquest of the Salassian Gauls, the terror of the Alps. In the Middle Ages Aosta (a corruption of *Augusta*) was ruled by the Challant Viscounts, and then by the Dukes of Aosta, who owed allegiance to the Savoys. But here the French influence remained stronger than in Piemonte, and you are more likely to hear French or a French dialect in the streets than Italian. Aosta is touristy, but in a relaxed way: it is part resort and part an everyday workplace.

As the centre of transport in the Valle d'Aosta, the city makes a good base; it also has its 'own' ski resort at Pila. On 31 January it holds the famous **Sant'Orso Fair**, a market dating back to the year 1000, where Aosta's woodworkers sell everything from ladders to fine sculpture. In July there's a series of organ concerts, and in October the finals of a peculiar Valdostana sport, the *Bataille des Reines*, the 'Battle of Cows', in which heifers butt heads.

Tourist Information

Aosta: Place Chanoux 8, ✆ 0165 236 627, ✆ 0165 34657; and in Rome, Via Sistina 9, ✆ 06 4744 1044, ✆ 06 482 3837. They provide information on hiking routes in the Aosta valleys, and publish a monthly booklet with useful information.

Place Emile Chanoux

Aosta is a hard town to get lost in, with its straight Roman streets branching out from the central **Place Emile Chanoux**, site of the French-style town hall, the tourist office and the IVAT (the local handicrafts association), where arts and crafts are displayed year-round. A short distance from the square tower are the mighty double arches of the **Porta Pretoria**, the original Roman gate, its impressive strength a compliment to the ferocity of the local Gauls. To the left of the gate stands the remains of the **Teatro Romano** (Roman Theatre), a four-storey section of the façade plus some of the central seating (*currently undergoing restoration*). Next door the **Tour Fromage**, or tower of the cheesemakers, holds a small contemporary art gallery. Through the Porta Praetoria, **Via Sant'Anselmo** is Aosta's main drag, named after St Anselm (1033–1109), Archbishop of Canterbury, the founder of Scholasticism and a Doctor of the Church, who was born in the street now awash in stuffed St Bernards and garishly labelled bottles of mysterious Alpine elixirs.

Via Sant'Orso to the left leads shortly to the Romanesque-Gothic hybrid **Collegiata dei Santi Pietro ed Orso** (*open April–Sept Tues–Sun 9–7; Oct–Mar Tues–Sun 9.30–12 and 2.30–5.30*), founded in the late 10th century. The church is famous for rare Ottonian frescoes dating from its construction, and for its little cloister (1133), its short columns topped by capitals of white marble, darkened with an artificial patina and carved with scenes both Biblical and mythological; cloisters were one of the few places where medieval sculptors could follow their fancies. The crypt contains the remains of Aosta's somewhat apocryphal patron, Sant'Orso (St Bear). Across the lane, the excavations belong to the **Basilica di San Lorenzo**, built in the 6th and destroyed in the 9th century (*closed for restoration*).

Via Sant'Anselmo ends at the **Arco di Augusto**, built at the founding of the city to celebrate the victory over the Salassi; the incongruous roof was added in the 18th century. On the other side of the arch and above the River Buthier, a single-span **Roman bridge** has outlasted the channel it once crossed, but is still used by Aostans to pass over the river-bed.

The Cathedral and Forum

From Place Emile Chanoux, Via Xavier de Maistre leads, on the right, to the scanty remains of the **Anfiteatro Romano** (Roman Amphitheatre) and the 12th-century **Torre del Balivi**. To the left is the **cathedral**, off Via Monseigneur de Sales, an ancient church rebuilt several times, with a neoclassical façade hiding a Gothic cross-vaulted interior. The 23 stained-glass windows are 15th–16th-century Swiss workmanship, while the choir contains finely inlaid 15th-century stalls and two excellent mosaics, one a 12th-century *Labours of the Months*, the other a 14th-century scene featuring 'ferocious beasts' from Mesopotamia. The huge suspended wooden cross with life-size Jesus is the work of local Piemontese craftsmen from the end of the 14th century. Next to the choir, behind the glass doors, is the well-arranged **Museo del Tesoro** (*open Tues–Sat 10–12 and 3–6, Sun 3–5.45; adm*), containing such outstanding treasures as an ivory diptych from the year 406, portraying the Emperor Honorius, the 13th-century effigy of Tommaso II of Savoy, visible in the choir, and Romanesque reliquaries and statues, all described in a free audio guide in English.

Opposite, in Piazza Giovanni XXIII, are the remains of the **Foro Romano** (*open April–Sept Tues–Sun 9–7; Oct–Mar Tues–Sun 10–12 and 2.30–4.30*), and the huge 302ft by 285ft **Cryptoporticus** or underground corridor that extended underneath. It may simply have been a storeroom or, perhaps, a walkway for the great and the good to perambulate on hot summer days—the temperature here is always several degrees cooler than outside. You can also make out the foundations of a Roman temple under the **Casa Arcidianale**.

Beyond the forum stands a nearly intact portion of the **Roman wall**, with **La Torreneuve**, built by the Challants. Other sections of the walls remain in the south, near the station, with three towers: Roman **Il Pailleron**, in a garden by the station; the impressive round **Torre Bramafam**, a Challant defensive work; and the **Torre del Lebbroso** (*open during exhibitions April–Sept daily 9–7; Oct–Mar daily 9.30–12.30 and 3.30–6.30*), which earned its sad name from a family of lepers who were incarcerated here from 1733 until the last survivor died in 1803. It is used today to house temporary exhibitions.

Around Aosta

Pila, 20km south of Aosta, is the nearest winter/summer resort, with chairlifts up Mt Chamolé (7546ft) that operate all year round, though much less frequently in summer. There are trails up the slopes of **Monte Emilius** (11,677ft), by way of Chamolé, that offer stupendous views over the ranges to the north.

More castles bristle over the valley west of Aosta, beginning with the solemn 13th-century **Castello di Sarre**, rebuilt in the 18th century. After the Risorgimento the kings of Italy, who spent 99.5 per cent of their time hunting, used it as a lodge, and filled the interior with trophies bagged in the surroundings. Two other restored medieval castles guard the pretty village of **St Pierre**, a bit further on; one is home to the **Museo Regionale di Scienzi Naturali** (*open Mar–Oct daily 9–7; adm*), the other, the 14th-century **Sarriod de la Tour**, is used for art exhibitions.

Aosta ✉ *11100*   ***Where to Stay and Eating Out***

Aosta is not only the central transport hub for the region, but it's more likely than most of the resorts to have rooms available if you haven't booked in advance.

In the centre, ★★★★**Europe**, Piazza Narbonne 8, ✆ 0165 236 363, ✆ 0165 40566 (*expensive*) is an excellent, friendly hotel with all mod cons, as well as a restaurant and a piano bar. One kilometre outside the centre, ★★★★**Valle d'Aosta**, Corso Ivrea 146, ✆ 0165 41845, ✆ 0165 236 660 (*expensive*) is a convenient, comfortable stopover used by travellers on the *autostrada*.

If you're driving, ★★★**Rayon de Soleil**, above Aosta in Saraillon, Via G. S. Bernardo, ✆ 0165 262 247, ✆ 0165 236 085 (*moderate*) is a pleasant, medium-sized hotel, with fine views, a garden and indoor pool. Back in town, the best choice is the oddly named ★★★**Bus**, Via Malherbes 18, ✆ 0165 43645, ✆ 0165 236 962 (*moderate*), located in a quiet street off Via Aubert, with rooms that are comfortable and tastefully decorated, and a good restaurant.

Next to the station, ★**Monte Emilius**, Via G. Carrel 9, ✆/✆ 0165 35692 (*cheap*), with its combination lovely/terrible views of mountains/railway tracks is a little gem of a hotel with some large, high-ceilinged Art-Decoish rooms with balconies. The restaurant is also good. A traditional favourite in the heart of town, **Piemonte**, Via Porta Pretoria 13, ✆ 0165 40111 (*moderate–cheap*) features excellent, home-style Piemontese and French cuisine—*bagna cauda* in the winter, boar steaks in the autumn, crêpes and apple pie, all at reasonable prices. *Closed Fri.*

Vecchia Aosta, Via Porta Pretoria 4, ✆ 0165 361 186 (*moderate–cheap*), built right into the Roman walls, has the most striking dining room in town. The food is good, too, featuring homemade pasta, cured venison and trout with almonds, and lots of wines to help it down. *Closed Wed.*

The **Vecchio Ristoro**, Via Tourneuve 4, ✆ 0165 33238 (*moderate–cheap*) is housed in a windmill that functioned until only a few years ago. The food is excellent—hot *antipasti*, smoked trout and salmon, and an especially good selection of local cheeses.

Closed Sun, and Mon lunch. For a nightcap, find **Papa Marcel's**, just off the main drag on Via Croix de Ville, the only place in town with any character, with graffiti scribbled all over the walls, and hundreds of bottles containing weird liquids on the shelves. A must.

The Western Valleys

Tourist Information

Cogne: Place Chanoux 36, ✆ 0165 74040, ✉ 0165 749 125.
Courmayeur: Piazza Monte Bianco, ✆ 0165 842 060, ✉ 0165 842 072.

Aosta to the Great St Bernard Pass

From Aosta at least two buses a day make the 34km trip to the most famous of Alpine passes, **Colle del Gran San Bernardo** (*closed Nov–May*), its importance now somewhat diminished by a tunnel (*open all year*). Before St Bernard, the pass was known as *Mont Jovis*, after a temple of Jupiter Poeninus; Celts, Romans and Holy Roman Emperors marched to and fro on a regular basis, and in 1800 Napoleon moved 40,000 troops through to defeat the Austrians at Marengo. The road up (SS27) is uncommonly pretty, affording splendid vistas down the valleys and back towards Aosta itself. **Etroubles** is the main resort en route, and **Sant Oyen**, in the midst of emerald meadows, is a quieter holiday centre, with skiing at Flassin.

The legendary 11th-century **Hospice of St Bernard** lies just over the Swiss border (*passports required*). St Bernard, archdeacon of Aosta, founded the monastery at the exposed summit of the pass (8100ft), and the canons from Marigny who run it made it their business to minister to weary travellers, many of them pilgrims or churchmen going to Rome. To help find people lost in the heavy snows the canons developed their famous hardy breed of dog. Magnificent specimens abound near the hospice, and when not engaged in saving the lives of intrepid skiers, they happily mug for the cameras of the intrepid tourist.

Val di Cogne and Gran Paradiso National Park

From Aosta and St-Pierre, the Val di Cogne stretches south towards the blunt peak of the Gran Paradiso massif (13,323ft). The valley's rich magnetite and iron mines were exploited long before its tourism potential; the latter began in earnest with the opening of the national park in the 1920s.

The mouth of the valley is defended by the Challant **Castello di Aymavilles** (*currently closed for restoration*), its four round towers dating from the 18th century. Further up, at **Pondel**, the stunning, torrential gorge of the Grand'Eyvia is spanned by a steep **Roman bridge**, still in use today. A breathtaking drive, through forested ravines and lush valleys, leads to the *comune* of **Cogne**, a pleasant, busy town that commemorates the traditional source of its livelihood with a handsome cast-iron fountain, erected in 1819.

Now a popular resort, Cogne is the main gateway to the **Parco Nazionale del Gran Paradiso**, which encompasses the entire massif. Set aside as a Savoy hunting reserve in the 19th century, the park was donated to the state by Vittorio Emanuele III in 1919. It played the lead role in preserving the ibex (or stambecco, or steinbock), a pretty deer-like creature with long, ridged horns, which numbered only 420 in 1945, all of them in the confines of the park. Since then their numbers have increased tenfold, and animals from the park have been reintroduced into many of their old Alpine haunts. Although ibex prefer high altitude and rugged crags, they may be seen around the valleys in the winter and early spring.

They share their paradise with the more numerous, shorter-horned chamois, who have a wider range and are more easily spotted—if not here, on local dinner menus. In November and December the males of both species may be seen furiously butting heads for the ladies. Among the birds you may be lucky enough to see a wall creeper, chough, golden eagle, ptarmigan, nutcracker or black grouse. The flowers are at their most spectacular in early June, all labelled in the **Giardino Alpino Paradisia** (*open June–Sept daily 9.30–12.30 and 2.30–6.30; adm*), laid out in 1955 in the lovely **Valnontey** near Cogne.

Cogne has seven campsites, hotels and eight Alpine refuges, used as hostels during ski season. The best one to aim for is **Vittorio Sella** (8478ft), a gorgeous walk through Cogne's vast meadow of Sant'Orso, up into the deep, flower-spangled vale of **Loson**, a favourite rendezvous of ibex and chamois now that the refuge is no longer a royal hunting lodge. You can return the next day to Cogne through Valnontey.

There are well-marked trek routes through the park, from flat meanders along valley floors to lung-bursting hikes up mountain sides; the Cogne tourist office can provide maps and advice. One of the easiest walks starts in Valnontey and continues up a gorgeous riverside trail towards the glaciers.

The western reaches of the park, the lush, unspoiled **Valsavarenche** and the **Val de Rhêmes** may be reached from Villeneuve on the Courmayeur road. In the Valsavarenche, the ideal base is **Dégioz**; from here a track leads up to the Vittorio Sella Refuge, while another, an ex-royal hunting road, goes to the **Nivolè Pass**, site of yet another hunting lodge, now the **Rifugio Albergo Savoia**; an alternative route diverges at Lake Djuan for the Entrelor Pass and the prettily situated village of **Rhêmes-Notre-Dame** in the Val de Rhêmes. The Valsavarenche bus terminus, at **Pont**, is the base for ascents of Gran Paradiso.

The Main Valley: Villeneuve to Pré-St-Didier

Every medieval Tom, Dick and Harry built a castle in these parts. **Villeneuve** is sprawled under the massive, ruined, 12th-century **Châtel-Argent**, while the next town, **Arvier**, sits under the slightly later **Château de la Mothe** and makes a helluva wine, *Vin de l'Enfer*. Here a road forks for the wild and rocky **Valgrisenche**, dominated by the melancholy **Castle of Montmayeur** high on its rock. The main villages in the Valgrisenche, **Valgrisenche** and **Planaval**, have the shimmering Rutor Glacier for a backdrop; just beyond the latter towers the massive Beauregard Dam and its artificial lake.

Back in the main valley, **Avise**, a charming village with two medieval castles, lies at the foot of a romantic gorge, where the **Pierre Taillée** has remains of the Roman road cut into the rock. On the far side you get your first memorable glimpse of Mont Blanc; above the road to the left, **Derby** has a fine collection of fortified medieval houses, a little Gothic church, and a waterfall, the **Cascata di Linteney**. To the right of the road the landmark is the 13th-century **Châtelard tower** in La Salle.

The medieval tower of **Morgex**, headquarters of the upper main valley, or Valdigne, was the administrative seat of the Savoys. The little resort of **Pré-St-Didier**, just beyond, lies at the confluence of the Dora de la Thuile and Dora Baltea rivers. Its warm chalybeate springs are used for skin complaints; its station is the last rail link in the Valle d'Aosta. From here you can pick up buses to La Thuile or Courmayeur.

Little St Bernard Valley

At Pré-St-Didier begins the scenic road up to the Little St Bernard Pass, threading forests and dizzily skirting the ravine of the Dora de la Thuile. The town of **La Thuile** is a growing winter resort, with excellent skiing on the slopes of Chaz Dura. In summer the most striking excursion is up to the **Colle San Carlo** and the **Tête d'Arpy**, with an azure lake and remarkable view of Mont Blanc.

Above La Thuile, Mont Blanc also forms a stunning backdrop to pretty **Lac Verney**, a mirror in a setting of emerald meadows. A bit beyond, the **Little St Bernard Pass** (7178ft; *open June–Oct*) is marked by a statue of St Bernard on a column, and a **cromlech** (neolithic stone burial circle), with the ruins of two structures on the side. Just over the French frontier, the ancient **Hospice du Petit-St-Bernard** was founded even before St Bernard, with the same purpose of sheltering destitute travellers. Bombed during the Second World War, it was ceded to France, and abandoned. In 1897, an abbot, Pierre Canous, planted an **alpine botanical garden** here, which, after years of neglect, has been re-established and reopened. From the pass it's 31km to the first French town, Bourg-St-Maurice.

Courmayeur

In more ways than one Valle d'Aosta reaches its climax in Courmayeur, one of the most stunning, best equipped and most congenial resorts in the Alps. Lying at the foot of Mont Blanc, it is perhaps Italy's most fashionable winter and summer resort, rivalling Chamonix in chic, but warmer both in its climate and atmosphere. The skiing is matchless, the scenery mythic in its grandeur, and the accommodation and facilities among the best in the Alps.

Besides the 100km of downhill ski runs at **Chécrouit-Val Veny**, served by nine cablecars, seven chairlifts, 13 ski lifts, and helicopters for jet-set thrills, Courmayeur offers magnificent

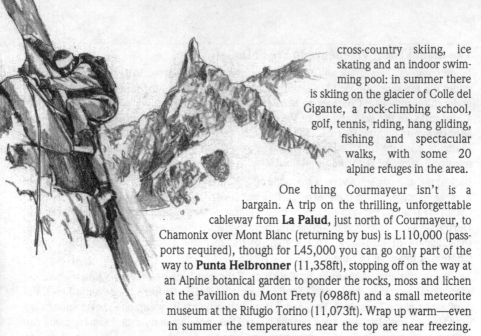

cross-country skiing, ice skating and an indoor swimming pool: in summer there is skiing on the glacier of Colle del Gigante, a rock-climbing school, golf, tennis, riding, hang gliding, fishing and spectacular walks, with some 20 alpine refuges in the area.

One thing Courmayeur isn't is a bargain. A trip on the thrilling, unforgettable cableway from **La Palud**, just north of Courmayeur, to Chamonix over Mont Blanc (returning by bus) is L110,000 (passports required), though for L45,000 you can go only part of the way to **Punta Helbronner** (11,358ft), stopping off on the way at an Alpine botanical garden to ponder the rocks, moss and lichen at the Pavillion du Mont Frety (6988ft) and a small meteorite museum at the Rifugio Torino (11,073ft). Wrap up warm—even in summer the temperatures near the top are near freezing. Alternatively, a one-way trip through the Mont Blanc tunnel is a mere L44,000; the entrance is near La Palud, just beyond the medieval fortress-village of **Entrèves**. Another scenic summer excursion is to take the Funivia Courmayeur from the east side of town to the **Plan Chécrouit**, and from there up to Col de Chécruit. This pass is the base for climbing **Mont Chétif** (1½ hours), the peak just before Mont Blanc, offering tremendous views into the mighty abyss of the **Aiguille Noire**. An alternative is to take another cable car from the Col de Chécruit to **Cresta d'Arp** (9039ft), with more fantastic views, and a ski run descending all the way to **Dolonne**. For a less adventurous outing there is a little **alpine museum** (*open May–June and Oct–Nov daily 9–12.30 and 3–6; closed Mon; adm*), at the top of town, housing the diaries, drawings and equipment of Alpine pioneers, and a collection of black and white photos of Alpine life in the 1930s and 40s.

Two gorgeous valleys run in opposite directions from Entrèves. The **Val Veny** may be ascended by bus as far as Lac Combal, the base for an ascent of Mont Blanc or a fairly easy hike to the Rifugio Elisabetta and, from there, a three-hour walk up to the **Colle de la Seigne** on the French border, with fabulous views in either direction. The **Val Ferret** is enchanting and serene, the site of a golf course, trout streams and the finest cross-country walks; there is accommodation in **Plampincieux**, a quiet resort in the pines.

Where to Stay and Eating Out

Cogne ✉ 11012

The family-run ★★★★**Bellevue**, Rue Grand Paradis 22, ✆ 0165 74825, ✉ 0165 749 192 (*very expensive*) has the best location of any hotel in Cogne, if not the whole of the Valle d'Aosta, with majestic views of a glacial valley—carpeted with meadow flowers in summer and littered with cross-country skiers in winter—from the hotel's excellent restaurant. The super-friendly staff is dressed in Cogne traditional costume; in the basement they have a swimming pool and a jacuzzi, and limousine service. *Open Christmas holidays–Oct.* Alternatively, there is the ★★★**Sant'Orso**, Via Bourgeois 2, ✆ 0165 74821, ✉ 0165 749 144 (*moderate*), which also enjoys splendid views at slightly more affordable prices, and has an excellent restaurant.

In an attractive chalet, **Lou Ressignon**, Via Mines de Cogne, ✆ 0165 74034 (*moderate*) serves good, honest Valdostan specialities—chamois (*camoscio*) with polenta for something out of the ordinary, topped off with a good homemade dessert. *Closed Tues.* **Brasserie du Bon Pec**, Rue Bourgeois 72, ✆ 0165 749 288 (*moderate*) is an excellent cosy little diner where big meaty grills and fondues are served by waiters in Cogne national dress. There is an extensive and expensive wine list. It's very popular, so book ahead.

Courmayeur ✉ 11013

In Courmayeur Christmas, Easter, July, August, and from the second week of February through to the end of March are high season, when reservations are a must. At other times, if a place is open, you'll find lower prices and more room.

The top choice ★★★★**Royal E Golf**, Via Roma 87, ✆ 0165 846 787, ✉ 0165 842 093 (*very expensive*) may look a little lopsided but inside the facilities and service are as balanced as you could wish. The views, especially from the excellent restaurant, are fantastic and rooms are beautifully furnished. There is an indoor pool and piano bar. *Open Dec–April and end-June–Sept.* ★★★★**Palace Bron**, ✆ 0165 846 742, ✉ 0165 844 015 (*very expensive*) is a luxury white chalet, little more than a kilometre above Courmayeur at pine forested Plan Gorret, with beautiful views over the Mont Blanc massif from nearly every room. It's convenient for the slopes, but far enough away to enjoy a rarefied tranquillity. Next to the hotel is an outdoor, lake-like pool; the restaurant and piano bar are elegant. *Open Dec–April and July–Sept.*

★★★**Del Viale**, Viale Monte Bianco, ✆ 0165 846 712, ✉ 0165 844 513 (*expensive*) is an old-fashioned alpine chalet with nice views. The cosy, folksy lobby and restaurant have stripped wooden floors and an open fire. Most rooms have a balcony or sun terrace. Friendly ★★★**Bouton d'Or**, Strada Statale 26, No.10, ✆ 0165 846 729, ✉ 0165 842152 (*moderate*), near the centre, has small but comfortably furnished rooms; some have balconies with views of Mont Blanc. The same family runs **Le Vieux Pommier**, Piazzale Monte Bianco 25, ✆ 0165 842 281 (*moderate*), a tourist favourite with a rustic hyper-Alpine interior and solid Valdostana cuisine. *Closed Thurs.* ★★★**Croux**, Via Circonvalazione 94, ✆ 0165 846 735, ✉ 0165 845 180 (*moderate*), in the centre of town, enjoys outstanding views. Its bedrooms are modern and well-equipped. *Open Dec–April and end-June–Sept.* **Venezia**, Via Delle Villette 2, ✆/✉ 0165 842 461 (*cheap*) has large rooms with fantastic views.

La Palud/Entrèves ✉ 11013

Hotels are more reasonable here. ★★**Astoria**, Strada La Palud 23, ✆ 0165 869 740, ✉ 0165 869 750 (*cheap*) is an excellent choice with big, modern rooms in a cosy old style. ★**Funivia**, Via San Bernardo, ✆ 0165 89924, ✉ 0165 89636 (*cheap*) also has big rooms, modern bathrooms, old wood furniture and priceless views. Just over in Entrèves, ★★★**La Brenva**, Strada La Palud 14, ✆ 0165 869 780, ✉ 0165 869 726 (*expensive*) was once a simple royal hunting lodge but has been a hotel since 1897. The décor has changed little since then, though the amenities are up-to-date. *The* place to dine, **Maison de Fillipo**, ✆ 0165 869 797, ✉ 0165 869 719 (*expensive*) has a fame that extends into France and Switzerland, and there are those who don't mind paying the tunnel fares just to come over to feast at this jovial temple of Alpine cuisine. And feast is no exaggeration, for if Philippe's all-you-can-eat doesn't bust your buttons, no place will. The décor is charming—rustic without fussiness—and the tables are laid out on three levels; in the summer you can dine out in the garden. The food, from the *antipasti* of salami and ham, to the ravioli filled with porcini mushrooms, the fondue, trout or game, and the grand dessert finale, is all delicious. *Closed Tues.*

East from Turin: Vercelli and Novara

East of Turin and north of the Po is a landscape that runs the gauntlet from flood plain to Alpine splendour. This section includes the province of Vercelli and part of Novara; for convenience, the northern part of Novara—from Lake Orta and Lake Maggiore to Domodossola and the Simplon Pass—is dealt with in the chapter on Lombardy and the Italian Lakes (*see* pp.222–32).

Getting Around

 This area is especially well served by **rail**. Frequent trains travel to Vercelli and Novara from Turin and Milan; both cities are also linked with Biella (1 hour), base of a network of **buses** into the Alpine valleys. The main rail and road approach to the Valsesia is from Novara (if coming from Turin, change trains at Romagnano) and go as far as Varallo (from Novara, 1½ hours), where you can catch a **bus** up to Alagna. Rail links from Vercelli continue south to Casale Monferrato, Asti and Alessandria, while Novara has trains to Lakes Orta and Maggiore and beyond.

Tourist Information

Vercelli: Viale Garibaldi 90, ✆ 0161 64631, ✉ 0161 64632. **Novara**: Corso F. Rosselli, ✆ 0321 623 398, ✉ 0321 393 291. **Biella**: Piazza V. Veneto 3, ✆ 015 351 128, ✉ 015 34612. **Varallo**: Corso Roma 38, ✆ 0163 51280, ✉ 0163 53091.

Vercelli and its rice paddies

Several million plates of risotto are born every year on the plain between Turin and Milan, a region that is no less than Europe's greatest producer of rice. Its capital, **Vercelli**, is surrounded by a seemingly endless patchwork of paddies divided by hundreds of irrigation canals, dating back to the 15th century. In summer, when they're newly flooded, they become magical, reflecting the clouds and sunset in an irregular checkerboard of mirrors, a landscape bordering on the abstract: uncanny and desolate, melancholy and beautiful.

Of all the cities in Piemonte, only Vercelli stirred from its feudal hibernation in the Renaissance, producing in the 16th century a school of painters, even though the most brilliant of them, Il Sodoma (born in 1477), soon escaped to more promising territory in Tuscany. Even so, as a minor 'city of art' Vercelli is an old, atmospheric place. If you have only an hour between trains you can take in its chief marvel, the **Basilica di Sant'Andrea**, which looms up just across from the station. The basilica was begun in 1219 by Cardinal Guala Bicchieri, papal legate and guardian and 'saviour' of Henry III. To thank Cardinal Bicchieri for his aid in obtaining the throne, Henry gave him the revenues from the Abbey of St Andrew in Chesterton, near Cambridge, and the cardinal used the money to finance another St Andrew's in Vercelli. Completed nine years later—a lightning clip in those days, thanks to the cardinal's resources—the basilica, though basically Romanesque, is famous in Italian architectural history as one of the first to display signs of the new Gothic style from the Île de France, first adopted by the Cistercian Order; it whispers in Sant'Andrea's twin bell towers, the flying buttresses, the vaulting in the nave and the plan of the church and cloister.

The change of materials halfway up the façade at first gives the same incongruous impression as a 1960s demi-wood station wagon. The three arched portals are Romanesque, with lunettes attributed to the great 12th-century sculptor Antelami. The lofty interior is majestic and striking in its simple red and white decoration. The cloister, with its cluster columns and sculptural details, is lovely, and offers the best view of the unusual cupola and the basilica's Romanesque and Gothic features. The massive detached campanile was added in 1407.

Vercelli's grand 16th-century **cathedral** is a short way to the left, in Piazza Sant'Eusebio; of the original Romanesque construction only the bell tower remains. It has an especially valuable library of codices, including 11th-century Anglo-Saxon poems perhaps brought to Vercelli by Cardinal Bicchieri. The one saintly member of the House of Savoy, the Blessed Amedeo IX, who died in Vercelli Castle in 1472, is buried in an octagonal chapel. From the cathedral, Via Duomo leads past the **Castello d'Amedeo** (to the left, behind Santa Maria Maggiore), then to Via Gioberti and Via Borgogna, site of the **Pinacoteca Borgogna** (*open Tues–Fri 3–5.30, Sat and Sun 9.30–12*), with paintings by Vercelli natives—most famously Sodoma, Gaudenzio and Defendante Ferrari, as well as works by other Italians.

Via Borgogna gives into old Vercelli's main street, **Corso Libertà**. At No.204 be sure to look in at the lovely courtyard of the 15th-century **Palazzo Centori**. The Corso continues to main Piazza Cavour, where markets are held under the Palazzo Municipio. Down Via Lucca, **San Cristoforo** is adorned with a famous series of frescoes (1529–33) by Gaudenzio Ferrari, including his masterpiece, the *Madonna of the Oranges*. In Via Verdi, off Piazza Cavour, Vercelli has an interesting archaeological and historical collection in the **Museo Leone** (*open Mar–Nov Tues and Thurs 3–5.30, Sun 10–12*), located in a 15th-century house and Baroque palace. From Piazza Cavour, Corso Libertà continues into the newer part of town; in Piazza Zumaglini, rice prices are decided in the Rice Exchange, or **Borsa Risi**; here, too, is the national rice board's headquarters.

Novara

Novara is an ancient city, but one that has preserved only a few traces of the past. The cobbled Corso Cavour and Corso Italia, lined with tearooms and fashionable shops, are pleasant for whiling away an hour or two, perhaps after digesting Novara's landmark, looming high above the surrounding rooftops: the three-tiered tower and dome of **San Gaudenzio**. The main body of the church was designed in the 16th century by Pellegrino Tibaldi, while the tower is a 19th-century addition by Italy's most phallic architect, Antonelli, who designed the similarly tall and pointy Mole in Turin. He crowned this particular creation with a spire and a shining figure of the saint who seems to poke the very sky. San Gaudenzio's equally unusual 8th-century campanile makes an interesting companion piece. Inside, look for Il Tanzio's nightmarish *Battle of Sennacherib* (1627).

Central Piazza della Repubblica has Novara's much restored **Broletto**, or lawcourts, in four separate buildings on a central courtyard, built between the 12th and 18th centuries. It shares the piazza with the **Duomo**, built in the 1860s by the inimitable Antonelli. This time, instead of building tall, he designed one of the largest doorways in Europe (38ft by 19ft). Parts of an earlier Romanesque cathedral survive, including the campanile, the 12th-century frescoed chapel of **San Siro**, the red brick cloister, and some mosaics in the chancel; in the main body are frescoes and paintings by Gaudenzio Ferrari and others of the Vercelli school, and a collection of 16th-century Flemish tapestries. The **Baptistry** dates back to the 5th century, and contains very unusual frescoes of the Apocalypse, added 500 years later.

Biella, the Santuario d'Oropa, and Around

Easily reached from Vercelli, Novara or Turin, the wool and textile town of Biella is divided into two—the lower half, **Biella Piano** and the upper, **Biella Piazzo**, linked since 1885 by a jaunty little incline railway (*daily 7am–midnight, Fri and Sat till 2am; L1500 return; pay at the top*). Biella Piano's chief monuments are clustered in the Piazza Duomo: the lovely little **baptistry**, dating back to the late 10th century and constructed from parts of old Roman buildings, the mighty nine-storey Romanesque **campanile** of a now-demolished church, and the town's white elephant, the Gothic **cathedral**, unfortunately prettified in the last century.

Biella Piano also has a fine Renaissance church—unusual in Piemonte—**San Sebastiano**, begun in 1504, with a remodelled 19th-century façade, housing a number of works by the Vercelli school, especially Bernardino Lanino's *Assumption*, and beautifully carved choir stalls. The **Museo Civico**, Via P. Micca 36 (*open 3–5.30; closed Wed*) houses archaeological finds, ceramics and paintings. Biella's social life, in the lower part of town, is centred around Via Italia, a pretty cobbled street where the great and the good come to promenade in the sunshine.

During the Renaissance wealthy textile merchants built their showy mansions up in Biella Piazzo, which retains much of its patrician air and offers fine views over the city and surrounding mountains. A three-storey **cotton mill** from 1859 stands near the centre, a reminder of what is still the region's lifeblood. Across the River Cervo, in San Gerolamo Park, the former villa of the great Alpine explorer and photographer Vittorio Sella is now the **International Museum of Alpine Photography**, founded in 1948, with his old equipment and photographs of the world's greatest peaks (*to visit, call © 015 23778*).

On the map the environs of Biella look like a plate of spaghetti, a confusing network of squiggly yellow valley roads winding between the mountains. The main attractions, all connected by bus, include the stately 16th-century castle in **Gagliànico**, 5km from Biella, and the most venerated hill shrine in Piemonte, the **Santuario d'Oropa**, 12km north, founded by St Eusebius in the 4th century when he returned from the Holy Land with the *Black Madonna and Child*, reputedly carved by St Luke. The sanctuary consists of three vast quadrangles, a new Baroque basilica, and a remnant of the original frescoed church, sheltering one of the most exotic statues in Italian Christendom, jet-black and embellished with a towering golden crown, a starry halo and costly jewels.

A cablecar near the sanctuary ascends **Monte Mucrone** (7661ft), with its lake, hiking in summer and skiing in the winter.

In the next valley to the east, **Piedicavallo** is a base for hikes into the Val Gressoney in Valle d'Aosta, or into the Valsesia (*see* below). A few kilometres south of Piedicavallo begins the **Strada Panoramica Zegna** (SS232), which winds across to the Valsesia, and is noted for its spectacular views of Monte Rosa.

In late spring thick clusters of rhododendrons and azaleas burst into a dazzling pageant of colour on Monte Burcina, west of Biella, in the village of **Pollane**. From here the road twists around to another popular hill sanctuary, **Graglia**, dedicated to Our Lady of Loreto. To the southwest of Graglia, at Donato, begins a district called **La Serra,** of steep green moranic ridge. Oaks, chestnuts, birch, and vineyards grow here in arcadian harmony, dotted with unspoiled villages. At the end of the ridge lies the clear, spring-fed **Lago di Viverone**, an unglamorous but soothing place to camp, swim, fish or mess about on a boat.

Varallo and the Valsesia

The lower part of this lovely Alpine valley is dotted with textile mills, but at **Varallo** the scene begins to change. Varallo is a fine, friendly town embraced by wooded slopes; the River Sesia froths and tumbles here, making for exciting white-water kayaking. Varallo has a good Pinacoteca, with works by the Vercelli school, sharing space with the Natural History in the **Palace of Museums** (*open June–Sept daily 10–12 and 3–6; closed Thurs*), as well as a fine church, **San Gaudenzio**, artistically piled up on top of a stair, housing a polyptych by Gaudenzio Ferrari. An entire wall of his work, depicting the Life of Christ, is in the church of **Santa Maria delle Grazie**, located at the foot of the steps up to Sacro Monte.

A very stiff walk (or cable car ride) will bring you to **Sacro Monte**, Varallo's five-star attraction, with singularly beautiful views over the lush woodlands. It was founded as the Sanctuary of New Jerusalem in 1491 by the Blessed Bernardo Caimi, who wanted to recreate the Holy Shrines of Palestine. The idea caught the fancy of St Charles Borromeo, the Archbishop of Milan, and when the two holy men were done, the result is nothing tub-thumping less than the Disneyland of the Counter-Reformation: 45 chapels, set in beautifully manicured grounds, containing the world's first dioramas—16th-century 3D scenes from the Bible with fresco backgrounds, featuring some 1000 statues and 4000 painted figures.

When you can pull yourself away from this sincere but slightly nutty extravaganza, visit the **Piazzale della Basilica**, a little gem of porticoes, palm trees and a fountain under a pavilion. The Basilica itself is a mass of gilded exploding Baroque; the crypt, its walls covered in heart-rending tributes to dead children, provides the final flourish of religious fervour.

North of Varallo extends the **Val Mastallone**, a scenic valley of deep ravines and Alpine scenery; **Rimella** and **Fobello**, the latter famous for its Walser lace-making and embroidery, with a lace museum and school, are two small resorts. The upper extension of the Valsesia, the **Val Grande**, is more touristy; the main resort at **Riva Valdobbia**, has Monte Rosa as a background and a parish church with curious exterior frescoes. A number of walks begin here, with the hike over the Colle Valdobbia to the Val Gressoney in Aosta the most popular. **Alagna**, the last town in the valley, is a popular summer and winter resort under Monte Rosa, with funiculars up into the massif. In the charming hamlet of Pedemonte, 3km from Alagna, the Walser population (who immigrated from the Swiss Valais in the 12th century) have converted one of their wooden 17th-century homes into the **Walser Museum** (*hours change by season*), furnished in the traditional manner.

Where to Stay and Eating Out

Vercelli ✉ 13100

Vercelli isn't exactly a popular stopover, although **★★★Il Giardinetto**, Via Sereno 3, ✆ 0161 257 230, 🖩 0161 259 311 (*moderate*) will do for a night, with eight modern rooms and an attractive little restaurant and bar. Nor is the province known for its cuisine, in spite of its rice; however, at **Il Paiolo**, Via Garibaldi 72, ✆ 0161 250 577 (*moderate*), you can dine well on hearty risottos. *Closed Thurs.*

Novara ✉ 28100

Central and elegant, the **★★★★Italia**, Via Solaroli 8/10, ✆ 0321 399 316, 🖩 0321 399 310 (*expensive*) is very modern, well furnished and comfortable and claims one of the best restaurants in Novara (*moderate*), with good rice dishes and some surprises, like chicken curry. At the family-run **★★★Parmigiano**, Via dei Cattaneo 4/6, ✆ 0321 623 231 (*moderate*), an old façade conceals a sparkling modern interior with simple rooms and an excellent restaurant—a good place to try out local specialities. The shrine of Novarese cuisine is the **Trattoria del Amicizia ai Tre Scalini**, Via Sottile 23, ✆ 0321 623 247 (*expensive*). The food—*antipasti* of the local *salame della duja*, *risotto al Barolo* or *pasta e fagioli*, and a wide variety of *secondi*—is excellent, and accompanied by a good list of Piemontese wines. *Closed Sun and Aug.*

Biella ✉ 13900

The **★★★★Astoria**, Viale Roma 9, ✆ 0161 402 750, 🖩 0161 849 1691 (*moderate*), Biella's grandest hotel, specializes in what it terms 'sober elegance', i.e. lots of comfort but little style. It has a bar, but no restaurant. **★★★★Augustus**, Via Italia 54 (in the centre), ✆ 015 27554, 🖩 015 29257 (*moderate*) is a no-nonsense business hotel with comfortable rooms.

In Biella Piazzo, near the funicular, **Ca' Verna**, Via Avogadro 10, ✆ 015 22724 (*cheap*) serves superb veal and pizzas. It's popular with the locals, and the general air of bonhomie is shared by the helpful staff. On the road to Oropa, **Il Baracca**, Via Santuario d'Oropa 6, ✆ 015 21941 (*expensive*) is the oldest and best place to eat in the area, with Piemontese treats like *bagna cauda, salame della duja*, rice dishes and mixed roast or boiled meats. *Closed Wed.*

Roppolo (Lago di Viverone) ✉ 13900

***Castello di Roppolo**, Via al Castello 2, ✆/🌐 0161 980 000 (*moderate*), near Lake Viverone, has 11 elegant rooms in a former medieval castle, in a lovely setting. It also houses the **Enoteca della Serra** wine cellar and restaurant, ✆ 0161 98501 (*moderate*), which offers a wide selection of Piemonte's finest wines and local specialities. *Open Mar–Oct Wed–Sun; Nov–Feb weekends only.*

Varallo ✉ 13019

*Monte Rosa**, Via Regaldi 4, ✆ 0163 51100 (*cheap*) is a wonderful little family-run hotel. Behind the red façade wait large old-fashioned, beautifully furnished rooms, with balconies and lovely views. The **Casa del Pellegrino**, ✆/🌐 0163 51656 (*cheap*), at Sacro Monte, is strong on atmosphere and character, if a little weak on comfort and normality, but then you are paying for the location.

Southeast Piemonte: Alessandria and Asti

When the Turinese or Milanese come to this region on weekends their thoughts are more on victuals and drink than on sights. Alba and Asti are the main wine-growing centres of Piemonte, producing its most famous wines in a supremely civilized landscape, characterized by lovely, rolling hills and winding roads, and dotted with small villages and fortifications. The region's other speciality, *tartufi* (white truffles), the pungent ambrosia of the Italians, are harvested in the autumn with a barrage of ecstatic festivals devoted to gluttony, and sold at daily auctions in the main towns.

Wines, and a Drinker's Itinerary

Piemonte is one of Italy's finest wine regions, and rare in that its most celebrated vintages—Barbaresco, Barolo, Dolcetto and Barbera—age well. To promote them the region has eight regional cellars (*enoteche regionali*) in historic castles and buildings along the 'wine roads' in the provinces of Asti and Cuneo: in **Grinzane**, ✆ 0173 262 159, in the castle that Cavour, the village mayor, used to call home (*open April–Sept 9–12 and 2.30–6.30; Oct–Mar 9–12 and 2–6; closed Tues and Jan*); **Barbaresco**, Via Torino 8/a, ✆ 0173 635 251, in the deconsecrated church of San Donato (*open 9.30–1 and 2.30–6; closed Wed, Jan and first week in July; wine-tasting L1000 per glass*); **Barolo**, Piazza Falletti, ✆ 0173 56277, in the 18th-century castle where the wine was born (*open 10–12.30 and 3–6.30; closed Thurs and Jan; adm L3000; wine-tasting—only at weekends—L3000 per glass*); **Mango**, at the Enoteca del Moscato d'Asti e dell'Asti Spumante in Mango Castle, ✆ 0141 89141 (*open 10.30–1 and 3–6; Dec–Mar 3–6; wine-tasting L1500 for Moscato, L2500 for other wines*); **Monferrato**, in the 17th-century Palazzo Callori, ✆ 0142 933 243 (*open Wed–Fri 9–1 and 2–5, Sat and Sun 10–12 and 3–7; closed Jan*); **Acqui Terme**, Piazza Levi 7, ✆ 0141 770 273/4, in the ancient cellars of the Palazzo Robellini (*open 10–12 and 3–6.30; closed Mon, Wed and Thurs morning*).

For more information on Piemonte's wine roads, contact the regional tourist board in Turin, Via Magenta 12, ✆ 011 43211.

Getting Around

Alessandria, Casale Monferrato, Acqui Terme, Asti and Alba are all linked together by **rail**, and Alessandria and Asti also have good connections to Turin, Genoa and Milan. To explore the scenic 'wine roads' (*strade dei vini*), though, you need a **car**.

Tourist Information

Alessandria: Via Savona 26, ✆ 0131 251 021, ✉ 0131 253 656. **Casale Monferrato**: Via L. Marchino 2, ✆ 0142 70243, ✉ 0142 781 811. **Acqui Terme**: Corso Bagni 8, ✆ 0144 322 142, ✉ 0144 322 143. **Asti**: Pza Alfieri 34, ✆ 0141 530 357, ✉ 0141 538 200. **Alba**: Pza Medford 3, ✆ 0171 35833, ✉ 0171 363 878.

Casale Monferrato and Alessandria

Between Vercelli and Alessandria, **Casale Monferrato**, Italy's biggest producer of cement, once held the more glamorous position as capital of the medieval and Renaissance duchy of Monferrato, though it retains few traces of the Paleologhi dukes who held court here—principally a fairly good Romanesque **cathedral** and some walls of the old **castle** across the piazza. Monferrato was one of the most important safe havens for Jews in Italy during the Renaissance and Counter-Reformation, and Casale's most striking monument is its Baroquely ornate **synagogue**, Via S. Olper 44 (*open Sun and public hols 10–12 and 3–5*), built in 1595, which now doubles as a Jewish museum.

Alessandria, the provincial capital, was founded in the 12th century by disgruntled nobility from Monferrato who opposed Emperor Frederick Barbarossa and named their new town after his arch-enemy, Pope Alexander III. These days Alessandria is best known as the city of Borsalino hats, famed as the world's finest. But, after checking out the fedoras, there's little to see besides the 12-pointed **Cittadella**, built in 1728 by the Savoys and one of the best-preserved from the period. North of Alessandria, **Valenza** produces gold and silver jewellery; the goldsmiths' association has a permanent exhibition of their craft in the centre of town.

Just eight kilometres south of Alessandria, on the Genoa road, Napoleon defeated the Austrians on 14 June 1800 in what he considered the greatest battle of his career, **Marengo**. The battlefield is marked by a column, and in the village there are monuments to Napoleon and General Desaix, who perished on the field, as well as a museum of the battle in the **Villa di Marengo** (*open Tues–Sat 10–12 and 2–6, Sun 2–6*). Another six kms further south lies **Bosco Marengo**, birthplace of Pope Pius V (1504–72), whose reign was notable for the great victory over the Turks at Lepanto. Pius built the magnificent church of **Santa Croce** in the village to serve as his tomb, a masterpiece of green marble and porphyry. The Romans, however, interred him in Santa Maria Maggiore.

Tortona and Acqui Terme

Tortona, east of Alessandria, was the Roman *Dertona*, and still has a sprinkling of Roman remains, most importantly two monumental tombs at the corner of Viale De Gasperi and Via Emilia. The **Museo Civico**, in Piazza Marconi, is housed in a 15th-century palace and contains Roman artefacts and medieval art. More Roman remains may be seen at the spa south of Alessandria on the SS30 road, **Acqui Terme** (*Acquae Statiellae*), most notably the four arches of the **Aqueduct** in the park near the hotel Antiche Terme. An **archaeological museum** (*open Tues–Thurs 9–1 and 4–7, Fri 9–1 and 4–10, Sat and Sun 10–2*), in the half-ruined Castello dei Paleologhi, contains mosaics and remains from the ancient baths. Next to the castle stands the fine Romanesque **cathedral**, with a good doorway and campanile.

The most memorable sight in Acqui, however, is the **Bollente**, a hot sulphuric spring that bubbles up under an octagonal pavilion, leaving the earth amid a diabolical cloud of steam.

Asti

Former rival of Milan, Asti is an old and noble city that well repays a visit. Although nowadays synonymous with fizzy wine, Asti is proudest of its poet, Vittorio Alfieri (1749–1803), who ran off with the young wife of the not-so-bonny Prince Charlie. Corso Alfieri is the main street, and all of the city's monuments are within a block of its length. At the Corso's end stands the 15th-century church and cloister of **San Pietro in Consavia**, housing a small archaeological collection (*open April–Sept Tues–Sat 9–12 and 3–7, Sun 3–7; Oct–Mar Tues–Sat 9–12 and 3–6, Sun 3–6*). Most intriguing, however, is its round **baptistry**, perhaps as old as the 10th century, supported by eight thick columns with cubic capitals.

Six streets further west, the Corso passes by the large **Piazza Alfieri**, with the tourist office and Public Gardens; behind the piazza is the **Campo del Palio**, the site of Asti's bare-back horse race, a tradition of neighbourhood rivalry dating back to 1275 and revived in 1967. As in Siena, the Palio combines medieval pageantry, daredevil riding, and much feasting and celebration afterwards; it takes place on the third Sunday of September, coinciding with Asti's great wine fair. A week before the Palio, in the *Festival della Sagra*, people from the surrounding villages parade in traditional 19th-century costumes, and recreate cooking and working practices from that era. Their produce is on sale in the Campo del Palio.

Just a short distance from Piazza Alfieri is the attractive Romanesque-Gothic **Collegiata di San Secondo**, home of the relics of Asti's patron saint, the Palio Astigiano (the banner awarded at the horse race) and a polyptych by Asti's greatest Renaissance artist, Gandolfino d'Asti. Medieval towers loom over the rooftops—the tall, elegant **Torre Troyana** across the Corso and, further down the Corso, the **Torre Comentina**, with the swallowtail merlins of the Ghibellines, and then the octagonal **Torre dei De Regibus**. Here, detour to the right for the tall **cathedral**, a 14th-century Gothic monument with Baroque frescoes, paintings by Gandolfino d'Asti and Holy Water stoups constructed from Roman and Romanesque capitals.

Back on the Corso there's a **museum** and wild-eyed bust devoted to Vittorio Alfieri, in his old house, Corso Alfieri 375 (*currently closed for restoration*). In the basement of the neighbouring Liceo, Via Gualtieri 1, you can visit the 8th-century **Crypt of Sant'Anastasio**, with notable carved capitals, and the **Museo Lapidario** (*open Tues–Sat 9–12 and 3–6, Sun 9–12*). On Via Mazzini, across from the Alfieri museum, the **Palazzo Malabayla** is the finest Renaissance palace in Asti.

The Corso ends by another medieval tower, the **Torre Rossa**, an unusual cylinder on a Roman foundation, with a checkerboard crown. Four km north, the **Chiesetta di Viatosto** is a pretty little Romanesque-Gothic chapel on a hill, with quattrocento frescoes inside and enchanting views over the fertile countryside to the Alps.

North of Asti: Monferrato

The province of Asti divides itself into two
sections, Monferrato in the north and the
Langhe in the south. The gastronomic
capital of Monferrato is **Moncalvo** (bus
from Asti), with famous wine and truffle
festivals. The towers and moats remain of
its castle, there's a good Gothic church,
San Francesco, and most spectacularly, a
view of the countryside from the large Piazza
Carlo Alberto. Just northeast of Moncalvo another
Black Madonna, similar to the one at Oropa, is vener-
ated at the **Santuario di Crea**. Its 23 chapels contain late 15th–17th-century frescoes and
statues; the highest chapel, del Paradiso, has more fine views over the vineyards. Another
town just northeast of Asti, **Castagnole Monferrato**, holds, on the second Sunday in
October, *La Vendemmia del Nonno* (Grandpa's Grape Harvest), with old-fashioned grape-
picking, barefoot wine-crushing, dancing and music. More sophisticated features include a
truffle auction, and stalls serving glasses of Barbera and Grignolina, as well as Ruch 130, a new
red dessert wine—accompanied by a huge buffet.

In the middle of the countryside near **Albugnano** (22km northwest of Asti, off the road to
Chivasso), the **Abbazia di Vezzolano** (*open April–Sept Tues–Sun 9.30–12.30 and 3–6,
Oct–Mar Tues–Sun 9.30–12.30 and 2–4*) is the finest Romanesque building in Piemonte,
founded according to legend in 773 by Charlemagne, who had a vision on the site while out
hunting. It has a remarkable façade from the early 12th century, adorned with blind arcades
and sculpture, and an even more remarkable rood screen that divides the nave in two and is
carved with two strips, the upper one depicting the *Four Evangelists* and the *Deposition,
Assumption* and *Incarnation of the Virgin*, while the lower one has a cast of solid medieval
characters sitting in a row, with their names draped over their chests like beauty contestants.
On the high altar are 15th-century terracotta figures of the *Virgin and Child*, worshipped by
kneeling figures of *St Augustine* and *Charlemagne*, all under a florid Gothic baldacchino. Part
of the **cloister** is even older than the church, with sculpted capitals, while the newer section
is adorned with frescoes of biblical scenes and Charlemagne. Between the abbey and Turin,
Chieri is a fine old town with an especially interesting Gothic **cathedral**, finished in 1436,
and built over Roman and early medieval foundations; its frescoed baptistry dates back to the
13th century.

Le Langhe and Alba

South of Asti lie the beautiful, fertile hills of Le Langhe, swathed with the intricate woven
patterns of the vines that produce Italy's finest red wines—Barolo, Barbera, Barbaresco,
Dolcetto and Nebbiolo. Little villages are clustered on the tallest hills, crowned by their castles
(many now regional *enoteche, see* above for details). One, **Montegrosso**, is the main
producer of Barbera wine; and **Costigliole d'Asti** and **Canelli**, surrounded by vineyards
producing muscat grapes, are the centre of Asti Spumante production. **Nizza Monferrato** is
the site of the **Museo Bersano**, Piazza Dante 24, © 0144 721 273 (*open Mar–Oct Mon–Fri
10–12 and 2–6*), with a collection of artefacts related to the history of wine.

On the banks of the Tanaro, **Alba** is the capital of Le Langhe, an austere medieval city of narrow winding alleys and brick towers. At the beginning of the 16th century it produced its greatest painter, Macrino, whose *Vergine Incoronata* (1501) hangs in the council chamber of the **Palazzo Comunale**, along with the *Piccolo Concerto* by Mattia Preti. The highlight of the 14th-century **Duomo** is the choir stalls, inlaid in 1500 by Cidonio. Traditionally a bitter enemy of Asti, Alba is now content to send up its old rival in a donkey Palio complete with clown jockeys the first Sunday in October. But Alba can be serious when needs be: its resistance fighters were the bravest in Italy and defended the 'Free Republic of Alba' from the Germans for 23 days in 1944.

Around Alba

Around Alba, hilltop villages, ruined castles and vineyards are set in lovely rolling country. A few kilometres south of the town the oldest Piemontese *enoteca*, in the castle of **Grinzane di Cavour**, is also the meeting point of the 'Order of the Knights of the Truffle and Wines of Alba', and contains a restaurant and a museum dedicated to wine-making, folk traditions, and the castle's most famous former resident, Count Camillo Cavour. **Barbaresco**, east of Alba, and **Barolo**, to the south, have respectively given their names to renowned red wines; in Barolo the 16th-century **Castello Falletti** is used as a wine museum and well-stocked *enoteca*. The village of **La Morra**, the belvedere of Le Langhe, is a good base for walks through the vineyards, and for visiting the former Abbey of the Annunciation, now the **Ratti Wine Museum** (*not as funny as it sounds, but open Mon–Fri 8.30–12 and 2.30–6*). Nearby **Verduno** is dominated by a 17th-century castle, in Juvarra's elegant Baroque style, that was used as a summer residence by King Carlo Alberto and is now a restaurant. Another castle, this one from 1340, guards the concentric village of **Serralunga d'Alba** to the east.

East of Alba, in **Brà**, odds and ends from Roman *Pollentia* (Pollenza) may be seen in the Gothic **Palazzo Traversa**, on Via Serra, and in **S. Chiara** (1742), designed by Bernardo Vittone, with its delightful Rococo interior. **Pollenza** itself retains a circular funerary monument, the foundations of the forum, theatre and amphitheatre (with seating for 17,000) which illustrate the fortune Roman *Pollentia* made in textiles. **Cherasco**, south of Brà, is smaller and more atmospheric—its **Torre Civica** has a rare clock of the phases of the moon. The local museum houses historical and archaeological items; the local castle is a comfortable residence built by the Visconti in the 14th century.

Activities

Organized rambles through the vineyards, villages and woods, on horseback or foot (known as 'trekking' in Italy), are popular here, ranging from a one-day stroll to a more strenuous three days, spending the night in castles along the way. For details, call © 0172 490 018/© 0172 495 300, ✆ 0172 495 110.

Where to Stay and Eating Out

Casale Monferrato ✉ 15033

La Torre, Via Gargoglio 3, © 0142 70295 (*expensive*) is a restaurant that the Turinese and Milanese drive out of their way to patronize. The offerings are based almost entirely on ingredients procured in the immediate environs, such as risotto with crayfish, spinach-filled tortelli, or breast of duck. *Closed Aug.*

Alessandria ✉ 15100

The most comfortable hotel, ★★★★**Alli Due Buoi Rossi**, Via Cavour 32, ℗ 0131 445 252, ✆ 0131 445 255 (*expensive*), also has the city's best restaurant. Located in the heart of town, the rooms are luxurious, and the meals feature the full range of Piemontese specialities. ★★★★**Domus**, Via T. Castellani 12, ℗ 0131 43305, ✆ 0131 23019 (*moderate*) is centrally located with small, modern rooms. ★★**Rex**, Via S. Francesco d'Assisi 48, ℗ 0131 252 297 (*cheap*) is bright and modern. **Il Grappolo**, Via Casale 28, ℗ 253 217 (*expensive*), at the top end of town, is a smart, modern restaurant installed in a 19th-century palazzo, with a fine selection of local wines.

Acqui Terme ✉ 15011

In Acqui Terme you can take the water or mud cure in the pampered environment of the ★★★★**Antiche Terme**, Viale Donati, ℗ 0144 322 101, ✆ 0144 324 909 (*cheap*), set in a pretty park, but nevertheless still a bargain. *Open June–end-Sept*. In the centre, **Carlo Parisio**, Via Mazzini 14, ℗ 0144 56650 (*expensive*) has an exquisite menu of Piemontese specialities—*bagna cauda*, stuffed vegetables, *agnolotti* and good roast meats. *Closed Mon and mid-July*.

Asti ✉ 14100

Reserve in advance for the Palio. Enjoying the best position in town, ★★★★**Reale**, Piazza Alfieri 6, ℗ 0141 530 240, ✆ 0141 34357 (*expensive*) has large, sumptuously decorated modern rooms all with balconies looking out on to the square, and is extremely good value. ★★★★**Aleramo**, Via E. Filiberto 13, ℗ 0141 595 661, ✆ 0141 30039 (*moderate*) is an excellent hotel. The top two of its six floors enjoy superb views over the town's rooftops. Just outside Asti (convenient for drivers), the ★★★★**Hasta**, Valle Benedetta 25, ℗ 0141 213 312, ✆ 0141 219 580 (*moderate*) is tranquil and very cosy, with tennis courts and a garden. It also has a good restaurant, featuring local dishes. ★★**Cavour**, Piazza Marconi 18, ℗/✆ 0141 530 222 (*cheap*), just off the Campo del Palio, is a clean, modern hotel with well-equipped rooms.

You can dine extremely well at **Gener Neuv**, Lungo Tanaro 4, ℗ 0141 557 270 (*very expensive*), overlooking the river, an elegant gourmet haven where you can enjoy a superb *menu degustazione*, based on Piemontese traditions and prepared in an imaginative and exquisite manner. The desserts are light and beautiful to behold, and the list of Piemontese wines is matchless. Reservations advisable. *Closed Mon and Aug*. Nearly as well known, **Falcon Vecchio**, Via San Secondo 8, ℗ 0141 593 106 (*expensive*) is in a wonderfully atmospheric old building. All its dishes are *tipici Astiani*—making it *the* place to try truffles or local meats. *Closed Sun eve and Mon*. Come the weekend, the **Monna Laura Pizzeria**, Via Cavour 30, ℗ 0141 530 113 (*cheap*) is buzzing with people who come for the well-prepared if standard fare.

Costigliole d'Asti ✉ 14055

Da Guido, Piazza Re Umberto 127, ℗ 0141 966 012 (*very expensive*) is one of the top restaurants in all Piemonte, where reservations long in advance are essential to partake of the beautiful masterworks of the kitchen, all made of the freshest local ingredients, with a predilection for porcini mushrooms and truffles. The wine cellar is one of the best endowed in the entire country. *Closed Sun and public holidays*.

Alba ✉ 12051

The best place to stay is the ★★★**Savona**, Via Roma 1, ✆ 0173 440 440, ✉ 0173 364 312 (*moderate*), which has recently been refurbished with very stylish, comfortable and modern rooms, as well as a restaurant and bar. ★★**Piemonte**, Piazza Rosetti 6, ✆/✉ 0173 441 354 (*cheap*) is nicely situated, though the rooms are small. There is a good selection of restaurants in Alba. One of the best, **Osteria dell'Arco**, Vicolo dell'Arco 2, ✆ 0173 363 974 (*moderate*) is in the very centre of town, in a historic building. The small, excellent-value menu includes a tasty tarragon risotto, stuffed guinea fowl and a good selection of wine. *Closed Sun and Aug.*

Barolo ✉ 12060

The classic place to dine from among a substantial selection of restaurants is **Del Buon Padre**, Via delle Viole 30, in the outskirts at Vergne, ✆ 0173 56192 (*moderate*), where the Piemontese cuisine is solid and simply very good, and the wines are divine. *Closed Wed.*

La Morra/Verduno ✉ 12064

The **Belvedere**, Piazza Castello 5, ✆ 0173 50190 (*moderate*) is where, according to many, Piemonte's finest *agnolotti* are served; it is also a lovely place to try *finanziera*, good mushroom and truffle dishes in the autumn and, naturally, fine wines. In Verduno, you can visit in Carlo Alberto's castle , the **Real Castello**, Via Umberto I 9, ✆ 0172 470 125 (*expensive*), and dine like a king on the region's favourite pasta, *tajarin* (tiny tagliatelle), roast guinea fowl and hazelnut torte. *Open mid-April–Nov.*

Southwest Piemonte: Cuneo and the Maritime Alps

Despite the long frontier this district shares with France, the difficult mountainous terrain has made this one of the least known corners of Italy. The French influence is strong, both in the dialect and kitchen. Isolation has also meant that traditions in handicrafts, costumes and festivals have lingered longer than almost anywhere else on the peninsula.

Getting Around

Cuneo is linked by **rail** with Turin via Saluzzo, and with Genoa via Ceva and Mondovì. It is also linked by one of Italy's most spectacular railways to southwest Piemonte's main mountain resort, Limone Piemonte, and then via French territory to Ventimiglia, a 98km stretch that only reopened in 1979 after suffering grave damage in the Second World War. The journey takes roughly three hours, with all its windings and hairpin bends over the mountains. **Bus** services also run from Cuneo to all the towns in the province and to Turin and Genoa.

Tourist Information

Saluzzo: Via Griselda 6, ✆ 0175 46710, ✉ 0175 46718. **Cuneo**: Corso Nizza 17, ✆ 0171 66615, ✉ 0171 695 440. **Limone Piemonte**: Via Roma 30, ✆ 0171 92101. **Mondovì**: Corso Statuto 39, ✆ 0174 40389, ✉ 0174 481 266.

South from Turin to Saluzzo

Students of the French Revolution will recognize the name of one of the first towns south of Turin, **Carmagnola**, as the origin of the popular Parisian song of that period, the 'Carmagnole'. The song was originally sung by Piemontese minstrels about an early 15th-century *condottiere* nicknamed Il Carmagnola; how it made Danton's hit parade is anyone's guess. **Racconigi**, a silk-making town further south, is the site of the **Castello Reale** of the Savoys, begun in 1676 and finished in 1842; behind the castle extends a beautiful park with ancient trees and a lake (*open Tues–Sun 9–1 and 2–7; the park is open every Sun 10–sunset; at all other times guided tours by appointment only, © 0172 84005; adm*).

Mellow old **Saluzzo** was the capital of a marquisate, founded in 1142, that knew its golden age in the 15th century; in the lanes below the castle it retains much of its character from those days. The church of **San Giovanni** (1280) has a good 14th-century Romanesque-Gothic campanile and contains among its treasures the tomb of Saluzzo's greatest Marquess, Ludovico II, who died in 1503. On Via San Giovanni, the charming 15th–16th-century **Casa Cavassa** is now used as the **Museo Civico**, which contains, amongst other things, a splendid carved altarpiece of the *Madonna of Mercy* by Hans Clemer (*open Tues–Sun 10–12.30 and 2–6; adm*). Four km south of Saluzzo, in **Manta**, the marquesses had one of their favourite castles. It's not much to look at, but contains in its baronial hall excellent frescoes by Giacomo Jaquerio of Turin, of nine heroes and nine heroines, believed by some to be portraits of the marquesses and their wives, all posing by the Fountain of Youth (1420s).

Western Valleys: the Po, Varaita and Maira

Buses calling at Saluzzo ascend the rugged Upper Valley of the Po just to the west. **Revello**, near the entrance to the valley, was fortified by the first Marquess of Saluzzo. Part of their palace has been incorporated in the Municipio, including their chapel, adorned with portraits of the marquesses and a Leonardoesque fresco of the *Last Supper*. The fine 15th-century **Collegiata** has a Renaissance marble portal by Matteo Sanmicheli. According to ancient tradition, when Charlemagne exiled the last Lombard king of Italy, Desiderius, in 774, he took refuge in **Ghisola**, a tiny, ancient hamlet near Paesana, at the valley crossroads.

Further up the valley, **Crissolo** is a small resort under the pointed peak of **Monviso** (12,600ft), the highest peak in the Maritime Alps. From Crissolo, with a guide and a sense of adventure, you can visit the stalactite-packed **Grotta del Rio Martino**. The valley road ends at the **Piano del Re**, the source of the Po, Italy's longest river (652km). If you've always wanted to drink a glass of Po, this is the place to do it; by the time it joins the Adriatic it becomes one of the most toxic substances in Europe. Above Piano del Re, you can walk through the **Pertuis de la Traversette** (9455ft), a 246ft tunnel dug in 1480 by the Marquess Ludovico II—a remarkable feat of Renaissance engineering undertaken to facilitate the passage of mule caravans between Saluzzo and the Dauphiny. The pass above Piano del Re is believed by some to have been used by even bigger freight—Hannibal's elephants.

Starting again from Saluzzo, from **Verzuolo** (south of Manta) you can take a lovely detour or an entire holiday in the luxuriant **Valle Varaita**, a Provençal-speaking valley that has retained many of its ancient ways. Aim for **Sampeyre**, manufacturer of ironwork and eiderdowns, where early frescoes have been discovered in **SS. Pietro e Paolo**. During Carnival, Sampeyre celebrates the *Baio*, a thousand-year-old pageant featuring historical characters and dramas in

Napoleonic-era costumes, topped with brightly ribboned hats. Another village, **Casteldelfino**, recalls in its name the 14th century when it was the capital of the Dauphin's Cisalpine lands; in good weather you can continue along the road to France, over the **Colle dell'Agnello**.

The **Valle Maira**, the next valley to the south, is known for its lush fruit orchards. It begins at **Dronero**, with an attractive 15th-century bridge, yet another one built by Old Horny. Nearby, **Villar San Costanzo** has a beautiful 12th-century crypt, a survivor of a Benedictine Abbey, entered through the church of **San Pietro in Vincoli**. Villar San Costanzo is also the base for visiting the weirdly shaped chimney rocks, or *ciciu* (puppets), on the Pragamonti ridge. Formed by glacial erosion eons ago, and standing anywhere from 6–26ft high, they look like giant mutant mushrooms and are especially haunting in winter or at night. The upper part of the Valle Maira, around **Acceglio**, is completely unspoiled.

Cuneo—Piemonte's Cheesy Wedge

A pleasant provincial capital, Cuneo stands at the confluence of the rivers Gesso and Stura, which here form a wedge, or *cuneo*, which lends the city its unusual triangular shape. If you're coming by rail, you'll pass over the impressive **Viadotto Soleri**, dating from the early 1930s. Mostly rebuilt in the 18th and 19th centuries, Cuneo is arranged around its vast porticoed main square, **Piazza Galimberti**, site of an enormous market every Tuesday. Of the churches, the most interesting is **San Francesco** (1227), with a good Gothic portal from 1481, now housing a small collection of Piemontese paintings from the 18th and 19th centuries and prehistoric, Roman and medieval artefacts (*open Tues–Sat 8.30–1 and 2.30–5.30, Sun on request*). In early November Cuneo hosts the Piemontese Cheese Exhibition, starring 'art cheeses'—Castelmagno, Brà, Murazzano, Rashera and more, which you can nibble on while sipping the vintages of Le Langhe.

Buses from Cuneo will take you up the surrounding valleys, the closest of which, the little **Valle Grana**, has the tiny village of **Monterosso Grana**, spread under its ruined watchtower, with a 15th-century frescoed chapel and a small ethnographic museum, and a school aimed at reviving the old crafts of furniture-making and weaving. **Pradleves** is a small resort, while **Castelmagno** makes its famous cheese. A serpentine road leads up and up to the **Santuario di San Magno**, dedicated to a Roman legionary martyred on this lonely site; its oldest section, the choir, dates back to the 15th century.

Borgo San Dalmazzo and its Three Valleys

South of Cuneo, **Borgo San Dalmazzo** is named after another Roman martyr, Dalmatius, but is more famous these days for its snails, the main attraction of the *Fiera Fredda* (the Cold Fair), an early December market founded by Emanuele Filiberto. Borgo's **Santuario della Madonna del Monserrato** is a miniature version of the famous Catalan shrine, accessible by foot in 20 minutes along a chapel-dotted Via Crucis. Fungi fans have a **Mushroom Museum** to peruse in the nearby village of Boves, © 0171 38005 (*open on request*).

A trio of valleys convene at Borgo San Dalmazzo. The longest, the **Valle Stura**, is a botanical paradise for its rare flowers, and throughout history was a major route of salt merchants and armies. Its chief town is medieval **Demonte**; on the mountain of Podio stand the ruins of the once mighty **Fortezza di Consolata**, destroyed by the French in 1796. Further up the valley, **Terme di Vinadio** is a small, hot sulphur spring-spa (*open summers only*); at Pietraporzio begins the **Stretta delle Barricate**, a narrow ravine closed in by sheer walls. **Argentera**, the last and highest *comune*, is a cool summer resort; between May and mid-October the pass into France above Argentera, the **Colle della Maddalena**, is open, lined with pastures and meadows and brimful of flowers.

The second valley, the **Valle Gesso**, leads into the heart of the Maritime Alps, the southernmost to have snow all year round, with three peaks—Argentera, Gelas and Matto—at over 10,000ft, all encompassed in the **Parco Naturale dell'Argentera**, along with many refuges and huts for hikes and ascents. In the middle of the park, the old Savoy spa, **Terme di Valdieri**, was rebuilt in the 1950s and is famed for its hot sulphur springs; waters flow down a series of steps covered with a rare, multi-coloured algae called 'muffa' (*Ulva labyrinthiformis*), which has special healing properties when applied to wounds.

East of Borgo San Dalmazzo, the **Valle Vermenagna**, the route taken by the railway and the SS20 road, is steep and wooded. From Vernante an 8km side road leads up to **Palanfre**, a small village on the fringe of an enchanting beech forest. The unusual circumstance of mountains over 10,000ft so close to the sea, and the high level of rainfall, combine to create a lush microclimate of extraordinary richness; over 650 different trees and flowers thrive within the limited confines of the **Parco Naturale di Palanfre**. Back in Valle Vermenagna, near the French border, Provençal-speaking **Limone Piemonte** is a popular winter sports centre, with the area's best nightlife in season. Its citrusy name actually derives from *leimon*, Greek for meadow, one of the village's most charming features. Amidst the new development stands the Gothic **San Pietro in Vincoli**, with examples of local 17th-century woodcarving.

There's another natural park at the head of the **Valle del Pesio**, the next valley, with interesting karstic formations and pine forests, spread under the loftiest peak, Marguareis. In the spring be sure to look for the **Piss del Pesio**, a spectacular 100ft jet of subterranean water into a void, which resembles just what it sounds like. The **Certosa di Pesio**, founded in 1173 and dominated by an oversize cloister, was abandoned after Napoleon, but is now once again used as a religious house, and the monks take in guests.

Mondovì

Like several other towns in Piemonte, Mondovì is divided into an older, upper half called Piazza, and a lower part known as Breo. Piazza's heart beats in the attractive, asymmetrical **Piazza Maggiore** where, in contrast to the Renaissance buildings, the **Chiesa della Missione** (1675–1733) adds an elegant Baroque touch; inside, 17th-century *trompe-l'œil* figures by Andrea Pozzo float in the vault. The **cathedral** (1763), also up in Piazza, has a chapel dedicated to Universal Suffrage, a notion introduced in Italy by five-times-Prime-Minister Giovanni Giolitti, a native of Mondovì. Down in mostly 18th-century Breo, the city's symbol, the 'Moor', sounds the hours atop the church of **SS. Piero e Paolo**. Two other noteworthy churches are in the mountainous environs: near Bastia Mondovì, the inside of the 11th–15th-century **San Fiorenzo** is covered with a series of 51 late-Gothic frescoes in the Provençal style, while just east of Mondovì the huge 16th–18th-century **sanctuary** in **Vicoforte** has an unusual, enormous dome and suitably impressive interior.

To the south, **Frabosa Soprana** is a popular winter and summer resort, with ski slopes; from here the road continues south to Bossea (bus from Mondovì), site of the **Grotte di Bossea** among the most interesting and important in Italy, with a wide variety of beautiful stalactite formations, narrow passages and huge caverns, an underground river and lakes, and a skeleton of a prehistoric bear, *Ursus spelaeus*. The caves maintain a year-round temperature of 9°C, and can be visited daily with a guide.

From the rail junction at **Ceva**, you can take a train south along the Tanaro as far as Ormea, by way of **Garessio**, a picturesque collection of four hamlets, with ski slopes, mineral water cures, and a summer palace of the Savoys, the **Castello di Casotto**. Pretty **Ormea** is a woodsy summer resort, its ruined castle once a nest of Saracen corsairs in the 10th and 11th centuries, when they controlled the Ligurian coast.

Where to Stay and Eating Out

Carmagnola ✉ 10022

Like the rest of Piemonte, the southwest corner is a happy hunting ground for the galloping, or even the bus-riding gourmet. **La Carmagnola**, Via Chiffi 31, ℰ 011 971 2673 (*very expensive*) is a lovely restaurant in a 17th-century Piemontese mansion, featuring dishes based on the freshest of ingredients; the delicious *menu degustazione* includes pheasant galantine in Sauternes and raspberry vinegar, and local specialities like *ossobuco* and *porcini* mushrooms in cream. The desserts and wines, from Le Langhe and Friuli, are exceptional. *Closed Mon and Aug.*

Saluzzo ✉ 12037

★★Persico, Vicolo Mercati, ℰ 0175 41213, ✆ 0175 248 075 (*cheap*), a stone's throw from the cathedral, is a nice bohemian hotel (complete with resident artist) with comfortable if slightly oddly furnished rooms, and a good restaurant (*moderate*). The wild boar stew is particularly recommended. In the birthplace of Saluzzo's great republican patriot, Silvio Pellico, **La Gargotta del Pellico**, Piazzetta dei Mondagli 5, ℰ 0175 46833 (*expensive*) is an exceptionally good restaurant—try the quail in pastry, or the *raviolini* with marjoram and mushroom butter, followed by superb desserts like pear mousse and Piemontese cheese. *Closed Tues, and Wed lunch.*

Cuneo ✉ 12100

One of the town's best hotels, the **★★★★Principe**, Piazza Duccio Galimberti 5, ℰ 0171 693 355, ✆ 0171 67562 (*moderate*) is right in the centre, and has 42 modern rooms. In the oldest quarter, **★★Ligure**, Via Savigliano 11, ℰ 0171 68942 (*cheap*) is a bit old and worn at the edges, but brightened with old-fashioned courtesy. Rooms vary in price, depending on the plumbing, and tasty meals of homemade pasta and roast meat or trout are equally cheap.

A favourite in old Cuneo is **Tre Citroni**, Via Bonelli 2, near Piazza Galimberti, ℰ 0171 602 048 (*expensive*), a family-run citadel of fine dining, with delightful *agnolotti* and roast lamb, among other dishes. Just north of Cuneo in Centallo, the excellent **Due Palme**, Via Busca 2, ℰ 0171 211 567 (*expensive*) serves mouthwatering *agnolotti*, lamb chops with porcini mushrooms, and duck *à l'orange*. For a real treat, head 9km south of Cuneo to Boves, where **Rododendro**, Frazione San Giacomo, ℰ 0171 380 372 (*very expensive*) is the wood-surrounded atelier of one of Italy's finest woman chefs. Her leek soup, truffles with eggs, and exquisitely tender

Chateaubriand have put the restaurant on Italy's gourmet map, with an extensive wine list of French and Italian bottles. *Closed Sun eve, Mon, and some of June.*

In the Cunean valleys there are many, often simple and rustic, places to stay and eat. Try **★★Tre Verghe d'Oro**, ✆ 0171 986 116 (*moderate*) in Pradleves in the Valle Grana, a long-established, old-fashioned mountain inn, which serves *gnocchi al Castelmagno* and other mountain specialities.

Limone Piemonte ✉ 12015

Near the slopes, **★★★Le Ginestre**, Via Nizza 68, ✆ 0171 92101, ◉ 0171 927 597 (*expensive*) is small, cosy and convenient. **★Mignon**, Via San Giovanni 3, ✆ 0171 92363 (*cheap*) has simple rooms and a good restaurant, where Piemontese specialities are complemented by a cosy atmosphere. Limone has no lack of restaurants—**Mac Miche**, Via Roma 64, ✆ 0171 92449 (*moderate*) offers a fairly standard but reliable Italian menu. *Closed Mon eve and Tues.* For excellent but less expensive food, try the family-run **La Crubarsela**, Via Comm. Beltrandi 7, ✆ 0171 92391 (*moderate*), just down from the tourist office, which serves fine local dishes in a homely setting, and has an unusually good wine selection. *Closed Mon.*

Liguria (the Italian Riviera)

'Riviera' in Italian simply means shore, but in Liguria the shore is THE Riviera, a rugged, rock-bound rainbow of coast linking France to Tuscany, endowed with what is surprisingly one of the rarer Italian commodities— beautiful beaches. Usually not large, buxom, sandy beaches, but rather refined, slender strands in magical settings, beneath steep cliffs and hanging gardens, backed by old fishing towns squeezed between the rock, or palm-fringed resorts that fit as comfortably as an old pair of shoes.

After Liguria, you'd have to continue all the way down to the Bay of Naples to find a shore of comparable interest and beauty. And if you're approaching from the haughty French Riviera, the Italian Riviera comes as a pleasant surprise, genteelly relaxed and laid back—no one cares if your socks don't quite match, or you've brought the children. There are splendid grand hotels, but they are outnumbered by small and unpretentious *pensioni*.

Although August is peak season these days, people first came to this fabled shore for its sunny and mild winter climate. Sheltered by the Maritime Alps and Apennines from the fogs and chills of the north, Liguria has a sensuous growth of lemons, oranges and flowers—one of the region's principal exports. The olive oil from its ancient groves is legendary. Bathed in a luminous, warm light, the Riviera's colours are dazzling, the reds, blues, yellows like glistening newborns. Yet just a few dozen hairpin turns up into the hinterland, and you're in another world altogether, lush and cool and green; Liguria is the most forested region of Italy.

The delights of sun and sea are only part of what the region has to offer. Long isolated from the rest of Italy because of the mountains, Liguria has a distinct identity all its own. Poor in resources, but full of intrepid, tenacious seamen and merchants, it has looked to the sea for its survival since the early Middle Ages. After the Crusades, the Republic of Genoa grew to become a seapower and east-west wheeler-dealer rivalled only by Venice, and in the 17th century it did so well financing Spain's treasure fleet that it became the wealthiest corner of Europe. All these experiences formed the Ligurian character—tough, feisty, shrewd, adventurous, independent and stubborn. Columbus, of course, came from Liguria, as did the great admiral Andrea Doria, and the Risorgimento heroes Garibaldi and Mazzini.

Not to be Missed

The **Via Aurelia** (SS1), successor to the Roman road, runs along the coast, offering the finest scenery, but the best thing to do is to base yourself in one place on the Riviera and explore from there. Highlights, from west to east, include the magnificent gardens of Villa Hanbury at **Ventimiglia**, the medieval hill towns of **Dolceacqua** and **Taggia**, and the ghost town of **Bussana Vecchia**, all near the old capital of fun, **San Remo**. Further along is the coral-fishers' village of **Cervo** and ancient **Albenga**, near the beautiful caves of **Toirano**. **Genoa** has an evocative old quarter and a great oriental museum, among others, and is worth at least a day.East of Genoa extends the magnificent promontory of **Monte di Portofino**, embracing the charming fishing town of **Camogli**, the ancient abbey of **San Fruttuoso**, and ultra chic and ultra lovely **Portofino** itself. Beyond are the celebrated **Cinque Terre** villages, hanging on or below cliffs, laced together by a stunning seaside footpath. Beyond the naval port of **La Spezia**, **Portovenere** is nearly as trendy as Portofino these days. The whole **Gulf of La Spezia**, 'the Gulf of Poets', is enchanting, and can easily be combined with a boat excursion to the Cinque Terre.

Food and Wine in Liguria

In Liguria look for ancient popular festivals and folk traditions, and for great regional cuisine, especially fish dishes prepared in a hearty style similar to neighbouring Provence—try *cacciucco*, Ligurian bouillabaisse, or *cappon magro*, pickled fish with vegetables, or *zuppa di datteri*, made with razor shell clams. Even the snacks are different, like *focaccia*, Ligurian pizza, made with a softer dough than the Neapolitan version, and with the ingredients baked inside, and *farinata*, a mixture of baked, ground chickpeas best eaten hot from the oven. Pasta (especially *trenette*, similar to linguini) is often served with Genoa's famous pesto sauce of basil, garlic, pine nuts, olive oil and parmesan, ground with a mortar and the pestle which gave it its name. And, although Liguria isn't one of Italy's great wine-growing regions, you may want to try its best, Pigato, a fine dry white, or Rossese, a fine dry red.

Riviera di Ponente: Ventimiglia to San Remo

The western Riviera enjoys one of the mildest winter climates in all Italy. Flowers thrive here even in February, and are cultivated in fields that dress the landscape in a brilliant patchwork (albeit increasingly shrouded in plastic), lending this stretch the well-deserved name of the 'Riviera of Flowers'. In the 19th century consumptive northerners flocked here every autumn, but you may want to avoid that particular season; in recent years, perhaps as a result of global warming, the area has been hit by tempestuous rains. In October 1998, San Remo endured its worst floods since 1875.

Getting Around

Trains run frequently up and down the coast; from Ventimiglia a line branches off for Cuneo, in Piemonte, one of the country's most scenic rail routes (*see* p.123). Inland, the hill towns are easily reached by bus from their nearest coastal towns.

Tourist Information

Ventimiglia: Via Cavour 61, ✆ 0184 351 183; **Dolceacqua**: Via Patrioti Martiri 58, ✆ 0184 206 666; **Bordighera**: Palazzo del Parco, Via Roberto 1, ✆ 0184 262 322, @ 0184 264 455; **San Remo**: Via Nuvoloni 1, ✆ 0184 571 571, @ 0184 507 649; **Arma di Taggia**: in the Villa Boselli, ✆ 0184 43733.

Ventimiglia

Ventimiglia is tricky: if you arrive by train it can seem seedy and dull. On the other hand, if you come by the coastal road from France it is pure enchantment, a garden-town by the sea where roses and carnations are the main crops, and in July they stage the 'Battle of the Flowers'.

Ventimiglia is also a garden of history, with the most ancient roots in Liguria. Between 100 and 200,000 BC, members of Europe's first sophisticated culture—the Neanderthal—lived in the **Balzi Rossi** caves, near the French frontier on the beach of Grimaldi. At the entrance to the caves, the **Museo Preistorico** displays the finds—seashell finery, tools, weapons and lumpy 'Venuses', the first sculptures, ever. The caves hold traces of elaborate burials, and the *Grotto del Caviglione* has an etching of a horse, of a breed now common only on the Russian steppes (© *0184 381 113; museum and caves open Tues–Sat 9–7; closed Mon*).

The same municipal bus from Ventimiglia serves Mortola Inferiore and the **Hanbury Gardens** (*open April–Sept 9–6; Oct–Mar 10–4; closed Wed*), a botanical paradise founded in 1867 by Sir Thomas Hanbury, who acclimatized some 5000 rare and exotic plants from Africa and Asia to co-exist with native Mediterranean flora; acquired by the state in 1960, the gardens are among the most important in Italy. Near the gardens, a section of the ancient Via Aurelia has a plaque listing VIPs who have passed this way, from St Catherine of Siena to Napoleon. The main road, passing underneath the gardens, leads to the customs post at Ponte San Ludovico, with its **castle** where Serge Voronoff performed his experiments, seeking the Fountain of Youth in monkey glands.

Ventimiglia's Roman incarnation, **Albintimilium**, 1km east of the modern town, was an important stop on the Via Aurelia; best-preserved among its ruins is the small 2nd-century AD **theatre** (*open Wed and Fri 3–7, Thurs and Sat 9–1*), while the finds are on view in the nearby **Museo Archeologico**, Via Verdi 41 (*open Tues–Sat 9.30–12.30 and 3–5, Sun 10–12.30; adm*). Ventimiglia itself is divided into old and new by the River Roja, the modern town built around the winter flower market and lined with typical seaside promenades, while the old town, with its twisting medieval lanes, has the attractive 11th–12th-century **cathedral** and **baptistry** for a focal point. Another Romanesque church, **San Michele**, was built from Roman columns and milestones. Guarding the coast to the west of town, the ruined 12th-century **Castel D'Appio** was the headquarters of the piratical Counts of Ventimiglia.

Dolceacqua

Among the valleys cutting inland from Ventimiglia, the Val Nervia is perhaps the most appealing (buses hourly from Ventimiglia). Aim for **Dolceacqua**, a picturesque village linked by the single arch of a medieval bridge, and crowned by the 16th-century **Castello di Doria**, reputedly haunted by lordly villains who took full advantage of their *droit de seigneur* with the local brides. On St Sebastian's Day (20 January) Dolceacqua holds a unique religious procession led by the 'tree man', who bears a huge tree branch hung with large, coloured communion hosts, a curious mixture of Christianity and ancient fertility rites.

The hills around Dolceacqua are terraced with vineyards producing *Rossese*, a good red wine available in the local cafés. Further up, **Pigna**, the 'Pinecone', looks like one, with its concentric walls, which shelter two fine churches with paintings by Giovanni Canevesio. Some 3km away, **Castelvittorio** has changed little since the 13th century, when its thick walls kept out arch enemy Pigna, with whom it conducted nonstop war in the Middle Ages.

Bordighera

Once a favourite winter retreat of chilblained Britons (who once outnumbered the locals), Bordighera is now one of the most jovial resorts on the Riviera, blessed with a good beach and regal promenades and a September festival of humour. As at Ventimiglia, the environs contain fields of cultivated flowers, but here the speciality is palms; since Sant'Ampelio supposedly brought the first date palm seeds from Egypt in 411, Bordighera has had a monopoly in supplying the Vatican with fronds during Easter week. Monet painted here in 1884, captivated by 'this brilliance, this magical light'. In the summer the tourist office runs free tours that point out the Giardino Moreno, Valle di Sasso and other places that caught his eye.

The tiny medieval nucleus of Bordighera, above the Spianata del Capo, is shoe-horned behind its gates; further up, the flower-bedecked **Via dei Colli** has excellent views of the shimmering coast. Below, the Romanesque church of **Sant'Ampelio** stands on its little cape above the grotto where the saint lived; from here you can walk along the pleasant Lungomare Argentina west to the spa, or east along the seaside Via Arziglia to Bordighera's palm and mimosa plantations at the **winter garden** and the **Giardino Madonna della Ruota**, a 45-minute walk. **Museo Bicknell**, Via Romano 39bis (© *0184 263 601; open Mon–Fri 10–12 and 3–5; closed first two weeks of Aug*) has plaster casts of the curious Neolithic rock-engravings from the Valle delle Meraviglie (part of France since the Second World War), discovered by the Reverend Clarence Bicknell. This whole neighbourhood is packed with British hotels and villas.

San Remo

San Remo is the opulent queen of the Italian Riviera, her grand hotels and villas as beautiful and out-of-date as antimacassars on an armchair. Yet even if the old girl isn't young, she's a corker with a Mae West twinkle in her eye. Other resorts may have more glamour, but few have more character. San Remo also has considerable bargains—the French pour over to purchase designer clothes and furnishings that cost 20 to 30 per cent more in Paris.

Set on a huge, sheltered bay, San Remo was long a watering hole for a variety of drifting aristocrats, most famously Empress Maria Alexandrovna, wife of Czar Alexander II. She played the Pied Piper to a sizeable Russian colony, including Tchaikovsky, who composed *Eugene Onegin* and the Fourth Symphony during his stay here in 1878. The duke of nonsense, Edward Lear, ended his lifelong travels in the Mediterranean here in 1888, as did the father of dynamite and famous prizes, Alfred Nobel, who died in 1896 in the **Villa Nobel**, on the east edge of town, by the Parco Ormond. Modern San Remo consists of three distinct parts: the shopping district, the rather dusty old town and the smart west end, where the grandest hotels are situated. To get the full flavour take the *passeggiata* down the lovely, palm-lined **Corso dell'Imperatrice**; here, springing out of luxuriant, semi-tropical foliage, are the incongruous onion domes of a **Russian Orthodox church** (*open year round Tues, Thurs and Sat 9.30–12.30 and 4–7; winter 3–6.30*), a dainty jewel box built in the 1920s by the exiled nobility and containing the tombs of the deposed members of the royal house of Montenegro.

This part of town reaches it zenith at the white brightly lit, Liberty-style **municipal casino**, a legacy from these golden days of fashion and still the lively heart of San Remo's social life, with its gaming rooms, roof garden cabaret and celebrated restaurant with a live orchestra (*open 10am–3am; roulette wheels in operation from 2pm–3am; there is a dress code in the French gaming rooms but not the American; adm Mon–Thurs L5000, Fri–Sun L15,000*). As you travel further east along Corso Matteotti, San Remo's main shopping street, you enter the lively, commercial heart of San Remo. In February the Corso's **Teatro Ariston** hosts the biggest event in the world of Italian pop, the unabashedly tacky *Festival della Canzone*, an extravagant five-day-long lip-synch ritual built of glitter and hype, where this once gloriously musical nation parades its contemporary talents with all the self-confidence of the Emperor in his new clothes. All year long, early risers can take in the intoxicating colour and scent of the **San Remo Flower Market** on Corso Garibaldi, just off Piazza Colombo—very much a working, wholesale market, but fascinating for visitors nonetheless.

The old town, **La Pigna**, is San Remo's 'casbah', a tangled, mystery-laden mesh of steep lanes and stairs weaving under archways and narrow tunnels, fortified around the year 1000 as a refuge against the Saracens. Get there by way of Piazza San Siro, site of the 12th-century, but much altered, **Duomo di San Siro**, with an unusual black crucifix by an unknown sculptor and the Baroque **Oratorio dell'Immacolata Concezione**. The large, covered food market is nearby on Piazza Eroi Sanremesi (*open Tues–Sat 8.30–1*). From here you can wend your way up through the casbah to the **Giardini Regina Elena**, which is rather dull but has fantastic views of the town and harbour. Standing majestically at the top of La Pigna is the 17th-century **Santuario Madonna della Costa** (*open April–Sept daily 9–12 and 3–6.30; Oct–Mar daily 9–12 and 3–5.30; buses run regularly from San Remo*). The madonna inside saved a local sailor from shipwreck, who subsequently donated the first gold coin to establish the shrine. On *Ferragosto*, 15 August, this event is celebrated with fireworks and a feast, in one of the Riviera's most attractive traditional festivals. The panoramic **Corso degli Inglesi** begins at the Casino, and passes the old funicular to **Monte Bignone**, the highest peak in the amphitheatre of hills around San Remo (4281ft); a committee has been formed to restore the funicular; until then you can drive or take a bus part of the way to the top, past the **Ulivi Golf Club** (© 0184 557 093), for great views of the Riviera.

Around San Remo

San Remo has several interesting neighbours, all easily reached by buses departing from the train station. Just to the west, the quiet seaside resort of **Ospedaletti** is shaded by luxuriant pines, palms and eucalyptus; Katherine Mansfield lived here in the early-1900s. Its name comes from the Knight Hospitallers of Rhodes, who had a pilgrims' hospice here in 1300. They also bestowed their name on the nearby hill town of **Coldirodi**, known for its **Rambaldi Art Gallery**, © 0184 670 131 (*open daily 10–12, Fri and Sat also 3.30–6; closed Mon and Wed; adm*), with great forgeries—of Veronese, Reni and Rembrandt (along with real paintings).

Then there's **Bussana Vecchia**, Italy's trendiest ghost town. On 23 February 1887 an earthquake killed thousands and turned Bussana into a picturesque ruin, while the inhabitants rebuilt a Bussana Nuova 2km closer to the sea. In a typical Italian contradiction, Bussana Vecchia officially no longer exists, but has a number of artistically minded inhabitants who are equally officially non-existent, but who have restored the interiors of the ruined houses and been hooked up with water, lights, phones and two mild-mannered llamas from Peru, and sell paintings and all sorts of arty-farty dust magnets. The earthquake knocked in the roof of the Baroque church (packed at the time for the Ash Wednesday service), but nearly all the parishioners managed to escape death in the side chapels; one survivor, Giovanni Torre detto Merlo, went on to invent the ice cream cone in 1902. The church is open to the sky, the stucco decorations sprout weeds, trees grow in the nave and apse, and cherubs smile down like broken dolls on a shelf.

Further inland, **Bajardo**, spread out over its conical hill with a backdrop of mountains and forests, was also devastated by the earthquake, but was rebuilt on the same site. Don't miss the ruined church, with intriguing 13th-century capitals carved roughly with the heads of Mongols, some of whom are believed to have accompanied the Saracens to Liguria. Bajardo celebrates the *Festival della Barca* on Pentecost Sunday, when a large tree trunk topped by a smaller pine tree is erected in the middle of the piazza, around which the people slowly dance and sing a tale of tragic love from the year 1200, when the Count beheaded his daughter rather than let her marry against his will.

To the east, **Arma di Taggia** has one of the finest sandy beaches in the area, lying at the mouth of the Valle Argentina; 3km inland, picturesquely medieval **Taggia** is the site of an antiques fair every fourth Saturday and Sunday of the month. The **Dominican Convent** (*open daily 9.30–12 and 3–5; closed Thurs*) contains a number of fine paintings of the 15th-century the Ligurian school; the monks introduced the olive trees that have made Taggia's fortune. Noble palaces with coats of arms line the streets in the walls, and a remarkable, dog-leg 16-arched **medieval bridge** crosses the Argentina. Come on the third Sunday of July for the ancient Festival of Mary Magdalen who, according to tradition, once paid Taggia a call, and is remembered by members of her red-capped confraternity with an eerie Dance of Death performed by two men, one playing the role of 'the man' and the other of Mary Magdalen, who dies and is brought back to life with a sprig of lavender.

There are a number of attractive hill villages above the Valle Argentina, most intriguing of which is **Triora**, the Riviera's very own Salem, a fortified 15th-century village where, in 1588, during a famine, 13 women and girls were denounced as witches before the Inquisition; five died before their accusers themselves were excommunicated. The **Museo Etnografico e della Stregoneria** (*open daily 3–6*) tells the story. The **Collegiata** has a beautiful *Baptism of Jesus* (1397) by Taddeo di Bartolo, and in the summer you can bungee jump too!

Where to Stay and Eating Out

San Remo has a hotel-finding service in the station, ✆ 0184 80172 (*closed Sun*). On the whole, though, you shouldn't have too much trouble finding a room outside of July and August. Note that many hotels still prefer guests to take full- or half-pension, particularly in high season.

Ventimiglia ✉ 18039

★★★**La Riserva**, ✆ 0184 229 533, ✆ 0184 229 712 (*moderate*), up in the olive groves at Castel d'Appio, 5km west of the town, is a fine family-run inn with magnificent views, a pool and very comfortable rooms. *Open April–Sept and Christmas*. The ★★★**Sea Gull**, Via Marconi 24, ✆ 0184 351 726, ✆ 0184 231 217 (*cheap*) is a comfortable establishment on the waterfront, with a private beach.

The premier restaurant in the Ventimiglia area, **Balzi Rossi**, Piazzale De Gasperi, ✆ 0184 38132 (*very expensive*) is right on the frontier at San Lodovico—with a dining room overlooking the sea. The cuisine blends the best of France and Liguria, and includes a legendary *terrina di coniglio*, scallops of sea bass, divine desserts and excellent wines. Reserve. *Closed Mon, and Tues lunch*.

Bordighera ✉ 18012

Modern, elegant ★★★★**Del Mare**, Via Portico della Punta 34, ✆ 0184 262 201, ✆ 0184 262 394 (*very expensive*) has a beautiful panoramic position, with private beach, sea-water pool, gardens and tennis. *Closed Nov–Christmas*. ★★★★**Cap Ampelio**, Via Virgilio 5, ✆ 0184 264 333, ✆ 0184 264 244 (*expensive*) overlooks the town and the sea, and offers designer furnishings, a heated pool and garden. ★★★**Britannique & Jolie**, Via Regina Margherita 35, ✆ 0184 261 464, 🖅 0184 260 375 (*moderate*) is a traditional favourite, with a garden near the sea. *Closed Oct–Nov.*

The most spectacular place to eat in Bordighera, inserted in the cliffs, is **La Reserve Tastevin**, Via Aurelia 20, at Capo Sant'Ampelio, ✆ 0184 261 322 (*expensive*). The views are fantastic, and so is the food, a delightful combination of ingredients from the sea and the Valle Argentina. *Closed Sun eve, Mon, and Nov.* Tiny but classy, **La Chaudron**, Piazza Bengasi 2, ✆ 0184 263 592 (*expensive*) will win your heart with delicious spaghetti with artichokes, and the Ligurian speciality, *pesce al sale* (fish baked in salt, skinned, then dressed with olive oil). Reserve. *Closed Sun and Mon.*

San Remo ✉ 18038

Near the Casino, the palatial turn-of-the-century *grande dame*, the ★★★★★**Royal**, Corso Imperatrice 80, ✆ 0184 5391, 🖅 0184 661 445 (*luxury*) is surrounded by lush gardens, with palms, flowers, tennis court and an enormous heated sea-water pool. Rooms vary from imperial suites to refurbished doubles. And, true to tradition, the hotel orchestra serenades guests in the afternoon and gets them dancing in the evening. One of the region's oldest hotels, the ★★★★**Astoria West End**, Corso Matuzia 8, ✆ 0184 667 701, 🖅 0184 663 318 (*very expensive*) sounds as if it belongs in New York, but instead sits in all its confectionery elegance—grand chandeliers, elaborate stucco ceilings and carved lifts—opposite the sea in San Remo. It also has luxuriant gardens with a pool. If you prefer something with a Liberty-style touch, ★★★★**Grand Hotel Londra**, Corso Matuzia 2, ✆ 0184 668 000, 🖅 0184 668 073 (*expensive*) can oblige. Built around the turn of the century, it has a lovely garden and pool, and fine original interior details. *Closed Oct–Nov.*

★★★**Paradiso**, Via Roccasterone 12, ✆ 0184 571 211, 🖅 0184 578 176 (*moderate*), set just back from the seafront above most of the hurly burly, is enveloped with flowers on the terrace and balconies. It has a distinguished, glass-enclosed restaurant. *Closed Nov–first half of Dec.* ★★★**Lolli Palace**, Corso dell'Imperatrice 70, ✆ 0184 531 496, 🖅 0184 541 574 (*moderate*) is a lovely little hotel with a decent restaurant. The sea-facing rooms are superb: bright and airy with great big bay windows and cute little balconies—all decorated in white and wood. Further along, at Corso dell'Imperatrice 27, ★★★★**Europa**, ✆ 0184 578 170, 🖅 0184 508 661 (*moderate*) is one of the few hotels to retain a *fin de siècle* character in its main rooms. Central ★★★**Eletto**, Via Matteotti 44, ✆ 0184 531 548, 🖅 0184 531 506 (*moderate–cheap*) is a very pretty 19th-century hotel, furnished with antiques and blessed with a welcoming little garden.

San Remo has a wide selection of reasonable pizzerias and restaurants concentrated around Piazza Eroi Sanremesi and Via Palazzo, between the seafront and the old town. For something special, try **Da Giannino**, Corso Trento e Trieste 23, ✆ 0184 504 014 (*very expensive*), for exquisite dishes based on fresh ingredients, including the regional speciality, *tagliolini al sugo di triglia* (wholewheat pasta with red mullet sauce), polenta with cheese and vegetable sauce, and pigeon with ginger, accompanied by an excellent wine list. *Closed Sun eve and Mon.* **Bagatto**, Via Matteotti 145, ✆ 0184 531 925 (*expensive*) is one of the brightest and most relaxed restaurants in San Remo, with tempting *antipasti*, *risotti* and other dishes using sun-ripened vegetables, as well as delicious seafood and lamb dishes. *Closed Sun and July.* Just outside San Remo, at Verezzo Cava, **Silvestro**, ℗ 0184 559 066 (*cheap*) offers an alternative to the constant barrage of seafood in the shape of delicious homecooked meat dishes, especially chicken and rabbit. *Closed Tues.*

Dolceacqua ✉ 18035

Sit under the plane trees at **Gastone**, Piazza Garibaldi 2, ℗ 0184 206 577 (*moderate*), a relaxed and friendly place, where you can try *cappon magro* and imaginative dishes such as *gnocchetti* with courgette flowers and shrimp. *Closed Mon eve and Tues.*

Arma di Taggia ✉ 18011

La Conchiglia, Via Lungomare 33, ℗ 0184 43169 (*expensive*) serves Ligurian delights based on seafood, local cheese and delicate olive oil—the prawn and white bean salad is delicious. There's a very good set lunch. *Reserve; closed Wed.*

Riviera di Ponente: Imperia to Savona

Imperia divides the 'Riviera of Flowers' from the more rugged, silvery 'Riviera of Olives'. Connoisseurs of olive oil rate Liguria's the tops in Italy, although of course there are plenty of other regions ready to dispute this most slippery of crowns.

Tourist Information

Imperia: Corso G. Matteotti 54/a, ℗ 0183 24947, ✆ 0183 24950. **Cervo**: Piazza Castello 1, ℗ 0183 408 197, ✆ 0183 403 133. **Alassio**: Via Gibb 26, ℗ 0182 640 346, ✆ 0182 644 690. **Albenga**: Via B. Ricci, ℗ 0182 558 444, ✆ 0182 558 740. **Finale Ligure**: Via San Pietro 14, ℗ 019 681 019, ✆ 019 681 804. **Savona**: Via Guidobono 125r, ℗ 019 400 2008, ✆ 019 400 3084.

Imperia

In 1923 two towns, Porto Maurizio and Oneglia, were married by Mussolini to form a slightly schizophrenic provincial capital, Imperia. The bustling oil port (olive oil, that is) of Oneglia was the birthplace of the great Genoese Admiral Andrea Doria, while the old quarter of Porto Maurizio has most of Imperia's charm, with steep lanes and steps and palatial hill, the Paraxio, though even here Imperia lacks the typical Riviera resort ambience, for better or worse.

The Porto Maurizio side of town has a **naval museum**, Piazza Duomo 11, ℗ 0183 651 541 (*open Sept–June Wed–Sat 4–7.30; July–Aug Wed–Sat 9am–11pm*), which contains ships' models and nautical instruments, and, in Oneglia, the **Museo dell'Olivo**, Via Garessio 13 (*open daily 9–12 and 3–6; closed Tues*), dedicated to the history and practice of olive-growing. Imperia is also the base for exploring old villages in the hinterland, like **Dolcedo**, the site of the most renowned olive groves in the region, with numerous *fantoios* (presses) that sell the local oil, as well as medieval bridges, one of which was built by the Knights of St John in 1292. In another valley, further east, the main SS28 leads to pretty **Pontedassio**.

East of Imperia are a string of popular resorts: **Diano Marina**, with its long beach and palms, and site of a small **Museo Civico** (*open daily April–Sept only*), which contains items from a 1st-century BC Roman shipwreck; modern **San Bartolomeo al Mare**; and, prettiest of the three, **Cervo**, a curl of white, cream and pale yellow houses sweeping up from the sea with a delightful, sunny, Moorish atmosphere. At the top of the curl stands the cream pastry Baroque **Chiesa dei Corallini** (the coral fishers), its concave façade emblazoned with a stag, or *cervo* in Italian. Although it hosts a chamber music festival in July and August, Cervo has only five small hotels near its shingle beach.

Andora, next along the coast, consists of a marine quarter with a beach and, up in the Merula Valley, a fortified hamlet, Castello Andora, reached by way of a medieval bridge, with a picturesque ruined castle, tower-gate and the lovely 13th-century Romanesque-Gothic church of **SS. Giacomo e Filippo**. On the other side of Capo Mele ('Cape Apples') lies the attractive old fishing town of **Laigueglia**, with a majestic Baroque church from 1754.

Alassio and Albenga

With its mild climate and fine beach, Alassio has long been a resort. Some old palazzi on its main street, the pretty 1597 church of **Sant'Ambrogio** with a Romanesque campanile, and a defence tower recall Alassio's pre-resort days. Visiting celebrities, beginning with Hemingway, have their autographs in ceramic plaques on the 'Muretto' ('little wall'), Alassio's Hollywood Boulevard; in August there's even a 'Miss Muretto' beauty contest. You can take an excursion boat to the tiny islet, **Isola Gallinaria**, a mile off the coast. Named after the wild hens which used to populate it, the island provided sanctuary for St Martin when he was fleeing Arian persecution in the 4th century. For over a thousand years it was home to a powerful abbey, of which only ruins remain; today it is a nature reserve, expecially popular with skin-divers. Another pleasant outing from Alassio is up to 13th-century Benedictine church of **Santa Croce**, with one of the best view-points in the area. From here you can walk the Roman road down to Albenga.

East of Alassio, **Albenga** was the Roman port of *Album Ingaunum*. It remained prosperous throughout the Middle Ages, until its harbour shifted away with the course of the Cento River; nowadays the town stands 1km from the sea and grows asparagus in the old river bed. Albenga's impressive collection of 13th-century towers, built during its days as a *comune*, stand like bridesmaids around the elegant 1391 campanile of the Romanesque **cathedral**. One (*c.* 1300) belongs to the Palazzo Vecchio del Comune, and now houses the **Museo Civico Ingauno** (*open Tues–Sun 10–12 and 3–6*), which contains finds from Roman to medieval times, and provides a good view from the top floor. Steps lead down from the piazza to Albenga's celebrated 5th-century **baptistry** (*open Tues–Sun 10–12 and 3–6*).

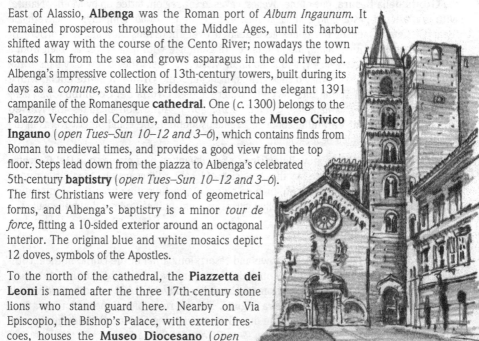

The first Christians were very fond of geometrical forms, and Albenga's baptistry is a minor *tour de force*, fitting a 10-sided exterior around an octagonal interior. The original blue and white mosaics depict 12 doves, symbols of the Apostles.

To the north of the cathedral, the **Piazzetta dei Leoni** is named after the three 17th-century stone lions who stand guard here. Nearby on Via Episcopio, the Bishop's Palace, with exterior frescoes, houses the **Museo Diocesano** (*open*

Tues–Sun 10–12 and 3–6), with 17th-century tapestries, paintings, reliquaries and illuminated manuscripts. The 13th-century **Loggia dei Quattro Canti**, nearby, marks the centre of the Roman town.

Another tower, on Piazza San Michele, belongs to the **Palazzo Peloso Cipolla** ('Hairy Onion Palace'), built in the 14th century, with a Renaissance-era façade; it now contains the **Museo Navale Romana** (*open Tues–Sun 10–12 and 3–6*), featuring amphorae and other items salvaged from a 1st-century BC Roman shipwreck discovered near the Isola Gallinaria, as well as 16th–18th-century blue and white pharmacy jars from Albisola.

To the west and along the Cento you can stroll through the scattered remains of *Album Ingaunum*—the old Roman road and tombs on the hill, the amphitheatre below, and the foundations of the city on the river banks. A short walk from here, along the Viale Pontelungo, will take you to part of the ancient Via Aurelia and the impressive 13th-century 495ft-long **Ponte Lungo**; apparently it only spanned the Cento for a few years before the river changed its course. Along the road, note the ruins of the 4th-century basilica of **San Vittore**, one of the oldest in Liguria.

Inland: the Paleolithic Grottoes of Toirano

Heading east from Albenga, **Ceriale** is a small seaside resort with a long beach lined with palms. **Borghetto Santo Spirito**, the next coastal town, is the junction (and bus pick-up point) for **Toirano**, a medieval village that seems spanking new compared with the relics of its Middle Palaeolithic inhabitants (80,000 BC), discovered in the limestone cliffs just up the valley. These Cro Magnons, like modern Italians, had excellent taste, and chose as their abode the **Grotta della Basura**, one of the loveliest caves in the region, tarted up by Mother Nature, with draperies of pastel-coloured stalactites. Apparently they had company: the cave has a 'Bear Cemetery', full of the bones accumulated over thousands of years; a 'Corridor of Imprints', where human hand, foot and knee prints mingle with bear claws, as if left from a mad prehistoric boogey-woogey; and a 'Room of Mystery', where they threw clay balls at the walls, perhaps just to see if they'd stick. The tour includes the **Grotta di Santa Lucia**, with a miraculous eye-curing spring, and the pretty water-sculpted **Grotta del Colombo** (*open daily 9–12 and 2–5; hour and a half guided tours; adm*). Admission includes the **Museo Preistorico della Val Varatella**, containing remains found in these and other caverns in the valley, and a reassembled bear skeleton.

Another medieval village nearby, **Balestrino**, is still defended by a picturesque **Del Carretto** castle; other castles constructed by the same clan of local lordlings may be seen further up at **Castelvecchio di Rocca Barbena**, high on a crag, its castle dating from the 11th century (but altered since), encircled by the walled village, with magnificent views down the valley.

The Coast: Loano to Noli

Loano is an attractive, palm-shaded town and resort, long a fief of the Doria; in their 16th-century **Palazzo Doria** (now the Municipio), you can see a rare 3rd-century AD mosaic pavement, and there are fine views from its Carmelite convent (1608). Another old seaside town and modern beach resort, **Pietra Ligure**, has the ruins of a Genoese fortress; from nearby Borgio, the next resort, you can dip inland to visit the **Grotta di Valdemino**, with more colourful stalactites (*open Tues–Sun 9–11.30 and 2.30–5; adm*).

Finale Ligure is the big news here, however, a lively resort spread between Finale Marina and the medieval village of Finalborgo, two kilometres inland. Finale is pocked with caves filled with the debris left by Palaeolithic man and woman—most famously the **Grotta delle Arene Candide**—and, although none are open to visitors, pottery, tools, tombs, Venuses and another huge bear skeleton are on display in the **Museo Civico**, housed in the cloister of Santa Chiara in Finalborgo *(open June–Sept Tues–Sun 10–12 and 3–6; Oct–May Tues–Sun 9–12 and 2.30–4.30)*. Finalborgo itself is spread under an impressive if derelict Del Carretti **castle** and the splendid 13th-century octagonal campanile of the **Basilica di San Biagio**. One of the prettiest excursions from Finalborgo is to make your way along the Roman **Via Julia Augusta**, which weaves through the Valle di Ponci northeast of Finale Pia, traversing five Roman bridges from 124 AD; one, the **Ponte delle Fate**, is in perfect nick.

Although it never made the big time like Pisa or Genoa, **Noli** thrived as a small maritime republic from 1192 to 1796, celebrated every September in a regatta between its four neighbourhoods. Lying between Capo Noli and Monte Ursino, Noli still has 8 of its original 72 medieval towers. Its most important monument is the 11th-century **San Paragorio**, founded in 820; its treasures include a 13th-century bishop's throne and a 12th-century crucifix called a *Volto Santo* because of the picture on it, said to be a true portrayal of Christ—similar to the more famous one in Lucca. Be sure to note Noli's antique street lamps. There's a good beach here, and an even better one nearby at **Spotorno**.

Savona

The provincial capital, Savona is a working city rather than a resort, as well as one of Italy's busiest ports; one of the most interesting things to do is hang around the docks and watch the aerial cablecars unload coal for the ironworks at San Giuseppe di Cairo. The harbour tower, the **Torre di Leon Pancaldo**, dates from the 13th century, but was renamed to honour Magellan's unlucky pilot who was born nearby. Other natives of Savona include the Della Rovere family, which gave the world two popes: Sixtus IV, who built the Sistine Chapel in the Vatican, and his nephew, Julius II, who hired Michelangelo to paint it.

The two also left their mark on Savona. Giuliano da Sangallo designed the **Della Rovere Palace** (now the law courts; Via Pia 28) for Julius; in the next street back the **cathedral** is full of fine Renaissance marbles and a carved choir, flanked by another **Sistine Chapel**, built by Sixtus and redone à la Rococo to house the marble tomb of his parents. The best art is tucked away in the **cathedral's treasury** *(open on request)*, with a fine *Adoration of the Magi* by the Hoogstaeten master, 14th-century English alabaster statues, and items donated by the popes. The cathedral's medieval predecessor was demolished by the Genoese in 1528 to build the **Fortezza Priamàr**—not to protect Savona, but to put a dampener on its considerable ambition. This now holds the **Pinacoteca Civico** *(open Mon–Sat 8.30–12.30)*, with Renaissance works by Donato de Bardi and Giovanni Mazone and others from the Baroque era; also modern Italian paintings in the **Museo Sandro Pertini**, donated by the old politician, and 20th-century works by Savonesi sculptress Renata Cuneo.

From Savona, rail lines branch off for Turin and Milan. The first route passes the traditional boundary between the Alps and the Apennines at **Bocchetta di Cadibona** and **Millesimo** (bus from Savona), a charming, fortified hill town, where even the bridge, the **Gaietta**, has a watch tower. Now a popular excursion destination, it has a clutch of artisans' workshops and pastry shops selling scrumptious rum chocolates called *millesimini*.

Savona to Genoa

Although the bathing quality declines the closer you get to the big city, there are some tempting stopovers: **Albisola**, Liguria's ceramics centre, or **Celle Ligure** and **Varazze**, both resorts, the latter still partly surrounded by walls that incorporate the façade (but nothing else) of the 10th-century church of **Sant'Ambrogio**. The rebuilt Sant'Ambrogio (1535), with a lovely medieval campanile, contains fine Renaissance and Baroque art. Further east, **Cogoleto**, according to one tradition, was the birthplace of Columbus. At least everyone in the village thinks so, and they've erected a statue to him in the piazza.

Pegli, a longtime weekend retreat of the Genoese, has been sucked into the metropolis but, like Nervi to the east, maintains its beauty and most of its tranquillity. The grounds of two seigneurial villas are now used as parks. One, the **Villa Doria**, belonged to the frescoed 16th-century Villa Centurione Doria, which now houses the **Museo di Storia Navale** (*open Tues–Sat 9–1 and 2–5*), with a fine collection of artefacts relating to Genoa's proud maritime traditions, including ships' models, paintings (among them a portrait of Columbus), compasses, astrolabes, weapons, armour and maps. Another park, the magnificent **Villa Durazzo-Pallavicini**, is an elegantly arranged 19th-century garden with statuary, rotundas, temples and ponds. The house itself contains an **archaeological museum** (*open Tues–Sat 9–5, Sun 9–12.30*), with pre-Roman and Roman finds from the Ligurian coast, including Genoa, and especially the Palaeolithic caves. The star exhibit is the 'Young Prince', discovered in the Grotta delle Arene Candide, with a seashell headdress and a dagger in his hand.

Where to Stay and Eating Out

Imperia ✉ 18100

★★★**Robinia**, Via Pirinoli 14, ✆ 0183 62720, ✉ 0183 60635 (*moderate*) is a pleasant if unexceptional choice, with its own beach, restaurant and 55 rooms, most with sea view. There are numerous one- and two-star hotels, mainly around Corso Matteotti. In Porto Maurizio, the **Lanterna Blù**, Via Scarincio 32, ✆ 0183 63859 (*very expensive*) serves fine dishes using ingredients from two local farms; be sure to try the hot seafood *antipasti. Closed Wed.* **Vecchio Forno**, Piazza della Chiesa, ✆ 0183 780 269 (*expensive*) is known for its ravioli filled with fresh herbs, as well as fresh fish, classically prepared, and a good wine list. Reserve. *Closed Wed, and two weeks in June.* Locals are proud of their prize-winning pizzeria, **Hobo's**, on Via Rambaldo in Porto Maurizio (*cheap*), where an exquisite *Quattro Stagioni* with a beer is L8500. In nearby Cervo, **San Giorgio**, Via Volta 19, ✆ 0183 400 175 (*expensive*) serves well-prepared Ligurian specialities like *trenette al pesto* or *verdure ripiene* (stuffed vegetables), in an art-filled setting. Reserve.

Alassio ✉ 17021

Alassio's finest hotel is probably the ★★★★**Grand Hotel Diana**, Via Garibaldi 110, ✆ 0182 642 701, ✉ 0182 640 304 (*very expensive*), with its own beach, beach restaurant, free bike-hire and indoor pool. The seafront rooms are nice and large with balconies. Out of a very extensive choice, the excellent ★★★**Milano**, Piazza Airaldi e Durante 11, ✆ 0182 640 597, ✉ 0182 640 598 (*moderate*) is right on the beach; its rooms are well equipped, with balconies and fine sea views; the restaurant serves various Ligurian specialities. **Bel Air**, Via Roma 40, ℗ 0182 642 578, ℡ 0182 640 238 (*cheap*) is wonderful value: its rooms are modern and it has its own beach.

What Alassio may lack in grand hotels it makes up for with a gourmet palace, **La Palma**, Via Cavour 5, ℗ 0182 640 314 (*expensive*), where you can choose between two *menus degustazione*, one highlighting basil, the sacred herb of Liguria, and the second Provençal-Ligurian specialities with an emphasis on seafood. Be sure to reserve. *Closed Wed.* In the heart of the old town, **La Cave**, Passeggiata Italia 7, ℗ 0182 640 693 (*expensive*) is an atmospheric old restaurant, serving typical Ligurian cuisine like *troffie al pesto* and fish soups. *Closed Wed.* For pizza in a traditional atmosphere, try **Della Quintana**, Via Gastaldi 5, ℗ 0182 643 301 (*cheap*), housed in a medieval building.

Garlenda ✉ 17033

****La Meridiana**, Via ai Castelli 11, ℗ 0182 580 271, ℡ 0182 580 150 (*very expensive*) is a golfer's paradise, amid pretty olive groves, ancient oaks and vineyards. A member of the Relais et Châteaux chain, it is a contemporary building constructed with traditional stone walls and wooden ceilings, with simple but attractive furnishings. As well as the golf course, there is a large pool, tennis courts and a riding school, and the sea is only 10km away. The really adventurous can take parachuting lessons at the little airport nearby, and the food is excellent. *Open all year.*

Finale Ligure ✉ 17024

Hotels in Finale Ligure mainly cater to families. ***Park Hotel Castello**, Via Caviglia 26, ℗ 019 691 320, ℡ 019 692 775 (*moderate*), near the top of the town, has more character than most and a pretty garden; it's also one of the few that remains open all year. For a change from the fairly anonymous modern establishments try ***Conte**, Via Genova 16, ℗ 019 600 670 (*moderate*), in its own secluded garden in a lovely setting. Inside, step back in time fifty years—old prints line the walls and period furniture sits in reception. All the rooms are different and large, and some have modern fittings. *San Marco**, Via Concezione 22, ℗ 019 692 533 (*cheap*) is fairly basic, with a good restaurant, right on the sea front.

The first-choice restaurant in Finale is **Raffa**, Via Concezione 64, ℗ 019 692 495 (*expensive*), run by Raffaele Ciuffo, who prides himself on choosing only the freshest fish, served in an intimate atmosphere. Don't leave without trying the speciality, *pescespada alla Raffa*. *Closed Wed.* **Al Cantuccio**, Via Torino 54, ℗ 019 691 394 (*cheap*) offers two fixed-price menus of local delicacies, one around L12,000 and the other at L30,000, accompanied by a good wine list.

Entertainment and Nightlife

During the summer this area is one of the liveliest on the Italian coast. Throughout summer, the **Musica nei Castelli di Liguria** classical music festival takes place in the many castles of the region. Full details are available from local tourist offices. Anyone with children should also keep in mind that Ceriale, just to the east of Albenga, has the only **aquapark** in the region, at Le Caravelle, Via Sant'Eugenio, ℗ 0182 931 755 (*open April–Sept daily 10–7*). Finale is the other hot-spot: plenty of

bars line the seafront, including Clipper, with an old-style atmosphere. Of the **discos**, Caligola, on Via Colombo, plays mainly dance; and El Patio, Lungomare Italia, provides less frantic music for a slightly older crowd; the **outdoor clubs**, Covo and Covo Nord Est, are trendiest of all.

Genoa

There's always a tingling air of danger, excitement, unexpected fortune or sudden disaster in real port cities. The streets are enlivened with sailors, travellers and vagrants of all nationalities, and there's always the volatility of the sea itself, ready to make or break a fortune. Of the country's four ancient maritime republics (Venice, Amalfi and Pisa are the others), only Genoa (Genova) has retained its salty tang and thrill. It is Italy's largest port, and any possible scenographic effect it could have, enhanced by its beautiful location of steep hills piling into the sea, has been utterly snuffed out by the more important affairs of the port: an elevated highway, huge docks, warehouses, stacks of containers and unloading facilites hog the shoreline for miles, so that from many points you can't even see the sea. And behind the docks wind the dishevelled alleys lined with typical piquant portside establishments that cater to weaselly men of indeterminate nationality, old pirates and discreetly tattooed ladies.

Counterbalancing this fragrant zone of stevedores is the Genoa that Petrarch called *La Superba*, the Superb City (or 'Proud', as in one of the Seven Deadly Sins) of palaces, gardens and art; the city whose merchant fleet once reigned supreme from Spain to the southern Russian ports on the Black Sea, the city that gave the Spaniards Columbus but which in return controlled the contents of Spain's American silver fleets, becoming the New York City of the 16th century, flowing with money, ruled by factions of bankers and oligarchs, populated by rugged individualists and entrepreneurs, and leaving a mark in the fashion industry with its silks and sturdy blue cotton trousers the French called *de Gênes*.

Genoa is a neon-flashing, kinetic antidote to the Riviera's resortarama. Even its impossible topography is exciting: squeezed between mountains and sea, the city stretches for 30 kilometres—there are people who commute to work by lift or funicular, tunnels bore under green parks in the very centre of the city, and apartment houses hang over the hills so that the penthouse is at street level.

The old quarter is a bustling warren of alleys, or *carugi*—miniature canyons under eight-storey palaces and tenements, streaming with banners of laundry. There are streets of Renaissance palaces and Art Nouveau mansions, art (although the Genoese produced few painters or sculptors of note, they amassed some fine collections), and one of the most amazing cemeteries on earth. And since the Colombus fair in 1992, Genoa has a new razzmatazz, concentrated in the Porto Antico and its many attractions.

History

Genoa's destiny was shaped by its position, not only as the northernmost port on the Tyrrhenian Sea, but one protected and isolated by a ring of mountains. It was already a trading post in the 6th century BC, when the Phoenicians and Greeks came to barter with the Ligurians. Later the city was a stalwart outpost of the Roman Empire, and as such suffered the wrath of Hannibal's brother Mago; rebuilt after his sacking, it remained relatively happy and whole until the Lombards took it in 641, initiating a dark, troubled period.

While the merchants of Amalfi, Pisa and Venice were creating their maritime republics in the 10th and 11th centuries, Genoa was still an agricultural backwater, far from the main highways of the Middle Ages, its traffic dominated by Pisa, its coasts prey to Saracen corsairs.

Adversity helped form the Genoese character. Once it rallied to defeat the Saracens in the 12th century, the city began a dizzy rise to prominence, capturing Sardinia and Corsica, and joining the Normans to conquer Antioch, where Genoa established its first of many trading colonies in the Middle East. In 1155 the walls had to be enlarged as the city expanded and competition with Pisa grew into a battle of blows as well as of trade. The turning point for their duel for supremacy in the western Mediterranean came in 1284, when Genoa soundly pummelled Pisa into naval obscurity at the battle of Meloria—a victory Genoa followed up by defeating a more troublesome rival, Venice, at the Curzonali Islands in 1298.

By this time Genoa had merchant colonies stretching from the coast of North Africa to Syria, along the Black Sea and in Spain, where Genoese captains became the first to sail to the Canaries and the Azores. Genoa itself was the most densely populated city in Europe, as its patricians constructed their towering houses that seemed so 'superb' to visitors; its fame was so widespread that Genoa served as a setting for a tale in the Arabian Nights, the only Western city to be so honoured.

The Famous Insult to the Genoese

It was during this period, in 1316, that one of the most beloved anecdotes of Genoese history occurred: a Genoese merchant, by name Megollo Lercari, was the guest of the Eastern Emperor at Trebizond, when he disagreed with one of the emperor's pages, who slapped him across the face. The emperor refused to let the Genoese strike back, though he apologized for the youth's behaviour. It was not enough. Seething, Megollo returned to Genoa, got up a private fleet, sailed back to Trebizond, and demanded the page. When the emperor refused, the Genoese besieged the city, capturing whoever they could and chopping off their ears or noses. Finally his subjects' despair made the emperor give in and he handed over the youth, and watched, first in trepidation and then amazement, as Megollo made the page stoop over, then gave him a smart kick in the seat of the pants. Honour thus regained, the merchant returned the youth, lifted the siege and sailed back to Genoa.

Genoa's first golden age was marred, however, as all subsequent ones would be, by civic strife and turmoil that were disgraceful even by Italian standards. The individualistic, stubborn Genoese refused to accept communal unity; nearly every enterprise was privately funded, down to the city's military expeditions. Genoa itself was divided into factions—nobles against each other, nobles against the mercantile classes, the merchants against the artisans—while the ruling families each dominated their own quarter, forming *alberghi*, or brotherhoods, of their partisans, and running their own prisons and armies.

In 1339 the popular classes, envying the government of Venice, won a victory by electing Genoa's first doge, Simone Boccanegra, the hero of Verdi's opera. Boccanegra raised taxes to support his habits: the nobles responded by inviting in the Visconti of Milan; Boccanegra was exiled to Pisa; the Visconti were thrown out; Boccanegra returned as Doge—Genoese civic history is an ignoble chronicle of one faction momentarily gaining the upper hand, and all the others doing everything to undermine it, even inviting in a foreign lord.

The Banco di San Giorgio

The real power in Genoa turned out to be a bank. When the city sank deep into debt during its prolonged war with Venice for the eastern Mediterranean (ending in Genoa's traumatic defeat at Chioggia in 1380), its creditors—Genoa's oligarchs —formed a syndicate, the Banco di San Giorgio, to guarantee their increasingly precarious loans. This the bank did by gradually assuming control of the city's overseas territories, castles, towns, and even its treasury. Genoa from then on, for all practical purposes, was run as a business proposition—once, in 1421, when the bank was short of cash, it sold Livorno to Florence for a tidy sum. The Genoese never had any reason to identify with their government, but, as Machiavelli noted, they were very loyal to their bank. Under its bankers, Genoa recovered from the defeat at Chioggia by transforming its economy from the mercantile to the financial sphere. The cinquecento found the city Europe's leading economic power, a position Genoa maintained thanks to the foresight of Andrea Doria (1468–1560), the 'Saviour of Genoa' and the greatest admiral of his day.

During the Wars of Italy between Charles V of Spain and Francis I of France, Doria drove Genoa's traditional French allies from the city and welcomed Spanish protection. He then wrote a new Republican constitution for the strife-torn city, institutionalizing the shared rule of the 28 *alberghi*. Charles V rewarded Doria with the title of Prince of Melfi, and he and other Genoese were given prominent posts throughout the Empire. Meanwhile the Banco di San Giorgio became fat and sleek financing the wars in the Low Countries for Charles V and Philip II, processing Spain's silver and taking over the international money market from Besançon and Antwerp: millions of *scudi* passed through Genoa every year. Doria was also Genoa's first great patron of the arts, introducing the Renaissance to the city that had formerly managed without it.

CORSO UGO BASSI

VIA S. UGO

CORSO FIRENZE

CORSO DOGALI

Castello d'Albertis/ Museo Etnografico

Stazione Principe

Piazza Acquaverde

Piazza d. Principe

VIA A DORIA

S. Giovanni di Prè

VIA BALBI

VIA S. BENEDETTO

Palazzo del Principe

Commenda

VIA DI PRÈ

VIA ADUA

VIA ANTONIO GRAMSCI

Palazzo Reale

VIA BUOZZI

Stazione Marittima

STRADA

To Lanterna

Bacino Porto Vecchio

Acquario

Bigo

Padiglione del Mare e della Navigazione

Porta Siberia

Molo Vecchio

San Marco

Città dei Bambini

VIA DEL MARCO

VIA MALAPAGA

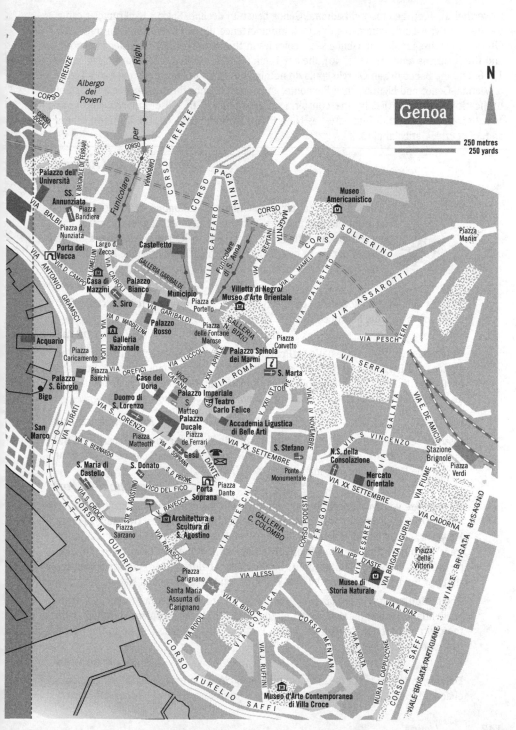

N

Genoa

250 metres
250 yards

CORSO FIRENZE

Albergo
dei
Poveri

CORSO FIRENZE

Il Righi

per

Funicolare

CORSO LOCALI

Funicolare

V. BRIGNOLE DE FERRARI

Palazzo dell'
Università

SS.
Annunziata

Piazza
Bandiera

Piazza d.
Nunziata

VIA BALBI

VIA ANTONIO GRAMSCI

Porta dei
Vacca

Largo d.
Zecca

Castelletto

GALLERIA GARIBALDI

CORSO PAGANINI

CORSO MAGENTA

CORSO FIRENZE

CORSO SOLFERINO

Museo
Americanistico

Piazza
Manin

VIA A. BERTINI

VIA CAFFARO

Funicolare
di S. Anna

Casa di
Mazzini

Palazzo
Bianco

VIA CAIROLI

VIA D. LOMELLINI

S. Siro

VIA GARIBALDI

Municipio

Piazza d.
Portello

Villetta di Negro/
Museo d'Arte Orientale

VIA G. MAMELI

VIA G. PALESTRO

VIA ASSAROTTI

Palazzo
Rosso

VIA D. MADDALENA

Piazza N. BIXIO
delle Fontane
Marose

GALLERIA

Acquario

Piazza
Caricamento

Galleria
Nazionale

VIA S. LUCA

Piazza
Banchi

VIA OREFICI

VIA LUCCOLI

Piazza
Corvetto

VIA PESCHIERA

VIA SERRA

Palazzo Spinola
dei Marmi

VIA XXV APRILE

VICO CASANA

VIA ROMA

S. Marta

VIALE IV NOVEMBRE

VIA GALATA

VIA E. DE AMICIS

Palazzo
S. Giorgio

Bigo

VIA S. LORENZO

VIA TURATI

Case dei
Doria

Duomo di
S. Lorenzo

Palazzo Imperiale

S.
Matteo

Teatro
Carlo Felice

Accademia Ligustica
di Belle Arti

VIA XXII OTTOBRE

San
Marco

SOPRAELEVATA

VIA S. BERNARDO

Palazzo
Ducale

Piazza
Matteotti

VIA P. SOPRANA

Piazza
de Ferrari

Gesù

V. DANTE

VIA XX SETTEMBRE

S. Stefano

N.S. della
Consolazione

VIA S. VINCENZO

Stazione
Brignole

Piazza
Verdi

VIA FIUME

VIA BRIGATA LIGURIA

VIA CADORNA

BISAGNO

S. Maria di
Castello

S. Donato

S. D. PRIONE

Piazza
Dante

Ponte
Monumentale

CORSO PODESTA'

Mercato
Orientale

VIA XX SETTEMBRE

VIA CESAREA

VIALE BRIGATA PARTIGIANE

VICO DEL FICO

Porta
Soprana

Piazza
Sarzano

STR. S. AGOSTINO

VICO DEL FICO

V. RAVECCA

Architettura e
Scultura di
S. Agostino

VIA FIESCHI

GALLERIA
C. COLOMBO

VIA FRUGONI

VIA IPP. D'ASTE

Piazza
della
Vittoria

VIA RAVASCO

VIA S. AGOSTINO

VIA S. CROCE

CORSO M. QUADRIO

Piazza
Carignano

Santa Maria
Assunta di
Carignano

VIA ALESSI

VIA N. BIXIO

VIA CORSICA

Museo di
Storia Naturale

VIA BRIGATA LIGURIA

VIA A. DIAZ

VIA RIVOLI

VIA J. RUFFINI

CORSO AURELIO SAFFI

CORSO MENTANA

VIA A. VOLTA

MURA D. CAPPUCCINE

CORSO A. SAFFI

Museo d'Arte Contemporanea
di Villa Croce

Nevertheless, after the crusty old admiral Genoa began to decline. Spain's bankruptcies came too frequently; Atlantic commerce overtook in importance the old Mediterranean trade; the Ottoman Empire gobbled up Genoa's last colonies in the east. The French besieged (1668), and the Austrians took briefly (1746), the city itself; Corsica, Genoa's last colony, revolted in 1768, and the Banco di San Giorgio could do nothing but sell it to France. By the 1815 Treaty of Vienna, Genoa and Liguria joined Piemonte, and almost at once the city became a hotbed of unification sentiment, led by the conspiring philosopher of the Risorgimento, Giuseppe Mazzini, and such patriot luminaries as Nino Bixio, Goffredo Mameli, the Ruffini brothers and, of course, Garibaldi himself.

Getting There and Around

by air

Genoa's international **airport**, Cristoforo Colombo, ✆ 010 601 5410, 6km from the city in Sestri Ponente, has direct flights to Britain and many European destinations as well as to Italian cities. **Buses** to the airport depart an hour before each flight from Stazione Brignole and Piazza de Ferrari.

by sea

You can sail away to exotic lands on a ferry from the **Stazione Marittima**, ✆ 010 246 3686, just below the Stazione Principe.

by rail

Genoa has two main train stations: **Principe**, in Piazza Acquaverde, just west of the centre, and **Brignole**, to the northeast. Principe in general handles trains from the north and France, while Brignole takes trains from the south, though most long-distance trains actually call at both. City bus no.37 links the two.

by long-distance bus

Intercity services and buses to the rest of the province and the Riviera depart from the Piazza della Vittoria, south of Stazione Brignole, or from Piazza Acquaverde, in front of Stazione Principe. For information, call ✆ 010 599 7414.

by public transport

Chances are you won't need to make much use of the city's public transport system, as most of Genoa's points of interest are in the centre between the two train stations. However, public transport is relatively cheap; an urban ticket, valid for ninety minutes travel on **bus, train, metro, lift or funicular**, is L1500. A day ticket with the same restrictions is L5000. **Tickets** must be purchased before embarking, from tobacco shops or the transport authority (ATM) information kiosks at the rail stations.

The **funiculars** run from Piazza del Portello and Largo della Zecca to the city's upper residential quarters; the one served by the latter, **Righi**, has a splendid outlook over the city and harbour. A **lift** from Piazza Portello will also take you up to the nearer belvedere at Castelletto.

by car and taxi

Driving in Genoa is not fun. The old quarter is closed to traffic and the street plan is chaotic, though one consolation is that the *Soprelevata*, the ugly elevated motorway that runs along the harbour, is never hard to find for a quick getaway. **Taxis**, on the other hand, are plentiful. For a radio taxi, call ✆ 010 5966.

Tourist Information

Porto Antico–Palazzina Santa Maria B5, ✆ 010 24871, ✉ 010 246 7658, *www. apt.genova.it* There are branch offices at Stazione Principe, ✆ 010 246 2633, and at the airport, ✆ 010 601 5247. For information about special events and what's on in general in Genoa, try the city's daily paper, *Il Secolo XIX*.

Genoa is one of several Italian cities with an unnecessarily complicated street-numbering system: any commercial establishment receives a red (r) number, but any residence a black or blue numberplate.

Stazione Principe to Via Garibaldi

Both of Genoa's two main stations are lovely—the Stazione Principe could serve as a setting for a fancy-dress ball. In its Piazza Acquaverde visitors are greeted by a **statue of Columbus**, a view of the port, and the stately Via Balbi. If you're catching a ferry, Via Andrea Doria will take you down to the Stazione Marittima, passing the **Palazzo del Principe** on the way, the only 'Royal' palace built during the secular history of the Genovese Republic. The royal in this instance was Andrea Doria whose decision in 1528 to commission Raphael's pupil, Perin del Vaga, to decorate the interior marked the beginning of Genoa's Renaissance (*open Sat 3–6, Sun 10–3; adm L10,000; guided tours outside opening hours,* ✆ *010 255 509*).

Afterwards, you might like to take in Genoa's most celebrated landmark, the **Lanterna**, a well-signposted 10-minute walk west around the port. The 384ft medieval lighthouse is now open for the first time in decades, and you can climb the 375 stairs to the top and admire the spectacular views of the city and coast (*guided tours by appointment only,* ✆ *010 246 5396, except Sun when you can just turn up at 2.30 at the Bigo—the giant crane; the first 100 people will be admitted*). In the old days a huge fire would be ignited on top to guide vessels into the port. Back near the Stazione Principe, **La Commenda** is Genoa's oldest hotel, where pilgrims lodged on their way to the Holy Land. In 1180 the Knights of St John built a hospital and adjacent two-storey church, **San Giovanni di Pré**, with a spire-clustered campanile.

Via Balbi is lined with late-Renaissance palaces, among them the yellow and red **Palazzo Reale** (*open Sun–Tues 9–1.45, Wed–Sat 9–7; adm exp*), with its hyper-decorated 18th-century ballroom and Hall of Mirrors, and a *Crucifixion* by Van Dyck, who spent several years in Genoa. Via Balbi gives on to Piazza della Nunziata, site of **SS. Annunziata** (16th-century), a church with a grubby façade which hides a voluptuous Rococo interior.

From the next square, **Largo della Zecca**, you have several options: browsing through the district's antique shops; a thrilling funicular ride to Righi, where you can dine at the top of the town; walking through the tunnel to Piazza Portello and taking the lift up to the Castelletto belvedere; or continuing round on Via Cairoli to Genoa's most famous street, **Via Garibaldi**. Via Garibaldi, the former *Strada Nuova* laid out in 1558, was for centuries Genoa's 'Millionaires' Row', with uninterrupted lines of 16th- and 17th-century palazzi. Many have since been converted into banks and offices, but the street's unique and elegant character has been carefully maintained.

Two of the palaces hold important art collections: the **Palazzo Bianco** (*open Tues, Thurs and Fri 9–1, Wed and Sat 9–7, Sun 10–6; closed Mon; adm*), at No.11, former residence of the Grimaldis, is no longer very white, but has the most noteworthy collection in the city, with a good assortment of Italian paintings, including Filippino Lippi's *Madonna with Saints*, Pontormo's *Florentine Gentleman*, Veronese's *Crucifixion*, and an even more impressive collection of Flemish art. Among the latter are Gerhard David's sweetly domestic *Madonna della Pappa*, paintings by Cranach, Van der Goes, Van Dyck and Rubens (who also worked for a while in Genoa); there is also a fine *San Bonaventura* by Zurbarán. The portrait of Andrea Doria by Jan Matsys has remarkable hands.

Across the street at No.18, the **Palazzo Rosso** (*currently undergoing renovation, but still open Tues, Thurs and Fri 9–1, Wed and Sat 9–7, Sun 10–6; adm*), retains some of its palatial fittings, as well as a picture gallery with an especially good collection of portraits by Van Dyck, Pisanello and Dürer, and works by Caravaggio and his follower Mattia Preti to Veronese and Guercino.

Opposite the Palazzo Rosso, the former **Palazzo Tursi** is now Genoa's Municipio, with the city's most beautiful courtyard and such municipal treasures as native son Paganini's violin, in the Sala della Giunta, and three letters from Columbus in the Sala del Sindaco. You can enter the courtyard of No.7, the **Palazzo Podestà**, with an elaborate fountain in the shape of a grotto. The façade of No.3, the 16th-century **Palazzo Parodi-Lercari**, was built by the descendants of Megollo Lercari, who recalled the 'Insult to the Genoese' at Trebizond with earless and noseless caryatids.

The Villa di Negro

Via Garibaldi ends at Piazza Marose, with more palaces, especially the 15th-century **Palazzo Spinola dei Marmi**, embellished with black and white bands and statues of the Spinola family. From here Salita Santa Caterina leads into the circular **Piazza Corvetto**, a major junction of the city bus lines and the entrance to the **Villa di Negro**, an urban oasis that takes full advantage of Genoa's crazy topography, with streams, cascades, grottoes and walkways, culminating at the top with the **Museo di Arte Orientale** (*open Tues, Thurs, Fri and Sat 9–1; adm*), Italy's finest museum of Oriental art, a lovely collection of statues, paintings and theatre masks, and an extraordinary set of Samurai helmets and armour, all well displayed in a sun-filled modern building.

At the corner of Piazza Corvetto and Via Roma you can stop off for a history-imbued coffee break at the early 19th-century **Caffè Mangani**. Via Roma continues down to tumultuous **Piazza de Ferrari**, on one side marked by the neo-classical **Teatro**

Carlo Felice, built in 1829, bombed in 1944, and then left crumbling until 1992, when it was restored and reopened for the Columbus celebrations; it now holds a full year-round programme of opera, dance and theatre, ✆ 010 538 1226. Across the piazza is the giant, black-and-white mass of the 16th-century Palazzo Ducale, since 1992 a shopping and exhibition centre (*see* below). Next to the Palazzo Ducale, Piazza de Ferrari and Piazza Matteotti are linked by a monumental staircase, formerly used for the city's processions.

From Piazza de Ferrari you can descend into Old Genoa; the most picturesque way is to head down Via Dante to Piazza Dante and through the tall twin-towered **Porta Soprana**, built in 1155 as part of the Barbarossa walls designed to protect the city from the Frederick of that name. Columbus' father was gatekeeper here; the explorer's 'boyhood home' is nearby, as are the ruins of the 12th-century cloister of **Sant'Andrea**, set out on the lawn.

The Old City

Within the Porta Soprana are the tall houses of old Genoa, sliced by corridor-like alleys, some so narrow that they live in perpetual shade. Partly bombed in the War and now mostly restored, leaning ever so gently towards the harbour below, many houses have white marble and black slate portals, permitted only to those families who performed a deed of benefit to the city, while corners and wall niches are decorated with hundreds of little shrines known as *madonnette*, the little Madonnas.

The old town is for exploring, although single women should exercise caution, especially after dark. To see the highlights of the quarter, take Via Ravecca down from Porta Soprana to the 13th-century Gothic church of Sant'Agostino, its ruined cloisters converted into the well-designed **Museo di Sant'Agostino** (*open Tues–Sat 9–7, Sun 9–12*), containing art and architectural fragments salvaged from Genoa's demolished churches. One of the finest works is the fragment of the tomb of Margherita of Brabant, wife of Emperor Henry VII, sculpted in 1312 by Giovanni Pisano. Margherita died suddenly in Genoa while accompanying her husband to Rome for his coronation, and Henry, whom Dante and many others had hoped would be able to end the feud between Italy's Guelphs and Ghibellines, died in Siena two years later, many believe of sorrow; his last request was that his heart be taken to Genoa to be interred with his wife. There are also Roman works, Romanesque sculpture, frescoes and the 14th-century wooden *Christ of the Caravana*.

From Sant'Agostino, the Stradone di Sant'Agostino leads to another good church, the 12th-century Romanesque **San Donato**, with an exceptionally lovely octagonal campanile, portal and interior, combining a mix of ancient and medieval columns. The nearby Via San Bernardo, one of the few straight streets in the old city, was laid out by the Romans. Their castle up the hill (take the Salita della Torre degli Embriaci) provided the foundations for Genoa's most venerable church, the evocative **Santa Maria di Castello**, incorporating Roman columns and stones in its Romanesque structure. The crusaders used Santa Maria's complex as a hostel. Fairest of its art is the 15th-century fresco of the *Annunciation* in the cloister, while the strangest is the *Crocifisso Miracoloso* in a chapel near the high altar—miraculous in that the Christ's beard is said to grow whenever Genoa is threatened with calamity.

Around Piazza Matteotti

Another entrance into the historic centre from Piazza de Ferrari is by way of Piazza Matteotti, dominated by the main yellow and red façade of the grandiose **Palazzo Ducale**. First built in the 16th century, it was greatly altered in the following century to serve as the city law courts. It stood neglected for years, but like the Carlo Felice theatre its was restored and renovated for 1992, and now you can walk through its attractive courtyards, one adorned with a fountain, or sample the restaurants, bars and shops, and visit the exhibitions (*Tues–Sun 9am–9pm; guided tours available of the monumental rooms, © 010 562 440; adm exp*). Sharing the square is the Baroque church of the **Gesù**, designed in the 1600s by Jesuit Giuseppe Valeriani. The interior is pure Baroque fantasia, all lavish stuccoes, frescoes and *trompe l'œil* stage effects that highlight its frothy treasures: a *Circumcision* and *St Ignatius Exorcising the Devil* by Rubens, and an *Assumption* by the 'Divino' Guido Reni.

Just off the square stands the jauntily black-and-white-striped **Duomo di San Lorenzo**, begun in the 12th century, and modified several times; the façade was last restored in 1934. Odds and ends from the ages embellish the exterior—two kindly 19th-century lions by the steps, and a carving of St Lawrence toasting on his grill above the central of three French-Gothic-style portals. On the north side there's a pretty 12th-century **Portal of San Giovanni**; on the south, Hellenistic sarcophagi, another Romanesque portal and a 15th-century tomb. The rather morose interior also wears jailbird stripes (two sides are currently undergoing renovation). The first chapel on the right contains a good marble *Crucifixion* of 1443, and a British shell fired from the sea 500 years later that hit the chapel but miraculously failed to explode. On the left, note the sumptuous Renaissance **Cappella di San Giovanni Battista**, with fine sculptures and marble decorations, and a 13th-century sarcophagus that once held the Baptist's relics.

The well-arranged **Museo del Tesoro** (*open Mon–Sat 9–12 and 3–6; guided tours only*), in the vaults to the left of the nave, contains a number of genuine treasures acquired during the heyday of Genoa's mercantile empire: a crystal plate said to have been part of the dinner service of the Last Supper, the blue chalcedony dish on which John the Baptist's head was supposedly served to Salomé, an 11th-century arm reliquary of St Anne, the golden, jewel-studded Byzantine *Zaccaria Cross*, and an elaborate 15th-century silver casket built to hold the Baptist's ashes.

The Salita del Fonaco follows the back of the Palazzo Ducale, then veers right for **Piazza San Matteo**, a beautiful little square completely clothed in the black and white bands of illustrious civic benefactors—and it's no wonder, for this was the public foyer of the Doria family, encompassed by their palazzi and their 12th-century church of **San Matteo**, inscribed with their great deeds and adorned with a charming early 14th-century cloister. Andrea Doria's palace was No.17 on the square, while No.14, belonging to Branca Doria, has a beautiful portal guarded by Genoa's patron St George.

Between Via San Lorenzo and Via Garibaldi

This northern section of the historic centre, built up mostly in the Renaissance, has survived somewhat better than the area around Porta Soprana, and has, amid its monuments, fine shops, pubs, restaurants and cafés. From Piazza San Matteo it's a short walk to the **Campetto**, a lovely square adorned with the ornate 16th-century **Palazzo Imperiale**; in the nearby Piazza Soziglia you can take a break at one of the oldest coffee-houses in Genoa, **Kainguti**, at No.98/r, or **Romanegro**, at No.74/r, both founded at the beginning of the 19th century. From Piazza Soziglia and the Campetto, pretty Via degli Orefici meanders down to the major intersection of medieval Genoa, **Piazza Banchi**, with its Renaissance Loggia dei Mercanti. From here Via Ponti Reale descends to the harbourside **Piazza Caricamento**, lined with the ancient arcades of Via Sottoripa and dominated by the gaudily decorated **Palazzo San Giorgio**. This was originally built in 1260 for the Capitani del Popolo, but was taken over in 1408 by the Banco di San Giorgio, so the shrewd bankers could scrutinize the comings and goings of the port. It's now occupied by the Harbour Board, but you can ask the guard to show you the rooms that have been refurbished in 13th-century style.

Seawards, on the other side of the *Sopraelevata* from the Piazza Caricamento, the whole of the old quay (*Molo Vecchio*), known locally as the Porto Antico, was the showcase for the 1992 celebrations. Redevelopment has continued apace; it is now home to an Antarctic Museum; the largest cinema complex in Italy; the **Citta dei Bambini** (*open daily 10–6; closed Mon; adm exp*), the *ne plus ultra* of educational playgrounds—full of climbing frames and giant plastic insects, as well as a building site where children can dress up in hard hats and overalls and push around plastic wheel barrows full of sand; and, housed in a converted ship, Europe's largest **aquarium** (*open Tues–Fri 9.30–6.30, Sat and Sun 9.30–8pm; ticket office closes an hour and a half earlier; adm very exp, children under 3 free*), with seals, dolphins, sharks and penguins, and reconstructions of coral reefs, visited by a million and a half people each year, making it Italy's third most attended 'museum'. There is also the **Gran Bigo**, or 'Great Crane', designed by Renzo Piano, which towers over the port; a panoramic, revolving lift goes to the top for the superb views (*tickets L6000*). Finally, there is the **Padiglione del Mare e della Navigazione** (Sea and Navigation Pavilion) (*open Mon–Fri 10.30–6, Sat and Sun 10.30–7; adm exp*), with artefacts from 16th- and 17th-century ships, and a reconstruction of a medieval shipyard.

Returning to the old city, **Via San Luca**, the main street passing through Piazza Banchi, was the principal thoroughfare of medieval Genoa and, in its day, home turf of another prominent Genoese family, the Spinola. They donated one of their palaces, just off Via San Luca in little Piazza di Pellicceria, with its 16th–18th-century decor and paintings to form the **Galleria Nazionale di Palazzo Spinola** (*open Tues–Sat 9–7, Sun 2–7*). The paintings, still arranged as in a private residence, include Antonello da Messina's sad, beautiful *Ecce Homo*, Joos Van Cleve's magnificent *Adoration of the Magi*, works by Van Dyck (*Portrait of a Child* and the *Four Evangelists*), and a statue of Justice, another fragment of Giovanni Pisano's tomb of Margherita di Brabante.

A little further to the north, back towards Largo Zecca, stands one of the chief shrines of 19th-century Italian history, the **Casa Mazzini**, Via Lomellini 11, where the romantic prophet of Italian unification, Giuseppe Mazzini, was born in 1805. It now houses Genoa's **Museo del Risorgimento** (*open Tues, Thurs, Fri and Sat 9–1*), with a collection centred on various relics of Mazzini himself.

East Genoa

East of the Piazza de Ferrari runs arcaded **Via XX Settembre**, the main thoroughfare of 19th-century Genoa, adorned here and there with Liberty-style touches. This is still the city's main shopping street, and it and the area around Stazione Brignole make up a lively neighbourhood, aglow with neon lights. Via XX Settembre is traversed by the Ponte Monumentale, which carries the Corso A. Podesta overhead. Next to the bridge a lane leads up to another of Genoa's striped medieval churches, **Santo Stefano**, which contains a *Martyrdom of*

St Stephen by a less flamboyant than usual Giulio Romano. Beyond the bridge the avenue continues to the large Piazza della Vittoria, a Fascist-era square presided over by a 1931 War Memorial Arch.

The Hills and Staglieno Cemetery

Some of the loveliest bits of Genoa are to be found up in the surrounding hills. The **Circonvallazione a Monte** is the scenic route, made up of several *corsi*, that skirts the slopes, a route followed by city bus no.33, from Stazione Brignole or Piazza Manin. The one attraction to stop for is at Corso Solferino 39, installed in the 17th-century Villa Grüber: the **Museo Americanistico F. Lunardi** (*open Tues–Sat 9.30–12 and 3–5.30, Sun 3–5.30*) housing an important collection of pre-Columbian art, especially strong in Mayan work. The hillside route continues along Corsos Magenta, Paganini, Firenze and U. Bassi, passing on the way the imposing medieval **Castello d'Albertis**, rebuilt in the 19th century.

Just over the mountains, along the Torrente Bisagno, lies Genoa's famous **Cimitero di Staglieno** (*open daily 8–5; bus no.34 from Piazza Acquaverde or Piazza Corvetto*). Founded in 1844, the cemetery covers 160 hectares, and even has its own internal bus system. The Genoese have a reputation for being tight-fisted, but when it comes to post-mortem extravagance they have few peers. Staglieno is a veritable Babylon of the dead, with miniature cathedrals, Romanesque chapels, Egyptian temples and Art Nouveau palaces and statuary—a fantastic, often surreal ensemble. In the centre of the hills, Genoa's great revolutionary idealist of the Risorgimento, Giuseppe Mazzini, is buried in a simple tomb behind two massive Doric columns, surrounded by laudatory inscriptions by Tolstoy, Lloyd George, D'Annunzio and others. After a life of plots, conspiracies and exile, Mazzini died in semi-exile in Pisa, hiding out under the assumed name of American abolitionist John Brown. Mrs Oscar Wilde is buried in the Protestant section.

Around Genoa

Nervi, one of the oldest resorts on the Riviera, is just east of Genoa, and has been incorporated into the metropolis and can be reached by bus no.17 from Piazza de Ferrari, or bus no.15 from the Piazza Caricamento. On the way, in Genova Quarto, is another monument to the Risorgimento, the **Museo Garibaldi** in Villa Garibaldi (*open daily 9–1; closed Thurs*), which houses some of the original red shirts of Garibaldi's Thousand (originally intended for slaughterhouse workers in South America), some of their bayonets and a variety of documents. In Nervi itself, two of the town's oldest Genoese villas have been converted to museums: the **Galleria d'Arte Moderna** in the Villa Serra Gropallo, Via Capolungo 3, contains a large collection of 19th- and 20th-century Italian art (*closed indefinitely for restoration; for information call © 010 282 641*). The other, the **Museo Giannettino Luxoro**, Viale Mafalda di Savoia 3 (*open Tues–Sat 9–1*), is further east in one of the Riviera's loveliest parks. It, too, has a small modern art collection, but is especially noteworthy for its decorative arts holdings: clocks (some of the first luminous timepieces), furniture, fabrics and lace.

There are also two popular excursions into the hinterland from Genoa: **Casella**, a small mountain resort reached by electric train from Piazza Manin, and **Torriglia** (reached by bus, or by car on the SS45 road towards Piacenza), with an impressive if utterly derelict medieval castle, a small resort offering skiing in winter and pretty walks in summer.

Genoa's premier cultural event is its annual **Boat Show**, a vast celebration of all things nautical held over ten days in early October. Each year half a million people come to look at over 2000 boats of all shapes and sizes displayed in and around the port's exhibition area. To get a closer look at the sea itself, take the **tour of Genoa's port**. Excursions are run by the Cooperativa Battellieri, ✆ 010 265 712, and by Alimar, ✆ 010 256 775; both companies depart from the Calata Zingari, near the Stazione Marittima.

Genoa ✉ 16100   *Where to Stay*

very expensive

****Starhotel President**, Via Corte Lambruschini 4, ✆ 010 5727, ✉ 010 553 1820, is currently the top hotel in the city, part of a complex in front of Stazione Brignole built specifically for the 1992 celebrations, and something like the ultimate in nineties luxury and design. Ultra-modern and super-sleek, it has 192 double rooms, vast suites, and a palatial reception area and gourmet restaurant.

The ****Bristol Palace**, Via XX Settembre 35, ✆ 010 592 541, ✉ 010 561 756, not far from Stazione Brignole, is an elegant choice with sumptuous antique furnishings, beautiful air-conditioned rooms and a pleasant English bar. The ****Brittania**, Via Balbi 38, ✆ 010 26991, ✉ 010 246 9242, is perhaps the best upper-range hotel near Stazione Principe. It is smart and slick, if garishly designed in black and red, and modern and comfortable. The top-floor rooms enjoy fantastic views, and though there's no restaurant, it does have a café, gym and billiard room.

expensive

****Astor**, Viale delle Palme 16, ✆ 010 329 011, ✉ 010 372 8486, is a fashionable and elegant hotel in an enchanting garden near the sea in Nervi, where you can escape the hurly burly of Genoa.

moderate

***Agnello d'Oro**, Via Monachette 6, ✆ 010 246 2084, ✉ 010 246 2327, is housed in a 17th-century property of the Doria family, near Via Balbi. Although most of the old-fashioned charm is concentrated in the lobby, the rooms are very comfortable. ***Bellevue**, Salita Provvidenza 1, ✆ 010 246 2400, ✉ 010 265 932, enjoys a wonderful view of the port. It has smart air-conditioned rooms, but no restaurant.

cheap

Cairoli, Via Cairoli 14/4, ✆ 010 246 1454, ✉ 010 246 1524. Among the more respectable and hygienic of the city's inexpensive choices, and very centrally located, it's more like a 3-star hotel, with sparkling, modern rooms and a relaxed, friendly and personal atmosphere. Excellent value.

Villa Bonera, Via Sarfatti 8, Nervi, ✆ 010 372 6164, ✉ 010 372 8565, outside the city in Nervi, is a very attractive option with 26 charming rooms in a 17th-century villa surrounded by a pretty garden.

★Major, Vico Spada 4, ✆ 010 247 4174, 📠 010 246 9898, is a cheaper alternative, in a great position just inside the *centro storico*, and close by Piazza de Ferrari and Via Garibaldi. The rooms are clean and modern, and a real bargain.

Eating Out

Besides various forms of pasta with pesto, the Genoese are fond of putting basil in numerous other dishes: *pansotti* are little ravioli filled with spinach and served in a walnut sauce; *torta pasqualina* consists of vegetables and hard-boiled eggs rolled in a pastry; *cima alla Genovese* is breast of veal filled with similar ingredients.

expensive

One of Genoa's most famous restaurants, **Toe Drue**, Via Corsi 441, ✆ 010 650 0100, is in the working-class district of Sestri Ponente, west of the centre. The name means 'hard table', and this very fashionable restaurant has kept the furnishings of the rustic inn that preceded it. On these hard tables are served an array of delightful and unusual Ligurian specialities, many featuring seafood. Reservations essential. *Closed Sun, and Aug.* **Gran Gotto**, Viale Brigata Bisagno (near Piazza della Vittoria), ✆ 010 583 644, is another of the city's classic eateries, featuring imaginative and delicately prepared seafood like turbot in radicchio sauce, warm seafood *antipasti*, famous *rognone* (kidney) dishes and delectable desserts. *Closed Sat lunch and Sun.* Near the centre, **Saint Cyr di Corti Elia**, Piazza Marsala 8, ✆ 010 886 897, has a short menu but what they do they do well. The food is always beautifully presented and the staff are charming. Try their Genovese *minestrone* with pesto. *Closed Sat lunch and Sun.* Near Piazza Banchi, **Trattoria del Mario**, Via Conservatori del Mare 35/r, ✆ 010 297 788, is an old favourite that offers the freshest of fish prepared in authentic Genoese style, and pasta with pesto as well as *cima*; the delicious seafood salad is a popular starter. *Closed Sat and Aug.* One of the best traditional choices in the old city, **Pancetti Antica Osteria**, Borgo Incrociati 22/r, ✆ 010 839 2848, offers *pansotti* (chickpea soup) and some other Ligurian classics that are rarely prepared elsewhere, accompanied by the region's best vintages. *Closed Mon.*

moderate–cheap

In the maze of the southern old city, **Archivolto Mongiardino**, no. 2 in the street of the same name, ✆ 010 247 7610, is the place to go for *aragosta* (lobster) and other excellent seafood dishes. *Closed Sun and Mon.* **Genio**, Salita San Leonardo 61, ✆ 010 588 463, off Via Fieschi, near Piazza Dante, is another popular restaurant serving great traditional Ligurian food, and offering a wider choice for non-seafood fans. *Closed Sun.*

Good inexpensive restaurants abound in Genoa, especially in the *centro storico*. Try the fresh fish in the **Trattoria da Pino**, in Piazza Caricamento, ✆ 010 362 395, one of Genoa's top greasy-spoon districts. **Ostaja Do Castello**, Salita Santa Margherita del Castello, ✆ 010 298 980, has some of the best cheap food in town, with good Genoese specialities. *Closed Sun.* And, just off Via XXV Aprile, near the Piazza de Ferrari, the wonderfully authentic **Trattoria da Maria**, Vico Testadora 14/r, ✆ 010 581 080, serves up filling three-course meals for under L20,000. *Closed Sat.*

Entertainment and Nightlife

In Paganini's home town there is bound to be plenty of music. The **Genoa Opera**, now back in the Teatro Carlo Felice in Piazza de Ferrari after years of being without a proper home, presents its main season from January to June, and in the summer sponsors the prestigious **Ballet Festival** in the park in Nervi. Every year Genoa competes with Venice, Pisa and Amalfi in the **Regatta of the Ancient Maritime Republics**, hosted by the previous year's winner.

The main centre of **café and bar** life is around Via XX Settembre, though a noisier and seamier choice of places waits around the port. Anyone feeling a need for a more English drinking ambience can find it at the **Brittania Pub** on Vico della Casana just off Piazza de Ferrari, which is very popular with both foreigners and Italians.

Riviera di Levante: Recco to Sestri Levante

East of Genoa, the coast, fairly tame up to this point, becomes a creature of high drama and romance. The beaches aren't as prominent, nor the climate quite as mild, but from the Monte di Portofino to the once nearly inaccessible fishing villages of the Cinque Terre, the mountains and sea tussle and tumble in a voluptuous chaos of azure, turquoise and piney green. Against these deep-coloured coves, cliffs and inlets rise the villages of weathered pastels and ochres, with silvery groves of olives gazing out over bobbing fleets of fishing craft, sailing boats and sleek white yachts.

Getting Around

The Genoa–Pisa **railway** hugs the coast, but in many places you can only get glimpses of the scenery between the tunnels. The most scenic road is the old coastal Via Aurelia (SS1), which is also the route used by most of the **buses**. Camogli, San Fruttuoso, Portofino, Santa Margherita and Rapallo are linked by **boat** services.

Tourist Information

Camogli: Via XX Settembre 33, ⊘/✉ 0185 771 066. **Portofino**: Via Roma 35, ⊘ 0185 269 024. **S. Margherita Ligure**: Via XXV Aprile 2/b, ⊘ 0185 287 485, ✉ 0185 283 034. **Rapallo**: Via A. Diaz 9, ⊘ 0185 51282, ✉ 0185 230346. **Chiávari**: Corso Assarotti 1, ⊘ 0185 325 198, ✉ 0185 324 796. **Sestri Levante**: Via XX Settembre 33, ⊘ 0185 457 011, ✉ 0185 459 575.

Recco and Camogli

Of all the nubs and notches in the Italian coastline, one of the best beloved is the squarish promontory of Monte di Portofino, which comes into view as you leave Nervi, and forms, on its western side, the Gulf of Paradise. **Recco**, at the crossroads to Camogli, was bombed into dust during the War, and has since been completely rebuilt, but **Camogli**, only a kilometre or so away on the promontory, was spared. Built on a pine-wooded slope, it is an old sea town, once home port of a renowned fleet that fought with Napoleon; its fishing and merchant vessels were equally prominent along the Riviera. Its name derives from *Casa Mogli* (home of wives), since the menfolk were almost always at sea. The old harbour, piled high with tall, faded houses with dark green shutters, is the site of the famous *Sagra del Pesce*, an ancient festival that takes place on the second Sunday in May, where Italy's largest frying pan (13ft across) is used to cook up thousands of sardines, which are distributed free to all comers—a display of generosity and abundance that carries with it the hope that the sea itself will be equally generous and abundant in the coming year.

A small promontory separates Camogli's little pebble beach from its fishing port. Near here, Castello della Dragonara, originally built in the Middle Ages to defend the port from Saracens, now contains the **Acquario Tirrenico** (*open April–Sept 10–11.45 and 3–6.45; Oct–Mar 10–11.45 and 3–5.45; adm L6000*), an aquarium with 22 tanks of Mediterranean creatures.

Camogli recalls its own history in the **maritime museum**, Via Gio Bono Ferrari 41 (*open April–Sept Wed–Mon 9–12 and 4–7; Oct–Mar Wed, Sat and Sun 9–11.45 and 3–5.40, Mon, Thurs and Fri 9–12*). The archaeological section (*open Wed–Mon 9–12*), contains artefacts from, and a reconstruction of, an Iron Age settlement discovered nearby; the maritime section contains an array of ship's models, nautical instruments, maps, paintings and documents that recall Camogli's thrilling days as a rough-and-tumble sea power.

From Camogli there is a regular boat service (run by Golfo Paradiso, Via Scalo 2, ✆ 0185 772 091, ✉ 0185 771 263) to the tiny fishing hamlet of **San Fruttuoso** on the seaward side of the promontory. The hamlet is inaccessible save by sea or on foot (from Camogli it's a three-hour hike; there are also boats from Portofino, Santa Margherita and Rapallo, so in summer it can be elbow-room only). On the way from Camogli the boats pass the **Punta Chiappa**, a point famous for the changing colours of the sea, though unfortunately—thanks to the quantity of rubbish floating around nowadays—the water is no longer as clear as it once was.

San Fruttuoso is named after its **abbey**, founded in 711 by the Bishop of Tarragona, who fled Spain from the Moors, bringing with him the relics of San Fruttuoso. The Benedictines subsequently took over, under the protection of Genoa's powerful Doria family; Andrea Doria added the **Torre dei Doria** in the 16th century, when Turkish corsairs plagued the coast in the name of the king of France. In 1981 the Dorias donated the abbey and surrounding land to the Italian National Trust; you can stroll through the abbey, and the pretty white 11th-century church with a Byzantine cupola and tiny cloister (*open Mar–April Tues–Sun 10–1 and 2–4; May–Oct till 6; Nov–Feb public holidays only*).

San Fruttuoso is surrounded by a lush growth of palms and olives, and from here it's a two-hour walk through these groves to Portofino. Another sight, best appreciated by skin-divers, is the 1954 bronze **Cristo degli Abissi** (Christ of the Depths), off shore, and eight fathoms under the sea, a memorial to those lost at sea and protector of all who work underwater.

Portofino

The stunning **Monte di Portofino** (2001ft) is easiest reached from **Ruta** and **Portofino Vetta** (buses from Camogli). Protected as a natural park, it offers several lovely walks, especially up to the summit (one hour from Ruta), with its priceless views of the Riviera and out to sea as far as Elba, or in another hour to the lighthouse on the cliffs (the Semaforo Nuovo), or in two hours to Portofino.

One of Italy's most
romantic little nooks, **Portofino**
itself was discovered long ago by artists, then by the
yachting set, who fell in love with its delightful little port framed by
mellowed, narrow houses, and then by the rich and trendy, who fell in love with its spectacular beauty and seclusion and made it a favourite setting for illicit trysts, far, they hoped, from the paparazzi. This exclusiveness still exists to a certain extent—it's certainly a difficult place to get to, especially if you have left the yacht at home. The nearest railway station is in Santa Margherita, 9km away; the only means of access a single coastal road—a steeply meandering ribbon of tarmac roughly one and a half cars wide. Buses make the journey (with constant horn accompaniment) from Santa Margherita Station every twenty minutes or so (L1700 one way). Despite this, and the fact that there are only a handful of hotels, Portofino's hard-fought seclusion vanishes every weekend and every day in summer when thousands of trippers pour in for an afternoon's window-shopping in the smart boutiques (some selling the district's famous lace), a drink in the portside bar or even a walk in the cyprus-lined hills. In the evening, though, the yachtsmen and the residents of the hillside villas descend once again to their old haunts and reclaim Portofino as their own.

Portofino's name is derived from the Roman *Portus Delphini*, which had a *mithraeum* (an initiatory sanctuary dedicated to the popular Persian god Mithras, a favourite of Roman soldiers) on its isthmus. This is now the site of the church of **S. Giorgio**, rebuilt after war damage in 1950 but still housing the relics of the defrocked St George; as often as not there's a cat sleeping under the altar. Further up, **Castello Brown**, built in the 1500s as a defence against the Turks, affords enchanting views of the little port (*open Tues–Sun 10–6; adm L4000*). Another lovely walk, beyond the castle, is to Punta del Capo and the **Faro**, the old lighthouse, taking in magnificent views of the Gulf of Tigullio through the pine forest. The other thing to do in Portofino is find a table at one of the two port-side drinking holes which have long competed for the biggest celebrities: **La Gritta American Bar** and **Scafandro American Bar**, both elegant, glamorous, studiously laid-back and very expensive.

Santa Margherita

Santa Margherita, with its beautiful harbour, is not as spectacular as Portofino, but friendly and lively, a popular winter hideaway for the British, and a summer resort with accommodation priced for all budgets. The main sight in town is the **Basilica di Santa Margherita**, a Rococo extravaganza with Italian and Flemish art. Just outside the town, towards Portofino, is the **Abbazia della Cervara**, where King Francis I was imprisoned after the Battle of Pavia. Boat excursions run to Portofino, San Fruttuoso and the Cinque Terre.

Rapallo and Inland

After Portofino, Rapallo, tucked in the innermost corner of the Gulf of Tigullio, is the most famous resort on the Riviera di Levante, enjoying a mild year-round climate, and counts among its blessings a fairly good beach, an 18-hole golf course, busy tourist harbour, indoor pool, tennis, riding school, stables, and marvellous natural surroundings. Rapallo was the long-time home of Max Beerbohm, who lived in the Villino Chiaro and attracted a notable literary circle; it is also a favourite venue for conferences—at the **Villa Spinola**, Italy and Yugoslavia signed the Treaty of Rapallo in 1920. This villa lies along the Santa Margherita road, as does **San Michele di Pagana** containing a *Crucifixion* by Van Dyck, and the site of large firework-popping festivals in July and September.

In Rapallo itself, the **castle**, surrounded by the harbour's waters, is now used for changing exhibitions. Further along the shore, there's a **Museum of Bobbin Lace** in the Villa Tigullio (*open daily 3–6, Thurs 10–11.30; closed Mon*), dedicated to Rapallo's proudest age-old craft. Rapallo's main attraction is its **funivia**, recently restored to full-working order (*Mar–Oct 8–sunset; Nov–Feb 8.30–5; cars leave every 30 minutes*). The seven-minute trip will take you up 7707ft, to the 16th-century **Santuario di Montallegro**, on the site where a vision of the Madonna appeared to a local farmer, with a Byzantine icon which miraculously flew here from Dalmatia and a spectacular view of the coast.

Inland from this stretch of coast there are two attractive hill resorts: one is **Uscio**, reached by the SS333 road from Recco, a health spa and manufacturer of large campanile clocks. From Rapallo and the Montallegro, a long, winding road arrives after about an hour at **Santo Stefano d'Aveto**, up in the Ligurian Apennines, where Rapallo's wintertime visitors head for a taste of snow and a bit of skiing at just over 1000m, as well as a scenic 8km cablecar excursion. Santo Stefano's landmark is the imposing **Castello Malaspina**.

Chiávari and Lavagna

East of Rapallo, **Zoagli** is a small seaside village that has produced patterned velvets ever since they were fashion's rage in the Middle Ages, although nowadays people prefer it for dressing their furniture instead of themselves; most of the velvet factories are open for visits. A seaside path cut into the rock offers lovely views over the gulf. **Chiávari**, the next town, was founded as a colony of Genoa in 1178, and is another specialized craft centre: in fine wooden and straw chairs, and macramé, an art brought back by the town's sailors from the Middle East, and still used to adorn towels and tablecloths with intricate fringes and tassels, although the easy money from tourism is leaving them by the wayside. Orchids are another local speciality, their blooms best seen at the annual show at the end of February.

The centre of life in Chiávari is **Piazza Mazzini**, with a lively morning market, tower and stern palaces and a monument dedicated to Liguria's favourite revolutionary. A few streets away, the **Palazzo Rocca**, Via Costaguta 2, has a beautiful garden designed by Bartolomeo Bianco (1629), and houses two museums: the **Civica Galleria** (*open Sat and Sun 10–12 and 4–7.30*), with works by the Genoese school, and the **Civico Museo Archeologico** (*open daily 9–1.30*), with items discovered in the nearby 8th–7th-century BC necropolis, demonstrating trade links with the Phoenicians, Greeks and Egyptians. Another place to aim for, **Caffè Defilla**, Via Garibaldi 4, founded in 1883, has excellent ice-cream and pastries. In Chiávari's newer quarters, there's a small pleasure port near the long sandy beach. A road leads from here to Santo Stefano d'Aveto.

Lavagna, separated from Chiávari by a bridge over the Entella, has an equally long beach. It was ruled in the Middle Ages by the Fieschi, who produced a 13th-century pope, Innocent IV, and Count Opizzo Fieschi, whose marriage to Bianca dei Bianchi in 1230 made such an impression on Lavagna that the anniversary (14 August) is re-enacted each year, finishing with the communal eating of the gargantuan *Torta dei Fieschi*. Innocent IV, on the other hand, is remembered in the beautiful early Gothic church he built, the **Basilica di San Salvatore dei Fieschi**, a half-hour's walk inland near Cogorno.

Sestri Levante

Sestri Levante overlooks a lovely, curving peninsula called the Isola, dividing the 'Bay of Silence' from what Hans Christian Andersen himself christened the 'Bay of Fables'. It has a picturesque sandy beach, and more than its share of touristic development. The magnificent garden on the peninsula belongs to Albergo dei Castello, where Marconi performed his first experiments with radio waves; below it stands the fine Romanesque church of **San Nicolò**, with views of the two bays. The **Galleria Rizzi**, Via Cappuccini 8, on the Bay of Silence (*open April–Oct Wed 4–7, Fri and Sat 9pm–11pm, Sun 10–1*), contains works by the Florentine, Emilian and Ligurian schools, ceramics and a small furniture collection.

From Sestri a bus heads inland along the tortuous SS523 to **Varese Ligure**, the chief town of the Val di Vara, an agricultural and market centre and summer resort. It has an unusual core, the perfectly circular Borgo Rotundo, laid out in the late 15th century by the Fieschi, who offered land to any merchant who would build a house in a ring around the market. The Fieschi also owned the recently restored 15th-century castle. North of Varese, the scenery is lush and rolling, dotted with minute slate-roofed hamlets.

Where to Stay and Eating Out

Recco ✉ 16036

Recco is a gourmet mecca, famous for its *focaccia* with cheese, and *trofie*, a helix-shaped pasta made of chestnut flour and wheat. The mayor runs two of the best places to eat: the celebrated **Manuelina**, Via Roma 278, ✆ 0185 74128 (*expensive*), where you can try *trofie* with pesto, and seafood prepared in a variety of styles for the *secondo*; and, next door, **Focacceria** (*expensive*), where you can dine on one of the town's specialities, or on Ligurian dishes such as *cima. Both closed Wed.* Another renowned restaurant in Recco is the hundred-year-old **Da-o Vittorió**, Via Roma 160,

℘ 0185 74029 (*expensive*), whose specialities include utterly superb *minestrone di verdura alla Genovese* and *trofie al pesto*. Recco has some of the best budget-price restaurants in the area, particularly along the seafront and Via Roma.

Camogli ✉ 16032

★★★★**Cenobio dei Dogi**, Via Cuneo 34, ℘ 0185 7241, 🖷 0185 772 796 (*luxury*), a former palace of Genoa's doges, is a lovely hotel at the water's edge with fantastic views of the gulf—on a clear day you can see the steady winking of Genoa's light-house. The bedrooms are light and airy, and there are two excellent restaurants, one on the hotel's private pebble beach, both open to the public; add various sun terraces, a flower-filled park, a heated pool and tennis courts. ★★★**Casmona**, Salita Pineto 13, ℘ 0185 770 015, 🖷 0185 275 930 (*moderate*), is a quiet, tidy place with a restaurant, and a shady little patio. ★★**Pensione La Camogliese**, Via Garibaldi 55, ℘ 0185 771 402, 🖷 0185 774 024 (*cheap*) is not far from the sea, and also has an attractive restaurant, with a veranda overlooking the port, and good, reasonably priced fish dishes. *Closed Wed.* **Vento Ariel**, Calata Porto 1, ℘ 0185 771 080 (*expensive*) is a tiny, charming place on the harbour that bases its existence entirely on the luck of the town's fishing fleet. Only fish and seafood are served, with daily set menus or *à la carte*. Reservations are essential in summer. *Closed Wed.*

San Fruttuoso ✉ 16032

There are two good seafood restaurants: **Da Giovanni**, ℘ 0185 770 047 (*expensive*), a small, charming place, which also doubles as an inexpensive hotel, and **La Cantina**, ℘ 0185 772 626 (*expensive*), on the beach, serving fish cooked to order.

Portofino ✉ 16034

The management of the ★★★★★**Splendido**, Viale Baratta 16, ℘ 0185 269 551, 🖷 0185 269 614 (*luxury*) believe they run the best hotel in Liguria, if not Italy. It's an arrogant assumption but one backed with testimonials from the likes of Churchill, Groucho Marx, Bogart, Bacall, Madonna and Bill Gates. The views alone, of olive-and-cyprus-clad hills gently framing the town, its tiny harbour and the deep blue sea beyond, are worth the astronomical fees. The bedrooms are sumptuous, the restaurant refined and the breakfast terrace, sheltered beneath a huge sub-tropical canopy, simply delightful. Swim in the heated outdoor pool or, for a mere L1,000,000 per day, go for a ride in the hotel's own speedboat. Its secluded location preserves its air of exclusivity; if you want to mingle with mere mortals, check in at the Spendido's smaller sibling, **Splendido Mare**, Via Roma 2, ℘ 0185 267 802, 🖷 0185 267 807 (*luxury*), which recently opened on the piazza by the harbour. This is a less grand, slightly cheaper version of the original with a delightful *al fresco* restaurant, the Chufley Bar. A shuttle service links the two hotels. *Both open Mar–Jan.*

★★★★**Nazionale**, Via Roma 8, ℘ 0185 269 575, 🖷 0185 269 578 (*luxury*), smack on the port, has a slightly faded charm, furnished with antiques or reproductions. The best rooms have Venetian furniture and overlook the harbour. It has no parking, which can be a big problem in Portofino. ★★★**Eden**, Vico Dritto 18, ℘ 0185 269 091, 🖷 0185 269 047 (*very expensive*) is far from cheap, but is the least expensive hotel in town, a charming 12-room establishment in the centre, endowed with a fine garden and good Ligurian restaurant.

Dining out in Portofino can be a rarefied experience. Most of the restaurants are clustered around Portofino's little piazza and port, including **Il Pitosforo**, Molo Umberto I 9, ✆ 0185 269 218 (*very expensive*), where the Ligurian cuisine is among the finest anywhere, whether you order *bouillabaisse*, spaghetti with prawns and mushrooms, the red mullet or sea bream with olives. A tree grows out of the middle of the dining room, and one whole wall is lined with a collection of spirits from around the world that will make any serious drinker's eyes glaze over in delight. Every night at 10pm, all the lights are switched off to highlight the magical view of the golden lights in the port. *Closed Tues.* **Da Puny**, Piazza Martire Olivetta 7, ✆ 0185 269 037 (*expensive*) serves delicious pasta and seafood dishes for starters, and well-prepared fish, like sea bass baked in salt. **Taverna del Marinaio**, Piazza Martire Olivetta 36, ✆ 0185 269 103 (*moderate*), although by no means cheap, is as reasonable as you'll find. The fish and pasta are excellent. *Closed Tues.*

Santa Margherita ✉ 16038

Two hotels have long rivalled one another in the luxury category: ★★★★★**Imperiale Palace**, Via Pagana 19, on the edge of town, ✆ 0185 288 991, ✆ 0185 284 223 (*luxury*), formerly a private villa, was converted into an hotel at the turn of the century; in 1922, in one of the palatial marble and gilt-encrusted public rooms, the Weimar Republic signed an agreement with Russia to re-open diplomatic relations. Antiques litter the hallways, public rooms and more expensive bedrooms, and concerts are held in the music room some afternoons. There's a heated outdoor pool, a lush tropical garden and a seafront terrace. *Open Mar–Oct.* The shining white ★★★★**Grand Hotel Miramare**, Via Milite Ignoto 30, ✆ 0185 287 013, ✆ 0185 284 651 (*very expensive*) is almost as palatial, though purpose-built as a posh winter hotel in the early 1900s. Surrounded by a lovely garden, with a heated salt-water pool, it has lovely air-conditioned rooms, many with fine views of the gulf from their balconies. The Miramare's water skiing school is one of the best in Italy.

★★★**La Vela**, Via N. Cuneo 21, ✆ 0185 284 771 (*moderate*), a former villa located a bit above town, has a friendly, intimate atmosphere and 16 rooms with good sea views. *Closed Nov–Christmas.* Best value in this category, though, is the very friendly and welcoming ★★**Fasce**, Via L. Bozzo 3, ✆ 0185 286 435, ✆ 0185 283 580 (*moderate*), part of the 'family hotel' chain. Its rooms are modern and immaculately maintained, and it also offers free bike hire and an excellent restaurant, where you can enjoy a full meal of delicious Ligurian specialities for not much more than L20,000 a head (*high season only*). *Closed Nov–Christmas.*

The finest restaurant in Santa Margherita, **Cesarina**, Via Mameli 2/c, ✆ 0185 286 059 (*very expensive*) is located under an arcade in the old part of town. The fresh and modern atmosphere matches such specialities as *zuppa di datteri* (razor clam soup) or Liguria's famous spaghetti with red mullet sauce. Reserve. *Closed Tues.* **L'Ancora**, Via Maragliano 7, ✆ 0185 280 599 (*moderate*) offers seafood specialities (an excellent *insalata di pesce*), and a good-value set tourist menu. *Closed Tues.*

Rapallo ✉ 16035

Rapallo has more hotels than any resort on the Riviera di Levante. The bright red ★★★★**Eurotel**, Via Aurelia Ponente 22, ✆ 0185 60981, @ 0185 50635 (*very expensive*), on the outskirts of town, has great views of the hills and harbour, large well-appointed rooms with balconies, smart lounge areas and a heated outdoor pool. In the centre, ★★★**Riviera**, Piazza IV Novembre 2, ✆ 0185 50248/9, @ 0185 65668 (*expensive*) is a converted villa near the sea. Remodelled inside, it has a popular glass terrace in the front and a garden at the rear.

Close to the seafront and right in the middle of town, ★**Pensione Bandoni**, Via Marsala 24/3, ✆ 0185 50423, @ 0185 57206 (*cheap*) is comfortable, simple hotel and good value. Among the olives, **Giancu**, Via S. Massimino 78, ✆ 0185 260 505 (*moderate*) is a fine family restaurant—complete with a playground. There's no playing around with the food, however—it's all good, traditional stuff. *Closed Wed.* The best cheap eateries are around Piazza Garibaldi and Via Venezia.

Chiávari ✉ 16043

In Leivi, 6km from Chiávari, **Ca' Peo**, Strada Panoramica, ✆ 0185 319 696 (*very expensive*) is one of the best restaurants on the Riviera. The atmosphere is elegant and charming, and the food imaginatively and delicately prepared, featuring radicchio from Treviso, truffles from Alba, porcini mushrooms and very fresh fish, followed by excellent desserts and accompanied by noble wines. Reservations are a must.

In Chiávari, **Felice**, Via L. Risso 71, ✆ 0185 308 016 (*moderate*) serves a delicious *zimino* (fish soup) and other Ligurian dishes; it's small, so reserve. *Closed Mon.*

Sestri Levante ✉ 16039

Occupying the tip of the Isola Peninsula, the ★★★★★**Grand Hotel dei Castelli**, Via Penisola 26, ✆ 0185 487 220, @ 0185 44767 (*very expensive*) was built in the 1920s on the site of a Genoese castle, using the castle's stone. The views of both bays and the sea crashing against the cliffs all around the hotel's park are magnificent, especially from the dining terrace. There's also a natural sea pool cut into the rock for safe swimming. *Open May–Oct.*

On the seafront is the supremely stately pink palace ★★★★**Villa Balbi**, Viale Rimembranza 1, ✆ 0185 42941, @ 0185 482 459 (*very expensive*), built in the early 1600s for the Brignole family, and full of unexpected treasures—a preserved library and a room decorated entirely in paintings of fish, as well as oak-beamed bedrooms and antique laden public rooms. Much of the original garden remains, including a large camphor tree growing through the roof of the restaurant. It also has a pool and a good private beach. *Open April–Oct.*

In the prettiest part of town on the Bay of Silence, ★★★**Helvetia**, Via Cappuccini 43, ✆ 0185 41175, @ 0185 57216 (*expensive*) is a welcoming little hotel with a large terraced garden. ★★★**Mira**, Via Rimembranza 15, ✆ 0185 41576, @ 0185 41577 (*moderate*) is a family-run hotel with rooms with a view, and a restaurant serving excellent fish specialities—*riso marinara* and *nasello alla mira*—on its covered terrace overlooking the sea. *Closed Mon.*

For excellent seaside dining, **Angiolina**, Piazza Matteotti 51, © 0185 41198 (*expensive*) is the place to go for an exquisite *zuppa di pesce* and other delicious denizens of the deep. *Closed Tues.* Seafood and traditional Ligurian cuisine comprise the menu at **Fiammenghilla Fieschi**, Via Pestella 6, © 0185 481 041 (*expensive*), a great place to try marinated swordfish, lobster, *focaccia* or *pansotti*; there is a very good Ligurian wine list. *Open evenings only.*

A few streets back from the 'Bay of Silence', **Polpo Mario**, Via XXV Aprile 163, © 0185 480 203, is a nice cosy family restaurant. It's very popular with locals, presumably because of the very generous portions.

Riviera di Levante: the Cinque Terre and La Spezia

Before sliding down to the comparatively dull and flat coast of Tuscany, the Riviera bows out with a dramatic flourish around the rugged, almost inaccessible cliffs of the Cinque Terre, the rocky peninsula of Portovenere, and La Spezia's lovely 'Gulf of Poets'. One particular plus point of this area is that prices, especially for accommodation, are noticeably more reasonable than elsewhere along the Riviera.

Getting Around

The easiest way to reach the Cinque Terre is by **train** from Genoa or La Spezia. Each of the five towns has a station, only a few minutes apart and separated by long tunnels; afterwards the train drills through the mountains straight to La Spezia and Sarzana, from where you can continue on towards Parma or Pisa.

The controversial coastal road to the Cinque Terre (*Litoranea delle Cinque Terre*; Italian engineers' bulldozers begin to twitch at the mention of the word 'inaccessible') hardly makes access easier: east of Sestri Levante, the narrow one-way tunnels lead to major traffic jams in the summer. Drivers should be aware, also, that the villages at the end of the winding cliff roads are tiny, and parking is a perennial problem.

There are **buses** from Piazza Chiodo in La Spezia to Riomaggiore and Manarola, Portovenere (every 15 minutes), Lerici, Sarzana and Florence.

There are also several **boat** lines serving the area, linking La Spezia, Lerici, Portovenere and the Cinque Terre; **NGP** goes as far as Portofino to the north, and Marina di Massa and Marina di Carrara in Tuscany; **Fratelli Rossignoli**, sails between Monterosso and Viareggio during summer. Ferries sail between La Spezia and Bastia, Corsica daily in summer, and less frequently at other times.

Tourist Information

Levanto: Piazza C. Colombo 2, © 0187 808 125. **Monterosso al Mare**: Via Fegina 38, © 0187 817 506. **La Spezia**: Viale Mazzini 45, © 0187 770 900, @ 0187 770 908; in the station, © 0187 718 997. **Portovenere**: Piazza Bastreri 1, © 0187 790 691, @ 0187 790 215. **Lerici**: Via Biaggini 6, © 0187 967 346. **Sarzana**: in the town hall, Piazza Matteotti, © 0187 6141, @ 0187 614 252.

Sestri Levante to the Cinque Terre

After Sestri Levante, the Apennines move in and crowd the coast, admitting here and there little glens and sandy strands—at sleepy **Moneglia** (from the Latin *monellia*, or jewel), with its quiet stretch of beach framed by two medieval castles, Monleone and Villafranca, **Deiva Marina**, near the pretty village of Framura, **Bonassola**, and, most importantly, **Levanto**, which has a good sandy beach, flower gardens, and several monuments from the 13th century—the **Loggia** (town hall), the church of **Sant'Andrea**, and chunks of its walls.

Next on the coast, **Monterosso al Mare** is the first of the towns of the **Cinque Terre** ('The Five Lands'), as they've been known since the Middle Ages. Perched wherever the cliffs and hills permitted enough space to build, surrounded by steep slopes corrugated by hundreds of terraces laboriously carved out of the earth and rock, the Cinque Terre towns are visually stunning. They also enjoy a fine, mild climate, and the vineyards that occupy the near-vertical terraces produce the region's finest (and most potent) wines—the ones labelled Sciacchetrà are made from raisins, and can be either dry or sweet. Formerly accessible only by sea or by a spectacular series of cliff-skirting footpaths, the towns have maintained much of their charm, even though nowadays they are far from being undiscovered.

Monterosso is the most touristy of the five, with beaches (free and 'organized'), hotels, rooms in private houses, and so on, and boats to hire for personal tours of the coast. Most of the facilities are in the new half of town, Fegina, separated from the old by a hill crowned with the **Convento dei Cappuccini** (1622) and a medieval tower; the 18th-century **Santuario di Soviore**, built over an older church, hosts a music festival in the summer. From Monterosso it's a momentary train ride or a lovely hour-and-a-half walk to the next town, **Vernazza**, founded by the Romans on a rocky spit, a striking vision from the footpath above. Its parish church, Santa Margherita of Antioch, was built in 1318.

The hour-and-a-half walk from Vernazza to **Corniglia** is one of the most strenuous, for Corniglia, unlike the other towns, is high up on the cliffs and not on the sea, though it does have the longest (though pebbly) beach. From Corniglia another hour's walk through splendid scenery leads to **Manarola**, a colourful fishing village built along steep lanes, all piled on a great black rock. It is linked in 20 minutes or so to **Riomaggiore** by the most popular section of the footpath, the 'Via dell'Amore', carved into the cliff face over the sea. Riomaggiore, one of the prettiest towns, also sees plenty of visitors, who crowd its lively cafés and rocky beaches.

La Spezia

The largest city in the region, the provincial capital, and a major naval base, La Spezia was bombed heavily in the Second World War and presents a modern but cheerful face to the world, standing at the head of one of Italy's prettiest gulfs. Mostly used by visitors as a base for visiting the Cinque Terre and Portovenere, it has a number of attractions in its own right—among them a promenade of swaying palms and lush public gardens.

The **Museo Civico**, Via Curtatone 9 (*open Tues–Sat 8.30–1.15 and 2.30–7.15, Sun 9–1*) contains an important archaeological section, with prehistoric finds from Palmaria's Grotta dei Colombi, pre-Roman and Roman material from Luni and, most notably, Ligurian stelae from the Bronze and Iron Ages. The excellent **naval museum**, in Piazza Chiodo, next to the Naval Arsenal (*open Tues–Thurs and Sat 9–12 and 2–6, Mon and Fri 2–6; adm*) contains a fine collection begun in 1560 by Emanuele Filiberto, with relics of the ships sent by the Savoys to the Battle of Lepanto, as well as models, figureheads and momentoes from Italy's naval battles. The **Museo Amedeo Lia**, Via Prione 234 (*open daily 10–6; closed Mon; adm exp*), housed in a former convent in the centre of town, contains works by Giovanni Mazone, Giacomo Recco and Titian.

Portovenere and Palmaria

South of La Spezia the road is delightful but winding (if you're prone to car sickness, take the boat), and passes by way of the pretty cove of **Le Grazie** before ending at **Portovenere**. With its long promontory, castle and pastel houses, Portovenere is fittingly named after the goddess of love herself, a protectoress of fishfolk. The temple of Venus stood at the tip of the promontory, until it was upstaged by a church dedicated to Christianity's top fisherman, **San Pietro**. This strange little church of black and white striped marble dates from 1277, while below are a few colourful remains of its 6th-century predecessor. It enjoys splendid views of Palmaria and the Cinque Terre coast; the lovely bay below once held the Grotta Arpaia, where Byron wrote *The Corsair*, and from where he swam across the gulf to Lerici and Shelley's villa. It collapsed in the 1930s.

The best thing to do in Portovenere is wander through its narrow, cat-crowded lanes (this is Italy's champion kitty city), past tall ancient houses on the waterfront with interesting details on the doorways, built by the Genoese, who fortified the town in the early 12th century (as the Pisans had fortified Lerici across the gulf).

A lane leads up to the lovely church of **San Lorenzo** (1130), with a bas-relief of St Lawrence being toasted on his gridiron over the door; inside is Portovenere's most precious relic, the *Madonna Bianca*, said to have floated to the town encased in a cedar log in the 13th century (the log, too, is on display). Further up, a steep but worthwhile walk leads to the 16th-century Genoese **castello**, with marvellous views (*open April–Oct daily 10–12 and 2–6; Nov–Mar daily 3–5*).

From Portovenere you can cross the 400m channel to **Isola Palmaria** and visit its famed **Grotta Azzurra**—though a much cheaper proposition is to book a passage from La Spezia. Palmaria, site of a Neolithic settlement, produces the black, gold-veined marble you may have noticed in Portovenere. The much smaller **Isola del Tino**, with a lighthouse and the ruins of an 8th-century monastery, and the even tinier **Tinetto**, lie further out.

Lerici

Lerici, on its own little bay, is the most important town on the east shore of the 'Golfo dei Poeti'. Tit for Portovenere's tat, its imposing **castello** (*open daily 9am–midnight; adm*), towering up on its promontory, was built by the Pisans, and enlarged by the Genoese in the 15th century; inside you can visit the Chapel of Sant'Anastasia (1250).

Lerici has a nice beach and mild winter climate, and its environs were beloved by Shelley, whose last home was the Casa Magni in **San Terenzo**, the charming fishing village across the bay; it was from here that he sailed, in 1822, to meet Leigh Hunt at Livorno, only to ship-wreck and drown by Viareggio.

To the south is the enchanting, tranquil, tiny cove and beach of **Fiascherino**, where D. H. Lawrence lived from 1913 to 1914; beyond is the unspoiled medieval hamlet of **Tellaro**. Another scenic road continues around the gulf and begins to climb up the Val di Magra to **Ameglia**, with its 10th-century castle, and the slate portals of the older houses.

Sarzana and Ancient Luni

From La Spezia, bridges cross the River Magra for **Sarzana**, once the easternmost edge of the Republic of Genoa: an ancient town guarded by a Medici citadel and the **Fortezza di Sarzello** (a mile east), a great stone steam iron built in the early-14th century by the tyrant of Lucca, Castruccio Castracani. The 14th-century **cathedral** contains one of the best works of Master Guglielmo: a *Crucifixion* of 1138; other churches of note include **Sant'Andrea** and **San Francesco**, which have good sculptures. To the north in **Fosdinovo**, the Malaspina castle which hosted Dante in 1306; he is also said to have visited the ruined 13th-century castle in **Castelnuovo Magra**. The church contains a *Calvary* by Brueghel the Younger.

Ortonovo lies near the site of the ancient Roman town and marble-shipping port of **Luni**, founded in 177 BC as a bulwark against the fierce Ligurians. The city survived until 1204, when its bishopric was moved to Sarzana and malaria led to its complete desertion.

Excavations have revealed a sizeable amphitheatre, forum, houses, temples and so on; on the site the **Museo Nazionale di Luni** (*open April–Sept Tues–Sun 9–12 and 3–7; Oct–Mar Tues–Sun 2–7; adm*) has marble statuary, coins, jewellery, portraits, etc., as well as a display of archaeological techniques used in excavating the site. If you're continuing down the coast from here, *see* 'The Tuscan Coast', p.613.

Where to Stay and Eating Out

Moneglia ✉ 16030

The bright pink **Villa Edera**, Via Venino 12, ✆ 0187 492 291, 📠 0187 49470 (*moderate*) is a nice, basic, quiet family-run hotel set in the hills a few minutes from the beach, directly next to the medieval Castello Monleone. It also has a lovely restaurant featuring homemade regional specialities.

Monterosso ✉ 19016

Monterosso has the best accommodation of the Cinque Terre, with the ★★★★**Porto Roca**, Via Corone 1, ✆ 0187 817 502, 📠 0187 817 692 (*very expensive*) as the top choice, located on the headland, with lovely views of the sea from all the rooms.

Probably the best budget option is ★★★**Degli Amici**, Via Burranco 36, ✆ 0187 817 574, ✇ 0187 817 424 (*moderate*), in the old part of town and 150m from the beach. The rooms are light and airy, some with balcony, and there's an excellent restaurant.

The best food is served at **Il Gigante**, Via IV Novembre, ✆ 0187 817 401 (*moderate*), with especially good Ligurian specialities—*pansotti, trenette al pesto* and fresh fish. *Closed Tues.*

Vernazza ✉ 19018

★**Sorriso**, Via Gavino 4, ✆ 0187 812 224 (*cheap*) is an honest little inn with a well-known restaurant. Partly carved out of the rock, **Gambero Rosso**, Piazza Marconi 7, ✆ 0187 812 265 (*moderate*) serves a delicious *tegame di acciughe*, a tasty dish made with anchovies, a Cinque Terre speciality.

On the square, **Da Capitano**, ✆ 0187 812 201 (*moderate*) serves fine fish fare—try the *linguine ai granchi*, washed down with the genial Captain's own wine.

Manarola ✉ 19010

★★★**Marina Piccola**, ✆ 0187 920 103, ✇ 0187 920 966 (*cheap*), with 10 simple rooms, is a good place to get away from it all, and it has a very nice restaurant. Rooms are better in the main hotel, rather than the annexe. The choice trattoria is **Aristide**, Via Roma, ✆ 0187 920 000 (*moderate*), serving a delicious *minestra* and exquisite fish dishes, also rabbit, game and other meat in season.

La Spezia ✉ 19100

★★★★**Jolly**, Via XX Settembre 2, ✆ 0187 739 555, ✇ 0187 22129 (*very expensive*), a modern and rather stylish member of the Italian hotel chain, has views stretching to the gulf. Near the station, the ★★★**Firenze & Continental**, Via Paleocapa 7, ✆ 0187 713 210, ✇ 0187 714 930 (*moderate*) is a comfortable hotel that's convenient for making rail hops into the Cinque Terre. Among the bargains the best is ★**Flavia**, Vicolo dello Stagno 7, off Via del Prione, ✆ 0187 27465 (*cheap*), not far from the station, with rooms for under L55,000.

Just off the seafront, the elegant **Parodi**, Viale Amendola 210, ✆ 0187 715 777 (*expensive*) has the best gourmet dishes in the city, with a tempting menu of market-fresh ingredients; and a great choice of wines and spirits, too, for a memorable night out. *Closed Sun.* There are a good number of low-price restaurants, much-patronized by the naval personnel who are everywhere in town, and mainly concentrated around Via del Prione. Try **Da Dino**, Via de Passano 17, ✆ 0187 736 157 (*cheap*), a charming, unpretentious place with an excellent-value fixed price menu. *Closed Sun eve and Mon.* **Incontro**, Via Sapri 10, ✆ 0187 24689 (*moderate*) is more upscale, with some unexpected dishes, such as asparagus wrapped in filo. *Closed Sun.*

Portovenere ✉ 19025

The large and modern ★★★★**Hotel Royal Sporting**, Via dell'Ulivo 345, ✆ 0187 790 326, ✇ 0187 777 707 (*expensive*) is the finest hotel, with a fantastic location overlooking sea and town, a salt-water pool, beach, garden and tennis courts. There is also a place to park, an important consideration in this little town. *Open April–Oct.* **★★Genio**, Piazza Bastreri 8, ✆ 0187 790 611 (*cheap*) has the cheapest rooms in Portovenere, and a nice little garden, too.

You can dine in a former fisherman's house in the picturesque Calata Doria, at **Al Gavitello da Mario**, ✆ 0187 900 215 (*expensive*). The menu is of course devoted to seafood, but prepared in unusual ways—for *primo*, try fish ravioli with prawn sauce, and for *secondo*, scampi with pear brandy. At the beginning of the promontory, **La Taverna del Corsaro**, Lungomare Doria 182, ✆ 0187 900 622 (*expensive*) has one of the most delightful locations in town, where you can savour delicacies like prawn in bell-pepper sauce and *zuppa di datteri* (razor clams). Family-run **La Spiaggia**, on the quay at Piazza Basteri 2, ✆ 0187 901 670 (*cheap*) serves some of the best fried squid rings in Italy and other fishy delights, along with a refreshing house wine.

Lerici and around ✉ 19032

★★★Shelley & Delle Palme, Lungomare Biaggini 5, ✆ 0187 968 204, ✉ 0187 964 271 (*moderate*) is one of the largest and most comfortable hotels on the 'Gulf of Poets'. On the left as you approach town, **★★★Byron**, Via Biaggini 19, ✆ 0187 967 104, ✉ 0187 967 409 (*moderate*) has small rooms compensated by fine views across the bay and, on the third floor, huge balconies. The best restaurant is **Due Corona**, Via G. Mazzini, ✆ 0187 967 417 (*very expensive*), beside the port, the deserving winner of two culinary awards. Seafood is, of course, a speciality; try their *cocktail di antipasti mare* and *grigliata mista. Closed Thurs.* **Paolino**, Via S. Francesco 14, ✆ 0187 967 801 (*expensive*) offers three choices—light, medium and full, depending on your appetite—with particularly good salads and pasta dishes.

In laid-back San Terenzo,**★★★Elisabetta**, Via Mantegazza 21, ✆ 0187 970 636 (*cheap*) is tiny but comfortable, with a garden, and **Palmira**, Via Trogo 13, ✆ 0187 971 094 (*expensive*) is a very popular trattoria that serves delightful *zuppa di vongole*, other seafood and meat dishes as well. *Closed Wed, and Sept and Oct.* On the cove of Fiascherino, **★★★Il Nido**, Via Fiascherino 75, ✆ 0187 967 286, ✉ 0187 964 225 (*moderate*) enjoys a lovely location, with enchanting views over the sea and beach. **Miranda**, Via Fiascherino 92, ✆ 0187 968 130 (*expensive*) serves mouthwatering seafood dishes like prawn flan in white truffle sauce and fish *gnocchi* with pesto.

Ameglia ✉ 19031

Ameglia, south of Lerici, is the site of the most famous hotel and restaurant in the area, **★★★★Paracucchi Locanda dell'Angelo**, at Ca' di Scabello, Viale XXV Aprile 60, ✆ 0187 64391/2, ✉ 0187 64393 (*moderate*). The hotel is modern, stylish and slick, and the sea is only a couple of minutes away. Chef Angelo Paracucchi has left the running of the restaurant (*very expensive*) in excellent hands; the menu changes often, but each dish is superb, and often amazingly simple. Great desserts, especially the fruit flambée, and excellent wine list. *Closed Sun eve, and Mon out of season.*

Lombardy and the Lakes

Of all the barbarians who desecrated the corpse of the Roman Empire, none were more barbaric than the Lombards (or Longobards), a tall Germanic tribe who bled much of the peninsula dry before settling down in the region that still bears their name. Even today the Milanese are taller than the average Italian, although whether it's because of their Lombard blood or general prosperity is anyone's guess. For since the Middle Ages Lombardy has been the economic powerhouse of Italy. The complaint that Milan makes money while Rome wastes it is almost as old as the city itself.

Milan, the pounding, racing economic heart of modern Italy, is the centre of gravity for the entire north. It always has been. The destinies of entire empires and kingdoms have been decided here, not to mention religions—Christianity was made the religion of the Roman Empire in Milan.

Lombardy has its gentle side as well. This was the homeland of Virgil, of composers Donizetti and Monteverdi, of the great violin masters, Amati, Guarneri and Stradivarius. And since the 18th century countless poets, composers and weary aristocrats have come for the peace and beauty of the Italian Lakes, one of the most charming districts in the country—which, although partially in Piemonte, Switzerland and the Veneto, have all been included here for convenience's sake.

Not to be Missed

Milan is far more than a centre of finances and fashion, but an art city in its own right, where you can easily spend three days, taking in nearby **Pavia** and its famous **Certosa** as a day trip. The famous gardens and villas of **Lake Como** (Villa Carlotta and Bellagio) or of **Lake Maggiore** (Stresa and the Borromean Isles) can also be seen in rather hurried day trips from Milan, though it's far more pleasant to stay on their shores. **Lake Garda**, a bit far for a day trip, rates as the liveliest for a prolonged stay, and is a good stopover if you're headed towards Venice; on Garda don't miss Sirmione and its Grotte di Catullo, or Gardone Riviera, with Gabriele D'Annunzio's kitsch palace. Both **Bergamo** and **Mantua** are top-notch art cities, the former for its medieval Città Alta and the Carrara Academy, the latter for the Renaissance palaces of the Gonzaga dukes. Silk-weaving **Como**, violin-making **Cremona** and Roman **Brescia** all have fine cathedrals and enough sights to occupy at least half a day.

Unknown Lombardy

Unknown, at least, to most foreigners. As well as the three main lakes, the lesser lakes of **Orta** and **Iseo** are also charmers. The Bergamasque valleys, the **Val Brembana** and the upper **Val Seriana** offer great Alpine scenery without the hype, while the beautiful **Val Camonica** above Lake Iseo is the home of the remarkable **National Park of Prehistoric Engravings**. The rugged Alpine valleys of Sondrio province, the **Valchiavenna** and the **Valtellina**, are dotted with castles and quiet villages; **Bormio**, at the top of the Valtellina, is one of Italy's top winter sports centres and the gateway to glacier-encrusted **Stelvio National Park**. More scenery lies to the north of Lake Maggiore, especially around **Domodossola** and the Romantic **Val Formazza**. Then there's **Sabbioneta**, an ideal Renaissance town near Mantua; the lovely frescoes of Masolino da Panicale in **Castiglione Olona**, east of Lake Maggiore; and the cathedral of **Monza**, with the treasure of the 6th-century Lombard Queen Theodolinda.

Most tourists don't come to Italy looking for slick, feverish Milan, and most of those who find themselves here take in only the obligatory sights—Leonardo's *Last Supper*, La Scala, the Duomo, the Brera, and the shops. Most Italians (apart from the almost 2,000,000 Milanese, that is) have little good to say about their second city, either: all the Milanese do is work, all they care about is money, and they refuse to indulge the myth of *la dolce vita.*

The Italians who deride Milan (most of whom work just as many hours themselves) are mostly envious, and the tourists who whip through it in a day are mostly ignorant of what this great city has to offer. Milan is indeed atypical, devoid of the usual Italian daydreams and living-museum mustiness. Like Naples it lives for the present, but not in Naples' endearing anarchy; as one of Europe's financial centres and a capital of fashion, Milan dresses in a well-tailored, thoroughly cosmopolitan three-piece suit. The skills of its workers, above all in the luxury clothing trades, have been known for centuries—as evoked in the English word 'millinery'.

And yet, as the Milanese are the first to admit, Milan has made its way in the world not so much by native talent as through the ability to attract it, from St Ambrose and Leonardo da Vinci to the designer of the moment. It has produced no great music of its own, but La Scala is one of the world's most prestigious places to sing; it has produced very few artists of its own but has amassed enough treasures to fill four superb galleries. Milan is the Italian melting pot, Italy's picture window on the modern world, where the young and ambitious gravitate to see their talents appreciated and rewarded. Here history seems to weigh less; here willowy Japanese models slink down the pavement with natty young gents whose parents immigrated from Calabria. Roiling, moiling, toiling, constantly evolving, Milan is *sui generis*; in Milanese dialect they have said, long before Gertrude Stein's 'a rose is a rose', *Milan l'e Milan*, Milan is Milan.

History

Milan was born cosmopolitan. Although located far from any sea or river, in the midst of the fertile Lombard plain, it occupies the natural junction of trade routes through the Alpine passes, from the Tyrrhenian and Adriatic ports and the River Po. This commercially strategic position has also put Milan square in the path of every conqueror tramping through Italy.

Mediolanum, as it was called for its first millennium and a half, first became prominent in the twilight of Rome when, as the headquarters of the Mobile Army and the seat of the Western government, it became the *de facto* capital of the Empire; Diocletian preferred it to Rome, and his successors spent much of their time here. The official Christianization of the empire began here in 313, when Constantine established religious toleration with his Edict of Milan.

St Ambrose (Sant'Ambrogio)

No sooner had Christianity received the imperial stamp of approval than it split into two hostile camps: the orthodox, early-Catholic traditionalists versus the followers of the Egyptian bishop Arius, who denied that Christ was of the same substance as God. An early bishop of Milan was an Arian and persecutor of the orthodox, and a schism seemed inevitable when he died. When the young consular governor Ambrose spoke to calm the crowd during the election of the new bishop, a child's voice suddenly piped up: 'Ambrose Bishop!' The cry was taken up, and Ambrose, who hadn't even been baptized, suddenly found himself thrust into a new job.

According to legend, when Ambrose was an infant in Rome, bees had flown into his mouth, attracted by the honey of his tongue. His eloquence as bishop of Milan (374–97) came in handy in preserving the unity of the Church. When the widow of Emperor Valentine desired to raise her son as an Arian, demanding a Milanese basilica for Arian worship, Ambrose and his supporters held the church through a nine-day siege, converting the empress's soldiers in the process. His most famous convert was St Augustine, and he set what would become the standard in relations between Church and Empire when he refused to allow Emperor Theodosius to enter church until he had done penance for ordering a civilian massacre in Thessalonika. Ambrose left such an imprint that to this day genuine Milanese are called Ambrosiani. Their church, which was practically independent from Rome until the 11th century, still celebrates Mass according to the Ambrosian rite and holds its own carnival of Sant'Ambrogio in March.

The Rise of the *Comune*

During the next few centuries 'Mediolanum' was shortened to Mailand, the prized Land of May, for so it seemed to the frostbitten Goths and Lombards who came to grab it. In the early 11th century Milan became Italy's first *comune* under the leadership of another great bishop, Heribert, who organized a *parlamento* of citizens and a citizen militia. The new *comune*—Guelph in defiance of imperial pretensions—at once began subjugating its Ghibelline rivals Pavia, Lodi and Como. To inspire the militia, Heribert also invented that unique Italian war machine, the *carroccio*, a huge ox-drawn cart that bore the city's banner, altar and bells into battle, to remind the soldiers of the city and church they fought for.

It was Lodi's complaint to Emperor Frederick Barbarossa about Milan's bullying that first brought old Red Beard to Italy in 1154. It was to prove a momentous battle between the emperor and Milan that would define the relationship of Italy's *comuni* towards their nominal overlord. Barbarossa besieged and sacked Milan in 1158; the Ambrosiani promised to behave, but attacked his German garrison as soon as he was back safely over the Alps. Undaunted, Barbarossa returned and for two years laid waste to the countryside around Milan, then grimly besieged the defiant city. When it surrendered he demanded the surrender of the *carroccio*, forced the citizens to kiss his feet with ropes around their necks, and invited Lodi and Como to raze the city to the ground, sparing only the churches of Sant'Ambrogio and San Lorenzo.

But this total humiliation of Milan, meant to *encourager les autres*, had the opposite effect; it galvanized Italy's *comuni* to form the Lombard League against the foreign oppressor (only Pavia hated Milan too much to join). On his next foray over the Alps in 1176, Barbarossa was soundly defeated by the Lombard League at Legnano and found his empire on the verge of total revolt. To preserve it, Barbarossa had to do a little foot-kissing himself in Venice, the privileged toe in this case belonging to Pope Alexander III, whom Barbarossa had exiled from Rome in order to set up another pope more malleable to his schemes. To placate the Lombard *comuni* the Treaty of Constance was signed in 1183, in which the signatories of the Lombard League received all that they desired: their municipal autonomy and the privilege of making war—on each other! The more magnanimous idea of a united Italy was still centuries away.

The Age of the Big Bosses

If Milan invented government by the *comune*, it was also one of the first cities to give it up. Unlike their counterparts in Florence, Milan's manufacturers were varied in their trades; they limited themselves to small workshops, and failed to form the companies of merchants and trade associations that were the power base of a medieval Italian republic. The first family to fill the vacuum at the top were the Torriani (della Torre), feudal lords who became the city's *signori* in 1247, only to lose their position to the Visconti in 1277.

The Visconti, created dukes in 1395, made Milan the strongest state in Italy, and marriages with French and English royalty brought the family into European affairs. Most ambitious of all the Visconti was Gian Galeazzo (1351–1402), married first to the daughter of the king of France and then to the daughter of his powerful and malevolent uncle Bernabò, whom Gian Galeazzo sent to prison before conquering northern Italy, the Veneto, Romagna and Umbria. His army was ready to march on Florence when he suddenly died of the plague. In his ruthlessness and his dependence on astrology, his love of art and letters (he founded the Certosa of Pavia, began the Duomo, held a lavish court and supported the University of Pavia), Gian Galeazzo was one of the first 'archetypal' Renaissance princes. The Florentines and Venetians took advantage of his demise to carry off pieces of his empire and, while his sons, the obscene Giovanni Maria (who fed his enemies to the dogs) and the gruesome, paranoid Filippo Maria, tried to regain their father's conquests, Milan's influence was eventually reduced to Lombardy.

Filippo Maria left no male heirs but he betrothed his wise and lovely daughter, Bianca, to his best *condottiere*, Francesco Sforza (1401–66). After Filippo's death the Golden Ambrosian Republic was declared by the Milanese, but it crumbled after three years, when Francesco Sforza returned peacefully to accept the dukedom. One of Milan's best rulers, he continued the scientific development of Lombard agriculture, navigable canals and hydraulic schemes, and kept the peace through an alliance with the Medici. His son, Galeazzo Maria, was assassinated, but not before fathering Caterina Sforza, the great Renaissance virago, and a son, Gian Galeazzo II.

Lodovico il Moro

It was, however, Francesco Sforza's second son, Lodovico il Moro (1451–1508), who took power and ran one of Italy's most sparkling courts, helped by his wife, the delightful Beatrice d'Este until her early death in childbirth. Lodovico hired Leonardo to paint the *Last Supper* and design engineering schemes and magnificent theatrical pageants. But Lodovico also bears the blame for one of the greatest political blunders in Italian history, when his quarrel with Naples grew so touchy that he invited Charles VIII of France to come and claim Naples for himself. Charles took him up on it and marched unhindered down Italy. Lodovico soon realized his mistake, and joined the last-minute league of Italian states that united to trap and destroy the French at Fornovo. They succeeded, partially, but the damage was done: the French invasion had shown the Italian states, beautiful, rich, in the full flower of the Renaissance, to be disunited and vulnerable. Charles VIII's son, Louis XII, took advantage of a claim on Milan through a Visconti grandmother and captured the city, and Lodovico with it. He died a prisoner in a Loire château, an unhappy Prospero, covering the walls of his dungeon with bizarre graffiti that perplexes visitors to this day. After more fights between French and Spanish, Milan ended up a province of Charles V's empire, ruled by a Spanish viceroy.

In 1712 the city came under the Habsburgs of Austria and, with the rest of Lombardy, profited from the enlightened reforms of Maria Theresa, who did much to improve agriculture (especially the production of rice and silk), rationalize taxes and increase education; her rule saw the creation of La Scala, the Brera Academy and most of central neoclassical Milan. After centuries of hibernation the Ambrosiani were stirring again, and when Napoleon arrived the city welcomed him fervently. With a huge festival Milan became the capital of Napoleon's 'Cisalpine Republic', linked to Paris via the new Simplon Highway.

The Powerhouse of United Italy

After Napoleon's defeat in 1814 the Austrians returned, but Milan was an important centre of Italian nationalist sentiment during the Risorgimento and rebelled against the repressive Habsburg regime in 1848. The city's greatest contribution during this period, however, was the novelist Manzoni, whose masterpiece *I Promessi Sposi* caused a sensation and instilled a sense of unity in a peninsula that had unravelled after the fall of Rome (*see* p.75).

After joining the new kingdom of Italy, Milan rapidly took its place as the country's economic dynamo, attracting thousands of workers from the poorer sections of Italy. Many of these workers joined the new Socialist Party, which was strongest in the regions of Lombardy and Emilia-Romagna. In Milan, too, Mussolini founded the Fascist Party and launched its first campaign in 1919. The city was bombed heavily during the war. In May 1945 Milan's own partisans liberated it from the Germans before the Allies arrived, and when Mussolini's corpse was hung up in the Piazzale Loreto the Milanese turned out to make sure that the duke of delusion was truly dead before beginning to rebuild their battered city on more solid ground.

Milan became, again, *the* centre of Italy's postwar economic miracle when it took off in the late fifties, drawing in still more thousands of migrants from the south. Despite a few hiccups, its wealth has continued to grow steadily ever since, while its political affairs were dominated from the seventies onwards by the Socialists and their ineffable boss Bettino Craxi.

Since the beginning of the 1990s, however, as anyone exposed to any of the Italian media has not been allowed to forget for even one minute, the whole structure has come crashing down, for it was in Milan, too, that the first allegations of the large-scale taking of *tangenti* (bribes) came to light, initially involving the Socialists, although the mud later spread to touch all the established parties. Craxi and his cronies have disappeared from the political map (Craxi disappeared from Italy altogether, and is holed up in Tunisia) and power in Milan is now disputed between a left/green alliance and Umberto Bossi's Lega Nord.

Getting There

The transport hub of northern Italy, Milan is well served by two international **airports**, several **train stations** and many long-distance **coach** services. Milan's expanding Metro network is, as well as one of the quickest means of getting from A to B, a very useful orientation aid, and stops (indicated Ⓜ) are listed in the text below.

from the airport

Milan's airports, **Linate** (8km from the centre) and the larger **Malpensa** (50km to the west), both receive national and international flights. As a rule, intercontinental flights use Malpensa while Linate handles most of the European and domestic traffic—but check. For flight information for both airports, call ✆ 02 7485 2200. STAM buses (*L4500*) run every 20mins between Linate and the Stazione Centrale (*5.40am–7pm*). City bus 73 (*L1500*) also runs to Linate from Piazza San Babila (Ⓜ *1*).

Air Pullman bus shuttles (✆ 02 4009 9260) link Malpensa to the Stazione Centrale and Linate in about an hour (*approximately once an hour 7am–10.15pm; L13,000*). A second shuttle bus runs from Piazza Castello and goes by way of the Trade Fair during exhibitions (*hourly 7.30am–12.30pm*). Beware that taxis from Malpensa to Milan cost a bomb.

Charters may use a third airport, **Orio al Serio**, by Bergamo, ✆ 035 326 325. STAB buses ✆ 035 318 472 (they're harmless, really) link it to Milan's Stazione Centrale (*L15,000*) and vice versa, leaving Stazione Centrale 3 hours before each charter flight.

by rail

Milan's splendiferous **Stazione Centrale** (Ⓜ *2 and 3*), designed in the 1930s with the travelling Fascist satrap in mind, dominates Piazza Duca d'Aosta northeast of the centre. Centrale (switchboard ✆ 02 63711) handles nearly all international trains, as well as most domestic routes.

Useful trams and buses from Centrale include tram 1 to Piazza Scala and Stazione Nord, and 33 to Stazione Garibaldi and the Cimitero Monumentale; bus 60 goes to Piazza del Duomo and Castello Sforzesco and bus 65 runs down Corso Buenos Aires, Corso Venezia and through the centre to Corso Italia. The **Left Luggage** is open 24 hours a day; **Lost and Found**, ✆ 02 6371 2667.

Stazione Garibaldi (Ⓜ *2*) is the terminus for car-train services, as well as trains for Pavia, Monza, Varese, Como and Bergamo. **Stazione Lambrate** (Ⓜ *2*), on the east side of the city, has connections to Genoa, Bergamo and towards the Simplon Pass. **Stazione Cadorna** (Ⓜ *Cadorna*) is the main station of Lombardy's regional Milan Nord railway (✆ 02 7202 2343), with connections to Como, Varese, Saronno, Erba and Laveno (Lake Maggiore).

by coach

Inter-city coaches arrive in the Piazza Castello (Ⓜ *Cairoli*). Contact the tourist office (*see* below) for information on destinations, schedules and prices.

Getting Around

Even though Milan looks like a bloated amoeba on the map, the city marks its age in rings, like a tree, and most of its sights are in the walkable innermost ring, the *Cerchia dei Navigli*. It's not difficult to find your way around—unless you've brought a car: the one-way system, no traffic zones and expensive parking make driving very unfun.

by bus and tram

The buses and dashing Art Deco trams and trolleys run by the Milan transport authority (ATM, ✆ 02 8901 0797) are convenient and their routes well-marked. Purchase **tickets** (L1500, or carnets of 10 tickets, L14,000) at tobacco shops, newsstands, metro stations or in the coin-gobbling machines at the main stops, and stamp them on board; a ticket is valid for 75 minutes' travel anywhere, regardless of how many transfers you make. Most bus routes run from about 6am to midnight, after which time special night bus routes operate with reasonable frequency.

Metro Line 1
(Red)

Metro Line 1
(Red)

V. LUIGI NONO

Cimitero
Monumentale

VIA PROCACCINI

VIA PAOLO SARPI

CORSO SEMPIONE

VIA CANONICA

VIA B. COLLEONI

VIA MELZI

V. EGINARDO

Fiera
Campignaria

Piazza VI
Febbraio

VIA BERTANI

V. BOEZIO

Piazza
Papa
Giovanni XXIII

VIA CANOVA

Piazza
Sempione

Arco
della Pace

Arena

V. BERENGARIO

VIA CASSIODORO

VIA VINCENZO MONTI

Parco

Civici Musei
d' Arte e
Pinacoteca
Sempione

VLE. EZIO

V. ROSSETTI

VIA PAGANO

Palazzo
dell' Arte

VIA MONTE ROSA

AMENDOLA FIERA

VIA TIZIANO

M

BUONARROTI

Castello
Sforzesco

M

VIA MASCHERONI

Largo
R. Zandonai

Piazza
Castello

BUONARROTI

M

Stazione
Nord

M

VIA M.

VIA GIOTTO

PAGANO

Stazione
Nord

Piazzale
Cadorna

DE ANGELI

M

V. R. SANZIO

WAGNER

M

Piazza
Conciliazione

M

CONCILIAZIONE

Santa Maria delle Grazie
(The Last Supper)

CADORNA

M

Piazza
Piemonte

CORSO VERCELLI

CORSO MAGENTA

Monestero
Maggiore/
Civico Museo
Archeologico

V. CIMAROSA

VIA DI P.TA VERCELLINA

VIA S. VITTORE

VIA G. CARDUCCI

VIA CAPPUCCIO

VIA G. B. VICO

Museo della Scienze
e della Tecnica

Sant' Ambrogio

VIA PAOLO GIOVIO

S. AMBROGIO

M

VIA OLONA

DE AMICIS

VIA G. WASHINGTON

Piazzale
Aquileja

V. ARIBERTO

VIALE PAPIANIANO

S. AGOSTINO

M

CORSO PORTA GENOVA

VIA VINCENZO FOPPA

Parco
Solari

VIA A. SOLARI

VIALE GORIZIA

G. D'ANNUNZIO

VIA SAVONA

Naviglio Pavese

Piazza
XXIV
Maggio

Stazione
Porta
Genova

M

PORTA GENOVA F. S.

NAVIGLIO GRANDE

RIPA DI PORTA TICINESE

to Autostrada A7

N

Milan

1/2km
1/2 mile

Metro Line 2
(Green)

If you plan to be riding around a fair bit, buy a one-day pass (L5000), or two-day pass (L9000), valid for buses, trams and the Metro. The ATM also publishes a very useful map showing all the bus routes and metro stops, the *Guida Rete dei Trasporti Pubblici*, available at the tourist office and the Stazione Centrale.

by Metro

The **Metropolitana Milanese** (Ⓜ) is well run, and a boon for the bewildered tourist. There are three lines: Red (Ⓜ*1*), Green (Ⓜ*2*) and Yellow (Ⓜ*3*). The Metro is open from 6am to midnight, and tickets are the same as those used for the buses and trams.

by taxi

Milanese taxis are yellow (but soon to be white) and their drivers generally honest and reliable. If it's not possible to flag a free cab down they can be found waiting at ranks in Piazza del Duomo, by the Stazione Centrale, and in other central piazzas. Alternatively, book a taxi on ✆ 02 8585, ✆ 02 6767 or ✆ 02 5353.

by car

Driving in Milan requires chutzpah, luck and good navigation skills. One-way streets are the rule, signs are confusing, parking impossible, and bringing a vehicle into the city centre between 7am and 7pm is illegal *unless* you have a foreign number plate. If you must bring a car into the centre, look for ATM car parks on the outskirts, or dump your car in one of the large parking lots at the *termini* of the metro lines.

Tourist Information

The main tourist office is in Piazza del Duomo on Via Marconi 1, ✆ 02 7252 4300, ✉ 02 7252 4360 (*open Mon–Fri 8.30am–8pm, Sat 9–1 and 2–7, Sun 9–1 and 2–5*). It has a branch office at the Stazione Centrale (*open Mon–Sat 8am–7pm, Sun 9–12.30 and 1.30–6*). Both will make free hotel reservations on the spot and provide good city maps and other practical information. **Tourist SOS**: Via Adige 11, ✆ 02 545 6551.

Piazza del Duomo

In the exact centre of Milan towers its famous **Duomo**, a monument of such imposing proportions (third largest in the world after St Peter's and Seville Cathedral) that on clear days it is as visible from the distant Alps as the Alps are visible from its dome. Bristling with 135 spires, defended by 2244 marble saints and one cheeky sinner (Napoleon, who crowned himself King of Italy here in 1805), guarded by 95 leering gargoyles, energized by sunlight pouring through the largest stained-glass windows in Christendom, Milan Cathedral is a remarkable bulwark of the faith. And yet for all its monstrous size, for all the hubbub of its busy piazza, traversed daily by tens of thousands of Milanese, the Duomo is utterly ethereal, a rose-white vision of pinnacles and tracery woven by angels. In Vittorio de Sica's *Miracle in Milan* (1950) it serves its natural role as a stairway (or rather launching pad) to heaven for the broomstick-riding heroes.

Gian Galeazzo Visconti began the Duomo in 1386 as a votive offering to the Mother of God, hoping that she would favour him with an heir. His prayers for a son were answered in the form of Giovanni Maria, a loathsome degenerate assassinated soon after he attained power; as the Ambrosiani have wryly noted, the Mother of God got the better of the deal. For, along with the money to build the church, Gian Galeazzo threw in the Candoglia quarries (source of the fine marble still used by the Cathedral Building company) and hired the finest architects and masons of the day, including the masters of Campione of Lake Lugano. However, before the cathedral was completed, the Gothic style—which the Italians never liked much to begin with—had become unfashionable, and the bewildered façade went through a Renaissance and a Baroque stage, then back to Gothic, with the end result, completed in 1809 under Napoleon's orders, resembling a shotgun wedding of Isabelline Gothic with Christopher Wren. In the 1880s there were plans to tear it down and start again, but no one had the heart, and the Milanese have become used to it. The subjects of the bas-reliefs on the bronze doors, all cast in this century, are a Milanese history lesson: the Edict of Constantine, the Life of St Ambrose, the city's quarrels with Barbarossa, and the history of the cathedral itself. To see what the original builders were about, walk around to the glorious Gothic **apse**.

The remarkable dimensions of the interior challenge the eyes to take in what at first seems like infinity captured under a canopy. Its tremendous volume is defined into five aisles by 52 pillars of titanic dimensions, crowned by rings of niches and statues, and is dazzlingly lit by acres of stained glass; the windows of the apse, embellished with flamboyant Gothic tracery, are among the most beautiful anywhere. In them you can see the mysterious alchemical symbol adopted as the Visconti crest, and now the symbol of the city: a twisting serpent in the act of swallowing a man.

All other decorations seem rather small afterthoughts, but you may want to seek out in the right transept Leoni's fine Mannerist tomb of Gian Giacomo de' Medici, better known as *Il Medeghino*, the pirate of Lake Como—erected by his brother Pope Pius IV. Near Il Medeghino's tomb is the most disconcerting of the cathedral's thousands of statues: that of San Bartolomeo being flayed alive, with an inscription saying that it was made by Marco Agrate and not by Praxiteles, just in case you were confused. Other treasures include the 12th-century Trivulzio Candelabrum, by Nicola da Verdun, as well as ivory, gold and silverwork in the Treasury, located by the crypt, where St Charles Borromeo (nephew of Il Medeghino) lies in state. Near the entrance of the cathedral is a door leading down to the **baptistry of St Ambrose** (*open daily 9.45–12.45 and 2–5.45; adm*), excavated in the 1960s, containing the octagonal font where the good bishop baptized St Augustine.

For a splendid view of Milan, take a walk through the enchanted forest of spires and statues on the **cathedral roof** (*open daily 9–5.30; steps or lift from outside the cathedral; adm*). The 15th-century dome by Amadeo, topped by the main spire with the gilt statue of *La Madonnina* (who at 14ft tall, really isn't as diminutive as she seems 300ft from the ground), offers the best view of all—on a clear morning all the way to the Matterhorn.

Palazzo Reale and Museo del Duomo

On the south side of the cathedral, the Palazzo Reale was for centuries the headquarters of Milan's rulers, from the Visconti down to the Austrian governors, who had the place redone in their favourite neoclassical style. In one wing, the **Museo del Duomo** (*open Tues–Sun 9.30–12.30 and 3–6; adm*) contains art and artefacts made for the cathedral, including some of the original stained glass and fine 14th-century French and German statues and gargoyles, tapestries, and a Tintoretto. Other rooms document the cathedral's construction, including a magnificent wooden model from 1519 and designs from the 1886 competition for the façade.

In the main core of the Palazzo Reale is the **Civíco Museo dell'Arte Contemporanea (CIMAC)** (*open Tues–Sun 9.30–5.30*). The concentration is on 20th-century Italian art, with early works by the futurists (especially Boccioni), as well as others by Modigliani, de Chirico, Morandi, de Pises, Melotti, Carrà, and current artists like Tancredi and Novelli; Kandinsky, Mondrian, Matisse, Picasso and Klee also check in. Behind the palace, on Via Palazzo Reale, note the beautiful 14th-century **campanile di San Gottardo**, formerly belonging to the palace chapel. The porticoes around Piazza del Duomo are occupied by some of the city's oldest bars; in the centre of the square Vittorio Emanuele II on his horse looks ready to charge into action.

The Galleria and La Scala

The king lent his name to Milan's majestic drawing room, the **Galleria Vittorio Emanuele**, a glass-roofed arcade linking Piazza del Duomo and Piazza della Scala. It was designed by Giuseppe Mengoni, who tragically slipped and fell from the roof the day before its inauguration in 1878. Here are more elegant bars (especially **Salotto**, serving perhaps Milan's best coffee) and some of the city's finest shops. In the centre, under a marvellous 157ft glass dome, is a mosaic figure of Taurus; the Milanese believe it's good luck to step on the bull's testicles.

Piazza della Scala, of course, is the address of one of the world's great opera houses, the **Teatro alla Scala**, its name derived from the demolished church of Santa Maria alla Scala. Inaugurated in 1778 with Salieri's *Europa Riconosciuta*, La Scala saw the premieres of most of the 19th-century classics of Italian opera; when bombs smashed it in 1943, it was rebuilt as it was in three years, reopening under the baton of its great conductor Arturo Toscanini. The **Museo Teatrale alla Scala** (*open June–Oct daily 9–12.30 and 2–5.30; Nov–May Mon–Sat only; adm*), entered through a door on the left, has an excellent collection of opera memorabilia (especially on Verdi) including scores, letters, portraits and photos of legendary stars, and set designs; there's even a section related to ancient Greek and Roman drama. From the museum you can look into the beautiful 2800-seat theatre, with its great chandelier; try to imagine the scene in 1859, when the crowded house at a performance of Bellini's *Norma* took advantage of the presence of the Austrian governor to join in the rousing war chorus.

An unloved 19th-century statue of Leonardo stands in the middle of the Piazza della Scala, while opposite the theatre the imposing **Palazzo Marino** is a fine 16th-century building hiding behind a 19th-century façade; now the Palazzo Municipale, it has one of the city's loveliest courtyards. A few steps away, on Via Catena, the unusual 1565 **Casa degli Omenoni** was built by sculptor Leone Leoni for his retirement, and is held up by eight uncomfortable telamones; around the corner of cobblestoned Piazza Belgiojoso, at Via Morone 1, the handsome old home of Alessandro Manzoni (1785–1873) is now a shrine, the **Museo Manzoniano** (*open Tues–Fri 9–12 and 2–4*), filled with items relating to the novelist's life and *I Promessi Sposi*, and an autographed portrait of his friend Goethe.

Museo Poldi-Pezzoli

In front of La Scala runs one of Milan's busiest and most fashionable boulevards, **Via Manzoni**. Verdi lived for years and died in a room in the Grand Hotel (No.29); at No.10 is the lovely 17th-century palace of Gian Giacomo Poldi-Pezzoli, who rearranged his home to fit his fabulous art collection, then willed it to the public in 1879. Repaired after bomb damage in the war, the **Museo Poldi-Pezzoli** (*open Tues–Sun 9.30–12.30 and 2.30–6, Sat till 7.30; April–Sept closed Sun pm; adm*) houses an exquisite collection of 15th- to 18th-century paintings, including one of Italy's best-known portraits, the 15th-century *Portrait of a Young Woman* by Antonio Pollaiuolo, depicting an ideal Renaissance beauty. She shares the elegant Salone Dorato, with the other jewels of the museum: Mantegna's Byzantinish *Madonna*, Giovanni Bellini's *Pietà*, Piero della Francesca's *San Nicolò* and, from a couple of centuries later, Guardi's *Grey Lagoon*. Other outstanding paintings include Vitale da Bologna's *Madonna*, a polyptych by Cristoforo Moretti and works by Botticelli, Luini, Foppa, Turà, Tiepolo, Crivelli, Lotto, Cranach (portraits of Luther and wife) and a crucifix by Raphael. The collection is also rich in decorative arts: Islamic metalwork and rugs—note the magnificent Persian carpet (1532) depicting a hunting scene in the Salone Dorato—medieval and Renaissance armour, bronzes, Flemish tapestries, Murano glass, sun dials, lace and more.

Via Monte Napoleone

Just up Via Manzoni is the entrance to Milan's high-fashion vortex, concentrated in the palace-lined **Via Monte Napoleone** and elegant **Via della Spiga**. Even if you're not in the market for astronomically priced clothes, these exclusive lanes make for good window-shopping and perhaps even better people-watching. It's hard to remember that up until the 1970s Florence was the centre of the Italian garment industry. When Milan took over—it had the airports Florence lacked—it added business savvy and packaging to the Italians' innate sense of style, creating a high-fashion empire rivalling Paris, London and New York.

There are three museums in the sumptuous 18th-century Palazzo Morando Bolognini, Via S. Andrea 6, between 'Montenapo' and Via della Spiga: the **Civico Museo di Milano** and the **Civico Museo di Storia Contemporanea** (*both open Tues–Sun 9–6*), the first with paintings of old Milan, the second devoted to Italian history between the years 1914 and 1945; the third, the **Civico Museo Marinaro Ugo Mursia** (*open Tues–Sun 9.30–5.30*) has a collection of nautical models, English figureheads, scrimshaw and mementoes, founded by a Milanese scholar obsessed with Joseph Conrad.

Near the intersection of Via della Spiga and Via Manzoni, the huge stone **Archi di Porta Nuova** are a rare survival of the 12th-century walls. Their moat was enlarged into a canal to bring in marble for building the cathedral; it was covered in the 1880s when its stench outweighed any economic benefit. (Bus no.96/97 from Piazza Cavour, makes the circuit of the former canal and the Castello Sforzesco, Santa Maria delle Grazie or Sant'Ambrogio.)

The Giardini Pubblici

From Piazza Cavour, Via Palestro curves between the two sections of Milan's Public Gardens. The romantic **Giardini di Villa Reale** (**Ⓜ** *Palestro*) were laid out in 1790 for the Belgiojoso family by Leopoldo Pollak, who later added the Villa Reale for Napoleon. The villa is now the **Civica Galleria d'Arte Moderna** (*open Tues–Sun 9.30–5.30*) where, at the time of writing, only the first floor (works by Picasso, Matisse, Modigliani, de Pisis, Tosi, Morandi and Renoir) and the Mariano Marini sculpture collection are open; Marini (*d.* 1980), the top Italian sculptor of the 20th century, spent most of his career in Milan, and in 1973 he gave the city many of his sensuous, acutely observed bronzes, as well as paintings and graphic works. When the rest of the gallery reopens, look for paintings by the self-consciously Romantic *Scapigliati* (the 'Wild-haired Ones') of Milan, Italian Impressionists, the Futurists and more. Other works are French: by Millet, Corot, Cézanne, Gauguin, Manet and Toulouse-Lautrec.

The **Giardini Pubblici** proper, a shady Arcadia between Via Palestro and the Corso Venezia, was laid out in 1782; artificial rocks compensate for Milan's flat terrain. A good place to take children, with its zoo, swans, pedal cars and playgrounds, it is also the site of Italy's premier Natural History Museum, the **Museo di Storia Naturale** (*open Tues–Fri 9.30–5.30, Sat, Sun and hols til 6.30*), near the Corso Venezia; another victim of the war, it has been rebuilt in its original neo-medieval style. Look out for the Canadian cryptosaurus, the Colossal European lobster, the Madagascar aye-aye and the 40-kilo topaz.

Corso Venezia itself is lined with neoclassical and Liberty-style palaces—most remarkably, the 1903 **Palazzo Castiglione** at No.47 and the neoclassical **Palazzo Serbelloni**, Milan's press club, on the corner of Via Senato. The district just west of the Corso Venezia was the city's most fashionable in the 1920s, and there are a smattering of rewarding buildings: the **Casa Galimberti**, with a colourful ceramic façade, at Via Malpighi 3, off the Piazza Oberdan; the good Art Deco foyer at Via Cappuccini 8; the eccentric houses on Via Mozart (especially No.11); and the romantic 1920s **Palazzo Fidia**, Via Melegari 2.

Lo Stile Liberty

'Liberty style' is the name given in Italy to Art Nouveau, the short-lived artistic and architectural movement that flourished in much of Europe around the turn of the century. It refers, curiously, to Liberty's, the London shop, whose William Morris-influenced, flower-patterned fabrics and ceramics were imported into Italy. The ethos behind the movement was an avoidance of architectural precedents, an embracing of 'naturalistic' ornament and smooth, flowing lines, and a desire to 'integrate' all the arts—hence the importance given not just to painting and fine art, but also to architecture and interior design. Decoration, an integral part of every work, was the key.

Liberty style was never as important in Italy as were its equivalents in France, Belgium, Austria or Catalunya—nor was it as extravagant—but it did for a time become the vogue among the newly wealthy middle classes of Italy's industrializing north. As the prosperity of this class grew in the 1900s, so too did demand for Liberty buildings and products—seen most notably in the hotels and villas around the lakes or Riviera. Perhaps the most important figure working in the style in Italy was Giuseppe Sommaruga (1867–1917), whose achievements include the Palazzo Castiglione, a pair of villas at Sárnico on Lake Iseo, and Hotel Tre Colli near Varese, characterized by their richly ornamental lines and an uninhibited use of space. In a similar more refined style is the architecture of Raimondo D'Aronco (1857–1932), who worked mainly on public buildings: his most famous work is the Palazzo Comunale in Ùdine.

Northwest of the Giardini Pubblici, **Piazza della Repubblica** has many of the city's hotels; the Mesopotamian **Stazione Centrale** (1931), blocking the end of Via Vittorio Pisani, is the largest train station in Italy. The nearby skyscraper, the **Pirelli Building**, is one that the Milanese are especially proud of, built in 1960 by Gio Ponti, while Pier Luigi Nervi designed the concrete structure. It's now the seat of Lombardy's regional government, and you can see most of the city from its terrace (call ahead, ✆ 02 67651). Further to the northwest, the Palazzo Martinitt houses the **Museo del Giocattolo e del Bambino**, Via Petteri 56 (Ⓜ *Lambrate; open Tues–Sat 9am–9.45pm, Sun 9–12.45 and 2.30–7.45; adm*), which has a beautiful display of toys dating back to 1700.

Brera and its National Gallery

Another street alongside La Scala, Via G. Verdi, leads into the Brera, one of the few old neigh-bourhoods to survive in central Milan. Although some of the old cobblestoned streets of Brera have maintained their original flavour (especially Corso Garibaldi), local trendies are busily turning the remainder into Milan's Greenwich Village, full of late-night spots and art galleries.

At the corner of Via Brera and the Via Fiori Oscuri ('Street of the Dark Flowers') is the elegant courtyard of the **Galleria Nazionale di Brera** (Ⓜ *Lanza* or *Monte Napoleone; open Tues–Sat 9am–9.45pm, Sun 9–12.45 and 2.30–7.45; adm; free on 1st and 3rd Sun, and 2nd and 4th Sat of each month; some sections may be closed*), one of the world's finest hoards of art. The collection was compiled by Napoleon, whose bronze statue, draped in a toga, greets visitors as they enter; a firm believer in centralized art as well as centralized government, he had northern Italy's churches and monasteries stripped to form a Louvre-like collection for Milan, the capital of his Cisalpine Republic, and threw open the doors in 1809.

Perhaps the best known of the Brera's masterpieces is Raphael's *Marriage of the Virgin*, a Renaissance landmark for its evocation of an ideal, rarefied world, where even the disap-pointed suitor snapping his rod on his knee performs the bitter ritual in a graceful dance step, all acted out before a perfect but eerily vacant temple in the background. In the same room hangs Piero della Francesca's last painting, the *Pala di Urbino*, featuring among its holy person-ages Federico da Montefeltro, Duke of Urbino, with his famous nose.

The Venetian masters are well represented: Carpaccio, Veronese, Titian, Tintoretto, Jacopo Bellini and the Vivarini, but especially Giovanni Bellini, with several of his loveliest Madonnas and his *Pietà*, and a joint effort with his brother Gentile of *St Mark Preaching in Alexandria*; there are luminous works by Carlo Crivelli and Cima da Conegliano; and several paintings by Mantegna, including his study in foreshortening, the *Cristo Morto*. Other works include *Christ at the Column* by Bramante, Caravaggio's *Supper at Emmaus*, the *Pala Sforzesca* by a 15th-century Lombard artist, depicting Lodovico il Moro and his family; a polyptych by Gentile da Fabriano; and fine works by the Ferrarese masters del Cossa and Ercole de' Roberti.

Outstanding among the non-Italians are Rembrandt's *Portrait of his Sister*, El Greco's *St Francis* and Van Dyck's *Portrait of the Princess of Orange*. When the Great Masters become indigestible, take a breather in the new 20th-century wing of the gallery, populated mainly by futurists like Severini, Balla and Boccioni, who believed that to achieve speed was to achieve success, and the metaphysical followers of De Chirico, who seem to believe just the opposite.

Brera's other principal monument is **San Simpliciano**, just off Corso Garibaldi to the north. Perhaps founded by St Ambrose, it retains its essential palaeo-Christian form in a 12th-century wrapping, with an octagonal drum. The apse has a beautiful fresco of the *Coronation of the Virgin* (1515) by Bergognone, and the larger of the two cloisters, from the mid 16th century, is especially charming with its twin columns.

Castello Sforzesco

Marking the western edge of the Brera quarter, the **Castello Sforzesco** (Ⓜ *Cairoli* or *Cadorna*) is one of Milan's best-known landmarks. Originally a fortress, the Visconti made it their base, and as a symbol of their power it was razed to the ground by the Ambrosian Republic in 1447. Three years later, Francesco Sforza rebuilt it; after air raids in the War damaged it and its treasures it was rebuilt again, this time disguising water cisterns in its towers.

Today it houses the excellent **Civici Musei d'Arte e Pinacoteca del Castello** (*open Tues–Sun 9.30–5.30*). The entrance, by way of a tower rebuilt on a design by Filarete (1452) and the huge Piazza d'Armi, is through the lovely Renaissance Corte Ducale, the Sforza residence. There are intriguing fragments of Milanese history—the equestrian tomb of Bernabò Visconti and a beautiful 14th-century monument of the Rusca family; reliefs of Milan's triumph over Barbarossa, and the city's gonfalon.

Leonardo designed the ilex decorations of the Sala delle Asse; the next room, the Sala dei Ducali, contains a superb relief by Duccio from Rimini's Tempio Malatestiano; the Sala degli Scarlioni contains the two finest sculptures in the museum, the *Effigy of Gaston de Foix* (1525) by Bambaia, and Michelangelo's unfinished *Rondanini Pietà*, a haunting work that the aged sculptor chiseled at off and on during his last nine years, repudiating all of his early ideals of physical beauty in favour of such blunt, expressionistic figures; the difference between this and his *Pietà* in St Peter's couldn't be greater.

Upstairs, among the Renaissance furnishings and decorative arts are the 15th-century Castello Roccabianca frescoes illustrating the medieval tale of Patient Griselda. The **Pinacoteca** contains a tender *Madonna with Child* by Giovanni Bellini, his brother-in-law Mantegna's more austere *Pala Trivulzio*, and the lovely *Madonna dell'Umiltà* by Filippo Lippi. Lombards, not surprisingly, predominate: Foppa, Solario, Magnasco (who spent most of his life in Milan), Bergognone (especially the serene *Virgin with SS. Sebastian and Gerolamo*) and Bramantino, with an eerie *Noli me Tangere*. There's a room of Leonardo's followers, and then the *Primavera,* by Milanese Giuseppe Arcimboldo (1527–1593), who was no one's follower at all, but the first surrealist—the Primavera is a woman's face made up entirely of flowers. From 18th-century Venice, Guardi's *Storm* looks ahead to another school—Impressionism.

The castle's third court, beautiful **Cortile della Rocchetta**, was designed by the Florentines Bramante and Filarete, both of whom worked for Francesco Sforza. The basement here is filled with an **Egyptian collection** and the **prehistoric collection** of items found in Lombardy's Iron-Age settlements, including 6th-century BC bronzes from the tomb of the warrior of Sesto Calende. The first floor houses a **museum of musical instruments**, with a beautiful collection of string and wind instruments, and a spinet played by Mozart. The **Sala della Balla**, where the Sforza danced, contains the *Tapestries of the Months* designed by Bramantino.

Parco Sempione and Cimitero Monumentale

Behind the Castello stretches the **Parco Sempione**, the city's largest, where you can find De Chirico's **Bagni Misteriosi** (Metaphysical Fountain); the 1930s **Palazzo dell'Arte**, used for exhibitions, especially the Triennial of modern architecture and design; the **Arena**, designed in

1806 after Roman models, where 19th-century dilettantes staged mock naval battles; and a triumphal arch, the **Arco della Pace**, marking the terminus of Napoleon's highway to the Simplon Pass. Originally intended to glorify Napoleon, the Austrians changed the dedication to peace. The **Casa Rustici**, Corso Sempione 36 (1931), designed by Giuseppe Terragni of Como on the proportions of the Golden Rule, is often considered Milan's finest modern building.

Further out (*tram 4 from Piazza Scala*), the **Cimitero Monumentale** (*open daily 8.30–5*) is the last rendezvous of Milan's well-to-do burghers. Their lavish monuments—Liberty-style temples and pseudo-ancient columns and obelisks—are only slightly less flamboyant than those of the Genoese, the Italian champs for post-mortem splendour. The cemetery keeper has guides to the tombs—Manzoni, Toscanini and Albert Einstein's father are here; the memorial to the 800 Milanese who perished in German concentration camps is the most moving.

West of the Duomo

Milan's greatest painting, Leonardo da Vinci's *Last Supper* (the *Cenacolo*), is in the refectory of the convent of **Santa Maria delle Grazie** (Ⓜ *Cadorna, then Via Boccaccio and left on Via Caradosso; open Tues–Sat 8–1.45 and 7–10, Sun 8–1.45 and 5–8; adm; expect a long queue*). The latest restoration of the fresco has just been completed, and visitors must pass through a sort of cleansing process, designed to protect the fragile image from any further deterioration. But before entering, get into the proper Renaissance mood by walking around the 15th-century church and cloister. Built by Guiniforte Solari, with later revisions by Bramante under Lodovico il Moro, it is perhaps the most beautiful Renaissance church in Lombardy, its exterior adorned with fine brickwork and terracotta. Bramante's greatest contribution is the majestic Brunelleschi-inspired tribune, added in 1492; he also designed the choir, the unusual crossing under the hemispherical dome, the sacristy and the elegant little cloister, all simple, geometric and pure.

The Last Supper

Leonardo painted three of his masterpieces in Milan, the two versions of the mystery-laden *Virgin of the Rocks*, and the *Last Supper*. The former two are in London and the Louvre; the latter would have been in Paris too, had the French been able to figure out a way to remove the wall. Unfortunately for posterity, the ever-experimental genius was not content to use proper, established fresco technique (where the paint is applied quickly to wet plaster) but painted with tempera on glue and plaster as if on wood, enabling him to return over and over to achieve the subtlety of tone and depth he desired.

The result was exceedingly beautiful, but almost immediately the moisture in the walls began its deadly work of flaking off particles of paint. Although it was considered a 'lost work' by the 17th century, various restorers have tried their hand at this most challenging task, with mixed success. In the Second World War the refectory was massively damaged by a bomb, and the *Last Supper* was only preserved thanks to piles of mattresses. Since 1977 restorers have been cleansing the work of its previous restorations, and stabilizing the wall; this process is now complete. Deterioration or no, the Last Supper still thrills. Painted at the moment when Christ announces that one of his disciples will betray him, it is a masterful psychological study, an instant caught in time, the apostles' gestures of disbelief and dismay captured almost photo-graphically. According to Vasari, the artist left the portrait of Christ purposely unfinished, believing himself unworthy to paint divinity; Judas was another problem, but Leonardo eventually found the proper expression of the betrayer caught guiltily unawares but still nefariously determined and unrepentant.

Monastero Maggiore and the Archaeology Museum

From Santa Maria delle Grazie, Corso Magenta leads back towards the centre; at the corner of Via Luini stands the Monastero Maggiore. The monastery's pretty 16th-century church of **San Maurizio** (*open Wed, Sat and Sun 9.30–12 and 3.30–6.30; closed June–Sept*) contains exceptional frescoes by Bernardino Luini, one of Leonardo's most accomplished followers. The former Benedictine convent (entrance at Corso Magenta 15) houses the city's Etruscan, Greek and Roman collections in the **Civico Museo Archeologico** (*open Tues–Sun 9.30–5.30*). As important as Milan was in the late Roman Empire (there's a model of the city inside), rela-tively little has survived the frequent razings and rebuildings. Other sections are Greek, Etruscan, Indian (from Gandhara), Goth and Lombard.

Sant'Ambrogio

Located just off San Vittore and Via Carducci (**Ⓜ** *Sant'Ambrogio*), the stern towers of the 12th-century gate, the **Pusterla di Sant'Ambrogio**, bristle, appropriately enough, with the armour, antique weapons and torture instruments of the **Museo della Criminologia e Armi Antichi** (*open daily 10–1 and 3–7.30; adm*). The Pusterla guards the last resting place of Milan's patron saint and the city's holy of holies, the beautiful church of **Sant'Ambrogio**. Founded by Ambrose himself in 379, it was enlarged and rebuilt several times (most notably by Archbishop Anspert in the 870s, when it became the prototype of the Lombard Romanesque basilica). Its current appearance dates from the 1080s.

The church (*open Mon–Fri 8–12 and 2.30–7, Sat and Sun 2.30–6*) is entered through a porti-coed **atrium**, which in 1140 replaced the original Carolingian paved court or *parvis*. It sets off

the simple, triangular façade with its rounded arches and towers; the one to the right, the Monks' Campanile, was built in the 9th century, while the more artistic Canons' Campanile on the left was finished in 1144. The bronze doors, in their decorated portals, date from the 10th century. In its day the finely proportioned if shadowy interior was revolutionary for its new-fangled rib vaulting; rows of arches divide the aisles, supporting the Matroneum (women's gallery). On the left, look for the 10th-century bronze serpent (the ancient symbol of health, or perhaps Moses' staff) and the richly sculpted **pulpit**, a masterpiece carved in 1080, set on an enormous late-Roman sarcophagus. The apse is adorned with 10th–11th-century mosaics of the Redeemer and saints, while the sanctuary contains two ancient treasures: a 9th-century *Ciborium* and a magnificent gold, silver, enamel and gem-studded **altarpiece** (835), both signed by 'Wolvinus magister phaber'. In the crypt below moulder the bones of Saints Ambrose, Gervasio and

Protasio. At the end of the south aisle the 4th-century **Sacello di San Vittore in Ciel d'Oro** ('in the sky of gold') contains brilliant 5th-century mosaics in its cupola and a presumed authentic portrait of St Ambrose.

After working on Santa Maria delle Grazie, Bramante spent two years on Sant'Ambrogio, contributing the unusual **Portico della Canonica** (entered from the door on the left aisle) and the two cloisters, now incorporated into the adjacent Università Cattolica; these display Bramante's new interest in the ancient orders of architecture, an interest he was to develop fully when he moved to Rome. In the upper section of the Portico is the **Museo della Basilica di Sant'Ambrogio** (*open Mon–Fri 10–12 and 3–5; closed Tues pm; Sat and Sun 3–5; adm*), housing illuminated manuscripts, the saint's bed, Romanesque capitals, ancient fabrics and vestments called the 'Dalmatiche di Sant'Ambrogio' dating back to the 4th century, tapestries, and frescoes by Luini and Bergognone. The 1928 **war memorial** in the Piazza Sant'Ambrogio was designed by Giovanni Muzio and inspired by Athens' Tower of the Winds.

Museum of Science and Technology

From Sant'Ambrogio, Via San Vittore leads to the Olivetan convent of San Vittore, repaired after the War to house the **Leonardo da Vinci Museo Nazionale della Scienza e Tecnica** (*open Tues–Sun 9.30–5, weekends til 6.30; adm*). Most of this vast and diverse collection, still arranged in its original 1950s format, is rather mysterious for the uninitiated, and if you're not keen about smelting and the evolution of batteries you may want to head straight for the **Leonardo da Vinci Gallery**, lined with wooden models and explanations of his inventions. Other rooms include musical instruments and displays on optics, radios, computers, clocks and astronomy; downstairs you can push buttons and make waterwheels turn. Another building is devoted to trains, and another to ships and naval history.

Milan's Financial District

For centuries, the area between Sant'Ambrogio and the Duomo has been the headquarters of Milan's merchant guilds, bankers and financiers, concentrated in the bank-filled **Piazza Cardusio** (Ⓜ *Cardusio*), Via degli Affari and Via Mercanti, just off Piazza del Duomo. Milan's imposing **Borsa** (stock exchange) in Piazza Affari was founded by Napoleon's viceroy Eugène de Beauharnais, and is now the most important in Italy. On Via Mercanti, the **Palazzo della Ragione** (1233), the old Hall of Justice, was given an extra floor with oval windows by Maria Theresa. On the side facing Piazza Mercanti, look for a beautiful early 13th-century equestrian relief; while facing Via Mercanti don't miss the bas-relief of a sow partly clad in wool, discovered when the foundations for the palazzo were dug. According to legend, a tribe of Gauls under their chief Belloveso defeated the local Etruscans in the 6th century BC and wanted to settle in the area. An oracle told them to found their town on the spot where they found a sow half-covered in wool, and to name it after her. The sow was duly found, and when the Romans conquered the Gauls, they translated the Celtic name into *Mediolanum*, 'half-woolly'.

The Ambrosiana

Still in the financial district, in Piazza Pio XI (off Via Spadari and Via Cantù), the Ambrosiana is Milan's most enduring legacy of its leading family, the Borromei. Cardinal Federico Borromeo (cousin of Charles) founded one of Italy's greatest libraries here in 1609, containing 30,000 rare manuscripts, including a 5th-century illustrated *Iliad*; Leonardo da Vinci's famous *Codex Atlanticus* and early editions of *The Divine Comedy* (*to arrange a visit, call © 02 8645 1436*).

After years of restoration, the Cardinal's art collection or **Pinacoteca** (*open Mon–Fri and Sun 10–6; adm*), housed in the same building, has recently been reopened. Although paintings have been added over the centuries, the gallery is essentially a monument to one man's taste—which showed a marked preference for the Dutch and for the peculiar, and ranges from the truly sublime to some of the funniest paintings ever to grace a gallery. Here are Botticelli's lovely *Tondo,* and his *Madonna del Baldacchino* nonchalantly watering lilies with her milk; a lovely portable altar by Geertgen tot Sint Jans, and the strange, dramatic *Transito della Vergine* by Baldassarre Estense.

Further along, an *Adoration of the Magi* by the Master of Santo Sangue is perhaps the only one where Baby Jesus seems properly thrilled at receiving the very first Christmas presents. A small room, illuminated by a pre-Raphaelitish stained-glass window of Dante, contains the glove Napoleon wore at Waterloo, a 17th-century bronze of Diana the Huntress, so ornate that even the stag wears earrings, and entertaining paintings by the Cardinal's friend Jan Brueghel the Younger, who put a pussycat in Daniel's den of lions. These are followed by more master-pieces: a *Page*, perhaps by Giorgione, Luini's *Holy Family with St Anne* (from a cartoon by Leonardo), Leonardo's *Portrait of a Musician*, a lovely portrait of Beatrice d'Este, and then Bramantino's *Madonna in Trono fra Santi*, a scene balanced by a dead man on the left and an enormous dead frog on the right. Challenging this for absurdity is the nearby *Female Allegory* by 17th-century Giovanni Serodine, in which the lady, apparently disgruntled with her lute, astrolabe and books, is squirting herself in the nose.

The magnificent cartoon for Raphael's *School of Athens* in the Vatican is as interesting as the fresco itself; the copy of Leonardo's *Last Supper* was done by order of the Cardinal, who sought to preserve the 'lost' work. A 16th-century *Washing of Feet* from Ferrara has one Apostle blithely clipping his toenails. Another room contains pages from Leonardo's *Codex Atlanticus*. The first Italian still-life, Caravaggio's *Fruit Basket*, is also the most dramatic; here too is Magnasco's *The Crow's Singing Lesson*. Further on, Titian's *Adoration of the Magi*, painted for Henri II of France, is still in its original frame.

San Satiro

On the corner of Via Spadari and busy Via Torino, a 19th-century façade conceals the remark-able church of **San Satiro** (officially Santa Maria presso San Satiro), rebuilt by Bramante in 1476, his first project in Milan. Faced with a lack of space in the abbreviated, T-shaped inte-rior, Bramante came up with the ingenious solution of creating the illusion of an apse with *trompe l'œil* stucco decorations. Bramante also designed the beautiful octagonal **baptistry** off the right aisle, decorated with terracottas by Agosto De Fondutis; to the left the 9th-century **Cappella della Pietà** is one of the finest examples of Carolingian architecture in north Italy, even though it was touched up in the Renaissance, with decorations by De Fondutis.

South of the Duomo: Porta Romana

This corner of Milan, the main traffic outlet towards the *autostrada* to the south, can be busy. Tram 13 will take you to **San Nazaro Maggiore** on Corso Porta Romana, a church that has undergone several rebuildings since its 4th-century dedication by St Ambrose. Its most original feature is the hexagonal **Cappella Trivulzio** by Bramantino, built to contain the tomb of the *condottiere* Giangiacomo Trivulzio, who wrote his own epitaph: 'He who never knew rest now rests: Silence.' Trivulzio did have a busy career; a Milanese who disliked Lodovico Sforza enough to lead Louis XII's attack on Milan in 1499, he became the city's French governor, then led the League of Cambrai armies in thumping the Venetians at Agnadello (1509).

On Corso Italia, another main artery south, **Santa Maria presso San Celso** (1490–1563) offers a fine example of the Lombard love of ornament. Within, beyond an attractive atrium, the interior is paved with an exceptional marble floor and decorated with paintings by Paris Bordone, Bergognone and Moretto; on the day of their marriage Milanese brides and grooms traditionally stop by to pray in the chapel of the Madonna. The adjacent 10th-century church of **San Celso** has a charming interior restored in the 19th century, and a good original portal.

South Milan: The Ticinese and Navigli Districts

Southwest of the centre, Via Torino leads into the artsy quarter named for the Ticino River, traversed by the Corso di Porta Ticinese (*tram 15 from Via Torino*). In the Ticinese you can find pieces of Roman *Mediolanum*, which had its forum in modern **Piazza Carrobbio**. There's a bit of the Roman circus on Via Circo, off Via Lanzone, and the **Colonne di San Lorenzo**, on the Corso: 16 Corinthian columns, now a favourite teenager hangout but originally part of a temple or bath, were transported here in the 4th century to construct a portico in front of the **Basilica di San Lorenzo Maggiore**. The oldest church in Milan, it acquired its octagonal form, encircled by an ambulatory and crowned with a dome, in the 4th century, predating the church it resembles most, San Vitale in Ravenna. Carefully spared by Barbarossa in the sack of Milan in 1164, it has since suffered severe fires, and in the 16th century, when it was near total collapse, it was rebuilt, conserving as much of the old structure as possible. Luckily, the beautiful **Cappella di Sant'Aquilino** (*adm*) has come down intact, with 4th- or 5th-century mosaics of Christ and his disciples, and an early Christian sarcophagus.

A green walkway, the Parco delle Basiliche, links San Lorenzo to the **Basilica di Sant' Eustorgio**, rebuilt in 1278 along the lines of Sant'Ambrogio, with a lofty campanile (1309). The pillars along the naves are crowned with good capitals, and the chapels, added in the 15th century, are finely decorated; one is dedicated to the Magi, where a Roman sarcophagus held the relics of the Three Kings until Frederick Barbarossa hauled them off to Cologne. The highlight of the church, however, is the pure Tuscan Renaissance **Cappella Portinari** (1468). Attributed to Michelozzo and often compared with Brunelleschi's Pazzi Chapel in Florence in its elegant cubic simplicity and proportions, the chapel is crowned by a lovely dome, adorned with stucco reliefs of angels. This jewel is dedicated to the Inquisitor St Peter Martyr (who was axed in the head near Lake Como in 1252), whose life of intolerance was superbly frescoed on the walls by Vincente Foppa and whose remains are buried in the magnificent marble *Arca di San Pietro Martire* (1339) by the Pisan Giovanni di Balduccio. Balduccio also added the relief of saints on the nearby 14th-century **Porta Ticinese,** built in the Spanish walls.

The colourful Navigli district (**Ⓜ** *Porta Genova, tram 8 or 19*) is named for its navigable canals, the **Naviglio Grande** (linking Milan to the River Ticino, Lake Maggiore and the Candoglio marble quarries) and **Naviglio Pavese** (to Pavia) that meet to form the docks, or *Darsena*, near Porta Ticinese. Up until the 1950s Milan, through these canals, handled more tonnage than seaports like Brindisi, and, like any good port, the Navigli was then a funky working-class district of warehouses, workshops, sailors' bars and public housing blocks. Although some of this lingers, the Navigli is now a relaxed, fashionably bohemian zone, where many of the city's artists work, where the restaurants are cheaper and you can hear jazz in the night.

Most shops are closed all day Sunday, Monday mornings, and in August.
Food stores close on Monday afternoons.

Milan is Italy's best shopping city hands down, especially for clothes and everything else capable of being designed in one way or another. Italians have always liked to put on the dog, *la bella figura*; it's in their blood. The hype machine has turned this into a national obsession. After an hour of window-shopping, however, only a die-hard fashion slave would disagree with Walter Benjamin's 'Monotony is nourished by the new.' The **big sales** begin the second week of January and around 10 July.

the Quadrilateral

Missoni, Valentino, Armani, Laura Biagiotti, Versace, Byblos, Krizia, Luciano Soprani, Dolce e Gabbana, Alberta Ferretti, Ferragamo, Prada, Gucci, Chanel, Helmut Lang, Fendi, Ferre, Gigli, Krizia, Moschino—you'll find them all in the Quadrilatero, defined by Via Monte Napoleone, Via della Spiga, Via S. Andrea and Via Borgospesso (Ⓜ *Monte Napoleone*). Nearly all the shops here have branch offices elsewhere in Milan and in other cities. You may just find the latest of the latest designs on Monte Napoleone, but be assured they'll soon show up elsewhere. The **jewellers** were actually here first, in the 1930s; have a look in the windows at **Buccellati** (No.4), considered by many the best jewellery designer in Italy, featuring exquisitely delicate gold work and jewels, each piece individually crafted. Other Quadrilateral shops worth a browse include **Lorenzi**, Monte Napoleone 9, the city's most refined pipe and male accessories shop. **Il Salumaio**, at No.12, has nearly every gourmet item imaginable.

the city centre

Besides the great Galleria Vittorio Emanuele, several minor *gallerias* branch off Corso Vittorio Emanuele, each a shopping arcade lined with good quality and reasonably priced shops. In Piazza del Duomo a monument almost as well known as the cathedral itself is Milan's oldest department store, **La Rinascente**; it's also the only one to have been christened by Gabriele D'Annunzio. The cafeteria on the top floor has great views over the cathedral. Other shops in the centre include **Guenzati**, Via Mercanti 1, which will make a velvet-lover's heart flutter. Near the Duomo, Via Spadari and Via Speroni are a food-shopper's heaven, beginning with the **Casa del Formaggio**, Via Speronari 3, where the best cheeses, from the most exotic to the most everyday, have been sold since 1894. **Rizzoli**, Galleria Vittorio Emanuele 79, is one of the city's best-stocked bookshops (with many English titles), owned by the family that founded the *Corriere della Sera*. In the Galleria del Corso, **Messaggerie Musicali** is one of the best in town for musical scores and recordings.The shops on busy Via Torino have some of Milan's more affordable prices, especially in clothes and footwear.

elsewhere in Milan

Brera offers some of Milan's most original shops and boutiques, as well as old standbys like **Surplus**, Corso Garibaldi 7, with a marvellous array of second-hand garments. On **Corso Buenos Aires** (Ⓜ *Lima*), one of Milan's longest and densest shopping thoroughfares, you can find something of every variety and hue; one unusual shop is **Le Mani d'Oro**, Via Gaffurio 5 (near Piazzale Loreto), which specializes in *trompe l'œil* objects and decorations. Another shopping street with excellent merchandise and reasonable prices is **Via Paolo Sarpi** (🚇 *Moscova*), formerly the city's Chinatown. For an excellent selection of books in English, try either **The English Bookshop**, Via Mascheroni 12, ✆ 02 469 4468 (🚇 *Conciliazione*), or **The American Bookstore**, Largo Cairoli, near the castle, 02 878 920 (🚇 *Cairoli*). If you're interested in the latest designs in furniture, Milan has a major concentration of showrooms and stores near the centre: well worth a look are **Artemide**, Corso Monforte 19; **De Padova**, Corso Venezia 14; **Dilmos**, Piazza San Marco 1; and **Alias**, Via V. Monti 2.

markets

The tourist office has a complete list of markets in Milan: most are open mornings from 9 to 1, with the exception of the huge **Saturday clothes markets** in Viale Papiniano (🚇 *S. Agostino*) and Via Osoppo (🚇 *Gambara*) that continue until 6pm. **Flea markets** include the Fiera di Senigallia in Viale D'Annunzio every Saturday from 8.30 to 5 (🚇 *S. Agostino*) and the Via Lorenzini market on Sunday mornings (🚇 *Lodi Tibb*). For **antiques**, there's the Mercatone dell'Antiquariato every last Sunday of the month, along the Naviglio Grande (🚇 *Porta Genova*), and the Mercato Antiquariato di Brera in Via Fiori Chiari on the third Saturday of each month (🚇 *Lanza*). On Sunday morning, a **postcard, stamp and coin market** is held in the Cordusio Arcade in Piazza Duomo (🚇 *Duomo*). Nearly all markets vanish in August.

Sports and Activities

A dip in one of Milan's public **swimming pools** can make a hot day of summer sight-seeing far more tolerable: two of the most convenient are situated in the **Parco Solari**, Via Montevideo 11 (🚇 *Sant'Agostino*), and the outdoor **Lido di Milano**, Piazzale Lotto 15 (🚇 *Lotto*). East of town, the **Parco dell'Idroscalo**, built around an artificial lake designed as a 'runway' for seaplanes in the 1920s, has a lovely complex of three pools known as Milan's Riviera (Viale dell'Idroscalo 1), reached by a special bus ID departing from San Babila. The **Luna Park** at Idroscalo has water slides and rides.

The best **golf** course in the Milan area is the **Golf Club Milano**, in the delightful Parco di Monza in Monza, a short distance north of the city (*see* p.201). A popular **bicycle excursion** from Milan is to pedal along the Naviglio Grande canal from the Darsena to the Ticino River (around 40km), passing by way of **Cassinetta di Lugagnano**, home of one of Italy's top restaurants (*see* p.198). Like the Venetians with their villas along the Brenta canal, the 18th-century Milanese built summer houses along the Naviglio. Only one, the 15th-century frescoed **Villa Gaia** in Robecco, is open—if you call ahead (✆ 02 947 0512). **Bicycles** can be rented for any period of time from Vittorio Comizzoli's shop, Via Washington 60, ✆ 02 498 4694 (🚇 *Wagner*).

Milan's two first-division football clubs, AC Milan and Inter, play on alternate Sundays during the September–May season at **San Siro** stadium, Via Piccolomini 5 (🚇 *Lotto*, then walk, or tram 24, or buses 95, 49 or 72). Tickets are available at the stadium or from Milan Point, Largo Corsia dei Servi 11, ✆ 02 782 768. For Inter matches you can also buy tickets at branches of Banca Popolare di Milano; for AC games from branches of the Banca Cariplo. American football (the 'Rhinos') and rugby are semi-professional and can often be seen at the **Giurati** sports centre. Milan has a good basketball team, which plays in the **Super Palatenda** sports facility on Via Sant'Elia.

In Milan you have the rather unappealing choice of paying a lot of money for an up-to-date modern room with no atmosphere, or paying less for a place where you may not feel very comfortable (or safe). Reserve in advance, because the exceptions to the rule are snapped up fast. Tourist offices (*see* p.182) provide a free hotel reservation service. In August much of Milan closes down, so it can be surprisingly easy to find a hotel. On the other hand, during the trade fairs (especially the fashion shows in March and autumn, and the April Fair) you may find no room at the inn.

luxury

*****Four Seasons**, Via Gesù 8, ✆ 02 77088, ✆ 02 7708 5000, is a beautiful hotel in a 17th-century monastery. The church is the lobby, breakfast is served in the refectory, and most of the spacious rooms (with enormous bathrooms) look over the cloister; there are great plush sofas around the blazing fire in winter; private garage.

*****Principe di Savoia**, Piazza della Repubblica 17, ✆ 02 6230, ✆ 02 659 5838, is the most elegant and prestigious of the CIGA hotels, originally built in 1927 and lavishly decorated. It is designed to please even the most demanding clients—when Margaret Thatcher and Jerry Lewis visited Milan, they stayed here. The hotel has its own airport bus and divine restaurant.

*****Grand Hotel et de Milan**, Via Manzoni 29, ✆ 02 723 141, ✆ 02 8646 0861, has been a favourite with everyone from Verdi to Hemingway since it opened in 1863. Nowadays the Grand is the headquarters of Naomi Campbell (whose favoured suite is decorated with Duchess of Windsor memorabilia) and Kate Moss. Rooms are furnished with antiques, and the atmosphere is grand and gracious.

very expensive

****Cavour**, Via Fatebenefratelli 21, ✆ 02 657 2051, ✆ 02 659 2263, is an elegantly furnished hotel in the Brera, a few blocks from Via Monte Napoleone. The modern ****De La Ville**, Via Hoepli 6, ✆ 02 867 651, ✆ 02 866 609, located between the Duomo and La Scala, has antique furnishings and courteous service, comfortable lounges, a bar and excellent restaurant; great weekend rates.

****Diana Majestic**, Viale Piave 42, ✆ 02 2951 3404, ✆ 02 201 072 (Ⓜ *Porta Venezia*) is a fashionable, Liberty-style hotel built at the turn of the century, with charming rooms, a garden and a lovely breakfast buffet. ****Excelsior Gallia**, Piazza Duca d'Aosta 9, ✆ 02 6785, ✆ 02 6671 3239, near the Stazione Centrale, has hosted visiting potentates since it first opened in 1932. Spruced up with briarwood furnishings and oriental rugs, its rooms are spacious and elegant; the Health Centre offers Turkish baths and beauty treatments, and the Baboon Bar (it got the name during the War; ask how) is a mellow place to spend an evening.

expensive

***Ariosto**, Via Ariosto 22, ✆ 02 481 7844, ✆ 02 498 0516, has more character than most (and is conveniently close to Ⓜ *Conciliazione*). An early 20th-century mansion, it has a lovely little courtyard, overlooked by the nicer rooms. ***Ariston**,

Largo Carrobbio, ✆ 02 7200 0556, 🖷 02 7200 0914, at the south end of Via Torino, is an environmentalist's dream: 100% cotton futons, hydro-massage water-saving showers, recycled everything and ion-emitting machines in every room; there's a no-smoking floor and bicycles to borrow. *Closed Aug.*

★★★**Manzoni**, Via Spirito Santo 20, ✆ 02 7600 5700, 🖷 02 784 212, is a pleasant hotel in one of the most privileged locations in Milan—on a quiet street in easy walking distance of Monte Napoleone and La Scala, with soundproofed rooms and a private garage. Book in advance. *Closed late-July–Aug.* ★★★**Soperga**, Via Soperga 24, ✆ 02 669 0541, 🖷 02 6698 0352, just east of the Stazione Centrale, is comfortable, soundproofed, and serves big breakfasts.

moderate

★★★**Gala**, Viale Zara 89, ✆ 02 6680 0891, 🖷 02 6680 0463, near Ⓜ *Zara*, is a fine moderate-sized hotel set in a quiet garden. *Closed Aug.* ★★★**Giulio Cesare**, Via Rovello 10, ✆ 02 7200 3915, 🖷 02 7200 2179, on a quiet street, is a decent, whole-some hotel with air-conditioning. ★★**Antica Locanda Solferino**, Via Castelfidardo 2, ✆ 02 657 0129, 🖷 02 657 1361 (*expensive–moderate*), an atmospheric 19th-century inn in Brera, is the most enjoyable at this price. All 11 rooms are different, though the baths are spartan; breakfast is brought to your room. Book well in advance. *Closed Aug.*

★★**London**, Via Rovello 3, ✆ 02 7202 0166, 🖷 02 805 7037, on a quiet street near Giulio Cesare and the castle: air conditioning, satellite TV and parking. *Closed Aug.* ★**Valley**, Via Soperga 19, ✆ 02 669 2777, 🖷 02 6698 7252, is a good budget hotel, a short distance from the Stazione Centrale, with comfortable rooms (some with baths).

cheap

★**Alba d'Oro**, Viale Piave 5, ✆ 02 7602 3880 (Ⓜ *Palestro*), 'the Golden Dawn', is small and safe; baths down the hall. ★**Casa Mia**, Viale Vittorio Veneto 30, ✆ 02 657 5249, 🖷 02 655 2228, is just north of the Giardini Pubblici (Ⓜ *Piazzetta Venezia*). ★**San Marco**, Via Piccini 25, ✆ 02 2951 6414, 🖷 02 2951 3243, has some rooms with bath (*moderate*); all have TVs (Ⓜ *Loreto*). ★**Speronari**, Via Speronari 4, ✆ 02 8646 1125, 🖷 02 7200 3178, just southwest of the Duomo, is adequate; rooms with bath cost a bit more. **Ostello Piero Rotta**, Via Salmoiraghi 2, ✆ 02 3926 7095, is Milan's modern youth hostel (near San Siro stadium and Ⓜ *QT8*). An IYHF card is required (can be bought on the spot). *Open all year 7–9.30 and 3.30–midnight; L26,000 per person per night, including breakfast; 3-bed room L90,000; maximum stay 3 days.*

Eating Out

You'll find some of Italy's finest restaurants in Milan, however, an average meal will cost you considerably more than it would almost anywhere else in Italy (but still less than in comparable London restaurants). Presume unless otherwise stated that all are **closed in August**; so few remain open that their names are listed in the paper. The best places to find cheaper restaurants are in the Ticinese, Brera and Navigli.

Saffron is Milan's fetish spice, and appears in most dishes *alla milanese*. The origins of its use go back to a Belgian stained-glass maker, working on the Duomo in 1574, who was called 'Saffron' by his fellows because he always sprinkled a bit of the stuff in his mixes to make the glass colours deeper and richer. The other glassworkers laughed and joked that he loved saffron so much that he would soon be adding it to his food. During the wedding of Saffron's daughter, his apprentice, meaning to play a prank, actually had the chef put saffron in the rice; everyone was astonished at the yellow concoction, but it was delicious, and the Milanese have been making their saffron *risotto alla milanese* ever since.

very expensive

Savini, in the Galleria Vittorio Emanuele, ✆ 02 7200 3433, is a bastion of Milanese tradition (since 1867), where you can try Lombard classics at the pinnacle of perfection: the often-abused *cotoletta* and risotto, and the earthy *cassoeula* and *ossobuco*. *Closed Sat lunch and Sun*. Another culinary bastion is **La Scaletta**, Piazzale Stazione Porta Genova 3, ✆ 02 5810 0290, the workshop of Italy's *nuova cucina* sorceress, Pina Bellini, who does exquisite things to pasta and risotto, fish and rabbit. Excellent desserts and wines finish off a truly memorable meal. Reserve. *Closed Sun and Mon*. **Peck**, Via Victor Hugo 4, ✆ 02 876 774, has meant the best in Milan for over a hundred years, either in its epicurean delicatessen at Via Spadari 9, or here at its modern cellar restaurant, which offers such a tantalizing array of delights that you hardly know where to begin. Their unctuous *risotto alla Milanese* is hard to beat. *Closed Sun and hols and 3 weeks in July, but open in Aug*. Elegant **Nino Arnaldo**, Via Carlo Poerio 3, ✆ 02 7600 5981, is the base of one of the city's most creative chefs: his pasta dishes are original and the limited dessert selection holds some real jewels—cinnamon ice cream and *zabaione*. *Closed Sat lunch and Sun*.

The **Antica Osteria del Ponte**, ✆ 02 942 0034, 20km from Milan along the Naviglio Grande in Cassinetta di Lugagnano, is a holy temple of Italian cuisine not to be missed by any serious gourmet, with heavenly dishes like ravioli filled with lobster and *zucchine*, fresh *foie gras*, cassata with pistachio sauce and perfect little pastries—nearly every dish based on Italian traditions. The décor is intimate and elegant. *Closed Sun and Mon*.

expensive

Aurora, Via Savona 23 (in the Navigli), ✆ 02 8940 4978, has lovely *belle époque* dining rooms and equally lovely Piemontese cuisine, with an emphasis on mushrooms and truffles, and a bewildering array of cheeses, although you might prefer the superb *tarte tatin*. Exceptional value, and lovely on summer evenings in the cool shade. *Closed Mon*. Pigs are trendy, and so is **Al Vecchio Porco**, Via Messina 8, ✆ 02 313 862, a pizzeria serving such delights as pizza with ricotta, tomatoes and olives, or the 'del Porco' with sausage, gorgonzola and egg. *Closed Sun lunch and Mon*.

moderate

Soak in the romantic old-world bistro atmosphere at **Ponte Rosso**, 23 Ripa Ticinese, ✆ 02 837 3132: the cuisine is simple but excellent. There's a fixed menu at lunch; at dinner choose from cannellini bean and radicchio soup, pasta with *zucchine* and saffron, or a scrumptious lemon tart. *Closed Sun*. Arrive early to avoid the queues at **Al Pont de Ferr**, 55 Via Ripa Ticinese, ✆ 02 8940 6277, to sample the smoked salami, and pigeon with mushrooms and polenta. *Closed Sat lunch, and Sun*. **Trattoria Toscana**, 58 Corso Porta Ticinese, ✆ 02 8940 6292, is a jolly place, with music and drinks in the garden; and gnocchi filled with ricotta, and swordfish with thyme. *Open till 3am. Closed Sat lunch and Sun.* Still in the Ticinese, **Trattoria all'Antica**, Via Montevideo 4, ✆ 02 837 2859, serves abundant simply prepared Lombard fare, with the freshest ingredients. *Closed Sun.* One of business Milan's secrets, **San Fermo**, Via S. Fermo della Battaglia 1, in the centre, ✆ 02 2900 0901, serves light, tasty economic lunches and affordable full dinners. *Closed Sun.*

cheap

Prize-winning championship pizzas, with a vast selection to choose from, are the speciality at **Da Rino Vecchia Napoli**, Via Chavez 4 (between Stazione Centrale and Parco Lambro), ✆ 02 261 9056; they also do good *antipasti*, gnocchi and fish dishes. Reserve. *Closed Sun lunch and Mon.* Another name in Milanese pizza lore is **Geppo**, Viale Brianza 30, ✆ 02 284 6548, with 50 to choose from, including a Milanese with saffron, rocket and porcini mushrooms (Ⓜ *Loreto*). *Closed Sun.* At lunchtime, the atmospheric **Osteria del Treno** (a former railway workers' club), Via S. Gregorio 46, ✆ 02 669 1706, has a good-value self-service that shouldn't be more than L25,000, although the excellent sit-down dinners are slightly dearer (Ⓜ *Lima*). *Closed Sat.* For vegetarian food, you can eat very well for around L20,000 at **Govinda**, 3/5 Via Valpetrosa, ✆ 02 862 417. *Closed Sun, and Mon lunch.* **Il Naviglio**, 5 Via Casale, ✆ 02 8940 0768, also serves good vegetarian food. *Closed Mon, and Tues evening.*

Entertainment and Nightlife

Check listings in the daily *Corriere della Sera*, and *La Repubblica*'s Wednesday *Tutto Milano* magazine. For clubs with live music check under the heading 'Ritrovi'; if you want to see a film in English, make sure it says *versione originale*. Other sources include the free *What's On in Milan* and *Milano Mese*, available at the main tourist office. **Tickets** are sold at the Virgin Megastore, Piazza Duomo 8; Ricordi, in the Galleria Vittorio Emanuele and Corso Buenos Aires 33; at La Biglietteria, Corso Garibaldi 81, and in a kiosk in Stazione Cadorna.

opera, classical music and theatre

For many people, an evening at **La Scala** is in itself the reason for visiting Milan. The season runs from 7 December, St Ambrose's Day, to mid-July; and mid-September through mid-November. For information on how to book by phone, ✆ 02 7200 3744; you can only order two tickets at a time. The tourist office in Via Marconi and the CIT office in the Galleria Vittorio Emanuele, call ✆ 02 863 701, have a certain number of tickets to sell to tourists. Finding a good seat at a moment's notice is all but impossible; ask your hotel's concierge, or show up an hour before the performance to see what's available; chances are it'll be a vertiginous gallery seat or standing room only.

More **classical music** is performed in the Giuseppe Verdi Conservatorio, Via del Conservatorio 12, ✆ 02 762 1101, or ✆ 02 7600 1854. *Closed July–mid-Sept.* The city sponsors **Renaissance and Baroque music concerts** in the church of San Maurizio, on Corso Magenta, and in San Marco, Piazza San Marco; *adm free or around L20,000*; the tourist office has programmes.

Milan is also the home of Italy's best theatre company, the **Piccolo Teatro**, Via Rovello 2, near Via Dante, ✆ 02 7233 3222. Founded after the Second World War and run for years by brilliant director Giorgio Strehler, the Piccolo is ideologically sound, with a repertory ranging from *commedia dell'arte* to the avant-garde. Tickets are priced low so anyone can go—but reserve as far as possible in advance. Sometimes the Piccolo performs at the much larger **Teatro Lirico**, Via Larga 14, near the Duomo, ✆ 02 809 665. The **Teatro Nazionale**, Piazza Piemonte 12, ✆ 02 4800 7700, puts on both plays and musicals. **Films** in English are shown regularly at the Anteo, Via Milazzo 9, ✆ 02 659 7732, Arcobaleno, Viale Tunisia, ✆ 02 2940 6054, and Mexico, Via Savona 57, ✆ 02 4895 1802.

jazz

Nearly all the jazz clubs are in the Navigli district, and the first three have restaurants as well. One of the best is **Scimmie**, Via Ascanio Sforza 49, ✆ 02 8940 2874, with diverse but high-quality offerings from Dixieland to fusion; in the summer the action moves to a canal barge. *Closed Tues.* The more informal **Capolinea**, Via Lodovico il Moro 119, ✆ 02 8912 2024, at the end of the no.19 tramline, has low prices and often excellent sessions; also check the listings for **Grillo Parlante**, Alzaia Naviglio Grande 36, ✆ 02 8940 9321. **Tangram**, Via Pezzotti 52, ✆ 02 8950 1007, schedules a mix of jazz, funk, rhythm and blues. *Closed Sun.* **Blues House**, 26 Via S. Uguzzone, ✆ 02 2700 3621, plays exclusively blues. *Closed Mon.*

cafés, gelaterie *and bars*

Milan has some good, lively bars that stay open late. The old rendezvous of artists and intellectuals in the twenties and thirties, **Jamaica**, Via Brera 26, is still open for business, as is another old bar, **Moscatelli**, Corso Garibaldi 93, an oasis for the fashion-weary.

Even the Milanese like to take an evening *passeggiata*, with a stop at the *gelateria*. Try the minuscule **Rossi**, Viale Romagna 23 (exquisite chocolates and tiramisù) (*closed Tues*); **Viel**, Foro Buonaparte 71, has the most surprising flavours (*closed Wed*); **Ecologica**, Corso di Porta Ticinese 40 (natural ingredients only) (*closed Wed*).

For a sophisticated drink try **Magenta**, Via Carducci 13 (near Ⓜ *Cadorna*), where models swan about in a young and trendy crowd. In the Navigli area two of the most popular bars are the **Grand Café Fashion**, Corso di Porta Ticinese, and **Cocquetel**, Via Vetere 14, with hundreds of cocktails. Homesick Brits will find heartier relief at the **Matricola Pub**, Viale Romagna 43, a Guinness-owned place with the black stuff on tap plus full pub lunches and 'English' breakfasts. *Closed Sun.* Another lively pub, **Pogue's Mahones**, Via Salmini 3, hosts occasional live Irish bands.

Brera's Corso Garibaldi/Corso Como area jumps at night: 'in' spots include **Atiemme**, Bastioni Porta Volta 15, in a former train station, with cocktails and music; nearby **Lollapaloosa**, Corso Como 15, is loud and Irish ; **Tropical Latino**, Corso Como 2, is loud and Mexican, with food, Mexican beer, and salsa. Arrive early to avoid queueing.

clubs and discos

The **club scene** in Milan, as in the rest of Italy, is often concerned more with appearance than having a good time. However, it is possible to discover some places where the emphasis is reversed—though you have to look hard. Generally, clubs open every day until 3am (though this is often extended at weekends), and the pricy admission fee entitles you to one free drink. At the time of writing, two discos are hot among fashion victims, models and designers: **Hollywood**, Corso Como 15. *Closed Mon.* **Shocking**, Via Bastioni di Porta Nuova 12. *Closed Sun.* The wonderful, bizarre and very chic **Plastic**, Viale Umbria 120, is small and shiny with a very eclectic clientele, drag-queen shows and fussy doormen; Thursday is gay night. *Open Thurs–Sat; adm.* Milan's foremost gay club, though, and the biggest in the country, is the often heavy **Nuova Idea**, Via de Castilla 30. *Open Thurs–Sun.* Another gay hotspot is **Sottomarino Giallo**, Via Donatello 2, with disco music for women only on Sat. *Closed Thurs.* Latin American sounds, live music, shows and dancing are on the evening menu at **Sabor Tropical**, 18 Via Molino delle Armi. *Closed Mon and Tues.*

Short Excursions from Milan

Monza

Only 15 minutes by train from the Stazione Porta Garibaldi, or 20 minutes by bus from Piazza IV Novembre, Monza is synonymous with the Italian Grand Prix, which is held in early September on the famous Monza race course. The course, built in 1922, lies in the heart of one of greater Milan's 'lungs', the beautiful Parco di Monza, formerly part of the Villa Reale of the kings of Italy. It includes the 27-hole **Golf Club Milano** as well as other recreational facilities in its acres and acres of greenery; the single sombre note is struck behind the 18th-century residence—an expiatory chapel built by Vittorio Emanuele III that marks the spot where his father Umberto was assassinated by an anarchist in 1900.

Monza itself is a pleasant if industrial town, once highly favoured by the Lombard Queen Theodolinda, who founded its first cathedral in the late 6th century after being converted from Arianism by Pope Gregory the Great. The present **duomo** on Via Napoleone dates from the 13th century, and bears a lovely if crumbling multi-coloured marble façade by the great Campionese master, Matteo (1390s), who also did some of the fine carvings inside. Theodolinda's life is depicted in a series of 15th-century frescoes near her tomb, honouring the good queen who left Monza its most famous relic, preserved in the high altar: the **Corona Ferrea** (Iron Crown of Italy) (*open daily 9–11.30 and 3–6.30, closed Mon; adm*), a crown believed to have belonged to the Emperor Constantine, named after the iron strip in the centre said to be one of the nails from the True Cross. In the old days, new Holy Roman Emperors would stop in Monza or Pavia to be crowned King of Italy, before heading on to Rome to receive the Crown of Empire from the Pope. The cathedral's precious treasury is displayed in the **museum** (*same hours; combined adm available*) and includes many objects that once belonged to Theodolinda: a processional cross given her by Gregory the Great, her crown and her famous silver hen and seven chicks, symbolizing Lombardy and its provinces.

Lodi

The southeast corner of the province of Milan, watered by the river Adda, is called La Bassa. La Bassa's main city, Lodi, was a fierce rival of Milan until the year 1111, when the Milanese ended the feud by decimating Lodi, leaving only the ancient church of San Bassiano intact; they then forbade the citizens of Lodi from returning. Even in the cruel and bitter period of inter-city rivalries Milan's treatment was unduly harsh, and in 1153 Lodi brought a formal complaint to the newly elected Emperor Frederick Barbarossa, hoping he would act as a referee. The emperor warned Milan to leave Lodi alone, and when the proud Ambrosiani mocked his threats he levied a terrible penalty, the brutal sacking of Milan. He also founded a new city of Lodi, but it showed its gratitude by joining Milan in the Lombard league as soon as the Emperor was safely back across the Alps—the first Italian city to learn that calling in foreign intervention was a Pandora's box best left closed. History, though, was to repeat itself over and over again before 1796, when another emperor, Napoleon, won an important battle over the Austrians here.

Besides the ancient church of **San Bassiano** in Lodi Vecchio (Old Lodi, 5km to the east), Lodi's greatest monument is its elegant Renaissance church of the 1490s, **La Incoronata**, containing paintings by Bergognone. It is located near the city's central arcaded Piazza della Vittoria, site of its Broletto and 12th-century Duomo.

Alfa Romeos and Saronno

Northwest of Milan, on the road and rail line to Varese, **Arese** has since 1910 been the home town of the *Associazione Lombarda Fabbrica Automobilistiche*, which became Alfa Romeo when Lombard magnates bought up the French Darracq manufacturer. Alfa, in turn, has recently been bought up by Fiat, but in Arese you can visit the six floors of the 'family album', the **Museo Storico di Alfa Romeo** (*ring ahead to visit, © 02 9339 2303*).

Further along towards Varese, Saronno is synonymous with *amaretto*, either in the cocktail glass or in the biscuits, but students of Renaissance art will recognize it at once for its **Santuario della Madonna dei Miracoli**, built by Giovanni Antonio Amadeo in 1498. The façade, with its trumpeting angels, was added in the 1500s by Pellegrini, while highlights in the interior include the dome's startling, innovative fresco, the *Concert of Angels* by Gaudenzio Ferrari (1534) and Bernadino Luini's frescoes in the chapel of the Madonna.

The Lombard Plain

The three provincial capitals of the Lombard plain are among Italy's most rewarding art cities: Pavia, the capital of the ancient Lombards and the region's oldest centre of learning, embellished with Romanesque churches and its famous Renaissance Certosa; Cremona, the graceful city where the raw medieval fiddle was reincarnated as the lyrical violin; and Mantua, the dream shadow capital of the wealthy Gonzaga dukes and Isabella d'Este.

Pavia

Pavia is a serious no-monkey-business town. It is one of those rare cities that had its golden age in the three-digit years, that misty half-legendary time that historians have shrugged off as the Dark Ages. But these were bright days for Pavia, when it served as capital of the Goths and saw Odoacer proclaimed King of Italy after defeating Romulus Augustulus, the last Roman Emperor in the West. In the 6th century the heretical Lombards led by King Alboin captured Pavia from the Goths and formed a state the equal of Byzantine Ravenna and Rome, making Pavia the capital of their *Regnum Italicum*, a position the city maintained into the 11th century; Charlemagne came here to be crowned (774), as did the first King of Italy, Berengar (888), and Emperor Frederick Barbarossa (1155). At the turn of the millennium the precursor of Pavia's modern university, the *Studio*, was founded, and among its first students of law was the first Norman Archbishop of Canterbury, Lanfranc, born in Pavia in 1005.

Pavia was the Ghibelline 'city of a hundred towers' and a rival of Milan, to whom it lost its independence in 1359. It was favoured by the Visconti, especially by Gian Galeazzo, who built the castle and founded the Certosa. It, with many other churches in the city, bears the mark of Pavia's great, half-demented sculptor-architect, Giovanni Antonio Amadeo.

Getting There

There are **buses** roughly every 45 minutes between Milan and Pavia, and this is also the best way to travel if you wish to visit the Certosa, some 8km north of Pavia. Buses arrive in and depart from Via Trieste, in the station-cum-shopping centre. Frequent **trains** link Pavia to Milan and Genoa, and there are less frequent services to Cremona and Mantua, Alessandria and Vercelli, and Piacenza. The train station is a 10-minute walk from the centre, at the end of Corso Cavour and Viale Vittorio Emanuele II.

Tourist Information

A couple of streets from the station, at Via Filzi 2, ✆ 0382 22156, ✉ 0382 32221.

The Duomo and San Michele

Through traffic has been banished from Pavia's core, which retains its street plan from the days when it was Roman *Ticinum*. The cardus (Corso Cavour) and the decumanus (Corso Strada Nuova) intersect by the town hall or **Broletto**, begun in the 12th century, and the **duomo**, a front-runner for the ugliest church in Italy. Begun in 1488, it owes its imposing design to Amadeo, Leonardo da Vinci, Bramante and a dozen others (proof that too many cooks spoil the broth), and its raw corrugated cardboard façade to an understandable lack of interest in ever finishing it. The last apses were added only in 1930.

Next to the cathedral, a stump recalls the singularly unattractive 12th-century **Torre Civica**, the sudden collapse of which in 1989 prompted serious attention to its more famous Pisan relation. From here, Strada Nuova continues down to the pretty **Covered Bridge**, a replacement for the original Renaissance model damaged in the last war. Off Strada Nuova, Via Maffi leads to 12th-century **San Teodoro**, where a fresco shows Pavia with its forest of towers and original bridge.

East of Strada Nuova, Via Capsoni leads to the Romanesque **Basilica di San Michele Maggiore**, founded in 661 but rebuilt in the 12th century after its destruction by lightning. Unlike the other churches of Pavia, San Michele is made of sandstone, mellowed into a fine golden hue, though the weather has been less kind to the intricate friezes that cross its front like comic strips, depicting a complete 'apocalyptic vision' with its medieval bestiary, monsters and human figures involved in the never-ending fight between Good and Evil. The solemn interior, where Frederick Barbarossa was crowned with the Iron Crown of Italy, contains more fine carvings on the capitals; the most curious, the fourth on the left, portrays the 'Death of the Righteous'. Along the top runs the women's gallery, while the chapel to the right of the main altar contains the church's most valuable treasure, a 7th-century silver crucifix.

The University and Castello Visconteo

The yellow neoclassical quadrangles of the **University of Pavia**, famous for law and medicine, occupy the northeast quadrant of the ancient street plan. First a *Studio,* it was officially made a university in 1361. In the 18th century Maria Theresa worked hard to bring the university back to life after scholarship had hit the skids, and financed the construction of the main buildings.

Three of Pavia's medieval skyscrapers or **Torri** survive in the middle of the university in Piazza Leonardo da Vinci; the roof in the Piazza shelters the crypt of the demolished 12th-century **Sant'Eusebio** church; nearby you can meet some of the university's 17,000 students at the Bar Bordoni, on Via Mentana. In Piazza San Francesco d'Assisi, northeast of the main university, the **San Francesco d'Assisi** was one of the first churches (1228) in Italy dedicated to the saint; it has an unusual façade, adorned with lozenge patterns and a triple-mullioned window.

At the top of Strada Nuova looms the **Castello Visconteo**, built in 1360 for Gian Galeazzo II, but partially destroyed in the Battle of Pavia on 24 February 1525 when Emperor Charles V captured Francis I of France, who succinctly described the outcome in a letter to his mother: 'Madame, all is lost save honour.' Three sides of the castle and its beautifully arcaded court-yard with terracotta decorations managed to survive, and now house Pavia's **Museo Civico** (*open Tues–Sun 10–12 and 2.30–4; Dec and Jan, July and Aug Tues–Sun 9–1 only*). The archaeological and medieval sections contain finds from Gaulish and Roman Pavia, as well as robust Lombard and medieval carvings and colourful 12th-century mosaics. The picture gallery contains works by Giovanni Bellini, Correggio, Foppa, Van der Goes and others.

San Pietro in Ciel d'Oro

Behind the castle, Via Griziotti (off Viale Matteotti) leads to Pavia's second great Romanesque temple, **San Pietro in Ciel d'Oro**, built in 1132 and named for its once-glorious gilded ceiling, mentioned by Dante in Canto X of the *Paradiso*. The single door in the façade is strangely off-centre; within, the **Arca di Sant'Agostino** is one of the greatest works of the Campionese masters, a magnificent 14th-century monument built to shelter the bones of St Augustine which were retrieved in the 8th century from Carthage by the Lombard king Luitprand, staunch ally of Pope Gregory II against the iconoclasts of Byzantium. Luitprand himself is buried in a humble tomb to the right, and in the crypt lies another Dark Age celebrity, the philosopher Boethius, executed by Emperor Theodoric of Ravenna in 524.

Outside the centre to the west (Corso Cavour to Corso Manzoni and Via della Riviera), it's a 15-minute walk to the plain, vertical, 13th-century **San Lanfranco**, containing the lovely *Arca di San Lanfranco*, sculpted by Amadeo in 1498, his last work (though Archbishop Lanfranc is actually buried in Canterbury); the same artist helped design the church's pretty cloister.

The Certosa di Pavia

'The greatest decorative masterpiece in all of Italy' as Jacob Burckhardt called it, the Certosa or Charterhouse of Pavia was built over a period of 200 years. Gian Galeazzo Visconti laid the cornerstone in 1396, with visions of the crown of Italy dancing in his head, and the desire to build a splendid pantheon for his hoped-for royal self and his heirs. Although many worked on the project (beginning with the Campionese masters of Milan cathedral), it bears the greatest imprint of Giovanni Antonio Amadeo, who with his successor Bergognone worked on its sculptural programme for 30 years and contributed the design of the lavish façade.

Napoleon disbanded the monastery, but in 1968 a small group of Cistercians reoccupied the Certosa. The monks live the same contemplative life as the old Carthusians, maintaining vows of silence. A couple, however, are released to take visitors around (*open in summer Tues–Sun 9–11.30 and 2.30–6; spring and autumn until 5; winter until 4; weekends are often very crowded*). If you arrive by the Milan–Pavia bus, the Certosa is a 1½km walk from the nearest stop, a beckoning vision at the end of the straight, shaded lane, surrounded by well-tended fields and rows of poplars, once part of the vast game park of the Castello Visconteo in Pavia.

Once through the gate and **vestibule**, frescoed by Luini, a large grassy court opens up, lined with buildings that served as lodgings for visitors and stores for the monks. At the far side rises the sumptuous **church**, a marvel of polychromatic marbles, medallions, bas-reliefs, statues and windows covered with marble embroidery from the chisel of Amadeo, who died before the upper, less elaborate level was begun. The interior plan is Gothic but the decoration is Renaissance, with later Baroque additions. Outstanding works include Bergognone's five saints in the chapel of Sant'Ambrogio (sixth on the left); the tombs of Lodovico il Moro and Beatrice d'Este by Cristoforo Solari; the beautiful inlaid stalls of the choir; and the tomb of Gian Galeazzo Visconti, all works of the 1490s. The old sacristy contains a magnificent ivory altarpiece (early 1500s) by Baldassare degli Embriachi, with 94 figures and 66 bas-reliefs.

From the church, the tour continues into the **little cloister**, with delicate terracotta decorations and a dream-like view of the church and its cupola, a rising crescendo of arcades. A lovely doorway by Amadeo leads back into the church. The **great cloister**, with its long arcades, is surrounded by the 24 house-like cells of the monks—each contains a chapel and study/dining room, a bedroom upstairs and a walled garden in the rear. The frescoed **refectory** contains a pulpit for the monks who read aloud during otherwise silent suppers.

Pavia ✉ *27100*   **Where to Stay and Eating Out**

Most people visit Pavia as a day trip from Milan, but you could do it vice versa to save money, although none of the hotels stand out. Next to the railway station, ★★★★**Moderno**, Viale Vittorio Emanuele II 45, ✆ 0382 303 401, 🖷 0382 25225 (*expensive*) is the most comfortable. Central ★★★★**Ariston**, Via A. Scopoli 10/d, ✆ 0382 34334, 🖷 0382 25667 (*expensive*) has a slightly more old-fashioned touch, with air-conditioning, for much less than you'd pay in Milan. ★★★**Excelsior**, Piazzale Stazione 25, ✆ 0382 28596, 🖷 0382 26030 (*moderate*) is also conveniently located. ★★**Aurora**, Via Vittorio Emanuele II 25, ✆ 0382 23664, 🖷 0382 21248 (*cheap*), near the station, has showers in all the rooms. The elderly but friendly ★**Splendid**, Via XX Settembre 11, ✆ 0382 24703 (*cheap*) has plenty of rooms, but all with hall showers.

Pavia is well-endowed with good restaurants. Specialities include frogs, salami from Varzi and *zuppa pavese* (a raw egg on toast drowned in hot broth). For excellent, innovative cuisine, eat at the small but chic **Locanda Vecchia Pavia**, Via Cardinal Riboldi 2, right under the cathedral, ✆ 0382 304 132 (*expensive*); its young chefs base the day's menu on what looks good in the market, with some surprising but delicious results like gratin of scallops and red mullet and truffle-filled ravioli. *Closed Mon and Wed lunch, and Aug.* Pavia's other temple of fine cuisine is **Al Cassinino**, Via Cassinino 1, © 0382 422 097 (*expensive*), on the Naviglio, just outside town on the Giovi highway. Done out in the style of a medieval inn, with rare antiques, dishes are whatever the market provides—try the fresh pasta with seasonal vegetables, or the pâté of sea bass and salmon. *Closed Wed and Christmas.*

Antica Osteria del Previ, Via Milazzo 65, © 0382 26203 (*moderate–cheap*), on the banks of the Ticino, is an old-fashioned place serving home-made salami, risotto with frog or radicchio and speck, and for *secondi* river-fish, frog and snails. *Closed Wed and lunch in summer.* The **Osteria del Naviglio**, Via Alzaia 39, © 0382 460 392 (*moderate–cheap*) has a vast selection of wines to be sampled with delicacies such as a *sformato* (a kind of hearty mousse) of potato and porcini or seasonal vegetables, or pappardelle with duck. Desserts are also excellent—try the sorbets or hazelnut *semifreddo. Closed Mon; open eves only.* In the 16th-century mill of the Certosa, **Vecchio Mulino**, Via al Monumento 5, © 0382 925 894 (*moderate–cheap*) serves up delicious food with ingredients garnered from the countryside—risotto with sweet peppers, tomato and oregano, crêpes filled with artichokes, and nearly every wine produced in Lombardy. *Closed Sun eves and Mon.*

Around Pavia: Lomello and Vigévano

West of Pavia and the Certosa lies the little-known Lomellina, a major rice-growing and frog-farming district, irrigated by canals dug by the Visconti in the 14th century. The feudal seat, **Lomello**, has some fine early medieval buildings, most notably a lovely little 5th-century polygonal Baptistry near the main church, the 11th-century Basilica di Santa Maria.

Also in the Lomellina is the old silk town of **Vigévano** (better known these days for its high-fashion shoes), the site of another vast castle of the Visconti and Sforza clans; it was the birthplace of Lodovico il Moro, and has been undergoing a lengthy restoration. Below it lies the majestic Piazza Ducale, designed in 1492 by Bramante (with help from Leonardo) as Lombardy's answer to Venice's Piazza San Marco. Originally a grand stairway connected the piazza to one of the castle towers; now the three sides are adorned with slender arcades, while on the fourth stands the magnificent concave Baroque façade of the cathedral, designed by a Spanish bishop, Juan Caramuel de Labkowitz. Inside there's a 15th-century Lombard polyptych on St Thomas of Canterbury, and a rich treasury (*open 3–5pm public holidays only, or upon request*), containing illuminated codices, Flemish tapestries and golden reliquaries.

Cremona

Cremona is famous for four things that have added to the sum total of human happiness: its cathedral, Claudio Monteverdi, nougat, and violins. It has been the capital of the last-mentioned industry since 1566, when Andrea Amati invented the modern violin from the medieval fiddle. Demand across Europe initiated a golden age of fiddle-making, when Andrea's son Nicolò Amati, and his pupils Stradivarius and Giuseppe Guarneri, made the best violins, ever. Walking around Cremona you can easily pick out the elegant curves and scrolls on the brick and terracotta palaces that inspired the instrument's baroque form, while the sweetness of the violin's tone seems to have something of the city's cuisine in it, not only nougat but *mostarda di Cremona*—candied cherries, apricots, melons and so on in a sweet or piquant mustard sauce. Today 50 *liutai* (violinmakers) keep up the tradition, using similar methods and woods (poplar, spruce, pear, willow and maple); a school and institute are devoted to the craft, and every third October (next in 2000) the city hosts a festival of stringed instruments.

Milan captured the once feisty *comune* of Cremona in 1344, and in 1441 gave the city to Bianca Maria Visconti as her dowry when she married Francesco Sforza. The city enjoyed a happy, fruitful Renaissance as the apple of Bianca's eye, producing Monteverdi, the father of opera, the prolific Campi family of painters, and Sofonisba Anguissola, the recently rediscovered Renaissance portrait painter admired by Michelangelo, Van Dyck and Philip II (who summoned her to work in Spain) for her ability to depict a sitter's soul.

Getting There and Around

Even Cremona's railway station is delightful: there are frequent **train** services from Milan (about two hours), Pavia, Mantua, Brescia and Piacenza, as well as three times a day from Bergamo. The station lies north of the centre, at the end of Via Palestro. **Buses** arrive at and depart from the bus station in Via Dante, next to the train station. Leave your **car** in the Via Villa Glori car park in exchange for free use of a bicycle.

Tourist Information

Piazza del Comune 5, ✆ 0372 23233, ✉ 0372 21722. If you're in the market for a violin or just want to visit a workshop, ask for their free list of *Botteghe Liutarie*.

Via Palestro to the Piazza del Comune

Cremona can be easily visited on foot, starting from the station and Via Palestro. Here, behind a remodelled baroque façade at No.36, **Palazzo Stanga Trecco**'s 15th-century courtyard is an excellent introduction to the Cremonese fondness for elaborate terracotta ornament. The **Museo Stradivariano**, nearby at No.17 (*open Tues–Sat 8.30–6, Sun 9.15–12.15 and 3–6; closed Aug; adm*), is an equally good introduction to the cream of Cremona's violins, featuring casts, models, items from the master's workshop and drawings explaining how Stradivarius did it. Just around the corner, the Palazzo Affaitati, Via U. Dati 4, (begun in 1561), houses a grand theatrical staircase added in 1769 and the **Museo Civico** (*same hours*), devoted to some amazingly dreary paintings by the Cremonese school (Boccaccino and the Campi family). The archaeology section includes a fine labyrinth mosaic with Theseus and the Minotaur (*c.* 2nd century AD) from the Roman colonia at Cremona; another section houses the cathedral treasury, with some fine illuminated codices and corals.

Via Palestro becomes Corso Campi, and at an angle runs into the boxy, Mussolini-era Galleria Venticinque Aprile, leading to **Piazza Roma**, a little park; here, along Corso Mazzini, is Stradivarius' red marble tombstone, transferred from a demolished church. Corso Mazzini forks after a block; near the split is Cremona's prettiest palace, the 1499 **Palazzo Fodri**, Corso Matteotti 17 (*now owned by the Banca d'Italia; ask the guard to unlock the gate*), with a court-yard adorned with frescoed battle scenes and terracottas.

Piazza del Comune: The Torrazzo and Duomo

Cremona's lovely medieval Piazza del Comune is seductive enough to compete in any urban beauty contest. By now you've probably caught at least a glimpse of the curious pointed crown of the tallest bell tower in Italy, the 370ft **Torrazzo** (*open April–Oct Tues–Sun 10.30–12 and 3–6; Nov–Feb Sat only 3–6; adm*). Only a bit shorter than Milan Cathedral, the Torrazzo was built in the 1260s, with battlements and bells, and a fine astronomical clock added in 1583 by Giovanni Battista Divizioli. The stout-hearted can ascend 487 steps to the top for an eye-popping view; the less ambitious can purchase a famous Cremona TTT postcard (Torrazzo, *torrone* and tits) to send home. The lower level houses a reproduction of a violin-maker's shop of Stradivarius' time, and in summer a man is on hand to show how it's done.

Linked to the Torrazzo in 1525 by the **Portico della Bertazzola**, the **duomo** is the highest and one of the most exuberant expressions of Lombard Romanesque, with a trademark Cremonese flourish in the graceful scrolls added to the marble front. Built by the Comacini masters after an earthquake destroyed its predecessor in 1117, the main door, the **Porta Regia**, is flanked by two nearly toothless lions, and four flat prophets, and crowned by a small portico known as the Rostrum, where 13th- and 14th-century statues of the Virgin and two saints silently but eloquently hold forth above a frieze of the months by the school of Antelami.

The cathedral was begun as a basilica, but as Gothic came into fashion it was decided to add the arms of a Latin cross; the transepts, especially the north one, are almost as splendid from the outside as the main façade. The interior is undergoing restoration, revealing primitive frescoes under opulent 16th-century works by Romanino, Boccaccino and Pordenone (who painted the *Crucifixion* under the rose window); the right transept has endearing sweet paintings on the ceiling and Flemish tapestries. Nervous reliefs attributed to Amadeo or Pietro da Rho decorate the pulpits, and the choir has exquisite stalls inlaid in 1490 by G. M. Platina, with views of Cremona and still lifes. In the crypt, with the tomb of Ombrono Tucenghi, patron saint of tailors (*d.* 1197), note the painting of old Cremona with its Manhattan skyline.

Completing the sacred ensemble in Piazza del Comune is the octagonal **Battistero di San Giovanni** (1167), with another pair of lions supporting the portico, and two sides of marble facing to match the cathedral. Across from the Duomo, the **Loggia dei Militi** (1292) was used as a rendezvous by the *comune*'s citizen militia; the outdoor pulpit between two of the arches is a relic of the charismatic medieval preachers like San Bernardino of Siena, whose sermons were so popular they had to be held outside.

Behind it, the lavish **Palazzo del Comune** (*open Tues–Sat 8.30–6, Sun 9.15–12.15 and 3–6; adm*) was begun in 1206 as the seat of the Ghibelline party and now serves as Cremona's town hall. To see are paintings salvaged from churches, a superb marble fireplace of 1502, and the **Saletta dei Violini**, with the town's collection, starring Stradivarius' golden 'Cremonese 1715', which retains its original varnish—as mysterious as the embalming fluids of ancient Egypt. Another of the master's secrets was in the woods; like Michelangelo seeking just the right piece of marble in the mountains of Carrara, Stradivarius would visit the forests of the Dolomites looking for trees that could sing. Other violins include 'Charles IX of France' by Andrea Amati, one of 24 violins commissioned in the 1560s by the French sovereign; the 'Hammerle', by Nicolò Amati (1658); Guarneri's 'Del Gesù' (formerly owned by Pinchas Zukerman); and his 1689 'Quarestini'.

Cremona

300 metres
250 yards

N

Station
Piazza Stazione
Bus Station
P
Piazza Risorgimento

VIA DANTE

VIALE TRENTO E TRIESTE

CORSO GARIBALDI

San Luca

VIA BERTESI

VIA G. FAERNO

Largo P. Sarpi

Palazzo Raimondi

Palazzo Stanga Trecco

VIA

Museo Stradivariano

Museo Civico

VIA U. DATI

PALESTRO

VIA A. MANZONI

VIA DEI MILLE

Palazzo Cittanova

Sant' Agata

CORSO GARIBALDI

Piazza Giovanni XXIII

VIA ASELLI

To San Sigismondo

Palazzo Trecchi

P

VIA VILLA GLORI

VIA MILAZZO

CORSO MATTEOTTI

Sant' Agostino

VIA PLASIO

CORSO CAMPI C. G. VERDI

Piazza Roma

Palazzo Fodri

CORSO MAZZINI

VIA G. DA CREMONA

Stradivarius' Tombstone

SOLFERINO

BOCCACC.

VIA CAVALLOTTI

Piazza Cavour

Palazzo del Comune

Torrazzo

VIA BOLDORI

Piazza del Comune

Duomo

VIA XX SETTEMBRE

Piazza della Pace

Battistero

VIA G. BONOMELLI

CORSO VITTORIO EMANUELE

Loggia dei Militi

VIA 11 FEBBRAIO

P

P

Teatro Ponchielli

Piazza Marconi

VIA TIBALDI

Piazza San Pietro

San Pietro al Po

VIA DEL GIORDANO

Back Towards the Station

Behind the Palazzo del Comune, Corso Vittorio Emanuele leads to the River Po. *En route* it passes one of Italy's earliest small-town stages, the **Teatro Ponchielli**, built in 1734 and rebuilt after a fire in 1808, named for Amilcare Ponchielli (*see* below) who premiered several of his operas here. A street to the right of the theatre leads back to Piazza San Pietro and **San Pietro al Po**, coated with 16th-century stuccoes and frescoes by Antonio Campi.

Cremona has several lofty churches with interiors that look like ancient Roman basilicas. One is the 14th-century **Sant'Agostino**, north of Corso Vittorio Emanuele, on Via Plasio. Its red-brick façade is adorned with terracotta decorations. There are good Renaissance frescoes by Bonifacio Bembo in the right aisle and a lovely *pala* of the *Madonna with Saints* (1494) by Perugino (*undergoing restoration at the time of writing*). Further up, Via Plasio joins Corso Garibaldi, site of the 11th-century **Sant'Agata**, hiding behind a neoclassical façade; the interior, a perfect Roman basilica, contains excellent frescoes by Giulio Campi of the singularly unpleasant *Martyrdom of St Agata*, and a masterpiece: the 13th-century wooden panel painted with the life of St Agatha. Opposite, Gothic **Palazzo Cittanova** (1256) was the headquarters of the Guelph; adjacent, note the flamboyant but phoney façade of the **Palazzo Trecchi**.

Continuing along, the pink and white **Palazzo Raimondi** (1496), Corso Garibaldi 178, houses the **Scuola Internazionale di Liuteria**, where students learn to make violins (*open by appointment, ✆ 0372 38689*); opposite stands the city's most peculiar palace, crowned with iron dragons. Near the station, **San Luca** has a beautiful terracotta façade and a detached octagonal temple of 1503, a votive offering for the end of a plague.

One last church, **San Sigismondo**, is 1km east beyond Piazzale Libertà, on Via A. Ghisleri (*take bus nos.2 or 3*). Built in 1463 by Bianca Maria Visconti to commemorate her marriage to Francesco Sforza, the interior is delicious proof that fake is better than real: rich pastel frescoes and *trompe l'œil* décors by Giulio, Antonio and Bernardino Campi, Camillo Boccaccino and Bernardino and Gervasio Gatti coat the interior. The choir stalls by Domenico and Gabriele Capra (1590) have just been restored; in the cloister look for a fresco of the *Last Supper* by Tommaso Aleni (1508). Bianca's marriage also occasioned the invention of nougat (*torrone*), made of almonds, honey and egg whites—the gastronomical equivalent to San Sigismondo.

Cremona ✉ 26100   ***Where to Stay and Eating Out***

Modern, comfortable, friendly and central, ★★★★**Continental**, Piazzale Libertà 27, ✆ 0372 434 141, 📠 0372 454 873 (*expensive*) sets the mood with its display of Cremona-made fiddles; parking available. By the main square, ★★★★**Impero**, Piazza della Pace 21, ✆ 0372 460 337 (*expensive*) offers stylish comfort in a streamlined Art Deco palace.

On a pedestrian-only street facing the cathedral, ★★★**Duomo**, Via Gonfalonieri 13, ✆ 0372 35242, 📠 0372 458 392 (*moderate*) has a nice restaurant (with a reasonably priced set menu) and comfortable rooms. For a bit less, try ★★★**Astoria**, Via Bordigallo 9, ✆ 0372 461 616, 📠 0372 461 810 (*moderate*), in a quiet street by the Duomo. Between the centre and the station, ★**Touring**, Via Palestro 3, ✆ 0372 36976 (*cheap*) is simple and old-fashioned with high ceilings and shared bathrooms. Right by the station, ★**Bologna**, Piazza Risorgimento 7, ✆ 0372 24258 (*cheap*) only has singles.

Behind the baptistry, **Aquila Nera**, Via Sicardo 3, *©* 0372 25646 (*expensive*) enjoys an enviable reputation for its regional dishes, starting with melt-in-your-mouth *antipasti, tortelli di zucca* and zesty *secondi* featuring meat or seafood. *Closed Sun eve, Mon and Aug*. An older more traditional restaurant on the west end of town, **Trattoria Mellini**, Via Bissolati 105, *©* 0372 30535 (*moderate*) features dishes to make animal-lovers foam at the mouth—casseroled donkey and baby horse, or raw baby horse with truffle. Less controversial fare includes a kind of risotto with salami and savoy cabbage, and fresh pasta with sausage. *Closed Sun eve, Mon and July*.

Porta Mosa, Via Santa Maria in Betlem 11, *©* 0372 411 803, is a tiny place serving delicious *tortelli* stuffed with squash, locally caught sturgeon steamed with herbs and capers, and a mean *tiramisù*. *Closed Sun, and mid-Aug–mid-Sept*. If your party can't decide between pizza, Thai or Chinese, **Hai Xia**, Corso Garibaldi 85, *©* 0372 39153 (*cheap*) serves all three, and all are delicious—especially the Thai. *Closed Mon*.

Around Cremona: Soncino and Paderno Ponchielli

Lying between the Po and the Oglio, the rich agricultural province of Cremona is well fortified with castles and towers that recall the glorious days when the Italian *comuni* had nothing better to do than beat each other up. The most imposing of the surviving castles, the **Rocca Sforzesca** (*open Tues–Sun 10–12; summer Sat and Sun 10–12.30 and 3–7; winter Sat and Sun 10–12.30 and 4.30–5.30*) rears up over **Soncino**, a walled town north of Cremona on the Oglio. Built in the 12th century, it was greatly enlarged in 1473 by Galeazzo Maria Sforza as an advance base against the Venetians, who were holed up in the Brescian town of Orzinuovi directly across the river. The moat and sinister beetling towers survive, as well as the dungeon, which in 1259 hosted the most brutal and hated man in Italy: the Veneto tyrant Ezzelino da Romano. Ezzelino was wounded when his own Ghibelline allies turned on him as he crossed the Oglio on his way to surprise Milan; at the age of 65, he kept his reputation as a tough *hombre* to the end, refusing to speak or receive medical treatment, ripping the bandages from his wounds with his teeth until he died in agony.

On a rather more cheerful note, admire the watermill under the castle walls, and the delicious painted terracottas and frescoes (*c.* 1500) by Giulio Campi and others inside **Santa Maria delle Grazie**. In the late 15th century the Sforzas invited Jewish refugees from Spain to settle in Soncino, one of whom, Israel Nathan, founded a press and printed his first ornate book in Hebrew in 1483, and the first complete Old Testament in Hebrew in 1488: the site of the press is now a little **Museo della Stampa** (*same hours as the castle*).

Between the two Italian towns that most sound like dairy products, Cremona and Crema, you'll find **Paderno Ponchielli**, birthplace of 'the Italian Tchaikovsky', Amilcare Ponchielli (1834–86). Italy has produced many one-opera composers, but Ponchielli can claim two that are performed with some frequency: *La Gioconda* and *Marion Delorme*; as the teacher of Puccini and Mascagni he was godfather of many others. His humble birthplace is now the **Museo Ponchiellano** (*open Mon–Wed 3–7, Sat and Sun by appointment, © 0374 67404*).

Crema

It was in 1159, during Frederick Barbarossa's third war with Milan, that the emperor, realizing that he lacked sufficient troops to besiege the big city, turned his German army on little Crema,

Milan's staunch ally. Four hundred Milanese came to Crema's defence, but Frederick wasn't in the mood for a fair fight. He hanged all of his adult hostages from Crema and Milan outside the gates, hoping to horrify Crema into surrendering, and when that didn't work he strapped the littlest ones to his moving siege towers, so that the Cremaschi could not repulse them without harming their own children. The histories tell how the parents asked their fellow citizens to kill them, to avoid witnessing their children's torture, while at the same time shouting to their children to be brave and boldly give up their lives for their country. In spite of Frederick's merciless tactics Crema held out for another six months, but at last, starving, it surrendered on the condition that the citizens could withdraw to Milan as their town was razed to the ground.

Three hundred years later, in 1449, Francesco Sforza offered the most loyal town of Crema to Venice when the Serenissima offered to support his dukedom. It proved to be a more pleasant occupation, enduring for three centuries and endowing Crema with a tidy elegance rare in the Lombard plain. To this day it has a white Istrian marble lion of St Mark on its gates and town hall, the latter by the pink brick **duomo**, a delightful Romanesque Gothic work built after Barbarossa sent the original up in flames. Its high 'wind façade' from the 1300s has windows finely decorated with curling vines, little turrets and blind arcading: next to it stands the whimsical, almost Moorish campanile of baked clay that so ravished John Addington Symonds.

Crema's streets are lined by neat, secretive façades that often hide pretty courtyards and gardens. There are quite a few tidy palaces, and the uncompleted but utterly romantic baroque **Palazzo Terni de' Gregori** (or Bondenti) in Via Dante, opposite the former convent of Sant' Agostino. This now houses the library and **Museo Civico** (*open Tues–Fri 2.30–6.30, Sat and Sun 10–12 and 4–6*), with Lombard armour, Risorgimento mementoes, two dramatic paintings of the *Miracles of Christ* by Alessandro Magnasco, and a really gross 17th-century *Martyrdom of San Erasmo*. Ask the curators to unlock the refectory to see the frescoes of the *Last Supper* and *Crucifixion* (1498) by Giovan Pietro da Cemmo. Just north of the walls, at the end of a long tree-lined avenue, stands the basilica of **Santa Maria della Croce** (1490–1500), a lovely Renaissance drum church inspired by Bramante, encircled by three orders of loggias.

West of Crema, **Rivolta d'Adda,** has an 11th-century church of San Sigismondo, dwarfed by its battlemented campanile and containing some good carvings. Rivolta also offers Jurassic-era fun in its **Parco della Preistoria** (*open Mar–Nov daily 9–dusk; adm*), where a zoo train chugs past 23 life-size reproductions of dinosaurs, prowling the wooded banks of the Adda.

Crema ✉ *26013*   **Where to Stay and Eating Out**

Crema has three hotels, all *expensive*: small ★★★★**Il Ponte di Rialto**, Via Cardorna 7, ✆ 0373 82342, 🖳 0373 83520, is the nicest; somewhat cheaper is the ★★★★**Palace**, Via Cresmiero 10, ✆ 0373 81487, 🖳 0373 86876.

As for food, the local speciality, *tortelli cremaschi*, is decidedly different: pasta filled with *amaretti*, raisins, citron, peppermint, nutmeg and cheese, served in melted butter, sage and cheese. Try it at **Trattoria Gobbato**, Via Podgora 2, ✆ 0373 80891 (*cheap*), a funky little place which has been feeding local railway workers for decades. It also serves great local salami, vegetable lasagne and hare with polenta. *Closed Mon; open daily July and Aug.*

Mantua's setting hardly answers to one's great expectations of Italy, sitting in the midst of a table-flat plain, on a wide thumb of land protruding into three swampy, swollen lakes formed by the River Mincio. Its climate is moody: soggy with heat and humidity in the summer and frosty under blankets of fog in the winter. The local dialect is harsh, and the Mantuans, when they feel chipper, dine on braised donkey with macaroni. Verdi made it the sombre setting of his opera *Rigoletto*. And yet this former capital of the art-loving, fast-living Gonzaga dukes is one of the most atmospheric old cities in the country—'a city in the form of a palace' as Castiglione called it—masculine, dark and handsome, with few of Cremona's sweet architectural arpeggios—poker-faced, but holding in its hand a royal flush of dazzling Renaissance art.

History

Mantua gained its fame in Roman times as the home town of Virgil, who recounts the legend of the city's founding by the Theban soothsayer Manto, daughter of Tiresias, and her son Ocnus. Virgil was born around 70 BC, and not much else was heard from Mantua until the 11th century, when the city formed part of the vast domains of Countess Matilda of Canossa. Matilda was a great champion of the pope against the emperor; her advisor, Anselmo, Bishop of Lucca, became Mantua's patron saint. Even so, as soon as Mantua saw its chance it allied itself with the opposition, beginning an unusually important and lengthy career as an independent Ghibelline *comune*, dominated first by the Bonacolsi family and then the Gonzaga.

Naturally defended on three sides by the Mincio, enriched by river tolls and enjoying the protection of the emperor, Mantua became prominent as a neutral buffer state between Milan and Venice. The three centuries of Gonzaga rule, beginning in 1328, brought the city unusual peace and stability, while the refined tastes of the marquesses brought out artists of the highest calibre: Pisanello, Alberti and Andrea Mantegna, who was court painter from 1460 until his death in 1506. Gianfrancesco I Gonzaga invited the great teacher Vittorino da Feltre to open a school in the city in 1423, where his sons and courtiers, side by side with the children of Mantua's poorer families, were taught according to Vittorino's advanced theories, which gave equal emphasis to the intellectual, the physical and the moral. His star pupil was Ludovico (1412–78), one of the most just princes of his day, who tried to recreate Mantua according to Florentine humanist principles. Ludovico's grandson, Gianfrancesco II, was a military commander who led the Italians against the French at Fornovo, but is perhaps best known in history as the husband of the brilliant Isabella d'Este, the foremost culture-vulture of her day as well as an astute diplomat, handling Mantua's affairs of state for her not very clever husband.

The family fortunes reached their apogee under Isabella's two sons. Federico II (1500–40), godson of Cesare Borgia, married Margherita Palaeologo, the heiress of Monferrato, acquiring that duchy for the family as well as a ducal title for the Gonzaga. He hired Raphael's assistant, Giulio Romano ('that rare Italian master', Shakespeare called him in *The Winter's Tale*), to design and adorn his pleasure dome, the Palazzo Tè. When he died, his brother, Cardinal Ercole, served as regent for his son Guglielmo, and both of these men, too, proved to be busy civic improvers. The last great Gonzaga, Vincenzo I, was a patron of Rubens, Fetti and Monteverdi, who composed the first modern opera, *L'Orfeo*, for the Mantuan court in 1607.

But times grew hard and in 1628 Vincenzo II sold off many of the Gonzaga's treasures to Charles I, including Mantegna's *Triumphs of Caesar*, now at Hampton Court. It's just as well that he did; two years later Mantua suffered a near mortal blow when the Gonzaga's claims to Monferrato came into conflict with the Habsburgs, who were never ones for legal niceties and sent troops to sack the city. The duchy, under a cadet branch, limped along until the Austrians snatched Mantua in 1707, eventually making it the southwest corner of their Quadrilateral.

Getting There and Around

Mantua, 25km from Verona's airport, is linked directly by **train** with Verona, Milan, Modena and Cremona, and indirectly with Brescia (change at Piadena). There are also **buses** (✆ 0376 327 237) to Lake Garda and towns in the province. Both the bus and train stations are near Piazza Porta Belfiore, at the end of Corso Vittorio Emanuele, about 10 minutes' walk from the centre.

Tourist Information

Piazza Mantegna 6, on the corner of Piazza dell'Erbe, ✆ 0376 328 253.

Piazza Mantegna

From the station, Corso Vittorio Emanuele and Corso Umberto I lead straight into the Renaissance heart of Mantua, where the narrow cobbled streets are lined with inviting porticoes. Rising above it all in Piazza Mantegna is the great basilica of **Sant'Andrea**, designed by Leon Battista Alberti in 1472 to house the Gonzaga's most precious relic: two ampoules of Christ's blood, said to have been given to St Andrew by St Longinus, the Roman centurion who pierced Christ's side. Ludovico Gonzaga had asked Alberti to create a truly monumental edifice to form a fitting centrepiece for the city, and Alberti came up with the goods. In Florence, Alberti had found himself constrained by his patrons' tastes, but in Mantua he was able to experiment with the ancient forms he loved. Sant'Andrea is based on Vitruvius' idea of an Etruscan temple, with a single barrel-vaulted nave supported by side chapels, fronted with a unique façade combining a triumphal arch and a temple. The lofty dome, designed by Juvarra, was completed in 1782. Andrea Mantegna (d. 1506) is buried in the first chapel on the left, with decorations by his followers and a rather stern self-portrait in bronze. The other chapels have fine altarpieces as well, especially the second one on the left, by Lorenzo Costa.

On the east side, the unfinished flank of the basilica is lined with the porticoes and market stalls of the delightful **Piazza dell'Erbe**. Sunk below the level of the modern pavement, the **Rotonda di San Lorenzo**, modelled on the Church of the Holy Sepulchre in Jerusalem, was built by Countess Matilda in 1082; an ambulatory supports a matroneum. Opposite the tourist office, **Casa di Boniforte da Concorezzo** has elegant stucco decoration, almost unchanged since it was built in 1455, while the 13th-century **Palazzo della Ragione** has a stout clock tower topped by an odd little temple and astronomical clock, added during Ludovico's restoration in 1475. The piazza is closed by the **Broletto** (1227), facing Piazza del Broletto; note the niche holding a 13th-century statue of Virgil seated near the door.

An archway leads into the grand cobbled **Piazza Sordello**, traditional seat of Mantua's bosses. On one side rise the sombre palaces of the Bonacolsi, the Gonzaga's predecessors, with their **Torre della Gabbia**, named for the iron cage they kept to suspend prisoners over the city (though the Mantuans claim it was only used once). At the head of the piazza stands the **duomo**, with a silly 1756 façade, topped by wedding-cake figures, that hides a lovely interior designed by Giulio Romano in 1545. Renaissance tapestries hang in the choir, and the

To Brescia

VIA DEI MULINI

VIALE MINCIO

Lago di Mezzo

Porta
Mulina

VIA TRENTO

VIALE MINCIO

Lago

Superiore

Statue of Virgil

Piazza
Virgiliana

VIA CAIROLI

Casa di
Rigoletto

To Padua
& Venice

Porta
S. Giorgio

Duomo

VIA LEGNAGO

Museo Gonzaga

VIA CAVOUR

Palazzo Bonacolsi /
Torre della Gabbia

Palazzo Ducale

Palazzo d'Arco

Piazza
Sordello

San Francesco

Basilica di
Sant'Andrea

Broletto

VIA F. LLI

VIA ACCADEMIA

VIA G. ARRIVABENE

BANDIERA

Casa di
Boniforte

Piazza
dell'Erbe

Stazione FF. SS.

Palazzo della Ragione

C.SO UMBERTO I

Piazza
Mantegna

Rotonda di
San Lorenzo

To
Cremona

CORSO VITTORIO EMANUELE II

Piazza
Cavallotti

VIA G. BERTANI

Teatro
Bibiena

LUNGO LAGO DEI GONZAGA

Lago

Inferiore

VIA ROMA

Bus
Station

CREMONA

VIA

VIA G. CARDUCCI

VIA SPERI

VIA DELLA

Piazza
Martiri Belfiore

VIA P. F. CALVI

VIA POMPONAZZO

VIA FONDAMENTA

Porto Catena

VIA GIOVANNI CHIASSI

VIA P. AMEDEO

VIA G. MAZZINI

VIA MASSARI

VIA TRIESTE

VIALE FIUME

VIALE PIAVE

VIA POMA

Palazzo di Giustizia /
Casa di Giulio Romano

VIA I. D'ESTE

VIA PIETRO FRATTINI

Piazza
Anconetta

VIALE ASIAGO

VIA DUGONI

CONCILIAZIONE

VIA GRIOLI

Casa di
Mantegna

VIA GIOVANNI ACERBI

VIA GIULIO ROMANO

CORSO GIUS GARIBALDI

VIALE GORIZIA

Piazzale
Gramsci

San Sebastiano

VIA N. SAURO

VIA G. RIPPA

VIA A. MORI

VIALE REPUBBLICA

VIALE MONTELLO

VIA MONTE GRAPPA

VIALE TE

VIALE RISORGIMENTO

VIALE MONTENERO

VIALE ISONZO

VIALE S. ALLENDE

Palazzo Tè

Ippodromo

VIALE TE

VIA BRENNERO

To Bologna

N

400 metres
400 yards

Mantua

215

enormous *Trinity* in the apse is by Domenico Fetti, another Roman painter who worked in Mantua in the early 1600s. The 15th-century house at No.23 has become the '**Casa di Rigoletto**' to satisfy the longings of Verdi buffs; opposite, a new archaeology museum is in the works.

The Palazzo Ducale

Open Tues–Sat 9–2 and 2.30–6, Sun 9–2; May–Sept Sun 9–2 and 4–10; to see the Camera degli Sposi, book in advance, © 0376 320 283; adm exp.

Opposite the Bonacolsi Palace stands the Gonzaga's, its unimpressive façade hiding one of Italy's most remarkable abodes, both in sheer size and the magnificence of its art. The insatiable Gonzaga kept on adding until they had some 500 rooms in three structures—the original **Corte Vecchia**, built by the Bonacolsi in 1290, the 14th-century **castello**, with its large towers overlooking the lake, and the **Corte Nuova**, designed by Giulio Romano. Throw in the Gonzaga's **Basilica di Santa Barbara** and you have a complex that occupies the entire northeast corner of Mantua. If you go in the winter, dress warmly—it's as cold as a dead duke.

Although stripped of its furnishings and most of its art, the Palazzo Ducale remains imposing, majestic and seemingly endless. One of the first rooms, the **chapel**, has a dramatic, half-ruined 14th-century fresco of the *Crucifixion*, attributed to Tommaso da Modena, while another contains a painting of a battle between the Gonzaga and the Bonacolsi in the Piazza Sordello, in which the Gonzaga crushed their rivals once and for all in 1328—although the artist, Domenico Monore, painted the piazza as it appeared in 1494.

Even more fascinating than this real battle is the vivid **fresco of Arthurian knights** by Pisanello. Recorded as damaged in the 1480s, the fresco was believed lost until 1969, when layers of plaster were stripped away to reveal the work commissioned by Gianfrancesco Gonzaga in 1442 to commemorate his receiving from Henry VI the concession to use the heraldic SS collar of the House of Lancaster, an insignia that forms the border, mingled with marigolds, a Gonzaga emblem. Beyond this are the remodelled **neoclassical rooms**, holding a set of Flemish tapestries from Raphael's *Acts of the Apostles* cartoons (now in the Victoria and Albert Museum). Woven in the early 1500s, these copies of the Vatican originals are in a much better state of preservation. Beyond, the **Sala dello Zodiaco** has vivacious 1580 frescoes by Lorenzo Costa; the **Sala del Fiume** is named for its views over the river; and the **Galleria degli Specchi** has mirrors and a note from Monteverdi on the days and hours of the musical evenings he directed there.

The Gonzaga were mad about horses and dogs, and had the **Salone degli Arcieri** painted with *trompe l'œil* frescoes of their favourite steeds standing on upper ledges; the family used to play a kind of guessing game with them, when curtains would be drawn over the figures. Sharing the room are works by Tintoretto and a family portrait by Rubens, court painter under Vincenzo I, a picture so large that Napoleon's troops had to cut it up to carry it off. The duke's apartments hold a fine collection of classical statuary: busts of the emperors, a Hellenistic torso of Aphrodite, and the 'Apollo of Mantova'. The **Sala di Troia** has vivid frescoes (1536) by Giulio Romano and Rinaldo Mantovano, while another ducal chamber has a 17th-century labyrinth painted on the ceiling, each path inscribed in gold with 'Maybe Yes, Maybe No.'

The oldest part of the palace complex, the 14th-century **Castello San Giorgio**, is reached by a low spiral ramp, built especially for the horses the Gonzaga could never bear to be without.

Here, in the famous **Camera degli Sposi**, are the remarkable frescoes painted by Mantegna in 1474, who like a genie captured the essence of the Gonzaga in this small bottle of a room. Restored to their brilliant original colours, the frescoes depict the life of Ludovico Gonzaga, with his wife Barbara of Brandenburg, his children, dwarves, servants, dogs and horses, and important events—greeting his son Francesco, recently made a cardinal, and playing host to Emperor Frederick III and King Christian I of Denmark. The portraits are unflattering and solid, those of real people not for public display, almost like a family photo album. The effect is like stumbling on the court of the Sleeping Beauty; only the younger brother, holding the new cardinal's hand, seems to suspect that he has been enchanted. The backgrounds of imaginary cities and ruins reflect Mantegna's other love, classical architecture, but add another element of unreality in their realistic vividness, as do his *trompe l'œil* decorations on the ceiling. From here the tour continues to the **Casetta dei Nani**, residence of the dwarfs, tiny rooms with low ceilings and shallow stairs, although there are party-poopers who say the rooms had a pious purpose, and were meant to bring the sinning dukes to their proud knees. The last stop is the **suite of Isabella d'Este**, designed by her as a retreat after her husband's death. Her fabulous art collection has long gone to the Louvre, but the ceiling's inexplicable emblems and symbols she devised with her astrologers remain like faint ghosts from a lost world.

Around Town

There are several sights within easy walking distance of the Palazzo Ducale. The **Teatro Accademico Bibiena**, Via Accademia 47, east of the Broletto (*open Mon–Sat 9.30–12.30 and 3–6; adm*) is a gem built by Antonio Galli Bibiena, a member of the famous Bolognese family of theatre builders. Mozart, aged 13, performed at the inaugural concert in 1770; father Leopold said it was the most beautiful theatre he had ever seen.

West of the Piazza Sordello, Via Cairoli leads to the city's park, **Piazza Virgiliana**, with a marble statue of Virgil from 1927 (in time for the poet's 2000th birthday) and the **Museo Gonzaga** (*open April–June Tues–Sun 9.30–12 and 2.30–5; July and Aug Thurs, Sat and Sun only; Nov–Mar Sun only; adm*), containing artefacts that once belonged to the family. Further west, in Piazza d'Arco, the **Palazzo d'Arco** (*open Nov–Feb Sat 10–12.30 and 2–5, Sun 10–5; Mar–Sept Tues–Fri 10–12.30 and 2.30–6, Sat and Sun 10–6; adm*) was rebuilt in 1784 for the arty counts from Garda's north shore and has been left more or less as it was, complete with furnishings, paintings, instruments, a superb kitchen and, in a room preserved from an older palace, frescoes of the zodiac, attributed to Giovanni Maria Falconetto of Verona (*c.* 1515). The nearby church of **San Francesco** (1304) was rediscovered in 1944, when a bomb hit the arsenal that had disguised it for a century and a half. Restored to its original state, it contains frescoes by the excellent Tommaso da Modena in the last chapel on the right.

South of the medieval nucleus, just off the main Via Principe Amedeo, the **Casa di Giulio Romano**, Via Poma 18, was designed by the artist himself in 1544 while working on the Palazzo Tè. He also gets credit for the quaint palace decorated with monsters nearby; the heavy **Palazzo di Giustizia** at No.22 was built in the 1620s. Mantegna also designed his dream house, the **Casa del Mantegna**, Via Acerbi 47, in the same neighbourhood (*open daily 10–12.30 and 3–6 when an exhibition is on; otherwise Mon–Fri 10–12.30*). Designed as a cube built around a circular courtyard, he intended it partially as his personal museum and embellished it with classical 'Mantegnesque' decorations. Opposite stands the neglected **San Sebastiano** (1460), a second church by Alberti, this one in the form of a Greek cross.

A Renaissance Pleasure Dome: the Palazzo Tè

Open Tues–Sun 9–6, Mon 1–6; adm exp.

At the end of Via Acerbi is Giulio Romano's masterpiece, the marvellous Palazzo Tè, its name derived not from tea, but from the rather less savoury *tejeto*, a local word for a drainage canal. On a swamp drained for a horsey Gonzaga pleasure ground, work began in 1527 when Federico II had Giulio Romano expand the stables to create a little palace for his mistress, Isabella Boschetti, of whom his mother, Isabella d'Este, disapproved. The project expanded over the decades to become a guest house suitable for an emperor. Charles V visited twice.

Giulio Romano had fled Rome in 1524 to escape prison for designing pornographic prints. In his Palazzo Tè, one of the very first great Mannerist buildings, he had the same desire to shock and upset the cool classicism exemplified by Alberti, and along the way he created one of the great Renaissance syntheses of architecture and art, combining *trompe l'œil* with a bold play between the structure of the rooms and the frescoes. Most of the art still has classical themes: the **Sala della Metamorfosi** is inspired by Ovid and Roman frescoes, which Giulio had discovered with his master Raphael in Nero's Golden House in Rome. Gonzaga emblems fill the **Sala delle Imprese**: putti holding a cup, a belt, a bird catching fish, a muzzle, a salamander (a symbol of Federico's love, which is consumed, but doesn't burn); the chariot of the sun is a first hint of Giulio's love of wacky perspectives. The next room has more life-size Gonzaga horses, and in the next, the **Sala di Psiche**, all glory bursts forth in the colours and exuberance of the scenes from *The Golden Ass*. The **Camera dei Venti** was Federico's study, designed with precious materials and a complex iconographic programme based on ancient astrological texts, each scene illustrating a prediction linked to a constellation.

Activities

Several **boat** companies operate on Mantua's lakes and the Mincio, including **Motonavi Andes**, Piazza Sordello 8, © 0376 322 875, ● 0376 322 869. A pleasant 1½hr trip past Gonzaga castles, a beautiful bridge designed by Nervi, water-lilies, water-chestnut farms and flocks of egrets costs L14,000, children L10,000; the company also sails to San Benedetto Po (*see* below)

Mantua ✉ *46100*   ### Where to Stay and Eating Out

Do book: Mantua's few hotels tend to fill up fast. ★★★★**San Lorenzo**, Piazza Concordia 14, © 0376 220 500, ● 0376 327 194 (*expensive*) is housed in a restored late-Renaissance building, with views over Piazza dell'Erbe and the dome of Sant'Andrea. The rooms have most comforts; guests have free access to a gym. ★★★★**Rechigi**, Via Calvi 30, © 0376 320 781, ● 0376 220 291 (*expensive*) is also in the historic centre; all rooms have satellite TV, air-conditioning and comfortable furnishings; there's ample parking and they hire out bikes.

★★★**Due Guerrieri**, Piazza Sordello 52, © 0376 321 533, ● 0376 329 645 (*moderate*) is housed in an older building overlooking the Palazzo Ducale; there's parking nearby. Near the station, ★★★**Bianchi Stazione**, Piazza Don Leoni 24, © 0376 326 465, ● 0376 321 504 (*moderate*) has recently been renovated. Also here, ★★**ABC**, Piazza le Stazione 25, © 0376 323 347, ● 0376 322 329 (*moderate–cheap*) has small cell-like rooms arranged around an inner courtyard with space for parking .**★Maragò**, just outside the centre at Virgiliana, ✆ 0376 370 313 (*cheap*) has 13 simple rooms, not all with bath, and parking.

Ostello Sparafucile, Lunetta di San Giorgio, ✆ 0376 372 465, is an exceptional hostel, just outside the city on the Lago di Mezzo. Occupying a 15th-century castle, popularly believed to be the headquarters of the baddie in *Rigoletto*, the interior has been remodelled, but without losing any of its character. Cheap meals are also available. *Closed 15 Oct–1 April; take bus nos.2 or 9 from Piazza Cavallotti.*

During the reign of the Gonzaga the Mantuans developed their own cuisine, which other Italians regard as a little peculiar. The notorious *stracotto di asino* (donkey stew) heads the list, but the Mantuans also have a predilection for adding Lambrusco to soup. Classic *primi* include *agnoli* stuffed with bacon, salami, chicken livers and cheese cooked in broth, *risotto alla pilota* (with onion, butter and grana cheese), or *tortelli di zucca* (pasta caps stuffed with pumpkin, mustard and cheese, served with melted butter). Catfish, eel, crayfish, pike (the delicious *luccio in salsa,* prepared with peppers and capers) and bass—and crispy-fried frog's legs are typical *secondi.*

Mantua is also the place to taste true Lambrusco; the foam should vanish instantly when poured. There are three main kinds: the grand *Lambrusco di Sorbana*, the mighty *Lambrusco di Santa Croce* and the amiable *Lambrusco di Castelvetro.*

The lovely **Aquila Nigra**, Vicolo Bonacolsi 4, ✆ 0376 327 180 (*expensive*), with its marble and frescoes, serves exquisitely prepared regional dishes and others; the pasta courses (ravioli filled with truffled duck, for instance) are a joy. A large choice of Italian and French wines, cheeses and delicious desserts like chestnut torte round off a special meal. *Closed Sun, Mon and Aug.* **Trattoria dei Martini**, Piazza d'Arco, ✆ 0376 327 101 (*expensive*) overlooks an inner garden and has a menu that changes according to season—tagliatelle with duck, lamb casseroled with herbs, or roast guinea fowl; around L60,000. *Closed Mon, Tues, and first part of Aug.*

In a superbly renovated 14th-century palace, **San Gervasio**, Via San Gervasio 13, ✆ 0376 327 077 (*moderate*) offers an excellent *menu mantovano* at L60,000 and has lunch bargains as well. *Closed Wed and Sun eve, and Aug.* In the summer, the tables fill up early at the **Ristorante Pavesi dal 1918**, Piazza delle Erbe ✆ 0376 323 627 (*moderate*), where they do a particularly good *gnocchi alla gorgonzola. Closed Thurs.* Away from the obvious tourist areas, **Quattrotette**, Vicolo Nazione, ✆ 0376 329 478 (*moderate*) squeezes in hordes of locals who cherish the dishes of vegetables and salads—*melanzana grillata, carciofi alla giudia* and *peperonata*—steaming hot bowls of pasta, and pasticceria. *Closed Sun.* **Al Garibaldini**, Via S. Longino 7, ✆ 0376 328 263 (*moderate*) is in the historic centre, in a fine old house with a shady garden for al fresco dining. The menu features especially good *risotti* and *tortelli di zucca*, fish and meat dishes. *Closed Wed and Jan.*

For no atmosphere but delicious Mantuan cooking at a very accessible price, try the **Al Lago**, Piazza Arche 5, ✆ 0376 323 300 (*cheap*). *Closed Mon.* **Due Cavallini**, Via Salnitro 5 (near Lago Inferiore, off Corso Garibaldi), ✆ 0376 322 084 (*cheap*) is the place if you want to bite into some donkey meat—though it has other less ethnic dishes as well. *Closed Tues and late-July–late-Aug.* **Il Portichetto**, Via Portichetto 14,

© 0376 360 747 (*cheap*) is run by a former left-wing activist who has turned his hand to cooking. The results are excellent. The menu revolves around river-fish—mixed *antipasti*, tagliatelle with perch or pike in *salsa verde*—and lots of vegetarian options. *Closed Sun eve and Mon.* **L'Ochina Bianca**, Via Finzi 2, © 0376 323 700 (*cheap*) has an ever-changing menu which might include smoked beef dressed with superb olive oil, deep-fried courgette (zucchini) flowers, delicate home-made pasta and meat dishes. *Closed Mon and Tues lunch.*

Around Mantua

Mantua's western lake, **Lago Superiore**, is noted for its delicate lotus blossoms, planted in the 1930s as an experiment. They have since thrived, and bloom in July and August around the city's park, the **Valletta Belfiore**, turning the lake violet and pink. Another park, **Bosco della Fontana** (*open Oct–Mar daily 9.30–5.30; April–Sept daily 8.30–7.30; adm weekends*) lies 5km to the north off the road to Brescia. Once a Gonzaga hunting reserve, with a moated little castle built as a hunting lodge in 1595, the Bosco's broad-leafed trees are a last relic of the ancient forest that once covered the Po plain. If you're in Mantua on 15 August be sure to visit the **Santuario della Madonna delle Grazie**, on the banks of Lago Superiore at Curtatone, where there's an unusual art competition for the *madonnari*—artists who draw sidewalk chalk portraits of the Madonna—among other diversions. Built as a votive offering by Francesco I after the plague of 1399, the church has a 15th-century frescoed ceiling, paintings by Lorenzo Costa, and a great hotchpotch of votive offerings, including a stuffed crocodile.

San Benedetto Po

Some 22km southeast of Mantua (connected in the summer by boats), San Benedetto Po grew up around the Benedictine abbey of **Polirone** (*open daily 8–12 and 2.30–7*), the 'Monte Cassino of the North', established in the year 1007 by the Canossa counts of Tuscany. It was especially favoured by the last of their line, the feisty Matilda (d. 1115), whose alabaster sarcophagus survives in the richly appointed **Basilica di San Benedetto**, rebuilt in the 1540s by Giulio Romano and linked to the 12th-century church of **Santa Maria**, which preserves a fine mosaic of 1151. There are three cloisters and a refectory with frescoes by Correggio, now part of the **Museo dell'Abbazia** (*open April–May 9–12.30 and 2.30–5; June–mid-Nov Sat 2.30–6, Sun 10.30–12.30 and 3.30–7; the rest of the year Sat 2.30–6, Sun 10–12 and 2.30–6; adm*).

Sabbioneta

An hour's bus ride southwest of Mantua on the Parma road, Sabbioneta was built as a capital and ideal dream city by the prince of Bozzolo, Vespasiano Gonzaga, member of a cadet branch of the Gonzaga family. Vespasiano was a firm believer that the city should be a rational expression in the measure of man, and had the streets of his 'Little Athens' laid out straight and square within its irregular hexagonal walls; his humanistic philosophy attracted many Jewish settlers, who founded a famous printing press. To see the interiors, contact the Pro Loco at the end of the brick atrium on Via V. Gonzaga 31, © 0375 52039 (*open April–Sept Tues–Sun 9.30–12.30 and 2.30–6; Oct–Mar till 5; ring ahead to book a tour in English; adm*).

The classical utopian vision of Vespasiano was out of fashion before Sabbioneta was even built, and its spark died with its creator, leaving a little museum city. Around central Piazza Castello,

Vespasiano constructed a long frescoed corridor, the **Galleria degli Antichi**, to display his classical statues (now in Mantua's Palazzo Ducale). At one end stands the **Palazzo del Giardino**, his pleasure palace, adorned with frescoes and stuccoes by the school of Giulio Romano. The next piazza contains the symmetrical **Palazzo Ducale**, with its five arches housing wooden equestrian statues of Vespasiano and his kin; other rooms, with fine frescoes and ceilings, include the **Sala d'Oro**, the **Sala degli Elefanti** and the **Sala delle Città Marinare**, with paintings of port towns. Behind the palace, the church of the **Incoronata** houses Vespasiano's mausoleum, with a bronze statue of the prince in classical Roman garb. The last stop on the tour is the small 1588 **Teatro Olimpico**, designed by Vincenzo Scamozzi after Palladio's theatre in Vicenza. Twelve plaster statues of the ancient Olympians grace the balcony, and some of the original Venetian frescoes have recently been rediscovered. Also in the centre of town is the 16th-century **synagogue**, derelict for the past 50 years.

Sabbioneta ✉ *46018* **Where to Stay and Eating Out**

In the centre, ****Al Duca**, Via della Stamperia 18, ✆ 0375 52474, 📠 0375 22021 (*cheap*) offers largish, comfortable enough rooms with en suite baths and TV. Of the many restaurants, the two best are just outside the city walls: the elegant **Parco Cappuccini**, Via Santuario 30, ✆ 0375 52002, 📠 0375 220 056 (*expensive*) occupies an 18th-century villa with a veranda looking onto the park, an inviting place to linger over classic Italian cuisine. *Closed Mon and Wed eve.* **Il Capriccio**, Via Solazzi 51 (the Mantua–Parma road), ✆/📠 0375 52722 (*moderate*) serves delicious creative dishes based on Mantuan tradition, with a L25,000 lunch menu. *Closed Tues eve and Wed.*

For a real treat, drive 20km north to Canneto sull'Oglio (just beyond Piadena), where you can feast at one of Lombardy's finest restaurants, **Dal Pescatore**, Località Runate 13, ✆ 0376 70304 (*very expensive; book well in advance*). In an elegant country villa filled with antiques and oriental rugs, Nadia Santini—Italy's most talented woman chef—enchants the privileged few (the dining room holds a maximum of 30 people) with her exquisite light cuisine using the best and freshest of produce, much of it picked that morning at the Santini family farm. Mantovan favourites like *tortelli de zucca* reach a kind of epiphany, served up with the best wines, the most civilized service and a bill at the end hovering around L110,000 per person excluding wine. *Closed Mon, Tues, much of Aug and two weeks in Jan.*

The Italian Lakes

Just to mention the Italian Lakes is to evoke a soft, dreamy image of romance and beauty, a Latin Brigadoon of gentlemen and gentle ladies strolling through gardens, sketching landscapes, and perhaps indulging in a round of whist on the villa veranda in the evening. The backgrounds to their fond pleasures are scenes woven of poetry, of snow-capped peaks tumbling steeply into ribbons of blue, trimmed with the silver tinsel of olives and the daggers of dark cypress; of mellowed villas gracing vine-clad hillsides and gold-flecked citrus groves; of spring's excess, when the lakes become drunken with colour, as a thousand varieties of azaleas, rhododendrons and camellias spill over the banks. For even though the Swiss border is just around the corner, the lakes cover enough area to create their own climatic oases of Mediterranean flora, blooming even at the foot of the starlit Alps.

Lake holidays faded from fashion in the post-War era, when a suntan became a symbol of leisure instead of manual labour and summer's mass trek to the seashore became as fixed a ritual as the drowning of lemmings. But the lakes are simply too lovely to stay out of fashion for long, and today a new generation is busily rediscovering what their grandparents took for granted. For better or worse, the Italians have ringed the lakes with finely engineered roads, making them perhaps too accessible, although all still have their leisurely steamers. Between July and September rest and relaxation, or even peace and quiet, may seem a Victorian relic, unless you book into one of the grander villa hotels. Quiet havens, however, still exist on the smaller, less developed lakes of Iseo and Orta, the east shores of Maggiore and Como.

Lake resorts are generally open between April and October. The best times to visit are in spring and autumn, not only to avoid the crowds, but because the lakes themselves are less subjected to winter mists and summer haze. In the restaurants, look for lake fish, served either fresh or sun-dried. The finest wines from the lake district come from the Franciacorta near Iseo, Bardolino on Lake Garda; reds from the Valtellina, and La Brianza near Lake Como.

Below, the lakes are described geographically from west to east, from Piemonte's Lake Orta and the valleys around Domodossola, through Lombardy's lakes and the Valtellina, Bergamo and Brescia, and then to Lake Garda on the border of the Veneto.

Lake Orta and Domodossola

The green waters of Lake Orta run still and quiet, and in the centre they hold a magical isle, illuminated on summer nights like a golden fairy-tale castle. A mere 13km long, Orta is a lake 'made to the measurements of man'. Nietzsche, who never fell in love, did so on its soft green shores. He didn't get the girl, but the world got *Thus Spake Zarathustra*. On a more mundane level, Orta's villages produce bathroom taps, saxophones, coffee pots and chefs; so many come from Armeno that the second Sunday each November it holds an annual reunion of cooks.

Getting Around

The main lake resorts, Orta San Giulio, Pettenasco and Omegna, are easily reached from Turin or Milan on **trains** heading north to Domodossola and the Simplon Pass. Orta is also easy to reach from Lake Maggiore: a rail line links Stresa to Arona and **buses** run from Arona to Orta, and from Verbania to Omegna.

Navigazione Lago d'Orta, ✆ 0322 844 862, provides a **boat** service at least twice a day between Oria, Omegna, Punta di Crabbia, Pettenasco, L'Approdo, Orta, Isola San Giulio, Pella, San Filiberto and Lagna. The company also offers a midnight cruise from Orta, Pella and Pettenasco on Saturday and Sunday in July and August.

Tourist Information

Orta San Giulio: Via Orlina, ✆ 0322 911 937; **Macugnaga**: Piazza Municipio, ✆ 0324 65110; **Domodossola**: Corso Ferraris 49, ✆ 0324 481 308, ✉ 0324 47974; **Santa Maria Maggiore**: Piazza Risorgimento 5, ✆ 0324 95091.

To the
Simplon Pass

SWITZERLAND

Domodossola

Piana di Vigezzo

F. Maggia

F. Ticino

Locarno

Ascona

Isole di
Brissago

Vira

Toceno
Craveggia
Villette

Oglia

Centovalli

Brissago

Druogno

Marone

S. Maria
Maggiore

Malesco

Mt. Limidario

Pino
Tronzano

Biegne

Trontano

La Cima

Finero

Cursolo Orasso S. Bartolomeo

Musignano

Villadossola

Beura

Mt. Togano

RISERVA NATURAL
VALGRANDE

Mt. Mottac

Cima di
Laurasca

Gurro

Valmara

Cavaglio-Spoccia

Val Veddasca

Maccagno

Cardezza

Sant' Anna

Cannobio

Colmegna

To Val di
Antrona

Falmenta

Cannobina

To Valle
Anzasca &
Macugnaga

Vogogna

Mt. Zeda

Trarego-Viggiona

E MT MOTTAC

Cannero
Riviera

Luino

Fornasette

Fiume Toce

Pran Cavallone

Cicogna

Aurano
Intragna

Oggebbio

Germignaga

Cremenaga

Campello
Monti

Forno

Mt. Massone

Valstrona

Massiola

Ornavasso

Mergozzo
Cossogno

Cambiasca

Miazzina

Premeno

Vignone

Bee

Ghiffa

Porto
Valtravaglia

Ponte Tresa

Grantola

N233

Mt. Orfano

Mergozzo
Bernardino

Arizzano

Castel S. Pietro

Mesenzana

Ghirla

Gravellona
Toce

Pallanza

Friolo

I. Madre

Intra
Verbania

Mt.
Camoscio

Baveno

I. Madre

Isole Borromee
Isola Bella
Stresa

Laveno

Mt. Nudo

Arcumeggia

Cittiglio

Cuveglio

Brinzio

Crusinallo

Mottarone

Cerro

S. Caterina
del Sasso

Orino

Parco di Campo
dei Fiori

Bisuschio

N344

Omegna

Brolo

Agrano

Vezzo

Gignese

Leggiuno
Lido di
Monvalle

Gavirate

Sta Maria
del Monte

Varese

Nonio

Cesara

Armeno

Brovello-
Carpugnino

Massino
Visconti

Belgirate

Bregano

Voltorre
Oltrona
Gropello
Calcinate

Malnate

Egro

Pella

Sovazza

Lesa

Biandronno

L. di Varese

Alzo

Pettenasco

Nebbiuno

Ispra

Solcio

Cazzago

Capolago

Lagna

Orta S. Giulio

Pisano

L. di
Monate

Osmate

Bodio

Castiglione
Olona

Pogno

Ameno

Meina

Ranco

Angera

Comabbio

L. di
Comabbio

Castelseprio

Gozzano

Arona

N32

A8

Valduggia

PARCO NATURAL
DEI LAGON

Sesto
Calende

Vergiate

A8 - A26

A26

Castelletto
sopra Ticino
Somma
Lombardo

Arsago
Seprio

Gallarate

A8

To Milan

Borgo
Ticino

Malpensa

Busto
Arsizio

Oleggio

Fiume Ticino

N

10 km
5 miles

Lakes Orta and Maggiore

223

Orta San Giulio, its Island and Omegna

Blithely set on its own garden peninsula, the lake's 'capital', Orta San Giulio, is a fetching little town. Lanes too narrow for cars (leave yours in the car park along the main road) all lead into handsome lakeside **Piazza Motta**, a cosy rendezvous nicknamed the *salotto* or drawing room, with the bijou 1582 **Palazzotto** as a centrepiece, decorated with faded frescoes. In April and May, Orta opens the season with a flower festival, the Ortafiori, when you can visit the superb gardens of the Villa Motta.

From Orta, steamboats run to the ports of Pella, Oira and Omegna, and to **Isola San Giulio**, once the lair of loathsome serpents and monsters. They were banished by Orta's St Patrick, St Julius, who arrived in 390 and founded the precursor to the island's **Basilica**. Most of what you see today dates from the 12th century, including the black marble pulpit, carved with the banished griffons and serpents. There are some good 15th-century frescoes by Ferrari and his school, and a marble sarcophagus of Lombard Duke Meinulphus, who had betrayed the island to the Franks and was beheaded by Agilulf; a decapitated skeleton was found inside in 1697.

On the northern tip of the lake, **Omegna** (Roman *Vomenia*) is the biggest town on the lake, where people make pots and pans, coffee pots and household appliances. The centre of town is pleasant enough, where the pretty Piazza del Municipio gives on to a bridge spanning the river that drains Orta, the Nigoglia—the only river in Italy to flow *towards* the Alps.

From Lake Orta to Domodossola: Valle Anzasca

From Omegna, the railway and *autostrada* continue into the northernmost reaches of Piemonte. Between Omegna and Domodossola, the enchanting **Valle Anzasca** diverges to the west (buses from Domodossola, or from the station at Piedimulera at the foot of the valley). Little villages lie scattered in the woods—tiny **Colombetti**, its slate roofs huddled under a cliff; **Bannio-Anzino**, the 'capital' of the valley, with modest skiing facilities and a 7ft-tall, 16th-century bronze Christ from Flanders in its parish church; **Ceppo Morelli**, with a famous, vertiginous bridge over the Anza; beyond Ceppo the road plunges through a gorge to the old mining town of **Pestarena**.

The various hamlets that comprise **Macugnaga**, the Valle Anzasca's popular resort, lie under the majestic frowning face of **Monte Rosa** (15,213ft). As in the Val Gressoney on the southern side of Monte Rosa, Macugnaga was settled by German-speaking Swiss from the Valais (the Walser) in the 13th century. A small museum in **Borca** is devoted to Walser folk-lore, while other old Swiss traces remain in the 13th-century parish church. Macugnaga has a number of ski lifts, and a chairlift that operates in the summer as well, to the magnificent **Belvedere** with views over the Macugnaga glacier; a cableway from Staffa to the **Passo**

Monte Moro (9407ft) is used by skiers in both the winter and summer seasons. From Macugnaga, fearless alpinists can attempt the steep east flank of Monte Rosa, one of the most dangerous ascents in the Alps; walkers can make a three-day trek over the mountains to Gressoney-St-Jean and other points in the Valle d'Aosta (trail map essential) (*see* p.99).

Domodossola

The largest town in the Valle d'Ossola, Domodossola lies at the foot of the **Simplon Pass** (*Passo del Sempione*), through which, after the Battle of Marengo, Napoleon constructed his highway from Geneva to Milan, completed in 1805. Exactly 100 years later the even more remarkable 19.8km Simplon Tunnel was completed—the longest in the world. Domodossola itself is a pleasant old town with an arcaded main square and a **Museo Civico**, with exhibits relating to the tunnel and the flight of the Peruvian Georges Chavez, the first man to fly over the Alps (29 September 1910), only to die in a crash near Domodossola.

A narrow-gauge electric railway, **La Vigezzina**, makes the picturesque journey in an hour and a half between Domodossola and Locarno on Lake Maggiore through the **Val Vigezzo**, a romantic beauty nicknamed the Valley of Painters. The place to stay if you're tempted to linger or paint a landscape is the main town, **Santa Maria Maggiore**; from nearby Maleco a road descends the Val Cannobina to Cannobio on Lake Maggiore.

Buses from Domodossola also plunge north into the spectacular scenery that leads up into the **Val Formazza**, colonized by German-speaking families from the Valais. Their charming, scattered, villages are small summer and winter resorts offering excursions to the Alpine lakes, especially from **Ponte** (with a chair lift), where the bus terminates. If you come on a Sunday or holiday from June until September (*9am–5pm*), or any day between 10 and 20 August, you can take in one of the most breathtaking waterfalls in all the Alps at the end of the road: the thundering 985ft veil of mist, the **Cascata del Toce**. At other times, like all of Italy's best waterfalls, its bounding, splashing energy spins hydroelectric turbines.

Where to Stay and Eating Out

Orta San Giulio ✉ 28016

Orta San Giulio is awash with lovely hotels, including one straight out of the *Arabian Nights*: ★★★★**Villa Crespi**, the lake's most luxurious, in a garden on top of town at Via C. Fava 8/10, ✆ 0322 911 902, ✉ 0322 911 919 (*very expensive*), a Moorish folly built in 1880 by Lombard cotton magnate Benigno Crespi and now painstakingly restored and furnished with period pieces. The eight suites and six bedrooms each have romantic canopied beds, marble baths and jacuzzis; the elegant dining room is equalled by the ravishing dishes prepared by top chef Natale Bacchetta: foie gras and *soncino* and pigeon stuffed with black truffles, for instance, accompanied by a wine and spirits list to die for: menus are surprisingly good value. *Closed Mon in winter.*

Down in Orta's centre, ★★★★**San Rocco**, Via Gippini 11, ✆ 0322 911 977, ✉ 0322 911 964 (*very expensive*) is located in a former 17th-century monastery with a pretty garden on the water. In Piazza Motta, brimming over with old-fashioned Italian character, ★★★**Orta**, ✆ 0322 90253, ✉ 0322 905 646 (*moderate*) has been run by the same family for over a century, with big rooms and bathrooms and a charming dining terrace directly on the lake. In 1882 Nietzsche and Lou Salomé spent their love-troubled week at the ★★★**Leon d'Oro**, Piazza Motta, ✆ 0322 911 991, ✉ 0322 90303 (*moderate*), and to this day the lake terrace is especially amenable to such breaks from philosophy; rooms are small but immaculate.

Set back on a quiet hill, ★★★**La Bussola**, Via Panoramica 24, ✆ 0322 911 913, ✉ 0322 911 934 (*moderate*) has 16 rooms and enjoys a magnificent panorama of the lake; there's a pretty garden with a pool and a good restaurant. Simple ★**Taverna Antico Agnello**, Via Olina 18, ✆ 0322 90259 (*cheap*) offers cosy rooms and a charming restaurant (*moderate*) where the menu changes with the season; reserve.

A couple of steps further down, ★★**Olina**, ✆ 0322 905 656, ✉ 0322 905 645 (*cheap*) has very pleasant rooms and an elegant restaurant where the *risotto al saffrone* and *bonito al pomodoro* are particularly good; menus with *antipasti* for L45,000. **Venus**, in Piazza Motta, ✆ 0322 90362, is always packed for lunch: fill up on polenta with mushrooms, fish and wine for L35,000. *Closed Mon.*

Pettenasco ✉ 28028

Right on Lake Orta, ★★★**Giardinetto**, Via Provinciale 1, ✆ 0323 89118, ✉ 0323 89219 (*moderate*) is a friendly family hotel with views of the Isola San Giulio. There are reduced rates for children, a pool, private beach and water sports facilities, and an excellent restaurant serving locally cured meats, tortellini with goats cheese and asparagus, and a soup of lake fish under a pastry crust. *Open April–Oct only.*

Valle Anzasca ✉ 28030

Most of the Valle Anzasca's accommodation is clustered in Macugnaga. The largest and most luxurious choice, ★★★**Zumstein**, Via Monte Rosa 63, ✆ 0324 65118, ✉ 0324 65490 (*moderate*) has attractive rooms near the centre of Staffa. *Closed May, Oct and Nov.* In the quiet *frazione* of Pecetto, ★★★**Nuova Pecetto**, ✆ 0324 65025, ✉ 0324 65891 (*moderate*) is charming and traditional with a garden and fine views of Monte Rosa. *Closed mid-Sept–Nov.*

★★**Chez Felice**, ✆ 0324 65229, ✉ 0324 65037 (*cheap*) is an unassuming villa with simple but charming rooms and the best restaurant in the valley (*moderate*) a haven of *nuova cucina*, where you can find salmon mousse with herbs, warm artichokes with a sauce of anchovies and capers, risotto with almonds, cheese and herb soufflé and, for afters, a magnificent array of local cheeses and exquisite desserts. *Closed Thurs; book if you're not staying at the hotel.*

Domodossola ✉ 28037

The most stylish hotel in town, ★★★**Corona**, Via Marconi 8, ✆ 0324 242 114, ✉ 0324 242 842 (*expensive*) has very comfortable rooms, and a garage. In the centre, **Trattoria Piemonte di Sciolla**, Piazza Convenzione 5, ✆ 0324 242 633 (*moderate*) comes highly recommended for its regional dishes such as polenta with milk and poppy seeds and its home-made desserts. *Closed Wed and late Aug.*

Lake Maggiore

*Have you not read in books how men when they
see even divine visions are terrified?
So as I looked at Lake Major in its halo
I also was afraid ...*

Hilaire Belloc, *The Path to Rome*

Italy's second-largest lake, Maggiore winds majestically between Piemonte and Lombardy, its northern corner lost in the snow-capped Swiss Alps. In Roman times Maggiore was called *Lacus Verbanus*, for the verbena that still grows luxuriantly on its shores. What really sets the lake apart, though, are the fabled Borromean Isles and their gardens, still the property of the Borromeo family of Milan, who also possess the fishing rights over the entire lake—as they have since the 1500s. Otherwise, the western shore, especially in the triad of resorts; Stresa, Baveno, and Verbania, are the most scenic places to aim for, with the best and most varied accommodation. Unless you reserve well in advance, however, avoid July and August.

Getting Around

Trains from Milan's Stazione Centrale to Domodossola stop at Arona and Stresa; others from Milan's Stazione Porta Garibaldi go to Luino on the east shore. A third option is the regional railway from Milano-Nord, which passes by way of Varese to Laveno. Trains from Turin and Novara go to Arona and Stresa; Stresa is also linked by train to Orta four times a day.

From Lake Orta, there are **buses** from Omegna to Verbania every 20 minutes. Buses that connect the two lakes also run from Stresa and Arona stations, others serve all the villages along the west shore.

Navigazione Lago Maggiore, © 0322 46651, runs **steamers** to all corners of the lake, with the most frequent services in the central lake area between Stresa, Baveno, Verbania, Pallanza, Laveno and the islands; **hydrofoils** buzz between the main Italian ports and Locarno (in Switzerland). Frequent services by steamer or hydrofoil from Stresa, Baveno and Pallanza sail to the Borromean Isles—a ticket for the furthest, Isola Madre, entitles you to visit all. **Car ferries** run year round between Intra and Laveno.

Tourist Information

Arona: Piazzale Duca d'Aosta, ©/◉ 0322 243 601; **Stresa**: Principe Tommaso 70, © 0323 30150, ◉ 0323 32561; **Baveno**, Corso Garibaldi 16, ©/◉ 0323 924 632.

Arona

Arona is the southernmost steamer landing, and even if you're just passing through it is hard to avoid **San Carlone**, a 115ft-high copper and bronze jug-eared colossus towering above the old town (*open April–Sept daily 8.30–12.30 and 2–6.30; Oct–Mar daily 9–12.30 and 2–5; adm*). San Carlone (St Big Chuck) is perhaps better known as Charles Borromeo (1538–84), born in the now-ruined **Castello di Arona**, and the statue was erected by his family in 1697. Nearby, the Borromeo chapel in **Santa Maria** contains a lovely 1511 altarpiece by Ferrari.

The World's Biggest Saint

Charles Borromeo, son of Count Gilbert Borromeo and a Medici mum, was the most influential churchman of his day, appointed 'Cardinal Nephew and Archbishop of Milan' at the age of 22 by his maternal uncle, Pope Pius IV. In Rome he was a powerful voice calling for disciplinary reform within the Church, and he instigated the Council of Trent, that decade-long Counter-Reformation strategy session in which he played a major role.

At one point the cardinals wanted to ban all church music, which had degenerated to the point of singing lewd ballads to accompany the *Te Deum*. Charles and his committee, however, decided to let the musicians have one more chance, and asked Palestrina to compose three suitable Masses that reflected the dignity of the words of the service (and Charles reputedly told the composer that the cardinals expected him to fail). To their surprise, and to the everlasting benefit of Western culture, Palestrina succeeded, and sacred music was saved.

After the death of his uncle-pope, Charles went to live in his diocese of Milan, the first archbishop to do so in 80 years. Following the codex of the Council of Trent to the letter (that's the book under the statue's arm), he at once began reforming his cosy clergy to set an example. The Milanese weren't exactly thrilled: Charles narrowly escaped an assassination attempt in the cathedral, when the bullet bounced off his heavy brocade vestments.

He was a bitter enemy of original thought and not someone you would want to have over for dinner; if New York has a Statue of Liberty, Arona has a Statue of Tyranny. For a queer sensation walk up through his hollow viscera (if he's been mended): his head can hold six people, who can peer out of his eyes. The plastic doodahs in the souvenir shop below are a trip in themselves.

More Borromeana awaits at **Angera**, across the lake in Lombardy and the first steamer call. Its mighty **Rocca di Angera** (*open April–June and Sept–Oct daily 9.30–12 and 2–5; July–Aug daily 9.30–12.30 and 3–7; adm*) commands the whole southern half of the lake. The 11th-century builders, the Della Torre, lost it to the Visconti, who had it frescoed in 1277 with battle scenes of their victory. The Borromei picked it up in 1439, and have lately added some detached frescoes from their palace in Milan, a huge wine press, and a vast doll museum.

Ranco ✉ *21020*　　　　　　　　　　　　**Where to Stay and Eating Out**

Surrounded by gardens, **★★★★Il Sole**, Piazza Venezia 5, ✆ 0331 976 507, 📧 0331 976 620 (*very expensive*) is a superb retreat from the world, north of Angera: a lovely old inn with a charming terrace and one of the finest restaurants on the lake. The exquisitely and imaginatively prepared lake fish and crayfish are worth the journey; they're complemented by a magnificent wine list and delicate desserts. *Closed Mon and Tues, Dec and Jan.*

Stresa: the 'Pearl of Verbano'

Beautifully positioned on the lake overlooking the Borromean Islands, under the majestic peak of Mottarone, Stresa is Maggiore's most beautiful town, bursting with flowers and sprinkled with fine old villas. Famous for its lush gardens, it soared in popularity after the construction of the Simplon Tunnel in 1906; Hemingway used its **Grand Hôtel des Iles Borromées** as Frederick Henry's refuge in *A Farewell to Arms*. Little triangular Piazza Cadorna, shaded by age-old plane trees, is Stresa's social centre, its number of habitués swollen by music-lovers attending the *Settimane Musicali di Stresa*, featuring orchestras from around the world from the last week of August through September. Two of Stresa's villas are open to the public: **Villa Pallavicino** (1850) and its colourful gardens, where saucy parrots rule the roost, along with a small collection of other animals (*open mid-Mar–Oct daily 9–6; adm*), and the **Villa Ducale** (1771), once the property of Catholic philosopher Antonio Rosmini (*d.* 1855); besides the gardens, there's a small museum (*open daily 9–12 and 3–6; donation requested*).

From Stresa you can ascend **Monte Mottarone** (4920ft), via the cableway beginning at Stresa Lido (*8.10, then every 20mins 8.40–11.40 and 12.40–5.10; L18,000, L10,000 ages 4–12*). The views are famous, on a clear day taking in not only all seven major Italian lakes, but also glacier-crested peaks from Monte Viso (far west) and Monte Rosa over to the eastern ranges of Ortles and Adamello. If you drive, walk or take the bus from Stresa, you can also visit the rock gardens of the **Giardino Alpinia** (*open April–15 Oct Tues–Sat 9–6, Sun and hols 9.30–6.30*), or **Gignese**, where the **Museo dell'Ombrello** (*open April–Sept Tues–Sun 10–12 and 3–6*) waits to tell you all about the history and making of umbrellas and parasols.

Stresa ✉ *28049*   ***Where to Stay and Eating Out***

Opened in 1863, **★★★★★Des Iles Borromées**, Corso Umberto I 67, ✆ 0323 30431, 📠 0323 32405 (*luxury*) is stylish in both its aristocratic furnishings and its modern conveniences. Overlooking the islands, with a lovely palm-shaded garden, the hotel has a pool, beach, tennis courts and a *Centro Benessere* ('well-being') where doctors will give you a check-up and exercises, and improve your diet. There's even a helipad. Some 40 years younger, **★★★★Regina Palace**, Corso Umberto I, ✆ 0323 933 777, 📠 0323 933 776 (*very expensive*) is a lovely, bow-shaped Liberty-style palace, tranquil in its park. It has a heated pool, tennis, beach, and splendid views. *Open mid-Mar–Oct.*

Another lake-front hotel, **★★★★Milan au Lac**, Piazza Marconi, ✆ 0323 31190, 📠 0323 32729 (*expensive*) has good-size rooms, many with balconies. *Open Mar–Oct.* **★★★Primavera**, Via Cavour 39, ✆ 0323 31286, 📠 0323 33458 (*moderate*) is a friendly hotel with a touch of style, and pretty balconies. **★★★Moderno**, Via Cavour 33, ✆ 0323 933 773, 📠 0323 933 775 (*moderate*) has rooms set round an inner patio. All have TV and minibar, and there are two very good restaurants. *Open Mar–Oct.* **★★★Du Parc**, Via Gignous 1, ✆ 0323 30335, 📠 0323 33596 (*moderate*) is a pleasant villa set in its own grounds below the railway tracks.

★★Elena, Piazza Cadorna 15, ✆ 0323 31043, 📠 0323 33339 (*cheap*) is a good budget option, with big modern rooms, most with balconies, all with satellite TV. It also has a garage. For even less, there's simple, central **★Fiorentino**, Via Anna Maria

Bolongaro 9, ☏ 0323 30254, 🖷 0323 933 822 (*cheap*), and the nice family-run **Orsola**, Via Duchess di Genova 69, ☏ 0323 31087 (*cheap*).

Book for Stresa's elegant gourmet haven, **L'Emiliano**, Corso Italia 52, ☏ 0323 31396 (*very expensive*), a temple of *nuova cucina* with a Bolognese touch and superb seafood specialities, local chicken baked with peppers, or salami with a tangy pear *mostarda*. The wine list includes sweet wines by the glass to go with excellent desserts. *Closed Tues, Wed lunch, Jan and Feb*. Find a table in the garden at **Piemontese**, Via Mazzini 25, ☏ 0323 30235 (*expensive*), to tuck into its divine spaghetti with melted onions, basil and pecorino, and its excellent fish dishes. *Closed Mon, Jan and half of Feb*. The **Irish Bar**, Via Passeggiata Margherita 9, ☏ 0323 31054, has been an institution in Stresa for 25 years, run by the hospitable Giovanni and Brigid Zawetta. Equally lively is the **Red Baron Pub**, at the top of Via Roma, an English-run place serving draught beer, great sandwiches and imaginative salads.

The Borromean Islands

Lake Maggiore became a private fief of the Borromei in the 1470s, and to this day they own some of the finest bits, including the sumptuous gardens and villas of the **Isole Borromee**. There are frequent boats from Stresa, Baveno, Pallanza and Laveno, or you can hire a boat and row there; the three islands have restaurants if you want to make a day of it.

The closest island to Stresa, **Isola Bella** (*guided tours Mar–Sept daily 9–12 and 1.30–5.30; Oct daily 9.30–12.30 and 1.30–5; adm exp*) was a scattering of barren rocks until the 17th century, when Count Carlo III Borromeo decided to make it a garden in the form of a ship for his wife Isabella (hence the name Isola Bella). Angelo Crivelli was put in charge of designing this pretty present, and arranged it in ten terraces to form a pyramid-shaped 'poop deck', to create the kind of perspectives beloved by baroque theatre. The project was continued by Vitaliano VI Borromeo (*d.* 1670), who added the grottoes and **palace**, completed by the Borromei according to the original plans between 1948 and 1959.

The Borromei opened the delightful, larger **Isola Madre** (*hours and adm as Isola Bella*) to the public in 1978. Here they planted a colourful and luxuriant botanical garden, dominated by Europe's largest Kashmir cypress; its camellias begin to bloom in January (*be sure to pick up the free guide to the plants*). On its best days few places are more conducive to a state of perfect languor, at least until one of the isle's bold pheasants, peacocks or parrots tries to stare you out. The 16th-century villa has a collection of 18th- and 19th-century puppet theatres, marionettes, portraits and furnishings. The third island, **Isola dei Pescatori**, is home to an almost too quaint and picturesque fishing village; a fourth islet called **San Giovanni**, just off the shore at Pallanza, is privately owned; its villa once belonged to Toscanini.

Beyond Stresa

Baveno is Stresa's quieter sister, connected by a beautiful, villa-lined road. It has been fashionable among the international set ever since 1879, when Queen Victoria spent a summer at the Villa Clara, now Castello Branca. A pretty road leads up **Monte Camoscio,** behind Baveno, while another leads back to the little Lake Mergozzo, a corner of Lake Maggiore that has been cut off in the last 100 years by silt from the river Toce. The main shore road carries on to **Pallanza**, which has a famously mild winter climate. Pallanza was united with Suna and Intra in 1939 to form **Verbania** (from the old Roman name of the lake), now the capital of a province. Here is the celebrated **Villa Taranto,** some 50 acres planted with 20,000 kinds of plants by a Scot, Captain Neil McEacharn. The aquatic plants, including giant Amazonian water lilies and lotus blossoms, the spring tulips and autumn colour are exceptional, as are some of the rarer species—the handkerchief tree, bottle bush, and copper-coloured Japanese maple. The house is used by the Italian prime minister for special conferences (*if he's not in, open April–Oct daily 8.30–7.30; adm exp*). Intra, Verbania's industrial quarter, is the departure point for a ferryboat across to Laveno, and buses up to the mountain resort of **Premeno.**

North of Intra, **Ghiffa** is a pretty, rural village with an attractive castle and 13th-century Lombard Gothic church. **Cannero Riviera**, further up the shore, is a quiet resort amid the citrus groves, facing two outrageously picturesque islets, former haunts by medieval pirates. **Cannobio**, the last stop before Switzerland, is an ancient town, one that, though in Piemonte, is famous for adhering to the Milanese Ambrosian Rite, itself revived by Cardinal Charles Borromeo in an effort to promote local pride. It has a fine Bramante-inspired **Santuario della Pietà**, with an altarpiece by Ferrari. The village lies at the foot of the Val Cannobina, where you can hire a boat to visit the pretty **Orrido di Sant'Anna** with its waterfall.

The Eastern Shore and Santa Caterina del Sasso

Interest on the Lombard shore is concentrated around the romantic, deserted Carmelite convent of **Santa Caterina del Sasso** (*open daily 8.30–12 and 2–6*), hanging on a sheer cliff over the water. The convent is visible only from the lake (if you're driving, follow the signs from the shore road after Leggiuno; boats call here between April and September). According to legend, in the 12th century a wealthy merchant and usurer named Alberto Besozzi was sailing on the lake when his boat sank. He prayed to St Catherine of Alexandria, who cast him upon this rock-bound shore. Alberto henceforth repented of his usury and lived as a hermit in a cave. When his prayers brought an end to a local plague, he asked that as an *ex voto* the people construct a church to St Catherine. Over the centuries, other buildings were added as the cave of 'Beato Alberto' became a popular pilgrimage destination, especially after a huge boulder fell on the roof, only to be miraculously wedged just above the altar, sparing the priest who was saying mass. The boulder finally crashed through in 1910 without harming anyone, because nobody was there; the monastery had been suppressed in 1770 by Joseph II of Austria. In 1986 the restoration of Santa Caterina was completed, revealing medieval frescoes (one in the Sala Capitolare shows 13th-century armed men). There's also a 16th-century fresco of the *Danse Macabre* in the Loggia of the Gothic convent.

Laveno, the most important town in the district, is well known for its ceramics. If you're taking the train from Milan or Varese, the Milano-Nord line will leave you right next to the lake. The best thing to do in Laveno is to take the cable car up to the **Sasso del Ferro** (3483ft), from where you can walk up for a marvellous view over the lake. Or come at Christmas-time, when Laveno can claim Italy's only underwater *presepio* (Christmas crib), floodlit and visible from terra firma.

The northern reaches of the lake on the eastern side are not very exciting. **Luino**, the largest town, was the birthplace of Bernardino Luini. To the north, **Maccagno Inferiore** and **Maccagno Superiore** are more pleasant places to take refuge from the crowds.

Sports and Activities

There are any number of beaches around the lake, though many are privately owned, often by hotels. There are 9-hole **golf courses** near Stresa, at Vezzo, and in the mountain resort of Premeno, reached by bus from Verbania.

Where to Stay and Eating Out

Isole Borromei ✉ 28049

The lovely and quiet ★★★**Verbano**, Isola dei Pescatori, ✆ 0323 30408, 🖷 0323 33129 (*moderate*) offers the chance to see the island after the hordes return to the mainland, and has a restaurant, where romantic views compensate for brusque service and very average food. Expect more of the views than the food at the Borromeo's restaurants too: the **Delfino**, on Isola Bella, ✆ 0323 30473, and **La Piratera**, on Isola Madre, ✆ 0323 31171 (*both moderate*).

Baveno ✉ 28042

The charming Monica and Marco run the bright ★**Elvezia**, up by the church at Via Monte Grappa 15, ✆ 0323 924106 (*cheap*), with a garden, tasty meals and parking.

Verbania-Pallanza ✉ 28052

Right on the lake, ★★★★**Majestic**, Via Vittorio Veneto 32, ✆ 0323 504 305, 🖷 0323 556 379 (*expensive*) is a grand old hotel, endowed with a good restaurant and plenty of amenities—indoor pool, tennis, park and private beach. *Open April–Oct.* ★★★**Belvedere**, Viale Magnolie 6, ✆ 0323 503 202, 🖷 0323 504 466 (*moderate*) is a good hotel for the price range, located near the steamer landing. ★★★**Pace**, Via Cietti 1, ✆ 0323 557 207, 🖷 0323 557 341 (*moderate*) offers excellent value, with modern rooms and old-style writing desks. *Open Mar–Oct.* ★**Villa Serena**, Via Crocetta 26, ✆ 0323 556 015 (*cheap*) enjoys a lovely position in a park near the lake. The best place to eat, **Milano**, Corso Zanitello 2, ✆ 0323 556 816 (*expensive*) is located in a fine old lake-front villa, with dining out on the terrace for a very romantic evening. The food is some of the finest on Maggiore: wonderful *antipasti* and lake fish prepared in a number of delicious styles. *Closed Tues.* Also on the lake front, the **Osteria dell'Angelo**, Piazza Garibaldi 35, ✆ 0323 556 362 (*moderate*) has lovely food— *crespelle* (little crêpes) stuffed with *scamorza* cheese, and various *risotti. Closed Mon.*

Cannero Riviera ✉ 28051

★★★**Cannero**, Lungolago 2, ✆ 0323 788 046, 🖷 0323 788 048 (*moderate*) has balconies overlooking the lake, a pool, better than average food in the restaurant, and a garage. Minimum stay three days. *Open mid-Mar–Oct.* The much simpler ★**Miralago**, Via Dante, ✆ 0323 788 282, 🖷 0323 787 075 (*cheap*) has views, but the bathrooms are down the hall. *Open Mar–Oct.*

Lake Varese and Castiglione Olona

Between Lake Maggiore and Milan lies the quiet **Lago di Varese**, 8½km long and the big sleepyhead of the 'minor lakes'. The main town, **Gavirate**, makes hand-carved pipes. Just south in **Voltorre**, the cloister of the 11th-century monastery of **San Michele** (now a cultural centre) has splendid, older carvings on the capitals, attributed to Lanfranco. From Biandronno boats depart for little Isolino Virginia, site of the **Museo Preistorico di Villa Ponti**, which chronicles a prehistoric lake settlement (3000 BC–Roman times).

The little Renaissance nugget of **Castiglione Olona**, southeast of the lake and 8km from Varese, is an islet of Tuscany in Lombardy, but it's an islet in a huge lake of suburban sprawl around an aeronautics plant; locate the ghastly new church and take the steep road down to the bottom of the valley to find the Borgo—the Castiglione Olona you want. It owes its quattrocento charm to Cardinal Branda Castiglioni (1350–1443), a son of the local nobility who went on to serve as a bishop in Hungary and briefly in Florence, where he was so enchanted by the blossoming Renaissance that he brought Masolino da Panicale (after his collaboration with Masaccio in Florence's Brancacci Chapel) and Lorenzo di Pietro (Il Vecchietta) home with him to do up Castiglione, and incidentally introduce the new humanism into Lombardy.

The Borgo, the Cardinal's 'ideal citadel', is essentially unchanged since 1440. In tiny central Piazza Garibaldi, the **Chiesa di Villa** was inspired by Brunelleschi, a cube surmounted by an octagonal drum, its exterior decoration limited to framing bands of grey and two giant statues on either side of the door, of St Christopher and St Anthony Abbot. Inside, nearly all the art dates from the 1400s: the Annunciation, the tomb of Guido Castiglioni by the school of Amadeo, and the four terracotta Doctors of the Church.

Opposite, the **Palazzo Branda Castiglioni** is now a museum (*open Tues–Sat 9–12 and 2.30–5.30, Sun 3–6*). The cardinal's bedroom has charming frescoes of children playing under the fruit trees by an unknown Lombard painter, while below are various emblems and sayings—mnemonic devices?—probably designed by the cardinal himself. Il Vecchietta frescoed the chapel (1437); in the study, Masolino painted a scene of Veszprem, Hungary, as described by the cardinal from memory.

Ancient plane trees line the steep Via Cardinal Branda that leads up to the Gothic **Collegiata** (*open Oct–Mar Tues–Sun 10–12 and 2.30–5; summer til 7; adm*), built in 1421 over the Castiglioni castle. The brick church contains beautiful frescoes, especially Masolino's *Life of the Virgin* in the vault, while Il Vecchietta painted the *Life of St Stephen*, and Paolo Schiavo frescoed the *Life of St Lawrence*; the *Crucifixion* in the apse is attributed to Neri di Bicci. In 1435 Masolino frescoed the entire **baptistry** (once the castle tower), a work commonly considered his life's masterpiece, the culmination of his evocatively lyrical and refined style.

The Olana valleys hold a pair of other surprises. The **Monastero di Torba** (*open Oct–Dec 10–1 and 2–5; Feb–Sept till 6; closed last 2 weeks of Dec, and Jan; adm*), set in the woods just off the road in Gornate Olana, was founded in the 5th century as a Lombard defence tower, but three centuries later it found a new use as a monastery. Acquired by the *Fondo per l'Ambiente Italiano*, the 8th-century frescoes in the tower have been restored, along with the original crypt and tombs. The tower defended **Castelséprio** to the south, a Lombard *castrum* designed on the Roman model. Destroyed in the 13th century, ruins of the walls, churches and castle moulder under the trees 1.5km from the centre, but the main reason to stop is little

Santa Maria Foris Portas: its unique 8th-century frescoes in an Eastern Hellenistic style were discovered during the Second World War by a partisan hiding here (*all part of a Zona Archeologica; open April–Sept Tues–Sat 9–6, Sun 9–4.45; Oct–Mar Tues–Sun 9–6*).

Lake Lugano

Zigzagged Lake Lugano with its steep, wooded fjord-like shores is more than half Swiss; the Italians, when they want to make a point about it, call it Lake Ceresio. Its most important town, Lugano, is the capital of the Canton of Ticino. The Swiss snatched it from Milan way back in 1512, and when the canton had a chance to return to Italy a couple of centuries later it stalwartly refused. Nevertheless, Italy maintains a wee island of territory in the middle of the lake, Campione d'Italia, which is just big enough to support a prosperous casino that more than welcomes Swiss francs. If you can't beat them, soak them.

Getting Around

Lugano's **airport** is served by Crossair, linked up to Swissair flights from London, Paris, Nice, Rome, Florence and Venice, as well as the major Swiss airports. From Varese **trains** go as far as Porto Ceresio on the west end of Lugano; from Milan trains to Como continue to Lugano by way of Chiasso, while Lugano itself is linked by a local train line (the FLP) to points west as far as Ponte Tresa.

Porlezza, on the east end of the lake, is linked by **buses** to Como or Menaggio; buses from Lugano or Como go directly to Campione d'Italia. All the lakeside towns are served by **steamers** on the *Società Navigazione Lago di Lugano* line, run with the precision of Swiss clockwork, except when the wind's up (© (4191) 971 5223; a variety of passes are available).

Tourist Information

Lugano: Riva Albertolli 5, © (4191) 921 4664, ✉ (4191) 922 7653.
Varese: Via Carrobbio 2, © 0332 283604.
Campione d'Italia: Via Volta 16, © (4191) 649 8182.

NB. Swiss phone numbers in this section are included with the country code.

Varese

A garden city of shoe-manufacturers, Varese serves as a departure point for lakes Maggiore or Lugano, Castiglione Olona or **Sacro Monte**, reached by bus from the station. Founded by St Ambrose in gratitude for Lombardy's deliverance from the Arian heresy, Sacro Monte's church of Santa Maria was lavishly Rococo-ed; pilgrims ascend along the Sacred Way, marked by 14 11th-century chapels dedicated to the Mysteries of the Rosary. There are fine views from Sacro Monte, and even finer ones if you continue up to the karst massif of the **Parco Naturale di Campo dei Fiori**. If you just have an hour or two to kill in Varese, head for the **Giardino Pubblico**, formerly the 18th-century park of the Este dukes of Modena; there's a hotchpotch of archaeology and art in the park's **Musei Civici** (*open Tues–Sun 9.30–12.30 and 2–5.30, Sun 9–12.30; adm*), housed in the Villa Mirabello.

Lakes Lugano and Como

10 kms
5 miles

N

SWITZERLAND

SWITZERLAND

Chiavenna
S. Cassiano
Samolaco
S. Fedelino
L. di
Mezzola
Novate Mezzola
Verceia
Livo
Peglio
Gravedona
Gera Sorico
Domaso
Colico
Piano di Spagna
Valtellina
Fiume Adda
Abbazia di Piona
Dongo
Musso
Dorio
Piona
Mt Bregagno
Mt Legnone
To
Sondrio
Morbegno
Rezzonico
Val Sanagra
Corrido
Dervio
Premana
Dasio
Porlezza
Loveno
Bellano
C. d. Margno
Albogasio
Drano Cima
L. di
Piano
Taceno
Margno
Pian d.
Betulle
Mt Oria
Cressogno
Menaggio
Tartavalle Terme
Mt Brè
Lugano
S.
Margherita
Mamete
Claino con
Osteno
Cadenabbia
Mezzegra
Varenna
Cortenova
Primaluna
Magliaso
Lanzo d'
Intelvi
Lenno
Tremezzo
Mt Foppe
Esino
Introbio
Ponte Tresa
S. Fedele
Intelvi
Salagra
Bellagio
*Piani di
Bobbio*
L.
Lugano
Campione
d'Italia
Castiglione
Ossuccio
Limonta
Lierna
Mt Grigna
Barzio
Brusimpiano
Ceresio
Maroggia
Mt Generoso
Comacina
L. di
Lezzeno
Madonna di
Ghisallo
Vassena
Maggio
*Piani di
Artavaggio*
Porto
Ceresio
Morcote
Melano
Argegno
Mt S. Primo
Oliveto
Mandello
Abbadia
Lariana
Piani Resinelli
Capolago
Brienno
Oveleso
Nesso
*Piani di
Lasnigo*
Onno
Ballabio
Bisuschio
Viggiù
Mt Bisbino
Torriggia
Laglio
*Piani di
Tivano*
Sormano
Valbrona
Pradello
*Piani
d'Erna*
Mendrisio
Rovenna
Carate
Pognana Lario
Canzo
Malgrate
L. di
Garlate
Cernobbio
Torno
Faggeto Lario
Asso
Lecco
Chiasso
Blevio
Brunate
Civate
Erve
Vercurago
Varese
Tavernerio
Erba
L. di
Annone
Carenno
Calolziocorte
Malnate
Albese
L. di
Pusiano
Còmo
Montorfano L.
di Alserio
Merone
Oggiono
Cantù
Galliano
Inverigo
B r i a n z a
Adda
Carate
Brianza
To Bergamo
Monza
To Milan
To
Milan

235

Lake Lugano

Lugano slowly drains its waters into Lake Maggiore through the Tresa, a river that forms the border between the Italian and Swiss halves of the village of **Ponte Tresa**. There's not much to see in either half beyond the steamer landing, but if from Varese you head instead to Lugano's other Italian landing at **Porto Ceresio**, you can take in along the way the 16th-century **Villa Cicogna Mozzoni** (*on the SS244, just north of Arcisate; open Sun and public hols April–Oct 9.30–12 and 2.30–7; open every afternoon in Aug; adm*) at Bisuschio, near the little resort of **Viggiú**; the villa has frescoes by the Campi brothers, and a fine garden.

From Porto Ceresio the steamer enters Swiss territory (bring your passport), passing the pretty village of **Morcote** on route to **Campione d'Italia**. In the Middle Ages, before state-sanctioned gambling was invented, the once-independent fief of Campione was celebrated for its master builders, who worked anonymously and are known to history only as the Campionesi Masters. They had a hand in most of Italy's great Romanesque cathedrals—in Cremona, Monza, Verona, Modena and Sant'Ambrogio in Milan—and such was their reputation that when the Hagia Sophia in Constantinople began to sag, the Byzantine Emperor hired the Campionesi Masters to prop it up. In their hometown they left only a small sample of their handiwork, **San Pietro** (1326). A later Baroque-coated church of the **Madonna dei Ghirli** (Our Lady of the Swallows) has a fine exterior fresco of the Last Judgement from 1400. Campione uses Swiss money and postal services and has no border formalities.

Lugano

Warm, palmy Lugano is an arty resort city piled between Monte Brè and Monte San Salvatore, a lovely setting that has been compared to Rio de Janeiro; in Switzerland at any rate it's as close as you can get to Paradise (a residential suburb, 10 minutes west by bus). To go with its sumptuous lake views, it has a sumptuous Renaissance gem, in waterfront Piazza Luini: the plain church of **Santa Maria degli Angioli**, frescoed by Bernardino Luini, his masterpiece; Ruskin, who wrote that Luini was 'ten times greater than Leonardo', saw these frescoes and wrote, 'Every touch he lays is ethereal; every thought he conceives is beauty and purity...' Lugano's **Villa Favorita** (*open Easter–Oct Fri–Sun 10–6; adm exp*) has a collection of paintings amassed by Baron Heinrich von Thyssen-Bornemisza: most of the Old Masters are at present showing in Madrid and Barcelona, but the villa retains a fine exhibition of European and American modern art. A popular excursion is to continue down the south arm of the lake to **Capolago** and take the rack railway up to the summit of Monte Generoso for the view.

East of Lugano the lake returns to Italy. **Santa Margherita**, on the south shore, has a cableway up to the panoramic Belvedere. **San Mamete**, a steamer landing on the north shore, is the prettiest village in the area, with its castle and the quiet Valsolda behind. **Osteno** has fine views of the lake, and boat excursions up the ravine of the River Orrido. From **Porlezza** you can catch a bus for Menaggio on Lake Como, passing tiny, enchanting Lago di Piano.

Where to Stay and Eating Out

Lugano ✉ CH6900, ✆ (4191–)

If money's no object, the 19th-century Relais & Châteaux ★★★★★**Villa Principe Leopoldo**, Via Montablano 5, ✆ 985 8855, ⊕ 985 8825 (*luxury*), in a beautiful hillside park overlooking the city, will keep you in the style you'd like to be accustomed to, complete with a health centre. Near the lake in the city centre, **★★★International au Lac**, Via Nassa 68, ✆ 922 7541, 🖷 922 7544 (*expensive*) is more than comfortable, with the added amenities of a pool, garden terrace and underground parking; if you're driving, the traditional, family-run **★★★Washington**, Via San Gottardo 55, ✆ 966 4136, 🖷 967 5067 (*moderate*), surrounded by gardens, is charming and boasts a good restaurant. Smack on the lake, far from the traffic, **★★Fisher's Seehotel**, Sentiero di Gandria 10, ✆ 971 5571, 🖷 970 1577 (*moderate*) is simple and pleasant. **★Montarina**, Via Montarina 1, ✆ 966 7272, 🖷 966 1213 (*cheap*), a villa set in a palm garden not far from the station, has pretty views over the lake, and free parking.

Lugano is chock-full of top-notch restaurants where you can seriously strain your overdraft facilities, but lunch at some of these temples of cuisine can be quite reasonable. Fashionable **Parco Saroli**, Via Stefano Franscini 6, ✆ 923 5314, serves excellent and unusual homemade pasta dishes, seafood, a wide choice of superb breads, cheeses, desserts and an award-winning wine list: for SF37.50 you can choose a pasta course, main course and dessert, and get a half-bottle of wine into the bargain; the *menu desgustazione* with six courses is SF65. *Closed Sun*. A delightful experience if you remember to book a day or two in advance, the intimate, utterly simple **Antica Osteria Gerso**, Piazzetta Solaro 24 at Massagno, ✆ 966 1915, serves a limited but discriminating menu: favourite dishes include onion soup with tangy pecorino cheese, *tortelli di zucca alle mandorle*, and duck with oranges, all accompanied by a fair wine choice from the adjacent *enoteca*; menu SF30. *Closed Sun and Mon*.

San Mamete (Valsolda) ✉ 22010

★★★Stella d'Italia, ✆ 0344 68139, 🖷 0344 68729 (*moderate*) is a lovely lake-side hotel with a lido, garden, good restaurant and waterside terraces. Each room has a balcony, and you can borrow the hotel's boat for outings. *Open April–Oct*.

Lake Como

Sapphire Lake Como has been Italy's prestige romantic lake ever since the earliest days of the Roman Empire, when the Plinys wrote of the luxuriant beauty surrounding their several villas on its shores. It was just the sort of luxuriant beauty that enraptured the children of the Romantic era, inspiring operas from Verdi, Rossini and Bellini, as well as enough good and bad English verse to fill an anthology. And it is still there, the Lake Como of the Shelleys and Wordsworths, the villas and lush gardens, the mountains and wooded promontories. The English still haunt their traditional English shore, but most of the visitors to Como these days are Italian, and there are times when the lake seems schizophrenic, its mellowed dignity battered by modern expectations of a Milanese Riviera. Even so, Como is large and varied enough to offer retreats where, to paraphrase Longfellow's ode to the lake, no sound of Vespa or high heel breaks the silence of the summer day.

Third largest of the lakes, 50km long but only 4.4km at its widest point, Como (or Lario) is one of the deepest lakes in Europe, plunging down 1345ft near Argegno. It forks in the middle like a pair of legs, the east branch known as the Lago di Lecco for its biggest town, while the prettiest region is the centre, where Como appears to be three separate lakes, and where towns like Tremezzo and Bellagio have been English enclaves for 200 years. One legacy of the

English are the seven excellent golf courses in the province, while the waters around Domaso are excellent for windsurfing. The further you go from the city of Como, the cleaner the lake.

Getting Around

 There are frequent FS **trains** from Milan's Stazione Centrale or Stazione Porta Garibaldi, taking you in 40 minutes to Como's main Stazione San Giovanni (information ✆ 031 261 494). Slower trains run on the regional Milano-Nord line to the lakeside station of Como–Lago. From Como, trains to Lugano and Lecco all depart from San Giovanni. **Buses** from Como run to every town on the lake.

A **steamer** (the 1926 *Concordia*), **motor boats** and **hydrofoils** are operated by *Navigazione Lago di Como*, based in Como at Piazza Cavour, ✆ 031 304 060, and in Lecco at Lungolario C. Battisti, ✆ 0341 364 036, where you can pick up schedules and tourist passes. The most frequent connections are between Como, Tremezzo, Menaggio, Bellagio, Varenna and Cólico, with additional services in the central lake, and at least one boat a day to Lecco. Note that hydrofoil tickets cost about half as much again as the more leisurely steamers. **Car ferries** run between Bellagio, Menaggio, Varenna and Cadenábbia. Some services stop altogether in the winter.

The City of Como

Tourist Information

Piazza Cavour 17: ✆ 031 269 712, ✉ 031 261 152, and in the Stazione San Giovanni: ✆ 031 267 214.

Magnificently located at the southern tip of the lake's left leg, Como is a lively little city that has long had a bent for science, silk and architecture. In AD 23 it was the birthplace of Pliny the Elder, compiler of antiquity's greatest work of hearsay, the *Natural History*, and later it produced his nephew and heir Pliny the Younger, whose letters are one of our main sources for information on the cultured Roman life of the period. From *c.* 1050 to 1335, when Como enjoyed a period as an independent *comune*, it produced a school of master builders, known generally as the Maestri Comacini, rivals to Lugano's Maestri Campionese.

Como's centre opens up to the lake at **Piazza Cavour**, with its cafés, hotels and steamer landing. Two landmarks in the public gardens just to the west offer an introduction to Como's more recent scientists and architects. The circular **Tempio Voltiano** (*open April–Sept Tues–Sun 10–12 and 3–6; Oct–Mar Tues–Sun 10–12 and 2–4; adm*), was built in 1927 to house the manuscripts, instruments and inventions of Como's electrifying son, the self-taught physicist Alessandro Volta (1745–1827), who lent his name to volts in a hundred languages. A bit further on, the striking **Monumento ai Caduti**—a memorial to the fallen of the First World War—was designed by the young Futurist architect Antonio Sant'Elia of Como (1888–1916), who himself died in action; the plans and drawings he left behind have estab- lished him as one of the most important visionary planners of the 20th century. The monument was actually built by Giuseppe Terragni (1904–34), a native of Como province and the most inspired Italian architect to work during the Fascist period; one wishes that he, like Sant'Elia, had lived a little longer. Ask the tourist office for their Terragni town plan.

From Piazza Cavour, Via Plinio leads back to Como's elegant salon, Piazza Duomo. The chief monuments are all attached: the **Torre del Comune** to the charming white, grey and red marble striped town hall, or **Broletto** (both built in 1215), one of the rare Romanesque symbols of civic might in the north; and this in turn is linked to the magnificent **duomo** (1396), the whole now looking spanking new thanks to a thorough cleaning for its 600th birthday. The Duomo is Italy's most harmonious example of transitional architecture, although Gothic dominates in the façade and lovely rose window and pinnacles. The sculpture and reliefs are by the Rodari family (late-15th–early-16th century), who also sculpted the lateral doors (the most ornate one, facing the Broletto, is called the Frog Door, although half the frog was chopped away by vandals). Perhaps even more unexpected than frogs are the two statues flanking the central door under delicate stone canopies: Pliny the Elder (on the left) and Pliny the Younger. And just what are such famous pagans doing on a cathedral? Although Pliny the Younger did write a letter to Trajan on the subject of Christians, praising their hard work and suggesting that they be left in peace, the fact is that Renaissance humanists regarded all noble figures of antiquity as honorary saints, especially if they were hometown boys.

Inside, the three Gothic aisles combine happily with a Renaissance choir and transept, crowned by a dome designed by the great late-Baroque master Filippo Juvarra in 1744. Nine 16th-century tapestries hang along the nave, lending an air of palatial elegance; a pair of Romanesque lions near the entrance are survivors from the cathedral's 11th-century predecessor. But most of the art is from the Renaissance: in the right aisle six reliefs with scenes from the Passion by Tommaso Rodari, and fine canvases by two of Leonardo's followers, Gaudenzio Ferrari (*Flight into Egypt*) and Luini (*Adoration of the Magi*); the latter's famous *Madonna with Child and Four Saints* adorns the high altar. The left aisle has more by the same trio: Rodari's *Deposition*, Ferrari's *Marriage of the Virgin* and Luini's *Nativity*.

For a contrast, go behind the Duomo and across the train tracks to Piazza del Popolo, where Giuseppe Terragni's ex-Casa del Fascio, now the **Palazzo Terragni**, stands out in all its functional, luminous beauty. Built in 1931, but completely unlike the typically ponderous buildings constructed under Mussolini, the Palazzo Terragni was 50 years ahead of its time, practically transparent, the masterpiece of the only coherent architectural style Italy produced in the 20th century. Its present occupants, the Guardia di Finanza, will let you in to visit.

From the cathedral, the main Via Vittorio Emanuele leads to Como's old cathedral, **San Fedele**, first built in 914. It has a unique pentagonal apse and doorway carved with chubby archaic figures and a griffon; the interior is lavishly decorated with 18th-century frescoes and stuccoes. Further up the street, in Piazza Medaglie d'Oro Comasche, the two sections of the **Museo Civico** (*open Tues–Sat 9.30–12.30 and 2–6, Sun 10–1; adm*) are the city's attic of artefacts from the Neolithic era up to the Second World War, with some Roman finds and detached frescoes along the way. From the Piazza Medaglie d'Oro Comasche, continue down Via Giovio to the **Porta Vittoria**, a striking skyscraper gate from 1192, its immaculate tiers of arches rising 72ft.

Near here, Como's small **Pinacoteca**, Via Diaz 84 (*same hours as the Museo Civico*) contains carved capitals and wonderful medieval paintings from the old monastery of Santa Margherita del Broletto. Two anonymous paintings are particularly notable: a placid *St Sebastian* shot through with arrows, and the poignant *Youth and Death*. Best of all, a short walk away from the Porta Vittoria, at the beginning of the Via della Regina (the road built by Lombard queen Theodolinda around Lake Como), is Como's Romanesque gem **Sant'Abbondio**, consecrated by Pope Urban II in 1095. The façade is discreet, and the twin campaniles of Norman inspiration, while the interior, with its lofty vaults and forest of columns forming five aisles, offers a preview of coming great events in Italian architecture. Its clean, unadorned majesty is relieved by the rich bands of reliefs around the windows of the nave and apse, imitating the intricate patterns of damasks from the Near East. The elegant apse is decorated with 14th-century frescoes: note the armoured knights coming to arrest Christ in Gethsemane. For great views take the funicular up **Brunate**, the hill overlooking Como (*every 15–30 minutes; call* ✆ *031 303 608, for exact times*). The station is on the Lungolario Trieste, by the beach.

Cantù, a short hop away on the train towards Lecco, has a rare 10th-century basilica, **San Vicenzo**, decorated with a remarkable fresco cycle painted just after the first millennium (check hours in the Como tourist office before setting out; the basilica is a 20-minute walk to the east of the station in Galliano; follow the signs).

Como ✉ *22100*   ***Where to Stay and Eating Out***

For character, charm and history, ★★★★**Le Due Corti**, Piazza Vittoria 15, ✆ 031 328 111, 🖷 031 328 800 (*expensive*) is *the* place to stay in Como. Converted from a monastery into a post house, rooms are arranged around the former cloister and all are individual, decorated with local fabrics, antique furniture and old prints. Concessions to modernity include air-conditioning, satellite TV, minibar and jacuzzis in some bathrooms. On the lake, the luxurious ★★★★**Palace Hotel**, Lungo Lario Trieste 16, ✆ 031 303 303, 🖷 031 303 170 (*expensive*) partly occupies the former palace of the Archbishop. Its rooms are big and modern, and some have fax machines. On Piazza Cavour, overlooking the lake, the grand old ★★★★**Barchetta Excelsior**, ✆ 031 3221, 🖷 031 302 622 (*expensive*) has many rooms boasting balconies over the lake. *Open all year.* Right in the heart of town is the elegant, recently reopened, 1902 ★★★★**Terminus**, Lungo Lario Trieste 14, ✆ 031 329 111, 🖷 031 302 550 (*expensive*), with a panoramic terrace on the lake. Just outside Como on the west shore, the 19th-century ★★★★**Villa Flori**, Via Cernobbio 12, ✆ 031 573 105, 🖷 031 570 379 (*expensive*) is classy and romantic. For an elegant splurge, join Como society at its **Ristorante Raimondi**, ✆ 031 573 105 (*expensive*), Como's finest, where exquisite renditions of classic Italian and Lombard cuisine are served on the lakeside terrace or in the luminous dining room. *Closed Mon.*

Near the lake, ★★★**Park Hotel**, Viale Fratelli Rosselli 20, ✆ 031 572 615, 🖷 031 574 302 (*moderate*) is medium-sized and welcoming, but without a restaurant. Another good choice, ★★★**Marco's**, Via Coloniola 43, ✆ 031 303 628, 🖷 031 302 342 (*moderate*) has 11 small rooms, all with TV, phone and balcony. You can dream about the corporate state at the ★★**Posta**, Via Garibaldi 2, ✆ 031 266 012, 🖷 031 266 398 (*cheap*), a hotel designed in 1930 by Terragni. There's also a youth hostel in Villa Olmo park, **Ostello dell'Olmo**, Via Bellinzona 6, ✆ 031 573 800.

Como is one of those towns where the restaurants tend to process clients with slipshod food and service, especially in summer. One that doesn't is the **Terrazzo Perlasca**, Piazza de'Gasperi 8, ✆ 031 300 263 (*expensive*), run by four brothers, two in the kitchen and two out front. The menu changes almost every day and features typical dishes like *filetto di laverello* and *fettuccine e funghi*, a peerless pasta with local mushrooms, all accompanied by wonderful views over the lake. *Closed Mon.* **Sant'Ana**, Via Filippo Turati 1/3, ✆ 031 505 266 (*expensive*) is also a good family establishment, dating back to 1907, more frequented by toilers in the silk trade than tourists, featuring well-prepared Lombard specialities: good risotto with radicchio and trout with almonds. *Closed Fri and Sat lunch, and late-July–late-Aug.* Another winner, the **Locanda dell'Oca Bianca**, Via Canturina 252 (on the road to Cantù) ✆ 031 525 605 (*expensive–moderate*) serves sit-up-and-take-note dishes from a variety of Italian regions out on its summer terrace. *Closed Mon out of season.* Or try the **Ristorante Teatro Sociale**, near the cathedral flank at Via Maestri Comacini, ✆ 031 264 042, serving a L30,000 tourist menu with wine.

Around Lake Como

Tourist Information

Cernobbio: Via Regina 33/b, ✆ 031 510 198; **Tremezzo**: Via Regina 3, ✆ 0344 40493; **Bellagio**: Piazza della Chiesa, ✆ 031 950 204; **Lecco**, Via Nazario Sauro 6, ✆ 0341 362 360, ● 0341 286 231; **Menaggio**: Piazza Garibaldi, ✆ 0344 32924.

Zigzagging back and forth from shore to shore, the steamer is the ideal way to travel around the lake, allowing you to drink in the marvellous scenery. The first steamer landing, **Cernobbio**, is an old resort, the 1816-17 retreat of Queen Caroline of England, who held her wild parties in what is now the fabulous Hotel Villa d'Este. Across the lake, near the steamer landing at **Torno**, stands the 16th-century **Villa Pliniana**, which so charmed Shelley that he tried to buy it; its name is derived from its peculiar intermittent spring described in a letter of Pliny the Younger. The area has been fertile soil for operas; Rossini composed *Tancredi* in the Villa Pliniana, while Bellini composed *Norma* and *La Sonnambula* in other villas nearby.

Back on the west shore, **Argegno** enjoys one of the most privileged positions on the lake, with views of the snow-clad mountains to the north and access to the west into the pretty Val d'Intelvi, which ascends to Lake Lugano. North of Argegno lies the pretty islet of **Comacina**, sprinkled with the ruins of ancient churches (and a restaurant, *see* below), the entrance to the lush and balmy mid-lake district of **Tremezzina**, where Como the 'mirror of Venus' hardly seems extravagant, especially in the spring. **Lenno**, the southernmost village, was the site of Pliny the Younger's villa 'Comedia'; in one of his letters he describes how he could fish from his bedroom window. It was in this idyllic setting, in front of a posh villa in nearby Mezzegra, that Mussolini and his mistress Claretta Petacci were executed by local partisans. They had been captured along the north shore of the lake, attempting to flee in a German truck to Switzerland. Claretta was killed trying to shield *Il Duce* from the bullets.

Beautiful villas are chock-a-block along the shore at **Tremezzo**, including two of the finest: the early 18th-century **Villa La Quiete** at Bolvedro, with its stone balustrades, and, from the same period, the celebrated **Villa Carlotta** (*open Mar and Oct daily 9–11.30 and 2–4.30; April–Sept daily 9–6; adm exp*), on the north end of Tremezzo. Originally built in 1747, the villa took its name from Princess Carlotta of the Netherlands, who received it as a wedding gift from her mother in the 1850s. But most of what you see was the work of the former owners, the Counts Sommariva, who laid out the magnificent gardens and park, where in April and May the thousands of azaleas, camellias and rhododendrons put on a dazzling display of colour. But no matter when you come you can also take in the neoclassical interior, filled with cool, virtuoso neoclassical statuary that the Sommarivas couldn't get enough of: a copy of Antonio Canova's *Cupid and Psyche* (the original is in St Petersburg), *Venus and Paris*, *Mary Magdalene* and *Palmedes* (rebuilt by Canova after someone understandably smashed it), and in the drawing room the Dane Bertel Thorvaldsen's marble frieze of *Alexander's Triumphant Entrance of Babylon*, commissioned by Napoleon but completed after Waterloo for the Sommarivas. After the Villa Carlotta, look for 'the leafy colonnade' of trees described by Longfellow which marks the entrance to **Cadenábbia**, still served by an Anglican church built in the 19th century when the English came here in droves.

Bella Bella Bellagio

High on the headland where the lake forks, enjoying one of the most scenic positions in all Italy, Bellagio (from the Latin *bi-lacus*) is a beautiful old town that has managed to maintain an air of quiet dignity through the centuries. A bus from the pier will take you to the **Villa Serbelloni**. Most scholars believe this stands on the site of Pliny's villa 'Tragedia', higher over the lake than his villa 'Comedia'; tragedy was considered a 'loftier' art, because in his day tragic actors wore higher heels. The villa is now the Study and Conference Centre of the Rockefeller Foundation, but there are two daily guided tours of the grounds between April and October (*Tues–Sun at 11 and 4; tickets are available from the tourist office up to 10mins beforehand; beware that the morning tour is often solidly booked by groups*). Another villa in Bellagio open for visits, the **Villa Melzi** (*open late-Mar–Oct daily 9–6.30; adm*), also has a fine garden and greenhouse, while the villa itself contains a collection of Egyptian sculpture.

Back on the west shore, **Menaggio** is another pleasant resort, with a lovely golf course and beach. It lies at the head of two valleys: the Val Menaggio, an easy route to Lake Lugano, and the **Valle Sanagra**, from where you can make one of the finest ascents on the lake, the day-long walk up to panoramic **Monte Bregagno**, departing from the Villa Calabi.

Varenna, on the east shore of the lake, is near Lake Como's most curious natural wonder, the **Fiumelatte**, Italy's second shortest river, running only 250m before hurtling down in creamy foam into Lake Como. For the Fiumelatte, as its name implies, is as white as milk. Not even Leonardo da Vinci, who delved deep into the cavern from which it flows, could discover its source, or why it abruptly begins to run in the last days of March and abruptly ceases at the end of October. Varenna also has a couple of lovely gardens open for tours: **Villa Monastero** (*open May–Oct daily 10–12 and 2–6.30; winter Sat and Sun only; adm*), built on the site of a 13th-century monastery with a garden especially known for its citrus trees, and **Villa Cipressi** (*same times and price; open all year*). High above Varenna, the ruined **Castello Vezio** was founded by Queen Theodolinda; you can drive up for the fantastic view. Another east shore village, **Bellano**, lies at the bottom of the steep gorge of the River Pioverna. It has a fine church, **Santi Nazzaro e Celso** (1348), by the Campionesi Masters (*open Easter–Sept daily 9.30–5.30; closed Wed*), and a walkway through the gorge over the river.

Across on the west shore, visitors to Venice will recognize the name **Rezzonico**, cradle of the family that built one of the grandest palaces on the Grand Canal. Further up, looming over Musso, the lofty, almost inaccessible **Rocca di Musso** was the stronghold of Como's notorious pirate, Gian Giacomo de' Medici, 'Il Medeghino', born during the Medici exile from Florence in 1498. He gained the castle from Francesco II, Duke of Milan, for helping to remove the French from Milan and assassinating the duke's best friend; he made it the base for his fleet that patrolled the lake and extorted levies from towns and traders. He ended his career as the Marquis of Marignano, helping Charles V oppress the burghers of Ghent. His brother became the intriguing Pope Pius IV, while his nephew was St Charles Borromeo.

Next on the lake, **Dongo**, **Gravedona** and **Sorico** once formed the independent republic of the Three Parishes that endured until the arrival of the Spaniards. In the Middle Ages the little republic was plagued by the attentions of the inquisitor Peter of Verona, who sent scores of citizens to the stake for daring to doubt that the pope was Christ's representative on earth. Peter got a hatchet in his head for his trouble—and a quick canonization from the pope as St Peter Martyr. Gravedona was and still is the most important town of the three; it has a 12th-century church, the small **Santa Maria del Tiglio**, believed to have been originally a baptistry, with frescoes of St John the Baptist; it has some fine carvings (the centaur pursuing a deer is Early Christian symbolism, representing the persecution of the Church), and an unusual tower. Nearby is another ancient church, **San Vicenzo**, with a 5th-century crypt.

Lecco and its Lake

The Lago di Lecco, the less touristy, east leg of Lake Como, resembles a brooding fjord, with granite mountains plunging down steeply into the water, a misty landscape beloved by Leonardo. **Lecco** itself is an industrial but pleasant city, lying at the foot of jagged Monte Resegone, where the River Adda continues its journey south (a typical entry in Pliny's *Natural History* records how the River Adda passes through the entire lake without mingling its waters). Lecco was the birthplace of Alessandro Manzoni (1785–1873) and the setting of his novel, *I Promessi Sposi* ('The Betrothed'), a 19th-century classic that embodies Manzoni's liberal, pro-unification attitudes. Literary pilgrims flock to the museum in Manzoni's boyhood home, the **Villa Manzoni**, now lost amid the urban sprawl at Via Guanella 7 (*from Piazza Manzoni, walk up Viale Dante; open Tues–Sun 9.30–2; adm*). Also to see in Lecco are the 14th-century fortified bridge over the Adda, built by the Visconti, which survives without its towers, and Lecco's **basilica**, adorned with 14th-century Giottoesque frescoes. The prettiest square in town is Piazza XX Settembre, just under the Visconti tower.

La Brianza

Between Lecco and Como are five baby-sized lakes in the pretty, wine-growing, furniture-making region called La Brianza. The first town, **Civate**, is the site of a famous Benedictine abbey, **San Calocero**, founded in 705, with 11th-century frescoes and nothing less than the keys of St Peter given him by Christ. Ask the sacristan at Civate's parish church for the key before setting out on the 1hr walk to 10th-century **San Pietro al Monte** (*open Sun after 8am, or contact Mario Canali, Via Monsignor Gilardi 3, © 0341 551 576*), with its remarkable frescoes of the Apocalypse, rare baldacchino from 1050 and ornate crypt. The adjacent **Oratorio di San Benedetto** has an unusual 12th-century painted altar.

Sports and Activities

There are superb walks and hikes of varying degrees of difficulty from virtually every one of the towns around the lake; local tourist offices can suggest possible itineraries. Boats too can be hired in most of the lakeside towns, and there are good public beaches in Como, at Villa Geno, and at the Lido in Menaggio.

Cernobbio ✉ 22012

The fabulous ★★★★★**Grand Hotel Villa d'Este**, ✆ 031 3481, ✆ 031 348 844 (*luxury*) is Lake Como's most glittering showcase. It was built in 1557 by Pelligrini for Cardinal Tolomeo Gallio, the son of a Como fisherman who went on to become one of the most powerful men in the Vatican—besides this villa, he had seven along the road to Rome so he never had to spend a night 'away from home'. Queen Caroline

was not the only crowned head to make use of the cardinal's old digs, and since 1873 it has been a hotel. Each room is furnished with antiques or fine reproductions, the public rooms are regal, the food is superb, prepared by a battalion of 40 chefs; the glorious gardens are in themselves a reason to stay. Add a floating swimming pool, another indoor pool, a fine golf course, squash, tennis, sailing, nightclub and more. Be warned that the rooms cost a king's ransom too, at L800,000 or more for a double; non-guests are welcome at the restaurant, where the average bill is L150,000. *Open April–Oct.*

If you haven't inherited a million bucks, there's the ★★★★**Asnigo**, Piazza S. Stefano, ✆ 031 510 062 ✆ 031 510 249 (*expensive*), a stunning hotel built in 1914 with a beautiful terrace overlooking Cernobbio and Como, and pretty rooms, friendly service and a good restaurant with a L33,000 daily menu. *Open all year.* ★★**Terzo Crotto**, Via Volta 1, ✆ 031 512 304 (*moderate*) has nine rooms, all with bath *and* an excellent restaurant (*dinners for around L50,000*). *Closed Mon and Tues lunch.* The rustic **Trattoria Gatto Nero**, Via Monte Santo 69, ✆ 031 512 042 (*expensive*) has lovely lake-views and delicious food. *Closed Mon, and Tues lunch.*

Comacina

The Isola Comacina is deserted except for a restaurant, the 50-year-old **Locanda dell'Isola Comacina**, ✆ 0344 55083. For one fixed price (*L50,000*) you are picked up in a boat at Cala Comacina or Ossuccio, and regaled with a set meal of *antipasti* followed by grilled trout, fried chicken, wine and dessert, a rendition of poetry and a return trip to the mainland. *Open April–Nov; closed Tues.*

Tremezzo ✉ 22019

Next door to Villa Carlotta, ★★★★**Grand Hotel Tremezzo Palace**, ✆ 0344 40446, ✆ 0344 40201 (*expensive*) offers the generous comforts of a large 19th-century hotel, with a garden, tennis, pool, lakeside restaurant and big rooms with good views. *Open Mar–mid-Nov.* Overlooking the lake and a shady garden, ★★**Villa Marie**, ✆ 0344 40427 (*moderate*) is an intimately Victorian hotel with 15 rooms. *Open April–Oct.*

Cadenábbia ✉ 22011

Right on the lake and charmingly old-fashioned, ★★★★**Bellevue**, ✆ 0344 40418, ✆ 0344 41466 (*moderate*) is a very pleasant place to stay, with plenty of sun terraces, a garden and pool. *Open mid-Mar–mid-Oct.* A cosy old hotel in Cadenábbia's piazza, ★★★**Britannia Excelsior**, ✆ 0344 40413, ✆ 0344 42068 (*moderate*) has lots of lakeside rooms with balconies, including cheap ones without bathrooms. *Open April–Oct.*

Bellagio ✉ 22021

Romantic Bellagio has several fine hotels, among them the magnificent, ornate ★★★★★**Grand Hotel Villa Serbelloni**, Via Roma 1, ✆ 031 950 216, 🖷 031 951 529 (*luxury*), set in a flower-filled garden at the very tip of the headland. The frescoed public rooms are glittering and palatial, and there's a heated pool and private beach, tennis, gym, boating and water-skiing, and dancing in the evening to the hotel orchestra. *Open April–Oct.*

The genial, family-run ★★★**Du Lac**, Piazza Mazzini, ✆ 031 950 320, 🖷 031 951 624 (*expensive–moderate*) occupies a 16th-century building near the centre, with a rooftop terrace and a rather traditional restaurant. The bar under the arcades is one of the nicest in town. Ask for a room with a view. ★★★**Firenze**, Piazza Mazzini 42, ✆ 031 950 342, 🖷 031 951 722 (*expensive*) is located in a villa right next to the harbour, owned by the same family for over a century. Many rooms have lake views, there's a cosy lobby with heavy beams and a Florentine fireplace, and a lakeside restaurant under an arbour. *Open April–Oct.*

Other choices include the lake-front ★★★**Excelsior Splendide**, ✆ 031 950 225, 🖷 031 951 224 (*moderate*), with a touching, faded Liberty-style charm, big old rooms (most with a view, though be sure to ask), a pool and its own garden. A few kilometres from the centre, in Loppia, the family-run ★★**Silvio**, Via Carcano 12, ✆ 031 950 322, 🖷 031 950 912 (*moderate*) is an absolute must for good value accommodation, peaceful surroundings and excellent home cooking. Fish, caught daily by father and son, and home-made pasta have already been approved by Pavarotti, Chancellor Kohl and Robert de Niro.

★**Roma**, Salita Grandi 1, ✆ 031 950 424, 🖷 031 951 966 (*cheap*) is just up from the lake, with views and large balconies on the top floor. *Open April–Oct.* **La Pergola**, Piazza del Porto, ✆ 031 950 263 (*cheap*), in the tiny fishing harbour of Pescallo, is a small, charming olde-worlde place with rooms overlooking the lake and a waterside restaurant. *Closed Tues out of season.*

In the centre of Bellagio at **Bilacus**, Salita Serbelloni 9, ✆ 031 95080 (*moderate*), you can sit on a romantic terrace, feasting on excellent, intense *spaghetti alle vongole*, saffrony mushroom risotto or simple grilled fish. *Closed in winter.* In the hamlet of San Giovanni, a pleasant half-hour walk through the Villa Melzi and beyond, is **Mella**, Via J. Rezia, ✆ 031 950 205 (*moderate*), *the* place to go for a feast of fish—starve yourself first—order the mixed fish *antipasto*, the mixed grilled fish and a bottle of lemony Soave. *Closed Tues and winter.*

Menaggio ✉ 22017

The modern ★★★★**Grand Hotel Menaggio**, ✆ 0344 30640, 🖷 0344 30619 (*very expensive–expensive*) stands in its own grounds on the lake. Rooms are fully equipped, most of them with a stunning view, and there's a pool. *Open Mar–Oct.* The ★★★★**Grand Hotel Victoria**, ✆ 0344 32003, 🖷 0344 32992 (*expensive*) was built in 1806; during recent renovation its original décor was carefully preserved and complemented with designer bathrooms, TVs and minibars. Near the centre, ★★**Corona**, ✆ 0344 32006, 🖷 0344 30564 (*moderate*) has lake-views and some inexpensive rooms without bath. Menaggio has a very fine youth hostel, **Ostello La Primula**, Via IV Novembre 38, ✆ 0344 32356 (*cheap*), with good cheap meals. *Open Mar–Oct.* For a friendly low-key restaurant with great pizzas and pasta at affordable prices, try **Alpino Ristorante Pizzeria**, Via Lago 13, ✆ 0344 32082, both calmer and better than the obvious tourist havens by the lake. *Closed Wed.*

Varenna ✉ 22050

★★★★**Royal Victoria**, Piazza S. Giorgio 5, ✆ 0341 830 102, ✆ 0341 830 722 (*expensive*), right on the lakeside in the midst of a 19th-century Italian garden, has 45 very comfortable rooms, all with en suite bath and minibar. *Open all year.* ★★★★**Du Lac**, Via del Prestino 4, ✆ 0341 830 238, ✆ 0341 831 081 (*expensive*) is right on the lake, with rooms and bathrooms that are very small though fully equipped, and have marvellous views. There's also a good lakeside restaurant. ★★★**Milano**, Via XX Settembre 29, ✆ 031 830 298 (*moderate*) is a lovely, family-run place in an exquisite setting, with eight rooms all with balconies and wonderful views. The ones to request (months in advance), are numbers 1 or 2, ideal for couples and incurable romantics.

Lecco ✉ 22053

Lecco has few hotels, but just a kilometre away at Malgrate, ★★★★**Il Griso**, Via Provinciale 51, ✆ 0341 202 040, ✆ 0341 202 248 (*expensive*) is a moderate-sized but elegant hotel with fine views of the lake from its terrace. There's a pool in the garden, and one of the region's best gourmet restaurants. *Reservations essential.* In town, ★★★**Moderno**, Piazza Diaz 5, ✆ 0341 286 519, ✆ 0341 362 177 (*moderate*) doesn't have much character, but the rooms are adequate with all mod cons.

Viganò Brianza

In La Brianza, the tiny village of Viganò, 9km south of Lake Annone, is worth a special trip for **Pierino Penati**, Via XXIV Maggio 36, ✆ 039 956 020 (*very expensive*). Delicious regional specialities and a superb wine list complement the chef's own innovations (*gnocchetti* in a saffron-scented prawn bisque, for instance), followed by excellent cheeses and desserts. *Closed Sun eve and Mon, Aug and Oct–Jan.*

Beyond Como: the Valli del Sondrio

North and east of Lake Como lies the mountainous province of Sondrio, sandwiched between the Orobie Alps and Switzerland. Its glacier-fed rivers flow in three directions: into Como and the Mediterranean, through the Danube to the Black Sea, and through the Rhine into the North Sea. Only four roads link the two main valleys, the Valchiavenna and the Valtellina, with the rest of Italy. The province is among the least-exploited Alpine regions, offering plenty of opportunities to see more of the mountains and fewer of your fellow creatures.

When the Spanish Habsburgs took Milan, the Valtellina, with its many Protestants, joined the Swiss Confederation. It was of prime importance to the Spaniards during the Counter-Reformation, assuring the route between Milan, Austria and the Netherlands. In 1620 the Spanish in Milan instigated the 'Holy Butchery' of 400 Protestants in the valley by their Catholic neighbours. The valley rejoined Italy only in the Napoleonic partition of 1797.

At Cólico on Lake Como's northeast shore, the **railway** from Milan and Lecco forks, one line heading north as far as Chiavenna, the other heading east as far as Tirano before veering north towards St Moritz. Sondrio is served by an efficient network of **buses**. Several lines run into Switzerland from Sondrio, Tirano and Chiavenna; there are direct coach connections to Sondrio from Milan.

Tourist Information

Chiavenna: Piazza Stazione, ✆/✉ 0343 36384; **Sondrio**: Via C. Battisti 12, ✆ 0342 512 500, ✉ 0342 212 590, with a horde of information on walking, climbing, mountain biking, riding, and skiing; **Bormio**: Via Stelvio 10, ✆ 0342 903 300, ✉ 0342 904 696; **Livigno**: Via Gesa 55, ✆ 0342 996 379, ✉ 0342 996 881, *aptminfo@livnet.it*

The Valchiavenna

In Roman times Lake Como extended as far north as **Samolaco**; between here and Cólico lies the marshy Piano di Spagna and shallow Lake Mezzola, an important breeding ground for swans. On the west shore of the lake stands the 10th-century Romanesque chapel of **San Fedelino**; on the east, **Novate Mezzola** is the base for walks in the enchanting **Val Codera**.

Chiavenna, the chief town in the district, is delightfully situated among the boulders of an ancient landslide in a lush valley. Amidst the rocks are natural cellars, the *crotti*, which maintain a steady, year-round temperature and have long been used for ripening cheeses and hams; some have been converted into wine cellars. The most important church, **San Lorenzo**, was begun in the 11th century and now guards its treasure: a 12th-century golden 'Pax' cover for the Gospels; also note the carved octagonal font (1156) in the Romanesque Baptistry. Above the Palazzo Baliani you can walk up to the **Parco Botanico Archeologico Paradiso** (*open Tues–Sat 2–6, Sun 10.30–12.30 and 2–6; winter Tues–Fri 2–5, Sat and Sun 10–12 and 2–5; adm*), an ancient pot-stone quarry where workers once cut out pots and stone for architectural details. Further up, **Parco Marmitte dei Giganti**, 'the giants' kettles', is named for its remarkable glacial potholes, the finest collection in Europe. The path up to the park passes *crotti* under the horse chestnuts and charming meadows; beyond the potholes a sign directs the way to the *incisioni rupestri*—etchings in the boulders left by centuries of passers-by.

East of Chiavenna in the Val Bregaglia, a magnificent waterfall, the **Cascate dell'Acqua Fraggia**, is just above **Borgonuovo**; 2000 leg-aching steps lead up past *crotti* to the ancient hamlet of Savogno atop the waterfall. In 1618 a landslide off Monte Conto buried the town of **Piuro**, next to Borgonuovo; you can visit the excavations of this humble 17th-century Pompeii, once an important pot-stone quarrying town. Before it was buried Piuro had fine mansions like the 16th-century **Palazzo Vertemate Franchi** in nearby **Prosto di Piuro** (*open Mar–Oct; guided tours only, Tues–Fri 10, 11, 2, 3 and 4, Sat and Sun 10, 11, 3, 4 and 5; adm*), its rooms decorated throughout with beautiful carved ceilings and lush mythological frescoes by the Campi brothers of Cremona.

North of Chiavenna, the **Valle San Giacomo** becomes increasingly rugged and steep, with dramatic landslides, glaciers and waterfalls. The village of **Campodolcino**, with a Roman bridge and a church with florid Rococo altars, shares the 45km 'Skirama' ski slopes with

Madesimo, watched over by a 43ft gilt statue of the **Madonna d'Europa**. **Madesimo**, further up, is a high-rise, high-altitude international resort (skiing, ice skating, trekking and riding)— before the 6948ft **Splügen Pass**, generally closed six months of the year.

The Valtellina

East of Cólico and Lake Como the thoroughly unpleasant, traffic-swollen SS38 enters the Valtellina, giving a false first impression: the rest of the great valley of the Adda, where villages and vineyards hang precariously on the faces of the mountains, is as pure and unadulterated and fresh as any, a great Alpine playground only a couple of hours from smoggy Milan.

The old, vine-wrapped villages and numerous churches along the lower valley are part of the **Costiera dei Cèch**, referring to its inhabitants, the Cèch, whose origin is as mysterious as the name. Their main town is **Morbegno**; from here buses make excursions south into two scenic valleys, the **Valli del Bitto**, with iron-ore deposits that made them a prize of the Venetians for two centuries, and the rural **Val Tartano**, a 'lost paradise' dotted with Alpine cottages, woods and pastures. The road through the valley was only finished in 1971, but many hamlets even today are accessible only by foot or mule. A third valley running north, the wild granite **Val Másino**, is traversed by the magnificent 'Sentiero Roma', and also serves as the base for the ascent of Monte Disgrazia (12,070ft), one of the highest peaks in the region. Near the village of Cataéggio, the landmark is an awesome granite boulder, the **Sasso Remenno**.

The provincial capital **Sondrio** (from *sundrium*, the land Lombard lords gave to their peasants) is mostly modern, built on the flood-prone Torrente Mallero which devastated the city in 1987. Many of Sondrio's surviving mansions have found new uses: one 18th-century palazzo holds the **Museo Valtellinese di Storia e Arte**, Via M. Quadrio 27 (*open Tues–Sat 10–12 and 3–6;* © *0342 526 270*), with art and frescoes salvaged from churches, and an exceptional collection of Rococo drawings, etchings and oils by the 18th-century Ligari family. At Via del Gesù 6, Palazzo Sertoli (with a fancypants *trompe l'œil* ballroom) houses the **Collezione Fulvio Grazioli** (*open Tues–Sat 9–10 and 2–3*), one of Italy's most important collections of rocks and minerals, nearly all from the Val Malenco (*see* below). Opposite Palazzo Sertoli, Via Scarpaletti leads up into old Sondrio, dominated by **Castello Masegra**, founded in 1041. On the other side of the Torrente Mallero, the **Palazzo Carbonera** (1533) is Sondrio's finest.

The best excursion from Sondrio is to head north into the **Val Malenco**, lined with deep chestnut forests and glacier lakes. It is a paradise for rock hounds—no valley in the Alps comes close to matching the 260 different minerals that have been found here; **Chiesa in Valmalenco** make a fine base for exploring or taking the 7-day Alta Via trail.

The Upper Valtellina

The highway rises relentlessly through the valley; but if you're driving, take the scenic 'Castel road' running north of the highway from Sondrio, past Tresivio and the melancholy ruins of Grumello Castle, then on to the old patrician town of **Ponte in Valtellina**. Ponte was the birthplace of astronomer Giuseppe Piazzi (1746–1826), discoverer of the first asteroid; the parish church of **San Maurizio** has an unusual bronze *cimborio* (1578), and frescoes by Luini.

Further east, charming **Teglio** gave its name to the entire valley (from *Tellina Vallis*). Its Renaissance **Palazzo Besta** is the finest in the region (*guided tours May–Sept 9, 10, 11, 12, 2.30, 3.30 and 4.30; closed 2nd and 4th Sun and 1st and 3rd Mon of the month; adm*). Built in 1539, the arcaded courtyard is embellished with *chiaroscuro* frescoes from the *Aeneid* and *Orlando Furioso*; inside, the Sala della Creazione has a world map dated 1549. Downstairs, the **Antiquarium Tellinum** (*same ticket*) houses the Stele di Caven or the Mother Goddess, an exceptional example of the prehistoric rock incisions common in these parts, which the locals once believed were made by the claws of witches. Among the old lanes in the centre, look for 11th-century **San Pietro**, with geometric decorations and a Byzantinish fresco of Christ Pantocrator in the apse; the **Oratorio dei Bianchi**, its exterior frescoed with a ruined 15th-century *danse macabre*; and the **Ca' del Boia**, with blackened arcades, once the home of a particularly adept executioner. These days Teglio takes pride in its wines and *pizzoccheri*, 'narcotic grey noodles with butter and vegetables', served up at the autumn *Sagra dei Pizzoccheri*. **Aprica,** to the east of Teglio, is a well-equipped winter/summer resort.

The vines begin to give way to lush apple orchards as you approach **Tirano,** a historic cross-roads: mule trains from Venice and Brescia would pass up the Valle Camonica and at Tirano either turn west to trade in the Valtellina or continue north into Switzerland and Germany. Today the town is the terminus of the FS trains from Milan and the narrow-gauge **Trenino Rosso del Bernina** that plunges and twists 70km through dramatic gorges to St Moritz; in July and August special open cars make it even easier to drink in the stupendous scenery. Once the site of a major annual Swiss-Italian fair, Tirano has a fine clutch of 16th- and 17th-century buildings in its centre, but its most famous, the **Santuario della Madonna di Tirano** (1505), is a kilometre away, marking the spot where the Virgin appeared, in September 1504. It became the focal point of Catholicism during the Counter-Reformation, and was exuberantly baroqued, painted and stuccoed and given an impressive wood-inlaid organ.

The Stelvio road continues up to **Grosotto,** with the 17th-century **Santuario della Beata Vergine delle Grazie,** with an even better 18th-century organ and, in the sacristy, a painting by Michelangelo's friend Marcello Venusti. The large old village of **Grosio,** another 2km on, was long the fief of the Visconti Venosta family, whose ruined castle sits on top of town. Just below the castle, however, is evidence that Grosio was important long before their arrival, in the curious stick-man engravings (2200–1000 BC) on the whaleback rock of its **Parco delle Incisioni Rupestri.** Art in Grosio took another step forward in the 16th century with the birth of Cipriano Valorsa, the 'Raphael of the Valtellina', who frescoed **San Giorgio** and his own house, the **Casa di Cipriano Valorsa.** The early 20th-century Villa Visconti Venosta contains the **Museo Civico** (*open summer Tues–Sun 10–12 and 2–5; winter Tues–Sat 10–12 and 2–4*); among the exhibits are Venetian-inspired costumes, with bright kerchiefs and Burano-embroidered aprons that the older women still wear. **Sóndalo,** the next town, has courtly 16th-century frescoes in its 12th-century church of Santa Marta.

Bormio and Stelvio National Park

The seat of an ancient county, not unjustifiably called the 'Magnifica Terra', **Bormio** is a fine old town with many frescoed palaces, recalling the days of prosperity when Venice's Swiss trade passed through. Splendidly situated in a mountain basin, it is a major ski centre: nearby **Santa Caterina Valfurva,** 'the skier's last white paradise', is a cradle of champions, most recently of Olympic gold medalist Deborah Compagnoni. Bormio is the main entrance into the **Parco Nazionale dello Stelvio,** Italy's largest national park, founded in 1935 and encompassing the grand Alpine massif of Ortles-Cevedale. A tenth of the park's area is covered with glaciers, including one of Europe's largest, the *Ghiacciaio dei Forni*. The peaks offer many exciting climbs, on **Grand Zebrù** (12,631ft), **Ortles** (12,811ft) and **Cevedale** (12,395ft) among other peaks. It also includes Europe's second-highest pass, the **Passo di Stelvio** (9048ft) through which you can continue into the South Tyrol between the months of June and October (*see* p.414–15); the pass is also an important winter and summer ski centre.

From Bormio the **Valdidentro** heads east up towards the **Valle di Livigno**, another ski area, noted for its traditional wooden houses and trout fishing. Before reaching the valley, however, you must pass through Italian customs—it's a bustling duty-free zone, though its Forcola di Livigno, another pass into Switzerland, is open in summer only.

Sports and Activities

Stelvio National Park is administered by Sondrio, Trentino and Bolzano provinces, all of which have **park visitor's centres**. Bormio's is at Via Monte Braulio 56, © 0342 910 100 (*open July–10 Sept daily 9–12 and 3–6*); they can tell you where to find the 1500km of marked trails, or the best place to see the park's chamois, the not very shy marmots, golden eagles, lammergeyers and ibex, reintroduced in 1968. The last bear was bagged in 1908, but hunting is now illegal, at least in Lombardy. Above Bormio's visitor's centre, the **Giardino Botanico Alpino Rezia** (*same hours*) contains many of the 1800 species of plants and flowers that grow in Stelvio.

Where to Stay and Eating Out

Prices in Sondrio's resorts are a relief compared to those in the Val d'Aosta and the Dolomites. Buckwheat is the stuff of life here, in the Valtellina's grey *polenta taragna* and the narcotic noodles, *pizzoccheri*; there are delicious cheeses like *bitto* and the low-fat *matûsh*, chestnut-fed pork, and fresh whipped cream on raspberries for dessert.

Morbegno ✉ 23017

A real charmer, the ★★★**Margna**, Via Margna 24, © 0342 610 377, @ 0342 615 114 (*moderate*) has been in business since 1886, but was completely remodelled and modernized; the excellent restaurant features the likes of crêpes filled with *bitto* cheese, risotto with wild mushrooms, and venison cutlets in juniper.

Sondrio ✉ 23100

Garibaldi is only one of the illustrious guests to have slept at ★★★★**Della Posta**, Piazza Garibaldi 19, © 0342 510 404, @ 0342 510 210 (*expensive*). Formerly the old stage post, this grand old hotel offers big rooms with lots of charm, as well as amenities like TV, phone and minibar. It also has a cosy reading room and an excellent restaurant.

Chiesa in Valmalenco ✉ 23023

★★★★**Tremoggia**, Via Bernina 6, © 0342 451 106, @ 0342 451 718 (*moderate*) is a welcoming place where rooms come with TVs and minibars, and the restaurant serves good cheesy *sciatt* and beef marinated in juniper. *Closed Wed and Nov.* In a peaceful setting, ★★★**Chalet Rezia**, Via Marconi 27, ©/@ 0342 451 271 (*moderate–cheap*) is a lovely little place with a covered pool, recommended by readers.

Ponte in Valtellina ✉ 23026

The Valtellina's best food is served in a 17th-century palace, **Cerere**, Via Guicciardi 7, © 0342 482 284 (*moderate*), which has long set the standard of classic Valtellina cuisine with dishes like *sciatt, pizzoccheri* and tagliatelle in a hearty sausage sauce; the wine list includes the valley's finest. *Closed Wed, Jan and July.*

Grosio ✉ 23022

★★★**Sassella**, ✆ 0342 847 272, ✉ 0342 847 550 (*moderate*) is a fine old hotel and restaurant, where all the rooms are fitted with private bath and TV. The restaurant (run by Pini Jim, the chef who feeds the Italian ski team) serves refined versions of *bresaola*, crêpes with mushrooms and local cheese, smoked trout and Valtellina wines; excellent inexpensive menu. *Closed Mon in winter.*

Bormio ✉ 23032

In the centre, ★★★★**Rezia**, Via Milano 9, ✆ 0342 904 721, ✉ 0342 905 197 (*very expensive–expensive*) is one of the town's cosiest hotels, furnished with locally hand-crafted furniture; the restaurant (*moderate*) is especially good, serving up delicious mushroom dishes in season. *Closed Mon.* Modern and upmarket, ★★★★**Palace**, Via Milano 54, ✆ 0342 903 131, ✉ 0342 903 366 (*very expensive*) offers tennis, a pool and very comfortable rooms, all with TV. *Closed in May.*

★★★★**Baita dei Pini**, Via Don Peccedi 15, ✆ 0342 904 346, ✉ 0342 904 700 (*expensive*) is central and pleasant, with very good rooms. *Open Dec–April and 15 June–Sept.* ★★**Everest**, Via S. Barbara 11 ✆ 0342 901 291, ✉ 0342 901 713 (*cheap*) has a garden and pleasant rooms, all with baths. *Closed Oct and Nov.* **Kuerc**, Piazza Cavour 8, ✆ 0342 904 738 (*moderate*), in the heart of the old town—and named after the ancient council of Bormio—is a good place to try local home cooking in an attractive setting.

Bergamo

At the end of *A Midsummer Night's Dream*, Bottom and his mechanic pals who played in 'Pyramus and Thisbe' dance a bergomask to celebrate the happy ending. Bergamo itself has the same happy, stomping magnificent spirit as its great peasant dance, a city that mixes a rugged edge with the most delicate refinement: it has given the world not only a dance but the maestro of *bel canto*, Gaetano Donizetti, the Renaissance painter of beautiful women, Palma Vecchio, and the great master of the portrait, Gian Battista Moroni.

Piled on a promontory on the edge of the Alps, the city started out on a different foot, founded by mountain Celts who named it 'Bergheim' or hill town. To this day the Bergamasques speak a dialect that puzzles their fellow Lombards; their language, courage and blunt up-front character are all a part of the essential *bergheimidad* that sets them apart. Although old Bergamo owes many of its grace notes to the long rule of Venice (1428–1797), the culture traffic was by no means one-way: Bergamo contributed not only artists, but the Serenissima's most brilliant and honourable *condottiere*, Bartolomeo Colleoni (1400–75), as well as many of Venice's servants, porters and stock comic characters.

The city prospered to the extent that in the 16th century another, separate Bergamo, Bergamo Bassa, grew up on the plain below; the two cities, high and low, contributed so many men to Garibaldi in its enthusiasm for the Risorgimento that it received the proud title 'City of the Thousand'.

Bergamo is an hour's **train** ride from Milan, and also has frequent connections to Brescia, but only a few trains a day to Cremona and Lecco; for information, call ℗ 035 247 624. Bergamo's **airport** has connections to Rome and Ancona. There are regular **bus** services (℗ 035 387 547) to Lake Iseo, as well as to Milan, Como, Lecco, Lake Garda, the Bergamasque valleys and Boario in the Val Camonica. Both train and bus stations are located at the end of Viale Papa Giovanni XXIII. If you're **driving**, park your car and leave it. Bergamo is purgatory to navigate, hell at rush hours (which is nearly always), and likely to leave you in limbo with no place to park.

Bergamo has two tourist offices, one by the train station (walk out of the station, turn left and look for the little 'i'), ℗ 035 242 226, ℗ 035 242 994; another a summer one in the Città Alta, Vicolo Aquila Nera 3, ℗ 035 232 730.

Up to the Piazza Vecchia

There are two Bergamos: the **Città Alta**, the medieval and Renaissance centre up on the hill, and the **Città Bassa**, pleasant, newer and more spacious on the plain below, most of its streets laid out at the beginning of this century. The centre of the Lower Town is the large, oblong **Piazza Matteotti** (from the station, walk up Viale Giovanni XXIII), with the grand 18th-century **Teatro Donizetti** and, on the right, the church of **San Bartolomeo**, containing a fine 1516 altarpiece of the *Madonna col Bambino* by Lotto. Further up Viale Vittorio Emanuele II is the funicular up to the Higher Town; once you're at the top, Via Gombito leads from the upper station in a short distance to beautiful **Piazza Vecchia**.

Architects as diverse as Frank Lloyd Wright and Le Corbusier have praised this square as one of Italy's finest, for its magnificent ensemble of medieval and Renaissance buildings, all over-looking a low, dignified lion fountain. At the lower end stands the **Biblioteca Civica** (1594), designed after Sansovino's famous library in Venice. Directly opposite, an ancient covered stair leads up to the 12th-century **Torre Civica**, with a 15th-century clock and curfew bell that still warns the Bergamasques to bed at 10pm; there is a lift to take visitors up for the fine views over Bergamo (*open April–Sept daily 9–12 and 2–8, Fri and Sat till 11pm; Oct and Mar daily 10–12 and 2–6; Nov–Feb weekends only 10–12 and 2–4; adm*). Next to the stair, set up on its large rounded arches, is the 12th-century **Palazzo della Ragione**, with a Lion of St Mark added recently to commemorate the city's golden days under Venice.

300 metres

250 yards

N

Accademia Carrara

VIA C. BATTISTI

VIA SAN GIOVANNI

VIA DELLA NOCA

VIA SAN TOMASCO

Galleria d'Arte Moderna e Contemporanea

San Bernardino in Pignolo

Sant'Alessandro della Croce

Porta Sant' Agostino

VIA PIGNOLO

Piazzale del Delfino

Convento di Sant'Agostino

VIALE VITTORIO EMANUELE II

VIALE DELL' MURA

Venetian Walls

Piazzale Sant'Agostino

VIA DELLA FARA

VIA PORTA DIPINTA

San Michele al Pozzo Bianco

Sant'Andrea

Rocca

VIA SOLATA

Funicular

VIA BOCCOLA

SAN LORENZO

VIA GOMBITO

VM. LUPO

To
Città Bassa

VIALE DELL MURA

VIA SANT'ALESSANDRO

Biblioteca Civica

Piazza Vecchia

Duome

Luogo Pio

Piazza Duomo

Santa Maria Maggiore

VIA VAGINE

Bapistry

VIA B. COLLEONI

Colleoni Chapel

VIA ARENA

CITTÀ ALTA

Palazzo della Ragione

Piazza Mascheroni

VIA SAN

Museo Donizettiano

VIA TRE ARMI

Cittadella

VIALE DELL MURA

Giardino Botanico

VIA BORGO CANALE

Casa Natale di Donizetti

To S.Vigilio &
Castello

Funicular

Bergamo: Città Alta

Through the dark, tunnel-like arches of the Palazzo della Ragione are glimpses of a second square resembling a jewel box. This is **Piazza del Duomo**, and the jewel box reveals itself as the sumptuous, colourful façade of the 1476 **Colleoni Chapel** (*open daily 9–12 and 2–6.30; Nov–Mar til 5.30; closed Mon*), designed for the old *condottiere* by Giovanni Antonio Amadeo while he worked on the Certosa at Pavia. The Colleoni Chapel is even more ornate and out of temper with the times, disregarding all the fine proportions and serenity of the Tuscans for the Venetian love of flourish. Amadeo also sculpted the fine tombs within, a double decker for Colleoni and his wife; the golden equestrian statue on top by Sixus of Nuremberg makes him look like a wimp compared to Verrocchio's version in Venice (*see* p.322). His young daughter Medea's tomb is much calmer, and was brought here in the 19th century from another church. The ornate ceiling is by Tiepolo, and there's a painting of the Holy Family by Goethe's constant companion in Rome, the Swiss artist Angelica Kauffman.

Flanking the chapel are two works by Giovanni, a 14th-century master of Campione: the octagonal **baptistry** (*open by appointment only, © 035 210 223*) and the colourful porch and equestrian statue of St Alexander on the otherwise austere **Basilica of Santa Maria Maggiore** (1137). The palatial interior, however, hits you like a gust of lilac perfume, with its sumptuous tapestries, but the best art—the 33 Old Testament scenes designed by Lorenzo Lotto and executed in *intaglio* by Capodiferro ('Ironhead') di Lovere—is off limits; only four are visible, on Sundays, although their locked wooden covers, with unfathomable allegories, are food for thought. Donizetti's tomb, near the back of the church, has mourning putti and a keyboard. The third building on the square is an insipid neoclassical **cathedral**.

The rest of the Città Alta deserves a stroll; walk along the main artery, Via Colleoni (the *condottiere* lived at No.9) to the old fortress of the Cittadella, which houses the city's **Museo di Scienze Naturale** (*open Tues–Sun 9–12.30 and 2.30–7.30; until 5.30 in winter*) and **Museo Civico Archeologico** (*open Tues–Sun 9–12.30 and 2.30–6*). Near the Cittadella is the bottom station of another funicular, up to **San Vigilio** where there is another fortress, the **Castello**, with superb views. Back at the Cittadella, quiet, medieval Via Arena leads around to the back of the cathedral, passing by way of the **Museo Donizettiano** (*open Tues–Sat 9.30–12.30 and 2.30–5, Sun 10–12 and 2–4*), with a collection of artefacts and instruments once owned by the great composer of *bel canto*, who died syphilitic and mad in 1848.

The Accademia Carrara

Open daily 9.30–12.30 and 2.30–5.30; adm; free Sun.

This is one of the top provincial art museums in Italy, and certainly one of the oldest, founded in 1796 by Count Giacomo Carrara and housed in this neoclassical palace since 1810. It has exquisite portraits—Botticelli's haughty *Giuliano de' Medici*, Pisanello's *Lionello d'Este*, Gentile Bellini's *Portrait of a Man*, Lotto's *Portrait of Lucina Brembati* with a vicious weasel under her arm and a sickly moon overhead, and another strange painting of uncertain origin, believed to be of Cesare Borgia, with an uncannily desolate background. Other portraits (especially the *Young Girl*, one of the most beautiful portraits of a child ever painted) are by Bergamo's Giovan Battista Moroni (1520–78), the master to whom Titian sent the *Rectors of Venice* for their portrait, saying that only Moroni could 'make them natural'. There are beautiful *Madonnas*, three superlative ones by Giovanni Bellini, others by Mantegna (who couldn't do children), Fra Angelico, Landi and Crivelli (with his cucumber signature). The anti-plague saint Sebastian is portrayed by three contemporaries in very different aspects—naked and pierced with arrows before a silent city, by Giovanni Bellini; well-dressed and sweetly contemplating an arrow, by Raphael; and sitting at a table, clad in a fur-trimmed coat, by Dürer. Other paintings are by Bergognone, Cariani, Fra Galgario, Palma Vecchio and Prevetali (all from Bergamo), the Venetians Carpaccio, Vivarini, Titian, Veronese, Tintoretto, Tiepolo and Guardi; also Cosmè Tura, Foppa, Luini, Savoldo, Moretto, Clouet, Van Dyck and Brueghel.

Bergamo ✉ *24100*   ***Where to Stay and Eating Out***

A few minutes from the funicular, ★★★★**Excelsior San Marco**, Piazzale della Repubblica 6, ✆ 035 366 111, ✉ 035 223 201 (*very expensive*) is the city's most comfortable hotel, with air-conditioned, modern rooms, and an excellent restaurant. ★★★★**Capello d'Oro e del Moro**, Viale Giovanni XXIII 12, ✆ 035 232 503, ✉ 035 242 946 (*expensive*) offers well-equipped modern rooms with satellite TV, lovely bathrooms, and a very good restaurant.

★★★**San Vigilio**, Via S. Vigilio 15, ✆ 035 253 179, up beyond the Città Alta—reached by the S. Vigilio cable car—was built earlier this century by a local bank for its employees' holidays. It has just seven rooms—five with magnificent views—and a nice olde-worlde atmosphere. In the Città Alta, ★★**Agnello d'Oro**, Via Gombito 22, ✆ 035 249 883, ✉ 035 235 612 (*moderate*) was built in 1600, although rooms are modern; the restaurant, a clutter of copper pots and masks, is excellent.★★**Sole**, Via Rivola 2, ✆ 035 218 238, ✉ 035 240 011 (*moderate*), on the corner of the Piazza Vecchia, is a shade noisier but homey. ★**Caironi**, Via Toretta 6, ✆ 035 243 083 (*cheap*) is a 20min walk from the station (or bus nos.5, 7 or 8). ★**Quarenghi**, Via Quarenghi 33, ✆ 035 320 331, ✉ 035 319 914 (*cheap*) is basic, with bathrooms down the hall, but it has parking. Near the station, ★**San Giorgio**, Via S. Giorgio 10, ✆ 035 212 043, ✉ 035 310 072, has quiet rooms, with bath and TV. Bergamo's **youth hostel**, Via G. Ferraris 1, ✆/✉ 035 361 724, is 2km from the station (bus no.14); L25,000 with breakfast.

Bergamo prides itself on its cooking: look for *casoncelli* (ravioli filled with tangy sausage-meat, in a sauce of melted butter, bacon and sage) and risotto with wild mushrooms. Many restaurants, surprisingly, feature seafood—Bergamo is a major inland fish market. In August, however, you might have to picnic. **Da Vittorio**, Viale Papa Giovanni XXIII 21, ✆/✉ 035 218 060 (*expensive*) specializes in seafood prepared in a number of exquisite ways, as well as a wide variety of meat dishes, polenta, risotto and pasta. *Closed Wed and three weeks in Aug*. The celebrated **Taverna del Colleoni** on the Piazza Vecchia, ✆ 035 232 596, ✉ 035 231 991 (*expensive*) features exquisite classical cuisine, including superb, delicate dishes such as ravioli filled with leek and potato in a toasted pine nut pesto. *Closed Mon and one week in Aug*.

Da Ornella, Via Gombito 3, ✆ 035 232 736, is the place to come for hearty rib-sticking winter dishes such as *polenta taragna* with rabbit and *casoncelli*. Near Donizetti's birthplace, **La Colombina**, Borgo Canale 12, ✆ 035 261402 (*cheap*) is almost the perfect restaurant, with stunning views from its terrace, and a pretty Liberty-style dining room. Try the salad of *taleggio* cheese with slivers of pear and the best *casoncelli* in town. Leave room for a slice of deep, dark caramelized apple cake. *Closed Mon and Aug*. For ice-cream, head for **Marianna**, by the Porta S. Alessandra, where you can sit on the terrace gorging on fig, apricot, rose petal or peach flavours.

The year after Bartolomeo Colleoni was appointed Captain General of Venice, he purchased the ruined **Castello di Malpaga** in Cavernago, 8km southeast of Bergamo, which he had restored for his old age; his heirs added a series of frescoes by Romanino or someone like him, commemorating a visit by Christian I of Denmark in 1474, portraying Colleoni hosting the banquets, jousts, hunts and pageants of Renaissance hospitality (*for information call © 035 840 003*).

At Trescore Balneario, 14km east of Bergamo on the road to Lovere, the chapel of **Villa Suardi** (*call © 035 943 376 to arrange a visit*) has an utterly charming fresco cycle by Lorenzo Lotto, painted in 1524 during his 15-year stint in Bergamo, when he was driven from his native Venice by the 'Triumvirate' of Titian, Sansovino and Aretino. The subject of the frescoes is the story of St Barbara, patroness of artillery-men, architects and gravediggers. Her apocryphal life reads like a fairy-tale—her pagan father locked her in a tower and, after various adventures, had her martyred for being a Christian, although he paid for his wickedness by being struck down by a bolt of lightning—and Lotto gave it just the treatment it deserved.

Southwest of Bergamo, **Caravaggio** was the birthplace of Michelangelo Merisi da Caravaggio, who left not a smear of oil paint behind, not even in the popular pilgrimage shrine of the **Santuario della Madonna del Fonte**, designed in a cool Renaissance style by Pellegrino Tibaldi (1575) on the site of a 1432 apparition of the Virgin. In Capriate San Gervasio, off the *autostrada* towards Milan, the **Parco Minitalia** (*open Mar–Oct daily 9–6; check winter opening hours with tourist office; adm*) cuts Italy down to size—1310ft from tip to toe, with mountains, seas, cities and monuments in their proper place. Due east of Bergamo, **Sotto del Monte** was the birthplace of the beloved Pope John XXIII, and is an increasingly popular pilgrimage destination; there's a **Museo Papa Giovanni** near his birthplace, filled with memorabilia (*open Tues–Sun 8.30–11.30 and 2.30–6.30*).

The Bergamasque Valleys

North of Bergamo two valleys plunge into the stony heart of the Orobie Alps. The western Val Brembana was the main route for Venetian caravans transporting minerals from the Valtellina; the eastern Valle Seriana is Bergamo's favourite summer retreat.

Tourist Information

San Pellegrino Terme: Viale Papa Giovanni XXIII 106, © 0345 21020.
Clusone: Piazza dell'Orologio, © 0346 21113.
Castione della Presolana: Piazza Roma, © 0346 60039, or © 0346 31146.

Val Brembana

North of Bergamo, just off the main road, in Almenno San Bartolomeo, the tiny, round 12th-century church of **San Tomè** (*open Sun and hols only 2–4; summer till 6*) is a jewel of Lombard Romanesque, composed of three cylinders, one atop the other, and prettily illuminated at night; its isolation makes it especially impressive. Zogno, further up the valley, has the **Museo della Valle Brembana** (*open Tues–Sun 9–12 and 2–5; adm*), with artefacts relating to the district's life and history and **La Grotta delle Meraviglie**, with a long gallery of stalactites and stalagmites. **San Pellegrino Terme**, next up the valley, means mineral water to millions of Italians. Lombardy's most fashionable spa, it developed at the turn of the century around two Baroque/Liberty-style confections, the Grand Hotel and the Casino. Excursions include a ride up the funicular for the view, and a visit to the 'Dream Cave', the **Grotta del Sogno**. According to legend, the humorously frescoed **Casa dell'Arlecchino** at Oneta in San Giovanni Bianco was the birthplace of Harlequin. The role, they say, was invented by a *commedia dell'arte* actor named Ganassa who lived there, who lumped together the experience of the many men and women who, like Harlequin, chose to forsake their poor hills to become servants in Venice or Bergamo. There are any number of lovely, forgotten hamlets like Oneta in these mountains; many of them lie in a mini-region called the Val Taleggio, on the other side of the spectacular gorge of the **Torrente Enna**.

The next town north, **Cornello dei Tasso**, may be down to 30 inhabitants, but it preserves as if in aspic its appearance as a medieval relay station, with an arcaded lane to protect the mule caravans. In the 13th century the business of expediting merchandise here was in the hands of the Tasso family, whose destiny, however, was far bigger than Cornello. One branch went on to run the post between Venice and Rome; another moved to Germany in the 1500s to organize for Emperors Maximilian I and Charles V the first European postal service and give us the word *taxi*. Their network of postal relay stations was still in use into the 19th century. Another branch of the family in Sorrento produced the loony, melancholy Renaissance poet Torquato Tasso. Cornello preserves the ruins of the Tasso ancestral home.

Beyond **Piazza Brembana** the road branches out into several mountain valleys. The most important and developed resort is **Foppolo**; besides winter sports it offers an easy ascent up the **Corno Stella**, with marvellous views to the north and east. Other ski resorts include **Piazzatorre** and **San Simone** near Branzi; **Carona** is a good base for summer excursions into the mountains and Alpine lakes. Another important village on the merchants' road, the prettily situated **Averara**, was the first station after the Passo San Marco; besides the covered arcade for the caravans, there are a number of 16th-century exterior frescoes.

Valle Seriana

Bergamo's eastern valley, the Valle Seriana, is industrial in its lower half and ruggedly Alpine in the north. At the bottom of the valley, some 8km from Bergamo, Alzano Lombardo is worth a brief stop for the **Basilica di San Martino**, containing one of Italy's most striking Rococo pulpits, covered with reliefs and soaring cherubs by Antonio Fantoni, along with some fine 17th-century inlaid and *intarsia* work. **Gandino** is another town to aim for; in the Middle Ages it was the chief producer of a heavy cloth called bergamasque. The finest structure in town is the **basilica**, a 17th-century garlic-domed church, with more works by Fantoni and a museum housing relics of the medieval textile industry.

Clusone, further up, is the capital and prettiest town of the Valle Seriana, with many frescoes, a beautiful 16th-century astronomical clock in Piazza dell'Orologio, and a market every Monday. Near the clock, the **Oratorio del Disciplini** is adorned with an eerie 1485 fresco of the *Danse Macabre* and the *Triumph of Death*, where one skeleton mows the nobility and clergy down with arrows, while another fires a blunderbuss. There are more frescoes inside, and a *Deposition* by Fantoni. Winter and summer resorts further north include the **Passo della Presolana** and **Schilpàrio**, both located near dramatic Dolomite-like mountain walls.

Lake Iseo and the Val Camonica

Lovely Lake Iseo (the Roman *Lacus Sebinus*) is the fifth in size, and a charming alternative for anyone wishing to avoid the hordes. Even back in the 1750s it was preferred by eccentric Italophiles such as Lady Mary Wortley Montagu, who disdained the English who 'herd together' by the larger lakes. Besides its wooded shores and backdrop of mighty mountains, Iseo bears triplet islands in its bosom, among them Monte Isola, the largest island in any European lake. Along the River Oglio, the main source of Iseo, runs the Val Camonica, a magnificent Alpine valley with nothing less than one of the world's greatest collections of prehistoric art.

Getting Around

Buses run frequently from Bergamo to the lake towns of Tavèrnola and Lovere. For a special treat, on summer Sundays and holidays, FS **trains** run from Bergamo to Palazzolo sul Oglio to link up to the little steam FBS train to Sàrnico, with direct connections on to the lake steamers; ✆ 035 910 900. Iseo town is served by frequent buses from Brescia, and a regional railway, the FNME, runs along the entire east shore of Lake Iseo from Brescia or the FS rail junction at Rovato, between Bergamo and Brescia. From Pisogne at the north end of the lake, several FNME trains a day continue up the Valle Camonica as far as Edolo. **Steamers** run by **Navigazione Lago d'Iseo**, Via Nazionale 16, Bergamo, ✆ 035 971 483, ply the lake between Lovere and Sàrnico, calling at 15 ports and Monte Isola. Timetables are posted by the quays.

Tourist Information

Iseo: Lungolago Marconi 2, ✆ 030 980 209, ✉ 030 981 361; **Boario Terme**: Piazza Einaudi 2, ✆ 0364 531 609, ✉ 0364 532 280; **Capo di Ponte**: by the highway, ✆ 0364 42080; **Edolo**: Piazza Martiri della Libertà 2, ✆/✉ 0364 71065; **Ponte di Legno**: Corso Milano 41, ✆ 0364 91122.

Franciacorta and Lake Iseo

Between Brescia and Iseo lies the charming wine-growing region known as **Franciacorta**, the 'free court', which, owing to its poverty, paid no taxes, a fact that endeared it to the villa-building patricians of Lombardy. Today the name of the region is also synonymous with one of Italy's best-known varieties of sparkling wine, as well as with mellowing old estates surrounded by vineyards producing a fine DOC red and Pinot Bianco. Places to stop include the **Villa Lana da Terzo** in Colombaro, where Italy's oldest cedar of Lebanon grows in the garden. The Romanesque Olivetan abbey church at **Rodengo** has three cloisters and frescoes by Romanino and Moretto, and in **Provaglio**, monks from Cluny founded **San Pietro in Lamosa** in 1083, overlooking an emerald peat bog called **Le Torbiere**, which blossoms into an aquatic garden of pink and white waterlilies in late spring; the tourist office in Iseo rents out rowing boats to enable you to paddle through.

Near Le Torbiere, **Iseo** is a charming little town and the main resort on the lake, with beaches and a venerable 12th-century church, Pieve di Sant'Andrea. **Clusane**, just south of Iseo, is crowned by an abandoned Castello di Carmagnola—it briefly belonged to the famous Venetian captain—and has a fishing fleet of white-, blue- and pink-rimmed boats called *naêcc*

Lake Iseo and the Val Camonica

Ponte di
Legno

Oglio

Tirano

Sondrio

Ponte in
Valtellina

Edolo

Ogliolo

Val di Corteno

Corteno Golgi

Val Malga

Alpi Orobie

Malonno

Cedegolo

Val di Saviore

Val Paisco

Parco Nazionale
Incisioni Rupestri

Capo di Ponte
Cemmo

Paspardo

Cimbergo

Nadro

Cerveno

Ceto

Val di Scalve

Oglio

Niardo

Borno

Breno

Cividate Camuno

Ossimo

Bienno

Berzo

Esine

Strada delle Tre Valli

Valle Seriana

Clusone

Angolo Terme

Lago Moro

Boario
Terme

San Pellegrino
Terme

Lovere

Ris. Nat Valle
del Freddo

Pisogne

Monte
Campione

Endine-Gaiano

Bianzano

Riva di
Solto

Zone

Lago di
Endine

Monasterolo
del Castello

Ris. Nat. Piramidi di Zone

Cislano

Marone

BERGAMO

Isla di Loreto

Monte Isola

Tavernola Bergamasca

Siviano

Sale Marasino

Chapel of Madonna della Cerìola

Peschiera Maraglio

Predore

Sulzano

*Parco
dell'Oglio
Nord*

Sarnico

Iseo

Ris. Nat. Torbiere

Clusane

Monastero di San Pietro

Colombaro

Provaglio d'Iseo

FRANCIACORTA

Erbusco

Passirano

N

Bornato

Rodengo-
Saiano

Rovato

BRESCIA

20 km

10 miles

✻ = Rock engravings (*incisioni rupestri*)

in the local dialect. They spend the day bagging the ingredients of *tinca al forno* (baked lake tench with polenta), a dish based on a recipe invented in 1800, and served in 20 restaurants, seating 4000—in a village with a population of 1500!

Steamers link Iseo town with **Sàrnico**, a smaller resort to the south, sprinkled with Liberty-style villas, and with the island of **Monte Isola**, a fair-size copy of Gibraltar soaking in its own tub, with just some 200 souls in genteelly decaying fishing villages; it has a number of inviting walks through olive and chestnut groves. Another steamer port, **Sale Marasino**, is one of the prettier spots on the lake, ringed by mountain terraces. From the nearby village of **Marone** you can hike up to the panoramic view point of **Monte Guglielmo** (6393ft, with an Alpine refuge), passing along the way **Zone** and its spiky 'erosion pyramids'. Next along the shore, the old village of **Pisogne** has the last train station on the lake shore, and bus connections to Lovere; its church of Santa Maria della Neve is covered with excellent frescoes by Romanino, who spent two years on the project.

Further north, **Lovere**, the oldest resort on Lake Iseo, has a 15th-century frescoed church, Santa Maria in Valvendra, and a handful of paintings in its **Galleria dell'Accademia Tadini** (*open May–Sept Tues–Sat 2–6*), especially a *Madonna* by Jacopo Bellini. The highlight of Iseo's west shore is **Riva di Solto**, with odd little bays and views across the water of the formidable Adamello Mountains. **Tavèrnola Bergamasca** has a local steamer to Sàrnico.

Val Camonica

From Pisogne the road and railway continue northeast into the lovely Val Camonica. Its name is derived from a Rhaetian tribe, the Camuni, whose artistic ancestors used the smooth, glacier-seared permian sandstone of their valley as tablets to engrave solar discs, labyrinths, mysterious figures, geometric designs, animals, weapons and people. What is especially remarkable is the unbroken length of time during which the engravings were made: the oldest are from the Neolithic era (before 2200 BC) and the latest date from the arrival of the Romans—a period spanning 25 centuries, from the random scratched symbols of the late Stone Age to the finely drawn, realistic and narrative figures of the Bronze and Iron Ages. Although it's impossible to understand the significance these etchings had for their makers, their magic must have been extraordinary: in the valley 180,000 have been discovered so far. Some are beautiful, some ungainly, some utterly mystifying, while a few are fuel for crackpot theories. UNESCO has put the Val Camonica on its list of sites to be protected as part of the artistic patrimony of humanity.

Some 12km from Pisogne, rock incisions from the 3rd millennium BC may be seen in a lovely park at Luine, near the spa of **Boario Terme**. Unfortunately the rock here has weathered, and the graffiti are often hard to decipher. Boario also offers the opportunity for a scenic detour up the **Valle d'Angolo** and its wild and narrow **Dezzo Ravine**. When the Romans conquered the valley their capital was **Cividate Camuno**, and it remembers their passing with mosaics and tomb stones in its small **Museo Archeologico** (*open Tues–Sun 8–2*). It also has a fine 12th-century tower, and in the environs churches with frescoes by the excellent quattrocento painter Da Cemmo, at **Esine** and **Bienno** (Santa Maria Annunziata).

Breno, the modern capital of the valley, lies under an imposing medieval castle; its 14th-century church of **Sant'Antonio** contains frescoes by Romanino, and its **Museo Civico Camuno** (*open Mon–Fri 8–12; adm*), in the town hall, has an ethnographic collection from the valley.

Capo di Ponte

In the centre of the Val Camonica, within a 6km radius of Capo di Ponte, are the most extensive and best-preserved prehistoric engravings: pick up a map in the tourist office. The most
accessible are in the **Parco Nazionale delle Incisioni Rupestri Preistoriche** (*open
Tues–Sun 9–1hr before sunset; adm exp*), where the Naquane rock attracted artists from the
Neolithic to Etruscan periods. Over a thousand figures, often superimposed, are etched on its
huge face: labyrinths, dogs, hunters; enigmatic processions, armed warriors and horsemen,
priests, a funeral; looms, carts, huts, even an Iron Age smithy. Certain symbols are repeated so
often as to suggest a code: 'blades', slashes and four-petalled, dotted 'Camuna roses'.

Capo di Ponte's **Centro Studi Preistorici** has a small museum, with plans of Camuni sites
(*open Mon–Fri 9–4*), while just up beyond a car park two great lumps of sandstone, the
Massi di Cemmo, once formed part of a longer megalithic alignment, covered with engravings of deer, oxen, other animals and human figures, all from the 3rd millennium BC.

A bit further up, **Archeodromo** (*open daily 8.30–12.30 and 1.30–6.30; adm*), the 'Centre of
Experimental Archaeology', has a reconstruction of an Iron-Age Camuni village; above this a
path leads to the lovely 11th-century Romanesque **San Siro**, its three tall apses rising over the
River Oglio (*to visit call Pro Loco at Capo di Ponte, © 0364 42080*). Across the river, the
equally beautiful Cluniac church of **San Salvatore** was built in the late 11th century in the
Burgundian style, its monastic grounds still protected by walls (*to visit, call © 0364 42389*).

A few kilometres south another great concentration of engravings was discovered in 1975 in
what is now the **Riserva Regionale Incisioni Rupestri Ceto-Cimbergo-Paspardo** (*open
Mon–Sun 9–12 and 2–6; adm*). The main entrance is in tiny **Nardo**, where a path leads up to
Foppe di Nardo, dotted with rocks etched from Neolithic to Etruscan times: scenes of solar
worship, stars, weapons, a village, footprints and what looks like a god by praying figures.

The reserve also encompasses Campanine, just under the ruined castle and village of
Cimbergo, where Iron-Age graffiti mingle with a Latin dedication to Jove and early Christian
symbols. Down on the main Val Camonica road below Ceto is the crossroads for **Cerveno**, up
in the hills to the west, where the chapels of the **Santuario della Via Crucis-San Martino**
contain 198 life-sized figures carved and painted in the 18th century, acting out the Passion of
Christ.

Further up the valley the scenery becomes grander as the Adamello group of the Brenta
Dolomites looms up to the right. Beautiful excursions into the range are possible from
Cedegolo into the **Val di Saviore**, with its mountain lakes Arno and Salarno under Mount
Adamello (11,660ft).

From **Malonno** you can drive along a scenic road through the chestnut woods of the **Valle
Malga**, with more lakes and easy ascents (Corno delle Granate, 10,204ft). Surrounded by
majestic mountains, **Edolo** stands at the crossroads of the valley and the Valtellina road to the
Passo di Tonale. It is a base for a whole range of excursions, and for the ski resorts of the **Valle
di Corteno**, **Ponte di Legno** (the most developed) and **Passo di Tonale**. From the Passo di
Tonale you can continue east into Trentino's Val di Sole (*see* p.402), while a road from Ponte
di Legno cuts north through Stelvio National Park to Bormio.

Iseo ✉ 25049

★★★★**I Due Roccoli**, in the hills above the town in Fraz. Invino, ✆ 030 982 2977, 🖷 030 982 2980 (*expensive*) occupies part of an old hunting lodge, amid its own large gardens. Rooms are beautifully designed and have either garden views or breathtaking views of the lake. There's a sun terrace, pool and an intimate dining room with an open log fire: service is impeccable and much of the superb food is harvested from the hotel's own farm. Favourite dishes include an *antipasto* of salad and truffles, a delicious *pappardelle verdi con funghi porcini* and, for dessert, a *mousse di cioccolato bianco* that's one of the best in the country. *Closed Oct–Mar; restaurant open to non-residents Thurs–Mon only.*

Other choices include ★★★**Ambra**, Piazza G. Rosa, ✆ 030 980 130, 🖷 030 982 1361 (*moderate*), on the lake and near the town centre. All its rooms have modern fittings, and most have bathrooms and balconies, but there's no restaurant. ★★★**Moselli**, in Pilzone, just outside Iseo, ✆ 030 980 001, 🖷 030 980 231 (*cheap*) is near the beach, in a garden. ★★**Milano**, Lungolago Marconi 4, ✆ 030 980 449, 🖷 030 982 1903 (*cheap*) offers smaller old-fashioned rooms, many with lake views, and a small restaurant and bar.

Il Volto, Via Mirolte 33, ✆ 030 981 462 (*moderate*) is an old-fashioned inn, naturally featuring lake fish (excellent with tagliolini) but also tasty land dishes such as roast pigeon in a mustardy cream sauce. *Closed Wed and Thurs lunch, and 2 weeks in July.* The best seafood in town is prepared in a variety of ways at **Al Desco del Vicolo Scaletta**, Piazza XX Settembre, ✆ 035 910 740 (*moderate*): the fresh tagliatelle with shrimp and scampi is a treat. *Closed Mon.* For a pizza or a glass of wine with *bruschetta* or a sandwich, try **Taverna L'Angolo Antigo Lantieri**, Via Lantieri 5, ✆ 035 913 331. And don't neglect the famous tench in Clusane just south of Iseo.

Monte Isola ✉ 25050

There are two wonderful inexpensive places in Siviano: at ★★**Bellavista**, ✆ 030 988 6106, rooms are comfortable, small and simple with outstanding views, and there's a nice little restaurant too; the quiet, romantic ★★**Canogola**, ✆ 030 982 5310 (*cheap*) in the trees by the lake, has only seven rooms, all with bath.

Sale Marasino ✉ 25057

By the lake, the ★★★★**Villa Kinzica**, ✆ 030 982 0975, 🖷 030 982 0990 (*expensive*) opened in July 1996 with every comfort, although there's a busy road just in front. An excellent bargain, ★★★**Rotelli**, ✆ 030 986 115, 🖷 030 986 241 (*moderate*) has magnificent views, a pool, tennis, sauna and gym and well-sized, modern rooms.

Boario Terme ✉ 25041

★★★★**Rizzi**, Via Carducci 5, ✆ 0364 531 617, 🖷 0364 536 135 (*moderate*) has the most comfortable rooms in town, all with TV, phone, safe etc. It has its own garden, with an outside veranda and a good restaurant featuring local dishes. *Open May–Oct.*

***Diana**, Via Manifattura 12, ©/® 0364 531 403 (*moderate*) is stylish and modern, with large bathrooms and wonderful views of the mountains, and a garden. The slightly old-fashioned ***Brescia**, Via Zanardelli 6, © 0364 531 409, ® 0364 532 969 (*moderate*) has fully equipped rooms, and a very stylish dining room with a pub/disco downstairs. ***Armonia**, Via Manifattura 11, © 0364 531 816, ® 0364 535 144 (*low moderate*) has simple rooms, all with TV and bath, and perhaps the most generous see-how-much-you-can-eat lunches and dinners in all Italy. A good budget option, in the station forecourt, **Ariston**, ©/® 0364 531 532 (*cheap*) offers small, clean rooms with modern fittings and old-fashioned hospitality.

Capo di Ponte ✉ 25044

Two simple, *cheap* choices here: **Graffiti**, Via Sebastiano Briscioli 42, ©/® 0364 42013, with en suite baths; and the slightly cheaper *Cumli, Via Italia 27, © 0364 42034, without; both have restaurants.

Brescia

Lombardy's second city, Brescia is a prosperous place but somehow it's no one's favourite, even though it has a full day's supply of art and architecture: Brescia's Roman and Lombard relics are among the best preserved in northern Italy. Perhaps it's the vaguely sinister aura of having been Italy's chief manufacturer of arms for the last 400 years. Perhaps it's because the Fascists saw fit to punch out the heart of the old city and replace it with a piazza as frosty and heavy as an iceberg. The Brescians detest it, but it's hard to avoid; they would do well to raze it. Give them credit, however, for preserving the rest of their historic centre by spawning Brescia Due, a mini-version of Paris's La Défense, to quarantine all their new office buildings.

History

Brescia was founded by the Gauls, remembered in its name Brixia, from the Celtic *brik* ('hill'). Brixia saw the inevitability of Rome early on, became a willing ally, and in 26 BC achieved the favoured status of a *Colonia Civica Augusta*, when it was embellished with splendid monuments. By the 8th century Brescia had recovered enough from the barbarian invasions to become the seat of a Lombard duchy under King Desiderius, whose daughter Ermengarda was wed by Charlemagne—the condition imposed by the Italians before they crowned him emperor. He later repudiated her, and the forlorn Ermengarda returned to Brescia to die in the Abbey of San Salvatore.

When Brescia joined the Lombard League against Barbarossa it had an eloquent voice to express its dissent: that of a Benedictine monk, Arnold of Brescia, who studied under Peter Abelard in Paris and went to Rome, preaching eloquently against the tyranny of the emperor and the corrupt, worldly materialism of the Church. In 1155 Barbarossa arrested the troublesome monk and handed him over to Pope Adrian IV, who burned Arnold alive at the stake. Firmly in the Guelph camp, Brescia held tight when Frederick II besieged it for 68 days, it briefly suffered under his lieutenant, the unspeakable Ezzelino da Romano, in 1258, then betrayed him; in 1421, when the detested Visconti horned in, the weary Brescians turned to Venice for relief and asked to be adopted. The Venetians didn't have to be asked twice; Brescia meant access to the unusually pure iron deposits in the valleys to the north. By the 16th century Brescia had become Italy's major producer of firearms, and the Serenissima imposed severe emigration restrictions to keep skilled workers from wandering.

Venice not only brought peace and prosperity, but initiated an artistic flowering as well. The Brescian Vincenzo Foppa (1485–1566) was a key figure in the Lombard Renaissance; his monumental paintings were among the first to depict a single, coherent atmosphere. The individualistic linear style of Girolamo Romanino (1485–1566) may stand somewhat apart, but Romanino's contemporary Alessandro Bonvincino (better known as 'the little Moor' or Moretto; 1498–1554), an ardent student of Titian, contributed the first Italian full-length portrait and taught Giovanni Battista Moroni of Bergamo. His contemporary, Giovanni Girolamo Savoldo, a Brescian who later worked in Venice, was neglected in his day but is now recognized for his lyricism. Recently Giacomo Antonio Ceruti (1698–1767) has been the centre of interest for his realist, unromanticized genre paintings of Brescia's humble, demented and down-and-out. His nickname was Il Pitocchetto ('the little skinflint').

Getting Around

Brescia is on the main Milan–Venice **rail** line, 55 minutes from Milan, an hour from Verona, and less to Desenzano del Garda, the main station on Lake Garda. There are also frequent services to Bergamo and Lecco, to Cremona and to Parma via Piadena. For FS rail information, call ✆ 030 37961. The regional FNME railway line wends its way north along the east shore of Lake Iseo and up the Val Camonica to Edolo.

There is an even more extensive **bus** network, with frequent links to the towns of Lakes Garda and Iseo and less frequently to Idro; also to Turin and Milan, Padua, Marostica, Bassano del Grappa and Belluno; to Trento via Riva and to Pinzolo and Madonna di Campiglio in Trentino, as well as to all points within the province. For information, call ✆ 030 44061. The **bus** and **railway stations** are located next to each other just south of the city centre on Viale Stazione. Bus C connects them to the centre, or you can walk there in 10 minutes up the Corso Martiri della Libertà.

Tourist Information

Corso Zanardelli 38, ✆ 030 45052, near the central Piazza del Duomo.

The Central Squares

Hurry, as the Brescians do, through the deathly pale **Piazza della Vittoria**, designed in 1932 by Marcello Piacentini: a frigid, Fascist square that melts each May, when it acts as the starting gate for the famous *Mille Miglia* vintage car race across Italy. Duck behind the post office to enter into a far more elegant display of power, the closed, Venetian-style **Piazza della Loggia**, named for the **Palazzo della Loggia**, Brescia's town hall, a neo-Roman confection begun in 1492 and designed in part by Sansovino and Palladio; its great white roof swells over the old city like Moby Dick on the prowl. Opposite the Palazzo della Loggia, the **Torre dell'Orologio** is a copy of the clock tower in St Mark's Square, complete with two bell-ringing figures on top. The Brescians must have been hopeless spendthrifts: the other chief buildings on the square are the old and new municipal pawn shops, the **Monte di Pietà Vecchia** (1489) and the **Monte di Pietà Nuova** (1590s); the Roman inscriptions embedded in the façade of the former constitute Italy's very first lapidary collection.

Looming up behind the clock tower rises the third-highest dome in Italy, the crown of the **duomo**, built in 1602 by Gianbattista Lantana. From the **Piazza Paolo VI** itself, however, the dome is hidden by a high marble front—a Lombard 'wind-breaker' façade. Over the door a bust of Brescia's great Cardinal Querini 'winks mischievously, as if inviting the faithful to enter'. You should take him up on it, not so much for the few paintings by Romanino (by the bishop's throne) and Moretto that try to warm the cold interior, as to visit the adjacent **Duomo Vecchio** or La Rotonda (*open April–Oct Wed–Mon 9–12 and 3–7; Nov–Mar Sat and Sun only 9–12 and 3–6*). Built in the 11th century over the ruined Basilica of San Filastrio and the ancient Roman baths, this singular old cathedral is the only one in Italy designed in the shape of a top hat, with a massive cylindrical tower rising from its centre, supported by eight pillars, the light diffused through its upper windows.

Inside, its simple form is broken only by a 15th-century raised choir; the altarpiece, an *Assumption* by Moretto, is one of his greatest works. The crypt of San Filastrio contains a mixed bag of Roman and early medieval columns, and mosaics from the baths. Several medieval bishops are entombed around the walls, most impressively Bishop Mernardo Maggi in his sarcophagus of 1308; the treasury holds two precious relics—the 16th-century *Stauroteca* containing a bit of the True Cross, and the 11th-century banner once borne on the *carroccio* of the Brescian armies.

On the other side of the new Duomo, the 12th-century **Broletto** was the old civic centre of Brescia and later became the seat of the Venetian governor; its formidable tower, the **Pegol**, predates it by a century. Just behind the new cathedral, the 18th-century **Biblioteca Queriniana**, Via Mazzini 1, contains rarities such as the 6th-century 'Purple Evangeliary' with silver letters, and Eusebius' 11th-century Concordances of the Gospels; Cardinal Querini, the founder, enriched his own collection at the expense of the Vatican Library.

Roman and Lombard Brixia

Flanking the Broletto, the ancient *Decumanus Maximus*, now Via dei Musei, leads to the heart of Roman Brixia. Its forum, now the narrow **Piazza del Foro**, lies under the mighty columns of the **Tempio Capitolino**, erected by Vespasian in AD 73 and preserved for posterity by a medieval mud-slide that covered it until its rediscovery in 1823. In 1955 an earlier, Republican-era Capitoline temple was discovered beneath Vespasian's, with unusual mosaics of natural stone. The Temple is divided into three *cellae*, which were probably dedicated to Jupiter, Juno and Minerva. They are now filled with the tombs and mosaics of the **Civico Museo Romano** (*open Tues–Sun 9–12.30 and 3–5; summer 10–12.30 and 3–6; adm*), a considerable collection thanks to the foresight of the 1485 municipal council, which forbade the sale of antiquities outside Brescia. The best treasures are upstairs: six gilded bronze busts of emperors and a 6ft bronze Winged Victory who, bereft of the object she once held, seems to be snapping her fingers in a dance. There's a gilt bronze figurine of a Gaulish prisoner, believed to be Vercingetorix, a beautiful Greek amphora from the 6th century BC and a facsimile of the 25ft-long Peutringer Map of Vienna, itself a 12th-century copy of a Roman road map.

Next to the temple is the unexcavated *cavea* of the **Teatro Romano**, while down Via Carlo Cattaneo, in Piazza Labus, you can make out the columns and lintels of the third building of the forum: the **curia**, or senate, imprinted like a fossil in the wall of a house.

From Piazza del Foro, Via dei Musei continues to the **Monastero di San Salvatore-Santa Giulia** (*open Tues–Sun 10–5; adm*), founded in the 700s by the wife of the Lombard king

Desiderius, and disbanded at the end of the 18th century. Its **Museo della Città** partly reopened in February 1996; during the work, a large Roman *domus* was uncovered under one of the three cloisters. The heart of the complex, the 8th-century **Basilica of San Salvatore**, was modelled on the 6th-century churches of Ravenna. In the nave, the capitals are either ancient Roman or made of stucco, an art at which the Lombards excelled. Some Carolingian frescoes remain under the arcades; others were painted by Girolamo Romanino in 1530. The semi-circular crypt, where the relics of St Giulia were laid in 762, was enlarged in the 12th century, with vigorous capitals sculpted by the school of Antelami: the one on the life of Giulia is a serene masterpiece. The same century saw the addition of another church, sturdy **Santa Maria in Solario**, crowned with an octagonal dome, its lower vaults supported on an ancient Roman altar, its upper level frescoed by Floriano Ferramola (1480–1528). In the 16th century a third church, **Santa Giulia**, was built; the nuns' choir has more frescoes by Ferramola.

The museum contains exceptional pieces. One is the 8th-century golden Lombard *Cross of Desiderius*, studded with 212 gems and cameos, including one from the 4th century of a Roman woman with her two children, peering warily into the approaching Dark Ages; the Brescians believe it is the great Galla Placidia of Ravenna. A 4th-century ivory coffer called the *Lipsanoteca* is adorned with beautiful bas-reliefs. One of the superb 5th-century ivory diptychs originally belonged to the father of the philosopher Boethius. Lombard jewellery, medieval art and Renaissance medals round off the collection.

The Cydnean Hill

The poet Catullus, who considered Brixia the mother of his native Verona, was the first to mention the Cydnean Hill that rises behind Via dei Musei. Named after the Celto-Ligurian king Cidno, the founder of Brixia, the site has been inhabited since the Bronze Age. It was the core of Gaulish and early Roman Brixia—along Via Piamarta are the ruins of the city's last surviving **Roman gate**, as well as the attractive 1510 **San Pietro in Oliveto**, named after the ancient silvery olive grove that surrounds the church. Up on top, an imposing Venetian gate in Istrian marble, still guarded by the Lion of St Mark, is the entrance to the **castello**, with its round Mirabella Tower, sitting on a Roman foundation. Built in 1443 during the brief reign of the Visconti, the donjon houses the **Museo Civico delle Armi Antiche Luigi Marzoli** (*open June–Sept Tues–Sun 10–5; Oct–May 9.30–1 and 2.30–5; adm*), one of Italy's most extensive collections of Brescia's bread-and-butter industry, with a special collection of 15th–18th-century firearms. The castle's Venetian granary houses the **Museo del Risorgimento** (*same hours*) with paintings, uniforms and weapons, with special honours going to Brescia's Ten Day revolt in 1849, bloodily suppressed by Austria.

The Pinacoteca and Around

From the Capitoline Temple, Via Crispi descends to Piazza Moretto, site of the **Pinacoteca Civica Tosio-Martinengo** (*open June–Sept Tues–Sun 10–5; Oct–May 9.30–1 and 2.30–5; adm*), housed in a 16th-century patrician palace. It showcases Brescia's local talent, including Foppa (*Madonna and Saints*), Savoldo, Moretto (his *Salomé* is a portrait of the Roman courtesan-poet Tullia d'Aragona), Romanino, Moroni and Ceruti; there's also a lovely *Adoration of the Magi* by Lorenzo Lotto, a *Senator* by Tintoretto, a *Portrait of Henri III* by Clouet and two early works by Raphael—a not altogether wholesome, beardless *Redeemer* and a lovely *Angel*, and an anonymous golden fairy-tale picture of *St George and the Princess*.

South on Via Crispi, there's more art in 16th-century **Santa Angela Merci** (by Tintoretto and Francesco Bassano) and at Via Monti 9, in the Istituto Paolo VI's **Museo Arte e Spiritualità** (*open Thurs–Sun 4–7*), devoted to contemporary religious art, something that Pope Paul VI sincerely believed wasn't an oxymoron. **Sant'Alessandro**, in Via Moretto, contains a pretty *Annunciation* by Jacopo Bellini; further north, in elegant, porticoed Corso Zanardelli, the **Teatro Grande** has a luscious foyer and five tiers of boxes; here, in 1904, Puccini's *Madam Butterfly* was wholeheartedly vindicated by the public after its disastrous premiere.

West Side Churches

The piquant quarters west of Piazza della Loggia are rich in interesting old churches. Just west of Via S. Faustino there are two strikingly unusual ones—**San Faustino in Riposo**, a cylindrical, steep-roofed drum of a church from the 12th century (near the intersection with Via dei Musei) and, further up on Contrada Carmine, the 14th-century **Santa Maria del Carmine**, crowned with a set of Mongol-like brick pinnacles; it contains frescoes by Foppa, among his finest work, and a 15th-century terracotta *Deposition* by Mazzoni (*open Tues–Sun 4–7*).

Just off Corso G. Mameli, Renaissance **San Giovanni Evangelista** has good works by Moretto, Romanino and the Bolognese painter Francia. Further along the Corso stands the giant **Torre della Pallata**, a survivor from the rough-and-tumble 13th century, with a travesty of a 16th-century fountain like a bunion on its foot. From here Via della Pace heads south to the venerable **San Francesco** (1265) with its cloister in red Verona marble and frescoes (a few by Romanino and Moretto), and the nearby **Santa Maria dei Miracoli** with a lovely 15th-century Lombard Renaissance marble façade that survived even though the interior was blown to smithereens in the last war. Further south, on Corso Matteotti, the 18th-century **Santi Nazzaro e Celso** houses the Averoldi polyptych (1522), considered the masterpiece of Titian's youth, with a gravity-defying, virtuoso *Risen Christ* in the centre. The chapels hold works by Moretto (*to get in, contact Signor Federici at nearby S. Maria dei Miracoli*).

Brescia ✉ *25100*   ***Where to Stay and Eating Out***

Brescia caters mainly to business clients, and its best hotels are comfortable if not inspiring. The city's premier hotel, ★★★★★**Vittoria**, Via X Giornate 20, ✆ 030 280 061, 🖷 030 280 065 (*very expensive*) has large, sumptuous rooms, palatial bathrooms of French *Rosa* marble, banqueting suites, and liberal use of marble and chandeliers throughout—but the severe Fascist-era architecture is a bit soulless. Near the centre by the castle, ★★★★**Master**, Via L. Apollonio 72, ✆ 030 399 037, 🖷 030 370 1331 (*expensive*) has some of the best rooms in town. A bit further out, ★★★★**Ambasciatori**, Via Crocifissa di Rosa 92, ✆ 030 399 114, 🖷 030 381 883 (*moderate*) is very modern, with a garage. ★★★**Cristallo**, Viale Stazione 12, ✆ 030 377 2468, 🖷 030 377 2615 (*moderate*) is an adequate, albeit nondescript, place near the station; ★★**Astron**, Via Togni 14, ✆/🖷 030 48220 (*cheap*) has clean, simple rooms.

Brescians are stolid conservatives at table: kid, stews, *risotti*, meat on a skewer and polenta have been in vogue since the Renaissance. You'll find them at elegant **La Sosta**, Via San Martino della Battaglia 20, ✆ 030 295 603 (*expensive*), set in an overhauled 17th-century stable; a second menu features prestige fish and Italian classics. *Closed Mon, Sun eve and Aug*.

The lovely medieval **Castello Malvezzi**, just north of the centre at Via Colle San Giuseppe 1, ✆ 030 200 4224 (*expensive*) serves delicious food, cooked by a French and an Italian chef, to go with a superb selection of wines. *Open eves only, closed Sun, Mon and most of Aug*.

The freshest of seafood with a Tuscan touch holds pride of place at **I Templari**, Via Matteotti 19, ✆ 030 52234 (*expensive*). *Closed Sat lunch and Sun*. Near the Duomo Vecchio, the intimate **Circolo delle Arti**, Via Trieste 3, ✆ 030 43008 (*moderate*) serves excellent southern Italian dishes; try the reasonably priced lunch menu. *Closed Tues*. **Bersagliera**, Corso Magenta 38 (*cheap*) is a good, popular pizzeria. At **La Vineria**, Via X Giornate 4, ✆ 030 280 477 (*cheap*) you can feast on excellent cured meats and salami, herby risotto, *casoncelli* and home-made tarts. *Closed Mon*.

Around Brescia

Besides Lakes Garda and Iseo, there are a number of worthwhile excursions into the mountains—as well as one to the south in the plain, to Montirone and its fine **Villa Lechi**, built in 1740 by Antonio Turbino, and little changed since the day when Mozart slept there. It has frescoes by Carlo Carloni and period furnishings, and the stables and park are well preserved.

To the north stretches the **Valtrompia**, a scenic agricultural valley. Its largest town, **Gardone Val Trompia**, produced firearms for Venice, and enjoyed the special protection of the Republic; it still makes hand-crafted sports rifles. North of Gardone the valley narrows as the road climbs to two summer resorts, **Bovegno** and **Collio**. Beyond Collio a new road continues up to the scenic **Passo del Maniva** and over to the Passo di Croce Domini.

Long, narrow **Lake Idro** lies over the mountains from Collio, at the head of the Val Sabbia. Surrounded by rugged mountains and rural villages, it is the highest of the Lombard lakes, and one of the best for trout fishing. Named after the small resort town of **Idro**, its sandy beaches are all low-key, family-orientated places. **Anfo** is another resort, while the most interesting lake settlement is **Bagolino**, on the trout-filled River Caffaro, with its peaceful medieval streets and the 15th-century church of San Rocco, frescoed in the 1400s by Da Cemmo. From Lake Idro you can continue up the Chiese River into Trentino's Valli Giudicarie (*see* p.401).

Lake Garda

The Italian lakes culminate in Garda, the largest (48km long, and 16km across at its widest point) and most dramatic, the Riviera of the Dolomites. With the profile of a tall-hatted witch, its romantic shores have enchanted poets from the days of Catullus and Virgil, who both knew it by its Roman name, *Lacus Benacus*. For travellers from the north, its olive and lemon groves, its slender cypress and exotic palm trees have long signalled the beginning of their dream Italy. No tourist office could concoct a more scintillating Mediterranean oasis to stimulate what the Icelanders call 'a longing for figs'—the urge to go south.

To Trento

Rovereto

Condino

Tiarno
Bezzecca
Varone
Arco

S. Antonio
Storo
L. Ledro
Molina di Ledro
Bastione
Riva del Garda
Torbole
N240
Mori

Bagolino

Mt. Caplone
Tremosine
Limone sul Garda
Tempesta
Brentonico Fontechel

Vesta
Magasa
Priezzo
Voltino
Bocca Tratto Spino
S. Valentino

L. Idro
Mt. Stino
Sermerio
Pieve
N149
Malcésine

Anfo
Vantone
Zumie
Valvestino
Tignale
Campione
Val di Sogno
Ala

Lavenone
Idro
Lemprato
L. Valvestino
Costa Mignone
Sommavilla
Porto di Brenzone
Mt. Cerbiolo
Avio
Mt. Castelberto

Mt. Zingla
Brenzone
Monte Baldo
Telegrafo
Belluno
Corno d'Aquilio
Mt. Tomba

Sabbio
Mt. Pizzocolo
S. Faustino
Gargnano
Castelletto Brenzone
Mezzavilla
Ferrara di M. Baldo
Peri
Monti Lessini
Tracchi

Vobarno
Cecina
Bogliaco
Senaga
Fosse
S. Anna
Erbezzo

Volciano
Toscolano
Pai
S. Zeno
Lumini
Breonio
Bosco Chiesanuova
Rovere Verona

Gavardo
Moderno
Gardone Riviera
Barbarano
Salò
Torri del Benaco
Caprino
Molina
Dolcè
Vaggimal
Prun
Ponte di Veja
To the Valley of the Sphinxes

Lake
S. Felice di Benaco
Pieve Vecchia
S. Vigílio
Garda
Costermano
Cerajno Monte
S. Giorgio
Villa
Stallavena

Polpenazze
Manerba
Gardoncino
Bardolino
Affi
Cisano
S. Ambrogio
Negrar
Pedemonte
Grezzana

Padenghe
Moniga
Garda
Lazise
Pastrengo
Valpolicella
Pescantina

To Brescia
Fabbrica
Lido di Lonato
Sirmione
Pacengo
Fiume Adige
Verona

Lonato
Desenzano del Garda
Colombare
Peschiera del Garda
Castelnuovo del Garda
To Vicenza

Calcinato
Rivóltella
Benedetto
A4

S. Martino della Battáglia
Sommacampagna

Solferino
Monzambano
Sigurtà Gardens
Villafranca di Verona

Volta
Valeggio sul Mincio
Fiume Mincio
N62

N
10 kms
5 miles
To Mantua

Lake Garda

269

Lake Garda is less status-conscious than the other lakes, and draws a wide range of visitors, from beach bums to package tourists and sailors and windsurfers come to test their mettle on Garda's unusual winds, first mentioned by Virgil: the *sover* which blows from the north from midnight and through the morning, and the *ora*, which blows from the south in the afternoon and evening. Storms are not uncommon, but on the other hand the breezes are delightfully cool in the summer. In the winter Garda enjoys a mild climate, less oppressed by clammy fogs and mists than the other lakes; the jagged peaks that rim it shimmer with snow and you can better take in the voluptuous charms that brought visitors to its shores in the first place.

Getting Around

There are two **train stations** at the southern end of Lake Garda, at Desenzano and Peschiera, both of which are also landings for the lake's **hydrofoils** (*aliscafi*) and **steamers**. **Buses** from Brescia, Trento and Verona go to their respective shores; Desenzano, the gateway to Lake Garda, is served by buses from Brescia, Verona and Mantua. Frequent buses connect Sirmione to Desenzano and Peschiera.

Other local bus lines run up and down the road that winds around the lake shores—a marvel of Italian engineering called *La Gardesana*, Occidentale (SS45) on the west, and Orientale (SS249) on the east. In summer, however, their scenic splendour sometimes pales before the sheer volume of holiday traffic.

All **boat services** on the lake are operated by *Navigazione sul Lago di Garda*, Piazza Matteotti 2, Desenzano, ✆ 030 9141 9511, where you can pick up a timetable; the tourist offices have them as well. The one **car ferry** crosses from Maderno to Torri; between Desenzano and Riva there are several hydrofoils a day, calling at various ports (2 hours the full trip), as well as the more frequent and leisurely steamers (4½ hours). Services are considerably reduced from October to March. Full fare on the 4-hour sail from Desenzano to Riva on the steamer is L15,400, and on the hydrofoil L20,700.

Tourist Information

Desenzano del Garda: Via Porto Vecchio 27, ✆ 030 914 1510, ✉ 030 914 4209; **Sirmione**: Viale Marconi 2, ✆ 030 916 114, ✉ 030 916 222; **Gardone Riviera**: Corso Repubblica, ✆ 0365 20347; **Gargnano**: Piazza Feltrinelli 2, ✆ 0365 712 224; **Limone sul Garda**: Piazzale A. De Gaspari, ✆ 0365 954 070, ✉ 0365 954 355; **Riva del Garda**, Giardini di Porta Orientale 8, ✆ 0464 554 444, ✉ 0464 520 308; **Arco**: Via delle Palme 1, ✆ 0464 532 155, ✉ 0464 532 353.

The South Shore: Desenzano and Solferino

Lively, colourful and delightful, **Desenzano del Garda**, on a wide gulf dotted with beaches, is Garda's largest town, built up in the 15th and 16th centuries (if you arrive by train, a bus will take you to the centre). Life centres around its busy portside cafés, presided over by a statue of Sant'Angela, foundress of the Ursuline Order, who seems appalled at all the carryings-on; another statue on the lake front, the whooshing **high speed monument**, celebrates an air speed record (709km per hour) set here in 1934 by Francesco Agello. On the lower end of the technological scale, Desenzano's Bronze Age (2200–1200 BC) inhabitants lived in pile dwellings, recently discovered in the peat bogs southwest of town and yielding the contents of the **Museo Archeologico Rambotti** in the cloister of Santa Maria de Senioribus, Via Anelli 7 (*open Tues, Fri, Sat, Sun and hols 3–7*). There are models of houses and, amongst the ornaments, little 'pearls' of amber: Desenzano was on the ancient trade route between the amber-rich Baltic and the Mediterranean, which endured until the end of the Roman period.

Desenzano, also on the Bergamo–Verona Via Gallica, became popular with the Romans towards the end of the empire, when the rich and powerful retreated from the growing anarchy to their massive country estates, maintained by hundreds of slaves and retainers—the origins of feudalism. One of the most important was Desenzano's **Villa Romana**, just in from the Lunglago at Via Crocifisso 22 (*open Mar–Oct Tues–Fri 8.30–7, Sun 9–5.30; Oct–Feb Tues–Fri 8.30–4.30, Sun 9–4.30; adm*). Although begun in the 1st century BC, the villa was given its present form in the 4th century, fitted with sumptuous heated baths, a triclinium (dining hall) with three apses, and other rooms covered with the most extensive mosaic floors in northern Italy; pick up the free archaeological itinerary pamphlet in English. Nearby, along Via Roma, **Santa Maria Maddalena** has 27 huge canvases by a transplanted Venetian, Andrea Celesti (*d. 1712*), and a strikingly different *Last Supper* by Giandomenico Tiepolo.

As well as Lake Garda, Desenzano is also the base for visiting the low, war-scarred hills to the south. The two most important battles occurred on the same day, 24 June 1859, when Napoleon III defeated Emperor Franz Joseph at **Solferino** and King Vittorio Emanuele defeated the Austrian right wing at **San Martino della Battaglia**, 8km away. It was the beginning of the end for the proud Habsburgs in Italy, but the Battle of Solferino had another consequence as well—the terrible suffering of the wounded so appalled the Swiss Henry Dunant that he formed the idea of founding the Red Cross.

At San Martino you can climb the lofty **Torre Monumentale** (*open Wed–Mon 9–12 and 2–5*), erected in 1893, which contains paintings and mementoes from the battle. Solferino is marked by an old tower of the Scaligeri of Verona, the **Spia d'Italia**, with a collection of uniforms; there's a battle museum by the church of **San Pietro**, containing 7000 graves, and a memorial to Dunant and the Red Cross, erected in 1959 (*all hours same as for the Torre*).

Sirmione

Sweet Sirmio! thou, the very eye
Of all peninsulas and isles,
That in our lakes of silver lie,
Or sleep enwreathed by Neptune's smiles

Thus spake Catullus, Rome's greatest lyric poet, born in Verona in 84 BC. Like many well-to-do Romans, he had a villa out on the narrow 4km-long peninsula of Sirmione that pierces Lake Garda like a pin, just over 280ft across at its narrowest point. Sirmione is the most visually striking resort on the lake.

On the very tip of the rocky promontory, the **Grotte di Catullo** (*Tues–Sat 9–7, Sun 9–6; closed Mon*), entwined with ancient olive trees are romantic ruins with a capital R, not of Catullus' villa, but of a Roman bath complex (Sirmione is famous even today for its thermal spa). The views across the lake to the mountains are magnificent; there's also a small **antiquarium** on the site, with mosaics and frescoes (*open Tues–Sun 9am–sunset; adm*).

The medieval centre of Sirmione is dominated by one of the most memorable of Italian castles, the fairytale **Rocca Scaligera** (*open Tues–Sat 9–12.30; adm*), built by Mastino I della Scala of Verona in the 13th century, and surrounded almost entirely by water. There's not much to see inside, but there are fine views from its swallowtail battlements. Also worth a look is the ancient Romanesque church of **San Pietro in Mavino**, with 13th-century frescoes. Cars are not permitted over the bridge into the town of Sirmione, and the best swimming is off the rocks on the west side of the peninsula.

Peschiera del Garda, Gardaland and the Sigurtà Gardens

East of Sirmione, Peschiera is an old military town near the River Mincio that drains Lake Garda. Fortified since Roman times, the imposing walls that you see today are actually 16th-century Venetian, reinforced by the Austrians when Peschiera was one of the corners of the empire's 'Quadrilateral'. Today Peschiera is mainly a transit point to the lake from the Veneto, but its massive purifying plant, the ultimate destination of what goes down every drain in every lakeside town (thanks to an underwater pipeline), still helps it to fulfil its ancient role as a defender, this time of the lake's status as the cleanest in all Europe.

Here, too, you can treat the children—at **Gardaland**, © 045 644 9777, Italy's largest, and most massively popular, Disney-clone theme park (*open late Mar–June and Sept–Oct daily 9.30–6.30; July–mid-Sept daily 9–midnight; adm; children under a metre-high (just over 3ft) free*). Attractions include the Magic Mountain roller coaster, Colorado boat ride, the Valley of the Kings, an African safari, some fairly scary space rides, a pirate ship, robots, a dolphin show and 'The World Of Barbie' (Her Sublime Plasticity continues to exert a subliminal effect on Italian womanhood: every little Italian girl owns at least ten Barbies).

The region south of Peschiera is known for its dry white wine, Bianco di Custoza, and for the pretty gardens and groves that line the Mincio all the way to the lakes of Mantua. The most amazing, the **Sigurtà Gardens**, 8km from Peschiera (*open Mar–Nov daily 9–6; adm*) were the 40-year project of Dr Count Carlo Sigurtà—'Italy's Capability Brown'—who, granted water rights from the Mincio, used them to transform a barren waste of hills into 500,000 square metres of Anglo-Italian gardens along 7km of lanes; 13 parking areas have been provided on the route so you can get out and walk as much as you like. The Sigurtà Gardens are near Valeggio sul Mincio, an attractive town in its own right, with a castle and massive bridge-dike built by the Visconti, and a pair of water fun parks.

Up the West Shore to Salò

From Sirmione the steamer passes the lovely headlands of Manerba and Punta San Fermo and the **Island of Garda**, the lake's largest, where there was a monastery once visited by St Francis. Long in ruins, it provided the base for a monumental 19th-century Venetian-Gothic-style palace, now owned by the Borghese family, one of whom, Scipione, made the famous drive from Peking to Paris in the early days of the automobile.

Salò (the Roman *Salodium*) enjoys one of the most privileged locations on the lake, but is best known internationally for having given its name to *Il Duce*'s last dismal stand, the puppet 'Republic of Salò' of 1943–45, formed after the Nazis rescued him from his prison in an Abruzzo ski lodge. It also has a number of fine buildings, including a late-Gothic cathedral with a Renaissance portal (1509), and paintings within by Romanino and Moretto da Brescia, and a golden polyptych by Paolo Veneziano. There's also a small museum, the **Museo del Nastro Azzuro** (*open Easter–Sept daily 5–7, Sun 10–1; closed Thurs*), containing information on the history of the region. **L'Ateneo**, in the Renaissance Palazzo Fantoni, contains a collection of 13th-century manuscripts and early printed books. North of Salò begins the **Brescia Riviera**, famous for its exceptional climate and exotic trees and flowers.

Gardone Riviera and D'Annunzio's Folly

North of Salò, sumptuous old villas, gardens and hotels line the lovely promenade at **Gardone Riviera**. Gardone became the most fashionable resort on Lake Garda in 1880, when a German scientist noted the almost uncanny consistency of its climate. One place that profits most from this mildness is the **Giardino Botanico Hruska** (*open Mar–Oct daily 9–6.30; adm*), a botanical garden with 8000 exotic blooms and plants, but in need of a good weeding.

Il Vittoriale

> *Open Oct–Mar Tues–Sun 9–12.30 (ticket office closes an hour earlier) and 2–6.30, Sat and Sun only until 6; April–Sept 8.30am–8pm; adm exp; you can buy a cheaper ticket for the museum and grounds only; expect queues.*

Above the garden waits **Il Vittoriale degli Italiani**, the home of Gabriele D'Annunzio (1863–1938). This luxurious Liberty-style villa in an incomparable setting, designed for a German family by Giancarlo Maroni, was presented to the writer by Mussolini in 1925, ostensibly as a reward for his patriotism during the First World War. D'Annunzio dubbed his new home 'Il Vittoriale' after Italy's victory in 1918; with Maroni's help he recreated it in his own image, leaving posterity a remarkable mix of eccentric beauty and self-aggrandizing kitsch.

More Italian than Any Other Italian

Born Gaetano Rapagnetta into a very modest family in the Abruzzo, the self-styled angel Gabriel of the Annunciation went on to become the greatest Italian poet of his generation, a leading figure in the *fin-de-siècle* Decadent school who managed to have nearly all of his works placed on the pope's Index. But Gabriele D'Annunzio scoffed at the idea that the pen is mightier than the sword. A fervent right-wing nationalist, he clamoured for Italy to enter the First World War, and when it was over he was so furious that Fiume (Rijeka), a town promised as a prize to Italy, was to be ceded by the Allies to Yugoslavia that he took it upon himself to invade Fiume with a band of volunteers (September 1919). In Italy D'Annunzio was proclaimed a hero, stirring up a diplomatic furore before being forced to withdraw in January 1921.

Luigi Barzini has described D'Annunzio as 'perhaps more Italian than any other Italian' for his love of gesture, spectacle and theatre—what can you say about a man who would boast that he had once dined on roast baby? Yet for the Italians of his generation, no matter what their politics, he exerted a powerful influence in thought and fashion; he seemed a breath of fresh air, a new kind of 'superman', hard and passionate yet capable of writing exquisite, intoxicating verse; the spiritual father of the technology-infatuated Futurists, ready to destroy the old bourgeois *Italia vile* of museum curators and parish priests and create in its stead a great modern power, the 'New Italy'.

He lived a life of total exhibitionism—extravagantly, decadently and beyond his means, at every moment the trend-setting, aristocratic aesthete, with his borzois and melodramatic affairs, with the actress 'the Divine' Eleanora Duse and innumerable other loves (preferably duchesses). Apparently he thought the New Italians should all be as flamboyant and clever, and he disdained the corporate state of the Fascists. For Mussolini, the still-popular old nationalist was a loose cannon and an acute embarrassment, and he decided to pension him off into gilded retirement on Lake Garda, correctly calculating that the gift of the villa would appeal to his delusions of grandeur.

D'Annunzio made the Vittoriale his personal monument, suspecting (correctly) that one day crowds would come tramping through to marvel at his cleverness and taste, if not sheer acquisitiveness: the villa is a pack rat's paradise, its every nook and cranny filled with quirky, desirable and hilarious junk, more or less all left as it was in 1938 when a sudden brain haemorrhage put an abrupt end to the poet's hoarding.

Once past the entrance gate, note the double arch, a copy of the bridge pier on the Piave, where the

Italians held the line against the Central Powers from 1917 to 1918. Like many jerks, D'Annunzio loved fast cars and two of his favourites are by the courtyard—one is the 1913 Fiat he drove in triumph to Fiume. The tour begins with the 'cool reception' room for guests D'Annunzio disliked—austere and formal compared to the comfy one reserved for favourites.

When Mussolini came to call he was entertained in the former; D'Annunzio escorted the dictator over to the mirror and made him read the inscription: 'Remember that you are of glass and I of steel.' Perhaps you can make it out if your eyes have had time to adjust to the gloom. Like Aubrey Beardsley and movie characters usually played by Vincent Price, D'Annunzio hated the daylight and had the windows painted over, preferring low-watt lamps.

The organs in the music room and library were played by his young American wife, who gave up a promising career to play for his ears alone. His bathroom, in spite of 2000 pieces of bric-à-brac, somehow manages to find space for the tub. In his bedroom, the Stanza della Leda, he kept a cast of Michelangelo's slave. In his spare bedroom, adorned with leopard skins, there's a coffin he liked to lie in to think cosmic thoughts.

He designed the entrance to his study low so that visitors would have to bow as they entered; here he kept a bust of la Duse, but covered, to prevent her memory from distracting his genius. The dining room, with its bright movie-palace sheen, is one of the more delightful rooms; but D'Annunzio didn't care for it and left his guests here to dine on their own with his pet tortoise, which he had had embalmed in bronze after it expired from indigestion, to remind his visitors of the dangers of overeating.

In the **museum**, located in the Art Deco Casa Schifamondo ('escape the world') that D'Annunzio built but never moved into, you can ponder his death bed and death mask, paintings and memorabilia. In the adjacent auditorium hangs the biplane our hero used to fly over Vienna to drop propaganda leaflets in the War.

The **private garden** occupies an 18th-century lemon terrace and has D'Annunzio's war memorial, with a throne and benches for nationalist legionary ceremonies, which must have been a hoot. The theatre, designed by Maroni after the Greek theatre in Taormina, has a magnificent view from the top seats, stretching from Monte Baldo to Sirmione; in July and August it hosts D'Annunzio's plays. There's a surreal touch nearby: the prow of the battleship *Puglia* from the Fiume adventure, jutting out—mast and all—through a copse of cypresses.

Walk above this to the **mausoleum**, the poet's last ego trip, a perverse wedding cake in glaring white travertine. In three concentric stone circles, the sarcophagi of the Fiume legionnaires surround the tomb of D'Annunzio himself, raised up on columns high above the others like a pagan sun-king, closer to his dark star than anyone else, the whole in hellish contrast to the mausoleum's enchanting setting.

Toscolano-Maderno and Gargnano

The double-barrelled *comune* of Toscolano-Maderno has one of the finest beaches on Lake Garda, and the car ferry to Torri. Toscolano traces its origins to the Etruscans, and Maderno was the site of Roman *Benacum*. In the 12th century many of Maderno's Roman bits were incorporated into the extremely elegant **Sant'Andrea**, a Romanesque beauty benignly restored in the 16th century by St Charles Borromeo; inside, the capitals, some retaining their original paint, are sculpted with fighting animals. The 18th-century parish church has a

Sant'Ercolano by Paolo Veronese and a *Martyrdom of St Andrew* by Palma Giovane. Toscolano was the chief manufacturer of nails for Venice's galleys and had a famous printing press in the 15th century; to this day the Cartiera di Toscolano mill is Garda's largest industry. The cool **Valle delle Cartiere**—the valley of the papermills—is a favourite excursion.

To the north, **Gargnano**, the last town before the towering cliffs, means sailing. Since 1950 it has hosted the colourful Centomiglia regatta the second week of September, attracting yachts from as far away as New Zealand. The Franciscans were among the first to live here in the 13th century; their church has been baroqued inside and the cloister's capitals have carvings of lemons and oranges, a reminder that the Franciscans were the first to cultivate citrus in Europe. In 1866 an Austrian flotilla fired cannons at the port; if you look closely you can see the scars. After the Borghese pile on Isola di Garda, the largest villa on the lake is just south of Gargnano: the 18th-century **Villa Bettoni** in Bogliaco, used as a set in a dozen films.

Limone sul Garda

North of Gargnano the lake narrows and the cliffs plunge sheer into the water and the Gardesana road pierces tunnel after tunnel like a needle. In the morning, when the wind's up, windsurfers flit across the waves like a swarm of crazed one-winged butterflies. On weekends their cars are parked all along the road around **Campione**, a tiny hamlet huddled under the cliffs. For tremendous views, take one of the several turnings inland that wind precipitously up to the cliffs: to **Tignale** or **Tremósine**, atop a 1000ft precipice.

The inland route from Tremósine rejoins the lake at **Limone sul Garda**, a popular resort with a teeny tiny port and a beach over 3km long. Its name comes from the Latin *limen* (border), although by happy coincidence Limone was one of the main citrus towns, and to this day its lemon terraces with their white square pillars are a striking feature of the landscape: D. H. Lawrence, who lived south of Limone for a spell, liked to see them as the ruins of ancient temples

Riva del Garda

North of Limone, the charming town of Riva sits snug beneath an amphitheatre formed by Monte Brione. An important commercial port for the bishops of Trento beginning in 1027, it was much sought and fought after, and ruled by Verona, Milan and Venice before it was handed back to the bishop-princes of Trent in 1521. In 1703, during the War of the Spanish Succession, the French General Vendôme sacked it and all the surroundings, leaving only a ghost of the former town to be inherited by Napoleon in 1796.

Riva revived as a resort during the days of Austrian rule (1813–1918) as the 'Southern Pearl on the Austro-Hungarian Riviera', a pearl especially prized by writers: Stendhal, Thomas Mann, D. H. Lawrence and Kafka were among its habitués. The centre of town, Piazza III Novembre, has a plain **Torre Apponale** (1220) and the **Palazzo Pretorio**, built by Verona's Cansignorio della Scala in 1376, while the lake front was defended by the sombre grey bulk of the 12th-century castle, the **Rocca**, surrounded by a swan-filled moat.

This now houses Riva's **Museo Civico** (*open Tues–Sun 9.30–6.30; July and Aug 9.30am–10.30pm, but hours change frequently*), with finds from the Bronze Age settlement at Lake Ledro, six statue-stelae from the 4th–3rd millennia BC, Roman finds, paintings, frescoes and sculpture. Riva's best church, the **Inviolata** (1603), is by an unknown but imaginative Portuguese architect, who was given a free hand with the gilt and stucco inside; it also has paintings by Palma Giovane.

Only 3km north, a dramatic 287ft waterfall, the **Cascata del Varone**, crashes down a tight grotto-like gorge by the village of Varone; walkways allow visitors to become mistily intimate with thundering water (*opening times according to season; adm*). From the west side of Riva the exciting Ponale Road (N240) rises to **Lake Ledro**, noted not only for its scenery but also for the remains of a Bronze-Age settlement (*c.* 2000 BC) of pile dwellings, discovered in 1929.

One has been reconstructed near the ancient piles around **Molina di Ledro**, where the **Museo delle Palafitte** houses the pottery, axes, daggers and amber jewellery recovered from the site (*open June–Sept daily 9–1 and 2–6; Oct and Nov Tues–Sun 9–1 and 2–5; Dec Sat and Sun only 9–12 and 2–5; Mar–May Tues–Sun 9–1 and 2–5*); the visit includes a botanical garden, dedicated to the plants cultivated by northern Italian farmers in the Bronze Age. From here you can continue to Lake Idro, through the shadowy gorge of the **Valle d'Ampola.**

One of the most dramatic sights on Garda is just behind Riva: the jagged crag and **Castello d'Arco**, dramatically crowned with ancient, dagger-sharp cypresses and the swallowtail crenellations. The path up is lovely and, despite the damage wrought by Vêndome's troops, there are a few frescoes left, including one of a courtly game of chess.

Arco itself, once heavily fortified and moated (the only surviving gate has a drawbridge), became, like Riva, a popular resort in the 1800s, prized for its climate. In the centre, a Baroque fountain dedicated to Moses splashes before the Palladian-inspired **Collegiata dell'Assunta** (1613) by Giovanni Maria Filippi, who went on to become court architect of Emperor Rudolph II in Prague. There's a public garden full of Mediterranean plants, and a pretty 19th-century **Casino**. **Dro**, up the Sarca Valley, is near the small lakes of Cavedine and Toblino; at **Le Sarche**, an ancient glacier deposited the *marocche*, a remarkable field of enormous boulders.

Where to Stay and Eating Out

Sirmione ✉ 25019

If you're driving, have the confirmation of your reservation handy to get past the castle guards. A neoclassical villa built by an Austrian general and converted into a hotel in 1954, *******Villa Cortine**, Via Grotte 12, ✆ 030 990 5890, ✇ 030 916 390 (*very expensive*) offers an immersion in romance, and perhaps the rarest amenity in the town—tranquillity. Its garden occupies almost a third of the entire peninsula, with exotic flora, venerable trees, statues and fountains running down to the water's edge. Inside, all is plush and elegant under frescoed ceilings, but it's ideal for a break from the real world, with private beach and dock, pool and tennis court. *Open April–Oct.*

Another top choice, *******Grand Hotel Terme**, Viale Marconi 7, ✆ 030 916 261, ✇ 030 916 568 (*very expensive*) has a private beach, pool, gym and a full health and beauty programme, as well as a lovely lakeside restaurant. *Open April–Oct.*

In the heart of the old town, *****Catullo**, Piazza Flaminia 7, ✆ 030 990 5811, ✇ 030 916 444 (*expensive*) offers good-sized rooms with beautiful views and modern amenities. *Open April–Nov.* In a medieval building, ******Eden**, Piazza Carducci 18, ✆ 030 916 481, ✇ 030 916 483 (*moderate*) has been beautifully remodelled with fine marbles, and co-ordinated bedrooms with princely bathrooms. Unusually, it does not have a restaurant. *Open Mar–Oct.*

Near the castle, **★★Grifone**, Via Bocchio 4, ℡ 030 916 014, ✆ 030 916 548 (*cheap*) is more attractive on the outside than in the rooms, but has a great location. *Open April–Oct.* **★★Speranza**, Via Casello 6, ℡ 030 916 116, ✆ 030 916 403 (*cheap*) has all the fittings of a three-star hotel, including air-conditioning and marble bathrooms, but at significantly lower prices. *Open Mar–Nov.*

One of Garda's finest restaurants is near the base of Sirmione's peninsula: the classy **Vecchia Lugana**, Via Verona 71, ℡ 030 919 012 (*expensive*). The food, based on lake fish, is exquisite, prepared with a light and wise touch—try the divine asparagus tagliatelle in a ragoût of lake fish, or the mixed grill of fish and meat; menus at L60,000 and L80,000. *Closed Mon eve and Tues.*

Near the Scaliger castle, **La Rucola**, Via Strentelle 7, ℡ 030 916 326 (*expensive*) has a great atmosphere to go with its particularly flavoursome specialities, many dishes judiciously prepared with fruit. *Closed Thurs.* **Marboré**, Via Vittorio Emanuele 71, ℡ 030 916 409 (*cheap*) serves tasty pizzas and simple L24,000 menus in a garden by the lake. *Closed Mon.*

Salò ✉ 25087

One of the loveliest places to stay on the lakes, **★★★★Laurin**, Viale Landi 9, ℡ 0365 22022, ✆ 0365 22382 (*expensive*) is an enchanting Liberty-style villa converted into a hotel in the 1960s, retaining the elegant period décor in the public rooms. The charming grounds include a swimming pool and beach access. *Closed Jan.*

At the **★★★★Duomo**, Lungolago Zanardelli 63, ℡ 0365 21026, ✆ 0365 21028 (*expensive*), the first-floor rooms are the ones to request—all lead out to a huge geranium-laden balcony overlooking the lake. Rooms are big and modern, and there's a fine restaurant.

Similar if less exalted accommodation is available at the lakefront **★★★Benaco**, Lungolago Zanardelli 44, ℡ 0365 20308, ✆ 0365 20724 (*moderate*), which also boasts a good restaurant. **★★★Vigna**, Lungolango Zanardelli 62, ℡ 0365 520 144, ✆ 0365 520 516 (*moderate*) has rooms that are none too individual, but comfortable and modern, and views that really steal the show.

For a good, reasonably priced and traditional meal try **Trattoria alla Campagnola**, Via Brunati 11, ℡ 0365 22153 (*moderate*). Garden-fresh vegetables are served with every dish, the pasta is home-made, and they make great use of wild mushrooms. At the **Osteria dell'Orologio**, Via Butterini 26, ℡ 0365 290 158 (*cheap*), a beautifully restored old inn, you can indulge in '*tonno del Garda*' (pork cooked in wine and spices), lake fish and skewered wild birds. *Closed Wed.* The same family run the slightly more expensive **Antica Trattoria delle Rose**, Via Gasparo da Salò 33, ℡ 0365 43220 (*moderate*). Go for *pasta e fagioli*, or lake fish with pasta. *Closed Wed.*

Gardone Riviera ✉ 25083

Gardone Riviera and its suburb Fasano Riviera have competing Grand Hotels, both attractive old pleasure domes. In Gardone, the **★★★★Grand Hotel**, Via Zanardelli 72,

℗ 0365 290 220, ✆ 0365 290 221 (*very expensive*), with its 180 rooms, was one of the largest resort hotels in Europe when built in 1881. Its countless chandeliers glitter as brightly as when Churchill stayed there in the late 1940s. Almost all the palatial air-conditioned rooms look on to the lake. Guests can luxuriate on the garden terraces, or swim in the heated outdoor pool or off the private sandy beach. The dining room and delicious food match the quality of the rooms. *Open mid-April–mid-Oct.*

Fasano's alternative, ★★★★**Fasano Grand Hotel**, ℗ 0365 20261, ✆ 0365 22695 (*very expensive*) was built in the early 19th century as a Habsburg hunting palace, and converted into a hotel around 1900. Surrounded by a large park, it's furnished with *belle époque* fittings; there are tennis courts, a heated pool and beach, and the restaurant is one of Lake Garda's best. *Open May–Oct.*

Another excellent choice, Fasano's ★★★★**Villa del Sogno**, Via Zanardelli 107, ℗ 0365 290 181, ✆ 0365 290 230 (*very expensive*) was its creator's 'Dream Villa' of the 1920s. Immersed in trees, there's a private beach (five-minutes' walk) and a pool in its flower-filled garden. *Open April–Oct.*

A Liberty-style palace set in gardens on the lake, ★★★**Villa Fiordaliso**, Corso Zanardelli 132, ℗ 0365 20158, ✆ 0365 290 011 (*very expensive*) has only seven rooms. You can request (for a price) the suite where Mussolini and Claretta Petacci spent their last few weeks. Located in a serene park, with a private beach and pier, it also boasts an elegant restaurant—the best in Gardone—featuring classic Lombard dishes; the *menu degustazione* are L65,000 and 90,000. *Closed Nov and Mon.*

At lakeside ★★★**Monte Baldo**, Via Zanardelli 104, ℗ 0365 20951, ✆ 0365 20952 (*moderate*), a well-aged outer appearance hides a fully refurbished and stylish interior. The hotel also has a pool. *Open April–Oct.* Above the main road overlooking the lake, with a garden sheltering it from the traffic, ★★★**Bellevue**, Via Zanardelli ℗ 0365 20235, ✆ 0365 290 088 (*moderate*) offers modernized rooms, all with private bath. *Open April–Oct.*

Halfway up to Il Vittoriale, ★**Hohl**, Via dei Colli 4, ℗ 0365 20160 (*moderate–cheap*) is another atmospheric 19th-century villa in a pleasant garden. None of the rooms has a bath, but they're quiet. In Fasano, ★★**Touring**, Via Zanardelli 147, ℗ 0365 21031 (*cheap*) is a solid year-round budget choice.

Gargnano ✉ 25084

In Villa, just outside Gargnano,★★★**Baia d'Oro**, Via Gamberera 13, ℗ 0365 71171, ✆ 0365 72568 (*expensive*) is a small but charming old place on the lake front with an artistic inn atmosphere. It has a private beach and picturesque terraces. *Open mid-Mar–Oct.* ★★**Du Lac**, Via Colletta 21, in Villa, smack on the water, ℗ 0365 71107, ✆ 0365 72594 (*moderate*) is a salmon-tinted charmer. *Open April–mid-Oct.*

Near the port, **La Tortuga**, Via XXIV Maggio 5, ℗ 0365 71251 (*expensive*) is a celebrated gourmet haven, specializing in delicate dishes based on seasonal ingredients and lake fish, perfectly prepared; there are also delicious vegetable soufflés, innovative meat courses, mouth-watering desserts and fresh fruit sherbets, and an excellent wine and spirits cellar; menus from L65,000 to L95,000. *Closed Mon eve, Tues and mid-Jan–Feb.*

Limone ✉ 25010

****Le Palme**, ✆ 0365 954 681, 📠 0365 954 120 (*moderate*) is housed in a pretty Venetian villa, preserving much of its original charm alongside modern amenities. Named after its two ancient palm trees, it has a fine terrace, tennis courts and a good fish restaurant. *Open April–Oct.*

Above the centre, ***La Limonaia**, Via Sopino Alto 3, ✆ 0365 954 221, 📠 0365 954 227 (*moderate*) enjoys a superb position, and has both an adult and a children's pool and playground. *Open Mar–Oct.* Agreeable and small, ***Sogno del Benaco**, ✆ 0365 954 026, 📠 0365 954 357 (*moderate*) has fairly standard rooms. Above the lake in an olive grove, *Mercedes**, Via Nanzello 12, ✆ 0365 954 073 (*cheap*) has a pool and lovely views. *Open April–Nov.*

Riva del Garda ✉ 38066

When German intellectuals from Nietzsche to Günter Grass have needed a little rest and relaxation they have for many decades flocked to Riva del Garda to check in at ****Hotel du Lac et du Parc**, Viale Rovereto 44, ✆ 0464 551 500, 📠 0464 555 200 (*very expensive*), modernized, spacious, airy and tranquil, and set in a large lakeside garden; facilities include indoor and outdoor pools, a beach, sailing school, gym, sauna and tennis courts. *Open April–Oct.*

At the turn-of-the-century ****Grand Hotel Riva**, Piazza Garibaldi 10, ✆ 0464 521 800, 📠 0464 552 293 (*expensive*), majestically positioned on the main square, 87 modern rooms look out over the lake; the rooftop restaurant combines fine food with incomparable views. It also has a private beach. *Open Mar–Oct.*

Right on the port in Riva's main square, ****Sole**, Piazza III Novembre, ✆ 0464 552 686, 📠 0464 552 811 (*expensive*) has plenty of atmosphere and a beautiful terrace; most rooms have private baths and look out over the lake, though they vary widely in size and quality.

By the harbour, ***Centrale**, Piazza III Novembre 27, ✆ 0464 552 344, 📠 0464 552 138 (*moderate*) has fully equipped, spacious rooms; almost as good and slightly cheaper, ***Portici**, Piazza III Novembre 19, ✆ 0464 555 400, 📠 0464 555 453 (*moderate*) has been competely refurbished and has modern rooms. *Open April–Oct.*

Built in 1400, *Restel de Fer**, Via Restel de Fer 10, ✆ 0464 553 481, 📠 0464 552 798 (*moderate–cheap*) has only five rooms and a good restaurant, with summer dining in the cloister.

If you seek peace and quiet, and a garden and pool in a panoramic spot, the family-run *Villa Moretti** 3km up in Varone, ✆ 0464 521 127, 📠 0464 521 751 (*cheap*) fits the bill. A good economy choice, *Villa Minerva**, Viale Roma 40, ✆ 0464 553 031 (*cheap*) is very pleasant and very popular.

Riva's hostel, **Ostello Benacus**, Piazza Cavour 9, ✆ 0464 554 911, 📠 0464 556 554, has beds for L19,000 per night. *Open Mar–Oct.*

The East Shore: Riva to Peschiera

Garda's east shore belongs to the province of Verona. The silvery groves that grace the hills gave it its name, the Riviera degli Olivi, but its most outstanding feature is Monte Baldo, a massive ridge of limestone stretching 35km between Lake Garda and the Adige Valley, cresting at 6989ft. Baldo is anything but bald: known as 'the botanical garden of Italy', it supports an astonishing variety of flora from Mediterranean palms to Arctic tundra; some 20 different flowers first discovered on Monte Baldo bear its name. The southern third of the Riviera degli Olivi is more grapey than olivey, the land of Bardolino.

Tourist Information

Malcésine: Via Capitanato 6/8, ✆ 045 740 0044, 📠 045 740 1633; **Torri del Benaco**: Via Gardesana 5, ✆ 045 722 5120; **Garda**: Lungolago Regina Adelaide 3, ✆ 045 627 0384; **Bardolino**: Piazza Matteotti 53, ✆ 045 721 0078.

Torbole

Back on Garda's northeast shore, **Monte Baldo** looms over Torbole and the Sarca, the most important river feeding the lake. An old fishing village and a pleasant resort, Torbole is famous in the annals of naval history. In 1437, during a war with the Visconti, the Venetians were faced with the difficulty of getting supplies to Brescia past the southern reaches of Lake Garda, then controlled by Milan. A Greek sailor made the suggestion that the Venetians sail a fleet of provision-packed warships up the Adige to its furthest navigable point, then transport the vessels over Monte Baldo on to Lake Garda. Anyone who has seen Herzog's film *Fitzcarraldo* will appreciate the difficulties involved, and the amazing fact that, with the aid of 2000 oxen, the 26 ships were launched at Torbole only 15 days after leaving the Adige. But after all that trouble, the supplies never reached Brescia. The same trick, however, perhaps even suggested by the same Greek, enabled Mohammed II to bring the Ottoman fleet into the upper harbour of Constantinople the following year and capture the city.

Malcésine and Monte Baldo

South of Torbole, the forbidding cliffs of Monte di Nago hang perilously over the lake (and attract scores of Lycra-bright human flies) before **Malcésine**, the loveliest town on the east shore. The Veronese lords always took care to protect this coast and in the 13th century, over the old Lombard castle, they built their magnificent **Rocca Scaligero** (*open April–Oct daily 9.30–8; winter Sat, Sun and hols only; adm*) rising up on a sheer rock over the water; inside are natural history exhibits, prehistoric rock etchings and a room dedicated to Goethe, who was accused of spying while sketching the castle. As well as the Scaliger castle, note the 16th-century **Palazzo dei Capitani del Lago** in the centre of Malcésine's medieval web of streets.

Every half-hour a pair of cablecars run vertiginously up **Monte Baldo** (*L18,000 return; call ✆ 045 740 0206, for information*); the views are ravishing, and the ski slopes at the top are very popular with the Veronese. Malcésine also has pretty walks through the olives, and the shore has lovely places to swim and sunbathe, especially around the cove called the Val di Sogno. To the south, the hamlet of **Cassone** straddles the Aril, the shortest river in the world.

Torri del Benaco and Garda

Further south, past a steep, sparsely populated stretch of shore, there are two pretty towns, one on either side of Punta di San Vigilio, that played minor roles in the 10th century. The first, laid-back **Torri del Benaco**, owes its name to a rugged old tower in the centre which served as the headquarters of Berengario, the first king of Italy, in his 905 campaign against the Magyars.

Later, it was defended by another **Scaliger castle** (1383), now a museum (*open April, May and Oct daily 9.30–12.30 and 2.30–6; June–Sept daily 9.30–1 and 4.30–7.30; adm*), with displays on olive oil, citrus and fishing, and rock engravings found in the area from *c.* 2000 BC, similar to those in the Valle Camonica—the best may be seen on the path to Punta di San Vigilio. The church of **Santa Trinità** has good 14th-century Giottoesque frescoes.

Laurence Olivier often stayed in enchanting **Punta di San Vigilio**, with its Sirens' rocks, occupied by the beautiful **Villa Guarienti**, designed by Sammicheli, the old church of San Vigilio, and a 16th-century tavern, now an inn (*see* below). On the other side of a green soufflé of a headland, the Rocca del Garda, lies **Garda** itself, a fine old town with Renaissance palazzi and villas. It gave the lake its name, from the Lombard *Warthe*, 'the watch'.

After Charlemagne defeated the Lombards, Garda became a county, and in 960 in its long-gone castle the wicked Count Berenguer secretly held Queen Adelaide of Italy prisoner, after he murdered her husband Lotario and she refused to marry his son. After a year she was discovered by a monk, who spent another year plotting her escape. She then received the protection of Otto I of Germany, who defeated Berengar, married the widow and became Holy Roman Emperor.

Bardolino

Bardolino, to the south, is synonymous with its lively red wine with a bitter cherry fragrance that goes so well with fishy *antipasti*; you can learn all you want to know about it at the Cantine Zeni's **Museo del Vino**, Via Costabella 9 (*open Mar–Oct daily 9–1 and 2–6*). There are two important churches in Bardolino itself: the 8th-century **San Zeno** and the 12th-century **San Severo**, with frescoes and a landmark campanile. **Cisano**, south of Bardolino, has a museum dedicated to the Riviera degli Olivi's other cash crop, the **Museo dell'Olio d'Oliva**, Via Peschiera 54 (*open daily 9–12.30 and 3–7; closed Sun and Wed pm*).

The next town, **Lazise**, was the main Venetian port and retains an ensemble of Venetian buildings, as well as another castle, this one built in the 9th century by the Magyars and rebuilt by the Scaligers. Just inland, at Bussolengo, the **Parco Natura Viva** is a private foundation devoted to the protection of endangered species, and is divided into a zoo, with a tropical aviary (*open year round daily 9–6*), and a drive-through safari park with animals from the African savannah (*open 15 Mar–Oct daily from 9.30*). Near here too is Gardaland—*see* p.272.

Where to Stay and Eating Out

Note that prices are considerably lower on this side of Garda.

Malcésine ✉ 37018

★★★★**Val di Sogno**, ✆ 045 740 0108, 🖷 045 740 1694 (*expensive*) is situated about three minutes out of town in a beautiful setting in its own grounds right on the lake shore. There is a pool, private beach, a lakeside restaurant, and modern rooms with balconies.

South of the centre, ★★★★**Park Hotel Querceto**, at Campiano, © 045 740 0344, ✆ 045 740 0848 (*expensive*) is a romantic place to stay, with lovely views, a pool, garden, and one of the best restaurants in the area, where the cuisine is light and tasty and adapted to the season. *Closed Nov–Mar.*

The inviting ★★★**Vega**, Viale Roma, © 045 657 0355, ✆ 045 740 1604 (*moderate*) offers big rooms, all with satellite TV, minibar and air-conditioning, and a beach. ★★★**Sailing Centre**, north of the centre at Molini Campagnola 3, © 045 740 0055, ✆ 045 740 0392 (*expensive–moderate*) has sailing and windsurf schools, pool, satellite TV and more. *Open end-Mar–end-Oct.*

The beautifully positioned ★★★**Malcésine**, Piazza Pallone, © 045 740 0173, ✆ 045 657 0073 (*moderate–cheap*) has a garden with swimming terrace, pleasant rooms, and an excellent value, if average, restaurant.

Right in the centre, you can sleep where Goethe snoozed in 1786 at the simple ★★**San Marco**, Via Capitanato, © 045 740 0115 (*cheap*); all rooms have a bath. ★**Miralago**, Viale Roma, © 045 740 0111 (*cheap*) is a good option with lake views. By the Porto Vecchio, **Da Pace** is a popular place with outdoor tables for seafood by the lake; around L40,000.

Torri del Benaco ✉ 37010

The comfortable ★★**Gardesana**, Piazza Calderini 20, © 045 722 5411, ✆ 045 722 5771 (*moderate*) is right on the harbour with splendid views of lake and castle. Breakfast and meals are served on the harbour patio. The simple and plain ★★★**Al Caval**, Via Gardesana 186, © 045 722 5666, ✆ 045 629 6570 (*moderate*) has a park and windsurf rentals, and the best restaurant in town (*moderate*), where the usual lake fish get special treatment in terrines and pasta dishes. *Closed Jan–Mar.*

Garda ✉ 37016

★★★★**Locanda San Vigilio**, the little inn hidden out by Sammicheli's villa on Punta di San Vigilio, © 045 725 6688, ✆ 045 725 6551 (*very expensive*) has seven romantic rooms, a beach and delicious food. *Open mid-Mar–mid-Oct.*

A lakeside villa, ★★★★**Du Parc**, Via Marconi 3, © 045 725 5343, ✆ 045 725 5642 (*expensive*) has recently been entirely refurbished and upgraded. *Open July–Aug.* The large, modern and quite luxurious ★★★★**Eurotel**, © 045 6270 3333, ✆ 045 725 6640 (*moderate*) has a fine garden and pool. *Open Easter–Oct.*

★★★**Flora**, Via Giorgione 22 and 27, ©/✆ 045 725 5348 (*moderate*) is situated slightly above the town in its own grounds, and is slick and modern with pine fittings, spacious rooms (all with balcony) and fantastic amenities—tennis, mini-golf and *two* pools. *Open Easter–Oct.*

Next door to the Flora, ★★★**Continental**, Via Giorgione 14, © 045 725 5100, ✆ 045 725 6288 (*moderate*) is also in its own grounds and well priced, but not quite as modern or comfortable—and with only one pool. *Open Easter–Oct.* ★**Vittoria**,

Lungolago Regina Adelaide, © 045 725 5065, ® 045 627 0752 (*cheap*) is the best cheap hotel in Garda, at the end of the lakefront walk. The rooms are big, and service is friendly. *Open Easter–Oct.*

On the landward side of Garda, **Stafolet**, Via Poiano 12, © 045 725 5427 (*moderate*) is worth asking directions to, for its wild duck and plump, spinach-filled *strangolopreti* ('priest stranglers'). Less distinguished, but good and cheap, **Al Pontesel**, Via Monte Baldo 71, © 045 725 5419, features stout local cooking.

Venetia

SWITZERLAND

Brenner Pass

Vipiteno

Brunico
S49

Malles Venosta

Merano

Bressanone
S12

S40

S38

Solda

Stelvio National Park

Ortisei
S22

Bolzano

Alto Adige

Canazei

Dolomites

Marmolada

Agordo

S42

Trentino

Cles

S48

Cavalese

S. Martino
di Castrozza

Pala di S.
Martino

S38

Madonna di
Campiglio

S39

Brenta Dolomites

S12

TRENTINO-
ALTO ADIGE

Cima d'Asta

S42

Trento

Borgo Valsugana

Croce d'Aune

S50

Feltre

S47

Riva del Garda

Arco

Rovereto

Asiago

Valdobbiadene

M. Grappa

VENETO

Asolo

A22

LOMBARDY

M.
Baldo

Bassano del Grappa

Maser

Marostica

Fanzolo

S45

Recoaro
Terme

Breganze

Castel-
franco
Veneto

Giazza
M. Lessini

Bolca

Schio

Thiene

S248

S53

Cittadella

Torri di
Benaco

S. Ambrogio di
Valpolicella

Lake Garda

A4

Brescia

S11

Bardolino

Negrar

Bosco
Chiesanuova

Vicenza

A31

Piombino
Dese

S57

Sirmione

Montecchio Maggiore

Dolo M

Peschiera di
Garda

S226

A4

Verona

Soave

S11

Lonigo

Padua

Stra

S11

San
Bonifacio

Abano Terme

A13

S16

S45

Valeggio
(Sigurta Gardens)

Villafranca
di Verona

Euganean Hills
Montegrotto Terme

Brenta

A21

Arqua Petrarca

A22

S12

Este

Monselice

Mincio

Montagnana

S10

Mantua

Badia
Polesine

Adige

Po

S62

Po

S482

S434

Fratta
Polesine

Rovigo

Adria

S420

S16

A1

A22

S12

Po

S9

A15

EMILIA-ROMAGNA

A13

Ferrara

Venetia

20 km
10 miles

N

AUSTRIA

Dobbiaco

S49

E66

Villach

Tre Cime
di Lavarede

Alpi   Carniche

A2

Cristallo

S52

Unterthörl

Julian Alps

E61

Cortina
d'Ampezzo

Auronzo di
Cadore

Sappada

Comeglians

Pontebba

Camporosso

Tarvisio

L. Predil

M. Civetta

Pieve di
Cadore

Sauris

Arta Terme

Ampezzo

Tolmezzo

M.Magante

Forni di
Sopra

Forni di Sotto

Venzone

Kobarid
(Caporetto)

Agordo

S51

Longarone

**FRIULI
VENEZIA-GIULIA**

Gemona
d. Friuli

Maniago

S. Daniele
di Friulio

Tarcento

Stupizza

SLOVENIA

Belluno

Alpago

Montereale

Tricesimo

S. Croce

Valcellina

Spilimbergo

Udine

Nevegal

Cansiglio

Cividale d. Friuli

Vittorio
Veneto

Sacile

Pordenone

S13

Codroipo

Cormòns

Nova Gorica

Conegliano

Sesto al Reghena

S-Vito al
Tagliamento

A23

Palmanova

Gorizia

S13

A27

A28

Piave

S53

A4

S14

Gradisca d'Isonzo

Monfalcone

Treviso

Latisana

Aquileia

Sistiana

Portogruaro

Duino

Abisina

Grotta-Gigante

S. Dona
di Piave

Livenza

Lignano
Sabbiadoro

Miramare

Vila Opicina

Lipica

S14

Lignano Pineta

Grado

Trieste

Caorle

Bibione

Golfo di Trieste

Muggia

Altino

Eraclea Mare

Koper

Lido di Jesolo

Cavollino

Mestre

A4

Mira

Dolo

S309

Venice

Brenta

*Golfo di
Venezia*

E751

CROATIA

Chioggia

Sottomarina

To Greece

To Pula

To Greece

Rosolina Mare

Isola Albarella

Adige

S309

Adria

Po

Taglio
di Po

Po Delta

Mesola

Porto
Tolle

Goro

Pula

287

Venetia, or the Tre Venezie in Italian, encompasses three double-barrelled regions—the Veneto, the autonomous region of Trentino-Alto Adige (including a good part of the Dolomites), and Friuli-Venezia Giulia, stretching east to Slovenia. As the local economic powerhouse for over a thousand years, the Venetian influences are strong everywhere; in wealth Venetia rivals Lombardy, in culture it rivals Tuscany itself: Venice, Verona, Vicenza, Treviso, Padua, Trento and Ùdine are major art cities. Lagoons and sandy beaches line the coast, while the Dolomites, arguably the most beautiful mountains in the world, are dotted with fairy-tale castles and vineyards, as well as resorts equipped for every summer and winter sport, including one, Cortina d'Ampezzo, with Olympic facilities. In between, landscapes are lush and green, and littered with thousands of villas built in the 16th–18th centuries, including 18 by Palladio, the master of the genre. Friuli is one of Italy's top wine regions, and has a variety of other attractions, especially its Roman-medieval capital Aquileia, the most important archaeological site in northern Italy, and the fascinating Lombard town of Cividale.

Because Venetia has so much to offer, especially for families (the seashore, Lake Garda and its theme parks, and the mountains) avoid coming in August if you possibly can, when the crowds and prices can be overwhelming. At any time of year you can get along without a car, although a car does come in handy for visiting villas or castles. Venice is the obvious place to start, and has frequent links to Padua and Treviso; Verona, with quick connections to Lake Garda is another good base, although Palladio-philes will want to stay in Vicenza. The Dolomites are served by an excellent bus system; Trento, Bolzano and Cortina are important hubs and have beautiful routes to explore in all directions. Ùdine makes a good base for Friuli-Venezia Giulia, with connections to Aquileia, Trieste and the coast.

The Best of Venetia in a Fortnight: a Circular Tour

Days 1–3: Venice and the Lagoon. **Day 4**: Padua, with an evening in Àsolo. **Day 5**: Àsolo and Villa Masèr, and on to Vicenza. **Day 6**: Vicenza. **Days 7–8**: Verona. **Day 9**: Lake Garda, night in Riva. **Day 10**: Trento. **Day 11**: Bolzano. **Day 12**: The Great Dolomites Road to Cortina. **Day 13**: A day in the mountains around Cortina. **Day 14**: Back to Venice, by way of Conegliano and Treviso. But you'll have more fun if you can give it three weeks! For a Friulian itinerary, *see* p.416.

Venice

Venice seduces, Venice irritates, but Venice rarely disappoints. She is a golden fairy-tale city floating on the sea, a lovely mermaid with agate eyes and the gift of eternal youth. On the surface she is little changed from the days when Goethe called her the 'market-place of the Morning and the Evening lands', when her amphibious citizens dazzled the world with their wealth and pageantry, their magnificent fleet, their half-Oriental doges, their crafty merchant princes, their splendidly luminous art, their silken debauchery and decline and fall into a seemingly endless carnival. One can easily imagine Julius Caesar bewildered by today's Rome, or Romeo and Juliet missing their rendezvous in the traffic of modern Verona, but Marco Polo, were he to return from Cathay today, could take a familiar gondola up the familiar Grand Canal to his house in the Rialto, astonished more by the motor-boats than anything else. Credit for this unique preservation goes to the Lagoon, the amniotic fluid of Venice's birth, her impenetrable 'walls' and the formaldehyde that has pickled her more thoroughly than many far more venerable cities on the mainland.

For a thousand years Venice called herself the Most Serene Republic (*la Serenissima*), and at one point she ruled 'a quarter and a half' of the Roman Empire. The descent to an Italian provincial capital was steep and bittersweet; and sensitive souls find gallons of melancholy, or, like Thomas Mann, even death, brewed into the city's canals that have nothing to do with the more flagrant microbes. In the winter, when the streets are silent, Venice can be so evocative that you have to kick the ghosts out of the way to pass down the narrower alleys.

But most people show up in the summer, and like their ancestors, have a jolly good time. For Venice is a most experienced old siren in her boudoir of watery mirrors. International organizations pump in the funds to keep her petticoats out of the water and smooth her wrinkles, while with a wink she slides a knowing hand deep into your pocket. Venice has always lived for gold, and you can bet she wants yours—and you might just as well give it to her, in return for the most enchanting, dream-like favours any city can grant.

When to Go

Venice (Venezia) is as much a character as a setting, and the same may be said of its weather. In no other city will you be so aware of the light; on a clear, fine day no place could be more limpid, no water as crystal bright as the Lagoon. The rosy dawn igniting the domes of St Mark's, the splash of an oar fading in the cool mist of a canal, the pearly twilit union of water and sky are among the city's oldest but evergreen clichés.

If you seek solitude and romance with a capital R, go in January. Pack a warm coat, water-resistant shoes and an umbrella, and expect frequent fogs and mists. It may even snow—in 1987 you could even ski jump down the Rialto bridge. But there are also plenty of radiant diamond days, brilliant, sunny and chill; any time after October you take your chances.

As spring approaches there is Carnival, a beautiful but rather bland attempt to revive a bit of old Venice; Lent is quiet, though in the undercurrent the Venetians are building up for their first major invasion at Easter. By April the tourism industry is cranked up to full operational capacity; the gondolas are un-mothballed, the café tables have blossomed in the Piazza, the Casino has re-located to the Lido. In June even the Italians are starting to go to the beach.

In July and August elbow room is at a premium. Peripheral campsites are packed and the queues at the tourist office's room-finding service stretch around the corner. The heat can be sweltering, the ancient city gasping under a flood of cameras, shorts, sunglasses and rucksacks. Scores head off to the Lido for relief; a sudden thunderstorm over the Lagoon livens things up, as do the many festivals, especially the Redentore and its fabulous fireworks in July. In the autumn the city and the Venetians begin to unwind, the rains begin to fall, and you can watch them pack up the parasols and cabanas on the Lido with a wistful sigh.

N

Venice

500 metres
500 yards

S. Michele

Gesuiti

FONDAMENTA NUOVE

Rio dei SS. Apostoli

Rio di S. Giovanni Crisostomo

SS. Giovanni
e Paolo

Fondaco dei
Tedeschi

Campo S.
Bartolomeu

S. Lio

Campo S.
Maria Formosa

S. Salvador

SALIZZADA
DI S. LIO

S. Maria Formosa

Rio di S. Francesco

S. Zulian

MERCERIE

Pal. Querini
Stampalia

CALLE DEI FABBRI

CALLE VALLARESSO

Teatro
Goldoni

Basilica

Piazza S.
Marco

Museo
Correr

Pal.
Ducale

Giardini
Reali

RIVA DEGLI SCHIAVONI

Pal. Dandolo
Gritti

Campo SS
Filippo e
Giacomo

S.
Zaccaria

GIUDECCA

Rio della Pietà

Rio del Vin

S. Giorgio
dei Greci

Rio di S. Lorenzo

Scuola di
S. Giorgio
degli Schiavoni

CASTELLO

Canale delle Galeazze

Arsenale

S. Pietro

VIA GARIBALDI

S. Giorgio
Maggiore

S. Giorgio
Maggiore

Canale di San Marco

Giardini
della Biennale

S. Elena

History

Venice has always been so different, so improbable, that one can easily believe the legend that the original inhabitants sprang up from the dew and mists on the mud banks of the Lagoon. Historians who don't believe in fairies say that Venice was born of adversity: the islands and treacherous shallows of the Lagoon provided the citizens with a refuge from **Attila the Hun** and the Arian heresies sweeping the mainland. Twelve Lagoon townships grew up between modern Chioggia and Grado; when Theodoric the Great's secretary Cassiadorus visited in 523 he wrote that they were 'scattered like sea-birds' nests over the face of the waters'.

In 697 the 12 townships united to elect their first duke, or doge. Fishing, trading—in slaves, among other things—and their unique knowledge of the Lagoon brought the Venetians their first prosperity, but their key position in between the Byzantine empire and the 'barbarian' kings on the mainland also made them a bone of contention. In 810 the **Franks**, who had defeated the Lombards in the name of the Pope and claimed dominion over the whole of northern Italy, turned their attention to the last hold-out, Venice: Doge Obelario de'Antenori, engaged in a bitter internal feud with other Venetian factions, and even invited Charlemagne's son **Pepin** to send his army into the city. The quarrelling Venetians, until then undecided whether to support Rome or Constantinople, united at the approach of Pepin's fleet, deposed the Doge, declared for Byzantium, and entrenched themselves on the Rialto. The shallows and queer humours of the Lagoon confounded Pepin, and after a gruelling six-month siege he threw in the towel. A subsequent treaty between the Franks and the Eastern Emperor Nicephorus (814) recognized Venice as a subject of Byzantium, with important trading concessions. As Byzantine authority over the city was never more than words, it in effect marked the birth of an independent republic.

The Venetians lacked only a dynamic spiritual protector; their frumpy St Theodore with his crocodile was simply too low in the celestial hierarchy to fulfil the destiny they had in mind. In 829 Venetian merchants, supposedly on secret orders from the Doge, carried off one of the Republic's greatest coups when they purloined the body of **St Mark** from Alexandria, smuggling him past Egyptian customs by claiming that the saint was pickled pork. To acquire an Evangelist for themselves was, in itself, a demonstration of the Venetians' new ambition.

Marriage to the Sea

As the East–West trade expanded, the Venetians designed their domestic and external policies to accommodate it. At home they required peace and stability, and by the beginning of the 11th century had squelched all notions of an hereditary dogeship by exiling the most hyperactive families; Venice would never have the despots who plagued the rest of Italy.

Raids by **Dalmatian pirates** spurred the Venetians to fight and win their first major war in 997, under Doge Pietro Orseolo, who captured the pirates' coastal strongholds. The Venetians were so pleased with themselves that they celebrated the event with a splendidly arrogant ritual every Ascension Day, **La Sensa** or 'Marriage of the Sea', in which the Doge would sail out to the Lido in his sumptuous barge, the *Bucintoro*, and cast a diamond ring into the sea, proclaiming 'We wed thee, O sea, in sign of our true and perpetual dominion.'

Venice, because of her location and fleet, supplied a great deal of the transport for the first three **Crusades**, and in return received her first important trading concessions in the Middle East. Arch-rival Genoa became increasingly envious, and in 1171 convinced the Byzantine

Emperor to all but wipe out the Venetian merchants in Constantinople. Rashly, the Doge Vitale Michiel II set off in person to launch a revenge attack upon the Empire, and failed utterly. On his return he was killed by an angry mob. The Venetians were always sore losers, but they learned from their mistakes: the Great Council, the **Maggior Consiglio**, was brought into being to check the power of the Doge and avert future calamities.

Vengeance stayed on the back-burner until the next Doge, the spry and crafty Enrico Dandolo, was contracted to provide transport for the **Fourth Crusade**. When the Crusaders turned up without their fare, Dandolo offered to forgo it in return for certain services: first, to reduce Venice's rebellious satellites in Dalmatia, and then, in 1204, to sail to Constantinople instead of Egypt. Aged 90 and almost blind, Dandolo personally led the attack; Christendom was scandalized, but Venice had gained, not only a glittering hoard of loot, but three-eighths of Constantinople and 'a quarter and a half' of the Roman Empire—enough islands and ports to control the trade routes in the Adriatic, Aegean, Asia Minor and the Black Sea.

To ensure their dominance at home, in 1297 the merchant élite limited membership in the *Maggior Consiglio* to themselves and their heirs (an event known in Venetian history as the **Serrata**, or Lock-out), their names inscribed in the famous **Golden Book**. The doges were slowly reduced to honorary chairmen of the board, bound up by an increasingly complex web of laws and customs to curb any possible ambitions; for the patricians, fear of revolution from above was as powerful as fear of revolt from below.

A Rocky 14th Century

First the people (1300) and then the snubbed patricians (the 1310 **Tiepolo Conspiracy**) rose up against their disenfranchisement under the *Serrata*. Both were unsuccessful, but the latter threat was serious enough that a committee of public safety was formed to hunt down the conspirators, and in 1335 this committee became a permanent institution, the infamous **Council of Ten**. Because of its secrecy and speedy decisions, the Council of Ten (in later years it was streamlined into a Council of Three) was more of a real executive than the figurehead doge; it guarded Venice's internal security, looked after foreign policy and, with its sumptuary laws, kept tabs of the Venetians' moral conduct as well.

Away from home the 14th century was marked by a fight to the death with **Genoa** over eastern trade routes. Each republic annihilated the other's fleet on more than one occasion before things came to a head in 1379, when the Genoese, fresh from a victory over the Venetian commander **Vittor Pisani**, captured Chioggia and waited for Venice to starve, boasting that they had come to 'bridle the horses of St Mark'. As was their custom, the Council of Ten had imprisoned Pisani for his defeat, but Venice was now in such a jam, with half of its fleet far away, that the people demanded his release to lead what remained of their navy. A brilliant commander, Pisani exploited his familiarity with the Lagoon and in turn blockaded the Genoese in Chioggia. When the other half of Venice's fleet came dramatically racing home, the Genoese surrendered (June 1380) and never recovered in the East.

Fresh Prey on the Mainland

Venice was determined never to feel hungry again, and set her sights on the *terra firma*—not only for the sake of farmland, but to control her trade routes into the west that were being increasingly harried and taxed by the *signori* of the Veneto. Treviso came first, then opportunity knocked in 1402 with the sudden death of the Milanese duke Gian Galeazzo Visconti, whose conquests became the subject of a great land grab. Venice picked up Padua, Bassano, Verona and Belluno, and in 1454 added Ravenna, southern Trentino, Friuli, Crema and Bergamo. In 1489 the Republic's overseas empire reached its greatest extent when it was presented with Cyprus, a somewhat reluctant 'gift' from the king's widow, Venetian noble-woman Caterina Cornaro, who received Àsolo as compensation.

But just as Venice expanded, Fortune's wheel gave a creak and conspired to squeeze her back into her Lagoon. The **Ottoman Turks** captured Constantinople in 1453, and although the Venetians tried to negotiate trading terms with the sultans (as they had previously done with the infidel Saracens, to the opprobrium of the West), they would be spending the next three centuries fighting a losing battle for their eastern territories. The discovery of the New World was another blow, but gravest to the merchants of Venice was **Vasco da Gama**'s voyage around the Cape of Good Hope to India in 1497, blazing a cheaper and easier route to Venice's prime markets that broke her monopoly of oriental luxuries; Western European merchants no longer had to pay Venice for safe passage to the East. In just 44 years nearly everything that Venice had worked for over 500 years was undermined.

On the mainland, Venice's rapid expansion had excited the fear and envy of Pope Julius, who rallied Italy's potentates and their foreign allies to form the **League of Cambrai** to humble the proud republic. They snatched her *terra firma* possessions after her defeat at Agnadello in 1509, but quarrelled amongst themselves afterwards, and before long all the territories they conquered voluntarily returned to Venice. Venice, however, never really recovered from this wound inflicted by the very people who should have rallied to her defence, and although her Arsenal produced a warship a day, and her captains helped to win a glorious victory over the Turks at **Lepanto** (1571), she was increasingly forced to retreat.

A Most Leisurely Collapse

The odds were stacked against her, but in her heyday Venice had accumulated enough wealth and verve to cushion her fall. Her noble families consoled themselves in the classical calm of Palladio's villas, while the city found solace in masterpieces of Venice's golden age of art. Carnival, ever longer, ever more licentious, was sanctioned by the state to bring in moneyed visitors, like Lord Byron, who dubbed it 'the revel of the earth, the masque of Italy'. In the 1600s the city had 20,000 courtesans, many of them dressed as men to whet the Venetians' passion. It didn't suit everyone: 'Venice is a stink pot, charged with every virus of hell,' fumed one Dr Warner, in the 18th century.

In 1797 **Napoleon**, declaring he would be 'an Attila for the Venetian state', took it with scarcely a whimper, ending the story of the world's longest enduring republic, in the reign of its 120th doge. Napoleon took the horses of St Mark to Paris as his trophy, and replaced the old *Pax tibi, Marce, Evangelista Meus* inscribed in the book the lion holds up on Venice's coat-of-arms with 'The Rights of Men and Citizens'. Reading it, a gondolier made the famous remark, 'At last he's turned the page.' Yet while many patricians danced merrily around his Liberty trees, freed at last from responsiblity, the people wept.

Napoleon gave Venice to **Austria**, whose rule was confirmed by the Congress of Vienna after the Emperor's defeat in 1815. The Austrians' main contribution was the railway causeway linking Venice irrevocably to the mainland (1846). Two years later Venice gave its last gasp of independence, when a patriotic revolt led by **Daniele Manin** seized the city and re-estab-lished the republic, only to fall to the Austrian army once again after an heroic one-year siege.

Modern Venice

The former Republic did, however, finally join the new kingdom of Italy in 1866, after Prussia had conveniently defeated the Austrians. Already better known as a magnet to visitors than for any activity of its own, Venice played a quiet role in the new state. Things changed under **Mussolini**: the industrial zones of Mestre and Marghera were begun on the mainland, and a road was added to the railway causeway. The city escaped damage in the two World Wars, despite heavy fighting in the environs; according to legend, when the Allies finally occupied Venice in 1945 they arrived in a fleet of gondolas.

But Venice was soon to engage in its own private battle, with the sea. From the beginning the city had manipulated nature's waterways for her own survival, diverting a major outlet of the Po, the Brenta, the Piave, the Adige and the Sile rivers to keep her Lagoon from silting up. In 1782, Venice completed the famous *murazzi*, the 4-kilometre-long, 20-foot-high sea walls to protect the Lagoon. But on **4 November 1966** a deadly combination of wind, torrential storms, high tides and giant waves breached the *murazzi*, wrecked the Lido and left Venice under record *acque alte* (high waters) for 20 hours, with disastrous results to the city's architecture and art. The catastrophe galvanized the international community's efforts to save Venice. Even the Italian state, notorious for its indifference to Venice (historical grudges die slowly in Italy) passed a law in 1973 to preserve the city, and contributed to the construction of a new flood barricade similar to the one on the Thames.

This giant sea gate, known as 'Moses', has now been completed, but arguments continue over whether it will ever be effective if needed, and what its ecological consequences might be. Seemingly threatened by a myriad of potential disasters—the growth of algae in the Lagoon, the effects of the outpourings of Mestre on its foundations, the ageing of its native population, or perhaps most of all the sheer number of its tourists—the city contrives to survive, as unique as ever, and proposals to give it more of a function in the modern world, as, for example, a base for international organizations, may serve to give it new life as well.

The Face of Venice

Venice stands on 117 islets, divided by over 100 canals that are spanned by some 400 bridges. The longest bridges are the 4.2km rail and road causeways that link Venice to the mainland. The open sea is half that distance across the Lagoon, beyond the protective reefs or *lidi* formed by centuries of river silt and the Adriatic current. The Grand Canal, Venice's incomparable main street, was originally the bed of a river that fed the Lagoon; the other canals, its tributaries (called *rio*, singular, or *rii*, plural), were shallow channels meandering through the mud banks, and are nowhere as grand—some are merely glorified sewers.

A warren of 2300 alleys, or *calli*, handle Venice's pedestrian-only traffic, and they come with a colourful bouquet of names—a *rio terrà* is a filled-in canal; a *piscina* a filled-in pool; a *fondamenta* or *riva* a quay; a *salizzada* is a street that was paved in the 17th century; a *ruga* is one lined with shops; a *sottoportico* passes under a building. A Venetian square is a *campo*, recalling the days when they were open fields; the only square dignified with the title of 'piazza' is that of St Mark's, though the two smaller squares flanking the basilica are called *piazzette*, and there's one fume-filled *piazzale*, the dead-end for buses and cars.

All the *rii* and *calli* have been divided into six quarters, or *sestieri*, since Venice's earliest days: **San Marco** (by the piazza), **Castello** (by the Arsenal) and **Cannaregio** (by the Ghetto), all on the northeast bank of the Grand Canal; and **San Polo** (by the church), **Santa Croce** (near the Piazzale Roma) and **Dorsoduro**, the 'hard-back', by the Accademia, all on the southwest bank. Besides these, the modern *comune* of Venice includes the towns on the **Lagoon islands**, the **Lido**, and on the mainland **Mestre** and **Marghera**, Italy's version of the New Jersey Flats, where most Venetians live today. There is some concern that historic Venice (population around 79,000, down from 200,000 in its heyday) may soon become a city of second homes belonging to wealthy northern Italians and foreigners.

Signs and Directions

The Venetian language, or Venet, sounds to the uninitiated like an Italian trying to speak Spanish with a numb mouth—and it turns up on the city's street signs. Your map may read 'San Giovanni e Paolo' but you should inquire for 'San Zanipolo'; 'San Giovanni Decollato' (decapitated John) is better known as 'San Zan Degola'. Still, despite the impossibility of giving comprehensible directions through the tangle of alleys (Venetians will invariably point you in the right direction, however, with a blithe *'sempre diritto!'*— 'straight ahead!'), it's hard to get hopelessly lost in Venice. It only measures about 1.5 by 3 kilometres, and there are helpful yellow signs at major crossings, pointing the way to San Marco, Rialto, and the Accademia, or the Piazzale Roma and the Ferrovia if you despair and want to go home. When hunting for an address in Venice, make sure you're in the correct *sestiere*, as quite a few *calli* share names. Also, beware that houses in each *sestiere* are numbered consecutively in a system logical only to a postman from Mars; numbers up to 5000 are not unusual.

Architecture

At once isolated but deeply linked to the traditions of East and West, Venice developed her own charmingly bastard architecture, especially in a style called Venetian Gothic, adopting only the most delightfully visual elements from each tradition. Ruskin's *The Stones of Venice* is the classic work on the city's buildings, which harsher critics—and Ruskin was one—disparage for being all artifice and show. The Venetians inherited the Byzantines' love of colour, mosaics, rare marbles and exotic effects, epitomized in the magnificently gaudy **St Mark's**. Venetian Gothic is only slightly less elaborate, and achieved its most notable products in the great palaces, most notably the **Palazzo Ducale** and the **Ca' d'Oro**, with their ogival windows and finely wrought façades.

The Renaissance arrived in Venice relatively late, and its early phase is called Lombardesque, after the **Lombardo** family (Pietro and sons Tullio and Antonio) who designed the best of it, including the small but flawless **Santa Maria dei Miracoli** and the rich **Scuola di San Marco**. Later Renaissance architects brought Venice into the mainstream of the classical revival, and graced Venice with the arcaded **Piazza San Marco**, the **Libreria** of Sansovino, the **San Michele** of Mauro Codussi (or Coducci), and two of **Palladio**'s finest churches, which stand out in clear contrast to the exuberant jumble that surrounds them. Venice's best Baroque works are by **Longhena**, the spiritual heir of Palladio.

To support all this on the soft mud banks, the Venetians drove piles of Istrian pine 16½ft into the solid clay—over a million posts hold up the church of Santa Maria della Salute alone. If Venice tends to lean and sink, it's due to erosion of these piles by the salty Adriatic, pollution, and the currents and wash caused by the deep channels dredged into the Lagoon for the large tankers sailing to Marghera. Or, as the Venetians explain, the city is a giant sponge.

Most Venetian houses are between four and six storeys high. On the tops of some you can see the wooden rooftop loggias, or *altane*, where the Renaissance ladies of Venice were wont to idle, bleaching their hair in the sun; they wore broad-brimmed hats to protect their complexions, and spread their tresses through a hole cut in the crown.

Venetian Art

Venice may have been a Renaissance Johnny-come-lately, but the city and its hinterland are rivalled only by Tuscany when it comes to the first notch painting. Before the 14th century the Venetians excelled primarily in mosaic, an art they learned from the Byzantines, shown at their very best in St Mark's and Torcello. In 1306 **Giotto** painted his masterpiece in Padua's Cappella Scrovegni and gave local painters a revolutionary eye-full. His naturalism influenced a school of artists in Padua and **Paolo Veneziano**, the first great Venetian painter of note, although many artists would continue painting decorative Gothic pieces for a long time to come, notably **Jacobello del Fiore**, **Michele Giambono** and the **Vivarini** family.

Things began to change in the mid 15th century, with the advent of two great masters. **Andrea Mantegna** (1431–1506), trained in Padua, influenced generations with his strong interests in antiquity, perspective and powerful sculptured figures. His more lyrical and humane brother-in-law, **Giovanni Bellini** (1440?–1516) founded the Venetian school. Bellini learned the technique of oil painting from **Antonello da Messina** during his visit in 1475, and he never looked back: his use of luminous natural light and colour to create atmosphere ('tonalism') and sensuous beauty are characteristics all of his followers adopted, if few ever equalled. Meanwhile Giovanni's brother, **Gentile Bellini,** and **Vittore Carpaccio** (1470–1523) avoided tonalism altogether in their charming and precise narrative works.

The Cinquento–Settecento

For the heavy hitters of Venice's 16th-century Golden Age, however, tonalism was a religion: while other Italians followed the Romans in learning drawing and anatomy, the Venetians went their own way, obsessed by the dramatic qualities of atmosphere. The tragically short-lived **Giorgione of Castelfranco** (1475–1510) was the seminal figure in the new manner: his *Tempest* in the Accademia is a remarkable study in brooding tension. Giorgione also invented 'easel painting'—i.e. art that served neither Church nor State nor the vanity of the patron, but stood on its own for the pleasure of the viewer.

Giorgione's colleague, Tiziano Vecellio, or **Titian** (1485/90–1576), was the greatest master of the Venetian school. Known for his bold, spiralling compositions, his rich colours and his luscious mythologies, he was a revolutionary in his old age, using increasingly free brush-strokes and even applying paint with his fingers. **Tintoretto** (1518–94), of the quick brushstrokes, took his Mannerist compositions to unforgettable extremes, while his contemporary, **Paolo Veronese** (1528–88), painted lavish *trompe l'oeil* canvases and frescoes that are the culmination of Venice at her most decorative. This was also the period of **Palma Vecchio**, the sensuous painter of Venetian blonde goddesses, **Cima da Conegliano**, author of some of the loveliest landscapes, and **Lorenzo Lotto**, of the famous psychologically penetrating portraits, who was run out of Venice by Titian and his buddies.

Venetia and its art enjoyed a revival in the twilight years of the 18th century, when its art was in great demand at home and abroad. Much of the thanks goes to **Giambattista Tiepolo** (1697–1770), the first to cast Baroque gloominess aside to create an effervescent, light-filled, brilliantly coloured style; he was also the last great fresco-painter in Italy. His chief follower was his son Giandomenico, although his influence can also be seen in the luminous palettes of **Antonio Canaletto** (1697–1768) and **Francesco Guardi** (1712–93) who produced the countless views of Venice that were the rage among travellers on the Grand Tour; even now most of their works are in Britain and France. **Pietro Longhi**, their contemporary, devoted himself to genre scenes that offer a delightful insight into the Venice of 200 years ago.

Getting There

by air

Venice's **Marco Polo Airport** is 13km north of the city near the Lagoon, and has regularly scheduled connections from London, New York (via Milan), Paris, Vienna, Nice, Zürich, Frankfurt, Düsseldorf, Rome, Milan, Palermo and Naples. For flight information in Venice, call ✆ 041 260 9260.

The airport is linked with Venice by water-taxi (✆ 041 966 870 or ✆ 041 523 5775), the most expensive option (L140,000); or by *motoscafi* to San Marco (Zecca) roughly every hour (L17,000 per person), connecting with most flights from March to October. If you're catching an early flight, you can reserve a departure (✆ 041 541 5058). There is also an airport ATVO bus to the Piazzale Roma (L7000) or, cheapest of all, the ACTV city bus no.5 (L1500), which passes by twice an hour.

by sea

Venice is loveliest approached by sea. There are daily car ferries between Venice, Corfu and Patras (2 days), and Alexandria (3½ days). An easier way to approach Venice on water is by taking the *Burchiello* from Padua along the Brenta Canal (*see* p.341).

by train

Venice's **Stazione Santa Lucia** (the **Ferrovia**) is the terminus of the *Venice Simplon-Orient Express* and less glamorous trains from the rest of Europe and Italy. All trains from Santa Lucia stop in Mestre, where you may have to change for some destinations. For rail information, call ✆ 1478 88088.

Water-taxis, *vaporetti* and gondolas wait in front of the station to sweep you off into the city. If you've brought more luggage than you can carry, one of Venice's infamous porters (distinguished by their badges) will lug it to your choice of transport, and if you pay his fare on the water-taxi, will take it and you to your hotel (official price for one or two pieces of luggage is L30,000 between any two points in the historic centre, extra bags L10,000). Sometimes you can track down a porter once you disembark at one of the main landings. Since rates for baggage handling are only regulated at the station, negotiate a price in advance.

by car

All roads to Venice end at the monstrous municipal parking towers in **Piazzale Roma** or its cheaper annexe, **Tronchetto**, ✆ 041 520 7555, the largest car park in Europe. You can leave your car there for L25,000 a day, or less for longer stays. In the summer, at Easter and Carnival, when the causeway turns into a solid conga-line of cars waiting to park, consider the Italian Auto Club's three alternative car parks (open to non-members): **Fusina**, ✆ 041 547 0055, with a shady, year-round campsite, located at the mouth of the Brenta Canal south of Marghera (car park open summer only; *vaporetto* no.16 to Venice); **S. Giuliano**, in Mestre near the causeway (bus service to Venice), and **Punta Sabbioni**, ✆ 041 530 0455, in between the Lido and Jesolo (ferry no.17 from Tronchetto).

Getting Around

vaporetti *and* motoscafi

Public transport in Venice means by water, by the grunting, canal-cutting *vaporetti* (the all-purpose water-buses), or the sleeker, faster *motoscafi*, run by the ACTV (✆ 041 528 7886). Note that the only canals served by public transport are the Grand Canal, the Rio Nuovo, the Canale di Cannaregio and the Rio dell'Arsenale; between them, you'll have to rely on your feet, which is not as gruelling as it sounds, as Venice is so small you can walk across it in an hour.

Single **tickets** (a flat rate of L6000) should be purchased and validated in the machines at the landing-stages (random inspections aren't very frequent, but if you get caught without a validated ticket you'll have to pay a L30,000 fine on the spot). As some landing stages don't sell tickets, it's best to stock up (most *tabacchi* sell them in blocks of ten). Or, if you intend being on a boat at least three times in a given day, purchase a **24-hour tourist pass**, for L18,000, valid for unlimited travel on all lines, or the **3-day pass**, for L35,000. If you plan to spend more than a few days in Venice, the cheapest option is to buy a *tesserino di abbonamento* from the ACTV office at Piazzale Roma (L10,000 and a passport photo—there's a machine at the Ferrovia) which is valid for three years and entitles you to buy monthly season tickets (L45,000) or single tickets at greatly reduced rates.

Lines of interest to visitors are listed below; most run until midnight. Precise schedules are listed in the tourist office's free monthly guide, *Un Ospite di Venezia.*

Line 1   (*accelerato*, the Italian euphemism for slow-coach) runs in an hour from Piazzale Roma and the Ferrovia down the Grand Canal to San Marco and the Lido, and vice versa, stopping everywhere. Every 10mins (every 20mins after 9pm).

Line 82   (orange) (*diretto*) does a speedier circular tour from S. Zaccaria (S. Marco), including the extension to the Lido, the Giudecca and S. Giorgio Maggiore. Every 10mins during the day, approximately once an hour at night.

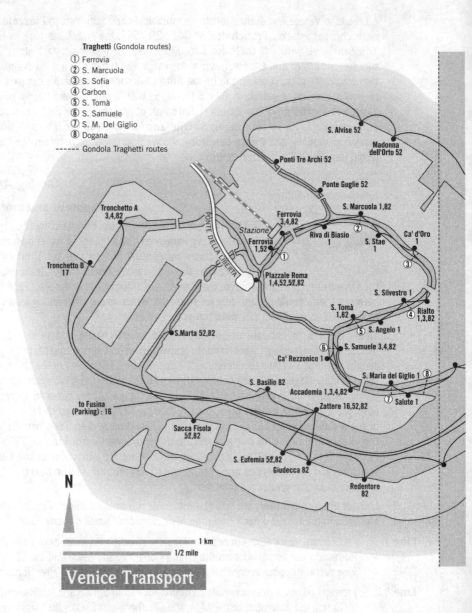

Traghetti (Gondola routes)
1. Ferrovia
2. S. Marcuola
3. S. Sofia
4. Carbon
5. S. Tomà
6. S. Samuele
7. S. M. Del Giglio
8. Dogana

------ Gondola Traghetti routes

S. Alvise 52

Madonna dell'Orto 52

Ponti Tre Archi 52

Ponte Guglie 52

S. Marcuola 1,82

Tronchetto A 3,4,82

Ferrovia 3,4,82

Riva di Biasio 1

S. Stae 1

Ca' d'Oro 1

Stazione

Ferrovia 1,52
1

Tronchetto B 17

Plazzale Roma 1,4,52,82

S. Silvestro 1

S. Tomà 1,82

Rialto 1,3,82
4

S.Marta 52,82

S. Angelo 1
5

S. Samuele 3,4,82
6

Ca' Rezzonico 1

S. Maria del Giglio 1
8

S. Basilio 82

Accademia 1,3,4,82

Salute 1
7

to Fusina (Parking) : 16

Zattere 16,52,82

Sacca Fisola 52,82

S. Eufemia 52,82

Giudecca 82

Redentore 82

N

1 km

1/2 mile

Venice Transport

PONTE DELLA LIBERTA

Regular Lines

1: *(accelerato)* Piazzale Roma–Ferrovia–Grand Canal–San Marco–Lido: stops every where; around the clock, every 10min (20mins after 9pm). The entire one-way journey takes an hour.

6: *(diretto motonave)* S. Zaccaria–Lido; every 20mins.

11: (the 'mixed' line) Lido–Alberoni (by bus)–Pellestrina (by boat)–Chioggia (by boat); about once an hour. (Not shown.)

12: Fondamente Nuove–Murano–Torcello–Burano–Treporti; about once an hour.

13: Fondamente Nuove–Murano–Vignole–S. Erasmo; about once an hour.

14: S. Zaccaria–Lido–Punta Sabbioni–Treporti–Burano–Torcello (every half-hour).

17: (car ferry) Tronchetto (Piazzale Roma)–Giudecca–Lido–Punta Sabbione; every 50mins.

52: (red 'barred') *(motoscafo)* Piazzale Roma–Giudecca–S. Zaccaria–Campo della Tana (the Arsenale)–Fondamente Nuove–Murano (all six stops)–S. Michele; every 20mins.

52: (green) *(motoscafo)* Lido–S. Zaccaria–Zattere–Piazzale Roma–Ferrovia–Fondamente Nuove–Murano; every 20mins.

82: (orange) *(diretto)* S. Zaccaria (S. Marco)–Lido–Giudecca–S. Giorgio Maggiore; a speedy circular tour; every 10min during the day, approx. once an hour at night.

82: (green) *(diretto)* S. Zaccaria–S. Giorgio Maggiore–Giudecca–Zattere–S. Marta; every 10mins.

N: *(servizio notturno)* Lido–S. Zaccaria–Accademia–S. Toma–Rialto–Piazzale Roma–Zattere–Zitelle–S. Giorgio Maggiore; every 20mins from about 11pm all night.

Summer only

3: Tronchetto–Grand Canal–S. Zaccaria–Tronchetto

4: S. Zaccaria–Grand Canal–Tronchetto–S. Zaccaria

16: (private service *L8000*) Zattere–Fusina car park; every 50mins.

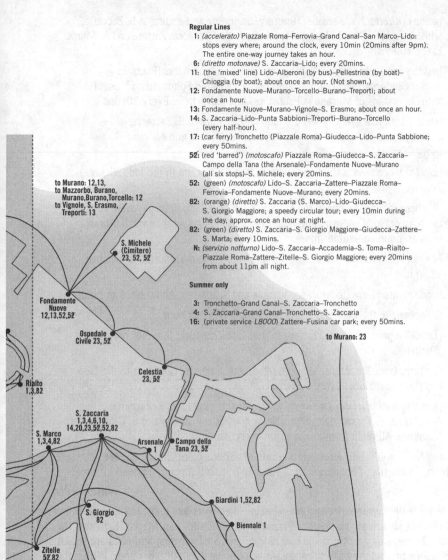

to Murano: 12,13,
to Mazzorbo, Burano,
Murano,Burano,Torcello: 12
to Vignole, S. Erasmo,
Treporti: 13

S. Michele
(Cimitero)
23, 52, 52

Fondamente
Nuove
12,13,52,52

Ospedale
Civile 23, 52

to Murano: 23

Rialto
1,3,82

Celestia
23, 52

S. Zaccaria
1,3,4,6,10,
14,20,23,52,52,82

S. Marco
1,3,4,82

Arsenale
1

Campo della
Tana 23, 52

S. Giorgio
82

Giardini 1,52,82

Biennale 1

Zitelle
52,82

S. Elena
1,23,52

to Punta
Sabbioni:
14

to Grazie,
S. Clemente:
10

to Lido,
Punta Sabbione :
17

to Lido:
1,6,14,52,82

to Lido :
1,52

Line 82 (green) (*diretto*) has a smaller itinerary, beginning and ending at S. Zaccaria, with stops at S. Giorgio Maggiore, all along the Giudecca, Zattere and S. Marta. Every 10mins.

Line 82 (red 'barred') a *motoscafo* linking various major landmarks (Piazzale Roma, Giudecca, S. Zaccaria, Campo della Tana and Fondamente Nuove) with the islands of Murano (all six stops) and S. Michele. Every 20mins.

Line 52 (green) a *motoscafo* between the Lido and all stops to S. Zaccaria, Zattere, Piazzale Roma, Ferrovia, Fondamente Nuove and Murano. Every 20mins.

Line 6 (*diretto motonave*) is the large steamer from S. Zaccaria to the Lido. Every 20mins.

Line 11 (the 'mixed' line) begins at the Lido on a bus to Alberoni, from where you catch a boat for Pellestrina, then another for Chioggia, or vice versa. About once an hour, sometimes more.

Line 12 Fondamente Nuove to Murano, Burano, Torcello and Treporti. About once an hour.

Line 13 Fondamente Nuove to Murano, Vignole and S. Erasmo. About once an hour.

Line 14 S. Zaccaria to the Lido and Punta Sabbioni. Every half-hour.

Line 16 (*L8000*) a private service, Zattere to the Fusina car park. Summer only, every 50mins.

Line 17 Car ferry from Tronchetto (Piazzale Roma) through the Giudecca to the Lido and Punto Sabbione. Every 50mins.

Line N (*servizio notturno*) does a sweep which includes the Lido, S. Zaccaria, Accademia, S. Toma, Rialto, Piazzale Roma, Zattere, Zitelle and S. Giorgio Maggiore. All night from about 11pm every 20mins.

At San Marco you'll find **excursion boats** to various points in the Lagoon; they are more expensive than public transport, but may be useful if you're pressed for time.

water-taxis

These are really more tourist excursion boats—they work like taxis, but their fares are de luxe. Stands are at the station, Piazzale Roma, Rialto, San Marco, Lido and the airport. These jaunty motor boats can hold up to 15 passengers, and fares are set for destinations beyond the historic centre, or you can pay L150,000 per hour. Within the centre the minimum fare for up to four people is L50,000; additional passengers are up to L10,000 each, and there are surcharges for baggage, holiday or nocturnal service (after 10pm), and for using a radio taxi (© 041 522 2303).

gondolas

Gondolas, first mentioned in the city's annals in 1094, have a stately mystique that commands all other boats to give way. Shelley and many others have compared them to a funeral barque or the soul ferry to Hades, and not a few gondoliers share the infernal Charon's expectation of a solid gold tip for their services. Like Model Ts, gondolas come in any colour as long as it's black, still obeying the Sumptuary Law of

1562. Once used by all and sundry, they now operate frankly for tourists (and Venetian weddings). Official prices are L120,000 for a 50-minute ride (L150,000 after 8pm). Before setting out, agree with the gondolier on where you want to go and how long you expect it to take to avoid any unpleasantness later on.

In addition, gondolas retired from the tourist trade are used for **gondola traghetti** services across the Grand Canal at various points between its three bridges— your only chance to enjoy an economical, if brief, gondola ride for L700. *Traghetto* crossings are signposted in the streets nearby. For appearance's sake you'll have to stand up: only sissies ever sit down on *traghetti.*

by bus

Piazzale Roma is Venice's bus terminus; there are frequent city buses from here to Mestre, Chioggia, Marghera and Malcontenta, regional buses every half-hour to Padua, and less frequently to other Veneto cities and Trieste. It has its own helpful tourist information office, ✆ 041 528 7886.

car hire

If you want to explore the mainland by car, several hire firms have offices at Piazzale Roma, the airports, or Mestre Station: **Avis,** (Marco Polo Airport) ✆ 041 541 5030; **Europcar,** (Piazzale Roma) ✆ 041 523 8616, (Treviso Airport) ✆ 0422 23396; **Maggiore,** (Marco Polo) ✆ 041 541 5040, (Mestre) ✆ 041 935 300.

Tourist Information

The main information office is in one corner of Piazza San Marco, to the far left as you face the square from the basilica (Ascensione 71/c, ✆ 041 522 6356). Branch offices at Palazzetto Selva, right by the S. Marco *vaporetto* stop (✆ 041 529 8730), the railway station (✆ 041 529 8727) and the bus station in Piazzale Roma (✆ 041 522 7402) offer accommodation services. There are also offices on the Rotonda Marghera (✆ 041 937 764), at Marco Polo Airport (✆ 041 541 5887) and on the Lido at Gran Viale 6 (✆ 041 526 5721). All distribute the free, fortnightly magazine *Un Ospite di Venezia,* with current events and other information in English.

For L5000, people between the ages of 14 and 29 can buy a ***Rolling Venice*** card, which gives discounts on the city's attractions, from films at the Film Festival to museums, hostels, shops, restaurants and reduced price tickets for the *vaporetti.* Apply at: the Assessorato alla Gioventù, Corte Contarina 1529, San Marco, ✆ 041 274 7650/1 (*Mon–Fri 9.30–1, Tues and Thurs also 3–5*); Agenzia Arte e Storia, Corte Canal 659, Santa Croce, ✆ 041 524 0232 (*Mon–Fri 9–1 and 3.30–7*); or Associazone

Italiana Alberghi per la Gioventù, Calle del Castelforte 3101, San Polo, ✆ 041 520 4414 (*Mon–Sat 8–2*). Take a photo and your passport.

If you lose something in the city, try the Municipio, ✆ 041 274 8111; or if you lost it on a train, ✆ 041 785 238; or on a *vaporetto*, ✆ 041 780 310.

Ambulance, ✆ **041 523 000**.

If you have an accident or become seriously ill, go to the *Pronto Soccorso* department of the **city hospital** in Campo Santi Giovanni e Paolo, Castello, or the **Ospedale del Mare**, 1 Lungomare d'Annunzio, Lido, ✆ 041 529 4111; if you need a doctor at night or on holidays ring the *Guardia Medica*, ✆ 041 529 4060.

Several *farmacie* are open all night on a rotating basis: the addresses are in the window of every pharmacy, or you can ring ✆ 041 523 0573 for a list.

Places that exchange money outside normal banking hours include:

American Express: S. Moisè 1471, ✆ 041 520 0844 (*open April–Oct Mon–Sat 8–8*); **CIT**: Piazza S. Marco 4850, ✆ 041 528 5480 (*open Mon–Sat 8–6*); **INTRAS**: Piazza S. Marco, by the clock tower (*open Mon–Sat 8.30–6*); **World Vision**: (Thomas Cook), Calle delle Ostreghe 2457, S. Marco.

The **main post office** is in the Fóndaco dei Tedeschi, near the Ponte Rialto (*open Mon–Sat 8.15–7.25*). There are also smaller offices at the foot of Piazza San Marco (Calle dell'Ascensione) and at the western end of the Zattere.

The Grand Canal

A ride down Venice's bustling and splendid main artery is most visitors' introduction to the city, and there's no finer one. The Grand Canal has always been Venice's status address, and along its looping banks the patricians of the Golden Book, or *Nobili Homini*, as they called themselves, built a hundred marble palaces with their front doors giving on to the water, framed by peppermint-stick posts where they moored their watery carriages.

The highlights, from Piazzale Roma to Piazza San Marco include: the 12th-century **Fóndaco dei Turchi** (with rounded arches, on the right after the Station Bridge), the Ottoman merchants' headquarters until 1838, and now the Natural History Museum. Nearly opposite, Mauro Codussi's Renaissance **Palazzo Vendramin-Calergi**, where Richard Wagner died in 1883, is now the winter home of the casino. Back on the right bank, just after the San Stae landing, the Baroque **Palazzo Pésaro** is adorned with masks by Longhena. And then comes the loveliest palace of all, the **Ca' d'Oro**, with a florid Venetian Gothic façade, formerly etched in gold, now housing the Galleria Franchetti (*see* p.323).

After the Ca' d'Oro, the **Ponte di Rialto**—one of the most famous bridges in Europe—swings into view. 'Rialto' recalls the days when the canal was the Rio Alto; originally it was spanned here by a bridge of boats, then by a 13th-century wooden bridge. When that was on the verge of collapse, the republic held a competition for the design of a new stone structure. The winner, Antonio da Ponte, was the most audacious, proposing a single arch spanning 157ft; built in 1592, it has defied all the dire predictions of the day and still stands, even taking the additional weight of two rows of shops. The reliefs over the arch are of St Mark and St Theodore.

To the right stretch the extensive **Rialto Markets**, and on the left the **Fóndaco dei Tedeschi** (German Warehouse), once the busiest trading centre in Venice, where merchants from all over the north lived and traded. The building (now the post office) was remodelled in 1505 and adorned with exterior frescoes by Giorgione and Titian, of which only sad fragments survive (now in the Ca' d'Oro).

Beyond the Ponte di Rialto are two Renaissance masterpieces: Sanmicheli's 1556 **Palazzo Grimani**, across from the S. Silvestro landing (now the Appeals Court), and Mauro Codussi's **Palazzo Corner-Spinelli** (1510), just before the Sant'Angelo landing stage. A short distance further along the left bank are the **Palazzi Mocenigo**, actually three palaces in one, where Byron lived for two years. A little way further on the same side, the wall of buildings gives way for the Campo San Samuele, dominated by the **Palazzo Grassi**, an 18th-century neoclassical residence, renovated by Fiat as a modern exhibition and cultural centre.

The lovely Gothic **Ca' Foscari**, on the right bank, just after the bend in the canal, was built in 1437 for Doge Francesco Foscari: two doors down, by its own landing-stage, is Longhena's 1667 **Ca' Rezzonico**, where Browning died. Further on the canal is spanned by the wooden **Ponte dell'Accademia**, built in 1932 to replace the ungainly iron 'English bridge'.

On the left bank, before the S. Maria del Giglio landing, stands the majestic Renaissance **Palazzo Corner** (Ca' Grande), built by Sansovino in 1550. On the right bank, Longhena's Baroque masterpiece **Santa Maria della Salute** is followed by the Customs House, or **Dogana di Mare**, crowned by a golden globe and weathervane of Fortune, which guard the entrance to the Grand Canal. The next landing-stage is San Marco.

Byron Goes Swimming

Byron arrived in Venice in 1816, his heart full of romance as he rented a villa on the Brenta to compose the last canto of his *Childe Harolde's Pilgrimage*. The city's canals at least afforded him the personal advantage of being able to swim anywhere (his club foot made him shy of walking); on one occasion he swam a race from the Lido to the Rialto Bridge and was the only man to finish.

It wasn't long before the emotional polish of *Childe Harolde* began to crack. To Byron's surprise, Venice didn't perfect his romantic temper, but cured him of it. He went to live in the Palazzo Mocenigo on the Grand Canal, in the company of 14 servants, a dog, a wolf, a fox, monkeys and a garlicky baker's wife, *La Fornarina*, who stabbed him in the hand with a fork—which so angered Byron that he ordered her out, whereupon she threw herself into the Grand Canal. Under such circumstances, all that had been breathless passion reeked of the ridiculous, as he himself admitted:

> *And the sad truth which hovers o'er my desk*
> *Turns what was once romantic to burlesque*

Venice, its women, its own ironic detachment and its love of liberty set Byron's mind free to write *Beppo: A Venetian Story*, spoofing Venice's *cavalieri serventi* (escorts/lovers—even nuns had them) while celebrating the freedom of its people. He followed this with two bookish plays on Venetian themes: *Marino Faliero* and *The Two Foscari*, and most importantly began his satirical masterpiece, *Don Juan*.

Meanwhile debauchery was taking its toll: an English acquaintance wrote in 1818 that 'His face had become pale, bloated and sallow, and the knuckles on his hands were lost in fat.' Byron became infatuated with a young Countess, Teresa Guiccioli, and left Venice to move in with her and her elderly husband in Ravenna. But, having tasted every freedom in Venice, Byron once more began to chafe; the Contessa was 'taming' him. He bundled up the manuscript of *Don Juan* and left, only to die of fever at the age of 36 in the Greek War of Independence.

Piazza San Marco

Venice's self-proclaimed Attila, Napoleon, described this as 'Europe's finest drawing-room', and no matter how often you've seen it in pictures or in the flesh, its charm never fades. There are Venetians (and not all of them purveyors of souvenirs) who prefer it in the height of summer, at its liveliest, when Babylonians from the four corners of the earth outnumber even the daredevil pigeons, while the café bands provide a Fellini-esque accompaniment. Others prefer it in the misty moonlight, when the hazy, rosy streetlamps make it unreal.

The piazza and its two flanking *piazzette* have looked essentially the same since 1810, when the Ala Napoleonica was added to the west end, to close in Mauro Codussi's long, arcaded **Procuratie Vecchie** (1499) on the north side and Sansovino's **Procuratie Nuove** (1540) on the south. Both, originally used as the offices of the Procurators (caretakers) of St Mark's, are now filled with jewellery shops. Two centuries ago they contained an equal number of coffee-houses. Only two survive—the **Caffè Quadri** in the Procuratie Vecchie, the old favourite of the Austrians, and **Florian's**, in the Procuratie Nuove, its hand-painted décor unchanged since it opened its doors in 1720, although with *espressos* at L7000 a head the proprietors could easily afford to remodel it in solid gold.

St Mark's Basilica/Basilica di San Marco

Open to visitors Mon–Sat 10–4.30, Sun and hols 2–5. No shorts, and women must have their shoulders covered and a minimum of décolletage, or risk being peremptorily dismissed from the head of the queue. There are separate admission charges for many of the smaller chapels and individual attractions; different sections are frequently closed for restoration. Disabled ramp access from Piazzetta dei Leoncini.

This is nothing less than the holy shrine of the Venetian state. An ancient law decreed that all merchants trading in the East had to bring back from each voyage a new embellishment for St Mark's. The result is a glittering robbers' den, the only church in Christendom that would not look out of place in Xanadu. Until 1807, when it became Venice's cathedral, the basilica was the private chapel of the doge, built to house the relics of St Mark after their 'pious theft'

Piazza San Marco

50 metres
50 yards

N

Campo
SS. Filippo
e Giacomo

CALLE DEGLI ALBANESI

RUGA GIUFFA

Aquarium

S. Apollonia
Cloister/Museo
Diocesano

C. SCOLASTICA

Ponte dei Sospiri
(Bridge of Sighs)

Prisons

RIVA

DEGLI SCHIAVONI

Rio   Canonica

Ponte
della
Paglia

FOND. DELLA CANONICA

C. DELLA CANONICA

C. LARGA SAN MARCO

Palazzo
Patriarcale

St Mark's
Basilica

Palazzo Ducale
(Doge's Palace)

Piazzetta
dei Leoncini

MOLO

Column of
St Mark

Torre
dell'Orologio

Loggetta

Piazzetta
San Marco

Column of
St Theodore

MERCERIE

Campanile

Procuratie
Vecchie

Libreria

Museo
Archeologico

Zecca

CALLE DEL CAPELLO NERO

Procuratie

Piazza
San Marco

Zecca

della

Giardinetti
Reali

S. Marco Giardinetti
3, 4, 82

delle

Procuratie
Nuove

Rio

Rio

Ala
Napoleonica

Museo Correr

CALLE DELL'ASCENSION

S. Marco Vallaresso

FOND. ORSEOLO

C.S. SELVADEGO

SALIZZADA S. MOISE

CALLE VALLARESSO

FREZZERIA

Names in *italics* refer to mosaics.

1 *Translation of the Body of St Mark* (1270)
2 *Venice Venerating the Relics of St Mark* (1718)
3 Central door, with magnificent 13th-century carvings in arches
4 *Venice Welcoming the Relics of St Mark* (1700s)
5 *Removal of St Mark's Relics from Alexandria* (1700s)
6 Pietra del Bando, stone from which the Signoria's decrees were read
7 *Scenes from the Book of Genesis* (1200) and 6th-century Byzantine door of S. Clemente
8 *Noah and the Flood* (1200s), tomb of Doge Vitale Falier (d. 1096)
9 *Madonna and Saints* (1060s); red marble slab where Emperor Barbarossa submitted to Pope Alexander III (1177); stair up to the Loggia and Museo Marciano
10 *Death of Noah and the Tower of Babel* (1200s)
11 *Story of Abraham* (1230s)
12 *Story of SS. Alipius and Simon, and Justice* (1200s)
14 Tomb of Doge Bartolomeo Gradenigo (d. 1342)
15 *Story of Joseph*, remade in 19th century
16 Porta dei Fiori (1200s); Manzù's bust of Pope John XXIII
17 *Christ with the Virgin and St Mark* (13th century, over the door)
18 Pentecost Dome (the earliest, 12th century)
19 On the wall: *Agony in the Garden and Madonna and Prophets* (13th century)
20 Baptistry, *Life of St John the Baptist* (14th century) and tomb of Doge Andrea Dandolo
21 Cappella Zen, by Tullio and Antonio Lombardo (1504–22)
22 On the wall: *Christ and Prophets* (13th century)
23 In arch: *Scenes of the Passion* (12th century)
24 Central Dome, the *Ascension* (12th century)
25 Tabernacle of the Madonna of the Kiss (12th century)
26 On wall: *Rediscovery of the Body of St Mark* (13th century)

27 Treasury
28 Dome of S. Leonardo; Gothic rose window (15th century)
29 In arch, *Scenes from the Life of Christ* (12th century)
30 Altar of the Sacrament; pilaster where St Mark's body was rediscovered, marked by marbles
31 Altar of St James (1462)
32 Pulpit where newly elected doge was shown to the people; entrance to the sanctuary
33 Rood screen (1394) by Jacopo di Marco Benato and Jacobello and Pier Paolo Dalle Masegne
34 Singing Gallery and Cappella di S. Lorenzo, sculptures by the Dalle Masegnes (14th century)
35 Dome, *Prophets Foretell the Religion of Christ* (12th century); Baldacchino, with Eastern alabaster columns (6th century?)
36 Pala d'Oro (10th–14th century)
37 Sacristy door, with reliefs by Sansovino (16th century)
38 Sacristy, with mosaics by Titian and Padovanino (16th century) and Church of St Theodore (15th century), once seat of the Inquisition, and now part of the sacristy: both are rarely open
39 Singing Gallery and Cappella di S. Pietro (14th century): note the Byzantine capitals
40 Two medieval pulpits stacked together
41 *Miracles of Christ* (16th century)
42 Dome, with *Life of St John the Evangelist* (12th century)
43 Cappella della Madonna di Nicopeia (miraculous 12th-century icon)
44 Cappella di S. Isidoro (14th-century mosaics and tomb of the Saint)
45 Cappella della Madonna dei Máscoli: *Life of the Virgin* by Andrea del Castagno, Michele Giambono, Jacopo Bellini
46 On wall: *Life of the Virgin* (13th century)
47 Finely carved Greek marble stoup (12th century)
48 *Virgin of the Gun* (13th century—rifle ex-voto from 1850s)
49 Il Capitello, altar topped with rare marble ciborium, with miraculous Byzantine Crucifixion panel

St Mark's Basilica

Note how crooked it is!
In the Middle Ages symmetry was
synonymous with death.

N

Sacristy

38

37
36
35

39

34

Sanctuary

43
33
33
30

32
31

44
42
41
24
29
28

47

45
46
48
25
26
27

23

49

16
22
18
19

20

15

17

20

15

9

14
12
11
10
8
7
21

Narthex

1
2
3
4
5
6

Piazzetta dei Leoncini

Piazza San Marco

in 828, a deed sanctioned by a tidy piece of apocrypha that had the good Evangelist mooring his ship on the Rialto on the way from Aquileia to Rome, when an angel hailed him with the famous 'Pax tibi...' or 'Peace to you, Mark, my Evangelist. Here your body shall lie.'

The present structure, consecrated in 1094, was begun after a fire destroyed the original St Mark's in 976. Modelled after Constantinople's former Church of the Apostles, five rounded doorways, five upper arches and five round Byzantine domes are the essentials of the exterior, all frosted with a sheen of coloured marbles, ancient columns and sculpture ('As if in ecstasy,' wrote Ruskin, 'the crests of the arches break into marbly foam...'). The spandrils of the arches glitter with gaudy, technicolour mosaics—the High Renaissance, dissatisfied with the 13th-century originals, saw fit to commission new painterly scenes, leaving intact only the *Translation of the Body of St Mark* on the extreme left, which includes the first historical depiction of the basilica itself. The three bands of 13th-century **reliefs** around the central portal, among Italy's finest Romanesque carvings, show Venetian trades, the Labours of the Months, and Chaos in the inner band.

Front and centre, seemingly ready to prance off the façade, the controversial 1979 copies of the bronze **horses of St Mark** masquerade well enough from a distance. The ancient originals (cast between the 3rd century BC and 2nd century AD, and now inside the basilica's Museo Marciano) were one of the most powerful symbols of the Venetian Republic. Originally a triumphal quadriga taken by Constantine the Great from Chios to grace the Hippodrome of his new city, it was carried off in turn by the artful Doge Dandolo in the 1204 Sack of Constantinople. Another prize from Byzantium are the four porphyry 'Moors' huddled in the corner of the south façade near the Doges' Palace; according to legend, they were changed into stone for daring to break into St Mark's treasury, though scholars prefer to believe that they are four chummy 3rd-century Roman Emperors, the Tetrarchs.

The Interior

The best mosaics, most of them from the 13th-century, cover the six domes of the **atrium**, or narthex, their old gold glimmering in the permanent twilight. The oldest mosaic in St Mark's is that of the *Madonna and Saints* above the central door, a survivor of the original basilica. A slab of red marble in the pavement marks the spot where the Emperor Barbarossa knelt and apologized to 'St Peter and his pope'—Alexander III, in 1177. This, a favourite subject of Venetian state art, is one of the few gold stars the Republic ever earned with the papacy; mistrust and acrimony were far more common.

The interior, in the form of a Greek cross, dazzles the eye with the intricate splendour of a thousand details. The domes and upper vaults are adorned with golden mosaics on the New Testament, the oldest dating back to the 1090s, though there have been several restorations since. Ancient columns of rare marbles, alabaster, porphyry and verdantique, sawn into slices of rich colour, line the lower walls; the 12th-century pavement is a magnificent geometric mosaic of marble, glass and porphyry. Like a mosque, the nave is covered with carpets.

The first door on the right leads to the 14th-century **baptistry**, much beloved by John Ruskin and famous for its mosaics on the life of John the Baptist, with a lovely Salomé in red who could probably have had just as many heads as she pleased. (*With luck this may have reopened by the time you visit.*) Attached to the baptistry, the **Cappella Zen** was designed by Tullio Lombardo in 1504 to house the tomb of one Cardinal Zen, who had left a fortune to the Republic on condition he be buried in St Mark's. Further along the right transept you can visit the **treasury** (*open daily 9.45–5; adm*), containing the loot from Constantinople that Napoleon overlooked—golden bowls and crystal goblets studded with huge coloured gems, straight from the cavern of Ali Baba.

Near the Altar of the Sacrament, at the end of the right transept, a lamp burns next to one pillar: after the 976 fire, the body of St Mark was lost, but in 1094 (after Bari had beaten Venice to the relics of St Nicolaus) the good Evangelist staged a miraculous reappearance, popping his hand out of the pillar during Mass. St Mark is now safely in place in a crypt under the high altar, in the **sanctuary** (*open daily 9.45–5; adm*). You can't visit his relics, but you can see the altar's retable, the fabulous, glowing **Pala d'Oro**, a masterpiece of medieval gold and jewel work. The upper section may originally have been in the Church of the Pantocrator in Constantinople, and the lower section was commissioned in that same city by Doge Pietro Orseolo I in 976. Over the years the Venetians added their own scenes, and the Pala took its present form in 1345.

In the left transept, the **Chapel of the Madonna of Nicopeia** shelters a venerated 10th-century icon hijacked from Constantinople formerly carried into battle by the Byzantine Emperors and renamed the *Protectress of Venice*. More fine mosaics are further to the left in the **Chapel of St Isidore** (stolen by the Venetian bodysnatchers from Chios—and in the mosaic he seems happy to go, grinning like a chimp). In the **Chapel of the Madonna dei Máscoli**, the mosaics on the *Life of the Virgin* (1453) by Tuscan Andrea del Castagno and Michele Giambono were among the first harbingers of the Renaissance in Venice.

Before leaving, climb the steep stone stair near the west door of the narthex to the **Museo Marciano**, **Galleria and Loggia dei Cavalli** (*open daily 9.45–5; adm*), for a closer look at the dome mosaics from the women's gallery and to visit the loggia, where you can inspect the replica horses and compare them with the excellently restored, gilded, almost alive originals sadly cooped up in the museum.

The Campanile

Open summer daily 9–7.30; winter daily 9.30–3.30; other months in between; adm.

St Mark's bell tower, to those uninitiated in the cult of Venice, seems like an alien presence, a Presbyterian brick sentinel in the otherwise delicately wrought piazza. But it has always been there, at least since 912; it was last altered in 1515, and when it gently collapsed into a pile of rubble on 14 July 1902 (the only casualty, a cat) the Venetians felt its lack so acutely they began to construct an exact replica, only a few hundred tons lighter and stronger, completed in 1912. It is 332ft tall, and you can take the lift up for a bird's-eye vision of Venice and its Lagoon; from up here the city seems amazingly compact. Although you have to pay for the view, misbehaving priests had it for free; the Council of Ten would suspend them in cages from the windows. Under the campanile, Sansovino's elegant loggetta adds a graceful note to the brick belfry. Its marbles and sculptures glorifying Venice took it on the nose when the campanile fell on top of them, but they have been carefully rebuilt.

The Correr Museum and Clock Tower

At the far end of the piazza, in the Procuratie Nuove, the **Museo Correr** (*open daily 9–7, last tickets at 6; adm exp, but includes entrance to Palazzo Ducale*) contains Venetian memorabilia—the robes, ducal bonnets and old-maidish nightcaps of the doges, the 20-inch heeled *zoccoli*, once the rage among Venetian noblewomen, and a copy of the statue of Marco Polo from the temple of 500 Genies in Canton. Upstairs, the fine collection of paintings includes two great works by Carpaccio, *The Courtesans* (or Ladies—in Venice it was notoriously hard to tell) and the *Young Man in a Red Beret*, with his archetypal Venetian face; Antonello da Messina's damaged but luminous *Pietà*, and others by Cosmè Tura and a young Giovanni Bellini; and the Bosch-esque *Temptation of St Anthony* by Il Civetta (the 'Little Owl').

At the head of the Procuratie Vecchie two bronze wild men, called the 'Moors', sound the hours atop the clock tower, the **Torre dell'Orologio** (*closed for restoration*), built to a design by Mauro Codussi in 1499 above the entrance to Venice's main shopping street, the Merceria. The old Italians were fond of elaborate astronomical clocks, but none is as beautiful as this, with its richly coloured enamel and gilt face, its Madonna and obligatory lion. The Council of Ten (which actually encouraged false rumours about itself, to make its job easier) supposedly blinded the builders to prevent them from creating such a marvel for any other city. Below, flanking the basilica's north façade, a fountain and two porphyry lions just right for children to ride, stand in **Piazzetta Giovanni XXIII**, named after the beloved Venetian patriarch who became pope in 1959.

Piazzetta San Marco

To the south of the basilica, the Piazzetta San Marco was the Republic's foyer, where ships would dock under the watchful eye of the doge. The view towards the Lagoon is framed by two tall Egyptian granite columns, trophies brought to Venice in the 1170s. The Venetians had a knack for converting their booty into self-serving symbols: atop one of the columns several Roman statues were pieced together to form their first patron saint, St Theodore with his crocodile (or dragon, or fish), while on the other stands an ancient Assyrian or Persian winged lion, under whose paw the Venetians slid a book, creating their symbol of St Mark.

Opposite the Doges' Palace stands the **Libreria**, built in 1536 by Sansovino and considered by Palladio to be the most beautiful building since antiquity, where light and shadow play in its sculpted arcades. Sansovino, trained as a sculptor, was notorious for paying scant attention to architectural details, and the library was scarcely completed when its ceiling caved in. The miscalculation cost him a trip to the Council of Ten's slammer, and he was only released on the special pleading of Titian. Scholars with permission from the director can examine such treasures as the 1501 *Grimani Breviary*, a masterwork of Flemish illuminators; Homeric *codices*, the 1459 world map of Fra Mauro, and Marco Polo's will. But not the famous library Petrarch willed to the Republic—the Venetians absentmindedly misplaced it.

Next to the library, at No.17, Venice's **Museo Archeologico** (*open Mon–Sat 9–9, Sat 9–midnight, Sun 9–8*) is one of the few heated in the winter. It has an excellent collection of Greek sculpture, including a violent *Leda and the Swan* and ancient copies of the famous *Gallic Warriors of Pergamon*, all given to the city by Cardinal Grimani in 1523. On the other side of the Libreria, by the waterfront, is another fine building by Sansovino, the 1547 **Zecca**, or Mint, which once stamped out thousands of gold *zecchini*, and gave English the word *sequin*.

The Palace of the Doges (Palazzo Ducale)

Open 15 April–Oct daily 9–7; winter daily 8.30–1; other months somewhere in between; adm exp—includes entry to the Museo Correr. Ticket office in the courtyard through Porta della Carta.

What St Mark's is to sacred architecture, the **Doges' Palace** is to the secular—unique and audacious, dreamlike in a half-light, an illuminated storybook of Venetian history and legend. Like the basilica, it was founded shortly after the city's consolidation on the Rialto, though it didn't begin to take its present form until 1309—with its delicate lower colonnade, its loggia of lacy Gothic tracery, and the massive top-heavy upper floor, like a cake held up by its own frosting. Its weight is partly relieved by the diamond pattern of white Istrian stone and red Verona marble on the façade, which from a distance gives the palace its wholesome peaches-and-cream complexion. Less benign are the two reddish pillars in the loggia (on the Piazzetta façade) said to have been dyed by the blood of Venice's enemies, whose tortured corpses were strung out between them.

Some of Italy's finest medieval sculpture crowns the 36 columns of the lower colonnade, depicting a few sacred and many profane subjects—animals, guildsmen, Turks, and Venetians. Beautiful sculptural groups adorn the corners, most notably the 13th-century *Judgement of Solomon*, near the palace's grand entrance, the 1443 **Porta della Carta** (Paper Door), a Gothic symphony in stone by Giovanni and Bartolomeo Bon.

Fires in 1574 and 1577 destroyed much of the palace, and at the time there were serious plans afoot to knock it down and let Palladio start again *à la* Renaissance. Fortunately, however, you can't teach an old doge new tricks, and the palace was rebuilt as it was, with Renaissance touches in the interior. One of these is just within the Porta della Carta: Antonio Rizzo's delightful arcaded courtyard and his finely sculpted grand stairway, the **Scala dei Giganti**, named for its two Gargantuan statues of *Neptune* and *Mars* by Sansovino.

Visitors enter the palace via another grand stairway, Sansovino's **Scala d'Oro**. The first floor, once the private apartments of the doge, is now used for special exhibitions (*separate adm*), while the golden stairway continues up to the *Secondo Piano Nobile*, from where the Venetian state was governed. After the fire that destroyed its great 15th-century frescoes, Veronese and Tintoretto were employed to paint the newly remodelled chambers with mythological themes and scores of allegories and apotheoses of Venice—a smug, fleshy blonde in the eyes of these two. These paintings are the palace's chief glory, and signboards in each room identify them in detail. Visiting ambassadors and other foreign official guests would be required to wait in the first room, the **Anticollegio**, so the frescoes (Tintoretto's *Bacchus and Ariadne* and Veronese's *Rape of Europa)* had to be especially impressive; in the next room, the **Sala del Collegio**, with several masterpieces by both artists, they would be presented to the hierarchy of the Venetian state.

Tintoretto's brush dominates in the **Sala del Senato**—less lavish, since only Venetians were admitted here—while the main work in the **Sala del Consiglio dei Dieci** is Veronese's ceiling, an *Old Man in Eastern Costume with a Young Woman*. Under this the Council of Ten deliberated and pored over the accusations deposited in the *Bocche dei Leoni*—the lions' mouths spread over the Republic. To be considered, an accusation had to be signed and supported by two witnesses, and anyone found making a false accusation would suffer the punishment that would have been meted out to the accused had it been true. Next to the Ten's chamber, the old **Armoury** (Sala d'Armi) houses a fine collection of medieval and Renaissance arms and armour.

From here the visit continues downstairs, to the vast and magnificent **Sala del Maggior Consiglio**, built in 1340 and capable of holding the 2500 patricians of the Great Council. At the entrance hangs Tintoretto's crowded, and restored, *Paradiso*—the biggest oil painting in the world (23ft by 72ft), all the Blessed looking up at Veronese's magnificent *Apotheosis of Venice* on the ceiling. The frieze along the upper wall portrays the first 76 doges, except for the space that would have held the portrait of Marin Falier (1355) had he not led a conspiracy to take sole power; instead, a black veil bears a dry note that he was decapitated for treason. The portraits of the last 44 doges, each painted by a contemporary painter, continue around the **Sala dello Scrutinio**, where the votes for office were counted. Elections for doge were Byzantine and elaborate—and frequent; the Maggior Consiglio preferred to choose doges who were old, and wouldn't last long enough to gain a following.

A Doge's Life: Gormenghast with Canals

Senator in Senate, Citizen in City were his titles, as well as Prince of Clothes, with a wardrobe of gold and silver damask robes and scarlet silks. Once the doge was dressed, the rest of his procession would fall in line, including all the paraphernalia of Byzantine royalty: a naked sword, six silver trumpets, a damask parasol, a chair, cushion, candle and eight standards bearing the Lion of St Mark in four colours, symbolizing peace, war, truth and loyalty. Yet for all the pomp the doge was the only man in Venice not permitted to send a private note to his wife, or receive one from her, or from anyone else; nor could he accept any gift beyond flowers or rose-water, or go to a café or theatre, or engage in any money-making activity, while nevertheless having to meet the expenses of his office out of his own pocket. Nor could he abdicate, unless requested to do so.

The office was respected, but often not the man. When a doge died he was privately buried in his family tomb before the state funeral—which used a dummy corpse with a wax mask. First, an 'Inquisition of the Defunct Doge' was held over the dummy, to discover if the doge had kept to his *Promissione* (his oath of coronation), if his family owed the state any money, and if it were necessary to amend the *Promissione* to limit the powers of his successor still further. Then the dead doge's dummy was taken to St Mark's to be hoisted in the air nine times by sailors, to the cry of 'Misericordia!' (Mercy), and then given a funeral service at Santi Giovanni e Paolo.

At the end of the tour the **Bridge of Sighs** (*Ponte dei Sospiri*) takes you to the 17th-century **Palazzo delle Prigioni**, mostly used for petty offenders. Those to whom the Republic took real exception were dumped into uncomfortable *pozzi*, or 'wells', in the lower part of the

Palazzo Ducale, while celebrities like Casanova got to stay up in the *Piombi* or 'Leads' just under the roof (*see* below).

The Secret Itinerary

In 1984 the section of the palace where the real nitty-gritty business of state took place, a maze of narrow corridors and tiny rooms, was restored. Because the rooms are so small the 1½-hour guided tour, the Itinerari Segreti is limited to 20 people, and the reason why it's not better known is that it's only available in Italian (*mornings at 10 and 12; book at least a day in advance at the director's office on the first floor, or ring © 041 522 4951*).

The tour begins at the top of the Scala d'Oro, with the snug wood-panelled offices of the **Chancellery** and the 18th-century **Hall of the Chancellors**, lined with cupboards for holding treaties, each bearing the arms of a Chancellor. In the justice department is the **Torture Chamber**, where the three Signori della Notte dei Criminali (night judges of the criminals) would 'put to the question' anyone suspected of treason, hanging them by the wrists on a rope that is still in place. This ended in the early 1700s, when Venice, along with Tuscany, became the first state in Europe to abolish torture.

Next is the ornate **Sala dei Tre Capi**, the chamber of the three magistrates of the Council of Ten, who had to be present at all state meetings. As this chamber might be visited by foreign dignitaries, it was lavishly decorated with works by Veronese, Antonello da Messina and Hieronymus Bosch. From here it's up to the notorious **Piombi**, which despite their evil reputation appear downright cosy, as prisons go. Casanova's cell is pointed out, and there's an elaborate explanation of his famous escape through a hole in the roof. Near the end of the tour comes one of Venice's marvels: the **attic of the Sala del Maggior Consiglio**, where you can see how the Arsenale's shipwrights made a vast ceiling float unsupported over the room below; built in 1577, it has yet to need any repairs.

San Marco to Rialto

The streets between the piazza and the market district of the Rialto are the busiest in Venice, especially the **Mercerie**, which begin under the clock tower and are lined with some of the city's smartest shops. It was down the Mercerie that Baiamonte Tiepolo, miffed at being excluded from the Golden Book, led his rebel aristocrats in 1310, when an old lady cried 'Death to tyrants!' from her window and hurled a brick at his standard-bearer, killing him on the spot and causing such disarray that Tiepolo was forced to give up his attempted coup. It was a close call that the Republic chose never to forget: the site, above the Sottoportego del Capello Nero, is marked by a stone relief of the heroine with her brick.

The Merceria continues to the church of **San Zulian**, redesigned in 1553 by Sansovino, with a façade most notable for Sansovino's statue of its pompous and scholarly benefactor, Tommaso Rangone. Sansovino also had a hand in **San Salvatore** in the next campo, adding the finishing touches to its noble Renaissance interior and designing the monument to Doge Francesco Venier. An elderly Titian painted one of his more unusual works for this church, the *Annunciation*, which he signed with double emphasis *Titianus Fecit*—'*Fecit*' because his patrons refused to believe that it was by his hand.

Humming, bustling **Campo San Bartolomeo**, next on the Mercerie, has for centuries been one of the social hubs of Venice, and still gets packed with after-work crowds every evening.

Its centre is graced by the **statue of Goldoni**, whose comedies in Venetian dialect still make the Venetians laugh; and by the look on his jolly face, he still finds their antics amusing. Follow the crowds up to the **Ponte di Rialto** (*see* 'The Grand Canal', p.305), the geographical heart of Venice, and the principal node of its pedestrian and water traffic.

The city's central markets have been just across the bridge for a millennium, divided into sections for vegetables and for fish. Near the former you may pay your respects to Venice's oldest church, little **San Giacomo di Rialto**, founded perhaps as long ago as the 5th century and substantially reworked in 1071 and 1601. In the same campo stands a famous Venetian character, the 16th-century granite hunchback, **Gobbo di Rialto**, who supports a little stairway and marble podium from which the decrees of the Republic were proclaimed.

San Marco to the Accademia

Following the yellow signs 'To the Accademia' from the Piazza San Marco (starting by the tourist office), the first campo belongs to Baroque **San Moisè** (1668), Italy's most grotesque church, with a grimy opera-buffa façade and rockpile for an altarpiece. For more opera and less buffa, take a detour up Calle Veste (the second right after Campo San Moisè) to monumental Campo San Fantin and **La Fenice** (1792), the Republic's last hurrah and one of Italy's most renowned opera houses, which saw the premieres of Verdi's *Rigoletto* and *La Traviata*. A fire by a contractor during renovations ripped it apart in 1996, so expect to see only scaffolding for a long time to come. Venice has a venerable musical tradition, albeit one that had become more tradition than music by the time of the era of grand opera—although Mozart's great librettist, Lorenzo da Ponte, was a Venetian.

Back on route to the Accademia, in the next campo stands **Santa Maria Zobenigo** (or del Giglio), on which the Barbaro family stuck a fancy Baroque façade in 1680, not for God but for the glory of the Barbaros; the façade is famous for its total lack of religious significance. The signs lead next to the Campo Francesco Morosini, named after the doge who recaptured the Morea from the Turks, but who is remembered everywhere else as the man who blew the lid off the Parthenon. Better known as **Campo Santo Stefano**, it's one of the most elegant squares in Venice, a pleasant place to sit outside at a café table—particularly at **Paolin**, Venice's best *gelateria*.

At one end, built directly over a canal, the Gothic church of **Santo Stefano** has the most gravity-defying campanile of all the leaning towers in Venice (most alarmingly viewed from the adjacent Campo Sant'Angelo). The interior is worth a look for its striking wood ceiling, soaring like a ship's keel, as well as its wooden choir stalls (1488).

Galleria dell'Accademia

Open daily; hours vary slightly throughout the year; summer Tues–Sat 9am–10pm, Sun 9am–8pm; adm exp, free for under-18s and over-60s if members of the EU. Get there early—a maximum of 300 visitors are allowed at a time.

Just over the bridge and Grand Canal from Campo Santo Stefano stands the Galleria dell'Accademia, the cathedral of Venetian art, ablaze with light and colour. The collection is arranged chronologically, beginning in the former refectory of the Scuola (**Room I**): among them, 14th-century altarpieces by Paolo and Lorenzo Veneziano, whose half-Byzantine Madonnas look like fashion models for Venetian silks. Later altarpieces fill **Room II**, most importantly Giovanni Bellini's *Pala di San Giobbe*, one of the key works of the quattrocento: the architecture repeats its original setting in the church of San Giobbe; on the left St Francis invites the viewer into a scene made timeless by the music of the angels at the Madonna's feet. Other beautiful altarpieces in the room are by Carpaccio, Basaiti and Cima da Conegliano (the subtle *Madonna of the Orange Tree*).

The next rooms are small but, like gifts, contain the best things: Mantegna's confidently aloof *St George*, the little allegories and a trio of Madonnas by Giovanni Bellini (including the lovely, softly coloured *Madonna of the Little Trees*) and Piero della Francesca's *St Jerome and Devotee*, a youthful study in perspective.

In **Room V** you will find Giorgione's *La Vecchia*, with the warning '*Col Tempo*' ('With Time') in her hand, and the mysterious *The Tempest*, two of the very few paintings scholars accept as being indisputably by Big George, but how strange they are! It is said Giorgione invented easel painting for the pleasure of bored, purposeless courtiers in Catherine Cornaro's Àsolo (*see* p.353–54) but the paintings seem to reflect rather than lighten their ennui and discontent.

Highlights of the next few rooms include Lorenzo Lotto's *Gentleman in his Study*, which catches its sitter off guard before he could clear the nervously scattered scraps of paper from his table, and Paris Bordone's masterpiece, *Fisherman Presenting St Mark's Ring to the Doge* (1554), celebrating a miracle of St Mark.

The climax of the Venetian High Renaissance comes in **Room X**, with Veronese's *Christ in the House of Levi* (1573), set in a Palladian loggia with a ghostly white imaginary background, in violent contrast to the rollicking feast of Turks, hounds, midgets, Germans and the artist himself (in the front, next to the pillar on the left). The painting was originally titled *The Last Supper*, and fell foul of the Inquisition, which took umbrage (especially at the Germans). Veronese was cross-examined and ordered to make pious changes at his own expense; the artist, in true Venetian style, saved himself both the trouble and the money by simply giving it the title by which it has been known ever since.

Room X also contains Veronese's *Annunciation*, and some early Tintorettos—*Translation of the Body of St Mark* and *St Mark Freeing a Slave*, in which the Evangelist, in true Tintoretto-esque fashion, nosedives from the sky. The last great painting in the room was also Titian's last ever, the sombre *La Pietà*, which he was working on when he died in 1576, aged about 90, from the plague; he intended it for his tomb, and smeared the paint on with his fingers.

Alongside several more Tintorettos, the following few rooms mainly contain works from the 17th and 18th centuries (Tiepolo, Sebastiano and Marco Ricci, Piazzetta, Longhi, Rosalba Carriera). Canaletto and Guardi, whose scenes of 18th-century Venice were the picture post-cards of the British aristocracy on their Grand Tour, are represented in **Room XVII**.

The final rooms of the Accademia were formerly part of the elegantly Gothic church of Santa Maria della Carità, and house more luminous 15th-century painting by Alvise Vivarini, Giovanni and Gentile Bellini, Marco Basaiti and Crivelli. **Room XX** has a fascinating series depicting the *Miracles of the True Cross* with Venetian backgrounds, painted by Gentile Bellini, Carpaccio and others. **Room XXI** contains the dreamily compelling and utterly charming *Cycle of S. Ursula* by Carpaccio, from the former Scuola di Sant'Orsola. Finally, the last room, **Room XXIV**, the former *albergo* of the church, contains two fine paintings that were originally made for it: Titian's striking *Presentation of the Virgin* (1538), and a triptych by Antonio Vivarini and Giovanni d'Alemagna (1446).

Dorsoduro

The Accademia lies in the *sestiere* of Dorsoduro, which can also boast the second-most-visited museum in Venice, the **Collezione Peggy Guggenheim** (*open Easter–Oct Wed–Mon 11–6; closed Tues; adm exp*), just down the Grand Canal from the Accademia in her 18th-century Venetian palazzo. In her 30 years as a collector, until her death in 1979, Ms Guggenheim amassed an impressive quantity of brand-name 20th-century art—Bacon, Brancusi, Braque, Calder, Chagall, Dali, De Chirico, Duchamp, Dubuffet, Max Ernst (her second husband), Giacometti, Gris, Kandinsky, Klee, Magritte, Miró, Mondrian, Moore, Picasso, Pollock, Rothko and Smith. Administered by the Solomon R. Guggenheim Foundation in New York, the collection can come as a breath of fresh air after so much high Italian art, and also sponsors temporary exhibitions, even in winter; look out for posters.

From here it's a five-minute stroll down to the octagonal basilica of **Santa Maria della Salute** (1631–81), on the tip of Dorsoduro (*open daily 9–12 and 3–6*). One of five votive churches built after the passing of plagues (Venice, a busy international port, was particularly susceptible), La Salute is the masterpiece of Baldassare Longhena, its snow-white dome and marble jelly rolls dramatically set at the entrance of the Grand Canal. The interior is a relatively restrained white and grey Baroque, and the **sacristy** (*adm*) contains the *Marriage at Cana* by Tintoretto and several works by Titian, including his *St Mark Enthroned Between Saints*. Almost next to the basilica, on the point, stands the distinctive profile of the **Dogana di Mare**, the Customs House (*see* 'The Grand Canal', p.305).

The **Fondamenta delle Zattere**, facing away from the city towards the freighter-filled canal and the island of Giudecca, leads around to the **Gesuati**, the only church in Venice decorated by Umbrian artists. For a more elaborate feast, take the long stroll along the Fondamenta (or take *vaporetto* line 5 to San Basegio) to Veronese's parish church of **San Sebastiano**, on Rio di San Basilio. Veronese, it is said, murdered a man in Verona and took refuge in this neighbourhood, and over the next 10 years he and his brother Benedetto Caliari embellished San Sebastiano—beginning in 1555 with the ceiling frescoes of the sacristy and ending with the magnificent ceiling, *The Story of Esther*, and illusionistic paintings in the choir (*the custodian is usually there on weekday mornings or Sun afternoons; tip him for turning on the lights*).

From San Sebastiano you can head back towards the Grand Canal (Calle Avogaria and Calle Lunga S. Barnaba); turn left up Calle Pazienza to visit the 14th-century church of the **Carmini**, with a landmark red campanile and lovely altars by Cima da Conegliano and Lorenzo Lotto. The **Scuola Grande dei Carmini** (*open Mon–Sat 9–12 and 3–6; adm; sometimes open for concerts*), next door, was designed by Longhena in the 1660s, and contains one of G. B. Tiepolo's best and brightest ceilings, *The Virgin in Glory*.

The Carmini is on the corner of the delightful **Campo Santa Margherita**. Traditionally the main marketplace of Dorsoduro, it's also a good spot to find inexpensive pizzerias, restaurants and cafés that are not aimed primarily at tourists. It is also close to **Ca' Rezzonico** (Rio Terrà Canal down to the Fondamenta Rezzonico), where Robert Browning died in 1889. Now home to the **Museo del Settecento Veneziano** (*open Oct–April daily 10–4, May–Sept daily 10–5; closed Fri; adm exp; currently only the first floor is open*), this is Venice's attic of 18th-century art, with bittersweet paintings by Giandomenico Tiepolo, wild Rococo furniture by Andrea Brustolon, a pharmacy, genre scenes by Longhi, and a breathtaking view of the Grand Canal. One of the palaces opposite belonged to Doge Cristoforo Moro, whom the Venetians claim Shakespeare used as his model for Othello, confusing the doge's name with his race.

San Polo and Santa Croce

From the Ponte di Rialto, follow the yellow signs to Piazzale Roma, passing the pretty **Campo** and church of **San Polo** (*open Mon–Sat 7.10–5.30, Sun 3–5.30; adm*), with Giandomenico Tiepolo's uncanny photograph-like *Stations of the Cross* in the Oratory of the Crucifix. The signs next take you before a venerable Venetian institution: the huge brick Gothic church of the **Frari** (*open Mon–Sat 9–6, Sun and hols 3–6; adm*), built between 1330 and 1469. Monteverdi, one of the founding fathers of opera, and choir director at St Mark's, is buried here, as is Titian, whose tomb follows the Italian rule—the greater the artist, the worse the tomb (see Michelangelo's in Florence). The strange pyramid was intended by Antonio Canova to be Titian's tomb, but it eventually became the sculptor's own last resting place. The Frari is celebrated for its art, and especially for the most overrated painting in Italy, Titian's *Assumption of the Virgin* (1516–18), in the centre of the Monk's Choir. Marvel at the art, at Titian's revolutionary Mannerist use of space and movement, but its big-eyed, heaven-gazing Virgin has as much artistic vision as a Sunday school holy card.

That, however, is not true of Giovanni Bellini's *Triptych of Madonna with Child and Saints* in the sacristy, or Donatello's rustic statue of *St John the Baptist* in the choir chapel. In the north aisle, Titian's later *Madonna di Ca' Pésaro* was modelled on his wife Celia and had a much wider influence on Venetian art than the *Assumption*. Also note the beautiful Renaissance *Tomb of Doge Nicolò Tron* by Antonio Rizzo in the sanctuary, from 1476.

The Scuola di San Rocco

Next to the Frari, the **Scuola di San Rocco** (*open summer daily 9–5.30; winter mornings only; adm*) belonged to the wealthy confraternity of San Rocco, a saint renowned for his juju against the Black Death. He was so popular among the Venetians that they stole his body from Montpelier and canonized him before the pope did. The *scuola* has a beautiful, lively façade by Scarpagnino, and inside it contains one of the wonders of Venice—or rather, 54 wonders—by Tintoretto, who worked on the project from 1562 to 1585 without assistance.

Tintoretto always managed to look at conventional subjects from a fresh point of view; while other artists of the High Renaissance composed their subjects with the epic vision of a Cecil B. de Mille, Tintoretto had the eye of a 16th-century Orson Welles, creating audacious, dynamic 'sets', often working out his compositions in his little box-stages, with wax figures and unusual lighting effects. In the *scuola*, especially in the upper floor, he was at the peak of his career, and painted what is considered by some to be the finest painting cycle in existence, culminating in the *Crucifixion*, where the event is the central drama of a busy human world. Vertigo is not an uncommon response—for an antidote, look at the funny carvings along the walls by Francesco Pianta. In the same room there are also several paintings on easels by Titian, and a *Christ* that some attribute to Titian, some to Giorgione.

Just north, beyond Campo San Stin, the **Scuola Grande di San Giovanni Evangelista** (*open in theory if you ring the bell Mon–Fri 9.30–12.30, but it's best to call ahead, © 041 522 4134*) deserves a look for its beautiful Renaissance courtyard and double-ramp stairway (1498), Mauro Codussi's masterpiece, noted for the rhythms of its domes and barrel vaults.

From Campo San Stin, if you start along Calle Donà and keep as straight as possible, you should end up at **Ca' Pésaro** on the Grand Canal, a huge 17th-century pile by Longhena that is occupied by the **Galleria d'Arte Moderna** (*due to re-open Dec 1999; call © 041 721*

127, to check), with a collection of works exhibited in the Biennale. Italian contemporary art is the mainstay, but some international figures are also represented, such as Gustav Klimt. Ca' Pésaro also houses a **museum of oriental art** (*open Tues–Fri 9–2, Sat and Sun 9–1; closed Mon; adm*), with a higgledy-piggledy collection of Asian artefacts collected in the last century. If you really want to escape the crowds, head further up the canal to the stuffed Lagoon fowl in the **Museo di Storia Naturale** (*due to re-open in 2000; call © 041 524 0885 to check*) in the Venetian-Byzantine **Fóndaco dei Turchi**.

San Marco to Castello

From Piazzetta San Marco, the gracefully curving, ever thronging **Riva degli Schiavoni** took its name from the Slavs of Dalmatia; in 1782 Venice was doing so much business here that the quay had to be widened. A few steps beyond the Palazzo Ducale, one of the city's finest Gothic palazzi was converted in 1822 to the famous **Hotel Danieli**, its name a corruption of the 'Dandolo' family who built it. The quay also has a robust **memorial to Vittorio Emanuele II** (1887) where two of Venice's over 10,000 lions shelter—as often as not with members of Venice's equally numerous if smaller feline population between their paws.

From Riva degli Schiavoni, Sottoportico San Zaccaria leads back to the lovely Gothic-Renaissance **San Zaccaria** (*open daily 10–12 and 4–6*), begun by Antonio Gambello in 1444 and completed by Mauro Codussi in 1515. Inside, look for Bellini's *Madonna and Saints*, where his tonalism verges on a colour version of Leonardo's *sfumato* style, and the refined Florentine frescoes by Andrea del Castagno in the chapel of San Tarasio. Another church, back on the Riva itself, **La Pietà**, served the girls' orphanage which the red-headed priest Vivaldi made famous during his years as its concert master and composer (1704–38). The church was rebuilt shortly afterwards by Giorgio Massari, with a remarkable oval interior in luscious cream and gold, and G. B. Tiepolo's extravagant *Triumph of Faith* on top. It has particularly fine acoustics—Vivaldi helped design it—and is still frequently used for concerts.

Due north of La Pietà stands the city's Greek Orthodox Church, 16th-century **San Giorgio dei Greci**, with its tilting tower and *scuola*, now the **Museum of Byzantine Religious Painting** (*open Mon–Sat 9–1 and 2–5, Sun 9–1; adm*). Run by the Hellenic Centre for Byzantine Studies, many of its icons were painted in the 16th and 17th centuries by artists who fled the Turkish occupation. In Venice the Greeks came into contact with the Renaissance; the resulting Venetian-Cretan school nourished, most famously, El Greco.

Close by, another ethnic minority, the Dalmatians—present in Venice from the 900s—began their tiny **Scuola di San Giorgio degli Schiavoni** in 1451 (*open daily 9.30–12.30 and 3.30–6.30; closed Mon; adm*). Its minute interior is decorated with the most beloved art in Venice: Vittore Carpaccio's frescoes on the lives of Dalmatia's patron saints—Augustine writing, watched by his patient little dog; Jerome bringing his lion into the monastery, George charging a petticoat-munching dragon in a landscape strewn with maidenly leftovers. Some of the greatest paintings by Carpaccio's more serious contemporaries, the Vivarini and Cima da Conegliano, hold pride of place in **San Giovanni in Brágora** (between San Giorgio degli Schiavoni and the Riva); the best work, Cima's *Baptism of Christ*, is in the sanctuary.

The Arsenale

From the Riva degli Schiavoni, the Fondamenta dell'Arsenale leads to the twin towers guarding the **Arsenale**. Founded in 1104, this, first of all arsenals, derived its name from the

Venetian pronunciation of the Arabic *darsina'a*, or work shop, and up until the 17th century these were the greatest dockyards in the world, the very foundation of the Republic's wealth and power. In its heyday the Arsenale had a payroll of 16,000, and produced a ship a day to fight the Turks. Dante visited this great industrial complex twice, and as Blake would later do with his Dark Satanic Mills, found its imagery perfect for his *Inferno*.

Today the Arsenale is occupied by the Italian military, but you can look at the **great gateway** next to the towers, built in 1460—almost entirely from marble trophies purloined from Greece. Among the chorus line of lions is an ancient beast that Francesco Morosini found in Piraeus, with 11th-century runes carved in its back in the name of Harold Hardrada, a member of the Byzantine Emperor's Varangian Guard who was later crowned king of Norway. Other very innocent-looking lions, eroded into lambs, were taken from the island of Delos in 1718 when the Turks weren't looking. The only way to get a look at the inside of the Arsenale is by taking the line 52 *vaporetto*, which goes through the middle of it.

Venice's glorious maritime history is the subject of the fascinating artefacts and models in the **Museo Storico Navale** (*open Mon, Tues, Wed and Sat 8.45–1.30, Thurs 2.30–5; closed Fri, Sun and hols; adm*)—most dazzling of all is the model of the doge's barge, the *Bucintoro*. The museum is just past the gateway to the Arsenale, near the beginning of Via Garibaldi; in a neighbouring house lived two seafarers, originally from Genoa, who contributed more to the history of Britain than that of Venice: Giovanni and Sebastiano Caboto.

Via Garibaldi and Fondamenta S. Anna continue to the Isola di San Pietro, site of the unmemorable **San Pietro di Castello** (*open Mon–Sat 10–5.30, Sun 3–5.30; adm*), until 1807 Venice's cathedral, its lonely, distant site a comment on the Republic's attitude towards the papacy. The attractive, detached campanile is by Codussi, and, inside, there is a marble throne incorporating a Muslim tombstone with verses from the Koran, which for centuries the Venetians claimed was the Throne of St Peter in Antioch. To the south are the refreshing pines and planes of the **public gardens**, where the Biennale takes place in even-numbered years in the artsy pavilions. This, and the **Parco delle Rimembranze** further on, were a gift from Napoleon, who knocked down four extraneous churches to plant the trees. From here you can take line 1 or 2 back to San Marco, or to the Lido.

San Marco to Santi Giovanni e Paolo

The *calli* that lead from the Piazzetta dei Leoncini around the back of San Marco and over the Rio di Palazzo will take you to the Romanesque cloister of Sant'Apollonia and the **Museo Diocesano** (*open Mon–Sat 10.30–12.30*), containing an exceptional collection of trappings and art salvaged from the city's churches. Through a web of alleys to the north, the 16th-century Palazzo Querini-Stampalia, home of the **Fondazione Querini-Stampalia** (*open Tues–Thurs and Sun 10–1 and 3–6, Fri and Sat 10–1 and 3–10; closed Mon; adm exp*), which has an endearing assortment of genre paintings—scenes of 18th-century Venetian convents, dinner parties, music lessons by Pietro Longhi and the naif Gabriel Bella, as well as works by Bellini, Palma Vecchio, Vincenzo Catena (a 16th-century merchant and the first known amateur to dabble in painting) and G. B. Tiepolo—all in a suitably furnished *palazzo*.

Santa Maria Formosa (*open Mon–Sat 10–5.30, Sun 3–5.30; adm*), in its charming campo just to the north, was rebuilt in 1492 by Codussi, who made creative use of its original Greek-cross plan. The head near the bottom of its campanile is notorious as being the most hideous thing in Venice, while inside, Palma Vecchio's *Santa Barbara*, modelled on the artist's daughter, is famed as the loveliest. Another celebrated work, Bartolomeo Vivarini's *Madonna della Misericordia* (1473), is in the first chapel on the right; the parishioners shown under the Virgin's mantle earned their exalted position by paying for the painting.

The next campo to the north is dominated by **Santi Giovanni e Paolo** (or *San Zanipolo*), after St Mark's the most important church on the right bank (*open daily 7–12.30 and 3–7.15*). A vast Gothic brick barn begun by the Dominicans in 1246, almost entirely rebuilt after 1333, and completed in 1430, no one would say it was beautiful, despite its fine front doorway. It was the pantheon of the doges; all their funerals were held here after the 1300s, and some 25 of them went no further, but lie in splendid Gothic and Renaissance tombs. Scattered among them are monuments to other honoured servants of the Venetian state, such as Marcantonio Bragadin, the commander who in 1571 was flayed alive by the Turks after he had surrendered Famagusta, in Cyprus, after a long siege; his bust sits on an urn holding his neatly folded skin. The adjacent chapel contains Giovanni Bellini's polyptych of *St Vincent Ferrer*, a fire-eating subject by the gentlest of painters; next is a small shrine containing the foot of St Catherine of Siena. The right transept has paintings by Alvise Vivarini, Cima da Conegliano and Lorenzo Lotto; the finest tomb is in the chancel: of Doge Andrea Vendramin, by Tullio and Antonio Lombardo (1478); the ceiling by Veronese in the **chapel of the rosary** in the north transept (damaged by fire in the last century) is from the long demolished church of the Umiltà.

Adjacent to San Zanipolo, the **Scuola Grande di San Marco** has one of the loveliest Renaissance façades in Italy, the fascinating *trompe l'oeil* lower half by Pietro and Tullio Lombardo, the upper floor by Mauro Codussi, finished in 1495. The *scuola* is now used as Venice's municipal hospital, but it is possible to enter to see the lavish coffered ceiling in the library with the permission of the *Direttore di Sanità.*

Opposite stands Verrocchio's dynamic equestrian **statue of Bartolomeo Colleoni**, the great and honest *condottiere* from Bergamo (1400–76). Proud of his emblem of *coglioni* (testicles—a play on his name), Colleoni envied Donatello's statue of Gattamelata erected by the Venetians in Padua (*see* p.346), and in his will he left the Republic 100,000 ducats if it would erect a similar statue of him in front of St Mark's. Greedy for the money but unable to countenance a momument to an individual in their sacred Piazza, the wily Venetians put the statue up before the *scuola* of St Mark. Verrocchio had only finished the plaster moulds when he died in 1488, leaving Alessandro Leopardi to do the casting. Verrocchio never saw a portrait of his subject, and all resemblances to Klaus Kinski are purely accidental.

Santa Maria dei Miracoli and the Ca' d'Oro

From Campo San Zanipolo, Largo G. Gallini leads to the perfect little Renaissance church of **Santa Maria dei Miracoli** (*open Mon–Sat 10–5.30, Sun and hols 3–5.30; adm*), built by Pietro Lombardo in the 1480s and often compared to an exquisite jewel box, elegant, graceful and glowing with a soft marble sheen, inside and out. Just to the south, two enclosed courtyards are known as the **Corte Prima del Milion** and the **Corte Seconda del Milion**, where Marco Polo used to live. The latter in particular looks much as it did when the great traveller lived there; 'Million', his nickname in Venice, referred to the million 'tall' tales he brought back with him from China. Nearby, Codussi's **San Giovanni Crisostomo** (1504) was his last work, a seminal piece of Renaissance architecture that contains Giovanni Bellini's last altar painting (*SS. Jerome, Christopher and Augustine*), as well as a beautiful high altarpiece by Sebastiano del Piombo.

Further towards the railway station up the Grand Canal, signposted off the Strada Nuova (Via 28 Aprile), stands the enchanting Gothic **Ca' d'Oro**, finished in 1440 and now housing the **Galleria Franchetti** (*open daily 9–2; adm*). In its collection are Mantegna's stern *St Sebastian*, Guardi's series of Venetian views, an excellent collection of Renaissance bronzes and medallions by Pisanello and Il Riccio, Tullio Lombardo's *Double Portrait*, and now fragments of the famous frescoes by Giorgione and Titian from the Fóndaco dei Tedeschi. The building itself is famous for the intricate traceries of its façade, best appreciated from the Grand Canal, and the courtyard, with a beautifully carved well-head by Bartolomeo Bon.

Due north, near the Fondamente Nuove, stands the unloved, unrestored church of the **Gesuiti** (*open daily 10–12 and 5–7*), built by the Jesuits when the republic relaxed its restrictions against them, in 1714–29: a Baroque extravaganza, full of *trompe l'œil* of white and green-grey marble draperies that would make a fitting memorial for Liberace. A previous church on this same site was the parish church of Titian, to which he contributed the *Martyrdom of St Lawrence*—the saint on a grill revered by Titian's patron, Philip II of Spain.

Cannaregio

Crumbling, piquant Cannaregio is the least visited *sestiere* in Venice, and here, perhaps, you can begin to feel what everyday life is like behind the tourist glitz—children playing tag on the bridges, old men in shorts messing around in unglamorous, unpainted boats on murky canals, neighbourhood greasy spoons and bars, banners of laundry waving gaily overhead.

Northern Cannaregio was Tintoretto's home base, and he is buried in the beautiful Venetian Gothic **Madonna dell'Orto** (*open Mon–Sat 10–5.30, Sun and hols 3–5.30; adm*). It also contains several of his jumbo masterpieces, such as the *Sacrifice of the Golden Calf*, in which Tintoretto painted himself bearing the idol—though he refrained from predicting his place in the *Last Judgement*, which hangs opposite. He also painted the highly original *Presentation of the Virgin* in the south aisle, near one of Cima da Conegliano's greatest works, *St John the Baptist*. The first chapel by the door has a *Madonna* by Giovanni Bellini.

From the Campo Madonna dell'Orto, take a short walk down the Fondamenta Contarini, where, across the canal, in the wall of the eccentric **Palazzo Mastelli**, you can see one of Venice's curiosities: an old, stone relief of a Moor confronting a camel. There are three more 'Moors' in the **Campo dei Mori**, just in front of the Madonna dell'Orto. The original identities of these figures has long been forgotten, although a fourth one, embedded in one corner of the square and with a metal nose like Tycho Brahe, is named Signor Antonio Rioba. He featured in many Venetian pranks of yore: anonymous satires or denunciations would be signed in his name, and new arrivals in the city would be sent off to meet him.

Also in the area is another church, **Sant'Alvise** (*currently under restoration*), which must be the loneliest church in Venice. Its main features are a forceful *Calvary* by Giambattista Tiepolo and a set of charming tempera paintings that Ruskin called the 'Baby Carpaccios', but are now attributed to Carpaccio's master, Lazzaro Bastiani, as Carpaccio himself would only have been about eight years old when they were painted.

Three *rii* to the south of Sant'Alvise is the **Ghetto**—THE Ghetto, that is, for, like '*Arsenal*', the Venetians invented it: *ghetto* derives from the word *getto* meaning 'casting in metals', and there was an iron foundry here which preceded the establishment of a special quarter to which all Jews were ordered to move in 1516. The name is poignantly, coincidentally apt, for in Hebrew 'ghetto' comes from the root for 'cut off'. And cut off its residents were in Venice, for the Ghetto is an island, surrounded by a moat-like canal, and at night all Jews had to be within its windowless walls. Cramped for space, the houses are tall, with very low ceilings, which, as many people have noted, eerily presages ghetto tenements of centuries to come. But the Venetians did not invent the mentality behind the Ghetto; Spanish Jews in the Middle Ages were segregated, as were the Jews of ancient Rome. In fact, Venetian law specifically protected Jewish citizens and forbade preachers from inciting mobs against them—a common enough practice in the 16th century. Jewish refugees came to Venice from all over Europe; here they were relatively safe, even if they had to pay high taxes and rents. When Napoleon threw open the gates of the Ghetto in 1797, it is said that the impoverished residents who remained were too weak to leave.

The island of the **Ghetto Nuovo**, the oldest section, is a melancholy place, its small campo often empty and forlorn. The **Scuola Grande Tedesca** is the oldest of Venice's five synagogues, built by German Jews in 1528, and is in the same building as the small **Museo Comunità Israelitica/Ebraica** (*open daily 10.30–5; closed Sat and Jewish holidays; adm exp for the guided tour at 30mins past the hour*). The informative tours (in English) organised by the museum visit this synagogue and two others, the **Scuola Spagnola**—an opulent building by Longhena—and the **Scuola Levantina**.

Light years from the Ghetto in temperament, but only three minutes away on foot, the **Palazzo Labia** (next to the 1580 **Ponte delle Guglie**), has a ballroom with Giambattista Tiepolo's lavish frescoes on the *Life of Cleopatra*. The palazzo is now owned by RAI, the Italian state broadcaster, and the ballroom is open for concerts (*or call © 041 524 812, well in advance to arrange an appointment between 3 and 4pm*). Away from the palazzo towards the railway station runs the **Lista di Spagna**, Venice's tourist highway, lined with restaurants, bars, hotels and souvenir stands that are not always as cheap as they should be.

San Giorgio Maggiore and the Giudecca

The little islet of San Giorgio Maggiore, crowned by Palladio's temple-fronted church of **San Giorgio Maggiore** (*vaporetto line 82; open daily 10–12.30 and 2.30–6.30; adm, including the campanile*), dominates the view of the Lagoon from Piazzetta San Marco, seeming to hang between the water and the sky, bathed by light with as many variations as Monet's series on the cathedral of Rouen. The white interior is relieved by Tintoretto's *Fall of Manna* and his celebrated *Last Supper* on the main altar, surrounded by finely carved Baroque choir stalls. A lift whisks you to the top of the **campanile** for a remarkable view over Venice and the Lagoon. The old monastery, partly designed by Palladio, is now the headquarters of the Giorgio Cini Foundation, dedicated to the arts and the sciences of the sea, and venue for frequent exhibitions and conferences.

La Giudecca (lines 52 and 82) actually consists of eight islands that curve gracefully like a Spanish *tilde* just south of Venice; prominent among its buildings are a string of empty mills and factories—the product of a brief 19th-century flirtation with industry—and for the most part the atmosphere is quiet and homely. Like Cannaregio, it's seldom visited, though people wander over to see Palladio's best church, **Il Redentore** (*open Mon–Sat 10–5.30, Sun 3–5.30; adm*). In 1576, during a plague that killed 46,000, the doge and the senate vowed that if the catastrophe ended, they would build a church and visit it once a year until the end of time. And so they do: on the third Sunday of each July a bridge of boats is constructed to take the authorities across from the Zattere. The Redentore provides a fitting backdrop to the pageantry; Palladio's temple front, with its interlocking pediments, matches the basilican interior, with curving transepts and dome; the shadowy semi-circle of columns behind the altar adds a strikingly mystical effect.

Shopping

Venice is a fertile field for shoppers, whether you're looking for bric-à-brac (just walk down the Lista di Spagna) or the latest in Italian design—but don't expect many bargains. Everything from fresh fish to inlaid wooden boxes and tourist junk can be found at the **Rialto markets**. There's also a large food market on Castello's **Via Garibaldi**, and smaller stalls in the *campi* and on barges along the smaller canals.

antiques

Campo San Maurizio, near Campo Santo Stefano, has the largest concentration of antique shops. **Antonietta Santomanco della Toffola**, Frezzeria 1504, S. Marco, has Russian and English silver, prints and antique jewellery and glass, while the establishments of the print dealer **Pietro Scarpa**, Campo S. Moisè 1464, and Calle XXII Marzo 2089, S. Marco, are as much museums as shops. Away from the San Marco area, **Salizzada**, S. Lio 5672, in Castello, has old prints of Venice, clocks, and many other curious odds and ends. **Xanthippe**, Dorsoduro 2773, near Ca' Rezzonico, is a highly eclectic shop specializing in the 19th century and Art Deco Venetian glass.

books

Fantoni Libre Arte, Salizzada di S. Luca 4121, S. Marco, has a monumental display of art books, while **Sansovino**, Bacino Orseolo 84, S. Marco (just outside the Procuratie Vecchie), also has a large collection of art and coffee-table books. The best stock of books in Italian about every aspect of Venice, including some rare editions, is in **Filippi**, Calle del Paradiso 5763, Castello. For books in English, try **Sangiorgio**, Calle Larga XXII Marzo 2087, S. Marco; **Alla Toletta**, Sacca della Toletta 1214, Dorsoduro; or **Serenissima**, Merceria dell'Orologio 739, San Marco.

fashion, fabrics and accessories

Most designer boutiques are located in the streets west of Piazza San Marco. **Missoni**, Calle Vallaresso 1312, S. Marco, near Harry's Bar, has some of Italy's most beautiful knitwear; **Krizia**, Mercerie del Capitello 4949, S. Marco, has more youth-orientated, colourful knits; **Laura Biagiotti**, Via XXII Marzo 2400/a, S. Marco; Venetian **Roberta di Camerino**, Lungomare Marconi 32, on the Lido; and Giorgio Armani, at **Giorgio Armani da Elysée**, Frezzeria 1693, S. Marco, and **Emporio Armani**, Calle dei Fabbri 989, S. Marco, with more accessible prices. For fashions by maverick Italian and French designers, try **La Coupole**, Via XXII Marzo, or its sister shop, **La Fenice**, Frezzeria 1674, for more everyday wear. Then there's **M. Antichità**, S. Marco 1691, offering velour dresses of Renaissance richness, and jewels to match.

Fashionable second-hand clothes await at **Aldo Strausse**, Campo S. Giustina, in Castello, but **Emilio Ceccato**, Sottoportico di Rialto, S. Polo, is the place to find something very typically Venetian—gondoliers' shirts, jackets and tight trousers. Meanwhile, at the **Camiceria San Marco**, Calle Vallaresso 1340, S. Marco, they will make up men's shirts and women's dresses to order for you within 24 hours.

For sensuous and expensive lingerie, visit **Jade Martine**, S. Marco 1645. The great place to find Venetian lace, whether for lingerie or tablecloths, is on Burano (*see* p.339–40), although beware that the bargains there are neither handmade nor even Buranese. Back in Venice itself, **Jesurum**, Piazza S. Marco 60/61, has a vast quantity of Venetian lace and linen of all kinds on display in a 12th-century former church behind St Mark's Basilica, as well as a selection of swimwear and summer clothes.

High-quality fabrics were one of Venice's traditional specialities, using skills that in many cases have been reinvigorated in recent years. **Trois**, Campo S. Maurizio, S. Marco 2666, is an institution selling colourful pleated Fortuny silks, invented in Venice and made to traditional specifications on the Giudecca. More modern designs in silks and fabrics can be found at **Valli**, Merceria S. Zulian 783, S. Marco.

For posh shoes, **La Fenice**, Via XXII Marzo 2255, S. Marco, has a good selection by French and Italian designers. The greatest name in Venetian leather is **Vogini**, Via XXII Marzo 1300, S. Marco, which has a comprehensive selection of bags and luggage, and a complete range by Venetian designer Roberta di Camerino.

Jewellery in Venice tends to be expensive and conservative—particularly in the many shops in and around San Marco. **Codognato**, S. Marco 1295, is one of the oldest jewellers in Venice, with some rare Tiffany, Cartier and Art Deco items; at **Missiaglia**, Piazza S. Marco 125, you can see some of the most elegant pieces produced by Venetian gold and silversmiths working today.

food and drink

As well as in the markets (*see* above), try **Pastificio Artigiano**, Strada Nuova 4292, Cannaregio, where for fifty years Paolo Pavon has created Venice's tastiest pastas, among them *pasta al cacao* (chocolate pasta) and lemon, beetroot and curry varieties. Similarly, **Il Pastaio**, Calle del Varoteri 219, in the Rialto market, offers pastas in over a score of different colours. **Colussi**, Rugheta S. Apollonia 4325, near Campo Santi Filippo e Giacomo, has an enormous range of Venice's bizarre pastries. For picnic ingredients, **Rizzo Pane**, Calle delle Botteghe, S. Marco, just off Campo F. Morosini, is an *alimentari* with everything you could possibly need.

gifts

Anyone seeking gifts will find plenty in Venice, though, again, prices sometimes need to be handled with care. At **La Scialuppa**, Calle Seconda dei Saoneri 2695, S. Polo, you can buy the wares of woodworker Gilberto Penzo, who makes beautiful *forcole* (gondola oar locks, made of walnut) and replicas of Venetian guild signs. **Calle Lunga 2137**, in Dorsoduro, is a workshop specializing in decorative wrought-iron, and **Fondamenta Minotto 154**, S. Croce, near S. Nicolò Tolentino and the railway station, has gold and brass items, such as Venetian doorknockers. For children, **Signor Blum**, Calle Lunga S. Barnaba 2864, Dorsoduro, has beautiful jigsaw puzzles and wooden toys. The **Consorzio Artigianato Artistico Veneziano**, Calle Larga S. Marco 412, S. Marco, has a selection of all kinds of handmade Venetian crafts.

As Burano is the centre for lace, so too Murano (*see* below) is still the place to go for glassware, but in the city one of the grand names in Venetian glass is **Pauly**, at the end of Calle Larga, near Ponte Consorzi, S. Marco, which has 30 rooms of both traditional and contemporary designs in a former doge's palazzo. At a less exalted level, **Paolo**

Rossi, Campo S. Zaccaria 4685, S. Marco, has attractive reproductions of ancient glassware, and **Arte Veneto**, Campo S. Zanipolo 6335, Castello, offers glass and ceramic trinkets that escape looking ridiculous. The oldest Venetian craft—mosaics—are also available, as individual *tessere* or larger items: try **Arte del Mosaico**, Calle Erizzo 4002, Castello, or **Angelo Orsoni**, Campiello del Battello 1045, Cannaregio. For exquisite handmade paper, blank books and photo albums try **Paulo Olbi**, Calle della Mandorla 3653 (by Campo S. Angelo), and for paper designs, silk ties and masks fusing Persian and Italian styles, **Alberto Valese-Ebrû**, Campo S. Stefano 3471, S. Marco (nearly opposite the church door).

Venice ✉ *30100*   *Where to Stay*

The rule of thumb in Venice is that in whatever class of hotel you stay, expect it to cost around a third more than it would on the mainland, even before the often outrageous charge for breakfast is added to the bill. Reservations are near essential from about April to October and for Carnival; many hotels close in the winter, although many that do stay open offer discounts. Single rooms are rare. If you arrive without reservations, the tourist offices at the railway station and Piazzale Roma have a free room-finding service (a deposit is required, which is deducted from your hotel bill), though they get very busy in season. Also, the tourist office in Piazza San Marco has a list of agencies that rent self-catering flats in Venice and neighbouring resorts.

luxury

★★★★★**Cipriani**, Giudecca 10, ✆ 041 520 7744, since 1963 has been one of Italy's most luxurious hotels, a villa isolated in a lush garden at one end of the Giudecca, that's so quiet and comfortable you could forget Venice exists, even though it's only a few minutes away by the hotel's 24-hour private launch service. An Olympic-size pool, sauna, jacuzzis in each room, tennis courts, and a superb restaurant are just some of its facilities, and no hotel anywhere could pamper you more.

★★★★★**Danieli**, Riva degli Schiavoni 4196, ✆ 041 522 6480, ✆ 041 520 0208, the largest and most famous hotel in Venice, is in the most glorious location, overlooking the Lagoon and rubbing shoulders with the Palazzo Ducale. Formerly the Gothic palazzo of the Dandolo family, it has been a hotel since 1822; Dickens, Proust, George Sand and Wagner checked in here. The setting is beautiful: silken walls, Gothic staircases, gilt mirrors and oriental rugs. The new wing, much vilified since it was built in the 1940s, is comfortable but lacks the charm and the stories.

★★★★★**Gritti Palace**, S. Maria del Giglio 2467, S. Marco, ✆ 041 794 611, the 15th-century Grand Canal palace that once belonged to the dashing glutton and womanizer Doge Andrea Gritti, has been preserved as a true Venetian fantasy, now part of the CIGA chain. All the rooms are furnished with Venetian antiques, but for a real splurge do as Somerset Maugham did and stay in the Ducal Suite. Another of its delights is the restaurant, the **Club del Doge**, on a terrace overlooking the canal.

very expensive

★★★★**Concordia**, Calle Larga S. Marco 367, ✆ 041 520 6866, ✆ 041 520 6775, the only hotel overlooking Piazza S. Marco, has been swishly renovated with a touch of

Hollywood in some of its furnishings, central air-conditioning, and substanial off-season discounts. ★★★★**Londra Palace** Riva degli Schiavoni 4171, Castello, ✆ 041 520 0533, ✆ 041 522 5032, is where Tchaikovsky wrote his *Fourth Symphony* (in room 108); it was also a favourite of Stravinsky. The hotel was created by linking two palaces together, and it has an elegant interior, views of the lagoon from over half the rooms, and exceptionally good service. There is also an excellent restaurant, **Les Deux Lions**. ★★★★**Saturnia & International**, Via XXII Marzo 2398, S. Marco, ✆ 041 520 8377, ✆ 041 520 7131, a lovely hotel in a romantic quattrocento palazzo, has preserved centuries of accumulated decoration. Very near S. Marco, it has a garden court, faced by the nicest and quietest rooms. Off-season discounts.

expensive

★★★**Accademia 'Villa Maravege'**, Fondamenta Bollani 1058, Dorsoduro, ✆ 041 521 0188, ✆ 041 523 9152, offers a generous dollop of slightly faded charm in a 17th-century villa with a garden, just off the Grand Canal. Its 26 rooms are furnished with a menagerie of antiques, some of which look as if they were left behind by the previous occupant—the Russian Embassy. Book well in advance. Off-season discounts.

★★★**La Fenice et Des Artistes**, Campiello de la Fenice 1936, S. Marco, ✆ 041 523 2333, ✆ 041 520 3721, is a favourite of opera buffs in Venice (though that's not much use until La Fenice re-opens). Inside there are lots of mirrors, antiques and chandeliers to make artistes feel at home. Fully air-conditioned.

★★★**Flora**, Calle Bergamaschi 2283/a, S. Marco, ✆ 041 520 5844, is a small, comfortable hotel on a little street that's remarkably quiet so near to the Piazza, with a charming garden and patio. Ask for a large room. Air-conditioning and off-season discounts. ★★★**Do Pozzi**, Corte do Pozzi 2373, S. Marco, ✆ 041 520 7855, ✆ 041 522 9413, with a bit of the look of an Italian country inn, has 29 quiet rooms on a charming little square, only a few minutes from Piazza San Marco. It's friendly and well run. Optional air-conditioning in all rooms. ★★★**Malibran**, S. Giovanni Crisostomo 5864, Cannaregio, ✆ 041 522 8028, in the Corte del Milion, is next to, or perhaps even incorporating, the house of Marco Polo.

★★★**Sturion**, Calle del Sturion 679, San Polo, ✆ 041 523 6243, ✆ 041 522 8378, a popular choice, is one of the least expensive hotels actually on the Grand Canal. It's advisable to book well ahead for one of its eight large, finely furnished rooms.

★★★**Agli Alboretti**, Rio Terrà Foscarini 884, Dorsoduro, ✆ 041 523 0058, ✆ 041 520 4048, is a charming little hotel, on a rare tree-lined lane near the Accademia. ★★★**La Calcina**, Zattere ai Gesuati 780, Dorsoduro, ✆ 041 520 6466, near the Gesuati church and overlooking the Giudecca canal, was Ruskin's *pensione* in 1877. Book well ahead.

moderate

★★**Falier**, Salizzada S. Pantalon 130, S. Croce, ✆ 041 710 882, ✆ 041 520 6554, a small hotel near Campo San Rocco, is elegantly furnished, with two flower-filled terraces to lounge around on when your feet rebel; one room has its own terrace. ★★**Messner**, Salute 216, Dorsoduro, ✆ 041 522 7443, is a nicely modernized hotel near the Salute, and very suitable for families. Great showers, awful coffee.

★★Mignon, SS. Apostoli 4535, Cannaregio, ✆ 041 523 7388, 🖷 041 520 8658, in a fairly quiet area, not far from the Ca' d'Oro, has a loyal following. It boasts a little garden for leisurely breakfasts, though the rooms are rather plain. **★★La Residenza**, Campo Bandiera e Moro 3608, Castello, ✆ 041 528 5315, 🖷 041 588 5042, is in a lovely 14th-century palace in a quiet square between San Marco and the Arsenale. The public rooms are flamboyantly decorated with 18th-century frescoes, paintings and antique furniture, though the bedrooms are simpler.

cheap

The largest concentration of cheap hotels in Venice is around the Lista di Spagna, running eastwards into Cannaregio from the train station, though they can be tacky and noisy. A more relaxed, pleasant and attractive area is in Dorsoduro, particularly around the Campo Santa Margherita.

★Casa Carettoni, Lista di Spagna 130, Cannaregio, ✆ 041 716 231, is the most pleasant and comfortable cheap hotel near the station; no breakfast is a plus, as you can do as Venetians do and take it in a nearby bar. **★Casa Petrarca**, Calle delle Fuseri 4393, S. Marco, ✆ 041 520 0430, is near the Piazza; Petrarch didn't really sleep in one of these six friendly rooms, but who cares?

★Casa Verardo, Ruga Giuffa 4765, Castello, ✆ 041 528 6127, 🖷 041 523 2765, is a classy, nine-room *locanda* with friendly owners. **★Sant'Anna**, Corte Bianco 269, Castello, ✆ 041 528 6466, is a fine little hotel popular with those who want to escape tourist Venice, located just north of the Giardini Pubblici. Only eight rooms, including some triples. **★Silva**, Fondamenta Rimedio 4423, Castello, ✆ 041 522 7643, is a bit hard to find—on one of the most photographed little canals in Venice, between the S. Zaccaria *vaporetto* stop and S. Maria Formosa. The rooms are fairly basic, but quiet, and the staff are friendly.

hostels and campsites

The tourist office has a list of all inexpensive hostel accommodation in Venice; schools are often pressed into use to take in the summer overflow, charging minimal rates to spread out a sleeping bag.

Camping is big business in the north-east corner of the Lagoon, around Cavallino, Jesolo and Punta Sabbioni. A good campsite not far from Venice, and open all year, is **Fusina**, Via Moranzani, Malcontenta, near Fusina, ✆ 041 547 0055, 🖷 041 547 0050. The *vaporetto* Line 16 from there to Venice runs every hour in summer, less frequently at other times.

Ostello Venezia, Fondamenta delle Zitelle 86, Giudecca, ✆ 041 523 8211. Venice's youth hostel enjoys a striking location, with views across to San Marco. They don't take phone reservations, and to be assured of a place in July or August you should write well in advance. At other times, you can chance it—the office opens at 6pm, but doors open at noon for waiting. IYHF cards required (available at the hostel); curfew 11.30pm. Bed and breakfast L25,000; meals L14,000.

Foresteria Valdese, Calle della Madonnetta 5170, Castello, ✆ 041 528 6797, is an old palazzo converted into a dormitory/*pensione* by the Waldensians. Check-in 9–1 and 6–8; beds in dorm L20,000, with breakfast; in rooms L24,000 per person. **Domus Cavanis**, Rio Terrà Foscarini 912, Dorsoduro, ℗ 041 528 7374, is a Catholic-run hostel open June–Sept only. Single (L45,000), double (L65,000) and triple (L90,000) rooms; students get about a 10% discount. Optional breakfast L7000.

Eating Out

The Venetians themselves are traditionally the worst cooks in Italy, and their beautiful city bears the ignominy of having the highest percentage of dud restaurants per capita. Not only is cooking in general well below the norm in Italy, but prices tend to be about 15 per cent higher, and even the moderate ones can give you a nasty surprise at *conto* time with excessive service and cover charges. The cheap ones, serving up 500 tourist menus a day, are mere providers of calories to keep you on your feet; pizza is a good standby if you're on a budget. The restaurants listed here have a history of being decent or better, so chances are they still will be when you visit.

luxury

Antico Martini, Campo S. Fantin 1983, S. Marco, ℗ 041 522 4121, is a Venetian classic, all Romance and elegance. It started out as a Turkish coffeehouse in the early 18th century, but nowadays is better known for seafood, a superb wine list and the best *pennette al pomodoro* in Venice. The intimate piano bar-restaurant stays open until 2am. Its romantic flavour is temporarily swallowed up by La Fenice's rebuilding operations directly outside. *Closed Tues, Wed midday, Dec and Feb.*

Danieli Terrace, in the Danieli Hotel, Riva degli Schiavoni 4196, Castello, ℗ 041 522 6480, has a rooftop restaurant renowned for classic cuisine (try the *spaghetti alla Danieli*, prepared at your table) and perfect service in an incomparable setting overlooking Bacino San Marco.

very expensive

La Caravella, Calle Larga XXII Marzo 2397, S. Marco, ℗ 041 520 8901, is in an annexe to the Saturnia Hotel (*see* above). For sheer variety of seasonal and local dishes, prepared by a master chef, few restaurants in Italy can top this merrily corny repro of a dining hall in a 16th-century Venetian galley. Try gilt head with thyme and fennel. Despite the décor, the atmosphere is fairly formal. *Open Oct–April; closed Wed.* **Do Forni**, Calle dei Specchieri 468, S. Marco, ℗ 041 523 2148, for many Italians as well as foreigners, is *the* place to eat in Venice. There are two dining rooms, one 'Orient Express'-style and the other rustic, always filled with diners partaking of its excellent seafood *antipasti*, polenta, and seafood. *Closed Thurs* in winter.

Harry's Bar, Calle Vallaresso 1323, S. Marco, ℗ 041 523 6797, in a class by itself—a favourite of Hemingway and assorted other luminaries—is as much a Venetian institution as the Doges' Palace. Best to avoid the formal restaurant upstairs and just flit in for a quick hobnob while sampling a sandwich or the justly famous house cocktails (a Bellini, Tiziano or Tiepolo—delectable fruit juices mixed with Prosecco), at a table downstairs near the bar. *Closed Mon.*

expensive

Dall'Amelia, Via Miranese 113, Mestre, ℗ 041 913 951, is of necessary inclusion despite its inconvenient mainland location—all Italian gourmets cross the big bridge to dine here at least once. The oysters are delicious and the *tortelli di bronzino* (sea bass) divine; it also has one of Italy's most renowned wine cellars. **Antica Besseta**, Salizada da Ca'Zusto (at the end of Calle Savio), S. Croce, ✆ 041 524 0428, is a family-run citadel of Venetian homecooking, where you can experience an authentic *risi e bisi*, or *bigoli in salsa*, scampi, and the family's own wine. *Closed Tues, Wed lunch, and part of July and Aug.*

Corte Sconta, Calle del Pestrin 3886, Castello, ✆ 041 522 7024, may be off the beaten track, but the reputation of this trattoria rests solidly on its exquisite molluscs and crustaceans, served in a setting that's a breath of fresh air after the exposed beams and copper pots that dominate the typical Venetian restaurant. The Venetians claim the Corte Sconta is even better out of season; be sure to order the house wine. *Closed Sun, Mon, and most of July and Aug.*

Hostaria da Franz, Fondamenta San Isepo (or Giuseppe) 754, Castello, facing the side of the church, ✆ 041 522 7505, is well out of the way, just north of the Giardini Pubblici, but well worth the trouble of getting lost *en route*. This is one of Venice's best: great oysters, *gnocchi* and seafood cooked the way it should be if all Venetians tried harder. The house wine is lovely. *Closed Tues.*

Antica Locanda Montin, Fondamenta di Borgo or Eremite 1147 (near S. Trovaso), Dorsoduro, ✆ 041 522 7151, has long been Venice's most celebrated artists' eatery, with a vast garden, but the food can range erratically in quality from first to third division. *Closed Tues evening, Wed, and half of Aug.*

Trattoria Vini da Arturo, Calle degli Assassini 3656, S. Marco, ✆ 041 528 6974, in an infamous little street near La Fenice, is a tiny trattoria that marches to a different drum from most Venetian restaurants, with not a speck of seafood on the menu. Instead, try the *papardelle al radicchio* or Venice's best steaks; its *tiramisù* is famous. *Closed Sun and half Aug.* **A La Vecia Cavana**, Rio Terrà dei SS. Apostoli 4624, ✆ 041 523 8644, is Cannaregio's smartest restaurant, where you can dine on Adriatic specialities. *Closed Tues.*

moderate

Altanella, Calle della Erbe 268, Giudecca, ✆ 041 522 7780, is a delightful old seafood restaurant with an attractive setting on the Rio del Ponte Longo and a sideways glimpse of the Giudecca canal thrown in. Any of the grilled fish will be superb, and the *risotto di pesce* and *fritto* are worth the trip in themselves. *Closed Mon evening, Tues, and half of Aug. Reserve.* **Antica Mola**, Fondamenta degli Ormesini 2800, Cannaregio (no ✆), near the Ghetto, has all the old favourites—grilled fish, risotto, *zuppa di pesce*—and tables by the canal. *Closed Wed.*

Antico Giardinetto da Erasmo, S. Croce 2315, ✆ 041 721 301, behind the church of S. Cassiano, stars delicious seafood cooked in a variety of styles. In good weather you can eat out in the little garden. *Closed Sat, Sun and Aug.* **Alla Madonna**, Calle della Madonna 594, S. Polo (off Fond. del Vin, Rialto), ✆ 041 523 3824, is a large, popular, and very Venetian fish restaurant. *Closed Wed and Jan.*

Da Remigio, Salizzada dei Greci 3416, Castello, ✆ 041 523 0089, is a neighbourhood favourite, with solid Venetian cooking. Very popular with the locals. *Closed Mon, and Tues eve.* **Tre Spiedi**, Salizzada S. Canciano 5906, Cannaregio, ✆ 041 528

0035, near the Campiello F. Corner and the central post office, has a cosy atmosphere to go with local specialities like *spaghetti alla veneziana* and *braciola bruno* (pork chops). *Closed Mon.*

cheap

Aciughetta, Campo SS. Filippo e Giacomo, Castello, ✆ 041 522 4292, is one of the best cheap restaurants and bars near the Piazza San Marco, with good pizzas and atmosphere to boot. *Closed Tues.* **Rosticceria San Bartolomeo**, Calle della Bissa 5424, San Marco, ✆ 041 522 3569, serves honest cooking for honest prices, a no-frills trattoria with an even cheaper snack bar downstairs.

San Tomà, Campo San Tomà 2864, San Polo, ✆ 041 523 8819, is a good trattoria-cum-pizzeria with convivial outdoor tables. **Da Crecola**, S. Giacomo dell'Orio 1459, S. Croce, ✆ 041 524 1496, set in a quiet corner by a canal, has outdoor tables, and good pasta dishes, like *tagliatelle alla gorgonzola*, 50 different kinds of pizza, and a delightfully *pétillant* house wine.

Casa Mia, Calle dell'Oca 4430, Cannaregio, ✆ 041 528 5590, near Campo SS. Apostoli, is a lively pizzeria full of locals, with six courtyard tables. *Closed Tues.* **Vino Vino**, Campo S. Fantin 1983, S. Marco, ✆ 041 522 4121, is a trendy offspring of the élite Antico Martini, where you can eat a well-cooked, filling dish (cooked by the same chefs!) with a glass of good wine at prices even students can afford. *Closed Tues, Wed midday, Dec and Feb.*

Entertainment and Nightlife

Sadly, in a city that's clearly made-to-order for revelry and romance, life after dark is notoriously moribund. The locals take an evening stroll to their *campo* for a chat and an *aperitivo*, before heading home to dinner and the TV—the hotblooded may go on to bars and discos in Mestre, Marghera or the Lido. Visitors are left to become even poorer at the **Municipal Casino**, out on the Lido from April to October, and at other times in the Palazzo Vendramin on the Grand Canal (*open 3pm–2am; dress up and take your passport*). You might prefer to spend less more memorably on a moonlit gondola ride–or just wander about. Venice is a different city at night, when the *bricole* lights in the Lagoon are a fitting backdrop for a mer-king's pageant.

Even so, there are a few places to go, and stacked against the absence of everyday nightlife there's Venice's packed schedule of special events. For an up-to-date calendar, consult *Un Ospite di Venezia*, free from tourist offices.

opera, classical music and theatre

Venice's music programme is heavily oriented to the classical. Opera (from December to May only), ballet, recitals and symphonic concerts, once at **La Fenice**, are now performed in a temporary pavilion at Tronchetto; tickets available through the Cassa di Risparmio, Campo S. Luca, ✆ 041 529 1111. At Venice's main theatre, **Teatro Goldoni**, Calle Goldoni 4650/b, S. Marco, ✆ 041 520 5422, the Goldoni repertory holds pride of place, but there are also other plays, as well as concerts; in summer performances are often moved to Campo S. Polo.

Two other concert venues, worth visiting as much for the décor as the music are the **Palazzo Labia**, Campo S. Geremia, Cannaregio (call ahead for tickets, ℭ 041 524 2812), and Vivaldi's lovely Rococo church of **La Pietà** (information and tickets, ℭ 041 520 8711), where prices are usually high but the acoustics are well-nigh perfect.

cafés and bars

The classic cafés of Venice face each other across Piazza San Marco: **Florian's** and its great rival **Quadri**, both beautiful, and both correspondingly exorbitant. More fashionable with smart Venetians today, particularly on Sundays, is **Harry's Dolci**, Fondamenta S. Biagio 773, on the Giudecca, noted for its elegant teas, ice-creams and cakes, as well as the Cipriani's **Cips**, open for scrumptious sandwiches and cakes. **Caffè Costarica**, Rio Terrà di S. Leonardo, Cannaregio, brews Venice's most powerful *espresso* and great iced coffee (*frappé*), and also sells coffees and beans.

Throughout the day Venetians frequently drop into bars and wine bars (*bacaro*) for a 'shadow' (an *ombra*, a tiny glass of wine generally downed in one go) and *cicheti*, the local equivalent of tapas. For the greatest variety, try Venice's oldest wine bar, **Al Volta**, Calle Cavalli di S. Marco 4081, S. Marco, with over 2000 Italian and foreign labels and a sumptuous array of *cicheti*. *Open 9–2.30 and 5–9; closed Sun.* **Do Mori**, a resolutely traditional Rialto bar, north of Ruga Vecchia San Giovanni, has delicious snacks (but no tables) to go with your *ombra*. *Open 8.30–9; closed Sun.*

Between 5pm and dinner is the time to indulge in a beer and *tramezzini*, finger sandwiches that come in a hundred varieties; some of the best are to be found at eccentric **Bar alla Toletta**, Calle della Toletta 1191, Dorsoduro, run by a temperamental middle-aged couple with a voracious appetite for jazz. The title of best *gelateria* in the city has by convention been accorded to **Paolin**, on the Campo Santo Stefano, S. Marco, above all for their divine pistachio. However, **Nico**, on the Zattere ai Gesuati, Dorsoduro, is also a must on anyone's ice-cream tour, if the late night queues are anything to go by.

jazz, clubs and nightspots

Venice's few late-night bars and music venues can be fun, or just posy and dull, and what you find is pretty much a matter of pot luck. **Paradiso Perduto**, Fondamenta della Misericordia 2540, Cannaregio, ℭ 041 720 581, is the city's favourite late-night bar/restaurant with inexpensive if variable food, and a relaxed atmosphere popular with locals and English visitors. Once known for live jazz, they now have a bit of trouble with their late-night licence, so live events are rare. *Open 6pm–midnight; closed Wed.*

A current favourite for young trendies is **Taverna l'Olandese Volante** (Flying Dutchman), Campo S. Lio 5658, Castello, ℭ 041 528 9349, Venice's answer to a pub, open late with snacks and simple food. The informal wine bar, **Osteria da Codroma**, Fondamenta Briati 2540, Dorsoduro, ℭ 041 520 4161, hosts a backgammon club, art shows and occasional live jazz. *Open 7pm–2am; closed Thurs.* Another bar/restaurant with music and dancing is **Ai Canottieri**, Ponte Tre Archi 690, Cannaregio, ℭ 041 715 408. *Open 7pm–2am; closed Sun.*

There are also a few fairly glitzy piano bars, such as **Linea d'Ombra**, Zattere ai Saloni, near the Salute, ☎ 041 528 5259. *Open 8pm–1am; closed Wed.* A favourite venue for Venetians is Marghera's **Al Vapore**, Via Fratelli Bandiera 8, ☎ 041 930 796, which hosts live rock and jazz. In July and August there's a disco on the Lido: **Acropolis**, Lungomare Marconi 22, ☎ 041 526 0466. The Lido is also the place to hie for a late-night game of billiards, *chez* **Al Delfino**, an 'American Bar' with music and snacks at Lungomare Marconi 96, ☎ 041 526 8309. *Open until 2am.* Or **Villa Eva**, Gran Viale 49, ☎ 041 526 1884, with music and snacks from midnight until 4am. *Closed Thurs except in the summer.*

The main late-night drinking holes are **Harry's Bar** (*see* above, 'Eating Out'), especially if someone else is paying; or **Osteria ai Assassini**, Calle degli Assassini, S. Marco, which has wines, beers, and good *cichetti. Open till midnight; closed Sun.* For more filling victuals, try **Vino Vino** (*see* above, 'Eating Out'). *Open till 2am.*

exhibitions and art festivals

Venice is one of Europe's top cities for exhibitions: major international shows fill the **Palazzo Grassi**, Campo S. Samuele, S. Marco, which Fiat has transformed into a lavishly equipped exhibition and cultural centre. High calibre art and photographic exhibitions also appear frequently at the **Palazzo Querini-Stampalia**, the **Peggy Guggenheim Collection** and **Ca' Pésaro**.

Then there's the **Biennale**, the most famous contemporary art show in the world, founded in 1895 and now held, in principle, in even-numbered years. The main exhibits of the forty or so countries officially represented are set up in the permanent pavilions in the Giardini Pubblici, but there is also an open section for younger and less-established artists, in venues across the city.

The city's other great cultural junket is the **Venice Film Festival**, held in the Palazzo del Cinema and the Astra Cinema on the Lido every year in late August and September. As well as spotting the stars, you can get in to see films if you arrive at the cinemas really early—tickets are only sold on the same day as each showing.

traditional festivals

Venice's renowned **Carnival**, first held in the ten days preceding Lent in 1094, was revived in 1979 after several decades of dormancy. It attracts huge crowds, but faces an uphill battle against the inveterate Italian love of *bella figura*—getting dressed up in elaborate costumes, wandering down to San Marco and taking each other's picture is as much as most of the revellers get up to. Concerts and shows are put on all over Venice, with city and corporate sponsorship, but there's little spontaneity or serious carousing, and certainly no trace of what Byron called the 'revel of the earth'. Even so, a **Carnival mask** can still make a good souvenir, either in papier mâché (*cartapesta*) or leather. There are mask shops all over Venice; for the traditionally crafted item, try **Giorgio Clanetti (Laboratorio Artigiano Maschere)**, Barbaria delle Tole 6657, Castello, near SS. Giovanni e Paolo.

In 1988 Venice revived another crowd pleaser, **La Sensa**, held on the first Sunday after Ascension Day, in which the doge married the sea (*see* p.292). Now the mayor plays the groom, in a replica of the state barge or *Bucintoro*. It's as corny and pretentious as it sounds, but on the same day you can watch the gondoliers race in the **Vogalonga**, or long row, from San Marco to Burano and back again.

Venice's most spectacular festival, **Il Redentore**, is held on the third Sunday of July, with its bridge of boats to the Giudecca (*see* p.324–25). The greatest excitement happens the Saturday night before, when Venetians row out for an evening picnic on the water, before the fabulous fireworks display over the Lagoon. For landlubbers the prime viewing spots are on the east ends of either the Giudecca or the Zattere.

More perspiration is expended in the **Regata Storica** (first Sunday in September) down the Grand Canal, a splendid pageant of historic vessels and crews in Renaissance costumes and hotly contested races by gondoliers. Another bridge of boats is built on 21 November, this time across the Grand Canal to the Salute, for the feast of **Santa Maria della Salute**, commemorating the end of another plague, in 1631. This event provides the only opportunity to see Longhena's unique basilica as it was meant to be, with doors thrown open on to the Grand Canal.

The Lagoon and its Islands

Pearly and melting into the bright sky, iridescent blue or murky green, a sheet of glass yellow and pink in the dawn, or leaden, opaque grey: Venice's Lagoon is one of its wonders, a desolate, often melancholy and strange, often beautiful and seductive 'landscape' with a hundred personalities. It is 56km long and averages 8km across, added up to some 448sq km; half of it, the Laguna Morta ('Dead Lagoon'), where the tides never reach, consists of mud flats except in the spring, while the shallows of the Laguna Viva are always submerged, cleansed by tides twice a day.

To navigate this treacherous sea the Venetians developed an intricate network of channels, marked by *bricole*—wooden posts topped by orange lamps—that kept their craft from running aground. When threatened, they only had to pull out the *bricole* to confound their enemies; the Lagoon was thus always known as 'the sacred walls of the nation'. Keeping the Brenta and other rivers from silting it up kept engineers busy for centuries.

Once the largest of the 39 Lagoon islands were densely inhabited, each occupied by a town or at least a monastery. Now all but a few have been abandoned. Occasionally one hears of plans to bring them back to life, only to wither on the vine of Italian bureaucracy. If you think you have a good idea, take it up with the Revenue Office (Intendenza di Finanza).

The Lido and South Lagoon

The Lido, one of the long spits of land that protects the Lagoon, is by far the most glamorous of the islands, one that has lent its name to countless bathing establishments and clubs all over the world. On its 12 kilometres of beach, poets, potentates and plutocrats at the turn of the century spent their holidays, making the Lido the pinnacle of *Belle Epoque* fashion, so brilliantly evoked in Thomas Mann's *Death in Venice*, and Visconti's subsequent film. The story was set and filmed in the **Grand Hotel des Bains**, just north of the fascist-style **municipal casino** and **Palazzo del Cinema**, host of the Venice Film Festival.

The Lido is still the playground of the Venetians and their visitors, with its bathing concessions, riding clubs, tennis courts and golf course. The free beach, the **Spiaggia Comunale**, is on the north part of the island, a 15-minute walk from the *vaporetto* stop at San Nicolò (go down the Gran Viale, and turn left on the Lungomare d'Annunzio), where you can hire a changing hut and frolic in the sand and sea.

Further north, beyond the private airfield, the **Porto di Lido** is maritime Venice's front door, the most important of the three entrances into the Lagoon, where you can watch the ships of the world sail by. This is where the Doge would sail to toss his ring into the waves, in the annual 'Marriage of the Sea'. It is stoutly defended by the mighty **Forte di Sant'Andrea** on the island of Le Vignole, built in 1543 by Venice's fortifications genius Sammicheli. In times of danger, a great chain was extended from the fort across the channel.

One of the smaller Lagoon islands just off the Lido, with its landmark onion-domed campanile, is **San Lazzaro degli Armeni** (*vaporetto no.20 from Riva degli Schiavoni; open to visitors daily 3–5pm*). It was Venice's leper colony in the Middle Ages, but in 1715 the then-deserted island was given to the Mechitarist Fathers of the Armenian Catholic Church after they were expelled from Greece by the Turks. Today their monastery is still one of the world's major centres of Armenian culture, and its monks, always noted as linguists, run a polyglot press able to print in 32 languages, one of the last survivors in a city once renowned for its publishing. Tours of San Lazzaro include a museum filled with relics of the ancient Christian history of Armenia, as well as memorabilia of Lord Byron, who spent a winter visiting the fathers and bruising his brain with Armenian. The fathers offer inexpensive prints of Venice for sale; or else they would appreciate a donation.

Sports and Activities

Despite dire reports about the state of the waters of the Adriatic, people still swim off the Lido without becoming mutants, but there is an alternative in the public **swimming pool** on Sacca Fisola, at the west end of the Giudecca, ℘ 041 528 5430. If you're interested in **sailing**, inquire at the Compagnia della Vela, near the Giardinetti in S. Marco, ℘ 041 522 2593, for information on lessons and boat hire.

The Lido has the attractive 18-hole Alberoni **golf course**, Via del Forte Alberoni, ℘ 041 731 015, and two **tennis clubs**, the Tennis Club Venezia, Lungomare Marconi 41/d, ℘ 041 526 0335, and the Campi Comunali di Tennis, ℘ 041 526 5689. You can also **ride** along the Lido, like Byron and Shelley, although it's no longer a romantic hooves-in-the-surf affair—inquire at Circolo Ippico Veneziano, Ca' Bianco, Lido, ℘ 041 526 1820. If you prefer to cycle along the Lido, **bikes** can be hired at Giorgio Barbieri, Via Zara 5.

★★★★★**Excelsior Palace**, Lungomare Marconi 41, Lido di Venezia, ✆ 041 526 0201, ✉ 041 526 7276 (*luxury*) is an immense confection, built in 1907 as the biggest and most luxurious resort hotel in the world and recently redesigned with as much flamboyance as ever. The outrageous exterior is part-Hollywood part-Moorish neo-Gothic. Its amenities include a private beach, swimming pool, tennis courts, golf, nightclub and private launch service to Venice; and you can ogle the stars at the film festival. The restaurant offers the classic turn-of-the-century Lido experience ✆ 041 526 0201 (*very expensive*), with everything you could possibly desire—including a traditional Venetian meal. *Closed mid-Nov–mid-Mar.*

★★★★**Des Bains**, Lungomare Marconi 17, Lido di Venezia, ✆ 041 526 5921, ✉ 041 526 0113 (*very expensive*), a grand old luxury hotel, now part of the Sheraton empire, preserves much of its *Belle Epoque* revelries in its magnificent Liberty-style salon, private *cabanas*, and large garden designed for dalliance. Thomas Mann stayed here on several occasions, and has Aschenbach sigh his life away on the private beach. There's also a salt-water swimming pool, tennis courts, perfect service, and a launch service into Venice. *Closed Dec–mid-Mar.*

★★★★**Quattro Fontane**, Via delle Quattro Fontane 16, Lido di Venezia, ✆ 041 526 0227, ✉ 041 526 0726 (*very expensive*) is the best of the smaller Lido hotels, formerly a seaside villa. Its cool walled-in courtyard is inviting and tranquil, and the public and private rooms are furnished with antiques. Tennis court. Book well in advance. *Closed Nov–Mar.*

★★★**Villa Parco**, Via Rodi 1, Lido di Venezia, ✆ 041 526 0015, ✉ 041 526 7620 (*expensive*) is a recently renovated villa a short way from the beach, with a fine little garden for a bit of privacy. Children are welcome.

From the Lido to Chioggia

Buses or ferries from the Lido, or quicker buses from Piazzale Roma, will take you to Chioggia at the southernmost end of the Lagoon. The seldom used bus/ferry route (leaving roughly every hour) allows you to take in **Malamocco**, a tranquil fishing village named after the first capital of the Lagoon townships. After Pepin nabbed it in 810, the capital moved to the Rialto, leaving the original Malamocco to sink poetically into the sea during a tremendous storm in 1106. Next to it, **Alberoni** is home to the Lido Golf Course and the ferry to the next island reef, Pellestrina. The **Murazzi**, or sea walls, begin here, the last great project of the Republic's Magistrato alle Acque. Built in response to increased flooding in the 18th century, the 4-km long Murazzi are made of huge, white Istrian blocks and built, as their plaque states: Ausu Romano–Aere Veneto ('With Roman audacity and Venetian money'). From 1782 until 4 November 1966 they succeeded in holding back the flood.

Dusty **Chioggia** is one of the most important fishing ports on the Adriatic, a kind of working-class Venice where the streets and canals are arrow straight and full of working craft, many with brightly painted sails. The morning fish market, brimming with exotic denizens of the deep, is one of the wonders of Italy. On the map the town on its islands even resembles a fish, gutted and spread out flat, its straight narrow lanes lined up like bones.

The Venetians like to poke fun at Chioggia, which they consider a grumpy old place, and they wind it up by calling the little Lion of St Mark on its column in Piazzetta Vigo the 'Cat of St Mark'. Almost nothing remains of the medieval town, thanks to Genoa and the 1380 Battle of Chioggia, but the church of **San Domenico**, contains Carpaccio's last painting, *St Paul*, signed and dated 1520, and a beautiful quattrocento crucifix on the altar.

Other monuments are strung all the way along the main **Corso del Popolo** (the fish spine): the 14th-century grain warehouse, the **Granaio**, has a relief of the Madonna by Sansovino on the façade; the **Duomo** was built by Baldassare Longhena after the original 14th-century cathedral burned in 1623. In the chapel to the left of the altar are some murky 18th-century paintings of martyrdoms, one of which is attributed to Tiepolo, although it's hard to swallow. However, the Gothic chapel of San Martino has a lovely polyptych (1349) that really might be by Paolo Veneziano.

And when you've had your fill of fish and the locals, you can stroll along the long bridge (or catch the bus at the cathedral) for a swim at Chioggia's lido, **Sottomarina**; from here it's a short drive down into the Po Delta, now a natural park (*see* p.351).

Eating Out

Chioggia ✉ 30015

Seafood-lovers flock to the cat—**El Gato**, behind the famous fish market in Campo S. Andrea 653, ✆ 041 401 806 (*expensive*), where the chef prepares the freshest of fish in the tastiest of Venetian styles. *Closed Mon and Tues lunch, Jan and mid-Feb.*

At the old-fashioned **Trattoria Buon Pesce**, Stradale Ponte Caneva 625, ✆ 041 400 861 (*moderate*), start with *gnocchetti alla marinara* and follow it with oysters, crab or whatever the waiter suggests. Best of all, prices are half what you'd pay in Venice.

Islands in the North Lagoon

Most Venetian itineraries take in the islands of Murano, Burano and Torcello, all easily reached by inexpensive *vaporetti*, as is the cypress-studded cemetery island of **San Michele** (*vaporetti nos.55 or 23*), with its simple but elegant church of **San Michele in Isola** by Mauro Codussi (1469), his first-known work and Venice's first taste of the Florentine Renaissance, albeit with a Venetian twist in the tri-lobed front.

It contains the tomb of Fra Paolo Sarpi, the monk-philosopher who led the ideological battle against the pope when the Republic was placed under the Great Interdict of 1607, in a major duel of secular and church authority. Venice eventually won the battle of will, thanks mainly to Sarpi, who also wrote the famous Protestant-sympathizing *History of the Council of Trent*, discovered the contraction of the iris, and shared notes on astronomy with Galileo.

The **cemetery** itself is entered through the cloister next to the church (*open daily 8.30–4*). The Protestant and Orthodox sections contain the tombs of some of the many foreigners who preferred to face eternity from Venice, among them Ezra Pound, Sergei Diaghilev, Frederick Rolfe (Baron Corvo) and Igor Stravinsky. The gate-keeper provides a basic map.

The rather dowdy old island of Murano (*vaporetti nos.52 or 23 from S. Zaccaria or nos.12 or 13 from Fondamente Nuove*) is synonymous with glass, the most celebrated of Venice's industries. The Venetians were the first in the Middle Ages to rediscover the secret of making crystal glass, especially mirrors, and it was a secret they kept a monopoly on for centuries by using the most drastic measures: if ever a glassmaker let himself be coaxed abroad, the Council of Ten sent their assassins after him in hot pursuit. Few did, however, because the Republic treated them with kid gloves.

Because of the danger of fire, all the forges in Venice were relocated to Murano in 1291, and the little island became a kind of republic within a republic—minting its own coins, policing itself, even developing its own list of NHs (*nobili homini*—noblemen) in its own *Golden Book*—aristocrats of glass, who built solid palaces along Murano's own Grand Canal.

But glass-making declined like everything else in Venice, and only towards the end of the 19th century were the forges once more stoked up on Murano. Can you visit them? You betcha! In fact a trip to the glassblowers' is the single most touristy thing to do in Venice. After watching the glass being made, there's the inevitable tour of the 'Museum Show Rooms'; these have the same atmosphere as a funeral parlour, all respect and solicitude, carpets and hush-hush—not unfitting, as some of the blooming chandeliers, befruited mirrors and poison-coloured chalices begin to make Death look good. There is no admission charge, as it is hoped you might buy, though there's not too much pressure to do so.

It wasn't always so kitschy. The **Museo Vetrario** (*open daily 10–5; closed Wed; adm exp*), in the 17th-century Palazzo Giustinian on Fondamenta Cavour, has some simple pieces from Roman times, and a choice collection of 15th-century Murano glass, especially the delightful 1480 *Barovier Nuptial Cup*; later glass tends to prove that Murano's glassblowers have long had a wayward streak. A multilingual exhibit explains the history of glassmaking.

Nearby, the Veneto-Byzantine **Santi Maria e Donato** (*open daily 8–12 and 4–7*), a contemporary of St Mark's, has a beautiful arcaded apse. The floor is paved with a marvellous 12th-century mosaic, incorporating pieces of ancient Murano glass, and on the wall there's a Byzantine mosaic of the Virgin. The relics of Bishop Donato of Euboea were nabbed by Venetian body-snatchers, but in this case they outdid themselves, bringing home not only San Donato's bones but those of the dragon the good bishop slew with a gob of spit; you can see four of them hanging behind the altar. Back on the Fondamenta dei Vetrai, the 15th-century **San Pietro Martire** has one of Giovanni Bellini's most serene masterpieces (*Madonna and Child with St Mark, St Augustine and Doge Barbarigo*), from 1488.

Burano (*vaporetto no.12*) is the Lego-land of the Lagoon, where everything is in brightly coloured miniature—the canals, the bridges, the leaning tower and the houses, painted with a Fauvist sensibility in the deepest of colours. Traditionally on Burano the men fish and the women make Venetian point, 'the most Italian of all lace work'—beautiful, intricate and murder on the eyesight. All over Burano you can find samples on sale (beware, however, much is really machine-made or imported), or you can watch it being made at the **Scuola dei**

Merletti in Piazza Galuppi (*open Tues–Sat 10–4; adm*), though '*scuola*' is misleading, as no young woman in Burano wants to learn such an excruciating art; the school was founded in 1872, when traditional lacemaking was already in decline. In the sacristy of the church of **San Martino** (with its tipsily leaning campanile) look for Giambattista Tiepolo's *Crucifixion*, which Mary McCarthy aptly described as 'a ghastly masquerade ball'.

From Burano you can hire a *sandola* (small gondola) to **San Francesco del Deserto**, some 20 minutes to the south. St Francis is said to have founded a chapel here in 1220, and the whole islet was subsequently given to his order as a site for a **monastery** (*visitors welcome daily 9–11 and 3–5.30*). In true Franciscan fashion, it's not the buildings you'll remember (though there's a fine 14th-century cloister), but the love of nature evident in the beautiful gardens. Admission is free, but donations are appreciated.

Torcello

Though fewer than 100 people remain on Torcello (*vaporetto no.12; no.14 takes twice as long*), this small island was once a serious rival to Venice herself. According to legend, its history began when God ordered the bishop of *Altinum*, a Roman town north of Mestre, to take his flock away from the heretical Lombards into the Lagoon. The new island town developed quickly, and for the first few centuries seems to have been the real metropolis of the Lagoon, with 20,000 inhabitants, palaces, a mercantile fleet and five townships; but malaria decimated the population, the *Sile* silted up Torcello's corner of the Lagoon, and the rising star of Venice drew its citizens to the Rialto.

Torcello is now a ghost island overgrown with weeds, its palaces either sunk into the marsh or quarried for their stone, its narrow paths all that remain of once bustling thoroughfares. One of these follows a canal from the landing stage past the picturesque Ponte del Diavolo to the grass-grown piazza in front of the magnificent Veneto-Byzantine **Cathedral of Santa Maria Assunta**, with its lofty campanile, founded in 639 and rebuilt in the Ravenna basilica-style in 1008. It is the oldest building in the Lagoon, and one of the most impressive.

The interior (*open daily 10.30–6; adm*) has the finest mosaics in Venice, all done by 11th- and 12th-century Greek artists, from the wonderful floor, to the spectacular, potent *Last Judgement* on the west wall and the unsettling, heart-rending *Teotoco*, the stark, gold-ground mosaic of the thin, weeping Virgin portrayed as the 'bearer of God'.

Next to the cathedral is one of the finest late-Byzantine churches still in existence, the 11th-century octagonal **Santa Fosca**, surrounded by an attractive portico. Near here stands an ancient stone throne called the **Chair of Attila**, though the details of its connection with the Hunnish supremo are suspiciously nebulous. Across from the cathedral the two main surviving secular buildings of Torcello, the Palazzo del Consiglio and Palazzo dell'Archivio, contain the small **Museo dell'Estuario** (*open daily 10–12.30 and 2–4; closed Mon and hols; adm*), with archaeological finds and artefacts from Torcello's former churches.

Cavallino and Jesolo

One suspects these beach resorts north of Venice owe part of their success to their total *lack* of any cultural 'obligations'. On the other hand, they have every facility for fun, from windsurfers and rollerblades to hire, water parks and even covered *bocce* courts. Two ports are linked to

Venice: **Punta Sabbioni** (*vaporetto no.14, from Riva degli Schiavoni*) and **Treporti** (*vaporetto no.12, the last port after Torcello, Murano and Burano*); frequent buses ply the strip between Jesolo and Punta Sabbioni. The **Litorale del Cavallino**, the 10km sliver of land that protects the northern part of the Lagoon, was long known as a semi-wild place of dunes and pine forests. There are still a few, among its 28 camping grounds and umpteen hotels and restaurants. **Lido di Jesolo**, north from Punta Sabbioni, is even more densely packed, attracting some six million tourists a year with its wide sandy beach; because of the Adriatic's periodic pollution problems, nearly all hoteliers have installed pools.

The Veneto

Memories of Venice are strong in the Veneto, but each city has a distinct personality, formed in the rambunctious Middle Ages when they were independent *comuni*. Padua, the brain of the Veneto, has nearly as much fine art as Venice, as well as a saint that in modern polls beats Mark hands down. Petrarch practically invented villa life when he retired to the Euganean Hills. Vicenza, the city of Palladio, is full of architectural bravura, with a score of famous villas within an hour's drive; Verona, the city of the Scaliger, is a rosy tinted medieval beauty on the Adige. The little minor art capital of Rovigo rules the Po flatlands; Treviso and its canals is a Venice in miniature; Belluno enjoys a beautiful setting in the foothills of the Dolomites.

From Venice to Padua: Villas along the Brenta

In *The Merchant of Venice*, Portia, disguised as a young lawyer, left her villa of Belmont on the Brenta Canal and boated down to Venice to preserve Antonio's pound of flesh. For about the same price you can trace her route in a day-long excursion on the stately, villa-lined Brenta in a modern version of the famous canal boat, the *Burchiello* (*end-March–end-Oct Tues, Thurs and Sat from Venice, Wed, Fri and Sun from Padua*). The journey may be booked through any travel agent or CIT office abroad, or in Padua (*see* p.342). Price includes admission into the three villas open to the public, lunch, guide, and coach back to the city of origin. You can also follow the Brenta, less romantically and far less expensively, along the S11, by car or the half-hourly bus to Padua from Piazzale Roma. However, to reach La Malcontenta you must take a different bus from Piazzale Roma that leaves only once an hour.

Often called an extension of the Grand Canal, the Brenta Canal was one of the choicest locations for Venetian patricians to go a-squiring in the country, and still be within easy communication with the city; over seventy villas lie on or just off the waterway. One of the first is Palladio's celebrated Villa Foscari (1560), or **La Malcontenta**, named, they say, for Foscari's wife, the sad lady in one of the frescoes (*between Fusina and Oriago; open April–Oct Tues and Sat 9–12 or by appointment, © 041 520 3966; adm exp; guided tours*). La Malcontenta epitomizes the classical dream world of the Renaissance and harmonic proportions that Palladio understood better than any other. Viewed from the canal, the villa is a vision begging for Scarlett O'Hara to sweep down the steps—not by chance: Palladio's *Quattro Libri dell'Architettura* was the Bible for the 18th-century builders in America.

Further up the canal, **Mira Ponte** is the site of the 18th-century **Villa Widmann-Foscari** (*guided tours Tues–Sun 9–6; adm exp*). If you only have time for one villa, don't make it this one—redone soon after its construction in the French Baroque style, the villa contains some of its original furniture and bright, gaudy murals by two of Tiepolo's pupils, but not much of real interest. Mira's post office occupies the **Palazzo Foscarini**, Byron's address from 1817 to 1819, while working on the fourth Canto of *Childe Harold*.

The grandest villa in the Veneto is further up at Stra: the **Villa Nazionale** (or **Pisani**), enlarged by Alvise Pisani to celebrate his election as Doge in 1735 (*guided tours June–Sept Tues–Sun 9–6; Oct–May Tues–Sun 9–1.30; adm*). Modelled after Versailles, it was completed in 1760, then purchased by Napoleon in 1807 for his viceroy in Italy Eugène Beauharnais; in 1934 Mussolini chose it as a suitable stage for his first meeting with Hitler. Inside, the villa has lost most of its decoration, but the ballroom makes up for the boredom with one of Giambattista Tiepolo's shimmering *Apotheosis of the Pisani Family*, a fresco as lovely as its subject matter is ridiculous. The park contains one of Italy's most fiendish garden mazes.

Padua

Although only half an hour from Venice, Padua (Padova) refuses to be overshadowed by the old dowager by the sea, and can rightly claim its own place among Italy's most interesting and historic cities. Nicknamed *La Dotta*, 'The Learned', it is home to one of Europe's oldest universities, founded in 1221 and attended by Petrarch, Dante and Galileo. Padua's churches, under the brushes of Giotto, Altichiero, Giusto de' Menabuoi and Mantegna, were virtual laboratories in the evolution of fresco. But what Padua attracts most of all are pilgrims of a more pious nature; its exotic landmark, a seven-domed mosque of a basilica, is the last resting place of St Anthony of Padua, whom the locals call simply *Il Santo*, the Saint. Although the northern half of Padua was bombed in the last war, some of the arcaded southern streets could still serve as a stage for *The Taming of the Shrew*, which Shakespeare set in this lively, student-filled city.

Getting There

Padua is easily reached by **train** from Venice, Bologna, Vicenza and other cities on the Milan–Venice line. Outside the station a booth dispenses tickets for the city buses. The **bus station** is a 10-minute walk away in Piazzale Boschetti, Via Trieste 40, ✆ 049 820 6844, with buses every half-hour to Venice, and good connections to Vicenza, Treviso, Este, Monsélice, Bassano and Rovigo. For the Venice–Padua **Burchiello launch** down the Brenta Canal (*see* above), contact Siamic Express, Via Trieste 42, ✆ 049 660 944, ✆ 049 662 830, *siamic@tin.it*

Tourist Information

Riviera Mugnai 8, ✆ 049 875 0655, ✆ 049 650 794, *apt@padovanet.it* Also in the railway station, ✆ 049 875 2077 (*open Mon–Sat 9–6, Sun 9–12*). If you plan to do the main attractions in Padua, save money with a **Biglietto Unico**, available from any one of the participating sites.

Giotto's Cappella degli Scrovegni and the Museo Civico Eremitani

Padua deserves at least a day but, if you only have a couple of hours, it's a short walk from the bus or railway station to the jewel in its crown: Giotto's extraordinary, recently restored frescoes in the **Cappella degli Scrovegni** (or *Madonna dell'Arena*), a church sheltered by the crusty shell of Padua's Roman amphitheatre. Enter with the same ticket as the adjacent **Museo Civico Eremitani** (*both open 9–6, till 7 in summer; closed Mon; adm exp*).

Piazzale
Stazione VIA DELLA PACE
VIA DELLA PACE
VIA FRA PAOLO SARPI
VIA PILADE BRONZETTI
VIA BEATO PELLEGRINO
VIA RAGGIO DI SOLE
Piazzale
Mazzini
VIA GIOTTO
VIALE CODALUNGA
CORSO DEL POPOLO
VIA U. FOSCOLO NICCOLO
TOMMASEO
Santa Maria
del Carmine
Pza.
Petrarca
TRIESTE Giardini
dell'Arena
Pza.
Boschetti
Porta
Savonarola
VIA D. CAMPAGNOLA
VIA SAVONAROLA
Cappella degli
Scrovegni
Museo
Civico
Canale
Piovego
RIV. MUGNAI
LARGO
EUROPA
CORSO GARIBALDI
VIA DANTE
VIA S. PIETRO
VIA BENEDETTO
Ple
S. Benedetto
MILANO
Piazza
Insurrez-
ione
Scuola di
San Rocco/
S. Lucia
Eremitani
Pza
Garibaldi
Porta
Altinate
CASSAN PORCIGLIA
VIA G. B. MORGAGNI
VIA CORSO
ORSINI
VIA VOLTURNO
VIA NICCOLO
Palazzo del Capitanio
e Torre dell'Orologio
VIA S.
LUCIA
Pza
Signori
Caffè
Pedrocchi
Pza
Cavour
Pza Frutti
VIA DEGLI ZABARELLA
VIA ALTINATE
VIA G. B. BELZONI
Loggia della
Gran Guardia
Municipio
Santa Sofia
VIA G. FALLOPPIO
VIA MILAZZO
VIA RIVIERA
VIA DEI TADI
Duomo e
Battistero
Pza
Duomo
Palazzo
della
Ragione
Pza
Erbe
8 FEBBRAIO
RIV. DEI PONTI ROMANI
VIA S. SOFIA
VIA SORIO
Porta
San Giovanni
RIVIERA P. PALEOCAPA
VIA DEL VESCOVADO
VIA S. ROSA
VIA MARSALA
VIA ROMA
RIV. TITO LIVIO
VIA ANTENORE
Palazzo
del Bò
VIA DEL SANTO
VIA SAN FRANCESCO
VIA CERNAIA
VIA EUGANEA
VIA S. G. BARBARIGO
Pza
Castello
VIA 20 SETTEMBRE
VIA S. CHIARA
RIV. RUZANTE
Loggia e
Odeo Cornaro
VIA Del Santo CESAROTTI
VIA OSPEDALE CIVILE
La
Specola
VIA UMBERTO
RIV. BUZANTE
Statue of
Gattamelata
VIA GATTAMELATA
VIA P. PAOLI
VIA A. CAVALLETTO
VIA R. MARIN
VIA CESARO
VIA B. L. BELUDI
Basilica di
Sant'Antonio
VIA JACOPO
FACCIOLATI
VIA GUGLIELMO MARCONI
VIA S. MARIA
VIA LUIGI CADORNA
CORSO VITTORIO EMANUELE II
Orto
Botanico
Prato
Della
Valle
VIA CAVAZZANA
VIA MICHELE SANMICHELI
VIA ALESSANDRO
VIA GOITTO
Piazzale
S. Croce
Porta
Santa Croce
VIA 58 FANTERIA
Basilica di
Santa Giustina
VIA GIORDANO BRUNO
VIALE FELICE CAVALLOTTI
VIA A. COSTA

N

500 metres
500 yards

Padua

343

The chapel was built by Enrico Scrovegni in 1303, in expiation for the sins of his father, Reginaldo the usurer. Fortunately, he left enough money behind for Enrico to commission Giotto, then at the height of his career, to fresco the interior with a New Testament cycle (1304–07). In sheer power and inspiration, Giotto's masterpiece was as revolutionary in its day as Michelangelo's Sistine Chapel would be 200 years later—a fresh, natural narrative composition, with three-dimensional figures solidly anchored in their setting. Dante visited Giotto while he worked, and as a compliment placed Reginaldo in the seventh ring of the *Inferno* (Canto XVII). Giotto, however, had no doubt where he was going; you'll find him fourth from the left in the front row of the elect in the *Last Judgement*.

Padua's vast **Museo Civico**, installed in the adjacent convent of the Eremitani, combines archaeology (coins and vases from the Veneto, and 14 rare funerary *stelae* from the 6th to 1st centuries BC) and acres of fine art. Here you'll find Giotto's *Crucifixion*, designed for the altar of the Cappella Scrovegni, works by his follower Guariento, founder of the medieval Paduan school, and others by nearly every Venetian who ever applied brush to canvas: Bellini, Tintoretto, Titian, Vivarini, Veronese, Tiepolo and down the line. Don't miss what must be the most camp portrait in all Italy: the 17th-century *Venetian Captain* by Sebastiano Mazzoni, framed among cupids, lions and a giant artichoke. The small Renaissance bronzes that fill the halls were a speciality of Padua, especially those by Il Riccio (Andrea Briosco).

Next to the museum, the church of the **Eremitani** (1306; *open Mon–Sat 8.15–12.15 and 4–6, Sun 9.30–12 and 4–6*) was shattered in an air raid in 1944. What could be salvaged of the frescoes has been painstakingly pieced together, most importantly Andrea Mantegna's remarkable Ovetari chapel, frescoed from 1454 to 1457 when he was in his early twenties; *The Martyrdom of S Christopher and St James* still astonishes, thanks to Mantegna's depiction of the cold might of Rome, and his wizardly use of perspective to foreshorten the action from below. Padua's oldest church, the 9th-century **Santa Sofia**, is to the east at the corner of Via S. Sofia and Via Altinate; much rebuilt in the 11th century, it has a lovely Byzantine apse.

Central Padua: The University and Palazzo della Ragione

A short walk from the Eremitani will take you to Piazza Cavour, the historic heart of Padua and site of what resembles an Egyptian-revival mausoleum with columned stone porches at either end. This is the **Caffè Pedrocchi**, built in 1831 by Giuseppe Jappelli, and famous in its day for never closing (it couldn't—it had no doors) and for the intellectuals and students who came here to debate the revolutionary politics of Mazzini. In Jappelli's adjacent neo-Gothic, bullet-scarred **Pedrocchino**, students turned words into deeds in 1848, clashing with the Austrian police.

Cater-corner on Via VIII Febbraio is the seat of the **University of Padua**, the 16th-century **Palazzo del Bo'** ('of the ox'), a nickname derived from a tavern that stood here in 1221. Galileo delivered his lectures from its old wooden pulpit; the Great Hall is coated with the arms of its alumni, and the claustrophobic **Anatomical Theatre** (1594) is believed to be the first permanent one anywhere, designed by Fabricius, tutor of William Harvey, who went on to discover the circulation of blood. Other professors included Vesalius, author of the first original work on anatomy since Galen (1555), and Gabriello Fallopio, discoverer of the Fallopian tubes (*guided tours Mar–Sept Tues, Thurs 9, 10 and 11,Wed, Tues and Fri 3, 4 and 5; adm*).

Around the corner, **Piazza Antenore** has two sarcophagi for a centrepiece. The one on columns supposedly contains what remains of Antenor, hero of the Trojan War and founder of ancient *Patavium*, according to the great Roman historian Livy. Livy himself was born in the nearby Euganean Hills, and the other sarcophagus commemorates his 2000th birthday. Perhaps he'll get something nicer for his 3000th!

Opposite the Palazzo del Bò and behind the 16th-century **Municipio**, with its uncomfortable fascist-era façade, the delightful **Piazza delle Erbe** and **Piazza delle Frutta** still see bustling markets every morning. They are separated by the massive **Palazzo della Ragione** (*open daily 9–6; closed Mon; adm*). Constructed as Padua's law courts in 1218 and then rebuilt in 1306, its upper storey, or *Il Salone*, is one of the largest medieval halls in existence, measuring 260ft by 88ft, the 85-ft ceiling like a 'vaulting over a market square', as Goethe described it. Its great hull-shaped roof was rebuilt after a fire in 1756—an earlier blaze, in 1420, destroyed the frescoes by Giotto, which were replaced a few years later with over 300 biblical and astrological scenes by Niccolò Miretto. Exhibitions are frequently staged in the Salone, but two exhibits never change: the *pietra del vituperio*, a cold stone block where debtors were made to sit bare-bottomed, and a giant **wooden horse**, built for a joust in 1466, its fierce glance complemented by testicles the size of bowling balls.

Just to the west, Padua's stately **Piazza dei Signori** saw many a joust in its day, and can still boast Italy's oldest astronomical clock, built by Giovanni Dondi (1344) in the tower of the **Palazzo del Capitaniato**. On the left is the fine Lombard-style **Loggia della Gran Guardia** (1523), while behind Dondi's clock you'll find the university's Arts Faculty, the **Liviano**, built in 1939 by Gio Ponti. The Da Carrara, Padua's medieval *signori*, lived here in the 1300s, and the Liviano incorporates their palace's **Sala dei Giganti** and its giant frescoes of ancient Romans, repainted by Domenico Campagnola in the 1530s; Altichiero added the more intimate 14th-century portrait of Petrarch sitting at his desk. Around the corner from the square stands Padua's rather neglected **duomo**, begun in the 12th century but tampered with throughout the Renaissance—Michelangelo was only one of several cooks who spoiled the broth here before everyone lost interest. The **baptistry** (*open daily 9.30–1 and 3–6; adm*), however, was beautifully frescoed by Florentine Giusto de' Menabuoi in the 1370s. The dome, with its multitude of saints in the circles of paradise, is awesome, but chilling.

St Anthony, Donatello, and the Biggest Square in Italy

Below the commercial heart of Padua rise the exotic domes of the **Basilica di Sant'Antonio** (*open daily 6.30am–7pm*). St Anthony of Padua was a Portuguese missionary inspired by St Francis, who was shipwrecked in Italy *en route* to the heathen lands, but stayed, preached, and was canonized only ten months after his death, in 1232. The basilica was begun in the same year and finished the following century. For pure fantasy it is comparable only to St Mark's, a cluster of seven domes around a lofty, conical cupola, two octagonal *campanili* and two smaller minarets—perhaps not what a friar vowed to poverty might have ordered, but certainly a sign of the esteem in which he is held.

Inside pilgrims queue patiently to press their palm against his tomb and to study the votive testimonials and photos (happy babies, wrecked cars) thanking the busy saint, who also runs Heaven's Lost Property Office. No one pays much attention to the 16th-century marble reliefs lining St Anthony's chapel, although they are exquisite works of the Venetian Renaissance: the fourth and fifth are by Sansovino, the sixth and seventh by Tullio Lombardo, and the last by Antonio Lombardo. Behind the chapel, the **Cappella di Conti** has richly coloured frescos by Giusto de' Menabuoi (1382).

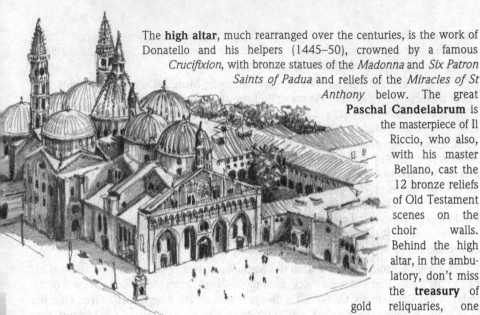

The **high altar**, much rearranged over the centuries, is the work of Donatello and his helpers (1445–50), crowned by a famous *Crucifixion*, with bronze statues of the *Madonna* and *Six Patron Saints of Padua* and reliefs of the *Miracles of St Anthony* below. The great **Paschal Candelabrum** is the masterpiece of Il Riccio, who also, with his master Bellano, cast the 12 bronze reliefs of Old Testament scenes on the choir walls. Behind the high altar, in the ambulatory, don't miss the **treasury** of gold reliquaries, one containing Anthony's tongue and larynx, found perfectly intact when his tomb was opened in 1981. In the right transept, the **Cappella di San Felice** contains more beautiful frescoes and a remarkable *Crucifixion*, painted in the 1380s by Altichiero. The basilica complex includes several other exhibitions and museums: one, the **Museo Antoniano** (*open daily 9–1 and 2–5; closed Mon; adm*) houses art made for the basilica over the centuries, including a lunette frescoed by Mantegna and a delightful 15th-century German reliquary in the shape of a ship.

Sharing the large piazza in front of the basilica, a bit lost among the pigeons and souvenir stands, is one of the key works of the Renaissance, Donatello's **statue of Gattamelata** (1453), the first large equestrian bronze since antiquity. The cool 'Honeyed Cat' *condottiere* from Narni, Umbria served Venice so well and honestly that the usually tightwadded Republic paid for this monument, which Donatello imbibed with a serene humanistic spirit, in marked contrast to Verrocchio's arrogant Colleoni statue in Venice. Flanking the piazza opposite Gattamelata, the **Oratorio di San Giorgio** (*closed for restoration*) has beautiful frescoes by two heirs of Giotto: Altichiero and Jacopo Avanzi. You can, however, visit the adjacent **Scuoletta del Santo**, with paintings on the *Life of St Anthony* by a variety of artists in the panelled upstairs room, including some, certainly not the best, by a teenage Titian (*open summer daily 9–1 and 2.30–6.30; winter 10–1 and 2–5; closed Mon; adm*).

A few streets south of Piazza del Santo, the **Orto Botanico** (*open April–Sept Mon–Sat 9–1 and 3–6; Oct–Mar 9–1; adm*) is Europe's oldest botanical garden, established in 1545; it retains the original layout, and even a few original specimens. At 'Goethe's palm', planted in 1585 and still flourishing, the poet speculated on his Theory of the Ur-plant, that all plants evolved from one universal specimen. Beyond, 'Italy's largest piazza', the **Prato della Valle** (1775), does service as parking lot and pantheon for 78 illustrious men (and one woman) associated with Padua. On one side stands the **Basilica of Santa Giustina** (*open daily 7.30–12* *and 3.30–7.30*), designed by Il Riccio, its domes similar to St Anthony's, but its façade unfinished and its interior still-born Baroque, if brightened by a Veronese altarpiece; don't miss, off the right aisle, the 5th-century **Sacellum di San Prosdocimo**.

Activities

Thanks to the students, there's always something happening. The tourist office's bi-monthly *Padova Today* lists events; every summer a series of concerts, exhibitions, open-air films and shows takes place. The Prato della Valle sees a large general market every Saturday, and an antique market every third Sunday of the month.

Padua ✉ 35100   **Where to Stay and Eating Out**

Note that the best restaurants in the centre are linked to hotels.

You can't miss the ★★★★**Donatello**, Via del Santo 102, ✆ 049 875 0634, 🖷 049 8675 0829 (*expensive*), by the basilica of Sant'Antonio—Donatello's *Gattamelata* points right to it.

Also in the historic centre, the newer, more comfortable ★★★★**Majestic Toscanelli**, Via dell'Arco 2, ✆ 049 663 244, 🖷 049 876 0025 (*expensive*) has every luxury, and a popular restaurant specializing in Brazilian dishes. ★★★★**Grande Italia**, Corso del Popolo 81, ✆ 049 876 111, 🖷 049 875 0850 (*expensive*) is in a beautiful Liberty building, conveniently opposite the railway station.

Small and cosy, ★★★**Leon Bianco**, Piazzetta Pedrocchi 12, ✆ 049 875 0814, 🖷 049 875 6184 (*moderate*) is right in the heart of Padua; from its roof terrace, where breakfast is served in summer, you can look down on the Caffè Pedrocchi. Cheaper and near the station, friendly ★★★**Al Cason**, Via Paolo Scarpi 40, ✆ 049 66236, 🖷 049 875 4217 (*moderate*) will make you feel at home, and fill you up with the classics in its restaurant.

★★**Sant'Antonio**, Via S. Fermo 118, ✆ 049 875 1393, 🖷 049 875 2508 (*cheap*), by the Porta Molino between the station and the centre, has a friendly, family atmosphere. ★**Pavia**, Via del Papafava 11, ✆ 049 661 558 (*cheap*) is deservedly popular, clean, central and friendly. The large, pleasant, city-run **Ostello Città di Padova** is at Via Aleardi 30, ✆ 049 875 2219, 🖷 049 654 210; IYHF cards required. To get there, take bus nos.3, 8 or 11 from the station to the Prato della Valle.

Not far from the centre, **Antico Brolo**, Corso Milano 22, ✆ 049 66455 (*expensive*) occupies an elegant 15th-century *palazzo* with a garden for outdoor dining; try the Chateaubriand with balsamic vinegar (*tourist menu L50,000*). *Closed Mon and Sun lunch, and some of Aug.* There's a good, much cheaper, pizzeria in the wine cellar.

At Torre, 2km from the Padua-Est *autostrada* exit, **Dotto di Campagna** Via Randaccio, ✆ 049 625 469 (*moderate*) offers elegant surroundings and cookery based on the finest ingredients; try their *risotti* or *pasta fagioli*. Tourist menu L38,000. *Closed Sun eve, Mon and Aug.* For classic Paduan homecooking, the crowds venture out to **Da Giovanni**, Via Maroncelli 22, ✆ 049 772 620 (*moderate*) (bus no.9 from the railway station). The homemade pasta is good, and so are the free-range capons. *Closed Sat lunch, Sun, and Aug.*

For 150 years, **Bertolini**, Via Antichiero 162, ✆ 049 600 357 (*cheap*), just north of the station, has been a favourite; go for the hearty vegetarian and seasonal dishes and homemade desserts. *Closed Sat.* Just outside Padua's western walls (take Corso Milano from the centre), **Bastioni del Moro**, Via Bronzetti 18, ✆ 049 871 006 (*cheap*) has had a recent facelift and serves up a delicious gnocchi with scallops and porcini mushrooms, although prices soar if you order fish; tourist menu L25,000. *Closed Sun.*

South of Padua: the Euganean Hills and Around

The landscape south of Padua is as flat as any of the prairies of the Po, with the exception of the lush Euganean Hills, a retreat of poets and the world-weary since Roman times; dotted with villas, spas, walking trails and country restaurants, they remain Padua's favourite playground. South of the hills wait a handsome trio of medieval towns: Monsélice, Este and Montagnana—all 'with pasts'—as people used to say of women who dared to have fun.

Getting Around

The Euganean Hills are easiest reached by **bus** from Padua. There are also regular **trains** from Padua to Monsélice, Este, Montagnana and Rovigo, which take about the same time as the buses, although you may have to change at Monsélice; trains via Montagnana continue to Mantua. Buses from Monsélice go to Arquà Petrarca.

Tourist Information

Ábano Terme: Via Pietro d'Abano 18, ✆ 049 866 9055, ⌨ 049 866 9053. **Montegrotto Terme**: Viale della Stazione 60, ✆ 049 793 384, ⌨ 049 795 276. **Monsélice**: Piazza Mazzini, ✆ 0429 72380. **Este**: Piazza Maggiore, ✆ 0429 3635 (with bikes to hire). **Montagnana**: Piazza V. Emanuele, ✆ 0429 81320.

The Euganean Hills

As soon as you leave Padua you'll spot them: the *Colli Euganei*, ancient volcanic islands, once surrounded by sea and now basking in the middle of the plain. Fertile, well-watered and defensible, they attracted the region's first settlers, the Paeloveneti, who made Este their chief stronghold. A few thousand years later, the Romans discovered the two key secrets of the Euganean Hills: wine (now DOC Colli Euganei) and hot mud. Livy, Suetonius and Martial all recommended the virtues of their springs, which flow from the ground at 87°C, and they have been appreciated ever since: some 130 hotels built over thermal swimming pools provide health or beauty cures at **Ábano Terme** and **Montegrotto Terme**, where the old Roman spa has been excavated. At nearby **Torréglia**, the vast **Villa dei Vescovi** (*open Mar–Nov Mon, Wed and Fri 10.30–12.30 and 2–6; adm*), was designed by Giovanni Maria Falconetto (1579) for holidaying bishops, and was a major influence on Palladio.

From Torréglia, there's a road west to **Teolo**, Livy's birthplace. Because of their unusual micro-climate, the Euganean Hills are home to some interesting flora, now protected in a regional park; from Teolo you can join a 42km circular nature trail around the district or visit the Benedictine **Abbazia di Praglia**, founded in 1117 but given the full Renaissance treatment by Tullio Lombardo, Bartolomeo Montagna, Giambattista Zelotti and others (*tours given by the monks every half hour: winter daily 2.30–4.30; summer daily 3.30–5.30; closed Mon*).

South of Torréglia towards Galzignano Terme, the **Villa Barbarigo** at **Valsanzibio** (*open daily 9–12 and 2–7.30, till sunset in winter; adm exp*) has the grandest gardens in the Veneto, laid out in the mid 1600s in the style of the Tivoli Gardens near Rome, with fountains, waterfalls, nymphaeums, pools and another wicked garden maze. Beyond, medieval **Arquà Petrarca** is the gem of the Euganean Hills, where the world-weary Petrarch, accompanied by his daughter Francesca and his stuffed cat, Laura II, retired in 1370. His charming villa, the **Casa del Petrarca** (*open daily 9–12.30 and 3–7; adm*), preserves much of its 14th-century furnishings; with the exception of a radio mast, the view from the poet's study remains the same. Petrarch died here in 1374, and now occupies a marble sarcophagus in front of the church.

Monsélice, Este and Montagnana

Spilling like an opera set down the southern slopes of the Euganean Hills, the natural citadel of **Monsélice** was first fortified by the Romans, and in 1239 by Ezzelino da Romano, the cruel tyrant of the Veneto. His beautifully restored Ca' Marcello is now part of the **Castello Cini** (*open April–11 Nov; guided tours daily at 9, 10, 11, 2, 3 and 4; summer daily at 9, 10, 11, 3, 4 and 5; adm*) and houses a superb collection of medieval and Renaissance arms and antiques. The castle lies near the base of Vincenzo Scamozzi's striking **Via Sacra delle Sette Chiese** (1605), zigzagging up the hill, past the sumptuous **Villa Nani**, the Romanesque **Duomo**, seven **chapels** built by Scamozzi and frescoed by Palma Giovane, and the elegant 16th-century **Villa Duodo** and **Esedra di San Francesco Saverio**, also by Scamozzi, now a university centre of hydraulic studies. A path continues up to the **Rocca,** built over a Lombard fort by Frederick II, Ezzelino's boss (*recently opened for visits Sat and Sun; to book, call © 0429 72931*).

Monsélice's old rival, **Este** (ancient *Ateste*), is only 9km to the west; its name was adopted by its 11th-century rulers, who moved on to greater glory in Ferrara. Like Monsélice, Este was a hotly contested piece of real estate, and bristles with the towers of the 1339 **Castello dei Carraresi**, now put out to pasture in a public garden. Abutting the garden, the 16th-century Palazzo Mocenigo houses the excellent **Museo Nazionale Atestino** (*open daily 9–7; adm*), covering the Paleoveneto civilization from the 10th century BC up to Roman times: don't miss the outstanding 7th-century BC *Situla Benvenuti*, a bronze vase decorated with warriors and fantastic animals; a superb collection of 6th–5th-century BC bronzes; and, a bit out of place, a luscious red-dressed *Madonna and Child* by Cima da Conegliano. Behind the castle, the **Villa De Kunkler** was Byron's residence from 1817 to 1818; here Shelley, his guest, penned *Lines written among the Euganean Hills*, after the death of his little daughter, Clara. Don't miss the startlingly tilted 12th-century campanile of **San Martino**, just off Piazza Maggiore, and Giambattista Tiepolo's altarpiece of *Santa Tecla versus the Plague* in the **duomo**.

Montagnana, 15km to the west, boasts some of the best-preserved medieval fortifications in Italy, the handiwork of Ezzelino da Romano and Padua's Carrara family. The walls extend two kilometres, defended by 24 intact towers—impressive but not effective; Venice lost and regained the town 13 times during the War of the Cambrai. The walls now form a picturesque backdrop to Montagnana's colourful Palio in September. Jutting out asymmetrically in the main piazza, the **duomo** has a portal by Sansovino, a *Transfiguration* by Veronese and a huge, anonymous painting of *The Battle of Lepanto*. Palladio mavens won't want to miss his **Palazzo Pisani**, by the Porto Padova.

Where to Stay and Eating Out

Ábano Terme ✉ 35031

All of the spa hotels in the Euganean Hills have private mineral-water pools, therapists and gardens, but none can match the class of Giuseppe Jappelli's 1825 ★★★★★**Grand Hotel Orologio**, Viale delle Terme 66, ✆ 049 866 9111, 🖷 049 866 9841 (*very expensive*), with a large park and landscaped pools that attract many guests seeking pampered tranquillity instead of magic mud. *Closed Dec–Feb*. The friendly ★★★**Verdi**, Via F. Busonera 200, ✆ 049 667 600, 🖷 049 667 025 (*moderate*) offers more pools and mud, for a quarter of the price. In nearby Torréglia, join the Paduans at their favourite traditional country restaurants: **Da Taparo**, Via Castelletto 42, ✆ 049 521 1060 (*moderate*) has a beautiful terrace overlooking the hills. *Closed Mon*. **Antica Trattoria Ballotta**, Via Carromatto 2, ✆ 049 521 2970, 🖷 049 521 1385 (*moderate*) has been in business since 1605. *Closed Tues*.

Arquà Petrarca ✉ 35032

At lovely **La Montanella**, Via Costa 33, ✆ 0429 718 200 (*expensive–moderate*), you can enjoy not only the garden and view over the village itself, but exquisite *risotti* and duck with fruit; select your wine, olive oil and vinegar from special menus. *Closed Tues eve, Wed, 2 weeks each in Aug, and Jan*.

Monsélice ✉ 35043

Modern ★★★**Ceffri Villa Corner**, Via Orti 7, ✆ 0429 783 111, 🖷 0429 783 100 (*moderate*) has a pool and well-equipped rooms, and a good restaurant featuring home-made pasta with a L30,000 tourist menu. Fungi fiends head to elegant **La Torre**, Piazza Mazzini 14, ✆ 0429 73752 (*moderate; expensive for truffles*) for gratification. *Closed Sun eve, Mon, and part of July and Aug*.

Montagnana ✉ 35044

★★★**Aldo Moro**, Via G. Marconi 27, ✆ 0429 81351, 🖷 0429 82842 (*moderate*) has fine rooms by the cathedral, and a good restaurant serving the local *prosciutto dolce del montagnanese*. IYHF card-holders can stay in the magnificent **Rocca degli Alberi Youth Hostel** ('Tree Castle'), at the Legnano Gate, built in 1362, ✆ 0429 81076, 🖷 0429 070 266 (*cheap*). *Closed mid-Oct–Mar*. Trattoria **Da Stona**, Via Carrarese 51, ✆ 0429 81532 (*cheap*) has tasty homecooking, *prosciutto dolce* and local wines; tourist menu L19,000. *Closed Mon*.

Little Mesopotamia

About 20km south of Monsélice, Rovigo is the capital of the province wedged between the mighty Adige and the mightier Po, known as the Polèsine or 'Little Mesopotamia'. Like ancient Mesopotamia it has been blessed and cursed by its rivers, which make it fertile but often spill over their banks, while miles of silt have left its ancient capital Adria high and dry.

Getting Around

From Rovigo there are frequent **buses** to Adria and the Delta towns; **trains** also run from Rovigo to Adria and Chioggia, Ferrara and Bologna. Rovigo's **bus station** is on the Piazzale G. di Vittorio; the **railway station** is on the Piazza Riconoscenza. The Palladian villa at Fratta Polèsine is accessible by bus from Rovigo (direction: Trecenta).

Tourist Information

Rovigo: Via J. H. Dunant 10, ✆ 0425 422 400, or ✆ 0425 361 481, ✆ 0425 30416.

Rovigo and Adria

The other inhabitants of the Veneto may sneer '*Rovigo no m'intrigo*', but this prosperous little provincial capital doesn't give a snap. For a landmark, Rovigo can match Bologna with its odd couple of leaning towers, the 11th-century **Torri Donà**, one tall, one stubby. Nearby (nothing is far), central Piazza Vittorio Emanuele II is a handsome trapezoid dotted with palaces, one containing the **Pinacoteca dell'Accademia dei Concordi** (*open Mon–Fri 9.30–12 and 3.30–7, Sat 9.30–12; July and Aug Mon–Sat 10–1*), founded by local scholars in 1580, with a fine collection of works by Giovanni Bellini, Lorenzo Lotto, Palma Vecchio and others.

From adjacent Piazza Garibaldi, follow Via Silvestri back to the octagonal **La Rotonda**, by Francesco Zamberlan, a pupil of Palladio, with a detached tower by Longhena and walls covered with 17th-century paintings glorifying Venetian bureaucrats.

From Rovigo it's 18km southwest to **Fratta Polèsine**, where Palladio's pretty temple-fronted **Villa Badoera** (1570) is now property of the city of Rovigo, with its frescoes of pseudo-Roman grotesques by Giallo Fiortino (*open April–Sept daily 10–12 and 3–7; Oct–Mar Tues–Sun 10–12 and 2–5; adm*).

Buses and trains from Rovigo also head east for **Adria**, a dusty place dominated by a radio mast, founded by the Etruscans and colonized by the Greeks in the 6th century BC, when it stood on the shore of the sea that took its name. The Venice of its day, Adria has but one canal now, and a **Museo Archeologico Nazionale**, Via G. Badini 59 (*open daily 9–7, Thurs, Fri and Sat also 8.30–11pm; adm*), with lovely Roman glass and a 3rd-century BC iron chariot of Gaulish workmanship, found entombed with three tiny horses.

The Po Delta

After travelling over 652km, the Po splits into six major branches, creating a reed-filled delta, a marshy wonderland of a thousand islets, filled with waterfowl and migratory birds from the north. Before its current status as the **Parco del Po**, a few resorts mushroomed up along the sandy, pine-shaded shores—namely **Rosolina Mare** and **Isola Albarella**, although both try hard to behave in an ecologically correct manner. There are several **boat cruises** to choose from that explore the delta, most of them departing from **Porto Tolle** or **Taglio di Po**; you can also arrange fishing outings. Contact the port authority in Porto Tolle, ✆ 0426 330 289.

Little Mesopotamia   351

Rovigo ✉ 45100

A few steps from the centre, the Liberty-style ★★★★**Villa Regina Margherita**, Viale Regina Margherita 6, ✆ 0425 361 540, 🖷 0425 31301, is the most stylish place to stay, with well-equipped rooms. **Tavernetta Dante dai Trevisani**, Corso del Popolo 212, ✆ 0425 26386 (*moderate*) serves that medieval Veneto favourite, *pappardelle all'anatra*, and other treats. *Closed Sun.*

The best place of all, however, is 8km south in Arquà Polèsine: **Degli Amici**, Via Quirina 4, ✆ 0425 91045 (*moderate*), where fresh and salt water fish share the menu with duck and goose, prepared in an old wood oven. *Closed Wed; in summer also closed Sat and Sun lunch.*

North of Padua: Up the Valley of the Brenta

Some of the Veneto's best-known sites are north of Padua, in the foothills of the Dolomites: Castelfranco, birthplace of Giorgione, and Àsolo, where the Queen of Cyprus held her fabled Renaissance court, and several outstanding villas, including Masèr, where Palladio and Veronese collaborated to create a unique work of art.

Getting Around

From Padua there are both **buses** and **trains** to Bassano del Grappa (40mins), via Castelfranco; from Vicenza change trains at Castelfranco, passing Cittadella on the way. From Venice, change in Treviso. From Castelfranco there are infrequent buses to Piombino Dese, on the local road to Venice.

From Bassano regular **buses** run to Possagno (roughly 30mins), which is also served by a bus from Castelfranco. Frequent buses on the Bassano–Treviso route serve Àsolo and Masèr; others, from Bassano and Vicenza, run to Maròstica (20 buses daily), Lonedo di Lugo, Thiene and Asiago. Bassano's **bus station** is in the Piazzale Trento, near the tourist office, ✆ 0424 30850; the **train station** is at the top of Via Chilesotti. Àsolo and Masèr are also linked by buses from Montebelluna.

Tourist Information

Castelfranco Veneto: Via Francesco Maria Preti 39, ✆ 0423 495 000.
Àsolo: Piazza G. D'Annunzio 2, ✆ 0423 529 046, 🖷 0423 524 137.

Castelfranco and Cittadella

Piombino Dese, just off the main SS307 from Padua to Castelfranco, is a sprawling rural *comune*, and a must-detour for Palladiophiles. Its 1554 **Villa Cornaro**, a block from the Piombino Dese train station (*open by appointment only, ✆ 0499 365 017*) is one of the master's most innovative and well-preserved structures, the first with a double loggia; inside, it was frescoed in 1717 by Mattia Bortoloni with biblical scenes. **Castelfranco Veneto**, further north, basks in the glory of having given the world Giorgione, in 1478. Big George in return gave Castelfranco a masterpiece: the **Duomo**'s *Castelfranco Madonna* (1504), a triangular composition of the Virgin, St Francis and the local soldier-saint Liberalis, their remote figures inhabiting the same ineffable, dreamlike world as his paintings in the Accademia in Venice. Next to the Duomo, the **Casa del Giorgione** (*open Tues–Sun 9–12 and 3–6; adm*) is deco-rated with a *chiaroscuro* frieze of scientific instruments attributed to Giorgione, and has copies of all the known works by this most elusive of painters.

Castelfranco itself is a walled city, built by Treviso in 1199 to counter the ambitions of Padua. The Paduans, tit for tat, founded the egg-shaped **Cittadella** 15km to the west; one tower in its mighty 13th-century walls was Ezzelino's infamous torture chamber (cf. *Paradiso* IX, 54). The Venetians added the fine lion with a kinky tail in the main square.

From Castelfranco you can also nip up to **Fanzolo**, 5km to the northeast, for another of Palladio's finest: **Villa Emo** (*open April–Sept daily 3–7, Sun and hols 10–12.30 and 3–7; Oct–Mar Sat and Sun only 2–6; adm exp*), and the only villa still owned by the family that commissioned it. Like most, this ranch was designed as a working farm, and was one of the first in Europe to grow maize (1536), used primarily to fatten pigeons before it was used for polenta to fatten Venetians. The main rooms were frescoed with brightly coloured mythologies by Giambattista Zelotti; the *barchesse* or storage wings are now a hotel (*see* below). Palladio also designed the long rows of workers' cottages that are slowly being restored.

Villa Barbaro at Masèr

Open Mar–Oct Tues, Sat, Sun and hols 3–6; Nov–Feb Sat and Sun 2.30–5; adm exp.

Montebelluna, also northeast of Castelfranco, was another favourite area for building summer villas, including the lovely Villa Barbaro at Masèr. Begun in 1568 for brothers Daniele and Marcantonio Barbaro (the former was Patriarch of Aquileia and one of Venice's most distin-guished humanistic scholars), Masèr is a unique synthesis of two great talents: Palladio and his friend Paolo Veronese.

Palladio taught Veronese about space and volume, and nowhere is this so evident as in these ravishing, architectonic, *trompe l'œil* frescoes, populated by the original owners and their pets, who linger as if the villa lay under the same spell as Sleeping Beauty's castle—an effect heightened by the slippers passed out to visitors at the door (to protect the original floors). Signora Barbaro and her sons gaze down from painted balconies; a little girl opens a door; a dog waits in a corner; painted windows offer views of imaginary landscapes; the huntsman in the far bedroom is Veronese, gazing across the row of rooms at his mistress.

Behind the villa, the nymphaeum is guarded by giants sculpted by Marcantonio himself. The striking, if crumbling, **Tempietto**, just across the road, is a miniature pantheon designed by Palladio in 1580 and decorated by Alessandro Vittoria.

Àsolo the 'Town of a Hundred Horizons'

The old walled hilltown of **Àsolo** was the consolation prize given by Venice in 1489 to Queen Caterina Cornaro after demanding her abdication from the throne of Cyprus. It could have been worse: Àsolo is one of the most enchanting spots in Italy, and Caterina's Renaissance court lent it a high degree of refinement and art. Pietro Bembo used it as a setting for his dialogues on love, *Gli Asolani*, and Giorgione strolled through its rose-gardens strumming his lute; the enforced idleness in Àsolo perhaps inspired his invention of art merely for the sake of pleasure. In the last century, Àsolo was also a beloved retreat of Robert Browning (his last volume of poems was entitled *Asolando*; 'Pippa Passes' was set here as well). Eleonora Duse and the great traveller Freya Stark lived and are buried here.

Some people never get beyond Àsolo's perfect piazza with its 16th-century **Fontana Maggiore**, but you can look at the **castello** with its watch tower (in both senses of the word—it tells the time) and what little remains of the garden where Queen Caterina lived in 'lace and poetry'; the courtyard has a modern *bocce* court. In 1700 the great hall was replaced with a theatre, but in 1930 the John Deere tractor heir bought and rebuilt it in his villa in Sarasota, Florida.

Near the castle, the frescoed **Loggia del Capitano** contains a museum dedicated to Queen Caterina, Browning and La Duse (*but closed until kingdom come for restoration*). The **Duomo** has works by Lotto, Jacopo da Bassano and Vivarini. For the famous view over Àsolo of 'a hundred horizons' climb (or drive—the road is halfway down the hill) up to the **Rocca**, built over a Roman fort (*open Sat and Sun; adm*).

Possagno, 10km north at the foot of Monte Grappa, was the birthplace of Antonio Canova (1757–1822), the ultimate neoclassical sculptor, the favourite of Napoleon and several popes. You can visit his house, and clay and plaster models, in the **Gypsoteca** (*open May–Sept Tues–Sun 9–12 and 3–6; Oct–April 9–12 and 2–5; adm*).

Most artists leave a work or two in their hometowns, but Canova left nothing less than a full-scale model of the Pantheon with the Parthenon stuck on front as his last resting place. The town itself describes the **Tempio** as 'one of the greatest monuments that man on earth has ever erected—in praise of God—to himself'. For L2000 you can climb up the dome (*open daily 9–12 and 2–5; closed Mon*); for free you can study the leaning bell tower, and try to figure out if it was built that way.

Where to Stay and Eating Out

Castelfranco Veneto ✉ 31033

★★★**Roma**, Via Fabio Filzi 39, ℭ 0423 721 616, ✆ 0423 721 515 (*moderate*) is outside the fortifications, but offers a good view of them. Next to the walls, **Alle Mura**, Via Preti 69, ℭ 0423 498 098 (*expensive–moderate*) is an elegant place, with well prepared seafood dishes, served in summer in a garden. *Closed Thurs*.

Just above Castelfranco at Salvarosa, you can also stay at little ★★★**Ca' delle Rose**, on the Circonvallazione Est, ℭ 0423 490 232, ✆ 0423 490 261 (*moderate*), and dine at its famous restaurant, **Barbesin**, ℭ 0423 490 446. The setting is as idyllic as the products of its kitchen, based entirely on fresh, seasonal ingredients; the veal with apples melts in your mouth. *Closed Wed eve and Thurs*.

In the same area, the hotel ★★★★**Fior**, Via dei Carpani 18, ℭ 0423 721 212, ✆ 0423 498 771 (*expensive*) occupies an old villa and park, with tennis, pool, sauna and all the trimmings.

Fanzolo ✉ 31050

Stay in the wing of Palladio's **★★★Villa Emo**, Via Stazione 5, ✆ 0423 476 414, ✉ 0423 487 043 (*expensive*): the handful of elegant rooms and suites come with a swimming pool in the grounds, peace and quiet guaranteed, and fine dining in the restaurant, open to non-guests (*expensive*). *Closed Mon, and Tues lunch.*

Àsolo ✉ 31011

Àsolo can boast one of Italy's most charming and romantic hotels, **★★★★★Villa Cipriani**, Via Canova 298, ✆ 0423 952 166, ✉ 0423 952 095 (*very expensive*), in a house dating from the 16th century that belonged to Robert Browning, decorated with Persian carpets owned by Eleonora Duse. The hotel has an enchanting garden filled with roses and song birds; some of its 32 rooms are located in its garden houses. The restaurant, in the tradition of Venice's Cipriani family, serves equally lovely meals.

Also in the centre, the famous **★★★★Al Sole**, Via Collegio 33, ✆ 0423 528 111, ✉ 0423 528 399 (*expensive*) has recently had a complete overhaul but hasn't lost any of its charm. One of Àsolo's oldest houses hosts the **Hosteria Ca' Derton**, Piazza D'Annunzio 11, ✆ 0423 52730 (*moderate*), featuring traditional specialities to match the setting. *Closed Mon.* Every celebrity that has passed through has had a drink at the **Caffè Centrale**, Via Roma 72; you should, too; it's a great place to watch the world go by.

Masèr and Around ✉ 31010

Just up the road from Palladio's villa, dine in enchanting surroundings at **Da Bastian**, Via Cornuda, ✆ 0423 565 400 (*moderate*); its pâté, risotto, tasty Venetian-style snails and desserts are renowned. *Closed Wed eve, Thurs, and some of Aug.*

Bassano del Grappa, Maròstica and Asiago

Carry on west for more Veneto essentials: Bassano del Grappa with its covered bridge, Maròstica, where they play chess with human players, more villas by Palladio and the mountains of Asiago. For getting around details *see* above p.352.

Tourist Information

Bassano: Largo Corona d'Italia 35, ✆ 0424 524 351, ✉ 0424 525 301.
Maròstica: Piazza Castello, ✆ 0424 72127, ✉ 0424 72800, *proloco@telemar.it*
Asiago: Via Stazione 5, ✆ 0424 462 661 ✉ 0424 462 445.

Bassano del Grappa

Sprawled over the foothills of the Alps where the Brenta begins its flow down the plain, the colourful bustling town of Bassano celebrated its first millennium in 1998. Palladio gets credit for its picturesque landmark, the **Ponte degli Alpini**, the unique covered wooden bridge. First constructed in 1599, the bridge has been rebuilt several times to the master's design—lastly in 1969, after it was swept away in the Brenta's flood. At one end, in the Palazzo Beltrame-Menarola, the grappa distillery Poli operates a **Museo della Grappa** where you can taste and buy (*open daily 9–1 and 2.30–7.30; closed Mon am*).

A Grappa Digression

Although a lot of grappa does come from Bassano del Grappa, its name doesn't derive from the town or its mountains, but from graspa, the residues left at the bottom of the wine vat after the must is removed; it can be drunk un-aged and white, or aged in oak barrels, where it takes on a rich, amber tone. First mentioned in a 12th-century chronicle, grappa, or *aqua vitae* ('the water of life'), was chugged down as a miracle-working concoction of earth and fire to dispel ill humours. In 1601 the Doge created a University Confraternity of Aqua Vitae to control quality; during the First World War, Italy's Alpine soldiers adopted Bassano's enduring bridge as their symbol and grappa as their drink. One of their captains described it perfectly:

Grappa is like a mule; it has no ancestors and no hope of descendants; it zigzags through you like a mule zigzags through the mountains; if you're tired you can hang on to it; if they shoot you can use it as a shield; if it's too sunny you can sleep under it; you can speak to it and it'll answer, cry and be consoled. And if you really have decided to die, it will take you off happily.

Bassano's centre is made up of a string of squares: medieval Piazzotto Montevecchio, where the old municipal pawn shop, or **Monte di Pietà**, is covered with the coats of arms of 120 Venetian *podestàs*. This is linked to piquant Piazza Libertà, hogged by the neoclassical façade of the mastodontic church of **San Giovanni**, while the next square, Piazza Garibaldi, is guarded, both physically and spiritually, by a medieval **Torre Civica** and the Gothic church of **San Francesco**. Its cloister contains the **Museo Civico** (*open Tues–Sat 9–6.30, Sun 3.30–6.30; adm; same ticket for the ceramics museum*), with an excellent archaeological section of finds from Magna Graecia, and paintings with an emphasis on the dark and/or stormy, especially by the Bassano family, and especially Jacopo (*see* his masterpiece, the twilit *Baptism of St Lucia*). Alessandro Magnasco weighs in with the uncanny *Burial of a Trappist Monk* and *Franciscan Banquet*, full of racing, wraith-like friars. There are calmer works as well: Michele Giambono's *Madonna* and a beautiful recently restored *Crucifix* by Guariento.

In the mid 17th century Bassano and the nearby town of Nove became the Veneto's top ceramic manufacturers, a status they maintain to this day, thanks to 56 firms. In the 18th-century Palazzo Sturm, just up Via Ferracina from the bridge, the **Museo della Ceramica** (*open April–Oct daily 9–12.30 and 3.30–6.30; closed Mon; winter Fri 9–12, Sat and Sun 3–7; same adm as Museo Civico*) has a display of the local ware, porcelain knicknacks and majolica.

The 'Grappa' was added to Bassano's name in 1928, not for its firewater, but in memory of the terrible fighting in the First World War at Cima Grappa, where the Italians held the line after Caporetto. The road up to **Cima Grappa** (5822ft), the Strada Cadorna, was built during the conflict and begins in Romano d'Ezzelino. On top, the **Galleria Vittorio Emanuele II** was the enormous trench dug by the Italian military to shelter its battery of guns; displays and a museum describe the conflict. The monumental cemetery holds the remains of 12,615 Italians; the slightly smaller Austro-Hungarian cemetery contains 10,590 dead (*open mid-May–Sept daily 10–2; Oct–May daily 10–12 and 1–4*).

West of Bassano

More colourful ceramics wait in **Nove**, where budding potters learn the ropes at the national school: part of the complex includes the **Museo Istituto Statale d'Arte per la Ceramica**, Via Giove 1 (*open school hours*); the far larger **Museo Civico della Ceramica** in the 19th-century Palazzo De Fabris (*open Tues–Sun 9–1; adm*) has works from the last three centuries by local masters and foreign artists, including Picasso.

Maròstica, 7km west of Bassano, is a striking storybook town enclosed in 13th-century walls, its upper castle sprawled over the hill and a lower castle, abode of the Venetian lord and now the town hall, sitting like a giant rook in the main piazza. This provides the perfect setting for the storybook event that has put Maròstica on the map: the *Partita a Scacchi*, the human chess match, which takes place on even-numbered years, the second weekend in September.

The game, played with its human (and horse) 'pieces' in medieval costume on a 72-square-ft board, commemorates the contest in 1454 for the hand of Lionora Parisio. Her father, the Venetian governor, refused to let her two suitors fight the traditional duel for humanitarian reasons 'in sad memory of the unhappy lovers Madame Juliet Capuleti and Master Romeo Montecchio' and even offered the loser his younger daughter.

The level of play matches the gorgeous costumes; each game is a reproduction of a grand masters' duel, although things can go wrong when the pieces misunderstand their commands, announced in archaic Venet. At other times all the Renaissance finery is on display in the castle's **Museo dei Costumi** (*open Sun 9–6; or by asking ahead at the Pro Loco; adm*).

Further west, in **Lonedo di Lugo**, near the town of Lugo (about 6km north of Breganze), there are two important villas by Palladio. **Villa Godi Valmarana Malinverni**, Via Palladio, 44 (*open Mar–May, Sept and Oct Tues, Sat, Sun and hols 2–6; June–Aug daily 3–7; adm*), built in 1540, was his very first, with the central portion, usually the most prominent and decorated part of his villas, recessed behind two large wings. The interior was frescoed by Padovano and assistants, and contains a fossil collection and rooms of Italian 19th-century painting.

The later and more classically elegant **Villa Piovene Porto Godi** is a couple of doors down, in a neoclassical park (*gardens only; open daily 2.30–7*).

In the centre of pleasant **Thiene**, 10km to the west, the quattrocento **Villa de Porta Colleoni** (*open mid-Mar–mid-Nov Sun only for tours at 3, 4 and 5; adm*) is an attractive castle-villa, with towers, battlements and Venetian Gothic windows; inside there are frescoes, antique ceramics and jumbo paintings of the former residents of the 18th-century stables on the grounds. Opposite note the flamboyant little church of the **Natività**, its roofline studded with flames of curly kale. Thiene's slender **Torre Civica** dates from the 1600s.

North of Thiene you can climb into the cool green high plain of **Asiago** (3257ft), known for its salubrious climate, cheese and pretty walks and skiing. Like all the villages, the main town Asiago had to be completely rebuilt after its use as a battlefield in the War to end all wars; its focal point is a massive pink stone Municipio, with an enormous tower and lion; in the park behind, a delightful fountain features Pan and all the animals of the forest. A ghastly number of war dead—12,795 identified, 21,491 nameless, 19,999 Austro-Hungarians—lie in the hilltop Sacrario, which also houses a small **Museo Storico** (*open daily 9–12 and 3–5*).

Bassano del Grappa ✉ 36061

In the centre, the traditional ★★★**Belvedere**, Piazzale Gen. Giardino 14, ✆ 0424 529 845, ✉ 0424 529 849 (*expensive*), in a 15th-century house, has the best rooms in town, and is convenient, if not always quiet; ask for one in the back. The elegant restaurant, Viale delle Fosse 1, ✆ 0424 524 988, serves Bassano's finest gastronomic delights, both Veneto and Italian classics, with the promised view. *Closed Sun.* Just east, at Mussolente, the lovely award-winning ★★★★**Villa Palma**, Via Chemin Palma 30, ✉ 36065, ✆ 0424 577 407, ✉ 0424 87687 (*expensive*) occupies an elegant 17th-century villa, with plush rooms full of high-tech gizmos, and a gourmet restaurant. Besides these, there's **Al Sole-Da Tiziano**, Via Vitorelli 41, ✆ 0424 523 206 (*moderate*), for a perfect risotto, duck and Bassano's favourite seasonal ingredients: mushrooms, asparagus and radicchio. *Closed Mon, and July.*

Maròstica ✉ 36063

Al Castello, ✆ 0424 73315 (*moderate*), in the upper castle, offers lovely views and lovely food, with an emphasis on fresh local ingredients; top it off with a *caffè corretto*, 'corrected' with one of a score of different grappas. The restaurant is run by the talented chef of ★★★**La Rosina**, Contrà Narchetti 4, 2km north in Valle San Floriano, ✆ 0424 75839, ✉ 0424 470 290 (*moderate*); another restaurant, in a superb hilltop setting, which also has comfortable modern rooms. *Closed Aug.* In Maròstica proper, ★★★**Europa**, Via Pizzamano 19, ✆ 0424 77842, ✉ 0424 72480 (*moderate*) is up to date, and its restaurant offers one of your few chances for paella in the region.

Asiago and Around ✉ 36012

Long established ★★★**Erica**, Via Garibaldi 55, ✆ 0424 462 113, ✉ 0424 462 861 (*moderate*) is a cosy bet for a summer or winter stay. *Open Dec–mid-April, June–mid-Sept.* In Kaberlaba, 5km from Asiago, little ★★★**Da Barba**, ✆ 0424 463 363, ✉ 0424 462 888 (*moderate*) offers magnificent views, a warm welcome and good food not far from the pistes. *Closed May and mid-Oct–Nov.*

Vicenza

'The city of Palladio', prettily situated below the Monte Bérici, is an architectural pilgrimage shrine and knows it; where other Italians grouse about being a nation of museum curators, the prim Vicentini glory in their city, the intellectual product of a gentry immersed in humanistic and classical thought (a gentry, they gently remind you, that was far better educated than those merchants by the lagoon, who ruled Vicenza in its heyday). Their pride was recently vindicated when UNESCO placed Vicenza on its list of World Heritage Sites.

Although heavily damaged during the Second World War, restorers have tidied up all the scars, for these days the rouble rolls in Vicenza. Its other name is the 'City of Gold', thanks to its gold-working industry, the most important in Europe; it is also the birthplace of the inventor of the silicon chip, Federico Faggin. Add machine tools, textiles and shoes to the list, and you have one of Italy's wealthiest cities.

Getting There

Vicenza is on the main **rail** line between Verona and Venice; there is also a branch line up to Thiene. The station is south of the centre, at the end of Viale Roma. The FTV **bus station**, ✆ 0444 223 115, is alongside it, with buses to Bassano and Maròstica, Asiago, Rovigo, Este, Lonigo and other destinations in the region.

Leave your car in one of the two attended car parks, one at the west end of the town by the Mercato Ortofrutticolo, and the other to the east, by the stadium. Both are linked to the centre by special bus service every five minutes.

Tourist Information

Piazza Matteotti 12; also Piazza Duomo 5, ✆ 0444 320 854, ✆ 0444 325 001.

Porta Castello to the Piazza Signori

From the station, Viale Roma enters the historic centre through the **Porta Castello**, with its powerful 11th-century tower. The palace with the columns the size of sequoias is the **Palazzo da Porto Breganze**, designed by Palladio and partly built by his pupil Scamozzi, before the very monumentality of the design defeated him. Scamozzi also built the less exciting **Palazzo Bonin** at No.13, after his master's designs.

From Piazza Castello, Contrà Vescovado leads to the Gothic **Duomo**, which was carefully pieced together after the War and houses a beautiful polyptych by Lorenzo Veneziano, painted in 1356, in the 5th chapel on the right. Excavations have revealed the Duomo's 8th-century ancestor and a stretch of Roman road and, under the square, a **Criptoportico**, a subterranean passage from a 1st century AD palace. Down Contrà Porti, turn at Via Pigafetta for the fine eclectic **Casa Pigafetta** (1444), birthplace of Antonio Pigafetta, who happened to be in Spain in 1519 when Magellan was setting out for the first of all world tours; Pigafetta went along, and wrote the definitive account of the voyage three years later; note his motto *'Il n'est rose sans espine'* by the door. Beyond, to the left, lies the Piazza dei Signori.

Piazza dei Signori

This kingly square is the heart and soul of Vicenza, its public forum from Roman times to this day. In the 1540s the Vicentines decided that the piazza's crumbling old medieval Palazzo della Ragione needed a facelift to match their Renaissance-humanist aspirations. Having rejected designs by such luminaries as Sansovino and Giulio Romano, they surprisingly hired a young unknown called Palladio to give it a facelift. The city would never be the same.

Vicenza's Perfect Architect

 A Paduan by birth, Andrea di Pietro della Gondola (1508–80) had worked in Vicenza as a stone mason from the age of 16. When he was 29, he met the great humanist Giangiorgio Trissino, who saw a spark in the young man no one else had noticed, and gave him a Renaissance education, took him on a two-year tour of Rome, and gave him a new name: Palladio. His first major commission, the Basilica, so captured the hearts of the Vicentines that they commissioned him to build their palaces and villas. He was, for them, the perfect architect, able to produce classical grandeur for very little money—mainly by using cheap brick coated with a marbly sheen of stucco. Towards the end of his career, he summed up everything he knew in *I Quattro Libri della Architettura*, of which Sir Reginald Blomfield, in his *Studies in Architecture*, wrote pointedly, 'With the touch of pedantry that suited the times and invested his writings with a fallacious air of scholarship, he was the very man to summarize and classify, and to save future generations of architects the labour of thinking for themselves.' The book contributed greatly to the Palladian movement in Britain and America that began in 1603, when Inigo Jones visited Vicenza, and reached its peak in the 1700s under its 'high priest', Lord Burlington, and its great admirer, Thomas Jefferson.

In 1549 Palladio began working on the building, ever since known as the **basilica** ('hall of justice', as in ancient Rome), and kept at it off and on until his death. Two tiers of rounded arches interspersed with Doric and Ionic columns give an appearance of Roman regularity, although Palladio had to vary the size of the arches to compensate for the irregularities in the Gothic structure. The roof is concealed behind a pediment lined with life-size statues; stare at them long enough and the urge to shoot them off like ducks in a penny arcade becomes almost irresistible (*open Tues–Sat 9.30–12 and 2.15–5, Sun 9–12.30; free if there's no exhibition*). To see what Palladio was disguising, go behind the basilica to the **Piazza delle Erbe**, home to Vicenza's daily market, and its **Torre del Tormento**, the medieval prison.

The basilica shares Piazza dei Signori with the needle-like **Torre di Piazza** (12th–15th century), and Palladio's **Loggia del Capitaniato** (1571), built to celebrate the victory at Lepanto. If its grand columns and arches seem confined in too narrow a space, it's because the loggia was meant to extend over several more bays. The neighbouring 16th-century **Monte di Pietà**, built in two sections, was frescoed in the 1900s with Liberty-style pin-up girls, some of whom still faintly survive moral outrage, war damage and Father Time.

As in Venice, this Piazza has two colomns: of the Redeemer (1640) and of St Mark (1473). A right turn here down Via San Michele leads to the Retrone, one of Vicenza's two rivers, spanned here by the **Ponte S. Michele** (1620). There are lovely views of the Retrone lapping the houses and, on the opposite bank, the **Oratorio di S. Nicola** is remarkable for the creepiest altarpiece in Italy, *La Trinità* by the 17th-century Vicentine painter Francesco Maffei, whose feverish brush infected the Oratorio's walls as well, with the assistance of Giulio Caprioni (*but unfortunately you have to find a guided tour to join to get in*).

Corso Palladio, Contrà Porti and Around

Returning to the Piazza dei Signori, step behind the Loggia dei Capitaniato to **Corso Palladio**, 'the most elegant street in Europe, not counting the Grand Canal in incomparable Venice'. Just to your rights is Vincenzo Scamozzi's masterpiece, **Palazzo Trissino**, with an Ionic portico and superb courtyard (begun in 1592, now the Municipio), the city's prettiest, and the late-Gothic **Palazzo Da Schio** (1470s), or 'Ca' d'Oro'. Palladio himself is only dubiously linked to a couple of works on the street named after him; to find his work, turn up **Contrà Porti**, another elegant street: **Palazzo Iseppo Da Porto**, at No.21, is one of his earlier works

(1552), influenced by Raphael. Next door, the sombre Gothic **Palazzo Porto-Colleoni** (No. 19) hides an internal garden courtyard and an airy asymmetrical loggia; next to it, the late-Gothic **Palazzo Porto-Breganze** (No.17) has a beautiful door added in 1481 and a precious mullioned window, the only one in Vicenza with Venetian reversed arches.

The vast medieval **Palazzo Thiene** (now the Banca Popolare), like the Basilica a facelift project for Palladio, who was to make it the most imposing residence in all Vicenza, like many of Palladio's projects, was never completed. The Contrà Porti side is a fine work by Lorenzo da Bologna; around the corner is Palladio's, with its weighty sculpted windows, rustication and Mannerist classicizing, his homage to Giulio Romano. Some of the interior retains its original and rather magnificent decoration; if the bank isn't too busy, ask to see the first floor's Rotonda with a domed vault and statues. Its neighbour on the corner of Contrà Riale, **Palazzo Barbaran-da Porto**, built from scratch by Palladio in 1570, will hold the **Museo Palladiano** in 1999, to coincide with a big exhibit on Palladio's influences in Europe (*for more information, contact the Institute for Palladian Studies, ☎ 0444 323 014*).

Diagonally across the Contrà Zanella from the Palazzo Thiene, the church of **Santo Stefano** contains one of Palma Vecchio's most beautiful paintings, *Madonna with SS. George and Lucy and Musical Angel*. More fine art waits just at the other end of the Contrà S. Stefano in the chapels of the early Gothic **Santa Corona**: it contains, among other works, Veronese's *Adoration of the Magi* (1573) and Giovanni Bellini's *Baptism of Christ*, a late masterpiece set in a rugged landscape. Alongside the church, the **Musei Santa Corona** contain natural history exhibits and the many Paleoveneti, Roman and Lombard relics discovered in the area (*open Tues–Sat 9–12.30 and 2.15–5, Sun 9–12.30; adm*).

At the north end of the Corso, Palladio's open, airy **Palazzo Chiericati** (1550–1650) is one of his masterpieces, and now home to the **Pinacoteca** (*open Tues–Sat 9–12.30 and 2.15–5, Sun and hols 9–12.30; adm*). The ground floor retains its original frescoes, including a hilarious ceiling by Domenico Brusasorci, who took it upon himself to portray the sun god and his steeds in just the position earthlings would see them at noon—all bums and bellies. Upstairs are 24 rooms of art from the 14th to the 20th centuries, by Paolo Veneziano, Memling, Bartolomeo Montagna, Cima da Conegliano, Lorenzo Lotto, Sansovino, Tintoretto, Van Dyck, Jan Brueghel the Elder, Bassano, Veronese, Tiepolo *père* and *fils*, and the irrepressible Francesco Maffei (*Glorification of the Inquisitor Alvise Foscarini*).

Teatro Olimpico

Open 16 Mar–15 Oct Mon–Sat 9.30–12.20 and 3–5.30; 16 Oct–15 Mar Mon–Sat 9.30–12.20 and 2–4.30; year round Sun 9.30–12.20; adm.

Across Piazza Matteotti from the museum, the Teatro Olimpico was Palladio's swansong, one of his most original works, a unique masterpiece of the Italian Renaissance, and the oldest operational indoor theatre in the world (1580). Palladio himself was a member of the group of 25 literati and dilettantes who formed the high-minded 'Olympic Academy' that built the theatre for their own plays and lectures. For the seating and stage, Palladio as always went back to his Vitruvius and the Roman theatres he had seen during his sojourns, while after his death Scamozzi added the stage set of a square and radiating streets in flawless, fake perspective—designed especially for the theatre's first production in 1585, Sophocles' *Oedipus Rex*, and meant to represent the city of Thebes. But here Thebes has become a pure ideal, a

Renaissance dream city, so perfect that no one ever thought to change the set, or bothered, as the Council of Trent banned theatrical representations not long after. Now, however, it has been brought back to life, and is used for plays and ballets.

Outside the Historic Centre

Vicenza's oldest church, **SS. Felice e Fortunato** (a 10-min walk from Piazza Castello), was built just after Constantine officialized Christianity. Since then the church has taken its licks from barbarians and earthquakes, but has been un-restored as much as possible to its 4th-century appearance, revealings mosaics in the right aisle and a martyr's shrine. Two other churches full of art are north of the Duomo and Corso Palladio, up **Corso Fogazzaro**, an atmospheric street lined with porticoes: first, the 13th-century Franciscan **San Lorenzo**, with a lovely marble portal, and further on, **Santa Maria del Carmine**, a Gothic church decorated with 15th-century bas reliefs and altars by Veronese and Jacopo Bassano.

Monte Bérico and the Villa Rotonda

Vicenza's holy hill, Monte Bérico, rises just to the south of the city. Buses make the ascent every half-hour from the bus station, or you can walk up under the half-mile-long **Portici**, built in the 18th century to shelter pilgrims climbing to the Baroque **Basilica di Monte Bérico** (*open Mon–Sat 7–12 and 2.30–7; Sun 7–7*). This commemorates two 15th-century appari-tions of the Virgin, and contains two first class paintings: *La Pietà* by Bartolomeo Montagna, and the *Supper of St Gregory the Great* by Veronese, hung in the refectory (down the steps to the left), and carefully pieced together after Austrian soldiers sliced it to shreds in 1848. Outside, there are superb views of the city and the Villa Rotonda.

From here, walk back down the Portici as far as Via M. D'Azeglio; not far down this road on the right is an alleyway leading to the **Villa Valmarana**, nicknamed 'dei Nani' after the stone dwarfs on the wall, arty ancestors of the modern garden gnome (*open May–Sept Wed, Thurs, Sat and Sun 10–12; 15 Mar–April 2.30–5.30; May–Sept daily 3–6; Oct–15 Nov 2–5; adm exp*). The villa's main attraction, however, is its sumptuous decoration by Giambattista Tiepolo, who frescoed the *Palazzina* with scenes of love versus duty from the *Iliad, Aeneid, Orlando Furioso* and *Jerusalem Delivered.* Son Giandomenico's more intimate, ironical scenes of rural life in the *Foresteria* (guest house) seem to undermine his father's Grand Manner right under his nose.

From here, a further five-minute walk along the Stradella Valmarana (alternatively, by bus no.8 from the railway station) brings you to the Villa Capra-Valmarana, better known as the **Villa Rotonda** (*gardens open 15 Mar–early-Nov Tues–Sun 10–12 and 3–6 (but confirm for Fri, Sat and Sun, © 0444 321 793); adm; interior open Wed only; adm exp*), designed by

Palladio for Cardinal Capra in 1551 and completed after his death by the faithful Scamozzi. Unlike Palladio's other villas, which were functional farmhouses with outbuildings, the Villa Rotonda was built for sheer delight, the occasional garden party and, although no one knew it at the time, as the perfect setting for Joseph Losey's film, *Don Giovanni*. One of the main interests of the Accademia Olimpica was mathematics, and the Villa is, if anything, an exercise in geometrical form—a circle in a cube, complemented by four symmetrical porches.

Around Vicenza: More Villas

The tourist office publishes a map listing the most important of the hundreds of villas of Vicenza province. Only a handful are open for visits, and the ones that are often have bizarre hours, so be sure to check before setting out. Most are in the north (*see* p.352–53) or south in the Colli Berici; otherwise, it's easy to take a bus from Vicenza out to **Montecchio Maggiore**, 13km west along the road to Verona, defended by two Scaliger castles that in Da Porto's 1529 tale of *Romeo and Juliet* belonged to the Montagues and Cappelletti. Just before the village, the 18th-century **Villa Cordellina-Lombardi** (*open April–Oct Tues–Fri 9–1, Sat, Sun and hols 9–12 and 3–6; adm*), built in 1760 by Giorgio Massari has colourful frescoes by a young Giambattista Tiepolo.

Vicenza ✉ *36100*   ***Where to Stay and Eating Out***

Vicenza has a rather limited assortment of hotels. Near the railway station, ★★★★**Campo Marzo**, Via Roma 21, ✆ 0444 545 700, 📠 0444 320 495 (*expensive*) has modern, comfortable rooms, with air-conditioning, and a garage. For comfort in a central location, complete with parking, try ★★★**Cristina**, Corso B. Felice 32, ✆ 0444 323 751, 📠 0444 543 656 (*moderate*).

If you're driving, 6km west of town, in Altavilla towards Montecchio Maggiore, ★★★★**Genziana**, Via Mazzini 75, Selva, ✉ 36077, ✆ 0444 572 398, 📠 0444 574 310 (*moderate*) is warm and welcoming and full of art; there's a pool too. *Closed some of Aug.* Up on the slopes of Monte Bérico, ★★**Casa Raffaele**, Viale X Giugno 10 (through an arch in the Portici), ✆ 0444 545 767, 📠 0444 542 2597 (*cheap*) is good value, with tranquillity and great views. On a quiet street in the historic district are ★★**Due Mori**, Contrà da Rode 26, near the Piazza dei Signori, ✆ 0444 321 888, 📠 0444 326 127 (*cheap*); and the more basic ★**Vicenza**, a few doors down, ✆/📠 0444 321 512.

Vicenza claims that its *baccalà alla vicentina* (salt cod, pommelled and baked with butter, onions, anchovies and cheese) is the most refined cod dish in Italy. Try it at **Nuovo Cinzia & Valerio**, Piazzetta Porta Padova ✆ 0444 505 213 (*expensive*), which also does tagliatelle with salmon or grilled sole, followed by home-made ice-cream and crisp biscuits. *Closed Sun eve, Mon and Aug.*

Luigi Da Porto, author of the original *Romeo and Juliet*, was born in a 15th-century palace that was converted into an inn some 200 years ago: the **Antica Trattoria Tre Visi**, Corso Palladio 25, ✆ 0444 324 868 (*moderate*), with its fireplace and rustic fittings, is a charming place to enjoy good Veneto cooking and homemade pasta. *Closed Sun eve, Mon and July.* Just west of the city walls, at family-run **Trattoria Framarin**, Via Battista Framarin 48, ✆ 0444 570 407 (*moderate*), you'll also find delicious home-made pasta and a warm welcome. *Closed Sun, and some of Aug.* Cheap choices include **Vecchia Guardia**, Contrà Pescherie Vecchie 11, © 0444 321 231, near Piazza dell'Erbe, for pizza and straightforward meals. *Closed Thurs.* There's also the basic, lively and very popular **Antica Casa della Malvasia**, Contrà delle Morette 5, near Piazza dei Signori, © 0444 543 704, for real home cooking.

Verona

> *There is no world without Verona walls*
> *But purgatory, torture, hell itself*
> *Hence banished is banish'd from the world;*
> *And world's exile is death.*

Romeo and Juliet, Act III

Well, love leads one to extremes. When Cupid's pilgrims descend on Verona they sigh over 'Juliet's balcony' and other places concocted in response to a demand for shrines to the unlucky teenage lovers. But the gorgeous rosy-pink city curling along the banks of the Adige has far more to offer than Romeo and Juliet and other star-crossed lovers singing their hearts out in its popular summer opera in the Roman Arena: evocative streets and romantic piazzas, sublime art, magnificent architecture, and all the gnocchi you can eat.

History

Blessed with a navigable river at the bottom of a busy Alpine pass, Verona was favoured by the Romans from the time of its colonization in 89 BC, a period when it produced Vitruvius, the spiritual father of Palladio and Renaissance architecture, and the lyric poet Catullus. The city maintained its status as a regional capital under the Ostrogoths and Franks, and in 1107 it became a free *comune*. This inaugurated the most violent era of Verona's history, when the city's nobility spiced Italy's Guelph and Ghibelline battles with a sideshow of purely domestic feuds and vendettas. Their notoriety inspired the story of *Romeo and Juliet* (first written by Luigi Da Porto in 1529), and led to the *comune* in despair actually inviting the 'son of Satan' himself, the tyrant Ezzelino da Romano, to take power, which he did until 1259, when the reins of the city were taken over by the Della Scala family.

The Della Scalas (or the Scaligeri) were a typical late-medieval Italian family of exquisite gangsters, combining a bloodthirsty passion for power with a taste for the arts. Their names were, however, uniquely canine: Cangrande I ('Big Dog'; 1311–29) both greatly expanded the family's claims in northern Italy and gave such generous hospitality to Dante that the poet dedicated his *Paradiso* to him (although one may well wonder if Dante's famous 'Letter to Cangrande' on how to read poetry ever arrived; any modern postman who saw the name 'Big Dog of the Stair' written on the door would have walked straight past). Cangrande's heir, Mastino II ('the Mastiff') consolidated his gains while his own successor, the fratricidal Cansignorio ('Lord Dog'; 1359–75) presided over the construction of the family's last great monuments. In 1387 the city was seized by the Milanese warlord Gian Galeazzo Visconti.

By the time of Visconti's death in 1402, Verona had had enough of *signori* and joined up with the Serenissima. After Venice's defeat in the Wars of the Cambrai, Verona opened its gates to the German army and didn't return to St Mark's fold until 1517. The jilted Venetians retaliated by making Verona foot the bill for a vast new system of walls designed by Sammicheli. However (and notably unlike Venice), Verona had the spunk to resist Napoleon in 1797—only to be partly destroyed for its presumption. Bombed in the Second World War, Verona quickly rebuilt and remains a *città d'arte* of the first rank. It has also, since the war, become one of the economic boom towns of modern Italy.

Getting Around

 Verona's **airport** Valerio Catullo, at Villafranca, has daily flights to London on British Airways, and others to Rome, Naples and Bari. For information call, ✆ 045 809 5666. Every 20 minutes buses link the airport to Porta Nuova station in Verona; there also three connections daily to the respective bus stations in Brescia, Mantua and Trento.

Verona is the junction of major **rail** lines from Venice, Milan, Bologna, Trento and Bolzano. The station, **Porta Nuova**, is south of the centre, a 15-minute walk from the Piazza Brà up Corso Porta Nuova; alternatively, city buses no.71 or 72 link the railway station with both Piazza delle Erbe and Piazza Brà. A machine dispenses bus tickets opposite the station. The provincial **bus depot** is across the street from Porta Nuova railway station (✆ 045 800 4129); there are frequent departures from here to Lake Garda and the mountains, and also to Mantua. The historic centre is closed to traffic from 7.30 to 10am and from 1.30 to 4.30pm, with the exception of cars going directly to hotels. There are **car parks** near the train station, Arena and Corso Porta Nuova, the main entry point if you are coming from the A4. **Bicycles** can be hired on the southeast corner of Piazza Brà, ✆ 045 504 901. For **taxis** call, ✆ 045 532 666.

Urban (ATM, ✆ 045 588 7111) and provincial (APT) buses offer an *Invito a Verona Pass* (available at the bus depot, tourist office or museums mid-June–Oct), a daily or weekly scheme that includes unlimited travel and museum admissions.

Tourist Information

In the side of Palazzo Barbiera, Via Leoncino 61, ✆ 045 806 8680 (next to the Arena), and Porta Nuova railway station, ✆ 045 800 861 (*both open daily; in winter closed Sun*). For the province: Piazza delle Erbe 38, ✆ 045 800 6997, ⊜045 801 0682, *veronapt@mbox.vol.it*
Youth information: Corso Porta Borsari 17, ✆ 045 801 0795.
Note: on the first Sunday of every month admission is free to the Arena, the Museo Castelvecchio, the Teatro Romano, Juliet's tomb and the Museo Lapidaro Maffeiano.

Porta Nuova to the Arena

The first thing most people see of Verona, whether arriving by rail or road, is Sammicheli's Renaissance gate, the **Porta Nuova**, now stranded on a traffic island at the head of the Corso Porta Nuova. This avenue leads straight under the **Portoni della Brà**, built under Gian Galeazzo Visconti's tenure, and into the heart of tourist Verona: the large, irregular **Piazza Brà**, a favourite promenade of the Veronese and tourists, milling about a broad swathe of café-filled pavements (the *Liston*) and the **Arena** (*open daily 9–7; closed Mon; during opera season 8.15–3.30; adm*). Built in the 1st century AD and, after the Colosseum, the best-

Piazza Vittorio Veneto
VIA DEI MILLE
VIA CARLO EDERLE
VIA ANZA NI
VIA QUATTRO NOVEMBRE
VIA PRATO SANTO
VIA TOMASO DA VICO
VIA M. TODESCHINI
VIA RISORGIMENTO
VIALE DELLA REPUBLICA
Ponte Risorgimento
To Milan
VIA PONTIDA
Arsenale
Piazzale Cadorna
Ponte Vittoria
San Zeno
VIA PORTA S. VENO
RIGASTE SAN ZENO
ADIGE
San Lorenzo
VIA SCARSELLINI
CORSO CAVOUR
Arco dei Gavi
Castelvecchio
STRADONE A. PROVOLO
VIA ROMA
STRADONE PORTA PALIO
V. MANIN
VIA G. MARCONI
CORSO PORTA NUOVA
VIA DELLA VAL VERDE
V.C. BATTISTI
VIA LOCATELLI
VIA DEL MINATORE
VIA FRANCO FACCIO
Porta Nuova
To Mantua and Airport
Porta Nuova Station
Campo Sportivo

Verona

250 metres
250 yards

N

Santo
Stefano
Ponte
Pietra
Castel San
Pietro
Museo
Archeologico
Teatro
Romano

San Giorgio
in Braida
Ponte
Garibaldi

Duomo
Galleria d'Arte
Moderna
S. Anastasia

Fondazione Museo
Miniscalchi-Erizzo

VIA PRATO SANTO
LUNGADIG PANVINIO

VIA PIANA
VIA DUOMO
VIA FORTE

VIA S.
MAMMASO
VIA EMILEI
CORSO PORTA
BORSARI
VIA STADE
S. ANASTASIA
VIA ANASTASIA

Piazza
dei
Signori
5
1 2 S. Maria
Antica
3
4

S. Maria
in Organo

Giardini
Giusti

VIA S. MARIA IN ORGANO

V. MURO
PADRI

SS. Nazaro
e Celso

Museums:
1 Casa Mazzante
2 Loggia del Consiglio
3 Casa di Giulietta
4 Palazzo della Ragione
5 Scaliger Excavations

Porta dei
Borsari
Palazzo
Bevilacqua
SS. Apostoli

VIA MAZZINI
VIA STELLA
VIA CAPPELLO
VIA LEONI

Arena
Piazza
Bra

San Fermo
Maggiore
Ponte
Navi
San Paolo

VIA LEONCINO

VIA S.
PAOLO

VIA VENTI SETTEMBRE

VIA NICOLA MAZZA

PORTA
VESCOVO

VIALE
VENEZIA
To Venice

Museo Lapidario
Maffeiano

STRAD.S.FERMO

ADIGE

VIA C.MONTANARI
VIA G. BERTONI

VIA PALLONE

Museo Civico
di Storia
Naturale

VIA DEL
MINATORE
V.C.TRINITA

Tomba di
Giulietta

LUNGADIGE
CAPULETI

VIA FRANCESCO TORBIDO

Cemetery

VIA DEL FANTE

LUNGADIGE GALTAROSSA

VIA FRANCO FACCIO

Ponte S.
Francesco

Campo
Sportivo

preserved amphitheatre in Italy, the elliptical Arena measures 456ft by 364ft and seats 25,000, and has been kept in an excellent state of preservation since the 16th century. Earthquakes, however, have downed the original outer arcade except for the four arches of the wing, or '*ala*'. As amphitheatres go, the Arena is exceptionally lovely in its pink and white stone, enough to make one almost forget the brutal sports it was built to host; since 1913, the death and mayhem has been purely operatic, with sets in Karnak proportions.

Opposite the Arena in Piazza Brà rises the 17th-century **Palazzo della Gran Guardia**, with a Visconti tower peeking over its shoulder; the **Museo Lapidario Maffeiano**, on the corner of Via Roma, at No. 28 (*open Tues–Sun 9–3; adm*) was one of the first such museums in the world, established in 1714, with an important collection of ancient inscriptions.

Piazza delle Erbe and Piazza dei Signori

From Piazza Brà, **Via Mazzini** (the first street in Italy to ban cars) is the most direct route to the core of medieval and Roman Verona, **Piazza delle Erbe**, occupying the old forum and still fulfilling its original purpose, selling fast food, souvenirs and overpriced vegetables. Four old monuments on the piazza's spine poke their heads above the rainbow lake of parasols—a Lion of St Mark; a 1368 fountain built by Cansignorio topped by a Roman statue known as the 'Madonna Verona'; an elegant Gothic stone lantern; and a 16th-century loggia called the 'Berlina', where malefactors used to be tied and pelted with rotten produce.

A colourful variety of buildings encases the square, including the charming **Casa Mazzanti**, formerly part of a Scaligeri palace and brightened with 16th-century frescoes, and the 12th-century **Torre dei Lamberti**, 275ft high, with a lift to the top from the courtyard of the Palazzo della Ragione (*open Tues–Sun 9–7; adm*). The smaller **Torre del Gardello**, at the other end of the square, was another work of Cansignorio. Six ancient gods pose atop the adjacent Baroque **Palazzo Maffei**, while the battlemented red-brick palace, built in 1301 for a merchants' association, still does duty as Verona's Chamber of Commerce after 700 years.

From bustling Piazza delle Erbe, the **Arco della Costa** ('of the rib'—named after a whale bone hung in the arch) leads into stately **Piazza dei Signori**, the civic centre, presided over by a rather severe 1865 statue of Dante, and the striped **Palazzo della Ragione**, with a Romanesque-Gothic courtyard (*Cortile del Mercato Vecchio*) and striking grand staircase. Behind Dante, the **Loggia del Consiglio** (1493), with yellow and red frescoes and statues of five ancient citizens of Verona (including Pliny the Elder, pinched from Como), is the city's finest Renaissance building. The adjacent crenellated **tribunale** (law courts), formerly a Scaliger palace, has a portal by Sammicheli; in the courtyard, and adjacent to Via Dante, you can peer down through glass into Verona's Roman streets, revealed in the 1980s' **Scaliger excavations**. The underground corridors are used for photo exhibitions (*open daily 10–7; closed Mon*).

The arch adjoining the Tribunale leads to the grandiose Gothic pantheon of the Della Scala, the **Scaliger Tombs** or *Arche Scaligere*. The three major tombs portray their occupants in warlike, equestrian poses on top, and reposing in death below, although a copy has replaced the statue atop the Tomb of Cangrande (d. 1329), built into the wall of the 12th-century church of **Santa Maria Antica**. Don't miss the crowned dogs next to Cangrande's effigy, holding up ladders, the family emblem. More ladder motifs can be seen in the fantastical pinnacles of the tomb of 'Lord Dog' Cansignorio (d. 1375), in the more sedate one of Mastino II (d. 1351), and in the web of their wrought-iron enclosure. The rather plain 14th-century house in the same Via delle Arche Scaliger belonged to the Montecchi family (Shakespeare's Montagues), and has been known ever since as the **Casa di Romeo**.

The tour groups, however, are all over at the **Casa di Giulietta**, Via Cappello 23, near the Piazza delle Erbe (*open daily 9–7; closed Mon; adm*). Although the association is slim (the 13th-century house was once an inn called 'Il Cappello', reminiscent of the Dal Cappello aka Capulet family), it was restored on the outside in 1935 to fit the bill, with lovely windows and *de rigueur* balcony; inside you can peruse lovelorn grafitti, ripe postcards and photos of Italian girlhood's new Romeo, Leonardo di Caprio. The well-fondled bronze statue of Juliet in the courtyard is a bit busty for a 13-year-old, but girls grew up faster back then.

Sant'Anastasia, Modern Art and the Duomo

North of the Scaliger Tombs, it's hard to miss Gothic **Sant'Anastasia**, Verona's largest church, begun in 1290 but never completed; in its woebegone façade, only the fine portal, with frescoes and reliefs of St Peter Martyr, gives an idea of what its builders intended. The interior, however, is beautiful but, just coming in from the sun, many people start at what appears in the dim light to be two men loitering under the holy water stoops; these are the *Gobbi*, or 'hunchbacks'. There are frescoes by Altichiero from 1390 in the Cavalli Chapel (note how the horse-head helmets the worshippers wear on their backs are similar to the dragon head on Cangrande's statue); terracottas by Michele da Firenze; paintings by the school of Mantegna in the Pellegrini chapel; and, best of all, in the sacristy, a fresco of *St George at Trebizond* (*1438*) by Pisanello, Italy's unrivalled maestro of international Gothic; his watchful, calculating princess seems more formidable than any dragon. Nearby, in Corso Sant'Anastasia, the medieval Palazzo Forti now houses the **Galleria d'Arte Moderna** (*open daily 9–7; closed Mon*), where frequent exhibitions share the walls with Italian masters (Hayez, Fattori, De Pisis, Boccioni, Birolli, Vedova and Manzù) of the 19th and 20th centuries.

A few streets down Via Duomo, almost at the tip of the river's meander, stands Verona's **duomo**, consecrated in 1187—Romanesque at the roots and Renaissance in the octagonal crown. The portal, supported on the backs of griffons, was carved by the 12th-century Master Nicolò of San Zeno (*see* below). Look for the chivalric figures of Roland and Oliver guarding the west door, and on the south porch a relief of Jonah and the Whale.

Inside, there's the beautifully carved Tomb of St Agatha (1353) in the Cappella Mazzanti and an *Assumption* by Titian in the first chapel on the left. Painted in 1540, it shows us a very different Virgin from the heaven-gazing goddess in Venice's Frari—this one looks down sympathetically at her friends on earth. The pretty cloister has a few remains of the Duomo's pre-Romanesque predecessor, and the ancient baptistry, **San Giovanni in Fonte**, has an eight-sided font big enough to swim in (1200) from a single piece of marble and decorated with beautiful reliefs. The chapter library, the **Biblioteca Capitolare**, Piazza del Duomo 10 (*open daily 9.30–12.30; also Tues and Fri 4–6; closed Thurs, Sun and July*), originated in the 5th century as a *Scriptorium* and justifiably claims to be the oldest library still operating in Europe; it contains a magnificent collection of medieval manuscripts.

North of the Adige: Veronetta

The north bank of the Adige is known locally as 'Veronetta', and it's worth a whole morning unto itself: if you cross over the Ponte Garibaldi, just down from the Duomo, the large dome of **San Giorgio in Braida** (1477) looms to your right, sheltering a number of first-rate paintings, especially Paolo Veronese's *Martyrdom of St George*. Follow the Adige down to **Santo Stefano**, an important Paleo-Christian church pieced together in the 12th century from 5th–10th-century columns and capitals, and brightened with 14th-century frescoes, some by Altichiero. In front, the **Ponte Pietra**, built by the Romans, was blown up in the Second World War, but partly reconstructed from its original stone dredged up from the Adige.

In ancient times, the citizens of Verona would trot over this bridge to attend the latest plays at the **Teatro Romano** (*open Tues–Sun 8–1.30; adm*), carved out of the cypress-clad hill of San Pietro in the time of Augustus. They still do: the cavea and arches are in good enough nick to host Shakespeare in the summer. A lift goes up to the **Museo Archeologico** (*same hours and ticket*), occupying a convent built on top of the theatre and containing small bronzes, portrait busts and a few mosaics. Above it, the **Castel San Pietro** was built by the Austrians over Roman fortifications, and has famous views over Verona at sunset.

South, on the Interato dell'Acqua Morta, **Santa Maria in Organo** has a façade (1533) by Fra Giovanni da Verona; the talented friar also made the charming *trompe l'oeil intarsia* choir stalls, lectern and cupboards (in the sacristy) depicting scenes of old Verona—as well as birds, animals and flowers.

Across the street that runs at the back of the church, behind the façade of the Palazzo Giusti, are the cool **Giardini Giusti** (*open daily 9am–dusk; adm*), described by the Bavarian Thomas Coryat as 'a second paradise, and a passing delectable place of solace'. That was in 1611, the date of the enormous cypresses, formal box hedge parterres, the fountains and grotto topped with a leering mask; the hillside was re-landscaped in the 19th century in the more romantic and informal English style.

Further south, **Santi Nazaro e Celso** (1484), on Via Muro Padri, contains 16th-century frescoes and a painting of the eponymous saints by Montagna, while **San Paolo** (rebuilt 1763), south on Via San Paolo, contains Veronese's beautiful *Madonna and Saints*, one of the few works he left in his home town before he had to move on to Venice, supposedly after committing a murder. On the river bank, at Lungadige Porta Vittoria 9, there's the elegant Palazzo Pompei, built in 1530 by Sammicheli and now housing the **Museo Civico di Storia Naturale** (*open Mon–Sat 8–7; Sun 1.30–7; closed Fri; adm*), with an excellent fossil collection.

San Fermo Maggiore and Juliet's Tomb

From Piazza delle Erbe, Via Cappello/Leoni leads past the picturesque ruins of the Roman **Porta dei Leoni** (incorporated in a building) to the splendid vertical apse of **San Fermo Maggiore**, an architectural club sandwich of two churches, one atop the other. The Romanesque bottom was begun in the 11th century by the Benedictines, while the upper Gothic church, with its attractive red and white patterns, was added by the Franciscans. The interior is covered with fine 14th-century frescoes, works by Caroto (*Madonna and Saints*), and a graceful *Annunciation* by Pisanello (1462).

The so-called **Tomba di Giulietta** (*open daily 8.15–7; closed Mon; adm*) is back near the river on Via del Pontiere, not far from the Piazza Brà. Even the Veronese admit no plausible connection, but the Romanesque cloister and the 14th-century red marble sarcophagus would make a fine set for the tragedy's last scene. A small **museum of frescoes** is an added attraction, including lovely 16th-century allegorical and mythological scenes by Paolo Farinati.

Piazza delle Erbe to Castelvecchio

From Piazza delle Erbe, Corso Porta Bórsari leads to an impressive Roman gate, **Porta dei Bórsari**, built in the 1st century AD and named after the *borsarii*, who collected duties on goods entering the city on the Via Postumia. Beyond the gate, the street becomes Corso Cavour, embellished with palaces from various epochs, including Sammicheli's refined 1588 **Palazzo Bevilacqua** (No.19), noted for its ornate, rhythmic alteration of large and small windows, columns and pediments.

Opposite, the lovely Romanesque **San Lorenzo** (1117) preserves its upper, women's gallery (*matroneum*), reached by way of its two cylindrical towers. Further down, Corso Cavour opens up into a small square with yet another Roman arch: the simple but elegant **Arco dei Gavi**, designed by Vitruvius in honour of a local family. The French demolished it in 1805, but in 1932 the local *fascisti* put it back together again.

Castelvecchio and its Museum of Art

Next to the arch, Cangrande II's fortress of **Castelvecchio** (1355) has weathered centuries of use by other top dogs, from the Venetians to Napoleon and the Nazis, to become Verona's excellent and well-arranged civic **museum of art** (*open Tues–Sun 9–7; adm*). The ground floor features a sarcophagus (1179) carved with vivid reliefs of SS. Sergius and Bacchus, as well as expressive 14th-century Veronese sculpture, especially a stark, painful *Crucifixion*. The museum is rich in lovely Madonnas, beginning with two straight out of fairy tales: the *Madonna of the Quail* by Pisanello, and the *Madonna of the Rose garden* by Stefano da Verona; there are fine paintings by Crivelli and Mantegna, followed by another beautiful *Madonna* by Giovanni Bellini, and Carpaccio's *SS. Caterina and Veneranda*.

Next comes Verona's mascot, the striking 14th-century equestrian **statue of Cangrande I** from the Arche Scaligere, displayed outside the first floor window. The pyjama-clad steed, complete with an equine hood ornament and deathly eyes, and the moronically grinning 'Big Dog' himself, with his ghastly dragon-helmet slung over his back, make an unforgettable pair, straight out of a malevolent pantomime. Beyond Cangrande are paintings by Veronese, Tintoretto, Giovan Francesco Caroto (including his well-known *Child with Sketch*, a happy insight into Renaissance childhood), both Tiepolos, Guardi and Longhi. Behind the castle, Cangrande II's **Ponte Scaligero**, spanning the Adige, repeats the attractive 'swallowtail' battlements of the Castelvecchio; like the Ponte Pietra, it was meticulously reconstructed from the original stones after the War.

The Basilica of San Zeno Maggiore

A 15-minute walk west from the Castelvecchio, mostly along the riverbank (or bus no.32 or 33 from Corso Porta Borsari), will take you to the superb **Basilica di San Zeno** (*open daily 7–12.30 and 3.30–6.30*), the belle of Verona's churches and one of the finest Romanesque buildings anywhere. First built in the 4th century, the church took its present form in the mid-14th century. Its magnificence demanded a legend: beneath its lofty campanile (finished in 1149) lies the tomb of a personage no less than the Frankish King Pepin the Short.

The rich façade of San Zeno has a perfect centrepiece: a 12th-century rose window of the *Wheel of Fortune* by Maestro Brioloto. Below, the beautifully carved porch (1138) by Masters Nicolò and Guglielmo shows scenes from the months, the miracles of San Zeno, the Hunt of Theodoric and other allegories. The **bronze doors**, with their 48 panels, are a 'poor man's Bible' and one of the wonders of 11th-century Italy, and still, after a millennium, have an unmatched freshness and vitality: in the Annunciation scene Mary covers her face in fear and anguish while the angel Gabriel does his best to comfort her; in the Descent into Hell, Christ and a large, leering Satan fight a tug-of-war for souls. Other scenes seem a bit strange to us, especially the one of two nursing mothers on the lower lefthand door, one suckling twin children, the other, what look to be twin crocodiles.

The vast interior, divided into three naves by Roman columns and capitals, has a beautiful Gothic ceiling, 13th- and 14th-century frescoes and, on the altar, the magnificent triptych of the *Madonna col Bambino tra Angeli e Santi* (1459) by Andrea Mantegna, a work that brilliantly combines the master's love of classical architecture and luminous colouring. Although the French returned the painting after Napoleon took it, they kept the predella as a souvenir; the originals are in the Louvre. In the crypt below, the body of St Zeno glows in the dark.

Verona ✉ *37100*   ***Where to Stay and Eating Out***

Be sure to reserve or call ahead if you come in July or August, when opera fans fill the city. Rooms are also tight in March, when Verona hosts an agricultural fair. Although Verona is more famous for its wine than its food, the locals are more than fond of their gnocchi, the 'traditional symbol of abundance'. The tall, light cake *pandoro* is a Veronese speciality that's sold all over Italy, especially at Christmas.

Goethe and Mozart slept at the ★★★★**Due Torri Baglioni**, Piazza Sant'Anastasia 4, ✆ 045 595 044, ✆ 045 800 4130 (*very expensive*), and would feel just at home today, at least in the rooms appointed in 18th-century antiques. The public rooms are resplendent, and the banquet rooms have circus frescoes. In a quiet street near the Arena, ★★★★**Colomba d'Oro**, Via C. Cattaneo 10, ✆ 045 595 300, ✆ 045 594 974 (*very expensive*) offers very comfortable air-conditioned rooms behind its old stone façade, and parking. A 16th-century palace houses the ★★★★**Accademia**, Via Scala 12, ✆/✆ 045 596 222 (*very expensive*), another excellent, atmospheric choice smack in the centre.

Centrally located near the Arena, the recently renovated ★★★**Giulietta e Romeo**, Vicolo Tre Marchetti 3, ✆ 045 800 3554, ✆ 045 801 0862 (*expensive*) is on a quiet street and offers fine rooms (and parking), but no restaurant. If you're arriving by train,

★★★Novo Hotel Rossi, Via delle Coste 2, ✆ 045 569 022, ✆ 045 578 297 (*expensive–moderate*) is very convenient and *simpatico*. For tranquil, modern and comfortable rooms near the Roman Theatre, try **★★★Italia**, Via Mameli 58, ✆ 045 918 088, ✆ 045 834 8028 (*expensive*).

150 yards from the Arena, **★★Sanmicheli**, Via Valverde 2, ✆ 045 800 3749, ✆ 045 800 4508 (*moderate*) has easy parking. Just south of the Castelvecchio, there's family-run **★★Scalzi**, Via Scalzi 5, ✆ 045 590 422, ✆ 045 590 069 (*moderate*). For cheaper rooms in the centre, try **★Catullo**, Via Valerio Catullo 1, ✆ 045 800 2786 (*cheap*).

If you have an IYHF card, however, you can't beat the **Ostello Verona**, Via Fontana del Ferro 15, ✆ 045 590 360 (*cheap*), just beyond Castel di San Pietro (take bus no.72 to the first stop across the river), a 16th-century villa with frescoes. Beds are up in the newer wing. The reception stays open year round, 24 hours a day, but you won't be allowed in until 5pm; get there early in summer.

The king of the Veronese restaurant scene is **Il Desco**, Via dietro San Sebastiano 7, ✆ 045 595 358 (*very expensive*), in a 15th-century palace, not far from the Ponte Nuovo. Expect exquisite dishes based on seasonal ingredients: gnocchi with ewe's milk cheese, red mullet with black olives and rosemary, goose liver in a sauce of sweet wine and grapes. *Closed Sun, hols, part of Jan and June.*

Run by the same family for over a hundred years, **Arche**, Via delle Arche Scaligere 6, ✆ 045 800 7415 (*very expensive*), located near the Scaliger tombs, has long been the place to go for a special meal in an aristocratic setting. The freshest of fish is brought in daily from Chioggia and imaginatively prepared by the maestro in the kitchen—the menu changes daily. *Closed Sun, Mon lunch, and Jan.*

An even older favourite, a couple of streets from Piazza delle Erbe, **I Dodici Apostoli**, Corticella San Marco 3, ✆ 045 596 999 (*expensive*) offers a traditional Renaissance setting—complete with frescoes of Romeo and Juliet. The name is derived from 12 18th-century 'apostles' of the kitchen who gathered here to dine. Some of the delicacies served today are adapted from Renaissance recipes; the *salmone in crosta* (marinated salmon in pastry) is famous. *Closed Sun eve, Mon, two weeks in June, and July.*

For a glamorous, gourmet experience, sit outside in Piazza dei Signori and have your every culinary care tended to by the elegant waiters of **Nuovo Marconi**, Via Fogge 4, ✆ 045 591910 (*expensive*). The food is as rooted in tradition as the surroundings: tagliolini with crab, gnocchi with pumpkin, and fine scampi and duck. *Closed Sun, part of June, and July.* The century-old **Bottega del Vino**, Via Scudo di Francia 3 (off Via Mazzini), ✆ 045 800 4535 (*expensive*) uses organically grown ingredients and pasta made on the premises; the wine list is enormous. *Closed Tues, except during opera season.*

Near Juliet's house, **Greppia**, Vicolo Samaritana 3, ✆ 045 800 4577 (*moderate*) serves up traditional and Veronese favourites in a quiet little square. *Closed Mon and June.* Prices are lower over the Adige in 'Veronetta': **Alla Strueta**, Via Redentore 4 (near the Roman Theatre), ✆ 045 803 2462 (*moderate*) was an old workers' osteria, now featuring delights on the order of smoked goose breast, gnocchi and especially Verona's cabbage classic *pastissada de cavalo*. *Closed Mon and Tues lunch, and Aug.*

In 'Veronetta', **Osteria Morandin**, Via XX Septembre 144 (just off Interrato dell'Acqua Morta) (*cheap*) is another old standby, with a good choice of wine and a few dishes or snacks to go along. *Closed Sun.* There are numerous other choices in the centre, offering competitive fixed menus, and countless snack possibilities.

Entertainment and Nightlife

Verona bills itself as the 'city for all seasons' and offers a wide-ranging cultural programme throughout the year. Big events take place in the Arena, especially the Stagione Lirica, the **opera and ballet** festival founded in 1913, with performances almost daily in July and August. If you're travelling on a tight schedule, it's best to reserve your seat before coming to Italy: for programme details and reservations, contact the **Ente Lirico Arena di Verona**, Piazza Brà 28, ✆ 045 805 1811; tickets sales are next to the Arena at Via Dietro Anfiteatro 6/b, ✆ 045 800 5151, ✉ 045 801 3287. At the same time Verona also hosts a **Shakespeare festival** (in Italian) in the Roman Theatre: same address as above for information and tickets.

From December to April there is **drama** in the Teatro Nuovo, and also more **opera and concerts** in the Teatro Filarmonico. From mid-December to mid-January Verona uses the arcades of the Arena for a massive show of Christmas cribs (*presepi*) from around the world. In the spring the city hosts one of Italy's oldest **carnivals**, first recorded in 1530; the last Friday of carnival is known as the 'Bacchanal of Gnocchi', presided over by the Papà dello Gnocco, who walks about with a giant dumpling on a fork. All listings are in the tourist office's free *Passport Verona*.

Around Verona: Soave, Valpolicella and Lessinia

Verona's province is awash in wine, the sloshing cradle of four of Italy's best-known DOC wines: white Soave and Bianco di Custoza, and red Valpolicella and Bardolino. And each has at least one *strada del vino* if you want to spend a lazy hour or two touring and tasting. Bianco di Custoza and Bardolino grow on the shores of Lake Garda (*see* p.273 and p.282), while east along the Vicenza road (SS11), vines literally engulf the old town of **Soave**, distinguished by the well-preserved crenellated **Scaliger castle** (*open daily 9–12 and 3–6; closed Mon; adm*), first built in the 10th century. On Via Roma, try a Soave Classico or the sweet Recioto di Soave, a dessert wine made from raisins at the **Enoteca del Castello**.

Valpolicella, northwest of Verona, has twin nuclei, **Negràr** and **Sant'Ambrogio**. The latter produces Verona's famous red marble in addition to red wine; nearby, in the lovely old hilltop hamlet of **San Giorgio**, the parish church was founded in the 7th century. The ciborium over the altar also dates from the 600s, and among the frescoes there's a fascinating 12th-century *Last Judgement*. Northern Valpolicella melts seamlessly into **Lessinia**, the foothills of the Dolomites, famous for rocks—in formations, flintstones and fossils. And falls—at **Molina**'s Parco delle Cascate. North, beyond **Fosse**, the slopes of Corno d'Aquilio are pierced by the **Spluga della Preta**, one of the world's deepest chasms, its floor 2906ft down. Lessinia's flint attracted the first people in *c*.500,000 BC. Finds from the period are in the prehistory museum at **Sant'Anna d'Alfaedo**, along with a 20ft fossilized shark. South of Sant'Anna, not far off the road to Fane, don't miss the **Ponte di Veja**, a spectacular, natural 170ft arch, the inspiration for the Malebolge bridge in Dante's *Inferno*. A winding road loops east to **Bosco**

Chiesanuova, Lessinia's modest winter sports centre. From here follow the road to **Velo Veronese**, the starting point for a visit to the **Valley of the Sphinxes** (*Valle delle Sfingi*), named for its striking chasms and landforms, made of layers of red ammonite.

In 17th-century Lessinia, flintlocks were big business. Many of these were made by Bavarians who had settled here in the 13th century. Their roots are remembered in their language, costumes, and the huge *tromboni*, a kind of arquebus that they blast on holidays. You can learn more about them at the museum in **Giazza**, one of Lessinia's prettiest villages with its medieval German houses. **Bolca**, southeast of Giazza, caused a sensation in the Renaissance when the discovery of a rich bed of fossilized fish was cited as scientific proof of Noah's Flood. They are also extremely beautiful and delicate, and in the local fossil museum.

Treviso

Although famous for radicchio and Benetton, Treviso is still one of the Veneto's best kept secrets, laced with little canals (or *canagi*) diverted from the River Sile, languorous with willows, lazy water wheels, swans and mossy walls, yet all humming with more than a little discreet prosperity. Like Verona, it formed its character in the century preceding its annexation by Venice (1389), when it was ruled by the Da Camino and embellished by one of Giotto's greatest pupils, Tommaso da Modena, who did little outside of Treviso.

Colours were an obsession in Treviso long before Benetton united them. Attractive building stone was scarce, so it became the custom to cover the humble bricks walls with plaster and frescoes—in the 1300s with simple colours and patterns and, by the 1500s, with heroic mythologies and allegories. Although faded and fragmented since then—on Good Friday 1944 an air raid destroyed half of Treviso in five minutes—one of the delights of visiting the city is to pick out frescoes under the eaves, or hidden in the shadows of an arcade.

Getting Around

Treviso **airport** (© 0422 230 393) is southwest of the town; bus no.6 runs from there to the railway station; Ryan Air links it several times a week to London Stansted. Both the **train** and **bus** stations (© 0422 412 222) are in Via Roma south of the centre. **Trains** run from Venice or Mestre to Treviso and Belluno, either directly or by changing at Padua or Conegliano; services are more frequent from Padua. One line goes via Conegliano and Vittorio Veneto; the other, longer but more scenic, via Montebelluna (also a getting-off point for Masèr and Àsolo) and Feltre.

Tourist Information

Piazza Monte di Pietà 8, © 0422 547 632, ✆ 0422 419 092, *tvapt@sevenonline.it*

Piazza dei Signori and the Duomo

From the bus or train station, it's a 10-minute walk over the Sile along the Corso del Popolo and Via XX Settembre to the Piazza dei Signori, the heart of Treviso. Here stands the city's only surviving *comunale* palace, the enormous brick **Palazzo dei Trecento**, 'of the Three Hundred', built in the 1200s and rebuilt nearly entirely after it was bombed in the war;

Treviso café society shelters underneath it. Adjacent, the **Palazzo del Podestà** was rebuilt in 1877, along with the Torre Civica looming over its shoulder. Behind the Palazzo dei Trecento, the **Monte di Pietà** (municipal pawn shop) contains the lovely Renaissance **Sala dei Reggitori** (*visit by appointment only, call © 0422 654 320*), with walls of gilt leather, a painted, beamed ceiling and canvases by Sebastiano Ricci and Luca Giordano.

The arcaded main street, Calmaggiore, leads from the square to the **duomo**, a Venetian Romanesque building with a cluster of domes (12th century); the adjacent baptistry gives an idea of what the cathedral looked like before its many alterations. Besides fine Renaissance tombs of local prelates, much of the cathedral's best art is concentrated in the **Cappella Malchiostro**, just right of the altar, designed by Tullio and Antonio Lombardo, with works by Paris Bordone (*Adoration of the Shepherds*) and Girolamo da Treviso (*Madonna del Fiore*). The frescoes are by native son Pordenone, while his mortal enemy Titian contributed *The Annunciation* on the altar; Vasari wrote that Pordenone always painted with his sword at his hip in case Titian showed up while he was working. Behind the cathedral, the **Museo Diocesano** (*open Mon–Thurs 9–12, Sat 9–12 and 3–6*) has one of Tommaso da Modena's masterpieces, the detached fresco, *Cristo Passo*.

Museo Civico and San Nicolò

From Piazza Duomo, Via Canova leads past the 15th-century **Casa Trevigiana** (*open for special exhibitions*), a reliquary of the city's architecture containing provocative bits salvaged from her ruins. Via Canova meets Borgo Cavour near the **Museo Civico Luigi Bailo** (*open Tues–Sat 9–12.30 and 2.30–5, Sun 9–12; adm*), with Bronze-Age swords and 5th-century BC bronze discs from Montebelluna; and an excellent collection of masters from the Veneto: Giovanni Bellini, Titian, Lotto, Jacopo Bassano, Cima da Conegliano, the Tiepolos, Rosalba Carriera, Guardi, Longhi—and Joshua Reynolds.

Borgo Cavour makes a grandiose exit through the great Venetian gate, **Porta dei Santi Quaranta** (1517), encompassed by an impressive stretch of the ramparts. However, if you turn instead down Via S. Liberale and turn right in Via Absidi, you'll come to Treviso's best church, Gothic **San Nicolò** with its attractive polygonal apse. The interior is a treasure house of lovely frescoes—from a huge *St Christopher* on the south wall to the charming pages by Lorenzo Lotto by the d'Onigo tomb. Tommaso da Modena contributed the saints standing to attention on the columns, but even better are his perceptive portraits of 40 Dominicans (1352), some using medieval reading glasses, in the **Capitolo dei Domenicani**, in the adjacent Seminario (*open April–Sept daily 8–6; Oct–Mar daily 8–12.30 and 3–5.30; ring the bell*).

San Francesco

Treviso's east end is seperated by one of its wider streams, the Cagnàn; on an little islet (take Via Trevisi–Via Pescheria from the Monte di Pietà), the lively and colourful **fish market** (1851) is open every morning except Sunday. San Nicolò's near twin, the tall brick, Romanesque-Gothic **San Francesco**, is just up Via S. Parisio, and has a fresco of the Madonna by Tommaso da Modena, as well as the tombs of Francesca Petrarch (d. 1384) and Pietro Alighieri (d. 1364), the children of Italy's two greatest poets, whose final meeting-place here in Treviso was purely a coincidence.

Back along the walls to the east, Viale Burchiellati leads shortly to the city's other great gate, Guglielmo Bergamasco's exotic **Porta San Tomaso** (1518). From here follow Borgo Mazzini to the deconsecrated church of **Santa Caterina**, with Tommaso da Modena's detached frescoes on *The Life of St Ursula*, a series that's just as delightful as Carpaccio's St Ursulas in the Accademia in Venice (*but closed for restoration*).

Treviso ✉ *31100*   **Where to Stay and Eating Out**

Near the station, modern ★★★★**Continental**, Via Roma 16, ✆ 0422 411 662, ✉ 0422 411 620 (*expensive*) is convenient and air-conditioned, and has a garage, although if you're driving you may prefer one of the 20 rooms just north of town in the attractive patrician ★★★**Scala**, Viale Felissent 1, near the exit for Conegliano, ✆ 0422 307 600, ✉ 0422 305 048 (*expensive*), set in a pretty park. In the centre, the hospitable and long-established ★★**Campeol**, Piazza Ancillotto 8, ✆ 0422 56601, ✉ 0422 540 871 (*moderate*) has good views. Near the Treviso Sud exchange on the A27 in Silèa, ★★★**La Fattoria**, Via Callalta 83, ✆ 0422 361 770, ✉ 0422 460 150 (*moderate*) has cosy rooms in a farm-villa. *Closed part of Aug.*

Besides cherries and Prosecco, Italy's finest bubbly, Treviso produces the Veneto's finest radicchio and *sopa coada*—a baked pigeon casserole. If money's no object, try it at **Alfredo**, Via Collalto 26, ✆ 0422 540 275 (*expensive*), long Treviso's most acclaimed restaurant, in a lovely, elegant Belle Epoque setting. The imaginative menu has an emphasis on seafood. Reserve. *Closed Sun eve, Mon and Aug.*

In a beautiful 12th-century building, **Al Bersagliere**, Via Barberia 21, ✆ 0422 579 902 (*moderate*) offers a full selection of delicious *antipasti*, *sopa coada* and other Venetian specialities such as squid in its own ink, risotto and Venetian-style liver. *Closed Sun, Sat lunch, and Aug.* **Beccherie**, Piazza Anchillotto 10, ✆ 0422 540 871 (*moderate*) is one of Treviso's bastions of local atmosphere and cooking—try *pasta e fagioli* with radicchio. *Closed Sun eve, Mon, and July.* **Toni del Spin**, Via Inferiore 7, ✆ 0422 543 829 (*moderate–cheap*) remains an old favourite for its Veneto dishes (*bigoli, risi e bisi*) topped off with American apple pie. *Closed Sun and Mon lunch.*

North of Treviso: the Marca Trevigniana

You can drive straight up to the Dolomites in less than two hours from Treviso, or spend a day exploring the fine towns of its province, the Marca Trevigniana, along the way.

Tourist Information

Oderzo: Piazza Castello 1, ✆ 0422 815 251, ✉ 0422 814 081.
Conegliano: Via Colombo 1, ✆/✉ 0438 21230.
Vittorio Veneto: Piazza del Popolo 18, ✆ 0438 57243, ✉ 0438 53629.

Oderzo and Conegliano

A delightful town crisscrossed by canals and devoted to wine-making, **Oderzo** may not be a household name, but in its Roman heyday, as *Opitergium* it was recorded as far away as Egypt. Piazza Vittorio Emanuele II marks the old forum, overlooked by the late-Gothic **Duomo**; in Via Garibaldi, the **Museo Civico Opitergino** (*open daily 9–12.30 and 3–5.30,*

Sun 3–6.30; closed Mon and Thurs; adm) has a good assortment of Roman finds and mosaics. Nearby, the **Pinacoteca Alberto Martini**, Via Garibaldi 63 (*open Mon–Fri and Sun 3–7*) has works by Oderzo-born surrealist painter Alberto Martini, as well as other contemporary Italian painters, mostly from Oderzo. Make the short detour north of Oderzo to picturesque **Portobuffolè**, a village of frescoed buildings and three very funny Venetian lions (especially the spooked one with a pie pan face, sticking out its tongue on the 15th-century Monte della Pietà, now the Cassa Marca). The oldest house, 13th-century **Casa di Gaia da Camino**, houses a bicycling museum.

Conegliano, a town neatly divided into old and new, with the Accademia cinema and its giant sphinxes in the centre, was the birthplace of Giambattista Cima (1460–1518)—'the sweet shepherd among Venetian painters' as Mary McCarthy called him—the son of a seller of hides, who often painted his native countryside in his backgrounds. If you haven't seen the originals, reproductions are displayed at his birthplace, the **Casa di Cima**, on quiet Via Cima 24 (*ring ahead, © 0438 21660*). An original and beautiful Cima, a *Sacra Conversazione* in an architectural setting (1493), forms the altarpiece of the 14th-century **Duomo**. In the 16th century Ludovico Pozzoserrato and Francesco da Milano collaborated on the frescoes of Old and New Testament scenes in the adjacent **Sala dei Battuti**, the hall of a flagellants' confraternity (*open daily 9–12, Sun 3–7, if you ring ahead, © 0438 22606; closed Wed*). Be sure to stroll down arcaded **Via Venti Settembre**, lined with old frescoed palaces; the **castle** on the hill, begun in the 10th century, has a small **Museo Civico** with paintings and other odds and ends (*open daily 10–12.30 and 3.30–7; closed Mon; adm*). Conegliano produces a delightful Prosecco which you can go a-tasting along the pretty 42-kilometre **Strada del Prosecco**— from the castle to **Valdobbiadene** to the west, then back east to Vittorio Veneto. On the way have a look at **San Pietro di Feletto**, its exterior frescoed in the 15th century by an unknown painter, who pictures Jesus in a unique fashion: lines from his wounds are connected to chickens, wine, people lying in bed and farm tools.

Vittorio Veneto

The Venetian pre-Alps saw heavy action in the First World War, and the hills around Asiago, Monte Grappa and the Piave are often crowned with dispiritingly huge Italian, British or French war cemeteries. **Vittorio Veneto**, north of Conegliano, was the site of Italy's final victorious battle (October 1918). The Vittorio's name, however, is for Vittorio Emanuele II; in 1866, to celebrate the birth of Italy, the two rival towns of Cèneda and Serravalle were united. The **Castello di San Martino**, dating back to the Lombards, hovers over **Cèneda**, where the main Piazza Giovanni Paolo I holds the **Loggia del Cenedese**, designed by Sansovino in 1538, now home to a museum of the battle (*open May–Sept daily 10–12 and 4–6.30; Oct–April daily 10–12 and 2–5; closed Mon; adm*); Albino Luciani (John Paul I) was a long-time bishop of Vittorio Veneto and founded the **Museo Diocesano** in the seminary, with works by Palma Giovane and Titian (*open by request*). Another church, **Santa Maria del Meschio**, has a beautiful altarpiece of the *Annunciation* by Andrea Previtali.

Serravalle begins with a clock tower up the poetic street (Via Dante/Virgilio/Petrarca) which links the two halves of Vittorio Veneto. Serravalle has conserved its atmospheric old palaces and houses, especially in Piazza Flaminio, where the 15th-century **Loggia Serravallese** houses, confusingly, the **Museo del Cenedese** *(open April–Sept daily 10–12 and 4.30–6.30; Oct–Mar daily 10–12 and 3–5; closed Tues; adm)*, with a collection of Roman finds, sculpture and minor paintings. The **duomo** has a fine altarpiece by Titian, the *Madonna col Bambino* (1547). Vittorio Veneto's playground is the lovely **Bosco del Cansiglio**, a vast forest of fir, larch and beech on a lofty karstic plateau set aside by Venice in 1548 as its 'Forest of St Mark's Oars'; Monte Cansiglio itself offers the closest downhill skiing to Venice.

Where to Stay and Eating Out

Oderzo ✉ 31046

The nicest place to sleep is 5km east at Gorgo al Monticano: the 15th-century ★★★**Villa Revedin**, Via Palazzi 4, ✆/☎ 0422 800 033, (*moderate*), set in a park; rooms are well-equipped and the breakfasts superb. In Oderzo, **Gellius,** Calle Pretoria 6, ✆ 0422 713 577 (*moderate*) offers the chance to dine in a Roman prison, but the food has improved dramatically in the last 2000 years. *Closed Mon, and Tues lunch.* In Portobuffolè you can sleep in the ducal ★★★★**Villa Giustinian**, Via Giustiniani 11, ✉ 31019, ✆ 0422 850 244, ☎ 0422 850 260 (*expensive*), built in 1695 and elegantly furnished, and encompassed by a large park. *Closed part of Aug.*

Conegliano ✉ 31015

Behind an exterior frescoed in the 1500s, ★★★**Canon d'Oro**, Via XX Settembre 129, ✆/☎ 0438 34246 (*moderate*) has a warm welcome and plush modern rooms, over-looking the town's main street. ★★★**Sporting Hotel Ragno d'Oro**, Via Diaz 37, ✆ 0438 412 300, ☎ 0438 412 310 (*moderate*), set in parkland on Conegliano's outskirts, boasts tennis courts, a sizeable pool, sauna and satellite TV.

Just outside Conegliano, the lovely **Tre Panoce**, Via Vecchia Trevigiana 50, ✆ 0438 60071 (*expensive–moderate*) occupies a seicento farmhouse crowning a hill of vine-yards, with outdoor tables in summer (if you're not driving, bus no.1 stops outside). Prepared with the freshest seasonal ingredients, you can try a number of little dishes by ordering the *menu veneto*, followed by delicious desserts. *Closed Sun evenings, Mon, and Aug.*

In town, in a 13th-century building, **Al Salisà**, Via XX Settembre 2, ✆ 0438 24288 (*expensive–moderate*) is extremely elegant, featuring succulent snails (*lumache*) and game specialities in season, especially venison. There's also a good local wine list, and special menus for lunch. *Closed Tues evenings, Wed, and Aug.* On the Strada del Prosecco, between Valdobbiadene and Vittorio Veneto in Follina, the elegant ★★★**Romantik Hotel Abbazia**, Via IV Novembre, ✉ 31051, ✆ 0438 971 277, ☎ 0438 970 001 (*expensive*) has lovely modern rooms, including jacuzzis in a 17th-century estate. They even hire out bikes or cars for excursions.

Vittorio Veneto ✉ 31029

★★★**Terme**, Via della Terme 4, ✆ 0438 554 345, ☎ 0438 554 347 (*moderate*) has good, comfortable rooms near the station. Dine on hearty mountain specialities at the popular **Postiglione**, Via Cavour 39, ✆ 0438 556 924 (*moderate*), in an old post house. *Closed Tues.* The finest dining in the region, however, is west in Tarzo: **Il Capitello**, Via S. Francesco, Cobranese, ✆ 0485 564 279 (*moderate*) features all that's exquisite, with a modern flair. *Closed Wed, Thurs lunch, Jan and Aug.*

A provincial capital at the junction of the Piave and Ardo rivers, Belluno is one of those small perfectly proportioned Italian cities: urban, urbane and yet never far from magnificent views over the countryside—here of the Venetian Dolomites.

Tourist Information

Belluno: Via Rodolfo Pesaro 21 ☏ 0437 940 083, ✉ 0437 940 073.
Feltre: Piazza Trento-Trieste 9, ☏ 0439 2540, ✉ 0439 2839.

Belluno

The old civic and religious centre of town, **Piazza del Duomo**, has two of Belluno's finest buildings, the ornate **Palazzo dei Rettori** (1491), residence of the Venetian governors, and the **Duomo**. Founded in the 7th century, and last redesigned by Pietro Lombardo, work dragged on the church until the 1600s, and tends to be overshadowed by the magnificent detached **campanile**, designed by Filippo Juvarra (1742); once restoration work is completed, you may be able to go up again for the bird's-eye views.

In Via Duomo, the **Museo Civico** (*open Tues–Sat 10–12 and 3–6, Sun 10–12; closed Mon*) is a treat for fans of extrovert womanizing Baroque painter Sebastiano Ricci, with some of his greatest work; it also provides a chance to learn about some interesting if obscure local painters from the 1300–1800s. Via Mezzaterra/Via Rialto follow the ancient Roman *castrum,* by way of atmospheric **Piazza del Mercato**, a picture perfect little square, with arcades and a fountain from 1410. To the south Via Mezzaterra ends at the 12th-century **Porta Ruga** and a postcard view of the Piave Valley and the mountains. Also have a look at the Gothic church of **Santo Stefano** (1468) in Via Roma, where a 15th-century relief of the Madonna in her merciful umbrella pose guards the door, leading into a handsome striped interior.

If you don't have time for a foray into the Dolomites, take the bus to the **Alpe del Nevegàl**, 12km south of Belluno, for gorgeous views and a chairlift to the Rifugio Brigata Alpina Cadore (5248ft), with an Alpine garden. From the refuge it's an easy three-hour walk up to the **Col Visentin**, where another refuge commands a unique panorama: north across the sea of Dolomite peaks and south to the Venetian Lagoon. The hills of the **Alpago** are another popular weekend destination, especially the **Lago di Santa Croce**, the focal point for its small villages: aim for **Pieve d'Alpago** in a lovely setting, famous for its restaurant.

Feltre: the Dead Man and SS. Vittore e Corona

West from Belluno the SS50 skirts the Piave on its way to hilltop Feltre. Sacked by the troops of Emperor Maximilian in 1510 during the War of the Cambrai, Feltre was immediately rebuilt and has changed little since, especially the houses along **Via Mezzaterra**, with their faded frescoes and dozens of marble plaques hammered into illegibility by someone who had it in for Feltre's memories. The jewel on Via Mezzaterra is the picturesque **Piazza Maggiore**, where a very quizzical Lion of St Mark stands vigil over the castle; the church of San Rocco has a fountain by Tullio Lombardo, and the superb 16th-century **Palazzo dei Rettori** (now the Municipio) is decked out with a Palladian portico. Inside, a wooden theatre built in 1684 saw the production of Goldoni's first plays. In the centre of Piazza Maggiore, a statue honours the famous educator, Vittorino da Feltre (*see* Mantua).

The Palazzo Villabuono, by the town's east gate, now houses the **Museo Civico**, Via L. Luzzo 23 (*closed for restoration at time of writing*) which has among its archaeological collection an altar to the *anna perrena* (the year), and among its paintings works by Gentile Bellini, Cima da Conegliano and Feltre's own contribution to the Renaissance, Lorenzo Luzzo, better known by his punk nickname, *Il Morto da Feltre*, the 'Dead Man', given to him because of his unusual pallor. The *Transfiguration*, the Dead Man's most acclaimed work, is nearby in the sacristy of the church of **Ognissanti**.

Five km from Feltre, signposted off the Treviso road (SS 473), the Romanesque **Santuario di SS. Vittore e Corona** (*open April–Sept daily 8–12 and 3–7; Oct–Mar daily 9–12 and 3–6*) is up a steep little road. Built in 1100 and almost unchanged since, it shelters the remains of Vittore, a Roman soldier martyred in Syria in 171, and Corona who converted at the sight of his martyrdom and got the same herself. Their bodies spent a few centuries on Cyprus before the Venetians brought them here in 1096. The apse is filled with their elevated sarcophagus, decorated with windblown acanthus (note the relief of Vittore on the underside); behind look for the capitals inscribed with Kufic script, reading 'the Universe is God'. The frescoes are by the schools of Tommaso da Modena and Giotto. In fact, a number of figures are copied directly from Padua's Scrovegni Chapel—Giotto himself sold the reproduction rights. Don't miss the *Last Supper*, where the artist tried to paint prawns but drew scorpions instead.

Where to Stay and Eating Out

Belluno ✉ 32100

Central ★★★**Astor**, Piazza dei Martiri 26-E, ☎ 0437 942 094, ✉ 0437 942 493 (*moderate*) has comfortable rooms. Not far from the station, ★★★**Delle Alpi**, Via J. Tasso 13, ☎ 0437 940 545, ✉ 0437 940 565 (*moderate–cheap*) has welcoming rooms and one of the best restaurants in town, specializing in seafood. *Closed Sun and some of Aug.*

Pieve d'Alpago ✉ 32010

Just outside Pieve in the hamlet of Plois, you'll find one of the top restaurants in all Venetia: **Dolada**, Via Dolada 9, ✆ 0437 479 141, ✉ 0437 478 068 (*very expensive*), overlooking Lago di Santa Croce. Wood panelling, candlelight and romance accompany unfussy, inspired food, in the best Italian tradition: home-made pasta, the celebrated *zuppa dolada*, superb fish, duck and lamb dishes, and an exceptional wine list. *Closed Mon lunch and Tues, exc in July and Aug).* It also has hotel rooms.

The Dolomites

...the most beautiful 'constructions' in the world.

Le Corbusier

There are mountains, and then there are the Dolomites. Born as massive corals in the primordial ocean, and heaved up from the seabed 60 million years ago, tempests and blizzards over the aeons have whittled away at the dolomitic limestone and porphyry o form an extraordinary landscape. Otherworldly and majestic peaks claw and scratch at the sky between the valleys of the Adige and the Piave rivers, each monumental range a petrified tempest of jagged needles, cloud-tickled pinnacles and sheer cliffs, dyed rose by the dawn and glowing red by the setting sun.

These most romantic and beautiful of mountains were named after a wandering French mineralogist with a fantastical name, Dieudonné Sylvain Guy Tancrède de Gratet de Dolomieu, who in 1789 was the first to describe their mineral content. Marmolada (10,959ft), the highest peak in the range (17 others top 10,000ft) has glaciers even in summer, but elsewhere the snow fields convert in July to a massive bouquet of wild flowers, streaked with blue gentians, yellow Alpine poppies and buttercups, edelweiss and pink rhododendron. The air and light in autumn are so sharp and fine they can break your heart.

Highlights of the Dolomites

There are so many lovely drives and walks in the Dolomites it seems preposterous to put one above the other. The **Great Dolomites Road** between Bolzano and Cortina (SS241 and SS48) justly deserves its fame—there's so much to see you may wish you really had a rubber neck. Other sensational areas are the **Pale di San Martino** and **Paneveggio Natural Park**; the passes of the **Sella Group**; along the western slopes of the **Brenta group**; and around **Cortina d'Ampezzo**: Misurina, Auronzo, the Val di Sesto and Val di Landro.

Man-made sights pale before the handiwork of angels, but the cities of **Trento**, **Bolzano**, **Bressanone**, **Vipiteno** and **Rovereto** are all worth a stop. The mountains are also endowed with literally hundreds of well-preserved **castles**, many with medieval frescoes; quite a few now house hotels or restaurants. Among the churches, there's the **abbey of Novacella** near Bressanone; the curious hermitage of **San Romedio** at Cles; the frescoes in San Rocco at **Tesero**, San Virgilio at **Pinzolo** and **Malles'** parish church and abbey.

When to Go

Prices skyrocket in the Dolomites during their high-season periods (Christmas holidays, end of January to Easter, mid-July to mid-September). To avoid high prices and the crowds, try to go in June, early July or late-September–October, when the alpine refuges are open but not packed to the gills, or immediately after the New Year holidays for skiing, when everyone else has to go back to work and the resorts offer big discounts. May and November are dead.

The High Trails and Other Walks

The Dolomites offer walks for everyone from semi-couch-potatoes to the rock-grappling daredevils, and eight **High Trails of the Dolomites** (*Alte Vie delle Dolomiti*) specially designed for those who fall in between. The trails range from 120km to 180km in length, and are designed to take the average walker two weeks—though it doesn't hurt to plan a few days on top of that for rests and detours. The High Trails have the virtue of keeping you on top of mountains and plateaus for most of their length. While they do not require any special climbing skill (trails with a vertiginous *via ferrata*, 'iron ladder', or other obstacles usually have detours for the less intrepid), they do demand a stout pair of hiking boots with good rubber soles (80 per cent of accidents are caused by slipping) and protection against sudden storms. A telescopic walking stick for descents, and a mobile phone in case of emergencies, are also recommended. Write to the tourist office in Belluno (*see* p.380) for maps and booklets.

Other memorable walks, requiring no special equipment, are two easy but ravishing paths above **Misurina** around Tre Cime di Lavaredo; above **Santa Cristina** to Sassolungo; around **Madonna di Campiglio** and **Molveno** in the Brenta Group; around **Colle Santa Lucia**; and above **Merano**. If you've had mountain experience, a famous trek begins in the **Val di Fassa** and runs to the bizarre Torri del Vaiolet on **Catinaccio/Rosengarten**. Many of the 200 Alpine refuges in Trentino are operated by the *Società degli Alpinisti Tridentini* (SAT), Via Manci 57, 38100 Trento, ✆ 0461 981 871, ✉ 0461 986 462.

There are two good sets of **maps** that include the above *Alte Vie* and other paths as well, and point out the location of the Alpine refuges: *Carta dei Sentieri e Rifugi*, Edizioni Tabacco Ùdine, and *Maps Kompass-Wanderkarten*, Edizioni Fleishmann-Starnberg. Both are scale 1:50,000, and are readily available at newsstands in the region. The relevant tourist offices have booklets on each trail in English that contain all the basic information you need to know before you go, including the telephone numbers of the refuges. They also give a good idea of the level of difficulty of each trail, so read them thoroughly before setting out. For more information *see* **Practical A–Z**, pp.34–5.

Skiing

The Dolomites are like a candy shop for winter sports junkies. As the sunny side of the Alps they enjoy good clear weather, and when it snows it falls delightfully dry and powdery. There

The Dolomites

To Innsbruck

Brenner Pass

SWITZERLAND

AUSTRIA

Passo
di Resia

Largo di
Resia

Burgusio
Laudes
Glorenza   Malles Venosta
Sluderno
Spondigna   Silandro   S38

Val di Senales

ALTO   ADIGE

Tirolo
Parcines   Merano
Naturno
S. Vigilio   Sarentino
Avelengo

Val Venosta
Laces
Tarres

Val l'Ultimo

Colle Isarco

Val Ridanna

Maiern
Vipiteno

S. Leonardo
in Passiria

Stelvio

Solda
Ortles

Gioveretto

National   Park

Bormio

Mt Cevedale   Bagni di Rabbi

Fondo
Malosco
Caldaro
Romeno
Sanzeno
Termeno

Bolzano

Appiano

Ora

Egna

Peio

Val di Sole
S42
Malè   Noce   Cles
Tuenno
Taio   Dermulo

Val di Non

Segonzano

Pelizzano   Folgarida

Ponte di Legno

Parco National
Adamello Brenta

Madonna di
Campiglio

Presanella

Pinzolo

Brenta

Tosa

Mezzocorona

S. Michele all'Adige

Andalo
Molveno
L. di
Molveno

Lisignano
Lavis

Val di Cembra

Cembra

Baselga
di Piné

Edolo

Mt Adamello

Val di Genova

Val di Daone

S. Lorenzo
in Banale   Stenico

Sarca

Vezzano

Pergine

Civezzano

Trento

Lavarone

Calliano

Folgaria

To
Sondrio

Tione
di Trento

Ponte Arche

L. di Toblino

Mt
Bondone

L. di
Caldonazzo

Lardaro

Breno

Chiese

Giudicarie

Riva
del Garda

Villa Lagarina
Isera

Volano
Rovereto

To
Brescia

L. Garda

To Verona
Avio

Adige Etsch

Adige

Val Lagarina

N22

S12

S45

384

is a variety of slopes of all levels of difficulty, and country trails, toboggan and bobsled runs, ice rinks and speed-skating courses; if all of the ski runs were ironed out flat they would stretch from the Brenner Pass to Reggio Calabria. There are other bonuses as well: ski schools in July, and indoor, heated pools in the middle of winter. The only problem comes in trying to choose where to aim for. For winter sports, **Cortina d'Ampezzo**, having hosted the Winter Olympics, has the best facilities, but **San Martino di Castrozza** and **Madonna di Campiglio** come in close behind, with **Auronzo, Canazei, Selva di Cadore, Sappada, Solda** and **San Candido** on their heels. Write ahead to the tourist offices in Belluno, Trento or Bolzano, or book a week's *Settimana Bianca* package (a week's room and board at a hotel, ski-pass and instruction) from CIT (Citalia) or other travel offices all over Italy. The *Dolomiti Superski* pass gives unlimited access (for about $50/£35 a day) to 464 lifts, 1180 km of ski runs for periods of one, two or three weeks, ✆ 0471 795 397, ✉ 0471 794 282. There's excellent information on the internet: *www.DolomitiSuperski.com*

Getting Around the Dolomites

Even the heirs of the Romans can make the **trains** go only so far. The line north of Venice, Treviso and Belluno passes through Pieve di Cadore before petering out in Calalzo di Cadore, 35km from Cortina d'Ampezzo (2½hours from Venice). The western Dolomites–Trento, Bolzano to the Brenner Pass are on the Verona– Munich (*Monaco* in Italian) line. Branch lines run from Bolzano to Merano and Malles Venosta, to the west, and from Bressanone to Brunico and San Candido to the east.

To make up for the lack of trains, the Dolomites are exceptionally well served by two **bus** companies—*Dolomiti-Bus* in the east (for example, with daily routes to Àgordo, Arabba, Falcade and Colle S. Lucia from Venice) and the cheerful but still *SAD Buses* in the west. Besides their normal runs, the companies add special scenic tours in July and August from the major centres.

The Eastern Dolomites: the Cadore

Although mostly Italian-speaking, much of the Cadore, the district north of Belluno along the upper Piave, was incorporated into Italy only after the First World War. Its somewhat over-ripe, fashionable heart is Cortina d'Ampezzo, host of the 1956 Winter Olympics, which did much to introduce the Dolomites to the world. The Alte Vie pass through this region as well, winding across some of the most renowned ridges and peaks in the range.

Tourist Information

Pieve di Cadore: Via XX Settembre 18, in Tai, ✆ 0435 31644, ✉ 0435 31645.
Santo Stefano di Cadore: Via Venezia 40, ✆ 0435 62230, ✉ 0435 62077.
Sappada: Borgata Bach 20, ✆ 0435 469 131, ✉ 0435 66233.
San Vito di Cadore: Via Nazionale 9, ✆ 0436 9119, ✉ 0436 99345.

The Piave Valley

The roads north along the River Piave from Belluno (SS50) and Treviso (SS51) meet at the junction of Ponte nelle Alpi before continuing up through scenery marked by the steep pyramids of **Monte Dolada** and **Piz Gallina**. A less benign mountain, **Toc** (6301ft), looms over the town of **Longarone**. In 1963 a landslide from its slopes crashed into the local reservoir, Lake Vaiont, creating a tidal wave that killed 1917 people in Longarone; a memorial church, unfortunately resembling a parking garage, documents the disaster and has a few poignant bits salvaged from the mud. A road runs along the path of the disaster, the lofty and narrow **Gola del Vaiont**, to the lake, 6km to the east. From Longarone there's also the option of turning west on the SS251 for the **Val Zoldana**, a lovely valley lining the River Maè, with typical hamlets in wood and stone, the cradle of Italy's best *gelato* makers. The valley road passes the stunning peaks of Civetta and Pelmo on the way to Selva di Cadore (*see* p.391).

The main road from Longarone skirts the high banks of the Piave north into the foothills of the Antelao and Marmarole and **Pieve di Cadore**. *Pieve* means parish, and from Roman times on this was the most important one in the Cadore, a status that grew with the reputation of that mighty wielder of the brush, Tiziano Vecellio (Titian), born here *c*.1483. His statue stands in the main piazza, just up from his birthplace, the pretty **Casa Natale di Tiziano** (*open daily 9.30–12.30 and 4–7; closed Mon; adm*), containing drawings, studies and some original furnishings. In the church of **Santa Maria Nascente**, the last chapel on the left holds his *Madonna with SS. Andrew and Titian*, starring his own family—his daughter as the Virgin, his son as Titian the Bishop, his brother as St Andrew and Titian himself looking in from the left. The most important building in Pieve doesn't leave room for any false modesty but calls itself the **Palazzo della Magnifica Comunità Cadorina** (*same hours as Titian's Birthplace*). Built in 1525, it now houses the local historical museum, with pre-Roman weapons and 2nd-century BC bronze figurines. Towards Tai, at the crossroads, the **Museo degli Occhaia** (*open daily 9.30–12 and 3.30–7; adm*) contains a collection of antique spectacles. But what Pieve is proudest of these days is Babbo Natale (the Italian Santa Claus), who has made the town his home, with a Christmas-letter-answering service for the bambini.

The road and the Piave continue north past the end of the rail line at **Calalzo**, where can you catch a bus for the resort **Santo Stefano di Cadore**, located in the beautiful **Comelico Valley**. From here you can continue northwest to Cortina, or take another beautiful road east towards the popular resort of **Sappada**, a town more Austrian in feel than Italian.

From Pieve di Cadore there is also a direct road to Cortina d'Ampezzo, the SS51, which winds through the **Valle del Boite** with its many rustic wooden chalets, between the Antelao massif, the 'King of Cadore' and **Pelmo**, one of the most unusual and striking peak clusters in the Dolomites. The road passes through **Borca di Cadore** and the more important resort of **San Vito di Cadore**, an excellent base for ascending Pelmo and nearby peaks.

Where to Stay and Eating Out

Sappada ✉ 32047

One reason for Sappada's popularity is its abundance of reasonably priced accommodation. A couple of good choices are **★★Corona Ferrea**, Borgata Kratten 17, 🕾 0435 469 103, ✆ 0435 469 103 (*cheap*), which has comfortable rooms, all with bath (*open July–20 Sept and 20 Dec–15 April*), and the small **★★★Sierra Hof**, Borgata Soravia 110, 🕾 0435 469 110, ✆ 0435 469 647 (*cheap*), near the centre of the village. In Cima Sappada, 4km away, **★★★Belvedere**, Piazza Cima 93, 🕾/✆ 0435 469 112 (*moderate*) has only 14 rooms, but does have its own sauna. It also offers one of the area's best restaurants: mountain specialities include several variations on venison and tasty desserts. *Open Dec–Mar and mid-June–Sept.*

San Vito di Cadore ✉ 32046

There are a number of comfortable hotels here: the best is ★★★★**Marcora**, Via Roma 28, ✆ 0436 9101, 🖷 0436 99156 (*very expensive*), in a fine setting with a pool. *Open 20 June–10 Sept and 20 Dec–20 Mar.* ★★★**Cima Belprá**, Via Calvi 1, at Chiapuzza, ✆ 0436 890 441, 🖷 0436 890 418 (*moderate–cheap*) is a welcoming place with the best restaurant in the whole area: **La Scaletta**, with beautiful views, and traditional polenta and beef dishes. *Closed Mon out of season, and Nov.*

Cortina d'Ampezzo

Cortina's the sort of place where David Niven and Audrey Hepburn in turtlenecks and sunglasses would sit about in a café, but it also enjoys the best location in the Dolomites: a lofty (4015ft–10,637ft), sunny, cross-shaped meadow at the junction of the Boite and Bigontina valleys, in the centre of a ring of extraordinary mountains—Tofane, the great mount 'owl' (scene of the 1997 World Cup); Cristallo; Sorapis, licked by stony flames; and the Cinque Torri, the 'five towers'. Devoted heart and soul to fun and the sporting life, Cortina is almost as well known for its night-time activities, when the *après ski* crowd fills its clubs to trip the light fantastic until the wee hours of dawn. But whatever worldly pleasure and delight this snowy fleshpot offers, it comes at a price, rating right up there with Capri, Portofino and Venice herself on the bottom line of the tab.

Getting Around

Cortina's **bus** station is just off Via Marconi, and is served by SAD (✆ 167 846 047), and Dolomiti buses (✆ 0435 332 155). Services are greatly augmented from June to September, when buses serve virtually every paved road in the region; SAD buses make the Great Dolomites route once a day. There's one bus a day direct from Venice or Treviso (✆ 042 15944). The nearest **train** stations are Dobbiaco, 32km north (on the Bolzano–Lienz line), or Calalzo di Cadore, 35km south; both have regular bus connections to Cortina.

Tourist Information

Piazzetta S. Francesco 8, near the central Piazza Venezia, ✆ 0436 3231, 🖷 0436 3235, *apt1@sunrise.it* They have an accommodation service, good maps of surrounding trails, and information about excursions. The local Alpine guide organization is next door, and open in July, August and September, ✆ 0436 868 505.

The Sporting Life

The 1956 Olympics endowed Cortina with superb winter sports facilities; here you can ski-jump, speed-skate, fly down bobsled and luge runs, and cut figures of eight in the ice stadium, not to mention the thousand and one downhill and cross-country ski runs in the vicinity. In the summer, it's an excellent base for hiking, rock-climbing, delta-planing, torrentialism and more, while in town there's a riding school, tennis and summer/winter swimming pools, and activities like the Ice Disco Dance in the Olympic Ice Stadium.

Cortina has its share of trendy shops, and a museum of contemporary art you can take in if it rains—the **Museo Ciasa de Ra Regoles**, Via del Parco, on the corner of Corso d'Italia (*open daily 10.30–12.30 and 4–7.30; closed Mon; adm*) which has sections on palaeontology and ethnography, and art by De Pisis, Morandi, De Chirico and others. Two cablecars from Cortina wait to whisk you up to the mountains, both at the end of the town bus lines: in the north, near the Olympic stadium, to **Tofana di Mezzo** (10,637ft) where there are privately run Alpine refuges, and in the west, to **Tondi di Faloria** (7685ft).

Cortina ✉ 32043   *Where to Stay and Eating Out*

Expect to run up against the full- or half-board requirement nearly everywhere in Cortina in its high season—which is mortifying to the pocketbook though not to the flesh; the local cuisine is usually as haute as the price.

If you're putting on the dog in Cortina, the place to do it is the ★★★★★**Miramonti Majestic**, Via Miramonti 103, ✆ 0436 4201, ✆ 0436 867 019 (*luxury*). Warm, traditional and rustic, it has pretty wooden balconies affording magnificent views. The well-designed rooms have all imaginable creature comforts, and there's an indoor pool, tennis courts, golf, exercise facilities and sauna. *Open July–Aug, and Christmas–Mar.*

If you'd rather be in the centre of the action, historic ★★★★**De La Poste**, Piazza Roma 14, ✆ 0436 4271, ✆0436 868 435 (*very expensive*) is a large Alpine chalet with classy rooms and balconies; the Poste's terrace and bar see much of Cortina's social round, especially in the evening; half-board mandatory in high season.

Ten minutes' walk from the centre, down at the bottom of the valley beside the river, another Alpine chalet, ★★★★**Corona**, Via Val di Sotto 10, ✆ 0436 3251, ✆ 0436 867 339 (*expensive*) is memorable for a modern art collection even more extensive than the one in the museum; it's also more convenient than most for the ski lift. *Open June–Sept and Dec–Mar.* Award-winning ★★★**Da Beppe Sello**, Via Ronco 68, ✆ 0436 3236, ✆ 0436 3237 (*expensive*) is warm and welcoming, and serves some of the best food in Cortina, with game specialities in season. *Open Nov–Easter and mid-May–mid-Sept.*

Elegant **El Toulà**, Via Ronco 123, ✆ 0436 3339, near Pocol (*expensive*), in a refurbished wooden farmhouse, specializes in perfect grilled meats, roast lamb, and desserts with a Tyrolean touch, accompanied by a renowned wine list. *Open Christmas–Easter and 15 July–30 Aug; closed Mon.* Its rival, **Tivoli**, Via Lacedel 34, ✆ 0436 866 400 (*expensive*), northeast of the centre, offers lovely views and innovative, ultra refined cuisine. *Closed Mon.*

★★★**Menardi**, Via Majon 110, ✆ 0436 2400, ✆ 0436 862 183 (*moderate*) is an 800-year-old farmhouse that's been run as an inn by the same family for the past century, furnished with antiques and bedecked with fresh flowers. *Open 20 June–20 Sept and 20 Dec–10 April.* ★★**Cavallino**, Corso d'Italia 142, ✆/✆ 0436 2614 (*moderate*) is small and friendly.

A brief walk up the hill behind town brings you to **Al Camin**, Via Alverà 99, ✆ 0436 862 010 (*moderate*), cosy with lots of wood and a fireplace, serving local versions of polenta and goulash. *Closed Mon.*

★★★**Imperio**, Via C. Battisti 66, ✆ 0436 4246, @ 0436 4248 (*cheap*) is an unpretentious hotel with no restaurant but adequate rooms. *Closed May.* As a second choice try the ★★**Montana**, Corso Italia 94, ✆ 0436 860 498, @ 0463 868 211 (*cheap*).

Excursions From Cortina

As a major crossroads, Cortina offers numerous forays into the surrounding mountains. For the classic Great Dolomites Road between Cortina and Bolzano, *see* p.410.

Tourist Information

Auronzo: Via Roma 10, ✆ 0435 9359, @ 0435 400 161.
Dobbiaco: Via delle Dolomoiti 3, ✆ 0474 72132, @ 0474 72730.
Àlleghe: Piazza Kennedy 17, ✆ 0437 523 333, @ 0437 723 881.
Àgordo: Via Sommariva 10, ✆ 0437 62105, @ 0437 65205.

Lake Misurina and around

For a beautiful short trip from Cortina, take the SS48 and SS48b over the lofty **Tre Croci Pass** to **Lake Misurina**, shimmering below the jagged peaks of Sorapis and the remarkable triple-spired **Tre Cime di Lavaredo**, 15km northeast of Cortina. The colours of Misurina are so brilliant they look touched-up on the postcards; as a resort it makes a quiet alternative to Cortina, especially if ice-skating is your sport. From Misurina it's a magnificent 7km drive up to the **Rifugio Auronzo**, located just beneath the Tre Cime di Lavaredo, where you can make the easy walk to the 1916 **Bersaglieri memorial**, honouring Italy's famous sharpshooters. More fine views await from **Monte Piana**, a lofty meadow 6km north of Misurina.

Circular routes from Misurina to Cortina

There are two possible circular routes from Misurina back to Cortina that make rewarding, full-day excursions. Both begin to the east on the SS48 via **Auronzo di Cadore**, past a peak known as the **Corno del Doge** for its resemblance to the Doge's bonnet. Auronzo, on the shores of an artificial lake, surrounded by fragrant spruce forests, makes another fine base, and has a cablecar and chairlifts up **Monte Agudo**.

From Auronzo you can circle south around Pieve di Cadore and the Valle del Boite (161km altogether; *see* above, p.387) or take the longer route around to the north (224km) through **Comelico** and the beautiful **Val di Sesto**. The route passes into the Alto Adige, through **San Candido/Innichen**, a pretty resort on the River Drava; it has a Benedictine monastery and a lovely Romanesque collegiate church, the 13th-century **SS. Candidus e Corbinian**, its altar decorated with a superb early 13th-century *Crucifixion* group in polychrome wood.

The turn back to Cortina (SS51) is at **Dobbiaco/Toblach**, one of the original Dolomite resorts, thanks to its magnificent setting and lake, and a railway station built by the Habsburgs. The large **castle** in the old part of town was built for Emperor Maximilian in 1500. In July Dobbiaco holds a series of concerts in honour of Mahler, who spent his summers here; in summer, too, you can visit the little **Museo Gustav Mahler**, 4km from the centre at Casa

Trenker (*ring the tourist office for hours*). From Dobbiaco the road heads south past wooded Lake Dobbiaco and enters the dramatic **Val di Landro**, where the Cristallo group looms over **Carbonin/Schluderbach**. Beyond are a pair of little lakes, and the lonely ruins of the **Castel Sant'Umberto**. The road then circles around castle-crowned **Podestagno**, before descending into the Ampezzo with the Le Tofane group storming up to the right.

Cortina to Colle Santa Lucia and Agordo

There are two routes to these mountains southwest of Cortina: the main one follows the Great Dolomites Road (*see* p.410) through the Falzarego Pass, before taking the SS203 southwards at Andraz; while an alternative, lesser-known but equally pretty route takes the smaller SS638 road through the **Passo di Giau**, where in recent years some of the most important Mesolithic tombs in Europe (5000 BC) were discovered. The artefacts of 'Mondeval man' can now be seen down in **Selva di Cadore**, in the **Museo Storico** (*open July and Aug daily 4–6.30*). Selva is a growing resort in the lovely Val Fiorentina, where a road crosses into the Valle di Zoldana and ends up at Longarone (*see* p.387). Above Selva, **Colle Santa Lucia**, is a pretty place with its old agricultural hamlets and a beautiful belvedere.

Continuing south from Colle the road passes **Caprile** and the mighty north wall of Civetta *en route* to **Alleghe** with its lovely **lake**, formed in 1771 by a landslide from Civetta. At **Cencenighe** you have the option of turning off for Falcade and San Martino di Castrozza (*see* p.398). **Agordo** (45km) is an attractive town and resort in the Val Cordévole, along one of the principal branches of the Piave. The Passo Duran above Agordo leads back to Cortina via the Valle di Zoldo and the village of **Dont** (another 21km)—there are splendid views of Civetta and Pelmo, and you can buy samples of local woodcarving.

Where to Stay and Eating Out

Misurina ✉ 32040

★★★**Lavaredo**, Via Monte Piana 11, ✆ 0436 39227, ✉ 0436 39127 (*moderate*) has tennis courts and a good restaurant. *Closed Nov–mid-Dec*. The ★★**Dolomiti des Alpes**, Via Monte Piana, ✆ 0436 39031, ✉ 0436 39216 (*cheap*), just above the lake, has a sauna-solarium. *Closed Oct–mid-Dec*.

Auronzo di Cadore ✉ 32041

★★★**Auronzo**, Via Roma 30, ✆ 0435 400 202, ✉ 0435 99879 (*moderate*) is a cosy old place on the lake shore, with tennis. *Open Dec–Mar and June–Sept*. Comfortable ★★**Juventus**, Via Padova 26, ✆ 0435 9221, ✉ 0435 99284 (*moderate*) is right on the beach. ★★**Vienna**, Via Verona 2, ✆ 0435 9394 (*cheap*) is near the lake with good views. East of Auronzo at Cima Gogna, **Cavaliere**, ✆ 0435 9834 (*moderate*) serves delicious suckling pig and risotto with herbs or mushrooms. *Closed Wed*.

Dobbiaco/Toblach ✉ 39034

Since 1911 the same family has run the recently renovated ★★★★**Cristallo**, Via S. Giovanni 37, ✆ 0474 972 138, ✉ 0474 972 755 (*expensive*), a fine resort hotel in a beautiful setting, with an indoor pool and sauna. *Open Christmas–Easter and June–mid-Oct*. Dine on refined mountain cuisine at **Winkelkeller**, Via Conte Künigi 8, ✆ 0474 972 022 (*moderate*). *Closed Wed, June and part of Oct*.

Selva di Cadore ✉ 32020

★★★**Giglio Rosso**, at Pescul, ✆ 0437 720 310, 📠 0437 521 110 (*moderate*) is a fine place both to stay and to eat, where the kitchen does a fine mulberry risotto and turkey in beer. *Open Dec–Mar and June–Sept.*

Àlleghe/Caprile ✉ 32022

The 130-year-old ★★★★**Alla Posta**, Piazza Dogliani 19, in Caprile ✆ 0437 721 171, 📠 0437 721 677 (*expensive*) is the most prestigious hotel, with an indoor pool, sauna and good restaurant. *Open 20 Dec–15 April and 15 June–30 Sept.* ★★★**Coldai**, Via Coldai 13, ✆ 0437 523 305, 📠 0437 523 438 (*moderate–cheap*) has lovely views over the lake, and pleasant rooms. *Closed May–mid-June, Oct and Nov.* The ★★**Marmolada**, Corso Veneto 27, ✆ 0437 721 107 (*cheap*) is simple but adequate—who wants to spend time indoors anyway? *Closed May and Oct.*

The Western Dolomites: Trentino

The autonomous province of Trentino encompasses the western Dolomites, as beautiful as the eastern mountains, especially the Val di Fassa and the isolated but hauntingly majestic Brenta Group, to the west of the Adige. Unlike the Alto Adige/Süd Tirol further north, Trentino is mostly Italian in language and heritage, sprinkled with a Ladin minority in the valleys. Trento itself is a fine little art city, worth a day on its own.

Tourist Information

No province in Italy has such an efficient and enthusiastic tourist board—it even has branches in **Rome** (Via del Babuino 20, 06 3609 5842, 📠 063 202 4134) and **Milan** (Piazza Diaz 5, ✆ 02 8646 1251, 📠 02 7200 2188). Between Verona and Trento the only tourist office is in **Rovereto**: Via Dante 63, ✆ 0464 430363, 📠 0464 435 528.

From Verona to Trento: Val Lagarina and Rovereto

Following the Adige up from Verona, the A22 and SS12 enter Trentino near **Avio**, dominated by the proud 14th-century **Castello di Sabbionara** (*open Tues–Sun 10–1 and 2–6, till 5 in winter; closed Jan; adm*). Its guardhouse preserves a wonderful fresco cycle of battling knights, while in the keep the frescoes depict scenes of courtly love.

Further up the Adige, past a sea of vineyards, **Rovereto**, 'the Athens of the Trentino', is an evocative old place, the second city of the Trentino, built around an imposing Venetian castle; between 1416–87 the city formed the northern extent of the Serenissima, before the Trentini, with the aid of the Tyroleans, shoved the Venetians back to Verona. This area was also hotly contested in the First World War, and the castle contains an extensive **war museum** devoted primarily to that conflict (*open Mar–Nov Tues–Sun 8.30–12.30 and 2–6; July–Sept 8.30–6.30; adm*). Cannons from each of the 19 belligerents were melted down to make the largest ringing bell in the world, the **Campana dei Caduti**, located in the southern quarter of Rovereto; it rings in memory of the fallen every day at sundown.

The Futurist Fortunato Depero (1892–1960) worked for many years in the town, and bequeathed it the **Museo Depero**, Via della Terra 53 (*open daily 9–12.30 and 2.30–6;*

closed Mon; adm), near the castle, a perfect and rather striking little museum designed by the artist himself as a showcase for his tapestries, puppets and paintings. Rovereto was also the home town of archaeologist Paolo Orsi, who willed his statues, busts and vases from Magna Graecia to the city. They are displayed, along with ethnographic items and a natural science collection, in the new **Musei Civici**, Borgo S. Caterina 43 (*open Tues–Sat 9–12 and 3–6*).

Just southeast of Rovereto, you can walk the 'Path of the Dinosaurs', marked by footprints planted 200 million years ago. The 'Path of Peace', a long-distance walk along the front line of the First World War, ends at Mount Zugna just to the south, by the Campana dei Caduti.

Across the Adige from Rovereto, **Isera** is the centre for the production of Marzemino, one of Trentino's finest red wines. To the north, visible from the road to Trento, the partly ruined but still imposing **Castel Beseno** (*open April–Oct daily 9–12 and 2–5.30; closed Mon; adm*) is the largest castle in the region, and has rooms frescoed with scenes of the months. Two small resorts on a 3280ft plateau below Monte Cornetto can be reached by the SS350 from Calliano: **Folgaria**, with its 17th-century Maso Spilzi, restored to its original appearance (*open June–Sept*), and the larger **Lavarone**, near the lake of the same name, where Freud spent three summers.

Where to Stay and Eating Out

Rovereto ✉ 38068

***Rovereto**, Corso Rosmini 82/d, ✆ 0464 435 522, 🖃 0464 439 644 (*expensive*) is a fine central hotel, with comfortable air-conditioned rooms in a variety of styles, and an excellent restaurant: **Novecento** (*moderate*), featuring regional dishes, as well as a vegetarian menu. *Closed Sun.* There's also an excellent, modern **Youth Hostel**, Via della Scuola 16, ✆ 0464 433 707 (*cheap*), near the railway station.

The best place to eat in Rovereto is **Al Borgo**, Via Garibaldi 13, ✆ 0464 436 300 (*expensive*), a sophisticated little restaurant in the heart of town. The menu features dishes like ham and spinach in puff pastry, risotto with lemon, or turbot with artichokes, and fantastic desserts, all accompanied by piano music in the evening. Rare in Italy, they bake their own bread. *Closed Sun eve and Mon, part of Feb and July.*

Lavarone ✉ 38046

Freud stayed at the ***Hotel du Lac** in Frazione Chiesa, ✆ 0464 783 112 🖃 0464 783 255 (*moderate*). An indoor swimming pool and tennis courts in addition to its pretty setting on the lake make it a fine place to forget your neurosis.

Trento

In the 16th century Emperor Charles V, ruler of much of Europe and the Americas, found his Germanic possessions in the throes of the Reformation, and his Catholic domains bracing for a hysterical reaction. Charles sought to heal the rift in his realm by asking Pope Clement VII to call a council to look into some urgently needed reforms. Clement demurred until Charles sacked Rome in 1527, but years would pass before one of his successors, Paul III, actually convoked the prelates, after quibbling about venue—Charles wanted it on Imperial turf, while the pope insisted on an Italian city. Italian Trento, ruled by a powerful bishop-prince in the Holy Roman Empire, proved to be the perfect compromise, thanks to the lobbying efforts of the city's great Renaissance patron, Bernardo Cles, Prince-Bishop from 1514 to 1539. By the time it started, the Council of Trent (1545–63) was too late to bring the Protestants back into the fold, although it did provide the doctrinal ammo for the Counter-Reformation.

The Council put Trento on Europe's map, but it doesn't put on airs. Lying at the foot of Monte Bondone, between the banks of the Adige and the Fersina, it is refreshingly unpretentious and charming; many of its gently winding streets are embellished with *al fresco* frescoes, and its bishop's palace has a fresco cycle of the months that alone is worth the trip.

Getting Around

The **bus** and FS **railway** station are almost next to each other on the Piazza Dante. Atestina buses go up all the valleys in Trentino, © 0461 983 627. For the Trento-Malè station, with trains up the Val di Non to Cles, turn left out of the main station and walk 500m to Via Seconda da Trento 7, © 0461 238 350.

Tourist Information

Via Alfieri 4, across Piazza Dante from the station, © 0461 983 880, © 0461 984 508. **Trentino** regional information: Via Romagnosi 3, © 0461 839 000, © 0461 260 245; freephone in Italy, © 1678 45034; *apt@provincia.tn.it*

To the Duomo

Trento's points of interest can easily be seen on foot. **Piazza Dante**, in front of the station, is a convenient place to start (and find a place to park); the statues of the eponymous poet and other Italian celebrities were erected here amid the public gardens in 1896 by Trento's irredentist societies, in defiance of their Austrian rulers. Next to the station itself, the attractive 12th-century collegiate church of **San Lorenzo** stands in a sunken lawn.

From San Lorenzo, Via Andrea Pozzo and Via D. Orfane lead to the gracious pink **Santa Maria Maggiore** (1520), a simple and elegant Renaissance church with ornate portals, commissioned by Bernardo Cles. It was large enough to be used for several sittings of the Council of Trent, and has a beautiful organ gallery by Vincenzo Grandi (1534) and, among its paintings, the *Dispute with the Doctors* by Giambattista Moroni from Bergamo.

One block east of S. Maria Maggiore runs **Via Belenzani**, forced through the medieval quarters by Bernardo Cles who wanted a proper straight street to the cathedral. It is lined with fine palaces: the best, **Palazzo Pona Geremia**, is entirely covered with recently restored 16th-century frescoes of the locals receiving the Emperor Maximilian and mythological subjects. Via Belenzani ends with the handsome porticoed **Casa Cazuffi**, decorated with monochrome frescoes from the 1530s. These overlook **Piazza Duomo** and the 18th-century **fountain of Neptune**, the region's sea god symbol—not an obvious mascot until you focus on the trident he wields and remember the city's Roman name, *Tridentum*.

The Duomo and Museo Diocesano Tridentino

Trento's beautiful **duomo** was designed in the 13th century and completed in 1515. Although it took 300 years to build, the style is all monumental Romanesque, richly decorated with galleries along its three apses and dome. The Council of Trent held its three major sessions here, and its decrees were blessed before the huge crucifix, still there in a right-hand chapel. The baldacchino over the high altar is a replica of St Peter's. Excavations unearthed a 6th-century basilica under the Duomo, first home of the relics of Trento's patron, San Vigilio.

Vigilio and the Ciusi-Gobj Masquerade

 Vigilius was a Roman patrician who studied in Athens then moved to Trent with his family, where he was made bishop. His persuasive powers converted his diocese, but when he went further afield to the Val Rendena and tipped over a statue of Saturn, he was stoned to death. He is celebrated every 20–26 June with an enthusiastic *Palio dell'Oca*, in which teams from each of the city's districts don 17th-century costumes and race down the Adige on rafts, trying to slip a ring over the neck of a papier-mâché goose suspended over the river. The climactic moment comes on 26 June, commemorating the same day back in the Middle Ages when Trento hired workers from Feltre to reinforce the walls. Food supplies being low, Trento's bishop realized that the city could not afford to feed the workers and sent them home—only the Feltrese returned in the night to raid the stores. The ensuing battle is re-enacted in costume in the Piazza Duomo—the *Ciusi* are from Feltre, and they have five chances to break the ranks of Trento's *Gobj* to make off with the prize: a hot pot of bubbling polenta.

Next to the cathedral, the **Palazzo Pretorio**, crowned with swallowtail battlements, and a medieval **Torre Civica** house the excellent **Museo Diocesano Tridentino** (*open daily 9–12.30 and 2.30–6, closed Sun; adm*), renovated, and opened by John Paul II in 1995. There are paintings of the Council of Trent; a 16th-century portrayal of a *Mass of St Gregory*, its nonchalant congregation including a large band of pious skeletons; three 12th-century ivory caskets made by Islamic craftsmen and other treasures; and four charming 15th-century wooden altarpieces from the Val di Non, portraying three local martyrs in scenes observed by a man in a beaver hat. The museum's greatest prize, a cycle of six early 15th-century Flemish tapestries by Peter Van Aelst—woven masterpieces of portraiture and detail—were brought to Trento by Bernard Cles. (*The ticket also includes access to the excavations.*)

Castello di Buonconsiglio and its Museums

From Via Belenzani, Via Roma/Via Gian Antonio Manci leads to the magnificent residence of the bishop-princes, **Castello di Buonconsiglio** (*open summer Tues–Sun 10–6; winter 9–12 and 4–5.30; adm exp*). Because of Trento's strategic location on the main highway to Rome, the medieval German Emperors sought to keep the city's favour by granting its bishops a near-regal temporal status. Their castle consists of two buildings—the 13th-century Castelvecchio, with its Venetian Gothic loggia, and the Magno Palazzo, added by Bernardo Cles (1528–36). Today they house the provincial museum of art: medieval manuscripts, statues (especially fine wooden sculptures from the 15th and 16th centuries) and paintings, although these are over-shadowed by the castle's own 16th-century frescoes by Marcello Fogolino, Gerolamo Romanino and Dosso Dossi, the latter who painted the Olympian gods to conform to Counter-Reformation modesty levels—the gods model turn-of-the-century bathing costumes, and the goddesses look like Tarzan's Jane. Best of all are the ravishing, detailed **frescoes of the**

months in the Torre dell'Aquila, painted around the year 1400. While the nobility sports and flirts in the foreground, peasants perform their month-by-month labours, tending their flocks, making cheese, planting and harvesting, and making wine. One scene has the oldest-known depiction of Trento, dominated by the castle itself.

Buonconsiglio also has an historical collection from the Napoleonic era to the Second World War; the idea for this museum was suggested in 1903 by local patriot Cesare Battisti, who, 13 years later, was executed for high treason in this same castle, by the Austrians. His and his companions' cells, the courtroom, and the ditch where they were shot and hanged, are shrines. You've probably already noticed Battisti's memorial—a marble circle of columns on the hill over the Adige. The present is served by the new **Galleria Civica d'Arte Contemporaneo** (*open daily 10–12 and 4–7; closed Mon; adm*), which hosts changing exhibitions.

More Museums: Art and Planes

Prince-Bishop Cristoforo Madruzzo did not feel quite at ease in the Castello di Buonconsiglio, and built a suburban residence on the Adige where he could get away from it all. This, the Palazzo delle Albere, 'of the poplars'—named for the trees that once lined the road out—now shelters the **Museo d'Arte Moderna e Contemporanea**, Via R. da Sansoverino 45 (*open daily 10–6; closed Mon; adm*), devoted to 19th–20th-century art, mostly Italian with a high concentration of Futurists, who offer a stark contrast to the Renaissance frescoes by Fogolino.

The **Museo dell'Aeronautica Gianni Caproni**, Via Lidorno 3, by Trento's airport (*open daily 9–1 and 4–6; closed Mon; adm*) began in 1929 as the private collection of Gianni Caproni, a native of Trentino and one of Italy's leading aviation engineers in the 1910s and 20s, and whose aviation factory in Trento only closed in the 1950s; the museum contains a number of unique specimens, as well as a model of Leonardo da Vinci's flying machine.

Around Trento: Monte Bondone and Lake Caldonazzo

The slopes of Trento's own mountain, Bondone, can be easily reached by road or cablecar (*Mon–Sat 7am–9pm, Sun 9am–6pm*), departing from the Ponte di San Lorenzo in Trento (behind the bus station) and climbing as far as **Sardagna**. At least three buses a day continue on to **Vaneze** and **Vason**, both ski resorts; from Vason another cablecar ascends to one of Bondone's three summits (6881ft). Further on, **Viotte** has an Alpine refuge and **Botanical Garden** (*open June–Sept daily 9–12 and 2–5*), one of the richest in Europe, founded in 1938 on the banks of two artificial lakes and planted with over two thousand species of high-altitude flora. Keep your eyes peeled for the pair of golden eagles who have recently nested nearby.

Another popular excursion is to head east up the Val Sugana along the Brenta to warm **Lago di Caldonazzo**, 'Trento's Lido', ideal for swimming, sailing and windsurfing. From lakeside **Vetriolo Terme** you can hike up to the summit of Panarotta for splendid views over Caldonazzo and its equally warm neighbour, **Lake Levico**.

Trento ✉ *38100*   ***Where to Stay and Eating Out***

Some of the bishops at the Council slept at the predecessor of the ★★★★**Accademia**, Vicolo Collico 4/6, near Santa Maria Maggiore, ✆ 0461 233 600, ✉ 0461 230 174 (*expensive*). The panelled rooms are air-conditioned; the restaurant is excellent, with a menu that changes monthly. ★★★★**Buonconsiglio**, Via Romagnosi 16/18, ✆ 0461 272 888, ✉ 0461 272 889 (*expensive*) is another fine, newly revamped choice in the historic centre.

Trento's celebrated **Chiesa**, in the 17th-century Palazzo Wolkenstein, Parco San Marco (near the Castello di Buonconsiglio) ✆ 0461 238 766 (*expensive*) is famous for its 'Apple Party Menu' in which Trentino's delicious apples appear in every dish; other specialities are smoked trout and cheese strudels, an extensive wine list and scrumptious desserts. Reservations essential. *Closed Sun, Mon lunch and Aug.*

Osteria a Le Due Spade, Via Don Rizzi 11, ✆ 0461 234 343 (*expensive*), in business since 1545, serves refined dishes in a delightful setting, decorated with mosaics. *Closed Sun, and Mon lunch.*

Two hotels with the same name offer chances for inexpensive sleeps in the centre: ★★**Venezia**, Via Belenzani 70, ✆ 0461 234 559 (*cheap*), on Trento's prettiest street; and ★**Venezia**, Piazza Duomo 45, ✆/✉ 0461 234 144 (*cheap*), with small, basic rooms with bath; ask for one overlooking the Duomo and fountain of Neptune.

★★★**America,** Via Torre Verde 50, ✆ 0461 983 010, ✉ 0461 230 603 (*moderate*) is a very comfortable choice from the 1920s, within walking distance of the train station. ★★★**Aquila d'Oro**, Via Belenzani 76, ✆/✉ 0461 986 282 (*moderate*), in the centre, has extremely comfortable rooms, as well as café tables spilling out into the street.

If you have a car, ★★★**Villa Madruzzo**, Via Ponte Alto 26, ✆ 0461 986 220, ✉ 0461 986 361 (*moderate*), 3km east of Trento in Cognola, is in a charming 19th-century villa in a leafy park, with comfortable rooms, fine views and a good traditional restaurant.

Right under the Castello di Buonconsiglio, the retro **Port'Aquila**, Via Cervara 66, ✆ 0461 230 420 (*moderate*) serves good *canederli* (Tyrolean gnocchi), polenta and other traditional dishes, served with well-aged Trentino vintages. *Closed Sun and Aug.* **Al Vo'**, Vicolo del Vo' 11 (off Via Torre Verde), ✆ 0461 985 374 (*moderate–cheap*) serves good regional dishes and unusual specialities. *Closed Sun and two weeks in July.*

The popular **Forst**, located in the middle of Trento in the 16th-century palace on Oss Mazzurana 38, ✆ 0461 235 590 (*cheap*) is the place to drink beer and Trentino's wines, eat a pizza *tirolese* (with mushrooms and *speck*) or a *piatta trentino* (a mixture of local specialities). *Closed Mon and July.*

East of Trento

The magic mountains wait, whether you turn east, west or north of Trento. San Martino di Castrozza and Paneveggio National Park are the main attractions to the east, along with two lovely valleys and a score of lovely lakes.

Tourist Information

Cavalese: Via F.lli Bronzetti 60, ✆ 0462 241 111, ✉ 0462 230 649. **Predazzo**: ✆ 0462 501 237, ✉ 0462 502 093. **Canazei**: in the Val di Fassa, ✆ 0462 601 113, ✉ 0462 602 502. **San Martino di Castrozza**: Via Passo Rolle 165, ✆ 0439 768 867, ✉ 0439 768 814. **Fiera di Primiero**: ✆ 0439 62407, ✉ 0439 62992.

Val di Fiemme and Val di Fassa

These two northeasternmost valleys of Trentino, running between the Pale di San Martino, Rosengarten and the western slopes of the Marmolada, are among the most stunning and well-known among the cross country skiing fraternity. From Trento the road ascends the Val di Cembra, passing through a striking region of rocks eroded into spiky 'pyramids' near **Segonzano**. The once autonomous **Val di Fiemme** begins at **Cavalese**, where the elected *Regolani* held their parliament by the parish church; you can still see their stone benches, the **Banc de la Reson**. The *Magnifica Comunità* of Cavalese still has considerable say in local affairs, running the Val di Fiemme from the grand old frescoed **Palazzo della Comunità**, rebuilt in the 1500s by Bernardo Cles. Inside, a **museum** (*open July, Aug and Christmas daily 4.30–7.30*) documents Fiemme's proud past, and has works by the 17th–18th-century Fiemme school, a group of harmless painters who travelled about the smaller courts of Europe. A cablecar from Cavalese ascends to **Mount Cermis** (7311ft).

Other places to aim for in the Val di Fiemme include **Tesero**, a delightful village with a 15th-century bridge, that hasn't surrendered its soul to tourism, and where furniture- and instrument-makers still ply their old trades. Perhaps too well. The chapel of **San Rocco** (1528) is frescoed with a 'Sunday Christ', surrounded by all the tools that are taboo on the Sabbath; were the locals inveterate workaholics or merely avoiding the collection plate? In **Predazzo** the **Civico Museo di Geologia**, founded in 1899 in Piazza SS. Filippo e Giacomo (*under restoration*) takes the subject of Dolomitic rocks and marine fossils in hand; the museum has set up a marked half- or full-day geological path at Doss Cappèl, reached by the Predazzo chair lift. Predazzo is the turn off for San Martino di Castrozza (*see* below).

Otherwise, continue straight into the beautiful **Val di Fassa; Moena**, the largest town and winter sports centre, is the 'boundary'. It has two churches of note: the large 12th-century **San Vigilio**, with paintings by local artist Valentino Rovisi, a pupil of Tiepolo; and **San Volfango**, richly frescoed by one of the anonymous, itinerant artists who travelled around the Trentino in the 15th century.

Seven *comuni* in the Val di Fassa preserve their Ladin language (a cross between Celtic and Latin introduced by Roman settlers) and culture, especially **Vigo di Fassa**, site of the Ladin Cultural Institute and several *tabià*—the Ladini's traditional wooden cabins. A 20-minute walk leads up to the pretty Gothic church of **Santa Giuliana a Vigo**, with quattrocento frescoes honouring the valley's patron saint. For a big thrill, take the three chairlifts from nearby Pozzo di Fassa up the flanks of Rosengarten, leaving you at the path to the **Torri del Vaiolet**, a strikingly sheer triple pinnacle.

Campitello di Fassa, the next town up the valley, has a funivia to the **Col Rodella** (8151ft)—a famous viewpoint and winter sports wonderland. Further up the Val di Fassa, **Canazei**, rebuilt after 1912 when a fire destroyed the town, is the fine base for exploring the other magnificent peaks in the area—Marmolada, Sassolungo and Sella. The passes above lead towards Arabba and Cortina, or north into the Val Gardena (*see* p.408).

San Martino di Castrozza and Paneveggio National Park

Predazzo is the main turn off for the stunning, pinnacle-crowned **Pale di San Martino**, 'the altars of St Martin' (10466ft) and the principal group of the southern Dolomites, and **San**

Martino di Castrozza, dramatically lying at its foot—the biggest and best-equipped resort south of Cortina d'Ampezzo (complete with helicopters, skating and a bobsled run). But don't expect much character—the Austrians demolished the medieval town in the First World War, leaving only the ancient church. Among the most popular excursions is the ascent by cablecar and chairlift to the summit of **Rosetta** (8997ft).

Most of the big scenery around San Martino lies within the **Parco Naturale Paneveggio–Pale di San Martino**, a superb wilderness of emerald meadows, rushing streams, wildflowers and wildlife. Access to the park is from the visitors' centre in **Paneveggio**, north of San Martino, beyond the **Passo di Rolle**. Two paths take in tremendous vistas, not only of the Pale di San Martino, but also the distinctive peaks of Marmolada, Pelmo and Civetta. The forests here provided Stradivarius and his colleagues with the resonant wood for their fiddles; the Venetians, more interested in masts, replanted trees a certain distance apart, to make sure the trunks were tall and straight, and punished tree-poachers with death. Rules are still strict: there are only a few camp sites and no one may stay longer than 24 hours.

The Pale di San Martino is encircled by a road of scenic grandeur. The southern route, via Agordo (SS347), passes through **Frassene**, then climbs through the forests of Gosaldo to the **Passo di Cereda** and **Fiera di Primiero**, with a 15th-century centre. Fiera stands at the crossing of two valleys, the Cismon and the Canali, and has good skiing; in the summer a popular outing is the hour's walk up to the sinister ruined **Castel di Pietra**, precariously balancing on a jagged rock— built, according to legend, by Attila the Hun.

Where to Stay and Eating Out

Cavalese ✉ 38033

One of the nicest hotels has the funniest name, ★★★**Villa Trunka Lunka**, Via Degasperi 4, ✆ 0462 340 233, 🖷 0462 231 433 (*moderate*), with only 24 rooms, and a sauna and solarium. Right on the pistes of Mt Cermis, superbly positioned at 6560ft, ★★★**Sporting-Club Grand Chalet des Neiges** ✆/🖷 0462 341 650 (*expensive–moderate*) also has a pool to go with its magnificent views. *Open mid-Dec–mid-April.*

For dinner, try **Cantuccio**, Via Unterberger 14, ✆ 0462 340 140 (*expensive–moderate*), where mushrooms are king and they make a mean rabbit in garlic cream and artichokes. *Closed Mon eve and Tues out of season.*

Moena ✉ 38035

Up above Moena at Passo di San Pelligrino, ★★★★**Monzoni**, ✆ 0462 573 352, 🖷 0462 574 490 (*expensive*) is a great place to stay: an old mountain refuge converted into a splendid hotel, with an emphasis on nightlife and fun. *Open Christmas–mid-April and mid-July–Aug.*

Moena is famous for its *puzzone* or 'stinky cheese', which in spite of its name tastes pretty good with toasted polenta. Try it (or something else) at **Malga Panna**, Via Costalunga 29, ✆ 0462 573 489 (*expensive*) which offers a variety of menus, including a *menu degustazione* of trout, rabbit, *tortelli ai porcini*, speck, venison and strawberries. *Open Dec–April and July–Sept; closed Mon.*

Canazei ✉ 38032

In a panoramic spot near the slopes, ★★★**La Perla**, Via Pareda 103, ✆ 0462 602 453, ▨ 0462 602 501 (*expensive*) is a comfortable spot, with a gym, indoor pool and sauna. *Closed Nov.* ★★★**Bellevue**, ✆ 0462 601 104, ▨ 0462 601 527 (*moderate*) has great mountain views and pleasant rooms. ★★★**Il Caminetto**, ✆ 0462 601 230, ▨ 0462 61527 (*expensive–moderate*) has an indoor pool.

San Martino di Castrozza ✉ 38058

Soak up turn-of-the-century Dolomite atmosphere at ★★★★**Des Alpes**, Via Passo Rolle, ✆ 0439 769 069, ▨ 0439 769 068 (*expensive*). *Open Christmas–Mar and July–mid-Sept.* Astride the Passo di Rolle north of San Martino, ★★★**Venezia**, ✆ 0439 68315, ▨ 0439 769 159 (*moderate*) has fantastic views stretching across the valley, near the National Park. Five minutes' walk up the hill behind San Martino brings you to the ★★**Suisse**, Via Dolomiti 1, ✆/▨ 0439 68087 (*cheap*), a simple but comfortable bed and breakfast.The best dining around is at **Malga Ces**, at Loc. Malga Ces, ✆ 0439 68223 (*moderate*) which serves *canederli* (Tyrolean gnocchi), polenta with venison, local cheeses and fruits of the forest. *Open Dec–mid-April and mid-June–Sept.*

West of Trento: the Brenta Dolomites

The Brenta Group, though a bit distant from the other Dolomites, is just as marvellous and strange, and a challenge for experienced alpinists, although there are numerous less demanding walks for ordinary folk as well. The Adamello-Brenta Park is the last refuge of brown bears in the Alps, but you'd have to be very lucky, if that's the word, to see one. The following section circles them—175 km round trip from Trento.

Tourist Information

Molveno: ✆ 0461 586 924, ▨ 0461 586 221. **Pinzolo**: ✆ 0465 51007, ▨ 0465 502 778. **Madonna di Campiglio**: Via Pradalago 4, ✆ 0465 442 000, ▨ 0465 540 404. **Folgarida**: ✆ 0463 986 113, ▨ 0463 986 594. **Malè**: Viale Marconi 7, ✆ 0463 901 280, ▨ 0463 901 563.

Around Monte Paganella

To reach Monte Paganella, the eastern flank of the Brenta group, first head north to **San Michele all'Adige**, home to the **Museo degli Usi e Costumi della Gente Trentina**, a fascinating ethnographic collection, occupying 40 rooms in a former Augustinian monastery (*open daily 9–12.30 and 2.30–6; closed Mon; adm*). Nearby **Mezzocorona** produces the 'prince of Trentino wines': Teròldego; and lies at the start of the wine road to Bolzano (*see* p.406–7).

From Mezzocorona follow the signs to three well-equipped resorts, served by four buses a day from Trento: **Fai della Paganella**, **Andalo** (both with cablecars to the summit of Monte Paganella—6970ft) and **Molveno**, near Lago di Molveno, and a good base for hiking. From Molveno the road continues south to **Ponte Arche**, passing Fiavé, where a 5000-year-old settlement of lake dwellers was discovered. East of Ponte Arche is picture postcard **Lake Toblino**, with its enchanting 12th-century castle (now a restaurant, *see* below), set on a tiny peninsula amid trees planted by Attila the Hun. Or so they say.

The Valli Giudicarie

The Brenta Group's southern flanks rise over the Giudicarie Valleys, a network encompassing several rivers and torrents, running from lake to lake—from Molveno down to Idro. Just south of Molveno, **San Lorenzo in Banale** has a road rising north up the **Val d'Ambiez** and the Rifugio al Cacciatore, providing a quick route for hikers to approach the highest peaks of the Brenta group.

Further down, the Giudicarie is defended by the lovely castle at **Stenico**, founded in the 12th century. It retains some faded but good Renaissance frescoes; part of it now houses the archaeological collections of the Trentino Provincial Museum (*guided tours Tues–Sun 9–12 and 2–5; adm*).

One of the Giudicarie's rivers, the Sacra, feeds Lake Garda. The main road follows it up to **Pinzolo**, an attractive town where the exterior of the cemetery church, **San Vigilio**, was frescoed in 1539 by Simone Baschenis with a vividly eerie medieval-style *Dance of Death*. Placid, business-like skeletons conduct princes, popes, soldiers and everyone else to their end, with a couplet of elegant poetry for each. More of Simone Baschenis' precise work can be seen inside the church and at **Carisolo**, 2km away, where he painted another *Danse Macabre* on **Santo Stefano**. Frescoes within tell of an apocryphal visit by Charlemagne.

Carisolo is just in the lovely **Val di Genova**, one of the most beautiful valleys in the Alps, once the haunt of ogres and witches, all of whom were turned to stone after the Council of Trent. Part of the **Parco Naturale Adamello-Brenta**, the Val di Genova is graced by the lofty **Cascate di Nardis**, a woodland waterfall flowing from the glacier on **Presanella** (10673ft)—in Pinzolo you can find a guide to make the ascent. To the east a chairlift (the world's fastest, they claim, so hold on to your hat) rises to the lower slopes of **Cima Tosa**, the highest peak of the Brenta Dolomites.

Madonna di Campiglio

From Pinzolo the SS289 zigzags up to the most important resort in the Brenta Dolomites, the superbly sited **Madonna di Campiglio**, with facilities that include a ski-jump, 31 lifts, speed-skating, skating rink and an indoor pool; in the summer it offers experienced climbers a chance to test their mettle on ice and a wild, rocky terrain; for walkers it has the most scenic trails. Even if you only have enough spunk to get into a chairlift, you can enjoy the marvellous views from the **Passo del Grostè**, some 7413ft above Madonna to the east, or from

Pradalago to the west. Get the tourist office's map to take the classic walk through the beautiful Val di Brenta and Valsinella just to the south. A far more difficult path, the fabulous **Via Bocchette**, takes in the region's most bizarre naked pinnacles and fantastic cliffs. North of Madonna the road passes through **Passo Campo Carlo Magno**, named after Charlemagne, who stopped here on his way to Rome to receive the Emperor's crown.

Val di Sole

Still circling the Brenta Group, the next valley, the **Val di Sole**, occupies the upper reaches of the Noce River and the Trentino sector of the Stelvio National Park (*see* p.414–15). Italy's 'Sun Valley' is a cosy region of soft green meadows with the lofty peaks of Monte Cevedale as a backdrop; many valley churches have exterior frescoes by Simone Baschenis or his kin, especially an *Annunciation* at Pellizzano and a *St Christopher* at Peio.

The scenic roads up the **Val di Peio** and **Val di Rabbi** lead into the Stelvio; there is a park **visitors' centre** in Bagni di Rabbi. **Malè**, the capital of the Val di Sole, is the site of an ethnographical museum, the **Museo della Civiltà Solandra** (*open mid-June–mid-Sept daily 10–12 and 4–7; closed Sun*), with handicrafts and agricultural and domestic implements; these days, the town is an important woodworking centre, and has good skiing in the winter.

Down the Val di Non: Lake Santa Giustina to Trento

The wooded Val di Non, the enchanting valley along the lower Noce, produces some of Italy's finest apples, especially Golden Delicious and 'Renetta del Canada', which look more like potatoes. The valley is especially lovely in the spring, when its apple blossoms, emerald meadows and snow-clad mountains glow with colour.

Cles, the main town of the Val di Non (linked by local train to Trento), stands on the large artificial lake of Santa Giustina. Prince-bishop Bernardo Cles was born in the 11th-century **Castello Cles**, but the most striking building is across the lake, 6km from **Sanzeno**: the remarkable **Santuario di San Romedio** (*open daily 7.30–6*), reached by way of a road up a narrow gorge. The hermit Romedio lived as a kind of Alpine St Jerome with his pet bear on the cliff, and his sanctuary consists of chapels in different styles stacked one atop another down the rock over the centuries, the end result somewhat resembling a doll's house in the forest. Don't miss the 11th-century barbaric reliefs on the portal, the disarming home-made ex-votos, or the ghastly souvenir shop.

South of Cles a 15km road leads to **Lago di Tovel**, lying deep in the folds of the Brenta Dolomites. Unlike other mountain lakes celebrated for their sapphire hue, Tovel was until recently famous for its ruby redness at certain periods when a rare algae, *Glendodinium sanguineum*, covered its surface. Nowadays Tovel is perhaps the only case in the world where one regrets to say that pollution has made the water turn blue.

From Lake Santa Giustina you can head east to Bolzano through the **Passo Mendola** (with a cablecar up to a tremendous view), or continue down the Val di Non past its orchards and old castles to **Vigo di Ton**, where the **Castel Thun**, was transformed into the most sumptuous palace in the whole Trentino. When restored, it will be part of the Provincial museum; its paintings, long ignored, were recently found to be major early 17th-century works by Crespi and the Bologna school. The road continues south to Trento via San Michele all'Adige.

San Michele all'Adige ✉ 38010

Da Silvio, Via Nazionale 1, Masetto de Faedo, ✆ 0461 650 324 (*moderate*) has an ultra-modern setting and imaginative kitchen; try the delicious *Altamira*, a selection of mixed meats grilled at your table, with your choice of sauces. *Closed Sun eve and Mon, part of Jan and June.*

Molveno/Toblino ✉ 38018

★★★Belvedere, Via Nazionale 9, ✆ 0461 586 933, ✉ 0461 586 044 (*expensive*) has fine rooms with exquisite views over the lake and mountains, an indoor pool, fitness centre and solarium. *Open Christmas, Feb and April–Oct.* Dine in the romantic 12th-century **Castel Toblino**, ✆ 0461 864 036 (*moderate*), amid frescoes and medieval weapons; run for over 30 years by the same family, the menu is based on trout, mushrooms and other Trentino treats. *Open Mar–Oct; closed Tues.*

Madonna di Campiglio ✉ 38084

Madonna di Campiglio is the one resort in the Brenta Dolomites with accommodation to please the most demanding customers, and prices are correspondingly high. You can shoot high altitude drives while staying at the **★★★★Golf Hotel**, up at the Passo Carlo Magno, ✆ 0465 441 003, ✉ 0465 440 294 (*very expensive*), one-time summer residence of the Habsburg emperors, now beautifully converted into a hotel. *Open mid-Dec–Mar and mid-June–mid-Sept.* Down in Madonna di Campiglio itself, the very attractive **★★★★Spinale Club**, Via Monte Spinale 39, ✆ 0465 441 116, ✉ 0465 442 189 (*very expensive–expensive*) is elegantly appointed, and has a large indoor pool and other sporting facilities; they also take special care of children. *Open Dec–April and June–Sept.* **★★★Palù**, Via Vallesinella 4, ✆ 0465 441 695, ✉ 0465 443 183 (*expensive*) is an older hotel with air-conditioning in summer and a blazing fireplace to sit around in the winter. *Open Dec–Easter and July–Sept.* Small and cosy, **★★Hermitage**, Via Castelletto 65, ✆ 0465 441 558, ✉ 0465 441 618 (*moderate*) has a fine panoramic terrace and good food. *Open Dec–mid-April and July–Sept.*

Alto Adige/Süd Tirol

Everything has two names on the sunny side of the Alps, in the bilingual province of Alto Adige/Süd Tirol. In isolated mountain valleys people speak German and little Italian, while others still converse in Ladin, a language that owes its origins to the days when Tiberius sent Roman soldiers to crush the Celts of the mountain valleys of Switzerland and the Tyrol. Some stayed, and their descendants became known as the Ladini, or Latins, who still speak Ladin, a mix of Latin and Celtic dialect. In the Middle Ages all were ruled by the bishop of Bressanone and the counts of Tyrol, based near Merano. After the abdication of the 'Ugly Duchess', Margaret of Tyrol, in 1363, the whole region passed to the Habsburgs. Northern influence was hence much stronger here than in Trentino, and when Napoleon gave the Süd Tirol to Austria it had no objection—unlike Trentino, which chafed to join Italy.

After the First World War Italy gained Trentino, and in the 1920s absorbed the lands up to the Brenner Pass as the natural frontier. Mussolini, a dedicated cultural imperialist, immediately invented Italian names for all the towns in the Alto Adige and tried to stick the language down the inhabitants' throats, until Hitler told him to lay off. Still, things were so bad that in 1939, when German citizenship was offered to anyone who didn't want to be Italian, most people left, leading to severe depopulation of rural areas. It was hardly an auspicious beginning, and if it weren't for the Italian vote from Trentino, the southern half of the autonomous region, separatism would have been a serious problem. As far as language goes, the figures are presently 69 per cent German-speaking, 27 per cent Italian and 4 per cent Ladin. Rome for its part has done much to mollify the region, granting it a great deal of autonomy and enough economic perks to make it one of the country's wealthiest areas.

Its position at one of the great historical crossroads between north and south, its brilliant Alpine scenery, its winter sports and renowned climatic spa at Merano, made the Süd Tirol a tourist destination long before the other Dolomite provinces. The region also has an exceptional collection of frescoes in its castles and churches, and produces fine wines, especially whites—there are some 40 vines for every inhabitant. Try the light and smooth Riesling Renano, dry and snappy Gewürtztraminer, Weissburgunder (Pinot Bianco), Welschriesling (Riesling Italico), Sylvaner (with a dry, delicate perfume) and Müller-Thurgau (light and fruity), all of which may be sampled along the wine road south of Bolzano.

Bolzano/Bozen

Bolzano, the lively, cultured capital of Alto Adige, with its high, narrow-gabled houses, beer cellars and arcaded streets is an excellent base for visiting the mountains on either side. Located on the banks of the Isarco and Talvera, which merge just downstream to form the Adige, Bolzano has been an important market town since the Middle Ages. And as of March 1998, the city has a new symbol, although one far far older than itself: Ötzi the Ice Man.

Getting Around

Trains for Trento, Bressanone, Vipiteno, Brenner and Innsbruck, to the north; Merano and Malles/Venosta, to the north-west; and Brunico, Dobbiaco and Lienz to the east, all depart from the FS station, a short distance from Piazza Walther down Viale Stazione. The **bus station** is across Via Garibaldi, ✆ 167 846 047, with connections to Cortina and to nearly every town in the Alto Adige.

Tourist Information

Piazza Walther 8, ✆ 0471 307 000, ✉ 0471 980 128. For the Alto Adige/Süd Tirol region: Piazza Parrochia 11, ✆ 0471 993 808, ✉ 0471 993 899, with an extremely efficient web site: *www.sudtirol.com* Alpine information service: ✆ 0471 993 809. Club Alpino Italiano (CAI): Piazza delle Erbe 46, ✆ 0471 971 694.

Piazza Walther, the Duomo and Via dei Portici

Bolzano's cultural fusion manifests itself unexpectedly in its pretty parlour, **Piazza Walther**. In the centre stands a statue of the great *minnesinger* from these parts, Walther von der

Vogelweide (1170–1230), and at his feet slouch travellers from around the world munching on Big Macs. In front of Walther stands Bolzano's Gothic **duomo**, with its green and yellow roof and pretty tower. The art, however, is a block behind the cathedral in the church of the **Domenicani** (*open Mon–Sat 9.30–5.30*), now the Music Conservatory, where the chapels of San Giovanni and Santa Caterina contain lovely 14th-century Giottoesque frescoes by artists from Padua, the best medieval work in the Alto Adige.

From here Via Goethe leads up to the jovial **Piazza delle Erbe**, Bolzano's commercial hub, where Neptune and his trident (nicknamed *Gabelwirt* 'Mine host with fork') watch over the daily fruit and vegetable market. On Via Argentieri, off Piazza delle Erbe, the 18th-century Palazzo Mercantile has a lovely courtyard; it now houses a **Museo Mercantile** (*open Mon–Fri 10–5; adm*), where a collection of period furniture and paintings attest to Bolzano's old flair for business.

This is still readily apparent if you return to Piazza delle Erbe to stroll up the city's main street, **Via dei Portici**, lined with smart shops. Via dei Portici passes the old heart of the city, Piazza del Grano (the former cornmarket) and ends in Piazza Municipio, where the ornate neo-Baroque Town Hall of 1907 holds court. Take Via dei Bottai, a street of beer cellars, to the Casa di Massimiliano (1512), the old Imperial customs' house, now the new **Museo Provinciale di Scienze Naturali** (*open Tues–Sun 9–5*), with displays on glaciers and the first people to move into the valleys after they melted. From here Via Vintler leads around to Piazza della Madonna and Via dei Francescani, where the church of the **Francescani** (*open Mon–Sat 10–12 and 2.30–6*) has a pretty Gothic cloister, a 14th-century fresco of the Franciscan Doctors, and a beautiful altarpiece of the Nativity, by woodcarver Hans Klocker (1500). The street leads back to Piazza delle Erbe.

Museo Archeologico dell'Alto Adige

On Via Museo, around the corner from Piazza delle Erbe. Open May–Sept Tues–Sun 10–6, Thurs 10–8; Oct–April Tues–Sun 9–5, Thurs 9–8; adm exp. Audio guides in English available for a small fee.

You might recall reading about the discovery in the papers. In 1991 Erika and Hermert Simon were walking along the Similaun Glacier northwest of Merano when they happened across a body. There hadn't been an accident or murder there in years. The man they found mummified in the ice had died 5,300 years ago, at the start of the Copper Age.

It was the first time ever that scientists had such an ancient body in such excellent condition, and after years of study and analysis, Ötzi, as he's been baptized, has become the magnet of this new museum which opened in March 1998. He was about 46 years old, they estimate, an experienced mountaineer who got caught in a sudden storm. He had tattoos on his torso and legs, that might have served as a kind of acupuncture map. A room reproducing the cold and humidity of the glacier was specially built to house him. And a curious, rather poignant sensation it is, peering through the window at the body of a man who could be one's grandfather, 250 generations removed.

Ötzi, in short, was a lot like us. They've made a model of what he looked like, dressed in all his gear, which is spread out in the next cases. His clothing is cunningly designed for the weather, using the materials at hand in 3700 BC, from bearskin hat to goatskin underwear, and a mantle woven of grasses; he had a bow and arrows, and in his pouch he carried bone tools and lucky talismans. The museum's other exhibits—prehistoric to Roman—pale somewhat after the Ice Man, but don't miss the statue steles carved by his near contemporaries nor the cast of the Mithraic altar of Bressanone (*see* p.412).

Museo Civico and Over the Talvera to Gries

Nearby, on the corner of vias Museo and Cassa di Risparmio, the **Museo Civico** (*open Tues–Sat 9–12 and 2.30–5.30, Sun 10–1; adm*) houses Gothic altarpieces by local masters Hans Klocker and Michael Pacher, Baroque art and ethnographic items. Via Museo ends at the bridge over the Talvera, a river lined with parks and promenades; to the right, in its own field, the stout-towered 13th-century **Castel Mareccio** no longer guards Bolzano, but hosts conventioneers. Just across the Talvera, the imposing fascist **Monumento alla Vittoria** celebrates Italy's victory in the First World War and was purposefully placed where the Austrian monument was slated to go; in 1978 Tyrolean nationalists attempted to blow it to smithereens. On Saturday morning it hosts an enormous market.

Corso Libertà leads through Mussolini's dreary industrial suburb (1937), purposefully built as a contrast to old Bolzano and everything it stood for. The Corso ends in **Gries**, an old health resort. The old **parish church** of Gries (*open April–Oct Mon–Fri 10.30–12 and 2.30–4*) houses a beautifully carved Gothic wooden altar with doors by Michael Pacher (1475) and a masterful 13th-century *Crucifix*. (Bus no.10 travels back from here to the centre.)

Around Bolzano

There are two fine walks around Bolzano. Beyond the Gries parish church, at the end of Via Knoller, begins the 1½km **Passeggiata del Guncina**, with an inn at the top for refreshments. A bit longer but more dramatic, the **Passeggiata Sant'Osvaldo** begins near the train station at Via Renico and descends by the head of the Lungotalvera promenade. Further up the Talvera, **Castel Roncolo** (*open Mar–Nov Tues–Sat 10–5*) has guarded the passage on its impregnable rock since 1237. The city gave it to Emperor Maximilian; it preserves 14th-century frescoes of chivalric knights, some of which were 'touched up' in 1508.

Three cablecars ascend from Bolzano, the most rewarding one from Via Renon, near the station, which climbs 4005ft up the slopes of Bonzano's playground, Mt Renon/Rittner to **Soprabolzano/Oberbolzen** (*cablecar runs daily 7am–8pm*). The views are splendid, but continue from here on the rack railway to **Collabo/Klobenstein**, and follow the path to the **Longomoso Pyramids**—rocks eroded to form a dense forest of needles and bizarre stone drapery. More fine views of the Dolomites can be had from **San Genesio/Jenesien**, a hamlet easiest reached by cablecar from Via Sarentino (just before the Castel Roncolo).

The Strada del Vino/Der Weinstrasse

Folks on the west bank of the Adige south of Bolzano have been making wine since before the Romans, and this lovely road through the vine-carpeted hills is so well known that the towns along it have taken its name. Specific places to aim for include **Castel d'Appiano**, one of *forty* castles and manor houses in **Appiano sulla Strada del Vino/Eppen an der Weinstrasse**. In 1158 one of its lords, Federigo d'Appiano, had the cheek to hijack a precious treasure the Pope was sending to the Holy Roman Emperor, only to have his castle obliterated in response.

The current castle was rebuilt shortly after, but the holy armies left the original chapel, **Santa Caterina**, untouched, with its beautiful frescoes from the dawn of the 13th century (*open daily April–1 Nov; closed Tues in July*).

The winemaking capital, **Caldaro sulla Strada del Vino/Kaltern an der Weinstrasse**, overlooks Lago di Caldaro, which is warm enough for a dip from May to September. The **Museo Provinciale del Vino** in Castel Ringberg (*open April–7 Nov Tues–Sat 9.30–12 and 2–6, Sun and hols 10–12*) is full of vinous lore and carved barrels. **Termeno sulla Strada del Vino/Tramin an der Weinstrasse** owes its fame to its blood-heating wine, Gewürztraminer Aromatico, of reputed aphrodisiacal qualities; try it at the **Cantina Hofstätter**, in Piazza del Municipio, which claims to possess the largest wine cask in Europe. Termeno's neo-Gothic church conserves a quattrocento choir with elegant Renaissance frescoes. Just outside of town, rising out of a sea of vineyards, tiny **San Giacomo in Castelaz** has remarkable frescoes spanning the 13th–15th centuries.

Where to Stay and Eating Out

Bolzano/Bozen ✉ 39100

Note that in the summer you may want to base yourself higher up; the humidity in the valley can turn Bolzano into a sauna. Best here is the CIGA chain's lavish ★★★★**Parkhotel Laurin**, Via 4 Laurino, ✆ 0471 311 000, ✆ 0471 311 148 (*very expensive*), built at the turn of the century in Viennese *Jugendstil*, located in a fine old park and rose garden near the centre. It has a heated swimming pool, and the public areas are furnished with fine antiques clustered around black marble fireplaces; don't miss the beautiful frescoed bar and exquisite dining in the restaurant **Belle Epoque**. Also in the centre, modern ★★★★**Luna-Mondschein**, Via Pieve 15, ✆ 0471 975 642, ✆ 0471 975 577 (*expensive*) is set next to a park, with cosy rooms, garage, and an indoor/outdoor restaurant serving Tyrolean classics.

★★★**Città-Stadt**, in Piazza Walther, ✆ 0471 975 221, ✆ 0471 976 688 (*moderate*) is in the very heart and soul of Bolzano, and there's parking. Outside the centre, the 11-room ★★★**Eberle**, Passeggiata Sant'Osvaldo 1, ✆ 0471 976 125, ✆ 0471 982 334 (*moderate*) offers guests peace and quiet, a pool, tennis, sauna and gym, in addition to cosy rooms and an excellent restaurant. ★**Croce Bianca-Weisses Kreuz**, Piazza del Grano 3, ✆ 0471 977 552, ✆ 0471 972 273 (*cheap*) is cheerful and welcoming; its lobby is a café that opens on to the pavement.

Like the language, the cuisine of Alto Adige/Süd Tirol is a bit more than half Germanic—instead of *prosciutto*, expect *speck* (prosciutto smoked over juniper) on pizza. Other specialities are Wiener schnitzel, sauerkraut, goulash, *knodel* (bread-crumb dumplings), *terlaner* (wine soup), with apple, cheese and poppy-seed strudels for dessert. This Bolzano cuisine, stylishly prepared according to the market, holds pride of place at **Amandè**, near the Ice Man at Viacolo Ca' de Bezzi 8 (off Via Cavour), ✆ 0471 971 278 (*expensive*). *Closed Sun.* **Da Abramo**, Piazza Gries 16, ✆ 0471 280 141 (*expensive–moderate*) offers contemporary elegance and very good Italian food; seafood is a speciality, and among their offerings are a divine risotto, turbot with rosemary, and escalopes in a white pepper sauce. *Closed Sun and some of*

Aug. In the centre, **Cesare**, Via Perathoner 15, ✆ 0471 976 638 (*moderate–cheap*) is a fine place to tuck into fresh pasta and succulent grilled meats. The jovial 400-year-old **Cavallino Bianco/Weisses Rossel**, Via dei Bottai 6, ✆ 0471 973 267 (*cheap*) is still extremely popular, with an eclectic menu stretching from ham and eggs to *Bolognerschnitzel* and a very tasty onion soup. *Closed Sat eve and Sun.*

Appiano sulla Strada del Vino/Eppen an der Weinstrasse ✉ 39057

Close to Bolzano and the wine road, ★★★★**Schloss Korb**, at Missiano, ✆ 0471 636 000, ✏ 0471 636 033 (*expensive*), a fairy-tale 11th-century castle surrounded by vines, has 53 spacious rooms, heated pools, tennis and a fine restaurant. *Open Easter–early-Nov.* The smaller, very elegant ★★★★**Schloss Freudenstein**, at San Michele, ✆ 0471 660 638, ✏ 0471 660 122 (*expensive*) enjoys another beautiful setting, and has a pool. *Open April–mid-Nov.* Also at San Michele, book a table at the award-winning **Zur Rose**, ✆ 0471 662 249 (*expensive*), for a gourmet epiphany based on Tyrolean tradition in a 12th-century house. *Closed Sun, Mon lunch and July.*

East of Bolzano: the Val Gardena and Rosengarten

Bolzano lies just to the west of the Süd Tirol's most celebrated Dolomite scenery, taking in the pinnacles of Pelmo, Civetta and Marmolada. Scores of Alpine refuges, chairlifts and cablecars, and fast buses from Bolzano to the valleys, make access easy.

Tourist Information

Val Gardena/Grödnertal: *www.val-gardena.com* **Ortisei/Sankt Ulrich in Gröden**: Via Rezia 1, ✆ 0471 796 328, ✏ 0471 796 749. **Santa Cristina**: Via Chemun 25, ✆ 0471 793 046, ✏ 0471 793198. **Selva di Val Gardena/Wölkenstein**: Via Meisules 213, ✆ 0471 795 122, ✏ 0471 794 245. **Corvara**: Ciasa de Comun 198, ✆ 0471 836 176, ✏ 0471 836 540, *www.altabadia.it* **Nova Levante/Welschnofen**: Lago di Carezza, ✆ 0471 613 126, ✏ 0471 613 360, *www.sudtirol.com/rosengarten*

Val Gardena/Grödnertal

The most accessible and certainly one of the most beautiful excursions from Bolzano is to take the Brenner road north into the Ladin-speaking Val Gardena, lying between the jagged Odle group and **Alpe di Siusi**, a magnificent plateau noted for its sunny skiing and world-class ski schools, and endless meadows of flowers in the late spring; there are numerous lifts up from the Val Gardena, or a road up from the resort town of **Siusi**. A classic but not strenuous hike from Siusi is the 4-hour trek up **Monte Pez**, including a stay at one of the grand dames of 19th-century Alpine refuges, the **Rifugio Bolzano di Monte Pez**.

The SS242 turns off the main highway and enters the Val Gardena at **Ponte Gardena/Waidbrück**, in the shadow of the medieval **Castel Trotsburg**, perched on a crag, with Gothic and late-Renaissance decor (*guided tours Easter–Oct daily at 10, 11, 2, 3 and 4; closed Mon; adm*). The largest town in the valley, elegant **Ortisei/St Ulrich**, and the next two villages, **Santa Cristina** and **Selva di Val Gardena/Wölkenstein**, are all well-equipped resorts with cablecars to the Alpe di Siusi; skiers should make time for the Saslonch-Ruacia piste which passes right below the 17th-century **Castel Fischburg**. Santa Cristina has lifts into the Odle group and up to the foot of the most distinctive peak in the region, the spiralling, dream-like **Sassolungo** (10430ft) to the south.

The Woodcarvers of the Val Gardena

 Ortisei has specialized in woodcarving for several centuries. Farmers began carving to while away the long winter evenings, using a soft pine from the valley's slopes. By the 17th century some began to neglect their land to hike over the mountains selling carved toys, ornaments, household furniture and implements. By 1820, 300 craftsmen were working in the valley, and a school was set up in 1872 to consolidate skills and encourage trade. Today there are more than 3000 woodcarvers up and down the Val Gardena. The tourist office issues a list of workshops that can be visited, and which sell to casual callers; the Chamber of Commerce of Bolzano issues a certificate with every piece of work, ensuring that it is entirely carved by hand. Ortisei's museum has a permanent exhibition of ancient and modern works, as does the local church. If you're inspired, Ortisei's school of woodcarving holds weekly courses in July and August: contact the tourist office for details.

From the crossroads in Selva di Val Gardena you have a choice of two spectacular routes, either over the fabulous **Passo di Sella** to Canazei in Trentino, where you can pick up the Great Dolomites Road (*see* below), or over the grand **Passo di Gardena** down into the **Alta Badia** to the east, another beautiful valley that has retained its Ladin culture. **Corvara in Badia** and **La Villa** are its main resorts, which were good enough to host the Alpine Ski World Cup. Another treat in the Alta Badia is the famous **Sella Ronda**, a circuit of the entire Sella group, entirely on skis, thanks to a series of refuges and lifts. To the north the SS244 leads to San Lorenzo near Brunico, while to the south the road descends to Arabba.

Catinaccio/Rosengarten

The other main group accessible from Bolzano, Catinaccio/Rosengarten, is enchanting—and enchanted. Its name first appears in a 13th-century Tyrolean epic describing how King Lauren of the Dwarves was made prisoner and dragged away from his mountain realm. Furiously Lauren put a curse on the roses that had betrayed him, that no one would ever see them again, neither by night nor by day. But he neglected to mention the dawn or the twilight, when the enchanted roses make the stony face of Rosengarten blush a deep red.

From Bolzano the road to Rosengarten (SS241) begins at Cardara/Kardaun, just east of town, and passes through the breathtaking narrow and deep red gorge—like a giant sore throat—of the **Val d'Ega**. As the road nears **Nova Levante/Welschnofen**, the main resort, the craggy peaks of the **Latemar** group loom up to the right, while the massive wall of Rosengarten rises to the left. You can reach the slopes of Rosengarten from Nova Levante or the Passo di Costalunga near gorgeous aquamarine **Lake Carezza**, a popular stop on the road from Nova Levante. For an even more spectacular approach, continue along the SS241, to **Pozza di Fassa** on the eastern slopes of Rosengarten.

The Great Dolomites Road: Bolzano to Cortina d'Ampezzo

The above stretch of road from Bolzano, the SS241 through the Val d'Ega to Rosengarten and Pozza, is the first leg of the fabled 110km Great Dolomites Road, laid out in 1909. Buses from Bolzano or Cortina make the journey, and you should take one—it's torture, it really is, to have to keep your eyes on the road. On the other hand, driving allows you to linger for as long as you like at the passes and other belvederes.

After Pozza di Fassa the road (now the SS48) continues up Trentino's Val di Fassa to **Canazei** (*see* p.398), the best base for the ascent of the Dolomites' mightiest peak, **Marmolada** (10,962ft). The road from Canazei climbs past the peculiar tower of **Sassolungo** and Sella glowering on the left, on its way to the **Passo Pordoi**, affording stupendous views of Sella and Marmolada. From the pass the road writhes down towards **Arabba**, a ski resort dwarfed by Sella, and **Pieve di Livinallongo**, below the odd-shaped **Col di Lana**, its summit blown off by an Italian mine in the First World War. The road then climbs again, past the haunting, eroding **Castello d'Andraz** (just after the settlement of Andraz) to the **Sasso di Stria** (Witch's Rock) and the tunnel at **Passo di Falzarego**, where a cablecar on threads ascends the vertiginous cliffs. From the pass the road begins the descent to Cortina, with views of the strange **Cinque Torri** (Five Towers) and nearly vertical slopes of Tofane, before reaching the top of the Valle del Boite, with beautiful views over Cortina (*see* p.387).

Where to Stay and Eating Out

Ortisei/Sankt Ulrich in Gröden ✉ 39046

The historic ★★★★**Adler**, Via Rezia 7, ✆ 0471 796 203, ⌨ 0471 796 210 (*very expensive–expensive*) is also the most glamorous, in a large park, with an indoor pool and tennis courts, beauty treatments and the best restaurant in town. *Open mid-Dec–mid-April and mid-May–Oct*. Just outside town, ★★★**La Perla**, Via Digon 1, ✆ 0471 796 421, ⌨ 0471 798 198 (*expensive*) is a year-round pleasure to visit, with its park and indoor pool. *Open mid-June–mid-Oct and mid-Dec–mid-April*.

Selva di Val Gardena/Wölkenstein in Gröden ✉ 39048

The small but very comfortable ★★★★**Alpenroyal**, Via Meisules 43, ✆ 0471 795 178, ⌨ 0471 794 161 (*expensive*) is one of the few hotels in the area that are open all year, with plenty of facilities to keep its guests fit and happy—indoor pool, whirlpool baths, sauna, solarium, beauty centre and fitness room. *Open mid-Dec–mid-April and June–Oct*. ★★**Europa**, Via Nives 50, ✆ 0471 795 157, ⌨ 0471 796 445 (*moderate*) is a typical little family-run mountain hotel. *Closed May and Nov*.

Santa Cristina in Valgardena/Sankt Christina in Gröden ✉ 39047

★★★★**Diamant**, Via Skasa 1, ✆ 0471 796 780, ⌨ 0471 793 580 (*very expensive*) has lovely mountain views, an indoor pool and sauna, and tennis courts, all in a quiet park. *Open mid-Dec–Mar and mid-June–mid-Oct*. There are several hotels up at Monte Pana, open for the summer and winter seasons: one, ★★★**Cendevaves**, ✆ 0471 792 062, ⌨ 0471 793 567 (*moderate*) has an indoor pool and good views.

Nova Levante/Welschnofen ✉ 39056

****Posta Cavallino Bianco, Strada Carezza 30, ✆ 0471 613 113, 📠 0471 613 390 (*expensive*) has a name that recalls the former postal relay station, though its facilities—indoor and outdoor pools, tennis, and much more—are contemporary and very comfortable. *Open mid-Dec–mid-April and mid-May–mid-Oct.* The good value *****Stella**, Strada Carezza 51, ✆ 0471 613 125, 📠 0471 613 525 (*moderate*) has nice rooms, an indoor pool and fitness room.

***Rosengarten, Via Catinaccio 43, ✆ 0471 613 262, 📠 0471 613 510 (*moderate*) is a lovely place to stay, and also the best place to eat in town, with the freshest local ingredients, herbs from the garden, and home-made pasta. *Closed Mon, Tues lunch and Nov.*

North Towards the Brenner Pass

North of Bolzano and Ponte Gardena lies the Val Isarco/Eisacktal, the main route to the Brenner Pass. Bressanone, Vitipeno and Novacella are the man-made highlights.

Tourist Information

Bressanone/Brixen: Via Stazione 9, ✆ 0472 836 401, 📠 0472 36067. **Brunico/ Bruneck:** Via Europa 22, ✆ 0472 555 722, 📠 0472 555 544. **Vipiteno/Sterzing:** Piazza Città 3, ✆ 0472 765 325, 📠 0472 765 441; *www.sudtirol.com/sterzing*

Val Isarco: Bressanone

On the way up from Bolzano the road passes the ancient town of **Chiusa/Klausen**, under the **Monastero di Sabiona**, founded in the 4th century: the 'Tyrol's Cradle of Christianity', immortalized in Albrecht Dürer's engraving, *The Great Fortune* (*Nemesis*) c. 1497. Nearly all rebuilt in the 17th century after a fire, you can visit the church, **Santa Croce** (*open daily 7–6.30*) with curious *trompe l'oeil* frescoes of landscapes and architecture painted in 1679. From Chiusa a side road climbs to the 16th-century **Castel Velturno** (*guided tours Mar–Nov daily at 10, 11, 2.30 and 3.30; closed Mon; adm*), the summer residence of the bishop of Bressanone, decorated with frescoes and wood intarsio.

Bressanone/Brixen is the most charming city in the Alto Adige, capital of the region for a millennium and seat of a powerful prince-bishop, similar to Trento's. Although the **duomo** was metamorphized into a dull Baroque church in the 18th century, the remodellers neglected the Romanesque cloister and its magnificent 14th-century frescoes, covering nearly every incident in the Bible. The bishops' palace has an exquisite arcaded, three-storey courtyard, and houses the **Museo Diocesano** (*open 15 Mar–Oct daily 10–5, closed Sun; adm*), with the cathedral treasure and a fine collection of *presepi* (Christmas cribs).

Three km north of Bressanone, the wine-making **Abbazia di Novacella** (*guided tours Easter–Oct Mon–Sat at 10, 11, 2, 3 and 4; Nov–Easter Mon–Fri 10 and 3, Sat at 11; adm*), begun in 1142, is a fascinating study in the evolution of architecture, with its 12th-century tower, Baroque church, beautiful frescoed 14th-century cloister and the round, crenellated 12th–16th century-chapel of San Michele.

The Pusteria

The Pusteria, the wide and pleasant valley running eastwards along the River Rienza towards Dobbiaco/Toblach, is dotted with typical Tyrolean villages and castles. Many of its churches contain works by the valley's 15th-century master woodcarver Michael Pacher, most notably the 13th-century parish church of **San Lorenzo di Sebato,** with an ancient crypt (*closed Mon and Tues*). The capital of the Pusteria, medieval **Brunico/Bruneck,** has two lovely old gates, along with a 13th-century bishop's castle; along elegant Via di Città, even the city pharmacy has frescoes. From here you can head up a wooded valley north to **Campo Tures**, clustered under the baronial **Castel di Tures**, guarding the entrance to the Val Aurina. Tours take in the hall of mirrors, two dozen rooms of tapestries, a chapel frescoed in 1482 by the school of Pacher and beautiful library (*tours Jan–Oct Tues, Fri and Sun at 4; June–Aug 10–11 and 2–4.30; adm*). Glacier alpinists come here for the **Vedrette Giganti** (or di Ríes), reached from Riva di Tures, and its waterfall, while extremists may carry on north up the Val Aurina to **Casere** and its hamlet, **Pratomagno**—the northernmost houses in Italy.

East of Brunico, **Monguelfo/Welsberg** is a resort under a 12th-century castle; from here a road turns south into the Val di Braies, where the **Lago di Braies**, fast in the Dolomites' embrace, is celebrated for its perfect stillness and intense green colour. East of Monguelfo the road continues to Dobbiaco (*see* p.390).

The Upper Val Isarco to the Brenner Pass

The main town between Bressanone and the pass, **Vipiteno/Sterzing** formerly belonged to the great banking dynasty, the Fuggers. The attraction it held for them was its mines, especially silver; although abandoned in 1979 they were lucrative enough in the Renaissance for the residents to build splendid battlemented houses after a fire devastated Vipiteno in 1443. The tall **Torre di Città** was built to celebrate the reconstruction; the mines are remembered in the **Museo Provinciale delle Miniere Jöchlsthurn** (*open Easter–15 Nov Tues–Sat 10–12 and 2–5; adm*). The best houses are along Via Città Nuova; pop into the courtyard of the Municipio to see an impressive Mithraic altar from the 3rd century BC. In Piazza Città, the **Museo Multscher** (*open April–Oct Mon 2–5, Tues–Fri 10–12 and 2–5, Sat 10–12; adm*) is devoted to elegant works by the 15th-century painter Hans Multscher. Three km southeast, the Counts Thurn und Taxis' 11th–14th century **Castel Tasso** has frescoed rooms and late-Gothic decorations (*guided tours Easter–Nov 1 daily at 9.30, 10.30, 2 and 3; closed Fri; adm*).

Further north, **Colle Isarco/Gossensass** is another resort, with skiing and hiking on Cima Bianca and in the Val di Fleres. Beyond this lies the **Brenner Pass** (4510ft), the lowest of the Alpine passes, and the route of countless invaders from the north; during the Second World War it was heavily bombed. From here it is 125km to Innsbruck.

Where to Stay and Eating Out

Bressanone ✉ 39042

Stay in the lap of luxury at ★★★★**Dominik**, Via Terzo di Sotto 13, ✆ 0472 830 144, ✉ 0472 836 554 (*very expensive*)—the spacious rooms have lovely views, and there's an indoor pool and sauna. *Open April–mid-Nov and Christmas holidays*. Another hotel recalls a gift from the King of Portugal, who in 1550 sent an Indian elephant to Emperor Maximilian for his menagerie. On route the pachyderme spent a week in Bressanone's post house, so impressing the locals that they had its portrait done, and there it remains to this day, on the front of the ★★★★**Elefant**, Via Rio Bianco 4, ✆ 0472 832 750, @ 0472 836 579 (*expensive*). Of the old Renaissance inn only the fresco remains, but the ceilings and walls still have antique panelling and beautiful tile stoves. Many of the rooms are furnished with antiques, though no one remembers which one the elephant slept in. There's also a swimming pool, tennis and pleasure garden, as well as a dairy and vegetable garden that provides many of the fresh ingredients for the Tyrolean dishes served in the Elefant's restaurant. *Open Mar–Nov and Christmas; restaurant closed Mon out of season.*

By the river, little turn-of-the-century ★★★**Bel Riposo**, Via dei Vigneti 1, ✆ 0472 836 548, @ 0472 836 548 (*moderate*) is charming and welcoming and has a gourmet restaurant, **Zum Auenhaus**, ✆ 0472 838 344, for ultra-refined Tyrolean cuisine. *Closed Mon.* ★★**Goldene Traube**, Via Portici Minori 9, ✆ 0472 836 552, @ 0472 834 731 (*cheap*) fills up fast. The old walls are ringed with cafés; one of them, the century-old **Fink**, Via Portici Minori 4, ✆ 0472 834 883 (*moderate*), has a restaurant upstairs, serving traditional Südtirolese cooking: saddle of venison, *polenta nera* (made from buckwheat) and other delicacies. *Closed Tues eve, Wed and July.*

Vipiteno/Sterzing ✉ 39049

In the 16th-century ★★★★**Aquila Nera**, Piazza Città 1, ✆ 0472 764 064, @ 0472 766 522 (*expensive–moderate*) you can relax in the heart of town and take a dip in the indoor pool. A favourite place to eat, **Pretzhof**, ✆ 0472 764 455, 8km away in Tulve, (*moderate*) will fill you up on delicious traditional dishes prepared with ingredients from the family's farm. *Closed Mon, Tues and some of June and July.*

Merano and The Upper Adige

A famous spa, vineyards and lots of castles follow the road and Adige up to to the Resia Pass, near the Austrian and Swiss frontiers.

Tourist Information

Merano: Corso Libertà 35, ✆ 0473 235 223, @ 0473 235 524; *info@meraninfo.it*

Merano

Just 28km up the Adige from Bolzano, Merano is an attractive town of gardens and flowers, a favourite spa for central Europeans with respiratory complaints since the 1830s. Basking in a balmy microclimate, the benefits of the waters, clean air and graded mountain walks are complemented by specific cures, such as the notorious grape cure in September and October (in juice form the other months); eating two pounds of Merano grapes a day, taking care to chew them well, apparently keeps the doctor away.

Apart from inflicting digestive disorders, Merano has other attractions: along the Adige, there's the striking Liberty-style Casino and **Kursaal** topped with dancing maidens, now a Congress centre. Two streets back, the arcaded Via dei Portici was the main street in the medieval town; the stern 15th-century Gothic **duomo** contains International Gothic frescoes in the style of Trento's Castello di Buonconsiglio.

Via Cassa di Risparmio leads back to the little 15th-century **Castello Principesco** (*open Tues–Sat 10–5, Sun 10–1; July and Aug also Sun 4–7; adm*), built by Archduke Sigismond and containing Gothic furnishings, arms, and swords. Opposite, you can take a chairlift up to Tirolo (*see* below) or pick up the 4km **Passeggiata Tappeiner**, the Meraners' favourite promenade, a botanical wonderland overlooking the city. At Via delle Corse 42—the next street over—the **Museo Civico** (*same hours*) has four Bronze-Age statue steles, Gothic sculptures and a *Pietà* by the school of Michael Pacher.

For centuries the landowners of these valleys were generally left alone to defend their turf, and as a result the area bristles with a large proportion of the Alto Adige's more than 350 castles. The big cheese, however, lived just above Merano in **Tirolo**, at **Castel Tirol** (*open April–Oct daily 10–5; closed Mon; adm*), balanced on the precipice. The castle gave its name to the region and to this day remains a symbol of Tyrolean identity, the headquarters of the independent Counts until 1363, when Margherita di Maultasch, the 'Ugly Duchess', ceded Tyrol to the Habsburgs. Adorned with medieval monsters and frescoes, it houses different exhibitions every year. Also in Tirolo, **Castel Fontana** (*open mid-Mar–Nov daily 9.30–5; closed Tues; adm*), a rather imaginary reconstruction of a 12th-century castle, has a collection of farm instruments and memorabilia related to poet Ezra Pound (d. 1972), who was found too crazy to stand trial for treason (he made pro-Mussolini radio broadcasts during the War) and retired here in 1958, after his release from a Washington hospital.

The Val Venosta

West of Merano, the Val Venosta follows the Adige west towards Austria. At **Naturno**, the little church of **San Procolo** has some fresco fragments that go back to the 8th century, the oldest in any German speaking territory (*open Tues–Sun 9.30–12 and 2.30–5*). In the upper valley, an hour's drive from Merano, **Sluderno/Schludrens**, was long ruled by the Trapps, whose magnificent 13th/16th-century **Castel Coira** (*open late Mar–1 Nov Tues–Sun 10–12 and 2–4.30; adm*) has gloriously painted Renaissance loggias and the largest private collection of armour in all Europe. At the other extreme, nearby **Glorenza/Glurns** is the smallest walled city in Europe, and looks much as it did in the 15th century.

At Sluderno the SS41 branches off west to Switzerland; the main road continues to ancient **Malles Venosta**, before turning north to Austria. Malles also has very old frescoes, colourful and Carolingian, in the chapel of **San Benedetto** (*key at the Weiskopf family, Via S. Bemedeo 31; open Mon–Sat 9–11.30 and 1.30–5; adm*). Just up in **Burgusio**, the beautiful 17th-century Benedictine **Abbazia di Monte Maria** has a gleaming white crown of towers and gables, in a woodland setting; the crypt from the original church has rare, excellently preserved 12th-century frescoes of Jerusalem (*guided tours 15 June–15 Sept daily at 10, 11, 3 and 4.30; Oct–May daily at 10.45 and 3; closed Sat pm and Sun; adm*). On the way to Austria the road passes the romantically ruined castle of **Lichtenburg** and the artificial **Lago di Resia**, with the church spire of a submerged village poking above its surface.

Parco Nazionale dello Stelvio

If you leave the main valley road (the SS40) at Spondigna, just before Sluderno, and stay on the SS38, you'll enter the **Stelvio National Park**, the largest in Italy and administered by the provinces of Sondrio, Trento and Bolzano, all of which have **visitors' centres** that can tell you where to find the trails, Alpine refuges and the best flowers and wildlife: chamois, marmots, eagles and the ibex, reintroduced in 1968. As well as offering endless possibilities for climbers, the park has fifty lakes, a hundred glaciers (a tenth of the 134,620 hectares is ice) and Europe's second-highest pass, the **Passo dello Stelvio** (*open June and October*). Through it the road makes its way down towards Bormio and the Valtellina (*see* pp.248–50).

Merano ✉ *39021*   ***Where to Stay***

You can sleep like a lord in a castle, near the centre: in the picturesque 12th-century ★★★★**Kurhotel Castel Rundegg**, Via Scena 2, ✆ 0473 234 100, 🖷 0473 237 200 (*very expensive*) has every luxury, including an indoor pool and fitness centre and a lovely park. Set among the vines above Merano, ★★★**Castello Labers**, Via Labers 25, ✆ 0473 234 484, 🖷 0473 234 146 (*expensive*), a castle-villa from the 1200s, is a little more modest, but has a pool and views, too. *Open April–Nov.*

Kafka preferred the artistocratic ★★★★★**Palace**, Via Cavour 2, ✆ 0473 211 300, 🖷 0473 234 181(*very expensive*), in the heart of Merano, set in beautifully main-tained grounds with a spa and beauty centre; the restaurant is considered the best in town. Another atmospheric choice, ★★★**Westend**, Via Speckbacher 9, ✆ 0473 447 654, 🖷 0473 222 726 (*moderate*), near the centre, has 22 lovely rooms in a 19th-century villa, tucked in a garden. Near the spa, ★**Pension Tyrol**, Via 30 Aprile 8, ✆ 0473 449 719 (*cheap*) is quiet, in a big garden, with free parking.

Merano's restaurants are concentrated around the Via dei Portici: for *typische Südtiroler* cooking, try **Laubenkeller** at No.118, ✆ 0473 237 706 (*moderate*). *Closed Thurs.* Or try **Sissi**, up by Castello Principesco, Via Galilei 44, ✆ 0473 231 062 (*expensive*), where the delicious food has a Piedmontese touch. *Closed Mon.*

Friuli-Venezia Giulia

For many British or American visitors, this elongated region east of Venice is terra incognita, a jumbly name that often turns up on the wine list in Italian restaurants. Trieste, at the far end of Italy, evokes cloudy images of pre- and post-War intrigue, a kind of Third Man on the Mediterranean. In between Trieste and Venice the imagination fails.

It doesn't help that the region is burdened with a history as messy as its name. In Roman days Aquileia was the most important city and seat of the oldest patriarchate outside Rome. Its authority was gradually usurped by Cividale del Friuli, the Lombard capital, in the Dark Ages, and then in the Middle Ages by Ùdine, before Venice took over in 1420. Trieste was Venice's bitter rival under the Counts of Gorizia and the Austrians. Napoleon threw the region in with the 'Kingdom of Illyria', a piece of real estate subsequently picked up by the Austro-Hungarian Empire, until 1918 when Italy inherited it, as well as all of Istria down to Fiume (modern Rijeka). After the Second World War, Tito took Trieste from the Germans; the western Allies then forced them to leave, occupying the city themselves as a neutral free port until 1954, when it was readmitted into Italy, leaving the rest of Istria to Yugoslavia. The region's troubles were hardly over: two disastrous earthquakes in 1976 (6.5 and 6.1 on the Richter scale) shook Friuli to the core, killing a thousand people, levelling entire towns, and leaving 70,000 buildings in need of major structural repair.

Weary of being marginal, Friuli-Venezia Giulia is now creating an identity of its own, but it's like trying to put together pieces from several different jigsaw puzzles. The population in the east speaks Slovenian, while the north has a sizeable German minority. In Trieste there are large Jewish, Greek and Serb minorities, and in the middle, around Údine, a majority Friulian ethnic group, like the Ladini in the South Tyrol, who speak a language similar to the Swiss Rhaeto-Romansch. In the 1990s, with the re-opening of Central and Eastern Europe, Friuli Venezia-Giulia is no longer eastern Italy's dead end, but an important link to its future.

Friuli-Venezia Giulia Highlights

The two essential attractions in the region are Roman/medieval Aquileia and Cividale del Friuli, with its unique Lombard relics from the Dark Ages. There are good beaches between Venice and Trieste: Càorle, Bibione, Lignano-Sabbiadoro and Grado. Mountain-lovers have the Carnia and Julian Alps. Trieste is a fascinating bit of Central Europe stuck on the Med, and its Carso hinterland is fascinating to explore, especially its Grotta Gigante. Leave a day for Údine, the chaming 'City of Tiepolo'. Portogruaro and San Daniele del Friuli are fine smaller towns, and at Codroipo, you can visit the villa of the last doge.

Wine in Friuli

The Friuli region has seven DOC regions. The best is the Collio (around Gorizia), famous for its whites, especially Pinot Bianco and Riesling. The Collio Orientale, a much larger region, also produces good whites and a brisk red, Refosco. Rochi di Cialla and Giovanni Dri are just two of the best-known labels. The other DOC regions—Aquileia, Isonzo, Carso, Latisana and Grave del Friuli—produce good reds; names to look out for are Schiopettino, Carso Terreno, and Riva Rossa.

From Venice to Lignano-Sabbiadoro

Getting Around

Trains from Venice along the coast run roughly every two hours (journey time to Trieste two hours). **Buses** are less frequent, though Càorle can most easily be reached by direct bus from Venice. An alternative is to take the train to S. Donà di Piave and the local bus to Càorle from there. For Lignano-Sabbiadoro, take the train to Latisana, linked by bus to the coast in about 30 minutes.

Tourist Information

Càorle: Calle delle Liburniche 11, ☎ 0421 81085, 🖃 0421 84251. **Portogruaro**: Borgo S. Agnese 37, ☎ 0421 273 230, 🖃 0421 274 600. **Lignano-Sabbiadoro**: Via Latisana 42, ☎ 0413 71821, 🖃 0431 70449, *www.fvgpromo.it.lugano*

Altino and Càorle

The SS14 from Venice passes first Marco Polo airport and then **Altino**, the modern name of Roman Altinum. Once renowned for its wealth, it was put to the sack by Attila the Hun—only the first of many hardships that led its inhabitants to give up and found a new city on the island of Torcello in the Venetian Lagoon. They took whatever Attila and the Lombards didn't wreck, so that all that remains in the **Museo Nazionale** (*open Tues–Sun 9–2*) are mosaics, items from tombs and a few odds and ends.

The route continues over the Piave near **San Donà di Piave**, a town that had to be completely rebuilt after the First World War; it was here that Hemingway, then an ambulance-driver for the Red Cross, was wounded in 1918, an experience that became the germ of *A Farewell to Arms*. From San Donà, a detour to the old fishermen's town and modern seaside resort of **Càorle** is tempting, for its isthmus, beaches and lagoon beloved of wildfowl, and cathedral, built in 1038, with a charming cylindrical campanile and a splendid Venetian *Pala d'Oro* (12th–14th centuries). **Bibione**, to the east, is an even bigger resort, with a long strand of sand.

Portogruaro and Around

Portogruaro is a seductive old town, dreaming away under its palm trees and jauntily tilted 193ft campanile, built in the 12th century. The **duomo** is a wallflower, but the neighbouring 14th-century **Loggia Comunale** is shaped like a mountain, the roofline crested with fantail Ghibelline battlements, which lend it a curiously organic appearance. The **Museo Nazionale Concordiese**, in Via del Seminario (*open daily 9–7; adm*) is crowded with an assortment of bronzes and coins, among other finds excavated in Concordia Sagittaria, just to the south. This was an arrow-manufacturing (*sagittae*) Roman colony, and has a Romanesque cathedral standing next to a ruined basilica (389) and a frescoed Byzantine baptistry of 1089.

In **Summaga**, 3km west of Portogruaro, the abbey of Santa Maria Maggiore, ✆ 0421 205 126, was built around a 6th-century votive chapel. The walls are covered with a fascinating cycle of 12th- and 13th-century frescoes, all recently restored; in the votive chapel, don't miss the fighting griffins and lions, chivalrous deeds, and virtues and vices.

More fond old things await in **Sesto al Règhena**, 9km north of Portogruaro, a quaint medieval village with a moat in the centre, originally part of the defences of **Santa Maria in Silvis** (*open daily 8–7*), a Lombard foundation that grew to become one of the most powerful abbeys in the area. The current basilica dates from the 12th century and is decorated with 14th-century frescoes, one showing Christ crucified on a voluptuous pomegranate tree. Among the bas-reliefs is a beautiful 13th-century *Annunciation*, while the crypt contains an 8th-century Lombard-Byzantine sarcophagus of St Anastasia. Lastly, to the west near **Fossalta di Portogruaro**, by the little church of Sant'Antonio in Vilanova, grows one of the oldest oak trees in Europe, already three hundred years old when they signed the Magna Carta.

Lignano-Sabbiadoro

From a few kilometres east of **Latisana**, where a new road (the SS354) branches off to the coast, you can follow the crowds south to the Laguna di Marano and the fastest-growing resort area on the Adriatic, **Lignano-Sabbiadoro**, the 'Austrian Riviera'. Set on the tip of the peninsula, with a lovely 9km sandy beach and scores of new hotels, apartments, bungalows and campsites, Lignano-Sabbiadoro and its two adjacent resorts of **Lignano-Pineta** (the prettiest section, under the pinewoods) and smart **Lignano Riviera** offer fun in the sun and Wienerschnitzel just like Mutter makes. Some of the smaller islands are dotted with *casoni*, steep thatched fisherman's cottages—some real, some recreated for visitors.

Where to Stay and Eating Out

Càorle ✉ 30021

Set on its own little port, ★★★**Diplomatic**, Via Strada Nuova 19, © 0421 81087, 🕮 0421 210 089 (*cheap*) is comfortable and has the area's best restaurant, **Duilio**, celebrated for its seafood. A charming setting, a huge wine list, and reasonably priced menus are particular attractions. *Closed Mon and Jan.*

Lignano ✉ 33054

Near the pines in Lignano-Pineta, ★★★★★**Greif**, Arco del Grecale 27, © /🕮 0431 422 261 (*very expensive*) is a large resort hotel with a pool and park, sauna and private beach. The more intimate ★★★★**Medusa Splendid**, Raggio dello Scirocco 33, © 0431 422 211, 🕮 0431 422 251 (*moderate*) also has a pool, very good rooms, and a garden. *Open mid-May–mid-Sept.* In Lignano Riviera, fashionable ★★★★**Eurotel**, Calle Mendelssohn 13, © 0431 428 991 🕮 0431 428 992 (*expensive*) enjoys perhaps the most beautiful setting in the area and offers lovely rooms, a heated pool and more. *Open mid-May–mid-Sept.* Good restaurants include the convivial **Bidin**, Via Europa 1, © 0431 71988 (*expensive*), with a separate *menu degustazione* for either fish or meat. *Closed Wed.* **Al Bancut**, Via Friuli 32, © 0431 71926 (*moderate*) features grilled fish. *Closed Tues eve and Wed.*

Pordenone and Around

Tourist Information

Pordenone: Corso V. Emanuele II 38, © 0434 21912, 🕮 0434 523 814.
Spilimbergo: Piazza Castello, ©/🕮 0427 2274.
San Daniele: Via Roma, ©/🕮 0432 940 765.

There's not a lot to say about Pordenone, provincial capital and manufacturer of domestic appliances. Its name is only familiar thanks to the Renaissance artist G. A. Sacchiense, who adopted it and whose works may be seen in the **Museo Civico**, housed in the pretty 15th-century Palazzo Richiere (*open Tues–Sun 9.30–12.30 and 3–6; adm*), and in the salmon pink **duomo**, where his odd masterpiece, the *Madonna della Misericordia* (1515) hangs. The lofty **campanile** is Pordenone's landmark, a refined tower of Romanesque brickwork of 1347. The bijou **Palazzo Comunale**, focal point of Pordenone's arcaded, palace-lined Corso Vittorio Emanuele, has a Venetian clock tower topped by two bell-ringing Moors, superimposed on a graceful 13th-century building. And that about sums it up.

Hanging over the willowy banks of the Livenza, **Sacile** (west of Pordenone) is famous for its bird festival (the *Dei Osei*), held on the last Sunday in August ever since 1351. Thousands of songbirds are assembled in the main piazza, and prizes are awarded to the birds and the person who can best imitate their songs.

Towards Ùdine: the Villa of the last Doge, Spilimbergo and San Danielee

On the road to Ùdine, Codroipo is the site of the **Villa Manin** (1738), nothing less than the biggest villa in all Venetia, the swan song—or swan blast, rather—of a way of life (*open Tues–Sun 9–12.30 and 3–6; winter 9–12 and 2–5*). When owner Ludovico Manin was elected Doge in Venice, his chief rival declared, 'A Friulian as Doge! The republic is dead.' The prediction was no sooner proved correct than Napoleon himself stayed at this massive ranch as a guest, if not a welcome one. A painting by David hangs in the room he slept in; also to see are air-headed frescoes, an elegant horseshoe exedra (a secular version of Bernini's colonnade in St Peter's Square), a museum of arms and carriages and a handsome park.

Medieval **Spilimbergo**, on the west bank of the Taglimento, has a discreet charm, a pretty 12th-century castle complex with exterior frescoes, a Gothic cathedral with a Romanesque portal and paintings by Pordenone, and a Mosaic school, founded in 1922 and open for tours (*by appointment, ✆ 0427 2155*). Off to the north of Spilimbergo, near Clauzetto, the **Grotte Verdi di Pradis** (*open July and Aug daily daylight hours; other months sunny Sundays only; adm*) is as weirdly green as its name; walkways follow the torrential Cosa up a high narrow gorge. In 1968 it was made a church, the 'National Temple of Speology'.

Surrounded by fields of maize and *prosciutteries*, **San Daniele del Friuli** is the 'Siena of Friuli', an ochre-tinted medieval market town famous for its sweet cured hams. Don't miss the recently restored frescoes by Pellegrino di San Daniele (1498–1522) in the church of **Sant' Antonio**, his masterpiece. There are other good churches to see, and the **Biblioteca Guarneriana**, Via Roma 1 (*open Tues–Sun 9–12*), founded in the 15th century by a canon of Aquileia, with lovely medieval manuscripts. Every August, at the *Aria di Festa*, hundreds of hams are lined up in the piazza for tasting.

Where to Stay and Eating Out

Pordenone ✉ 33170

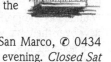

The elegant ★★★★**Villa Ottoboni**, Piazzetta Ottoboni 2, ✆ 0434 208 891, ✆ 0434 208 148 (*expensive*) is near the centre, and offers fully furnished rooms; the attached restaurant dates from the late-15th century. For comfortable modern rooms, ★★★**Park**, Via Mazzini 43, ✆ 0434 27901, ✆ 0434 522 353 (*moderate*) is a good choice in the centre of town.

Dine at **Da Zelina**, in an early-Renaissance palace in Piazza San Marco, ✆ 0434 27290 (*moderate*), on succulent meat dishes, and pizzas in the evening. *Closed Sat lunch, Mon and part of Aug.*

Spilimbergo ✉ 33097

★★**Michielini**, Viale Barbacane 3, ✆/✆ 0427 50450 (*cheap*) is an old family-run hotel in the centre of town, with a good restaurant; alternatively, in the medieval castle at **Torre**, Piazza Castello, ✆ 0427 50555 (*moderate*) dine on the likes of ravioli filled with pumpkin in mushroom sauce and strudels; anyone fond of wine will have a field day with the selection in its cellar. *Closed Sun eve and Mon.*

Palmanova, Aquileia and Grado

In a beeline from north to south, you have the planned military town, the ancient capital and the modern seaside resort—the only one in the Adriatic entirely facing south—offering a strikingly varied and full day.

Getting Around

For Aquileia and Grado take the train to Cervignano del Friuli and then a bus, or a direct bus from Trieste. Ùdine has frequent buses to Palmanova, Aquileia and Grado.

Tourist Information

Aquileia: Piazza Capitolo, © 0431 919 491 (*summer only*).
Grado: Viale Dante Alighieri 72, © 0431 899 309, ✆ 0431 899 209.

Palmanova

In the Renaissance, despite all Alberti's theories on town planning, only a handful of new towns were ever constructed. One of the most remarkable, **Palmanova**, was built in 1593 by the Venetians as their eastern bulwark against the Austrians and Turks, and populated by 'volunteers'. Perhaps because it was never actually needed for anything, Palmanova remains intact, a perfect example of 16th-century 'ideal' radial military planning and a geometrical *tour de force*: the star formed by its walls has nine points. Even though most of the walls and moat are now overgrown, their stone softly moulded into serpentine hills and gullies, they are still defended by young conscripts. At the **Museo Storico**, Borgo Ùdine 4 (*open daily 10–12 and 3–6; closed Wed; adm*), ask about the torchlight tour of the walkways within the walls.

Aquileia

If Palmanova is unique in its plan, Aquileia, directly south, is unique in that it was the only major Roman city in Italy to die on the vine. While most other Roman metropolises are still notable towns or cities, Aquileia has dwindled from an estimated 200,000 in its heyday to 3,500 inhabitants, who no longer receive emperors but tend vineyards and the tourists who flock to see the most important archaeological site in northern Italy.

Founded as a Roman colony in 181 BC, Aquileia ('Eagle') earned its name from the eagles that flew over the town while plans were being laid for Augustus' German campaign. It proved to be a good augury. Augustus himself was in and out of Aquileia and received Herod the Great here. Christianity found an early foothold in the city; the Patriarchate of Aquileia was founded in 313, the very same year that Constantine the Great issued the Edict of Milan, tolerating the religion, and its patriarch was given jurisdiction that extended to the Ukraine. It didn't last long; after Aquileia was sacked by Attila (452) and the Lombards (568), the patriarch moved to a safer home in Grado, an island on the outer port of Aquileia. When Aquileia wanted the title back in the 7th century, Grado refused to surrender it, and for 400 years rival patriarchs sat in Grado and in Cividale del Friuli, the Lombard capital. When they were reconciled in 1019, Aquileia's great basilica was rebuilt, but it was the city's last hurrah. Aquileia's port on the Natissa silted up, malaria chased out the population, and the patriarchate moved to Cividale, and then Ùdine, and was demoted to an archbishopric.

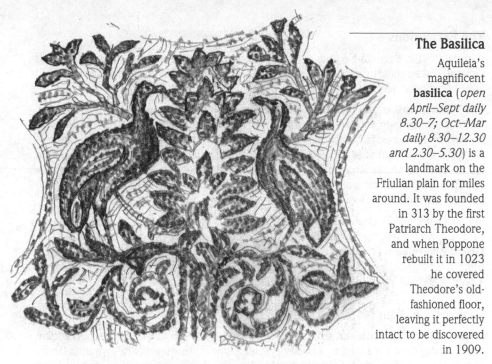

The Basilica

Aquileia's magnificent **basilica** (*open April–Sept daily 8.30–7; Oct–Mar daily 8.30–12.30 and 2.30–5.30*) is a landmark on the Friulian plain for miles around. It was founded in 313 by the first Patriarch Theodore, and when Poppone rebuilt it in 1023 he covered Theodore's old-fashioned floor, leaving it perfectly intact to be discovered in 1909.

The pavement is vast—837 sq yards—the largest Paleochristian mosaic in the west, a vivid and often whimsical carpet of portraits, animals and geometric patterns happily mingling with Christian and pagan scenes. Original frescoes from 1031 survive in the apse, showing Patriarch Poppone dedicating the basilica, accompanied by Emperor Conrad II and Gisela of Swabia.

Set next to the wall, the 11th-century marble **Santo Sepolcro** is a reproduction of the Holy Sepulchre in Jerusalem. Next to this, the so-called **Cripta degli Scavi** (the excavations around the belltower) contains more mosaics from 313, sandwiched in between pagan Roman mosaics and others from the 8th century. The **crypt** proper, under the altar, is adorned with colourful 12th-century Byzantine-style frescoes (*one adm for both crypts*). The **Museo del Patriarcato**, opposite the basilica (*open April–Oct daily 9.30–12.30 and 3–6; closed Mon*), contains fancy medieval reliquaries, sculptures and other works from the Basilica, including bas-reliefs of Christ with St Thomas of Canterbury, carved only a few years after his martyrdom, showing just how fast news of church politics travelled in the 1170s.

The Museo Archeologico

Open April–Sept Tues–Sun 9.30–7, Mon 9–2; Oct–Mar Tues–Sun 9–2; adm.

On the same road, but down to the left, an old palace houses a fascinating collection of artefacts from Roman Aquileia, including a fine set of highly individualized Republican portrait busts; unlike the Greeks who idealized in marble (or perhaps were just better looking), the Romans insisted that all their warts, cauliflower ears and crumpled noses be preserved for posterity. Among the bas-reliefs there's a smith with his tools, amber and gold ornaments, and a thousand household items that breathe life into ancient Aquileia. The Aquileians could be lighthearted: there are flies made of gold, and a wee bronze figurine of a springing cat.

The Excavations

A circular walk, beginning on the Via Sacra behind the basilica, takes in most of Aquileia's excavations; an unfortunate proximity to that quarrying magpie Venice, has shorn them of most of their grandeur.

The Via Sacra first passes by **Roman houses** and **Palaeo-Christian oratories** (some with mosaics intact), then continues up through the considerable ruins of the ancient harbour, marked by cypresses: in the 1st century AD this was a bustling commercial port. Continue straight and bear right after the crossroads on Via Gemina to the **Palaeo-Christian Museum** (*same hours as Museo Archeologico*), with reliefs and sarcophagi, and a walkway over the undulating mossy mosaics of a huge 4th-century basilica; ancient Aquileia required not one but two enormous churches.

Return by way of Via Gemina to Via Giulia Augusta. To the right you can see the old Roman road, and on the left, the **Forum** with its re-erected columns. Just off a fork to the right, the **Grand Mausoleum** (1st century AD) was brought here from the distant suburbs. The meagre ruins of the amphitheatre, the baths and the **Sepolcreto** (five Roman family tombs) are on Via XXIV Maggio and Via Acidino, north of the village's central Piazza Garibaldi.

Grado: Up to Your Neck in Sand

Aquileia had an inner port and an outer port, or *grado*, on the island that still bears its ancient name. Today Grado is linked by a causeway, and reigns as the queen of its own little lagoon and archipelago. The narrow alleys of the old town, the **Castrum Gradense**, are called *calli* as in Venice, and most are as happily traffic-free. In the 6th century the Patriarch of Nova Aquileia, as he fashioned himself, moved to the **duomo** (Basilica of Sant'Eufemia). Here Corinthian capitals sit atop exotic marble pillars, and the 11th-century domed pulpit is carved with four Evangelists; the painted baldachin could easily be the tent of the sheik of Araby.

The mosaic floor is from the 6th century, although its scriptural adages and geometrical patterns may seem austere after the garden of delights in Aquileia's basilica. One scene on the altar depicts *Castrum Gradense* and its islands; in the back glows a silver *pala* donated by the Venetians in 1372. An alley of sarcophagi separates Sant'Eufemia from the octagonal 5th-century Baptistry, with a full immersion font, and another smaller basilica, the 5th-century **Santa Maria delle Grazie**, with its original altar screeens and mini-theatre for the clergy behind the altar—a common feature of early-Byzantine basilicas.

Grado owes its origin as a beach resort to medicine. Keen to bring children with TB to the seaside, doctors sought a fresh-water spring on the peninsula of Grado. In 1892 a spring was duly discovered, and Emperor Franz Josef at once included Grado on his official list of curative resorts in the Habsburg empire. A new town grew up to accommodate the nobility, who have since been replaced by athletes, models and business people undergoing specific treatments, including the 'sand cure'—being buried up to one's neck in warm sand.

If the free beaches are dirty or crowded, walk east to **Pineta**, or catch the boat to **Barbana**, an island in the lagoon with a resident religious community (*boats run frequently every day in summer; Nov–May Sat and Sun only*). There are also daily sea connections to Trieste and the Istrian coast in summer (*see* p.424) and to the fishing village of **Porto Buso**.

Aquileia ✉ 33051

★★★**Patriarchi**, Via Julia Augusta 12, ℰ 0431 919 595, ℯ 0431 919 596 (*moderate*) overlooks the excavations; all rooms are air conditioned. **La Colombara**, Via S. Zilli 34, ℰ 0431 91513 (*moderate*), 2km out on the Trieste road, serves up some of the finest cuisine in the area, specializing in seafood prepared in a number of excellent ways, accompanied by good wines from the Collio. *Closed Mon and June.*

Grado ✉ 34073

Grado has plenty of nice hotels. ★★★★**Antica Villa Bernt**, Via Colombo 5, ℰ 0431 82516, ℯ 0431 82517 (*expensive*), a refurbished villa from the 1920s, has just 22 lovely air-conditioned rooms. *Open April–Oct.* ★★★★**Savoy**, Via Carducci 33, ℰ 0431 897 111, ℯ 0431 83305 (*expensive*) has a thermal pool, garden, parking and very comfortable rooms. *Open June–Oct.* ★★★**Cristina**, Viale Martiri della Libertà 11, ℰ 0431 80989, ℯ 0431 8594 (*cheap*) is a typical beach hotel, with a shady garden. *Open May–Sept.*

In the winding streets around the cathedral, **All'Androna**, Calle Porta Piccola 4, ℰ 0431 80950 (*expensive*) has a daily changing menu of fresh fish, and home-made bread and pasta. *Closed Tues out of season, and Dec–Mar.* Overlooking Roman excavations, **De Toni**, Piazza Duca D'Aosta 37, ℰ 0431 80104 (*moderate*) offers fresh fish, prepared in a variety of local styles, along with a long wine list. *Closed Wed.*

Trieste

Once the main seaport of the Austro-Hungarian Empire, two world wars left Trieste to become the woebegone widow of the Adriatic. With the fall of the Berlin Wall, all this has changed: Trieste is now a very merry widow, courted across Central Europe and quickly regaining its old cosmopolitan lustre, something that the inhabitants accept as simply another twist in a knotted history. The streets and shops bubble with Slovene, Serbo-Croat, German, Hungarian and Czech, and a bewildering variety of car licence plates clog up the very Central European 19th-century streets. Trade is picking up, too: not from tourists who once passed through on their way to points east, but from Slovenes and Hungarians flashing new-found wealth, and Austrian and Czech businessmen seeking new Mediterranean markets.

Don't come to Trieste for art or beautiful buildings: its capitalist swag has been firmly invested in banks, shipping-lines and stocks. Instead, come to sense the energy and excitement of a city shaking off decades of nostalgic sloth, and picking up the threads of its most vibrant time, the beginning of this century. Or you could just come for the breasts: plastered with naked statues, Trieste must have more perky size Ds than any other city in the world.

History

Founded as the Celtic port of *Tergeste*, Trieste first became an important city under Augustus. From the 9th to the 13th centuries it maintained a precarious independence under its prince-bishops; in the 14th and 15th centuries it was Venice's chief rival in the Adriatic.

Austria, always longing for a port, is deeply woven into Trieste's history. It first offered the city its protection in 1382, and in 1719 Charles VI granted it free port status, initiating a golden age. Trieste returned to Austrian rule after the fall of Napoleon in 1815, although bereft of free-port status. Their heavy-handed government turned the majority Italian population into ardent 'Irredentists' (the 'Unredeemed'), turbulently desiring union with Italy.

Italian troops were welcomed in 1918, but Italian government all too soon proved to be another disappointment for Trieste, when Mussolini tried to force the heterogeneous population into a cultural strait-jacket. The real disaster came in the aftermath of the Second World War, when Trieste found itself permanently divorced from its Istrian hinterland in Slovenia and Croatia. Tito only gave up his claims to Trieste itself in 1954, and the border was not finally settled until 1975. In the mid-1960s, the city, lacking direction, decided to create a new role for itself as a scientific and research centre—Trieste has institutes of theoretical physics, genetic engineering, experimental geophysics and marine biology, among others.

At the turn of the last century Trieste sparkled not with scientists, but literati. Sir Richard Burton, translator of the *Arabian Nights*, was consul here from 1870 until his death in 1890. James Joyce, after eloping with Nora Barnacle, taught English in Trieste from 1904 to 1915 and 1919 to 1920; here he wrote *The Dubliners* and began *Ulysses* (fans can pick up a Joycean itinerary at the tourist office, marking all his old haunts). Joyce befriended and translated Ettore Schmitz (Italo Svevo), a member of Trieste's once-thriving Jewish community. And unknown to either of them, Rainer Maria Rilke was living and working nearby at Duino.

Getting There

by air

Trieste's **airport**, served by daily flights from Rome and Milan, and weekly flights from London on British Airways, is at Ronchi dei Legionari, ✆ 0481 773 224, 30km to the north near Monfalcone; the airport bus departs from the main bus station in Piazzale Libertà. **Alitalia:** Piazza Sant'Antonio 1, ✆ 040 631 100.

by sea

The *Marconi* links Trieste to Grado and Lignano, Piran (Slovenia) and Umag, Porec, Rovinj and Pula (Croatia) (*Wed–Mon from late-May–Sept*). Remember to take a passport for Slovenia and Croatia. Tickets from Piazza Unità d'Italia 6, ✆ 040 367 529, or Piazza Duca degli Abruzzi 1/a, ✆ 040 363 737. In the summer, **ANEK** runs ferries to Igoumenitsa, Patras and Corfu in Greece, ✆ 040 363 242. **Sem Ferries** sail to Split on the Dalmation Coast once a week (Via Milano 4, ✆ 040 760 033). Harbourmaster: Riva Tre Novembre 13, ✆ 040 366 666.

by rail

There are frequent trains to Venice, Gorizia, Ùdine, as well as to Austria, Slovenia and other destinations in Eastern Europe, from the **Stazione Centrale**, on Piazza della Libertà 8.

by long-distance bus

The main **bus station** is in front of the Stazione Centrale, in Piazza della Libertà, ✆ 040 425 001. It has bus services to Venice, Treviso, Padua, Belluno, Trento, and

Cortina and Sappada in the Dolomites; long-distance coaches to Milan, Mantua and Genoa; and international services to Ljubljana, Rijeka and Zagreb.

Getting Around

Trieste's many long, straight Habsburger streets make it easy to find your way around, and **buses** are quite frequent. Most routes run from or by the central bus station; for information call, ✆ 167 016 675.

There is also a **funicular** railway (*tranvia*) every 22 minutes from Piazza Oberdan to Villa Opicina above the city. For a radio taxi, ✆ 040 307 730. Cars have been banished from much of the city centre and parking can be diabolical; just surrender your *macchina* to one of the garages or car parks (near Piazza della Libertà and Piazza Unità d'Italia) and get it over with.

Tourist Information

Via San Nicolò 20, ✆ 040 679 6111, ✉ 040 679 6299; also at the Stazione Centrale, ✆ 040 420 182, *www.fvgpromo.it* **Friuli-Venezia Giulia regional tourist office**: Via G. Rossini 6, ✆ 040 363 952, ✉ 040 365 496. **British consulate**: Vicolo delle Ville 16, ✆ 040 302 884.

Along the Port to Piazza dell'Unità d'Italia

If you only have an hour or two at Trieste's train or bus station, you can pop over to the **Galleria Nazionale d'Arte Antica**, Piazza della Libertà 7 (*open daily 9–1.30; closed Sun; adm*), with a second-division collection of Italian paintings from the 15th–19th centuries, and a charming *Diana and Actaeon* by Lucas Cranach the Elder. Otherwise, take Corso Cavour into the **Borgo Teresiano**, the neoclassical commercial centre laid out in 1750 by Maria Theresa's planners with a pair of rulers, and planted with neoclassical architecture.

The street passes over the **Canale Grande**, an inlet with moorings for small craft; the adjacent Piazza Ponterosso is the site of the daily **market**. At the head of the canal stands the temple-fronted church of **Sant'Antonio** and, near it, the blue-domed Serbian Orthodox **Santo Spiridone**, an exotic orchid in the regimented garden. Just over the canal, overlooking the sea on Riva Tre Novembre, Trieste's oldest coffeehouse, **Caffè Tommaseo** (1830) has recently been restored, along with its Belle Epoque furnishings.

Trieste's whale of a heart, **Piazza dell'Unità d'Italia**, is one of Italy's largest squares. It faces the harbour, framed by the **Palazzo del Comune**, topped by two Moors who ring the bell in the clock tower; on one side the **Palazzo del Governo** glows in its bright skin of neo-classical mosaics, on the other broods the **palace of Lloyd Triestino**, now the seat of Friuli-Venezia Giulia's regional government. In one corner, a pile of rocks and statuary purported to represent the *Four Continents* (1750), may send you staggering off for a drink at the piazza's **Caffè degli Specchi**, in business since 1839 and once an Irredentist meeting place.

Trieste keeps its art a few blocks south of Piazza Unità d'Italia, around Piazza Venezia. The **Museo Revoltella**, Via Diaz 27 (*open daily 10–1 and 3–7.30; closed Tues and Sun pm; July and Aug also open 8pm–midnight; adm*), was founded by Baron Pasquale Revoltella, one of the financiers of the Suez Canal (which was a big boon to Trieste's port). Full of original furnishings, it contains 18th- and 19th-century paintings by Triestine artists that evoke the city's golden days, as well as modern works by Morandi and De Chirico. Up a block, on Largo Papa Giovanni XXIII, the **Museo Sartorio** (*open daily 9–1; closed Mon; adm*), housed in an 18th-century villa, offers a glimpse into Triestine bourgeois life in the 19th century, along with a mix of new and old art, including a triptych by Paolo Veneziano.

Up the Capitoline Hill

Catch bus no.24 from the station or Piazza dell'Unità to ascend Trieste's very own Capitoline Hill, the nucleus of the Roman and medieval city. In the 5th century the Triestini raised the first of two basilicas here to their patron San Giusto. An adjacent basilica, built in the 11th century, was linked to the earlier church in the 14th century, thus giving the **Cathedral of San Giusto** (*closed 12–3*) its curious plan. The doorway, under a splendid Gothic rose window, is framed by the fragments of a Roman sarcophagus: six funerary busts gaze solemnly ahead like a corporate board of directors, while a Roman frieze embedded in the adjacent, squat campanile resembles a fashion plate for armour. The interior has some fine mosaics, especially the 13th-century *Christ with SS. Giusto and Servulus*, as well as good 12th-century frescoes. Buried on the right is Don Carlos, the Great Pretender of Spain's 19th-century Carlist Wars, who died as an exile in Trieste in 1855.

Next to San Giusto are fragments of the Roman forum and a 1st-century basilica, of which two columns have been re-erected. The excellent view over Trieste from here is marred by a 1933 **Monument to the Fallen**, which admirably extols the principal fascist virtues of strength and vulgarity The 15th-century **Castello di San Giusto** was begun by the Venetians and finished by the Austrians, and offers more views from its ramparts and a small **Museo Civico** (*open Tues–Sun 9–1; adm*), full of armour and weapons.

Just down the lane from the cathedral is the **Civico Museo di Storia e Arte e Orto Lapidario** (*open Tues–Sun 9–1, Wed 9–7pm; adm*), housing finds from ancient Tergeste, and a famous 5th-century deers' head rhyton from ancient Tarentum. The Orto Lapidario contains a red granite Egyptian sarcophagus and the tomb of J. J. Winckelmann, the famous art historian who was murdered in Trieste in 1768 by a cook. On the way down to the centre, have a look at the 1st-century **Roman theatre** on Via Teatro Romano.

More Caffès and Museums

The Grand Cafés, once the symbol of Triestine society and filled with fervent cross-cultural conversation, ideas and spies, have mostly vanished, or deal primarily in nostalgia. Joyce was an habitué of the **Caffè Pirona**, Largo Barriera Vecchia 12, north of the castle hill and south of Piazza Goldoni (at the bottom of the 'Giant's Stair' from the Castello); the locals say he conceived Ulysses over its *pinzas* and *putizzas*. On the other side of Piazza Goldoni, **Caffè San Marco**, Via Cesare Battisti 18, opened in 1914 but was rebuilt after it was blown up in the First World War, complete with Venetian murals that betrayed the owner's pro-Italian sentiments. According to the *Triestini*, the masked figures in the oval over the bar portray Vittorio Emanuele and Mussolini. One street away, on Via S. Francesco, stands the most beautiful **synagogue** in Italy, and the biggest in Europe, built in 1910 on ancient Syriac models.

In sombre counterpoint, Trieste had the only concentration camp in Italy used for mass exterminations, the **Risiera di San Sabba** at the southern extreme of the city (Ratto della Pileria

1), a rice-husking factory that was taken over by the Nazis in September 1943 to 'process', among others, 837 Triestine Jews. The building now houses a small **museum** (*bus no.8; museum open Tues–Sun 9–1*). In the same area, the **Museo Ferroviario**, in the Campo Marzio (*open daily 9–1; closed Mon*) has a display of retired locomotives. It also runs summer excursions in period trains: three-hour electric train journeys around the city, and steam train excursions around the region and neighbouring countries; ✆ 040 379 4185.

Excursions from Trieste

You can't go too far without running into Slovenia. For a short jaunt, take the **Opicina Tranvia**, built in 1902, up the cliffs from Piazza Oberdan for the fine panorama from the **Vedetta d'Opicina**. Another popular excursion is to Miramare, some 7km up the beach-lined **Riviera di Barcola** (bus no.36 from Piazza Oberdan or Stazione Centrale). On the way stands the **Faro della Vittoria**, a lofty lighthouse and 1927 war memorial to sailors, crowned by a heavy-sinewed, big-busted Valkyrie in a majorette's costume.

Miramare: Habsburg Folly by the Sea

Open April–Sept daily 9–6; Oct–Mar daily 9–4; July–early Sept also Thurs–Sat 8.30–10.30pm; adm exp. Park open daily in summer 8–7; winter 8–4; free.

Set on its own little promontory by the sea, the castle of Miramare hides a dark history behind its charming 19th-century façade. It was built by the Habsburg Archduke Maximilian and his Belgian wife Carlotta, and visitors are greeted by a stone sphinx with a cryptic smile that seems to ask the world: why did Maximilian leave this pleasure palace, and like a *dummkopf*, let Napoleon III's financiers con him into becoming Mexico's puppet emperor in 1864, and why did he linger around there to face a firing squad three years later? Was he an idealist like his apologists claim, or too much of a Habsburg to know any better?

Carlotta, after desperately trying to rally European support for her husband, went mad after his execution and survived him for another 50 years in Belgium; while Miramare acquired the ominous reputation of laying a curse on anyone who slept within its walls, when another Habsburg—the Archduke Ferdinand—stayed here on his way to assassination in Sarajevo. When the Americans occupied the palace in 1946, their commander insisted on sleeping out in the park in a tent.

You can hear the whole sad story in the sound and light show 'Miramare's Imperial Dream' (*in Italian only; shows July, Aug and Sept Mon, Tues and Wed 9.30 or 10.45pm; ring © 040 679 6111, for possible performances in English*). The charming park was designed by Maximilian, who made a better botanist than emperor of Mexico; the gardens and coastal waters are now managed by the World Wildlife Federation and shelter the rare Stella's otter and marsh harriers.

The Carso

Most of Trieste's slender province lies within the Carso, named from its karst or pliable limestone, easily eroded by the rain into remarkable shapes—and here, pale cliffs that form Italy's most dramatic Adriatic coastline north of Monte Còrnero. Inland the karst has been buffeted by the 90mph bora into petrified waves of rock dotted with *dolinas* (swallow holes), while, underground, aeons of dripping water have formed vast caverns, ravines and subterranean lakes and rivers. Vineyards grow wherever there's room, and elsewhere the landscape is dominated by sumac, which autumn ignites into a hundred shades of scarlet.

Between Miramare and the industrial shipbuilding town of Monfalcone lies the fishing village of Duino, with its 15th-century **Castello Nuovo**, perched on a promontory over the sea. Castello Nuovo has long been owned by the Princes von Thurn und Taxis, one of whom played host to Rilke here from 1910 to 1911, when the poet began his *Duino Elegies*. The castle is now the seat of a school, and off limits, but you can follow the beautiful 2km **Rilke walk** along the promontory, beginning in nearby **Sistiana**, a pretty resort with a yacht harbour in its own little bay; peregrine falcons nest on the cliffs.

Born in a karstic abyss in Slovenia, the **Timavo River** continues underground for 30km before reappearing near the winsome Romanesque church of **San Giovanni al Timavo**, above Duino. The main attraction in the Carso is the **Grotta Gigante** (*bus no.45 every half hour from the Piazza Oberdan; guided tours April–Sept daily 9–12 and 2–7; closed Mon exc in July and Aug; Oct–Mar daily 10–12 and 2–4.30; closed Mon; adm exp*). The name for once is no exaggeration: this is the largest cavern in the world open to visitors; its main hall could swallow the entire basilica of St Peter's. A pair of stalactites measuring 346ft are the biggest, anywhere. The ceiling is so high that drops of water disintegrate before reaching the floor, forming curious leaf-shaped stalagmites. A belvedere overlooks a sheer 360ft drop. The cave is in Sgonico, site of a beautiful botanical garden, the **Carsiana** (*open May–Sept Sat and Sun*).

Bus no.40 from Piazza Oberdan offers an excursion through some fine scenery to the perilous Karstic cliffs in the **Val Rosandra**, south of Trieste. Bus no.20 heads along the coast from Trieste to **Muggia**, a higgledy-piggledy Venetian fishing port at the end of Italy. The lion in its square looks most disapproving, however, and holds a closed book. The pretty tri-lobed Duomo has a peculiar relief over the door, showing God holding a grown-up Jesus on his lap; the frescoes inside date from the 13th century. The best views around are enjoyed by the **Basilica di Santa Maria Assunta**, a 10th-century frescoed church overlooking Muggia.

The **opera season** at Trieste's Teatro Comunale Verdi runs from November to March; in summer the theatre and the Sala Tripcovich in Piazza della Libertà sees an **International Operetta festival** (for schedules and bookings call ✆ 040 672 2500, ✇ 040 672 2249). **Carnival** is celebrated with a Venetian flair in Muggia, with a lavish parade that's well beyond what you would expect in a small town.

Trieste ✉ *34100*   ***Where to Stay and Eating Out***

On Trieste's finest square is the city's finest hotel, ★★★★**Duchi d'Aosta**, ✆ 040 760 0011, Piazza dell'Unità d'Italia 2, ✇ 040 366 092 (*very expensive*), in a neo-Renaissance palace erected in 1873. Now owned by the CIGA chain, it exudes a dignified Belle Epoque ambience; upstairs the luxurious rooms are fitted with all modern comforts. It has an excellent restaurant, **Harry's Grill**, and there is parking outside or in the garage.

★★★**Novo Impero**, Via S. Anastasia 1, ✆ 040 364 242, ✇ 040 365 023 (*expensive*) is located near the train station, a short walk from the centre; some rooms are cheaper.

By the historic hill, ★★★**San Giusto**, Via C. Belli 3, ✆ 040 762 661, ✇ 040 760 6585 (*moderate*) is modern, with everything you need.

★★**Al Teatro**, Via Capo di Piazza G. Bartoli 1 (near Piazza dell'Unità), ✆ 040 366 220, ✇ 040 366 560 (*moderate*) served as British headquarters after the Second World War, and is a bit of a nostalgic trip back to old Trieste. Comfortable ★★★**Milano**, Via Ghega 17, ✆ 040 369 680, ✇ 040 369 727 (*moderate*) is near the station. Or take the tranvia up to Opicina and the ★★★**Nuovo Daneu**, Via Nazionale 11, ✆ 040 214 241, ✇ 040 214 215 (*moderate*), which has a good restaurant and indoor pool.

There are many less expensive choices in the centre of Trieste (look around Via Roma, Via della Geppa or Via XXX Ottobre). ★**Alabarda-Flora**, Via Valdirivo 22, ✆ 040 630 269, ✇ 040 639 284 (*cheap*) is clean, comfortable and good-value. The **Youth Hostel** is idyllically but inconveniently placed overlooking the sea at Viale Miramare 331, ✆/✇ 040 224 102, 8km north of Trieste near Miramare. Take bus no.36.

Trieste is a good place to eat dumplings instead of pasta—Slovenian influences are strong. Nearly every restaurant makes *jota*, a minestrone with beans, potatoes and sauerkraut. The middle-European influence is especially noticeable in the desserts: the lovely strudels, the *gnocchi di susine* (plums) and *zavate*, a warm cream pastry.

The place to partake of *cucina triestina* is the **Antica Trattoria Suban**, Via Comici 2, ✆ 040 54368 (*expensive*), in the suburb of San Giovanni (and quite hard to find, so take a taxi). Founded out in the country in 1863, it has since been absorbed by urban growth, but this wonderful old inn maintains its old feel and its fine views over Trieste. Suban offers a famous *jota*, *sevapcici* (Slovenian grilled meat fritters), sinful desserts and good wines. Readers warn, however, that the quality depends on the presence of the regular chef; when booking ask if he's on duty, and if not, wait till he is. *Closed Mon lunch, Tues, part of Jan, and Aug.*

Towards Miramare, **Hosteria Bellavista**, Via Bonomea 52, ℭ 040 411 150 (*expensive*) is a wine-lover's paradise, with hundreds of bottles from around the world to go with delicate renditions of Trieste's favourites, and lovely views. *Closed Sun, Mon lunch, and some of Jan.*

Take a taxi into the hills for **Scabar**, way down Via dell'Istria at Erta di S. Anna 63, ℭ 040 810 368 (*moderate*), for fish and mushroom dishes; the day's special is usually fantastic. *Closed Mon, Tues, Feb and mid-July–Aug.* Convenient to Piazza Unità d'Italia and the museums, **Città di Cherso**, Via Cadorna 6, ℭ 040 366 044 (*moderate*) serves delicious seafood Friulian-style, topped off with heavenly desserts. *Closed Tues, some of July and Aug.*

Buffet da Pepi, Via Cassa di Risparmo 3, ℭ 040 366 858 (*cheap*) was founded in 1903 and has been thriving ever since, serving up Trieste's specialities. *Closed Sun.* The waiters still write the orders on the tablecloths at **Re di Coppe**, Via Geppa 11, ℭ 040 370 330 (*cheap*), serving up a classic *jota* and meats. *Closed Sat, Sun, and mid-July–mid-Aug.*

Gorizia and around

The frontier town of Gorizia was for centuries ruled by a powerful dynasty of counts, who were always ready to stir up trouble against Venice, with the approval of the Kings of Hungary. When the last count died in 1500, the city was briefly controlled by Venice before being taken over by the Habsburgs. As in Trieste, the Austrians gave Gorizia broad, straight boulevards and parks and pronounced the result an 'Austrian Nice' (minus the seashore).

The city saw fierce fighting in the First World War, but it was after the Second World War that Gorizia became Italy's Berlin, divided between Italy and Slovenia in such a thoughtless manner that it almost choked. Things were improved in 1979, when residents were granted a 16km zone around the city to transact their affairs freely. In 1991 Gorizia saw the first shots of the Balkan War, when Slovenia declared independence and the Yugoslav army was sent in to wrest back the lucrative border posts. Today, as independent Slovenia prospers, the town has flashy boutiques catering for cross-border traffic.

Tourist Information

Gorizia: Via Diaz 16, ℭ/✉ 0481 533 870.
Gradisca d'Isonzo: Palazzo Torriani, Via M Ciotti, ℭ 0481 99217, ✉ 0481 99880.

Borgo Castello

Crowning Gorizia, Borgo Castello is a little medieval village within the city, all enveloped by a Venetian fortress of 1509. In the centre stands the **Castle of the Counts of Gorizia**, first mentioned in 1001, but completely rebuilt after the First World War. It now houses the **Museo del Medioevo Goriziano** (*open Tues–Sun 9.30–1 and 3–7.30; adm*), with a display dedicated to Gorizia's complicated history. Just below stands the pretty church of **Santo Spirito** (1386) and the Casa Formentini, now the **Museo Provinciale** (*open daily 10–8; closed Mon; adm*), featuring local artists, especially Giuseppe Tominz, painter of the bourgeoisie of Gorizia and Trieste (d. 1866), don't miss his self portrait with his brother (fully grown) sitting on his lap, about to receive Giuseppe's fully laden palette on the back of his frock coat. Best of all are the basement rooms, dedicated to the Isonzo front and its trenches, evoking the horror and some of the black humour of the First World War.

In 1990 Guglielmo Coronini, the last Count of Gorizia, died, and now his home, **Villa Coronini Cronberg** (1594), Viale XX Settembre 14, is open for tours (*Tues–Sat 10–1 and 4–8, Sun 10–12 and 4–8; adm*). There's the bedroom where Charles X, the last King of France, died in 1836 and the Count's paintings—by Tintoretto, Strozzi, Magnasco, Rubens, Monet, Rosalba Carriera and, of course, Giuseppe Tominz; prints by Titian and Rembrandt and Japanese masters, and more; you can also wander through the villa's English park.

Wine Around Gorizia

The hills around Gorizia, the **Collio**, are a lost bit of Tuscany as well as the most prestigious wine region in Friuli, producing exquisite white wines since the Middle Ages. The pleasant, leafy town of **Gradisca d'Isonzo** straddles the blue-green River Isonzo, neat and tidy with pastel houses and little 17th-century palazzi. It also offers the chance to taste any or all of the Friulian wines at the **Enoteca Regionale Serenissima**, in business since 1965 (*open daily 10–1 and 4–11pm; closed Mon*). **Cormòns**, another major wine town, was the only one in Italy to erect a statue to Emperor Maximilian. Visit its **Cantina Prodottori Vini del Collio e Isonzo**, © 0481 60579 (*closed Sun*), which produces a Vino della Pace, made from vines gathered from around the globe, and sent out annually to the world's heads of state.

Where to Stay and Eating Out

Gorizia ✉ 34170

Just north of Gorizia at San Floriano del Collio, a 17th-century manor house is now the ★★★★**Golf Hotel**, Via Oslavia 2, © 0481 884 051, @ 0481 884 052 (*expensive*): 15 rooms furnished with antiques and every amenity; pool, tennis and golf, too. In town, the ★★★**Palace**, Corso d'Italia 63, © 0481 82166, @ 0481 31658 (*moderate*) has large modern rooms. In Borgo Castello, you can sup in medieval splendour at the **Lanterna d'Oro al Castello**, © 0481 82007 (*moderate*). The menu features Friuli specialities like *prosciutto di San Daniele*, venison, kid and boar. *Closed Mon.*

Cormòns ✉ 34071

The nicest place to sleep in the Collio, ★★★**Felcaro**, Via S. Giovanni 45, © 0481 60214, @ 0481 630 255 (*moderate*) is spread out over several buildings, with a pool, tennis courts, fitness centre, and a fine restaurant, specializing in game dishes to go with its enormous wine list (*moderate*). In a charming rural setting on a hill, ★★**La Subida**, Monte 22 © 0481 60531, @ 0481 61616 (*cheap*) has a handful of rooms, many sleeping up to five, with a pool, tennis and riding; the restaurant, **Il Cacciatore**, serves excellent regional dishes, with extensive borrowings from nearby Slovenia. Excellent Collio wines, too (*expensive–moderate*). *Closed Tues, Wed and Feb.*

Legend states that Ùdine's *castello* sits on a mound erected by Hunnish warriors who carried the soil in their helmets so that Attila could watch the burning of Aquileia. The story is apocryphal, as Ùdine went on to take Aquileia's place as seat of the patriarchate from 1238 to 1751. In 1420 its leading family gave it to the Serenissima. In the Second World War it was the last city in Italy to be liberated (May 1945).

Ùdine is something of a best-kept secret; artistically, you'll see much that looks Venetian and much by lagoonland's greatest 18th-century painter, Giambattista Tiepolo, thanks to his first important patron, Patriarch Dionisio Delfino, who kept GB here with commissions between 1726 to 1730, a period when he took up the brilliant colours that became his trademark.

Getting Around

Gorizia, Cormòns and Ùdine are all on the line from Trieste; a private local railway line links Ùdine with Cividale (20min). Ùdine's **railway station** (with connections to Venice, Trieste and Gorizia) is on Viale Europa Unità; the **bus station** is not far away on the other side of the same street, © 0432 506 941.

Tourist Information

Piazza 1 Maggio 7, © 0432 295 972, ✉ 0432 504 743.

Piazza della Libertà

The heart of Ùdine, Piazza della Libertà, has been called 'the most beautiful Venetian square on *terra firma*'. Its most striking building, the candy-striped **Loggia del Lionello,** a mini-doges' palace, was built by a goldsmith in 1448 and faithfully reconstructed after a fire in 1876; a second loggia, the **Loggia di San Giovanni** (1533), supports a clock tower and a bell rung by two Venetian-inspired 'Moors'. There is the usual Venetian column topped by a Lion of St Mark, accompanied by statues of Heracles and Justice, with Bette Davis eyes. The **Municipio**, all in white Istrian stone, is a fine piece of Art Deco by Raimondo D'Aronco (1910–31) that manages to blend right in.

Palladio's rugged **Arco Bollari** (1556) is the gateway to the sweeping **portico**, built in 1487 to shelter visitors to the Castello, former seat of the Patriarch and the Venetian governor. Rebuilt in 1517, and restored after the earthquake, it houses the **Civici Musei** (*open daily 9.30–12.30 and 3–6; closed Mon; adm, but free Sun am*); sections include archaeology, designs and prints, and paintings: a large and excellent collection, with especially good works by Carpaccio, Giambattista Tiepolo and Luca Carlefarijs of Ùdine (1662–1730).

Down in the City

Just east of Piazza Libertà along Via Vittorio Veneto, the oft-altered **duomo** has a charming 14th-century lunette over the door with figures so weathered they look like gingerbread. The interior, a dignified Baroque symphony of grey and gold, has two frescoes by Tiepolo. In the *campanile*, the small **Museo del Duomo** is adorned with excellent 1349 frescoes of the *Funeral of St Nicolas* by Vitale da Bologna, and a 14th-century sarcophagus. Even after

Tiepolo become world famous he never forgot his first fans, and in 1759 when he was at the height of his powers he returned to fresco the **Oratorio della Purità**, added to the cathedral in 1680; he also painted the altarpiece of the *Immaculate Conception*; the *chiaroscuro* frescoes on the walls are by his son Giandomenico.

Near the Duomo on Piazza Venerio, 14th-century **San Francesco** has good frescoes in the apse. From here take a left on Via Savorgnana for the more ornate **San Giacomo**, with its clock tower and life-size figures gazing over the arcaded **Piazza Matteotti**, Ùdine's old market square. Note the outdoor altar over the door of San Giacomo, used to celebrate mass on market days—as convenient for shoppers in its day as a drive-in church in California.

And there's more on the Tiepolo trail: from Piazza Libertà take Via Manin to Piazza Patriarcato and the **Palazzo Arcivescovile**, now the **Museo Diocesano** (*open Wed–Sun 10–12 and 3.30–6.30*), with an entire gallery of Old Testament scenes frescoed by GB in the 1720s. More recent art (Severini, Carrà, De Chirico, De Kooning, Segal, Lichtenstein, Dufy, and the brothers Afro, Mirko and Dino Basaldell of Ùdine) is in the **Galleria d'Arte Moderna** (*open daily 9.30–12.30 and 3–6; closed Mon; adm, but free Sun am*): take bus no.2 from the station.

Cividale del Friuli

Tourist Information

Corso Paolino d'Aquileia 10, ✆ 0432 731 461, ✆ 0432 731 398.

Only a hop and a skip from Ùdine in the valley of the Natisone, Cividale del Friuli is a fine old town with an impressive pedigree. Caesar founded it in 50 BC and named it for his family, *Forum Iulii*, a name condensed over the centuries into 'Friuli'. The Lombards invaded in 568, liked what they saw, and made Cividale the capital of their first duchy. The Patriarch of Aquileia (*see* below) moved here in 737, initiating a magnificent period, documented by Paulus Diaconus, the Lombard historian born in Cividale and one of the brightest beams of light we have on the 'Dark Ages' in northern Italy.

The Duomo and Archaeology Museum

The centre of Cividale is a series of squares around the old forum. In the most important, **Piazza Duomo**, you'll find the rebuilt 13th–15th-century **Palazzo Comunale**, a statue of founder Julius Caesar and the **Duomo** (*open daily 9.30–12 and 3–7, till 6 in winter*), begun in 1453 and given its plain but attractive Renaissance façade by Pietro Lombardo. It contains unique treasures: the 12th-century silver altarpiece, the *Pala di Pellegrino II*, with its 25 saints and two archangels; a fine gilded equestrian monument (1617); and the Renaissance sarcophagus of Patriarch Nicolò Donato.

Off the right aisle, the **Museo Cristiano** contains the octagonal Baptistry of Callisto and the Altar of Ratchis, dating back to 749, when there was still considerable confusion about lion anatomy (the one on the Baptistry is part fish, part hedgehog) and how hands and arms are attached to the human body. In the scene of the Magi, Mary and baby Jesus frown as if they didn't like their presents—what's a baby going to do with a pot of myrrh anyhow? Yet compare its barbaric charms with the Tempietto (*see* below).

Next to the Duomo, the **Museo Archeologico Nazionale** (*open April–Sept daily 9–7, Mon 9–2; Oct–Mar daily 8.30–2; adm*) is housed in Palladio's Palazzo Pretorio. This vast treasure trove has Roman items, especially the unique Zuglio bronzes—an enormous shield with a man's portrait in the centre—as well as objects from Lombard tombs of the 6th and 7th centuries: crosses, *fibulae*, swords and shield-holders (*ambone*). There are ivory pieces for a game called *ad tabulam*, the 8th-century Carolingian *Pax del Duca Orso*, adorned with an ivory crucifix and studded with jewels; a 5th-century *Evangelical of St Mark*, autographed by Lombard nobles who thought it was written in the apostle's hand; and architectural bits from the Romanesque Duomo—mermaids, monsters and a man in a funny hat.

The Ipogeo Celtico and Tempietto Longobardo

Corso Ponte d'Aquileia descends to the pretty turquoise Natisone and the lofty 1442 **Ponte del Diavolo**. In the Middle Ages it was a common folk belief that bridges were magical, and stories grew up on how they were erected overnight by the Devil in exchange for the first soul that ventured across in the morning. But of course Satan is a sucker in every instance; the wily Cividalesi sent over a cat at dawn.

Just up from the bridge is the mysterious **Ipogeo Celtico**, Via Monastero 21 (*the bar All'Ipogeo has the key; on Mon pick it up at the tourist office instead*). This creepy pit, the perfect setting for a nasty cult, may have served as a funeral chamber in the 3rd century BC, although no one's sure, because there's nothing to compare it to. The Romans and Lombards used it as a prison, where unfortunates would have had to look at the three monstrous carved heads that peer out of the walls, seemingly from the dawn of time.

Follow the Natisone up to the happier **Tempietto Longobardo**, or Santa Maria in Valle (*open summer daily 9–1 and 3–6.30; winter daily 10–1 and 3.30–5.30; adm*), the finest 8th-century work in Italy, despite the fact that it had to be restored in the 13th century after an earthquake shattered three-quarters of its ornamentation and all of its mosaics. The stuccoes that remain, however, are a love letter from the Dark Ages: ravishing, uncanny and perhaps even miraculous: a sextet of gently smiling saints and princesses in high relief, standing at either side of a beautiful and intricately carved window, all positioned over an even more intricately carved arch with a vine motif. Artistically, Europe wasn't to see the like again for 400 years.

Udine ✉ 33100

****Astoria Italia**, Piazza XX Settembre 24, ✆ 0432 505 091, 🖷 0432 509 070 (*expensive*) is the grande dame of the city's hotels, located in the heart of town; it has a fine restaurant. The elegant turn-of-the-century ***La' di Moret**, Viale Tricesimo 276, ✆ 0432 545 096, 🖷 0432 545 096 (*moderate*), north of the centre, has won awards for its rooms; and the restaurant features great seafood, Friuli style. *Closed Sun eve and Mon.* Just outside the centre, 5 minutes' walk from the train station, ***San Giorgio**, Piazzale Cella 2, ✆ 0432 505 577, 🖷 0432 506 110 (*moderate*) has modern, air-conditioned rooms. Cheap hotels are here, too, including the 'Where are you going?' **Quo Vadis**, Piazzale Cella 28, ✆ 0432 21091, 🖷 0432 21092.

The oldest restaurant in Udine, **Alla Vedova**, Via Travagnacco 9, ✆ 0432 470 291 (*moderate*) is off the SS13 to Tarvisio; but what better way to spend an evening than at a table near the hearth (or outdoors in the summer), dining on wild duck risotto? The house's red Refosco is famous. *Closed Sun eve and Mon.*

Another historic inn, the **Vitello d'Oro**, at central Via Valvason 4, ✆ 0432 508 982, 🖷 0432 508 982 (*expensive*) serves traditional specialities, with an emphasis on fish. *Closed Wed and three weeks in July.* Charming **Vecchio Stallo**, Via Viola 7, ✆ 0432 21296 (*cheap*) is Udine's best value for money; good food, and wine by the glass. *Closed Wed.* For an exceptional meal, head 7km north to Tricesimo and its gourmet haven, **Boschetti**, Piazza Mazzini 9, ✆ 0432 851 230 (*very expensive*)—try *pappardelle* with porcini, scallops with French beans in almond oil, or steamed salmon with vegetables, followed by exquisite desserts. *Closed Sun eve, Mon and half of Aug.*

Cividale del Friuli ✉ 33043

Ivy-covered ***Locanda al Castello**, Via del Castello 20, ✆ 0432 733 242, 🖷 0432 700 901 (*moderate*), in the suburb of Fortino, is not in a castle but a former fortified Jesuit Seminary, and now offers Cividale's most atmospheric rooms, as well as a fine restaurant. *Closed Nov and Feb.*

The romantic **Locanda Pomo d'Oro**, in an 11th-century hostel, Piazza S. Giovanni 20, ✆/🖷 0432 734 189 (*cheap*) is the best option in town. **Alla Frasca**, Via di Rebeis 8/a, ✆ 0432 731 270 (*moderate*) offers a charming Renaissance atmosphere to go with tasty Friulian dishes, including a *menu di funghi* that offers truffles and mushrooms with everything. *Closed Mon.*

North of Udine: the Julian and Carnia Alps

The mountainous north of Udine is now linked to the city by a bright new *autostrada*. It has yet to bring in the crowds. The Julian Alps are Slovene-speaking, their church towers crowned with colourful garlic domes. If the peaks lack the romance of their Dolomite neighbours, they also lack their crowds and lofty prices.

Tarvisio: Via Roma 10, ✆ 0428 2135, ✉ 042 82972.
Tolmezzo: Piazza Centa 14, ✆/✉ 0433 44898.
Forni di Sopra: Via Cadore 1, ✆ 0433 886 767, ✉ 0433 886 686.

Into Friuli's Mountains

Just off the *autostrada*, **Gemona** and **Venzone** were the epicentre of the powerful 1976 earthquake. Rather than move on, both were rebuilt with meticulous care, a labour of love that after 23 years is almost completed. Set in the Julian foothills, Gemona del Friuli's gem is a 13th-century cathedral with a façade featuring a remarkable St Christopher, sculpted by a Nordic artist in 1331. Nearby Venzone, a smaller, double-walled town, began as a crossroads stop on the Julia Augusta road. A display under the painted ceiling of the loggia has astonishing before and after photographs.

The *autostrada* continues northeast into the Julian Alps. The mountains south of **Tarvisio** (near the Austrian and Slovenian borders) cradle an up-and-coming resort, **Sella Nevea**, near two pretty lakes. Tri-national ski passes are available.

The Carnia Mountains rise to the west, next door neighbours to the Dolomites. **Tolmezzo**, an 18th-century producer of damasks and taffetas, is the main town and transportation hub of the mountains. In a 16th-century palace in Piazza Garibaldi, the Museo Carnico (*open daily 9–1 and 3–6; closed Mon*) has a fine ethnographic collection, covering mountain life from the 14th to the 19th centuries. Beyond Tolmezzo the scenery grows increasingly delightful. From **Comeglians** there is a lovely scenic road up to **Sappada** in the Cadore (*see* p.387). West of Tolmezzo, at **Ampezzo**, you can pick up the road to isolated **Sauris** with its beautiful lake. The road west to Pieve di Cadore passes **Forni di Sotto**, a village rebuilt after the Nazis burnt it to the ground in reprisal for partisan activities, and **Forni di Sopra**, in a beautiful setting, with a fine 15th-century triptych in the Romanesque church of San Floriano.

Emilia-Romagna

Between the sparkling wines of Lombardy, the elegant Soave of the Veneto and the full-bodied Chianti of Tuscany, Emilia-Romagna seems like a glass of warm beer. It is mostly flat, on the southern plain of the Po, hot and humid in the summer, and cold and fog-bound in the winter. Most tourists see it only from the train window when chugging between Venice and Florence.

But for anyone interested in cracking the surface of this glossiest and most complex of nations, Emilia-Romagna is an essential region to know. For this is Middle Italy: agricultural, wealthy, progressive, a barometer of Italian highs and lows—the birthplace of the country's socialist movement, but also of Mussolini and Fascism. In Emilia-Romagna hard-working cities like Modena, Parma and Bologna share space with Rimini, Italy's vast, madcap international resort, with Ravenna, the artistic jewel of the region with its stupendous Byzantine mosaics, and with traditional Apennine villages. Emilia-Romagna is the cradle of innovative film directors—Fellini, Bertolucci and Antonioni; of musical giants like Verdi, Toscanini, Pavarotti, Tebaldi and Bergonzi; and of such diverse talents as Marconi, Correggio, Savonarola, Ariosto, Pavarotti, Parmigianino and Ferrari.

As a united region, Emilia-Romagna is a child of the Risorgimento. Emilia, west of Bologna, was named after the Via Aemilia, built by M. Aemilius Lepidus in 187 BC between Piacenza and Rimini, running almost dead straight for hundreds of kilometres along the course of the Apennines. Nearly all of Emilia's cities grew up at intervals along the road, like beads on a string. Romagna, east of Bologna, recalls the period from the 5th century to 751 when this was 'Rome', when Ravenna was the last enclave of the Roman Empire in the west, ruled by the exarchs of the Eastern Roman Empire in Byzantium. By the Middle Ages these cities had gone their own way, controlled by dukes or *signori*—the Farnese, Este, Malatesta, Bentivoglio and Da Polenta—who claimed allegiance to the pope, and held the front line between the Papal States and the Venetians and Milanese.

In Emilia-Romagna you'll find, besides the remarkable art of the Byzantines and Ostrogoths in Ravenna, exceptional Romanesque churches (Parma and Modena), two of Italy's crookedest towers (Bologna), beautiful Renaissance art (Parma, Bologna and Ferrara) and the Renaissance's strangest building, the Malatesta Temple in Rimini. You can ski, hike, ride or hang-glide in the Apennines, sunbathe in style on the Adriatic, visit the ancient Republic of San Marino or Italy's ceramics capital at Faenza, or attend grand opera in Parma, Reggio, Bologna or Modena. You'll also find Italy's best food —this is the home of Parmesan cheese and Parma ham, tortellini, lasagne, spaghetti bolognese, and a hundred different kinds of sausages, balsamic vinegar and eels. It is also the home of Lambrusco which, if it's the right stuff, should foam like a beer when it's first poured, only to reveal a sparkling, elegant and full-bodied wine below.

Emilia-Romagna

Emilia-Romagna Highlights

Ravenna with its marvellous churches and mosaics is a must see, followed in short order by **Bologna**, perhaps Italy's most underestimated great art city, which can easily fill three days, followed by lovely **Parma**, with its cathedral, Farnese palace museums and Correggios, and **Ferrara**, the captial of the arty Este dukes. Then comes **Modena's** cathedral and museum, **Faenza's** great ceramics museum, **Rimini's** Malatesta temple and beach madness, **Busseto** for Verdi fans and **Piacenza**, **Reggio Emilia**, and the pigmy republic of **San Marino**. You may need a breather in the country. From Piacenza you can visit the attractive Roman ruins at **Velleia**, or ancient **Bobbio**, a monastery founded by an Irish monk. Parma is encircled by fine castles, especially **Torrechiara** and **Soragna**, or there's the Farnese's 'little Versailles' in **Colorno**. North of Reggio Emilia, **Luzzara**, home to Italy's museum of *naïf* painting. Ferrara is near the wetlands of the **Po Delta** and the medieval **abbey of Pomposa**.

The Gourmet in Emilia-Romagna

Nothing sums up this area so well as food and, beside the wonderful experiences waiting in restaurants, it's easy to find tastes to take home. Cheese, meat, wine, liqueurs or sweets travel well. Most Parmesan cheese, called *grana* on account of its grainy quality, is actually *Parmigiano-Reggiano*, and is produced around Parma, Modena and Reggio Emilia. A true Parma ham is first left to dry in the sweet air of the Magra Valley, to lose its excessive saltiness and gain the scent of pine and olives, then taken down the Cisa Pass to take the chestnutty air of the Apennines. Yet even more revered is *culatello*, a sausage made from a pig's buttocks, which can be prepared only in the humid lowlands of the Po Valley.

Nocino is a liqueur which tradition states must come from Sassuolo, near Modena, and be made from unripe walnuts picked on St John's Day, 24th June. Alcohol is poured over the crushed nuts, then sugar, cinnamon, cloves and lemon rind are added; the mixture is left for forty days before being sieved through cotton. The other great specialities of Modena are balsamic vinegar—the finest of which is as prized and precisely regulated as any DOCG wine—and cherries, from Vignola. In Bologna delicatessens sell fresh tortellini, stuffed with any combination of ricotta cheese, minced beef or veal, bread, chicken, nutmeg and fresh herbs. Bologna is also famous for its desserts and pâtisserie, the most specialized of which is *torta di riso*, a sweet, thick rice pudding.

Piacenza

Competing with the more famous charms of nearby Parma and Cremona, Piacenza is the unassuming wallflower of Renaissance cities. Nevertheless, it can boast of two of the most gallant horses in Italy, a Botticelli, and an amazing liver. A Roman colony established in 218 BC at the conjunction of the Via Aemilia and the Po, Piacenza was an important *comune* in the 12th and 13th centuries, and a member of the Lombard League in 1314. It spent much of its history under the Farnese thumb, as part of the Duchy of Parma. In 1848, after a plebiscite,

Piacenza became the first city to unite with Piedmont in the new nation of Italy, earning itself the nickname of *Primogenita* or 'first-born'.

Getting Around

The **train station** on Piazzale Marconi, a 10-minute walk from the centre, has frequent links to Milan, Parma and Cremona. The **bus station**, ℗ 0523 337 245, in Piazza Cittadella, near the Palazzo Farnese, has buses to Cremona, Bobbio (10 a day), Grazzano Visconti, Castell'Arquato and other towns in the province. Buses to Velleia (1hr 40min) are infrequent; if you go make sure you don't get stranded.

Tourist Information

Piazzetta dei Mercanti 10 (flanking Piazza Cavalli), ℗/✉ 0523 329 324.

Piazza Cavalli

Piacenza's excellent Piazza Cavalli (to get there from the station, cut across the park to vias G. Alberoni and Roma, then turn left on Via Carducci) takes its name from its two bronze **horses** with flowing manes, masterpieces of the early Baroque, cast in the 1620s by Francesco Mochi. Riding them are two members of the Farnese clan: Alessandro, the 'Prince of Parma', Philip II of Spain's governor in the Low Countries during the Dutch War of Independence (not a position that won him any popularity contests, despite the fine statue), and his son Ranuccio. The piazza also contains the Gothic **Palazzo del Comune** (*open to visitors during temporary exhibitions*), built in 1280, with swallowtail crenellations, mullioned windows and a rose window, and the 13th-century church of **San Francesco**, noted for its Gothic interior.

Rising up at the end of the main Via XX Settembre, the Lombard-Romanesque **Duomo** (1122–1233) is an imposing pile; a picturesque confusion of columns, caryatids and galleries viewed from the side and apse. The transitional interior (Romanesque to Gothic) has a striking striped marble floor and good 15th-century frescoes. From here Via Chiapponi leads to **Sant'Antonino**, Piacenza's oldest church, with an 11th-century octagonal lantern believed to be the first built in Italy, and a fine Gothic porch called the *Paradiso*. Just southwest on vias San Siro and Santa Franca, opposite a picturesque but derelict Art Nouveau theatre, is the **Ricci-Oddi Gallery** (*due to reopen end of 1999*), a well-arranged collection that shows what Italian artists were up to between the years 1800 and 1930.

The Palazzo Farnese

From Piazza Cavalli, Corso Cavour leads to the pachydermic, uncompleted Palazzo Farnese, local headquarters of the ducal family (begun in 1558). Inside is the **Museo Civico** (*open Tues, Wed and Fri 9–12.30, Thurs 9–12.30 and 3.30–5.30, Sat 9–12.30 and 3–6, Sun 9.30–12 and 3.30–6.30; adm*). Botticelli's lovely *Tondo* is the highlight of the paintings, and in the archaeological section you can see the most famous Etruscan bronze of them all: the *Fegato di Piacenza*, a model of a sheep (or some say human) liver, designed for apprentice augurs, diagrammed and inscribed with the names of the Etruscan deities. The Etruscans regarded the liver as a microcosm of the sky, ruled over by various gods, and looked in it for blemishes to see which deity had anything to communicate. Another section of the museum contains medieval arms, and another 18th- and 19th-century coaches.

About 2km southwest of the city is **San Lazzaro Alberoni** (*visits by appointment only,*
© 0523 613 198). This college contains a fine collection of Flemish tapestries and, among its
16th–18th-century Flemish and Italian paintings, Antonello da Messina's *Christ at the
Column*—an unusual composition and the Renaissance's most sorrowful Christ.

Environs of Piacenza

The rarely visited hills and mountains south of Piacenza offer several possibilities for excursions or road stops. The main SS45 to Genoa follows the Trebbia Valley to **Bobbio** (46km),
where St Columbanus founded a monastery in 612, shortly before his death. Columbanus,
one of several scholarly Irishmen who came to the illiterate continent as missionaries in the
Dark Ages, had also founded the great abbey of Luxeuil (Vosges), but had been forced to leave
because of his outspoken views of the Frankish count. The **basilica**, rebuilt in the 15th
century, has traces of Columbanus' church and his Renaissance sarcophagus. The **Museo di
San Colombano** (*open Sat 4.30–6, Sun 11–12 and 3–6; adm*) contains a famous 4th-
century ivory bucket with reliefs, and Romanesque statuary and painting; in the town of
Bobbio, clustered around the monastery and castle, there are many fine old stone houses.

Emilia's best-preserved Roman town, prettily situated on a hillside, is **Velleia**, 33km south of
Piacenza between Bobbio and Salsomaggiore. It was never very large, but retains its forum,
temple, amphitheatre and mysterious large carved stones that resemble bathplugs. Most of the
finds are now in Parma, though bits and pieces remain in Velleia's **antiquarium** on the site
(*open daily 9am–sunset*). If you're driving you can cut over the hills from here to Lugagnano
and **Castell'Arquato**, a lovely walled hill town built around an asymmetrical **Palazzo
Pretorio** (1293) and a picturesque Romanesque church of the same period. Just as
picturesque, closer to Piacenza but not as authentic, **Grazzano Visconti** was recently rebuilt
in the medieval style. The village is a good place to purchase ornamental wrought iron.

Piacenza ✉ *29100*   ***Where to Stay and Eating Out***

Piacenza's most prestigious hotel, ★★★★**Grande Albergo Roma**, Via
Cittadella 14, © 0523 323 201, 📠 0523 330 548 (*expensive*), is
just off Piazza Cavalli, with old-fashioned service, comfortable
air-conditioned rooms and a good restaurant. The rooms at the
★★★**Nazionale**, Via Genova 35, © 0523 712 000, 📠 0523 456
013 (*moderate*) are more modern. Near the station, ★**Moderno**, Via
Tibini 31, © 0523 29296, 📠 0523 384 438, is basic (*cheap*). *Closed Aug.*

Piacenza can claim an exceptional gourmet restaurant, the delightful **Antica Osteria
del Teatro**, Via Verdi 16, near Sant'Antonino, © 0523 384 639 (*expensive*), where
local recipes merge delectably with French *nouvelle cuisine* under the chef's magic
touch. *Closed Sun eve, Mon and Aug.* **Peppino**, Via Roma 183, © 0523 329 279
(*moderate*), near the Duomo, specializes in fish with Sicilian influences: swordfish
cooked with sultanas, pine nuts and wild fennel, *tortelloni di branzino* (filled with sea
bass); and rich *zabaglione*. *Closed Mon and most of Aug.* **La Pireina**, Via Borghetto
137, © 0523 338 578 (*cheap*), a traditional trattoria near the old city walls, serves
local dishes in an unpretentious way: *tortelli d'erbette* (stuffed with spinach and
ricotta), *tagliolini al ragù*, *faldia* (breaded horse steak). *Closed Sun and Aug.*

North of the Via Aemilia between Piacenza and Parma lies the flat Po Valley known as the *Bassa*, a favourite landscape in Italian films. Down the Via Aemilia itself, 30km east of Piacenza, the **Abbey of Chiaravalle della Colomba** (*open daily 9–12 and 2–7*), 4km north of Alseno, has a Romanesque church and beautiful brick cloister. More of the same awaits at **Fidenza**, Roman *Fidentia Iulia*, known for centuries as Borgo San Donnino until Mussolini resurrected its more imperial-sounding name. Of interest, it has a 13th-century **Duomo**, with a beautiful porch by the followers of Antelami, the master of Parma's Baptistry.

South of Fidenza, **Salsomaggiore** ('Big Salt'), with its 109 hotels, is the largest and best-known of a cluster of saline water spas specializing in arthritic and rheumatic cures. It was popular with Italian royalty at the turn of the century, and is now favoured by opera singers. Its baths, the **Terme Berzieri**, are concentrated in a half-baked Liberty-style palace, while the **Palazzo dei Congressi** on Viale Romagnosi was once the grand hotel, owned by Cesar Ritz; past clients included Caruso, Toscanini and Queen Margherita of Italy. The lobby is still one of the grandest in Italy—a Liberty-arabesque fantasy with fabulously colourful frescoes by Galileo Chini. Another important spa nearby is **Tabiano Bagni**, with stinky sulphur springs.

Busseto and its Swan

Some 15km north of Fidenza on the road to Cremona, Busseto is the attractive, neatly rectangular walled town that gave the world Joe Green—Giuseppe Verdi. To Italians Verdi is not just another great composer, but the genius who expressed the national spirit of the Risorgimento in music: Italy's answer to Richard Wagner. Opera buffs can take in the complete 'Swan of Busseto' tour, beginning in the house at **Roncole**, 9km southeast of Busseto, where the composer was born in 1813, son of a grocer and tavern-keeper (*open April–Sept Tues–Sun 9.30–12.30 and 3–7; Oct and Nov Tues–Sun 9.30–12 and 2.30–5; adm*). While in Roncole, you can also visit the parish church where little Giuseppe was baptized and played the organ.

In Busseto proper a statue of Verdi relaxes in an armchair near the medieval castle, or **Rocca**, built by Oberto Pallavicino, who became the subject of Verdi's first opera, *Oberto*. The Rocca contains the **Teatro Verdi**, modelled after La Scala, built in the composer's honour in 1845; Verdi frequently attended performances. The Rocca's Palazzo Pallavicino is now the **Museo Civico** (*castle, theatre and museum open same hours as Verdi's birthplace; adm*), full of Verdian memorabilia. With the proceeds from *Rigoletto*, Verdi built the **Villa Verdi**, in Sant'Agata di Villanova, 3km north of Busseto (*open April–Oct; guided tours by appointment © 0523 830 210; adm*); it has a replica of the hotel room in Milan where Verdi died in 1901.

The Castles of Parma

Some of the remarkable castles in the province of Parma lie between Busseto and Parma. The **Palazzo di Soragna** (*open April–Oct Tues–Sun 9–11 and 3–6; Nov–Mar Tues–Sun 9–11 and 2–4.30; adm*), begun in the 8th century as a castle, was converted into a palace ten centuries later by its current owners, the Princes of Meli Lupi, and was frescoed by the likes of Parmigianino and Gentile da Fabriano. In Fontanellato the fairy-tale **Castello di Sanvitale** (*open Tues–Sun 9.30–11.45 and 3–6; Nov–Mar Tues–Sun 9.30–11.45 and 3–5; adm*) is much more castle-like, surrounded by a moat and adorned inside with frescoes; the rich, sensuous *Diana and Actaeon* in the boudoir is by Parmigianino. Another imposing fortress nearby, **Castel Guelfo** (*visible from the outside only*), once belonged to the Ghibelline Pallavicini family of Busseto, but was renamed as an insult by its Guelph captors in 1407.

In **Colorno**, just north of Parma on the road to Mantua, one of the Farnese dukes, Ranuccio II, converted an old castle into a 'miniature Versailles' in 1660. It has beautiful gardens, an orangerie—and tunnels. The later Bourbon rulers must have been nervous, for they installed escape hatches leading all over the countryside, one supposedly running all the way to Parma (*open to visitors by appointment, © 0521 312 545/© 0521 313 719*).

Where to Stay and Eating Out

Salsomaggiore ✉ 43039

The ★★★★★**Grand Hotel et de Milan**, Via Dante 1, © 0524 572 241, @ 0524 573 884 (*very expensive*) is the plushest place in town to take the waters, with lovely rooms and a heated pool in a pretty garden. *Open April–Oct.* ★★★**Valentini**, Viale Porro 10, © 0524 578 251, @ 0524 578 266 (*moderate*) also has its own spa and swimming pool, set in a quiet park. *Closed 10 Nov–20 Dec.* There is also a large choice of cheap hotels, like the central ★**Albergo Livia**, Piazzale Berzieri 6, © 0524 573 166 (*cheap*).

The classic place to eat is **Al Tartufo**, Viale Marconi 30, © 0524 573 696 (*expensive*); besides *tartufi* (truffles), you can try the chef's famous grilled mushrooms. **Alle Querce da Giorgio**, Via Parma 85, © 0524 578 281 (*moderate*) is a peaceful restaurant by the side of a lake filled with trout and carp. The patron suggests a menu, which will probably feature *porcini* mushrooms, truffles and home-made pasta. *Closed Mon*.

Busseto ✉ 43011

The finest place to stay in Busseto is, naturally, named after one of Verdi's operas, and is owned by the family of a tenor who often performs in them, Carlo Bergonzi: ★★★**I Due Foscari**, Piazza Carlo Rossi 15, © 0524 92337, @ 0524 91625 (*moderate*). It's small, very comfortable and has modern air-conditioning; but make sure you book ahead. It also has a fine restaurant, featuring solid, traditional Parmigiano dishes.

Fontanellato ✉ 43012

Locanda Nazionale, Via A. Costa 7, © 0521 822 602 (*cheap*) has six simple rooms overlooking the castle; the restaurant (*moderate*) serves excellent home-made pasta (try the *maltagliati* with asparagus) and *tagliata* (steak) cooked with balsamic vinegar.

Sacca di Colorno

Stendhal-Da Bruno, Via Sacca 80, © 0521 815 493 (*moderate*) is the perfect complement to a visit to the Farnese palace, inhabited in Stendhal's time by Marie Louise. Fish is the speciality here—eels and small fry from the Po, and denizens of the deep brought in daily from Chioggia; and great home-made desserts and wine.

Parma

Le Monde rates Parma as the best of all Italian cities to live in. Besides its general air of well being and contentment, Parma's many admirers can cite her splendid churches and elegant lanes, her art and antiquities, the lyrical strains of grand opera that waft from her Teatro

Regio—a house that honed the talents of the young Arturo Toscanini—and the glories of its famous cheese and ham at table, as reasons not only to visit, but to return again and again. Parma is the place to see the masterpieces of Benedetto Antelami (1177–1233), the great sculptor trained in Provence and whose Baptistry here introduced the Italians to the idea of a building as a unified work of architecture and sculpture. Parma's distinctive school of art began relatively late, with the arrival of Antonio Allegri Correggio (1494–1534), whose highly personal and self-taught techniques of *sfumato* and sensuous subtlety deeply influenced his many followers, most notably Francesco Mazzola, better known as Parmigianino.

History

Parma is a fine example of how Italians can adapt and even prosper in the face of continual political uncertainty. After starting out as a small Roman way-station on the Via Aemilia, the fledgling medieval town of Parma found itself insecurely poised on the edge of the spheres of influence of pope and emperor, a conflict echoed internally by the factions of the Da Correggio and Rossi families. Throughout the Middle Ages and Renaissance, Parma changed hands among the Visconti, Della Scala, Este, Sforza and others before its incorporation in the Papal States in 1521. Even this endured only until 1545, when Pope Paul III required a tax farm for his natural son, Pier Luigi Farnese, and created the Duchy of Parma and Piacenza to fit the bill.

Pier Luigi's own ambitions led shortly to his assassination by a Spanish-led conspiracy, but all in all the duchy gave Parma a measure of stability. In 1748, with the extinction of the male Farnese line, it passed to a branch of the French Bourbons, who ruled it until the Napoleonic era. The year 1815 saw the arrival of Parma's best-loved ruler, Napoleon's widow Marie Louise, who was given the duchy by the Congress of Vienna. In 1859 mass unrest forced her to abdicate; a year later, after a plebiscite, the city was incorporated into the Kingdom of Italy.

Getting Around

Parma has a small **airport**, © 0521 982 626, northwest of the city, with services to Rome and a few other destinations, mostly in Italy (plus flights to London in the summer). The city is easy to reach by rail, on the main line from Turin and Milan to Bologna, Florence and Rome. The **train station** is north of the centre, on Via Monte Altissimo, at the end of Via Garibaldi; buses no.1 and no.8 link it to the city centre. The **bus station**, © 0521 273 251, is between the railway station and the Palazzo della Pilotta.

Tourist Information

Via Melloni 1/6, © 0521 218 889, ✉ 0521 234 735 .

Palazzo della Pilotta

Arriving by train or bus in Parma one of the first buildings you notice is also, unfortunately, the most pathetic: the ungainly, unfinished and, since 1944, bomb-mutilated **Palazzo della Pilotta**, built for the Farnese. It was named after *pelote*, a ball game once played in its court-yard. But looks are deceiving—for within this patched-together shell are Parma's greatest treasures. A grand staircase leads to the **Museo Archeologico Nazionale** (*open Tues–Sun 9–6.30; adm*), founded in 1760 and containing finds from the excavations at Roman Velleia. The single most important exhibit is the **Tabula Alimentaria**, a large bronze tablet that records the contributions of private citizens to the dole in Trajan's time, as well as many fine

Parma

N

200 metres
200 yards

Stazione FS

Piazzale C.A. Dalla Chiesa

VIALE BOTTEGO

Ponte Circonvallazione

VIALE PIACENZA

Palazzo Ducale

VIALE PASINI

VIALE TOSCHI

VIA VERDI

Parco Ducale

Bus station

Ponte Verdi

Palazzo della Pilotta

Piazza Pilotta

Camera di S. Paolo

VIA KENNEDY

Piazzale Santa Croce

Casa di Toscanini

Piazza Serventi

Torrente Parma

Piazza della Pace

VIA MASSIMO D'AZEGLIO

Piazza Ghiaia

Teatro Regio

VIA GARIBALDI

Pza Duomo

VIA CAVOUR

VIALE DEI MILLE

VIALE DELLA VITTORIA

VIA COCCONCELLI

Ponte di Mezzo

Piazza Corridoni

S.S. Annunziata

Madonna della Steccata

VIA IMBRIANI

Pal. d. Governatore

Piazza Picelli

STRADA D. QUARTIERE

S. Maria del Quartiere

VIALE DELLA COSTITUENTE

STRADA BIXIO

Piazza Garibaldi

Università

VIA FARINI

Piazza Matteotti

Piazzale Boito

STRADA FARINI

VIALE DELLA VITTORIA

VIALE DEI MILLE

To Cimitero della Villetta

Piazza Rondini

Ponte Caprazucca

VIA MARIA LUIGIA

VIALE BASETTI

STRADA BIXIO

VIALE GORIZIA

BORGO

FELINO

446

bronzes, Etruscan and Greek ceramics, and statuary from the collections of ducal anti-quarians.On the second floor, the **Galleria Nazionale** (*open daily 9–1.45; adm exp*) was founded even earlier, in 1752. To reach it, you first pass through the fine wooden **Teatro Farnese**, built in 1618 by Palladio's pupil, Giambattista Aleotti; in 1944 a bomb tore most of the theatre into splinters and sawdust, but it has since been carefully reconstructed.

Most of the gallery's paintings are from Emilia-Romagna and Tuscany. Early Renaissance works are by the Tuscans Gaddi, Giovanni di Paolo and Fra Angelico, and the Emilians Simone dei Crocifissi and Loschi (whose *St Jerome* holds a toddler of a lion paternally by the paw). Further along there's a lovely portrait sketch by Leonardo, *La Scapigliata*, paintings by Cima da Conegliano, and Sebastiano del Piombo's portrait of the handsome if calamitous Medici pope, Clement VII. Some of Correggio's most celebrated works are here—the tender *Madonna di San Gerolamo* and the *Madonna della Scodella* —as well as Parmigianino's *Marriage of St Catherine* and the flirtatious *Turkish Slave*; non-Italians include Peter Brueghel the Younger, Van Dyck, and Holbein's portrait of the sharp-featured Erasmus. In a room of their own are portraits of the Farnese clan, and Canova's statue of Marie Louise on her throne.On the same floor as the gallery, the **Palatine Library** (*open Tues–Sat 9–12*) has a vast collection of incunabula, codices, manuscripts and editions published by the city's famous printer, Bodoni, who gave his name to the popular type he invented.

Piazza della Pace and Around

Once a car park, Parma's main piazza has become the victim of a controversial planning project which, in typical Italian fashion, is going nowhere fast. The ground has been cleared and the piazza is at present surrounded by an ugly high fence. The idea was to turn the area into some kind of park, but as soon as work began builders came up against the inevitable important archaeological remains. Now the project has been suspended while the Parmigiani and politicos argue about what is to become of the Piazza. In the meantime, the fat and not so fat

447

ladies still sing at the piazza's celebrated **Teatro Regio** (*entrance in Via Garibaldi; tours Mon–Sat 10, 11 and 12, except at rehearsal times*), built by Marie Louise in 1829. This is one of operatic Italy's holy-of-holies, and the best place to hear the region's favourite son, Verdi. Its audiences are contentious and demanding, and each year tenors and sopranos from all over the world submit either to avalanches of flowers or catcalls from the famous upper balconies, the *loggioni*. Toscanini began his career playing in its orchestra, since re-named in his honour.

Just off the piazza and Via Melloni is the **Camera di S. Paolo** (*open daily 9–1.45; adm*), in the ex-convent of San Paolo. In 1519 its worldly abbess, Giovanna Piacenza, hired Correggio to fresco her refectory with sensuous mythological scenes; he portrayed the abbess herself as the goddess Diana over the fireplace. The decorative scheme in the vault is unique, with sixteen putti set over sixteen mythological emblems, of mysterious import. The abbess wasn't the only woman in the Renaissance to hide her meaning in secret code (*see* p.217, Isabella d'Este's rooms in Mantua). Another room contains frescoes and grotesques by Araldi (1514).

Piazza Duomo

Strada Pisacane connects Piazza della Pace to Piazza Duomo, the heart of medieval Parma and the site of its superb cathedral and baptistry. The **Duomo** (*open daily 9–12.30 and 3–7*) is ambitious, angular Romanesque, embellished with rows of shallow arches; three tiers cross the façade, creating an illusion of depth around the central window, and the pattern continues in the rich decoration of the apses and dome. Reliefs of the Months decorate the central portal (1281); frescoes cover every inch of the interior, which has two masterpieces: a bas-relief of the *Deposition from the Cross* by Antelami and, in the dome, Correggio's *Assumption* (1526–30), celebrated for its almost three-dimensional portrayal of clouds, angels and saints.

The octagonal **baptistry** (*open daily 9–12.30 and 3–6; adm*), built of pale rose-coloured marble from Verona, is one of the jewels of the Italian Romanesque, designed in 1196 by Antelami, who also carved the remarkable ribbon frieze that encircles the exterior. The meaning behind all the winged cats, archers, griffons and sea serpents is as elusive as Correggio's ceiling at San Paolo; many are repeated in mirror images. Antelami is also responsible for the doorways dedicated to the Virgin Mary and the Last Judgement, and the statues in the niches. Inside are his famous reliefs of the Months, and Spring and Winter. The 13th-century tempera paintings are by an unknown but masterly hand—be sure to bring enough lire coins to light them up.

Save some lire, however, for **San Giovanni Evangelista**, the church just behind the cathedral (*open daily 7–12 and 3.30–8*). Under its Baroque skin it shelters one of the key works of the High Renaissance, Correggio's *Vision of St John* fresco in the dome. Unfortunately, when the church was remodelled in 1587, the rest of Correggio's ceiling was destroyed, though a fresco of St John writing down his vision survives over the door north of the altar. Other frescoes are by Parmigianino. Near the church you can visit the historic **'Spezieria di S. Giovanni** on Borgo Pipa (*open daily 9–1.45; adm*), which has been dispensing drugs since 1298 and contains old jars, pots, 16th-century decoration and medieval pharmaceutical instruments.

Piazza Garibaldi

In company with the other old gents of Parma, Garibaldi and Correggio, or at least their statues, spend the day in the modern centre of the city, **Piazza Garibaldi**. Here, too, stands the yellow 17th-century **Palazzo del Governatore**, with its intricate sundial. Behind the palazzo, the church of **Madonna della Steccata** (*open daily 9–12 and 3–6*) was built in 1539 on Bramante's original design for St Peter's. The chapels in its sumptuous interior contain excellent 16th-century frescoes by Parmigianino and his contemporaries.

Paganini, Toscanini and Stendhal

There are three musical and literary pilgrimages to make in Parma. The first is to the **tomb of Paganini**, the embalmed wizard of catgut and bow who lies decked out in virtuoso splendour in Villetta cemetery, after the rest of Europe, suspecting his talents were diabolic, refused him Christian burial (*15min walk from the centre, on the west side of the river; open May–Sept daily 7.45–12.30 and 6–7; Oct and Feb–April daily 7.45–12.30 and 2.30–5.30; Nov–Jan daily 7.45–12.30 and 2–5*). The **birthplace of Arturo Toscanini** (1867–1957) is at Via Rudolfo Tanzi 13, between the Ponte di Mezzo and the Parco Ducale; it contains memorabilia and a copy of every record he ever made (*open Tues–Sat 10–1 and 3–6, Sun 10–1; adm*).

Stendhal aficionados will be glad to know that there really is a **Charterhouse of Parma**, the Certosa (*open Mon–Fri 8–12 and 2–5, Sat and Sun 8–12, but hours vary*), although it bears no resemblance to his imagination's invention. Located 4km east of town (bus no.10), it was founded in 1281 but totally rebuilt in the 17th century, and now serves as a military school. The cloister is out of bounds, but you can visit the church's frescoed interior.

Four Castles

Further afield there are Parma's famous castles (*see* p.444–45, for those to the west of the city), each reachable by bus from Parma. In the foothills to the south (on the Langhirano road) towers **Torrechiara** (*open April–Sept Tues–Fri 9–1.45, Sat and Sun 9–6.15; Oct–Mar Tues–Sun 8.30–1.45; adm*), a castle of brick and fantasy almost unchanged since the 15th century, and defended by four mighty towers. Inside there is an elegant courtyard and frescoes by an artist named Bembo, who exceeded himself in the 'Golden Room'. Another castle, the

15th-century **Bardi**, perches atop its own hill southwest of Parma and has beautiful beamed ceilings and 16th-century frescoes (*open Mar–June/Sept–Oct Sat 2–6, Sun and hols 10–6; July and Aug daily 10–7; Nov Sat 2–7, Sun and hols 10–5; adm*). On the local road to Reggio Emilia via Montecchio lies **Montechiarugolo** (*call ahead, ☎ 0521 686 600*). Built in 1406 in the style of Torrechiara, it contains fine Renaissance paintings. At **Compiano**, in the mountains on the SS513, the half-ruined castle has something surprisingly rare in Italy—ghosts.

Shopping

The market in Piazza Ghiaia, by the river, is the most convenient place to stock up for a picnic or pick up specialities to take home. Otherwise, try **Specialità di Parma**, Via Farina 9/c, an emporium magnificently stocked with delicacies. Parma has its share of antique shops, around Via N. Sauro; fashion shops are clustered around Borgo Angelo Mazza. A world food fair, the **Cibus**, is held in even years. For tours of the plants that make Parma's *prosciutto* and cheese, call the cooperatives: the Consorzio Prosciutto, ☎ 0521 243 987, and Consorzio Parmigiano, ☎ 0521 292 700.

Parma ✉ 43100   ### Where to Stay and Eating Out

The pig is like the music of Verdi; nothing in it of waste.

old Parma saying

Parma's trade fair grounds are bustling in May and September, when you should reserve a couple of months in advance.

It is just like the Parmigiani to link their two ruling passions, music and food; a perfect onion is greeted with the same rapt silence as a perfect dish of pasta, dusted with freshly grated parmesan cheese. Local dishes to look out for are *stracotto* (braised beef), *carpaccio* (raw beef), the various methods of serving *carciofi* (artichokes)—in fritters, pasta dishes and in crêpes—and the stuffed pasta dishes: *tortelli 'd'erbetta'* (stuffed with ricotta and spinach), *'di zucca'* (with pumpkin) or *'di patate'* (with potato).

★★★★**Grand Hotel Baglione**, Via La Piacenza 12/c, ☎ 0521 292 929, ✆ 0521 292 828 (*very expensive*) is the top hotel, slightly outside the centre, whose rooms have every mod con. ★★★★**Park Hotel Stendhal**, Via Bodoni 3, ☎ 0521 208 057, ✆ 0521 285 655 (*expensive*), in the heart of town alongside the Piazza Pilotta, is rather old, but still with good facilities.

★★★**Torino**, Via A. Mazza 7, ☎ 0521 281 046, ✆ 0521 230 725 (*moderate*) is centrally located, with comfortable rooms and very friendly staff. In the knot of small streets behind the Duomo, ★★★**Button**, Borgo Solina 7, ☎ 0521 208 039, ✆ 0521 238 783 (*moderate*) has small but very comfortable rooms.

★**Brozzi**, Via Trento 11, ☎ 0521 272 717 (*cheap*), near the station, is a popular budget hotel with a good restaurant. The youth hostel, **Ostello Cittadella**, Parco Cittadella 5, ☎ 0521 961 434, is housed in the Farnese's 17th-century pentagonal fortress, which now serves as a municipal park (bus no.9 from the station). IYHF card required.

La Greppia, Via Garibaldi 39, ✆ 0521 233 686 (*very expensive*), housed in a former stable, has a delicious selection of *pasta di verdure* (made with spinach or tomatoes), original vegetable dishes and good *secondi*, all prepared before your eyes in the glass kitchen. *Closed Thurs, Fri and July.* Large and cheerful,

Parizzi, Strada della Repubblica 71, ✆ 0521 285 952 (*expensive*) is an ideal place to dip into Parma's specialities: delicious *prosciutto di Parma* and salami, followed by crêpes or asparagus in pastry, and for *secondo*, *scaloppe Parizzi*, with fontina and ham, and great desserts. Reserve. *Closed Sun eve, Mon and most of Aug.*

Near the Duomo, **Angiol d'Or**, Vicolo Scutellari 1, ✆ 0521 282 632 (*expensive*) has seating outside and delicious *tortelli all'erbetta*, and pasta with sea bass. *Closed Sun, Mon and Aug.*

Vecchio Molinetto, Via Milazzo 39, ✆ 0521 253 941 (*moderate*), near the Villetta cemetery, is an unpretentious place offering good honest local cuisine—great risotto baked with veal, and *involtini alla Molinetto*. *Closed Mon and Aug.* In the centre, traditional **Sant'Ambrogio**, Vicolo Piaghe 1/a, ✆ 0521 234 482 (*moderate*) serves particularly good pasta and local meats.

Other excellent and central places in which to get to grips with the local cuisine are **Croce di Malta**, Borgo Palmia, ✆ 0521 235 643, and **Trattoria dei Corrieri**, Strada del Conservatorio 1, ✆ 0521 234 426 (*cheap*), in an old postal relay station. The menu usually features salami and ham *antipasti*, pasta *alla parmigiana*, and filling and tasty *bollito misto* (boiled meats).

Entertainment and Nightlife

Opera mobilizes a more enthusiastic local audience in Parma than just about anywhere else. The main season at the Teatro Regio runs from December to March, with some concerts during the rest of the year; there are also occasional performances at the Teatro Farnese.

Parma also hosts two **music competitions**, one for conductors, at the end of August, and another for operatic singers, in October. September sees the **Verdi Festival**; for information, contact Fondazione Verdi Festival, Via Farini 34, ✆ 0521 289 028, ✉ 0521 282 141. Throughout the summer concerts are also held in the castles—the tourist office provides a full list of forthcoming events.

Reggio Emilia

A bright, prosperous agricultural city, Reggio Emilia was the Roman *Regium Lepidi*. From 1409 to 1796 Reggio was ruled by the Este family of Ferrara, during which time its most famous son, Ludovico Ariosto (1474–1533), author of *Orlando Furioso*, was born. Nowadays it is noted for its numerous ballet schools, its balsamic vinegar and its version of Parmesan cheese, Parmigiano-Reggiano, which tastes exactly the same as Parma's to any sane person.

Piazza Prampolini 5, © 0522 451 152, ● 0522 436 739.

Piazza Prampolini

Reggio grew up on the Via Aemilia, which now divides the old and new parts of the city. In the older, southern half, Piazza Prampolini is the civic and ecclesiastical heart of Reggio, with its peculiar **Duomo** topped by a single octagonal tower. Most of its Romanesque features were remodelled away in the 16th century, although fine statues of Adam and Eve remain on the façade, and in the tower niche there is a copper Madonna flanked by the cathedral donors. On the same piazza, the **Palazzo Comunale**, begun in 1414, was where the *Tricolore* was proclaimed the Italian national flag in 1797 during the second congress of Napoleon's Cispadane Republic, a very short-lived entity that covered the area between Reggio, Mantua, Ferrara and Bologna. Behind the cathedral and beyond the main market in Piazza San Prospero—another wonderful place to see and stock up on local produce—the 16th-century church of **San Prospero** is noted for its fine choir, with frescoes and inlaid stalls.

North of the Via Aemilia

At the heart of Reggio's new broad streets, vast Piazza Cavour has the 19th-century **Teatro Municipale**, the town's opera house, crowned by a surplus of musing statuary; performances of opera, concerts and plays (from December to March) are of a high quality, if not quite as prestigious as the Regio in Parma. The **Museo Spallanzani** (*open Tues–Sat 9–12, Sun 9–12 and 3–6*), near a powerful monument to the Martyrs of the Resistance, has various collections— Natural History, archaeology in the **Museo Chierici** (with the buxom Neolithic 'Chiozza Venus'), the **Museo del Risorgimento** and Resistance. In Reggio's public garden, behind the theatre, there is an imposing funerary monument of a Roman family (50 BC), discovered in Boretto. Near here is the very eclectic **Galleria Parmeggiani** (*open Tues–Sat 9–12, Sun 9–12 and 3–6*), with a 16th-century Moresco doorway brought over from Valencia.

In San Maurizio, 3km east of Reggio, **Villa Il Mauriziano** was the home of Ariosto's family, and some of the rooms have been restored to their appearance when the poet came to visit from Ferrara (*open Tues–Sun 9–11; for visits outside these hours, call © 0522 456 5271*).

Around Reggio

Some 15km northeast of Reggio, **Correggio** is a pretty town with old arcaded streets, which suffered an earthquake in October 1996; all buildings but the Palazzo dei Principi have now re-opened. It is the birthplace of the painter Antonio Allegri, better known as Correggio (d. 1534); his home on Borgo Vecchio was reconstructed in 1755. The **Palazzo dei Principi** (*call © 0522 693 296, to see if it's reopened*), begun in 1506, contains the Museo Civico, with a *Christ* by Mantegna and some lovely cinquecento Flemish tapestries. The Renaissance church of **San Quirino** is attributed to the Farnese's favourite architect, Vignola. Northwest in **Novellara**, the 14th-century Gonzaga dukes built a fine castle; this now serves as the town hall and museum, with medieval and Renaissance frescoes and a collection of chemists' jars.

Near the banks of the Po, **Gualtieri**, the Lombard *Castrum Walterii*, has a Spanish-style *plaza mayor*, **Piazza Bentivoglio**, and the 16th-century brickwork **Palazzo Bentivoglio**. The latter has some fine frescoes, particularly those in the *Sala dei Giganti*. Another old Lombard town, **Guastalla** (*Wartstal*), was a capital of the Gonzaga, and conserves many 16th-century memories: a statue of Condottiere Ferrante Gonzaga, the **Basilica della Pieve**, a fine Romanesque church begun in the 10th century, and the Teatro Ruggeri (1671). Further down the Po, on the outskirts of **Luzzara**, the former convent has been converted into the charming **Museo Comunale dei Pittori Naïf**, with a permanent collection of *naïf* art (starring Antonio Ligabue of Gualtieri) founded by Cesare Zavattini, *cinema verità* director, and collaborator of Vittorio De Sica.

Back towards the west along the river, **Brescello** is adorned with a statue by Sansovino of Ercole II d'Este in the guise of his namesake Hercules. The town is famous in Italian popular culture as the hometown of Giovanni Guareschi's *Don Camillo*, the priest of the post-war era (immortalized in films by Fernandel), eternally, fraternally at war with the Communist mayor Peppone. For obsessive fans, the Reggio tourist board produces a Guareschi guide.

All of these villages are accessible by bus or train from Reggio; for **Canossa**, south of Reggio, you'll have to drive, or else walk 7km from the nearest bus stop. Its name will ring a bell with anyone who ever studied medieval history—it was the original family seat of the powerful feudal family of Da Canossa, whose most famous member was the mighty, charismatic Countess Matilda. In 1077, after Emperor Henry IV deposed Pope Gregory VII and the pope in turn excommunicated the emperor, Matilda, a partisan of the Guelfs, was instrumental in bringing Henry to Canossa on his knees in the snow to apologize to Gregory. It was a turning point; for the next two centuries, popes would hold the moral high ground over the kings and barons of Europe. Today Canossa is scenic and tranquil, with a ruined castle as a dim reminder of the days of Countess Matilda; every now and then historical pageants are staged inside.

Where to Stay and Eating Out

Reggio ✉ 42100

The ******Astoria Mercure**, Viale L. Nobili 2, ✆ 0522 435 245, ✉ 0522 453 365 (*expensive*) offers fine views over the municipal gardens. It has its own garage, comfortable, air-conditioned rooms and great service. The *****Park**, Via de Ruggiero 1, ✆ 0522 292 141, ✉ 0522 292 143 (*moderate*) is small, comfortable and friendly, 4kms from the centre of town, in a tranquil setting with garden and restaurant, and a minibus service into town. The ****Morandi**, Via Aemilia S. Pietro 64, ✆ 0522 454 379, ✉ 0522 451 209 (*cheap*) is fairly basic, but central. The youth hostel, **Ostello Tricolore**, Via dell'Abbadessa 8, ✆ 0522 454 795 (*cheap*) is modern, well-equipped and near the station.

Caffè Arti e Mestieri, Via Aemilia S. Pietro 14, ✆ 0522 432 202 (*expensive*) is an elegant restaurant situated in an old theatre in the centre of town, serving interesting *antipasti*, pasta with baby squid and courgette flowers, creative meat and fish courses, and wonderful desserts—figs cooked in honey and balsamic vinegar. The lovely garden is a green oasis in the heat of the summer. *Closed Sun and Mon.* **Canossa**, Via Roma 37, ✆ 0522 454 196 (*moderate*) is a fine place to try the various hams of this area, served together as an *antipasto*; other specialities include *cappelletti* in broth, and *tortelli* made on the premises. *Closed Wed.* For pizza, paella and tagliatelle with peppers, at tables out on the street, try **La Casseruola**, Via S. Carlo 5, ✆ 0522 453 837 (*cheap*). *Closed Wed.* In an arcade leading off Piazza Prampolini is a thriving pizzeria, **Sotto Broletto**, Via Broletto 1, ✆ 0522 439 676 (*cheap*). *Closed Thurs*.

Guastalla ✉ 42016

North of Reggio, Guastalla has the most in the way of accommodation. *****Old River**, Viale Po 2, ✆ 0522 838 401, @ 0522 824 676 (*moderate*) offers excellent air-conditioned rooms (which can be crucial in August) in a pleasant green setting, and parking. ***Pacian**, Via Trieste 3, ✆ 0522 824 195 (*cheap*) has inexpensive rooms. There's a youth hostel outside town at Viale Po 11, ✆ 0522 824 915. *Open Mar–Oct.*

Modena

Modena puts on a class act—'Mink City' they call it, the city with Italy's highest per capita income, a city with 'a psychological need for racing cars' according to the late Enzo Ferrari, whose famous flame-red chariots compete with the shiny beasts churned out by cross-town rival Maserati. Sleek and speedy, Modena also has a lyrical side of larger-than-life proportions: Luciano Pavarotti was born here, and its scenographic streets take on an air of mystery and romance when enveloped in the winter mists rising from the Po.

Known in Roman days as *Mutina*, Modena first came to note in the 11th–12th centuries under Countess Matilda, powerful ally of the pope. When it became an independent *comune*, however, Modena's Ghibelline party dominated in response to the Guelph policies of arch rival, Bologna. In 1288 the city came under the control of the Este dukes of Ferrara, and the Este Duchy of Modena endured until 1796. A feebly independent duchy was recreated by the Vienna Congress in 1815, only for Modena, like Parma, to be swept into the Kingdom of Italy by the wave of nationalistic feeling in 1859/60.

Getting Around

There are frequent **rail** connections with Bologna, Parma and Milan, and also to Mantua via Carpi. The station is on Piazza Dante, a 10-minute walk from the centre (or take bus no.1 or no.3). The **bus station** at Via Bacchini, ✆ 059 308 801, has frequent connections to Bologna, Ferrara and destinations in Modena province (to Vignola every hour; six a day to Fanano and Sestola ; eight a day to Fiumalbo via Pievepelago).

Tourist Information

The efficient city tourist office is at Piazza Grande 7, ✆ 059 206 660, @ 059 206 659.

Duomo di San Geminiano

Via Aemilia is Modena's main thoroughfare, and it is in the centre of this city where the old Roman highway picks up one of its loveliest gems, the cobbled and partially porticoed **Piazza Grande**, site of Modena's celebrated Romanesque **Duomo di San Geminiano**. Begun with funds from Countess Matilda in 1099, the cathedral was designed by master-builder Lanfranco and completed in the 13th century. Curiously, its main features are Ghibelline-Lombard; Lanfranco followed the bidding of Modena's burghers to show their independence, both from Matilda and the powerful Abbey of Nonantola (*see* below). Complementing the Duomo's fine proportions are the magnificent carvings by the 12th-century sculptor Wiligelmo above the three doors. His friezes on either side of the main Lion Portal illustrate scenes from the medieval mystery play on the Book of Genesis, the *Jeu d'Adam*. Wiligelmo's South Portal depicts the life of Modena's 4th-century patron, St Geminiano. The weights and measures carved into the façade recall the days when the daily market was held in the square. Wiligelmo's contemporary, the 'Master of the Metopes', executed the eight fascinating relief panels of mythological creatures and allegorical subjects on top of the buttresses—monsters relegated to the ends of the cathedral just as they are relegated to the ends of the earth. These are copies; the originals, which deserve a much closer look, are in the adjacent **Museo Lapidario** on Via Lanfranco (*for admission call ✆ 059 216 078, or plead with the sacristan*). Yet another 12th-century sculptor put King Arthur in the lunette over the Porta della Pescheria.

Later 12th-century work, including the rose window, was done by the Campionesi masters of Lake Lugano, who added the final touches to Lanfranco's charming interior, with its rhythm of arches supported by slender columns and ponderous piers. The crypt under the raised altar is supported by lion pillars and adorned with remarkable tinted bas-reliefs of the Passion by the Campionese masters. The mighty, if slightly askew, campanile, called the **Ghirlandina**, houses a famous trophy—an ancient wooden bucket stolen during a raid on Bologna in 1325, and the subject of a 17th-century mock-heroic epic, *La Secchia Rapita.* The Bolognese make periodic attempts to steal it back; according to rumour, they have it now, and the one you see is only a replica. At the base of the campanile is a photo memorial to Modena's martyred partisans.

Palazzo dei Musei

The other main sight in Modena is the Palazzo dei Musei (with your back to the cathedral, turn left along Via Aemilia), housing the **Biblioteca Estense** (*open Mon–Sat 9–1*). Among its famous collection of illuminated manuscripts is one of the most fabulous anywhere, the *Bible of Borso d'Este*, made for the Duke of Modena, a gorgeously coloured 1200-page marvel illustrated in the 15th century by the Emilians Taddeo Crivelli and Franco Rossi. Upstairs, the **Galleria Estense** (*open Tues, Fri and Sat 9–7, Wed and Thurs 9–2, Sun 9–1; adm*) was founded by Francesco I d'Este, whose excellent bust by Bernini greets visitors at the entrance. His taste and budget weren't quite as elevated as that of some other dukes, but here's your chance to see a Tommaso da Modena outside of Treviso, as well as some good early Emilian works, bronzes by Il Riccio of Padua, a good Flemish collection, works by Palma Vecchio, Tintoretto, Cima da Conegliano and Veronese, and Velázquez' *Portrait of Francesco I d'Este.*

On the way back to Piazza Grande, stop by to see the *Deposition* by Guido Mazzoni (1476) in **San Giovanni Battista**. From Piazza, Grande Via C. Battisti leads to the huge Baroque **Palazzo Ducale**, now the National Military Academy and off limits unless you happen to stumble into Modena on the Sunday nearest 4 November. Between this behemoth and the station the main landmark is the neo-Romanesque **Tempio Monumentale**, erected in 1923.

Eleven kilometres east of Modena, the important **Abbey of Nonantola** (*open daily 7.30am–8pm*) was founded in 652 by the Lombard abbot Anselmo, rebuilt in the 12th century and later given the Baroque one-two. The portal, however, retains its beautiful carving by the workshop of Wiligelmo. The church contains relics of the 4th-century St Sylvester, pope under Constantine, while the crypt contains 64 columns with carved capitals, and the tomb of another pope, St Adrian III, who died here in 885 *en route* to the Diet of Worms.

The Modenese Apennines and Carpi

From Modena you can break away from the flatlands of the Po by heading south into the Apennines, which achieve majestic proportions on the Tuscan border. The region has perfect updrafts for hang-gliding and sailplanes, especially around **Pavullo** and **Montecreto**. In April the emerald-green foothills around **Vignola** and **Savignano** are covered with the lacy blossoms of Vignola's famous cherry trees; from here continue further south to **Guiglia** and the peculiar pinnacles of Rocca Malatina in the **Parco Naturale di Sassi**. Just south of Guiglia, don't miss the 11th-century church at **Pieve Trebbio**, with primitive capitals inside. Motorheads won't want to miss **Maranello**, where the **Galleria Ferrari** is dedicated to the legendary marque, with scale models, trophies, vintage cars and a reconstruction of Enzo Ferrari's office (*open Tues–Sun 9.30–12.30 and 3–6; adm exp*). **Sassuolo**, southwest of Modena, is the centre of Italy's ceramic tile industry, which has been booming since Italian designers have discovered that people spend money on decorating their bathrooms and kitchens as well as their persons. It also produces Nocino (*see* p.441).

The most striking scenery is up at **Sestola**, a winter and summer resort near the highest peak of the Northern Apennines, **Monte Cimone** (7100ft). From Sestola you can visit the pretty glacial **Lago della Ninfa** and the **Giardino Esperia** at the Passo del Lupo, a botanical frontier where Alpine and Apennine species grow side by side. Another excursion from Sestola is to **Pian Cavallaro**, and from there to the summit of Monte Cimone for a unique view—on a clear day you can see both the Tyrrhenian and Adriatic seas, and all the way north to the Julian Alps and Mont Blanc.

You can also make the ascent from **Fiumalbo**, just below the Passo Abetone that separates Emilia from Tuscany. Two mountain lakes are just south of Fiumalbo: **Lago Santo** and **Lago Bacio**. Not as pretty, but more unusual, is the small **Lago Pratignano**, in the meadows south of Fanano, a little to the east of Sestola. In the spring its banks are strewn with unusual wild flowers and carnivorous plants—bring your waders.

North of Modena buses and trains run to **Carpi**, a wealthy, workaholic town dominated by the vast **Piazza dei Martiri**. Beside it stands the 16th-century **Castello dei Pio**, which holds the **Museo al Deportato**, remembering the prisoners and civilians deported to Germany from a Nazi camp that stood outside the town (*open Thurs, Sat and Sun 9–12.30 and 3–6.30*).

Activities

Vignola celebrates its **Cherry Blossom Festival** in April, with horse races, bicycle tours and other events. On 15 August there's a traditional festival at Pievepelago, and in nearby Riolunato the *Maggio delle Ragazze* and *Maggio delle Anime*, both celebrated in May. For exact dates, contact the tourist office in Sestola, Via Passerini 18, © 0536 62324. The **Pavarotti singing competition** takes place in Modena in June.

Where to Stay and Eating Out

In the heart of Emilia's pig country, Modena prides itself on *salumeria* and *prosciutto*; minced pork fills its tortellini and its famous main course, *zampone* (pig's trotter), which is boiled and sliced. Modena's famous balsamic vinegar, *aceto balsamico*, as valuable as frankincense in the Middle Ages, is distilled from Trebbiana grapes which, after a few years of diligently pouring it from one barrel to another, achieves a delicate taste between sweet and sour. Modena is also the best place to taste true Lambrusco, which must be drunk young (a year or so old) to be perfectly lively and sparkling.

Modena ✉ 41100

Palatial ★★★★**Canalgrande**, Corso Canalgrande 6, ✆ 059 217 160, 🖂 059 221 674 (*expensive*) has richly decorated public rooms, with crystal chandeliers, frescoes and plush bedrooms. Ancient trees grace the pretty garden. Near the station, ★★★**Daunia**, Via del Pozzo 158, ✆ 059 371 182, 🖂 059 374 807 (*moderate*) has a terrace, comfortable rooms and parking. The recently refurbished ★★★**Centrale**, Via Rismondo 55, ✆ 059 218 808, 🖂 059 238 201 (*moderate*) is near the cathedral. ★**Sole**, Via Malatesta 45, ✆ 059 214 245 (*cheap*) has basic, spacious rooms, without baths.

The cathedral of Modenese cuisine, **Fini**, Largo San Francesco, ✆ 059 223 314 (*very expensive*) was founded in 1912, and has an almost endless menu of hearty regional pasta (the *pasticcio di tortellini* is exceptional), *zampone* or *bollito misto*, and appetizers (hams, sausages and salami), all deliciously prepared. *Closed Mon, Tues and most of Aug*. The very elegant **Borso d'Este**, Piazza Roma 5, ✆ 059 214 114 (*very expensive*), opposite the Palazzo Ducale, offers a light, experimental menu: shrimp and artichoke salad, risotto with radicchio and marrow flowers, duck in balsamic vinegar, imaginative desserts, and French and Italian wines. *Closed Sun and Aug*.

A brief drive from the centre, **Vinicio**, Via Aemilia Est 1526, ✆ 059 280 313 (*expensive*) adapts local cooking to lighter, modern tastes—tortellini with ricotta and spinach, and meats prepared with balsamic vinegar. *Closed Sun and Mon*. The most Modenese restaurant in Modena is **Bianca**, Via Spaccini 24, ✆ 059 311 524 (*moderate*), which prepares all the local favourites just like mamma. *Closed Sat midday, Sun and Aug*. **Alla Redecocca**, Piazzetta Redocca 8, ✆ 059 242 750 (*cheap*) is an excellent trattoria, serving local dishes without fuss or expense. *Closed Tues*.

At weekends, Modenese gourmands embark into the Apennines: stop at any roadside restaurant and you'll find simple meals of smoked meats, cheeses, raw vegetables and freshly baked breads, known as *crescente* after their distinctive shapes—like a flat, baked muffin or of thin dough fried in fat. During the week it'll be a lot quieter.

North of Modena towards **Carpi**, stop at **Da Lancellotti**, Via Grandi 120 in Soliera, ✆ 059 567 406 (*expensive*), whose chef grows his own vegetables and edible, aromatic flowers that flavour all the food. *Closed Sun and Mon*.

Sestola ✉ 41029

★★★★**San Marco**, Via delle Rose 2, ✆ 0536 62330 (*expensive*) has air-conditioned rooms and tennis courts in a lovely garden. The nearby ★★★**Tirolo**, Via delle Rose 19, ✆ 0536 62523 (*cheap*) also has tennis courts and very comfortable rooms. *Open June–Sept and mid-Dec–mid-May*. **Il Faggio**, Via Libertà 68, ✆ 0536 61566 (*moderate*) serves local ingredients—including venison and wild boar. *Closed Mon*.

Entertainment and Nightlife

In Modena the **concert, ballet and opera season** at the Teatro Comunale runs from September to May. In addition, Pavarotti gives a concert in his home town's Piazza Grande in mid-September. It's expensive and booked up well in advance, but crowds still come to sit in the neighbouring bars, and listen to the music while watching the show on TV.

Bologna

'You must write all the beautiful things of Italy,' said the Venetian on the train, but the man from Bologna vehemently shook his finger. 'No, no,' he insisted. 'You must write the truth!' And it is precisely that—a fervent insistence on the plain truth as opposed to the typical Italian *bella figura*—that sets Bologna apart. A homespun realism and attention to the detail of the visible, material world are the characteristics of the Bolognese school of art (recall Petrarch's comment that while only an educated man is amazed by a Giotto, anyone can understand a Bolognese picture).

The city's handsome, harmonic and well-preserved centre disdains imported marble or ornate stucco, preferring honest red brick. Bologna's municipal government, long in the hands of the Italian Communist Party (now the PDS), is considered the least corrupt and most efficient in the whole country. In the 11th century it was the desire for truth and law that led to the founding of the University of Bologna, whose first scholars occupied themselves with the task of interpreting the law codes of Justinian in settling disputes over investitures between pope and emperor. And it is Bolognese sincerity and honest ingredients in the kitchen that has made *la cucina bolognese* by common consent the best in all Italy.

La Dotta, *La Grassa* and *La Rossa* (the Learned, the Fat and the Red) are Bologna's sobriquets. It may be full of socialist virtue, but the city is also very wealthy and cosy, with a quality of life often compared to Sweden. The casual observer could well come away with the impression that the reddest things about Bologna are its telephone booths and its street names like Via Stalingrado, Via Yuri Gagarin and Viale Lenin. But Bologna is hardly a stolid place—its bars, cafés and squares are brimming with youth and life, and there's a full calendar of concerts from rap to jazz to Renaissance madrigals, as well as avant-garde ballet, theatre and art exhibitions; in 2000 Bologna will be one of several 'European Culture Capitals', and the city's buildings are getting a major spring cleaning for the occasion.

History

Born as the prosperous Etruscan outpost of Felsina, and renamed Bononia by the Gauls, Bologna grew up at the junction of the Via Aemilia and the main road over the Apennines from Florence. Dominated by Ravenna for centuries, Bologna broke away in the 11th century and became an independent *comune* in the 12th and 13th centuries, a golden age when it was one of the Guelph leaders of the Lombard League. As such it warred with Ghibelline Modena, and defeated that city in the Battle of Fossalta in 1249, capturing the talented Enzo, King of Sardinia and natural son of Emperor Frederick II. Defying custom, Bologna refused to ransom him and kept him in a nice little castle until he died in 1272.

Bologna became part of the Papal States in 1278, though for the next few centuries real power was held by 'first citizens', most famously the Bentivoglio (Wish-you-well) family (1401–1506). They heralded a flowering of local culture, despite a sensational family saga of assassination, high-living and questionable legitimacy—the paternity of Annibale, father of the great art patron Giovanni II, was decided by a throw of the dice. Giovanni II ruled for 43 years until ousted by Pope Julius II, after which Bologna was ruled directly by a papal legate.

Bologna witnessed one of the turning points in Italian history in 1530 when Charles V insisted on being crowned Holy Roman Emperor in its basilica of San Petronio instead of in Rome, which his troops had sacked three years previously. Charles felt that going to Rome would seem like an act of contrition, and such was the low standing of papal authority that when he told Pope Clement VII that he did not need to seek crowns, but that crowns sought him, the humbled pope only agreed. Charles' coronation, both as Emperor and King of Italy, was celebrated with tremendous pomp, but marked the deathknell for the Renaissance and the beginning of three centuries of foreign domination for Italy. Luigi Barzini notes that from then on the Italians put away their bright clothes and began to wear black in the Spanish style, as if they were in mourning—just as the Fascisti donned black shirts under Mussolini.

Modern Bologna

In the 19th century Bologna was the birthplace of Guglielmo Marconi, who carried out his first experiments with radio at the Villa Grifone, and of the composer Ottorino Respighi (1879–1936), whose music was popularized abroad by his fellow-Emilian Toscanini. It was also at this time that Bologna took the lead in the Italian socialist movement—as well as in enduring the brunt of the Fascist reaction in the 20th. And although it was on the Germans' 'Gothic Line' (1944–45), and the scene of fervid partisan activity, Bologna emerged from the War relatively unscathed.

The historic centre is one of the best preserved and maintained in Italy, to the credit of the city's policy of 'active preservation'—old houses in the centre are gutted and renovated for municipal public housing, maintaining the character and diversity of the old quarters. Nor is this the first time that Bologna has found a creative solution to its housing needs: every street is lined with arcades, or *portici*. The original ones date from the 12th century, when the *comune*, faced with a housing shortage caused by 10,000 university students, ordered rooms to be built on to existing buildings over the streets. Over time the Bolognese became attached to its porticoes and the shelter they provided from the weather; now it claims 35km of *portici*, more than any other city in the world.

Getting There

by air

Bologna's G. Marconi **airport** is to the northwest in the Borgo Panigale, ✆ 051 647 9615; the 'Aerobus' runs from there to the railway station. Bologna has flight connections with major Italian and European cities, as well as Sicily and Sardinia.

by rail

Bologna is one of the prime nodes of the FS network, with frequent and fast trains to Venice, Florence, Milan, Ravenna, Rimini and just about anywhere else in Italy from the **Stazione Centrale** in Piazza delle Medaglie d'Oro, information ✆ 1478 88088. It is to the north of the city centre, about a 10–15-minute walk from Piazza Maggiore; alternatively, bus no.11 and no.27 go straight there. Because of the ultra-Right bombing here in August 1980, that killed 85 people, Bologna is the one station in Italy where your bags will be inspected minutely if you leave them at the *Consegna*.

by long-distance bus

The **bus station** is near the FS at Piazza XX Settembre, ✆ 051 350 301, and has services every hour for Ferrara, Imola, Modena and Ravenna, and less frequent services to many other destinations in the region.

Piazza
VII Novembre

VIA DON MINZONI

Piazza
Dei Martiri

VIA DELLE LAME

VIA RIVA DI RENO

VIA MARCONI

Piazza
Di Porta
S. Felice

VIA S. FELICE

VIA RIVA DI RENO

P

VIA N. SAURO

Piazza
Di Porta
Sant'Isaia

VIA DEL PRATELLO

VIA UGO BASSI

Tombe dei
Glossatori

Piazza
S. Francesco

S. Francesco

VIA PORTA NOVA

VIA BATTISTI

P

S.
Salvatore

VIA SANT' ISAIA

Piazza
Malpighi

Piazza
Di Porta
Saragozza

VIA SARAGOZZA

VIA BARBERIA

250 metres
250 yards
N
Bologna

Stazione Centrale
Piazza Medaglie D'Oro
Bus Station
Piazza XX Settembre
Piazza Dei Martiri
Montagnola Park
Piazza Di Porta Mascarella
VIA DEI MILLE
P Piazza VIII Agosto
VIA IRNERIO
Pinacoteca Nazionale
Piazza Di Porta S. Donato
VIA GALLERIA
VIA DELL'INDIPENDENZA
VIA RIGHI
VIA DELLE BELLE ARTI
S. Martino
VIA MARSALA
Teatro Comunale
Piazza Verdi
VIA ZAMBONI
Università
Pal. Fava
Duomo
VIA OBERDAN
S. Giacomo Maggiore
VIA UGO BASSI
Piazza D. Nettuno
Pal. dir Re Enzo
Torre Garisenda
Piazza di P. Ta Ravegnana
VIA SAN VITALE
Piazza Di Porta S. Vitale
VIA RIZZOLI
Piazza Roosevelt
Pal. Comunale
Piazza Galileo
Pal. d. Podestà
Piazza Maggiore
S. Maria della Vita
S. Bartolomeo
Torre degli Asinelli
Pal. d. Mercanzia
VIA CLAVATURE
Casa Isolani
STRADA
Pal. dei Giganti
VIA D'AZEGLIO
VIA ARCHIGINNASIO
Museo Civico Archeologico
Piazza Minghetti
P
S. Stefano
MAGGIORE
S. Petronio
Piazza Galvani
Archiginnasio
VIA FARINI
VIA FARINI
VIA SANTO
S. Maria dei Servi
VIA GUERRAZZI
VIA SAN PETRONIO VECCHIO
VIA CARBONESI
Piazza Cavour
Piazza Di Porta Maggiore
Pal. Bevilacqua
Piazza S. Domenico
S. Domenico
CASTIGLIONE
STEFANO
Piazza Carducci
VIA TAGLIAPIETRE
VIA MIRAMONTE
Piazza D. Tribunali
Piazza Di Porta S. Mamolo
Piazza Di Porta Castiglione
Piazza Di Porta S. Stefano

461

Most of Bologna's sights are within easy walking distance of one another, but the city also has an efficient local **bus** system. Offices that dispense tickets, bus maps and information are at the main bus station in Piazza XX Settembre, at a booth outside the railway station, and at 1/1 Piazza Re Enzo, near Piazza Maggiore, ✆ 051 242 150.

Bologna's Tangenziale ring road encircles a typically Italian imbroglio of pedestrian and one-way streets with no place to park. If you insist on driving, you may find a parking space in Piazza XX Settembre, where it is also possible to hire **bicycles** inside the Porta Galliera, at No.7, ✆ 051 630 2015 (*open Mon–Fri 6.30–11 and 12–9, Sat 6.30–11 and 12–3*). For a **taxi**, call ✆ 051 372 727, or ✆ 051 534 141.

Tourist Information

The main tourist information office is right in the centre of the city, Piazza Maggiore 6, ✆ 051 239 660 (*open Mon–Sat 9–7, Sun 9–1*). There's also an office at the railway station, ✆ 051 246 541 (*open Mon–Sat 9–12.30 and 2.30–7*), and at the airport.
Ambulance, ✆ **333 333**.
Hospital: Ospedale Sant'Orsola, Via Massarenti 8, ✆ 051 636 3111.
24-hour pharmacy: Piazza Maggiore, next to the tourist office; or check the list outside to see which pharmacies are on duty that night, or call ✆ 192 for information.
At **Credito Romagnolo**, Via Rizzoli 34, there is a 24-hour cash-exchange machine.
Main post office: Piazza Minghetti, not far from the Archiginnasio.

Piazza Maggiore

The centre stage of Bolognese public life is Piazza Maggiore and its antechamber, **Piazza Nettuno**, graced with the virile and vaguely outrageous **Fountain of Neptune**, 'who has abandoned the fishes to make friends with the pigeons', designed in the 16th century by Tomaso Laureti of Palermo and executed by Giambologna. Adjacent, and occupying part of both squares, are the 13th-century **Palazzo di Re Enzo** (where they kept Frederick II's son) and the **Palazzo del Podestà**, begun about the same time and remodelled in 1484 by Aristotele Fioravanti, who went on to design part of the Kremlin. The corners of the **Voltone** (the big portico in front) contain 16th-century statues of Bologna's four patron saints.

Filling the western side of the Piazza Maggiore, the crenellated **Palazzo Comunale** incorporates the 1287 Casa Accursio (the arcaded section), and the 1425 annexe by Fioravante Fioravanti, father of Aristotele. Over the door presides a bronze statue of Pope Gregory XIII, calendar-reformer and a native of Bologna. Under a canopy to the left is a beautiful terracotta Madonna by Nicolò dell'Arca, a Renaissance sculptor from Puglia who left his best work in Bologna. Inside are two museums (*both open Tues–Sun 10–6; adm*)—the **municipal art collection**, reached via Bramante's grand staircase (1505), with works by the Bolognese school, and the **Museo Morandi**, devoted to Bologna's great contemporary painter, Giorgio Morandi (1890–1964). He hardly ever left the city and, although a friend of the futurists and metaphysicists in Ferrara, kept to himself, quietly producing some of this century's best paintings. The subject matter—boxes, a vase of flowers—is mundane, but under Morandi's fierce gaze is transformed with startling intensity. There are also landscapes of Grizzana, where Morandi spent his summers, his personal art collection and a reconstruction of his studio .

Opposite the Palazzo del Podestà, the **Basilica di San Petronio** by Antonio da Vicenza (1390), is the largest structure on the square, yet had the Bolognese had their way, this temple to their patron would have been even larger than St Peter's in Rome. However, the Cardinal Legate ordered them to spend their money on the university instead, leaving even the façade unfinished; the white and red marble stripes recalling the city's heraldic emblem only made it up to the door. The remarkable main door has bas-reliefs by Jacopo della Quercia of Siena, begun in 1425. Like Ghiberti's doors to the Baptistry in Florence (for which job della Quercia had been an unsuccessful candidate), they are landmarks in the visual evolution of the early Renaissance, and seem strangely modern—almost Art Deco in sensibility.

The lofty interior saw the crowning of Charles V and, according to tradition, the conversion of a visiting monk named Martin Luther who became so nauseated by papal pomp and pageantry that he decided to go ahead and start the Reformation. In 1655 the astronomer Cassini traced the meridian on the floor and designed the huge astronomical clock which tells the time with the shaft of light admitted through an oculus in the roof. Two of the chapels (third and fourth on the left) are noteworthy—one with 15th-century frescoes of Heaven and Hell, the other containing Lorenzo Costa's *Madonna and Saints*. In the museum at the end of the aisle are models of Bologna's pipe dreams for the basilica and its façade (*open daily 10–12; closed Tues*).

Missing from the front of San Petronio, however, is Michelangelo's colossal bronze statue of Pope Julius II, commissioned by that pope in 1506 after he regained the city for the Papal States. Julius also built a large castle in the centre of Bologna. Both were torn to bits by the population as soon as the pope's luck changed; and to rub salt into his wounded pride the bronze was sold as scrap to his arch-enemy, Alfonso I of Ferrara, who melted it down to cast an enormous cannon—which he fondly named 'Julius'.

Via dell'Archiginnasio

Bologna's excellent **Museo Civico Archeologico**, Via dell'Archiginnasio 3 (*open Tues–Sat 9–2, Sun 9–1 and 3.30–7; adm*) is just to the left of San Petronio. Into its dim and dusty wooden cases is crammed one of Italy's best collections of antiquities—beautifully wrought items from the Iron Age Villanova culture, native Italics who were eventually conquered by the Etruscans, and artefacts from Bologna's beginnings as Etruscan *Felsina*. Felsina may have been a frontier town, but it is richly represented here with tomb art, gravestones shaped like chesspieces and the embossed bronze urn, the *Situla di Certosa*, similar to others found in Tuscany. The Etruscans traded extensively with the Greeks, whose Attic vases are one of the highlights of the museum. There are a few items from Gallic Bononia, Roman artefacts (a lovely copy of Phidias' bust of Athena Lemnia), and an excellent Egyptian collection.

Further down the street is the seat of the old university, the **Archiginnasio** (*open Mon–Sat 9–1*), its walls covered with the escutcheons and memorials of famous alumni. Bologna's university is the oldest in Europe, but was not provided with a central building until 1565. After 1803 this became the municipal library, but the porter will admit you to the ornate old **anatomical theatre**, shattered by a bomb in the Second World War and painstakingly rebuilt in 1950. The monument in the piazza in front of the Archiginnasio commemorates Luigi Galvani, the 18th-century Bolognese discoverer of electrical currents in animals, who gave his life and name ('galvanize') to physics. Just off Piazza Maggiore on Via Clavature, stop in **Santa Maria della Vita** to see the terracotta *Lament Over the Dead Christ* by Nicolò dell'Arca, a work harrowing in its grief and terror, a 15th-century version of Edvard Munch's *Scream*.

Two Leaning Towers

In the passage under Via Rizzoli (the main street flanking Piazza Maggiore), you can see the remains of the old Roman Via Aemilia. To the east, the end of Via Rizzoli is framed by the beautiful **Piazza Porta Ravegnana** and a pair of towers that might have wandered off the set of *The Cabinet of Dr Caligari*. After the initial shock wears off, however, fondness invariably sets in for this odd couple, the Laurel and Hardy of architecture. The taller one looks respectable only because the other is so hilarious.

The **Due Torri** were built in 1119 in a competition between two families. The winner, the svelte 318ft **Torre degli Asinelli** (*open summer daily 9–6; winter daily 9–5; adm*), is the highest in Bologna, which once had 180 such skyscrapers. It tilts about 3 feet out of true, though the 500 steps that lead to the top are more likely to make your head spin than the tilt. The view over Bologna is worth the trouble, however. Its side-kick, the **Torre Garisenda**, sways tipsily to the south, 10ft out of true; the Garisenda contingent failed to prepare a solid foundation and, when they saw their tower pitching precariously, they threw in the towel. In 1360 it became such a threat to public safety that its top was lopped off, leaving only a squat 157ft stump; inscribed in its base you can read what Dante wrote about it in the *Inferno*.

From the towers five streets fan out to gates in the eastern walls of the old city. One of these, the palace-lined **Strada Maggiore**, follows the route of the Via Aemilia, passing **San Bartolomeo**, notable for its two works by Bolognese masters: Albani's *Annunciation*, in a chapel on the south aisle, and Guido Reni's *Madonna*. In the 19th century Italians considered the 'Divine Guido' as their greatest artist; since then he has taken a precipitous and admittedly deserved fall from fashion. At Strada Maggiore 13, the **Casa Isolani**, home of the British Council, is one of the best-preserved 13th-century houses left in Bologna; at No.44 the 18th-century **Palazzo dei Giganti** (or Davia) (*open Tues–Sat 9–2, Sun 9–1*) contains the Museum of Industrial Art and the Galleria Davia-Bargelli, housing Vitale da Bologna's famous *Madonna with Teeth,* the patroness of dentists and perhaps the most characteristic and earnest work of the earnest Bolognese school. At this point the *portici* of the street intermingle with those of the arcades of the city's Gothic jewel, **Santa Maria dei Servi**, which contains among its works of art a rare *Madonna* by Cimabue (in the apse) which you'll need to illuminate to see.

Santo Stefano

Via Santo Stefano, another street radiating from the two towers, may be reached from Santa Maria dei Servi on Via Guerrazzi (where, at No.13, the 14-year-old Mozart was elected to the Accademia Filarmonica). Via Santo Stefano has a curious quartet of churches, with a cloister and two chapels thrown in, all part of the monastery of **Santo Stefano** founded by St Petronius, who reproduced here the layout of Jerusalem's holy places. Three of the churches of this unique and harmonious Romanesque ensemble face Piazza Santo Stefano—the largest is the **Crocifisso**, begun in the 11th century, with an altar in its façade and an ancient crypt below its raised choir. To the left is polygonal **San Sepolcro**, containing the tomb of San Petronio, modelled after the Holy Sepulchre and adorned with bas-reliefs. **SS. Vitale e Agricola**, further to the left, is Bologna's oldest church, built in the 5th century, with bits and pieces of old Roman buildings, and alabaster windows.

Beyond it is the **Cortile di Pilato**, containing an 8th-century Lombard bathtub that somehow gained the sinister reputation of being the basin in which Pontius Pilate washed his hands. From here you can enter the fourth church, the 13th-century **Trinità**, with a lovely 11th-century cloister, and a museum, with works by Simone de' Crocifissi and others (*all open daily 9–12 and 3.30–6*). Up Via Santo Stefano towards the Due Torri is the lovely Gothic **Palazzo della Mercanzia** (1384); it has an ornate loggia by the architect of San Petronio, Antonio da Vincenzo.

Via Zamboni

Again from the towers, Via Zamboni leads shortly to Piazza Rossini. Rossini, composer of the *Barber of Seville* and *William Tell*, studied from 1806 to 1810 at the **Conservatorio G. B. Martini** (*open Mon–Sat 9–1*), and spent much of his life in a nearby palazzo. The Conservatory houses original scores by Mozart, Monteverdi and Rossini, and a portrait by Thomas Gainsborough. Also on the square is **San Giacomo Maggiore**, begun in 1267. It was the parish church of the Bentivoglio, one of whom, Giovanni II, hired Lorenzo Costa to paint the frescoes in the **Cappella Bentivoglio**—the *Triumph of Death*, the *Apocalypse* and *Madonna Enthroned*—with Giovanni II and family in their midst.

In these pictures the Bentivoglio seem benign enough, but the Bolognese hated them and tore their palace apart brick by brick when they were deposed. The fresco itself was commissioned in thanksgiving for Giovanni's escape from hired assassins. The fine altarpiece in the chapel is by Francesco Francia, a native of Bologna, while the high-mounted tomb opposite, of Anton Galeazzo Bentivoglio (1435), is by Quercia. Be sure to ask the sacristan to let you into the **Oratory of Santa Cecilia**, frescoed by Costa and Francia. The **Teatro Comunale**, further up Via Zamboni in Piazza Verdi, was built by Antonio Bibiena in 1763 over the Bentivoglio Palace. The Bibiena clan of theatre- and stage-designers were in demand all over Europe in the 17th and 18th centuries, and did much to popularize the typical Baroque tiers of boxes, which the Teatro Comunale preserves behind its 1933 façade.

The University

Beyond the theatre is the **University**, which was moved in 1803 from the too-central Archiginnasio (where the students could cause trouble) into Pellegrino Tibaldi's Mannerist **Palazzo Poggi**, topped by the eclectic observation tower, or *speculum*, and adorned with Tibaldi's frescoes of Ulysses. Famed for medicine, astronomical studies (Copernicus studied here) and the sciences, Bologna was and is known best for jurisprudence, ever since its founding by the Glossatori (who 'glossed' or annotated Justinian's codes). One student, Vacarius, founded the law school at Oxford in 1144.

The university has a number of small museums, including one dedicated to the university itself at Via Zamboni 33, which also has the museum of **astronomy**; the **Orto Botanico**, Via Irnerio 42; the museum of **human anatomy**, Via Irnerio 48, which houses a bizarre collection of 18th-century medical models; or, for a sobering look at Fido *sans* skin, there's the museum of the **anatomy of domestic animals**, Via Belmeloro 12 (*opening hours vary; for information call © 051 259 021; closed Sat*).

Pinacoteca Nazionale

Via Belle Arti 56; open Tues–Sat 9–2, Sun 9–1; summer Fri and Sun also 8.30pm–11.30pm; adm.

Across from the university, Bologna's most important art is stored here: 14th-century Bolognese artists, of whom Vitale da Bologna emerges as the star with his intense *St George and the Dragon*; Giotto, the Vivarini brothers and Cima da Conegliano of Venice are also here, with works by the Ferrara school (Costa, Cossa and Ercole de' Roberti, especially the tearful *Magdalene*). Later Bolognese paintings are by Francesco Francia, Aspertini and Tibaldi. Raphael's *S. Cecilia in Estasi* was moved here from a local church; near it are pictures by Perugino, Giulio Romano and Parmigianino. Beyond them are works from Bologna's 16th–18th-century eclectic revival—the Carracci brothers, Guido Reni and Guercino.

Via Belle Arti, heading back towards the centre, passes several fine palaces and ends at the intersection of Via Mentana. Turn left for 15th-century **San Martino**; Paolo Uccello painted a fresco here which was believed completely lost until 1981, when a delightful fragment was discovered. The church also contains fine works by Francia and Costa.

North and West of Piazza Maggiore

Via dell'Indipendenza is the main street linking Piazza Maggiore to the station. In its northern reaches is the attractive **Montagnola Public Garden** and bustling **Piazza VIII Agosto**, site of a busy popular food, clothes and second-hand goods market on Fridays and Saturdays.

On Via dell'Indipendenza near Piazza Nettuno is Bologna's 10th-century cathedral, **San Pietro**, rebuilt in the Baroque era. As with Venice's San Pietro di Castello, this symbol of the papacy received scant affection—the basilica of the city's own patron saint was far more important. Hence San Pietro is not too interesting, unless you are a devotee of St Anne, whose skull is the chief treasure, a gift of Henry VI of England. The Romanesque campanile is a survivor of the original church; for a taste of medieval Bologna with all its towers stroll down Via Altabella.

Opposite the cathedral, Via Manzoni leads to the Palazzo Fava, site of the **Museo Civico Medioevale e del Rinascimento** (*open Mon and Wed–Fri 9–2, Sat and Sun 9–1 and 3.30–7; closed Tues; adm*), with a collection of armour, ceramics, majolica plates, tombs of medieval scholars, ivory works, glass and a 13th-century English Cope. In addition, several rooms of the old palazzo have recently been opened to the public, where Annibale Carracci and other Bolognese painters frescoed scenes from the *Aeneid* and classical mythology. Via Ugo Bassi, the westerly section of the Via Aemilia, leads to narrow and lively **Piazza Malpighi**, home to one of Bologna's city gates, the 13th-century **Tombs of the Glossatori**, and the lovely Gothic **San Francesco**, with its old towers and beautiful 14th-century marble altar screen sculpted by Pier Paolo dalle Masegne. Back towards the centre, Via C. Battisti runs south from Via Ugo Bassi to the 17th-century **San Salvatore**, with a striking Mannerist *Marriage of St Catherine* (1534) by Girolamo da Carpi, his masterpiece.

South of Piazza Maggiore

From the Archiginnasio continue south down Via Garibaldi to **San Domenico**, built in 1251 to house the relics of St Dominic, founder of the Order of Preaching Friars. Dominic built a convent on this site and died here in 1221 and, although the exterior and interior of his church have been frequently remodelled, his tomb, the **Arca di San Domenico**, is a master-work. Many chisels contributed to it, including Nicolò Pisano and his school, who executed the beautiful reliefs of the saint's life; Nicolò dell'Arca, who gained his name from this work, added the cover of the sarcophagus and the statues on top; and a 20-year-old Michelangelo sculpted SS. Petronius and Proculus and an angel. Among the other works, look for a bust of St Dominic by Nicolò dell'Arca, and the beautiful wooden inlaid choir stalls.

From San Domenico, Via Marsili leads to Via D'Azeglio, with the **Palazzo Bevilacqua**, a 15th-century Tuscan-style palace where the Council of Trent took refuge from a plague in Trent in 1547. Just north of here is the lovely brick and terracotta façade of **Spirito Santo**, Via Val D'Aposa 6. Via Marsili, now Via Urbana, continues to the **Collegio di Spagna**, the Spanish college founded for Spanish students in 1365 by Cardinal Albornoz. In the Middle Ages Bologna had many such colleges, but this one (an official corner of Spanish territory) is the only one to survive. Cervantes studied here, as did St Ignatius. From here Via Saragozza wends down to the **Porta Saragozza**, starting point for the portico to beat all porticoes— winding 4km up the hill to the **Santuario della Madonna di San Luca**. The church was built to house an icon attributed to St Luke, and the 666-arch portico was added between 1674 and 1793.

There are fantastic views of the Apennines from the sanctuary (if you can't face the whole hike, bus no.20 from Via dell'Independenza covers some of the route). Other famous viewpoints in the hills south of Bologna are from **San Michele in Bosco**, a hospital in a former convent (bus no.30), and from **Villa Aldini** (bus no.52A), built on the site where Napoleon admired the panorama of the city skyline. From this villa you can walk down towards the Porta San Mamolo and the fine 15th-century church of the **Annunziata**.

Shopping

Via Rizzoli and Via dell'Independenza are the main centres for fashion and other chic outlets. Probably Bologna's most interesting buy, however, is food, at the bustling **markets** at Via Ugo Bassi 2, and Via Clavature, just off the Piazza Maggiore (*open Mon–Sat mornings*). There's a market selling just about everything in Piazza VIII Agosto and along Via dell'Independenza (*Fri and Sat*). The windows of Bologna's general **food stores** present a dazzling array of delicacies; there is a string of them in the streets around Piazza Maggiore, particularly towards the Two Towers.

Bologna ✉ *40100*   ***Where to Stay and Eating Out***

In Italy's gastronomic capital eating out is a pleasure, whether you plump for a meal at a five-star restaurant or head for one of the city's late-night inns or *osterie*. Locally they call it *cucina petroniana*, and it gave Italy tagliatelle, tortellini and lasagne, which the Bolognese like to tint green with spinach. *Alla bolognese* means with a meat and tomato sauce that only Bologna knows how to prepare *just so*. The city is known for the best pâtés in Italy, its veal dishes and, of late, for its innovations in the kitchen. For an authentic Bolognese repast order a fruity amber-coloured Albana, white Trebbiano or dry Sauvignon to accompany your *antipasti*; a Bianco dei Colli with your tagliatelle, or a heartier Barbera Bolognese for pasta dishes from the oven; with veal dishes, a Merlot dei Colli; and if you order seafood, an energetic Pignoletto from the Colli.

Embedded in Bologna's history, and right in the centre, is the ★★★★**Grand Hotel Baglioni**, Via Independenza 8, ✆ 051 225 445, ✆ 051 234 840 (*luxury*), with frescoed ceilings and luxurious, if ancient, rooms, plus an underground garage and baby-sitting service. Morandi's paintings were first exhibited here, in 1914. ★★★★**Corona d'Oro**, Via Oberdan 12, ✆ 051 236 456, ✆ 051 262 697 (*luxury*), on a narrow cobbled street right in the heart of the old city, is stylish and comfortable, occupying an old palazzo from 1300. The impressive and spacious *fin de siècle* reception has just been restored. ★★★★★**Royal Carlton**, Via Montebello 8, ✆ 051 249 361, ✉ 051 249 724 (*very expensive*) is an ultra-modern palace in the centre, with flamboyant designer rooms. The lobby and bar are striking, and there's a garage. Recently revamped, ★★★**Commercianti**, Via Pignatteri 11, ✆ 051 233 052, ✉ 051 224 733 (*very expensive*) is a little hotel near San Petronio. The nicest rooms, with attic ceilings, ancient beams and the odd piece of fresco, are at the top.

For a swimming pool you'll have to venture outside the city walls to the ★★★★**Holiday Inn**, Piazza della Costituzione, ✆ 051 372 172, ✉ 051 357 662 (*expensive*). A minute from the Piazza Maggiore, the recently redecorated ★★★**Roma**, Via D'Azeglio 9, ✆ 051 226 322, ✉ 051 239 909 (*expensive*) is a fine choice in medieval Bologna, with large rooms. In a pleasant square beside San Petronio, ★★★**Orologio**, Via IV Novembre 10, ✆ 051 231 253, ✉ 051 260 552 (*expensive*) has cosy rooms in an aged palazzo, and good views.

Tucked away by the university, ★★**Rossini**, Via Bibiena 11, ✆ 051 237 716, ✉ 051 268 035 (*moderate*) has comfortable rooms and friendly management. Just off Piazza Maggiore in a nest of shopping streets, ★**Apollo**, Via Drapperie 5, ✆ 051 223 955 (*moderate*) has small rooms; the market outside starts up early, but you couldn't be better placed. Two good central, clean and friendly choices, are ★**Panorama**, Via Livraghi 1, ✆ 051 221 802 (*cheap*) (no en suite baths), and ★**Marconi**, Via Marconi 22, ✆ 051 262 832 (*cheap*). There are two **youth hostels**, both inconveniently located 6km east of the city centre at Via Viadagola 5, ✆ 051 501 810, and Via Viadagola 14, ✆ 051 519 202 (bus no.93 from Via Irnerio). IYHF cards are required and there is an 11.30pm curfew.

Notai, Via dei Pignattari 1, ✆ 051 228 694 (*very expensive*), near the cathedral, is a Bolognese classic, with a piano bar upstairs and an elegant Victorian dining room below, unusual pasta dishes and unorthodox but succulent variations on local favourites. It also has Bologna's best wine list. *Closed Sun.* Another favourite, **Franco Rossi**, Via delle Donzelle 1/a, off Via dell'Independenza, ✆ 051 238 818 (*very expensive*) has a very friendly atmosphere, and traditional specialities—tagliatelle and risotto, duck with green peppercorns, or devilled scampi. *Closed Sun and July.* Near San Petronio, **Battibecco**, Via Battibecco 4, ✆ 051 223 298 (*very expensive*) is an elegant restaurant attracting a lunchtime business crowd. Fish is the speciality, but you can opt for one of the vegetarian risottos (with aubergine or porcini mushrooms), duck breast cooked in *aceto balsamico*, or fillet with a Barolo sauce. *Closed Sun.*

Bologna's most celebrated restaurant, **Pappagallo**, in the pretty Piazza della Mercanzia 3, ✆ 051 232 807 (*expensive*) has an enchanting dining room where Alfred Hitchcock and Albert Einstein were wont to twirl their forks. The *menu degustazione* is firmly rooted in local tradition: *tortellini in brodo* or *tagliatelle al ragù bolognese* are fixtures. *Closed Sun and Mon midday.* On the north side of the centre, **Il Tartufo**, Via del Porto 34, ✆ 051 252 662 (*expensive*) features both traditional Emilian dishes and new creations like rabbit with black truffles or lamb in balsamic vinegar. *Closed Sun.* **Serghei**, Via Piella 12, ✆ 051 233 533 (*moderate*), not far from the university, is a typical little rustic Bolognese family-run trattoria. The menu, unchanged for years, features home-made pasta (meat-filled *tortellini* in tasty broth, rocket-filled *agnolotti*), pork cooked in milk, *osso buco*, and a wonderful ricotta tart to finish. *Closed Sat eve and Sun.*

Da Cesari, Via de' Carbonesi 8, ✆ 051 237 710, has been around for more than thirty years, but you might find innovative dishes on the menu: ravioli stuffed with rabbit and smoked ricotta, alongside standards like tripe *alla parmigiana*. *Closed Sun, and Sat in June and July.* Just off Via S. Stefano, **Trattoria Sale e Pepe**, Via de' Coltelli 1/12, ✆ 051 228 532 (*moderate*) serves unusual dishes with a Neapolitan touch, and great desserts; and a good cheap lunch menu. *Closed Sat lunch and Sun.* **Da Bertino**, Via Lame 55, ✆ 051 522 230 (*moderate*) offers tasty simple Bolognese cuisine; and take-away. *Closed Sun.*

For budget restaurants try near the university, particularly around Piazza Verdi and Via Belle Arti. Such is the strength of the local food cult that they will rarely disappoint. **Osteria del Matusél**, Via Bertoloni 2/2 (*cheap*), near the university, offers hearty, filling meals: thick soup, macaroni and hunks of meat. *Open till 12.45am; closed Sun.* The **Centro Naturista**, Via Albari 6, ✆ 051 235 643 (*cheap*) offers vegetarian and healthy fare, and an alternative crowd.

Lively **Osteria la Botte**, Via Sant'Isaia 30 (*cheap*) has a fine list of wines accompanied by a small but delicious choice of daily dishes. Founded in 1468, **Osteria del Sole**, Vicolo Ranocchi (*cheap*), just off Piazza Maggiore, has long wooden tables where you can eat your own food bought at the surrounding market and sample the excellent wine. *Weekdays only, open until 9pm.* (Also *see osterie*, below).

Entertainment and Nightlife

Not surprisingly, a thousand-year-old university city like Bologna stays up later than most other Italian cities. People here eat late— often around 10pm—and there are plenty of bars and cafés open till 3am. During college terms you only have to take a look at the student bars and the posters in their windows to find out about concerts, films, exhibitions, performances and clubs; or check out the listings in Bologna's local paper, *Il Resto del Carlino* (which does *not* mean 'the remains of little Charles', as many foreigners suspect, but the change from an old coin called a Carlino—instead of change you could have a newspaper). The local fortnightly magazine, *La Mongolfiera*, usually has better listings on more youth-orientated events.

One reflection of Bologna's progressive open-mindedness is that it contains the headquarters of Italy's largest **gay organization**, **Arci-Gay**, and is the only city in the country to have a municipally supported gay centre, the **Cassero**, Porta Saragozza 2, which sponsors films and discussions during the week, and discos at weekends. There are several **women's organizations** in the city; **Ufficio Progetto Donna**, Via S. Margherita 13, ✆ 051 271 457, issues lists.

opera, classical music, theatre and cinema

The **drama** season at the Teatro Duse runs from November to May, while **operas** are performed at the Teatro Comunale from December to May. During the winter **films** are also shown in their original language at **Tiffany**, Piazza di Porta Saragozza 5 (*Wed*), and at **Adriano**, Via S. Felice 52 (*Mon*). Throughout the year the **Cinema Lumière**, Via Pietralata 55, shows mainly art-house movies, many of which have never been dubbed into Italian in the first place. In June especially, but also in July and August, dance performances and concerts are presented in Piazza Maggiore. As an alternative to the usual Italian mid-summer shutdown, Bologna's enterprising local authorities also organize the *Bologna Sogna* festival throughout July and August, featuring concerts, theatre and open-air cinema.

cafés, bars and osterie

Pasticceria Impero, Via Indipendenza 39, is a good place for breakfast; the speciality of the house are *certosini*, cakes with pine nuts, candied fruit, almonds and honey. For fine-quality *gelati*, try **Moline**, Via delle Moline 6, near the university (*closed Tues*), or more central **Frulé**, Via Clavature.

No visitor should leave Bologna without drinking in one of the traditional *osterie*; most serve food, many have live music and stay open late into the night. **Osteria dell'Orsa**, Via Mentana 1, near the university, has live jazz and good food; **Bentivoglio**, Via Mascarella 4, is a huge, smart cellar for live music, with snacks or full meals, and an endless wine list; and the great, lively **Osteria del Montesino**, Via del Pratello 74, serves good *crostini* and stays open till 2am, or 4am on Fri and Sat. *Closed Tues*. There are also sleeker, more modern bars, such as **Bar Rosa Rose**, Via Clavature 18, a popular early-evening meeting point just off Piazza Maggiore.

clubs and discos

As often happens in Italy, many of the bigger clubs are outside the city centre. One of the best-established is **Bestial Market**, Via delle Scale 21, outside the Porta San Felice on the edge of the centre, a very student-orientated venue that offers a wide mix of techno and other dance music, and occasional live gigs. **Porta di Mare**, Via Sampieri, near the Two Towers, is a rare centrally located lively music and dance venue. **Candilejas**, Via Bentini 20, is a funky sometimes Latin-orientated club in the suburb of Corticella (nightbus no.62 from Piazza Nettuno). In summer the ever-generous Bologna city council sponsors cheap, open-air **raves**, usually in the city outskirts.

East of Bologna

Between Bologna and the Adriatic are a hotchpotch of attractions—Italy's most important trotting course and the Imola motor-racing course, the fine medieval town of Brisighella, Italy's most important ceramics town, Faenza, and Forlì, decorated by Mussolini.

Getting Around

Between Bologna and Rimini **trains** are fast, frequent and occasionally packed, particularly in August. A slow local train runs from Faenza to Florence and stops at Brisighella; to continue to Florence you may have to change at Borgo San Lorenzo. Bagno di Romagna and other towns near the Tuscan frontier can be reached by **bus** from Forlì or Florence.

Forlì: Corso della Repubblica 23, ✆ 0543 712 435. **Faenza**: Piazza del Popolo 1, ✆ 0546 25231. **Bagno di Romagna**: Via Lungo Savio 14, ✆ 0543 911 046, ▤ 0543 911 026. **Brisighella**: Piazzetta Porta Gabolo, ✆ 0546 81166 (*summer only*).

Imola

Nearest to Bologna, Imola is synonymous with the **San Marino Grand Prix**, held on the race track here, and for a restaurant, the **San Domenico**, a pilgrimage shrine for grand gourmets. Otherwise, in the 18th-century **cathedral** you can pay your respects at the tomb of Imola's patron saint Cassian, a schoolteacher whose martyrdom was particularly unpleasant: he was stabbed with the pens of his students. **Castello di Imola**, to the south of the Via Aemilia, was defended by Caterina Sforza, widow of the Lord of Imola, until its capture by Cesare Borgia in 1500. In **Dozza**, a few kilometres back towards Bologna, a 13th-century castle houses the **Enoteca Regionale Emilia-Romagna**, ✆ 0542 678 089, ▤ 0542 678 073 (*open April–Oct Mon–Sat 10–12 and 3–6, Sun and hols 10–12 and 3–7; Nov–Mar Mon–Sat 2–5, Sun and hols 2–6*), where you can sample 450 wines selected from the region's 67,500 producers.

Faenza

'Faience ware' was born in the 16th century in Faenza with the invention of a new style of majolica: a piece was given a solid white glaze then rapidly, almost impressionistically, decorated with two tones of yellow and blue. It caused a sensation, and was in such demand throughout Europe that Faenza became a household name.

Today Faenza has regained much of its 16th-century lustre as a ceramics centre. There are 500 students enrolled in its *Istituto d'Arte per la Ceramica* and some 60 artists from around the world run workshops in the town. The **Associati Ente Ceramica**, Voltone Molinella 2, ✆ 0546 22308, issues a list of studios that you may visit and buy from: particularly worth seeing are Carlo Zauli, Via della Croce 6, ✆ 0546 22123; Ivo Sassi, Via Bondiollo 11, ✆ 0546 663 069; and Goffredo Gaeta, Via Carena 3, ✆ 0546 22816. Among several buildings and palaces adorned with majolica the most splendid is the Liberty-style **Palazzo Matteucci** in Corso Mazzini. Every year from September to October Faenza hosts an international ceramics exhibition; the theme is contemporary in odd years, and antique in even.

The **Museo Internazionale delle Ceramiche**, Viale Baccarini 19 (*open Mon–Fri 9–7, Sat and Sun 9.30–1 and 3–7—if you're carrying on to Ravenna it's worth buying the* biglietto cumulativo, *which includes the major monuments there*) was founded in 1908 and restored after its bombing in the War. It houses a magnificent collection of ceramics, centred on 16th- and 17th-century Italian works; pieces from Faenza adorned with giraffe-necked Renaissance ladies were typical nuptial gifts. There are fine Liberty-style pieces by Domenico Baccarini and Francesco Nonni, and downstairs you'll find pieces by Picasso, Matisse, Chagall and Rouault.

Brisighella

Some 12km south of Faenza on the Florence road, Brisighella is a charming village and thermal spa in the Lamone Valley. The sharp cliffs overhead are crowned by the splendid towers of the 12th-century **Rocca** and the **Torre dell'Orologio**, the latter originally a respectable guard tower with a clock slapped on its front in the 18th century. Brisighella produces much of the clay fired in Faenza's kilns—next to the village you can see the gashes left in the hills by the old quarries. So precious was this cargo borne by mule caravans that a protected, elevated passageway, the **Via degli Asini** (Mule Road), was built through the centre of town which, in case of attack, could be sealed up at either end. In the Rocca you can visit the **Museo del Lavoro Contadino** (*open 15 April–15 Oct Tues–Fri 10–12 and 3.30–5.30; Oct–April Sat 2.30–4.30, Sun 10–12 and 2.30–4.30; adm*), devoted to the region's traditional peasant culture, life and work. Several ceramics workshops still operate in Brisighella; from the end of June to the first week of July the city hosts an elaborate **Medieval Festival**, with music, games, feasts, plays, and absolutely gorgeous costumes.

Forlì

The *Forum Livii* on the Via Aemilia was elided over the years into Forlì, a city split between an attractive old town and the architectural legacy of Mussolini, who was born in nearby Predappio. The centrepiece of old Forlì is the striking 12th-century **Basilica di San Mercurio**, with a good campanile, a fine 13th-century lunette of the Magi by the school of Antelami, and an interesting interior. The **Duomo** on Corso Garibaldi has a temple façade; inside, note the painting of 15th-century firemen. On Corso della Repubblica, the **Pinacoteca Saffi** (*open Mon–Fri 9–2 and 3–8, Sat 9–2; closed Aug*) has works by local artist Marco Palmezzano, Fra Angelico, and others, and Flemish tapestries and ceramics. Nearby, **Santa Maria dei Servi** contains the finely sculpted tomb of Luffo Namai (1502). South of the centre, Forlì's castle, the picturesque 15th-century **Rocca di Ravaldino**, belonged to Caterina Sforza, and was the birthplace in 1498 of her son Giovanni de' Medici ('Giovanni delle Bande Nere', a famous *condottiere* and father of Cosimo I, first Duke of Tuscany). It now serves as a prison.

The Local Palio

Siena's *palio* (traditional horse race) may be the most famous, but it's neither unique in Italy, nor the only one to claim the longest history. However, whereas Siena's has continued virtually uninterrupted for centuries, the others, particularly in Emilia-Romagna, have resurrected themselves over the past few decades, and so lack the pomp, vast crowds and deep emotional response of that gallop around the Campo. The palios in Montagnana, Ferrara, Faenza (last two Sundays in July) or Forlimpopoli may be less vital, violent, cosmopolitan and crooked, but they do have other charms: no tourists, few police, small crowds, and a chance to see an Italian community expressing its self-love. Older traditions do remain (the tug of war to decide placings at the race's start), but the lack of formality and crowds allow a relaxed atmosphere; kids in medieval finery will spend the afternoon tearing round the streets, beating on drums.

Siena provides the framework which lesser palios copy. The day begins with a procession in medieval costume, probably led by the town's standard, followed by a delegation from each district: 'landowners' on horseback, young married couples holding hands, a matron in the middle of a crowd of urchins, a criminal in the stocks, massed ranks of young men clasping spears and pushing a catapult, a cart piled with geese, and troupes of teenage *sbandierati* twirling long, silken flags from one hand to the other, tossing them into the air and, as they unfurl, catching them again.

By comparison the race itself is chaotic. Bales of hay line wooden barriers which shield the crowds from the thundering horses. Each bareback rider carries a *nerbo*, a whip with which he may hit any horse or opponent, and wears a small coat named *giacchetto*, from which we derive the English word 'jockey'. The horses, fired up, take several minutes to form a regular starting-line. The race is brief and furious. Its aftermath depends on where you are: in Montagnana, near Rovigo (*see* p.349), the victor will be carried home for a beer and barbecue. In Siena supporters will try to kill the losers for having lost and the victor for having won; the entire city weeps for joy or shame at the outcome; casks of wine are splintered open on the pavement and goblets handed out to any passer-by.

Into the Apennines

South of Forlì three principal routes lead into Tuscany. Some of the best scenery is in the Montone Valley, the main route to Florence, along the SS67, passing the Renaissance planned village of **Terra del Sole**, begun in 1564 in the form of a perfect rectangle. Ruined medieval castles haunt the next towns of **Dovadola** and **Rocca San Casciano**. Dante's beloved Beatrice spent several summers in the very pretty old medieval town of **Portico di Romagna**; the Portinari house where she stayed can still be seen in the main street. Near the Tuscan frontier the 9th-century abbey in **San Benedetto in Alpe** sheltered Dante after his unsuccessful bid to return to Florence from exile (*Inferno*, Canto XVI, 94–105). In San Benedetto you can hire horses to explore the region's valleys, especially the lovely **Valle dell'Acquacheta** with its bucolic, stepped waterfall. The rapid Brusia River is popular with canoeists and kayakers, and this is a marvellous area for hill walking.

The narrow alternative route just east (SS9 *ter*) passes through the Sangiovese wine country around **Predappio**, where Mussolini was born in 1883; in 1957 his remains were re-buried in the local cemetery near those of his wife Rachele, and are something of a pilgrimage site for creeps. Mussolini made Predappio the seat of the local *comune*, and embellished it with public buildings, leaving the old *comune*, **Predappio Alta**, alone beneath its overgrown castle. In Predappio Alta, you can taste the local ruby-red Sangiovese or 'blood of Jove' at the **Cà de Sanvès** (*open daily 10–12 and 3–midnight; closed Tues*).

From Forlimpopoli, with its well-preserved medieval castle, a third road heads south for **Bertinoro**, an old town famous for its wine and hospitality. Such were the squabbles over guests that a column was erected in front of the 14th-century **Palazzo Comunale** and hung with rings, one belonging to each family. Whichever ring a stranger tethered his horse to decided which family got to be his host. Nearby **Polenta** has a fine 9th-century Byzantine-Romanesque temple. The main SS310 from Forlì continues into the scenic heavily forested Upper Bidenta Valley. There are ski facilities at Monte Campigna, near the old Tuscan town of **Santa Sofia**. Much further south, near **Balze**, there's more skiing at Monte Fumaiolo, on whose slopes the Tiber begins its 418km journey to Rome. **San Piero in Bagno** and **Bagno di Romagna**, with thermal and mud baths, are popular summer resorts in the region.

Cesena and Crossing the Rubicon

In the 14th–15th centuries Cesena, site of the European Trotting Championships in August, was one of the jewels of the Malatesta clan. Their castle still dominates the town, while a

1452 basilica built for Domenico Malatesta Novello is the main sight, housing the **Biblioteca Malatestiana** (*open Mon–Sat 9–12.45 and 4–6, Sun 10.30–12.30; closing depends on daylight since there is no electric light inside; adm*), with a priceless collection of manuscripts. Between Cesena and Rimini at **Savignano**, the road crosses a poor excuse for a stream that most authorities accept as the shadowy Rubicon, which divided what was then Gaul from what was then Roman Italy, and which Julius Caesar crossed with his army, thereby defying the Senate and declaring his intention to take over the Roman state. Today it separates respectable Emilia-Romagna from the international bikini beach boogaroo at Rimini.

Where to Stay and Eating Out

Imola ✉ 40026

Ristorante San Domenico, Via G. Sacchi 1, ✆ 0542 29000 (*very expensive*) is venerated by gastronomes from around the world. Consistently rated in the top five in the country, this temple of Italian cuisine offers a constantly changing menu of the day, sublimely prepared with the lightest and most delicate of touches. The dining room is as beautiful as the desserts, and the wine list is exquisite enough to shatter a credit card. *Closed Mon, Sun evening and most of Aug*.

Now breathing on San Domenico's sacred heels, **Naldi**, Via Santerno 13, ✆ 0542 29581 (*expensive*) offers tempting and innovative variations on Emilia-Romagna recipes—pâtés with black truffles, tortellini in walnut cream, stuffed chicken breasts—in a charming setting.

Osteria del Vicolo Nuovo, Via Coldronchi 6, ✆ 0542 32552 (*moderate*), in a 16th-century cellar, serves dishes based on local traditions: cheese soufflé with porcini mushrooms, home-made pasta—gnocchi with porcini, tortellini with asparagus—rabbit roasted in San Giovese wine, tongue with *salsa verde. Closed Sun and Mon*.

Faenza ✉ 48018

In the centre, ★★★★**Vittoria**, Corso Garibaldi 23, ✆ 0546 21508, ✆ 0546 29136 (*expensive*) has 19th-century furnishings and a dining room with a fine frescoed ceiling. If you're driving, ★★★★**Cavallino** (*moderate*) is outside Faenza at Via Forlivese 185, ✆ 0546 634 411, ✆ 0546 634 440, and has a garage, garden and restaurant. For cheaper accommodation, there are many *affittacamere* (rooms for rent) in private houses. Call the tourist office for details. **Le Volte**, Corso Mazzini 54, ✆ 0546 661 600 (*moderate*) is hidden in the basement of the Galleria Gessi. Surrounded by antique furniture, you can eat *tortelloni al radicchio*, duck breast roasted with cabbage and pepper, or rack of lamb in a herb crust. *Closed Sun*. **La Pavona**, Via Santa Lucia 45, ✆ 0546 31075 (*moderate*), on the edge of town, has a pleasant outdoor pergola and serves traditional cooking with a twist—lots of vegetarian dishes—accompanied by an excellent wine list. *Closed Wed.*

Brisighella ✉ 48013

South of the village, on a hill in open countryside, **Relais Torre Pratesi**, Via Cavina 11, ✆ 0546 84545, ✆ 0546 84558 (*expensive*) occupies a 15th-century tower and farmhouse which have been carefully restored to create a comfortable, even luxurious, hotel. The views are superb and the restaurant good. At ★★★★**Gigiolè**, Piazza

Carducci 5, ℘ 0546 81209 (*expensive*), the rooms have recently been brought up to four-star standard, but the *raison d'être* continues to be the superb food created by a chef who has researched Romagna's medieval culinary traditions—ravioli stuffed with rabbit and mint, veal with wild fennel, and mulberry pudding. *Closed Mon.* **La Grotta (Osteria con Uso di Cucina)**, Via Metelli 2, ℘ 0546 81829 (*moderate*) offers three menus—the bargain, the regional and the *degustazione.* It's rated one of the best restaurants in Emilia-Romagna, and the prices are amazing. *Closed Tues.*

Forlì ✉ 47100

****Principe**, Viale Bologna 153, ℘ 0543 701 570, ℮ 0543 702 270 (*moderate*), just outside the centre, has comfortable modern rooms; its restaurant serves good land and seafood. Within 10km of Forlì are two gourmet restaurants. Outside Forlimpopoli in Selbagnone, **Al Maneggio**, ℘ 0543 742 042 (*very expensive*) is located in a delightful garden. Elegant simplicity is the rule here—superb *gamberoni*, risotto, desserts and wines. *Closed Sun evenings and Mon.* At Castrocaro Terme, **La Frasca**, Via Matteotti 38, ℘ 0543 767 471 (*very expensive*) offers wonderful local cuisine— white bean and mushroom soup, red mullet with coriander, and hundreds of cheeses. Superb wine list. *Closed Mon, two weeks in Jan and two weeks in Aug.*

Bagno di Romagna ✉ 47021

****Hotel Tosco Romagnolo**, Piazza Dante Alighieri 2, ℘ 0543 911 260, ℮ 0543 911 014 (*expensive–moderate*) is a charming place to stay, relax and dine in one of Italy's most enchanting dining rooms; the food is based on Tuscan and Romagna country traditions, served with excellent wines. *Open Easter–15th Nov.*

Ferrara

There's been a certain mystique attached to Ferrara ever since Jacob Burckhardt called it 'the first modern city in Europe' in his classic *Civilization of the Renaissance in Italy.* Whether or not Burckhardt was right can be debated endlessly; what is certain is that the famous 'additions' to the medieval city in the Renaissance were far too ambitious. Ferrara, even in the most brilliant days of the Este family, never mustered more than 30,000 citizens—not enough to fill the long, straight, rational streets laid out within the 9km circuit of the walls.

But what was a failure in the Renaissance is a happy success today; if Italian art cities can be said to come and go in fashion, Ferrara is definitely in, popularized by a well-received international campaign to save its unique walls. Thanks to the rather tyrannical Este, the charming city they enclose was one of the brightest stars of the Renaissance, with its own fine school of art led by Cosmè Tura, Ercole de' Roberti, Lorenzo Costa and Francesco del Cossa. Poets patronized by the Este produced three of the Italian Renaissance's greatest epics—Boiardo's *Orlando Innamorato* (1483), Ariosto's better-known continuation of the same story, *Orlando Furioso* (1532), and Tasso's *Gerusalemme Liberata* (1581), all praising the ducal family.

History

Ferrara grew up on a formerly navigable branch of the Po River and until the 17th century based its economy on river tolls, the salt pans of the Comacchio and the rich agricultural land of the Delta. It was always ruled by one family or the other, but it was the rise of the Este in

1250 that made Ferrara a great city, an outpost of papal power in the north. The Este clan produced and married some of the most interesting characters of the Renaissance: there was Nicolò II (1361–88), the friend of Petrarch; Alberto (1388–93), who founded the University of Ferrara; Nicolò III (1393–1441), reputedly the father of hundreds of children on both banks of the Po, as well as being the villain who perpetrated one of the tragic love stories of his day—he found that his young wife Parisina and his son by another woman were lovers, and had both of them executed.

The legitimate sons of Nicolò III—Leonello, Borso and Ercole I (1471–1505)—were responsible for the city's great cultural flowering. Ercole I had the first addition to the city (known as the Herculean Addition) designed by his architect Rossetti; his offspring, Isabella (wife of Francesco Gonzaga), Beatrice (married to Lodovico Sforza, *Il Moro*), and Cardinal Ippolito, were among the most cultured and influential people of their day. His heir, Alfonso I (1505–34), married the beautiful and unjustly maligned Lucrezia Borgia, who ran a brilliant and fashionable court, patronizing Ariosto and Titian, while her husband spent his days casting huge cannons. Their son, Ercole II (1534–59), married Renée, daughter of Louis XII of France, and a Calvinist, who sheltered John Calvin in Ferrara under an assumed name; eventually relations with Rome became so touchy that she had to be sent away.

The last Duke, Alfonso II (1559–97), patron of the unstable Tasso, was considered the best-educated and most courtly ruler of his day. When he died without issue, Ferrara, sick and tired of paying the bills, was glad to see the last of the Este, and be ruled by a papal legate. The city soon became a backwater, and its population declined. In this century, however, the modern 'Metaphysical School' of painting (De Chirico, Carrà, De Pises, Morandi, and others) had its origins in the city, inspired at least in part by the great frescoes in the Palazzo Schifanoia.

Getting Around

Ferrara's **railway station** is just outside the city walls, a 15-minute walk west of the centre along Viale Cavour (or take local bus no.1, no.2 or no.9). There are frequent rail connections to Bologna, Venice and Ravenna. The **bus station** is near the corner of the Rampari di San Paolo and Corso Isonzo, ✆ 0532 599 492; a fine network of lines serves the coast, Bologna, Modena, Ravenna, Rovigo and other local destinations.

Pancake flat, Ferrara has the second-largest ratio of **bicycles** to humans in Europe (after Copenhagen). Hire one at the *deposito* just outside the train station, ✆ 0532 772 190, or try Itinerando, Via Kennedy, just off Piazza Travaglio, ✆ 0532 202 003.

Tourist Information

The office is inside the Castello Estense, ✆ 0532 299 303, ✉ 0532 212 266.

The Castle and the Cathedral

At the very centre of Ferrara towers the imposing **Castello Estense** (*open Tues–Sun 9.30–5; adm*), which would look like a Victorian factory building were it not for the moat and drawbridges. It was begun in 1385 by Nicolò II after a revolt, but later the Este transformed it into their chief residence, its crenellations replaced by white marble balustrades, and its great halls adorned with art. A few decorated rooms survive: the *Salone* and *Saletta dei Giochi* (the games room, the latter belonging to the children) and the fine *Sala dell'Aurora* (the dukes' bedroom) and *Camerina dei Baccanali* are the most interesting. The tour includes Renée's Calvinist chapel, the dungeon where Ugo and Parisina languished before their beheading, and the prison where Giulio and Ferrante, brothers of Alfonso I, spent their lives after attempting a coup. Even the life of the most cultured duke wasn't all peaches and cream.

From the Castello, Corso dei Martiri leads first to the **Palazzo Comunale**, built in 1243 and adorned with statues of Nicolò III and Borso; next to it in Piazza della Repubblica stands a statue of Savonarola, a native of Ferrara. Opposite the palazzo is the handsome rose-coloured **Duomo**, begun in 1135 by Wiligelmo and finished a century later. Its glory is a marble portico, carved with a magnificent 13th-century *Last Judgement* by an unknown sculptor; a certain Maestro Nicolò executed the bas-reliefs of *St George* in the lunette over the door. The candy-striped campanile is from the 15th century; the arcade on the north side retains its original twisted columns. The interior was remodelled in the 17th century, but you can see the best art in the **Museo della Cattedrale** (*open Tues–Sat 10–12 and 3–5*), including the marble *Madonna of the Pomegranate* by Jacopo della Quercia, two organ shutters by Cosmè Tura, painted with an *Annunciation* and a *St George*, and a relief of the months. The picturesque portico flanking the Duomo in Piazza Trento e Trieste was added in 1473.

Renaissance Palaces

From behind the cathedral in Via Voltapaletto, Via Savonarola will take you to the **Casa Romei** (*open Tues–Sun 9–2; adm*), a fine example of the typical Renaissance palace, built for a banker who won the sweepstakes by marrying an Este in 1445. As well as its charming frescoes, fireplaces and elegant courtyards, there are expressive detached frescoes moved here from Sant'Andrea and other disused churches. Further down Via Praisolo, behind the church of San Girolamo, the **Corpus Domini** church (*open Mon–Fri 9.30–12 and 3.30–5.30*) contains the austere tombs of Alfonso I, Alfonso II and Lucrezia Borgia. Nearby, up Via Ugo Bassi, the late-Renaissance **Palazzina di Marfisa d'Este** is in a garden at Corso della Giovecca 170 (*open Mar–Oct daily 9.30–1 and 3–6; Nov–Feb daily 9.30–1 and 2–5; adm; free first Mon of the month*). Marfisa, a friend of Tasso, was beautiful and eccentric, and the subject of several ghost stories; it seems that she enjoyed post-mortem rides through Ferrara at midnight in a wolf-drawn carriage. The interior of her little palace, with its unusual *grotteschi* frescoes on the ceiling, has been restored and fitted with period furnishings.

Palazzo Schifanoia

Ferrara's most famous palace, the 1385 Palazzo Schifanoia (*open daily 7am–7pm; adm; free first Mon of the month*), is a couple of streets away at Via Scandiana 23 (follow Via Ugo Bassi to Via Madama). Schifanoia means 'disgust with boredom', and it would be hard to stay bored in the utterly delightful **Salone dei Mesi**, painted for Borso d'Este by Ferrara's finest—Cosmè Tura, Ercole de' Roberti and Francesco del Cossa. The scenes of mythological and allegorical subjects peopled by charming 15th-century aristocrats are believed to have been inspired by Petrarch's *Triumphs*—in each month a different god is seen to 'triumph', most famously Venus in the month of April, with a rare scene of a Renaissance kiss. The palace has several other rooms with beautiful ceilings, and houses an eclectic collection of medieval art (note the alabaster *Passion of Christ* from Nottingham) and ancient art.

Palazzo di Lodovico il Moro

Turn right at the walls at the end of Via Scandiana and continue to Via XX Settembre for No.124, the elegant Palazzo di Lodovico il Moro designed by Biagio Rossetti and named after Beatrice d'Este's Milanese husband, although it never belonged to him. It has frescoes on the ground floor by Raphael's pupil, Garofalo, and upstairs an excellent **Museo Archeologico Nazionale** (*open Tues–Sun 9–2; adm*), with artefacts from the necropolis of the Graeco-Etruscan seaport of Spina, including Attic vases, a splendid gold diadem and two pirogues carved from tree trunks in the later Roman period. Nearby in Via Beatrice d'Este, the convent of **Sant'Antonio in Polèsine** has fine frescoes dating back to the 13th century and inlaid choir stalls. Just outside the walls (through the Porta Romana), **San Giorgio** was Ferrara's cathedral until the 12th century, and is worth a look for the sumptuous 1475 **tomb of Lorenzo Roverella**, Pope Julius II's physician. On the way back towards the centre, on Via delle Scienze, the 13th-century **Palazzo Paradiso** was the former seat of the university and is now the site of the Ariosto library, with the complete manuscript of *Orlando Furioso* and Ariosto's tomb.

The Herculean Addition

North of the Castello Estense stretches the Herculean Addition, laid out by Biagio Rossetti for Ercole I, which more than doubled the size of 15th-century Ferrara. Not long after the fall of the Este dynasty travellers noted that many of the streets here were abandoned and over-grown, and even today they feel somewhat melancholy and quiet.

Rossetti's showpiece, **Palazzo dei Diamanti**, in the very centre of the Addition, takes its name from the 8,500 pointed, diamond-shaped stones that stud the façade—diamonds being the emblem of the Este. It houses the **Pinacoteca Nazionale** (*open Tues–Sun 9–2; adm*), a fine collection by the Ferrara school—Tura, Cossa, Costa, Roberti, the sweet Raphaelesque Garofalo (a favourite of the 18th century) and Dossi—and detached frescoes from churches and palaces. There's also a Carpaccio *Death of the Virgin*, and 19th- and 20th-century art on the ground floor.

The Diamond Palace lies at the junction of two main streets; down one, Corso Biagio Rossetti, Via Ariosto leads off to the right to the **Casa di Ariosto** (*closed for restoration*), which the poet built for himself. 'Small,' he described it modestly, 'but suited to me.' To the east of the Diamond Palace, the **Palazzo Massari**, Corso Porta Mare 9 (*open daily 9–1 and 3–6; adm; free first Mon of the month*) houses the **Galleria d'Arte Moderna**, a collection of slides and reproductions of major works by Ferrara's Metaphysical School. Pass through it to reach the **Palazzina dei Cavalieri di Malta**, seat of the Knights of Malta from 1826 to 1834, and now seat of a collection of 19th-century and Liberty-style art.

In stark contrast to the Addition, the ghetto where the Jews (including many refugees from Spain) were confined from 1627 to 1859 is a labyrinth of narrow, cobbled streets, brick arches and alleyways on the south side of town. A new **Jewish Museum** (*open for guided tours*

Sun–Thurs 10–2) has opened in Via Mazzini, where once there were three synagogues. Since 1485 this has been the focus of Jewish life in Ferrara; it was purchased by a rich financier from Rome employed at the Estensi court, who left it in his will 'forever for the common use of the Jews'. The **Cimitero Israelitico**, along the walls by Via Porta Mare, was founded in the 17th century; strewn with wild flowers, it is one of the prettiest spots in the city.

The Walls

Ferrara's well-preserved 9km circuit of red-brick walls is most easily seen by bicycle. They date from the 15th and 16th centuries, and the best stretch is between the Porta Mare and the former Porta degli Angeli, built by Rossetti on the north side of the city. Cycle paths run along their length, linking with routes out to the Po.

Around Ferrara

The region around Ferrara is flat and somewhat dreary. **Argenta**, southeast of the city, is mainly visited for a restaurant (*see* below). Its attractive quattrocento church of San Domenico houses a small art gallery, with works by Garofalo and others. Between Ferrara and Modena, **Cento**, under its 14th-century castle, was the birthplace of Disraeli's ancestors and painter Giovanni Francesco Barbieri, better known by his nickname Guercino 'Squinty' (1591–1666); a collection of his work is in the Pinacoteca Civica, Via Matteotti 10.

Activities

Ferrara has its own **palio** (traditional horse race), every year on the last Sunday in May. The **Ferrara Buskers' Festival** is held in the last week in August, when buskers from all over the world come to perform in the streets in the centre of town. *Ferrara Musica* is an international season of concerts and opera which runs from September to May. Venues include the stunning Teatro Comunale.

Ferrara ✉ *44100*   ***Where to Stay and Eating Out***

Ferrara's most famous dish (and Lucrezia Borgia's favourite) is *salama da sugo*—a sausage that is cured for a year, then gently boiled and eaten with a spoon. The bakers of Ferrara are famous for their X-shaped bread, *ciupèta*; little caps of pasta, *cappelletti*, often filled with pumpkin, are another local speciality. When Renée of France came to Ferrara she brought her own vines, the origin of the delicious *Vino di Bosco*.

★★★★**Ripagrande**, Via Ripagrande 23, ✆ 0532 765 250, ✉ 0532 764 377 (*expensive*), housed in the Renaissance Beccari-Freguglia palace, has the most memorable accommodation in Ferrara. Its ground floor retains its Renaissance décor and heavy-beamed ceiling, and there's a fine restaurant. The rooms are modern, equipped with kitchenettes, sitting rooms, air-conditioning and TV. There's parking, and bicycles for hire. ★★★★**Astra**, Viale Cavour 55, ✆ 0532 206 088, ✉ 0532 247 002 (*expensive*) is a long-established hotel with a fine restaurant.

Beautiful ★★★★**Villa Regina**, Via Comacchio 402, ✆ 0532 740 222, ✉ 0532 761 085 (*moderate*), just outside the city in a converted villa, is set amid luxurious parkland. Right beside the castle, the modern, slick ★★★**Touring**, Viale Cavour 11, ✆ 0532 206

200 (*moderate*) has air-conditioning and parking. *****Europa**, Corso Giovecca 49, ℗ 0532 33460, in the medieval city in a 17th-century palace, also has parking.

San Paolo, Via Baluardi 9, ℗ 0532 762 040, ⊛ 0532 762 040 (*cheap*), near the city walls beside Piazza Travaglio, is incredible value for money. ***Casa Degli Artisti, Via Vittoria 66, ℗ 0532 761 038 (*cheap*), right in the centre of town, is on a quiet side street near the Duomo.

Trigabolo, Piazza Garibaldi 4/5, ℗ 0532 318 318, in Argenta (*very expensive*) is another gourmet enclave in an unlikely spot, which the locals rave about. In its elegant dining room you can feast on ravioli stuffed with artichokes with basil sauce, cannoli with turbot in clam sauce, goose liver with pears, or veal with lettuce, cream and almonds. A great wine list and rich desserts top it all off. *Closed Tues and first three weeks in July.*

Back in the city, **Aldobrando**, Corso Porta Mare 45, ℗ 0532 752 648 (*expensive*) bases its menu solidly on Ferrara's cuisine, especially *salama da sugo*. *Closed Sun.* **Centrale**, Via Boccaleone 8, ℗ 0532 206 735 (*expensive*), in a side-street behind the Palazzo Comunale, offers an interesting variety of tortelloni, beef with truffles, and desserts made on the premises. *Closed Sun and Wed evening.* **Da Guido**, Via Vignatagliata 61, ℗ 0532 761 052 (*moderate*) is an intimate trattoria with specialities such as fresh artichokes, breast of duck with apple sauce, and seafood. *Closed Tues and July.* At **La Provvidenza**, Corso Ercole d'Este 92, ℗ 0532 205 187 (*moderate*), flanked by trees, the menu features fish (Thurs and Fri), or *salama da sugo* and charcoal grilled meats. *Closed Mon.* The **Osteria Degli Angeli**, Via Volte 4, ℗ 0532 764 376 (*moderate*), is in one of the oldest streets in Ferrara. *Closed Mon.*

Slightly outside the centre, family-run **Tenuta S. Teresa**, Via Gramicia 83, ℗ 0532 750 337 (*cheap*) produces hearty home cooking; it has a bustling atmosphere, and an open fire in the winter. *Closed Mon.*

Entertainment and Nightlife

A university town, Ferrara is quite lively at night; check the local newspaper, *La Nuova Ferrara* for listings. Ferrara has a unique place to drink: **Al Brindisi**, Via degli Adelardi 11, near the cathedral. It occupies the same locale as the ancient Taverna da Chiucchiolino, opened in 1435, and although the furnishings are much newer, the atmosphere is often just as jovial as it was in the 15th century. For coffee and delicious pastries, try the **Caffè Europa**, Via della Giovecca 51. To find the hip young things of Ferrara, go to **Bar Ariosto**, in Piazza Ariostea. The bar **Centro Storico**, near the Duomo, has a vast spread of nibbles to go with your evening *aperitivo*.

The Coast: from the Po to Ravenna

For most people the main attractions along this coast are the Po Delta and magnificent Romanesque abbey of Pomposa, though there are plenty of Italian family lidos in the vicinity if you're tempted to join the summer ice-cream, pizza and parasol brigades.

Buses from Ferrara radiate to the flatlands of the coast.

Comacchio: Piazza Floegatti 28, ✆ 0533 310 161. **Lidi di Comacchio**: Viale Carducci 32, Lido degli Estensi, ✆ 0533 327 464. **Pomposa**: ✆ 0533 719 110.

The Southern Po Delta

Alfonso II d'Este was the first to start draining the marshes south of the Po Delta. Much of the land was planted with rice; a large part of the rest now belongs to the **Parco del Delta del Po**, one of Italy's most important wetlands, and a birdwatcher's paradise. Part of the primordial coastal pine forest survives intact in the **Bosco di Mésola**, now a nature reserve (*visitors are admitted Sun and holidays only 8am–sunset*). Not far to the west, near Italba, this varied and ever-changing coastline offers something completely different—a marooned 100-acre patch of dunes, once part of the coast, called the 'Moraro'. Excursion boats plying the narrow canals between the reeds explore the mouth of the Po di Goro and the Valle di Gorino, departing from the picturesque fishing hamlets of Gorino, Goro or Mésola; for information, contact **Freccia del Delta**, ✆ 0533 999 817, or **Principessa**, ✆ 0533 999 815, in Gorino.

The Abbey of Pomposa

The main coast road from the north, SS309, follows the old Roman coastal road, the Via Romea. Just south of the Po di Goro it passes through **Mésola**, with an old hunting lodge, the 'Delizia Estense' of Alfonso I d'Este, then continues down to the haunting and serene Abbey of Pomposa, an 8th-century Benedictine foundation, formerly on its own islet; in this atmosphere of total tranquillity the monk Guido d'Arezzo invented the modern musical scale in the early 11th century. Uninhabited since the 17th century, the abbey is dwarfed by its **campanile**, adorned with mullioned windows, which progress tier by tier from a narrow slit on the bottom to a grand *quadrifore* (four arches) on top. The **church** (7th–11th centuries) has a lovely Byzantine atrium and an interior embellished with colourful 14th-century frescoes, many by the charming Vitale da Bologna; there are other frescoes by his school in the monks' Chapter House. The abbot governed from the beautifully austere 11th-century **Palazzo della Ragione** (*all open daily 7–12 and 2–7*).

The resorts along the sandy **Lidi di Comacchio** begin at the **Lido di Volano** on the other side of the wetlands of the Valle Bertuzzi, where the setting sun ignites the waters in a thousand colours. Of the resorts, the **Lido delle Nazioni** and **Porto Garibaldi** are the most interesting and best equipped. The name of the latter recalls that the defeated hero attempted to escape from here after the collapse of the Roman Republic in 1849, in a desperate guerrilla movement that cost the life of his pregnant wife Anita. The most important town in the area is **Comacchio**, with its famous monumental triple bridge, the **Trepponti**, spanning three of the town's canals. Comacchio is famed for its eels, farmed in the Valli di Comacchio—if you're in the area between September and December you can watch the fishermen scoop them up. Just west of Comacchio stood the Graeco-Etruscan **Spina**, for centuries the main port of Felsina (Bologna), but now miles from the sea.

Innocently tucked away among the art towns of Emilia-Romagna there is one famous city that has nothing to do with Renaissance popes and potentates, Guelphs or Ghibellines, sports cars or socialists. Little, in fact, has been heard from Ravenna in the last thousand years. Before that time, however, this city's career was simply astounding—heir to Rome itself, and the leading city of western Europe for centuries. For anyone interested in Italy's shadowy progress through the Dark Ages, this is the place to visit.

There's a certain magic in three-digit years; history guards their secrets closely, giving us only occasional glimpses of battling barbarians, careful monks 'keeping alive the flame of knowledge' and local Byzantine dukes and counts doing their best to hold things together. In Italy, the Dark Ages were never quite so dark. This can be seen in Rome, but much more clearly here, in the only Italian city that not only survived but prospered all through those troubled times. In Ravenna's churches, adorned with the finest mosaics ever made, such an interruption as the Dark Ages seems to disappear, and you experience the development of Italian history and art from ancient to medieval times as a continuous and logical process.

History

On an important route to Dalmatia and the Danube, Ravenna and its port Classis first became prominent during the reign of Augustus. With their nearly impregnable setting, surrounded by marshes, the military advantage was clear, and Classis became Rome's biggest naval base on the Adriatic. As conditions in Italy grew unsettled in the 5th century, the relative safety of Ravenna began to look very inviting to frightened emperors.

Honorius moved the capital of the Western Empire here in 402—just in time, with Alaric's sack of Rome coming eight years later. Honorius' sister, Galla Placidia, ruled the city in the emperor's absence, and began to embellish it with churches and monuments befitting its new status. When the Visigoths attacked Ravenna, Galla Placidia was taken hostage, and married the Visigothic king Ataulf. They got on well together in Toulouse, and before his assassination she rode at his side everywhere, even in battle. She returned eventually to Ravenna, and ruled it until her death in 450.

By the 6th century, with sheep grazing in the Roman Forum, Ravenna had become accepted as the metropolis of Italy. The Ostrogothic kings, Odoacer and Theodoric, made it their capital; during the reign of the latter the last flowering of Latin letters took place, under the influence of his famous councillors: Boethius, Symmachus and Cassiodorus. Boethius, one of the Fathers of the Church, wrote his *Consolation of Philosophy* in Theodoric's dungeon, where the king had consigned him after suspecting the philosopher of intrigues with Constantinople.

The terrible wars for control of Italy, between the Ostrogoths and the Eastern Emperor, were beginning. Ravenna was spared the destruction the Byzantine generals Belisarius and Narses spread through the rest of Italy; after their victory the city became the seat of the *exarchs*, the Byzantine viceroys who were to rule increasingly smaller bits of Italy over the next 500 years. It was this period that would see the city's golden age.

The Greek exarchs, never popular among their new subjects, performed the occasional service of obtaining Constantinople's aid in keeping the Lombards at bay. While tolerating the exarch's presence, the people of Ravenna were coming to rely increasingly on their own resources; when help from the east failed to appear, it was their own militia that defended the city against invaders. So, in the worst times, the city survived as a sort of cultural time-capsule, protected by its own efforts—and its swamps—still maintaining trade and cultural relations with the east, and carrying on the best traditions of classical culture single-handedly..

In 751 the Lombards finally succeeded in taking Ravenna, chasing out the last exarch. Only six years later, however, Pepin the Short's Frankish army snatched it back, and the city was placed under the rule of the popes. Ravenna declined slowly and gracefully in the following centuries. Venice took over its role as leading port of the Adriatic as Classis silted up and was abandoned. The newer cities of Romagna, such as Ferrara and Faenza, assumed a larger role in the region's economy, and even Ravenna's ancient school of Roman law was transferred to Bologna, there to become the foundation of Europe's first university.

Despite its declining fortunes, Ravenna still managed to rouse itself in 1177, becoming a free *comune*. During the 13th century government fell into the hands of the Da Polenta family, famous for offering refuge to Dante in his exile from Florence. Dante finished the *Divine*

Comedy in Ravenna, and died here in 1321. In 1441 Ravenna came under the rule of Venice, and enjoyed a brief period of renewed prosperity which lasted until the popes came back in 1509; the economic decadence brought by papal rule has been reversed only since the 1940s. Parts of the city were heavily damaged in the Second World War, but in the last few decades, with the construction of a ship channel and new port, the discovery of offshore gas deposits and the introduction of large chemical industries, Ravenna has become a booming modern city—just coincidentally one with a medieval centre full of Byzantine mosaics.

Getting There and Around

Ravenna is not on the main Adriatic **railway** line, but there are several trains a day from Florence, Venice, Ancona and Bologna (change at Faenza or Ferrara from other cities). The station is in Piazza Farini (and the **bus station** is just across the tracks), east of the old town next to the ship channel, a short walk from the centre.

City buses from the train station or Piazza del Popolo will take you to Classe or the nearby lidos. The no.2 bus from the station goes past Mausoleo Teodorico, otherwise it's a half-hour walk out on a busy highway. Bus no.4 and no.44 from the station go to S. Apollinato. You can hire **bicycles** in Piazzale Stazione, or in the ACI car park near San Vitale.

Tourist Information

Via Salaria 8, © 0544 35404, @ 0544 482 670. Single block tickets (*biglietto cumulativo; L10,000*) are available that cover several sites; the ticket that includes San Vitale, S. Apollinare and the Battistero Neoniano, is worth buying if you're going to all of them, and the comprehensive ticket including Faenza's ceramics museum is a bargain.

San Vitale

Open summer daily 9–7; winter daily 9–4.30; Mar and Oct daily 9–5.30.

At first this dark old church may not seem like much, but as soon as the now-automatic lights come on, the 1400-year-old mosaics ignite into an explosion of colour. The mosaics of San Vitale, Ravenna's best, are one of the last great works of art of the ancient world. The octagonal church, begun in 525 during the reign of Theodoric, is itself a fine example of the surprisingly sophisticated architecture from that troubled age. By the time it was finished, in 548, the city was in the hands of Belisarius' Byzantine army; the famous mosaic portraits of Justinian and Theodora can be taken as the traditional imperial style of political propaganda.

Outside Ravenna nothing like this church was built, or could have been built, in the 6th century. Far from being the sorry recapitulation of old forms and styles you might expect, San Vitale was a breathtakingly original departure in architecture—not the last work of the Romans, but the first of the Romanesque.

Take some time to admire the interior, with its beautiful interplay of octagons, arches, gables and exedrae—pure proportional geometry done in plain solid brick. Inside, the curious double capitals on the columns are no design conceit, but an important 5th-century invention; the trapezoidal *impost block* on top is a capital specially designed to support the weight of arches. Holding up the second-floor galleries and large octagonal cupola was an unusual design problem; these capitals and the eight stout piers around the dome were the solution. We do not know whether San Vitale's architects were Latins or Greeks, but the year after it was begun work commenced on the similar church of SS. Sergius and Bacchus in Constantinople, the prototype for the Hagia Sophia 10 years later.

In its structure the great dome in Constantinople owes everything to the little dome of Ravenna: the innovation of the galleries, for example, in which the women were segregated, and the elongated apse cleverly combining the central plan favoured by eastern Christians with the basilica form needed for a court's religious ceremonies. Nowhere in Constantinople, however, or anywhere in the east, will you find anything as brilliant as San Vitale's **mosaics**. Much was undoubtedly lost during the iconoclastic troubles of the 8th century; though iconoclasm was fiercely resisted in Italy—it was one of the first causes of the rupture between the Roman and Greek churches—and most of Ravenna's art was fortunately left in peace.

The colours are startling. Almost all the other surviving Byzantine mosaics, in Sicily, Greece and Turkey, are simple figures on a bright gold ground, dazzling at first but somewhat monotonous. There is plenty of gold on the walls of San Vitale, but the best mosaics, in the **choir**, have deep blue skies and rich green meadows for backgrounds, highlighted by brightly coloured birds and flowers. (The usual nomenclature is misleading; the 'choir' is the site of the main altar, while the clergy sat on the bench around the apse.)

The two **lunettes** over the arches flanking the choir, each a masterpiece, show the two events in the Old Testament that prefigure the Transfiguration of Christ: the hospitality of Abraham and the sacrifice of Isaac, and the offerings of Abel and Melchisedek, set under fiery clouds with hands of benediction extended from Heaven. Around the two lunettes are scenes of Moses and Jeremiah; note, above the lunettes, the delicately posed pairs of angels holding golden crosses—almost identical to the fanciful figures from earlier Roman art displaying the civic crown of the Caesars. At the front of the choir the **triumphal arch** has excellent mosaic portraits of the Apostles supported by a pair of dolphins; the galleries have portraits of the four evangelists.

The **apse** is dominated by portraits of Justinian and Theodora—mostly, of course, of Theodora, the dancing girl who used her many talents to become an empress, eventually coming to wear poor Justinian like a charm on her bracelet. Here she is wearing a rich crown, with long strings of fat diamonds and real pearls. Justinian, like Theodora, appears among his retinue offering a gift to the new church; here he has the air of a hung-over saxophone player, badly in need of a shave and a cup of coffee. His cute daisy slipper steps on the foot (a convention of Byzantine art to show who's boss) of his General Belisarius, to his left. The likenesses are good—very like those in Constantinople—suggesting that the artist may have come from there, or at least have copied closely imperial portraits on display at Ravenna.

It can easily be imagined how expensive it was in the 5th century to make mosaics like these. It is said that the Hagia Sophia in Constantinople had over two hectares of them, and even the treasury of Justinian was not bottomless; consequently most of San Vitale remained undecorated until the 17th-century bishops did the rest in a not-too-discordant Baroque. The bishops' floor has been pulled up to reveal the original, of inlaid marble in floral and geometric patterns, the direct ancestor of medieval pavements in the churches of Tuscany and the south.

The Mosaics

Either light was born here,
Or reigns here imprisoned.

Latin inscription, Sant'Andrea chapel

 In Byzantine times the greatest gift an emperor could bestow on any dependent town was a few tons of gold and enamel *tesserae* and an artist. Before Christianity, mosaics were a favourite Roman medium for floors only. Some reached the level of fine art (examples are in the Naples museum, or the great villa at Piazza Armerina, Sicily), but more often the productions were on the level of the famous 'Beware of the dog' mosaic in Pompeii. It was the early Christians, with a desire to build for the ages and a body of scriptures that could best be related pictorially, who made mosaics the new medium of public wall art in the 6th century. Mostly it was an affair of the Greeks, who still had the talent and the resources for it; and it's most likely that Greek artists from the court of Constantinople created the mosaics in the churches and baptistries of Ravenna.

Western Christian art was born here, developing from the simple images—the Good Shepherd and the Cross and Stars—to the iconic Christ in Sant'Apollinare Nuovo and the beautiful scriptural scenes in San Vitale. Never, though, did the early mosaicists turn their back on the idea of art; with the ideals of the ancient world still in their minds, they naturally thought of art and religion as going hand in hand, and found no problem in serving the cause of both. Using a new vocabulary of images and the new techniques of mosaic art, they strove to duplicate, and surpass, the sense of awe and mystery still half-remembered from the interiors of the pagan temples. Try to imagine a church like San Vitale in its original state, with candles—lots of candles—flickering below the gold ground and gorgeous colours. You may see that same light that enchanted the Byzantines—the light of the Gospels, the light from beyond the stars.

Mausoleo di Galla Placidia

Same hours as S. Vitale.

This small chapel, set in the grounds of San Vitale and originally attached to the neighbouring church of Santa Croce, never really held the tomb of Ravenna's great patroness—she is buried near St Peter's in Rome, and it's anyone's guess who occupies the three huge stone sarcophagi, traditionally the resting places of Galla Placidia and two emperors, her second husband Constantius III and her son Valentinian. Galla Placidia did construct the chapel, a small, gabled and cross-shaped building that is almost 7ft shorter than when it was built; the ground level has risen that much in 1400 years.

The simplicity of the brick exterior, as in San Vitale, makes the brilliant mosaics within that much more of a surprise. The only natural light inside comes from a few tiny slits of windows, made of thin sheets of alabaster. The two important mosaics, on lunettes at opposite ends of the chapel, are coloured as richly as San Vitale. One represents St Lawrence, with his flaming gridiron; the other is a beautiful and typical early Christian portrait of Jesus as the Good Shepherd, a beardless, classical-looking figure in a fine cloak and sandals, stroking one of the flock. On the lunettes of the cross-axis, pairs of stags come to drink at the fountain of life; around all four lunettes, floral arabesques and maze patterns in bright colours cover the arches and ceilings.

Everything in the design betrays as much of the classical Roman style as the nascent Christian, and the unusual figures on the arches holding up the central vault seem hardly out of place. They are SS. Peter and Paul, dressed in togas and standing with outstretched hands in the conventional pose of Roman senators.

The vault itself, a deep blue firmament glowing with hundreds of dazzling golden stars set in concentric circles, is the mausoleum's most remarkable feature. In the centre, at the top of the vault, a golden cross represents the unimaginable, transcendent God above the heavens. At the corners, symbols of the four evangelists provide an insight into the origins of Christian iconography. Mark's lion, Luke's ox and Matthew's man occupy the places in this sky where you would expect the constellations of the lion, the bull and Aquarius, 90 degrees apart along the zodiac. For the fourth corner, instead of the objectionable scorpion (or serpent, as it often appeared in ancient times) the early Christians substituted the eagle of St John.

The Museo Nazionale

The medieval and Baroque cloisters attached to San Vitale now house the large collection of antiquities found in Ravenna and Classis (*open Tues–Sat 8.30–7, Sun 8.30–10pm; adm*). There's a little bit of everything: good Roman plumbing, a boy's linen shirt from the 6th century, and no end of coins and broken pots. The well-labelled coin collection is interesting even to the non-specialist, providing a picture history of Italy from Classical times into the early Middle Ages. Exceptional works of art include the 6th-century Byzantine carved screens, and a possibly unique sculpture of Hercules capturing the Cerynean hind. This, too, is from the 6th century, perhaps the last piece of art made in ancient times with a classical subject, possibly a copy of an earlier Greek work. Lovely, intricately carved ivory chests and plaques from the Middle Ages and Renaissance, with charming tableaux of medieval scenes such as tournaments and banquets, fill an entire room. To understand Ravenna and its buildings better, be sure to see the fascinating architectural models of the Neonian Baptistry (*see* below).

Ravenna's Centre

Piazza del Popolo at the centre of Ravenna was built by the Venetians during their brief period of rule, along with the twin columns bearing statues of Ravenna's two patrons, San Vitale and Sant'Apollinare. A little way south, off porticoed **Piazza San Francesco**, a modest neoclassical pavilion was built in the 18th century over the **tomb of Dante**. Ravenna is proud of having sheltered the storm-tossed poet in his last years, and the city will gently remind you of it in its street names, its tourist brochures, its Teatro Alighieri and its frequent artistic competitions based on themes from the *Divina Commedia*. Coming here may help explain just what Dante means to Italy; in all the country's more recent wars, for example, soldiers have come here for little rituals to 'dedicate their sacrifice' to the poet's memory. Today there are always wreaths or bouquets from organizations of all kinds and private citizens from all over Italy. Beside the tomb is the **Museo Dantesco** (*open Tues–Sun 9–12; adm; free on Sun*), with a collection of paintings, sculptures and books connected with the poet. Behind the tomb, the church of **San Francesco** was founded in the 5th century but rebuilt in the 11th and thoroughly baroqued in the 1700s. Greek marble columns and a fine 4th-century altar survive, and in the church itself and the Braccioforte oratory (behind the iron gate, by Dante's tomb) are fine early Christian sarcophagi, one familiarly called the 'Tomb of Elijah'.

North of Piazza del Popolo, Ravenna has a fine example of a medieval leaning tower: the tall, 12th-century **Torre Pubblica**, now supported by steel struts. This one seems good evidence for those who believe such things to be intentional. Despite the angle of the tower, the windows near the top were built perfectly level. Byron lived in nearby Via Cavour during his affair with Countess Teresa Guiccioli; his home now houses the Carabinieri. In a little square between Via Paolo Costa and Via Armando Diaz, the **Arian Baptistry** (*Battistero degli Ariani*) (*open summer daily 8.30–6; winter daily 8.30–6; adm*) recalls church struggles of the 6th century. Theodoric and his Ostrogoths, like most of the Germanic peoples, adhered to the Arian heresy, a doctrine that mixed in elements of pagan religion and was condemned by more orthodox Christians as denying the absolute divinity of Christ. Like all heresies, this one is really the story of a political struggle, between the Gothic kings and the emperor in Constantinople. Unlike Justinian, a great persecutor, the Goths tolerated both faiths; the baptistry belonged to the adjacent Santo Spirito church (rebuilt in the 16th century), once the Arians' cathedral, while the Athenasians (orthodox) worshipped at what is now the cathedral of Ravenna. The Arian Baptistry preserves a fine mosaic ceiling, with the 12 Apostles arranged around a scene of the Baptism of Jesus. The old man with the palm branch, across from John the Baptist, represents the River Jordan.

There is another leaning tower—an even tipsier one—nearby on Viale Farini, two streets up from the railway station. It is the 12th-century campanile of **San Giovanni Evangelista**, a much-altered church that was begun by Galla Placidia in 425. Bombings in the last War destroyed the apse, with its original mosaics, but some parts of the 13th-century mosaic floor, with scenes of the Fourth Crusade and some fantastical monsters, can be seen in the aisles.

Sant'Apollinare Nuovo

Open summer daily 9.30–7; winter daily 9.30–6; Mar and Oct daily 9.30–4.30; adm.

After those of San Vitale, the mosaics of this 6th-century church are the finest in Ravenna. Theodoric built it, and after the Byzantine conquest and the suppression of Arianism it was re-dedicated to St Martin, another famous persecutor of heretics. The present name comes from the 9th century, when the remains of Sant'Apollinare were moved here from the old Sant'Apollinare in Classe. The tall, cylindrical campanile, a style that is a trademark of Ravenna's churches, was added in the 10th century.

Unlike San Vitale, Sant'Apollinare was built in the basilica form, with a long nave and side aisles. The two rows of Greek marble columns were probably recycled from an ancient temple. Above them are the mosaics on panels that stretch the length of the church. On the left, by the door, you see the city of Classe, with ships in the protected harbour between twin beacons, and the monuments of the city rearing up behind its walls. On the right, among the monuments of Ravenna, is the Palatium, Theodoric's royal palace. The curtains in the archways of the palace cover painted-over Gothic notables and probably Theodoric himself, effaced by the Byzantines. Beyond these two urban scenes are processions of martyrs bearing crowns: 22 ladies on the left side, 26 men on the right. The female procession is led by colourful, remarkable portraits of the Magi (officially enrolled as Saints of the Church, according to the inscription above), offering their gifts to the enthroned Virgin Mary. Above these panels, more mosaics portray Old Testament prophets and doctors of the Church, as well as scenes from the life of Jesus. These mosaics, smaller and not as well executed, are from Theodoric's time. Next to Sant'Apollinare are the remains of the 6th-century building traditionally called the **Palace of Theodoric** (*open summer daily 8.30–7; winter 8.30–5*). More likely this was a later governmental building of some sort; it may have been the palace of the Byzantine exarchs. Inside its tower there is a display of mosaics discovered while excavating the area.

The Battistero Neoniano and the Museo Arcivescovile

Open summer daily 9–7; winter daily 9.30–4.30; Mar and Oct daily 9.30–5.30; adm.

An earthquake in 1733 wrecked Ravenna's **cathedral**, west of Piazza del Popolo, and there's little to see in the replacement but another round medieval tower. Somehow the disaster spared the 'Orthodox' or **Neonian Baptistry**, named after the 5th-century bishop Neon who commissioned its splendid mosaics. A modern Ravenna architect named Raffaello Trinci has added glass cross-sections, which elaborate the proportions and geometrical theory behind the Byzantines' 'new' architecture of the 6th century, a recasting of ancient sacred geometry that was to have a great influence on the cathedral builders of the Middle Ages. Unlike the Arian Baptistry, here almost the entire decoration has survived: a scene of the Baptism of Jesus and portraits of the 12 Apostles on the ceiling under the dome, while below the eight walls bear four altars and four empty thrones. The *etimasia*, the preparing of the Throne for Jesus for the Last Judgement, is an odd bit of Byzantine mysticism; interestingly enough, classical Greek art often depicts an empty throne as a symbol for Zeus, only with a pair of thunderbolts instead of a cross. In the 1500 years since its construction the ground level here has risen over 10ft—so has the baptistry's floor. In the side niches are a 6th-century Byzantine altar and a huge, thoroughly pagan marble vase. The 13th-century marble font is big enough for the immersion baptism of adults.

The **Archiepiscopal Museum**, behind the cathedral, comes as a real surprise. Its little-known treasures include the ivory throne of Bishop Maximian, a masterpiece of 6th-century sculpture thought to have been a gift from Emperor Justinian, and an 11th-century reliquary, the silver 'Cross of Sant'Agnello'. Among the fragments of sculpture and mosaics are works saved from the original cathedral. The large marble disc by the wall, divided into 19 sections, is an episcopal calendar, regulated to the 19-year Julian cycle to allow Ravenna's medieval bishops to calculate the date of Easter and other holy days.

The biggest surprise, however, is finding that the nondescript Archbishop's Palace in which the museum is located is, in parts, as old as anything in Ravenna. A little door at the back leads to a small chapel called the **Oratorio di Sant'Andrea**, built around 500 during the reign of Theodoric. The mosaics on the vaults are among Ravenna's best: in the antechamber a fanciful scene of multicoloured birds and flowers, and an unusual warrior Christ in full Roman armour and wielding the cross like a sword, treading a lion and snake underfoot. In the chapel itself, four angels and the four evangelists' symbols surround Christ's monogram on the dome, and the apse bears a beautiful starry sky around a golden cross, like the one at the Galla Placidia mausoleum. The best mosaics, however, are the excellent portraits of saints decorating the arches. Early Christian representations of the saints are often much stronger than the pale, conventional figures of later art. Such portraits as these betray a fascination with the personalities and the psychology of saints; such figures as St Felicitas or St Ursicinus may be forgotten now, but to the early Christians they were not mere holy myths, but near contemporaries, the spiritual heroes and heroines responsible for the miraculous growth of Christianity, the exemplars of a new age and a new way of life.

Mausoleo Teodorico

Via Cimitero, near the industrial zone; open summer 8.30–7; winter 8.30–6; adm.

For the real flavour of the days of the Roman twilight, nothing can beat this compellingly strange, sophisticated yet half-barbaric building outside the old city. To reach it, walk north from the railway station, past the new port and the Venetian fortress called the **Rocca di Brancaleone**, which now has a park inside. Theodoric's tomb, perhaps the only regular 10-sided building in Italy, is in another small park. Downstairs, there is a cross-shaped chamber of unknown purpose. The second storey, also decagonal though smaller, contains the porphyry sarcophagus, now empty. It is a comment on the times that scholars believe this is a recycled bathtub from a Roman palace..Theodoric was hardly broke, though; he could afford to bring the stone for his tomb over from Istria—and note the roof, a single slab of stone weighing over 300 tons. No one has yet explained how the Goths brought it here and raised it—or why.

Classe

If you have the time, there is another important monument to Ravenna's golden age to be seen at the ruins of Classe, 5km from town; any local train towards Rimini or the regular bus service can take you there. Sant'Apollinare in Classe, in fact, is literally all that remains of what was once the leading port of the northern Adriatic. The little River Uniti began to silt up Classe's harbour in classical times; when the port ceased to be a Roman military base and the funds for yearly dredging were no longer there, the city's fate was sealed. By the 9th century Classe was abandoned. The people of Ravenna carted away most of its stone and encroaching forests and swamps erased the rest. Today the former port is good farmland, 6km from the sea.

Sant'Apollinare *(open daily 9–12 and 2–6)*, a huge basilica-form church completed in 549, survives only because of its importance as the burial place of Ravenna's patron. The exterior, in plain brick, is another finely proportioned example of Ravenna's pre-Romanesque, with another tall cylindrical campanile. Inside it's almost empty, with only a few early-Christian sarcophagi lining the walls. The beautiful Greek marble columns have well-carved capitals in a unique style. Above them are 18th-century portraits of all Ravenna's bishops—important to this city where for centuries the bishops defended local autonomy against emperors, exarchs and popes.

The real attraction, however, is the mosaics in the apse, an impressive green-and-gold ground allegorical vision of the **Transfiguration of Christ**, in a flower-strewn Mediterranean landscape, with Sant'Apollinare in attendance and three sheep representing Peter, James and John, who were with Christ on Mount Tabor. As at San Vitale, there are scenes of the sacrifices of Abel, Melchizedek and Abraham, opposite a mosaic of the Byzantine Emperor Constantine IV bestowing privileges on Ravenna's independent church. Archangels Gabriel and Michael appear in Byzantine court dress, under a pair of palm trees, the 'tree of life'.

Elsewhere around Classe there's little to see; bits of Roman road, pine groves, some foundations. Excavations began only in 1961, and continue today. Sant'Apollinare is near the centre of an immense necropolis with some half-million burials. Some interesting things could turn up here in coming years (*visiting hours at the excavations, daily 9am–dusk*).

Activities

The **Ravenna Festival** is an important music festival which runs from mid-June to mid-July. Internationally renowned musicians perform concerts, recitals and opera in some of the city's historic churches and palaces. For information call, ✆ 0544 32577.

Ravenna ✉ 48100   ## Where to Stay and Eating Out

At the top of the list, on a quiet street near San Vitale, ★★★★**Bisanzio**, Via Salaria 30, ✆ 0544 217 111, 🖷 0544 32539 (*expensive*) is modern, luxurious and serene, with only 36 rooms. ★★★**Diana**, Via G. Rossi 4, ✆ 0544 39164, 🖷 0544 30001 (*moderate*) is a comfortable hotel with all mod cons in every room. Ageing gracefully,★★★**Centrale Byron**, Via IV Novembre 14, just off Piazza del Popolo, ✆ 0544 33479, 🖷 0544 551 070 (*moderate*) has some very nice rooms and some very plain ones. Despite appearances Byron never lived here. ★★★**Columbia**, Viale Italia 70, ✆ 0544 446 038, 🖷 0544 447 202 (*moderate*) is a beautiful modern hotel in attractive Marina Romea, to the north and a little way out of the city—but like all the places here it's a 10-minute walk from the beach.

Ravenna has plenty of budget rooms but most are around the port, a long walk from the centre along Via delle Industrie. In a more convenient, if not particularly pleasant, location is ★★★**Roma**, Via Candiano 26, ✆ 0544 421 515, 🖷 0544 420 505 (*cheap*), by the railway station. A nicer option is ★**Al Giaciglio**, Via Rocca Brancaleone 42, ✆ 0544 39403 (*cheap*). The restaurant serves good home cooking, using only fresh ingredients, and offers a *cheap* lunch menu that changes daily. If you wish to loll on the beach after a day perusing the mosaics, there's a bargain on the Lido at Classe: ★★★**Adler**, Viale Caboto 121, ✆ 0544 939 216, 🖷 0544 939 222 (*cheap*), with a pool and private beach. The **youth hostel**, Via Nicolodi 12, ✆ 0544 420 405, is, again, on the east side of the tracks, a 10-minute walk down Via Candiano from the station (or take bus no.1). *Open Mar–Oct.*

Ravenna is dull after dark, but does harbour some good restaurants. At **Tre Spade**, Via Faentina 136, ✆ 0544 500 522 (*expensive*), in the suburbs west of the centre, they like to innovate and never miss a step. Most of Ravenna comes here for the seafood, but you can be adventurous and try the vegetable/pastry concoctions, stuffed pigeon or some pasta combinations never seen before on this planet. *Closed Sun eve, Mon* *and Aug*. **La Gardela**, Via Ponte Marino 3, ✆ 0544 21714 (*moderate*) is small and air-conditioned, and makes its own tortelloni; follow it with scaloppine with taleggio and rocket, and sample their large collection of grappas. *Closed Thurs*. In the same area, in a beautiful building with painted ceilings, **Ca' de Ven**, Via Corrado Ricci 24 (*moderate*) is an *enoteca* with a huge selection of Emilia-Romagna wines and snacks. Suitably calm and dark, it's a great local favourite, the perfect place to while away an afternoon after a morning with the Byzantines.

Near S. Vitale, **Taverna San Romualdo**, Via S. Alberto 364, ✆ 0544 483 447 (*moderate*), is a typical rustic Romagnolo *osteria* which serves hearty dishes and is excellent value for dishes such as *tortellacci* stuffed with nettles and served with mascarpone and pine nuts, minestrone flavoured with truffles, octopus stewed in balsamic vinegar and served tepid with rocket and cannellini beans, and nougat *semi-freddo* with chocolate sauce. *Closed Tues*. **Renato Guidarello**, with entrances at both Via Mentana 33, and Via Gessi 9, ✆ 0544 213 684 (*cheap*) has a pleasant, traditional atmosphere and local cuisine, with fish still the main item every Friday. For a light lunch, try the elegant **Caffè del Teatro**, Via Mariani 1. *Closed Sun*.

The Adriatic Riviera

From Ravenna and Classe the long stretch of small resorts that began at Comacchio straggles on towards the beach-Babylon of Rimini. These tiny lidos are slow-paced, if packed with Bolognese families in the summer. Those nearest Ravenna suffer somewhat from industrial pollution, but there has been a big effort to keep the beaches clean. **Marina Romea**, a spit of land with a broad beach and a pine forest, is perhaps the nicest; all are an easy day's outing from Ravenna. The first big centre on the coast is **Cervia-Milano Marittima**, the next, **Cesenatico**, was built around a pretty, canal-like harbour designed for Cesare Borgia in 1502 by Leonardo da Vinci. The **Museo della Mariniera** in the harbour itself is a floating maritime museum, a display of the traditional fishing and trading boats used in the northern Adriatic.

Rimini

At first glance Italy's biggest resort may strike you as strictly cold potatoes, a full 15km of peeling skin and pizza, serenaded by the portable radios of ten thousand teenagers and the eternal whines and giggles of their little brothers and sisters. To many Italians, however, Rimini means pure sweaty-palmed excitement. In the sixties, following the grand old Italian pastime of *caccia alle svedesi*, a staple of the national film industry was the Rimini holiday movie, in which a bumbling protagonist with glasses was swept off his feet by some incredible Nordic goddess, who was as bouncy as she was adventurous. After many complications, embarrassing both for the audience and the actors, it could all lead to true love.

For the bumbling protagonists of real life, whether from Milan or Munich, all this may only be wishful thinking but they still come in their millions each year. As a resort Rimini has its advantages. Noisy as it is, it's a respectable, family place, relatively cheap for northern Italy, convenient and well organized. Also, tucked away behind the beachfront is a genuine old city, dishevelled, damaged in the Second World War, but inviting, and offering one first-rate Renaissance attraction.

Getting Around

On this stretch of coast, the FS Adriatic **rail** line works almost like a tram service, with lots of trains and stops near the beaches in all the resorts. In summer there are regular flights from Milan and countless foreign charters to Rimini's little **airport**, behind the beaches at Miramare. Rimini city **buses** run regularly in summer. A 24-hour 'Orange Ticket' is available, giving unlimited travel within Rimini and between Bellaria and Riccione. From Rimini Station, on Piazzale Cesare Battisti, there are buses to nearby towns (10 a day to San Marino—14 in summer). For **taxis**, call ✆ 0541 50020. Cultural day-trippers who shudder at Rimini's beach madness can dip in easily—the Tempio Malatesta is only a 10-minute walk from the station.

Tourist Information

In summer Rimini and its 'burbs have as many information offices as ice-cream stands. The main ones are at Piazzale C. Battisti, next to the station, ✆ 0541 51331, and on the beach at Piazza Fellini 3, ✆ 0541 56902, ✆ 0541 56598. Next to both you'll find the **Promozione Alberghiera**, the local accommodation service (*see* below).

The Tempio Malatestiano

Open daily 7–12 and 3.30–7; winter till 6.

Sigismondo Malatesta ('Headache'), tyrant of Rimini, went into the books as one bad hombre. According to Jakob Burckhardt, 'the verdict of history...convicts him of murder, rape, adultery, incest, sacrilege, perjury, and treason, committed not once, but often.' The historian adds that his frequent attempts on the virtue of his children, both male and female, may have resulted from 'some astrological superstition'. In 1462 Pope Pius II accorded him a unique honour—a canonization to Hell. The Pope, who was behind most of the accusations, can be excused a little exaggeration. He wanted Sigismondo's land, and resorted to invoking supernatural aid when he couldn't beat him at war. Modern historians give Sigismondo better reviews, finding him on the whole no more pagan and perverse than the average Renaissance duke, and less so than many popes. The family had ruled at Rimini since the 1300s—ironically it was a pope who first put them in business. Early dukes, like Malatesta 'Guastafamiglia' ('Destroyer of Families') were hard men, and good role models for Sigismondo, but they succeeded for a time in spreading their rule as far as Cesena and Fano. By Sigismondo's time, money and allies were suddenly lacking, and the family was deposed by the unspeakable Alexander VI in 1500.

The shortage of funds was also responsible for the abandonment in 1461 of Sigismondo's personal monument, the eclectic and thoroughly mysterious work that has come to be known as the Malatesta Temple. Whatever Sigismondo's personal habits, he was a learned man and a good judge of art. To transform this unfinished 13th-century Franciscan church into his Temple he called in Leon Battista Alberti to redesign the exterior and Agostino di Duccio for the reliefs inside. Scholars have been puzzling for centuries over Sigismondo's intentions. Although the temple has been Rimini's cathedral since 1809 it is hardly a Christian building, full of undecipherable sculptural allegories with everywhere the entwined monograms of Sigismondo and his wife Isotta degli Atti; in part it seems a tribute to this famous lady, who is buried here along with Sigismondo.

Alberti's unfinished exterior, grafting Roman arcades and pilasters on to the plain Franciscan building, grievously feels the lack of the planned cupola that might have tied it all together. The big arches on the sides were meant to hold sarcophagi of Rimini's notable men; only a few were ever used. Inside these arches, four pairs of chapels hold the **sculptural reliefs** made by Agostino—among the greatest works of the Renaissance. These low reliefs, on blue backgrounds like a della Robbia cameo, depict angels and child musicians, the Arts and Sciences, St Michael, putti, Sigismondo himself and the Triumph of Scipio. Some of the best are the allegorical panels of the planets and signs of the zodiac; note especially the enchanting *Moon*, Cynthia in her silver car, and a scene of 15th-century Rimini beneath the claws of the Crab. Among the other works in the Temple are a fresco by Piero della Francesca of Sigismondo and his patron, St Sigismund of Burgundy, and a painted crucifix by Giotto. The tombs of Sigismondo and Isotta, with their strange device (the omnipresent monograms S and I together like a dollar sign) and elephants (the Malatesta heraldic symbol) are also fine works.

Old Rimini was the home town of the late Federico Fellini, and you may recognize some of the street scenes from *Amarcord*. Some ruins survive as reminders of Roman *Arminium*, a thriving Adriatic port and a rival to Classe: the foundation of an amphitheatre near the southern walls, and the **Arco di Augusto** in the southern gate near the post office. This arch marked the meeting of the Via Aemilia and the Via Flaminia. The Roman high street, the *cardo*, is now called Corso di Augusto; from here it passes through central **Piazza Tre Martiri**—which retains some arcades in the shop fronts from the days when it was the Roman forum—and continues on to the north gate and the five-arched **Bridge of Tiberius** (AD 21), badly patched up after damage in the Greek-Gothic wars.

A few streets further over the bridge, the church of **San Giuliano** contains a painting of that saint's martyrdom, Paolo Veronese's last work. From here towards the sea, along the river-bank, stretches Rimini's colourful fishing port. Back at the centre, on Piazza Cavour, the **Palazzo del'Arengo** has been Rimini's town hall since 1207; it faces the bulky castle of the Malatestas, the Rocca Sigismondo, which now houses the **Museo delle Culture Extraeuropee** (*open Mon–Fri 8–1, Tues and Thurs also 3–6*), with ancient and folk art from Africa, Asia and the Americas. Two streets away, the **Museo Comunale**, Via Gambalunga 27 (*open Mon–Fri 8–1, Tues and Thurs 8–1 and 3–6, Sat 8.30–12.30, Sun 3–6*) has Roman mosaics and paintings by Ghirlandaio and Giovanni Bellini.

Some Beach Statistics

Rimini is not the place for those who want to be alone.

tourist brochure

The subject makes Rimini's holiday barons and the hotel consortium mildly uneasy. 'There's room for everybody,' they say, and in a way they're right. The resort has 15km of broad beaches, and about 1600 hotels with some 55,000 rooms. At the usual resort ratio, that means about 85,000 beds. It could be a problem in the really busy season. If all the beds are full—plus another 25,000 day-trippers, campers and holiday apartment tenants—that makes 110,000 souls, or 7333 per kilometre of beach front. There are plenty of other things to do in Rimini, fortunately, but with only 5½inches of shore per bum, if everyone tries to hit the water at the same time the results could be catastrophic.

This really need never happen. Many of these people at any given time will be in Rimini's 751 bars, 343 restaurants, 70 dance halls and discos, 49 cinemas, or three miniature golf courses, or at one of the many sailing and wind-surfing schools, or the dolphin show (on the beach near the port). Other attractions include **Fiabilandia**, an amusement park for the little ones, with a Mississippi riverboat, a Fort Apache and the genuine King Kong (on SS16 south of Rimini; bus no.8 and no.9 go there). North of town there's **Italia in Miniatura** which, besides mouse-sized cathedrals and castles, offers you performing bears, go-carts and 'bumper boats' (on the coast road, towards Viserba), and there are long water-slides to be found at Riccione.

More Beaches

Holiday madness continues through the string of resorts south of Rimini. **Riccione**, **Misano Adriatico**, **Cattolica** and **Gabicce Mare** are all huge places, and in the summer they can be as crowded and intense as Rimini itself. None of them have any particular charm, and it's hard to tell one from another—they're really more or less suburban extensions of Rimini; Riccione has the aura of fashion, if you want to keep up with the Italians. The Adriatic Riviera begins to fade when the wide beaches of the Romagna give way to the more rugged coast of the Marche, but soon picks up again when the hills recede (to continue this route, *see* p.500).

Rimini ✉ *47900*　　　　　　　　　　　　　　　　*Where to Stay and Eating Out*

A holiday in Rimini usually means a standard package. Expect a pleasant, unimaginatively furnished room with a balcony; in the high-season you'll probably have to take half-board. You may as well take pot luck by calling on the local hoteliers' association, the **Promozione Alberghiera**, Piazza Tripoli, ✆ 0541 390 530, or in the railway station, Piazzale Fellini 3, ✆ 0541 53399, and let them find you a vacancy. You do not come to Rimini for scenery, charming inns or fine cuisine, but to join the crowd and seek out endless fun. If that sounds good, make sure to get a place in the centre where the action is. Tell them precisely what you want and they'll find it for you. They do not cover all hotels; those mentioned below are not on their list, but are close to the beach and the town.

An old-fashioned Grand Hotel might seem out of place in Rimini, but there's one in the centre—the ★★★★★**Grand Hotel**, Via Ramusio 1, ✆ 0541 56000, ✉ 0541 56866 (*luxury*), on Parco dell'Indipendenza at Marina Centro. This turn-of-the-century palace helped make Rimini what it is today, and its rooms are almost indecently luxurious, all the brass well-polished, and the chandeliers well-dusted. It's the only hotel in Rimini with its own dance orchestra, as well as a pool, a private beach, and nice gardens.

★★★★**Ambasciatori**, Viale Amerigo Vespucci 22, ✆ 0541 55561, ✉ 0541 23790 (*expensive*), just back from the sea, is a splashy modern building with a private beach, designed to attract a youngish crowd. The ★★★**Admiral**, Via R. Elena 67, ✆ 0541 381 771, ✉ 0541 389 562 (*moderate*) is another sharp ultra-modern palace, with a rooftop terrace and spacious balconies for most rooms. ★★★**Apogeo**, Via Oriani 10, ✆ 0541 381 366 (*moderate*) has a small swimming pool. Of the hundreds in the *cheap* bracket, ★★**Primavera**, Viale Lagomaggio 113, ✆ 0541 380 206, and ★★**Pensione Primula**, Viale Trento 12, ✆ 0541 23712, are both in a good position with comfortable rooms. The **youth hostel**, Via Flaminia 300, ✆ 0541 373 216, is south of Rimini in Miramare (bus no.124). IYHF cards are required and reservations are virtually always necessary. *Open May–Sept.*

When it comes to restaurants, there's nothing to complain about (this is still Emilia-Romagna, after all). **Lo Squero**, Lungomare Tintori 7, ✆ 0541 27676 (*expensive*), near the Grand Hotel, has an outdoor terrace overlooking the beach: shellfish are a speciality. *Closed Tues.* **Taverna degli Artisti**, Viale Vespucci 1, ✆ 0541 28519, (*expensive*), with its colourful menu, is also best known for seafood, along with some imaginative light pasta openers and something unexpected—a little *degustazione* of whisky; they have almost every brand from around the world.

In the old town, **Dallo Zio**, Via S. Chiara 16, ✆ 0541 786 160 (*moderate*) is an excellent seafood palace that's very popular with locals and tourists alike, offering marine lasagna, fishy vol-au-vent and other surprises. *Closed Wed.* Near Piazza Malatesta, **Osteria di Santa Colomba**, Via Agostino di Duccio 2, ✆ 0541 780 048 (*moderate*) is an old favourite (they say Napoleon slept here), with simple traditional fare—the best possible antidote to the cosmopolitanism of beach Rimini may be a plate of pasta with chickpeas. *Open dinner only; closed Sun.*

Osteria de Borg, Via Forzieri 12, ✆ 0541 56074 (*cheap*), in the San Giuliano area, serves imaginative dishes—good soups, *tortellini* stuffed with carrot, or *strozzapreti* with broccoli and spicy sausage. **Pic-Nic**, Via Tempio Malatestiano 30, ✆ 0541 21916 (*cheap*) owes everything to cosmopolitanism, with an eclectic range of pizza—*noisy pizza, atomic pizza*, pizza with roast beef (*all'Inglese*)—and goulash. *Closed Mon.* Along the seafront several thousand more pizzerias will try and tempt you; try **Rimini Key**, Piazzale B. Croce (*cheap*), for good-value pizza and set menus.

Entertainment and Nightlife

music, theatre and cinema

For listings, pick up the tourist office's *Instantaneo*. In season art exhibitions cater for rainy days, and the city of Fellini also hosts a continual series of cinema events—themed festivals, cartoon seasons and open-air extravaganzas—centred on the semi-official Rimini Film Festival in September. In late summer and autumn Rimini stages the **Sagra Musicale Malatestina**, a festival of classical music (information, ✆ 0541 26239). The nearby town of Santarcangelo holds an annual **theatre festival** in July, with dynamic, innovative work (information, ✆ 0541 626 185).

clubs and discos

Rimini and its even-more-in-vogue neighbour Riccione make up the undisputed clubland capital of Italy, a magnet for ravers from all over Italy and abroad. On summer weekends crowds descend from all the cities within a 200km radius, and on mornings-after the road back to Bologna is often scattered with the battered cars of partygoers who didn't make it home. For listings and information on clubs, one-nighters and anything else coming up, check *Il Resto del Carlino* and the magazine *Chiamami Città*, or search for posters.

The main place for cruising the clubs is along the seafront, from about 10pm onwards, though there's also another little knot of activity away from the beach in Covignano. If you get fed up with walking, a night bus runs along the length of the seafront between Riccione and Bellaria, and to Covignano.

Of the Riviera's best-established and most popular clubs, **Pascià**, Via Sardegna 30, Riccione, is a large, stylish venue offering a bouncy mix of house, techno and other Euro-dance sounds. The most fashionable club of all is **Paradiso**, Via Covignano 260, with a regular diet of Euro-dance but also special events every week involving visiting DJs, performances and the gamut of musical styles. Also in Covignano an open-air rave, **Bandiera Gialla**, is held every weekend in summer.

San Marino

As a perfect counterpart to the sand-strewn fun fair of Rimini, just 23km inland you may visit the world's only sovereign and independent roadside attraction. Before Rimini became the Italian Miami Beach, the 26,000 citizens of San Marino had to make a living peddling postage stamps. Now, with their medieval streets crowded with day-trippers, the San Marinese have been unable to resist the temptation to order some bright medieval costumes, polish up their picturesque mountain villages, and open up some souvenir stands and 'duty free' shops. Their famous stamps, though nothing like the engraved numbers of 40 years ago, are still prized by collectors, and recently the country has begun to mint its own coins again after a lapse of 39 years; nevertheless the citizens of San Marino, who may just have the highest average income in Europe, still make their living almost entirely from tourism.

Getting Around

There are frequent buses to San Marino from Rimini.

Tourist Information

San Marino town: Contrado Omagnano 20, ✆/📠 0549 882 412.

The World's Smallest Republic

Also the oldest republic. According to legend San Marino was founded as a Christian settlement on the slopes of Monte Titano by a stonecutter named Marinus, fleeing from the persecutions of Diocletian in the early 4th century. 'Overlooked', as the San Marinese charmingly put it, by the empire and various states that followed it, the little community had the peace and quiet to evolve its medieval democratic institutions; its constitution in its present form dates from 1243 when the first pair of 'consuls' was elected by a popular assembly. The consuls are now called Captains Regent, but little else has changed in 700 years.

Twice, in 1503 and 1739, the Republic was invaded by papal forces, and independence was preserved only by a little good luck. Napoleon, passing through in 1797, found San Marino amusing and half-seriously offered to enlarge its boundaries, a proposal that was politely declined. Garibaldi, fleeing from Rome after the end of the nationalist revolt of 1849, sought refuge here and was allowed in, though the Republic, jittery at the approach of an Austrian army, kicked him out before dawn the next morning. It redeemed itself by becoming an island of peace and taking in thousands of refugees in the Second World War.

Entering San Marino from Rimini at the hamlet called Dogana (though there are no border formalities now), you pass through a string of villages in a green and pretty countryside. San Marino, no midget like the Vatican City, is all of 12km long at its widest extent. At the foot of Monte Titano, rising dramatically above the plain, is **Borgomaggiore**, the largest town, with a cablecar up to the capital and citadel of the republic, also called **San Marino**. Here, among medieval streets, are wonderful views over Rimini and the coast. Nothing is really as old as it looks; the **Palazzo del Governo**, full of Ruritanian guardsmen, is a reconstruction of 1894. Here the Grand Council meets and the Captains Regent have their offices. Some new museums have been conjured up for the tourists—Stamp and Coins, Garibaldi, Weaponry, Wax and torture instruments—but the best thing to do is walk through Monte Titano's forests to the three (rebuilt) medieval **tower fortresses** on the three peaks that give San Marino its famous silhouette; famous to philatelists anyhow, and long the symbol of the republic.

Around San Marino

Two other mountain towns near San Marino are most easily visited from Rimini: **Verucchio** is a pleasant medieval village that retains some of its gates and churches, as well as a 10th-century fortress that became the stronghold of the tyrants of Rimini, the **Rocca Malatesta**. There is a small **Museo Archeologico** at the lower end of town, with unusual ceramics from the 1400 BC Villanova culture.

San Leo, on the western side of San Marino (actually in the Marche), according to legend, was founded by a companion of Marinus, but lost its independence long ago. The rough-walled, 9th-century church called the **Pieve** is worth a look, but San Leo's real attraction is the **castle**, built for the Montefeltro dukes in the 15th century. Like their palace at Urbino, this fortress is a perfect representative building of the Renaissance: balanced, finely proportioned in its lines, a building of intelligence and style—hung on a breathtakingly sheer cliff. Once this mountain held a temple of Jupiter; as *Mons Feretrius* (referring to Jove's lightning) it gave its name to the Montefeltro. A later fortress on this site was briefly 'capital of Italy' in the 960s, during the reign of King Berengar II. The current one, long used as a papal Alcatraz, hosted the 18th-century confidence man Cagliostro for four years, when the pope commuted his death sentence for heresy to life imprisonment in conditions that drove him mad. Now the castle has a small picture gallery and Cagliostro memorabilia.

San Marino ✉ *47031* **Where to Stay and Eating Out**

Italian currency is valid everywhere, but make sure you don't get too many San Marino coins in change; once you get back to Italy they will only be good for souvenirs. On San Marino's citadel, in the middle of the old town, ★★★★**Titano**, Contrada del Collegio 21, ✆ 0549 991 006, ✉ 0549 991 375 (*moderate*) is a restored century-old building where half the rooms have great views over the countryside. Not far away, ★★★**La Rocca**, on Salita alla Rocca, ✆ 0549 991 166 (*cheap*) has a TV in each of its 10 rooms, a pool, and balconies with good views.

The best restaurant in the centre can be found snuggling up to the Hotel Titano. **Buca San Francesco**, Piazzetta Placito Feretrano, ✆ 0549 991 462 (*moderate*) has nothing out of the ordinary, but its soups, tortellini and *scallopine alla sanmarinese* are good. Of the many cheaper restaurants in the town, the best is probably the **Trattoria Panoramica**, on Salita alla Rocca, ✆ 0549 992 305 (*moderate*), with an outdoor terrace overlooking San Marino and the surrounding hills.

Le Marche

A *march*, or *mark*, in the Middle Ages meant a border province of the Holy Roman Empire, usually an unsettled frontier held by one of the Emperor's fighting barons. With no better name than that, one might expect this Italian region to be somewhat lacking in personality. In fact, this has always been the odd bit of central Italy. In ancient times it was also a border zone, shared by Umbrians, Piceni, Gauls and Sabines. Today, the Marchegiani still have a little identity problem, but it doesn't keep them awake at night. Their land, tucked between the Apennines and the Adriatic, is one of the greenest, prettiest and most civilized corners of Italy, with two lovely Renaissance art towns in Urbino and Ascoli Piceno, lots of beaches and scores of fine old towns in the valleys that lead up to the impressive snowy peaks of the Sibelline Mountains, one of the highest sections of the Apennines.

Not to be Missed

You can shoot through the Marche in two hours, or get lost for weeks exploring the hilltowns of its mountain valleys. Along the coast, overbuilt resorts are everywhere; the nicest for a stay are **Pésaro**, **Senigállia** and **Fano**, or in the beautiful strip just south of the bustling port of **Ancona** called the **Cónero Riviera**. Nearly perfect Renaissance **Urbino**, of course, is the main attraction, but **Ascoli Piceno** in the south is a lovely, scarcely visited, art city in its own right, and even non-Catholics should stop to see the great Renaissance art at **Loreto**. You'll have to make an extra effort to visit the hill towns, strung along the valleys, but **Jesi** and **Camerino** won't disappoint, nor the magnificent caves at **Frasassi**.

Pésaro and Urbino

Just across the border from Emilia-Romagna, the impressive 11th–14th-century **Castello di Gradara** (*open daily 9–2; adm*) marks the entrance to the Marche. Tradition has it that this was the scene of the story of Francesca da Rimini and Paolo Malatesta, tragic lovers consigned to hell by the heartless Dante in the fifth canto of the *Inferno*—a story exploited to the max by the management, as it's in easy tour bus striking distance of Rimini. From there, the road quickly arrives at the provincial capital of Pésaro.

Getting Around

Pésaro's **railway station** is on the south edge of town at Viale Roma, about ½km from the centre. At least 10 **buses** a day go to Urbino, some via Fano and (usually) Fermignano; most leave from the bus station in Piazza Matteotti, and all leave from or stop at the Pésaro train station. Urbino has connections to most of the interior villages and towns in Pésaro province.

Tourist Information

Pésaro: Via Mazzolari 4, ✆ 0721 30258, and Viale Trieste 164, ✆ 0721 69341.
Urbino: Piazza Rinascimento 1, ✆ 0722 2613, near the Palazzo Ducale.

to Bologna

Rimini

Cattólica

Perticara

Talmello

Novaféltria

Sant' Agata
Féltria

San Leo

Pennabilli

Tavoleto

SAN MARINO

Gabicce Monte

Casteldimezzo

Fiorenzuola di Focara

Gradara

Pesaro

Macerata Féltria

Sassocorvaro

Piandimeleto

Fano

Borgo
Pace

Sant'
Angelo in Vado

Urbino

Fossombrone

Mercatello

Urbánia

Fermignano

Mondavio

Corinaldo

Senigállia

Acqualagna

Gola di
Furlo

Pérgola

M A R C H E S

Cagli

Erèmo di Fonte
Avellana

Arcévia

Sassoferrato

Sierra San
Quirico

Rosaro

Jesi

Ostra Falconara

Chiaravelle

Ancona

Portonovo

Monte Conero

Sirolo

to Greece

Mergo

Ósimo

Numana

Genga

Grotta di Frasassi

Gola di
Rossa

Filottrano

Castelfidardo

Porto Recanati

to Città di
Castello

Gubbio

Fabriano

Cingoli

Montefano

Loreto

Cerreto d'Esi

Poggio San
Romualdo

Montecassiano

Helvia Recina

Recanati

to Arezzo

Matélica

San Severino
Marche

Macerata

Civitanova
Marche

PERUGIA

Esahatoglia

Chiascio

Corridonia

Monte
San Giusto

Porto Sant'
Elpídio

Tevere

Assisi

Camerino

Tolentino

Urbisaglia

Chiaravalle
di Fiastra

Sant'Elpido
a Mare

Porto
San Gíorgio

San
Ginesio

Massa
Fermane

Mogliano

Falerone

Fermo

Torre di Palme

Foligno

Faleria

Sarnano

Serrigliano

Monterubbiano

Pedaso

Cupra Marittima

to Terni

Visso

Parco
Nazionale

Amándola

Monte Rinaldo

Grottammare

Santuario della
Madonna Dell'Ambro

Montefortino

Offida

San Benedetto
del Tronto

Gola dell'Infernaccio

Montemónaco

Ascoli
Piceno

Acquaviva
Picena

Monti Sibillini

Lago di
Pilato

M. Vettore
▲ 2476m

N

Arquata
del Tronto

to Pescara

Porto d'Ascoli

to Rieti

Land over 200 metres

25km
15 miles

Le Marche

501

Pésaro

In the Middle Ages the five big ports of the central Adriatic were known as the Pentapolis—Rimini, Fano, Senigallia, Ancona and Pésaro. Pésaro, like Rimini, has developed into a large resort, but a much tidier and more pleasant one. It is proud to be the home town of Gioachino Rossini; you can visit his **birthplace**, Via Rossini 34 (*opening hours vary; inquire at the tourist office*), near the cathedral, see his piano and manuscripts at the **conservatory** he founded, on Piazza Olivieri, or take in one of his operas at Pésaro's unusually grand opera house, the **Teatro Rossini**, during the Rossini Festival in late summer.

The Sforzas of Milan ruled Pésaro until they sold it to the della Rovere, the family of Julius II, in 1512. The big **Palazzo Ducale** in the centre of town was completed in 1510. In those years Pésaro rivalled Faenza as a producer of fine ceramics; you can see examples at the **Museo Civico**, Via Toschi Mosca (*opening hours vary; call © 0721 387 357 for information; adm*). Besides the majolica plates there are a few good pictures—and one very great one, a *Coronation of the Virgin* by Giovanni Bellini. Another museum, the **Museo Oliveriano** (*open Sept–June Mon–Sat 9–12; July and Aug Mon–Sat 5–8*), has a collection of archaeological finds left by the Romans and the various tribes they squashed.

Pésaro is a lovely town to walk through, both in its older quarters and in the newer streets by the beach. They are full of trees and little villas from the turn of the century—many in the Liberty style, including the outrageous **Villino Ruggieri** the centre of the beach front in the Piazzale della Libertà, with its cornice supported by terracotta lobsters, designed by an architect named Oreste Ruggiero in 1907. Pésaro's castle, the **Rocca Costanza**, near the sea, was built by Luciano Laurana, the designer of the palace at nearby Urbino.

Urbino

From Pésaro—and from almost nowhere else—it is easy to reach the isolated mountain town of Urbino. With its celebrated ducal palace, and the memory of the honourable and refined Duke Federico who built it, Urbino is one of the key monuments of the Italian Renaissance. Today its boosters go perhaps too far—'the ideal city of the Renaissance' and 'most beautiful palace in the world', with a lack of modesty that would have disappointed Federico da Montefeltro. Even so, Urbino does represent more clearly than any Italian town a certain facet of the Renaissance: elegance, learning and intelligent patronage combined in a small place. Urbino's golden age may not have long outlasted the reign of Duke Federico, but, as an example of what a community can be, it exerts a fascination to this day.

The Court of Duke Federico

Throughout the Middle Ages Urbino's fortunes were attached to those of the house of Montefeltro, mountain warlords from San Leo who gradually extended their influence in the northern Marche. Most of them were *condottieri* working throughout Italy for various masters. In 1443 Oddantonio da Montefeltro earned the title of Duke for his services. His half-brother and successor, Federico (reigned 1444–82), was the most successful of all the family *condottieri*, a crafty and respected warrior who earned the money for his famous palace serving the cause of the Pope and Alfonso of Naples. In his later days, with more of a chance to stay at home, Federico became one of the quattrocento's great patrons, as well as a slow but close student of the Classics and the new humanities; he learned Greek and Latin, and assembled one of the best libraries in Europe. Much of the legend of Urbino at this time comes from Baldassare Castiglione, in whose book *The Courtier* Urbino's court was idealized as the height of civilized existence.

Federico ruled Urbino paternally and well, always liberal to those of his subjects in need, peering into every detail of his little state's economy and social life, and educating the sons of the poor. It is also said that he banished gambling and cursing, and made the people of Urbino exert themselves to keep the place clean. His admirable wife, Battista Sforza, was a duchess beloved of her subjects, a lady capable of delivering an impromptu speech in impeccable Latin to welcome any surprise visitor. Their son, Guidobaldo I, was as enlightened a ruler as his father, and clever enough to survive after an occupation by Cesare Borgia's Papal army in 1497. However, when Guidobaldo died without an heir, the duchy fell to a member of the della Rovere family, a relative of Julius II.

Urbino's time as an independent state lasted less than two hundred years. The last of the della Rovere dukes willed the town and its territories to the popes in 1626, and it was left as a quiet backwater, ruled with the same lazy neglect as the rest of the Papal States. Urbino had, though, a moment of high drama in 1944. Many of the works of art of central Italy had been taken there for safekeeping as the war had spread to the Italian mainland. During the German retreat in August, one of their commanders planted enough explosives under the town walls to blow the whole place to kingdom come. Only a small number went off, and the remainder were defused by the British after the liberation—a job that took over a week.

The Palazzo Ducale

So many architects helped Federico build his dream house, it is difficult to divide the credit. Alberti may have been an original adviser, and the Dalmatian Luciano Laurana is generally given credit for most of the work, but the finest part of it, the twin-turreted façade, is by Ambrogio Barocchi, and no one is quite sure who did the elegant arcaded courtyard. That every Italian schoolchild should know this to be 'the most beautiful palace in the world' is an interesting reflection both on the Italians and on the quattrocento. Federico's palace is not finished, not symmetrical, and not really even very grand; its aesthetic is utterly foreign to the tastes of the centuries that followed.

For all that, it is a great building, and a test of one's faith in the genuine Renaissance—the 15th-century high noon of life and art, as opposed to the cinquecento of Spaniardism, surrender and neurotic excess. Many critics have regarded it, though unfinished, as the culmination of Renaissance architecture, not yet entirely enslaved to perspectivism or imitation of the ancients, but a creation of freedom and delight. The palace was comfortable for the Montefeltri to live in, and an exquisite decoration for the city of Urbino.

The palace **façade**, overlooking the hills on the edge of town, consists of three levels of balconies between two slender towers; the decorative trim is done in a fine Dalmatian limestone that eventually hardened to look like marble. To enter the palace today you have to go round the back through the courtyard, called the **Cortile d'Onore**, a prototype for so many other palace courtyards around the western Mediterranean. Much of the interior is occupied by the **Galleria Nazionale delle Marche**, a splendid collection whose finest works were originally the property of Duke Federico (*open Mon 9–2, Tues–Sat 9–7, Sun 9am–10pm; summer also Fri and Sat 8.30pm–11.30pm; adm exp*).

Piero della Francesca's amazing *Flagellation* is perhaps the best-known work in Urbino, an endlessly disturbing image that has troubled art scholars for centuries. Standing before a pavilion of fantasy classical architecture, three gentlemen in contemporary dress hold a serious discussion, indifferent to the scourging of Christ going on behind them—a bloodless scourging, for that matter. Piero had already written one of the great Renaissance treatises on theoretical perspective; a complex system of foreshortening is here the major feature of the work. The combination of a surreal, dream-like scene and a drily scientific visual presentation gives the painting its enigmatic quality—as critics have often noted, this is one of the places where art crosses the line into sorcery. Almost as strange a display of perspectivist wizardry is another work, often attributed to Piero or Laurana, the *Ideal City*. The scene is a broad, paved square, lined with buildings in the new style, dominated by a large circular temple in the centre. Here again, perspective is the star of the work. Disturbingly, there are no people present—no living things at all save a few potted plants on the balconies.

Not to be outdone by Piero, Paolo Uccello offers a similarly mysterious *Miracle of the Profaned Host*, and Luca Signorelli is represented by two inspired works, the *Crucifixion* and *Pentecost*. Other paintings not to miss: a *Crucifixion* by Antonio Alberti de Ferrara, taking care to show off contemporary fashions, in armour as well as court dress; the *Annunciation* by Vicenzo Pagani (and a pagan-looking work it is, too); *La Muta*, a portrait of a lady by Raphael; also fine works by Luca della Robbia, Giovanni Santi, Crivelli, Verrocchio and Alvise Vivarini. The Spanish artist Pedro Berruguete contributes the famous *Portrait of Duke Federico*; the tough old warrior, with his broken nose, symbolically still wears armour as he pores over a heavy book, with his little son Guidobaldo at his knee; note the badge of the Order of the Garter, conferred on Federico by King Edward IV of England.

Some of the surviving interior decoration of the palace is wonderful too—carved mantelpieces and window frames in many rooms, and, above all, the intarsia (inlaid wood) **study** of Duke Federico. The designs, by Botticelli, Bramante and Francesco di Giorgio Martini, portray the 'Life of a Scholar', with many *trompe l'œil* effects. The paintings of philosophers and illustrious men are by Berruguete. Nearby, reached by a spiral staircase inside one of the façade's towers, are the **Cappella del Perdono**, with an ornate ceiling of hundreds of angel heads in stucco, and an equally fancy chamber called the **Tempietto delle Muse**. The palace's upper floor has rooms full of 16th- and 17th-century paintings, and portraits of the poor Italians dressed in black like their Spanish overlords. *Chiaroscuros* of the *Life of St Paul* by Claudio Ridolfi, 18th-century ceramics, and woodcuts by a Marchegiano artist of the 1900s named Adolfo di Carolia, make the climb upstairs worth while. The basement houses a display on the restoration of the palace; there are bits of the duke's plumbing and cooking pots, with other curiosities found during the restoration, such as the sundial-birdbath from the roof garden (sadly, long destroyed), and a big book with a conspicuous dedication to *James III, Re di Gran Bretagna*. The Old Pretender was a guest here twice in the 1700s.

The Town and the Walls

Urbino today is above all a university town and, despite its small size, is a lively place full of students from many countries. Though its streets and roads are often steep, the town and its surrounding hills make an enchanting spot for walks. Adjacent to the ducal palace, the **cathedral** is a work of the 1790s, completely rebuilt after an earthquake that caused the collapse of its dome; there is a small collection of religious art and artefacts in the **Museo Diocesano Albani** (*open daily 9–12 and 3–6*). On Via Barocci, off Via Mazzini, the street that leads up from Urbino's main gate, the little **Oratorio di San Giovanni** (*open Mon–Sat 10–12.30 and 3–5.30, Sun 10–12.30; adm*) has strikingly colourful frescoes by the brothers Jacopo and Lorenzo Salimbeni (1416), artists from San Severino Marche, near Macerata, who showed a distinctive approach to early-Renaissance painting, still heavily under the influence of Giotto. Their work includes a *Crucifixion*, an enthroned *Madonna*, and a cycle on the life of John the Baptist. On the same street, the **Oratorio di San Giuseppe** has a carved *presepio* (crib) by Urbino artist, Federico Brandani. The town's most famous son, though, was Raphael, born here in 1483, and his birthplace is now restored as a museum. The **Casa di Raffaello** (*open Mon–Sat 9–1 and 3–7, Sun 10–1; check winter hours with tourist office; adm*) has works by other artists, some pieces of furniture, and a *Madonna* attributed to Raphael himself, but nothing major by the artist.

All of Urbino's 16th-century walls are intact, and the garden enclosed by one of the corner bastions, the **Fortezza Albornoz**, has a fine view of the palace and town. A pleasant half-hour walk out from the western end of town will take you to the pretty church of **San Bernardino**, attributed by some to Bramante, another son of the Urbino area; inside are the simple but impressive black marble tombs of the Montefeltro dukes.

Where to Stay and Eating Out

Pésaro ✉ 61100

One fine old establishment tops the list—★★★★**Vittoria**, Piazzale della Libertà 2, ℐ 0721 34343, ✉ 0721 65204 (*expensive*), a renovated century-old villa in the centre of the beach strip, filled with period furnishings. But Pésaro has many modern, understated three-star hotels, which seem to cost (high season) around L65–90,000 for a decent double room. It's hard to recommend one over the other: the ★★★**Principe**, Viale Trieste 180, ℐ 0721 30222, ✉ 0721 31636 (*moderate*), quite a distance from the centre, has a good, popular restaurant. The 17th-century ★★★**Villa Serena**, Via San Nicola 6, ℐ 0721 55211 (*moderate*), just outside town, has fireplaces in every room, antique furniture, and remarkably reasonable prices, as well as a good restaurant.

In the historic centre, **Lo Scudiero**, Via Baldassini 2, ℐ 0721 64107 (*expensive*) occupies the cellar of a 17th-century palace. Specialities include some imaginative dishes with seafood and pasta—ravioli with sole, or *tagliatelle marine*. Roast lamb is another dish they do well. **Da Alceo**, Via Panoramica Ardizio 101, ℐ 0721 51360 (*expensive*), right on the sea, offers great fresh fish dishes and home-made pasta and desserts, and has a good friendly atmosphere. *Closed Mon.* Also on the seafront, **Teresa**, Viale Trieste 180, ℐ 0721 30222 (*expensive*) has exceptional specialities such as a risotto made with wild herbs, and fried calamari with sage. *Closed Mon.* For a fine fish dinner there's **Nuovo Carlo**, Viale Zara 54 (*moderate*)—often crowded, and not without reason. **Antica Osteria La Guercia**, Via Baviera 33, ℐ 0721 33463 (*cheap*), right on the corner of the Piazza del Popolo, is the oldest in town, and serves all the classics, including home-made *strozzapreti*. *Closed Sun.*

Urbino ✉ 61029

Hotels in Urbino can be extremely crowded in the summer, and even spring. There aren't many, so book ahead. Perched next to the city walls, the most luxurious place in town short of the palace itself is the ★★★★**Bonconte**, Via delle Mura 28, ✆ 0722 2463, 🖩 0722 4782 (*expensive*). ★★**Italia**, Corso Garibaldi 32, ✆ 0722 2701 (*cheap*) is very good, and only a few steps away from the ducal palace. The ★★**San Giovanni**, Via Barocci 13, ✆ 0722 2827 (*cheap*) is in an old *palazzo*, and has a good restaurant.

In a fancy restored granary, **Vecchia Urbino**, Via dei Vasari 3, ✆ 0722 4447 (*expensive*) serves excellent tagliatelle with sole or truffles, and a savoury *millefoglie ducale*; and there's a good list of local wines. *Closed Tues*. **Trattoria Leone**, ✆ 0722 329 894 (*moderate*), right in Piazza della Repubblica, has traditional dishes, with surprise specialities such as *coniglio al porchetta* on the menu. **Il Cortegiano**, Via Puccinotti 13 (*moderate*), near the cathedral, may look more pricy, but like other Urbino restaurants it offers local food and roasts for about L35,000. *Closed Mon*.

Towns and Villages Around Urbino

Urbino can be used as a base for excursions into the rolling hills and mountains of the northern Marche, dotted with towns as serene and lovely as those in Tuscany, though much less known. **Fermignano**, where Bramante may have been born (that honour is also claimed by Urbánia), is one of the most conveniently placed, about 9km south of Urbino. At its centre, under a graceful medieval tower and bridge, there is a little waterfall on the Metauro River. From Fermignano, you can follow the Metauro Valley east through a rocky ravine called the **Gola del Furio**. The Romans, under Vespasian, dug the tunnel to reach **Fossombrone**, then known as *Forum Sempronii*, after the reformer Sempronius Gracchus. Scenographically built on tiers under a Montefeltro palace, Fossombrone is full of tattered palaces and churches, but with nary a tourist in sight.

To the west, the Metauro Valley will take you to **Urbánia**, another residence of the Montefeltro dukes; originally called Castel Durante, it was renamed after Pope Urban VIII. Urbánia retains a smaller Ducal Palace with a museum, a picture gallery and the remains of Duke Federico's famous library, with many antique globes and maps (*open June–Aug daily 10–12 and 3–7; closed Mon; or by request*, ✆ *0722 319 985*).

Beyond Urbánia all roads lead towards the summits of the Apennines, and villagers dream of the truffles, just like their counterparts across the mountains in Umbria. The *Sagra del Tartufo* in October is the big event of the year in **Sant'Angelo in Vado**, another exceptionally pretty town on the Metauro; from here the road begins the climb over the mountains to Arezzo and Perugia. To the north, **Piandimeleto**, **Sassocorvaro** and **Tavoleto** are three villages built around genteel Renaissance castle-palaces; Sassocorvaro's is an unusual, striking round one, built by Francesco di Giorgio Martini, with a small museum. For beautiful **San Leo**, in the northernmost corner of the Marche, *see* p.498.

Back on the Coast: Pésaro to Ancona

South of Pésaro, the string of Adriatic resorts continues through Fano and Senigállia, which are not just resorts, however, but fine old towns, both members of the medieval Pentapolis.

Fano: Viale Cesare Battisti 10, ✆ 0721 803 534.
Senigallia: Piazza Morandi 2, ✆ 071 792 2725.

Fano

Older even than the Romans, Fano takes its name—once *Fanum Fortunae*—from a famous temple to the goddess Fortuna. Back then it was the most important of the Marche's coastal cities, the terminus of the Via Flaminia from Rome. Today, in the central Piazza XX Settembre, Fortune still smiles on Fano from the 16th-century **Fontana della Fortuna**. The elegant loggia behind it belongs to the **Corte Malatestiano** (*open July–Sept Tues–Sat 8.30–12.30 and 5–7, Sun 9–12; Oct–June Tues–Sat 8.30–12.30, Sun 9–12; adm*), a palace built in the 1420s and enlarged in 1544 when Fano was ruled by the tyrants of Rimini. The picture gallery stars works by Michele Giambono, Giovanni Santi and Guercino. The church of **Santa Maria Nuova**, two blocks south on Via dei Pili, has altarpieces by Giovanni Santi and Perugino, with a small predella panel attributed to Santi's young son Raphael. From Roman days Fano preserves a stately gate built in the year AD 2, the **Arco di Augusto**. San Michele Church, to the right of the gate, has a relief on its façade showing how the arch looked before it was heavily damaged in 1463. The eventually successful besieger who bombarded it was none other than Duke Federico of Urbino, working at that time for the pope; the defender—Sigismundo Malatesta of Rimini. Fano's **lido**, modern and a little overbuilt, is typical of the resorts on the Adriatic, but the long broad beach continues down the coast for miles, through the resort suburbs of Torrette and Marotta, and there's room for all.

Senigállia

Senigállia, the next town on the coast, was the site of an important trade fair in the Middle Ages. Besides its long 'velvet beach', one of the nicest on the Adriatic if all divided up by the hotels, its main landmark is an elegant though serviceable fortress, built by the della Rovere in 1480, the Rocca Roveresca (*open April–Sept Tues–Sat 9–1 and 5–10, Sun 9–1; winter Tues–Sat 9–1 and 3–7, Sun 9–1; adm*).

Where to Stay and Eating Out

Fano ✉ 61032

Fano is full of typical moderately priced Italian seaside hotels: try ★★★**Excelsior**, Lungomare Simonetti 21, ✆/🌐 0721 803 558; ★★★**Piccolo**, Viale Cairoli 1, ✆ 0721 800 626, 🌐 0721 8305; and ★★**Astoria**, Viale Cairoli 86, ✆ 0721 803 474. There's a youth hostel, the **Ardizio**, ✆ 0721 55798 (*cheap*), near the beach north of town. *Open mid-May–Sept.* The fishermen's co-operative runs a little place where you can put away an enormous pile of little fishes for under L25,000—**Pesce Azzurro**, on Lungomare Sarsonia (*cheap*). *Pesce azzurro*—'blue fish'— refers not to one specific variety, but to many kinds of (very tasty) small fish that were once common in these waters. *Closed Mon, and Oct–Mar.*

Senigállia ✉ 60019

Among the countless hotels and campsites, ★★★**La Vela**, Piazza N. Bixio 35, ✆ 071 792 7444 (*moderate*) is a nice place with a garden and tennis courts; its biggest advantage, though, is that it's the furthest hotel from the railway line. **Riccardone's**, Via Rieti 69, © 071 64762 (*expensive*) has tables outside and local dishes made from the freshest ingredients. Let the chef direct you through the menu, featuring such delicacies as squid with artichokes or a wonderful mixed grill of fresh fish. *Closed Mon.* By the water, **Uliassi**, Banchina di Levante 6, © 071 65463 (*moderate*) serves dishes (using the freshest of fish) with an innovative touch. Try the generous *antipasti*, and the monkfish (*Coda di Rospo*) with *caponata* of aubergine. *Closed Mon.*

Inland: The Valle dell'Esino

The mountain valleys, stretching in parallel down to the sea, neatly divide the Marche's geography. South of the Metauro, the Esino is the next important valley, most easily reached from Falconara, south of Senigállia. The first town is **Jesi** (Roman *Aesis*), set on a narrow ridge between crumbling, picturesque Renaissance walls with houses built on and over their tops.

In 119 Jesi was the birthplace (in a tent, in the piazza) of none other than the Emperor Frederick II *Stupor Mundis*, and on the entrance of the **Palazzo del Comune** is engraved the text of a letter from Frederick confirming the town's ancient privileges. In the next square, the 16th-century **Palazzo Ricci** has an odd waffle-iron façade like the Gesù Nuovo in Naples. Two streets over to the west, the **Palazzo della Signoria** is another fine Renaissance building, with a small museum of paintings and archaeological finds. Jesi's real treasure, however, is a lavishly stuccoed Rococo gallery and a set of paintings by Lorenzo Lotto, including the strange *Annunciation* in the **Pinoteca Comunale**, located in the Palazzo Pianetti on Via XX Settembre (*open Tues–Sun 10–1 and 5–7; adm*). Outside the walls, the church of **San Marco** has exceptional 14th-century Giottoesque frescoes.

Beyond Jesi, the Valle dell'Esino is squeezed into another limestone gorge, the **Gola di Rossa**; a road off to the right leads to the village of **Genga** and the **Grotte di Frasassi** (*open daily 8–8; guided tours every 90min, Sun every 10min; adm*). One of them, already a popular attraction, is the 'cave of the winds', with a glistening display of glistening pastel stalactites and calcareous pools that go on for over a kilometre. Another cave, called the **Grotto del Santuario**, has an octagonal 18th-century chapel built inside it. Nearby, close to the Genga railway station, is the 10th-century church of **San Vittore delle Chiese**. Another rather difficult 17km past Genga takes you to the lovely hill village of **Arcevia**, where there is an altarpiece by Luca Signorelli in the church of San Medardo.

Fabriano, near the border with Umbria and a stop on the Rome–Ancona railway, was another victim of the 1997 earthquake. Although little actually crumpled, many buildings were left unsound; expect to see a good deal of scaffolding and braces over the next few years. Fabriano was famous in Renaissance times for paper-making (the watermark was invented here), and as the home of a school of painting, influenced by Gentile da Fabriano, the wizard of International Gothic (d. 1427). Works by the school can be seen in the **Pinacoteca Civica** on Piazza Umberto di Savoia, along with a good collection of Renaissance works (*open Tues–Sat 10–12 and 3–6, Sun 10–12; summer Tues–Sun 10–12 and 3.30–6.30; adm*). A fine arcaded square, the **Piazza del Comune**, marks the centre of town, with a Palazzo del Comune and fountain very reminiscent of those in Perugia. **San Domenico**, Fabriano's most important church, has frescoes by local artists of the 14th century, most notably those in the Chapel of S. Orsola. Its convent now houses a **museum of papermaking** (*open Tues–Sat 10–6, Sun 10–12 and 2–5; adm*), run by the local papermill, for—in a way that's very typical of the tenacity of craftwork in many Italian towns—Fabriano still makes its living from paper. The most important use for speciality paper is, of course, banknotes; besides supplying the Italian treasury, Fabriano paper changes hands every day from Kashmir to the Congo. At the museum much of the equipment of the old craft has been assembled, and demonstrations are given of how it's done.

For a real detour off the beaten track, press on south to **Matelica**, with another fine town square and a picture gallery, the **Museo Piersanti** (*open May–Oct Tues–Sun 10–12 and 5–7; Nov–April Sat and Sun 10–12 and 4–6*), with an exceptional triptych by Antonio da Fabriano and some saints by Giovanni Bellini. **Cerreto d'Esi**, nearby, has remains of a Byzantine gate and a leaning tower, said to have been built in the time of Justinian.

Ancona

Just before the city, the mountains once more reach the sea, giving the mid-Adriatic's biggest port a splendid setting, a crescent-shaped harbour under the steep promontory of Monte Guasco; here colonists from Syracuse founded the city in the 5th century BC. It was the furthest north the Greeks ever went in the Adriatic, and the colony was never a great success until Roman emperors, especially Trajan, built it up. Ancona recovered from the centuries of decay to become the leading city of the Pentapolis in the 12th century, and lived on quietly thereafter, coming under papal rule in 1532. Our own century, however, has been murderous to Ancona. The Austrians bombarded it in 1915, and the British and Americans did a much more thorough job in 1944. Then came a major flood, a serious earthquake in 1972, and after that a landslide that caused parts of the old town to be abandoned. For all its troubles, Ancona has come up smiling. The port is prospering, and even though most of the population now live in newer districts to the south and west, the city is finally devoting its attention to the restoration of the historic centre.

Getting There

by air

Ancona's Raffaello Sanzio airport is 10km north at Falconara, ✆ 071 282 7233/7234, and has regular flights from Rome and Milan, as well as charters year-round from Russia, Ukraine and Lithuania, and London in the summer. The terminal for airport buses is Piazza Roma 21, in front of Alitalia, ✆ 071 207 5892.

by sea

There are plenty of **ferry** services from Ancona to Corfu, Igoumenitsa, Patras, Piraeus, and Crete in Greece; to Albania; to Split and Dubovnik in Croatia, and Turkey. Contact the tourist office for schedules; in summer book tickets well in advance from your travel agent at home.

by rail

Ancona lies at the intersection of the Adriatic coast route and Ancona–Rome lines, with no long waits for trains in either direction. The **station** is west of the port at Piazza Roselli (buses nos.1 or 3 to or from Piazza Repubblica by the port). A few trains continue to the Ancona Marittima station on the port.

by bus

Buses to Portonovo and the Cónero Riviera, to other towns in the province and to Bologna, Rome and other long-distance destinations all leave from the bus station in

Piazza Cavour. Many buses also stop at the railway station. Ancona's few sights are not far from each other, but they are uphill—if you're not up to making the long climb up to the cathedral, the no.11 bus from Piazza Cavour or Piazza Repubblica will save you the trouble.

Tourist Information

Via Thaon de Revel 4, © 071 33249, ◎ 071 31966; branch offices in the railway station, © 071 41703, and in the Palazzo Provincia on Corso Stamira, © 071 29882. In summer only there's also a booth in the port, © 071 201 183, and in the Cónero resorts of **Numana**, Piazza Santuario, © 071 933 0612, and **Sirolo**, Piazza Vittorio Veneto, © 071 933 0611.

Around the Port

It's surprising anything is left at all, but most of Ancona's monuments have survived the recent misfortunes, even if many are a little the worse for wear. The business centre has gravitated a few streets inland, around broad **Piazza Cavour**; from here Corso Garibaldi leads down to the sea. At its western end, the long curve of the port is anchored by the **Mole Vanvitelliana**, a pentagonal building that resembles a fortress, but really served as Ancona's *lazaretto* or quar-antine hospital in the 18th century. At the other end, the tall, graceful **Arch of Trajan** was built in AD 115, in honour of Ancona's imperial benefactor; even though the sculptural reliefs have disappeared, it is one of the better preserved Roman arches in Italy. Nearby, the 18th-century Pope Clement XII imitated Roman glory by having an arch put up to himself; the **Arco Clementino**, like the *lazaretto*, was the work of Vanvitelli, the court architect of the Bourbons at Naples, best known for his palace at Caserta. At the centre of the port, the 15th-century Venetian Gothic **Loggia dei Mercanti**, the merchants' exchange, is the best souvenir of Ancona's heyday as a free maritime city.

To see the oldest quarters of Ancona you'll have to climb a little, starting up Via Gramsci and passing under the Renaissance decorative arch of the **Piazza del Governo**. Off in a little square to the left, **Santa Maria della Piazza** has a fine late-Romanesque façade with figures of musicians, soldiers and odd animals carved by a 'Master Phillippus'. Another two cross-streets up take you to **San Francesco delle Scale**, with another Gothic portal, and a late-Renaissance palace that houses the **Pinacoteca Comunale** (*open Tues–Sat 9–7, Sun and Mon 9–1; adm*). It contains a masterpiece by the eccentric but endearing Carlo Crivelli, tidiest of all Renaissance painters—a *Madonna col Bambino*, complete with Crivelli's trademark apples and cucumbers hanging overhead. There is also a good *Madonna* by Lotto, formerly in the Santa Maria church, and yet another by Titian, floating smugly on a cloud.

On Monte Guasco

Further up, the street changes its name to Via del Guasco, and bits of decorative brickwork from Roman Ancona's theatre peek out in between and under the buildings. This was the area hardest hit by the earthquake and landslide, and restoration work is going on everywhere. One building that may never be completely finished is the one on Via Ferretti that houses the **Museo Nazionale delle Marche** (*open July–Sept Tues–Sun 9–7, Mon 8.30–1.30; Oct–June daily 8.30–1.30; adm*), an important archaeological collection with exceptional Greek vases, sculpture and metalwork. The wartime bombings blew up its first home, and the second was jolted severely in the earthquake and closed entirely to visitors for many years,

N

Ancona

500 metres
500 yards

Adriatic Sea

Monte Guasco

Arco Clementino

Arco di Traiano

Cathedral di San Ciriaco

Museo Nazionale delle Marche

Roman Amphitheatre

Palazzo del Senato

Port

San Francesco delle Scale

VIA PIZZECOLLI

LUNGOMARE VANVITELLI

VIA FANTI

Ferry Terminal
(for ferries to Croatia, Albania and Greece)

Pinocoteca Comunale

Loggia dei Mercanti

Palazzo del Governo

San Domenico

MARSALA V. GOITO

SS. Sacramento

Fontana Calamo

Sant' Agostino

CORSO G. GARIBALDI

VIA CARDUCCI

CORSO VA STAMIRA

To Monumento ai Caduti

VIA E. CIALDINI

VIA F. PODESTI

VIA F. TORRIO

VIA MONTEBELLO

VIA GIANNELLI

VIA XXIX SETTEMBRE

VIA EINAUDI

Mole Vanvitelliana

VIA SANZIO

Citadella

Parco Comunale

VIA S. STEFANO

VIA VITTORIO

VIA DI CIRCONVALLAZIONE

VIA GUIGLIELMO MARCONI

VIA GIAMB. PERGOLESI

VIA RAFFAELLO

VIA MARTIRI DELLA RESISTENZA

Train Station

Piazza Rosselli

VIA FLAMINA

VIA DE GASPARI

VIA CORSO ALBERTO

VIA D. RICOSTRUZIONE

VIA GIORDANO BRUNO

Piazza U. Bassi

though it has now partially reopened. Also damaged in 1972 was the 13th-century **Palazzo del Senato**, around the corner: Ancona's capital when it was a self-governing *comune*.

Ancona's **cathedral** crowns Monte Guasco, a site that in antiquity held a famous temple of Venus. To reach it you either climb a long stairway flanked by gardens, the **Scalone Nappi**, or drive up from the port, where an ugly new road has replaced the neighbourhoods lost in the landslide. Unusually for a church this far north, the 11th-century cathedral shows a strong influence of the Apulian Romanesque, and but for the long, rounded transepts the building would not look out of place in any of the cathedral towns around Bari. The sculpted portals and detached campanile were both added about 1200. Inside, there isn't much to see; the marble columns came originally from the Temple of Venus, and there is an unusual carved altar screen from the 12th century. The cathedral is dedicated to St Cyriacus, an early bishop and martyr—not a real martyr, but a clever piece of propaganda from the time of the virtuous but non-Christian Emperor Julian the Apostate.

The Cónero Riviera

The same arm of the Apennines that stretches down to shelter Ancona's port also creates a short but uniquely beautiful stretch of Adriatic coast. South of Ancona, the cliffs of Monte Cónero plunge steeply into the sea, forcing the railway and coastal highway to bend inland, and isolating a number of beautiful beaches and coves only a few kilometres from the centre of Ancona, and now a national park. The little resort town of **Portonovo**, on the northern slopes of Cónero, can be reached by bus from Ancona in half an hour. There is a small beach, and a church of the 1030s in the same style as Ancona cathedral. **Santa Maria di Portonovo**, with the same blind arcading around the roofline and a distinctive cupola in the centre, is one of the better Romanesque churches in the north. Dante mentioned it, as 'the House of Our Lady on the Adriatic Coast', in the 21st canto of the *Paradiso*. The southern end of Cónero is marked by the often very crowded but attractive resorts of **Sirolo** and **Numana**. Both Sirolo and Numana have beaches nearby, but the best in the area are in places that can only be reached by small boat, like the beach of **Due Sorelle** or the stretch of jagged white cliffs called **Sassi Bianchi**.

Where to Stay and Eating Out

Ancona ✉ 60100

The city's best, ★★★★**Grand Hotel Palace**, Lungomare Vanvitelli 24, ✆ 071 201 813, 🖃 071 206 4832 (*very expensive*), is by Trajan's Arch: a small, very comfortable hotel with a good restaurant, and a roof garden with views over the port. For a little tranquillity, ★★**Viale**, Viale della Vittoria 23, ✆ 071 201 861 (*moderate*) is a good choice, nearly 1km from the centre. ★★★**Rosa**, Piazza Fratelli Rosselli 3, ✆ 071 41388 (*moderate*), near the railway station, also has good standard rooms. There's a clutch of uninspiring budget-range hotels in this area. For something nicer, try ★**Centrale**, Via Marsala 10, ✆ 071 54388 (*cheap*), a basic but comfortable hotel in the city centre.

Passetto, on Piazza IV Novembre, ✆ 071 33214 (*expensive*) is an excellent seafood restaurant—*zuppa di balleri*, made from a kind of mussel that only lives around the Cónero coast, is the speciality. *Closed Wed.* **La Moretta**, Piazza del Plebiscito 52, ✆ 071 202 317 (*expensive*) has long been a favourite with locals for its excellent *stoccafisso all'anconetana* (wind-dried cod) and *spaghetti agli scampi. Closed Sun.* Like any self-respecting port, Ancona has dozens of *trattorie* where you can put away some less grandiose marine delights at inconceivably low prices. The **Osteria del Pozzo**, on Via Bonda (*cheap*), in the centre of the port, offers a fine mixed seafood grill (*about L20,000*). **La Cantineta**, around the corner on Via Gramsci, ✆ 071 201 107 (*cheap*) offers a foretaste of Greece, complete with Greek seamen fingering worry-beads. It's one of the most popular places, with delicious *stoccafisso* and lemon sorbet.

Portonovo ✉ 60020

★★★★**Fortino Napoleonico**, Via Poggio 60, ✆ 071 801 124, ✆ 071 801 314 (*expensive*), as its name implies, incorporates part of a fortress built during the Napoleonic Wars, but it's modern inside, very quiet, and has its own beach and a pool. It is also one of the finest places to dine in the region (*very expensive*), with two beautiful dining rooms and immaculate service. Their *menu degustazione* has eight superb courses, including stuffed olives and scampi, sole stuffed with spinach, cream and smoked salmon, shrimps with fennel and orange, gnocchi with caviar. Nearby, ★★★**Emilia**, Via Poggio 149/a, ✆ 071 801 145 (*expensive*) is a pretty modern place with a pool and tennis courts. The owners invite artists to stay for free in exchange for a painting, so the hotel is covered with pictures, including one by Graham Sutherland. Its restaurant, ✆ 071 801 109 (*expensive*) has a sea terrace and a menu devoted to fish. **Da Anna**, on the beach, ✆ 071 801 343 (*cheap*) is a restaurant not to be missed if you're anywhere near the Cónero. The proprietor goes out daily to catch the fish, and his wife does the cooking. The atmosphere and the cuisine couldn't be better, and the prices could be much worse. *Open Easter end Oct.*

Numana ✉ 60026

How the hotel-keepers in Numana get away with charging what they do is a mystery. One that's worth the bill is the ★★★**Gigli Eden**, Via Morelli 11, ✆ 071 933 0652 (*moderate*) which offers nice rooms with a view, two pools, tennis and acres of grounds. There's also a secluded private beach, though it's a bit of a climb back up.

The Southern Marche: Down the Coast

After Monte Cónero, the Adriatic won't show you another stretch of beautiful coastline until the Gargano Peninsula in Puglia. All through the southern Marche, the seaside is dotted with humble but growing resort towns, all pleasant enough but nothing special: **Porto Recanati**, **Civitanova Marche**, **Porto Sant'Elpidio**, **Porto San Giorgio** and **Pedaso**. If you're looking for a chance to dip inland, the best places would be the pilgrimage shrine of Loreto or the fine old town of Fermo, 6km west of Porto San Giorgio.

Getting Around

There are frequent **trains** along the coast between Ancona and Pescara. Loreto is also on this line—the station is outside the town, but there is a regular connecting bus. There is also a line that cuts inland from Civitanova Marche to Macerata, and meets the Ancona–Rome line near Fabriano. A car comes in handy here, but there are **buses** to most destinations from Ancona, Macerata or Ascoli Piceno.

Loreto: Via Solari 3, ✆ 071 970 276. **Porto San Giorgio**: Via Oberdan 8, ✆ 0734 678 461. **Fermo**: in the Piazza del Popolo, ✆ 0734 228 738.

Sweet Music: Castelfidardo and Osimo

Many of the inland towns of the Marche can provide object lessons in the growth and strength of Italy's 'new model' small-scale economy. Just where you least expect it, you'll find a modest, often family-run plant, producing goods that are among the best in their trade. Fermo, for example, and the villages around it, produce a quarter of all the shoes made in Italy. South of Ancona, **Castelfidardo** lives almost entirely on the manufacture of accordions. It is claimed locally that this least academic of musical instruments was invented here in the 1870s; an **Accordion Museum**, in Via Mordini (*open daily 9.30–12 and 3–6; adm*) waits to fill in any gaps in your knowledge. **Ósimo**, 3km up the road, is more up-to-date; it makes most of Italy's electric guitars and keyboards. Its neighbours aren't impressed; they call people from Ósimo '*senza teste*' because of the twelve headless Roman statues in the town hall. Ask to visit the mayor's office, to see the beautiful if retro (for 1464) polyptych by the Vivarini brothers. At the highest point in town, the 13th-century **cathedral**, has quirky medieval monsters and snakes around its doors and rose window, and in the crypt, a 4th-century Luni marble sarcophagus; the baptistry has a fantastic 17th-century bronze font and ceiling.

Loreto

The inventor of the accordion, the story goes, got his inspiration when an Austrian pilgrim on his way to Loreto left behind a button concertina as a gift after staying for the night. The town of Loreto puts up billboards all over Italy inviting us to visit, but few foreigners apart from the devout ever take the hint. That is a pity, for, like Urbino, Loreto is a small but concentrated dose of fine art from the Renaissance. Its story is a mystery of the faith. During the 13th century the Church found itself threatened on all sides by heretical movements (the Albigensians, most famously) and free-thinkers. The popes responded with violent repression, but also tried in more subtle ways to assimilate and control these movements; creating the Franciscans was one approach, and the encouragement of the cult of the Virgin Mary was another. Conveniently enough, a legend of a miracle in the Marche gained wide currency. Mary's house in Nazareth, after being divinely transported to a hill in Istria, decided to fly off again in 1294, this time landing in these laurel woods (loreti) south of Ancona. Supposedly the house had bestirred itself in protest over Muslim reoccupation of the Holy Land; the popes were thumping the tub for a new Crusade, and Loreto was just coincidentally located on the route to the Crusader ports on the Adriatic.

Loreto's Santuario della Santa Casa

Beginning in the 1460s, the simple church originally built to house the *Santa Casa* was reconstructed in a massive building programme that took well over a century to complete. Corso Boccalini, lined with the inevitable souvenir stands, leads from the town centre up to the Sanctuary—and a very sudden surprise it is, too, when you turn the corner and enter the enclosed **Piazza della Madonna**, with the church, a great fountain by Carlo Maderno (one of the architects of St Peter's) and an elegant **loggia** by Bramante, enclosing the square. The sanctuary's understated façade is typical early-Roman Baroque, if a little ahead of its time

(1587). No one is perfectly sure whom it should be ascribed to, since so many architects had a hand in the work. Giuliano da Sangallo built the cupola (almost a copy of Brunelleschi's dome in Florence), Bramante did the side chapels, and Sansovino and Sangallo the Younger also contributed. One of the best features is the circle of radiating brick **apses** on the east end, turreted like a Renaissance castle. The only unfortunate element in the ensemble is the ungainly neoclassical **campanile**, added by Vanvitelli in the 1750s. Don't blame the architect; the tower had to be squat and strong to hold the 15-ton bell, one that has little trouble making itself heard for miles around once it gets going.

Chapels line the walls inside, embellished by the faithful from nations around the world. The sedate Spanish chapel is one of the better ones, and the English chapel holds a memory of the lyric poet Richard Crashaw, a refugee from Protestantism who served as canon here until his death in the 1640s. A good deal of Loreto's art was pilfered by Napoleon and consequently most of the paintings in the interior are post-1800; the two **sacristies** in the right aisle have frescoes by Melozzo da Forlì and Luca Signorelli. Under the dome is the object of the pilgrims' attention: the **Santa Casa**, a simple brick building, sheathed in marble by Bramante, and decorated with beautiful reliefs by Sansovino, Sangallo, della Porta and others, showing scenes from the *Life of Mary*. Next to the sanctuary there is a small **museum** (*open Tues–Sun 9–1 and 4–7; adm*), featuring works by Lorenzo Lotto.

Fermo

The Sabine town of *Firmum*, later a close ally of Rome, has gained importance and lost it several times; during the 10th century it was the capital of a duchy that included all the southern Marche, and later it was the seat of a university. A singular relic of Roman times can be visited under the Via degli Aceti: the **Piscina Epuratoria**, an enormous underground reservoir of 30 chambers built in AD 140–160 and designed to both hold and clarify rain- and spring-water. The 15th-century façade of the **Palazzo Comunale** is adorned with a mildly eerie statue of Pope Sixtus V, once Fermo's bishop, inviting you in to a fine collection of art in the **Pinacoteca Civica** (*open Tues–Sun 9.30–12.30 and 4.30–7.30; Aug also Thurs 9pm–midnight; adm*), including a moving and intense *Nativity* by Rubens; local records recall a Fermo priest commissioning it in 1608 for the grand sum of 1700 *scudi*. In the museum of the 14th-century **cathedral**, they'll show you a chasuble of Moorish silk that belonged to St Thomas à Becket—though they can't really explain how they got it.

Where to Stay and Eating Out

Loreto ✉ 60025

Hotels in Loreto are invariably clean and respectable, with a crucifix above every bed. A good many of them are run by religious orders. ★★★**Casa del Clero Madonna di Loreto**, ✆ 071 970 298, ✉ 071 970 102 (*moderate*) is a typical example. For a slightly more secular atmosphere, try ★★**Centrale** Via Solari 7, ✆ 071 970 173.

It might be worth a stay in Loreto in order to have dinner at the town's one outstanding restaurant, **Orlando Barabani**, Via Villa Constantina 89, at Loreto Archi, ✆ 071 977 696 (*moderate*); specialities include roast small game—quail, pigeon and thrushes— along with snails or *coniglio con porchetta*. Closed Wed.

Fermo ✉ 63023

Overlooking the town's lovely historic centre, facing the cathedral, ★★★**Casina delle Rose**, Piazzale Girfalco 16, ✆ 0734 224 636, 🖷 0734 228 932 (*moderate*) is a comfortable hotel with a reasonable restaurant. Another attractive choice is the ★★**Regina Mundi**, ✆ 0734 226 700 (*moderate*), outside the centre at S. Petronilla.

The Pocket Province of Macerata

You won't find a more out-of-the-way corner in central Italy. Although this hilly enclave lacks great attractions, all of its towns put up a good front, with stout medieval walls or a pretty Romanesque tower to lure you in for a short stop. Many of its villages and towns also have fine works of art in their little museums.

Getting Around

Trains run from Ancona to Macerata and Tolentino, branching off the main coast line at Civitanova Marche. **Buses** to most destinations in the province operate from the Giardini Diaz in Macerata.

Tourist Information

Macerata: Piazza della Libertà 12, ✆ 0733 234 807. **Tolentino**: Piazza Libertà 19, ✆ 0733 973 002. **Camerino**: Piazza Cavour 9, ✆ 0733 2534.

Macerata, Recanati and Tolentino

Macerata, the modest provincial capital, is a pleasant medieval-looking town of 45,000. About one-sixth of them could fit into the town's landmark, a huge colonnaded hemicycle and outdoor theatre called the **Arena Sferisterio**, built in the 1820s—maybe the grandest setting for opera south of Verona. Macerata makes good use of it in their **opera festival** in July, one of the most popular summer music events in Italy. In recent years the programme has featured many major international names, and it's often necessary to book in advance; the tourist office has details. On Piazza Vittorio Veneto, the **Pinacoteca Civica** complex (*open Tues–Sat 9–1 and 5–7.30, Sun 9–12*) houses a *Madonna* by Crivelli (no cucumbers, but a lovely work just the same) and archaeological finds from a nearby Roman town, *Helvia Ricina*. If you're fond of *presepi* (Christmas cribs) and can't make it to Naples, Macerata has a little private **Museo Tipologico del Presepio**, on Via Maffeo Pantaleoni (*open by appointment, call Cavaliere Cassese, ✆ 0733 49035*). There's also an excellent collection of 20th-century Italian art (Manzu, De Chirico, De Pises, Balla, etc.) in the 16th-century **Palazzo Ricci Gallery**, Via Ricci 1 (*open Tues and Sat 4.30–6.30*).

Recanati, on the road between Macerata and Loreto, was the birthplace of Italy's greatest modern poet, Giacomo Leopardi. They have made a discreet cottage industry out of him, and you can visit his birthplace in the **Palazzo Leopardi** (*open daily 9–12 and 3–6; adm*), along with a small museum and library. Relics of another favourite son, tenor Beniamino Gigli, fill the town's **Pinacoteca** (*open Tues–Sat 9–1 and 5–7, Sun 9–1; adm*), it also has works by Lorenzo Lotto, including what may be the silliest *Annunciation* ever painted. Recanati is high up on a hill, and has wonderful views as far as Loreto and the Adriatic. South of Macerata the valley of the Chienti carries you deeper into the province, towards the Monti Sibillini. At **Corridonia**, just southwest of Macerata, there is an interesting 6th-century Byzantine church,

San Claudio al Chienti, with a pair of round Ravenna-style campaniles. **Tolentino**, further up the valley of the Chienti on the SS77, is one of the larger towns, prosperous and modern and not much to look at until you reach the medieval centre and its **Basilica of San Nicola**, from the 1300s, but now sumptuously Baroque. An artist known only as the 'Maestro di Tolentino' left a beautiful series of frescoes in the **Cappellone**; intense, inspired work that bears comparison with the best trecento painting in Tuscany.

Around the garden cloister, there's a **museum** (*open daily 8.30–12 and 3–6.30; adm*), with silverwork, ceramics, a giant *presepio* and fascinating collection of ex-votoes testifying to St Nicholas of Tolentino's spiritual prowess. Tolentino has a fascinating **clock tower**, in Piazza della Libertà, one that will tell you the phases of the moon, the canonical hour and the day. For something different, Tolentino has the world's first **museum of caricatures** (*open Tues–Fri 3–6, Sat and Sun 9.30–12.30 and 3–6; or by appointment, © 0733 901 325*), in the nearby Palazzo Sangallo, with hundreds of cartoons from around the world.

Camerino and the Monti Sibillini

Camerino, up-river on its ridge, passed the time during the Middle Ages in endless fighting with arch-enemy Fabriano just to the north. Home to a small university since the 1300s, Camerino has two good picture galleries, the **Museo Diocesano** (*open Tues and Sat 10–1*) and the **Museo Civico** (*open 9–12 and 4–7, Sat 9–12, closed Sun*); in both the best works are by local quattrocento painter Girolamo di Giovanni. The striking ruined castle east of town is the **Rocca Varano**, from the 13th century. Beyond Camerino there are only narrow mountain roads over the Apennines to Foligno and Spoleto in Umbria.

Further south, the mountains grow higher, reaching a climax in the dark, dramatic range called the **Monti Sibillini**, with the second highest peak in the Apennines, **Monte Vettore** (8121ft), which often has snow until June. Around these there are skiing areas at **Ussita** and **Arquata del Tronto**, both with a wide choice of long runs. Arquata del Tronto, a lovely village beneath a hilltop castle, lies along the surest route over the mountains, the SS396, an often spectacular road that leaves the SS4 from Ascoli Piceno to the 4920ft pass, the **Forca Canapine** (or you can take the dull new tunnel), before descending to Umbria.

The route provides a balcony over all the southern Apennines, and is full of wild flowers in late spring. No one is sure how the 'Mountains of the Sibyls' got their name; ancient writers record no such oracular priestesses in these parts. Italy, though, is full of stories about them, and supposedly these mountains are behind the legend of Venusberg in Wagner's *Tannhäuser*.

Macerata ✉ *62100*   ***Where to Stay and Eating Out***

Accommodation is scarce in Macerata. For something really special, it's worth driving 9km north of town to ★★★★**Villa Quiete**, Località Valle Cascia, outside Montecassiano, © 0733 599 559, (*expensive*), an 18th-century country house, furnished with antiques, in beautiful grounds with a pool and good restaurant. ★★★**Da Rosa**, Via Armaroli 94, © 0733 23670 (*moderate*) is a fine place to stop over during the opera festival. Macerata is the place to try *vincisgrassi*, a dish with many variations, a more refined version of lasagna, sometimes with béchamel sauce. The name comes from the 19th-century Austrian General Windischgrätz, who must have liked it a lot.

Macerata's best restaurant is **Da Secondo**, Via Pescheria Vecchia, © 0733 260 912 (*moderate*), where besides *vincisgrassi* you can order the famous *fritto misto* of lamb and vegetables. Reserve. **Da Silvano**, Piaggia della Torre (*cheap*) serves excellent pizza and other more local dishes.

Ascoli Piceno

Urbino, at the northern end of the Marche, and Ascoli, at the southern, compete for your attention as almost polar opposites. Urbino gets most of the praise, and partisans of Ascoli may find that somewhat unfair. Unlike the northern town, paternalistically led by its enlightened dukes, Ascoli, with its long heritage as a free *comune*, has always had to do for itself. The difference shows; Ascoli is beautiful, but in a gritty, workaday manner, like Florence. It has taken some hard knocks in its 2500 years, which have helped make it a city of character.

History

For the Piceni, a powerful tribe that lived in the southern Marche and had the woodpecker as its totem beast, Ascoli probably served as the centre of their confederation. To the Romans, *Asculum Picenum* was an early ally, but later a major headache. Asculum fought Rome in the Samnite Wars, and actually initiated the pan-Italian revolt of the Social Wars. The Romans took the city in 89 BC and razed it to the ground, soon afterwards refounding it with a colony of veterans. The street plan of Ascoli today has hardly changed since then; it is one of the most perfect examples in Italy of a rectilinear Roman *castrum*. In the Dark Ages, Ascoli's naturally defensible position between steep ravines helped avert trouble. Its citizens, too, showed admirable determination, defeating Odoacer's Goths on one occasion and the Byzantines and Saracens on several others. Despite periods under the rule of others—Lombards, Franks, Normans and various feudal lords—Ascoli emerged by the 1100s as a strong free *comune*. Reminders of this most glorious period of the city's history are everywhere, in the 13th-century Palazzo del Popolo, the clutch of tall, noble towers like those of San Gimignano, and in Ascoli's famous festival, the **Quintana**, a jousting contest that happens the first weekend in August, according to rules laid down in 1378. Ascoli lost its freedom immediately, and its prosperity gradually, with the coming of papal rule in the 15th century, only recovering some of its wealth and importance in the last 100 years.

Getting Around

Ascoli is not the easiest place to reach without a car. The only **train** service is a dead-end branch off the Adriatic coast line, from San Benedetto del Tronto and Porto d'Ascoli. The station (several trains a day), is on Viale Marconi, in the new town.

Buses for Pésaro, Ancona, Rome and destinations within the province leave from Viale Alcide di Gasperi, behind the cathedral; the Brumozzi Travel Agency on Corso Trieste, near Piazza del Popolo, has information on both trains and buses. For the Rome bus, see the Cameli Agency, Via Dino Angelini 127, west of the cathedral.

Tourist Information

Ascoli: Piazza del Popolo 1, © 0736 257 288.
San Benedetto del Tronto: Via delle Tamerici 5, © 0735 592 237.

Piazza del Popolo

Like Rome, Ascoli is built of travertine. Also like Rome, it has more traffic than it can handle, and consequently the first impression will be of a grey, sooty town that shows its age. It's all the more a wonder, then, that the central **Piazza del Popolo** can be so effortlessly one of the most beautiful squares in Italy. This is no grand architectural ensemble, not monumental, nor even symmetrical. But the travertine paving shines almost like marble, and the low arcades that surround it give the square architectural unity and provide a fit setting for two fine buildings. The first, the **Palazzo del Popolo**, was begun in the 1200s and redone in the late 16th century, with a façade by Ascoli's best-known artist, Cola dell'Amatrice. At the narrow end of the Piazza, the church of **San Francesco** (*c.* 1260) turns its back on the square—not really an insult, since the apse and transepts are the best part of the building, a classic, austere ascent of Gothic bays and towers under a low dome added in the late 15th century. Over the south door is a statue of Pope Julius II. The façade, around the corner, isn't much to look at; a strange, flat square of travertine decorated with a tiny plain rose window, like a wall with an electrical outlet on it. It does have a good sculpted portal, guarded by a pair of sarcastic-looking lions. The southern end of the façade adjoins the **Loggia dei Mercanti**, built by the Wool Corporation—a typical medieval-style manufacturers' cooperative guild—in the early 1500s. On the northern side, the cloister has become Ascoli's busy and colourful **market**.

Via del Trivio, in front of San Francesco, is the centre of activity; follow it northwards to Ascoli's oldest and prettiest neighbourhoods, on the cliffs above the River Tronto. Most of the city's surviving **towers** are here. Ascoli has as many of these medieval family-fortresses as San Gimignano in Tuscany, but they are not as well known; the tallest is the **Torre di Ercolani** on Via Soderini. Piazza Ventidio Basso, the medieval commercial centre, has two interesting churches: **SS. Vicenzo ed Anastasio**, which has an unfinished Renaissance façade with Romanesque carvings around the portal, and the Gothic **San Pietro Martire**. The former is famous for a miraculous well in the crypt (a cure for leprosy).

At the northern tip of Ascoli, a doughty single-arched Roman bridge, the 1st-century **Ponte di Solesta**, still carries traffic across to the northern suburbs. If you cross it, and walk along the riverbank to the east, you will see signs for the church of **Sant'Emidio della Grotta**, on the street of the same name, an elegant 1623 Baroque façade that closes off the front of a cave; here St Emidio, Ascoli's patron, was martyred, and the site became the city's earliest place of Christian worship. All around the northern edge of Ascoli, the lovely valley of the Tronto makes a perfect picnic spot. Parts of Ascoli's walls, still visible in many places, still show the characteristic diamond-shaped brickwork of Roman construction, and at the western entrance to town, on Corso Mazzini, a Roman gate survives, the **Porta Gemina**.

Piazza Arringo

Ascoli's **cathedral**, dedicated to Sant'Emidio, is a 12th-century building similar to San Francesco but with a new façade from the 1530s, also by Cola dell'Amatrice. In a chapel on the south side you can see the inevitable cucumber in an altarpiece by Carlo Crivelli, one of his finest works. The 10th-century octagonal **baptistry** stands resolutely in the middle of Ascoli's busiest street while, facing the cathedral behind the fierce dragons in the twin Renaissance fountains, is the **Palazzo Comunale**, its Baroque façade concealing the 13th-century town hall.

Inside, in the **Pinacoteca** (*open April–Oct Mon–Fri 9–1 and 4.30–7, Sat 9–1, Sun 4–8; Nov–Mar Mon–Sat 9–1, Sun 9.30–12.30; adm*) there are works by Cola dell'Amatrice and other local artists, as well as by Simone de Magistris, Titian, Guido Reni, Van Dyck and, of course, Crivelli, and collections of ceramics and musical instruments. Across the square, the **Museo Archeologico** (*open May–Sept Tues–Sat 9–7, Sun 9–1.30; Oct–April daily 8.30–1.30; adm*) has good bronzes by the Piceni, stones they used to hurl at the Romans, carefully inscribed with curses, and a plan of the city in Roman times. A walk through the streets north of Piazza Arringo will take you past the palaces of medieval Ascoli, with many curious carvings and inscriptions; one, the **Palazzo Bonaparte** on Via Bonaparte, was built by a prominent family of the 1500s that local legend claims as the ancestors of the famous Bonapartes. Napoleon himself said he didn't know if it was true or not. The **Palazzo Malaspina**, Corso Mazzini 224, is one of the more elaborate buildings, and now houses a museum of contemporary art (*open daily 9–1; closed Mon*).

The Ascoli Coast

Here, too, the coast is lined with small resorts, starring **San Benedetto del Tronto**, one of the most popular and smartest on the whole Adriatic Riviera—once a Benedictine monastery and now a modern resort with thousands of palms decorating its beaches, discos and restaurants. **Grottammare** is a slightly cheaper version, a little further up the coast.

Where to Stay and Eating Out

Ascoli ✉ 63100

Accommodation is scarce. The ★★★**Gioli**, Via Alcide De Gasperi 14, ✆ 0736 255 550 (*moderate*), near the cathedral, has parking—a real blessing—and a small garden. ★★**Pavoni**, Via Navicella 135, ✆ 0736 342 575 (*cheap*) has 10 simple comfortable rooms. The youth hostel—the **Ostello de' Longobardi**, Via Guiderocchi 5, ✆ 0736 259 007 (*cheap*), in a medieval tower on the northern edge of town—is very friendly. To most Italians Ascoli means one thing, *olive all'ascolano*. These breaded and fried stuffed olives are wonderful, but one of the most tedious dishes imaginable to prepare, and you won't often find them outside Ascoli. The best place to try them is the **Cantina Al Pennile** on Via Spalvieri (*moderate*), in the eastern suburbs: a long-time Ascoli institution, and a real bargain. Closer to the centre, olives and other specialities await you at **Tornasacco**, Piazza del Popolo 36, off Piazza Arringo, ✆ 0736 25151 (*moderate*): tagliatelle with lamb sauce, and very good local cheeses. *Closed Fri.* **Kursal**, Corso Mazzini 221, ✆ 0736 253 140 (*moderate*), in the centre, has a variety of *risotti*—asparagus, salmon and caviar, or truffles—as well as other local specialities. Ascoli is also good for inexpensive family-run *trattorie*. Pick one out at random, or seek out **Da Giovanna** on Rua Marcolini, a block west of Piazza Arringo (*cheap*), where you can have an agreeably satisfying dinner for under L25,000.

San Benedetto ✉ 63039

San Benedetto has a vast choice of moderately priced hotels. The ★★★★**Ambassador** Via Cimarosa 5, ✆ 0735 659 443 (*expensive*) has a pool, tennis courts and sea views. **Messer Chichibio**, Via Bezzecca 19, ✆ 0735 584 001 (*moderate*) is one of the few quality restaurants left in this tourist haven, serving fresh fish dishes and regional food.

Abruzzo and Molise

Abruzzo and Molise

30km
10 miles

N

Adriatic

Sea

To Split

Pineto
Silvi Marina
Montesilvano Marina
Città
S. Angelo
Pescara
Moscufo
Francavilla al Mare
Chieti
Ortona
San Giovanni
in Venere
Fossacesia
Marina
Serramonacesca
Lanciano
A B R U Z Z O
Guardiagrele
Vasto
Caramanico Terme
Atessa
Termoli
▲ Mt Morrone
*Montagna
della Maiella*
Campomarino
Sulmona
Bomba
Pacentro
Guglionesi
Portocannone
Grotta di Cavallone
Taranta Peligna
Acquaviva
San Martino
Tavola Rotondo
Collecroce
in Pensilis
Campo di
Giova
Torrebruna
Ururi
To Foggia
Castiglione
Montefalcone
nel Sannio
Scanno
Pescocostanzo
Pescopennataro
Larino
Rivisondoli
Capracotta
Roccaraso
Agnone
Bonefro
Castel di Sangro
Pietrabbondante
Colletorto
P U G L I A
Barrea
M O L I S E
*Largo di
Barrea
d'Abruzzo*
Montenero
Valcocchiaro
Alfedena
Santa Maria della
Strada
Pescolanciano
**Abbey San Vincenzo
al Volturno**
Frosolone
Cerro al
Volturno
Campobasso
Atina
Carpinone
Baranello
Isernia
Ferrazzano
Scapoli
The M A T E S E
S85
Monteroduni
Boiano
Venafro
Campochiaro
Cassino
*Lago di
Matese*
Saepinum
Volturno
Piedimonte Matese
To
Benevento
To Naples
C A M P A N I A

*Tremiti
Islands*

523

In Italy's long and narrow peninsula, dense with cities, art and ruins, *autostrade* and pizzerias, and sultry sunglassed *signorinas,* Abruzzo and Molise come as a breath of fresh air. Sparsely populated, marginal to the great affairs of state, these two regions stand out for their majestic natural beauty and vast tracts of unspoiled wilderness that encompass the highest peaks of the Apennines and the habitat of Italy's unique species of bear. Because of the harsh and rugged terrain, with only small pockets suitable for agriculture, the region's economy has traditionally been pastoral, but with an emphasis on crafts—ceramics, gold, wood, iron-work, weaving and lace-making. And though many Abruzzo towns wear the proud badges of modernity, the Abruzzese have little care to compete with Milan and Rome—instead, like Candide, they tend their own garden and hone their skills, even if they use them to tailor suits as well as to embroider tablecloths. Yet from this mountain-bound land of country tradition came two of Italy's most urbane, sophisticated and passionate poets, Ovid and Gabriele d'Annunzio, and its greatest modern philosopher, Benedetto Croce. It is also, for some reason, the most passionately enthusiastic about rugby— L'Aquila has been Italy's national champion several times.

History

In prehistoric times the coast of Abruzzo formed part of a little-known Bronze Age culture, the Middle Adriatic, that produced the enigmatic Warrior in Chieti's archaeology museums. Culture was less advanced up in the hills, but the different Italic tribes who gathered here— the Praetutii, the Vestini, the Paeligni and others, of whom almost nothing is known beyond their names—formed a formidable challenge to Roman expansion before being overwhelmed by the legions in the Social Wars of 91–82 BC. The Lombards gave what is now the Abruzzo to the Duchy of Spoleto, and Molise to the Duchy of Benevento.

The Normans, under King William I of Sicily, picked up the region from the English Pope Adrian IV, and Emperor Frederick II, who inherited the Norman possessions in Italy, made the Abruzzo an independent province. Frederick had grand plans for the region, but they died with him as the Abruzzo was swallowed up by the Angevins, then kings of Naples. Like Umbria, Lazio and most of the Marche, Abruzzo and Molise then began to stagnate—the only difference being that these regions stagnated under the kings of Naples, rather than under the popes. It was the Bourbons who divided the Abruzzo into four territories—Abruzzo Citeriore, Ulteriore Primo, Ulteriore Secondo and Molise—which is why you'll often see the region's name in the plural (the Abruzzi). But if Abruzzo was neglected and sucked dry by the Neapolitans, its lot under the kings of Italy was scarcely any better, and thousands of people migrated to North America, Britain and other parts of Europe—among them the father of Dante Gabriele Rossetti and the ancestors of Madonna. Only after the Second World War, with the small boom of its compact seaside resorts, the development of small-scale industries and the building of new roads by the *Cassa per il Mezzogiorno*, and the growing interest in the unsullied charms of its landscape, has the tide of emigration been stemmed.

Belted with mountains, Molise is an atavistic and introspective *banlieu*, designated its own region not so much for historical as for cultural reasons, although it formed a county of its own back in the 13th century, when its name, of unknown derivation, was first used. This rather charming patch of the Abruzzi that got away has its own customs and dialect—a direct result of its impossible geography and the large settlements established there in the 15th and 16th centuries by Slavs and Albanians. Molise is one of the last regions in Italy where women still don their traditional costumes to please themselves and not the shutter-happy hordes.

Itineraries

The coast, like that of the Marche, is mostly cold toast, though there are some fine sandy beaches and pretty hills here and there. It is easily accessible; **Pescara**, the region's biggest resort, is a destination for international charter flights, and only an hour and a half's drive by *autostrada* from Rome. **Termoli** in Molise is another big resort. Inland, mountains and magnificent scenery provide the main attractions, in the famous **Gran Sasso** and lesser-known **Maiella** and **Matese** ranges, and in the **National Park of the Abruzzo**—all paradises for hiking and climbing, and boasting the best downhill and cross-country skiing in Central Italy. Of the towns, there is pretty old **L'Aquila**, the regional capital (and best base for visiting the Gran Sasso), and the ceramics town of **Castelli**, just under the Gran Sasso; medieval **Sulmona** and **Scanno** near the National Park; **Penne** and **Atri**, near the coast, and medieval **Tagliacozzo** and the Roman ruins of **Alba Fucens** on the road to Rome. Molise has an exceptional Roman town, **Saepinum**, and mountain villages preserved in aspic like **Boiano**, bell-casting **Agnone** and lofty **Capracotta**. Abruzzo also preserves enough Romanesque monuments to warm the cockles of any medievalist's heart, several of which are superlative: **San Giovanni in Venere** on the coast; **Santa Maria di Collemaggio** in L'Aquila; the two churches of **Bominaco**; and **San Clemente in Casauria**, on the Via Valeria.

Food and Wine

Abruzzo pasta is sold all over Italy, but the great local speciality is *maccheroni alla chitarra* (so called because it is cut with an implement shaped a little like a guitar). Inland Abruzzo is mountainous, and well suited to sheep-rearing; lamb dishes (especially grilled or roasted) are popular here, while the local variant of *pecorino* cheese, made from sheep's milk, is often served with pasta. Like all coastal areas of Italy, the coastal areas of Abruzzo has its own squid speciality—squid stuffed with anchovies, breadcrumbs and garlic. The food of the Molise uses many of the same basic ingredients as Abruzzo cooking, except that here you're likely to come across more offal, and virtually everything tends to be flavoured with little, hot, red peppers, called *diavolini* ('little devils') by the Molisani. Montepulciano d'Abruzzo is the best-known wine of the area. It's a smooth, dry red which, like many Italian wines, is best drunk within three years.

Down the Coast: from Giulianova and Pescara to Termoli

Small inexpensive seaside resorts, jam-packed with Italian families in the summer, and some beautiful works of art and churches of the Romanesque era, are the main attractions along the Adriatic Coast and its hinterland. If you're not into Italian-style seaside holidays—where you pay for a beach chair, umbrella and changing facilities in neat little rows, in order to have the privilege of watching everyone else do the same thing—you may have difficulty finding stretches of beach where you can just sit on the sands under the pines.

Getting Around

Pescara's **airport** now has a daily flight to and from London Stansted via Milan (Air One, ✆ 085 432 4225), plus charter connections with other European cities. In summer, **boats and hydrofoils** link Ortona to Vasto, and Vasto to Termoli, the Tremiti Islands and Rodi Garganico in Puglia. Termoli is the main port for the Tremiti (*see* **Puglia** p.882–83), with hydrofoils and motorboats daily. Services by train and bus along the coast are good. There is a direct **rail** line from Rome to Chieti and Pescara, via Sulmona, and between Bologna and Lecce, the length of the coast. ARPA, ✆ 06 442 33928, the Abruzzo bus company, connects Chieti with Pescara (three times a day).

Tourist Information

Loreto Aprutino: Via dei Normanni 8, ✆ 085 829 0484. **Penne**: Piazza Luca da Penne, ✆ 085 827 0436. **Pescara**: Via Nicola Fabrizi 171, ✆ 085 421 1707. **Chieti**: Via B. Spaventa 29, Palazzo INAIL, ✆ 0871 63640. **Ortona**: Piazza della Repubblica 9, ✆ 085 906 3841. **Vasto**: Piazza del Popolo, ✆ 0873 367 312. **Termoli**: Via M. Bega, ✆ 0875 706 754.

Giulianova, Roseto and the Lower Vomano Valley

Between the Marche and Pescara, the Adriatic is lined with the same kind of small, Italian family resorts south of Ancona; places like Alba Adriatica, Giulianova, Roseto degli Abruzzi, Silvi and Pineto all offer big beaches, modern hotels, amusement arcades and playgrounds. The most interesting of these is **Giulianova**, with its medieval old town set back behind the beachfront sprawl. Within the old walls stands the town's best monument, the Romanesque **Santa Maria a Mare**, with unusual bas-reliefs on its façade (*currently closed for restoration*), and the Renaissance **cathedral**. The SS80 turns inland here for Teramo (*see* below).

Roseto degli Abruzzi, another resort out of the same mould, lies near the mouth of the Vomano, one of the principal rivers coming down from the Gran Sasso, and has fine views up the valley to the naked limestone peaks of the Corno Grande. From Roseto you can head up the valley (on the SS150) to see two Romanesque gems. One is the 11th-century **San Clemente a Guardia Vomano**, near Notaresco, whose builders made good use of Roman ruins, fitting them together like a jigsaw. The church houses an unusual and lovely 12th-century *ciborium*. The other is the abbey of **Santa Maria di Propezzano**, near Morro d'Oro, where the Abruzzese fondness for simple forms has created a handsome asymmetrical façade and a charming two-storey cloister. The interior is embellished with 12th- and 13th-century frescoes, the cloister with scenes by the 17th-century Polish artist Sebastiano Majewski. A side road to the north leads to **Canzano**, famous for turkey in aspic, *tacchino alla canzanese*.

Pineto and Atri

Pineto, another little resort with a pretty pine-lined beach, has for its landmark the **Torre di Cerrano**, built by Charles V against the Ottoman threat and now a merchant marine research station. Pineto is a starting point for visiting **Atri** (10km inland) by car or bus—though buses go from Pescara and Teramo, if you're coming from further afield. Atri stands on the site of the ancient Sabine city and Roman colony of *Hatriaticum*, founded under the sign of the wood-pecker, the bird of Mars. Atri disputes with Adria in the Veneto the honour of having lent its name to the Adriatic Sea, a controversy that raged among ancient scholars like Pliny, Livy and Strabo; Atri tried to boost its claim by engraving the fact on its singular coins—the heaviest ever minted in western Europe, guaranteed to put a hole in the pocket of any toga.

The Roman sites in the town include the remains of ancient baths, in the crypt of Atri's majestic 13th-century **cathedral**. This building has an austerely elegant square façade and matching campanile, and in the choir there are excellent quattrocento frescoes by Andrea de Litio, the Piero della Francesca of the Abruzzo, who gave his scenes of *The Life of the Virgin* surreal landscapes of knobby hills and imaginary towers. In the cathedral **museum** (*irregular opening hours; © 085 870 579; adm*) there are ivories, polyptychs and statues, majolicas by Grue of Castelli (*see* p.534) and mosaics and fragments from the 9th-century church that preceded the cathedral. During the Middle Ages and Renaissance, Atri was controlled by the Acquaviva dukes, whose frowning 14th-century **Palazzo Ducale** (now the town hall and post office) contains a cheerful courtyard. The outskirts of Atri boast some strange geology: once-inhabited caves, eroded rock formations (*calanchi*) and 'Danteesque pits'.

South of Pineto, the SS16bis heads inland from Montesilvano Marina, a satellite resort of Silvi, towards a clutch of interesting villages. In **Loreto Aprutino**, the church of **Santa Maria in Piano** (*open summer daily 9–7; winter daily 9–4*) contains 14th–15th-century frescoes—the *Life of St Thomas Aquinas* and *The Particular Judgement*, portraying Heaven's elect marching to the pearly gates on a bridge the width of a hair. Loreto also has the **Museo Civico della Civiltà Contadina** (*open Tues–Sun 5–7, Sun also 10–12; winter 4.30–6.30, Sun also 10–12*), a collection of tools, traditional craft work and rather naïve tableaux of peasant life, and a new **archaeological museum** (*open Sat 4.30–7.30, Sun 10–12.30 and 4.30–7.30*).

The pale-pink town of **Penne**, further west, was an important town of the Vestini, and today preserves a rare if eclectic urban harmony, its narrow winding streets dotted with Renaissance mansions. Its sights include the ancient crypt of the **cathedral**, itself destroyed in the Second World War and rebuilt, and **Santa Maria in Colleromano** (*ring the bell if closed*), a 15-minute walk from the centre, with good 14th–15th-century statues. In **Moscufo**, further south, **Santa Maria del Lago** merits a visit for its unique 12th-century pulpit adorned with painted reliefs.

Pescara

Pescara wears many hats—it's Abruzzo's biggest resort, most prosperous town, a fishing port and provincial capital. In ancient times its port was shared by several Italic tribes and later by the Romans, who made it the terminus of the Via Tiburtina–Via Valeria (the modern SS5). In 1864 Gabriele D'Annunzio was born here, the son of a local merchant, and his birthplace, or **Casa Natale**, on Corso Manthonè (*closed for restoration*), has a charming little courtyard. Pescara has an outdoor theatre built in D'Annunzio's honour, which is the venue for a Jazz Festival in the first half of July. The **Museo delle Genti d'Abruzzo** (*open Tues–Sun 9–12; adm*), on Via delle Caserme, a comprehensive up-to-date collection, is dedicated to everyday life and popular traditions in the Abruzzo over the centuries.

Pescara's golden egg, though, is its 16km-long sandy beach, almost solid with hotels, cafés and fish restaurants between the Pescara River and Montesilvano; whatever old buildings it had were decimated in the fierce fighting that took place along the coast in the Second World War. Still, this is no Rimini; families bake together in the day, and stroll about eating ice-cream in the evening. If you need excitement, there are riding stables, go-karts, tennis courts and, for some real thrills, the **Fish Museum**, in Pescara's bustling fish market on Lungofiume Paolucci (*but the aquarium is empty; usually open Mon–Sat 9–1; free adm while under restoration*).

Chieti

For something a bit weightier than gills and beachballs, head up to Chieti, about 13km up the Pescara River. Another provincial capital, Chieti was the Roman *Theate Marrucinorum*, a name that its bishop, Pietro Carafa, made use of when founding the Theatine Order in 1524. Bishop Carafa went on to become Paul IV, the most vicious and intolerant of popes, but it's no reflection on Chieti, which avoids such extremes.

The **Museo Nazionale Archeologico di Antichità** (*open daily 9–7; adm*), in the Villa Comunale, is Chieti's star attraction, and one of the region's most important museums: the chief repository of pre-Roman and Roman artworks unearthed in the Abruzzo, including the shapely 6th-century BC *Warrior of Capestrano*, dressed like a Mexican bandit and accompanied by an as yet untranslated inscription—the language of the mysterious Middle Adriatic Bronze-Age culture. There is a room of other items found in Bronze-Age tombs, and others containing Hellenistic and Roman sculptures, tombs, portraits, coins, jewellery and votive offerings, many discovered in Alba Fucens, in the Abruzzo National Park, and Amiternum, near L'Aquila. Next door, the documentation of material from Abruzzo's many Upper Palaeolithic caves is displayed with ancient ceramics and artefacts from Italic necropolises.

Out of doors, Chieti retains a couple of traces of *Theate Marrucinorum*—the remains of three little temples on Via Spaventa, near the post office—while in the eastern residential quarters stand the **Terme Romane** (*to visit, ask the staff at the Museo Archeologico, © 0871 331 668*), or baths, of which a mighty cistern is the most impressive feature. Best of all are the lovely views, stretching from the sea to the Gran Sasso and Maiella Mountains.

Ortona and Lanciano

South of Pescara, beyond the pleasant resort of **Francavilla al Mare**, lies Abruzzo's largest port, **Ortona**. Over the years Ortona has taken more than its share of damage, earthquakes and warfare, particularly in the autumn of 1943, when the Germans were well-entrenched along a line north of the River Sangro, and thousands of lives were lost in the six-week Battle of the Sangro and Moro rivers before they were rooted out. There are two large British military cemeteries in the vicinity, one near the River Moro, about 3km south of Ortona, and the other just south of Torino di Sangro Marina, between Ortona and Vasto.

From Ortona you can take a narrow-gauge local train for an inland loop (although admittedly the bus is much faster), seeing Guardiagrele and Lanciano on the way. **Guardiagrele** was a famous goldsmiths' centre in the Renaissance, the birthplace of the renowned Nicola da Guardiagrele in the 15th century, who made the silver crucifix in the treasury of **Santa Maria Maggiore** (*open mid-July–Aug daily 10–12.30 and 4–7.30; other times call ahead, © 0871 82117*). This church has a huge exterior fresco of St Christopher by Andrea de Litio, which was believed to bring good luck to any traveller who saw it.

Lanciano, a medieval market town that once attracted merchants from all over the Mediterranean to its wool and cloth fairs, retains more grey stone monuments from its golden days: **Porta San Biagio**, the only medieval gate to survive, and the **cathedral**, uniquely sited on a Roman bridge. Pilgrims have long come to **San Francesco** for its relics of an 8th-century miracle—some drops of blood and a little piece of human heart—when the bread and wine of the Mass supposedly really did transubstantiate into flesh and blood for a sceptical monk. Above the church is the 11th-century fortress of the **Torri Montanare**, which has great views of the hills and mountains further inland. Lanciano is also the starting point for one of the most spectacular drives in the Abruzzo—the SS84 to Roccaraso, near the Abruzzo National Park.

San Giovanni in Venere and Vasto

Back on the coast, above the railway station of the small resort of **Fossacesia Marina**, stands one of Abruzzo's most remarkable monuments—**San Giovanni in Venere**. 'Venere' refers to Venus, over whose temple this church was erected; temples to the love goddess were often placed in similar spots, high over the sea. Begun as early as the 8th century, the church was rebuilt in 1015 and converted into a Cistercian abbey in 1165. There are several Puglian-Sicilian touches in the church, perhaps introduced by Frederick II's architects—in the decoration of the narrow windows, the robust figures of the bas-reliefs, and the design of the magnificent marble *Portale della Luna*, the 'Portal of the Moon' (1230). Be sure to walk around the church to see the beautiful apses. Inside, the ceiling is supported by cruciform piers, and there are some old, if not very interesting, frescoes dating back to the 12th century. The large crypt, entered from the aisles, contains ancient columns from the temple of Venus.

Further south, salty old **Vasto**, home town of the father of Dante Gabriele and Christina Rossetti, stands on a low natural terrace above its beach and port, the former attracting large numbers of French as well as Italian tourists. Its narrow streets end at the weathered but distinctive 13th-century castle, with a cylindrical tower. Vasto is proud of its painter, Filippo Palizzi (1818 99), whose works can be seen in the church of San Pietro, and in the local **Museo Civico** (*open Mon–Sat 10–12*).

Termoli

Crossing over the River Trigno, you enter Molise, which is, in the main, even more rural and unspoiled than Abruzzo, although this may not be immediately apparent from the busy beaches along the coast. **Termoli** gets top billing here, a bright little fishing town with a long sandy beach, palms and oleanders. The diva of the old town, or at least the part that survived a Turkish raid in 1566, is the 13th-century **cathedral**, its façade undulating with blind Puglian-style arcades; but it also boasts a **castle** and walls from the same period, both built by the Emperor Frederick II. After enjoying the view from the castle there's nothing more demanding to do than relax on the beach and try to decide which seafood restaurant to try in the evening. If Termoli's too crowded, there's another modest resort down the coast, **Campomarino**. A little further south, and the road enters Puglia (*see* p.879).

Where to Stay and Eating Out

Most of the hotels date from the past couple of decades; some prices have rocketed recently, but they are a bargain compared with the rest of Italy.

Giulianova ✉ 64022

★★★★**Gran Hotel Don Juan**, Lungomare Zara 97, ✆ 085 800 8341, ✉ 085 800 4805 (*very expensive*) is the smartest hotel on this stretch of coast. Located on its own beach, it has a pool, tennis courts and garden. *Closed Oct–April.* The smaller ★★★**Promenade**, Lungomare Zara 119, ✆ 085 800 3338, 🖷 085 800 5983 (*moderate*) has similar amenities but not so much style. *Closed Oct–mid-May.*

The Abruzzo's most celebrated seafood restaurant is **Beccaceci**, Via Zola 28, ✆ 085 800 3550 (*expensive*), which serves its own long-established seafood and pasta inventions—try the *linguine alla giuliese* or the squid stuffed with prawns. *Closed Sun eve, Mon and 27 Dec–10 Jan.* For traditional cuisine, **Osteria della Stracciavocc**, Via Trieste 124, ✆ 085 800 5326 (*moderate–cheap*) serves outstanding pasta and seafood. *Closed Mon, Tues lunch and two weeks in Sept.*

Pescara ✉ 65100

Pescara has by far the most hotels and restaurants on the coast, but tranquillity is a rare commodity in the summer, and full-board is bound to be required in July and August. The top hotel, ★★★★**Carlton**, Viale Riviera 35, ✆ 085 373 125, 🖷 085 421 3922 (*moderate*) is a very comfortable resort palace on the sea, with a private beach that almost absorbs the racket. ★★★**Bellariva**, Viale Riviera 213, ✆ 085 471 2641 (*moderate*) is unpretentious and good for families. ★★★**Salus**, Lungomare Matteotti 13/1, ✆ 085 374 196 (*cheap*) has good standard rooms and a private beach.

Elegant **Guerino**, Viale della Riviera 4, ✆ 085 421 2065 (*expensive*) is the city's best seafood restaurant, with a seafront terrace: the tasty Adriatic speciality of fillets of John Dory with *prosciutto* go down especially well. *Closed Tues and 22 Dec–5 Jan.* **Duilio**, Via Regina Margherita 11, ✆ 085 378 278 (*moderate*) features seafood in nearly every delicately prepared dish. *Closed Sun evenings, Mon and Aug.*

La Terrazza Verde, Largo Madonna 6, ✆ 085 413 239 (*moderate*) doesn't serve fish at all. In a panoramic setting with a beautiful garden terrace high up in the hills, it serves delicious gnocchi and duck, a popular dish in Abruzzo, prepared in a variety of ways. *Closed Wed.* **Trattoria Roma**, tucked away at Via Trento 86, ✆ 085 295 374 (*cheap*) is a good place to find hearty Abruzzese cooking. It's very popular with locals, and the menu changes daily; there's always at least one good fish choice. *Closed Sun.*

Montesilvano Marina ✉ 65016

The large, modern and comfortable ★★★★**Serena Majestic**, Viale Kennedy 12, ✆ 085 83699, 🖷 085 836 9859 (*moderate*) is on the beach, with gardens, tennis courts and a pool. One of the best-value hotels on the coast, ★★★**Piccolo Mondo**, Via Marinelli 86, ✆ 085 445 2647 (*cheap*) has been totally renovated; with just 20 rooms, and a roof terrace and garden, it's a good choice for a family holiday.

Chieti ✉ 66100

Two km out of town, ★★★★**Dangio'**, Strada Solferino 20, Loc. Tricalle ✆ 0871 347 356, 🖷 0871 346 984 (*moderate*) is the best place to stay, with comfortable rooms and a gourmet restaurant, **La Regine** (*expensive*). *Closed Sun eve and Mon lunch.* For a fairly priced, fairly cooked meal try **Venturini**, Via De Lollis 10, ✆ 0871 330 663 (*cheap*), an institution whose speciality is a mushroom risotto with mozzarella. *Closed Tues.* **Nonna Elisa**, Loc. Brecciarola, Via Bentivoglio 2 (take Viale Maiella), ✆ 0871 684 152 (*cheap*) offers a delicious, strictly *abruzzese* experience. *Closed Mon.*

Guardiagrele

Villa Maiella, Via Sette Dolori 30, © 0871 809 362 (*cheap*) is one of the most popular restaurants in the area: with an imaginative menu based on traditional recipes, careful, enthusiastic service and excellent wine. *Closed Mon and 2nd half of July.*

San Giovanni in Venere

Parco dei Priori, Via San Giovanni in Venere 41, next to the abbey, © 0872 608 171 (*expensive–moderate*) is located in a well-restored 18th-century villa, and serves lovely seafood, including excellent lobster. *Closed Mon.*

Vasto

Vasto is a bit of a gastronomic capital on the coast. At **All'Hostaria del Pavone**, Via Barbarotta 15, © 0873 60227 (*moderate–cheap*), you can taste a wonderful *scapece* (tiny fishes, first fried then marinated in saffron and vinegar)—a dish that has nourished generations of sailors—as well as many other fish specialities. *Closed Tues.*

Termoli ✉ 86039

★★★★**Corona**, Corso M. Milano 2/a, ©/● 0875 84043 (*moderate*) is a medium-sized traditional hotel in the centre of town; the Liberty-style dining room serves good food. *Closed Sun.* Little 9-room ★★★**Cian**, Lungomare Colombo 48, © 0875 704 436 (*cheap*) is a good budget choice, on a rock above the coast, with lovely views. **Lo Squaloblu**, Via de Gasperi 49, © 0875 81399 (*expensive–moderate*) is an excellent restaurant serving exquisitely cooked (and also raw) molluscs and crustaceans, and duck, followed by a delicious variety of local cheeses. *Closed Mon and several weeks between Dec and Jan.* The modest **Da Noi Tre**, Corso Fratelli Brigida 34, © 0875 703 639 (*cheap*) serves good fish. *Open daily in summer; in winter closed Mon and several weeks between Dec and Jan.* 5km north of the centre, on the SS16 Adriatica Highway, **Torre Saracena**, © 0875 703 318 (*expensive– moderate*), in an ancient watchtower on the beach, features the freshest of fish, prepared in some surprising ways. *Closed Mon and Nov.*

Teramo

Getting Around

Teramo is fairly easily reached by **train**, on a spur from the coastal line at Giulianova. **Buses** on both the *autostrada* and local roads also quickly link Teramo to the coast, to Ascoli Piceno and to L'Aquila.

Tourist Information

Via del Castello 10, © 0861 244 222 (*open Mon–Sat 9–1*).

From Giulianova the SS80 heads 20km inland to Teramo, midway between the coast and the Gran Sasso. Originally a Roman city, Teramo knew its happiest days in the 14th century under the Angevins, and even though it wears mostly 20th-century fashions today, it preserves several fine monuments. The **cathedral** stands out with its remarkable Cosmati-decorated portal and Romanesque saints; around them a miscellany of lions, collected from here and there, lend feline elegance to the façade, which is as simple, square and ungabled as any in Abruzzo. The cathedral's Ghibelline crenellations recall the days when Teramo was the fief of its bishop, who still possesses the title of 'Prince of Teramo', although he no longer makes much use of a special papal dispensation from more rough and ready days that allowed him to wear armour under his robes and keep his sword handy by the altar. The pretty campanile is from the 15th century; inside there is a silver altar frontal with 30 scenes from the Bible, a masterpiece by Nicola da Guardiagrele (1448) who also made the silver statues of Mary and Gabriel by the main door. The 15th-century polyptych is by the Venetian Jacobello del Fiore.

Near the cathedral lie the ruins of the **Teatro Romano** and, a short distance further on, the original cathedral, **Santa Maria Aprutiensis** (6th–12th-century)—its name recalling the Italic tribe of the Praetutii who gave their name to *Aprutium* (and hence to Abruzzo). Santa Maria (also called Sant'Anna), built of bits of Roman columns and other ancient fragments, is Teramo's attic of odds and ends—Lombard carvings, a 6th-century triforium and ancient angelic frescoes. Another block east is the well-preserved 14th-century **Casa dei Melatini**. In the Franciscan convent of **Madonna delle Grazie**, to the east by Piazza della Libertà, is a painted wooden statue of the *Madonna and Child* by one of the Abruzzo's best sculptors, Silvestro dall'Aquila (15th century). More 15th-century Abruzzese art is on display in the **Museo Civico e Pinacoteca**, Via Adelfico (*open Mon–Sat 10–1 and 3–7; adm*). If you're driving, take the road to the **Osservatorio Astrofisico** for good views of the Gran Sasso.

The Virtù of Teramo

Teramo has its own culinary speciality called *virtù* that's customarily cooked on the first of May. Judging from its ingredients, it began as a way of using up winter stocks and adding the first of the new season's goodies—traditionally local women each contributed an ingredient. It's a cross between a soup and a stew—a type of minestrone, in fact—based on a stock to which are added twelve different kinds of dried peas, beans and lentils, along with celery, sausage and different bits and pieces of pig, such as trotters and ears, all well-salted and seasoned with herbs.

Around Teramo

Heading north from Teramo towards Ascoli Piceno on the SS81, the road passes **Campli**, just to the east, a small town with several Romanesque and Gothic monuments. The rather formidable **Palazzo del Comune** was built in the 14th century but much altered in 1520. The Romanesque church of **San Francesco** is a fine embodiment of the Abruzzese ideal that less is more; inside are some 14th-century frescoes. Its former convent now houses a **Museo Archeologico** (*open daily 8.30–1.30 and 3.30–7.30*), containing artefacts from the 6th–3rd-century BC Italic necropolis at Campovalano, a kilometre away. Nearby there's the abbey and church of **San Pietro**, founded in the 8th century and rebuilt in the 13th; the frescoed figures on the piers inside were designed to be part of the congregation (*to visit both the necropolis and San Pietro, call the owner of the Alimentari in Campovalano's main square, ☎ 0861 56306, during business hours*). A few kilometres north of Campli rises the superbly positioned Renaissance town of **Civitella del Tronto**, crowned by an impregnable castle that the Bourbons managed to hold right to the bitter end in 1861. First built around the year 1000, it has half a kilometre of travertine walled terrace, lending it its distinctive crew-cut skyline.

Teramo's most attractive hotel is the ★★★★**Sporting**, Via De Gasperi 41, ✆ 0861 412 661, 📠 0861 210 285 (*moderate*), because of its garden, although it's on the outskirts of town. ★**Castello**, Via del Castello 62, ✆ 0861 247 582 (*cheap*) is basic but adequate, with 17 rooms. **Il Duomo**, Via Stazio 9, ✆ 0861 241 774 (*moderate*) serves up local specialities throughout the year: *maccheroni alla chitarra*, and meat dishes, including grilled kid. *Closed Mon, and second and third week of Aug.*

The Gran Sasso: 'The Big Rock of Italy'

The Gran Sasso offers Alpine grandeur only an hour by motorway from Rome, and as such is an immensely popular ski and hiking resort. There are plans to designate it a nature park but, until then, environmentalists and developers will continue to disagree on its future. If you plan to do any hiking pick up a map either from the tourist office or from the **Club Alpino Italiano** (CAI) in L'Aquila, Via del Mulino, ✆ 0862 24342 (*open daily 7am–8pm*).

Tourist Information

Centro Turistico del Gran Sasso: Corso Vittorio Emanuele 49, L'Aquila, ✆ 0862 22146 has information on sights and other outdoor activities in the region's mountains, as does the local office of the **Club Alpino Italiano** (*see* above).

Approaching the Gran Sasso from the east, and Castelli

South of Teramo the SS150 divides into two arms embracing the Gran Sasso—the main road that joins up with the SS80 from Teramo and continues up the narrow Val di Vomano to the north—the most scenic road in the region (*see* p.535)—and another that follows the higher **Valle di Mavone** to the south. The latter (SS491) is an excellent approach to the mountains, with the highest peak of the Apennines, the **Corno Grande** (9551ft) looming ahead.

Several curiosities along the SS491 offer tempting detours—near Castelcastagna there's **Santa Maria di Ronzano**, a three-nave church embellished with frescoes dated 1181, among the finest examples of Lombard art in Central Italy. Between Montorio al Vomano and Isola del Gran Sasso you can take in the village of **Tossicia**, with a pretty medieval nucleus lying between two mountain streams; the tiny church of **Sant'Antonio Abate** has a grand 1471 Renaissance portal by the Venetian Antonio Lombardo. Works by one of Italy's best-known *naif* painters, Annunziata Scipione, may be seen in nearby **Azzinano**.

The scenery is stunning as the road reaches **Isola del Gran Sasso**, a fine stone village and a good base for hikes up to the **Campo Imperatore** (*see* p.534); it has another Romanesque church, **San Giovanni ad Insulam**, as well as a more recent shrine to the modern patron saint of Abruzzo-Molise, San Gabriele dell'Addolorata, a young Franciscan monk from Assisi who died in the monastery here in 1862. His relics draw pilgrims by the bus-load—processed through a huge, disconcerting steel-and-concrete basilica designed in shopping mall moderne.

To the southeast of Isola, dramatically positioned at the foot of the great wall of Monte Camica, is **Castelli**, another good mountain base. Castelli is the great centre in the Abruzzo for ceramics, an industry that achieved art and glory in the 17th-century workshops of the

Grue and Gentili families. The ceramic tradition is still continued in various workshops in the town and in the August ceramics fair, where part of the fun is tossing reject plates over the river. Castelli's **Chiesa Madre** contains a majolica *pala* by Francesco Grue, as well as 12th-century wooden statues. More of the Grues' work (as well as that of other local craftsmen) may be seen in the **Museo della Ceramica Abruzzese** (*open Oct–May Tues–Sun 10–1, Sun also 3–5; June–Sept Tues–Sun 10–7; adm*). The Museo also serves as a tourist office, © 0861 979 398, and they organize guided tours around Castelli. Most splendiferous of all, however, is the rural church of **San Donato**, which Carlo Levi rightfully dubbed 'The Sistine Chapel of Italian Majolica', for its ceiling (visible from the outside through a grate) of a thousand ceramic tiles—the only ceiling like it in Italy, an impressive 360 square feet covered with a colourful patchwork of different folk motifs—plenty of rabbits, skulls, portraits, notices of various kinds, geometric patterns and so on (1615–17). Also on the outskirts is the derelict Romanesque church of **San Salvatore**, with a charming medieval pulpit.

Approaches from L'Aquila and the west

If you're coming from L'Aquila, catch the bus from Corso Vittorio Emanuele to the Funicular at **Fonte Cerreto**, near **Assergi**, the village at the mouth of the Gran Sasso Tunnel—alternatively, if you have a car and the roads are clear, drive up the SS17bis by way of **Bazzano** (site of an interesting 12th-century church, **Santa Giusta**). Both the funicular and the road will take you to the **Campo Imperatore** (6973ft), a beautiful, gentle upland basin, filled with flowers in the late spring and ski bunnies in the winter.

Mussolini's Least Favourite Hotel

Near the upper funicular station stands the *Albergo di Campo Imperatore*, which once sheltered a real would-be emperor. After the ad hoc Italian government of Marshal Badoglio had deposed Mussolini and begun to seek peace with the Allies in 1943, there remained the delicate question of what to do with the former Duce. After being shuttled off to a Tyrrhenian island, he was brought to this hotel, at the time inaccessible by road, which set the stage for the SS Commando Otto Skorzeny's daring rescue on 12 September 1943. German paratroopers slipped in and out by flying in a Fieseler Storch—an aeroplane the size of the average bedroom—into which Skorzeny somehow managed to squeeze the portly Mussolini before escaping. Hitler then set up a new headquarters for his associate on Lake Garda, the capital of the ill-fated Italian Social Republic. This episode fooled the Allies, and has fooled historians for decades. Only recently has it been established that Skorzeny's exploit wasn't necessary at all: the Germans might have picked him up in a car. It was all a publicity stunt, part of Hitler's campaign to glorify the SS at the expense of the regular German army, which was getting beaten on all fronts, and whose political loyalty was already suspect.

Many of the trails through the Gran Sasso begin at the hotel, including one up past the Duca degli Abruzzi refuge to the **Corno Grande** (9551ft), a spectacular eight-hour walk. There are also three ski lifts in the Campo Imperatore, and four nearby at Monte Cristo. South of L'Aquila there is more good skiing as well as bobsledding at **Campo Felice**, above the picturesque village of **Rocca di Cambio**, the highest in Abruzzo at 4700ft.

The Upper Vomano Valley: Teramo to L'Aquila

At **Montorio al Vomano** the SS150 joins the main SS80, the scenic road which, like the more efficent but less panoramic *autostrada*, links Teramo with L'Aquila. Montorio, topped by its grand but never-completed Spanish castle, has an eclectic church, the **Collegiata di San Rocco**, with a façade that has been added to whenever funds were handy; within, the carved wooden Baroque altar and tapestries are the main attraction.

Further up the valley the twin, blunt, snow-shrouded peaks of the Due Corni del Gran Sasso look over the shoulder of **Fano Adriano**, an old town and now a small winter and summer resort, with skiing and hiking at **Pratoselva**. The village's name means 'Hadrian's Temple', although none of this remains; the 12th-century **San Pietro** is modern Fano's finest church, with a Renaissance façade from 1550. **Pietracamela**, even higher up in the lap of the Gran Sasso (3296ft), is a base for hikes over the Sella dei Due Corni to the Campo Imperatore, and for skiing at the Gran Sasso's biggest resort, **Prati di Tivo**, a fine lofty meadow of beech forests. During the peak season a helicopter takes expert skiers to otherwise inaccessible runs.

The SS80 towards L'Aquila continues past the **Lago di Campotosto**, an irregular man-made lake stocked with fish, and then winds around the western flank of the Gran Sasso. About 10km before L'Aquila it comes to **Amiternum**, the ruins of a Sabine city mentioned in the *Aeneid*. Later a Roman colony, it was the birthplace of the poet Sallust. A small theatre, amphitheatre, houses with mosaics and frescoes, and other relics, were brought to light in 1978 (*ring the custodian's bell; adm*). Nearby, medieval **San Vittorino** has, under the 12th–16th-century church of **San Michele** (*closed on and off for restoration; call Don Sigismondo, © 0862 461 695, to schedule a visit*), something out of the ordinary in this part of the world: catacombs, although, unlike the great ones in Rome, these have been embellished with 15th-century frescoes. A procession is held through them on the last Sunday in May; at other times you may have to ask at the church to be able to see them.

The Gran Sasso ✉ *67100*   **Where to Stay**

Mussolini's least favourite hotel, at the top of the cablecar route, ★★★★**Albergo di Campo Imperatore**, © 0862 400 000, 🖅 0862 606 688 (*moderate*) is very comfortable. Another hotel that was used to hold Mussolini in 1943, little ★★**La Villetta**, by the lower funicular station at Fonte Cerreto, © 0862 606 171 (*cheap*) is a pretty, friendly hotel that makes a good base for visiting the mountains. Up in Prati di Tivo, ★★★★**Miramonti**, © 0861 959 621, 🖅 0861 959 647 (*moderate*) is a comfortable, modern resort hotel with a garden, pool and tennis courts. *Open 20 Dec–10 April and 20 June–10 Sept.*

L'Aquila

L'Aquila, the regional capital, is an intriguing town in its own right, as well as making an ideal base for travelling around the rest of the Abruzzo. The name means 'the eagle', the symbol of empire, and it's not surprising to learn that the city was founded by Emperor Frederick II in 1240 as a bulwark against the popes. L'Aquila is one of the few cities in Italy of any importance not to have ancient precedents; instead, to populate his new town, Frederick relocated the inhabitants of surrounding castles and hamlets—99 of them in all, according to tradition, who each built their own church in the new town. But what made L'Aquila's fortune was its loyalty to Queen Giovanna II in 1423, when the city was besieged for over a year by the Aragonese. The queen thanked the city for its steadfastness by granting it privileges that helped it to become, for several centuries, the second city in the Kingdom of Naples, a wool and livestock market town and a producer of silk and saffron. It attracted Adamo di Rottweil, a student of Gutenberg, who founded a printing press here in 1482, one of the first in Italy.

L'Aquila's good fortune made it cocky, and in 1529 it rose up against its rulers in Naples. The Spanish viceroy quickly put an end to its pretensions and punished the Aquilani by forcing them to pay for a huge new citadel to discourage any further revolts. Much of what the Spaniards didn't destroy in their reprisal fell in the earthquake of 1703. And yet, despite its vicissitudes, L'Aquila has managed to keep a considerable portion of its labyrinthine old quarter, its walls and even some of its exceptional 13th-century monuments.

Tourist Information

Via XX Settembre 8, ✆ 0862 22306 (*open Mon–Sat 8–2 and 3–7*).

Getting Around

Trains connect L'Aquila (with no great hurry or frequency) to Rieti in Lazio and Terni in Umbria, as well as to Pescara by way of Sulmona, the main junction for rail routes in the central Abruzzo. L'Aquila is also less than two hours from Rome by **bus** on ARPA (Rome, ✆ 06 442 33928; L'Aquila, ✆ 0862 22146; Pescara, ✆ 085 421 5099), with 18 departures a day (11 on Sundays) from outside Stazione Tiburtina; in Rome you must buy tickets before boarding at Via Teodorico 28 (*open daily 6.30am–9.30pm*).

A 99-headed Fountain

L'Aquila's famous **Fontana delle 99 Cannelle**, built in 1272, stands in a pink-and-white chequered courtyard in a corner of the walls near the Porta Rivera, not far from the railway station on the western side of the old city. The fountain's water flows through the mouths of 93 mouldering grotesque heads (and six unadorned spouts), each representing one of the hamlets that were brought together to form the city of L'Aquila. The fountain has three sides (the one to the left is a more recent addition, built in the 16th century). While you're there, try to figure out how the two sundials work on the façade of the little church opposite.

From the fountain, Via San Jacopo ascends to join Via XX Settembre, the main entry-point into the city if you're approaching from Rome. If you follow Via XX Settembre straight into a small piazza laid out as a park, turn right at the next street and then left on to the Viale di Collemaggio you will reach L'Aquila's greatest Romanesque church, **Santa Maria di Collemaggio**, founded in 1270 by the hermit Pietro Morrone. The church has one of the most sumptuous and attractive façades of any in Abruzzo, its three rounded portals decorated with spiral mouldings and niches for saints, who have mostly vanished. Above the portals runs a pretty ribbon frieze, and above that are three rose windows of different patterns, the centre one a masterpiece of the stonecarver's art. The elegant interior has been stripped of its centuries' accumulation of art and debris, leaving the fancy Renaissance tomb of Celestine V as its chief decoration. Pietro Morrone was an utterly holy man but rather naïve and, in 1294, to his surprise, he was crowned pope here by cardinals who hoped to use him as their instrument. After a few months it became evident that the new Pope Celestine V wasn't quite turning out as expected and he was subtly 'encouraged' in Naples' Egg Castle (*see* p.805) to resign St Peter's throne—the only pope ever to do so voluntarily. Soon after his death, however, one of his successors canonized him, and here he rests as St Peter Celestine. He gained an additional somewhat embarrassing claim to fame in 1988 when his relics were stolen and held to ransom, only to be returned without further ado when it became clear to the body snatchers that no one thought Celestine was worth the asking price. A privilege Celestine V granted the church during his brief office is a Holy Door, an uncommon feature, which is opened annually on 28 August for the faithful to pass through and receive the still-distributed papal indulgence.

Around Piazza Duomo

From Via XX Settembre and the park, Corso Federico II leads into Piazza Duomo, L'Aquila's main market square ever since 1304 when Charles of Anjou granted the town the right to hold one here—you'll find produce and handicrafts on sale daily from dawn to 1pm. Frequently shattered by earthquakes, the **Duomo** itself is dressed in a dull neoclassical façade, a wallflower next to the piazza's 18th-century Baroque **Santuario del Suffragio**, with opulent curves and a death's head above the entrance. The neighbourhood around Piazza del Duomo is one of L'Aquila's most attractive. On Via Santa Giusta, the 13th-century church of **Santa Giusta** has a good portal and rose window embellished with 12 droll figures, while all around it the streets are full of Baroque palaces. On Via Sassa, the church of **San Giuseppe** contains a 15th-century equestrian tomb by Ludovico d'Alemagna, while **Palazzo Franchi**, at No.56, contains a lovely Renaissance courtyard with a double loggia. From Piazza Duomo, Corso Vittorio Emanuele leads to the **Quattro Cantoni**, the 'Four Corners', the city's main crossroads. To the left, on Corso Umberto, lies Piazza del Palazzo, the palazzo in question being the **Palazzo di Giustizia**, from where Margherita of Austria, a daughter of Charles V born on the wrong side of the blanket, ruled as Governess of Abruzzo. The bell in the palace's tower sounds 99 strokes every day at dusk.

San Bernardino

On the other side of the Quattro Cantoni, Via San Bernardino leads to the masterpiece of Abruzzese Renaissance, the church of **San Bernardino**. The great revivalist preacher, San Bernardino da Siena, spent several years in the Franciscan convent in L'Aquila before he died, whereupon one of his disciples, St John of Capestrano, founded this church as his memorial. Work began in 1452, but the perfectly balanced, elegant façade was only finished by Cola dell'Amatrice in 1542. It is best seen from the bottom of the stair in front of the church; we are in Abruzzo, so the roof is gable-less. The 1703 earthquake smashed the vast interior, which was rebuilt in flagrant Baroque; the magnificent gilt wood ceiling, incorporating San Bernardino's IHS monogram, is by Ferdinando Mosca. San Bernardino's mausoleum and the *Tomb of Maria Periera* are both works by Silvestro dall'Aquila, a pupil of Donatello. The second chapel on the right contains a *pala* by Andrea della Robbia, grandson of the more famous Luca.

The Castello and Museo Nazionale d'Abruzzo

To the north the Corso Vittorio Emanuele runs out into the shady Parco del Castello and, above it, the grand, moated **castello**. Built in 1535 by Pier Luigi Sacrivà, it is a showpiece of military architecture unwillingly financed by the citizens of L'Aquila, with a grand doorway, crowned by Charles V's two-headed eagle. The castle contains the **Museo Nazionale d'Abruzzo** (*open Tues–Sat 9–7, Sun 9–1; adm*), the region's finest, with a well-arranged collection of archaeological treasures and art salvaged from abandoned local churches. The biggest exhibit is on the ground floor, to the right of the entrance: the *Elephas Meridionalis*, a reconstructed prehistoric pachyderm, discovered near L'Aquila in 1954. Here too are Roman portraits, statues, tombs, tympanums, reliefs, tools and so on; on the first floor the medieval section has a vast collection of religious art—superb polychrome wooden statues, including a *St Sebastian* and a *Madonna and Child* by Silvestro dell'Aquila and a fine 15th-century panel painting of *St John of Capestrano*. Other fine triptychs show a Sienese-Umbrian influence. On the next floor you'll find works by Neapolitan painters like Mattia Preti and Andrea Vaccaro, as well as by Abruzzese artists like Pompeo Cesari. The third and final floor contains 20th-century works, mainly by local artists; concerts are held regularly in the castle's auditorium.

From L'Aquila to Popoli

The SS17 runs southeast from L'Aquila along the southern flanks of the Gran Sasso, passing quiet villages like **Calascio**, with its impressive ruined citadel 4920ft up, or **Castel del Monte**, further up still, with an interesting medieval core. On the other side of the SS17, **Fossa** has 12th-century frescoes of the *Day of Judgement* in its church of **Santa Maria ad Cryptas** that are said to have inspired Dante (*if closed, call Don Giuseppe, © 0862 751 226*).

Tiny **Bominaco** (near Caporciano) is the site of the most celebrated monuments in this corner of Abruzzo, two churches that belonged to a fortified Benedictine Abbey (*call the custodian, Sig. Cassiani, © 0862 93604, to arrange a visit*). The monastery dates from some shadowy three-digit year; **San Pellegrino** is said to have been founded by Charlemagne, though it was rebuilt in 1263. The interior, rectangular with an ogival vault, is covered with the colourful, stylized frescoes of the period: a pictorial calendar of the months and major feast days, scenes from the New Testament, saints and geometrical patterns. The sanctuary is set apart by a marble transenna carved with a griffon with a cup, and another with a fearsome dragon—not your ordinary church fare. The saint is buried under the sanctuary and it is said that you can hear his heart beating through a hole by the altar.

Santa Maria Assunta has none of the ancient strangeness of San Pellegrino, but is a 12th-century gem, beautifully endowed with carved doors, windows, capitals and a pulpit. Just to the west of Bominaco are the caves of the **Grotte di Stiffe** (*50-min guided tours June–Sept daily 10–1 and 3–8; Oct–May shorter evening hours; adm exp; call © 0862 86142, to arrange a tour in English*), where half a mile of illuminated walkway takes you along an underground river beneath eerie stalactites.

From Navelli the road makes a dramatic writhing descent to Popoli (*see below*), on the Via Valeria and the Rome–Pescara *autostrada*, or you can turn eastwards to **Capestrano**, birthplace of San Bernardino's saintly follower, St John of Capestrano (1386–1456). The swallows come back here, too, if not on the same tight schedule as their Californian cousins.

L'Aquila ✉ *67100*   ***Where to Stay and Eating Out***

As elsewhere in the Abruzzo, prices are notably low compared to the Italian norm. The region's eating establishments are more original than its hotels, especially if you come in May when the locals are cooking up pots of *virtù* (*see above*).

***Castello**, Piazza Battaglione Alpini, ✆ 0862 419 147 (*moderate*) is a classy hotel opposite the castle. ***Duomo**, Via Dragonetti 6, ✆ 0862 410 893 (*moderate*), in a 17th-century palace off Piazza Duomo, has 28 rooms, some with a view of the square. ***Duca degli Abruzzi**, Viale Papa Giovanni XXIII 10, ✆ 0862 28341 (*moderate*) has comfortable rooms. The not-so-central *Orazi**, Via Roma 175, ✆ 0862 412 889 (*cheap*) has 10 rooms. Traditional Abruzzese cuisine is a speciality at **Ernesto**, Piazza Palazzo, ✆ 0862 210 94 (*moderate*): home-made pasta dishes featuring truffles or saffron, *stracotto* (beef stewed in Montepulciano wine) and *cacio e ova* (stewed in a sauce of eggs and *pecorino*). Reserve. *Closed Sun, Mon and two weeks in Aug.* Family-run **Aquila da Remo**, Via San Flaviano 9, ✆ 0862 22010 (*moderate*) has good solid cooking in a simple setting. *Closed Fri and two weeks in July.* Slightly cheaper, **Del Giaguaro**, Piazza Santa Maria Paganica 4, ✆ 0862 28249 (*cheap*) is conveniently placed, and offers good local cuisine. *Closed Mon evenings, Tues and two weeks between July and Aug.* **Dei Gemelli**, Via Guelfaglione 27, ✆ 0862 27574 (*cheap*), near the Duomo, is worth a detour for its wonderful home-made pasta. *Closed Sun.*

Southern Abruzzo and the National Park

For many people the highlight of the Abruzzo is its National Park, the second largest in Italy and of special interest for its rare fauna and flora. For mountain-lovers there's also the Montagna della Maiella, a range nearly as impressive as the Gran Sasso and considerably less touristy. Man-made sights include *Alba Fucens*, Abruzzo's best archaeological site, and intriguing old towns like Sulmona, Scanno, Pescocostanzo and Tagliacozzo.

Getting Around

As a major **rail** junction, and with **bus** services to most of the area, Sulmona is the best base for exploring; but bus and train connections are infrequent, so you have to be well-organized. Buses run fairly frequently from L'Aquila to Avezzano, and from there to Pescasséroli, the administrative centre of the Abruzzo National Park. There's a direct early morning ARPA bus to Pescasséroli from Rome, which returns to Rome in the evening (*mid-June–mid-Sept*). Spectacular **roads** include the SS5bis from L'Aquila to Celano, SS84 from Lanciano to Roccaraso, and SS83 from Pescina, near Celano, through the National Park.

Tourist Information

Tagliacozzo: Via Vittorio Veneto 6, ✆ 0863 610 318. **Sulmona**: Corso Ovidio 208, ✆ 0864 53276. **Scanno**: Piazza Santa Maria della Valle 12, ✆ 0864 74317.

The Via Valeria: Pescara to Rome

Inland from Chieti, the old Roman Via Valeria/Via Tiburtina accompanies the A25 up the Pescara Valley. Near the village of Torre de' Passeri, more Romanesque awaits at **San Clemente in Casauria**, founded by Emperor Louis II (Charlemagne's great-grandson) in 871. The Cistercians took over and rebuilt the church in the 12th century, endowing it with a magnificent three-arched porch and intricately carved capitals, and a stunning portal with reliefs that form a fitting frame for the ornate bronze doors. The same sculptors may also have carved the *baldacchino* and pulpit in the Romanesque interior; Louis II's original crypt was preserved in the reconstruction of the church, and is reached by steps from the aisles.

Popoli stands at the confluence of the Aterno and the Sagittario, where they meet to form the River Pescara. The town's largest church, Romanesque **San Francesco**, is topped with statues and pierced by an unusual rose window. The 14th-century **Taverna Ducale**, decorated with escutcheons, was not where Popoli's Cantelmi dukes drank, but where they stored the tithes from their subjects. It has survived in better shape than their castle which looms over Popoli. **Corfinio**, to the west, was called Pentima until Mussolini gave it back its ancient name—for here stood the Paeligni capital *Corfinium*, famous in history as the united headquarters of the Italic tribes in the Social Wars of the 1st century BC. They renamed the city *Italica*, the first instance in history that the name signified a union of the peninsula's peoples, hoping it would soon take over from Rome as capital. Now even its ruins are meagre; there's a small archaeology museum in the convent of **Sant'Alessandro** (*for admission, inquire at the church*). Near Corfinio the SS17 leaves the Via Valeria to continue south to Sulmona (*see* below), while the *autostrada* veers south to avoid the scenic gorges of the Aterno River and the lofty pass at Forca Caruso. Back on the old Roman road, **Celano** is a pretty hill town spread out beneath the skirts of its four-square **Piccolomini Castle**. Celano was the birthplace of the Blessed Tommaso da Celano, a disciple of St Francis, and his first biographer; he also composed the '*Dies Irae*', the eerie medieval hymn of the dead most often heard these days in the finale of Berlioz' *Symphonie Fantastique*. Nearby you can visit the stunningly steep and narrow gorge, the **Gole di Celano**, or head north on the scenic SS5bis towards L'Aquila, by way of the mountain resort town of **Ovindoli** and Rocca di Cambio.

Avezzano and *Alba Fucens*

The region south of Celano is known as the Marsica, after its ancient inhabitants, the Marsi, who lived on the shores of Lake Fucino. Marsica's modern capital, **Avezzano**, has little to commend it, having been toppled by an earthquake in 1915 and bombed during the Second World War. Its one monument, the **Castello Orsini**, has a portal with a relief celebrating the Victory of Lepanto. In the **Palazzo Comunale** there's a small museum of inscriptions and architectural fragments from the cities of the Marsica (*closed for restoration*). Avezzano is a main departure point for the Abruzzo National Park (*see* below).

If the ancient Marsi were to return to their homeland today, they would be amazed to find their lake—once the largest in Central Italy—replaced by the fertile basin called the **Piana del Fucino**. But they would also tell you that their *Lacus Fucinus* had been a bit of a mess, with an inadequate outlet and prone to flooding. To drain it, Emperor Claudius ordered what became the greatest underground engineering work of antiquity (AD 54)—a 6km-long tunnel intended to spill the lake's waters into the River Liri. However, for all the amazing skill that went into the work, the tunnel didn't work very well and was eventually blocked up. In 1240 Frederick II tried to have it unblocked, but failed, and only in 1875 did British, Italian, French and Swiss engineers finally drain the lake, reclaiming thousands of hectares.

Of all the ancient cities of the Marsi, the only one to leave behind many traces is *Alba Fucens* (*open daily till dusk*), near modern **Albe**, completely rebuilt after the 1915 earthquake (8km from Avezzano, and linked by buses). Alba was founded as a Roman colony in 300 BC to keep an eye on the area's tribes—hence the mighty walls. Ancient Alba occupies three hills, and its ruins intermingle with the ruins of medieval Alba. Much has been excavated, including the amphitheatre, the forum, the basilica, the weedy theatre, the baths and a long section of the original Via Valeria. Near the amphitheatre is the well-preserved Romanesque church of **San Pietro** (*irregular opening hours*), adorned with Cosmati work.

Tagliacozzo

To the west of Albe, Tagliacozzo is a pretty, ancient town on the slopes of Monte Bove, only an hour by bus from Tivoli and Rome. Named after Thalia, the Muse of Theatre, it is known for the battle that took place on 12 August 1268, which ended the reign of the Swabians and heirs of Frederick II. As Dante described it, the Germans under Conradin were caught unawares and disarmed by the clever plans and intrigues of the Angevins, led by William di Villehardouin. The site of the battle is marked by the ruined church of **Santa Maria della Vittoria**, at Scurcola Marsicana, east of Tagliacozzo. In the town itself, the church of **San Francesco**, with a fine rose window and portal, contains the relics of Tommaso da Celano. Tagliacozzo's secular architecture is, however, more interesting than its churches, beginning with the 14th-century **Palazzo Ducale**, a grand building on a grand piazza; the loggia on the first floor shelters fine though damaged frescoes by Lorenzo da Viterbo. The quarter around the genteel old **Piazza dell'Obelisco**, with its Renaissance obelisk, has many picturesque houses and peeling palaces from the 14th and 15th centuries. The town's theatrical connections do not lie only in its name: near the Palazzo Ducale, the small **Teatro Thalia** hosts an open-air festival of theatre, music and dance every summer, usually in July.

Sulmona

South of the Via Valeria, Sulmona, beautifully located in a green basin surrounded by mountains, was the capital of another obscure Italic tribe, the Paeligni, but is best remembered as the birthplace of Ovid (43 BC–AD 17), who is commemorated with a large 20th-century statue in Piazza XX Settembre. Much later Sulmona became the capital of its own province, created by Frederick II. It became a minor centre of learning and religion, home of the main abbey of the Celestine Order, and of Pietro Angeleri, who lived in the hermitage of Monte Morrone (and was also known as Pietro Morrone), before being brought down to L'Aquila to be crowned Pope Celestine V (*see* p.536–37). In the early Renaissance its craftsmen were celebrated for their gold-work, although since then they have learned a sweeter skill—what the Italians call *confetti*.

Confetti Nuts

To Italians *confetti* means the sweets covered in sugar of all kinds of colours that are given out to guests at a wedding. They have been a speciality of the Abruzzo since the Middle Ages and, although the original *confetti* were sugared almonds, today they come in a variety of fillings that include chocolate or hazelnuts. The capital of *confetti* is Sulmona, where any number of shops in the historic centre sell confectionery made up to look like flowers or ornate gold and silver ornaments, and have lavish window displays to match. **William di Carlo**, which has its factory and showroom near the station, reckons that it is the oldest *confetti*-manufacturer in the town.

The main street, Corso Ovidio, holds Sulmona's loveliest monument, the church and palace of **Santa Maria Annunziata**, a Gothic and Renaissance ensemble first begun in 1320. Although the three portals on the palace's façade were done at different periods, the result is as harmonically sweet as *confetti*: here is a finely carved, floridly Gothic left portal, crowned by a statue of St Michael, while the middle portal is pure symmetrical Renaissance in form; the comparatively plain portal on the right was the last built, in 1522. Doctors of the Church and saints stand sentry along the façade, while above them runs an intricate ribbon frieze, and above that are three lacy Gothic windows.

Two small **museums** (*open daily 9.30–1*) contain work of the goldsmiths of Renaissance Sulmona (*free*) and sculpture and paintings from the 16th–18th centuries (*adm*). The church's Baroque façade was rebuilt after the 1703 earthquake, yet it still complements the adjacent palace. Concerts are held in the palace courtyard each summer.

Running through the centre of Sulmona is an unusual Gothic **aqueduct** (1256), which supplied water to the towns and its mills; a good place to see it is the huge Piazza Garibaldi, site of the 1474 **Fontana del Vecchio**, named after the bust of a jovial old man on top. Across the road from the fountain stands the lovely carved Romanesque portal of **San Francesco delle Scarpe** ('with shoes' because here the Franciscans wore shoes instead of sandals), but it's a portal and nothing more, the rest having tumbled in one of Sulmona's earthquakes. Outside town, towards Monte Morrone, are some Roman ruins (steps, platform, a mosaic pavement and a stretch of road), part of a **Temple of Hercules**, that locals have for centuries referred to as 'Ovid's villa', though any connection with the poet has now been disproved.

Around Sulmona

There are picturesque hill towns in the vicinity of Sulmona, like **Pacentro**, 9km to the east, its lanes winding around the battlemented towers of the ruined Cantelmo Castle. Beyond Pacentro the SS487 heads up in a serious way into the rugged Maiella Mountains, and a few winding kilometres further east, near Passo San Leonardo, reaches a T-junction where you can turn north towards **Caramanico Terme** (a pretty hill town and sulphur-water spa) and the Via Valeria, or south past the **Campo di Giove**, a winter sports centre with a cablecar up the slopes of a mountain called the Round Table (7885ft), towards the dramatic SS84 and the Sangro Valley.

Pescocostanzo, **Rivisondoli** and especially **Roccaraso** (all stops on the Sulmona–Isernia railway) are well-endowed with sports facilities. Charming Pescocostanzo once owed allegiance to Vittoria Colonna, poet and friend of Michelangelo, and made lace before it became a ski resort; its lovely **Collegiata di Santa Maria del Colle** (*usually open daily for services only*), has excellent wood carvings, dating back to the 11th century.

On the SS84 between Roccaraso and Lanciano (and accessible by bus from either end), is **Taranta Peligna**, which has a new cablecar that rises up to what must be the most spectacular cave in Central Italy, the **Grotta del Cavallone** (4674ft) (*open April–Sept; guided visits last 1½ hrs; to make sure it's open, call the Roccaraso tourist office, © 0864 62210, open Mon–Sat 9–1 and 4.30–6.30*), used as a setting in D'Annunzio's play *La Figlia di Jorio*. The cave's name, the 'Big Horse', comes from the profile carved by nature on the wall at the grandiose entrance of the grotto: other rooms are adorned with stone flowers or lace, alabaster streaks that remind Italians of ham (in the 'Sala del Prosciutto') and fairies, while the 'Sala del Pantheon' is full of curious stalagmite monsters and deities.

To the west of Sulmona lies **Cocullo**, famous for its bizarre 'Procession of Serpents', held on the first Thursday of every May. Live snakes are draped over a statue of Cocullo's patron, San Domenico, as well as over the more inspired locals, who thus form a procession through the streets, uncannily coiling and writhing. There is a story that St Dominic rid the area of poisonous snakes, but scholars have a sneaking suspicion that the festival is a living folk memory of the cult of the goddess Angizia, the enchantress of snakes.

Scanno

From Cocullo (or Anversa degli Abruzzi) the SS479 ascends the lovely **Valle del Sagittario**, passing through the steep Gorge of the Sagittario and alongside the pretty trout-filled Lago di Scanno. Perched high above the lake, the village of **Scanno** is one of the most popular destinations in the Abruzzo, a picturesque place that fascinated 18th-century travellers who wondered at its customs and costumes, more reminiscent of Asia Minor than Italy. Even today the women of Scanno sometimes wear their traditional dress, with their turban-like headdresses; the best time to see the costumes is in the mid-August festival, when Scanno celebrates its very unusual marriage customs. For magnificent views of the sunset over the lake and mountains, drive up the zigzagging road from here to **Frattura**, or take the chairlift up to Monte Rotondo, Scanno's small winter resort.

Parco Nazionale d'Abruzzo

West of Cocullo is the SS83 for the **Abruzzo National Park**. Founded in 1923 and enlarged in 1976, the park covers 400 square kilometres of some of the loveliest scenery in the Apennine range, a little paradise of flowery meadows and forests of beech, pine, oak, ash, maple and yew, the last home of *Ursus arctos marsicanus*, the brown Abruzzo bear, and the Abruzzo chamois; here too are Apennine lynxes, boars, wolves, badgers, red squirrels, eagles, falcons, woodpeckers, owls and many unusual species of songbirds, all protected by law from the enthusiastic Italian hunter.

After passing through the beautiful **Passo del Diavolo**, the road reaches the largest village in the park, **Pescasséroli**, birthplace of Benedetto Croce (1866–1952), the greatest Italian philosopher of the past two centuries.

The **park visitors' centre**, Via Consultore 1, © 0863 91955, has well-made trail maps and information on where to find the flora and fauna (*open daily 9–12 and 3–7*); also visit the small museum (*open daily 10–1 and 3–7; adm exp*). If you want to camp, apply to the Ufficio di Zona del Parco, inside the Visitors' Centre, or stay in one of the nearby camp sites. Bear in mind that at Easter and in July and August it's hard to find vacancies without a reservation.

A pleasant excursion from here even for non-committed hikers is the 2-hour walk up to the **Valico di Monte Tranquillo** (route C3 on the map). In mid-summer and in winter you can also ride Pescasséroli's cablecar up to the summit of Monte Vitelle. Further south, **Opi** and **Barrea** are other pretty villages in the park, near the Lago di Barrea and the Camosciara, where most of the park's graceful chamois live.

Just outside the park the fine scenery continues around **Alfedena**, built on the site of the Samnite town of *Aufidena*—across the river from the modern village you can see the ancient walls and necropolis. A 3km track also leads up from here to the lake of Montagna Spaccata.

Most hotels here only open in the summer and winter. Although not very attractive, Avezzano has the largest choice, many of them along the SS5.

Avezzano

Vecchi Sapori, Via Montello 3, ✆ 0863 416 626 (*moderate–cheap*) is a good, fairly priced restaurant with local specialities, including particularly fine pasta and lamb dishes, and fish on Friday.

Tagliacozzo ✉ 67069

The ★★★**Miramonti**, ✆ 0863 6581, ✆ 0863 6582 (*cheap*) has 21 comfortable rooms and a garden.

Sulmona ✉ 67039

★★★**Europa Park**, on SS17 (off Bivio Badia), just north of town, ✆ 0864 251 260, ✆ 0864 251 317 (*moderate*) is Sulmona's largest and most comfortable hotel, with a tennis court, bar and good restaurant. ★**Italia**, Piazza San Tommaso 3, ✆ 0864 52308 (*cheap*) is atmospheric and comfortable.

Another **Italia**, Piazza XX Settembre 22, ✆ 0864 33070 (*expensive–moderate*) prepares winning variations on traditional local cuisine—home-made pasta and lamb with rosemary. *Closed Mon.* **Clemente**, Vico del Vecchio 11, ✆ 0864 52284, serves up home-made sausages and delicious local dishes: fresh pasta with lamb sauce, saffron or wild mushrooms, roast kid, and good desserts. *Closed Thurs.*

Roccaraso ✉ 67037

★★★**Excelsior**, Via Roma 28, ✆ 0864 602 351 (*moderate*) is one of the classier hotels in the area. *Open mid-Dec–mid-Jan and April–Aug.*

Scanno ✉ 67038

★★★**Del Lago**, ✆ /✆ 0864 74343 (*moderate*) is a small, tranquil hotel with a garden in a lovely setting on the lake. *Open mid-Dec–mid-Jan and Mar–Oct.* Scanno is slightly more expensive than the surrounding area, but the hotel ★★**Margherita**, Via D. Tanturri 100, ✆ 0864 74353 (*cheap*) is good value. **Gli Archetti**, Via Silla 8, ✆ 0864 74645 (*moderate*) offers refined old elegance, and dishes made from home-grown ingredients; try the grilled lamb with pears. *Closed Tues Oct–May.*

Pescasséroli ✉ 67032

★★★★**Grand Hotel del Parco**, ✆ 0863 912 745, ✆ 0863 912 749 (*expensive*) is the grandest hotel in the area, with a beautiful setting, a garden and a heated pool. *Open Christmas–Mar and 15 June–Sept.* Another good choice in the National Park is 'the penguin', ★★★**Il Pinguino**, Via Collacchi 2, ✆ 0863 912 580, ✆ 0863 910 449 (*moderate*), with rooms that are far too snug for a real Antarctican.

Isolated, mountainous and even more sparsely populated than Abruzzo, Molise is one of the least-known regions of Italy. It belonged to the tenacious Samnites of old, and Italians still sometimes call it *Sanno*; at some point in the murky early Middle Ages it became the county of Molise and then, like the other *Abruzzi*, it was joined to the Kingdom of Naples. In the 14th and 15th centuries Slav and Albanian refugees from the Turkish invasion found new homes; their languages contributed to the great variety of regional dialects, and there are still cases today of neighbouring villages unable to understand one another.

Although an improved network of roads and even a *superstrada* has ended most of Molise's isolation, the rugged, mountainous terrain makes the going slow no matter how you travel. But it's just as well, for it is a region to drink in slowly, to sip instead of gulp down. This is very much backwoods Italy; the biggest events in the region are village rodeos, and the most famous attractions are ancient remains. However, unlike so much of Italy, the constant glare of flashbulbs has not made Molise fade into a picture of itself; you will not recognize much, if any, of it. In its freshness it is one of Italy's last frontiers.

Getting Around

Isernia is linked by **train** with Naples, Rome, Sulmona, Pescara and Campobasso; other trains from Naples to Campobasso pass through Benevento, then continue on to the coast at Termoli, via Larino. **Buses**—from Naples, Rome, Cassino and Vasto to Campobasso and Isernia—are on the whole much quicker, and less aggravating. The bus service for outlying villages is fair, departing from either Isernia or Campobasso.

Tourist Information

Isernia: Via Farinacci 1, © 0865 3992.
Campobasso: Piazza della Vittoria 14, © 0874 415 662.

Isernia

Heading down the SS17 from Sulmona and Castel di Sangro, you enter the dismal little capital of Isernia. This was the Samnite town of *Aesernium*, where the Italic tribes either first united against Rome, or fled after the Romans captured their capital of Corfinium in the Social Wars—at any rate Isernia modestly puts forth a claim of being 'the first capital of Italy', although even that boast pales before the fame of its onions (fêted every 28–29 June) and its lace. Over the centuries Isernia has been severely damaged by earthquakes—the last of them only in 1984—and was badly bombed in 1943, so there is little to see of its old town other than the 14th-century **Fontana Fraterna**, which has somehow managed to survive. It was built using bits of Roman masonry and bears an inscription that reads *AE PONT*—which led to a popular belief that Aesernium gave the world Pontius Pilate.

Today, however, the town's main attraction is much much older—a Palaeolithic village that was accidentally uncovered in 1979. At one million years old this is the most ancient evidence of human life yet discovered in Europe. No human remains were found, but there are a variety of other relics such as weapons, fireplaces, face paint and so on, and plenty of remains of the ancestors of the elephant, deer, rhinoceros, bison, bear and hippopotamus. They are well-presented, and accompanied by reconstructions of life in the prehistoric villages, with multi-lingual explanations and computerized displays, in the **Museo Nazionale della Pentria e Isernia** on Piazza Santa Maria (*open Tues–Sat 8–2 and 5–7, Sun 8–2*).

North of Isernia

The *comuni* in the high altitudes north of Isernia have been compared to the isolated villages of Tibet, each perched on its lonely hilltop. Highest in all the Apennines at 4661ft is **Capracotta**, a village immersed in mountain pastures, often buried under banks of snow in winter, so much so that residents sometimes have to use their upper-floor windows as doors—a fitting place for the first Italian ski club, founded in 1914. Nearby **Agnone**, the 'Athens of the Samnites', has been known for the past thousand years for its bells. One factory, the **Marinelli Pontifical Foundry**, still survives—the oldest in Italy, supplier to the Vatican and nearly every country in the world. Bells are still cast according to the ancient formula; while the molten bronze is being poured into the mould a priest is on hand to chant the medieval litanies that have always guaranteed a successful, clear-toned bell. You can see the foundry at work and visit its small **museum**, Via d'Onofrio 14, ✆ 0865 78235 (*by appointment on weekdays*). Besides bells, Agnone is known for its coppersmiths, whose workshops line the main streets of town; also be sure to note the Romanesque portal on the **cathedral**.

South of Agnone, **Pietrabbondante** has some of the most extensive Samnite ruins yet discovered. The site was a religious sanctuary and includes a well-preserved Greek theatre and a couple of temples, all built in the 2nd century BC. The ruins are located in a green field filled with flowers (*open Tues–Sun 9am–dusk*). **Pescolanciano**, on the way back towards Isernia, is dominated by its picturesque **Castello d'Alessandro**, founded in the 13th century and topped in later years by a pretty arcade.

West of Isernia

Spaghetti Western fans in Molise in mid-August can whoop it up at an Italian 'rodeo' at **Montenero Val Cocchiara**, northwest of Isernia; as usual in Italy, food is as much of an attraction as the events, and in this case it's barbecues. In the pre-cowboy days of the Lombards, the Benedictines built the abbey of **San Vincenzo al Volturno** to the south near **Castel San Vincenzo**. Often altered, damaged and rebuilt, the abbey was last restored in the 1950s; the **Crypt of San Lorenzo** managed to escape the assorted disasters and preserves 11th-century frescoes. (*The complex is usually closed, but try ringing the convent's bell.*)

The most impressive castle in Molise, **Cerro al Volturno** (*call ✆ 0865 955 246, for opening hours*) was built by the same Benedictines in the 10th century, but was rebuilt at the end of the 15th century. Appearing to grow organically out of a massive rock over the town, the castle is inaccessible except by a narrow path; in the 1920s the supporting cement bulwarks on the hill were added, all impressive enough to star on a L200 stamp. There aren't many souvenirs to buy in Cerro, but further south, in **Scapoli**, you can visit the bagpipe (*zampogna*) market in the last week of July, and choose your goat-bellied instrument from among the olive- and cherry-wood models on display. The bagpipe has a long (and still living) tradition among the shepherds of the Molise; they still take them down to play in the streets of Rome and Naples for Christmas. The market also features pipes from Scotland, Sardinia, Hungary and other regions and countries. Alternatively, you can explore the world of bagpipes inside the **Museo della Zampogna**, in the *municipio* (*open daily 9–12 and 3–7; adm*).

On the road south towards Campania, **Venafro** was made famous by Horace for its olive oil. Although now more than a little run down, it is also one of the most interesting towns in Molise. Cyclopean walls run along the road into town, and in the Middle Ages the Roman **amphitheatre** was turned into an oval piazza and the arcades into the front doors of the houses. Portable remains of Roman *Venafrum* are now in the **Museo Archeologico** (*open Tues–Sun 9–1; adm*) in the former convent of Santa Chiara. Another church, the **Annunziata**, has preserved its Romanesque interior if not exterior, and contains a series of 15th-century English alabasters. Venafro's derelict castle (14th–16th-centuries) and the 15th-century fortified ducal **Palazzo Caracciolo** are still waiting for funds to be restored.

Where to Stay and Eating Out

The few hotels that grace Molise tend to be either new and sterile, or old and worn at the heels. At table, the Molisani are a solidly old-fashioned and often spicy crew, favouring dishes like stuffed lamb heads (*testine d'agnello*), kid tripe, a kind of hillbilly pizza topped with greens and boiled pork (*pizza con le foglie*), smelly mountain cheese and polenta with red beans, olive oil, hot peppers and garlic (*polenta maritata*).

Isernia ✉ 86170

***La Tequila**, Via G. Tedeschi 85, just outside the centre in the new San Lazzaro neighbourhood, ✆ /✆ 0865 412 345 (*moderate*) has a pool. **Taverna Maresca**, Corso Marcelli 186, ✆ 0865 3976 (*moderate–cheap*) is a fine old restaurant in the old quarter. *Closed Sun, Aug, Christmas and Easter.*

Capracotta ✉ 86082

Up in the mountains and out of the way, the *****Montecampo**, Contrada Santa Lucia, ✆ 0865 949 128 (*cheap*) is a basic but pleasant 13-room hotel.

Agnone ✉ 86061

***Sammartino**, Largo P. Micca 44, ✆ 0865 78239 (*cheap*) is a comfortable hotel with an excellent restaurant, ✆ 0865 77577, where you can dine on first-rate grilled meat, including Molise's succulent baby lamb.

At **Da Casciano**, Viale Marconi 29, ✆ 0865 77511, you can taste a rare dish, the lamb *sotto la coppa* (cooked under the ashes), and finish with the unforgettable *ostie*, local pastry made with walnuts, chocolate, honey and wine must. *Closed Tues.*

Venafro

Just out of town on the SS85, **Il Quadrifoglio**, ✆ 0865 909 886 (*moderate*) has a surprise—the freshest of seafood (Venafro is a stop for the seafood trucks from the Adriatic to Rome), as well as lamb and other Molise dishes.

The Matese

South of Isernia and Campobasso is a lovely curve of snow-swept peaks and forests called the Matese, of which the southern half lies in Campania. Few Italians, much less foreigners, penetrate its quiet villages, where women in traditional dress sit out in the streets over their round *tomboli* making delicate lace. The lakes of the Matese are full of waterfowl, its streams brim with fish, and its forests are home to squirrels, wildcats, wolves and other creatures seldom seen in the rest of Italy; its glens produce *porcini* mushrooms by the ton.

The scenery is spectacular, especially around the largest of the district's several lakes, the **Lago del Matese**, with its resort of **Piedimonte Matese**, both in Campania. The road back to Molise (the SS158dir) runs through the Passo del Prete Morto ('Dead Priest Pass'); the northern slopes of the Matese are equally lovely, with a wonderful quality of light that gives **Campochiaro** its name. This medieval village still retains its walls and tower; a huge Samnite temple complex has been unearthed in the vicinity. Just to the west is the lofty little town of **Boiano**, the former Samnite stronghold of *Bovianum*. The upper part of town, called Città, retains Megalithic-era walls and the ruins of a Lombard castle. The views are great, and become fabulous if you're up to a rather stiff two-hour climb to the summit of **Monte la Gallinola** (6307ft)—on a clear day you can see as far as the Bay of Naples.

Saepinum

In 295 BC the Samnite city of *Saipins* was laid waste by the Romans. The few inhabitants who were neither killed nor taken into slavery went on to found a new town for themselves, a Roman colony called *Saepinum*. As a quiet provincial town it managed to avoid most of history until the 9th century, when the Saracens destroyed it. Later in the Middle Ages, when times were surer, the site was resettled, two miles uphill from the ruins (now modern **Sepino**), and old Saepinum was slowly covered by the dust of the ages and quarried here and there for its stone. Dilettantes began excavating the ancient town in the 18th century, and nowadays groups of archaeologists come to uncover more of it every summer. A bus runs from Campobasso to Sepino about every two hours (*for details, call © 0874 412 125*).

The charm of Saepinum comes partly from its remote and lovely setting in the Matese, making it one of the most evocative Roman sites in all Italy—the best example of a small provincial city. In Saepinum there is very little marble, no plush villas as in Pompeii and Heraculaneum, but neither are there any modern intrusions beyond a few farmhouses, making use of a column here, an architrave there; it is an ancient Anytown in the empire, in its layout and amenities a miniature version of nearly every colony founded by Rome.

The defensive **walls** encompassing Saepinum, built in the diamond patterns of *opus reticulatum*, are over 1km long and defended by 27 bastions—the best preserved of which, over 35ft high, stands near the theatre. Four gates lead into the central axis of the city; from the car park at Porta di Terravecchia you pass through the walls on the *cardus maximus*. This street retains its original paving stones, as you approach the central crossroads with the *decumanus*, the main street of every Roman town.

Here, as usual, you'll find the **forum** and civic buildings. The slender Ionic columns on one corner belonged to the **basilica**, the main meeting place and courts of a Roman city, with its podium for orators and lawyers. Just off it is an octagonal atrium, surrounded by the foundations of shop counters—Saepinum's central market. Across from the forum itself on the *decumanus* are, first, on the corner, the elections office (*Comitium*), the *Curia* (town hall), a temple, believed to have been dedicated to the cult of an emperor, and then the *Terme* (baths) and the well-preserved Griffon fountain.

The *decumanus* continues past a house called the **Casa dell'Impluvio Sannitico**—its atrium containing a fountain and Samnite-style *impluvium* (container to collect rain water) with an inscription in Oscan, the pre-Roman language of the region—to the Porta di Benevento, marked by a figure of Mars. Beyond the gate stands the funeral monument, with its inscriptions lauding the virtues of the deceased Caius Ennius Marso, one of the town's leading citizens.

In the opposite direction the *decumanus* passes through Saepinum's main commercial district, lined with shops, taverns and private residences. It ends at the most complete gate, the impressive **Porta Boiano**, with steps to the top for an excellent view of the excavations. Figures of prisoners (or slaves?) stand on plinths on either side, and its inscription informs us that Tiberius and his brother Drusas paid for the walls. Beyond this gate is a monumental **mausoleum** of Numisio Ligure. Along the walls are the remains of a private bath complex; beyond is the well-preserved **theatre**, with a crescent of medieval farmhouses that were built into the upper *cavea*; in its heyday the theatre seated 3,000 spectators. The stage is now occupied by another farmhouse, which contains an interesting **museum** (*closed for restoration*).

Campobasso

The capital of the County of Molise, Campobasso was once best known for its engraved cutlery—its knives, scissors and razors are still highly regarded—and wolfmen, but is now better known as the site of the National School for Carabinieri (which has managed to keep the wolfmen under control) and its June procession, the *Sagra dei Misteri di Corpus Domini*. In the 17th century Campobasso's old Corpus Domini processions were banned by the bishop for making spectators laugh; and they stayed banned until 1740, when a local sculptor named Di Zinno came up with the idea of building metal contraptions to support real people in the soaring Baroque postures of the angels and saints he carved for churches. The bishop accepted these as serious augmenters of the faith, and indeed they are, for it seems as if faith alone is holding up the bevy of six-year-old angels and saints suspended on the 13 floats or 'Mysteries' that are solemnly paraded through the streets to the accompaniment of the local bands. A long-planned **museum** of Samnite antiquities, Via Chiarizia (*open daily 9–1 and 3–7; closed Sun*) has finally opened and is well worth a look. The older, upper part of town has a couple of Romanesque churches, **San Giorgio** and **San Leonardo**, and the **Castello Monforte** (now a weather station) on top.

From Campobasso buses head out to scenic villages nearby, like **Ferrazzano**, with a castle and belvedere, and **Baranello**, an ancient town, the heir of the Samnite Vairanum. Baranello has a little **Museo Civico** (*open Mon–Sat 8–2; call office of Comune, © 0874 460 406, to arrange visit*) containing Samnite artefacts, 17th- and 18th-century Neapolitan kitsch paintings, Chinese porcelains and other *objets d'art* donated by a collector. Nearby, on the River Biferno, you can watch a still-functioning water wheel grind the grains that go into Molise's folksy cuisine.

Larino

Between Campobasso and Termoli on the coast, the small town of **Larino** (the Samnite *Larinum*) is prettily located amid hills of olive groves. The most important monument here, the **cathedral**, was built in 1319 and embellished with an ornate portal in its Puglian-style façade; the nearby church of **San Francesco** has some good 18th-century frescoes. Near the cathedral take a look inside the 'museum' of **Palazzo Comunale** (*open Mon–Fri 9–1*), three rooms which house beautiful Roman polychrome mosaics from the 2nd and 3rd century AD. A larger collection of art and artefacts is waiting to be put on display in Villa Zappone.

Meanwhile the *Ara Frentana*, a cylindrical Roman altar, is visible by the road leading to the train station. This was once the centre of the ancient Samnite town, and has a ruined amphitheatre—which in summer hosts concerts, plays and other events. Between May 25 and May 27, Larino holds a religious festival, the *Festa di San Pardo*, with a procession of 150 finely decorated ox carts. On the evening of the 25th the carts go from the cathedral to a Palaeo-Christian basilica dedicated to the three martyrs Primiano, Siriano and Cassio, to bring the statue of Primiano back to the cathedral for a late-night mass. The spectacle is at its best during the return trip (2km), as the carts are escorted by thousands of people holding torches.

Albanian and Slavic Villages

In the district around Larino there are several diehard communities of Albanians and Slavs, who still maintain their language, traditions and festivals. **Ururi**, west of Larino, is an Albanian town, as is **Portocannone**, which conserves in its Romanesque church an icon of the *Madonna of Constantinople*, brought over by settlers. The most interesting of the Slavic villages is **Acquaviva Collecroce**, where a dialect called 'Stokavo' is spoken. In the campanile of the church of **Santa Maria Esther** there is a medieval curiosity: a stone carved with the palindromic magic square of the words SATOR TENET AREPO, an ancient charm.

Where to Stay and Eating Out

Campobasso ✉ 86100

★★★★**Hotel Roxy**, Piazza Savoia 7, ✆ 0874 411 541(*moderate*) is plush and modern, with a discotheque for those wild Campobassani nights. ★★★**Skanderbeg**, Via Novelli 3, ✆ 0874 413 341 (*moderate*) is another good choice, offering modern comforts with touches of Molise tradition. ★★**Tricolore**, Via San Giovanni in Golfo 110, ✆ 0874 63190 (*cheap*) is a little family-run hotel in one of the prettier parts of town.

There are several good restaurants: **Aciniello**, Via Torino 4, ✆ 0874 94001 (*moderate–cheap*) is simple but genuine in its atmosphere and cuisine, and offers dishes like *pizza rustica* and rabbit. *Closed Sun and two weeks in Aug*. For something more refined and less strictly local, try the **Vecchia Trattoria da Tonino**, Corso Vittorio Emanuele II 8, ✆ 0874 415 200 (*moderate*); the wine list includes some of the finest local Molise labels. *Closed Sun*. One of the best restaurants in the region is in the pretty village of Ferrazzano—**Da Emilio**, Piazza Spenzieri 18, ✆ 0874 416 (*moderate*), where you can dine out on the terrace on meals with a delightful Emilia-Romagna touch. *Closed Tues, last two weeks in Jan and first two weeks in July*.

Larino

Larino doesn't have much in the way of hotels or restaurants, but the ★★★**Campitelli**, Via Mazzini 16 (near the amphitheatre), ✆ 0874 822 666 (*cheap*) is modern and functional, and has a good restaurant.

Tuscany

No region could be more essentially Italian. Its Renaissance culture and art became Italy's in common, and its dialect, as refined by Dante, cast a hundred others into the shadows to become the Italian language. Nevertheless, Tuscany seems to stand a bit aloof from the rest of the nation; it keeps its own counsels, never changes its ways, and faces the world with a Mona Lisa smile that has proved irresistible to northerners since the days of Shelley and Browning.

Today Britons, Dutchmen, Germans and Americans jostle each year for the privilege of paying two or three million lire for a month in a classic Tuscan farmhouse, with a view over a charmed, civilized landscape of cypresses and parasol pines, orderly rows of vines and olives, and a chapel on the hill with a quattrocento fresco. In Florence and the other cities, they stand in queues like refugees, waiting to enter the churches and museums that are the shrines of Tuscan art.

For a province that has contributed so much to western civilization since the Middle Ages, Tuscany's career remains slightly mysterious. Some have attempted to credit its cultural prominence to an inheritance from the ancient Etruscans, but most of modern Tuscany was never more than provincial throughout Etruscan and Roman times. Out of the Dark Ages, inexplicably, new centres of learning and art appeared, first in Pisa and Florence, and then in a dozen other towns, inaugurating a cultural Renaissance that really began as early as the 1100s.

As abruptly as it began, this brilliant age was extinguished in the 16th century, but it left behind a new province of Europe, finished, solid and well formed. Tuscany can be excused a little complacency. Though prosperous and enlightened, fully a part of modern Italy today, the region for

553

centuries has seemed perfectly content to let the currents of culture and innovation flow elsewhere. There's no sense in painting when anything new would have to hang next to Da Vincis and Botticellis, no incentive to build in a city full of churches and palaces by the medieval masters. After the surprising wave of bad taste that brought the Renaissance to a close, Tuscany was shamed into an introspectiveness and cultural conservatism of almost Chinese proportions.

Of course these centuries, during which Tuscany has quietly cultivated its own garden, have not been without some advantages. Its cities and their art treasures have been preserved with loving care. So has the countryside; if anything the last few hundred years have emphasized the frugal, hard-working side of the Tuscan character, the side that longs for the rural life, counts its pennies, and finds tripe with chickpeas a perfectly satisfying repast. All this at times makes a striking contrast with the motorways, the new industry around the cities, and the hordes of tourists descending on Florence, Pisa and Siena.

Not to be Missed

If you're coming for the first time, you will probably be chiefly interested in the three great art cities: **Pisa**, with its Field of Miracles and memories of its exotic career as an early medieval power; **Siena**, where the Midddle Ages begin to look disconcertingly attractive; and, most of all, the Renaissance city of **Florence**.

If there's time for more, you may consider picture-pretty **Lucca**, **Pistoia** and **Arezzo**, or some of the wonderful hill towns in the south, places like **San Gimignano** or **Montepulciano**, which offer small doses of the best of Tuscan culture in a lovely setting.

There's little to see on Tuscany's lonely coastline, and if you're passing through on the way to Rome or Umbria the inland routes will be the best bet. All the approaches over the Apennines from Emilia-Romagna offer delightful scenic drives—and plenty of curves and climbs. The best is the SS12 from Modena over to Lucca, with a branch off to Pistoia and Florence. From Genoa, if you have time, consider the roundabout routes through the Apuan Alps and the Serchio Valley from La Spezia to Lucca, as opposed to the coastal *autostrada*.

Florence

Venice, they say, moves one to dream a bit; Rome to contemplate the endless panorama of popes and Caesars; Naples convinces you that all is vanity. Florence (Firenze) on the other hand, a town long famed for good common sense and healthy scepticism, is different. It will not tempt you to easy conclusions; it is as romantic as a reference library. Florence, they say, moves one to argue.

So let's begin. Most writers have always assumed a certain point of view. You may think Florence is a museum city, they'll tell you, but you'll be wrong. Florence on the contrary is a thriving, progressive town that refuses to live in the past, insisting on earning its own way in the 20th century. Once it made Galileo's telescope, and today it still exports precision optical instruments. In the 1400s it led Europe in fashion as well as art; today its busy seamstresses on back streets do much of the work for the designers in Milan.

This argument is nice, but unfortunately untrue; despite its noise, ice-cream, light industry and horrendous traffic, Florence is a museum city, and if you don't care to look at pictures, you'd do better just to stay on the train. But what a museum town it is! Florence's collections easily surpass those of any other Italian city, and just from the odd bits in the back rooms its curators are able to mount a score of blockbuster special exhibitions each year. Most impressive of all is the fact that nearly all the art in them was made by the Florentines themselves, testimony to the city's position during two centuries as the great innovator of western culture.

History

The Etruscans, who founded Florence perhaps as early as 1000 BC, were typically coy about providing any further details; the city's early history remains a puzzle. Like so many cities, however, Florence seems to begin with a bridge. Dante and many other writers invoke the *marzocco*, the battered ancient icon that sat in the middle of the Ponte Vecchio and any number of bridges that preceded it, until a flood swept it away in the 14th century. Often pictured as a lion (like the replacement for the original made by Donatello, now on display in the Bargello), the *marzocco* may really have been a mounted cult image of the god Mars. Nothing could be more fitting, for in the centuries of its greatness Florence was full of trouble.

The city's apprenticeship in strife came during the endless Italian wars of the 4th–2nd centuries BC, when Rome was consolidating its hold on the peninsula. Sulla razed it to the ground during the Social Wars, and the town seems to have struggled back only gradually. Julius Caesar helped it along by planting a colony of veterans here in 59 BC. Roman Florence prospered, trading throughout the whole Empire. Its street plan survives in the neat rectangle of straight streets at the city's core. The town had an impressive forum right in the middle, at what is now Piazza della Repubblica.

If almost nothing remains from Roman times, it is only because Florence has been continuously occupied ever since, its centre constantly replanned and rebuilt. There were some hard times, especially during the Greek–Gothic wars of the 6th century and the Lombard occupation, but the city regained importance in the time of Charlemagne, becoming for a while the seat of the 'march' of Tuscany. Here, in what must have been one of the most fascinating eras of the city's history, once again we are left without much information. Florence, for whatever reason, was one of the first inland cities to regain its balance after the fall of the Empire. During the Dark Ages the city was already beginning to develop the free institutions of the later republic, and establishing the trading connections that were later to make it the merchant capital of Europe. About 1115, upon the death of the famous Countess Matilda of Tuscany, Florence became a self-governing *comune*.

The Florentine Republic

From the beginning, circumstances forced the city into an aggressive posture against enemies within and outside its walls. Florence waged constant war against the extortionist petty nobles of the hinterlands, razing their castles and forcing them to live in the city. As an important

Guelph stronghold, Florence constantly got itself into trouble with the Emperors, as well as with Ghibelline Pisa, Pistoia and Siena, towns that were to become its sworn enemies. In its darkest hour, after the crushing defeat at Montaperti in 1260, the Sienese almost succeeded in convincing their allies to bury Florence. A good sack would have been fun; Florence by the mid-13th century was possibly the richest banking and trading centre anywhere, and its gold florin had become a recognized currency across Europe.

In truth, Florence had no need of outside enemies. All through its history the city did its level best to destroy itself. Guelph fought Ghibelline with impressive rancour, and when there were no Ghibellines left the Guelphs split into factions called the Blacks and Whites and began murdering each other. In a different dimension, the city found causes of civil strife in the class struggles between the popolo grosso—the 'fat commons' or wealthy merchant class—and the members of the poorer guilds.

Playing one side against the other was the newly urbanized nobility. These brought their gang-ster habits to town with them, turning Florence into a forest of tall brick tower-fortresses and carrying on bloody feuds in the streets that the city officials were helpless to stop. Despite all the troubles, this was the era of Dante (d. 1321, in exile in Ravenna) and Giotto (d. 1337), the beginning of Florence's cultural golden age. Banking and wool (the leading commodity in the pre-industrial economy) were booming, and the florins kept rolling in no matter which faction was on top.

In 1282, and again in 1293, Florence tried to clean up its violent and corrupt government by a major reform; the *Ordinamenti della Giustizia* finally excluded the nobles from politics. It didn't work for long. Political strife continued throughout the 14th century, along with eternal wars with Lucca, Pisa and Siena, and some novel catastrophes. In 1339 Edward III of England repudiated his enormous foreign debt and Florence's two largest banks, the Bardi and Peruzzi, went bust.

Plagues and famines dominated the 1340s; the plague of 1348, the Black Death, killed three-fifths of the population (and provided the frame story for Boccaccio's *Decameron*). The nobles and merchants then took advantage of the situation to establish tight boss rule. You can still see their Guelph Party building on Via Porta Rossa, where the spoils were divided—the original Tammany Hall. A genuine revolution in 1378 among the *ciompi*, the wool trade proletariat, might have succeeded if its leaders had been half as devious and ruthless as their opponents.

Florence's continuing good luck again saw it through, however, and prosperity gradually returned after 1400. In 1406 Pisa was finally conquered, giving Florence a seaport. Florentine armies bested the Visconti of Milan twice, and once (1410) even occupied Rome. At the dawn of the Renaissance not only Florence's artists, scholars and scientists were making innova-tions—the city government in the 1420s and '30s invented the progressive income tax and the national debt.

The Rise of the Medici

Although the family is said to have begun as pharmacists (*medici*), by 1400 the House of Medici was the biggest merchant concern in Florence. With the resources of the Medici Bank behind him, Cosimo de' Medici installed himself as the city's political godfather, coercing or buying off the various interests and factions. In 1449 his son Lorenzo inherited the job, presiding over the greatest days of the Renaissance and a sustained stretch of peace and prosperity. Opposition, squashed originally by Cosimo, stayed squashed.

Lorenzo's military campaigns proved successful on the whole, and his impressive propaganda machine gave him an exaggerated reputation as a philosopher-king and patron of the arts. Lorenzo almost ruined the Medici Bank through neglect, but then made up his losses from public funds. His personal tastes in art seem to have been limited to knick-knacks, big jewels and antique bronzes, but his real hobby was nepotism. His son Giovanni, later to be made Pope Leo X at the age of 38, became a cardinal at 14.

Two years after Lorenzo's death in 1494, the wealthy classes of Florence finally succeeded in ending Medici rule when they exiled Lorenzo's weak son and successor, Piero. The republic was restored, but soon came under the influence of a remarkable Dominican demagogue, Girolamo Savonarola. Thundering out a fierce fundamentalist line, his preaching resulted in the famous 1497 'Bonfire of Vanities' on the Piazza della Signoria, when the people collected their paintings, fancy clothes, carnival masks and books and put them to the flame (a Venetian merchant offered instead to buy the whole lot from them, but the Florentines hurriedly sketched a portrait of him too, and threw it on the pyre).

Savonarola was more than a ridiculous prude. His idealistic republicanism resulted in some real democratic reforms, and the friar reserved his strongest blasts for the corruption of the church; not a bad idea in the time of Alexander VI, the Borgia pope. When Savonarola's opponents, the Arrabbiati ('infuriated'), beat his supporters, the *Piagnoni* ('snivellers'), in the 1498 elections, the way was clear for Alexander to order the friar's execution. Savonarola burned on 22 May 1498, on the spot where the 'Bonfire of Vanities' had been held, and his ashes were thrown into the Arno.

The Medici returned in 1512, thanks to Pope Julius II and his Spanish troops, and Lorenzo's nephew Giulio de' Medici was able to re-enter the city. When Giulio was elected Pope Clement VII in 1523 he attempted to continue running the city at a distance, but yet another Medici expulsion would take place after his humiliation in the sack of Rome in 1527, followed by the founding of the last Florentine republic.

By now Florentine politics had become a death struggle between an entire city and a single family. The last republic lived nervously in an atmosphere of revolutionary apocalypse; meanwhile Clement intrigued with the Spaniards for his return. An Imperial army arrived in 1530 to besiege the city and, despite heroic, last-ditch resistance, Florence had to capitulate when its commander sold out to the Pope and turned his guns on the city itself. In 1532 the Medici broke the terms of the surrender agreement by abolishing all self-government, obtaining the newly-minted title of Grand Dukes of Tuscany from Emperor Charles V.

To all intents and purposes Florentine history ends here. Cosimo I Medici (d. 1574) ruled over a state that declined rapidly into a provincial backwater. When the last Medici, fat Gian Gastone, died in 1737, the powers of Europe gave the duchy to the House of Lorraine. With the rest of Tuscany, Florence was annexed to Piedmont-Sardinia in 1859, and from 1865 to 1870 it served as the capital of united Italy.

Today, despite repeated attempts to diversify the local economy through the creation of new industrial areas on the outskirts, Florence largely lives on the sheer weight of its past creativity. It suffered badly in the Second World War, when the retreating German army blew up all the bridges over the Arno except the Ponte Vecchio, and destroyed many medieval buildings along the river's edge. Still worse damage was caused by the great floods of November 1966, which left several dead and many buildings and artworks in need of restoration work that is still continuing today.

The most recent damage came in May 1993, when a bomb planted by the Mafia exploded near the Uffizi, killing the family of a caretaker, destroying a Renaissance library, and substantially damaging parts of the Uffizi itself, particularly the Vasari Corridor. The perpetrators were tried in 1998 and, as a result, 14 life sentences were given, including the conviction of Toto Riina, the 'Boss of Bosses'.

Florentine Art

Under the assault of historians and critics over the last two centuries, 'Renaissance' has become such a vague and controversial word as to be nearly useless. Nevertheless, however you choose to interpret this rebirth of the arts, and whatever dates you assign it, Florence inescapably takes the credit for initiating it.

This is no small claim. Combining art, science and humanist scholarship into a visual revolution that often seemed pure sorcery to their contemporaries, a handful of Florentine geniuses taught the western eye a new way of seeing. Perspective seems a simple enough trick to us now, but its discovery determined everything that followed, not only in art but in science and philosophy as well.

The city's talents showed early, with the construction of the famous baptistry, perhaps as early as 700. From the start Florence showed a remarkable adherence to the traditions of antiquity. New directions in architecture—the Romanesque after the year 1000—had little effect; what passed for Romanesque in Florence was a unique style, evolved by a very self-confident city.

This new architecture (*see* the baptistry, San Miniato, Santa Maria Novella), based on elegantly simple geometry with richly inlaid marble façades and pavements, was utterly unlike even the creations of nearby Pisa and Siena, and began a continuity of style that would reach its climax with the work of **Brunelleschi** and **Alberti** in the 1400s.

Likewise in painting and sculpture, Florentines made an early departure from Byzantine-influenced forms, and avoided the International Gothic style that thrived so well in Siena. Vasari's famous *Lives of the Artists* (1547) lays down the canon of Florentine artists, the foundation of all subsequent art criticism.

It begins with **Cimabue** (*c.* 1240–1302), who, according to Vasari, first began to draw away from Byzantine stylization towards a more 'natural' way of painting. Cimabue found his greatest pupil **Giotto** (1266–1337) as a young shepherd boy, chalk-sketching sheep on a piece of slate. Brought to Florence, Giotto was soon to eclipse his master's fame and achieved the greatest advances on the road to the new painting, a plain, idiosyncratic approach that avoided Gothic prettiness while exploring new ideas in composition and expressing psychological depth in his subjects.

Even more importantly Giotto, through his intuitive grasp of perspective, was able to go further than any previous artist in representing his subjects as actual figures in space. In a sense Giotto invented space, and it was this advance that so astounded his contemporaries.

Vasari, for reasons of his own, neglected the artists of the Florentine Trecento, and many critics have tended to follow slavishly—a great affront to the master artist and architect **Andrea Orcagna** (d. 1368; works include the Loggia dei Lanzi and the Orsanmichele tabernacle) and others including **Taddeo and Agnolo Gaddi** (d. 1366 and 1396) whose frescoes can be compared to Giotto's at Santa Croce.

The Quattrocento

The next turn in the story, what scholars self-assuredly used to call the 'Early Renaissance', comes with the careers of two geniuses who happened also to be very good friends. **Donatello** (1386–1466), the greatest sculptor since the ancient Greeks, inspired a new generation of not only sculptors but also painters to explore new horizons in portraiture and three-dimensional representation.

Brunelleschi (1377–1446), neglecting his considerable talents in sculpture for architecture and science, not only built the majestic cathedral dome, but threw the Pandora's box of perspective wide open by mathematically codifying the principles of foreshortening. The new science of painting occasioned an explosion of talent unequalled before or since, as a score of masters, most of them Florentine by birth, each followed the dictates of his own genius to create a range of themes and styles hardly believable for one single city in a few short decades of its life. To mention only the most prominent:

Lorenzo Ghiberti (d. 1455), famous for the bronze doors of the baptistry; **Masaccio** (d. 1428), the eccentric prodigy much copied by later artists, best represented by his naturalistic frescoes in Santa Maria del Carmine and Santa Maria Novella; **Domenico Ghirlandaio** (d. 1494), Michelangelo's teacher and another master of detailed frescoes; **Fra Angelico** (d. 1455), the most spiritual, and most visionary of them all, the painter of the *Annunciation* at San Marco.

Paolo Uccello (d. 1475), one of the most provocative of all artists, who, according to Vasari, drove himself bats with too-long contemplation of perspective and the newly discovered vacuum of empty space; **Benozzo Gozzoli** (d. 1497), a happier soul, best known for the springtime *Procession of the Magi* in the Medici Palace; **Luca Della Robbia** (d. 1482), greatest of a family of sculptors, famous for the *cantoria* of the Cathedral Museum and exquisite blue and white terracottas all over Tuscany; **Antonio Pollaiuolo** (d. 1498), an engraver and sculptor with a nervously perfect line.

Fra Filippo Lippi (d. 1469), who ran off with a brown-eyed nun to produce **Filippino Lippi** (d. 1504)—both of them exceptional painters and sticklers for detail; and finally **Sandro Botticelli** (d. 1510); his progress from the secret garden of pure art, expressed in his astounding early mythological pictures, to conventional holy pictures, done after the artist fell under the sway of Savonarola, marks the first signs of trouble and the first failure of nerve in the Florentine imagination.

Leonardo, Michelangelo and the Cinquecento

With equal self-assurance the critics used to refer to the early 1500s as the beginning of the 'High Renaissance'. **Leonardo da Vinci**, perhaps the incarnation of Florentine achievement in both painting and scientific speculation, lived until 1519, but spent much of his time in

Milan and France. **Michelangelo Buonarroti** (d. 1564) liked to identify himself with Florentine republicanism, but finally abandoned the city during the siege of 1530 (even though he was a member of the committee overseeing Florence's defence).

His departure left Florence with no important artists except the surpassingly strange **Jacopo Pontormo** (d. 1556) and **Rosso Fiorentino** (d. 1540). These two, along with Michelangelo, were key figures in the bold, neurotic, avant-garde art that has come to be known as 'Mannerism'. This first conscious 'movement' in western art can be seen as a last fling amid the growing intellectual and spiritual exhaustion of 1530s Florence, conquered once and for all by the Medici. The Mannerists' calculated exoticism and exaggerated, tortured poses, together with the brooding self-absorption of Michelangelo and many others, are the prelude to Florentine art's remarkably abrupt downturn into decadence, and prophesy its final extinction.

There was another strain to Mannerism in Florence: following the cold classicism of Raphael of Urbino, less disturbed, less challenging than Michelangelo or Pontormo. With artists like **Agnolo Bronzino** (d. 1572), the sculptor **Bartolomeo Ammannati** (d. 1592), **Andrea del Sarto** (d. 1531), and **Giorgio Vasari** himself (d. 1574), Florentine art loses almost all imaginative and intellectual content, becoming a virtuoso style of interior decoration perfectly adaptable to saccharine holy pictures, portraits of dukes, or absurd mythological fountains and ballroom ceilings.

In the cinquecento, with plenty of money to spend and a long Medici tradition of patronage to uphold, this tendency soon got out of hand. Under the reign of Cosimo I, indefatigable collector of *pietra dura* tables, silver and gold gimcracks, and exotic stuffed animals, Florence gave birth to the artistic phenomenon modern critics call kitsch. In the cinquecento Florence taught vulgarity to the Romans, degeneracy to the Venetians and preciosity to the French. Oddly enough the city had as great an influence in its age of decay as in its age of greatness. The cute, well-educated Florentine pranced across Europe, finding himself praised as the paragon of culture and refinement. Even in England—though that honest nation soon found him out:

> *A little Apish hatte, couched fast to the Pate, like an Oyster,*
> *French Camarick Ruffes, deepe with a witnesse, starched to the purpose,*
> *Delicate in speach, queynte in arraye: conceited in all poyntes:*
> *In Courtly guyles, a passing singular odde man...*

> *Mirror of Tuscanism,* Gabriel Harvey, 1580

It's almost disconcerting to learn that Florence gave us not only much of the best of our civilization, but even a lot of the worst. Somehow the later world of powdered wigs and chubby winged *putti* is unthinkable without 1500s Florence. Then again, so is all the last 500 years of art unthinkable without Florence, not to mention modern medicine (the careful anatomical studies of the artists did much to help set it on its way) or technology (from the endless speculations and gadgets of Leonardo) or political science (from Machiavelli).

The Florentines of course found the time to invent opera too, and give music a poke into the modern world. And without that little discovery of the painters, so simple though perhaps so very hard for us in the 20th century to comprehend—the invention of space—Copernicus, Newton, Descartes and all who followed them would never have discovered anything.

But Florence soon tired of the whole business. The city withdrew into itself, made a modest living, polished its manners and its conceit, and generally avoided trouble. Not a peep has been heard out of it since 1600.

Not to be Missed

If you wanted to see everything worth seeing, it would take at least two weeks, and museum admissions alone would set you back some L350,000. For an abbreviated tour, be sure to see the **cathedral**, **baptistry** and **cathedral museum**, and Florence's two great museums, the **Uffizi** and the **Bargello**, leaving time for a walk around the Ponte Vecchio and a stop at **Orsanmichele**. Around the edges of the old centre, the churches of **Santa Croce**, **Santa Maria Novella**, **Santa Maria del Carmine** and the monastery of **San Marco** contain some of the best of Florentine painting. Finally, try to make it up to **San Miniato**, for the beautiful medieval church and the view over the city. Those with more time to spend can consider the florid 16th-century art in the **Palazzo Vecchio** and **Pitti Palace**, Gozzoli's frescoes in the **Medici Palace**, the very good **Archaeology Museum** and **Museum of Science**, and Brunelleschi's **Santo Spirito**. And for devotees of the Michelangelo cult, there's the real David in the **Accademia**, the **Medici Chapels** at San Lorenzo and the **Casa Buonarroti**.

Getting to and from Florence

by air

Pisa's Galileo Galilei airport used to be the principal airport for the area, until Florence's **Vespucci airport** was lengthened in 1996. Now it bustles with more international traffic than Pisa. For flight information, call ✆ 055 373 498, or ✆ 055 306 1700 (recorded message). It is 6km out at Peretola and is connected to the city by a regular bus service to Stazione Centrale (Santa Maria Novella) (15mins). A taxi ride to the centre will cost about L25,000 plus relevant surcharges. If you need to get to Florence from Pisa airport take the special train service to Stazione Centrale which takes one hour and leaves every hour or so, every day.

by rail

The main station (**Stazione Centrale**) is Santa Maria Novella, call ✆ 055 235 2061, for reservations, which the state railways often refers to as Firenze S.M.N. It is right in the centre of Florence, and the piazza it faces, Piazza della Stazione, and adjacent Piazza Santa Maria Novella, are also a major terminus for local bus routes. Some long distance trains also stop at **Campo di Marte**, on the eastern side of the city (served by bus nos.6, 12 and 20, or 91 at night).

by long-distance bus

It's possible to reach nearly every city, town and village in Tuscany from Florence. The tourist office has a complete list of services, but here are some of the most popular: **SITA**, Via S. Caterina di Siena 15, near the train station, ✆ 055 483 651, operates to Firenzuola, Greve and the Mugello Valley, and also to Siena, Pisa and Perugia; **LAZZI**, Piazza Stazione 47r, ✆ 055 351 061 (*Mon–Fri*) goes to Empoli, Incisa Valdarno, Prato, Pistoia and Lucca, and also to other European countries; and **COPIT**, Piazza Santa Maria Novella, ✆ 055 214 637, has services to Vinci. For 24-hour recorded information, call ✆ 166 845 010.

Florence

250 metres
250 yards

N

Lazzi Buses

Stazione Centrale

Sita Buses

Piazza della Stazione

Cappella degli Spagnuoli

Cenacolo di Foligno

Piazza dell' Unità Italiana

Santa Maria Novella

Piazza Santa Maria Novella

Croce del Trebbio

Ognissanti

Palazzo Antinori

San Pancrazio

Palazzo Rucellai

Piazza Goldoni

Palazzo Corsini

Piazza S. Trinita

Santa Trinita

SS Apostoli

Piazza di Cestello

San Frediano in Cestello

Porta San Frediano 100m

Piazza del Carmine

Ponte Santa Trinita

Santa Maria del Carmine

Santo Spirito

Piazza Santo Spirito

Ponte Vecchio

Casa Guidi

Piazza dei Pitti

Piazza S. Felicità

Santa Felicità

Grotta di Buontalenti

Museo La Specola

Piazza San Felice

Pitti Palace

Anfiteatro

Kaffeehaus

Boboli Gardens

Forte di Belvedere

Fontana di Nettuno

Museo delle Porcellane e Giardino del Cavaliere

Cenacolo di Sant' Apollonia

Piazza del Mercato Centrale

Opficio delle Pietre Dure

Cappelle Medicee

San Lorenzo

Palazzo Medici-Riccardi

Piazza Madonna

Biblioteca Laurenziana

Duomo

Museo dell'Opera del Duomo

Piazza di San Giovanni

Battistero

Piazza del Duomo

Museo Nazionale di Antropologia ed Etnologia

Santa Margherita de' Cerchi

San Gaetano

Piazza della Repubblica

Casa di Dante

Palazzo Strozzi

Piazza Strozzi

Arte della Lana

Palazzo Davanzati

Post Office & Telephones

Mercato Nuovo

Orsanmichele

Bargello

San Martino

Badia

Palazzo Pazzi-Quaratesi

Palazzo di Parte Guelfa

Piazza della Signoria

Palazzo Gondi

San Firenze

Loggia dei Lanzi

Uffizi

Palazzo Vecchio

Piazzale D. Uffizi

Museo di Storia della Scienza

Fiume

Museo Bardini

Piazza dei Mozzi

Palazzo dei Mozzi

VIA SANTO ZANOBI
VIA XXVII APRILE
VIA GUELFA
VIA SAN GALLO
VIA CAVOUR
VIA RICASOLI
VIA DE' GINORI
VIA NAZIONALE
VIA PANICALE
VIA TADDEA
VIA DELL'ARIENTO
SANT' ANTONINO
VIA FAENZA
BORGO LA NOCE
VIA DE' MARTELLI
VIA DE' PUCCI
VIA DE' SERVI
VIA DE' BUFALINI
V.D. MELARANCIO
GIGLIO
VIA DE' CONTI
BORGO SAN LORENZO
VIA DEI PANZANI
VIA DEI BANCHI
VIA DEI CERRETANI
VIA DELLE BELLE DONNE
VIA DEI FOSSI
VIA DELLA SCALA
VIA DELLA SPADA
VIA DELLE OCHE
VIA DEL CORSO
VIA DEL PROCONSOLO
VIA DEGLI AGLI
VIA DE' PECORI
VIA ROMA
VIA DELLO STUDIO
VIA DELLA SPEZIALI
VIA DEL CORSO
VIA DE' CERCHI
VIA DANTE ALIGHIERI
VIA STROZZI
VIA D. CAMPIDOGLIO
BORGO SAN JACOPO
VIA POR S. MARIA
VIA CALIMALA
VIA CALZAIUOLI
VIA DELLE TERME
VIA CONDOTTA
VIA LAMBERTESCA
VIA DEI NERI
VIA DE' CASTELLANI
VIA DE' ANGUILLARA
VIA DE' BENCI
VIA DE' PANDOLFINI
V. DELL' VIGNA VECCHIA
V. D. VIGNA VECCHIA
BORGO DEI GRECI
VIA ISOLA DELLE STINCHE
SS. APOSTOLI
V.D. VIGNA NUOVA
VIA DEL PARIONE
LUNGARNO CORSINI
LUNGARNO ACCIAIOLI
LUNG. GUICCIARDINI
LUNG. DIAZ
BORGO SS. APOSTOLI
BORGO SAN FREDIANO
LUNGARNO SODERINI
LUNGARNO AMERIGO VESPUCCI
PONTE AMERIGO VESPUCCI
PONTE ALLA CARRAIA
VIA DEI SERRAGLI
VIA S. MONACA
VIA SANT' AGOSTINO
VIA DI S. SPIRITO
VIA DEL PRESTO S. MARTINO
BORGO TEGOLAIO
VIA MAGGIO
VIA ROMANA
VIA DE' GUICCIARDINI
VIA DE' BARDI
COSTA DI SAN GIORGIO
LUNGARNO TORRIGIANI
COSTA DI SAN GIORGIO
CORTI
VIA DEL VASARIO
PONTE ALLE GRAZIE
VIA DI BELVEDERE
VIA DEI BELLE
VIA DELLE OCHE
VIA DEI CALZAIUOLI
BORGO OGNISSANTI
VIA DEL MORO
VIA PORCELLANA
VIA MAGGIO
BORGO SAN LORENZO
VIA DE' RONDINELLI
VIA GHIBELLINA
Palazzo Rucellai

All roads into the city meet up with an inner ring of roads, the *Viali*, which goes around the historic centre, much of which is closed to traffic. There are large car parks all around the *Viali*, particularly around the **Fortezza da Basso** and **Piazza Libertà** at the 'Parterre', which are quite expensive though still not as much as the ones that are actually within the centre itself.

Getting Around

Nearly everything you'll want to see is within easy walking distance, and large areas in the centre are pedestrianized. When you do need to get directly from A to B the city has an efficient local bus service.

Most of the more useful routes for visitors start from the main railway station: bus no.7 goes to San Domenico and then all the way to Fiesole; no.10 to the Duomo, San Marco and Settignano; no.13 to Piazzale Michelangelo and the Belvedere—especially useful if you want to avoid that long climb; no.37 goes to Galluzzo and the Certosa.

For a radio **taxi**, call ✆ 055 4798, or ✆ 055 4390. The really adventurous can **rent a bicycle** from Alinari, Via Guelfa 85r, ✆ 055 280 500, or Florence by Bike, Via della Scala 12r, ✆ 055 264 035; or a **scooter**, from Alinari, or Motorent, Via San Zanobi 9r, ✆ 055 490 113.

Just to make life difficult, Florence has two sets of address numbers on every street— red ones for business, blue for residences; your hotel might be either one.

Tourist Information

Via Manzoni 16, ✆ 055 290 832, a little out of the way, near Piazza Beccaria; there's a central branch office at Via Cavour 1r, just north of the Duomo. There's also a very genial booth outside the station, at the end of the bus ranks, ✆ 055 212 245, and a new office at Borgo Santa Croce 19, ✆ 055 234 0444, ✉ 055 226 4524. In **Fiesole** there is an office at Piazza Mino 37, ✆ 055 598 720.

Piazza del Duomo: The Baptistry

This ancient, mysterious building, the egg from which Florence's golden age was hatched, makes as good a place to start as any. Medieval Florentines were always too busy to look back, and now and then they lost track of themselves. The men of the quattrocento believed their baptistry to have been originally a Roman building, a Temple of Mars. After all the research that has gone into the question in the last few centuries the best guesses put the actual building in the 9th century—but maybe as far back as the 7th. The distinctive black-and-white marble facing, the tidily classical pattern of arches and rectangles that deceived Brunelleschi and Alberti, were probably added in the 10th or 11th century. The masters who built it remain unknown, but their strikingly original exercise in geometry provided the model for all Florence's great church façades. When it was new there was nothing remotely like it in Europe; to visitors from outside the city it must have seemed almost miraculous.

Every 21 March, New Year's Day on the old Florentine calendar, all the children born over the last 12 months would be brought here for a great communal baptism, a habit that helped make the baptistry not merely a religious monument but also a civic symbol, in fact the oldest and fondest symbol of the republic, which the Florentines never finished embellishing. Under the octagonal cupola the 13th- and 14th-century gold-ground mosaics show a strong Byzantine influence, though some (*The Life of John the Baptist*) may be the work of Cimabue.

To match them there is a beautiful inlaid marble floor decorated with the signs of the zodiac. Even more than the exterior, the patterned black-and-white marble of the interior walls is remarkable, combining influences from the ancient world and modern inspiration for something entirely new. It isn't cluttered inside; only a 13th-century Pisan-style baptismal font and the tomb of anti-pope John XXIII, by Donatello and Michelozzo, stand out.

Art historians used to date the coming of the 'Renaissance' to 1401, with the famous competition for the baptistry's **bronze doors**, when Lorenzo Ghiberti defeated Brunelleschi and others for the commission. The south door had already been completed by Andrea Pisano, with scenes from the life of John the Baptist in Gothic quatrefoil frames, and in his north door Ghiberti attempted no new departures. After 1425, however, he began the great east doors (the ones with tourists piled up in front) which were to occupy much of his time for the next 27 years. These are the doors Michelangelo is said to have called the 'Gates of Paradise', and undoubtedly they made a tremendous impression on all the artists of the quattrocento, using the same advances in composition and perspective and the same wealth of detail as the painters. Unfortunately the panels currently displayed are replicas, as the originals are being restored (four are now exhibited in the **Museo dell'Opera del Duomo**, *see* below).

The Old Testament scenes begin with the creation of Adam and Eve in the upper left corner, finishing with Solomon and Sheba in the Temple on the lower right-hand panel. On the frames, busts of contemporary Florentine artists peer out from tiny circles. It is a typical exhibition of Florentine pride that Ghiberti should put his friends among the prophets and sibyls that adorn the rest of the frames. Near the centre, the balding figure with arched eyebrows is Ghiberti himself.

The Duomo

For all its prosperity Florence was one of the last cities to plan a great cathedral. Work began in the 1290s, with the sculptor Arnolfo di Cambio in charge, and the Florentines from the beginning attempted to make up for their delay with audacity and size. Arnolfo laid the foundations for an octagonal crossing 156ft in diameter, then died before working out a way to cover it, leaving future architects with the job of designing the biggest dome in the world. Surprisingly the Duomo shows little interest in contemporary innovations and styles; a visitor from France or England in the 1400s would certainly have found it drab and architecturally primitive.

Visitors today often do not know what to think; they circle confusedly around its grimy, ponderous bulk (this is one of very few cathedrals in Italy that you can walk around completely). Instead of the striped bravura of Siena or the elegant colonnades of Pisa they behold an astonishingly eccentric pattern of marble rectangles and flowers—like Victorian wallpaper or, as one critic better expressed it, a 'cathedral wearing pyjamas'.

The west front cannot be blamed on Arnolfo; his original design, only one-quarter completed, was taken down in the late 16th century in a Medici rebuilding programme that never got off the ground. The Duomo turned a blank face to the world until 1888, when the present neo-Gothic extravaganza was added. After this façade the austerity of the interior is almost startling. There is plenty of room; contemporary writers mention 10,000 souls packed inside to hear the brimstone and hell-fire sermons of Savonarola. Even so the Duomo hardly seems a religious building—more of a *Florentine* building, with simple arches and the counterpoint of grey stone and white plaster, full of old familiar Florentine things. Near the entrance there are busts of Brunelleschi and Giotto along the right side. For building the great dome Brunelleschi was accorded a great honour—he is the only Florentine to be buried in the cathedral.

On the left wall, posed inconspicuously, you will see the two most conspicuous monuments to private individuals ever commissioned by the Florentine republic. The older one, on the right, is to Sir John Hawkwood, the famous English *condottiere* whose name the Italians mangled to Giovanni Acuto, a legendary commander who served Florence for many years. All along he had the promise of the Florentines to build him an equestrian monument after his death; it was a typical Florentine trick to cheat a dead man—but still they hired the greatest master of perspective, Paolo Uccello, to make a picture that looked like a statue. Twenty years later they pulled the same trick again, commissioning another great illusionist, Andrea del Castagno, to paint the non-existent equestrian statue of another *condottiere* named Nicolò da Tolentino.

A little further down, near the entrance to the dome, Florence commemorates its own secular scripture with a fresco of Dante by Michelino, a vision of the poet and his *Paradiso*. Two singular icons of Florence's fascination with science stand at opposite ends of the building: behind the west front a bizarre clock, also painted by Uccello, and in the pavement of the left apse a gnomon fixed by the astronomer Toscanelli in 1475. A beam of sunlight strikes it every year on the summer solstice.

There is surprisingly little religious art. Luca della Robbia contributed terracotta lunettes above the doors to the sacristies; the scene of the Resurrection over the north sacristy is one of his earliest and best works. He also did the bronze doors beneath it, with tiny portraits on the handles of Lorenzo il Magnifico and his brother Giuliano de' Medici, targets of the Pazzi conspiracy in 1478. In this ill-fated attempt to dispose of the Medici Giuliano was stabbed during Mass, but Lorenzo managed to escape, taking refuge in this sacristy. In the middle apse there is a beautiful bronze urn by Ghiberti containing relics of the Florentine St Zenobius. The only really conventional religious decorations are the frescoes in the dome, high overhead, mostly the work of Vasari.

Brunelleschi's Dome

Open Mon–Fri 8.30–6.20, Sat 8.30–5; adm.

Losing the competition for the baptistry doors was a bitter disappointment to Brunelleschi but a good piece of luck for Florence. His reaction was typically Florentine: not content with being the second-best sculptor, he began to devote all his talents to a field where he thought no one could beat him. He launched himself into an intense study of architecture and engineering, visiting Rome and probably Ravenna to snatch secrets from the ancients. When proposals were solicited for the cathedral's dome he was ready with a brilliant *tour de force*. Not only would he build the biggest dome of that era, and the most beautiful, but he would do it without any need for expensive supports while work was in progress, making use of a cantilevered system of bricks that could support itself while it ascended. Even today architects marvel at Brunelleschi's systematic way of tackling the job. Problems with weather and air pressure were foreseen and managed; hooks were inserted to hold up scaffolding for future cleaning or repairs.

Not only had Brunelleschi recaptured the technique of the ancients, he had surpassed them, with a system simpler and better than that of the Pantheon or Hagia Sophia. To the Florentines it must have come as a revelation; the most logical way of covering the space turned out to be a work of perfect beauty. Brunelleschi, in building his dome, put a crown on the achievements of Florence—after five hundred years still the city's pride and its symbol. To climb it, take the door on the left aisle near the Dante fresco; the complex network of stairs and walks between the inner and outer domes provides a thorough lesson on how Brunelleschi did it, and the views from the top are priceless.

Giotto's Campanile

Open April–Oct daily 9–6.50; Nov–Mar daily 9–4.20; adm.

There's no doubt: the dome steals the show on Piazza del Duomo, putting one of Italy's most beautiful bell towers in the shade both figuratively and literally. The dome's great size—366ft to the gold ball atop the lantern—makes the campanile look small, though 280ft is not exactly tiny. Giotto was made director of the cathedral works in 1334, and his basic design was completed after his death (1337) by Andrea Pisano and Francesco Talenti. It is difficult to say whether they were entirely faithful to the plan. Giotto was an artist, not an engineer; after he died his successors realized the thing was about to topple, a problem they overcame by doubling the thickness of the walls.

Besides its lovely form, the campanile's major fame rests with Pisano and Talenti's sculptural relief—a veritable encyclopaedia of the medieval world-view with prophets, saints and sibyls, allegories of the planets, virtues and sacraments, the liberal arts and industries (the artist's craft is fittingly symbolized by a figure of Daedalus). All these are copies; the originals can be seen in the cathedral museum (*see* below). If after climbing the dome you can take another 400 steps or so, the terrace on top offers a slightly different view of Florence. Some lesser-known monuments line the southern edge of the Piazza del Duomo. The **Loggia del Bigallo**, headquarters of one of Florence's still-operating charitable confraternities, was the place where mothers dropped off children they couldn't support. Inside there is a small museum of works commissioned by the confraternity in the 1400s (open by request, ☎ 055 215 440). A little way to the east, **Dante's Seat** is the ancient stone bench where, according to local legend, the poet would take the air, observing his fellow citizens and the building of the Duomo.

Museo dell'Opera del Duomo

Open April–Oct Mon–Sat 9–6.50, Sun 9–2; Nov–Mar Mon–Sat 9–6.20, Sun 10–1; adm exp.

Relatively few tourists find their way to the cathedral museum, hidden away in an inconspicuous building behind the central apse, but it contains some of the finest works of art in Florence, along with fascinating relics of the Duomo's past: brick moulds, tools, and a block and tackle from the original construction; models of the dome, and even Brunelleschi's death mask. Arnolfo di Cambio's sculpture from the original façade is here, along with drawings that show how it would have looked. There are a dozen big models of proposed reconstructions from the 1580s in various hack Mannerist styles—the façade could have been much, much worse. Florentines were never enthusiastic about the worship of relics, and long ago they shipped San Girolamo's jawbone, John the Baptist's index finger and St Philip's arm across the street to this museum.

In the 1430s Donatello and Luca della Robbia were commissioned to create a matching pair of *cantorie*, marble choir balconies. Both works, in exquisite low relief, rank among the Renaissance's greatest productions: Donatello's features dancing putti in a setting of quattrocento decorative motifs, and della Robbia's a delightful horde of children dancing, singing and playing instruments, a truly angelic choir. From the campanile, besides the reliefs of Pisano, there are some fine Old Testament figures by Donatello, as well as his gruesome wood statue of Mary Magdalen, something the Florentines no longer wished to see in their baptistry.

In the 1980s Michelangelo's last Pietà also joined the company, a strange, unfinished work that so exasperated the artist that he finally took a hammer to it, breaking Christ's left arm and leg. The tall, hooded figure supporting Christ—Nicodemus—dominates the composition; according to Vasari its face is that of Michelangelo himself. The finished, polished sections of the work, Mary Magdalen and part of the body of Jesus, are not Michelangelo's work at all, but that of a student, who also did his best to patch the arm.

Orsanmichele

Florence likes things neat and in their place. To balance Piazza del Duomo, the religious centre, there is Piazza della Signoria, the civic centre, with an equally formidable array of architecture and art, directly to the south at the other end of Via dei Calzaiuoli, long the city's main artery. On your way there, through the crowds navigating past the Via's fashionable jewellery shops and knick-knack sellers, you pass the unusual church of Orsanmichele.

This stately square building, built up to the street, is easy to miss; it doesn't look anything like a church, and in fact began its life as a grain market, with an open loggia at street level and emergency storehouses above where grain was kept against a siege. In 1304, when the market was relocated, the building was left to the city's powerful guilds, the *Arti*, as a trade and meeting hall. In 1380 Simone Talenti was hired to close in the arches of the loggia and make the 'Oratory of St Michael' (as the building was familiarly known because of the ancient chapel that had preceded it) into a church, although throughout the following century it continued to be closely associated with the guilds, the leaders of each of which strove to outdo the other by commissioning sculptures from the finest artists of the day.

All around the exterior the guilds erected statues of their patron saints: a remarkable collection, including Donatello's famed *St George* (now a copy; the original is in the Bargello) and *St Mark*, a work much admired by Michelangelo. *Saints Stephen* and *Matthew* are by Ghiberti. *Doubting Thomas* is by Verrocchio. The dim interior, full of stained glass and painted vaults, is ornate and cosy, with more of the air of a guildhall than a church. It makes a picture-book medieval setting for the wonderful **tabernacle**, a free-standing chapel with fine reliefs and sculpted angels by Andrea Orcagna (1350), precious stones and metalwork (every guild contributed something if it could), and a *Madonna* by Bernardo Daddi.

Piazza della Signoria

Now that the city has finally chased the cars out of this big medieval piazza it serves as a great corral for tourists, endlessly snapping pictures of the Palazzo Vecchio. In the old days it would be full of Florentines, the stage set for the tempestuous life of their republic. The public assemblies met here, and at times of danger the bells would ring and the piazza quickly fill with citizen militia, assembling under the banners of their quarters and guilds. Savonarola held his Bonfire of Vanities here, and only a few years later the disenchanted Florentines ignited their Bonfire of Savonarola on the same spot. (You can see a painting of the event at San Marco.)

The three graceful arches of the **Loggia dei Lanzi**, next to the Palazzo Vecchio, were the reviewing stand for city officials during assemblies and celebrations. Florentines often call it the *Loggia dell'Orcagna*, after the architect who designed it in the 1370s. In its simple classicism the Loggia anticipates the architecture of Brunelleschi and all those who came after him. The city has made it an outdoor sculpture gallery, with some of the best-known works in Florence: Cellini's triumphant *Perseus* (*under restoration*) and Giambologna's *Rape of the Sabines*, his bronze equestrian statue of Cosimo—standing imperiously at the centre of the piazza—as well as some of his other works, and a chorus of Roman-era Vestal Virgins.

All the statues in the piazza are dear to the Florentines for one reason or another. Some are fine works of art; others have only historical associations. Michelangelo's *David*, a copy of which stands in front of the Palazzo near the spot the artist intended for it, was meant as a symbol of republican virtue and Florentine excellence. At the opposite extreme, Florentines are taught almost from birth to ridicule the **Neptune Fountain**, a pompous monstrosity with a giant marble figure of the god. The sculptor, Ammannati, thought he would upstage Michelangelo, though the result is derisively known as *Il Biancone* ('Big Whitey'). Bandinelli's statue of *Hercules and Cacus* is almost as big and just as awful; Cellini called it a 'sack of melons'.

Palazzo Vecchio

Open Mon–Wed, Fri and Sat 9–7, Sun 8–1; closed Thurs; adm exp.

Florence's republican government was never perfect. In the better times chronic factionalism was barely kept in check, usually by the utter destruction or exile of one side or the other. Typically, however, the Florentines managed to give their aspirations a perfect symbol. The proud republic would accept nothing less than the most imposing 'Palazzo del Popolo' (as it was originally called) and Arnolfo di Cambio was able to give it to them. Even though the

308ft tower was for a long time Florence's tallest, Arnolfo avoided the sort of theatrical façade he was planning for the Duomo. The **Palazzo Vecchio** is part council hall, part fortress and part prison, and looks to fit all three roles well. Its rugged façade, copied in so many Florentine palaces, is not quite as frank and plain as it looks; all its proportions are based on the Golden Section of the ancient Greeks, rediscovered by medieval mathematicians. You may also accuse it of politically playing both sides—with square Guelph crenellations on the cornice and the swallowtail Ghibelline style on the tower.

The palace is often called the Palazzo della Signoria, the name it had under the rule of the Medici. After the final consolidation of their new government, the Duchy of Tuscany, the Medici turned the Palazzo Vecchio upside down. The house where Guelphs and Ghibellines once brawled in the council hall, and where lions were kept in the basement as a totem animal for the state, now became a florid Mannerist bower fit for a duke. Cosimo de' Medici's pet architect, Giorgio Vasari, oversaw the work in the 1550s and 1560s. Though the Medici did not reside there for long, the Palazzo was always used for state functions.

Today the Palazzo has somewhat recovered its old purpose. It serves as Florence's city hall, and the council holds its meetings in the **Salone dei Cinquecento**, built by the republic in 1495. At that time Leonardo da Vinci and Michelangelo were commissioned to fresco the two longer sides, a contest of talents that everyone in Florence looked forward to. For a number of reasons it never came off; only a small part of Leonardo's fresco was ever completed, and Vasari painted over it sixty years later. Even the designs for both men's concepts have been lost. Michelangelo's statue of Victory, originally intended for the tomb of Pope Julius II in Rome, was installed here by Vasari in the 1560s.

Despite the Palazzo's functional role as a base for the city administration, nearly all of the more historic rooms are open to the public (*free*), so you can look round the ferociously over-decorated **Cortile**, or courtyard, redone by Vasari. Inside, upstairs on the first floor, there is the fascinating **Studiolo di Francesco I**, a little retreat created for Duke Cosimo's son, who liked to dabble in poisons, where Vasari and his assistants painted a vast allegory of mythology, science and alchemy; more Vasari in the Chambers of Leo X and Clement VII (including a famous scene of the 1527 siege); and even more Vasari in the 'Quartiere degli Elementi'. Rooms with frescoes glorifying the Medici go on and on, but try not to miss the rooms of Eleanor of Toledo (Cosimo I's consort) done by Bronzino, or the **Sala del Giglio**, with a fine ceiling by the da Maiano brothers and *Judith and Holofernes* by Donatello.

Bargello: Museo Nazionale

Open daily 8.30–1.50; closed alternate Sun and Mon; adm.

For hundreds of years this medieval fortress-palace on the Via del Proconsolo, behind the Palazzo Vecchio, served as Florence's prison; today the inmates are men of marble—Italy's finest collection of sculpture, a fitting complement to the paintings in the Uffizi. When it was begun, about 1250, the Bargello was the Palazzo del Popolo, though by 1271 it was home to the foreign *podestà* installed by Charles of Anjou. When the Republic was reconstructed under the *Ordinamenti*, the decision was made to erect a bigger and grander seat of government—the Palazzo Vecchio. Just as that structure served as the model for so many Florentine palaces, so the Bargello was the model for the Palazzo, a rugged, austere work with a solid air of civic virtue about it. The Medici made a jail of it, but a thorough—and perhaps somewhat imaginative—restoration of the interior in the 19th century got it ready for its current job of housing the **Museo Nazionale**.

After the plain façade the delightful arcaded courtyard comes as a surprise, full of interesting architectural fragments, plaques and coats of arms in a wild vocabulary of symbols. In the first-floor galleries there are some early works of Michelangelo, including the *Bacchus*, and also Giambologna's *Mercury*—a work so popular it has entered everyone's consciousness as the way Mercury should look. There are also a number of works by Cellini, including his preliminary model for *Perseus* and his bust of *Cosimo I*. Upstairs, passing through the **Loggia**, now converted into an 'aviary' for Giambologna's charming bronze birds, you come to the **Salone del Consiglio**. This 14th-century hall contains many of the greatest works of Donatello: the fascinatingly androgynous *David*, the *St George* from Orsanmichele and the enigmatic Cupid or *Amor Atys*. These three alone make up a powerful case for considering Donatello the greatest of Renaissance sculptors. The alert watchfulness of *St George* created new possibilities in expressing movement, emotion and depth of character in stone, a revolution in art that was obvious even to Donatello's contemporaries. The *David*, obviously from a different planet from Michelangelo's *David*, explores depths of the Florentine psyche the Florentines probably didn't know they had. The same could be said of the dangerous-looking little boy Cupid. No one knows for whom Donatello made it, or who it is really meant to represent. With its poppies, serpents and winged sandals, it could easily be the ancient idol people in the 18th century mistook it for. Like Botticelli's mythological paintings it reflects the artistic and intellectual undercurrents of the quattrocento, full of pagan philosophy and eroticism, a possibility rooted out in the terror of the Counter-Reformation and quite forgotten soon after.

Among the other artists represented in the hall are Luca della Robbia, Verrocchio, Bernini, Michelozzo and di Duccio. The two bronze panels made by Brunelleschi and Ghiberti for the baptistry doors competition are preserved here; judge for yourself which is the better. Above, on the second floor, the collection continues with works mainly by Antonio Pollaiuolo and Verrocchio. The Bargello also houses an important collection of the decorative arts—rooms full of pretty bric-à-brac such as combs, mirrors, jewel caskets, reliquaries, Turkish helmets, vases and silks, wax anatomical figures and majolica from Urbino. Some of the most beautiful pieces are in a collection of medieval French ivory—intricately carved scenes like the 'Assault on the Castle of Love' and other medieval fancies. The Bargello's **chapel** has frescoes by an unknown follower of Giotto.

Dante's Florence

Dante would contemplate his Beatrice, the story goes, at Mass in the **Badia Fiorentina**, a Benedictine church on Via del Proconsolo across from the Bargello, with a lovely Gothic spire to grace this corner of the Florentine skyline. The church has undergone many rebuildings since Willa, widow of a Margrave of Tuscany, began it in around 990, but there is still a monument to Ugo, the 'Good Margrave' mentioned in Dante, and a painting of the *Madonna Appearing to St Bernard* by Filippino Lippi.

Between the Badia and Via dei Calzaiuoli, a little corner of medieval Florence has survived the changes of centuries. In these quiet, narrow streets you can visit the **Casa di Dante** (*open Mon, Tues and Thurs–Sat 9.30–12.30 and 3.30–6.30, Sun 9.30–12.30; closed Wed*), which was actually built in 1911 over the ruins of an amputated tower house, although scholars all agree that the Alighieri lived somewhere in the vicinity. Nearby, the stoutly medieval **Torre del Castagna** is the last extant part of the original Palazzo del Popolo, predecessor to the Bargello and Palazzo Vecchio. After giving up on Beatrice, Dante married his second choice, Gemma Donati, in the **Santa Margherita** church on the same block. Another church nearby, **San Martino del Vescovo**, has a fine set of frescoes from the workshop of Ghirlandaio—worth a look inside if it's open.

Florence As It Was

If, tramping the long and tired streets of this city, you still haven't discovered the Florence you came to find, stop in at the **Museo di Firenze Com'Era** (Museum of Florence As It Was), Via dell'Oriuolo 24 (*open Mon–Wed, Fri and Sat 9–2, Sun 9–1; closed Thurs; adm*), north of the Bargello and not far from the Duomo. In the first room, almost covering the entire wall, is the *Pianta della Catena*, most famous and most beautiful of the early views of Florence. Made in 1490 by an unknown artist (the handsome fellow pictured in the lower right-hand corner), it is really a copy of the original, lost during the Second World War in a Berlin museum. This fascinating painting captures Florence at the height of the Renaissance. Not much has changed; the great churches are without their façades, the Uffizi and Medici chapels have not yet appeared, and the Medici and Pitti palaces are shown without their later extensions.

This museum is not large—it has only a number of plans and maps, as well as a collection of watercolours of Florence's sights from the last century. One surprising fact that becomes clear from a visit here is that today's fussy and staid Florentines are much less interested in Renaissance Florence than in the city of their grandparents. For some further evidence check around the corner on Via Sant'Egidio, where remodelling has uncovered posters from 1925 announcing plans for paying the war debt and a forthcoming visit of the Folies Bergère. The Florentines have restored them and put them under glass.

The Uffizi Gallery

Open Tues–Sat 8.30am–10pm; Sun and hols 8.30–8; closed Mon; adm exp.

Poor Giorgio Vasari. His roosterish boastfulness and conviction that his was the best of all possible artistic worlds, set next to his very modest talents, have made him almost a comic figure in some art criticism. Even the Florentines don't like him. But on one of the rare occasions when he tried his hand as an architect he gave Florence something to be proud of. The Uffizi ('offices') were meant as Cosimo's secretariat, incorporating the old mint and archive buildings, with plenty of room for the bureaucrats needed to run the efficient, modern state Cosimo was building. The matched pair of arcaded buildings with restrained, elegant façades conceals a revolutionary but little-known innovation. Iron re-inforcements inside the façades make the huge amount of window area possible, and keep the building stable on the soft ground below; it was a trick that would almost be forgotten until the building of the Crystal Palace and the first American skyscrapers. The Uffizi is also a noteworthy piece of Renaissance urban design, an intelligent conception that unites the Piazza della Signoria with the Arno.

Almost from the start the Medici began to store their huge art collections in parts of the Uffizi. The last of the Medici, Duchess Anna Maria Lodovica, willed the entire hoard to the people of Florence in 1737. Give yourself a day or two to spend on the most important picture gallery in Italy, and come early in the day, especially in summer, when queues sometimes stretch around the arcades and beyond by 11am.

The size of the collection in the Uffizi is not overwhelming, but every work is choice. All the Florentine masters are represented, and the Medici even deigned to purchase a few foreigners. Here is a brief list of the works most worth seeing: near the entrance, amid halls of Medici clutter, the series of *Illustrious Men* (which includes the Cumean Sibyl!) in the dry precise style of **Andrea del Castagno**; then some fine trecento works by **Duccio di Buoninsegna** and **Cimabue**. If you can't make it to Siena this trip, be sure to see the works of that city's school, especially **the Lorenzetti brothers** and **Simone Martini**.

From the early quattrocento Florentine painters there is **Uccello**'s *Battle of San Romano*; even with only one third of the original present this is one of the most provocative of all paintings, a surreal vision of war with pink, white and blue toy horses. **Piero della Francesca** contributes a *Portrait of Federico da Montefeltro* with his famous nose (*see* 'Urbino', p.502); among the works by **Filippo** and **Filippino Lippi** there is a powerful grey *St Jerome*. **Botticelli** gets one big room to himself, in which are displayed his uncanny, erotic masterpieces including *The Birth of Venus*, *Primavera* and *Pallas and the Centaur* (another subtle allegory of the Medici triumph—the rings on Athena's gown were a family symbol), as well as some of his religious paintings and the disturbing *Calumny*, an introduction to the dark side of the quattrocento psyche.

Be sure to visit Room 15 and **Leonardo**'s *Annunciation*, an intellectual revelation that is one of the foremost achievements of Florentine art. Nearby are works by **Verrocchio** (Leonardo's teacher) and **Luca Signorelli**, and a formidable sea monster in **Piero di Cosimo**'s *Perseus and Andromeda*. In the Tribuna, a gaudy chamber designed by Bernardo Buontalenti, the Medici kept a valuable collection of Hellenistic and Roman sculpture, as well as portraits of *Cosimo* and *Eleanor of Toledo* by **Bronzino**. There's a surprising amount of German and Flemish painting, including **Dürer**'s *Adoration of the Magi* and *Adam and Eve*, both looking as much like Italian painting as he could make them—and **Cranach**'s *Portraits of Luther and Melanchthon*, spying on the Catholics. Venetians aren't as well represented, but there is the *Judgement of Solomon* by **Giorgione** and a *Sacred Allegory* by **Giovanni Bellini**.

Michelangelo always maintained that sculpture and fresco were the only arts fit for a man; oil painting he disdained, and just coincidentally he wasn't very good at it. The *Sacra Famiglia* here is the only canvas he ever finished. Next come some portraits by **Raphael, Rosso Fiorentino** and **Pontormo**; and the brightly coloured paintings of **Andrea del Sarto** (assuming that the restoration process has been completed). **Titian**'s overdressed Spaniards and well-upholstered girls get a room to themselves. The collections continue through painters of the 17th and 18th centuries—works of **Rembrandt** (two self-portraits), **Rubens, Van Dyck**, even **Goya**; the one exceptional picture here is the *Boy Playing at Cards* by **Chardin**.

In 1565 Francesco I commissioned Vasari to link the Palazzo Vecchio and the Uffizi to the Pitti Palace across the river, so he could pass through without rubbing elbows with his subjects. After 400 years, Florence just wouldn't look right without this covered passageway, the *Corridoio Vasariano*, leapfrogging around the back of the Uffizi, then over the top of the

Ponte Vecchio, through the rooftops on the other side and into the Pitti. The corridor contains a unique collection of artists' self-portraits, by Vasari himself, Velasquez, Rubens, Hogarth and many French artists. (*Admission with Uffizi ticket; check opening hours with tourist office.*)

Given the amount that Florence and the rest of Tuscany contributed to the birth of science it is only fitting to have the **Museo di Storia della Scienza** (Museum of the History of Science), Via Castellani (*open Mon, Wed and Fri 9.30–1 and 2–5, Tues, Thurs and Sat 9.30–1; adm exp*), in the heart of the city, just behind the Uffizi. Even in the dark centuries Florence never abandoned its scientific interests; the collection began with an institute founded by the Medici in the 1730s, the Accademia del Cimento, whose motto was 'Try and try again'. Pride of place goes to Galileo's instruments, including his first telescope, in addition to a large number of astrolobes, early microscopes, models of the planets, and armillary spheres, many of which are beautiful works of art in their own right. The last rooms contain wax anatomical models, a 15th-century Medici fetish.

Ponte Vecchio and Ponte S. Trinità

No one knows how long the Arno has been spanned at this point. The present bridge, built in 1345, replaced a wooden construction from the 970s, which in turn was the successor to a span that may have gone back to the Romans. Like medieval bridges in London and many other European cities, the new 14th-century bridge had shops and houses built all along it. By the 1500s it had become the street of the butchers; after Vasari built Cosimo's secret passage over the top the duke evicted the butchers (he didn't like the pong) and gave their places to the goldsmiths. They have kept their spot ever since, and hordes of shoppers from around the world descend on it each year to scrutinize the Florentine talent for jewellery. This is the most prestigious shopping location in Florence, and the jewellers are happy to stay—they could not be deterred even by the 1966 flood, when a fortune in gold was washed down the Arno.

In the summer of 1944 the river briefly became a German defensive line during the slow painful retreat across central Italy. Before they left Florence the Germans blew up every one of the city's bridges, saving only the Ponte Vecchio. Somehow the city managed to talk them out of it, and instead buildings on both sides were destroyed and the rubble piled up to block the approaches. Florence's most beautiful span, the **Ponte Santa Trinità**, had to go, however. The Florentines like their city just as it is, and immediately after the war they set about replacing the bridges exactly as they were. In the case of Santa Trinità it was quite a task. Old quarries had to be reopened to duplicate the stone, and old methods used to cut it (modern power saws would have done it too cleanly). The graceful curve of the three arches was a problem; they cannot be constructed geometrically and considerable speculation went on over how the architect (Ammannati, in 1567) had done it. Finally, remembering that Michelangelo had advised Ammannati on the project, someone discovered that the same form of arch could be seen on the decoration of Michelangelo's Medici Chapels, constructed most likely not by mathematics and common engineering, but by pure artistic imagination. Fortune lent a hand in the reconstruction; of the original statues of the 'Four Seasons', almost all the pieces were fished out of the Arno and reconstructed. Spring's head was missing, however, and controversy raged for a decade over whether to replace it or leave it as it was, until some divers found it, completely by accident, in 1961.

Around Piazza della Repubblica

On the map it is easy to pick out the small rectangle of narrow, straight streets at the heart of Florence; these remain unchanged from the little *castrum* of Roman days. At its centre the old forum deteriorated through the Dark Ages into a shabby market square, surrounded by the Jewish ghetto. So it remained until Florence, in a fit of post-Risorgimento ambition, decided to make it a symbol of the city's reawakening. The square was given a new design and a thorough facelift, and a grand arch was built, with a big inscription: THE ANCIENT CITY CENTRE RESTORED TO NEW LIFE FROM THE SQUALOR OF CENTURIES. Unfortunately the results were the same as in the new façade for the Duomo; Piazza della Repubblica is one of the ghastliest squares in Italy. Just the same, it is a popular place with tourists and natives alike, full of cafés with outside tables, and something of an oasis among the severe, unwelcoming streets of old Florence.

Those streets are worth walking. Dreary as they look at first sight, they are part of the soul of Florence. Also they are full of surprises; walk down Calimala, an important shopping street south of the Piazza, and you will encounter the **Arte della Lana**, behind Orsanmichele and connected to it by an overhead passageway. The 'Wool Corporation', richest of the guilds save that of the bankers, was really a sort of manufacturers' cooperative; its headquarters, built in 1308, was restored in 1905 in a delightful William Morris style of medieval picturesque. Nearby, further towards the river, is one of Florence's oldest marketplaces, covered by a beautiful loggia built in the 1500s. The **Mercato Nuovo**, where vendors hawk purses, toys and every sort of trinket, was in medieval times a merchants' exchange; it was also the place where the *carroccio*, the decorated wagon that served as a rallying point for the citizen armies during battles, was kept in time of peace. Florentines often call this the *Loggia del Porcellino*, after the drooling bronze boar put up as a decoration in 1612, a copy of a Greek sculpture in the Uffizi.

Between Via delle Terme and Via Porta Rossa the 14th-century **Palazzo Davanzati** recreates the atmosphere of a wealthy merchant's house of the 1400s as the **Museo della Casa Fiorentina Antica** (*closed for restoration; exhibition on ground floor open 8.30–1.50; closed alternate Sun and Mon*). Though some of the furnishings are from a century or two later, the late-medieval atmosphere is certainly present and, if historically accurate, a tribute to the taste of the honest burghers of the time. Some of Florence's oldest and most typical town houses lie between here and the river. Off Via Pellicceria, behind the Mercato Nuovo, is the 14th-century Guelph Party Building, often the real seat of power in the city, built with money confiscated from exiled Ghibellines.

Closer to the Arno stands **SS. Apostoli**, with a tabernacle by Andrea della Robbia; in the narrow streets around it you'll find the Piazzetta del Limbo, where unbaptized babies were buried in the Middle Ages. Further along the river, Gothic **Santa Trinità** has a dull façade added in the 1590s. One of the chapels has colourful frescoes by Lorenzo Monaco, who also did the altarpiece; another, the Sassetti Chapel, was decorated by Ghirlandaio. Ostensibly a series on the life of St Francis, scholars always comment on the frescos as a document of Florence's social history. All the Medici, Sassetti and their friends are present in finely detailed portraits, subtly arranged to show the city's new hierarchy of political and economic power.

For more Ghirlandaio continue on to the 13th-century **Ognissanti** (All Saints' Church), with another heavy façade added later. The man who named a continent, Amerigo Vespucci, is buried by the second altar on the right. Botticelli and Ghirlandaio both contributed versions of St Jerome for the cloister (*open daily 9–12.45*), and the latter's *Cenacolo* in the refectory (*open Mon, Tues and Sat 9–12*) is one of his better known works, a Last Supper that is more a garden party, with lemon trees and exotic birds, as well as a sulky Judas, third from the right.

Conspicuous Consumption *alla Fiorentina*

The streets west of Piazza della Repubblica have always been the choicest district of Florence. Via Tornabuoni, the fanciest shopping street, is as well-known in fashion as Via Montenapoleone in Milan or Via dei Condotti in Rome. In the 15th century this was the area most of the new merchant élite chose for their palaces. Today's bankers build great skyscrapers for the firm and settle for modest mansions themselves; in medieval Florence, things were reversed. The bankers and wool tycoons really owned their businesses, and in absolute terms probably had more money than anyone had ever had before. While their places of business were usually quite simple, for themselves they constructed imposing city palaces; all in the same conservative style, and competing with each other in size like some Millionaire's Row of Victorian-era America.

The style, derived from the Palazzo Vecchio, began at the **Palazzo Rucellai** on Via della Vigna Nuova (*closed for lengthy restoration*), a building designed by Alberti in 1446 for a prominent manufacturer and patron of learning. Much has been made of this building as a turning point in architecture; its real innovation is a consistent and skilful use of the classical 'orders', the system of proportion learned from Vitruvius. Of the other palaces in the neighbourhood north of Piazza S. Trinità, two stand out—the 1465 **Palazzo Antinori**, at the northern end of Tornabuoni, and the **Palazzo Strozzi**, two streets south. The Strozzi is the daddy of them all, the accustomed design blown up to heroic proportions; though three storeys like the rest, here each floor is as tall as three or four normal ones. Filippo Strozzi, head of a family of bankers who often felt strong enough to challenge the leadership of the Medici, built it in 1489 at the height of the clan's fortunes. Fifty years later his grandchildren were all exiles, bankers and advisers to the king of France. Both the Antinori and Strozzi palaces were the work of Benedetto da Maiano; the Strozzi houses a large library, and often hosts art exhibitions.

Santa Maria Novella

Santa Maria Novella, begun by the Dominicans in 1246, was always associated with the great families; in the 1600s the wealthy families of the neighbourhood would hold an annual carriage race around the two fat obelisks in the piazza in front. Between them they bestowed so much money to embellish it that by the 1500s the church had become a museum in itself, with important works of many late-medieval and Renaissance artists.

The brilliant black-and-white patterned façade, still the finest in Florence, shows the continuity of the city's style from medieval times. The lower half is part of the original work, finished before 1360, but the rest had to wait for one of the Rucellai family to commission Alberti to finish the job. It's his best work in Florence, a synthesis of classical architecture and

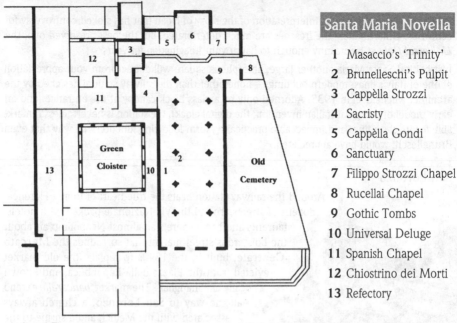

Santa Maria Novella

1 Masaccio's 'Trinity'
2 Brunelleschi's Pulpit
3 Cappèlla Strozzi
4 Sacristy
5 Cappèlla Gondi
6 Sanctuary
7 Filippo Strozzi Chapel
8 Rucellai Chapel
9 Gothic Tombs
10 Universal Deluge
11 Spanish Chapel
12 Chiostrino dei Morti
13 Refectory

medieval Florentine tradition, with volutes and arabesques that seem already to prefigure the Baroque. An odd touch is the image of the sun at the apex, the only image or symbol of any kind in Alberti's plan. Lower down, Cosimo I added the two unusual sundials over the left- and right-hand arches.

Inside, above the portal, is a *Nativity* by Botticelli. From there, proceeding clockwise around the church: a pulpit with reliefs by Brunelleschi; Masaccio's *Trinità* fresco, perhaps one of the earliest works with the temerity to depict God the Father; and then a *Resurrection* by Vasari. In the left transept, the Gondi Chapel has Brunelleschi's only wood sculpture, a crucifix—Vasari tells the story of how he made it to show Donatello a Christ with proper dignity, after complaining that his friend's crucifix (now in Santa Croce) made the Redeemer 'look like a peasant'. A great series of frescoes of the *Lives of St John and the Virgin* by Ghirlandaio surrounds the main altar. All his students helped him complete it—little Michelangelo included. Some equally fine frescoes by Filippino Lippi adorn the Filippo Strozzi Chapel in the right transept, where Strozzi is buried; the architect who designed his palace, da Maiano, also carved his tomb.

There's little of interest in the right-hand chapels, but just outside the left transept are some of the best parts of this surprisingly large monastic complex. Another Strozzi Chapel, this one from the 1360s, has a fine early fresco series of the *Last Judgement* by Nardo di Cione, brother of Orcagna. The Spanish Chapel, commissioned by Cosimo I's Spanish wife Eleanor of Toledo, offers a chilling touch of Counter-Reformation with a series of frescoes detailing the history of the Dominicans: the *domini canes* ('dogs of the Lord') sit at the pope's feet, symbolizing the order that ran the Inquisition and sniffed out heretics and freethinkers. In the background an interesting view of the Duomo as a fairly pink confection may in fact represent the original plans of Arnolfo di Cambio. Best of all, however, is the famous **Green Cloister** (*open Mon–Thurs and Sat 9–2, Sun 8–1; adm*), decorated with the most important frescoes by

Paolo Uccello, a mysterious interpretation of the story of Noah that has stoked controversy for centuries. Unfortunately the frescoes are much deteriorated, but the best preserved one, the *Universal Deluge*, is uncanny enough to haunt your imagination for years.

Just behind Santa Maria another large, amorphous square will detract from your appreciation of one of Italy's finest modern buildings—none other than the railway station, designed by the architect Michelucci in 1935. Adorned only by a glass block canopy at the entrance (and an early model of that great Italian invention, the digital clock), the station is nevertheless remarkable for its clean lines and impeccable practicality; form following function in a way that even Brunelleschi would have appreciated.

San Lorenzo

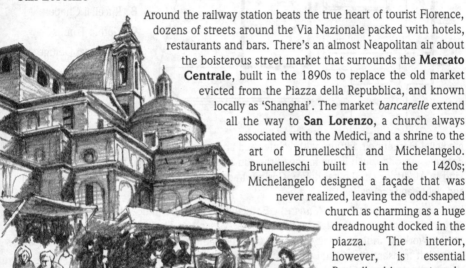

Around the railway station beats the true heart of tourist Florence, dozens of streets around the Via Nazionale packed with hotels, restaurants and bars. There's an almost Neapolitan air about the boisterous street market that surrounds the **Mercato Centrale**, built in the 1890s to replace the old market evicted from the Piazza della Repubblica, and known locally as 'Shanghai'. The market *bancarelle* extend all the way to **San Lorenzo**, a church always associated with the Medici, and a shrine to the art of Brunelleschi and Michelangelo. Brunelleschi built it in the 1420s; Michelangelo designed a façade that was never realized, leaving the odd-shaped church as charming as a huge dreadnought docked in the piazza. The interior, however, is essential Brunelleschi, a contemplative repetition of arches and columns in grey and white, while nothing else in Florence prepares you for the two pulpits in the nave, the last violent, near-impressionistic works of Donatello. Off the left transept, the **Old Sacristy** is a beautiful vaulted chamber with calmer sculptural decoration by Donatello.

Outside the church, a separate entrance on Piazza Madonna degli Aldobrandini leads to the famous **Medici Chapels** (*open Mon–Sat 8.30–5, Sun 8.30–1.50; closed alternate Sun and Mon; adm exp*) and their celebrated sculptures by Michelangelo. First, however, you will have to pass through the Prince's Chapel, under a huge eight-sided dome that dwarfs the rest of San Lorenzo, begun in 1604 following a design by a dilettante architect member of the Medici family. Several of the Medici dukes are buried in this dreary, trashy rotunda, the true monument of the ducal period and a sobering demonstration of just how soon Florence's great age of art declined into provincialism and preciosity. It certainly cost enough—the entire lower walls and floor are done in *pietra dura* with rich marbles from around the world, a job not completed until this century.

From here a corridor to the left leads to the **New Sacristy**, designed by Michelangelo in a severe style to match the Old Sacristy on the other side. The two tombs, of Giuliano Medici, Duke of Nemours, and Lorenzo, Duke of Urbino, the ruler to whom Machiavelli dedicated *The Prince*, are decorated with an allegorical sculptural scheme that has caused much discussion over the centuries. Giuliano is portrayed as a soldier representing the Active Life, with figures representing Day and Night reclining on his sarcophagus below. Lorenzo, as the Contemplative Life, sits and contemplates, overlooking figures of Dawn and Dusk (true to life in one respect; the passive Lorenzo was a disappointment to Machiavelli and everyone else). The male figures, at least, are among Michelangelo's triumphs. The women, Dawn and Night, come off less well. Michelangelo never had much use for the ladies—he wouldn't even use female models—and, whatever role they played in his personal mythology, he portrays them here as imperfect men, male forms with flabbier musculature and breasts stuck on like superfluous appendages.

In front of San Lorenzo a separate entrance leads to the **Biblioteca Laurenziana** (*currently closed for restoration*), designed for the Medici by Michelangelo and built by Ammannati, an important landmark in architecture: it was Michelangelo's first commission (along with the Medici Chapels), and one of the first steps on the slippery slope to Mannerism.

Palazzo Medici Riccardi

San Lorenzo became the Medici's church because it stood just round the corner from the family palace—a huge, stately building on Via Cavour constructed by Alberti and Michelozzo about the same time as the Palazzo Rucellai. The family's coat-of-arms, which you've probably already noticed everywhere in Florence, is prominently displayed in the corners. The seven, sometimes six, red boluses probably come from the family's origin as pharmacists (*medici*), and opponents called them 'the pills'. Medici supporters, however, made them their battle cry in street battles: 'Balls! Balls!'. The main reason for visiting is one of Florence's hidden delights: the **chapel** (*open Mon, Tues and Thurs–Sat 9–1 and 3–6, Sun 9–1; closed Wed; adm*), with extravagantly colourful frescoes by Benozzo Gozzoli. The *Procession of the Magi* is hardly a religious painting, a merry scene full of portraits of the Medici and others among the crowd following the Three Kings. The artist included himself, with his name on his hat. In the foreground of one of the panels, note the black man carrying a bow. Blacks (also Turks, Circassians, Tartars and other non-Europeans) were common enough in Renaissance Florence. Though originally brought as slaves, by the 1400s not all were still servants. Contemporary writers mention them as artisans, fencing masters, soldiers and, in one famous case, as an archery instructor, who may be the man pictured here. For an extraordinary contrast pop into the **gallery** (up the second set of stairs) with its 17th-century ceiling by Neapolitan Luca Giordano, showing the last, unspeakable Medici floating around in marshmallow clouds.

Fra Angelico's San Marco

Open daily 8.30–1.50; closed alternate Sun and Mon; adm.

Despite all the others who contributed to this Dominican monastery and church, it has always been best known for the work of its most famous resident. Fra Angelico lived here from 1436 until his death in 1455, spending the time turning Michelozzo's simple **cloister** into a complete exposition of his own deep faith, expressed in bright playroom colours and angelic pastels. Fra Angelico painted the frescoes in the corners of the cloister, and on the first floor there is a small museum of his work, collected from various Florentine churches, as well as a number of early 15th-century portraits by Fra Bartolomeo, capturing some of the most sincere spirituality of that age. The *Last Supper* in the refectory is by Ghirlandaio.

Other Fra Angelico works include the series of the *Life of Christ*, telling the story sweetly and succinctly, and a serenely confident *Last Judgement* in which all the saved are well-dressed Italians, holding hands. They get to keep their clothes in heaven, while the bad (mostly princes and prelates) are stripped to receive their interesting tortures.

Climbing the stairs to the monk's dormitory, right at the top your eyes meet the Angelic Friar's masterpiece, a miraculous *Annunciation* that offers an intriguing comparison to Leonardo's *Annunciation* in the Uffizi. The subject was a favourite with Florentine artists, not only because it was a severe test—expressing a divine revelation with a composition of strict economy—but because the Annunciation, falling near the spring equinox, was New Year's Day for Florence until the Medici adopted the Pope's calendar in the 17th century.

In each of the monks' cells Fra Angelico and students painted scenes of the Crucifixion, all the same but for some slight differences in pose; walking down the corridor and glancing in the cells successively gives the impression of a cartoon. One of the cells belonged to Savonarola, who was the prior here during his period of dominance in Florence; it has simple furniture of the period and a portrait of Savonarola by Fra Bartolomeo. Michelozzo's Library, off the main corridor (*currently closed for restoration*), is as light and airy as the cloisters below; in it is displayed a collection of choir books, including one illuminated by Fra Angelico.

If you liked Andrea del Castagno's work in the Uffizi, just around the corner from San Marco is a work many consider to be his best, the *Last Supper*, in the **Cenacolo di Sant'Apollonia**, Via XXVII Aprile 1 (*open daily 8.30–1.50; closed alternate Sun and Mon*).

Piazza Santissima Annunziata

This square, the only Renaissance attempt at a unified ensemble in Florence, is surrounded by arcades on three sides. The earliest of its buildings, one of Brunelleschi's most famous works, is also a monument to Renaissance Italy's long, hard and ultimately unsuccessful struggle towards some kind of social consciousness. Even in the best times Florence's poor were treated like dirt; if any enlightened soul had been so bold as to propose even a modern conservative 'trickle down' theory to the Medici and the banking élite, their first thought would have been how to stop the leaks. Babies, at least, had it a little better. The **Spedale degli Innocenti** (*open Thurs–Tues 8.30–2; adm*), built in the 1440s, was Florence's foundling hospital, and still functions as an orphanage today. Brunelleschi's beautiful arcade, decorated with the famous *tondi* of infants in swaddling clothes by Luca della Robbia, was one of the early classicizing experiments in architecture. There's a small picture gallery containing Ghirlandaio's *Adoration of the Magi* and several other works.

To complement Brunelleschi's arches the old church of **Santissima Annunziata** was rebuilt, and Michelozzo gave it a broad arcaded portico facing the street. Behind the portico the architect added the *Chiostrino dei Voti*, a porch decorated with a collection of early 16th-century frescoes, including two by Andrea del Sarto. The best of these, faded as it is, is a finely detailed *Nativity* by Alessio Baldovinetti, one of the quattrocento's under-appreciated masters. It is the gaudiest church in Florence; its freshly gilded elliptical dome, its unusual polygonal tribune around the sanctuary, and megatons of *pietra dura* have helped it become the city's high-society parish, where even funerals are major social events. The **Tempietta**, the candlelit chapel in the rear, also by Michelozzo, shelters a miraculous painting of *The Annunciation*.

The Accademia

Open Tues–Sat 8.30am–10pm, Sun 8.30–8; adm exp.

It may not be Florence's most interesting museum, but in summer the queues at the Accademia, just off the Piazza Santissima Annunziata, are often as long as those at the Uffizi. What people are most anxious to get a look at is of course Michelangelo's *David*. Just over a hundred years ago Florence decided to take this precocious symbol of republican liberty in out of the rain. The artist completed it for the city in 1501, when he was 26, and it was this work that established the overwhelming reputation he had in his own time.

Looking entirely contented with his own perfection, he stands in a classical exedra built just for him (behind protective glass). As the political symbol the republic commissioned he may be excessive—the irony of a David the size of Goliath is disconcerting— but as a symbol of the artistic and intellectual aspirations of the Renaissance he is unsurpassed. Other works by Michelangelo include the famous *non finiti*: the *Prisoners* and *St Matthew*, tortured forms still waiting for Michelangelo to come back and finish liberating them from the stone.

There is plenty of indifferent painting in the Accademia, but persevere for such works as the *Deposition from the Cross* by Perugino, the sweet and small *Madonna del Mare* by Botticelli; and Uccello's *Thebaid*. Some of the best works are in a room of lesser-known masters of the quattrocento, especially Mariotto di Cristoforo and the 'Maestro del Casione Adimare', the latter known only for the painted chest displayed here, a delightful scene of a marriage in Florence in the 1450s that has been reproduced in half the books ever written about the Renaissance. There is also a collection of musical instruments.

Museo Archeologico

Via della Colonna 36; open Tues–Sat 9–2, Sun 9–1; adm.

One of the most devious tricks of the Florentine museum torture is to keep your interest by changing the subject; just when you can't take another transcendent Renaissance painting, they politely offer a chance to see the greatest collection of Etruscan art in Tuscany. Nor is that all; the Egyptian and pre-historic collections in the Archaeological Museum are also exceptional. Again, the Medici are responsible; the museum began with purchases by Cosimo and Lorenzo il Magnifico. The Etruscans fill room after room, but the star attractions are two exquisite bronzes: the *Arringatore*, or Orator, a civic-minded and civilized-looking gentleman whom the inscription tells us was named Aurus Metellus; and the *Chimera*, a remarkable beast with the three heads of a lion, goat and snake. This 5th-century BC Etruscan work, dug up near Arezzo in 1555 and immediately snatched by the Medici, had a great influence on the Mannerist artists.

Greek art is also represented; Etruscan and Roman noble families were wont to buy up all they could afford. There is an excellent *kouros*, a young man in the archaic style from 6th-century BC Sicily, an almost complete ancient chariot, some good vases, and an unusual recent find: a 4th-century BC silver urn called the *Baratti Amphora*, made in Antioch and covered with scores of small medallions showing mythological figures. Scholars believe that the images and their arrangement may encode an entire system of belief, the secret teaching of one of the mystic-philosophical cults common in Hellenistic times, and they hope some day to decipher it.

Santa Croce

Santa Maria Novella was the Dominicans' church, and so naturally the Franciscans had to have one just as big and grand. The original church, said to have been founded by St Francis himself, went by the board in Florence's colossal building programme of the 1290s. Arnolfo di Cambio planned its successor, largely completed by the 1450s, but a job of 'restoration' by Vasari in the 1560s ruined much of the original interior. The façade, in the accustomed Florentine black-and-white marble, nevertheless has something of the Victorian Gothic about it—just as it should, since it was only added in the 1850s, a gift from Sir Francis Sloane.

No one has yet succeeded in doing anything with the vast, hideous piazza in front of it. However, it has become the venue every June for *Calcio in Costume*, a ball game similar to rugby, believed to be descended from a Roman sport that has its origins in the exercises of the citizen militias of the Florentine Republic. It's good fun to watch the usually immaculate Florentines in their Renaissance duds mixing it up in the dirt (fighting is more than permitted, as long as it's one to one).

The interior is a different story; like Santa Maria Novella it is a museum in itself. Starting clockwise from the left side: near the door is the **tomb of Galileo**, whose remains were moved here only after the Church grudgingly consented to allow him a Christian burial in 1737. For a while it was the custom to bury great Italians here, as a sort of Tuscan Westminster Abbey, and you'll

see plenty of tombs along both sides, mostly of thoroughly forgotten men of the 19th century. Two chapels down, the *Monument to Carlo Marsuppini* is a mine of good quattrocento sculpture, mostly by Verrocchio and Desiderio da Settignano. Look in the Bardi Chapel in the left transept for the *Crucifix* by Donatello (the one Brunelleschi said looked like a peasant). Many of the small vaulted chapels that flank the high altar contain important late (1330s) works by Giotto, his assistants and his followers. In the second **Bardi Chapel** is a series of frescoes on the *Life of St Francis* that can be compared with the more famous ones at Assisi.

The **Peruzzi Chapel** frescoes detail the *Lives of St John the Evangelist and St John the Baptist*. These works had a tremendous influence on all the later Florentine artists, but by the 18th century they were considered eyesores and whitewashed for 150 years—hence their fragmentary state. Two of Giotto's immediate artistic heirs, the Gaddi, also contributed much to Santa Croce. Agnolo Gaddi did the stained glass around the high altar, as well as the fascinating series of frescoes on the *Legend of the Cross*—how Seth received a branch from St Michael and planted it over Adam's grave, how the tree that grew from it was shaped into a beam for a bridge, then buried by Solomon when his guest the Queen of Sheba prophesied that it would someday bring about the end of the Jews. The beam was dug up and shaped into Christ's Cross, later found by St Helena, Constantine's mother, and then stolen by a Persian king and eventually recovered by the Emperor Heraclius. In the **sacristy**, off to the right, there are more fine frescoes by Agnolo Gaddi's father Taddeo, and yet more Gaddis in the Castellani Chapel (Agnolo) and Baroncelli Chapel (Taddeo).

Back down the right side of the church, Donatello's **Tabernacle** has a beautiful relief of the *Annunciation*. Then some more **tombs**: Rossini, Machiavelli, Michelangelo, and Dante. Michelangelo's is the work of Vasari, who thought himself just the fellow for the job. Vasari's vandalism ruined most of the chapels on this side, once embellished with frescoes by Orcagna and other great trecento painters.

The Pazzi Chapel

Open April–Sept daily 10–12.30 and 2–6.30; Oct–Mar daily 10–12.30 and 3–5; closed Wed; adm; one charge for both Pazzi Chapel and museum.

One of Santa Croce's chapels is well worth its entrance fee. Brunelleschi saved some of his best work for small places. Without knowing the architect and something about the austere religious tendencies of the Florentines the Pazzi Chapel is inexplicable: a Protestant reformation in architecture unlike anything ever built before. The 'vocabulary' is essential Brunelleschi: simple pilasters, arches and rosettes in grey stone and white plaster. The only decoration is a set of modest terracotta apostles by Luca della Robbia, coloured roundels of the Evangelists by Donatello, and a small stained-glass window by Alessio Baldovinetti. Even so, this is enough. The contemplative repetition of elements makes for an aesthetic that posed a direct challenge to the international Gothic of the time.

Across the broad cloister, the monks' refectory and several adjoining rooms now house the **Museo dell'Opera di Santa Croce**, with more works by della Robbia, bits from a large fresco by Orcagna wrecked by Vasari's remodelling, one of Donatello's statues from Orsanmichele—the gilded bronze *St Louis of Toulouse*—and a famous, mournful *Crucifix* by Cimabue, one of the early landmarks of Florentine painting, but only partially restored after damage in the 1966 flood.

Around Santa Croce

The east end of Florence, a rambling district packed with artisans and small manufacturers, was the artists' quarter in Renaissance times. Close to the river, it suffered grievously in the 1966 floods and to some extent has never quite recovered. Few things around this district are very old, but just west of Piazza Santa Croce you will see a series of streets—Via Bentacorti, Via Torta and Piazza Peruzzi—making an almost complete ellipse. These mark the course of the inner arcade of Roman Florence's amphitheatre; some stones can still be seen among the foundations of the old palaces. To the south, on Via dei Benci near the Arno, is a collection that Herbert Horne, a turn-of-the-century English art historian and Florentinophile bequeathed to Italy as the **Museo Horne** (*open Mon–Sat 9–1; summer Tues also 8.30pm–11pm; adm*), with odds and ends, ceramics, and works by Giotto, Gozzoli and Desiderio da Settignano.

Michelangelo never actually lived in the **Casa Buonarroti**, Via Ghibellina 70 (*open daily 9.30–1.30; closed Tues; adm exp*). The artist's continuing fascination with real estate has given critics since Vasari something to gossip about; he picked this property up for some of his relatives, and later generations made it into a Michelangelo museum. Besides some drawings and models, the collection contains some of the artist's early works, the *Battle of the Centaurs*, and a beautiful bas-relief called the *Madonna of the Stairs*. From here, three blocks north along Via Buonarroti will take you to the city's most colourful corner, the Sant'Ambrogio market and the *mercatino* in **Piazza dei Ciompi**. This is Florence's famous flea market, where dozens of vendors wait to sell you endearing junk in all shapes and sizes behind the typically Florentine 'Fish Loggia', designed by Vasari and moved here when the old market in Piazza della Repubblica was demolished. Just to the east is the church of **Sant'Ambrogio**, which has been thoroughly baroqued inside, but you can seek out good frescoes by Orcagna and Baldovinetti.

Across the Arno—the Palazzo Pitti

Once across the Ponte Vecchio a different Florence reveals itself—not too different, but at least a more pleasant place to walk around: greener, quieter and less burdened with traffic. The **Oltrarno**, as it is called, is not a large district. A chain of hills squeezes it against the river, and their summits afford the best views over the city. Across the bridge, the Medici's catwalk passes almost over the top of **Santa Felicità** church, best known as a monument to the quirky Mannerist painter Jacopo Pontormo. This artist, a recluse who lived atop a tower he built for himself, often pulling up the ladder to keep his friends at bay, frequently got himself into trouble with his neighbours for keeping the place full of dead animals and even human bodies, from which he studied form and anatomy. His work in Santa Felicità includes his acknowledged masterpiece, the *Deposition*, with its luminous, distorted figures and exaggerated expressions, as well as frescoes of the Annunciation and the Evangelists.

As the Medicis consolidated their power in Florence, they made a point of buying up all the important properties of their former rivals, especially their proud family palaces. The most spectacular example of this ducal eminent domain was the acquisition by Cosimo I of the **Pitti Palace**, built in 1457 by a powerful banker named Luca Pitti. The palace and its extensive grounds, now the Boboli Gardens, were purchased by Cosimo in the 1540s; he and his wife, Eleanor of Toledo, liked it much better than the medieval Palazzo Vecchio, and soon moved in for good. The palace remained the residence of the Medici, and later the House of Lorraine, until 1868. The original building, said to have been designed by Brunelleschi, was only as wide as the seven central windows of the façade.

Succeeding generations of Medici and Lorraines found it too small for their burgeoning collections of bric-à-brac, and added several stages of symmetrical additions, resulting in a long bulky profile, resembling some sort of Stalinist ministry on its bleak asphalt piazza. The grand dukes kept it better landscaped. Piazza Pitti was a prized address in the old days—the greatest of all Florence fans, the Brownings, lived across from the palace, and so for a time did Dostoevsky.

Altogether there are no less than eight separate museums in the Pitti complex, including collections dedicated to clothes, ceramics and carriages—a tribute to Medici acquisitiveness in the centuries of decadence, a period from which, in the words of Mary McCarthy, '...flowed a torrent of bad taste that has not yet dried up...if there had been Toby jugs and Swiss weather clocks available, the grand dukes would certainly have collected them.' Their picture collection, the **Galleria Palatina** (*open Tues–Sat 8.30am–10pm, Sun 8.30–1; adm exp*), will hold a place in your memory not so much for its Titians and Raphaels as for the thick gilt frames around them and the berserk opulence of the frescoed ceilings overhead.

There are plenty of bad pictures, but also some fine portraits by Titian, Van Dyck and Raphael, as well as some of Botticelli's later religious works, and plenty of Medici portraits (from Cosimo I to the dilapidated Gian Gastone). For a surprise, there are contemporary portraits of Queen Elizabeth I and Oliver Cromwell, both looking a little ill-at-ease in such surroundings.

While Florence was briefly the capital of Italy in the 1860s, the Savoy kings installed themselves in the Pitti, leaving behind a set of garish chambers inexplicably restored, and usually open to the public. The **Appartamenti Monumentali** (*guided tours daily at 9.30, 10.30, 11.30 and 12.30; it is not always possible to visit all the apartments*) are worth a look for connoisseurs of 19th-century French tapestries and furnishings.

Those serious about trinkets will find a wonderland at the Pitti: the **Museo degli Argenti** (*same hours as the Galleria Palatina; adm also valid for the costume and carriage museums*), a surprisingly vast collection of gold and silver work, engraved precious stones, cameos, ivory and crystal; the **Museo delle Carrozze**, with the fancy carriages of the Medici and the Lorraines. The **Galleria d'Arte Moderna** (*temporarily closed*) has the best collection extant of the 19th-century school called *Macchiaioli* ('Splatterers' might be the best translation)— Tuscan painters who tried to revive moribund Italian art by transplanting Impressionism from France. Finally, the hardest part of the Pitti to get into may be worth the trouble if you're fond of Spanish painting. Until it finds a permanent home, the **Contini Bonacossi Collection** resides in the Meridiana pavilion (*open by appointment only, © 055 238 8652*). This recent bequest includes works of Cimabue, Duccio and Giovanni Bellini, some sculpture and china, and also paintings by El Greco, Goya and Velázquez—the last represented by an exceptional work, *The Water Carrier of Seville*.

Boboli Gardens

Open daily 9–one hour before sunset; adm.

It is the loveliest park in the centre of Florence, the only park in the centre of Florence, and if you're visiting in the summer, the sooner you become acquainted with it the better. The Boboli is the only escape from the sun, humidity and crowds of July and August. Cosimo I began the planning and landscaping in the 1550s. The tone for what was to be the first Mannerist park was set early on by the incredible **Grotta del Buontalenti**, near the entrance behind the Pitti Palace. This artificial grotto is sheer madness, Gaudiesque dripping stone with peculiar creatures seeming to grow out of it. Inside are fantastic painted landscapes, surrounded by leopards, bears, satyrs and others harder to define.

There's a **museum of porcelain**, in a little palace called the Casino del Cavaliere, and t he groves and walks of the Boboli are haunted by platoons of statuary, some Roman and some absurd Mannerist work, like the fat baby Bacchus riding a turtle. There's a genuine obelisk, in the centre of a miniature Roman circus, and a fountain from the Baths of Caracalla. Some of the best parts of the gardens are the furthest away: shady paths and flower beds towards the south, near Florence's southern gate, the Porta Romana.

Santo Spirito and Santa Maria del Carmine

The centre of the Oltrarno district, Piazza Santo Spirito usually has a small market going under the plane trees, as well as restaurants and a quiet café or two. The church, **Santo Spirito**, boasts a severe 18th-century façade that conceals one of Brunelleschi's triumphs: a character-istic, contemplative interior of grey and white surrounded by ranks of semi-circular chapels. Even though later architects tinkered grievously with the plan after Brunelleschi's death, many consider this to be one of his best churches. Among the paintings in the chapels are works by Filippino Lippi (south transept, a *Madonna and Child*) and Orcagna (a fresco of the Crucifixion, in the refectory of the adjacent monastery).

With its walls of rough stone—the projected façade was never completed—**Santa Maria del Carmine** looks more like a country farmhouse than a church. Most of it was destroyed in a fire and reconstructed in the 1700s, but the **Brancacci Chapel** (*open Mon and Wed–Sat 10–5, Sun 1–5; adm*), another of the landmarks of Florentine art, somehow survived, and has been restored. Three artists worked on the chapel frescoes: Masolino, beginning in 1424, his pupil Masaccio, working alone from 1428, and Filippino Lippi, who completed the work in the 1480s. Scholars never tire of disputing the attributions of the various scenes, especially those that could be either Masolino's or Masaccio's. It doesn't matter; 'Little Tom' and 'Shabby Tom' both contributed greatly to the visual revolution of quattrocento painting. Both were revolutionary in their understanding of light and space, though art historians these days make more of a fuss over the precocious, eccentric Shabby Tom, who died at the age of 27 shortly after his work here. Some of the scenes—the *Expulsion of Adam and Eve*, the *Tribute Money*, and scenes from the life of St Peter—are among Masaccio's masterpieces. Almost every artist of the later 1400s and 1500s came here to do sketches and study how Shabby Tom did it; some of Michelangelo's sketches after Masaccio still survive.

The Forte di Belvedere

For the best views over Florence, and the best chance to get away from the city's dust and noise, you can climb up to the heights around Oltrarno. It's a pleasant walk whether you do it the short way, up Costa San Giorgio and through the old city walls, or the longer route towards Piazzale Michelangelo. This leads through an interesting, little-known corner of the city around Via dei Bardi and Via San Niccolò, two fine old streets with a scattering of Renaissance palazzi, and good frescoes by Alessandro Baldovinetti in the church of **San Niccolò sopr'Arno**.

At the top of a winding road and a long set of steps, Piazzale Michelangelo is a popular lookout point adorned with yet another full-size copy of the *David*. Beneath it, Via del Belvedere leads up between the walls and some country villas to the **Belvedere Fort** (*open daily 8–8*), from 1590, dominating the city's defences along the southern heights. This fort and adjacent walls replaced the earlier ones (those Michelangelo helped design) that survived the siege of 1529. The central building of the Belvedere has been restored to hold special art exhibitions, as well as bits of frescoes rescued from some of the lesser-known churches. Even if nothing is on, the view makes the climb worthwhile.

San Miniato

Despite the fact that the lovely Romanesque façade of this church can be glimpsed from almost anywhere in Florence, few visitors are ever moved to see it up close. As a result, you may have one of Florence's best churches all to yourself. Built in 1015 over an earlier church, on the spot where the head of obscure St Minias bounced after the Romans decapitated him, the exterior echoes the black-and-white geometric style of the baptistry. The playful patterns are continued inside, framing a richly coloured 13th-century mosaic of Christ Pantocrator in the apse. Despite its distance from the city centre this has always been a church dear to the hearts of the Florentines.

At the top of the façade you'll notice the gold eagle symbol of the Calimala, the medieval cloth merchants' guild. These rich businessmen had the church in their care, and over the centuries they bestowed on it many lovely things. Inside, be sure to see the wonderful inlaid marble floor, with signs of the zodiac and fantastical animals; also the **Cappella del Crocifisso**, a joint effort by Michelozzo and Luca della Robbia. The fine pulpit and choir screen date from the early 1200s, and the Chapel of the Cardinal of Portugal contains work by Baldovinetti (who also restored the apse mosaic), della Robbia, Pollaiuolo and Rossellino.

Peripheral Attractions

Most of these, inevitably, are museums. If it is possible that somehow, somewhere, there lives an indefatigable culture-tourist capable of taking on the major sites of Florence and still asking for more, the city will be glad to oblige.

The utterly peculiar **Villa Stibbert**, Via Stibbert 26, is north of the centre off Via Vittorio Emanuele (*open summer Fri–Wed 10–1 and 3–6; winter varies; adm; free on Sun; guided tours on the hour; at other times you may wander around freely*). To get there, take bus no.31 from the station. The life's vocation of an eccentric English collector (d. 1906) who fought with Garibaldi and later settled here, the villa, inside and out, is a sumptuous Victorian version of how the Florentine medieval style ought to have looked, populated by scores of mannequins parading in arms and armour of all nations and periods—from Portugal to Indonesia. Besides tin suits, there are large bulky footfaraws, lace, snuff boxes, and plenty of what a local guide intriguingly describes as 'brass and silver basins, used daily by Stibbert'.

Fans of Andrea del Sarto, Browning's 'Perfect Painter', can go a little out of their way to see two of his best works, a *Last Supper* in the **Cenacolo of San Salvi**, Via San Salvi 16 (*open Tues–Sun 8.30–1.50; adm*), and a set of *chiaroscuro* frescoes on the life of St John at the **Chiostro dello Scalzo**, Via Cavour 69 (*same hours as San Salvi*). There are architectural fragments, bric-à-brac, della Robbias, musical instruments—and beautiful medieval paintings and sculpture—at another former private collection, the **Museo Bardini**, Piazza de' Mazzi 1, in the Oltrarno near Via dei Bardi (*open Mon, Tues and Thurs–Sat 9–2; Sun 8–1; adm*).

As for science museums, Florence has more than any city in Italy. Many are gathered in the complex at Via la Pina 4, including a **botanical garden**, a museum of **mineralogy and lithology**, and a **botanical museum** full of wax flowers. All of these collections began with the inquisitive Medici grand dukes. They were also behind one of Florence's real curiosities, the stuffed hippo in the **La Specola Zoological Museum** (*open Thurs–Tues 9–1; adm*).

Fiesole

No ordinary suburb, **Fiesole** can claim to be the mother city of Florence itself. In fact the town is of Etruscan origin, the northernmost member of the federation of city-states called the Dodecapolis. *Faesulum* dwindled in the heyday of Roman-era Florence, but in the Dark Ages its secure hilltop site ensured its survival. When times became a little bit safer its families began moving back down to the Arno to rebuild Florence. For centuries now Fiesole has played the role of Florence's aristocratic suburb; its cool breezes and belvedere views make it the perfect retreat from the torrid Florentine summers.

There's no escaping the tourists, however; we foreigners have been tramping up and down Fiesole's hill since the days of Shelley. They're used to us by now, and a day trip here is for many visitors an obligatory part of a stay in Florence. The no.7 city bus from the Piazza della Stazione will have you there in less than half an hour, stopping in Piazza Mino da Fiesole, the town centre.

Mino da Fiesole is a favourite son, a quattrocento sculptor whose best work can be seen in the early 11th-century **Duomo** on the piazza; the tomb of Bishop Salutati off the right aisle contains his altarpiece with the Madonna and saints. Behind the cathedral on Via Dupré is the **Museo Bandini** (*open winter daily 9.30–5; summer daily 9.30–7; closed Tues; adm*), a must for anybody who loves the iridescent della Robbia terracottas on Tuscany's churches and would like a chance to see some up close. The museum has an entire roomful, along with a collection of 14th- and 15th-century Tuscan paintings.

Not much is left of Etruscan or Roman Fiesole, but you can visit the small **Teatro Romano**, excavated in 1911 and often used for plays and concerts in the summer; the archaeological area, on the hillside near the Bandini Museum on Via Partigiani, also includes scanty remains of baths and temples, and a small museum (*open April–Sept daily 9–7; Oct–Mar daily 10–4; closed Tues; adm*).

Perhaps the best sights Fiesole has to offer, though, are the perfect views over Florence and the surrounding area from old streets like Via Francesco on the edge of town. Walks around the outskirts reveal some lovely countryside and a few surprises: the **church of San Domenico** at San Domenico di Fiesole, a couple of kilometres from town, has three paintings by Fra Angelico, who lived for a while in the adjoining monastery. Nearby on Via di Badia, the **Badia Fiesolana**, Fiesole's original cathedral, has an unfinished 11th-century geometric façade like that of San Miniato or Santa Maria Novella, and an interior in the manner of Brunelleschi.

Shopping

Although central Florence sometimes seems like one solid boutique, the city is no longer the queen of Italian fashion. Nevertheless, the big **fashion** names of the 1960s and 70s, and the international chain stores of the 80s, are well represented in smart Via Tornabuoni, Via Calzaiuoli and in the streets around the Duomo.

The **jewellery** shops that line the Ponte Vecchio are forced by the nature of their location into competition, and you can get good prices for Florentine brushed gold, cameos and antique jewellery (much of it actually made in Arezzo these days). They do not set up shop here just to exploit tourists—they've been on the bridge for over 300 years. It is worth looking around Via della Vigna Nuova and Via del Parione for **leather goods**.

For bargains and surprises, try Florence's famous and boisterous **street markets**, usually open every day. The big San Lorenzo market, which has spread all over the neighbourhood around San Lorenzo church, is where ordinary Florentines probably buy most of their clothes. In this little bit of Naples transplanted to Tuscany, the range of choice is equal to three department stores; you'll see plenty of fake designer labels, and even some real ones.

Further west in Santa Croce, in the Piazza dei Ciompi, the *mercato delle pulci* (flea market) carries on daily, with a wide array of desirable junk, beneath Vasari's Fish Loggia; the shopkeepers, being Florentines, are a little smug and not inclined to bargain. More serious **antique** shops tend to cluster in the streets between Via Tornabuoni and the Ognissanti, and on Via Maggio.

The **Mercato Nuovo**, or *Mercato del Porcellino*, right in the centre of town, still performs its age-old function of selling Florentine straw goods—hats and bags—though tourist trinkets have taken over most of the stalls. There is also a small market in Piazza Santo Spirito in the Oltrarno (*mornings*) and a larger one in the Cascine Park (*Tuesday mornings*). Some of the real finds are in the towns around Florence: **glassware** in Empoli, and **ceramics** (including the inevitable della Robbia reproductions) in Impruneta and Montelupo.

Hotels in Florence tend to be expensive, and the problems of finding a room become chronic in July and August. But don't be discouraged; the Florentines are old pros in the tourist business, and even if you're daft enough to drop in during August without booking, you'll find plenty of help in locating a bed. There are several hotel consortiums that can find you something; most have some rooms in all price ranges. The first night's room fee or a similar amount will usually have to be paid when booking, as a deposit, and will then be deducted from your final bill.

The largest of the local hotel agencies is **ITA**, in Stazione Centrale, ✆ 055 282 893 (*open daily 9–9*), and in the AGIP service station at Peretola, to the west of Florence on the A11, ✆ 055 421 1800; there are also offices in the Chianti-Est service area on the A1, and in the Fortezza da Basso, by the car park, ✆ 055 471 960 (*Mar–Nov only*). You can't book by phone. Queues at their offices are often huge. Otherwise try **Florence Promotelhs**, Viale A. Volta 72, ✆ 055 570 481. An alternative to staying in the centre of Florence is to look for a hotel in Fiesole, which is cooler, and quieter at night, when you can appreciate the wonderful views over the city far below, twinkling like a mass of fairy lights. In addition, anywhere within half an hour of Florence you will find fine old villas and monasteries that have been turned into quiet, luxury hotels; though often in the most unlikely places, they are very popular with those in need of fresh air and tranquillity.

luxury

*****Excelsior**, Piazza Ognissanti 3, ✆ 055 264 201, ✆ 055 210 278, the former Florence address of Napoleon's sister Caroline, is immaculately staffed and neo-classically plush, with lots of marble and lush plants, a stylish bar and first-rate restaurant. The bedrooms are decadently luxurious, and the smart roof garden has views down the Arno.

*****Helvetia & Bristol**, Via dei Pescioni 2, ✆ 055 287 814, ✆ 055 288 353, has just 52 luxurious bedrooms, each one different, and each exquisitely furnished with antiques and rich fabrics; service is discreet and the atmosphere understated. Stravinsky, Bertrand Russell and Pirandello have stayed here. There is also a superb restaurant.

*****Villa San Michele**, Via Doccia 4, ✆ 055 59451, ✆ 055 598 734, is in a breathtaking location just below Fiesole. This 14th-century monastery has a façade and loggia reputedly designed by Michelangelo. Carefully reconstructed after bomb damage in the Second World War, it has become one of the most beautiful hotels in Italy, set in a lovely Tuscan garden, complete with a pool. The prices are seriously astronomical, but the food is wonderful. *Closed mid-Nov–mid-Mar.*

very expensive

****Monna Lisa**, Borgo Pinti 27, ✆ 055 247 9751, ✆ 055 247 9755, is one of Florence's most charming, well-situated small hotels, a well-preserved Renaissance palace owned by the descendants of sculptor Giovanni Dupre. The furnishings and works of art are family heirlooms. Try to book one of the tranquil rooms overlooking the garden. There is private parking. ★★★★**Kraft**, Via Solferino 2, ✆ 055 284 273, ✉ 055 239 8267, two minutes' walk from the Teatro Comunale, has cheerful, sunny rooms. There are great views from the top floor, a rooftop pool, and a restaurant.

expensive

★★★**Loggiato dei Serviti**, Piazza SS. Annunziata 3, ✆ 055 289 592, was designed for the Servite fathers by Antonio da Sangallo the Elder, who added a loggia to match Brunelleschi's Spedale degli Innocenti across the square. It features the best of Florentine taste, Italian and English antiques, a lovely garden, and parking nearby.

★★★**Beacci Tornabuoni**, Via Tornabuoni 3, ✆ 055 212 645, is another excellent small hotel, on the top three floors of an elegant Renaissance palace. The rooms are comfortable and you can admire the views from the roof terrace. ★★★**Morandi all Crocetta**, Via Laura 50, ✆ 055 234 4747, ✉ 055 248 0954, is a popular, 10-room hotel in the university area northeast of Piazza San Marco. Run by an Irish family, the building was a convent in the 16th century, and some of the comfortable rooms still have the odd fresco. Two have private terraces.

moderate

★★★**Pensione Bencista**, Via B. da Maiano 4, ✆ 055 59163, in San Domenico di Fiesole (on the no.7 bus route), in a sprawling villa dating back to the 14th century, has antiques in many of its rooms, and a garden and fine views. ★★**Pensione Alessandra**, Borgo SS. Apostoli 17, ✆ 055 283 438, ✉ 055 210 619, in a 1507 palazzo designed by Baccio d'Agnolo, near the Ponte Vecchio, has 25 rooms, the best with waxed parquet floors and antique furniture.

The family-run ★★★**Casci**, Via Cavour 13, ✆ 211 686, ✉ 055 239 6461, is in a 15th-century palazzo (once home to Rossini). The atmosphere is relaxed and cheerful, the breakfast room has a frescoed ceiling, and some of the rooms look on to a garden. Good value. The ★★★**Classic Hotel**, Viale Machiavelli 25, ✆ 055 229 351, ✉ 055 229 353, just above Porta Romana on the way to Piazzale Michelangelo, is a pink-washed villa in a shady garden. Rooms are furnished with a mixture of old and new, walls are white, parquet floors are polished. There is even the odd fresco. Excellent value for money.

cheap

Most of Florence's budget (or budget-ish) hotels are grouped together around the railway station. Most send touts to the station and, if you're getting stuck, at least check the prices they are offering. Except in high season it's usually possible to bargain. ★**Firenze**, Piazza dei Donati, ✆ 055 214 203, near the Duomo, is the classiest cheap hotel in Florence. Book in advance, and ask for one of the newer rooms. ★**Scoti**, Via Tornabuoni 7, ✆ 055 292 128, is a cheap and simple *pensione* run by new, friendly owners (Doreen is Australian). Large rooms have up to four beds and there's bags of atmosphere—and floor-to-ceiling frescoes in the sitting room.

Residenza Johanna, Via Bonifacio Lupi 14, ✆ 055 481 896, ✉ 055 482 721, north of Piazza San Marco, is a non-hotel, with no porter and DIY breakfast, but it's pretty and comfortable. ★**Il Granduca**, Via Pier Capponi 13, ✆ 055 572 803, between piazzas Donatello and della Libertà, is one of the nicest cheap hotels, with a garden and garage. Besides hotels, a number of **institutions** and **private homes** let rooms—there's a complete list in the back of the annual provincial hotel book (*Elenco degli Alberghi*), available from tourist offices.

Eating Out

For better or worse, the real Florentine specialities rarely turn up on many restaurant menus, and you'll probably finish your stay without ever learning what a Florentine cook can do with cocks' combs, calves' foot and tripe. Florence in its loftier moods likes to call itself the 'birthplace of international *haute cuisine*', but in fact the city's contribution to the Italian kitchen is minimal; everyone knows its only really popular dish, *bistecca alla Fiorentina*—thick grilled steaks seasoned with salt and pepper. Nevertheless, like any sophisticated city with lots of visitors, Florence has plenty of fine restaurants; even in the cheaper places, standards are high, and if you don't care for anything fancier there will be lots of good red Chianti to wash it down.

very expensive

Florence is blessed with one of the finest gourmet restaurants in Italy, the **Enoteca Pinchiorri**, Via Ghibellina 87, ✆ 055 242 777, near the Casa Buonarroti. The owners inherited the building, a wine shop, some 10 years ago, and have converted it into a beautifully appointed restaurant, with meals served in a garden court in the summer; they've also accumulated an astonishing collection of some 80,000 bottles of the best Italian and French wine. The cooking, a mixture of *nouvelle cuisine* and traditional Tuscan recipes, wins prizes every year. Be warned that you can leave behind as much as L200,000 per person here. *Closed Sun, Mon midday, and Aug.*

Cibreo, Via dei Macci 118r, ✆ 055 234 1100, overlooking Sant'Ambrogio market, has simple décor—food is the main concern: tripe *antipasto*, *prosciutto* from the Casentino, pumpkin soup, leg of lamb stuffed with artichokes, a delicious lemon *crostata*. There's an excellent selection of Italian or French wines, and Armagnac. *Closed Sun and Mon, Easter and mid-July–mid-Sep.* **Alle Murate**, Via Ghibellina 52r, ✆ 055 240 618, is an elegant but relaxed restaurant very popular for its 'creative traditional food'. There are two set menus, one of Tuscan dishes and the other offering something a little different. Recommended dishes include spaghetti with sea bass, steamed octopus with mashed potato, lamb's brain salad, pigeon stuffed with peppers and potatoes. *Open for dinner; closed Mon.*

expensive

If *cucina nuova fiorentina* sounds intriguing, try it on the veranda at **Caffè Concerto**, Lungarno C. Colombo 7, ✆ 055 677 377, overlooking the Arno. It remains open late, for light midnight suppers. *Closed Sun.* The informal **Coco Lezzone** (old Florentine dialect for big, smelly cook), Via del Parioncino 26r, off Lungarno Corsini, ✆ 055 287 178, serves excellent Tuscan classics using the highest quality ingredients. **Pane e Vino**, Via San Niccolò 70r (in the Oltrarno, just in from Ponte alla Grazie), ✆ 055 247 6956, is an informal restaurant which started life as an *enoteca* and still has a superb wine list. The very good value seven-course *menu degustazione* changes daily; with any luck, the superb porcini mushroom flan will be available. *Closed Sun.*

Il Latini, Via dei Palchetti 6r, ℰ 055 210 916, near Santa Maria Novella, is noisy, chaotic and great fun. Huge hams hang from the ceiling, and diners share the long tables, sampling good local fare at modest prices. You cannot book. **Ila Vecchia Bettola**, west of the Carmine in Viale Ariosto 32–4r, ℰ 055 224 158, is a noisy trattoria with marble-topped tables and wooden benches. The menu changes daily, but you can nearly always find their classic *tagliolini con funghi porcini*; the grilled meats are tasty and succulent. *Closed Sun.*

Ristoro di Cambi, Via Sant'Onofrio 1r, ℰ 055 217 134, in the Oltrarno, is popular with the Florentine intelligentsia. The food is genuinely Florentine, the décor rustic. The soups—classic *ribollita* and *pappa al pomodoro*—are tasty and warming, and the *bistecca alla fiorentina* the real McCoy. *Closed Sun.* **Baldovino**, Via Giuseppe 22r (Piazza S. Croce), ℰ 055 241 773, owned by a young Scotsman, serves anything from a salad, a filled foccaccia or a pizza (baked in a wood-burning oven) to a full menu of pastas, fish and meat. The wine list is interesting; he also runs a wine bar just across the road.

Central Florence, by popular demand, is full of *tavole calde*, pizzerias, cafeterias and snack bars, where you can grab a sandwich or a salad instead of a full sit-down meal (one of the best pizza-by-the-slice places is just across from the Medici Chapels).

La Casalinga, Via Michelozzo 9r, is an excellent but inexpensive traditional restaurant just by Piazza Santo Spirito in Oltrarno, serving hearty Tuscan food. Popular with students and young tourists, despite the cranky waiting staff. **Da Mario**, Via Rosina 2r, is a similar, not quite as cheap but sometimes friendlier little restaurant near the railway station. Arrive early for lunch to avoid the queues.

Trattoria Cibreo, Via de' Macci 118r, is an annexe at the back of the smart Cibreo (*see* above), and a real find. The food is more or less the same, just served on less expensive porcelain. *Closed Sun and Mon.* **Le Belle Donne**, Via delle Belle Donne 16r, ℰ 055 238 2609, is easy to miss, just off Via Tornabuoni. There is an emphasis on vegetable dishes, although it's not exclusively vegetarian. It's always crowded, so book. *Open Mon–Fri*.

The cheapest meal in Florence, though, will almost certainly be found at the lunch counter, the **Tavola Calda**, in the Sant'Ambrogio market, where, once you've fought your way through the crowds of market traders, you can get a full three courses for around L20,000, served with a complete absence of the usual restaurant courtesies.

Entertainment and Nightlife

opera, classical music, theatre

Florence is not renowned for its nightlife, but it does have plenty of theatre and music. The city's main cultural festival, the **Maggio Musicale**, combining opera and classical concerts, runs from April to June, with events at a variety of venues; the main **opera** season runs from September to December. For information inquire at tourist offices, or call ✆ 055 211 158. There is a festival in Fiesole each summer, the **Estate Fiesolana**, featuring concerts, dance, film screenings and theatre. Also, at almost any time of year, there is a busy concert calendar in Florence including many of the world's best-known musicians.

The city also takes **theatre** seriously, and at any given time you are likely to find the likes of Pirandello, Shakespeare, Brecht—even Niccolò Machiavelli—playing alongside contemporary works. *Firenze Spettacolo* and the English language *Events*, available from the city tourist office, has full listings of upcoming events.

cafés and bars

 Florence has plenty of stylish and pretty expensive bars, mostly around the main shopping and tourist streets such as the Via Tornabuoni. For a more relaxed atmosphere—and lower prices—try San Marco, the main student area, or in Oltrarno.

The city's most classic and elegant *gran caffè is* **Rivoire**, on the Piazza Signoria, a fine place to watch the milling throng once you've got over the prices. Also elegant, and a traditionally fashionable venue for fine-quality snacks, is **Procacci**, Via Tornabuoni 64, bizarrely an Italian bar that doesn't serve coffee.

For a livelier, younger clientèle, the long-established meeting-point in San Marco is the **Gran Caffè San Marco**, on the Piazza of the same name. Nearby, **La Mescita**, Via degli Alfani 70, is a good-value snacks and wine bar. For ice-cream, Florence's most lavish range of varieties is on offer at **Festival del Gelato**, Via del Corso 75r, but the most famous is **Vivoli**, Via Isola delle Stinche 7r (between the Bargello and S. Croce). *Closed Mon.*

clubs and discos

Although Florence after dark isn't exactly humming, in the last few years a number of new clubs, discos and music bars have opened up. The best way to find out about what's going on is to buy *Firenze Spettacolo*, look out for posters, particularly in the San Marco area, or inquire at one of the many English pubs. A funky time can usually be had at **Stonehenge**, Via dell'Amorino 16, near S. Lorenzo, which serves rock and cocktails (*10pm–after 1am*). **Central Park**, Parco delle Cascine, is a summer club with live music, three dance floors, shows and snacks. (Possibly the trendiest place in Florence.) The **Jazz Café**, Via Nuova de' Caccini 3, has a pleasant but smokey atmosphere, with live jazz (*Fri and Sat nights*), and a free jam session (*Tues*). *Closed Sun and Mon.* **Satanassa**, Via Pandolfini 26r, is a gay club with a disco and cocktail bar, *closed Mon*; **Tabasco**, Piazza Santa Cecilia 3r, was Italy's first gay bar.

Florentine Excursions

The countryside around Fiesole presents a lovely, thoroughly civilized landscape of villas and gardens, cypresses and parasol pines. Outside **Settignano**, back towards Florence, you'll pass the Villa Poggio Gherardo, which the Florentines like to say was the rendezvous for the genteel storytellers of the *Decameron*, and also the interesting church of **San Martino a Mensola**, with some parts as old as the 9th century, and paintings by Agnolo and Taddeo

Gaddi inside. Settignano has fine views over Florence and its valley. In recent times the area was best known as the home of the art historian and legendary Florentinophile Bernard Berenson; his **Villa I Tatti** now belongs to Harvard University. South of Florence is one of the typically grand fortress-monasteries of the Carthusian order, begun in the 1340s. The **Certosa di Galluzzo**, near the SS2 highway to Siena, contains works by the della Robbias and Pontormo. A few monks look after the place, and they keep up the tradition of cooking up bottles of potent chartreuse; they will be glad to sell you one in their old pharmacy.

Like their Bourbon cousins in France, the Medici dukes liked to pass the time by building new palaces for themselves. In their case, however, the reason was less self-exaltation than pure and simple real-estate speculation; the Medici always thought generations ahead. As a result the countryside around Florence is littered with Medici villas, most privately owned but some open to the public. **Villa la Petraia** (*villa open daily 9–4.30; closed the second and fourth Monday of the month; spring and summer open later; adm*), in the northern suburbs near the Via Gramsci, has beautiful gardens and a fountain statue of Venus of Giambologna.

More lovely gardens, typical of late-Renaissance landscaping, can also be seen in the same area, the suburb of Castello, at the **Villa di Castello**. Here the attraction is a fascinating example of the Medici's penchant for the offbeat and excessive, an artificial cavern called the **Grotta degli Animali**, filled by Ammannati and Giambologna with statues of every animal and fish known to man, along with mosaics made of seashells. Kitsch, perhaps, but a truly great example of kitsch in the best Medici tradition. (*Gardens only open 9–4.30 Tues–Sun; summer open later.*) Further out at Quinto Fiorentino, you can visit two unusual 7th-century BC Etruscan tombs. **La Montagnola**, Via Flli. Rosselli 95 (*open Tues, Thurs, Sat and Sun 9–12 and 2–5*), and **La Mula**, Via della Mula 2 (*temporarily closed for restoration work*), have no art, but the chambers under their 26ft artificial hills bear an odd relationship to much older cultures elsewhere in the Mediterranean—domed tholos tombs as in Mycenaean Greece, corbelled passages like the navetas of Mallorca, and entrances that look like the sacred wells of Sardinia.

From Florence through Prato and beyond, the towns strung along the *Autostrada del Sole* make up an almost continuous conurbation of power lines and industrial landscapes that blast your sensibility out of its quattrocento daydream and leave it somewhere in New Jersey. At **Sesto Fiorentino**, the famous 250-year-old Richard Ginori china and porcelain firm has a big collection of work dating back to 1737, including some special pieces made for the Medici—the **Museo Doccia**, Via Pratese 31 (*open Tues, Thurs and Sat 9.30–1 and 3.30–6.30; adm*).

The Plonk That Made Firenze Famous

Before the days of rampant wine-consciousness, Chianti was just the stuff in the straw-clad bottles, the inevitable accompaniment in Italian restaurants across the English-speaking world. Today, even if everybody knows what remarkably good, honest wine it is, some of it ranking among Italy's best, Chianti doesn't let the praise go to its head. It is still cheap, unpretentious, and a way of life in much of Tuscany. Actually, Chianti is grown from around Pistoia all the way to Chiusi, but the best, Chianti Classico, has its home in the original and extremely pretty **Chianti** region between Florence and Siena.

The Wine of the Iron Baron

Wine has been produced in the hills south of Florence since the cows came home, but what we know as Chianti was born in the 19th century, of a husband's jealousy. The 'Iron Baron' Bettino Ricasoli was extremely wealthy but not very good-looking. After serving as the second prime minister of unified Italy, he married and took his lovely bride to a ball in Florence. A young man asked her to dance. The Baron at once ordered her into their carriage and drove straight to the ancient family seat in Brolio in the Monti dei Chianti—an isolated castle that the poor woman would rarely leave for the rest of her life. To pass the time the Baron experimented in his vineyards, and over the years evolved a joyful, pleasing blend of Sangiovese and Caniolo grapes, with a touch of Malvasia. At the same time the famous dark green flask clad in straw (the *strapeso*) was invented. The Baron's Chianti and its distinctive bottle took the Paris Exposition of 1878 by storm. As imitators flooded the market, the boundaries of Chianti Classico were drawn in 1924, and the black cockerel, symbol of the Lega dei Chianti in 1385, was made its trademark, distinguishing it from Tuscany's six other Chianti-growing districts.

If you take the Via Chiantigiana (SS222) between Florence and Siena you'll find many vineyards to explore and wine-tastings to enjoy, especially at Greve, midway down the SS222, or at the Castello di Brolio itself, 10km south of Gaiole on the N484 (*open daily 9–12 and 3–sunset*).

The gateway to the Chianti from Florence, **Impruneta**, prefers making bricks and terracotta to growing grapes, but it's worth a stop for the **Basilica di Santa Maria**, with beautiful works by Michelozzo and Andrea della Robbia in two of its chapels. Up in the mountains to the east, the area around San Polo is famous for the cultivation of irises. **Greve**, the unofficial capital of the Chianti, has an unusual arcaded triangular piazza, and attracts big crowds for the Chianti Classico Market Show in September.

North of Florence

The lush green valley of the **Mugello** and the hills around it border four different provinces; it's a little-known corner of Tuscany, even though its villages get their share of summer foreigners in holiday homes. **Vicchio** is a humble town—the birthplace of both Giotto and Fra Angelico; there is a small collection of medieval art in the town museum *(for admission, ask at the* Comune). To the west, past Borgo San Lorenzo, **San Piero a Sieve** sits beneath the huge, mouldering pentagonal San Martino fortress, built by Michelozzo for the Medici; the village church has a lovely baptismal font by Andrea della Robbia. Michelozzo also designed another Medici villa, a pretty building on the site of an earlier fortress at nearby **Caffagiolo** (1451).

Up in the mountains to the north, **Scarperia**'s interesting Palazzo Pretoria was a governors' palace built by the Florentines in the early 14th century, its façade covered with the coats of arms of all the town's many governors. The church of the **Madonna dei Terremoti** (Our Lady of the Earthquakes) has frescoes attributed to Filippo Lippi. **Firenzuola**, with its narrow, arcaded streets, is a lovely town, a good place to stop if you're on your way to Bologna.

From Florence to Pisa

There are two routes to choose from, whether you're going by train or car. Surprisingly, the valley of the Arno is the less populated and less busy route, and always has been. Trade and traffic prefer to follow a northern route through the large towns of Prato, Pistoia and Lucca.

Getting Around

The fastest **train** line between Florence and Pisa is via Empoli, but there is also a frequent service through Prato, Pistoia and Lucca and then to Pisa or Viareggio. In Pistoia the railway station, with connections to Florence, Pisa and occasionally Bologna, is on the southern edge of town, two blocks from the town walls on Via XX Settembre. Most **buses** to other Tuscan cities leave Pistoia from Piazza San Francesco, at the west end of town, inside the walls off Corso Gramsci.

Empoli and the Arno Valley

Montelupo, with a castle overlooking the Arno, is a pretty town given to the manufacture of delicately painted ceramics, famous throughout Tuscany. Further down the valley comes **Empoli**, known for its Collegiata on the central Piazza Farinata degli Uberti, with a black-and-white geometrical façade in the best medieval Florentine style. The adjacent Collegiata Museum *(open Tues–Sun 9–12 and 4–7; adm)* contains a famous *Pietà* by Masolino, a pair of saints by Pontormo, and works by Lippi, Rossellino and della Robbia. There are a pair of possible detours from Empoli: south to **Castelfiorentino** up in the hills, with its crumbling castle and a Pinacoteca in Santa Verdiana (paintings on the life of St Francis); or north to **Vinci**, a village in a lovely quattrocento landscape, where fans of Leonardo can visit his birthplace, and lovers of gadgets can have a good time with the intricate models of the master's inventions in the Museo Leonardiano *(open daily 9.30–7; winter 9.30–6; adm)*—the bicycle, tank and helicopter, and dozens of other things he left detailed plans for in his notebooks. The museum is housed in the 13th-century Guidi Castle, which also has a small art collection. Closer to the main Pisa and Livorno road, **San Miniato**, home of the national kite-flying festival (first Sunday after Easter), is a fine town set in some of the fairest and most typically Tuscan countryside. It has yet another good picture gallery, in the Museo Diocesano (*open Easter–Oct Tues–Sun 9–12 and 3–5; in winter Sat and Sun only; adm*).

Prato

Living in Florence's shadow for a thousand years has not dampened Prato's spirit as much as you would expect. A town of almost 200,000, with a textile industry that has been important in Europe for 600 years, Prato could certainly express some weariness at having seen its wealth and talent constantly drained off to glorify its imperious neighbour. Twice Florence conquered the city, and on one occasion the Florentines simply bought it. Twice, in 1470 and 1512, the Pratese rebelled, but were crushed each time. The gruesome sack of the city in 1514, an atrocity with which the Spaniards and the Medici Pope Leo X meant to intimidate all Italy, quietened Prato down considerably. Now, almost 500 years later, Prato's industries are thriving once more, and the town makes a point of showing that it, too, has some culture. Coming in by rail (the station, with its park and bridges over the Bisenzio, makes a blissful introduction to the city) one of the first things you'll see is a great puffy sculpture by Henry Moore in a roundabout.

Tourist Information

Via L. Muzzi 51, ✆ 0574 35141, near the Duomo; Via Cairoli 48/52, ✆ 0574 24112.

Santa Maria delle Carceri

Entering old Prato by Viale Piave, the defiantly swallowtail crenellations of the **Castello dell'Imperatore** mark a strange Ghibelline interlude in Prato's past. Frederick II (*see* **Puglia** p.877) built it in 1237, his only such castle in northern Italy. Its clean lines must have seemed very sharp and modern in the 13th century, but the castle's location inside the walls hints that the purpose was less to protect Prato from the Florentines than to protect imperial officials from the Pratese. There isn't much inside, but the city often uses it for special exhibitions.

Behind the castle stands the unfinished black-and-white marble façade of **Santa Maria delle Carceri**, begun in 1485 by Giuliano Sangallo. Brunelleschian architecture was always a fragile blossom, as shown clearly by the failure of this sole serious attempt to transplant it outside of Florence. It was an audacious enterprise: Sangallo, a furiously diligent student of Vitruvius and Alberti, attempted a building based entirely on philosophical principles. Order, simplicity and correct proportion, as in Brunelleschi's churches, were to be manifest, with no frills allowed.

Sangallo, the favourite of Lorenzo the Magnificent, unfortunately proved a better theorist than architect; Santa Maria came out tedious and clumsy. The interior is better than the outside, a plain Greek cross very much in the Brunelleschi manner with a frieze and tondos by Andrea della Robbia. The name of the church—*carceri* means prisons—refers to a miracle, a speaking image of the Virgin painted on a nearby prison wall, that led to the building of the church.

The Duomo

North of the church, Via Pugliesi and Via Garibaldi pass several medieval towers on their way to the Piazza del Duomo. Prato's **Cathedral of St Stephen**, in flagrant green-and-white stripes like the Duomo at Siena, was begun in the 13th century and finished in bits and pieces over the next 200 years. Its best features are an exotic, almost Moorish-looking campanile, a della Robbia lunette of the Madonna with St Stephen over the door, a big clock that makes you smile when you notice it sitting where the rose window ought to be, and above all the **Pulpit of the Sacred Girdle** (*Pulpito del Sacro Cingolo*), a perfectly felicitous ornament, something beautiful and special that the Pratese can look at every day when they walk through the piazza. Michelozzo designed it (1428) and Donatello added the delightful reliefs of dancing children, along the lines of his *cantoria* in the cathedral museum in Florence. Mary's girdle came to Prato during the First Crusade; the outdoor pulpit was built so that it could be displayed to the people, five times a year on major church holidays.

In the cathedral, the prime attraction is in the choir: two series of lucent, precise **frescoes** by Filippo Lippi illustrating the stories of St Stephen and John the Baptist (the nun who would later run off with Lippi is said to be the model for Salomé). A separate entrance on the side of the building leads to the **Museo dell'Opera del Duomo** (*open Mon and Wed–Sat 9.30–12.30 and 3–6.30, Sun 9.30–12.30; adm*), where you can see the original Donatello reliefs from the pulpit—copies had to be made to face the weather outside—in addition to works by Filippino Lippi, an early painting by Uccello and a sophisticated *Madonna* by the quattrocento 'Master of the Nativity of Castello'. Outside the museum, stop for a look at the Romanesque cloister, done in patterns of the same green-and-white stone as the exterior.

More Museums

On the sleepy streets of old Prato you'll find only a few reminders of the city's businesslike past. **Piazza Mercatale**, by the river, is an attractive, huge, very Tuscan square, full of peeling yellow paint and flowers. Near the centre of town, on Via Rinaldesca, you'll pass the house of Renaissance Prato's most flamboyant tycoon, Francesco di Marco Datini. If there were an accountants' hall of fame, Datini would surely be one of the stars. He helped invent that dismal science, and also gets credit, according to the Pratese, for the 'invention of the promissory note'. Datini put his talents to good use, piling up an indecent fortune, fooling in politics, and dropping huge sums for charity. His **Palazzo Datini** (*c.* 1350) shows bits of the frescoes that once covered the entire façade—scenes from his own life.

Two streets to the north, the rugged, four-square **Palazzo Pretorio** was Prato's seat of government in the days of independence, and now serves as home to the **Galleria Comunale** (*open Mon, Wed–Sat 9.30–12.30 and 3–6.30, Sun 9–1; adm*), a rich collection containing works by the Lippis, Bernardo Daddi and many lesser-known Renaissance artists. Also on Piazza del Comune, Prato celebrates its medieval and modern textile industry in the **Museo del Tessuto** (*open daily 10–1 and 3.30–6.30; closed Tues; adm*), with a unique collection of fabrics and looms dating back to the 5th century AD. The museum is only here temporarily; there are plans to expand it eventually into a new home in one of the city's old textile mills outside the walls. From there, Via C. Guasti takes you four blocks to the big 13th-century church of San Domenico. Its cloister houses a museum of **mural painting** (*open 9–12; closed Tues; if not open, call © 0574 31208*), a small collection of frescoes taken from local churches and palazzi.

Around Prato

Carmignano, like Prato, was an ancient *comune* that lost its freedom to the Florentines. The town isn't much, but at the church of **San Michele** you can spend a long time looking at the masterpiece of crazy Jacopo Pontormo, *The Visitation*. The soulful, ethereal women, their feet barely touching the ground, make an unforgettable image. You can see more Pontormo, in a sunnier vein, along with other frescoes by Andrea del Sarto and Filippino Lippi, just east of town at the 1479 Medici villa of **Poggio a Caiano** (*open daily 9–1.30; closed second and third Mon; adm*), built by Giuliano da Sangallo for Lorenzo il Magnifico, a stately, almost Palladian villa with a big clock on top—as if the Medici ever cared what time it was. Besides the art, the villa has lovely woods and gardens all around.

Where to Stay and Eating Out

Prato ✉ 50047

Villa Rucellai, Via di Canneto 16, ✆ 0574 460 392 (*moderate*) is a superb, if slightly faded, Renaissance villa which has been home to the Rucellai family for generations. Just a couple of km from ugly, industrial Prato, the gardens are a haven (even if the view is not great), and the atmosphere that of a family home. Furnishings are simple but comfortable. ★★**Stella d'Italia**, Piazza Duomo 8, ✆ 0574 27910 (*cheap*) is Prato's old-fashioned, once grand hotel, looking on to the cathedral, with slightly faded rooms. On a quiet square near the Stazione Porta al Serraglio, ★★**Toscana**, Piazza Ciardi 3, ✆ 0574 28096 (*cheap*) is the best budget choice.

One reason for staying in Prato is its restaurants. **Il Pirana**, Via Valentini 110, ✆ 0574 25746, south of Viale Veneto, the main street between the central station and Piazza San Marco (*very expensive*) has an entirely justified reputation as one of the best seafood restaurants in inland Tuscany; try the scampi. Opposite the Metastasio Theatre, **Osvaldo Baroncelli**, Via Fra Bartolomeo 13, ✆ 0574 23810 (*expensive*) is an unpretentious, small establishment with an innovative chef who turns out dishes like tagliatelle with artichokes, veal *scaloppa* with truffles or stuffed celery, and duck stuffed with its own kidney. *Closed Sun, and Wed eve.* **Lapo**, Piazza Mercatale 141, ✆ 0574 23745 (*cheap*) is unspectacular, but good and usually crowded.

Carmignano ✉ 50100

Near Carmignano, ★★★★**Paggeria Medicea**, Viale Papa Giovanni XXIII 3, Artimino, ✆ 055 871 8081, 📠 055 871 8080 (*expensive*) is a villa with some unusual amenities—a hunting reserve and a lake stocked with fish, also a pool and tennis court, and pleasant modern rooms, many with balconies, all air conditioned.

Pistoia

Many have found it a gloomy town. Pistoia does seem to get more than its share of fog and clouds, and laughter in its plain, narrow streets seems a bit out of place. Pistoia has been around since it was *Pistoria* in Roman times, and it has usually been bad luck for somebody. The Catiline conspiracy, the famous attempted coup against the Roman Republic in 62 BC, ended when the legions tracked down the escaped Catiline and his henchmen near Pistoia. In the Middle Ages Pistoia had a dark reputation among its neighbours for violence and treachery. The Black versus White Guelph struggles that obsessed Florence for so long actually began here. Dante, himself a victim of that feud, never let a chance go by in the *Divine*

Comedy to curse and condemn the fateful city. In 1329 Florence captured Pistoia once and for all. The city carried on, living well off its old speciality, iron-working. True to its reputation, Pistoia supplied the warriors and conspirators of Europe with fine daggers. Later, keeping up with technology, the city gave its name to that new invention, the pistol.

Today Pistoia, the centre of a plain full of gardens and greenhouses, is better known for its flowers. Its people laugh at their odd history; bring it up and they'll be ready to blame it all on those obnoxious Florentines. Pistoia's somnolence over the last 600 years has left it with an historic centre almost entirely intact, many fine buildings, and a wealth of art.

Tourist Information

Pistoia: in Piazza Duomo, in the Bishop's Palace, ✆ 0573 21622.
Montecatini Terme: Viale Verdi 66, ✆ 0572 772 244.

Piazza del Duomo

Old Pistoia is almost perfectly diamond-shaped, surrounded by 16th-century walls with the old moats preserved on the northern and eastern sides. Right in the middle you'll find the L-shaped **Piazza del Duomo**, an excellent example of medieval urban design. The façade of the **Duomo**, with its Pisan arcades and stripes over a Florentine tympanum by Andrea della Robbia, makes an uneasy balance between the two architectural traditions. The tall, impressive campanile tips the balance towards Pisa, with a touch of the exotic in its Moorish-inspired arches. Inside, the real attraction is the enormous **altar of St James**, about a ton of solid silver, begun in 1287 and added to over the next two centuries.

Directly across from the cathedral is the striped, octagonal **baptistry** dating from 1350 (*open daily 9–12.30 and 3–6, Sun 9–12.30; closed Mon*), credited to Andrea Pisano—one of the outstanding Gothic buildings of Tuscany, with an especially fine sculptural trim on the exterior and an unusual conical dome under the roof. The 12th-century Palazzo dei Vescovi contains Etruscan and Roman finds in an **archaeological itinerary**, and the old cathedral is now included in the **Museo San Zeno**, with paintings and a reliquary by Ghiberti (*tours of both offered Tues and Thurs at 9, 10, 11.30 and 3.30, Fri 8.30, 10, 11.30, 2.30, 3.30 and 4.45; joint adm*). On the façade of the **Palazzo del Comune**, a head in black marble is set into the wall, the face of a Moorish king captured on a freebooting expedition to Mallorca. Besides the mayor, it houses the **Museo Civico** (*open Tues–Sat 9–7, Sun 9–4; adm*), which provides you with an introduction to the often weird 13th- and 14th-century 'Pistoian School' and much else; don't miss the hallucinatory battle scenes by Francesco Graziani.

From behind the cathedral, Via F. Pacini takes you north to another Pistoian surprise, the refined, arcaded façade of the **Ospedale del Ceppo**, done in the manner of the famous Ospedale degli Innocenti in Florence. As in Florence, the della Robbias were called upon to provide the decoration, but besides the simple terracotta medallions there is a unique terracotta frieze across the entire façade—in resplendent Renaissance technicolour. The frieze, by Giovanni della Robbia and later artists in the 1510s and 1580s, portrays the works of the hospital and allegorical virtues. A little way to the east, the 12th-century **Sant'Andrea** contains a real treasure, an exquisite pulpit by Giovanni Pisano, lifted on columns over figures of the four Evangelists and surrounded with reliefs full of intricately carved figures: a fitting introduction to the more famous works of the Pisano family in Pisa.

Two other churches on the northern side of Pistoia are worth a look. **San Francesco al Prato**, on the piazza of the same name, has an exceptional collection of 14th-century frescoes, and the **Madonna dell'Umiltà**, on the central Via della Madonna, is a curious, octagonal High Renaissance building. In the 1460s Giorgio Vasari was called upon to complete this long-unfinished church; he added a dome so heavy that the church has been threatening to collapse ever since.

More Stripes

From Piazza del Duomo, one block south and another east will put you in Piazza San Leone; the stubby tower here once belonged to perhaps the rottenest of all the Pistoians, a 13th-century noble thug and sworn enemy of the Church named Vanni Fucci; Dante found him in one of the lower circles of Hell, cursing and making obscene gestures up at God. **San Giovanni Fuoricivitas**, just around the corner of Via Cavour, must surely win a prize for being the stripiest church in Christendom. Turning its side to the street, and bristling with lozenge windows and blind arches, the 12th-century work looks more Pisan than anything you'll see in Pisa.

Inside (if anyone ever opens it) there is another fine pulpit, by a pupil of Pisano, and a della Robbia plaque of the *Visitation*. **San Domenico**, nearby on Corso Silvano, is less flamboyant on the outside, but the church and adjacent convent have some good frescoes, as does the **Cappella del Tau** across the street. Some of the pictures here, scenes from the story of Adam and Eve, are little-known works by Masolino.

There is another good Gothic façade on **San Pietro**, another street over to the east. The best stripes of all, however, may be on the zebras in the **Pistoia Zoo** (*open April–Sept 9–7; Oct–Mar 9–5; adm exp*), 4km west of town on Via Pieve a Calle. Italians don't usually care for zoos (though the Medici always kept big menageries) and this one may be the best in the country, even though it's only 20 years old.

Montecatini Terme

Only 15km west of Pistoia, this is perhaps Italy's best-known spa, a party centre for crowned heads and their sycophants in the 1890s and popular ever since. The waters, good for just about anything according to Montecatini's boosters, are the town's sole reason for being. To please its elevated clientele, Montecatini in the 19th century built itself into quite an elegant place, with a large park at the centre and imposing establishments such as the Versailles-like **Tettuccio**, where string quartets once serenaded those who came to take the waters.

Many of the other establishments are almost as good and, even if you prefer stronger stuff than mineral water for your cures, you can come for the florid 1890s architecture and genteel atmosphere. The other favourite recreation of Montecatini visitors is taking the **cablecar** up to the pretty village of Montecatini Alto.

Further west towards Lucca, **Pescia** is another garden centre, with a famous wholesale flower market. The church of San Francesco there has a painting of St Francis done shortly after his death—believed to be an accurate portrayal by an artist who knew him. In **Collodi** you'll see a park with a monument to Pinocchio; his creator, Carlo Collodi, took his pen name from his family's native town.

Pistoia ✉ 51110

***Il Convento**, Via S. Quirico 33, ✆ 0573 452 651, ✆ 0573 453578, 5km east at Pontenuovo (*moderate*) preserves its convent exterior if not all of its interior, in a quiet setting with views over Pistoia; there's also a pool and one of the city's better restaurants.

In Pistoia itself, there's the old and comfortable ***Leon Bianco**, Via Panciatichi 2, ✆ 0573 26675, ✆ 0573 26675 (*moderate*), with views over the campanile. **Villa Vannini**, Villa di Piteccio, ✆ 0573 42031, ✆ 0573 26331, 6km north of Pistoia and well off the beaten track (*moderate*) is a delightful villa run by the personable Signora Vannini. Rooms are very comfortable for their price bracket and furnished with elegant antiques. The food is excellent, and the walking in nearby woods exceptional. Cheap accommodation is rare in Pistoia; **Appenino**, Via XX Settembre 21, ✆ 0573 32243 (*cheap*), near the station, has simple, adequate rooms.

Just outside Pistoia in a beautiful 18th-century villa, **Locanda degli Elfi**, Loc. San Felice, ✆ 0573 41490 (*expensive*) offers fine fish and traditional local dishes. **Rafanelli**, Via Sant'Agostino 47, ✆ 0573 532 046 (*moderate*), just outside the town at Sant'Agostino, serves Tuscan home cooking (*maccheroni* with duck, game dishes or lamb) in a country villa setting. *Closed Sun eve, Mon and Aug*. **La Casa Degli Amici**, Via Bonellina 111, ✆ 0573 380 305, is a local favourite, serving wonderful fried rabbit with artichoke, and duck with orange (*moderate–cheap*).

Montecatini Terme ✉ 51016

Italy's choicest spa has no fewer than six hotels that claim the title of 'Grand' and half a dozen others that only decline to for discretion's sake. One of the grandest, the *****Grand Hotel Bellavista**, Viale Fedeli, ✆ 0572 78122, ✆ 0572 73352 (*very expensive*) offers golf, tennis, indoor pool, luxurious rooms, sauna, a health club and an infinite number of opportunities for self-indulgence. But for genuine Belle Epoque charm, *****Grand Hotel La Pace**, Viale della Torretta 1, ✆ 0572 75801, ✆ 0572 78451 (*very expensive*) is renowned throughout Europe, with a similarly impressive array of luxuries, and an elegant restaurant. *Open Mar–Oct*. There are plenty of good, if expensive, middle-range hotels. *Belsoggiorno**, Viale Cavallotti, ✆ 0572 78859 (*cheap*) is a good bargain, up in Montecatini Alto, with rooms overlooking a garden.

Enoteca da Giovanni, Via Garibaldi 25, ✆ 0572 71695 (*expensive*) is a unique and much-honoured restaurant—game dishes (hare, venison, wild duck) turn into impeccable *haute cuisine* surprises at the hands of a genuine master chef; you won't even notice the price. **Locanda Narciso**, Via Marruota 79, south of the tracks, ✆ 0572 72765 (*moderate*) offers good solid Tuscan cooking. *Closed Thurs*.

Lucca

The famous walls—'much like the walls of Berwick-on-Tweed', the Lucchese for some reason like to say—do not seem very formidable, more like a garden wall than something that would keep the Florentines at bay. Behind them you can see only pine trees and neat stucco buildings with the inevitable green shutters. The walls and the surrounding areas, once the outworks of the fortifications, are now full of lawns and trees, making a sort of green belt for the little city. The Lucchese ride their bikes and walk their dogs around the ramparts, and often stop to admire the view. Lucca at first glance may seem too bijou and tidy to be true. It is a dream city—not like Venice, but in a quiet, very domestic sort of way. After its long and brave history it has certainly earned the right to a little quiet. The annual hordes of Tuscan tourists leave Lucca alone for the most part, though there seems to be a small number of discreet visitors who come back every year. They don't spread the word, apparently trying to keep one of Italy's most beautiful cities to themselves.

Lucca's rigid grid of streets betrays its Roman origins. The town survived continuously through the bad centuries, and emerged in the age of the *comuni* as one of the leading trading towns of Tuscany, specializing in the production of silk. In the early 1300s, perhaps the height of the city's wealth and power, a remarkable adventurer named Castruccio Castracani appeared in the spotlight. Castracani, who for years had lived in exile—part of it in England—returned in 1314 when Pisan and Ghibelline troops captured Lucca. Within a year he had chased the Pisans out and seized power for himself, and by 1325 he had built for Lucca a little empire that included both Pisa and Pistoia. After routing the Florentines at Altopascio in that year he was making plans to snatch Florence too, but died of malaria just before the siege was to begin—another example of Florentine good luck. Internal bickering between the powerful families put an end to Lucca's glory days almost immediately, and the city barely escaped being gobbled up by one or other of its neighbours. As a competently functioning republic Lucca used tact and tenacity to survive even after the arrival of the Spaniards. After the Treaty of Cateau-Cambresis Lucca amazingly found itself standing together with Venice as the only truly independent Italian states. Like Venice the city was an island of relative tolerance and enlightenment during the Counter-Reformation, and it shared Venice's fate in 1805 when Napoleon arrived, and ordered its political extinction.

Getting Around

The **train** station, ✆ 0583 47013, is just south of the walls on Piazza Ricasoli, with lots of trains on the Pisa-Florence line. **Buses** leave from Piazzale G. Verdi, just inside the walls at the western end of the city: LAZZI buses run to Florence, Pistoia, Pisa, Prato or Viareggio, and CLAP buses to towns in Lucca province, including the upper Serchio Valley in the Apuan Alps. Call ✆ 0583 584 876, for information.

Tourist Information

Vecchia Porta San Donato, in Piazzale Verdi, ✆ 0583 419 689, near the bus station. It has **bicycles** available for hire in summer.

The Walls

Lucca's walls owe their considerable charm to Renaissance advances in military technology. The city began them in 1500, urged to the effort by the beginning of the Wars of Italy. The councillors wanted fortifications entirely up to date, to counter new advances in artillery, and their (unknown) architects gave them the state of the art, a model for the new style of fortification that would soon be transforming the cities of Europe. Being Renaissance Tuscans, they also made them a little more elegant than perhaps was necessary. The walls were never

Lucca

300 metres
300 yards

N

VIALE CARLO DEL PRETE

VIALE CARLO DEL PRETE

BALUARDO
SANTA
CROCE

PASSEGGIATA DELLE MURA URBANE

VIA DELLE CON

Palazzo
Pfanner

Sant'
Agostino

Piazza
S. Agostino

VIA DEGLI ASILI

VIA C. BATTISTI

VIA SAN GIORGIO

VIALE LAZZARO PAPI

VIA SAN TOMMASO

Porta
San Donato

Piazzale
S. Donato

i

Pinacoteca
Nazionale

VIA SANTA GIUSTINA

Piazza
S. Salvatore

VIA CALDERIA

VIA
S. LUCIA

Piazza di
Palazzo
Dipinto

Puccini
Museum

M

VIA
ROMA

VIA FILLUNGO

i

VIA DEL TORO

VIA DI POGGIO

San
Michele
In Foro

BALUARDO
SAN
DONATO

VIA GALLI TASSI

VIA SAN

PAOLINO

Piazza
S. Michele

VIA BECCHERIA

San
Giusto

VIA DE MANIN

to
Viareggio

VIALE ALFREDO CATALANI

Porta Vittorio
Emanuele

Piazzale
G. Verdi

San
Paolino

Palazzo
Pretoria

VIA
PESCHERIA

Piazza
Napoleone

VIA XX
SETTEMBRE

VIALE
GAETANO
LUPORINI

Piazzale
Boccherini

VIA

VITTORIO EMANUELE

Palazzo
Ducale

VIA VITTORIO VENETO

P

Piazza
del Giglio

to Pisa

MANIFATTURA
DEI
TABACCHI

VIA DEI TABACCHI

Piazza
S. Romano

San
Romano

CISCU

BALUARDO
SAN PAOLINO

PASSEGGIATA DELLE MURA

VIA GIUSEPPE

VICOLO

GARIBALDI

VIALE GIOSUÈ CARDUCCI

VIA FRANCESCO

CARRARA

Porta San
Pietro

VIALE EUROPA

to Pisa

Piazzale
del
Risorgimento

VIALE D. REPUBBLICA

VIALE DI SAN CONCORDIO

to Pisa

to Bagni di Lucca

VIALE AGOSTINO MARI

VIALE P. BATONI

BALUARDO SAN MARTINO

Piazzale Martiri della Libertà

BALUARDO CESARE BATTISTI

PASSEGGIATA DELLE MURA

Piazza Maria del Borgo

VIA MICHELE ROSI

VIALE GUGLIELMO MARCONI

VIA FILLUNGO

VIA SANTA GEMMA GALGANI

VIA DELLA ZECCA

VIA DEI FOSSO

San Frediano

VIA D. CAVALLERIZZA

Piazza S. Frediano

VIA BUSDRAGHI

San Pietro Somaldi

Roman Amphitheatre

Piazza S. Pietro Somaldi

San Francesco

Piazza S. Francesco

BALUARDO SAN SALVATORE

VIA DELL'ANFITEATRO

VIA D. FRATTA

VIA DELLA QUARQUONIA

Santa Maria dello Stellario

Museo Nazionale Guinigi

VIA FILLUNGO

VIA ANTONIO MORDINI

Piazza del Carmine

VIA DI

VIA DELL'ANGELO CUSTODE

VIA SAN NICOLAO

VIA DEL FOSSO

Villa Bottini Gardens

VIA SANTA CHIARA

VIA BRUNERO PAOLI

to Florence, Montecatini Terme

VIA SANT' ANDREA

Torre delle Ore

VIA FALINELLI

Torre Guinigi

Piazzale Don Aldo Mei

San Cristoforo

VIA ROMA

Piazza Bernardini

VIA SANTA CROCE

Porta San Gervasio

Santa Trinità

VIA ELISA

VIALE G. PACINI

Piazza dei Servi

Santa Maria Fortisportam

Piazza Santa Maria Forisportam

VIA SAN NICOLAO

BALUARDO CAIROLI

VIA DEL BATTISTERO

VIA A. VALLISNERI

Piazza Antelminelli

VIA DELLA ROSA

VIA DEL GIARDINO

BOTANICO

Giardino Botanico

San Giovanni

Museo della Cattedrale

VIA DEL DUOMO

Piazza San Martino

Duomo

Santa Maria della Rosa

VIA DEL FOSSO

PASSEGGIATA DELLE MURA

BALUARDO SAN REGOLO

GARIBALDI

BALUARDO SAN COLOMBANO

VIALE GIUSEPPE GIUSTI

VIALE REGINA MARGHERITA

Piazzale Ricasoli

Train Station

severely tested. Today, with the outer ravelins, fosses and salients cleared away (such earth-works usually took up as much space as the city itself), Lucca's walls are just for decoration, with a double row of shady trees planted on top to make an elevated garden boulevard that extends clear around the city. St Peter's Gate, near the station, still has its portcullis, and Lucca's proud motto LIBERTAS is inscribed over the entrance.

San Martino

Lucca's **Duomo**, perhaps the outstanding work of the Pisan style outside Pisa itself, was begun in the 11th century and only completed in the 15th. A porch with three arches, each a different size, makes the façade somewhat unusual. Above is a typical Pisan design of three levels of colonnades, and behind the arches are exquisite 12th- and 13th-century reliefs and sculpture—the best work Lucca has to offer. See especially the *Adoration of the Magi* by Nicola Pisano, and a host of fantastical animals and hunting scenes, the 12 months and their occupations, even *Roland at Roncevalles*, all by unknown masters.

Inside, a large marble tabernacle in the left aisle contains the *Volto Santo* ('Holy Image'), a painted wooden crucifix brought from Byzantium to Italy in 782 during the Iconoclast move-ment. According to legend, the crucifix was carved by Nicodemus, and accurately represents the face of Jesus. The image takes part in a candlelight procession each 13 September. A door from the right aisle leads to the sacristy, where you can see Lucca's real icon, Jacopo della Quercia's remarkable **tomb of Ilaria del Carretto**, a tranquil effigy complete with family dog. Opposite the cathedral is the **Museo della Cattedrale** (*open daily 10–6; winter Mon–Fri 10–3, Sat and Sun 10–6; adm*), with a second work by della Quercia, *St John the Evangelist*, as well as other treasures from the cathedral and the adjoining church of San Giovanni.

From the cathedral, in a quiet corner of town near the southern wall, Via Duomo takes you to twin piazzas full of trees, the focus of Lucca's evening *passeggiata*, **Piazza del Giglio** and **Piazza Napoleone**. After Napoleon seized Lucca, he gave it to his sister Elisa Baciocchi. This queen for a day occupied the old seat of the republican council and, after Waterloo when Lucca was given to a branch of the Bourbons, the 16th-century building became the **Ducal Palace**, the name it still has today.

San Michele in Foro

Many people mistake this church, set on a piazza right in the centre of Lucca, for the cathe-dral. Built about the same time, and with a similar Pisan façade, it is almost as impressive. The name comes from its location on what was Roman Lucca's forum. The ambitious façade rises high above the level of the roof, like the false fronts on buildings in Wild West towns of the 1880s. Every column in the Pisan arcading is different; some doubled, some twisted like corkscrews, inlaid with mosaic Cosmati work, or carved into medieval monsters. The graceful, rectangular campanile is Lucca's tallest and best.

West of San Michele, in a neighbourhood perfumed by the big tobacco factory near Porta Vittorio Emanuele, the 17th-century Palazzo Mansi contains the **Pinacoteca Nazionale** (*open Tues–Sat 9–7, Sun 9–2; adm*), with mostly 16th–17th-century paintings, works by Bronzino, Andrea del Sarto, Pontormo and Tintoretto. East of the church, **Via Fillungo** and its surrounding streets make up Lucca's busy shopping area, a tidy nest of straight and narrow alleys where the contented cheerfulness that distinguishes Lucca from many of its neigh-bouring cities seems somehow magnified. Near Via Fillungo's northern end, the 12th-century church of **San Frediano** stands out, thanks to the big mosaic panel on its façade, showing Christ and the Apostles in an elegant, flowing style. Inside is a beautiful covered baptismal font with a terracotta of the *Annunciation* by Andrea della Robbia.

Across Via 'Fillungo, narrow arches lead to the **Anfiteatro Romano**. Not a stone of which remains—the marble was probably carted off for San Michele and the cathedral—but Lucca is a city that changes so gradually and organically that the outline of the amphitheatre was perfectly preserved. Where the grandstands were, you now see a complete ellipse of medieval houses, with a piazza where the gladiators once slugged it out. Down Via S. Andrea you'll pass a number of resolutely medieval palaces, including that of the Guinigi family; long the leading power-brokers of Lucca, the Guinigi once even went so far as to imitate the Visconti and Medici and seize power for themselves from 1400 to 1430. Their stronghold, the **Torre Guinigi** (*open April–Sept daily 8.30–7.30; Oct–Mar daily 10–4.30; adm*), next to the palace, is one of Lucca's landmarks, the best example of the odd Italian fancy of towers with big trees growing out of the top. One of the most elaborate of the medieval family fortresses; it's worth the climb up for the view over the city and the Apuan Alps.

Continuing eastwards you pass the Via del Fosso; the canal running down the middle was the moat (*fosso*) of Lucca's oldest fortifications. Another Guinigi house, a suburban villa before the extension of the walls, contains the **Museo Guinigi** (*open Tues–Sat 9–7, Sun 9–2; adm*), with a good selection of painting and sculpture from this side of Tuscany. Sculptures from the 9th to the 15th century show the logical development of the Pisan-Luccan style, along with some original columns from the façade of San Michele, and an inspired *Annunciation* and other works by a sculptor named Matteo Civitoli, who deserves to be better known. Lucchese Renaissance painting, with a fond reluctance to give up the Middle Ages, is also well represented.

North of the city there are two showy but refined 17th-century villas: **Villa Mansi** at Segronugo (*open daily 9.30–12 and 3–7.30; winter daily 10–12.30 and 2.30–6; adm*); and the **Villa Torregiani**, nearby at Marfia, the country home of Elisa Bonaparte Baciocchi during her reign (*villa open Mar–Oct daily 10–1 and 3–7; closed Tues; adm exp*). Both have extensive English gardens.

Lucca ✉ *55100*   **Where to Stay and Eating Out**

In Lucca, try a dry white wine called *Montecarlo*, produced only in a small area east of the city; it's one of Tuscany's best.

There are no very special hotels in Lucca, but at Massa Pisana, on the Pisa road, you can stay in the ★★★★★**Principessa Elisa**, © 0583 379 737, @ 0583 379 019 (*very expensive*), Castruccio Castracani's own palace, built for the great Lucchese *generalissimo* in 1321. Often rebuilt since, it is modern inside and currently wears the façade of a stately Rococo mansion, surrounded by acres of gardens with a pool. *Open Mar–Nov.*

In Lucca try the slightly frayed, green-shuttered and delightful ★★★**Universo**, Piazza del Giglio, © 0583 493 678 (*moderate*), right in the centre of the old town; Ruskin and nearly everyone else who followed him to Lucca has slept here. Some rooms are much nicer than others.

★★★**Piccolo Hotel Puccini**, Via di Poggio 9, © 0583 55421, @ 0583 53487 (*moderate*) is small, comfortable and central. The less expensive places in Lucca can be great bargains; witness the friendly, well-run ★★**Diana**, near the cathedral on Via del Molinetto, © 0583 492 202 (*cheap*), with some of the nicest rooms in this price range in Italy. The modern, comfortable and rarely crowded **youth hostel** is 2km north of town on Via del Brennero, in Salicchi, © 0583 341 811 (*cheap*) (bus no.6 from the station). IYHF cards required. *Open 10 Mar–10 Oct.*

Solferino, Via delle Gavine 50, in San Macario in Piano, © 0583 59118 (*expensive*), 6km west of Lucca on the Viareggio road, has an extensive menu: duck with truffles, wild boar and grilled seafood. It's been run by the same family for four generations, and famous throughout Tuscany for almost as long. Simple Tuscan country specialities are also in evidence, but this is one place where you might want to splurge. At **La Mora**, Via Sestodi Moriano 104, © 0583 406 402 (*expensive*), north of town in Ponte a Moriano in an old posthouse, you can dine under the pergola in summer; try ravioli with asparagus or truffles, or gourmet roast lamb according to season.

In the centre, across from the Hotel Universo, **Il Giglio**, © 0583 494 058 (*expensive–moderate*) is Lucca's best seafood palace—river trout is a speciality as well. **Il Buca di Sant'Antonio**, Via della Cervia 1, © 0583 55881 (*moderate*) has been an inn since 1782, and offers old recipes like smoked herring and kid on a spit, alongside newer dishes like ravioli with ricotta and sage. For good cheap food, seek out Via Conce, in the northwest corner within the walls, where you can enjoy some surprising dishes at **Da Giulio in Pelleria**, © 0583 55948 (*cheap*), which is popular enough to warrant reservations, with top-quality 'peasant' fare. *Closed Sun and Mon.* **Buatino**, Via del Borgo Giannotti 508, © 0583 343 207 (*cheap*), just outside Porta Santa Maria, serves classic Lucchese dishes—tasty and succulent roast pork, simple grilled chicken and, of course, *zuppa di farro*. Prices are even lower at lunchtime. *Open for lunch and dinner; closed Sun.*

The Apuan Alps and the Serchio Valley

All across northern Tuscany the mountains have never been very far away. In the region's northwest corner they stretch to the very edge of the sea itself. These are no piddling foothills; two peaks within 45km of Lucca are 6560ft high. Not many tourists find their way up the Serchio—it may be the only truly worthwhile corner of Tuscany that hasn't been overrun. But if you simply can't look at another cathedral or picture gallery, and would like a spell in some striking yet civilized mountain scenery, this is the place.

Getting Around

Buses run to most destinations in the valley from Lucca, but some services are slow.

Bagni di Lucca: Piazza Municipio 101, © 0583 805 508.
Barga: Piazza Angelico, © 0583 73499 (*open April–Sept only*).

Lucca to Bagni di Lucca

North of Lucca you quickly arrive at **Diecimo**, a name that has survived from Roman times—10 Roman miles from the city. Its fine Renaissance campanile stands out starkly among the surrounding hills. Next, **Borgo a Mozzano** is famous for its beautiful little hog-back bridge, the *Ponte Maddalena*, with arches in five different sizes, and a legend attached to it of how the devil built it in one night. The credit really goes to Countess Matilda of Tuscany who, besides the bridge, endowed the villages around Borgo with a set of solid Romanesque churches.

A little further up river beyond the turn, still on the SS12, **Bagni di Lucca** has an interesting early 19th-century suspension bridge (1840) hung on iron chains, the *Ponte alle Catene*. Bagni is a town worth visiting: a spa that enjoyed a brief spell of high society's favour in the 19th century and was then quietly forgotten. It has elegant old establishments to take the waters (one like a miniature Roman Pantheon), a pretty site along the river, charming villas and gardens, and even a Victorian-Gothic-Alhambresque Anglican church; among the many English visitors in the old days were Shelley, Byron and Browning. Bagni's casino (1837) invented roulette to clean them out. Up in the mountains above Bagni, **San Cassiano** has a picturesque medieval bridge and a little-known 13th-century Pisan-style church, with a delicate carved façade. From Bagni, you have a choice of continuing along the SS12 towards **Abetone**, Tuscany's only big ski resort, under Monte Cimone (the highest peak in the area), or else turning back to head up the Serchio, into the region called the Garfagnana.

The Garfagnana and the Lunigiana

Barga, the main town along the Serchio Valley, is a little mountain *comune* that managed to keep its independence until 1341. It has an unusual 13th-century cathedral, begun in the year 1000 and set high on a terrace, with a plain, squarish façade that makes it look more like a medieval Palazzo del Popolo. Be sure to step in and see the 13th-century pulpit, by a Como sculptor named Guido Bigarelli. The pillars that support it, resting on a pair of lions devouring some poor fellows, are in the Pisan style, but the reliefs around the pulpit itself are unique, startling naïve-sophisticated versions of familiar scriptural scenes.

From Barga you can detour 17km to the **Grotta del Vento** (*open daily April–Sept; guided tours of one hour at 10, 11, 12, 2, 3, 4, 5 and 6; Oct–Mar open daily, same hours, but only part of the cave is visited; adm exp; for information, call © 0583 722 024*), up in the mountains, a long cavern hung with fat stalactites and set in a barren, eerie landscape of eroded limestone. Try to visit in the morning when it's less crowded.

The castle at **Castelnuovo Garfagnana**, further up the valley, properly decorative in the best 14th-century manner, was once commanded by the poet Ariosto, then in the service of the Estes of Ferrara. Further north, past **Piazza al Serchio**, the road leaves the Serchio behind and crosses over a pass into a region called the Lunigiana, the mountain hinterlands of the long-disappeared Roman port town of **Luni**. This rugged territory covered with chestnut forests has often given its governors fits; at the turn of the century it was a stronghold of rural anarchy, and in 1944 the partisans made it one of the bigger free zones in the north. It must always have been like this, for these mountains are jammed full of castles: **Monti**, **Fivizzano**, **Bagnone** and **Fosidinovo** have the best ones, and on the back roads of the region you'll find a number of tiny mountain lakes and Romanesque country churches. This hidden corner conceals a genuine prehistoric mystery.

Up in **Pontrémoli**, the northernmost town in Tuscany, the stout grey 14th-century Piagnaro Castle has been restored as a museum to hold over a score of large, carved 'statue-steles' of an unknown culture that flourished in Lunigiana about 1500–100 BC. The steles, sort of menhirs with personality, include some shaped into stylized warriors with daggers or axes; others are women with little knobby breasts. Dozens have been discovered in the Lunigiana, all in isolated areas. Similar things turn up in southern Corsica and in Languedoc. Interestingly, the records say Christianity only began to make headway here after 700 AD. Most of the steles at Pontrémoli have their heads knocked off, a sure sign that the Pope's missionaries were here.

Where to Stay and Eating Out

If you are passing through, either Bagni di Lucca or Barga makes a pleasant place to stay a few days to recharge your batteries.

Bagni di Lucca ✉ 55022

There are some quiet, modest old hotels: ★★★**Silvania**, at Lugliano, ✆ 0583 805 363, 🖝 0583 867 754 (*moderate*) is very tranquil; the ★★**Svizzero**, Via Casalini 30, ✆ 0583 87114 (*moderate*) is ineffably Tuscan, a strange place where the clock has stopped at about 1840, and so has the owner. Toscanini stayed in the small ★**Roma**, Via Umberto I 110, ✆ 0583 87278 (*cheap*), with a shady little garden at the back. **Da Vinicio**, Via del Casino, ✆ 0583 87250 (*moderate*) is a chaotic and popular pizzeria that also serves good roast pigeon and seafood.

Barga ✉ 55051

Outside Barga there's a huge 234-room resort hotel, ★★★★**Il Ciocco**, 6km north in Castelvecchio Pascoli, ✆ 0583 7191, 🖝 0583 723 197 (*expensive*), with an indoor pool, tennis courts, and, in short, the works. In the town itself, the lovely ★★★**Villa Libano**, Via del Sasso 6, ✆ 0583 723 774, 🖝 0583 723 059 (*moderate*), set in a courtyard next to the town's park, has a pleasant restaurant, with tables in the garden.

Fivizzano ✉ 54013

★★**Il Giardinetto**, Via Roma 151, ✆ 0585 92060 (*cheap*) is a delightful place to sleep and eat overlooking the Piazza Medicea. The rooms are comfortable and, as the name implies, there's a little garden to lounge in. *Closed Oct.* The restaurant (*moderate*) serves tempting hot and cold *antipasti*, as well as pasta and game dishes, and a flan with spinach and cheese, made from a Renaissance recipe.

Anything more than a simple trattoria is hard to come by in the Serchio Valley, but if you make it as far north as Pontrémoli, try the town's special pasta, *testaroli*, and the roast meats, stuffed vegetables and other local dishes at **Da Bussé**, Piazza del Duomo 31, ✆ 0187 831 371 (*moderate*). *Closed Fri.*

The Tuscan Coast

The ancient Etruscans weren't shy; these early free traders happily accepted goods, art and ideas from all over the Mediterranean world. For the last thousand years, however, for all its accomplishments, modern Tuscany has been a moody, introspective region, and usually a little dismissive towards what goes on in the rest of the world. The Tuscan coastline somehow reflects this: there is one big port, and a few little resorts, but on the whole Tuscany turns a blank face to the sea.

Getting Around

The main Rome–Genoa **rail** line runs a few kilometres inland all along the coast, making communications easy. **Buses** to most of the smaller destinations without a train station run from Massa or Viareggio.

Tourist Information

Carrara: Viale XX Settembre, ✆ 0585 844 403.
Marina di Carrara: Piazza Menconi 6/b, ✆ 0585 632 519, among the resorts.
Marina di Massa: Lungomare Vespucci 24, ✆ 0585 240 063.

Carrara and Massa

Carrara, of course, owes its living and its fame to the marble masses of the Apuan Alps that surround it. Carrara marble has added the lustre to ancient Rome, Renaissance Rome and art museums and banks the world over. The town is still busy, with scores of marble sawmills and 'artistic workshops' turning out everything from sculptures for new churches to reproductions of famous statues. Some Carraran marble went into the city's distinctive **cathedral**, with a tall belltower and an exquisite 13th-century rose window. The quarries in the surrounding hills are an unforgettable sight; usually they extend almost to the peaks, a shining white scar on the mountains with a narrow access road zigzagging perpendicularly to the top. This part of the Apuan Alps is haunted by Michelangelo, in his old clothes and smelly goatskin boots, taking his horse into the most inaccessible corners to discover new veins of perfect white stone. Michelangelo loved to spend time here with his rock, and he claimed with his usual modesty to have 'introduced the art of quarrying' into the area. Carrara's quarries are in no danger of running out; you wonder if they're joking when they gravely mention that there are only a few cubic kilometres of good stone left.

Massa, the small city to the south that shares the honour of provincial capital with Carrara, was the seat of a duchy during the Renaissance; the only thing in town to see is their 17th-century Palazzo Cybo-Malaspina, with a beautiful ornate courtyard. **Pietrasanta**, an attractive town about 10km further south, has a Renaissance cathedral and many marble works. The villages inland from Carrara, Massa and Pietrasanta have some of the best scenery in the Apuan Alps; mountain hiking is popular here, and there are a number of marked trails to follow.

Viareggio

From the Ligurian border almost as far as the mouth of the Arno, the coast is dotted with small resorts. **Forte dei Marmi**, built under a fortress of the Tuscan grand dukes, is perhaps the most interesting, a once-posh residential resort that had its moment of fashion in the 1860s.

The others, very popular with people from Milan and other big Italian cities, are just as polluted as the Riviera to the north, but less so than the beaches around the Arno and Livorno. In the summer, all are very crowded. **Viareggio**, the largest of them, is a town that goes back to Roman times; in addition to tourism it tries to make an honest living for itself from fishing and a dockyard. Everyone in Italy knows Viareggio for its big carnival, with a parade of grandiose, topical floats. Though it only began in the 1890s, it rivals Venice and Rome as the most popular place to be around Shrove Tuesday. The Gay Nineties bequeathed to Viareggio a number of Art Nouveau hotels and beachfront pavilions. These, plus the two beautiful shore promenades and the large pine groves that surround the town, make it one of the more pleasant resorts on the Tyrrhenian Sea.

A few kilometres to the south, **Torre del Lago Puccini** is a beauty spot built around a small lake, and you can visit the **Villa Puccini**, the home where the composer (of whom they're so fond that they renamed the town) wrote most of his operas (*open daily 10–12.30 and 3–6; summer 10–12 and 3–7.30; closed Mon; adm*). Every summer there's also a small-scale **Festival Pucciniano**, with opera performances in an open-air theatre which is built out on to the lake—the stage is actually on the water.

Where to Stay and Eating Out

Carrara ✉ 54033

The best hotel is called, naturally, **★★★Michelangelo**, Corso F.lli Rosselli 3, ✆ 0585 777 161 (*moderate*), with modern rooms and parking. There are also quite a few good restaurants—and if you're lucky you may find a bottle of Candia, the white wine eked from Carrara's mountain terraces. **Soldaini**, Via Mazzini 11, ✆ 0585 71459 (*expensive*) offers simple dishes from other Italian regions, exquisitely prepared. **Roma**, Piazza Battisti, ✆ 0585 70632 (*moderate–cheap*) is a favourite for good, simple Tuscan cooking. *Closed Sat* .

Forte dei Marmi ✉ 55042

Forte dei Marmi lacks Viareggio's bustle and cosmopolitan air, but many Italians prefer its calmer atmosphere and less crowded beaches; hotels here are more modern, and prices are increasing all the time. **★★★★Raffaeli Park**, Via Mazzini 37, ✆ 0584 787 294/787 115 (*expensive*) has ample facilities including a private beach, pool and garden. The **★★★Raffaeli Villa Angela**, Via Mazzini 64, ✆ 0584 787 472, ✉ 0584 787 115 (*moderate*) has very good facilities, including a private beach and a pool.

Viareggio ✉ 55049

Viareggio isn't quite the smart resort it once was, but still retains some of its posh 19th-century places—often with unfortunate modernizations. One of the most extravagant is the **★★★★Grand Hotel Excelsior**, Viale Carducci 88, ✆ 0584 50726, ✉ 0584 50729 (*very expensive*), built in 1923. The original décor of the public rooms is well preserved. *Open April–Oct.* Close by, the **★★★★Grand Hotel Royal**, Viale Carducci 44, ✆ 0584 45151, ✉ 0584 31438 (*expensive*) was built in a kind of neo-Renaissance eclectic style, with an impressive lobby, and an indoor pool. *Open April–Oct.* Or try the **★★★Liberty**, Lungomare Manin 18, ✆ 0584 46247, ✉ 0584 46249 (*moderate–cheap*). *Open April–Oct.* There are scores of one- and two-star hotels all along the beachfront.

The Tuscan Coast

to Genoa

to Parma

Campo Cecina

La Spezia

Carrara

Massa

Marinella

Marina di Carrara

Marina di Massa

Cinquale

Forte dei Marmi

Marina di Pietrasanta

Lido di Camaiore

Viareggio

Torre del Lago

Seravezza

Stazzema

Capriglia

Capezzano

V. Carducci

Pietrasanta

Camaiore

Valle Freddana

Massarosa

Lucca

Lago di Massaciuccoli

Pistoia

to Bologna

Prato

Florence

A11

S436

S69

† Certosa di Pisa

Gombo

San Piero a Grado

Marina di Pisa

Pisa

Arno

A1

Tirrenia

Livorno

Ardenza

Montenero

I. di Gorgona

A12

S206

S1

Castiglioncello

Rosignano

Vada

Marina di Cecina

Cecina

Bolgheri

Castagneto-Carducci

Volterra

S68

S429

to Arezzo

Poggibonsi

Siena

T U S C A N Y

S223

I. di Capraia

Porto

San Vincenzo

Campiglia Marittima

Suvereto

Massa Marittima

S439

Golfo di Baratti

Populonia

Piombino

Follonica

Golfo di Follonica

Punta Ala

S1

Vetulonia

S322

Braccagni

II Roselle

Portoferraio

Porto Azzurro

Isola d'Elba

Castiglione della Pescaia

Marina di Grosseto

Grosseto

S33

Alberese

Scansano

Magliano in Toscana

to Pitigliano

Manciano

I. Pianosa

Parco Monte dell'Uccellina

Talamone

S74

N

Porto Santo Stefano

Orbetello

Ansedonia

Capalbio

to Rome

S1

I. di Montecristo

Monte Argentario

Port Ercole

Giglio Castello

Giglio Campese

Giglio Porto

I. del Giglio

I. di Giannutri

Land over 200 metres

30km

20 miles

One might suspect that the hordes of Italians who descend on Viareggio every summer do so mainly to eat; the resort has a disproportionate number of good restaurants. Heading the list, **L'Oca Bianca**, Via Aurelia 312, © 0584 388 477 (*very expensive*), north of the centre, is the place to go for Mediterranean lobster (*aragosta*), all kinds of fish, and elaborately prepared and served gourmet concoctions. Try the *menu degustazione* (*L90,000*)—you could spend considerably more *à la carte. Closed Tues.*

A good place to go wine-tasting is **Il Puntodivino**, Via Mazzini 229, © 0584 310 446 (*moderate*); the wines and champagnes come from all over Italy and France; the food is local—prawns with *prosciutto*, or anchovies with fennel. *Closed Mon.* The tiny, simple **La Darsena**, Via Virgilio 172, © 0584 392 785 (*moderate–cheap*), tucked away among the famous shipyards, serves marvellous fresh seafood at exceptionally low prices. Lunch is a real bargain, and booking is essential.

Pisa

Unless you spend all your time around the raucous narrow streets around the market and the university, Pisa may strike you as an uncannily quiet, almost empty place. But this is no museum city; Pisa has a hundred thousand reasonably active and noisy people who do not choose just to live in the past. Still, the city itself seems somehow too big for them. There are no ruins, but definitely an air of unfulfilled ambitions, of a past greatness nipped in the bud.

Change the scene to about 1100, when, according to the chroniclers, Pisa, the 'city of marvels', the 'city of ten thousand towers', had a population of some 300,000. If you believe those numbers we have some fine stories about Prester John and the Sultans of Cathay to tell you, too—but the medieval writers are to be excused for their extravagance. Excepting Venice, of course, nothing like this enormous, exotically cosmopolitan city had been seen in Christian Europe since the fall of Rome. Its merchants made themselves at home in every corner of the Mediterranean, bringing back new ideas and new styles in art in addition to their fat bags of profit. Pisa in the early Middle Ages made good use of these cultural exchanges, contributing as much as any city to the rebirth of western culture.

History

In the Middle Ages Pisa liked to claim that it began as a Greek city, founded by colonists from Elis. Most historians, however, won't give them credit for anything earlier than about 100 BC, when a Roman veterans' colony was settled here. Records on what followed are scarce, but Pisa, like Amalfi and Venice, must have had an early start building a navy and establishing trade connections. By the 11th century, the effort had blossomed into opulence; Pisa had built itself a small empire, including Corsica, Sardinia and for a while the Balearics. About 1060 work was begun on the great cathedral complex and many other buildings, inaugurating the Pisan Romanesque.

The First Crusade, when Pisa's Archbishop led the entire fleet in support of the Christian Knights, was an economic windfall for the city, but when the Pisans weren't battling the Muslims of Spain and Africa, they were learning from them. Influences from Andalucian mosques turn up in most Pisan Romanesque work, and a steady exchange of ideas brought much of medieval Arab science and philosophy into Europe through Pisa's port. The influence of Pisan architecture, the highest development of the Romanesque in Italy, spread from Sardinia to Puglia; in addition, when Gothic arrived in Italy Pisa was among the few cities to take it seriously. In science, Pisa contributed a great though somewhat shadowy figure, the mathematician Niccolò Fibonacci, who either rediscovered the principle of the Golden Section or learned it from the Arabs, and also introduced Arabic numerals to Europe. Pisa's scholarly tradition over the centuries was crowned in the 1600s by its most famous son, Galileo Galilei.

Pisa was always a Ghibelline city, the greatest ally of the Emperors in Tuscany if only for expediency's sake. When a real threat came, however, it was not from Florence or any of the other Tuscan cities, but the rising mercantile port of Genoa. After years of constant struggle, the Genoese devastated the Pisan navy at the Battle of Meloria (an islet off Livorno) in 1284. It meant the end of Pisan supremacy, and all chance of recovery was quashed by an even more implacable enemy: the Arno. Pisa's port was gradually silting up, and when the cost of dredging became greater than the traffic could bear, the city's fate was sealed. The Visconti of Milan seized the economically enfeebled city in 1396, and nine years later Florence snatched it from them. Excepting the period 1494–1505, when the city rebelled and kept the Florentines out despite an almost constant siege, Pisa's history was ended. The Medici dukes did the city one big favour, supporting the University and even removing Florence's own university to Pisa. In the last 500 years of Pisa's long, pleasant twilight, this institution has helped the city stay alive and vital, and in touch with the modern world.

In April 1999 workmen discovered eight well-preserved Roman ships buried in the mud of what was once Pisa's harbour—to find so many in one place is extremely rare, and archaeologists are hoping that they might have stumbled upon an exciting source of new information.

Getting Around

Pisa's **Galileo Galilei airport** is the second busiest airport in the region (after Florence), with its own railway station with direct connections to Florence and other cities. Most trains also stop at Pisa-Centrale station, about a 10-minute journey. For airport information, call ✆ 050 500 707.

Pisa's **Stazione Centrale** is south of the Arno, on Piazza della Stazione (for information call, ✆ 050 28546). It is about a 20-minute walk from the centre; alternatively, take city bus no.1 from outside the station, which will take you directly to the Field of Miracles and the city centre. Many trains (Florence–Pisa or Genoa–Rome lines) also stop at Stazione San Rossore, near the cathedral and the Leaning Tower.

All intercity **buses** leave from near Piazza Vittorio Emanuele, the roundabout north of the Stazione Centrale: CPT buses for Volterra, Livorno and the coastal resorts (to the left on Via Nino Bixio, ✆ 050 505 511/✆ 050 884 111); and LAZZI to Florence, Lucca and La Spezia (on Via d'Azeglio, ✆ 050 42688). Many long-distance and local buses also stop at Piazza Manin, just outside the walls by the Leaning Tower.

Tourist Information

The main office is right near the cathedral, at the east end of Piazza del Duomo, ✆ 050 560 464. There are also offices at the Stazione Centrale, ✆ 050 42291, and at Via Benedetto Croce 26, ✆ 050 40096.

to Genoa

VIA DELLE CASCINE

Stazione
San Rossore

Piazza
Griffi

P

P

VIA CONTESSA MATILDE

Arena
Garibaldi

VIA ANTONIO ROSMINI

Campo Santo

Baptistry

Duomo

VIA ANDREA   PISANO

Piazza
D. Manin

PIAZZA DEI MIRACOLI

Leaning
Tower

Museo del Duomo

i

Roman
Baths

Porta
Lucca

VIA CARD.

PIETRO MAFFI

Museo delle
Sinopie

M

Piazza
Arcivescovado

Palazzo
Arcivescovado

M

P

VIA BONANNO   PISANO

VIA PISANO

VIA CARD. CAPPONI

VIA CARD. CAPPONI

Orto

VIA PORTA BUOZZI

VIA DON G. BOSCHI

VIA ROMA

VIA GIOSUE CARDUCCI

VIA PAOLO SALVI

VIA GHINI

VIA MILLE

Palazzo
dell'
Orologio

Palazzo
della
Carovana

VIA DELLA FAGGIOLA

VIA MARTIRI

VIA RISORGIMENTO

Botanico

Museums of
Mineralogy
and Zoology

M

VIA A. VOLTA

VIA SANTA MARIA

San Sisto

Piazza
dei
Cavalieri

Santo Stefano

VIA S. FREDIANO

VIA G. OBERDAN

VIA G. DINI

Santa
Cecilia

VIA NICOLA

VIA TRIESTE

VIA P. PAOLI

Domus
Galilaeana

San
Frediano

VIA ARANCIO

Piazza
Dini

VIA D. CAVALCA

San
Michele in
Borgo

San
Nicola

Piazza
Dante Alighieri

P

VIA VIENA

VIA SERRA

VIA VOLTURNO

P

Piazza
Solferino

Museo Nazionale
di Palazzo
Reale

Piazza
F. Cartara

Università
degli Studi

PACINOTTI

Piazza
Vettovaglie

Piazza
Garibaldi

Palazzo
Reale

Arno

Santa Maria
della Spina

LUNGARNO GAMBACORTI

Ponte
di Mezzo

Arsenale

Fiume

LUNGARNO R. SIMONELLI

Ponte
Solferino

LUNGARNO SONNINO SIDNEY

Piazza
A. Saffi

Palazzo
Gambacorti

San
Sepolcro

i

Ponte della
Cittadelle

VIA S.

VIA PAOLO

VIA S. ANTONIO

VIA S. FRANCESCO

Logge
di Banchi

VIA SAN

Porta
a Mare

San Paolo
a Ripa
d' Arno

Sant'Agata

VIA FRANCESCO NIOSI

CRISPI

CORSO ITALIA

VIA DEL CARMINE

Santa Maria
del Carmine

VIA PIETRO GORI

VIA S. GIOVANNI AL GATANO

VIA DI PORTA A MARE

VIA NINO BIXIO

Domus
Mazziniana

LAZZI
Buses

VIA D'AZEGLIO

VIA GIUSEPPE MAZZINI

VIA SANCASCIANI

VIA G. BRUNO

VIA LIVORNESE

VIA CESARE BATTISTI

Sant'Antonio
de Padova

VIALE BENEDETTO CROCE

to Livorno

ACIT
Buses

Piazza
Vittorio
Emanuele II

P

VIALE   BONAINI

N

250 metres
250 yards

Piazza
della
Stazione

P

Stazione
Centrale

Pisa

The Field of Miracles

Almost from the time of its conception, this title, *Campo dei Miracoli*, was the nickname given to medieval Italy's most ambitious building programme. As with Florence's cathedral, too many changes were made over two centuries of work to tell exactly what the original intentions were. But of all the unique things about this complex, the location strikes one first. Whether their reasons had to do with aesthetics or land values— probably a little of both—the Pisans built their cathedral on a broad expanse of green lawn at the northern edge of town, just inside the walls. The cathedral was begun in 1063, the famous Leaning Tower and the baptistry in the mid 12th century, at the height of Pisa's fortunes, and the Campo Santo in 1278.

If you plan to visit all three monuments and the museums here, the reduced-price joint ticket, the *biglietto cumulativo*, for L12,000, is worthwhile, rather than paying separately.

The Baptistry

Open daily 9–sunset;
summer daily 8am–7.40pm.

The biggest of its kind in Italy; those of many other cities would fit neatly inside it. The original architect, with the felicitous name of Master Diotisalvi ('God save you') saw the lower half of the building done in the typical stripes-and-arcades Pisan style. A second colonnade was meant to go over the first, but as the Genoese gradually muscled Pisa out of its trade routes, funds ran short. In the 1260s Nicola and Giovanni Pisano redesigned and completed the upper half in a harmonious Gothic crown of gables and pinnacles. The Pisanos also added the dome over the original prismatic dome of Diotisalvi, still visible from the inside. Both of these domes were impressive achievements for their time—among the largest attempted in the Middle Ages. Inside, the austerity of the simple, striped walls and heavy columns of grey Elban granite is broken by two superb works of art. The great **baptismal font** was the work of Guido Bigarelli, the 13th-century Como sculptor who made the crazy pulpit in Barga. There is little figurative sculpture on it, but the 16 large marble panels are finely carved in floral and geometrical patterns of inlaid stones, a northern variation on the Cosmati work of medieval Rome and Campania. Nicolà Pisano's **pulpit**, made about 1260, was one of the first of that family's masterpieces, and established the form for their later pulpits, the columns resting on fierce lions, the relief panels crowded with intricately carved figures in impassioned New Testament episodes.

The baptistry is famous for its uncanny acoustics; if you have the place to yourself, try singing a few notes from the centre of the floor. If there's a crowd, the guards will be just waiting for someone to bribe them to do it.

The Cathedral

Open April–Sept daily 7.45–12.45 and 3–7; Oct–Mar daily 7.45–12.45 and 3–5.

One of the first and finest works of the Pisan Romanesque, the cathedral façade, with four levels of colonnades, came out a little more ornate than Buscheto, the architect, planned back in 1063. These columns, with the similar colonnades around the apse and the Gothic frills later added around the unique elliptical dome, are the only showy features on the calm, restrained exterior. On the south transept, the late 12th-century **Porte San Ranieri** has a fine pair of bronze doors by Bonanno, one of the architects of the Leaning Tower. The biblical scenes are enacted under real palms and acacia trees; naturally, the well-travelled Pisans would have known what such things looked like.

In the interior little of the original art survived a fire in 1595. The roof went, as well as the Cosmati pavement, of which a few spots still remain. But some fine work survives: the great mosaic of Christ Pantocrator in the apse is a work of Cimabue; the **pulpit**, done about 1300 by Giovanni Pisano, is the acknowledged masterpiece of that family.

The men of 1595 used the fire as an opportunity to get rid of this nasty old medieval relic, and the greatest achievement of Pisan sculpture sat disassembled in crates, quite forgotten until this century. Pisano's pulpit is startling, mixing classical and Christian elements with a fluency never seen before his time. St Michael, as a *telamone*, shares the honour of supporting the pulpit with Hercules and the Fates, while prophets, saints and sibyls look on from their appointed places. The relief panels, jammed with expressive faces, diffuse an electric immediacy equal to the best work of the Renaissance. Notice particularly the Nativity, the Massacre of the Innocents, the Flight into Egypt and the Last Judgement.

The Leaning Tower

Closed since 1990 until further notice; perhaps forever.

Most likely, the stories claiming the tilt was accidental were pure fabrications, desperate tales woven by the Pisans to account for what, before mass tourism, must have seemed a great civic embarrassment. The argument isn't very convincing. That the tower would start to lean when only 328ft tall seems hard to believe; half the weight would still be in the foundations. Even less credible would be that they doggedly kept building it after the lean commenced. The architects who measured the stones in the last century to get to the bottom of the mystery concluded that the tower's odd state was absolutely intentional. Trying to tell that to someone from Pisa, however, will be received as if you had suggested lunacy is a problem in his family.

The leaning campanile is hardly the only strange thing in the Field of Miracles. The more time you spend here, the more you will notice: little monster-griffins, dragons and such, peeking out of every corner of the oldest sculptural work, skilfully hidden where you have to look twice to see them; or the big bronze griffin sitting on a column atop of the apse (a copy), the Muslim arabesques in the Campo Santo, or the perfect classical Corinthian capitals in the cathedral nave, next to the pagan images on the pulpit. The elliptical cathedral dome, in its time the only one in Europe, shows that the Pisans not only had audacity but the mathematical skills to back it up. You may have noticed that the baptistry too is leaning—about 5ft in the opposite direction. And the cathedral façade leans outwards about an inch and a half, hard to notice but disconcerting if you see it from the right angle. So much in the Field of Miracles gives evidence of a very sophisticated, strangely modern taste for the outlandish, it may have been that the medieval master masons in charge here simply thought that plain perpendicular buildings were becoming just a little trite.

Whatever, the campanile is a beautiful building and something unique in the world—also a very expensive bit of whimsy, with some 190 marble and granite columns. For the past few decades, it has proved particularly expensive to the local and national governments, as they have struggled to shore up the tower. During the 1980s the angle of its lean, which had been changing by minute amounts for years, began to increase at an unprecedented rate, and in 1990 the tower was closed to visitors—amid howls of protest from local businesses, who thought their tourist trade would be utterly destroyed—while scientists and experts from around the world put forward a whole series of proposals for stabilizing the monument. Tens of billions of lire have already been spent on trying to save what has become one of Italy's most universally recognized landmarks. But digging under the 14,000 tonne tower is perilous; in September 1995, while workers were freezing the ground to mute vibrations, suddenly to their horror the tower heaved a groan and tipped another tenth of an inch. Work is ongoing—expect the Field of Miracles to look like the Field of Hard Hats for a while yet.

The Campo Santo and the Museums

Open April–Sept daily 8–7.30; Oct–Mar daily 9–4; adm.

If one more marvel in the Campo dei Miracoli is not excessive, there is this remarkable cloister-cemetery, a rectangle of gleaming white marble, unadorned save for the blind arcading around the façade and the beautiful Gothic tabernacle of the enthroned Virgin Mary over the entrance. With its uncluttered, simple lines, the Campo Santo seems more like a work of our own century than of the 13th. The cemetery began, according to legend, when the battling

Archbishop Lanfranc, who led the Pisan fleet into the Crusades, came back with boatloads of soil from the Holy Land, in which the prominent citizens of the town could be given extra-blessed burials. The building around the site was built about a century later, in the 1270s. Over the centuries an exceptional hoard of painting and sculpture accumulated here. Much of this went up in flames on a terrible night in July 1944, when an Allied incendiary bomb hit the roof and set it on fire. Many priceless works of art were destroyed and others, including most of the frescoes, damaged beyond hope of ever being perfectly restored.

The biggest loss, perhaps, was the set of frescoes by Benozzo Gozzoli—the *Tower of Babel*, *Solomon and Sheba*, *Life of Moses*, the *Grape Harvest* and others; in their original state they must have been as fresh and colourful as his famous frescoes in Florence's Medici Palace. Even better known, and somewhat better preserved, are two 14th-century frescoes of the *Triumph of Death* and the *Last Judgement* by an unknown artist (perhaps Andrea Orcagna of Florence) whose failure to leave his name unfortunately put him down to posterity as the 'Master of the Triumph of Death'. In this memento of the century of plagues and trouble, the damned are variously cooked, wrapped up in snakes, poked, disembowelled, banged up and chewed on; still, they are some of the best paintings of the trecento, and somehow seem less gruesome and paranoid than similar works of centuries to come (though good enough to have inspired that pop classic, Lizst's *Totentanz*).

For another curiosity, there is the **Cosmography** of Piero di Puccio, a diagram of the 22 spheres of the planets and stars, angels, archangels, thrones and dominations, cherubim and seraphim, and so on; in the centre, the small circle trisected by a T-shape was a common medieval map pattern for the known earth. The three sides represent Asia, Europe and Africa, and the three lines the Mediterranean, the Black Sea and the Nile. Among the sculpture in the Campo Santo, there is a group with Emperor Henry VII sitting among his court like some exotic oriental potentate, taken from what survived of his tomb.

The collection of the **Museo del Duomo** (*open daily 9 until sunset; summer daily 8–7.40; adm*) is exhibited in the chapter house, in the southeast corner of the Campo dei Miracoli, near the Leaning Tower. The first rooms contain the oldest works, including two strange Islamic pieces, the strange 11th-century **griffin** originally on the top of the cathedral, believed to have first come from Egypt, and a bronze basin. Most of the statues by the Pisanos exhibited here were brought in from the elements only when they were so worn and bleached as to be barely recognizable, and resemble a convention of mummies. However, in Room 5 there is Giovanni Pisano's superb *Madonna del Colloquio*, one of the finest of the family's sculptures, and in Room 10 his lovely ivory *Madonna and Child*. The museum continues upstairs with intarsia, Roman and Etruscan odds and ends, some rare illuminated scrolls, and the *Pisan Cross*, carried by the Pisan soldiers on the First Crusade. Many of the damaged frescoes from the Campo Santo were moved to the **Museo delle Sinopie** (*open daily 9 until sunset; summer daily 8–7.40; adm exp*), across the Piazza from the cathedral, after the war, along with the *sinopie* discovered underneath when they were removed from the walls. Many of these simple sketches are works of art in their own right, and together with drawings and photos made before the bombing they help to give an idea of how the frescoes once looked.

North Pisa

With the cathedral off on the edge of town, Pisa has no real centre. Still, the Pisans are very conscious of the division made by the Arno; every year on 27 June the two sides fight it out on the Ponte di Mezzo in the *Gioco del Ponte*, a sort of medieval tug-of-war where the opponents try to push a big decorated cart over each other. From the Field of Miracles, Via Cardinale Maffi leads east to some ruins of **Roman baths** near the Lucca gate; two interesting churches in the neighbourhood are **San Zeno**, in a corner of the walls, with some parts as old as the 5th century; and **Santa Caterina**, a Dominican church with a beautiful, typically Pisan façade. Inside there is an *Annunciation* and a sculpted tomb by Nino Pisano, as well as a large painting from the 1340s of the *Apotheosis of St Thomas Aquinas*, with Plato and Aristotle in attendance and defeated infidel philosopher Averroes below.

There is a long street that begins near the Campo dei Miracoli as Via Carducci and changes its name along its route, becoming the old, arcaded **Borgo Largo** and **Borgo Stretto**. This is Pisa's traditional main artery, the most fashionable shopping street and the centre for the evening *passeggiata*. The twisting alleys of the lively market area are just off to the west, along with the **University**, still one of Italy's most important, and the **Piazza dei Cavalieri**. In 1562 Duke Cosimo I started what was probably the last crusading order of knights, the Cavalieri di Santo Stefano. The crusading urge had ended long before, but the Duke found this a useful tool for indulging the anachronistic fantasies of the Tuscan nobility—most of them newly titled bankers—and for licensing out freebooting expeditions against the Turks. Cosimo had Vasari build the **Palazzo della Carovana** for the order, conveniently demolishing the old Palazzo del Popolo, the symbol of Pisa's lost independence. Vasari gave the Palazzo an outlandishly ornate *graffito* façade; the building now holds a college of the university.

Next to it, the **Palazzo dell'Orologio** was built around the 'Hunger Tower' (left of the big clock), famous from Dante's story in the *Inferno* of Ugolino della Gherardesca, the Pisan commander who was walled in here with his two young sons after his fickle city began to suspect him of intrigues with the Genoese.

Santo Stefano, the order's church, is also by Vasari, though the façade is by a young dilettante of the Medici family; inside are some long, fantastical war pennants that the order's pirates captured from the Muslims in North Africa.

Museo di San Matteo

Open Tues–Sat 9–7, Sun 9–2; closed Mon; adm.

Much of the best Pisan art from the Middle Ages and Renaissance has been collected here, in an old convent that also once served as a prison. Most came from Pisan churches, so there is a predominance of straightforward religious subjects. The Pisano family is, of course, well represented, including one magically beautiful *Madonna* in medieval Pisan dress, a wooden sculpture by Andrea Pisano. Besides the Pisan statues, reliefs, ivory work and sarcophagi, there are paintings by such artists as Masaccio (*St Paul*), Fra Angelico, Ghirlandaio, Simone Martini, Gozzoli and Brueghel.

South of the Arno

Pisa's stretch of Arno is an exercise in Tuscan gravity, two mirror-image lines of blank-faced yellow and tan buildings all the same height. Only one landmark breaks the monotony, but it is something special. Near the Solferino Bridge, **Santa Maria della Spina** sits on the bank like a precious, tiny Gothic jewel box. Though one of the few outstanding achievements of Italian Gothic, originally it wasn't Gothic at all. Partially rebuilt in 1323, its new architect—perhaps one of the Pisanos—turned it into an extravaganza of pointy gables and blooming pinnacles. All of the sculptural work is first class, especially the figures of Christ and the Apostles in the 13 niches facing the streets. The chapel takes its name from a thorn of Christ's crown of thorns, a relic brought back from the Crusades.

Not far to the west, near the walls where the famous 'Golden Gate'—Pisa's door to the sea—once stood, remains of the old Citadel and Arsenal are still visible across the river. On the southern side, **San Paolo a Ripa del Arno** has an interesting 12th-century façade similar to the cathedral. San Paolo stands in a small park, and it is believed to have been built over the site of Pisa's original cathedral: perhaps building cathedrals in open fields was an old custom. Behind it, the unusual and very small 12th-century chapel of **Sant'Agata** has eight sides and an eight-sided prismatic roof. A similar building can be seen at the other end of south Pisa, the octagonal **San Sepolcro** off Lungarno Galilei, built originally for the Knights Templar.

Around Pisa

Just outside Pisa there are good Romanesque Pisan churches in the villages of Calci, Vicopisano and San Casciano. The **Certosa di Pisa** (*open April–Sept Tues–Sat 9–6, Sun 9–12; Oct–Mar Tues–Sat 9–5, Sun 9–12; adm*), a typically lavish 18th-century Charter-house, has a prominent site north of the Arno and a huge low building in some sort of 1920s Spanish-Californian exhibition style. West of the city at **Gombo** is a small beach where in 1822 Percy Shelley was brought ashore after being drowned, in the company of a British lieutenant, when a storm struck their small boat on the way to Livorno. His body was burned here too, as Trelawney, Leigh Hunt and Byron looked on.

Pisa ✉ *56100*   ***Where to Stay and Eating Out***

In Pisa, walks on the wild side of Tuscan cuisine seem more common than elsewhere—eels, brains, tripe, wild mushrooms, 'twice-boiled soup' and some dishes that cannot be found in any dictionary, and that waiters cannot satisfactorily explain. Don't be intimidated; there's always more common fare on the menu, and occasionally the more outlandish items turn into surprisingly refined treats.

Close to the Campo dei Miracoli, the ★★★★**Grand Hotel Duomo**, Via S. Maria 94, ✆ 050 561 894, 🖷 050 560 418 (*expensive*) is a modern but richly appointed luxury hotel with a roof garden and a garage; all the rooms are air conditioned.

Right in the centre on Lungarno Pacinotti, the ★★★**Royal Victoria**, ✆ 050 940 111 (*moderate*) is a tasteful hotel, its charm a little faded, with rooms overlooking the Arno. Many of the middle-range hotels are in the streets around the train station, south of the Arno, like the ★★★**Terminus e Plaza**, Via Colombo 45, ✆ 050 500 303 (*moderate*). If you're driving, you may want to stay at the ★★★**California Park Hotel** in San Giuliano Terme, ✆ 050 890 726 (*moderate*), just north of the city on the SS12r—a large hotel in a park with a pool. *Open Mar–Oct.*

Inexpensive hotels are spread around town, and most of them are usually full of local students; it's always best to call first, or else go up to the Campo dei Miracoli and try ★★**Di Stefano** Via Sant'Apollonia 35, off Via Carducci, ✆ 050 553 559 (*cheap*); the ★**Gronchi** on Piazza Archivescovado, ✆ 050 561 823 (*cheap*); the friendly ★**Helvetia**, Via Don Boschi 31, ✆ 050 553 084 (*cheap*); or ★**Albergo Giardino**, Piazza Manin, just outside the walls, ✆ 050 562 101 (*cheap*). All are relatively convivial places with plenty of rooms within easy walking distance of the cathedral.

The **Ristoro dei Vecchi Macelli**, Via Volturno 49, ✆ 050 20424 (*expensive*), on the north bank of the Arno, near Ponte Solferino, is a gourmet stronghold with highly imaginative dishes based on coastal Tuscan traditions. *Closed Wed and Sun lunch.* It's hard to believe that you are in Italy at **Cagliostro**, Via del Castelletto 26/30, ✆ 050 575 413 (*expensive*), an extraordinary restaurant/ *caffè*/ *enoteca*/art gallery/night club and general trendy hang-out, but the cooking is 'Tuscan Creative', with other dishes thrown in from around Italy. Lunch is more modest (and cheaper).

Da Bruno, Via Luigi Bianchi 12, ✆ 050 560 818 (*moderate*), outside the walls a few blocks east of the Campo dei Miracoli, is where you can see if you like simple Pisan cooking—things like polenta with mushrooms and *baccalà*. *Closed Mon eve and Tues.* Pisa is well endowed with unpretentious trattorias, many of them near the centre around the university. On Via San Frediano 16, **Osteria dei Cavalieri**, ✆ 050 580 858 (*moderate*) has seafood, vegetarian and meat fixed-price menus, and good game dishes such as rabbit with thyme. *Closed Sat lunch and Sun.* Cosy **Osteria La Grotta**, Via San Francesco 103, ✆ 050 578 105 (*moderate*) has a simulated grotto and comforting food: meat-lovers should try the Gran Padellata del Maremmano, a rich stew of three different kinds of meat cooked with spicy sausage and vegetables. *Closed Sun.*

Il Nuraghe, Via Mazzini 58, ✆ 050 44368 (*moderate*) has specialities such as ricotta ravioli, and snails. The chef here is Sardinian, so Tuscan and *Sarde* specialities rub shoulders. *Closed Mon.* Seafood delicacies hold pride of place at **Lo Schiaccianoci**, Via Vespucci 104, east of the station, ✆ 050 21024 (*moderate*). *Closed Sun.* In the centre of the city, near the Piazza dei Cavalieri, **Cateni**, Via della Faggiola 1, ✆ 050 552 725 (*moderate*) is an excellent, comfortable and very friendly family-run traditional restaurant, with wonderful gnocchi and fish.

Numero Undici, Via Cavalca 11, ✆ 050 54429 (*cheap*) is a diminutive trattoria with no frills—you order from the counter and take your plate to the table—but prices are rock bottom and the limited menu delicious. *Closed Sat lunch and Sun.* **Lo Spuntino**, Vicolo dei Tinti, ✆ 050 580 240 (*cheap*) is rather touristy and a bit hard to find (it's in an alley just off Via Oberdan), but the pizzas, *primi* and *secondi* are fine and good value. *Closed Fri.* One km from the Pisa Sud *autostrada* exit, **Re di Puglia**, Via Aurelia Sud 7, Loc. Mortellini, ✆ 050 960 157 (*cheap*) occupies a converted farmhouse and primarily uses produce fresh from the farm. Tuck into homemade pasta with mutton, rabbit or goat, and follow this with meat cooked on the huge grill. *Dinner only, also lunch on Sun. Closed Mon and Tues in winter.*

Getting Around

Livorno's **train** station is about 2km from the port, but there are regular city **buses** from there to the port and Piazza Grande in the centre. **Ferries** go from Livorno to the islands of Elba, Gorgona and Capraia (Toremar, usually at least twice daily, © 0586 896 113), to Bastia in Corsica (Corsica Ferries, © 0586 898 979, Corsica Marittima, © 0586 210 507) and to Olbia in Sardinia (Sarda Navigazione, © 0586 409 925, Moby Lines, © 0586 890 325). All offices are in the Stazione Marittima in the port. Ferries to Elba are heavily booked up in mid-summer and it can be easier to get the boat from Piombino, closer to Elba (*see* below).

Tourist Information

Livorno: Piazza Cavour 6, © 0586 89811; portside offices at Porto Mediceo and Terminal Calata Carrara (*summer only*). **Elba**: Calata Italia 26, Portoferraio, © 0565 914 671. **Grosseto**: Via Monterosa 206, © 0564 454 527. **Porto Santo Stefano**: Corso Umberto 55, © 0564 814 208.

Livorno

A few kilometres out to sea beyond Livorno's harbour, a medieval stone tower marks the tiny islet of Meloria, the place where the Genoese navy put an end to Pisa's importance as a Mediterranean power in 1284. And when the silting up of its river harbour put an end to Pisa as a great port, fate had this spot in mind to replace her. Livorno was founded in 1571 by Cosimo de Medici; over the next 200 years, while nearly all the rest of peninsular Italy was in economic decline, Livorno thrived as the nation's third port, after Genoa and Naples. It was an interesting town; after Duke Ferdinand decreed religious liberty for it, persecuted Jews, Greeks, English Catholics and even Spanish Moors settled here, along with political refugees from all over Europe. From the beginning there was a strong connection with England: an English engineer, son of the Duke of Leicester, designed the port, and trade connections were strong. Englishmen became so familiar with Livorno in the 17th century that they bestowed on it the bizarre anglicization of Leghorn.

Livorno, though the home town of the artist Modigliani, hasn't much to show for its 400 years, but its modern, ambitious outlook has earned it an important role in seagoing container traffic and a position as Tuscany's second city. There isn't much to see, but the city has plenty of ferries to jump on, and a reputation for seafood that is entirely deserved.

While you're waiting at the port, have a look at Livorno's landmark, the **monument to Ferdinand I**, better known as the 'Quattro Mori' for the four bronze Moors in chains around the pedestal, exceptional sculptures by a 17th-century artist named Pietro Tacca (four Moors' heads are the symbol of Sardinia). The best part of Livorno is the 'Venice' neighbourhood near the port, sliced through by small canals. Otherwise the city wears a strangely blank look, pure north-Tuscan taciturnity undiluted by medieval or Renaissance charm. It's pleasant enough, and the people are on the whole good cheerful Communists, but even when the streets are crowded Livorno can seem like a city seen in a dream.

The Tuscan Archipelago

Mostly this means Elba, one of Italy's number one holiday playgrounds, though there are also six smaller islands, tracing a broad arc along the coast from Livorno to Orbetello. Some of them might also be desirable holiday destinations, but for the Italian government's bad habit of using them as prisons.

Elba, reached by ferry from Piombino or Livorno, attracts over two million visitors each year, to unspectacular, family-style holidays on its miles of beaches. The scenery, reminiscent of nearby Corsica, is often impressive; pink granite, green *macchia* and forests, and a severely mountainous coast. In ancient times Elba was best known for its iron ore, and more recently for the brief sojourn of Napoleon (1814–15). Everyone visits his thoroughly depressing palace in the otherwise lovely island capital of **Portoferraio**. Other sights are few, but you can enjoy the mountains and beaches and wash down a fish dinner with Elban *Aleatico* or *Moscato*, two of Tuscany's best wines.

As for the other islands, from north to south: **Gorgona** once had villas of wealthy Romans but now is just a gloomy prison. The larger **Capraia**, once a penal colony, has more Roman ruins, cliffs, and now five hotels. Below Elba come **Pianosa**, another prison (and rather improbable setting for the US base in *Catch 22*); and **Montecristo**, a beautiful, uninhabited nature reserve, accessible only for day trips from Elba; and **Giglio**, the only real resort island, which boasts superb scenery and bird life, several hotels, three little villages, one of them medieval— Giglio Castello—and fine small beaches. Finally, **Giannutri**, a pretty, tiny island without roads, just big enough to hold some villas and one holiday village.

Gorgona and Capraia can be reached by a regular ferry service from Livorno and Elba; Giglio and Giannutri from Porto Santo Stefano, near Orbetello.

South of Livorno

The rugged coast south of Livorno is dotted with small beaches that can become tremendously crowded all through the summer: around **Castiglioncello**, a pretty spot when things are slow, then Rosignano Solvay, Marina di Cecina, San Vincenzo, Follonica and Punta Ala, all along the coastal plain. There are Etruscan tombs, not especially interesting, at **Populonia**, one of the big Etruscan cities of which few traces remain. It stands on a mountainous promontory, at the other end of which is **Piombino**, a town full of steel works that is also the most convenient ferry port for Elba.

Grosseto, today a fair-sized provincial capital, has no ancient memories—of course it doesn't, having been underwater until late-Roman times. Grosseto does have Medici fortifications and a small archaeological museum (*call © 0564 455 432, for hours and information*). Its plain, now reclaimed from swamps and made into rich farmland, marks the beginning of the **Maremma**, a low-lying region that extends almost as far as Rome. Once one of the centres of Etruscan civilization, malaria and Roman misrule led to its almost complete abandonment.

For centuries the Maremma remained a ghostly, disease-ridden marsh, though modern drainage and reclamation projects much like those in the Pontine Marshes to the south have made good farmland of it once more. Parts have been maintained in their original state as a nature park—including the **Monti dell'Uccellina**, a range of ragged hills set among parasol pine forests on the coast south of Grosseto. This is a favourite rest stop for migratory birds going to and from Africa—hence the name (*uccello* is Italian for 'bird'). Nine walks have been laid out, and there are tours in English in summer (*call the visitors' centre at Alberese, ✆ 0564 407 098, to find out when; adm limited to 500 people a day; open 9–one hour before sunset; adm*). There are no roads, but you can explore this stretch of coast by boat from **Talamone**, a little fishing port at its southern tip.

Near the end of Tuscany's coast is a geographical curiosity, **Monte Argentario**. Once, perhaps thousands of years ago, Argentario was an island, the member of the Tuscan archipelago closest to the shore. It gradually became joined to the mainland by three narrow sand bars, now solid and covered with trees. There's a story that sailors gave the Argentario its name in classical times, noticing the flashes of silver from the olive leaves that still cover the mountain slopes. The placid lagoons between the sand bars make up another renowned nature and bird reserve, and those who are prepared to walk out along the southernmost strip are also rewarded by the discovery of remarkably unspoilt beaches. **Orbetello**, on the central strip, was once a fashionable resort, though today this charming town must make way for trendy **Porto Ercole** and **Porto Santo Stefano**, two pretty fishing villages that in summer are a bit overburdened with Florentines and Romans on holiday.

Where to Stay and Eating Out

Livorno ✉ 57100

The ★★★**Gran Duca**, Piazza Micheli 16, ✆ 0586 891 024 (*moderate*), Livorno's most interesting hotel, built into a surviving section of the walls, has some rooms which look out over the Quattro Mori and the busy port. Being a port town, there's an abundance of cheaper hotels. Many can be found across the wide piazza from the train station, though none is especially distinguished. A good one is the old-fashioned ★★**Corsica**, Corso Mazzini 148, ✆ 0586 882 280 (*cheap*).

If you're stuck in Livorno, you can pass the time amenably eating fish. Probably the best restaurant is **La Chiave**, Scali della Cantine 52, ✆ 0586 888 609 (*expensive*)—try their *tagliolini* with octopus and basil. *Closed Wed.* Another good place to sample Livornese fish dishes is **L'Antico Moro**, Via di Franco 59, ✆ 0586 884 659 (*expensive*). Some of the best restaurants are to the south of the city in the seaside suburb of Ardenza. **Da Oscar**, Via Franchini 78, ✆ 0586 501 258 (*moderate*) has been a favourite for decades; there is a good selection of wines to go with the *linguine* and clams, excellent *risotti* and grilled *triglie* and *orate*. *Closed Mon.* At the wine bar **Cantina Nardi**, Via L. Cambini 6, ✆ 0586 808 006 (*cheap*) you can eat for under L30,000 at lunchtime, surrounded by hundreds of wine bottles. *Closed Sun.*

Elba ✉ 57100

There are quite a few hotels on Elba, mostly in Portoferraio, but they still get very heavily booked up in summer. ★★★★**Villa Ottone**, at Ottone, ✆ 0565 933 042 (*expensive*) is in a 19th-century villa right on the beach, with a shady garden and tennis court. The small ★★**La Conchiglia**, ✆ 0565 987 010 (*moderate*) is on probably Elba's best beach, at Cavoli, west of Campo nell'Elba. ★★**Andreina**, at La Cala, west of Marciana Marina, ✆ 0565 908 150 (*cheap*) is blissfully out of the way. It's a good idea to consult the tourist office, who have lists of hotels, **private rooms** and **apartments** to rent.

Orbetello ✉ 58015

The ***Piccolo Parigi**, Corso Italia 169, ℰ 0586 867 233 (*cheap*) is a delightful, friendly place in the middle of town.

Porto Ercole ✉ 58018

*****Il Pellicano, Cala dei Santi, ℰ 0564 833 801, ✆ 0564 833 418 (*luxury*) stands on the cliffs behind the town, with a garden, views over the sea and its own beach in a little cove. It has all imaginable amenities, including a pool and a first-class restaurant. Prices for the best rooms are close to L600,000 (rates are notably lower off-season). **La Lampara**, Lungomare Andrea Doria 67, ℰ 0564 833 024 (*moderate*) is an outstanding restaurant with tables outdoors on the port, where the cooking is more or less Neapolitan—so of course there's pizza as well as excellent grilled fish.

Porto Santo Stefano ✉ 58019

Best here is *****Filippo II**, ℰ 0564 812 640 (*moderate*), close to the beaches at Poggio Calvella. For dinner, the impeccably elegant and swanky **Dal Greco**, Via del Molo 1, ℰ 0564 814 885, on the yacht harbour (*expensive*) is still a good bargain at about L60,000. A *terrina di pesce* is the star attraction, along with lobster and a wide choice of other dishes. *Closed Tues.*

Siena

Understanding Florence, Siena's arch-enemy and artistic rival over the centuries, requires some work—a few bulky tomes of history and art criticism for starters, and an effort of the imagination beyond that. For Siena, on the other hand, you need only come to the city and look around. Draped on its hills, Siena reveals itself as a flamboyant ensemble of medieval buildings in honest brown (*siena*-coloured) brick; on the lower slopes, gardens and olive groves fill almost half the space within the old city wall, and above it all Tuscany's tallest tower and its gayest, most dazzling cathedral compete like beauties at the fair. Medieval Siena created beauty almost effortlessly, and its fierce civic pride tolerated nothing less than the building of a city that in itself is a single great work of art.

History

A Roman foundation, Siena emerged in the age of the *comuni* as one of the leading powers of central Italy, achieving its total independence in 1125. Like Florence, Siena lived on wool and banking; the clothing industry was never very large, but the bankers managed to make themselves indispensable to kings and princes all over Europe.

Ghibelline by convenience, Siena found itself almost constantly at war with Guelph Florence. The greatest moment in its history came in 1260, when news arrived of a huge army raised by Florence and other Tuscan cities coming to demand Siena's surrender. The city militias—reinforced by about 5000 Florentine political exiles—marched out and met the Florentines at Montaperti, beating them so badly that Florence was entirely at their mercy; only the attitude of the Florentine exiles prevented the Sienese from razing Florence to the ground, a famous story told by Dante in the *Inferno*. Nevertheless, as Florence's military and economic equal, Siena enjoyed a golden age that ended in 1348, when the Black Death carried off a third of the

to Florence and Motorway

V. VITT. EMANUELE

Porta Camollia

to Train Station

VIALE SARDEGNA

VIALE GIUSEPPE MAZZINI

VIA DON GIOVANNI MINZONI

VIA CAMPANSI

VIA

VIA RICASOLI

VIA BIAGIO DI MONTLUC

VIA DI CAMOLLIA

Chiesa di Fonte Giusta

V. N. SAURO

VIA GARIBALDI

VIA DOMENICO BEC

VIA SIMONE MARTINI

Porta Ovile

VIA

VIALE ARMANDO

VIALE R. FRANCI

La Lizza

VIALE MACCARI

LA LIZZA

Santo Stefano

VIA DEL PIAN D'OVILE

VIA DELLA STUFA SECCA

VIA DI VALLEROZZI

VIA DEL COMUNE

San Francesco

Piazza S. Francesco

VIALE V. VENETO

Fortezza

Piazza della Libertà

Medicea

VIA XXV APRILE

VIALE DELLO STADIO

VIALE F. TOZZI

Piazza Gramsci

Piazza Matteotti

VIA DEL MONTANINI

San Donato

VIA DEGLI ORTI

VIA ROSSA

VIA DE BARONCELLI

Piazza dell' Abbadia

Oratorio di San Bernardino

TERZO DI CAMOLLIA

VIALE V. VENETO

VIALE DEI

Bus Station & Hotel Information

VIALE

Palazzo Salimbeni

Santa Maria di Neve

Museo Archaeologico

Piazza San Domenico

VIA DELLA SAPIENZA

Casa di S. Caterina

Piazza Salimbeni

VIA DEL MORO

Santa Maria di Provenzano

VIA DELLE TERME

VIA BANCHI DI SOPRA

Palazzo Tolomei

TERZO

VIA S. BANDINI

1 Loggia della Mercanzia
2 Croce del Travaglio
3 Fonte Gaia
4 Palazzo del Magnifico
5 Cathedral Museum
6 Baptistry

San Domenico

Fontebranda

VIA S. CATERINA

VIA DELLA GALLUZZA

VIA S. CATERINA

Piazza Indipendenza

1 ● 2 ℹ

● 3

Palazzo Piccolomini

VIA BANCHI DI SOTTO

Logge del Papa

VIA DEL TORRIONE

San Martino

Porta Fontebranda

VIA FONTEBRANDA

VIA FRANCIOSA

Il Campo

Palazzo Pubblico

Piazza del Mercato

VIA DI SALICOTTO

VIA DEL SOLE

VIA ESTERNA DI FONTEBRANDA

6

Piazza del Duomo

Duomo

Piazza Selva D.

4

5

Piazza J.D. Quercia

Palazzo Chigi-Saracini

VIA DI CITTA

VIA DEL CASATO DI SOTTO

Pinacoteca Nazionale

San Giuseppe

VIA DI PORTA GIUSTIZIA

TERZO DI CITTA

VIA DI STALLOREGGI

VIA DEL CAPITANO

VIA S. PIETRO

San Pietro alle Scale

VIA DEL POGGIO

Prato di Sant' Agostino

VIA S. AGATA

Sant'Agostino

VIA P. MASCAGNI

PRIMO DEL OMBRO

VIA DEL MANTELLINI

VIA DI QUIRICO

VIA TOMMASO PENDOLA

Palazzo Pollini

Accademia di Fisiocvittici

Orto Botanico

VIA P. A. MATTIOLI

Porta Laterina

VIA DEL LATERINO

VIA ETTORE BASTIANINI

Santa Maria del Carmine

VIA S. MARCO

VIA DELLA DIANA

VIA DELLE SPERANDIE

VIA DELLE CERCHIA

Porta Tufi

Porta San Marco

Siena

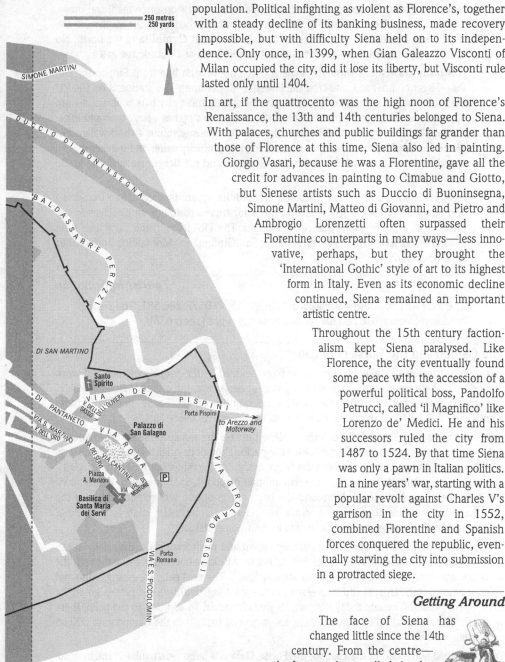

```
250 metres
250 yards
```

N

SIMONE MARTINI

DUCCIO DI BONINSEGNA

BALDASSARRE PERUZZI

DI SAN MARTINO

Santo Spirito

VIA DELL'OLIVIERA

SASSI

DI PANTANETO

VIA S. MARTINO

V. DELL'ORO

VIA DEI SERVI

V. DELLE CANTINE

VIA DI MONTONE

VIA DEI PISPINI

Porta Pispini

to Arezzo and Motorway

Palazzo di San Galagno

Piazza A. Manzoni

P

Basilica di Santa Maria dei Servi

VIA GIROLAMO GIGLI

Porta Romana

VIA E.S. PICCOLOMINI

population. Political infighting as violent as Florence's, together with a steady decline of its banking business, made recovery impossible, but with difficulty Siena held on to its independence. Only once, in 1399, when Gian Galeazzo Visconti of Milan occupied the city, did it lose its liberty, but Visconti rule lasted only until 1404.

In art, if the quattrocento was the high noon of Florence's Renaissance, the 13th and 14th centuries belonged to Siena. With palaces, churches and public buildings far grander than those of Florence at this time, Siena also led in painting. Giorgio Vasari, because he was a Florentine, gave all the credit for advances in painting to Cimabue and Giotto, but Sienese artists such as Duccio di Buoninsegna, Simone Martini, Matteo di Giovanni, and Pietro and Ambrogio Lorenzetti often surpassed their Florentine counterparts in many ways—less innovative, perhaps, but they brought the 'International Gothic' style of art to its highest form in Italy. Even as its economic decline continued, Siena remained an important artistic centre.

Throughout the 15th century factionalism kept Siena paralysed. Like Florence, the city eventually found some peace with the accession of a powerful political boss, Pandolfo Petrucci, called 'il Magnifico' like Lorenzo de' Medici. He and his successors ruled the city from 1487 to 1524. By that time Siena was only a pawn in Italian politics. In a nine years' war, starting with a popular revolt against Charles V's garrison in the city in 1552, combined Florentine and Spanish forces conquered the republic, eventually starving the city into submission in a protracted siege.

Getting Around

The face of Siena has changed little since the 14th century. From the centre—the famous piazza called simply the **Campo**—the city unfolds like a three-petalled flower along three ridges, a natural division since medieval times, with the quarter called the **Terzo di Città**, including the cathedral, to the southwest; the **Terzo di San Martino** to the southeast; and the **Terzo di Camollia** to the north. No cars are allowed in, but there are **car parks** at the Fortezza and outside the gates.

Not many **trains** pass through; Siena is only on a branch line from Empoli (on the Pisa–Florence line) to Chiusi (on the Florence–Rome line). The station is on the Via Mazzini, about 2km north of the old city. However, most city **bus** routes run from opposite the station (on the other side of the road—the stop has a large map and information board) to the Piazza Matteotti, the main local bus terminus a short walk north of the Campo. If there are four or more of you it is probably easier and quicker to take a **taxi** into the centre. All bus and rail information and rail tickets are available at the SETA agency, no.56 on the Campo.

A short distance from Piazza Matteotti, on the little square in front of San Domenico and along the Viale dei Mille, are the stops for **buses** to towns and villages in the province and also for long-distance destinations. The TRA-IN (*sic*) and Lazzi lines have several buses a day to Florence, Volterra, San Gimignano, Montalcino and smaller local destinations.

Tourist Information

The local APT has offices at Piazza del Campo 56, ☎ 0577 280 551. The Siena hoteliers' co-operative also has its own bookings office (*see* p.638).

The Campo and the Corsa del Palio

It is hard to imagine a lovelier square, or one more beloved by the people who live and work around it. Laid out on the site of the Roman forum of *Sena Julia*, the original settlement here, the unique, semicircular Campo, was paved in brick in the 1340s. Today, lined with pavement cafés all along its steep northern arc, it is still the centre of everything.

Twice each year, on 2 July and 16 August, Siena puts on the noisiest medieval blowout in Italy, the horse race around the Campo called the **palio**. Though its origins go back to the days of the *comune*, the palio in its present form began in the 1600s; riders from 10 of the city's 17 quarters (each *contrada* known by its totem animal: elephant, snail, unicorn, giraffe, owl, caterpillar, etc.) careen recklessly around the edge of the piazza while thousands jam the centre and any available open space to watch. The riders mean business; losers have a year of insults and rotten tomatoes to look forward to in their home district.

With no rules (not even against bribery!), they crowd and push frantically. Especially at the two right angles they must navigate, the sight of not only jockeys but horses flying through the air is not uncommon. Often less then half actually finish. The post-palio carousing, while not up to medieval standards, is still impressive; in the winning *contrada* the parties go on for days. Siena's tranquil beauty today conceals its true character. In addition to the palio, there was once also a festival called *Gioca del Pugno*—a general fistfight in the Campo with 300 on each side.

On the curved north end of the Campo, the **Fonte Gaia** is a large rectangular fountain decorated with mythological reliefs by Jacopo della Quercia (all copies; the originals are in the Palazzo Publico). In the 14th century the Sienese dug up a beautiful Greek statue of Venus by

Lysippus and built a pedestal for her atop the fountain. After the plague, the priests succeeded in convincing the people that the pagan statue had called down God's wrath. The statue was smashed to bits, and a band of Sienese dressed as peasants smuggled the pieces over the border with Florence and buried them, to transfer the bad luck to their enemies.

Palazzo Pubblico

Open Mar–Nov Mon–Sat 9.30–7.45, Sun 9–1; Dec–Feb daily 9.30 –1.45; adm exp.

This is the civic pride of Siena expressed in brick and marble, a huge building that still serves as the seat of the city council, as well as being the repository of much of the best Sienese art. Above it rises the tallest secular tower of medieval Italy, the graceful, needle-like construction that Henry James called Siena's 'Declaration of Independence'. The **Torre di Mangia** takes its odd name from a legendary glutton (and relative of the artist Duccio) whose job it was to ring the bell—there's a little statue of him in one of the courtyards. At the foot of the tower, the equally graceful marble loggia leads to the 'Cappella di Piazza', built to give thanks for Siena's deliverance from the Black Death.

Most of the Palazzo was built in the early 14th century. At the top you'll notice the familiar Christian symbol of the letters IHS inside a radiant sun. This was the mark of the 14th-century religious reformer San Bernardino, who often preached before huge crowds in the Campo. San Bernardino wanted to persuade the constantly warring nobles to replace their own heraldic devices with this holy sign—without much success. Around the façade are other devices from Siena's history: the city's black-and-white coat of arms, the wolf (according to legend Siena was founded by a son of Remus), and the balls of the Medici dukes. Inside, the ground floor is all city offices, and you'll need to climb the long stairs to see the rooms open to the public.

Among the old municipal chambers are the **Sala di Risorgimento**, with florid 1890s frescoes of Garibaldi and Vittorio Emanuele II in action, and an 'allegory of Italian liberty'; a **Council Room,** with Gobelin tapestries and figures of political virtue from antiquity by an interesting 15th-century Sienese painter named Beccafumi; and more of the same—classical gods, Caesar, Pompey and Judas Maccabaeus—around the pretty **chapel**, frescoed with a giant St Christopher (before setting out on a journey it was good luck to glimpse this saint, and in Italy and Spain he is often painted as large as possible so no one could miss him).

The **Sala del Mappamondo**, named after a lost cosmographical fresco, has a number of 13th-century frescoes, including the famous scene of the resolute *condottiere* **Guidoriccio da Fogliano,** off to besiege a castle. It has traditionally been attributed to Simone Martini (*c.* 1330), the greatest of Sienese fresco artists, though the attribution has recently been called into question. Unquestionably his is the fabulous *Maestà* in the same room, a dignified Madonna surrounded by saints, believed to be his earliest work. The Palazzo's greatest treasure, however, is the unique series of frescoes by Ambrogio Lorenzetti in the **Sala della Pace**, the *Effects of Good and Bad Government.* Here medieval allegory is applied to politics; two rival princes sit in state, one with Justice, Wisdom and Compassion for his counsellors, the other with such characters as Pride, Wrath and Avarice. On the long walls of the chamber two mirror-image cities are portrayed, the well-governed one (with Siena's cathedral discreetly painted in) is clean, orderly and happy, with smiling shopkeepers who look to be making nice profits; the other—urban blight, crime, oppression, corruption, housing problems and slipshod municipal services, the very picture of a 1300s South Bronx.

For views over Siena you may climb more stairs up to the **Loggia**, where the original reliefs from the Fonte Gaia are kept—or more stairs than you have ever seen, up the 328ft **Torre di Mangia** (*open daily 10–3.30, or as late as 7.30, depending on the season; adm*), for a view that is absolutely, positively worth the slight risk of cardiac arrest and the long queues (only 20 people are allowed in at a time).

Behind the Palazzo, steps lead down to the **Piazza del Mercato**, Siena's cheerful market-place. At the opposite end of the Campo narrow stairs under arches lead up to the **Croce del Travaglio**, the meeting place for the main streets from the three corners of the city. Here stands the 15th-century arcade known as the **Loggia della Mercanzia**, where guilds trans-acted business and Italy's most respected commercial tribunal once sat in judgement.

Terzo di Città and the Cathedral

From Via di Città, winding behind the Campo, a narrow street off to the right called Via dei Pellegrini leads to what seems at first to be a huge striped bastion in the wall. Siena's glorious **cathedral** sits atop the highest point in the city. The apse spills down the slope, its crypt at the street level of the rest of the city. Perhaps to save space and money, the architects tucked their **baptistry** under here. It contains some of the best art in Siena, though dim and hard to see even when the lighting machine is working.

The **baptismal font**, one of Siena's crown jewels, has relief panels by Donatello (*Herod's Banquet*), Ghiberti (*Baptism of Christ*) and Jacopo della Quercia (*Birth of John the Baptist*). Donatello also contributed the six bronze angels and some of the other statuary. Across the street from the baptistry, the **Palazzo del Magnifico** was home to Siena's 15th-century power brokers, the Petrucci.

A flight of steps leads up to the Piazza del Duomo, but at the top you must first pass through a portal in a huge, free-standing wall of striped marble arches. Siena's cathedral, 289ft long, might have seemed big enough, but the news that Florence was beginning a bigger one came as an insult to the city's pride. In 1339 the Council adopted an incredible plan to rebuild the cathedral; the old one was to be preserved as a transept, and a new nave, almost double the length of the old one, would be built out from the southern end. Had it ever been completed, it would have surpassed even St Peter's in Rome, the biggest in the world. Only nine years later, however, the Black Death struck, and Siena soon found itself without the means to continue. The northern wall and façade still stand, their arches bricked in and incorporated into other buildings. What was to be a cathedral nave is now a piazza, and a symbol for the end of a city's ambitions.

Even after all the other grand Tuscan cathedrals, Siena's comes as a revelation. It may not be a transcendent expression of faith, and it may not be an important landmark in architecture, but it certainly is one of the most delightful ornaments in Christendom. One suspects even sober-minded art critics are tempted to buy one of the illuminated plastic models in the souvenir shops, to take home and put on top of their television sets. The tall campanile stands striped like an ice-cream parfait—stripes darker and bolder than in Pisa or Lucca. The façade, even more confectionery-like, was largely the work of Giovanni Pisano, who added many of the statues of saints, prophets and pagan philosophers on the three great portals. The upper half was completed later, in the 1390s, and the glittering mosaics in the gables were added by artists from Venice only in the last century.

Inside, one hardly knows where to look first. Above the striped columns and walls the ornate Gothic vaulting is painted as a blue firmament with golden stars and angels—note the long rows of finely detailed heads of saints, running all along the nave. The most spectacular feature, however, is under your feet. Beginning in the 1360s, and continuing over the next two centuries, Siena's finest artists were commissioned to create inlaid marble scenes for the **pavement**, nearly an acre of them covering the entire cathedral floor. The subjects are fascinating. Entering from the west door, for example, you see a portrait of Hermes Trismegistus, the legendary patron of alchemists whose 'works', brought from Byzantium, caused such a stir in medieval Europe. Further down come the 10 Sibyls of antiquity, and a few images straight out of a deck of tarot cards: snakes and newts, a wheel of fortune, Socrates and Crates, and other symbols too arcane to think about. Many of the best have become somewhat fragile, and are now covered up for most of the year.

The **stained glass**, some of it from designs by Duccio, is also not to be missed, along with a **pulpit** by Nicola Pisano, with reliefs of philosophers and allegories of the Liberal Arts. Also, in the left aisle, there is the **Altare Piccolomini**, with some early work by Michelangelo (the statues of four saints on the lower level) and in the transept on the same side of the church there are two beautiful Renaissance sculptural ensembles, that of Bishop Giovanni Pecci, by Donatello, and another, of a cardinal, by Tino di Camaino.

The Piccolomini family, prominent in Siena for centuries, eventually attained European renown. Some were famous generals for the emperor in the Thirty Years' War (Schiller wrote a trilogy of plays about them), and during the Renaissance two of them made it to the Vatican—Popes Pius II and Pius III. The latter, in 1495, created the **Biblioteca Piccolomini** (*open daily 10–1 and 2.30–4.45; summer daily 9–7.15; adm*), just off the left aisle of the cathedral, to hold the library of the former, who was his uncle. Pius II, Aeneas Silvius Piccolomini, was a genuine Renaissance man: a poet, diplomat, historian, antiquarian, religious reformer and great geographer; Columbus studied his works closely.

Pius III hired Pinturicchio to cover the library walls with frescoes of his famous uncle's life. We see Aeneas Silvius in the courts of James II of Scotland and Emperor Frederick III, proclaiming a crusade and canonizing Catherine of Siena, among others. Pinturicchio's frescoes are spectacularly colourful, incorporating dozens of careful portraits of the famous and not-so-famous of the age, with loving attention to current court fashions in dress and coiffure. No better image of *la dolce vita* at the height of the Renaissance could be imagined. Aeneas Silvius' books have been carted off somewhere, but one of his favourite things still holds pride of place in the centre of the library: a beautiful marble vase with the Three Graces, a Roman copy of a work by Praxiteles that was studied closely by a good number of Renaissance artists.

Museo dell'Opera del Duomo

Open mid-Mar–Nov daily 9–1; April–Sept daily 9–7.30; adm.

For a close-up look at the façade of the cathedral, the only place to go is the cathedral museum, also known as the Museo Metropolitana, where most of the original sculptural work has been preserved. Some of these rank among the best Italian Gothic and Renaissance sculpture, especially statues of saints by Nicola Pisano and Jacopo della Quercia, remarkable for their kinetic possibilities—they seem ready to hop down from their pedestals and start declaiming if they suspect for a minute you've been skipping Sunday mass. Besides them, there are some original bits of the cathedral's pavement that had to be replaced, as well as some leftover pinnacles and other architectural details.

Upstairs, the collection of Sienese paintings includes Duccio di Buoninsegna's masterpiece, the former cathedral altarpiece called the *Maestà*, with an enthroned Virgin on one side and scenes from the Passion on the other. Duccio's animated composition and expressive faces here clearly surpass the work of his more celebrated contemporary, Giotto. The cathedral treasure contains lavish golden monstrances and reliquaries, and in one corner a simple, exquisite bouquet of gold flowers—the kind of gift popes would send along with their ambassadors in the 13th and 14th centuries. Part of the museum is built into the unfinished 14th-century cathedral. From the top floor you can climb up to the **Facciatone** ('big façade') for a view over the cathedral and the city.

Ospedale di Santa Maria della Scala

The neighbourhood around the cathedral is Rhinoceros country. To be specific, you're in the neighbourhood of the *Selva* (forest); that beast is its symbol. Opposite the old cathedral façade one entire side of the piazza is occupied by the great **Ospedale di Santa Maria della Scala**, believed to have been founded in the 9th century and for centuries one of the largest and finest hospitals in the world. Slowly the hospital functions have been moved out (one of the last patients to die here was Italo Calvino), and now they're converting it into a museum, dedicated to all the arts and the city's history, destined to be one of the largest in the world. Don't ask when it will be finished; as a *cantiere didattico*, part of the point is that the process of museum building itself is part of the attraction. For now, go inside (*open daily at changing hours; you should be safe visiting between 10.30 and 4.30; adm*) to see the frescoes in the **Sala dei Pellegrini**, with 15th-century frescoes of everyday hospital activities (Santa Maria was the seat of many revolutionary advances, such as doctors washing their hands back in the 1300s). The **Museo Archeologico**, already installed, has an Etruscan and Roman collection.

If you take the little stairs just west of the cathedral you'll find yourself in the **Piazza della Selva**, where a bronze rhinoceros commemorates some past Palio victory. South of the cathedral on Via San Pietro, Siena's **Pinacoteca** (*open Tues–Sat 9–7, Sun 8–1, Mon 8.30–1; adm*) occupies the restored 14th-century Palazzo Buonsignori, and has an excellent collection of Sienese art from its beginnings to the 17th century. The earliest works, on the top floor, include fine pieces by Guido di Siena, often called the founder of Sienese painting, and his followers. Most were brought here from churches around the city. As always, the works of Pietro and Ambrogio Lorenzetti stand out, for their dramatic faces and poses, and for their original approach to colour.

On the other floors, Madonnas and saints line up in room after room. Very few are without interest, though; the serious spirituality of all its painters, paradoxically expressed in rich settings and gorgeous colours, is a constant feature of the Siena school. Something else readily apparent is Sienese civic pride; almost all the painters have a fondness for painting their town in the background, even in a Nativity. Among later Sienese painters, Beccafumi is well represented, along with Il Sodoma, who initiated the Mannerist tradition in Siena, as well as acquiring his name from a still-popular vice. More Sodoma (an *Epiphany*) and some other fine paintings can be seen in the Piccolomini Chapel of **Sant'Agostino**, a 13th-century church two blocks south of the Pinacoteca, on Via della Cerchia.

Terzo di San Martino

Beginning again at the Loggia della Mercanzia, Via Banchi di Sotto leads down into the southeast 'third' of Siena, through the quarters of the Unicorn and the Elephant. Just off the Campo, the 1460 **Palazzo Piccolomini** has for centuries been the home of Siena's archives. The surprise attraction here is old Siena's **account books**. From the 1200s it became a tradition to have the city's best artists paint the covers—fascinating scenes of such prosaic subjects as medieval citizens coming to pay their tax, city workers receiving their pay, and honest monks at their tables trying to make the figures square.

Another elegant loggia, the **Logge del Papa** built by Aeneas Silvius (Pius II), stands on the next small piazza on the Banchi di Sotto. In the narrow streets down to the Piazza del Mercato there is another palio victory statuette—an elephant, for the Torre district—in the pretty Piazzetta Franchi on Via Salicotto. The **Basilica Servi di Maria** is this *terzo*'s biggest church, with good frescoes in the right transept by Pietro Lorenzetti.

Terzo di Camollia

The biggest and busiest of the *terzi*, this one runs northwards along Via Banchi di Sopra, Siena's fashionable shopping street and, for centuries, the town's main drag, where the entire population appears to make an evening *passeggiata* down to the Campo and back. Along it there are some of the palaces of the great medieval banking families. **Palazzo Tolomei** (1200–50) is the oldest, but much larger is the **Palazzo Salimbeni**, around a small piazza of the same name further up the street. The latter is the head office of Siena's bank, the *Monte dei Paschi di Siena*, founded in 1472. At the bottom of the hill behind it is the large church of **San Francesco**, with more frescoes by the Lorenzettis.

The quarter of the Goose, west of Banchi di Sopra, is a warren of narrow streets associated with the life of St Catherine of Siena, co-patron of Italy and one of medieval Italy's great mystics and religious reformers. Caterina Benincasa, born in 1347, 24th of 25 children in a poor family, began having visions at an early age and, like St Francis, she received the stigmata. Besides her devotional writings, for which she was recently proclaimed a Doctor of the Church, she kept a busy interest in the affairs of her day; as a woman she was able constantly to insult the popes over the crooked Church they ran without coming to any harm.

The **Santuario e Casa di Santa Caterina** (*open winter daily 9–12.30 and 3.30–6; summer daily 9–12.30 and 2.30–6*) still stands, on Costa Sant'Antonio just below San Domenico, and has been restored as a shrine and museum. **San Domenico** itself, a lofty 13th-century church at the end of Viale Curtatone, has her head in a golden reliquary, along with wonderfully hysterical frescoes of her life by the aforementioned Sodoma. San Domenico may seem a plain church from the outside, but you'll have a good view of its Sienese Gothic subtleties from below, at the **Fonte Branda**, a medieval fountain that was once the city's only source of water.

On the western edge of the city, the triumphant Duke Cosimo I of Florence built a fortress in 1560 to keep watch over the conquered city. The **Fortezza Medicea**, however, has nothing threatening about it; this most genteel of fortifications seems less a military work than a nobleman's villa and garden. The Sienese, who have long memories, have nevertheless turned the grounds into a park called Piazza della Libertà.

Sienese Pastimes

If you have more time to spend in Siena, there are plenty of ways to do it enjoyably. Just walking around the city is a treat. Nearly any old church you find open will be worth a look inside; more than most cities, Siena has preserved its medieval interiors and their art intact. South of the cathedral, you can take a walk in the country without leaving town, in the valleys between the *terzi*. Most of the medieval walls, and eight of the gates, survive.

If you want to learn more about the *contrade* and the palio, each of the 17 neighbourhood organizations (which are really legally chartered communities, a fascinating survival of the 'tribes' into which Roman and pre-Roman cities were organized) maintains its own museum. They are happy to show you around with some advance warning; the tourist office can give you a list of addresses and phone numbers, and will sometimes arrange visits for you.

Just outside the city, with fine views over Siena and its countryside, the monastery of **L'Osservanza** was founded by San Bernardino in the 1420s. Severely damaged in 1944, the church and cloister have been lovingly restored according to the original plans; there are works inside by Sano di Pietro and other Sienese painters, as well as Andrea della Robbia.

Siena ✉ *53100*   ***Where to Stay and Eating Out***

The city's hotels run an **information and reservations booth** in Piazza San Domenico, ✆ 0577 288 084, where all the long-distance buses stop. If you arrive by train without a reservation, take the local bus up to Piazza Matteotti, and then walk down the steps on one side of the piazza and along Via Curtatone to reach the booth.

Quite a few visitors to Siena find they have no room for lunch or dinner, having spent the day sneaking into pastry shops for slices of *panforte*, an alarmingly heavy concoction laced with fruits, nuts and secret Sienese ingredients. The chief producer by a long way is **Nannini**, who has several café-shops along the Banchi di Sopra. For that matter, anything in Siena's pastry shops is worth trying. They are all artists—this is one of the cities where you will see gargantuan creations of cake and crystallized fruit in the shop windows, as colourful as a Lorenzetti fresco, set out for all Siena to admire before they are carted off to some wedding party.

Most of Siena's best hotels are outside the walls, where the views and rural charm more than compensate for the slight inconvenience. At the top of the list is one of Italy's most remarkable establishments, built in the 14th century on a hill south of Siena. At ★★★★**La Certosa di Maggiano**, Via di Certosa 82, ✆ 0577 288 180, ✆ 0577 288 189 (*luxury*), the emphasis is on surprise luxuries—a heated pool, air conditioning that works, a quiet chapel and cloister, a salon for games, tennis courts, an excellent restaurant and a library that would be an antiquarian's dream. The cloister and the rest of this medieval complex are intact, and contain a bar and a restaurant open only to hotel guests. Of course, all this doesn't come cheap. For a second choice, ★★★★**Villa Scacciapensieri**, 3km north of the city at Strada Scacciapensieri 10, ✆ 0577 41441, ✉ 0577 270 854 (*very expensive*) has sunset views over Siena. A quiet country house, divided into 29 spacious rooms, it also has a pool and a fine restaurant, with tables on the terrace.

Just inside the walls, the ★★★**Palazzo Ravizza**, ✆ 0577 280 462 (*expensive*) occupies an old town house on Pian dei Mantellini, below the Duomo near the Porta Laterana. It has 30 rooms and a restaurant, plus free parking and a pretty terrace.

There are a number of reasonable hotels near the centre: ★★★**Duomo**, Via Stalloreggi 34, ✆ 0577 289 088 (*moderate*), south of the Duomo; the well-run ★★**Canon d'Oro**, Via Montanini 28, ✆ 0577 44321, ✉ 0577 280 868, near the Piazza Matteotti (*moderate*); and ★★★**Garden**, Via Custoza 2, ✆ 0577 47056, ✉ 0577 46050 (*moderate*), which has a swimming pool.

Genuinely inexpensive hotels are hard to find—especially at the start of the university terms when they're full of students. ★★**Il Giardino**, Via Baldassare Peruzzi 43, ✆ 0577 285 290 (*cheap*), near the Porta Pispini, is highly recommended, with good views and a pool. The centrally located ★**Tre Donzelle**, Via delle Donzelle, ✆ 0577 280 358 (*cheap*) is also pleasant.

Antica Botteganova, Strada Chiantigiana 29, ✆ 0577 284 230 (*expensive*), just outside Siena on the road to Gaiole (SS408), offers earthy Sienese cooking, such as veal cooked in Chianti Classico, at reasonable prices. *Closed Sun.* **Al Marsili**, Via del Castoro 3, just off the Piazza del Duomo, ✆ 0577 47154 (*expensive*) is another of Siena's best, in a singularly elegant setting—not very traditional, with dishes like gnocchi in duck sauce, but it's hard to complain. *Closed Mon.*

Tullio ai Tre Cristi, ✆ 0577 280 608 (*moderate*) has been on Vicolo Provenzano, near San Francesco, since about 1830; perhaps the most authentic of Sienese restaurants, its menu includes things like *ribollita*, tripe with sausages, and roast boar from the Maremma. *Closed Mon.* **Osteria le Logge**, Via del Porrione 33, just off the Campo, ✆ 0577 48013 (*moderate*) serves succulent *risotti* and pasta, as well as exotic *secondi* like *faraona* (stuffed guinea-fowl) and a fine wine list; it has been a popular tourist haunt for years. *Closed Sun.*

There are plenty of pizzerias and some cheap trattorias, many of them a little way away from the Campo. Not far from the Palazzo Pubblico, however, is **La Torre**, Via Salicotto 17, ✆ 0577 287 548 (*cheap*), a fun, lively place, popular with students. **Il Cavallino Bianco**, Via di Città 20, ✆ 0577 44258 (*cheap*) serves regional food and pizza, but its main bonus is that it stays open until late. *Closed Wed.*

The **Malborghetto**, Via Porta Giustizia 6, ✆ 0577 289 258 (*cheap*), on the Piazza del Mercato, is also a pleasant pizzeria; tables outside have a fine view of the rear of the Palazzo Pubblico. **Osteria La Chiacchiera**, Via Costa Sant'Antonio 4, ✆ 0577 280 631 (*cheap*) is a friendly little trattoria serving traditional Sienese cooking: *pici*, *ribollita*, kidneys, cockscombs (*cibreo*), tripe, hearty stews or a simple *bistecca*.

The Southern Hill Towns

Southern Tuscany may not be exactly what you think. There will still be plenty of typical, carefully tended Tuscan farmland, arranged as if by an artist with every garden, orchard, wood and vineyard in its proper place, but among the variety of landscapes in this small corner of Italy you will find marshland and rugged hills, and even lonely, deserted corners like the half-eroded heaths the Tuscans call the *Crete*. Some of the hill towns in this region go back to the Etruscans, and many can show you fine buildings and works of art from the age of the *comuni* or the Renaissance. Any number of them would make memorable day trips from Siena on the way to Rome or the coast.

West of Siena

Getting Around

Buses run to most villages in the region from Piazza San Domenico in Siena (*see* above). To get to San Gimignano it's possible to take a **train** to Poggibonsi (on the Empoli–Siena line) and then a bus from there, but it can be quicker just to take a bus direct from Siena. There is no rail service to Volterra, but an infrequent branch line service runs from Cecina on the coast to nearby Saline di Volterra.

However, there are frequent bus services to Florence, Pisa, Siena and Massa Marittima, all from Piazza XX Settembre in Volterra. **Parking** is difficult in most of these towns, but, as in San Gimignano, there are usually large car parks on the perimeter roads around the *centro storico*, and it's best to walk in from there.

Tourist Information

San Gimignano: Piazza del Duomo 1, ✆ 0577 940 008.
Volterra: Via G. Turazza 2, ✆ 0588 86150, behind the Duomo.

Colle di Val d'Elsa

This lovely village, set along a steep ridge, makes a perfect introduction to the hill towns. Though it has scarcely more than 10,000 people, Colle di Val d'Elsa boasts a wall with a grand Renaissance gate on the Volterra road, a 16th-century **cathedral** and three museums, including the **Museo d'Arte Sacra** (*open Oct–Mar Tues–Fri 3.30–5.30, weekends and holidays 10–12 and 3.30–6.30; April–Sept Tues–Fri 5–7, weekends and holidays 10–12 and 4–7; adm*), in the old bishop's palace, with Sienese and Florentine works in addition to the frescoes commissioned by a jolly 14th-century bishop—no martyrs or crucifixions, but scenes of the hunt.

Colle di Val d'Elsa was the birthplace of Arnolfo di Cambio, the master architect of Florence; his house is marked with a plaque. On the way to the town from Siena, the *Autostradale* passes **Monteriggioni**, an old Sienese castle with huge towers mentioned by Dante, and nearby **Abbadia a Isola** up in the hills, with frescoes from the late 1400s.

San Gimignano

In many of the smaller towns of Italy you can sense a false start, a free, self-reliant *comune* of the Middle Ages that could build a wall and defend itself, yet eventually found itself lacking either the money or the will to turn itself into a Florence or a Siena. When they ceased to grow, many crystallized into their medieval form and never changed. None did this more completely than San Gimignano. Approaching the town the startling skyline can be seen poking out from the surrounding hills from miles away: a dozen, lofty square towers, some over 148ft tall, haphazardly arranged like the boxy skyscrapers of a Dallas or Calgary.

The main museums and attractions of San Gimignano offer a *biglietto cumulativo* giving admission to all of them for L16,000. They also all operate the same opening times (*currently open April–Sept daily 9.30–7.30; Mar and Oct Tues–Sun 9.30–5.30; Nov–Feb Tues–Sun 9.30–12.30 and 2.30–5.30*), but these vary from year to year.

The Palazzo del Popolo

Unlike its 20th-century imitators, San Gimignano is an utterly charming town. Since the Middle Ages its population has dwindled to less than 9000, and those that are left are kept busy feeding day-trippers from Florence. Its medieval beauty and serenity have made San Gimignano perhaps the trendiest tourist destination in Tuscany (seven hotels, all three-star) but it wears its strange fate well.

The usual entrance is the southern **Porta San Giovanni**, at Piazza Martiri di Montemaggio, where you can park your car. Going up through the walls into the old town, Via San Giovanni leads you past another ancient gate, the Arco dei Bacci, to the church of San Giovanni, a Pisan-style building constructed for the Knights Templar, and then to the triangular Piazza della Cisterna, with the town's well and a few of its medieval towers. If you can imagine it, San Gimignano in the 13th century was said to have had 76 of these family fortresses. Pisa's and Florence's numbered in the hundreds. Most cities eventually made regulations against them, or demolished them. For whatever reason, San Gimignano was a special case; even in the 1400s it was known as the 'city of towers'.

By city ordinance none could be taller than the 164ft **Torre della Rognosa**, part of the **Palazzo del Podestà** on the adjacent Piazza del Duomo. This was a Ghibelline tower; Frederick II built it and the Palazzo as the seat of the imperial officials. Civic pride, however, dictated an even taller one be built for the **Palazzo del Popolo**, designed perhaps by Arnolfo di Cambio in about 1300.

The tower remains San Gimignano's tallest, and the only one you may climb; the Palazzo also has a beautiful, rustic-looking courtyard with bits of frescoes surviving around its walls, and upstairs the **Museo Civico**, with an *Annunciation* by Filippo Lippi and other works by Florentine and Sienese artists. Other rooms of the Palazzo have interesting frescoes, including the Sala di Dante, an audience hall so called because Dante once spoke here, as a Florentine ambassador attempting to talk the citizens into joining the Guelph League. Dante wasn't the only Florentine to pay a call; in the quattrocento San Gimignano seems to have been almost a kind of resort for the big city; besides the artists who left behind so many fine works, Savonarola, Machiavelli and others all spent time here.

The Collegiata

This is the name of San Gimignano's biggest church (1466–70), plain on the outside but a delightful, smaller version of Siena's cathedral within: the same striped arches, starry vaults, and a superlative collection of frescoes on its walls, including a *Crucifixion* by Barna di Siena full of angels, devils, evil Romans and fainting women, among other New and Old Testament scenes, and a *Last Judgement* by Taddeo di Bartolo.

A ticket from the Museo Civico will get you into the **Capella di Santa Fina**, with an introduction to what is surely the most moronic saint story in all Italy. There are many competitors for this honour, but consider little Fina going to the well for water, and accepting an orange from a young swain. When she returned home, her mother told her how wicked she was to take it, and the poor girl became so mortified over her great sin that she lay down on the table and prayed for forgiveness without ceasing for five years. After this, St Gregory appeared to call her soul to heaven, and the table burst into bloom with violets. Domenico Ghirlandaio got the commission to paint all this; he pocketed the money and did a splendid job, with sweet faces and springtime colours. Note San Gimignano's famous towers in the background.

In a courtyard to the left of the Collegiata, the **baptistry** has another work of Ghirlandaio, an *Annunciation*. The **Museo d'Arte Sacra e Museo Etrusco** occupy two sides of the courtyard—one with more 13th–15th-century sculpture, painting and illuminated choir books, and the other with finds from Etruscan tombs excavated in the area.

Behind the Collegiata, you can walk around the half-ruined fortress, the **Rocca**, or else continue northwards to Piazza Sant'Agostino and **Sant'Agostino**, famous for a series of frescoes by Benozzo Gozzoli on the life of St Augustine. The merriest of all Renaissance painters has a good time with this one, as shown in the charming panel where the master of grammar comes to drag sullen little Augustine off to school.

Lastly, also included in the *biglietto cumulativo* is an **ornithological museum**, a fairly fusty collection of stuffed birds bequeathed to the town by a local aristocrat in 1919, and housed in the **Oratory of St Francis**, with some 16th-century frescoes by Lorenzo Ciardi, in Via Queccerchio below the Rocca.

Volterra

Volterra has a talent for making visitors a bit uneasy. Its situation, among bleak, windy hills, could be the scene for some medieval Tuscan Wuthering Heights. The city itself seems taciturn and grey, brooding on its ancient memories. *Velathri* was a powerful city, the north-western corner of the Etruscan Dodecapolis. Its 5.5km circuit of walls encloses an area three times the size of the present town.

Volterra's periphery is as interesting as the town itself; besides the **Etruscan walls**, traceable for most of their length, there are the *balze*, the barren, eroded ravines that probably began as Etruscan mining cuts. They have already swallowed up medieval churches and exposed some ancient ruins, and they are still growing. It was this erosion that led to the discovery of the Etruscan necropoli around Volterra.

Not many substantial ruins have survived, but you can see the remains of a **Roman theatre** and **baths** just outside the northern wall by the Porta Fiorentina, and also some ruins in the 'archaeological park' near the **Fortezza Medicea**, a big castle built in the 1470s on what was the Etruscan acropolis. Just to the north of the fortress, the **Museo Etrusco Guarnacci**, Via Don Minzoni (*open 16 Mar–30 Oct daily 9–7; rest of the year daily 9–2; adm exp; joint ticket with the other museums*) has a huge collection of funerary urns found in the *balze* tombs since the 1700s. Most of them, with the familiar reclining figures of the deceased on top, are carved with battle scenes or images from Greek mythology.

Volterra's most conspicuous ancient relic, however, is the **Etruscan arch** in the southern wall, over Via Porta all'Arco. Much rebuilt in Roman times, the gate has three black stone protuberances, once probably images of the Etruscan versions of Jupiter, Juno and Minerva, now completely worn away. Near the other end of Via Porta all'Arco, Piazza dei Priori is the medieval centre, with the 1208 **Palazzo dei Priori**, the oldest town hall in Tuscany.

The imperial **Palazzo Pretorio** is nearly as old; around the corner on Via Sarti, the **Pinacoteca Comunale** (*open Tues–Sun 9–7; Nov–15 Mar 9–1; adm*) has a small collection of very fine 15th-century paintings, including a great *Annunciation* by Luca Signorelli, though the prize of the collection is the precise, intense and unforgettable *Deposition* (1521) by Rosso Fiorentino, a seminal work on the threshold between the Renaissance and Mannerism.

Behind Piazza dei Priori is the 15th-century **cathedral**, standing behind a large octagonal baptistry from the 1280s; inside the Duomo, in a chapel off the left aisle, is a fresco of the Three Kings by Gozzoli and a tabernacle over the high altar by Mino da Fiesole. In the **Museo d'Arte Sacra** (*open daily 9–1; 16 Mar–Oct daily 9–1 and 3–6; adm exp*), you can see a della Robbia bust of Volterra's patron, San Lino (Linus), successor to Peter as bishop of Rome—the first pope. Etruscan and Roman Volterra made its living by mining; one of the most important resources was alabaster, still one of the mainstays of the local economy. Volterra is full of workshops where artists turn this luminous stone into vases and figurines—some of the work is very good. You can seek out the shops yourself (they are everywhere; just look for the coating of fine white dust on the buildings) or stop at the artists' co-operative on Via Turazza.

Massa Marittima and San Galgano

South of Volterra, along the SS439, you'll pass over one of the loneliest and least-known corners of Italy. The **Colline Metallifere**, as the name implies, have been attractive to miners (and nobody else) since Etruscan times. The iron the Etruscans found here and on the nearby island of Elba made them rich; today the ore is mostly worked out, but there is still plenty of borax and other minerals. After the pass called **Ala dei Diavoli**, the 'Devil's wing', you can detour west on to the SS398 to see the real kingdom of borax at **Lago Boracifero**, near Monterotondo Marittimo. It's a bizarre landscape, and it smells bad too; miniature geysers and steamy pits bubble up boric salts amid grey and yellow slag piles. Lately it's been looking even stranger. In places the ground has become covered with webs of steampipes, ever since the *comune* discovered its geothermal resources could power everything in town almost for free.

Across the metal hills, **Massa Marittima** is the unlikely setting for one of Tuscany's finest cathedrals, a big 13th-century Pisan Romanesque building set on a stepped pedestal at the end of a broad piazza. There is a beautiful altarpiece in one of the chapels, a *Madonna della Grazie* attributed to Duccio; the tomb of San Cerbone, Massa's patron, is down in the crypt, with 14th-century reliefs of the saint's life.

Massa has three museums: the well-organized but not especially interesting Museo Archeologico and the small Pinacoteca are both situated in the 1230 Palazzo del Podestà (*open April–Sept Tues–Sun 10–12.30 and 3.30–7; Oct–Mar Tues–Sun 9–1 and 3–5; adm*). The art gallery has another notable *Madonna*, by Ambrogio Lorenzetti. The Mining Museum, in an old quarry on the edge of town, is currently closed for restoration.

If you take the SS441/SS73 road between Massa Marittima and Siena be sure not to miss the ruined abbey of **San Galgano**, about halfway in between, near the village of Monticiano. A Cistercian community from France settled here in the 1100s, and work commenced in 1218 on what must have been the grandest purely French Gothic building in Italy.

The monastery was dissolved in the 1600s, and since then the roof and the marble façade have gone, leaving as romantic a ruin as you could ask for: beautiful pointed arches and stone columns, with grass for a pavement and the sky for a roof. Parts of the vaulting remain and, besides the romanticism, San Galgano affords a rare opportunity to look at the bare structure of a Gothic building; it will increase your appreciation of the 13th century.

The Sword in the Stone

On some of the altarpieces in churches and museums in Siena you may have noticed the odd figure of a saint in what appears to be a scene from the *Morte d'Arthur*. This is San Galgano, a dissolute young soldier who received a vision of St Michael and thrust his sword into a stone, leaving his old ways to become a holy hermit. As Michael directed, after Galgano's death a circular chapel was built around the sword.

This is the **Cappella di Montesiepi**, on a hill above San Galgano abbey, and here you will find the sword still in its stone, sticking up from the pavement in the centre of the chapel. Whatever role this legend had in someone's religious secret agenda, like all the sites associated with St Michael it is exceedingly strange, a relic from the great age of western mysticism. There are some frescoes by Ambrogio Lorenzetti on the saint's life, but note also the strange shallow dome, done in 22 concentric stripes of brick and stone and probably representing the heavenly spheres of the medieval cosmology, as in the famous fresco in Pisa's Campo Santo.

San Gimignano ✉ 53037

The **★★★Leon Bianco** is an excellent hotel on Piazza della Cisterna ✆ 0577 941 294 (*moderate*). If you would prefer the tranquillity of the very lovely countryside, **★★★Le Renaie**, north of town at Pancole, is about 7km towards Certaldo, ✆ 0577 955 044 (*moderate*), and has a garden, pool and tennis. Friendly **Locanda Il Pino**, Via Cellolese 4, ✆ 0577 940 415 (*moderate–cheap*) has comfortable, high-quality rooms. Its restaurant (*moderate*) offers traditional Tuscan food, with the usual emphasis on game and fairly heavy dishes. **Convento di Sant'Agostino**, Piazza Sant'Agostino, ✆ 0577 940 383 (*cheap*), a religious house, rents out basic but atmospheric rooms (to men and women, including couples) subject to certain restrictions, such as a curfew.

One of San Gimignano's most popular and memorable restaurants is **Le Terrazze** in the Hotel La Cisterna, Piazza Cisterna, ✆ 0577 940 328 (*expensive*). The *medaglione al Vinsanto* is a surprise treat, or else try the *osso buco alla toscana* or *zuppa sangimignese*. *Closed Tues eve and Wed lunch.* **Osteria delle Catene**, Via Mainardi 18, ✆ 0577 941 966 (*moderate*) has good regional food: *ribollita alla sangimignese*. *Closed Wed.* The **Taverna Paradiso**, Via San Giovanni 6, ✆ 0577 940 302 (*cheap*) is a simple enjoyable pizzeria. *Closed Fri.* The **Gelateria di Piazza**, in Piazza Cisterna, is an award-winning *gelateria*, whose luscious ice-creams are among the best in Italy.

Volterra ✉ 56048

★★★Villa Nencini, Borgo S. Stefano, ✆ 0588 86386 (*moderate*) is a 16th-century villa with lovely views, just north of the city centre. Within the walls, the **★★★★San Lino**, Via San Lino 26, near Porta San Francesco, ✆ 0588 85250 (*moderate*) has quite simple accommodation, despite its star rating, but is the only place with parking. Closer to the centre, the **★★★Etruria**, Via Matteotti 32, ✆ 0588 87377 (*moderate*) has one of Volterra's best restaurants—offering roast boar and game dishes in season.

Restaurants in Volterra specialize in roast boar and the like, good medieval cuisine entirely in keeping with the spirit of the place. **Il Porcellino**, Vicolo delle Prigioni 8, ✆ 0588 86392 (*moderate*) combines seafood and familiar Tuscan favourites with local treats like roast pigeon and boar with olives. *Closed Tues.* For a quick bite, **Taverna dei Priori**, Via G. Matteotti 19, ✆ 0588 86180 (*cheap*), essentially a *tavola calda*, has sandwiches, salads and cooked food. *Closed Wed.*

Massa Marittima ✉ 58024

Massa is increasingly popular as a place to stay—especially with the Germans and the Swiss—and its few hotels are often full. **★★Duca del Mare**, Via D. Alighieri 1, ✆ 0566 902 284 (*cheap*), and **★★Girafalco** on Via Massentana, ✆ 0566 902 177 (*cheap*), are both just below the town centre, with gardens and fine views. In town, **★Cris**, ✆ 0566 903 830, Via degli Albizzeschi (*cheap*) is still cheaper, and adequate. Try the **Taverna del Vecchio Borgo**, Via Butigni 12, ✆ 0566 903 950 (*moderate*), which has an extensive list of *grappas*. Nearby in Località Ghirlanda, **Da Bracali** ✆ 0566 902 318 (*moderate*) offers variations on the local cooking, and some seafood dishes. *Closed Mon evenings and Tues.*

Getting Around

There are regular **buses** from Siena to most destinations in the area. The only town directly accessible by **train** is Chiusi, on the Florence–Rome line, which also has good bus connections to Chianciano and Montepulciano. There is a railway station called Montepulciano, but it is 10km northeast of the town, and only very local trains stop.

Tourist Information

Chianciano: Piazza Italia 67, © 0578 63167.
Abbadia San Salvatore: Via Mentana 95, © 0577 778 608.

Monte Oliveto Maggiore and Montalcino

As the SS2 rolls towards Rome it passes through another empty region of chalk hills and cliffs called the *Crete*. East of the highway, **Asciano** is a medieval walled village with another small collection of Sienese artists in its Museo d'Arte Sacra (*entrance on request, © 0577 718 207*), next to the Collegiata church.

Some 9km to the south, the **Monte Oliveto Maggiore** monastery complex was founded by Giovanni Tolomei, a member of one of Siena's leading families who abandoned banking and civic strife for the life of a hermit. With such backing it comes as no surprise that Monte Oliveto became one of the most elegant retreats in Tuscany. A few fortunate monks—artisans who specialize in the restoration of old books—still keep the place going. Set in a striking grove of cypresses, something of an oasis among the bare chalk hills, the monastery has a lovely fortress-gate decorated with della Robbia terracottas, a simple, exceptionally well-proportioned early 15th-century church, and a library with some skilful wooden *intarsia* pictures by Giovanni da Verona.

The real prize, though, is the **great cloister**, with a cycle of 36 frescoes (*currently undergoing a much-needed restoration*) from the life of St Benedict, whose monastic rule Giovanni Tolomei and his new Olivetan order were attempting to restore in all its purity. Nine are by Luca Signorelli; they show the artist's usual perfection of line and characteristic colouring. The rest are the work of Sodoma, seemingly attempting to work in the style of Signorelli, but with a Mannerist tendency to more excited poses and expressions, extravagant architectural backgrounds, and the inclusion of his badger and other pets in the scenes.

South of the monastery, **Montalcino**, an easy day trip from Siena by bus, has a strong castle, the Rocca, that was the last word in 14th-century military architecture. It defended the town well. After the siege of Siena in 1552, a party of bitter-enders escaped here to found the 'Republic of Siena at Montalcino'—perhaps the first ever republican government-in-exile. With the help of the Rocca they held out for several years against the minions of Spain and the Medici, one of the last strongholds of Italian liberty.

Today the town is better known for its red wines, the dark, pungent *Brunello* and the slightly less prestigious but also very good *Rosso di Montalcino*, some of Tuscany's best. There is also a good collection of Sienese painting in Montalcino, in the **Museo Civico e Diocesano**, just reopened after restoration (*open summer Tues–Sun 9.30–1 and 3.30–7; winter Tues–Sun 10–1 and 3–5; adm*), in Piazza Cavour, and just south of the town another abandoned monastery, the 12th-century **Abbazia di Sant'Antimo**. It has left behind an especially beautiful Romanesque church, with a luminous interior partially done in alabaster. Another good Romanesque church, from the 1080s, can be seen in the nearby village of **San Quirico**, back on the main road.

Pienza

Italians like to carry on, more perhaps than is necessary, about Pienza, a small town in the sheep country east of Montalcino that became one of the most characteristic early-Renaissance experiments in architecture and design. Before 1460 it was only the humble little village of Corsignano, but in that year Pope Pius II (Aeneas Sylvius Piccolomini) decreed that the town of his birth was to be glorified into a city of art, which he modestly renamed after himself. The new city got off to a flying start with Pius' commissioning of Bernardo Rossellino to design a cathedral and palace around a central piazza.

The **cathedral** has a simple three-arched entrance, decorated only with the Piccolomini arms and the keys of St Peter; ironically the best features are pure Gothic in inspiration, high pointed vaulting and some pretty traceried windows. They chose a bad spot for it; the cathedral has been settling and threatening to collapse since it was built, and occasionally sulphur fumes seep out of the floor. Around the cathedral square (Piazza Pio II), Rossellino's **Palazzo Piccolomini** (*open April–Sept daily 10–12.30 and 3–6; Oct–Mar daily 10–12.30 and 2–4; adm*) is nearly a copy of Alberti's design for the Rucellai Palace in Florence, which Rossellino helped build. The best part is around the back, a three-storey loggia and a garden.

The Piccolomini had large estates around Pienza; Aeneas Silvius was born here only because the family had temporarily exiled itself from Siena, after a revolt that excluded nobles from public office. Several other palaces went up in the wake of the Piccolomini, including the **Palazzo dei Canonici**; most of its contents are displayed in the new **Museo Diocesano**, Corso Rossellini (*open daily 10–1 and 2–6; adm*), which also contains an important collection of paintings, sculptures and tapestries. Pienza never fulfilled the ambitions of its founder; today it is just another Tuscan village known for its piazza and also for its *cacio*; the self-proclaimed 'Capital of Sheep Cheese' has been making it since the days of the Etruscans.

Montepulciano

Inhabitants of this town, the Roman *Mons Politianus*, are called *Poliziani*, and that is the name by which we know its most famous son. Angelo Ambrogini, as Poliziano, was a favourite at the court of Lorenzo the Magnificent and one of the greatest classical scholars of his day, as well as a playwright and poet (Botticelli's mythological paintings may have been inspired by his *Stanze per la Giostra*).

Like Pienza, Montepulciano has its share of Renaissance monuments, most notably Antonio da Sangallo's church of **San Biagio** (1518), 1km south of the town in the countryside. This superb though unfinished building captures some of the highest aspirations of Renaissance architecture. The graceful loggia of the adjacent **Canonica** (parish house), also by Sangallo, makes a fitting architectural complement.

In the town, the also unfinished **Duomo** has a beautiful altarpiece by Taddeo di Bartolo, and other works by Florentine and Sienese artists. The two cities fought over Montepulciano for centuries. Florence finally prevailed in both politics and art; the **Palazzo Comunale** (begun *c.* 1360), facing the Duomo, is a smaller copy of Florence's Palazzo Vecchio, with a façade by the Florentine Michelozzo, who also contributed a fine Renaissance façade for **Sant'Agostino** on Via Sangallo.

In the 16th century the town became something like Florence's southern outpost, and was equipped by the city's favoured architects, Sangallo the Younger and Vignola, with a set of walls, public buildings and palazzi. Today they exude a rather faded grandeur, and seem quite out of proportion for a small town. There are plenty of good palaces, several by Sangallo, along the main street, the Corso. Note his **Palazzo Bucelli** at No.73, with a foundation made entirely of carved Etruscan burial urns, filled with cement and stacked like bricks. Montepulciano is also much visited today for its powerful red wine, *Vino Nobile di Montepulciano*, which is on sale at any number of *enoteche* run by the producers themselves all around the town.

South of Montepulciano, **Chianciano Terme** is a large, bright and busy spa, whose motto *Chianciano—fegato sano* (Chianciano for a healthy liver) draws in many an imbibing Tuscan for an annual flush. It's not only the perfect cure for too much *Vino Nobile*, but usually has overnight accommodation in a pinch.

Chiusi

If anyone ever read you Lord Macaulay's rouser about Horatio at the Bridge when you were a child you will remember the fateful name Lars Porsena of Clusium, leading the Etruscan confederation to besiege Rome in the brave days of old. Thanks to Horatio, of course, Rome survived and made a name for itself; you can come here to see what happened to Clusium—or *Camars* as the Etruscans actually called it.

Modern Chiusi isn't much, but it has a market on Mondays and a first-class archaeological museum, the **Museo Nazionale Etrusco** (*open Mon–Fri 9–2, Sat and Sun 9–1; adm*), with lots of burial urns—many decorated with scenes from Homer—and examples of the black pottery called *bucchero* that was an Etruscan speciality. Several tombs can be visited off the road to Chianciano Terme; the **Tombe delle Scimmie**, which has some wall paintings, is the most interesting.

From Chiusi, the SS478 will take you back southwestwards to the southern end of Siena province, passing **Radicofani**, a startling sight with its tall castle perched atop a weirdly eroded barren hill. Further south comes the region of **Monte Amiata**, Tuscany's highest peak (5701ft), with Europe's second largest mercury mine; Amiata is an extinct volcano, and full of unusual minerals. There is a small ski resort at **Abbadia San Salvatore**, as well as the remains of a 12th-century Cistercian abbey that was the predecessor to San Galgano.

The southernmost corner of Tuscany is a strange and empty quarter, thriving in the days of the Etruscans but at no time since. Ruins of Etruscan tombs and walls can be seen at **Saturnia** and **Pitigliano**; the synagogue in Pitigliano is also worth a visit. **Sorano**, north of Pitigliano, is the natural conclusion to this somewhat disturbing region; it is almost a ghost town, most of it abandoned after landslides in the 1920s.

Almost every town in this southern hill country has rooms to rent: ask around. Chianciano Terme has a number of fairly stuffy spa hotels.

Montalcino ✉ 53024

Just outside Montalcino, ★★★**Al Brunello**, in Loc. Bellaria, ℭ 0577 849 304 (*moderate*) is an attractive place to stay in a garden setting. Near Montalcino, **Il Pozzo**, Piazza del Pozzo, in Loc. S. Angelo in Colle, ℭ 0577 864 015 (*moderate*) is worth a detour for a full-blown traditional meal at a very reasonable price. Sample glasses of *Brunello* with a plate of excellent ham, cheese or sandwiches, at the **Fiaschetteria Italiana**, Montalcino's ornate and wonderfully preserved 19th-century café, with tables on the main square, the Piazza del Popolo.

Pienza ✉ 53026

There is only one hotel as such, the simple but comfortable ★★★**Corsignano**, Via della Madonnina, ℭ 0578 748 501 (*moderate*); rooms are also available at the **Ristorante dal Falco**, Piazza Dante, ℭ 0578 748 551.

Montepulciano ✉ 53045

The rather elegant 16th-century ★★**Marzocco**, ℭ 0578 757 262, near the centre, is the best of Montepulciano's few hotels. Two good restaurants are the **Cittino**, on Vicola Via Nuova, ℭ 0578 757 335 (*moderate*), and the **Trattoria Diva**, Via Gracciano nel Corso 92, ℭ 0578 716 951 (*moderate–cheap*). You can have a tasty light lunch for L20,000 at the **Osteria dell'Aquacheta** on Via del Teatro (about halfway up the Corso), or at the **Caffè Poliziano** on the Corso—an establishment worth visiting at least for a cup of coffee to enjoy the towering views.

However, the best restaurants are outside town. In Montefollonico, a lovely village with panoramic views back towards Montepulciano, **La Chiusa**, located in an old *frantoio* (olive press) in Via Madonnina, ℭ 0577 669 668 (*very expensive*) has been acclaimed as the best restaurant in southern Tuscany, with a seven-course *menu degustazione* and an exhaustive wine list. *Closed Tues.*

Chiusi makes a good stop for lunch if you're travelling between Florence and Rome; at **Zaira**, Via Arunte 12, ℭ 0578 20260 (*moderate*), there are rabbit, duck and game dishes on the menu, accompanied by a good wine list. *Closed Mon.*

From Florence to Arezzo

Like all the northern part of Arezzo province, the routes along the Arno are lined with typically Tuscan small towns that managed not to be left behind in the Middle Ages. On the contrary, it is a highly industrialized region; lignite and felt hats are important, but new factories and power lines seem to be going up all the time. At **Incisa Val d'Arno** the cliffs close in towards the river; from here you have the choice of the fast route, the A1 *autostrada* direct to Arezzo, or dallying through the pretty villages in the hills above either bank of the Arno along the SS69.

San Giovanni Valdarno, the birthplace of Masaccio and a long-time Florentine fortress on the border with hostile Arezzo, is the largest and perhaps most interesting town in this area, with its arcaded piazza around the Palazzo Comunale, a building thought to be the work of Florence's Arnolfo di Cambio. The loggias that surround it are covered with the coats of arms of its Florentine governors. In the 15th-century **Basilica di Santa Maria delle Grazie** there is a priceless *Annunciation* by Fra Angelico, an early work that seems like a study for his famous Annunciation at San Marco in Florence.

In **Montevarchi**, there is a little museum where you can see a mastodon skeleton, a relic of the area's prehistory. **Terranuova Bracciolini** is an old Aretine fortress town, its walls still standing. In the hills north of the Arno, **Loro Ciuffena** and **Castiglion Fibbochi** are two more typical, pretty towns where little has changed—save the industry around the outskirts— since the 16th century. **Grópina**, near Loro Ciuffena, has a Romanesque church with a truly bizarre relic of the Dark Ages: a stone pulpit carved with wolves, eagles and unusual patterns; it may be from the time of the Lombards or even earlier.

Arezzo

Compared with the other cities of Tuscany, Arezzo looks a little down-at-heel and rustic, as if the art and sophistication of the Renaissance had somehow passed it by. The medieval air is part of its charm, and easily explainable: Arezzo lost its prosperity along with its independence when Florence annexed it in 1384. The lack of fine buildings, however, conceals a mildly glorious past. Arezzo was one of the richest cities of the Etruscan Dodecapolis; the famous bronze chimaera in the Florence archaeology museum was found here. The long list of famous Aretini begins in Roman times with Maecenas, the fabulously wealthy friend of Augustus and patron of Horace and Virgil. In the Middle Ages Arezzo was a typical free *comune*, a rival to Florence and a city of great cultural distinction. Guido d'Arezzo, the inventor of musical notation and the scale, was born here, as was Petrarch. Later came Giorgio Vasari and Pietro Aretino, the uninhibited writer and poet whose celebrated poison pen allowed him to make a fortune by *not* writing about contemporary princes and popes—the most genteel extortionist of all time. In the game of Tuscan power politics Arezzo was at its strongest in the early 14th century, under the rule of a remarkable series of warrior-bishops, of whom the best remembered is the fierce Guido Tarlati (d. 1327).

Today Arezzo is a very prosperous place. It should be, having perhaps the biggest jewellery industry in Europe, with hundreds of firms stamping out chains and rings, and bank vaults full of gold ingots. The old centre, however, hasn't really shared in this prosperity. Most people have moved out, and more and more shop fronts are given over to the city's other industry— antiques. Arezzo has become a curiosity shop, especially during the **antiques fairs**, held on the first Sunday of every month in Piazza Grande. It has also found a new role as a film set, providing a picturesque setting for Roberto Benigni's *La Vita e Bella*.

Getting Around

From Florence, Perugia and Cortona, the **train** is the easiest way to reach Arezzo; the station is at the southern end of town, where Via Guido Monaco crosses Viale Piero della Francesca and the old city walls. Many smaller towns, such as San Giovanni Valdarno, Poppi,

Bibbiena, Sansepolcro and Castiglion Fiorentino can also be easily reached by train. **Buses** for Cortona and other towns in Arezzo province, as well as for Siena, leave from the bus station, directly opposite the railway station on Viale Piero della Francesca, © 0575 382 169. Schedules are posted for all lines.

Tourist Information

Piazza della Repubblica 28, © 0575 377 678.

The Piazza Grande

The medieval-looking houses around **Piazza Grande** make a perfect setting for Arezzo's annual medieval festival, the *Giostra del Saracino*, in early September, where the colourful old costumes are dusted off and the town sports tilt at a wooden figure called the 'King of the Indies'. The antiques fairs are also held here. Giorgio Vasari built the long **Loggia** in the manner of an ancient Greek stoa, and contributed the clock tower to the **Palazzo della Fraternità dei Laici**, an odd building, half-Gothic and half by Bernardo Rossellino. If you thought this was the town hall, you've been fooled. The palazzo is really the home of a layman's brotherhood founded in the 1200s, and Arezzo's old Palazzo del Popolo exists only in ruins, behind Vasari's Loggia on Via dei Pileati. Like Pisa's, it was destroyed by the Florentines after they captured the city.

Also on Via dei Pileati, the **Casa di Petrarca** is a replacement for the original, destroyed during the Second World War; it stands near the 14th-century **Palazzo Pretorio**, decked with the coats of arms of imperial and Florentine governors. One block south you'll see the singular façade of Arezzo's finest church, **Santa Maria della Pieve**. This church turns its back on Piazza Grande, showing only a graceful arched apse. In the front, a distinctive irregular campanile and four levels of columns make a unique mountaineer's version of the Pisan-Luccan Romanesque style, done in rough-hewn stone with hardly any two columns or capitals alike. Under the arch at the front portal, note the interesting early medieval reliefs of the 12 months: April with its flowers, February with its pruning hook, and the pagan two-headed god Janus for January. The interior is dim and stark, but there is a good altarpiece by Pietro Lorenzetti, with a Madonna and saints modelling Tuscan fashions of the 14th century.

The Cathedral and Art Museum

Narrow streets from Piazza Grande lead up to the **Passeggio del Prato**, a big, English-style park with lawns and monuments. All of Arezzo slopes gradually upwards from the railway station, ending abruptly here; from the cliffs on the edge of the Prato there is a memorable view over the mountains, extending towards Florence and Urbino. Overlooking the park is a half-ruined Medici fortress of the 16th century; at the other end, you'll see the back of the **cathedral** with a lovely Gothic belltower (less than a hundred years old). This Duomo, built in bits and pieces over the centuries, is worth a look inside for the 16th-century stained glass windows, done by a French master named Guillaume de Marcillat, whose work resembles illuminated frescoes by a Gozzoli or Luca Signorelli. In the north aisle the 1327 **tomb of Bishop Guido Tarlati** is a fascinating early predecessor of the heroic sculptural tombs of the Renaissance, perhaps designed by Giotto; 16 relief panels tell the story of his life, his battles and his good works—all under a big Ghibelline eagle, like a party badge. The Duomo also has terracottas by Andrea della Robbia and a fresco by Piero della Francesca.

From here Via Ricasoli leads west towards the **Museo d'Arte Medievale e Moderna** (*open Mon–Sat 9–7, Sun 9–1; adm*), where you can get to know some good local artists not often seen elsewhere, such as Spinello Aretino, his son, Parri di Spinello, and Bartolomeo della Gatta. Renaissance ceramics from Urbino, Deruta and Montelupo are also well represented. Around the corner on Via XX Settembre you can swallow a heavy load of Mannerist excess at the **Casa di Vasari**. In the frescoes for his own house the indefatigable Vasari and his workshop went far beyond anything they ever did for Duke Cosimo (*open Mon–Sat 9–7, Sun 9–1; ring the bell*).

San Francesco

For many, the real allure of Arezzo is behind the doors of this dowdy, barnlike, typically Franciscan church (*open daily 8.30–12 and 2–6.30*). Beginning in 1452, Piero della Francesca created here one of the greatest of all Renaissance fresco cycles, the *Legend of the Cross*. As with Giotto's cycle at Santa Croce in Florence, the story is taken from Jacopo da Voragine's *Golden Legend*. Though faded, and damaged in many places, the work still shows Piero's use of glowing colours and complex perspectives, especially in such virtuoso achievements, still novel in his day, as night scenes (the *Annunciation* and *Constantine's Dream*) and grimly lifelike portrayals of battles. Even Vasari was impressed, though the best compliment he can manage in the *Lives of the Artists* is that Piero's drawing of horses was 'almost too excellent for those times'.

Out on the southern edge of Arezzo, near the station on Via Margaritone, are the remains of a **Roman amphitheatre**, made into a quiet park. A former monastery, built on a curve over the amphitheatre's foundations, has been restored to house the **Museo Archeologico** (*open Mon–Sat 9–1, Sun 9–1; closed second and third Sun of the month; adm*). Not much has survived from the thriving Etruscan and Roman city of *Arretium*, but there are some mosaics and sarcophagi, Greek vases and Etruscan funerary urns. Finally, you can take a 15-minute walk from Via Mecanate out through Arezzo's southern suburbs to see a simple but exceptionally pretty Renaissance church. **Santa Maria delle Grazie**, built by Benedetto di Maiano in 1470, has a Florentine-style loggia for a porch in front, and a della Robbia tabernacle.

Arezzo ✉ *52100*   **Where to Stay and Eating Out**

Arezzo isn't going to blind you with science in the kitchen, though you can enjoy Tuscany's best railway cuisine in the station bar.

If you're travelling by car, ★★★**Minerva**, Via Fiorentina 4, ✆ 0575 370 390 (*moderate*) may be the most convenient place to stay; it's a few streets west of the city walls, but it has pleasant rooms, an excellent, unpretentious restaurant, and parking. In town most of the rooms available are close to the station.

There is a wonderful view from the roof terrace of the ★★★**Continentale**, Piazza Guido Monaco 7, ✆ 0575 20251 (*moderate*), a fine, older hotel. Its competitor, ★★★**Europa**, Via Spinello 43, ✆ 0575 357 701 (*moderate*), opposite the station, is similarly modern and plain, but many of its rooms have air conditioning. ★★★**Truciolini**, Via Pacinotti 6, ✆ 0575 984 104 (*moderate*) has rooms with air conditioning, and parking.

Budget hotels are cheaper than elsewhere in Tuscany. ***Michelangelo**, Viale Michelangelo 26, ✆ 0575 20673 (*cheap*), near the station, is one of the best: friendly and well-kept. The **youth hostel** is at Via Francesco Redi 16, ✆ 0575 29047 (*cheap*).

One restaurant that tries hard (it even has a piano bar—perhaps a little incongruous after a day in medieval Arezzo) is **Le Tastevin**, Via de' Cenci 9, ✆ 0575 28304 (*moderate*); specialities include a fine *carpaccio*, and good *penne* with pepper sauce, and its cellar features wines from around the world. Tourists favour the **Buca di San Francesco**, Via S. Francesco 1, ✆ 0575 23271 (*moderate*), opposite Piero's frescoes, but don't let that discourage you—it has an honest-to-goodness medieval atmosphere and tasty Tuscan cooking to match, though slightly adapted for the uninitiated.

For a meal in the country, the **Osteria La Capannaccia**, Loc. Campriano 51/c, ✆ 0575 361 759 (*moderate*) is one of the best restaurants nearby, where the specialities are those of the Aretine countryside—simple dishes like *minestra di pane*, roast meats, and wines from the Colli Aretini—at very reasonable prices.

A good, if basic, local trattoria is **La Scaletta**, Piazza del Popolo 1 (*cheap*), right in the centre of Arezzo. **Il Ruspante**, Via Roma 34 (*cheap*) is a good-quality pizzeria with a wood oven.

Around Arezzo

Tourist Information

Bibbiena: Via Berni 29, ✆ 0575 593 098.
Cortona: Via Nazionale 72, ✆ 0575 630 353.

North of Arezzo: the Casentino and the Valtiberina

If you are going to or coming from Florence by car, the SS70 and SS7171 make an attractive alternative route to the *autostrada* up the Arno Valley. This route follows the Arno too, but up to its source and then over the Consuma pass to Florence. It traverses the region called the **Casentino**, a hard-working, backwoods corner of Tuscany full of grapes, olives, small family businesses, chestnut groves, cattle and monasteries.

Starting from Arezzo the first important town is **Bibbiena**, a typical hill town from which you can make a detour to **Chiusi della Verna**, up in a range of hills that bravely calls itself the 'Alpe di Catenaia'. St Francis lived here for many years, as a hermit on the wooded slopes of Monte Penna, and it was here in 1224 that he received the stigmata, an event recorded in the frescoes of the basilica at Assisi and scores of other churches around Italy. **La Verna**, an unusual rocky outcrop 3km above Chiusi della Verna, was the site of his hermitage; a Franciscan sanctuary still occupies the rock. They are always happy to receive visitors; in the Chiesa Maggiore and two smaller chapels you can see one of the largest collections of Andrea della Robbia terracottas—some of his best work, including a brilliant *Annunciation*. From the monastery it is an easy walk through pine groves up to the summit of Monte Penna.

North of Bibbiena the valley road divides. The SS71 northeastwards will take you to another famous monastic retreat, **Camaldoli**, set in thick forests over 3608ft up the mountains, the home of an order founded by San Romualdo in the early 11th century. The monks still live in separate cottages, sworn to complete isolation. The narrower SS70 carries on up the Arno Valley. **Poppi**, 8km up from Bibbiena, is the real attraction of this route: a beautiful little town of arcaded streets and squares with a stalwart, erect Palazzo Pretorio modelled after the Palazzo Vecchio in Florence.

From Bibbiena the road past Chiusi della Verna leads east over the mountains to the next valley, that of the Tiber. Both the Tiber and Arno are near their sources here, and in places they flow less than 15km apart. A few bumpy kilometres south of Chiusi della Verna, **Caprese Michelangelo** does not let any opportunity go by to remind you of its famous son. Besides changing its name, the tiny hamlet has restored the artist's purported birthplace, the old town hall where his father was a Florentine governor. Now a museum (*open on request*), it has full-size reproductions of Michelangelo's works, Michelangelo memorabilia, and questionable tributes from modern sculptors.

Further down the Tiber Valley **Sansepolcro**, similarly, lives on as a shrine to *its* favourite son, Piero della Francesca, with two of his most famous paintings in the town hall's Museo Civico (*open daily 9.30–1 and 2.30–6; until 7.30 in summer; adm exp. The building suffered some damage in the 1997 earthquake, but most rooms are still open*). The *Resurrection*, an intense, almost eerie depiction of the triumphant Christ rising over his tomb and the sleeping soldiers guarding it, shares pride of place with the *Misericordia Polyptych*, a gold-background altar-piece dominated by a giant-sized Madonna, sheltering under her cloak members of the confraternity who commissioned the picture. Other works present are from Luca Signorelli, Pontormo and Matteo di Giovanni; more Renaissance painting, by both Sienese and Florentine artists, can be seen in Sansepolcro's Romanesque **cathedral**. For yet another Piero della Francesca, stop at the cemetery chapel on the SS221 just west of **Monterchi**, south of Sansepolcro near the border with Umbria: his *Madonna del Parto*, a rare portrayal of a weary, pregnant Virgin, is a popular icon for expectant mothers, and the drive there is spectacular, especially when the sunflowers are in bloom.

South of Arezzo: the Valdichiana

Much of this area is a broad plain called the Valdichiana, all swamps and lakes before a 19th-century reclamation plan, and now full of prosperous farms. On both sides you'll find some of the most beautiful villages in this part of Tuscany—none with much history of their own, but comfortable, essentially Tuscan towns worth a stop and a walk around if you're on your way to Rome or Perugia. **Monte San Savino**, the home town of the architect Sansovino, is one of these; he designed the market loggia and other buildings around the town. Nearby **Lucignano** will run you in circles—ellipses really; the village has a unique plan of concentric ellipses, with four picturesque piazzas in the centre. The Palazzo Comunale, now the Museo Civico, has a number of interesting frescoes (*open April–Sept Tues–Sun 9.30–1 and 3–7.30; Oct–Mar Tues–Sun 9.30–1 and 3–6.30; adm*).

Just as distinctive is **Marciano della Chiana**, an old fortress town of gates and towers. Across the Valdichiana, **Castiglion Fiorentino** was known as Castiglion Aretino until the Florentines snatched it in 1384. It, too, has a museum in its Palazzo Comunale, with 15th- and 16th-century art, and some good frescoes in the Collegiata church. The town takes its name from the big castle of **Montecchio** on the opposite hill, a landmark visible all over the Valdichiana, now abandoned. For a while in the 1400s it was the stronghold of the *condottiere* Sir John Hawkwood, he of the famous 'monument' in Florence Cathedral.

Cortona

Cortona may not be entirely undiscovered, but it is still one of the real jewels among the hill towns. Set among terraced slopes covered with olives and vines, almost a kilometre above sea level, it's a web of crooked streets that climb precipitously to the old fortress—even halfway up, if there's a space between the houses, you will be able to see Lake Trasimeno below. Cortona was an Etruscan city, one of the Dodecapolis, and ragged, monolithic Etruscan stonework can still be seen at the foundations of its wall. As a medieval *comune*, it held its own against Siena, Arezzo and Perugia until 1490, when King Ladislas of Naples captured the city and sold it at a good price to the Florentines.

As in Arezzo, Florentine rule meant a long decline for Cortona, and consequently much that is genuinely medieval has survived. Some old streets, like Via del Gesù, have brick or stuccoed houses with the upper floors propped out over the street on timbers—the very picture of an old Italian town from any quattrocento painting. Cortona also retains one superb medieval square, the **Piazza della Repubblica**, an asymmetrical masterpiece of urban design in a very small space. The building with the clock is the 13th-century **Palazzo Comunale**.

Directly behind it, facing the adjacent Piazza Signorelli, the **Palazzo Pretorio** houses the fascinating **Museo dell'Accademia Etrusca** (*open April–Sept Tues–Sun 10–1 and 4–7; Oct–Mar Tues–Sun 9–1 and 3–5; adm*). Not everything here is Etruscan, but the fine Greek vases and Egyptian artefacts testify to the city's wealth and trade contacts long ago. Among the Etruscan art the star exhibit is an odd bronze lamp that looks for all the world like an Aztec calendar stone. There are paintings, too, by Lorenzetti of Siena, Pinturicchio, and Luca Signorelli, born in Cortona.

Behind the Academy, yet another tiny piazza leads to the **Duomo**, rebuilt to an uninteresting design in the 1560s. The **Museo Diocesano** (*open April–Sept Tues–Sun 10–1 and 4–7; Oct–Mar Tues–Sun 9–1 and 3–5; adm*), however, has excellent paintings, including an *Annunciation* by Fra Angelico, who spent 10 years in Cortona, as well as a famous *Deposition* and other works by Luca Signorelli; also some Duccio di Buoninsegna and Pietro Lorenzetti, and a Roman sarcophagus with reliefs of the Battle of Lapiths and Centaurs that was closely studied by Donatello and Brunelleschi.

Up and Down Cortona

If you have the urge to do some climbing you can visit **San Francesco** (1240), where both Luca Signorelli and Brother Elia, St Francis' businesslike successor, are buried. The town's four gates are set at the four points of the compass. The northern **Porte Colonia** has an Etruscan-Roman arch; the southern, on Via Nazionale, has a little terrace with the best view over Lake Trasimeno. Climb higher, to an area within the walls devoted to olives and vegetable gardens, and there will be even better views from the 19th-century **Basilica Santa Margherita** and the overgrown **Medici Fortress** at the top of Cortona's hill, built on the site of the ancient Etruscan acropolis, and a great place for a picnic.

Outside Cortona, down on the plain near the city's modern suburb of Camucia, be sure to stop to see **Santa Maria del Calcinaio** (1485), with elegant Renaissance symmetry by Giorgio Martini, on a simple central plan with an octagonal drum and dome. The stained glass is by Guillaume de Marcillat, who worked at Arezzo Cathedral. Nearby there are some Etruscan tombs: the intriguingly named, circular **Tanella of Pythagoras** and the **Tanella Angori**.

Sansepolcro ✉ 52037

******La Balestra**, Via del Montefeltro 29, ✆ 0575 735 151, ✆ 0575 740 282 (*moderate*) has modern, comfortable rooms and parking, plus an excellent restaurant which offers fine local cooking, with delicious home made pasta; for *secondi* try the lamb chops with zucchini flowers. The ****Orfeo**, Viale Diaz 12, ✆ 0575 742 061 (*cheap*), on the main road around the town walls, is basic but clean and reasonable.

Paola e Marco Mercati dell'Oroscopo, Loc. Pieve Vecchia, ✆ 0575 735 051 (*expensive*) mixes traditional and creative cooking: flamed king prawns in garlic sauce, chocolate tart with zabaglione and mascarpone. They also have a hotel (*moderate*), with 12 rooms. *Open evenings only; closed Sun.* The **Fiorentino**, Via Pacioli 60, ✆ 0575 740 350 (*cheap*) is an excellent-value local restaurant, also an hotel.

Monte San Savino ✉ 52048

******Castello di Gargonza**, 7km west of Monte San Savino off the SS73, ✆ 0575 847 021, ✆ 0575 847 054 (*moderate*) is an entire walled village converted into an hotel, with 20 rooms in restored houses, a pool and forests all around; the restaurant, with local specialities, is also very good.

Cortona ✉ 52044

******Il Falconiere**, 3km away at San Martino a Bocena, ✆ 0575 612 679, ✆ 0575 612 927 (*luxury*) is refined, frescoed and furnished with antiques and canopied beds, as well as a pool and first class restaurant (*expensive*) serving delicious meat and fish dishes. *Closed Wed in winter*. In town, *****San Luca**, Piazza Garibaldi 2, ✆ 0575 630 460 (*moderate*) is simple but comfortable, and many of the rooms have wonderful views. *****Portale**, Via Umbro Cortonese 39, ✆ 0575 691 008 (*moderate*) has a good restaurant. ***Athens** (named after Athens, Georgia, not Greece), Via S. Antonio, ✆ 0575 630 508 (*cheap*) is often packed.

Tonino, Piazza Garibaldi, ✆ 0575 630 500 (*expensive*) is Cortona's most elegant restaurant, with wonderful hot and cold *antipasti*, followed by traditional pasta dishes and the Valdichiana's tender beef. *Closed Mon eve and Tues*. Intimate **La Grotta**, is hidden away off the main square at Piazzetta Baldelli 3, ✆ 0575 630 271 (*expensive–moderate*) and a local favourite. *Closed Tues*. For good, well-prepared fare try **Trattoria dell'Amico**, Via Dardano 12, ✆ 0575 604 192 (*cheap*).

Umbria

The Umbrians tell it this way: in the centre of the world there is a sea, in the centre of the sea lies a peninsula, in the centre of the peninsula there is a region, in the centre of the region there is a town, in the centre of the town there is a bar, in the centre of the bar stands a billiard table, in the centre of the billiard table there are four markers, and in the centre of these markers lies the centre of all creation.

The town is Foligno, and the Umbrians, as unabashedly parochial as only Italians can be, are only partly in jest. Their rural little city-region, the 'Green Heart of Italy', is also her introspective soul, scarcely touched by the onrush of contemporary events. Umbria is rarely in the news; it bowed out of time long ago, a medieval backwater that stagnated for centuries under papal rule. As Americans say of North Carolina, it is 'a vale of humility between two mountains of conceit', and Tuscany and Rome are veritable Everests of conceit, casting long shadows even back in the days of the Umbrii, an Italic tribe that gave the region its name. The Umbrii were best known for their pacifism in a bossy peninsula. Rather than fight the Etruscans, they assimilated their ways, and used their alphabet whenever they had something to say (which, as far as anybody knows, was only once). Later, in the Etruscan twilight, the Umbrii were one of the few tribes passive (or smart) enough to accept the Romans without spilling buckets of blood.

Mild-tempered, isolated from outside influences—Umbria is the only Italian region that neither touches the sea nor shares a frontier with another country—the Umbrians tend to be complacent in their cocoon and conservative in their ways, refusing even to improve the recipe for the medieval paving stones they call bread. But for many this basic lack of interest in the outside world, combined with Umbria's gentle beauty, makes the region an ideal retreat for the spirit. St Francis of Assisi's doctrine of mystical love for all creation seems to come out of the soft bluish-green hills of Umbria, which has proved a fertile land for saints, producing a bumper crop, not only St Francis and St Clare, but St Benedict, the founder of monasticism; St Rita, the saint of impossibilities; and St Valentine, the patron of lovers. Umbrians visit their relics the way we would call on a fond uncle or aunt.

Umbria is lush and green, even in the middle of its blistering summer. Its medieval towns, hilltop tiaras of pinkish-grey stone, are evocative and lovely, and their churches and museums contain artworks that rival those of big sister Tuscany. But perhaps the greatest gift Umbria has to offer to the modern visitor is its stillness. You can see it in the soulful, introspective works of the Umbrian school of painting, in early Peruginos and gilded Pinturicchios—but especially in the paintings of Piero della Francesca, born on the Tuscan-Umbrian frontier, whose figures, having achieved mathematical perfection, are beyond all time. 'Umbria', as the friendly nun said on the bus, 'speaks in silences.'

20 kms
10 miles

N

Urbino

Ancona

Pergola

Sansepolcro

Città di Castello

Pietralunga

Scheggia

MARCHE

Macerata

Gubbio

TUSCANY

Fossato di Vico

Gualdo Tadino

Umbertide

Cortona

Castel Rigone

Passignano

Nocera Umbra

Assisi

Amandola

To Isola Maggiore
Florence
Castiglione d. Lago

Magione

Perugia

St Maria degli Angeli

Ascoli Piceno

Ponte San Giovanni

Torgiano

Spello

Lake Trasimeno

Bettona

Mt Vettore

Fontignano

Deruta

Foligno

Città di Pieve

UMBRIA

Montefalco

Trevi

Castelluccio
Norcia

Marsciano

Piano Grande

Fabro

Tempio del Clitunno

Ficulle

Allerona

Castel Viscardo

Todi

Spoleto

Scheggino

Cascia

Orvieto

Prodo

Lake Corbara

Monteluco

Castel Giorgio

Civitella del Lago

Acquasparta

San Pietro in Valle

Baschi

Carsulae

Bolsena

San Gemini

Torreorsina

Ferentillo

Arrone

Opolino

L. di Bolsena

Lugnano
in Teverina

Terni

Cascata delle Marmore

Labro

Amelia

Piediluco

Penna in Teverina

Narni

Antrodoco

Orte

Rieti

L'Aquila

Viterbo

L. di Vico

(Tiber)

Tevere

LAZIO

L. di Bracciano

Civitavecchia

To Rome

Umbria

659

Not to be Missed

Compact and full of interest, but not really on the way to or from anywhere, Umbria's best sights can be easily visited in a loop. Every tourist office in Umbria distributes a free map showing every one-horse town and backroad—just pick one up and explore. Although repairs are underway after the **September 1997 earthquake**, much of eastern Umbria is still under scaffolding; Foligno and Assisi were hard hit, and if there's something you really want to see, it's best to ring the tourist office ahead to see if it's been reopened.

The big medieval art five—**Perugia**, **Assisi**, **Orvieto**, **Gubbio** and **Spoleto**—are Umbria's top attractions, but the smaller hill towns like **Todi**, **Narni** and **Deruta** are charming destinations as well. Each little town has its treasure—in lovely **Spello** there are frescoes by Pinturicchio; **Città della Pieve** has its Peruginos, and **Montefalco** a magnificent fresco cycle by Gozzoli. The Romans endowed Umbria with a lovely waterfall, the **Cascata delle Marmore**; an ancient spa at **Clitunno**; and an evocative ruined city, **Carsulae**. What the region lacks in coast is compensated for with two lovely lakes, **Trasimeno** and **Piediluco**.

Getting Around

Besides the FS state **railways**, Umbria has its own private line, the FCU (*Ferrovia Centrale Umbria*). This humblest of railroads runs from Sansepolcro in Tuscany to Città di Castello, Umbertide, Perugia, Todi and Terni. The FS's Rome–Ancona main line reaches Terni, Spoleto and Foligno; at Foligno you can change trains for the branch line to Perugia. From Terni trains head south for Rieti and L'Aquila in Abruzzo. Trains between Rome and Florence stop at Orte (where you can change for Terni), at Orvieto and at Terontola (the junction for Perugia).

Towns not reached by train, like Gubbio, are served by **buses**, though service isn't frequent, especially at weekends. This is one region where you should seriously consider hiring a **car**.

Lake Trasimeno

Approaching Umbria from Tuscany, this section begins where that one left off, near the banks of Lake Trasimeno, easily reached by train from Cortona. The fourth-largest lake in Italy after Lombardy's big three, Trasimeno has a subtle charm: sleepy, placid and shallow, kissed by gently rolling hills covered with olives and vineyards. Special flat-bottomed boats skim over its waters, fishing for eels; the lake is doing its darnedest to become a peat bog. Of late, the villages around Trasimeno have become popular with English expatriates, searching for new pastures away from crowded Chiantishire.

Getting Around

Rail travel can be awkward: Castiglione del Lago is a stop on the Florence–Rome line, but only on slower trains. Most do stop at Terontola, the junction for Perugia, Tuoro and Passignano; from Siena change at Chiusi for Castiglione or Città della Pieve. Perugia is the main **bus** terminus for the area. Connections from Cortona and Siena are less frequent. Contact tourist offices for timetables.

On the lake itself a regular **boat** service links Castiglione, Tuoro and Passignano with each other and with Isola Maggiore. Connections are frequent in summer, but there are only one or two boats a day in winter. For sailing times, contact ✆ 075 827 157.

Tourist Information

Castiglione del Lago: Piazza Mazzini 10, ✆ 075 965 2484, 🖷 075 965 2763.
Passignano sul Trasimeno: Via Roma 36, ✆ 075 827 635.

The Lake Towns

In 217 BC the peace of Trasimeno's north shore at **Tuoro** was shattered when Hannibal ambushed the pursuing Romans, a battle that ended with the dismal destruction of two legions of the SPQR. It is said 15,000 legionaries perished—their rivers of blood are commemorated in the name of the hamlet **Sanguineto**, and their whitened bones in **Ossaia** (from *ossa*, bones). After their defeat at Trasimeno the Roman military machine grimly threw even more legions to their death against Hannibal at Cannae, before giving the Carthaginians the run of the peninsula, defeating them by refusing to fight. **Passignano**, nearby, enjoys a favoured location on its own promontory and walled old quarter. From here a road ascends to **Castel Rigone**, a restful little town with a fine Renaissance church called the Tricine.

On the west bank of Trasimeno, **Castiglione del Lago**, with its picturesque promontory, is the biggest resort, with a castle and beaches. Boats sail from here or Passignano to pretty **Isola Maggiore**, of fishermen and lacemaking womenfolk. In 1211, while visiting the island, St Francis threw back a pike a fisherman had given him, only to be followed across the lake by his grateful 'brother fish' until the saint blessed him—events commemorated in the island church of San Michele. A pretty path encircles the island, a good spot for a picnic.

Castiglione is also a good base for visiting Etruscan Chiusi in Tuscany and **Città della Pieve**, the latter the home town of Pietro Vannucci (1446–1523), better known as *Il Perugino*. He left several works in his home town: a lovely fresco of *The Adoration of the Magi* in Santa Maria dei Bianchi (*ring the doorbell marked* custode *to visit*) and some paintings in the Duomo (*open daily 8–12 and 3.30–6*). Perugino is a disturbing character, and you will find his art sometimes beautiful, but perhaps more often unsatisfying. Although a forerunner of the High Renaissance, the teacher of Raphael and a master of technique, Perugino was the most bitter of Renaissance artists. Born into a desperately poor family, he became a miser, riding from job to job with saddlebags full of money. Midpoint in his career he became an atheist; even so, he cranked out two more decades of richly rewarded but vacuous religious scenes before dying, stubbornly unconfessed on his deathbed (extremely rare in the 16th century), rejecting any future with the sweet-faced angels he depicted for others.

Medieval Perugians were so fond of fish from Trasimeno that Nicola Pisano jokingly sculpted some on the fountain in front of the cathedral.

Passignano ✉ 06065

★★★**Lido**, Via Roma 1, ✆ 075 827 219, ✆ 075 827 251 (*moderate*) has nice rooms on the lake. Above Passignano in Castel Rigone, ★★★★**Relais La Fattoria**, Via Rigone 1, Castel Rigone, ✆ 075 845 322, ✆ 075 845 197 (*moderate*) is a pretty hotel, converted from a cluster of 17th-century buildings, with spectacular views over the lake, a pool, and a good restaurant serving local specialities: fillets of perch and *spaghetti al sugo di Trasimeno* (a sauce of mixed lake fish).

The **Fischio del Merlo**, Via A. Gramsci 14, ✆ 075 829 283 (*moderate*) is an attractive trattoria, serving good lake fish. So too is **Trattoria del Pescatore**, Via San Bernardino 5, ✆ 075 827 165 (*moderate*). The **Cacciatori**, Via Nazionale 11, ✆ 075 827 210 (*expensive*) is a lakeside restaurant with slightly higher pretensions—the fish is excellent here, but prices can be steep. *Closed Wed in winter*.

Castiglione del Lago ✉ 06061

Hotels in Castiglione are simple, but ★★**Trasimeno**, Via Roma 174, ✆ 075 965 2494, ✆ 075 829 267 (*moderate*) has a pool and a bar. **La Cantina**, Via Vittorio Emanuele 89/a, ✆ 075 965 2463 (*moderate*) makes good pasta dishes with a *ragù* of fish or eels; their other speciality is game, like pheasant and quail, when in season. *Closed Mon*.

Isola Maggiore ✉ 06061

Isola Maggiore is the best place in Umbria to get away from it all: ★★★**Da Sauro**, Via Guglielmi, ✆ 075 826 168, ✆ 075 825 130 (*moderate*) is a gracious, uncomplicated place (only 12 rooms), and a real bargain, with a brilliant restaurant that specializes in fish from the lake: eels, carp and such, along with traditional Umbrian dishes.

Città della Pieve ✉ 06062

Le Cantine del Vescovo, Via Pietro Vannucci 37, ✆ 0578 299 200 (*moderate*) turns out more creative versions of the usual Umbrian fare. *Closed Mon*. A popular alternative in this area is to stay in local farmhouses. Contact **Agriturismo Azienda La Dogana**, Via Dogana 107, Tuoro del Trasimeno ✉ 06100, ✆ 075 230 158, ✆ 075 823 0252; the **Azienda Agraria I Cucchi**, Voc. I Cucchi, Petrignano del Lago, ✆ 075 952 8116, ✆ 075 500 3101; or the **Locanda del Galluzzo**, Via Case Sparse 12/a, Loc. Trecine, ✆ 075 845 352.

Perugia

What a town for assassinations!

H.V. Morton

Balanced on a commanding hill high above the Tiber, Perugia is a fascinating medieval acrobat adroitly able to juggle several roles at the same time: those of an ancient hill town, a magnificent *città d'arte*, and a slick, cosmopolitan modern city, famous for its two universities and its chocolates. It is a fit capital for Umbria, with splendid monuments from the Etruscan era to the late Renaissance, artistically stacked side by side; its gallery contains the region's finest paintings, but in its medieval alleyways cats sleep undisturbed.

History

An ancient Umbrian centre, conquered or assimilated by the Etruscans relatively late (around 500 BC), *Peiresa* grew to become one of the 12 cities of the Etruscan Federation, and was peacefully integrated into the Roman world in 310 BC. It had the misfortune to be the refuge of Mark Antony's brother in one of the civil wars, and was subsequently besieged and accidently burned to the ground by one of its own residents when it finally surrendered to Augustus' forces. Augustus had the city rebuilt and renamed *Augusta Perusia*.

Early in the Middle Ages Perugia became an autonomous and rather rascally city that liked nothing better than a punch-up with its neighbours. Strife, external and internal, was to be a constant until the 19th century, and if the city was well fortified against assaults, the towers and palaces of its citizens were equally well fortified against one another. The most prominent family from the 13th century on, the Baglioni, were prevented from taking power by their chief rivals, the Oddi. Their feud was interrupted by the *condottiere* Braccio Fortebraccio ('Arm Strongarm', the Popeye of his day; his escutcheon shows spinach sprouting in a helmet), who took the city in 1414 with the pope's army, and ruled it well.

After Fortebraccio's enforced peace, the Oddi and Baglioni were at it again. Even in the murderous Renaissance the Baglioni were notorious for their audacious liquidations of Oddi and rivals within their own family. One Baglioni gangster even tried to assassinate Pope Julius II when he came to visit Perugia, a failed attempt regretted by Machiavelli because it would have made the family immortal—for its iniquity. But the Baglioni had more immediate concerns than fame; as the Renaissance papacy became powerful, the popes' legates were eroding their old privileges. When Pope Paul III raised the price of salt in 1540, it was the excuse Perugia needed to revolt in what is known as the Salt War. While the city vainly awaited aid from Florence, the papal army captured it. To add still more salt to the wound, Paul III used the Baglioni palaces as the foundation for his fortress, the Rocca Paolina.

As a protest, to this day, Perugians, and indeed all Umbrians, eat bread made without salt (they often swear it tastes better!). From then on, until the Risorgimento, Perugia, like the rest of Umbria, was firmly held in the unnourishing bosom of the Papal States, states that were, as Goethe remarked, kept 'alive only because the earth refuses to swallow them'.

Getting Around

Perugia has an **airport**, 12km west of the city, but it has flights only to Milan and, in summer, to Sardinia. For information, call ✆ 075 692 9447/✆ 075 592 8017. The main FS **rail** station in Piazza Vittorio Veneto is just below the city and has connections to Terontola (for Lake Trasimeno, Arezzo and Florence) and Foligno (for Assisi, Spoleto, Terni and Rome). Halfway up the hill, Stazione Sant'Anna is the FCU rail station for Todi, Umbertide and Sansepolcro, ✆ 075 29121.

The provincial **bus** terminus, ✆ 075 751 145, has services to Gubbio, Rome, Urbino, Norcia and other destinations in the region; it's in Piazza dei Partigiani, linked to Piazza Italia by escalators (*scala mobile*) that are among the most scenographic anywhere (*see* below). If you're **driving**, parking can be a headache: most of the city is closed to traffic, and garages and car parks charge by the hour. You'll find them in Piazza Italia, Piazza Piccinino, and at Piazza Pellini, Mercato Coperto and Piazza Partigiani, all connected to the centre by elevator or escalator.

Tourist Information

Perugia has tourist offices at Piazza IV Novembre, © 075 572 3327, and at the FS station. The main **post office** is in Piazza Matteotti, © 075 572 0395. Unless otherwise noted, all **churches** in Perugia are open 8–12 and 4–sunset.

Summer **art courses** are offered by the Accademia di Belle Arti Pietro Vannucci, Piazza S. Francesco al Prato 5, © 075 573 0631; **Italian summer courses** are held at the University for Foreigners, Palazzo Gallenga, Piazza Fortebraccio 4, © 075 57461; write ahead for details.

Up to Piazza Italia

Most people ascend into Perugia from the west on Via XX Settembre. Between the FS and Sant'Anna stations, Largo Cacciatori delle Alpi gives on to Piazza dei Partigiani, from where elevators ascend to the Piazza Italia, fully inside the city. On the way you can stroll through a surreal, shadowy medieval quarter—all located underground. These streets were vaulted over to support the **Rocca Paolina**, the popes' fortress, designed after the Salt War by Sangallo, and a much-hated symbol of papal authority that was joyfully ripped apart in 1860 when Perugia joined the new Italian Kingdom.

Only a bulwark remains of the handsome but useless structure, pierced by the beautiful Etruscan gate called the **Porta Marzia**, dating from the 3rd century BC; Sangallo liked it enough to take it apart and reconstruct it. Porta Marzia leads into **Via Baglioni Sotteranea** (*open daily 8–7*), the main underground street. By literally burying the Baglioni palaces, Pope Paul III effectively put a halt to that murderous family's influence; today, this silent, sunless land of good medieval brick is their memorial.

On top of the Baglioni palaces lie the **Giardini Carducci**, a terraced public garden with an excellent view of the Umbrian countryside. Next to the gardens stand the dignified public buildings and hotels of **Piazza Italia** that replaced the Rocca Paolina; the proud griffon, emblazoned on the **Prefettura**, is the symbol of both the old and new *comune*.

Corso Vannucci

Two of Perugia's principal streets radiate from Piazza Italia: Via Baglioni and pedestrian-only **Corso Vannucci**, a splendid curve lined with the fortified palaces of Perugia's no-account nobility. Their forbidding residences are now elegant cafés and shops; their street has been renamed after Perugino (Pietro Vannucci) who in 1499 was commissioned to fresco the hall and chapel of the **Collegio del Cambio**, or Bankers' Guild (*open Mar–Oct Tues–Sat 9–12.30 and 2.30–5.30, Sun 9–12.30; Nov–Feb Tues–Sun 8–2; adm*). The hall is adorned with fashionably clothed allegorical figures. Perugino painted a self-portrait in the middle of the left wall, and his pupil, Raphael, then a mere pup of 17, painted the figure of Fortitude. The same ticket is good for the **Collegio della Mercanzia**, decorated with almost Moorish style 15th-century carvings and inlays, located at the far end of the Palazzo dei Priori.

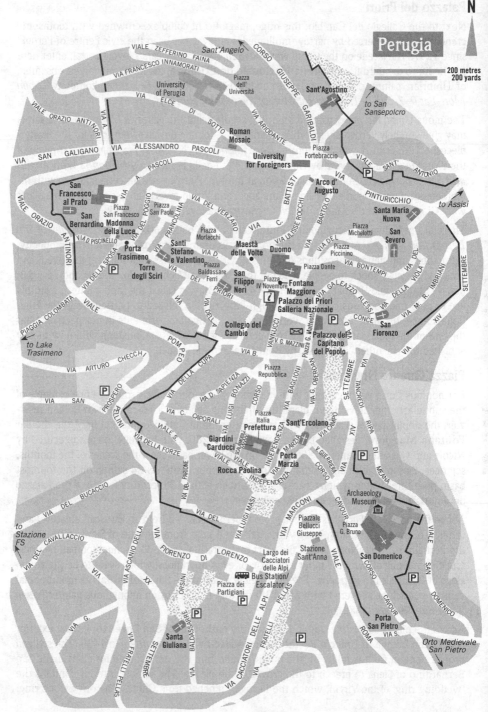

N

Perugia

200 metres
200 yards

Sant'Angelo

CORSO GIUSEPPE GARIBALDI

VIALE ZEFFERINO FAINA

VIA FRANCESCO INNAMORATI

Piazza dell'Università

University of Perugia

VIA ELCE DI SOTTO

VIA ARIODANTE

Sant'Agostino

to San Sansepolcro

VIALE ORAZIO ANTINORI

VIA A.

Roman Mosaic

Piazza Fortebraccio

VIA SANT' ANTONIO

VIA SAN GALIGANO

VIA ALESSANDRO PASCOLI

University for Foreigners

VIALE SANT'

Arco d' Augusto

PINTURICCHIO

to Assisi

VIALE ORAZIO

VIA A. PASCOLI

San Francesco al Prato

San Bernardino Madonna della Luce

Piazza San Francesco

Piazza San Paolo

VIA DEL POGGIO

VIA DEL VERZARO

VIA C. BATTISTI

VIA ULISSE ROCCHI

BARTOLO

Santa Maria Nuova

Piazza Micheletti

San Severo

Piazza Morlacchi

VIA FRANCOLINA

Maestà delle Volte

Duomo

VIA DELLA VIOLA

ANTINORI

Porta Trasimeno

Santi Stefano e Valentino

Piazza Baldassare Ferri

San Filippo Neri

Piazza Dante

Piazza Piccinino

VIA BONTEMPI

VIA DELLA SPOSA

Torre degli Sciri

VIA D. PISCINELLO

VIA D. PRIORI

VIA DELLA

Piazza IV Novembre

Fontana Maggiore

Palazzo dei Priori
Galleria Nazionale

VIA GALEAZZO ALESS

VIA M. R. IMBRIANI

XIV

SETTEMBRE

PIAGGIA COLOMBATA

VIALE

VIA POMPEO

VIA DELLA CUPA

Collegio del Cambio

VANNUCCI

CONCE

San Fiorenzo

to Lake Trasimeno

VIA ARTURO CHECCHI

Palazzo del Capitano del Popolo

VIA B.

Piazza G. MAZZINI

Piazza G. MATTEOTTI

Piazza D.

VIA D.

PROSPERO

VIA SAN

FELLINI

VIA D. SAPIENZA

VIA C. CAPORALI

VIA LUIGI BONAZZI

Piazza Repubblica

CORSO VANNUCCI

VIA G. OBERDAN

SETTEMBRE

RIPA DI MEANA

Piazza Italia

Prefettura

Sant'Ercolano

Archaeology Museum

VIALE S.

VIALE DELLA FORZE

Giardini Carducci

VIALE INDEPENDENZA

VIA MARZIA

Porta Marzia

V. GUERRIA

CORSO

XIV

TANCREDI

Piazza G. Bruno

VIA DEL PARIONE

Rocca Paolina

INDEPENDENZA

VIA DEL

VIA MARCONI

San Domenico

to Stazione FS

VIA DEL BUCACCIO

VIA DEL CAVALLACCIO

VIA ASCANIO DELLA

VIA FIORENZO DI

LORENZO

VIA LUIGI MASI

Piazzale Bellucci Giuseppe

Stazione Sant'Anna

CAVOUR

VIALE SAN

DOMENICO

Largo dei Cacciatori delle Alpi

Bus Station/ Escalator

VIA G.

VIA BALDASSARRE ORSINI

Piazza dei Partigiani

VIA CACCIATORI DELLE ALPI

VIA FRATELLI PELLAS

Porta San Pietro

VIA S.

CORSO CAVOUR

Santa Giuliana

VIA FRATELLI PELLAS

SETTEMBRE

Orto Medievale San Pietro

665

Palazzo dei Priori

Next to the Collegio del Cambio, this huge, magnificent complex, crowned with toothsome crenellations and pierced by narrow mullioned windows, has been the civic centre of Perugia since 1297. The façade on the Corso was added in 1443, and wears a lovely portal; enter here for the lift to the third-floor **Galleria Nazionale dell'Umbria**, the finest and largest ensemble of Umbrian paintings anywhere, with many Florentines to keep them company (*open Mon–Sat 9–7, Sun 9–1; closed 1st Mon of the month; adm exp*).

The pious Umbrians *never* painted anything secular, and the gallery's Madonnas and saints may give you holy vertigo after a while. If you feel it coming on, save your eyes for the masterpieces: a 13th-century wood sculpture, *Deposition from the Cross*; Fra Angelico's triptych of the *Dominicans*; a *Madonna* by Gozzoli; and Piero della Francesca's *Madonna With Angels and Saints* polyptych. In the *Annunciation* at the top, Piero creates an eerie stillness with his mathematical purity—on either side of the angel and Virgin rows of arches recede into a blank wall. Giovanni Boccati's *Madonna dell'Orchestra* is a lovely, musical work.

There are paintings by Perugino and Pinturicchio, who both worked on the *Miracles of San Bernardino of Siena*. At his best Perugino eschews drama and tension, preferring simplicity, gentle lines and static compositions often filled with a 'sweetness' that Raphael mastered, and which gives sugar-shock to people who cut their teeth on Michelangelo. The second Perugian native, Pinturicchio (Bernardino di Betto; 1454–1513), was called the 'rich painter', from his use of gold and gorgeous colours. Although Pinturicchio refused to participate in the High Renaissance, his most interesting works here are his small experiments in perspective. Near the end of the gallery are some good 16th-century views of Perugia, bristling with now mostly vanished towers; other city scenes, by Bonfigli, are in the chapel.

Piazza Quattro Novembre

Harmonious Corso Vannucci ends with melodic rapture in this lovely square, a fine example of the subtle art of medieval town planning. Built long ago over a 1st-century AD Roman reservoir, the sloping piazza is adorned with the most beautiful Gothic fountain in Italy, the circular **Fontana Maggiore**, designed by Fra Bevignate in 1280, with bas-relief panels executed by Nicola and Giovanni Pisano. The 50 panels on the lower basin show the scenes of the months, sciences, Aesop's fables and Roman history; the upper basin has 24 saints; on the topmost basin pose three water-nymphs. Facing the fountain is the 13th-century façade of the Palazzo dei Priori, with stairs leading up to its main door.

Above the portal are Perugia's original griffon (perhaps crafted from an Etruscan creature) and the lion of the Guelph party, hung with chains and bolts from the gate of Siena, captured by the Perugini in 1358. Not a few of the wars of central Italy seem like school football rivalries, one club making off with the other's mascot, or even doorknobs, which seem to be the equivalent of Perugia's proud trophy. The door below leads to the **Sala dei Notari**, a monumental vaulted council hall covered with fine 13th-century frescoes by an anonymous painter (*open Tues–Sun 9–1 and 3–7*).

Across the piazza stands the Gothic 15th-century **cathedral of San Lorenzo**, its best exterior feature the **Loggia di Braccio Fortebraccio,** added by the *condottiere* in 1423. The stylized bronze pope in front is Julius III: the pulpit behind him was constructed for charismatic San Bernardino of Siena to preach to the crowd in the piazza. The sombre interior contains the 'wedding ring' of the Virgin, which the Perugini pinched from Chiusi. The onyx stone ring, size XXXL, is kept in a reliquary with 15 locks (in case the Chiusini try to steal it back) in the **Cappella del Santo Anello**, and displayed on 30 July. On the same side of the church look for the bas-reliefs by Agostino di Duccio. Much of the cathedral's other art is in the **Museo dell'Opera** (*closed for restoration*), including a *Madonna* by Signorelli and a gonfalon with a portrait of the city, painted as an ex-voto after the plague of 1526.

Oratorio di San Bernardino

Flanking the Palazzo dei Priori, medieval Via dei Priori leads down past Perugia's only surviving tower, the 13th-century **Torre degli Sciri** (the others were victim of the city's internal warfare), and an Etruscan arch remodelled as the medieval **Porta di San Luca**. Turn at the Renaissance church of **Madonna della Luce** for Piazza San Francesco. Perugia was never a lucky city for St Francis: as a young rake he spent a year in prison after a Perugian raid on Assisi, and became ill (events that led to his conversion); and his 13th-century church, **San Francesco al Prato**, with its lovely Cosmatesque work, was partly ruined in a landslide. Next to it, however, stands a Renaissance gem, the **Oratorio di San Bernardino** (1461), its façade rich with colourful marbles and Agostino di Duccio's exquisite bas-reliefs. They are in the same almost Art Deco spirit as his more famous ones in Rimini, with especially good angels that wouldn't look out of place in the Rockefeller Center. If it's open, go in to see the 3rd-century AD sarcophagus used as the altar. An alternative route back to Piazza IV Novembre, by Via del Poggio, Via Tartuga and Via Aquilone, will take you past the beautiful **Teatro Morlacchi**, designed in 1788 by Alessio Lerenzini. After Piazza Cavallotti you can walk through a medieval architectural triumph of interwoven arches and asymmetrical vaults, **Via Maestà delle Volte**.

North Perugia

From Piazza Dante, next to the cathedral, Via del Sole leads up to the fine old **Piazza Michelotti**, the highest point in the city, with good views. Just below the piazza, Via dell'Aquila descends to **San Severo**, an ancient church baroqued in the 18th century, but preserving intact a Renaissance chapel containing Raphael's first important commission, a fresco of *The Holy Trinity* painted in 1505 (*open April–Sept daily 10–1.30 and 2.30–6.30; Oct–Mar daily 10.30–1.30 and 2.30–4.30; adm*). Via Ulisse Rocchi, also beginning in Piazza Dante, heads down to what has become Perugia's symbol, the **Arco di Augusto**, a magnificent gate built over a span of 2000 years—the lowest section by the Etruscans and the upper part by the Romans after the siege by Augustus (whose new name for the city *Augusta Perusia* is still legible over the arch), while on top of all is a pretty loggia added in the 16th century.

Beyond the gate lies Piazza Fortebraccio and the 18th-century Palazzo Gallenga Stuart, home of the **University for Foreigners** (*Università Italiana per Stranieri*), founded in 1921 as a centre for studies in Italian language and culture. Behind the university, steps lead down to Via Sant'Elisabetta and the Istituto di Chimica, built around a beautiful 2nd-century AD **Roman mosaic** portraying the myth of Orpheus (*open Mon–Fri 8–8, Sat 8–1*). To the north, in a former Olivetan monastery, is the main **University of Perugia**, founded in 1307.

At the northernmost edge of Perugia (take Via Garibaldi or Via Z. Faina) stands a tower built by Fortebraccio and a remarkable, 5th-century round church, **Sant'Angelo**, dedicated to St Michael and standing on the site of an ancient temple, of which 24 columns were re-used in the church. Another church at the other end of Via Garibaldi, **Sant'Agostino**, contains lovely inlaid choir stalls by Baccio d'Agnolo and frescoes from the 14th–16th centuries.

South Perugia

Perugia's second main street, Via Baglioni, widens below Piazza IV Novembre to form Piazza Matteotti, built over the Etruscan walls and lined with early Renaissance palaces. From here, Via Oberdan descends to Perugia's oddest church, **Sant'Ercolano** (1297–1326), a tall octagonal with a railway station clock and lace curtains in the upstairs window. The Porta Marzia is nearby, while Corso Cavour descends to Piazza G. Bruno and huge **San Domenico**, founded in 1305 and rebuilt in 1632, with an immense 15th-century stained-glass window, the beautiful 14th-century **tomb of Pope Benedict XI** and terracottas by Agostino di Duccio.

San Domenico's monastery contains the excellent **Museo Archeologico Nazionale dell'Umbria** (*open daily 9–1.30 and 2.30–7, Sun 9–1; adm*), with material from prehistoric Umbria, especially the Iron-Age settlement at Belverde sul Monte Cetona. Much comes from Etruscan cemeteries—a lovely 3rd-century BC incised bronze mirror, gold filigree jewellery, sarcophagi, a stone slab—the famous *Cippus Perusinus*—with one of the longest Etruscan inscriptions found, funerary urns, vases (one showing a hero who looks just like a dentist about to examine a monster's teeth), bronzes, armour, and a *kottabos*, thought to have been used in Etruscan party games. The Romans contribute busts, statues and tombs. Further down, Corso Cavour passes through **Porta San Pietro**, a 15th-century gate by Agostino di Duccio, then, as Borgo XX Giugno, continues to **San Pietro**—begun by the monks of Montecassino in 926 and remodelled since, but maintaining its ancient basilican form in the interior. It has a colourful ceiling and works by Perugino (in the nave and sacristy), beautiful inlaid choir stalls and stone pulpits; an inlaid door leads out to a terrace with a stunning view towards Assisi. Across the street you can take a breather in the 18th-century **Giardini del Frontone**.

Around Perugia

Near Ponte San Giovanni, east of Perugia, signs lead to its finest Etruscan tomb, the 2nd-century BC **Ipogeo dei Volumni,** in a modern yellow shelter (*open Mon–Sat 9.30–12.30 and 3–5, Sun 9.30–12.30; July and Aug 9.30–12.30 and 4.30–6.30; adm; 5 people at a time, for 5 min each*). The hypogeum is shaped like an Etruscan house, with an underground 'atrium' (under a high gabled roof). The main room holds the travertine urns containing the ashes of four generations of the family. The oldest one, that of Arnth, is a typical Etruscan tomb with a representation of the deceased on the lid; that of his 1st-century AD descendant, Publius Voluminius, demonstrates a rapid Romanization, decorated with unusual stucco high-reliefs.

Deruta

About 10km south of Perugia, Deruta is Umbria's most famous ceramics centre, having produced its colourful majolica since the Middle Ages. Shops in the streets are adorned with contemporary examples of the art, while pieces from the past may be seen in the **Pinacoteca Comunale** and **Museo delle Maioliche**, in the Piazza dei Consoli (*open Tues–Sun 9.30–12.30 and 3–6; adm*), along with some lovely detached frescoes from local churches.

Activities

If you're travelling with children, Perugia has a large, brightly lit **fun-fair** and Umbria's modest but sincerely meant 'Disneyland', the **Città della Domenica**, just west of the city, with a miniature Africa, a serpentarium, bumper cars, and more (*© 075 754 941; open April–Sept and Oct–Mar Sat and Sun only*).

The ★★★★★**Brufani**, Piazza Italia 12, ✆ 075 573 2541, ✉ 075 572
0210 (*very expensive*) is a renovated, traditional 19th-century hotel
with fine views over the countryside and an attractive central courtyard.
The rooms are very comfortable, and it has a garage.

Also in Piazza Italia, ★★★★**La Rosetta**, ✆/✉ 075 572 0841 (*expensive*) is deservedly popular, with a wide variety of rooms from various
periods. It has a celebrated restaurant, and the rooms are cosy and quiet. When
Goethe passed through he checked in at the ornate ★★★★**Della Posta**, Corso
Vannucci 97, ✆ 075 572 2413, ✉ 075 572 8925 (*expensive*), Perugia's oldest, with
renovated rooms, and a garage.

Between Perugia and Deruta, in Torgiano, ★★★★★**Le Tre Vaselle**, Via Garibaldi 48,
✆ 075 988 0147, ✉ 075 988 0214 (*expensive*) is a Relais et Châteaux villa set in the
Lungarotti family vineyards, an exquisite place offering lovely rooms and excellent
facilities; a wine museum, run by the wife of the owner (*open 9–12 and 3–8; adm*);
and one of Umbria's finest gourmet restaurants, serving the villa's own-label wine.

Enjoying a good location just off Corso Vannucci, ★★★★**Fortuna**, Via Bonazzi 19,
✆ 075 572 2845, ✉ 075 573 5040 (*moderate*) has more comfort than charm (and a
garage). Further from the centre, but worth the extra few minutes' drive, is the memorable ★★★★**Giò Arte e Vini**, Via Ruggero d'Andreotto 19, ✆/✉ 075 573 1100
(*moderate*), a hotel dedicated to the noble art of wine drinking. Each room is furnished
with rustic Umbrian furniture and a display case filled with bottles of wine. Guests are
encouraged to taste them and purchase from the amply stocked cellars on departure.
The restaurant is another treat. Every evening the *sommelier* chooses three different
wines and, for a surprisingly modest fee, diners can quaff to their hearts' content.

The friendly and convenient ★★**Aurora**, Viale Indipendenza 21, ✆ 075 572 4819
(*cheap*) is only a minute's walk from Piazza Italia, on the main road up from the
station. Rooms are rather spartan, but comfortable enough for a short stay. ★**Etruria**,
Via della Luna 21, ✆ 075 572 3730 (*cheap*) is a simple place just off Corso Vannucci.
The local youth hostel is the **Centro Internazionale Accoglienza per Giovani**, Via
Bontempi 13, ✆/✉ 075 572 2880 (*cheap*), by San Severo, with midnight curfew.
IYHF cards not required.

Some of the best restaurants are in the aforementioned hotels, especially La Rosetta,
Brufani and Le Tre Vaselle. For a taste of old Umbria, try the **Osteria del Bartolo**, Via
Bartolo 30, ✆ 075 573 1561 (*expensive*), where beautifully prepared dishes have
been re-created from ancient recipes. *Closed Sun.* Just north of the Duomo, *enoteca*
Aladino, Via della Prome 11 (the extension of Via del Sole) ✆ 075 572 0938 (*expensive*) is one of the most popular restaurants in the city, specializing in sunny Sardinian
and other fresh Mediterranean dishes to go with its fine choice of wines. *Closed Mon.*

On 'Witch Street,' in the medieval quarter west of Corso Vannucci, **La Taverna**, Via
delle Streghe 8, ✆ 075 572 4128 (*moderate*) serves simple dishes like succulent roast
lamb and game, and a wide variety of pasta with truffles and mushrooms. *Closed
Mon.* Another fine old inn is **Falchetto**, Via Bartolo 20, ✆ 075 573 1775 (*moderate*),
near the cathedral. The kitchen features Umbrian specialities—salumeria, *crostini*,

tagliatelle with truffles, *pasta e fagioli*, grilled lamb and trout, and tasty desserts. *Closed Mon.* **La Lanterna**, Via Ulisse Rocchi 6, ✆ 075 5736 064 (*moderate*) is a pretty trattoria, furnished in wood and terracotta and turning out good game dishes such as *cinghiale al ginepro* (wild boar with juniper berries) and *capriolo ai mirtilli* (venison with bilberries). *Closed Wed.*

At **Ubu Re**, Via Baldeschi 17, ✆ 075 573 5461 (*moderate*), close to the cathedral, the chef has a lighter touch, but here too there are good variations on the usual Umbrian theme, including an excellent *coscio di agnello alle olive* (leg of lamb cooked with olives). *Closed Mon, Sat, and Sun midday.* **Il Cantinone**, Via Ritorto 6, ✆ 075 573 4430 (*moderate*), also near the cathedral, offers *spaghetti all'amatriciana* and *filetto tartufato*—fillet of steak smothered with a black truffle sauce. *Closed Tues.*

In a Renaissance palace, **Paiolo**, Via Augusta 11, ✆ 075 572 5611 (*cheap*) has good-value good food, and delicious pizzas. *Closed Wed and part of Aug.* If you watch the prices, you can dine very well for around L25,000 at **Osteria Il Gufo**, Via della Viola 18 (by San Fiorenzo), ✆ 075 573 4126 (*cheap*), which serves seasonal dishes with a flair. *Evenings only, closed Sun and Mon.* **Cambio**, Corso Vannucci 29, ✆ 075 572 4165 (*cheap*) serves reasonable meals and simple lunches. *Closed Wed.*

If you want to make a picnic, Perugia's best bread is baked in some 30 different ways at **Ceccarani**, Piazza Matteroti 16. **Sandri**, on Corso Vannucci, is one of the prettiest pastry shops in Italy, with a frescoed ceiling and divinely artistic confections.

Entertainment and Nightlife

The principal Perugian occupation is the evening *passeggiata* down Corso Vannucci, with a stop for a bite at the Bar Ferrari, perhaps, before hanging out in Piazza IV Novembre. Other activities include July's **Umbria Jazz** festival, which draws lights like Wynton Marsalis to Perugia's stadium. In September the **Sacra Musicale Umbra** features sacred music in Perugia's churches.

Assisi

Rome may be the Eternal City, capital of an empire and Whore of Babylon; Florence the birthplace of the Renaissance, of modern western culture and the Italian language; and Foligno's billiard table the centre of the cosmos; but Assisi is the gentle soul of Italy, imbued with the spirit of the country's patron saint, known affectionately as *Il Poverello*, the Little Poor One. The importance of St Francis (1182–1226) in the history of Christianity cannot be over-estimated; he was the first to crack the strict hierarchy of the established Church; a democrat who preached a natural, everyday religion of love, and who had a simple, humble faith without dogma that had such a deep, mass appeal that the Church quickly institutionalized his teachings. Francis' own life, as an imitation of Christ, became part of the new iconography of the great religious revival he initiated.

Born to a wealthy cloth merchant named Pietro Bernardone, he was baptized Giovanni, but always called Francesco by his francophile father. Francis grew up speaking Provençal, the language of his Occitan mother, and spent a merry, wild youth as a troubadour. He was captured in Assisi's war against Perugia, and spent a year in prison reflecting on the vanity of the world. When released, he gave everything he owned to the poor, tended lepers and preached his message of poverty, humility and joy, attracting a band of followers. Although Francis refused to take priestly orders, he received authorization for his community from Innocent III in 1209.

Francis spent much of his career preaching and wandering, travelling through Spain to Morocco, accompanying the Crusaders to Egypt and the Holy Land. His songs and canticles, drawing on his troubadour days, were among the first vernacular verses composed in Italy, and the foundation for a 13th-century literary movement, of which the most famous work was the *Fioretti*, 'The Little Flowers', believed to be in part written by Francis himself. In 1221 the Franciscan Rule of poverty, chastity and obedience was sanctioned by Honorius III. Francis subsequently received the stigmata, and died two years later.

More than any other saint, Francis crosses ecumenical boundaries; in 1987, when Pope John Paul II invited representatives of all the world's religions to pray together, he chose Assisi as the host city. But Assisi is not only Italy's greatest pilgrimage shrine after Rome, it's a beautiful medieval town as well, built high on a spur of Monte Subasio, overlooking the velvet green Umbrian countryside. Don't become too distracted by the crowds or souvenir shops peddling toy monks, child-size crossbows and other baubles (no Italian shrine would seem right without them); but for a taste of the Assisi that Francesco and Chiara would recognise, stroll through the city's steep, dimly lit lanes at midnight, when all is silent and still.

There are two periods when Assisi is anything but silent, or still. Easter week, when its processions and mystery plays bring thousands of people to the city; and the *Calendimaggio* (first ten days in May), a medieval celebration that commemorates Francis's troubadour past with songs, dances, torchlit processions and competitions between Upper and Lower Assisi.

Tragically, as everyone knows, an earthquake in September 1997 brought the roof of the basilica down, killing two friars and two journalists who were examining the damage caused by the first shock of the day. Although the lower basilica reopened in late November 1997, the upper church will not be ready until 2000—the Franciscans have their fingers crossed—in time for the great Jubilee, when Assisi expects several million extra pilgrims.

Basilica di
San Francesco

Porta
San Giacomo

Piazza Superiore
di San Francesco

Casa dei
Maestri Comacini

VIA METASTASIO

VIA

Piazza Inferiore
di San Francesco

Arcades

VIA

SAN

FRANCESCO VIA DEL SEMINARIO

VIA FRATE ELIA

Oratorio dei Pellegrini

Porta
San Francesco

VIA FONTEBELLA

Monte
Frumentario

Piazza
Garibaldi

Perugia

VIA DEL FOSSO CUPO

Porta
San Pietro

Piazza
Pietro

VIA BORGO S. PIETRO

Santa Maria degli Angeli,
Train Station

San Pietro

VIALE

VIA

MARCONI

VITTORIO

N

Assisi

200 metres
200 yards

Getting Around

Assisi is a 30-minute **train** ride from Perugia or Foligno, where you'll have to change if you've come from Rome or Ancona. The station (℗ 075 804 0272), however, is 5km from the centre, in the suburb of Santa Maria degli Angeli; connecting buses will take you up to Piazzale Unità d'Italia, just below the basilica. Assisi is also linked by **bus** from Piazza Santa Chiara and Piazza Matteotti with Perugia, Foligno and Ascoli Piceno. There are three large **car parks** around the fringes of the old city, most of which is closed to traffic: in the Piazzale Unità d'Italia, below the basilica; near the Porta Nuova, below Santa Chiara, off the Foligno road; and at Piazza Matteotti, within the walls, below the Duomo.

Tourist Information

Piazza del Comune 12, ℗ 075 812 534/075 812 450, ℗ 075 813 727,
aptas@krenet.it

*At the time of writing
nearly everything in Assisi is closed for restoration,
with the exception of the lower basilica, the Museo
Civico, the Roman Forum and Santa Maria degli Angeli; check
with the tourist office to see what has reopened when you arrive.*

The Basilica di San Francesco

*Lower church only open daily 7–12 and 2–sunset; April–Oct daily 7–sunset; closed
Sun morning during services.*

Before Francis died he asked to be buried with the criminals on 'Infernal Hill' outside the city
walls. His lieutenant, Brother Elia, was not about to go against his wishes, but he waited until
Francis was canonized in April 1228, and the next day began work on an ambitious two-
storey basilica on the hill, now re-christened the Hill of Paradise. Not all of the order agreed
that such a project was fitting for a holy man wedded to poverty, but brother Elia and Pope
Gregory IX, who laid the cornerstone, won the day, creating not only the chief Franciscan
memorial, but a rare work of art as well.

The two churches that make up the basilica are believed to have been designed by Brother Elia himself, who created here what was to become a model for numerous other Franciscan churches, especially in the lines of the simple Gothic upper church. The **lower church** much resembles a crypt with its low dark vaults, although once your eyes adjust to the dim light you can see that they are covered with beautiful frescoes by the masters of the 13th and 14th centuries (bring plenty of coins to illuminate them). In the first chapel to the left there are relics of the saint—an autographed letter, his humble habit and sandals, and Honorius III's Papal Bull authorizing the Franciscan Rule. The first chapel to the left of the frescoed nave contains magnificent frescoes on the *Life of St Martin* by Simone Martini, painted around 1322, while the third chapel on the right contains frescoes on the *Life of Mary Magdalen*, attributed to Giotto (1314). The frescoes attributed in Assisi to Giotto (from *c.* 1295), constitute one of the longest-raging controversies in art history. The Italian faction is convinced that the frescoes in the lower and upper churches are the climax of Giotto's early career, while most foreign scholars believe Giotto didn't paint them at all. In any case, Martini's 'International Gothic style' poses a serious artistic challenge to the great precursor of the Renaissance. Giotto is also credited with the four beautiful allegorical frescoes over the high altar: Poverty, Chastity, Obedience and the Glory of St Francis. In the left transept are fine works by Pietro Lorenzetti of Siena, among the best in the basilica, especially the lovely *Madonna della Tramontana*, with *St Francis and St John*, a *Crucifixion* and a *Descent from the Cross*. In the right transept is Cimabue's *Madonna and Saints*, with a famous portrait of St Francis (1280), believed to be an accurate likeness; a female saint nearby, by Simone Martini, is believed to be St Clare.

In the **crypt** lie the tombs of Francis and four of his closest followers, discovered in 1818 having been secretly sealed off in the 15th century to protect them from Assisi's devious, relic-snatching enemy, Perugia. From the transepts stairs lead up to a terrace and the **Museo-Tesoro della Basilica** (*open daily 9.30–12 and 2–6; Nov–Mar closed Sun; adm*) containing whatever wasn't pillaged over the centuries—a beautiful Venetian cross, a French ivory Madonna from the 13th century, a Flemish tapestry of St Francis, and more.

In comparison with the lower church, the **Upper church**, facing its emerald-green lawn, is strikingly bright and airy, and dazzles with its colour. When, hopefully, it reopens in 2000, you'll once more be able to see its two major series of medieval frescoes; the earthquake left them cracked and broken in places, but more or less intact. The lower set on the *Life of St Francis* is by Giotto or his school, and the upper, with Old and New Testament scenes, is attributed to Pietro Cavallini. What makes most Italian scholars attribute the St Francis frescoes to Giotto is the artist's mastery of composition; Giotto amazed his contemporaries by his ability to illustrate the physical and spiritual essentials of a scene with simplicity and drama, cutting directly to the core. The scenes begin with the young *St Francis Honoured by a Simple Man*, who lays down his cloak and foretells his destiny; he returns his clothes to his father, who in his anger and disappointment has to be restrained; Pope Innocent III has a dream of Francis supporting the falling Lateran; the demons are expelled from Arezzo by Brother Sylvester; Francis meets the Sultan of Egypt, and creates the first Christmas crib, or *presepio*, at Greccio; he preaches to the attentive birds, then to Pope Honorius III; he appears in two places at the same time, and next, receives the stigmata from a six-winged Christ. He dies, bewailed by the Poor Clares, and is canonized.

The transepts were painted in 1277 by Giotto's master, Cimabue, though these works had deteriorated into mere shadows of their former selves even before the earthquake turned them to crumbs; what can be salvaged will, and by hook or by crook some kind of Cimabue clones will eventually refill the rebuilt transepts, good enough to give most of us non-experts a feeling for what was lost, perhaps even of the great *Crucifixion*. Behind the basilica, propped up on huge arches, the enormous convent is now used as a missionary college.

To the Piazza del Comune

From the basilica, Via San Francesco leads up past many fine medieval houses to the centre of Assisi. On the way there are several buildings of note: no.14, the Mason's Guild, or **Casa dei Maestri Comacini** (since most of those who built the basilica came from Como); at no.11, the pretty, frescoed **Oratorio dei Pellegrini**, a 15th-century gem surviving from a hospice built for pilgrims; and at no.3, the **Monte Frumentario**, a 13th-century hospital, converted into a granary. Next to it is a 16th-century fountain, still bearing the warning that the penalty for washing clothes here is one *scudo* and confiscation of the laundry. Near the entrance to the piazza is the **Museo Civico**, located in the crypt of a now-vanished church, with a small collection of Etruscan urns. A passageway from the museum leads into the ancient Roman Forum, which lies directly under the piazza. Currently work is going on to excavate the forum completely, underground—leaving the square above intact.

This square, the long, attractive **Piazza del Comune**, was built up after the barbarians destroyed the forum. It has always been the main axis of Assisi, and is embellished with the 13th-century buildings of the old *comune* (the **Torre and Palazzo del Comune** and the **Palazzo del Capitano del Popolo**), and what at first looks like a decrepit bank building, but is in reality a Roman **Temple of Minerva**, its Corinthian columns and travertine steps incorporated into the church of Santa Maria. When Herr 'Anti-Middle Ages' Goethe came to Assisi it was to see this façade—and nothing else. The Palazzo del Comune also contains the **Pinacoteca Civica**, with a small collection of Umbrian Renaissance art. To the left of the Palazzo, the **Chiesa Nuova** was built by Philip III of Spain on property owned by St Francis' father; the **Oratorio di San Francesco Piccolino** (of 'Little baby St Francis') is believed to mark the saint's birthplace.

Upper Assisi: the Cathedral and the Castle

From the Piazza, Via San Rufino leads up to the **Cattedrale di San Rufino**, with its huge campanile and beautiful Romanesque façade, designed by Giovanni da Gubbio in 1140 and adorned with three fine rose windows and the kind of robust medieval carvings of animals and saints that Goethe disdained. The interior was redone in the 16th century and is of little interest, but you can see the porphyry font where Saints Francis and Clare were baptized, as well as Emperor Frederick II, who was born in Jesi in the Marche. It is an amazing coincidence that the two leading figures of the 13th century should have been baptized in the same place. The holy water must have had a special Muslim essence to it, for both Francis and Frederick (*see* 'Lucera' and 'Castel del Monte' pp.877 and 886–87) were influenced by Islam: Francis and his Order of Minor Brethren had much in common with a Sufi order of 'Greater Brethren' founded by Najmuddin Kubra, who also had an amazing influence over animals. Francis, before finding religion, had been a Provençal-speaking troubador, a vocation that had its roots in Moorish singers in Spain, and when he left Italy it was to go to Spain, Egypt and the Holy Land, journeys his biographers found hard to explain; Egypt's Sultan Malik el-Kamil welcomed him when he came to visit, and when Francis returned to the Crusaders' camp he tried to persuade them not to attack. The themes of Francis' poetry, especially the canticles, are very similar to those of Rumi, the great love-poet and founder of the Whirling Dervishes.

From the cathedral a stepped lane leads up to the **Rocca Maggiore**, Assisi's well-preserved castle, built in 1174 and used by Corrado di Lutzen (who cared for the little orphan Emperor Frederick II), then afterwards destroyed and rebuilt on several occasions. It offers excellent views of Assisi and the countryside. From the Rocca you can visit more of Roman *Asisium*— the remains of the **amphitheatre** in the public gardens, and the **theatre** in Via del Torrione. The **Porta Perlici** near the amphitheatre dates from 1199, and there are some well-preserved 13th-century houses on Via del Comune Vecchio.

Basilica di Santa Chiara

When Santa Chiara (St Clare, 1193–1253) was 17 she ran away from her wealthy and noble family to become a disciple of St Francis, and head of the Franciscan Order for women, the Poor Clares. Gentle, humble and well-loved, she once had a vision of a Christmas service in the Basilica of St Francis while at the monastery of San Damiano, over a kilometre away, a feat that brought Pope Pius XII in 1958 to declare her the patroness of television. (Unfortunately the plastic statues of St Clare, with two holes in the back for your TV antennae, are now hard to find, even in Assisi trinket land.)

Her basilica, below Piazza del Comune (by way of Corso Mazzini), is a pink-and-white striped beauty with a lovely rose window, made memorable by the huge flying buttresses that support its outward side, masterpieces of medieval abstract art. The basilica was built on the site of old San Giorgio, where Francis attended school and where his body lay for two years before being moved to his own basilica. The interior was decorated with fine frescoes by followers of Giotto, although many are now in fragments. The chapel on the right contains the famous *Crucifix of San Damiano* that spoke to St Francis, commanding him to 'Rebuild my Church', while the adjacent chapel of the Holy Sacrament, has fine Sienese frescoes; these two chapels were part of San Giorgio. The nearby portrait of St Clare, with scenes from her life, is by the Byzantine-ish, 13th-century Maestro di Santa Chiara, while St Clare's body, darkened with age, lies like Sleeping Beauty in a crystal coffin in the neo-Gothic crypt.

From Santa Chiara, Via Sant'Agnese leads to the very simple church of **Santa Maria Maggiore**, built in 1163 on the site of a Temple of Apollo, traces of which are still visible in the crypt. Near here was discovered the house of Sextus Propertius, the Roman poet of love (46 BC–AD 14), complete with wall paintings, which may open to the public some fine day. Between here and the Piazzale Unità d'Italia, stroll along Via Cristofani and Via Fontebella, the latter adorned with wrought-iron dragons and another old fountain.

On the Outskirts of Assisi

The seminal events of Francis' life all took place in the countryside around Assisi. From Santa Chiara a gentle 1km walk leads down to **San Damiano**, a small, simple, asymmetrical church, where Francis heard the voice of the crucifix that changed his life and composed his masterful *Canticle of All Things Created*. He brought Clare here to live with her sisters in frugal contemplation. Once, when they were interrupted by the Saracen army of Frederick II about to attack Assisi, St Clare, holding the Sacrament, drove the infidels away and kept the city free from harm, an event celebrated every 22 June.

Another Franciscan shrine, the peaceful **Eremo delle Carceri**, lies along the scenic road up Monte Subasio, a pleasant walk or drive 4km east of Assisi. This was Francis' forest hermitage, where he would walk through the woods, and where he preached to the birds from a simple stone altar; here you can see his humble bed hollowed from the rock. The handful of Franciscans here live a traditional Franciscan existence, off the alms they receive.

Santa Maria degli Angeli, near the railway station, is a large unwieldy nutshell of a basilica built in 1569 to protect a sacred kernel—the tiny **Porziuncola**, an ancient chapel belonging to the Benedictines in the 6th century, where angels were wont to appear. The chapel was given by the Benedictines to St Francis in return for a yearly basket of carp from the River Tescio, still faithfully paid by the Franciscans. St Francis founded his first friary here, the remains of which have been partially excavated under the high altar; here St Clare took her vows of poverty as the spiritual daughter of Francis; here Francis died, 'naked on the bare earth', in the infirmary, now the **Cappella del Transito**, with a statue of St Francis by Andrea della Robbia. The garden contains the roses that St Francis threw himself on while wrestling with temptation, staining their leaves red with blood, only to find that they lost their thorns on contact with his body. Still thornless, they bloom every May. Francis' cave has been covered with the frescoed Cappella del Roseto, and there's an old pharmacy and **museum** (*open Easter–Oct daily 9–12 and 2.30–4.30*), with a portrait of St Francis by an unknown 13th-century master, another sometimes attributed to Cimabue, a *Crucifix* by Giunta Pisano, and items relating to Franciscan missionary work. The big feast day in the basilica, the *Festa del Perdono*, was initiated by Francis after he had a vision of Christ at the Porziuncola, who asked what would be most helpful for the soul. Francis asked for forgiveness for any who crossed the threshold; and indulgences are still given out every 1st and 2nd August.

Assisi ✉ *06081*   ***Where to Stay and Eating Out***

Tourists have been coming to Assisi for longer than to any town in Umbria, and it does its best to please. There are plenty of rooms, but still not enough for Easter or *Calendimaggio*, nor July and August, when you should definitely book.

The traditional, formal ★★★★**Subasio**, Via Frate Elia 2, ✆ 075 812 206, ✉ 075 816 691 (*expensive*) is linked to the Basilica of St Francis by the portico. Many of the rooms have views over the mystical countryside from vine-shaded terraces, and it has a medieval vaulted restaurant and a garage. St Francis never slept here, but Charlie Chaplin did. ★★★★**Fontebella**, Via Fontebella 25, ✆ 075 812 883, ✉ 075 812 941 (*expensive*), in a 17th-century *palazzo*, is nearer the centre, with comfortable bedrooms, elegant public rooms, a garden and garage. ★★★★**Giotto**, Via Fontebella 41, ✆ 075 812 209, ✉ 075 816 479 (*expensive*), near the basilica, has very pleasant, modern rooms, a garden and garage.

Near Piazza del Comune at the end of a narrow alley, the ★★★**Umbra**, Via degli Archi 6, ✆ 075 812 240, ✉ 075 813 653 (*moderate*) is a little family-run inn, quiet, sunny and friendly with a walled garden. Rooms can be a bit small, but many have balconies overlooking the countryside. The restaurant deserves special mention as one of the most attractive in Assisi, with the best regional cuisine—*risotto* with white truffles from Gubbio; in summer meals are served in the garden. ★★★**Dei Priori**, Corso Mazzini 15, ✆ 075 812 237, ✉ 075 816 804 (*moderate*) is housed in a gracious old palazzo, well-restored and very conveniently placed, just off Assisi's main piazza. ★★★**Hermitage**, Via del Pozzo 1, ✆ 075 812 764, 🖥 075 816 691 (*moderate*) is a comfortable hotel in a good central position, a short walk from the basilica. Nearly a kilometre away—a 10-minute walk from the west gate of Assisi—in a pretty country setting, the old stone ★★**Country House**, S. Pietro Campagna 178, ✆/🖥 075 816 363 (*moderate*) has lovely rooms furnished with items from the owner's ground-floor antiques shop. Still further afield, at Ospedalicchio di Bastia (SS147 towards Perugia), the friendly ★★★**Lo Spedalicchio**, Piazza B. Buozzi 3, ✆/🖥 075 801 0323 (*moderate*), converted from a medieval fortified house, nicely preserves many of its original features, but with added creature comforts, a garden and an excellent restaurant.

Near the amphitheatre, ★★**Ideale per Turisti**, Piazza Matteotti 1, ✆ 075 813 570, 🖥 075 813 020 (*cheap*) is a fine, small hotel with a garden and views. ★**Anfiteatro Romano**, Via Anfiteatro 4, ✆ 075 813 025, 🖥 075 815 110 (*cheap*) is a good quiet choice near Piazza Matteotti, with just seven rooms. American nuns run **S. Antonio's Guest House**, Via G. Alessi 10, ✆ 075 812 542 (*cheap*), in a 12th-century villa. Guests who arrive in the morning can also have a good cheap lunch here, but no dinner. Beware the early curfew. If everything is full, try the large pilgrimage houses in Santa Maria degli Angeli, especially the ★★**Cenacolo Francescano**, Via Piazza d'Italia 70, ✆ 075 804 1083, 🖥 075 804 0552 (*cheap*), with 130 adequate rooms, a short walk from the train station; or go to the tourist office for a list of smaller religious houses and rooms in private houses, of which there are dozens. There is a youth hostel at Rivotorto, 3km south of Assisi—**Victor**, ✆/🖥 075 806 5562.

The well-known **Buca di San Francesco**, Via Brizi 1, ✆ 075 812 204 (*expensive*), below street level in a cavernous medieval cellar, serves delicious cannelloni, home-made pasta with porcini mushrooms, pigeon cooked Assisi-style, or *filet al Rubesco* (fillet of steak cooked in red wine), and a good choice of Umbrian wines. *Closed Mon, Jan, Feb and most of July.* Another venerable choice, **Il Medioevo**, Via dell'Arco dei Priori 4, ✆ 075 81068 (*expensive*) has an elegant medieval atmosphere and tasty *antipasti* with Umbrian *prosciutto* and *faraona all'uva* (guinea-fowl with grapes). *Closed Wed, most of Jan and mid-July.* **La Fortezza**, Via della Fortezza, ✆ 075 812 418 (*moderate*), near the Piazza del Comune, has delicious *cappelletti al tartufo nero o funghi* (truffle or mushroom-filled pasta caps), roast guinea-fowl, or rabbit in asparagus sauce. *Closed Thurs.* A lovely stop on the road up to the breathtaking sanctuary of Eremo delle Carceri is **La Stalla**, Via Eremo delle Carceri, ✆ 075 812 317 (*moderate*), a typical country trattoria, converted, as its name suggests, from an old barn. Good hearty fare is served here at very reasonable prices, washed down with jugs of local wine. *Closed Mon.*

Near the temple of Minerva, **Piazzetta dell'Erba**, Via S. Gabriele dell'Addolorata 15/b, ✆ 075 815 352 (*cheap*) features delicious daily specials at kind prices. *Closed Mon.* Don't miss the rich strudels and chocolate-and-nut breads in the speciality **bakery** in Piazza del Comune, near the Temple of Minerva.

Towns Around Assisi: Bettona and Spello

There are a couple of pretty towns easily reached from Assisi. **Bettona**, a small hill town to the southwest, still retains a considerable portion of its Etruscan walls, and in its stern Palazzetto

Podestarile a small **Pinacoteca**, robbed a few years ago of its two Peruginos, but still containing works by Dono Doni and Andrea della Robbia. The key is kept in the police station.

Rosy-tinted **Spello**, an outstanding medieval hill town towards Foligno, was the Roman *Hispellum* and still retains its republican-era main gate, the **Porta Consolare**. But Spello's special claims to fame are its frescoes by Pinturicchio (1501) in the Cappella Baglioni in the Romanesque church of **Santa Maria Maggiore** (*open daily 7.30–12.30 and 2.30–6*), painted with the same brilliant palette that he used in Siena's Piccolomini Library; the *Annunciation* is especially lovely. Even the floor, made of Deruta majolica tiles, is bright and colourful. Pinturicchio also painted the altarpiece in **Sant'Andrea**, up the street, a church that's also famous for its 13th-century Umbrian *Crucifix*. Further up, there are excellent views from the **Torre Belvedere**, near the scant remains of the Roman acropolis and the medieval castle. Around Spello you'll find two other Roman gates in the walls: the **Porta Venere** and **Porta Urbica**, near the pretty 12th-century church of **San Claudio**.

Spello ⊠ 06038   *Where to Stay and Eating Out*

***La Bastiglia**, Via dei Molini, ℘/☏ 0742 651 277 (*moderate*) has pleasant rooms and a beautiful terrace and views. ***Altavilla**, Via Mancinelli 2, ℘ 0742 301 515, ☏ 0742 651 258 (*moderate*), run by the Prioetti family, also has a pleasant terrace and 24 well-furnished rooms. **Il Molino**, Piazza Matteotti, ℘ 0742 651 305 (*moderate*) has fine, mellow dining under the vaulted ceiling—home-made pasta or traditional Umbrian meats cooked over the flames. *Closed Tues.* For beautifully prepared game try the popular **Trattoria del Cacciatore**, Via Giulia, ℘ 0742 651 141 (*moderate*). *Closed Mon.* At **La Cantina**, Via Cavour 2, ℘ 0742 651 775 (*moderate*), the menu changes according to the season; you may be offered *oca al sagrantino e castagne* (goose braised with chestnuts) or *agnello al limone* (lamb with lemon). *Closed Wed.*

North of Perugia

The two main attractions north of Perugia are artsy Città di Castello and medieval Gubbio, the former linked by train with Perugia, the latter by bus. There is little worth stopping for in between—typical rural Umbrian countryside, low hills, tobacco fields and flocks of sheep.

Getting Around

Città di Castello is on the FCU local **rail** line from Perugia. There are no trains to Gubbio, but some 10 **buses** a day along the beautiful SS298 from Perugia, stopping at the Piazza Quaranta Martiri in Gubbio, where schedules are posted. There are also buses from here to Fossato di Vico, 20km south, the closest train station on the Rome–Ancona line, and to Città di Castello, Arezzo, Florence and Rome. There is a **bus information office** in Gubbio: Via della Repubblica 13, ℘ 075 922 0066.

Tourist Information

Città di Castello: Via Raffaele di Cesare 2/b, ℘ 075 855 4817, ☏ 075 855 2100.
Gubbio: Piazza Oderisi, ℘ 075 922 0693/0790, ☏ 075 927 3409.

Città di Castello

An ancient Umbrian town on the Upper Tiber, Città di Castello is now one of Italy's major tobacco towns, though one that preserves its civic monuments from the 1300s (the **Palazzo del Governo** and **Palazzo Comunale**, with a lofty vaulted hall). The part-Romanesque, part-Renaissance **Duomo** has a tilted Ravenna-style campanile, a Rosso Fiorentino, a 6th-century treasury and a lovely 12th-century silver altarpiece in its **museum** (*open April–June Tues–Sun 10.30–1 and 3–5.30; July–Sept 10–1 and 4–6.30; adm*). Another church, **San Domenico**, has ruined frescoes and a copy of Raphael's *Crucifixion* (the original is now in the National Gallery, London).

Città di Castello's best pictures, however, are in the **Pinacoteca** of the Palazzo Vitelli, Via della Cannoniera 22 (*open Tues–Sun 10–1 and 3.30–7; closed April and May; adm*), a harmonious Renaissance palace by the younger Antonio da Sangallo, with exterior graffiti by Vasari. The gallery includes fine Renaissance works, with civic standards by Luca Signorelli and Raphael, Ghirlandaio, the della Robbia family and Ghiberti. The **Collezione Burri**, in the Palazzo Albizzini, has paintings by local contemporary painter Alberto Burri (*open Tues–Sat 10–12 and 3–6, Sun 9–1; adm*).

Gubbio

It's hard to think of any other Italian town as resolutely medieval as good grey Gubbio, the sombre stone 'City of Silence', with its orderly Roman street plan draped over the steep, lower slopes of Monte Ingino. As one of Umbria's most visited hill towns, its dark magic has become grist for the tourist mill, but you'd have to be very particular to think Gubbio is spoiled. Like many other towns in the area, it is a ceramics centre, inheriting the tradition if not the secrets of the 16th-century Mastro Giorgio, who discovered a beautiful ruby lustre to add to his majolica. Mastro Giorgio's secret died with him, but Gubbio's potters still make fine ware, black like that of the Etruscans, or in lovely muted colours.

Gubbio was an important town of the ancient Umbrii, known as *Eugubium*. Long an independent *comune*, it was plagued in the Middle Ages by wolves, one of which in particular terrorized the populace. St Francis heard of it and, ignoring the townspeople's pleas for his safety, went out and had a word with it, brought it to the town, and made a public agreement that in exchange for regular meals it would stop preying on Gubbio, an agreement sealed with a shake of the paw. The wolf kept its part of the bargain, and is immortalized in a bas-relief over the door of a little church in Via Mastro Giorgio. Gubbio was captured by Urbino in 1384, and from that time on its fortunes followed those of the Marche. It has retained two exceedingly medieval festivals, however, which fill the solemn streets with colour and exuberance, most tumultuously the festival of the *Ceri* on 15 May in honour of San Ubaldo, Gubbio's patron, who persuaded Frederick Barbarossa not to attack the town in 1155; the festa itself is first documented a couple of years later, although it may have borrowed something from a lost pagan rite. The *ceri* (or 'candles') are tall, wooden, phallic towers, each topped by a wax saint representing a clan—San Ubaldo, San Giorgio and Sant'Antonio Abate. The *ceri* are baptized with a jug of water, and then carried on supports by teams of ten men. The climax of the day comes when the teams race pell-mell through the crowds up to the mountaintop church of San Ubaldo, a steep race that San Ubaldo invariably wins. On the last Sunday in May crossbowmen from Sansepolcro come to compete in the *Palio dei Balestrieri*, a contest dating back to 1461.

Gubbio, from the Bottom Up

Approaching Gubbio from the west, the first thing you see is the large, well-preserved 1st-century AD **anfiteatro Romano**, used these days for summer performances of classical plays and Shakespeare. Lower Gubbio proper is entered by way of green **Piazza dei Quaranta Martiri**, named in memory of the 40 citizens executed on this spot by the Nazis in reprisals for partisan activities in the vicinity. To the right, the church of **San Francesco** has a fine triple apse and some good frescoes, especially the 15th-century series on the Madonna in the left apse by Gubbio's own Ottaviano Nelli. Lining the other side of the piazza is the **Tiratoio**, or Weavers' Loggia, a 14th-century arcade under which newly woven textiles could be stretched to shrink evenly—one of the few such loggias to survive.

From the piazza, picturesque medieval lanes line the banks of the rushing Camignano. Many of the houses and modest palazzi date back to the 13th century, here and there adorned with carved doors or windows, or an extra door called the *Porta del Morto*, used solely to remove the dead. The main street, Via dei Consoli, passes by one of Gubbio's finest buildings, the 13th-century **bargello**, the police station and governor's office; its fountain used to be Gubbio's main water source. Further up, the street widens to form magnificent **Piazza della Signoria**, its belvedere hovering over a steep drop and a stunning view of the town below.

The king of the piazza is the beautiful **Palazzo dei Consoli**, a lofty, graceful 14th-century town hall attributed to Gubbio's best architect, Gattapone. Supported on the hill by a mighty substructure of arches, the palazzo is graced with an elegant loggia, a slender campanile, Guelph crenellations, and asymmetrically arranged windows and arches. Inside are two museums: the **Museo Archeologico**, with an Etruscan and Roman collection, and the **Museo Civico** (*both museums open winter daily 10–1 and 2–5; summer daily 10–1 and 3–6; adm*), with archaeological odds and ends and a unique treasure, the bronze *Eugubian Tablets*, discovered in the 15th century near the Roman theatre. These are the only extant records ever found in the Umbrian language, five written in Etruscan characters, the other two in Latin letters—they concern priestly rites and auguries. A stiff climb up the stairs leads to the gallery, with some of Gubbio's ceramics and a collection of art spanning the centuries. Most memorable, however, is the grand view from the loggia. Further up stands Gubbio's simple **Duomo**, built in the 13th century and most notable for the pattern of its stone vaulting and its 12th-century stained-glass windows. It has several good paintings, but the best art is in the museum: a beautiful 16th-century Flemish cope, magnificently embroidered and presented to the cathedral by Pope Marcellus II, a native of Gubbio. Opposite, the **Palazzo Ducale** (*open Mon–Sat 9–1.30 and 2.30–7, Sun 9–1.30; adm*) was designed for Federico da Montefeltro by Luciano Laurana, as a more compact version of the ducal palace in Urbino. The courtyard is well worth a look.

From the Duomo you can make the stiff climb up Monte Ingino to **San Ubaldo**, but it's much easier to take the funicular up from the Porta Romana on the southeast side of town. In San Ubaldo you can examine the three *Ceri*, and see that it's no wonder that the Gubbites need a considerable amount of Dutch courage to run up the mountain lugging these towers on their shoulders. There's a café where you can while away the afternoon, or walk a bit further up for even more spectacular views from the **Rocca** (2913ft).

Two churches near Porta Romana, near the lower funicular station, contain some of the finest works by Gubbio's Ottaviano Nelli. In **Santa Maria Nuova** is the lovely and joyous *Madonna del Belvedere*, Nelli's masterpiece, from 1403 (*if the church is closed, knock on the door marked* custode *in Via Dante for the key*). The 13th-century **Sant'Agostino**, just outside the gate, has some fine frescoes by Nelli and his students in the apse.

Where to Stay and Eating Out

Città di Castello ✉ 06012

Central ★★★★**Tiferno**, Piazza R. Sanzio 13, ✆ 075 855 0331 (*expensive*) is the best place both to stay and dine, with good comfortable rooms, a garage, and one of the best restaurants in the area—ravioli with shrimps in orange sauce, or pigeon with white grapes. ★★★**Delle Terme**, Via delle Terme, Loc. Fontecchio, ✆ 075 852 0614, ✆ 075 855 7236 (*moderate*) is at Fontecchio, a natural spa just outside Città di Castello. Pliny the Younger used to come here to take the waters, but you may be content with the open-air pool. *Open April–Nov.* ★★**Europa**, Via V. E. Orlando 2, ✆ 075 855 0551 (*cheap*), and ★★**Umbria**, Via dei Galanti, ✆ 075 855 4925 (*cheap*) are both good, clean, if uninspiring, hotels.

Il Bersaglio, Via E. Orlando 14, ✆ 075 855 5534 (*moderate*), just outside the walls, offers a wealth of pasta dishes, well-prepared meat and game and especially good truffles and wild mushrooms. Tucked down a small alley, **Amici Miei**, Via del Monte 2, ✆ 075 855 9904 (*moderate*) serves good honest Umbrian food with typical pasta dishes and a tempting array of home-made desserts. *Closed Wed.* A 10km drive along the SS257 (the Adriatica) to Fraccano will take you to a small trattoria, **SS Adriatica**, ✆ 075 855 3870 (*moderate*), of the kind fast disappearing in Italy. Choose from a limited but excellent menu of the day—good pasta, and meat grilled in front of you.

Gubbio ✉ 06024

The place to stay in style is the ★★★★**Park Hotel ai Cappuccini**, Via Tifernate, ✆ 075 9234, ✆ 075 922 0323 (*expensive*), a beautifully restored Franciscan monastery, 3km out of town, set in its own grounds with a pool, sauna and fitness centre. ★★★**Bosone**, Via XX Settembre 22, ✆ 075 922 0688, ✆ 075 922 0552 (*moderate*) is conveniently located in a picturesque setting. Rooms are comfortable enough, and there's a garage. ★★★**San Marco**, Via Perugina 5, ✆ 075 922 0234, ✆ 075 927 3716 (*moderate*) has modern comforts, a pretty garden terrace at the back, and parking.

★★**Dei Consoli**, Via dei Consoli 59, ✆ 075 927 3335 (*cheap*), well positioned near Piazza della Signoria, is small and simple. It has a good restaurant in a medieval cellar, with tasty *spiedini* (meat on a spit). ★★**Gattapone**, Via G. Ansidei 6, ✆ 075 927

2489, 📠 075 927 2417 (*cheap*), in the central medieval zone, has a small garden at the back. If you don't mind its monastic flavour, the **Casa Beniamino Ubaldi**, Via Perugina 74, ✆ 075 927 7773, a modern seminarians' college just outside the city walls, rents out spotless rooms—probably the best deal in town—and there's a bar.

You can dine at the **Fornace di Mastro Giorgio**, Via della Fornace di Mastro Giorgio, ✆ 075 922 1836 (*expensive*), in the workshop where the master ceramicist created his famous ruby glaze. The cuisine combines the best traditions of Puglia and Umbria, with seafood (rare in Umbria) on Thursday and Friday, and delicacies like *tagliolini alle alici* (with anchovies) or Umbrian pigeon with olives, and delicious desserts. *Closed Mon, and Sun eve.* **Taverna del Lupo**, Via Ansidei 21/a, ✆ 075 927 4368 (*expensive*) is a beautiful medieval place, where you can dine on boar sausage, game, *risotto dei tartufi* (Gubbio is a land of white truffles), delicious lasagne with prosciutto and truffles, and *Frico*, a local speciality of mixed meats with cress. *Closed Mon.*

La Balestra, Via della Repubblica 41, ✆ 075 927 3810 (*moderate*) features unusual *antipasti*, including herring (*aringa*), *fondutina con tartufo*, home-made pasta, and a good selection of meats. *Closed Tues.* On a clear day, the **Funivia**, on Monte Ingino above Gubbio, ✆ 075 922 1259 (*moderate*) offers fabulous views as well as delicious pasta with truffles or *porcini*, and tasty *secondi* like grilled lamb or stuffed pigeon, good desserts and local wines. *Closed Wed.* **S. Francesco e Il Lupo**, Via Cairoli 24, ✆ 075 927 2344 (*cheap*) features local products—*prosciutto*, porcini mushrooms and truffles—or pizza. **Del Bargello**, Via dei Consoli 37, at Largo Bargello, ✆ 075 927 3724, serves polenta, *agnolotti*, *agnello scottadito* (burn your fingers lamb) and other grilled meats. *Closed Sun.*

Via Flaminia: Gualdo Tadino to Spoleto

Whether you're travelling by car, bus or train, the eastern Umbrian towns along the ancient Via Flaminia (SS3) offer both lovely scenery and monuments, including some unexpected artistic treasures. Admittedly most people don't know about Foligno's cosmic billiard table, but many have heard of Spoleto's renowned **Two Worlds Festival**, the concept of which has given birth to a twin Spoleto festival in Charleston, North Carolina. Spoleto is also one of Umbria's loveliest hill towns, while Nocera Umbra, Trevi, Montefalco and Clitunno are small but worthy destinations in between.

Getting Around

The Rome–Ancona **railway** follows the Via Flaminia up from Spoleto all the way up to Gualdo Tadino, before veering east towards Jesi and Ancona. There are also **buses** linking Spoleto to Gualdo Perugia, Città di Castello and Gubbio. During the Due Mondi festival, there are special trains and buses between Rome and Spoleto to accommodate the crowds of festival-goers from the capital.

Tourist Information

Foligno: Porta Romana, ✆ 0742 354 459/✆ 0742 354 165.
Spoleto: Piazza della Libertà, ✆ 0743 220 311, 📠 0743 46241.

Gualdo Tadino and Nocera Umbra

Gualdo Tadino is a lofty little town where the Byzantine eunuch general Narses defeated the Goths in 552, a battle essential in preserving the Marche for the Eastern Church. It has a handful of good paintings in its **Pinacoteca**, housed in the church of San Francesco; some are by 15th-century native Matteo da Gualdo. From Gualdo the road descends the Valle del Topino ('Mousey') to **Nocera Umbra**, Roman *Nuceria Camellaria* and the region's most important spa and bottler of mineral water, a pretty, green little place. Another former church of San Francesco houses the local painting collection, with works mainly by Umbrian painters, especially an excellent *Nativity* by L'Alunno, the master of Foligno.

Foligno

Foligno is an ancient and important town, the Roman *Fulginia*, and it was one of the earliest printing centres in Italy, producing the first book in Italian in 1470. But this century has been rough on Foligno—it was bombed to smithereens in the war, although some of the old quarter has survived, especially the central Piazza della Repubblica. This in turn was walloped in Sepember 1997 when Foligno, the centre of the cosmos became the epicentre of the quake.

The 14th-century Palazzo dei Signori, the Trinci, is now used as a **Pinacoteca** (*open Tues–Sun 10–6; adm*); in the chapel, however, you can see more works by Gubbio's Ottaviano Nelli. The nearby **Duomo** has retained an impressive south front of 1201, which rates as one of the most unorthodox in Italy: among the zodiac, monsters and medieval bestiary is a portrait of Emperor Frederick II, arch enemy of the popes, and even a little Islamic star and crescent. The oldest thing in Foligno is the Romanesque **Santa Maria Infraportas**, with 12th-century frescoes in the Byzantine style.

More interesting than Foligno itself are the sites that surround it, all linked to the city by bus, with the exception of the 13th-century **Abbazia di Sassovivo** (*open daily 9–sunset*), with its magnificent and serene cloister, an hour's walk to the east. To the southwest lie three charming hill towns: **Bevagna**, with two Romanesque churches; tiny medieval **Gualdo Cattaneo** and the old town of **Montefalco**, called the 'Balcony Rail (*Ringhiera*) of Umbria' because of its lofty, commanding position. The pride of Montefalco is its rich 15th-century fresco cycle on the *Life of St Francis* by Benozzo Gozzoli, painted in the apse of the church-museum of **San Francesco** (*open spring and autumn Tues–Sun 10.30–1 and 2–6; summer 10.30–1 and 3–7; winter 10.30–1 and 2.30–5; adm*). Above the church the attractive, round **Piazza della Repubblica** affords excellent views of the countryside, especially from the tower of the Palazzo Comunale. Most of Montefalco's other churches contain good frescoes as well, especially **Sant'Agostino**, near the frescoed main gate **Porta Sant'Agostino**, and **San Fortunato**, beyond the Porta Spoleto, which boasts a few Gozzolis of its own.

Trevi, just on the eastern side of the main road, is another charming hill town, wrapped in olive groves that produce Umbria's rich green oil (buses link the train station with the town up above). Its name, like that of the famous fountain in Rome, derived from *Tre Via*, or Three Roads. Its tight, narrow streets contain some good medieval buildings and the 15th-century church of **Madonna delle Lacrime**, sheltering a good *Adoration of the Magi* by a sceptical 76-year-old Perugino. The Palazzo Lucarini now hosts the **Trevi Flash Art Museum** (*open Wed–Sun 10–1 and 3–6.30; adm*), a joint endeavour of *Flash Art* magazine and the *comune*, offering a permanent collection of contemporary Umbrian, Italian and foreign artists, as well as changing exhibitions. The convent of the church of San Francesco is the new home of the **Museo Civico** (*open April–Sept Tues–Sun 10.30–1 and 2.30–6; July and Aug 10.30–1 and 3.30–7; Oct–Mar Fri, Sat and Sun only 10.30–1 and 2.30–5; adm*) and its paintings: a *Madonna* by Pinturicchio (a copy of the one in London's National Gallery), a *Deposition* by the school of Sodoma, and a fine *Incoronazione di Maria* by Spagna.

Further south, just off the Via Flaminia, the **Fonti di Clitunno**, ancient *Clitumnus*, is famous for its snow-cold clear spring and pool. The ancient Romans built villas on the surrounding hillside, and bred pure white oxen on its dark green banks; they built a temple here to the river god. In the 4th or 5th century the temple was converted into a church, the delightful **Tempietto di Clitunno** (1km further), with simple frescoes from the 7th century (*open Tues–Sun 9–12 and 4–7; ring the bell*). From here buses continue to Spoleto.

Spoleto

Set among thickly wooded hills, ancient Spoleto is one of the most attractive towns in Italy, one that provides, in its numerous well-preserved monuments, a nearly complete history of the peninsula. At night, when its chief landmarks are illuminated and the city lights twinkle, it becomes a magical place, a setting fit for the dynamic **Festival dei Due Mondi** (Two Worlds Festival), founded by composer Gian Carlo Menotti and the late Thomas Schippers in 1958, and now Italy's most important performing arts festival. The annual influx of international culture has left a mark on this once drowsy hill town: monuments have been restored, art galleries and trendy shops line the medieval streets, and prices, during the three weeks of the festival (some time between mid-June and mid-July) get knocked way out of line.

Ancient Umbrian *Spoletium* was settled by the Romans in 242 BC, a few decades before an over-confident Hannibal came knocking at the gates, expecting an easy victory after his rout at Lake Trasimeno. But Spoletium held firm and repulsed him, and Hannibal, who intended to move on to Rome from there, took his elephants to graze in the Marche instead. The Goths under Totila wrecked the city, while the Lombards, slowly piecing it back together, made it a powerful duchy, so powerful that in 890 Duke Guido III made an armed play for the imperial crown against the heirs of Charlemagne; later the duchy became a fief of Countess Matilda of Tuscany, the Guelphiest of Guelphs, and in the 13th century it was incorporated into the Papal States. In 1499 it was ruled by Lucrezia Borgia, a 19-year-old recently married to the second of her three husbands by her intriguing father. By all accounts Lucrezia did well, but was sent off two years later to marry Alfonso d'Este of Ferrara.

If you arrive in Spoleto by train you are greeted, not by an Umbrian hill town, but by a huge iron sculpture by Alexander Calder, a relic of the 1962 festival now used to shade a taxi stand. Buses every 10 minutes link the station to central **Piazza della Libertà**, with the tourist office and the nearby **Teatro Romano**, some 380ft in diameter, built in the 1st century AD and restored for festival performances. The stage structure was removed in the Middle Ages and replaced by the pleasant Convent of Sant'Agata. More Roman memories are nearby, beyond the Piazza Fontana: the **Arco di Druso**, built in the year AD 23 to celebrate a victory over the barbarians. This once marked the entrance to the Roman forum, now Piazza del Mercato, but before you get there take the steps down to the 12th-century **Crypt of San Isacco**, with its curiously primitive frescoes. The church above, **Sant'Ansano**, was built into a Roman temple, remains of which may be seen near the altar. In Piazza del Mercato the landmark is an 18th-century fountain by Carlo Fiaschetti.

The next square, pretty Piazza Municipio, contains a **Roman house** believed to have once been the address of Emperor Vespasian's mother, with an atrium, bedrooms and baths, some with surviving mosaics. The house can be visited, together with the **Pinacoteca Comunale** in the nearby Palazzo Comunale (*open Tues–Sun 10–1 and 3–6; adm*), with works by native son Giovanni di Pietro (known as Lo Spagna), L'Alunno and other Umbriani.

The Rocca and Ponte delle Torri

From the Piazza del Municipio, Via Saffi climbs up to the Piazza Campello, with a 17th-century fountain called the **Mascherone** after its grotesque face. Above this looms the **Rocca**, the impressive six-towered castle built by Gattapone for the 14th-century papal legate, Cardinal Albornoz. It is built of third-hand stone, first used in the Roman amphitheatre and later cannibalized by the Goth supremo Totila for his fortress. The Rocca was a popular papal resort frequented by Julius II, accompanied on occasion by Michelangelo who loved the peace of the surrounding hills. Until 1983 it was used as a prison, but is currently closed for restoration as the new home for Spoleto's Pinacoteca.

For now, the best thing to do is stroll along the garden walk that encircles the Rocca, with great views of Spoleto below. The **Porta della Rocca** leads down to Master Gattapone's masterpiece, and one of the great engineering works of the trecento, the **Ponte delle Torri**, a bridge and aqueduct of 10 towering arches linking Spoleto with the slopes of Monteluco, spanning a 260ft ravine and the Tessino River far below. Gattapone built the bridge on a Roman foundation; it leads to the towers that gave it its name, and to the road for San Pietro and San Francesco (*see* below).

Sant'Eufemia and the Duomo

Below the Rocca on Via Saffi stands the pure and lovely 12th-century **Sant'Eufemia** (*open 8–12.30 and 2.30–6; in summer till 8*), with a dignified façade and beautiful Romanesque interior of ancient capitals and columns, a *matroneum* (women's gallery) and picturesque vaults. Next door is the dramatic **Via dell'Arringo**, a grand stairway descending to **Piazza del Duomo**, which must have been what sold Menotti on Spoleto when he travelled about, seeking a venue for the Two Worlds Festival: it doubles perfectly as an outdoor auditorium for concerts, with the cathedral and Umbrian hills as a backdrop. Thomas Schippers, co-founder of the festival, was so fond of the concerts and piazza that he asked to be buried here when he died, in 1977. The elegant **Duomo** was consecrated in 1198 by the most powerful of medieval popes, Innocent III, having been rebuilt after Emperor Frederick Barbarossa—the greatest of papal enemies—had razed its predecessor. It has several unusual features: eight rose windows of varying sizes, like buttons, adorn its horizontally divided façade, surrounding a gold-ground Byzantine-style mosaic of 1207. Its campanile is built out of Roman odds and ends, and very un-Italian flying buttresses help to hold it up. Although the interior was unfortunately re-done in the 17th century, it contains several treasures, most piously the *Santissimo Icone*, with a picture of the Madonna, brought to Spoleto from Constantinople. Pinturicchio painted the frescoes in the first chapel, the Eroli, and the apse contains lovely frescoes on the *Life of the Virgin* by Fra Filippo Lippi, who portrayed himself among the mourners in the scene of the Virgin's death. The fun-loving monk from Florence died in Spoleto while working on the project, and it was finished by his chief helper, Fra Diamanti; when Lorenzo de' Medici asked that Lippi's body be returned to Florence, the Spoletini refused, and Lorenzo had to be content with ordering a fine Florentine tomb for him, now in the right transept.

Lower Spoleto

On the opposite side of town (Via del Duomo to Via Filitteria) there's another grand theatre, the **Teatro Nuovo**, used both for the festival and for the even older September Festival of Experimental Opera. Nearby, the colourful church of **San Domenico** was built in the 1200s, and contains some interesting if fragmentary frescoes. From San Domenico walk down to the tall-towered 13th-century **Porta Fuga**, and then along Via Cecili, where you can take in an excellent stretch of Spoleto's **walls**, an intriguing record of the town's history, beginning at their 6th-century BC 'Cyclopean' base of huge polygonal rough blocks built by the ancient Umbrii, and going all the way up to the 15th-century additions on the top.

The street ends at Piazza Cairoli; from here Via dell'Anfiteatro descends past the ruined **amphitheatre**, now part of a barracks, to Piazza Garibaldi, with the fine 12th-century church of **San Gregorio** and the Roman **Ponte Sanguinario** ('bloody bridge'), so called because of all the Christians who were martyred here. From the bridge, signs point the way to the cemetery church of **San Salvatore**, a 15-minute walk. Built in the 4th century, it has an unusual façade, and preserves much of its original vertical lines and simplicity despite subsequent rebuildings. The elegant, fluted Corinthian columns in the interior were incorporated from a Roman temple.

Monteluco

Beautiful, forested Monteluco is Spoleto's holy mountain, lying just to the east of town, connected by bus from the Piazza della Libertà, or by walking from the Ponte delle Torri. If you're walking, take the right-hand fork for the Romanesque church of **San Pietro**, only a few minutes away, with a romp of a façade dating back to the dukes of Spoleto; if you've visited the medieval cathedrals of the north you'll recognize the animals, real and imaginary, that the Lombards delighted in portraying: here is a fox playing dead to capture some too-curious chickens, battles with lions, oxen, eagles, a wolf in monk's clothing, and the rest.

The other (left) fork in the road demands some vigorous walking through beautiful holm oak forests to reach the 12th-century church of **San Giuliano**, with a façade incorporating some 6th-century elements of its predecessor. Anchorites and hermits, refugees from the wars in the Holy Land, settled here in the 7th century; in the 13th century St Francis and San Bernardino of Siena came to meditate here, at the tiny monastery of **San Francesco** near the summit of Monteluco, a serene spot enjoying a lovely view of the surrounding countryside. Monteluco now has more summer villas and hotels than hermitages, but it's still a cool and tranquil place to spend an afternoon, and a good place to look for accommodation.

Where to Stay and Eating Out

Foligno ✉ 06034

★★★**Villa Roncalli**, Via Roma 25, ✆ 0742 391 091 (*moderate*) is a fashionable, central villa-hotel in a shady garden, with comfortable rooms and a garage. Near the station, the family-run ★★**Belvedere**, Via Ottaviani 19, ✆ 0742 353 990, ✉ 0742 356 243 (*moderate–cheap*) is more than adequate for bed and breakfast. For dinner, try **Da Remo**, Viale C. Battisti 11, ✆ 0742 340 679 (*moderate*) serving tasty *strangozzi* (fat, home-made spaghetti) and roast kid cooked in Sagrantino wine. *Closed Sun evenings and Mon.* Wine-lovers can enjoy their favourite tipple with cheeses and other snacks at cosy **Bacco Felice**, Via Garibaldi 73, ℰ 0742 341 019. East of Foligno, ★**Lieta Sosta**, Via Adriatica 228/a, loc. Colfiorito, ℰ/✉ 0742 681 321 (*cheap*) has seven rooms and a pool. Its restaurant offers fine country dining.

Montefalco ✉ 06036

★★★★**Villa Pambuffetti**, Via della Vittoria 20, ℰ 0742 378 823, ✉ 0742 379 245 (*expensive*) is a delightful 19th-century villa owned by a local noble family who now run it as a beautifully kept inn, with 15 rooms, all decorated differently, some with family antiques. The villa is set in a lovely park with a pool. ★★**Ringhiera Umbra**, Via G. Mameli, ℰ 0742 379 166 (*cheap*) is cheap but comfortable, a pretty *pensione* with a good restaurant. Montefalco is perhaps best known for a couple of red wines, Sagrantino and Rosso di Montefalco. Sagrantino is quite special, with a delicate aroma of blackberries; both are sold in many shops around town. **Coccorone**, Vicolo Fabbri, ℰ 0742 379 535 (*moderate*), off the central square, is an elegant, understated place with tempting crêpes and *tagliatelle al tartufo* for *primo*, and dishes like *faraona ai salmi* (braised guinea-fowl) and grilled pigeon for *secondi. Closed Wed.* For a similar price, **Il Falisco**, Via XX Settembre, ℰ 0742 379 185 (*moderate*) offers well-cooked local specialities such as *filetto al sagrantino. Closed Mon.*

Trevi ✉ 06039

★★**Del Pescatore**, Via Chiesa Tonda 50, ℰ/✉ 0742 78483 (*cheap*) is a *pensione* with nine pleasant rooms and an excellent restaurant: the **Taverna del Pescatore**, ℰ 0742 780 920 (*moderate*), run by another branch of the same family, with a menu based on meat or fish, both very good value and beautifully prepared. *Closed Wed.*

Clitunno ✉ 06042

Besides its own virtues, Clitunno is a quiet alternative to Spoleto if you've come for the festival. ★★**Le Fontanelle**, Via d'Elci 1, ℰ 0743 521 091 (*moderate*) is a lovely place surrounded by refreshing greenery. Rooms are comfortable, and the restaurant serves Umbrian specialities like country *prosciutto*, *strangozzi* and platters of tender lamb and chicken. **Il Vecchio Mulino**, Via del Tempio 34, Loc. Pissignano, ℰ 0743 521 122, ✉ 0743 275 097 (*moderate*) is an oasis of peace on the river (in spite of being near the main Perugia–Spoleto road)—an old, creeper-clad mill house, appropriately surrounded by water, with comfortable rooms and a lovely garden. At the Fonti di Clitunno, ★★**Ravale**, Via Virgilio, ℰ 0743 521 320 (*moderate*) has simple rooms as well as a modestly priced *ristorante-pizzeria.*

Spoleto ✉ 06049

During the Two Worlds Festival accommodation is tight in Spoleto and in the surrounding area, so reserve in advance. The tourist office in Spoleto has a list of private rooms to rent, but again, don't count on finding one on the spot: plan ahead.

Spoleto has several fine hotels, including spectacular, tiny ★★★★**Gattapone**, Via del Ponte 6, ℰ 0743 223 447, ✉ 0743 223 448 (*expensive*), in a stone house clinging to the slope near the Rocca and the Ponte delle Torri, with fabulous views; even during the festival rush it remains serene. Its eight rooms are spacious and finely furnished; another house next door contains the restaurant. ★★★★**Dei Duchi**, Viale Matteotti 4, ℰ 0743 44541, ✉ 0743 44543 (*expensive*), centrally located near the Piazza della

Libertà, is a well-designed contemporary hotel with fine views over Spoleto; it is popular among visiting artists and performers. ***Charleston**, Piazza Collicola 10, ✆ 0743 220 052, @ 0743 222 010 (*moderate*) is in a pretty 17th-century *palazzo*, with 18 comfortable rooms in the *centro storico*. Run by the same family, ***Clarici** Piazza della Vittoria 32, ✆ 0743 223 311, @ 0743 222 010 (*moderate*), in the lower part of town, is more modern, but still decorated with taste and style. Central **Dell'Angelo**, Via Arco di Druso 25, ✆ 0743 222 385 (*cheap*) has seven rooms.

About 12km south of Spoleto on the SS3 towards Terni is the **Pecoraro**, at Strettura, ✆ 0743 54431 (*cheap*), a very pretty and above all welcoming *pensione* where guests are treated like members of the family by owners Sandro and Illy Montefalchesi. There is also a small pool, and memorable home cooking and home-made grappas.

At **Il Tartufo**, Piazza Garibaldi 24, ✆ 0743 40236 (*expensive*), Umbrian truffle dishes are the speciality, utilizing the black truffles of the Valnerina in various combinations of pasta and eggs; other dishes include grilled lamb and kid, and veal. *Closed Wed.* Outside Spoleto, on the SS3 to Terni, the **Madrigale**, ✆ 0743 54144 (*expensive*) offers a gourmet *menu degustazione* of Umbrian specialities. *Closed Tues.*

Sabatini, Corso Mazzini 54, ✆ 0743 221 831 (*moderate*) serves good traditional Umbrian fare, indoors and out. *Closed Mon.* At **Il Panciolle**, Via Duomo 3, ✆ 0743 45598 (*moderate*), diners feast on truffles and meat grilled over the open fire. There are also seven nicely decorated rooms for rent. *Closed Wed.* In the heart of Spoleto, the **Trattoria del Festival**, Via Brignone 8, ✆ 0743 220 993 (*moderate*) has a pretty dining room with arched ceilings, and a blazing fire in winter. The chef has a winning way with truffle dishes and desserts. *Closed Fri.* For a good glass of wine and tasty snacks, try **La Cantina**, Via Filitteria 10/a, ✆ 0743 44475 (*moderate*). *Closed Mon.*

Monteluco ✉ 06049

In more tranquil Monteluco, the ***Michelangelo**, ✆ 0743 40289, @ 0743 47890 (*moderate*) has large rooms and very friendly staff. *Open April–Oct.* **Ferretti**, Loc. Monteluco 20, ✆ 0743 49849, @ 0743 222 344 (*cheap*) is a *pensione* with plenty of charm, looking out on to the pretty tree-shaded piazza. **Trattoria S. Giuliano**, ✆ 47797 (*moderate*), near the church of San Giuliano, is a lovely place overlooking Spoleto, with seasonal Umbrian dishes like *bruschetto*, *strangozzi*, mushrooms, game and asparagus omelettes. *Closed Wed.*

Entertainment and Nightlife

The Two Worlds Festival dominates the life of Spoleto in June and July. Major international music, dance and theatre companies, ensembles and performers are featured, and the festival has had a high reputation for launching new talent. It is also a major social event, particularly for Romans—the audiences for the major performances are sharply dressed, and prices very high. In the last few years, though, in response to criticism that the festival had become too top-heavy, the programme has sought to give greater prominence to more avant-garde work, and there are plenty of fringe shows alongside the official programme. For information and tickets, write well in advance to the **Associazione Festival dei Due Mondi**, Teatro Olimpico, Piazza

Gentile da Fabbriano 15, Rome. In Spoleto, information, programmes and tickets can be obtained by writing, phoning or visiting the festival headquarters, **Associazione Festival dei Due Mondi**, Piazza Del Duomo 9, ✆ 0743 45028.

The Valnerina

The Nera, one of the main tributaries of the Tiber, flows from the mighty Monti Sibillini along the southern edge of Umbria. Many of its sights are still Italian secrets; its black truffles, waterfalls and saints enjoy a national reputation, but the rest is touristically *terra incognita*.

Getting Around

Terni and Narni are the only towns in this area served by **rail**. Both are on the Rome–Ancona line, and from Terni there are also trains to Rieti and L'Aquila in Abruzzo. From Spoleto's Piazza della Repubblica **buses** depart frequently for Cascia and Norcia; others go to Scheggino, where you can catch a Terni provincial bus down the rest of the valley to Terni, Narni or Orvieto.

Tourist Information

Norcia: in the Municipio, ✆ 0743 828 044. **Cascia**: Via G. da Chiavano 2, ✆ 0743 71401, 🖷 0743 76630. **Terni**: Viale C. Battisti 7/a, ✆ 0744 423 047, 🖷 0744 427 259. **Amelia**: Via Orvieto 1, ✆ 0744 981 453, 🖷 0744 981 566.

Norcia

Little Norcia gave the world St Benedict (480–543), the father of monasticism, and his twin sister St Scolastica. It has also been known at times for witches, barber surgeons (who, in the 16th century, were the only ones capable of properly castrating a boy with operatic potential), cheeses and boar hams (in Umbria, a *norceria* is a cheese-charcuterie shop). An ancient place, mentioned by Virgil, it looks more Spanish than Italian, and, although earthquakes have slapped it around, old Norcia survives around central Piazza San Benedetto. It has a stern statue of St Benedict for a centrepiece, the 14th-century church of **San Benedetto**, built over the late-Roman house where the famous twins were born, and the handsome **Palazzo Comunale**, with a 13th-century campanile and door, next to all shops decked with bristling hams. The other side of the square is occupied by the **castle**, designed in 1554 by Vignola for Pope Julius III, now housing a modest museum of Umbrian art.

Above Norcia lies the beautiful **Piano Grande**, an unusual flat meadow measuring 16 square kilometres and surrounded by rolling hills and mountains that seem covered with huge swathes of coloured velvet in May and June. It is a rarefied landscape (used by Franco Zeffirelli in his 'Franciscan film' *Brother Sun, Sister Moon*), where herds graze and fields produce the famous minute lentils of **Castelluccio**, the old village in an upper corner of the plain. Castelluccio had 700 inhabitants in 1951, and now has around 40; winter conditions are so bad that the village is often cut off. From the summit of Monte Vettore (8121ft), the tallest peak in the area, you can see both the Adriatic and Tyrrhenian seas on clear days. In the winter there's skiing at Forca Canapine, on the south side of Piano Grande.

Cascia, in the Corno Valley south of Norcia, is an even more popular pilgrimage destination, thanks to Santa Rita, the 'Saint of Impossibilities', who was born near here in 1381, and suffered a rotten husband (hence all the tired Italian housewives you see) and a smelly wound in the middle of her forehead, but had to wait until the Fascist era to get a sanctuary.

Down the Valnerina: Crayfish and Mummies

Back in the main valley on the SS209, **Scheggino** is a small but pretty town on the River Nera, laced with tiny canals full of trout and a rare species of crayfish (*gamberettini*) imported from Turkey. It is also the fief of Italy's truffle tycoons, the Urbani family. Further down the valley a sign indicates the turn-off for the **abbey of San Pietro in Valle** (*open daily 10.30–1 and 2.30–5*), founded in the 8th century by Faroaldo II, Duke of Spoleto. Set far up above the road, with views across the valley to an abandoned citadel, the church has a lovely 12th-century campanile embedded with Roman bits, and a two-storey cloister with a Roman sacrificial altar in the centre. Inside, the nave is covered with frescoes from 1190, an unusual example of the Italian response to the Byzantine style. The altar is a rare example of Lombard work, sculpted on both the front and back; one of their early saints is interred to the right in a lovely 3rd-century Roman sarcophagus. On either side of the altar are 13th-century frescoes by the school of Giotto, with a pretty Madonna. In the back the cylindrical Etruscan altar is now used for monetary rather than animal offerings. Among the stone fragments arranged on the wall there's a real rarity—a bas-relief of a monk with oriental features, believed to depict one of two Syrian monks who set up a hermitage here in the 7th century.

The abbey is in the *comune* of **Ferentillo**, defended by two 14th-century fortresses that rise up like matching bookends. In **Precetto**, the oldest section of town, the crypt of **Santo Stefano** (*open daily 10–12.30 and 2.30–5; knock on door marked* custode *opposite church*) contains something most people don't expect to find in Umbria: **mummies**. Accidentally preserved by the soil and ventilation, you can see the poor mummified Chinese newlyweds who came here in the last century for a honeymoon and got cholera instead, two gruesome French prisoners who were hanged in the Napoleonic era, and a grinning pyramid of skulls; a desiccated vulture mummy points the way inside with its wing. Sad to relate, the mummies are now imprisoned in glass display cases, ruining much of their charm.

Picturesque **Arrone**, spilling over its rock, was once run by feudal lordlings, the bitter enemies of the abbots of Ferentillo. Their tower, sprouting a tree, is the local landmark. From Arrone, the road leads up to Piediluco and **Polino**, also endowed with a feudal tower and a monumental fountain; above Polino the Colle Bertone affords panoramic picnicking sites.

Cascate delle Marmore and Lake Piediluco

Between Arrone and Terni the road passes below another pretty hill townlet, **Torreorsini**, before reaching the 416ft-high, green and misty **Cascata delle Marmore**, one of Europe's tallest waterfalls—when it's running. Surprisingly, the Cascata is an artificial creation; in 271 BC Curius Dentatus, best known as the conqueror of the Sabines, first dug the channel to drain the marshlands of Rieti, diverting the River Velino into the Nera. Although the falls are usually swallowed up by hydroelectric turbines, the big waters are let down on weekends and in summer; after dark they are brilliantly illuminated (*Nov–15 Mar Sun and holidays 3–4; 16 Mar–April and Sept–Oct Sat 6–9, Sun 10–12 and 3–9; May–15 July Sat 5–10, Sun 10–1 and 3–11; 16 July–31 Aug Mon–Fri 5–6.30, Sat 5–10, Sun 10–1 and 3–11*).

There are two places from which to view the falls—from down below on the SS209, or from the belvedere on top, in the village of Marmore. A path through the woods connects the two, though it's steep, prone to be muddy in the off season, and much nicer to walk down than up (the path at the bottom begins 100 yards downstream from the falls). There are some pleasant places to swim near the bottom, but you can't use them when the falls are on. A siren goes off 15 minutes before the falls are turned on to warn swimmers not to linger. Both places are easily reached by bus from Terni, 6km away.

Above Marmore, **Lake Piediluco** zigzags in and out of the wooded hills, one of which is crowned by a 14th-century fortress. There are a couple of beaches, but unfortunately the lake is better to look at than swim in—the water is cold and dangerous. Perched high above the east shore of the lake is the pale old village of **Labro**, former nest of noblemen on the run, now almost completely taken over by Belgian expats. Just below the lake the Arrone road passes by **Villalago**, which has an outdoor theatre used during the Umbria Jazz Festival and other summertime events, and lovely gardens for picnicking.

Terni

Because doves mate on his day (or so they say), the first bishop of Terni, San Valentino, became the special patron of lovers and the greeting card industry. Curiously, the stodgy Terni-ites themselves have only recently picked up on the notoriety of their old bishop, and at the St Valentine's Market you may even see a pink heart or two as you go to pay your respects to his headless body in the basilica. Terni has little else to offer, besides trains and buses to other places, and shots of viper juice (or *Viparo*, the local *aperitivo* that has all the qualities of flat rum and Coke); as one of Italy's chief steel and armaments manufacturers—the gun that shot Kennedy was made in Terni—the city was condensed into rubble by air raids during the Second World War. It was during the original building of the steelworks that bulldozers uncovered one of the largest and richest Etruscan necropoli, although all the finds have been carted off to Rome's Villa Giulia Museum. The ancient Romans called it *Interamna Nahars*—a real mouthful that was traditionally considered the birthplace of the historian Tacitus, although scholars now quibble that Terni actually produced a more meagre Tacitus, Claudius Tacitus, emperor for a day. These days the city is a Cinecittà wannabe in Italian film; much of Roberto Benigni's *La Vita è Bella*, was made here.

Of Roman Terni only part of the **amphitheatre** remains, now employed as a pensioners' *bocce* court in the city's prettiest area, off the main Corso del Popolo. Visible from the Corso and Piazza Europa, the tiny round church of **San Salvatore**, locally known as the Sun Temple, was built in the 5th century, with a nave added in the 12th. Nearby stands the **Palazzo Spada** (1546) by Antonio da Sangallo the Younger, the best of Terni's surviving palaces. Across Via Garibaldi from the Manassei is the Palazzo Manassei, which houses the **Pinacoteca Comunale** (*open Mon–Sat 10–1 and 4–7; adm*), with Umbrian paintings, a *Marriage of St Catherine* by Gozzoli and, best of all, a large collection of works by Terni's own Orneore Metelli (1872–1938), a shoemaker and great naïve artist.

San Gemini, 13km north of Terni, is known for its mineral springs, located in a pretty park of old oaks. Four kilometres further on lie the evocative ruins of the Roman city of **Carsulae**, destroyed by the Goths and never rebuilt. Lying unfenced out in the open Carsulae is made lovely by its pretty environs: you can stroll along the original Via Flaminia, past the ruins of a theatre, amphitheatre, a mausoleum, temples and an arch dedicated to Trajan. Further north,

Acquasparta, within its medieval walls, has more locally famous curative waters and a small zoo; in the summer it hosts a German *lieder*-singing contest.

Narni

Narni, on a cliff over the Nera, is a picturesque hill town, tumbling in a jumble under its well-preserved castle, built in the 1300s by the ubiquitous Cardinal Albornoz. It was a Roman colony, and birthplace of Emperor Nerva, who lasted somewhat longer than Terni's emperor. Narni has several gems—in its **Duomo**, founded in the 12th century, there's a lovely early medieval screen of marble and Cosmati work. In the attractive 13th-century **Palazzo del Podestà** (*open Mon–Sat 8–7, Sun and hols 9–12*) hang a Ghirlandaio, a Gozzoli, and other paintings; with the nearby **Loggia dei Priori** by Gattapone it forms a fine setting for Narni's springtime medieval pageant, the *Corso dell'Anello*—the Tournament of the Ring—in which the various quarters of the town compete in a festival traditionally held on the second Sunday in May, one of the most spectacular and evocative festas in Umbria.

Narni has several other interesting churches: the pretty 12th-century **Santa Maria in Pensole**, the 14th-century **San Francesco**, built over one of St Francis' huts, and the 15th-century **Sant'Agostino**, on the other side of town. Down by the river and Narni's railway station are the romantic ruins of the **Ponte d'Augusto**, the 1st-century bridge that carried the Via Flaminia over the Nera.

Amelia

North of Narni, halfway between the Nera and the Tiber, lies the ancient agricultural town of Amelia. Both Cato and Pliny wrote that *Ameria* was centuries older than Rome, and as towering evidence of the fact stand its ancient **Pelasgian-Umbrian Walls**, dating back to the 5th century BC, built of massive polygonal blocks, 10ft thick and 23ft high. The **Duomo**, founded in 1050, with its original campanile, contains two Turkish banners captured at the Battle of Lepanto. Near the Tiber, **Lugnano in Teverina** has a 12th-century church, **Santa Maria Assunta**, a Romanesque gem with a curious porch and bas-reliefs, topped by an eagle instead of a cross; inside there's a good triptych by L'Alunno. **Penna in Teverina**, near Orte, is an old fortified town with a castle much disputed by Rome's eternal Punch and Judy factions, the Colonna and Orsini families, until the Colonna simply sold it to the Orsini. Some members of the family liked the area so much that they constructed a **Palazzo Orsini** with a fine 18th-century Italian garden attached. Other relics of that century are the *Mammalocchi*, allegorical figures in travertine standing at the entrance to another estate. On the first Sunday in October, wine is miraculously made to pour from Amelia's fountains.

Where to Stay and Eating Out

Norcia ✉ 06046

★★★**Nuovo Hotel Posta**, Via C. Battisti 10, ✆/℻ 0743 817 434 (*moderate*) has reasonable rooms. Its restaurant serves the famous, hearty, robust local fare of Castelluccio lentils, boar salami, *tortellini alla norcina* (with ricotta and sausage), and lamb with truffles, topped off by a tumbler of Norcia's nasty grappa flavoured with truffles. ★★★**Grotta Azzurra**, Via Alfieri, ✆/℻ 0743 816 513 (*moderate*) offers equally good rooms and an enjoyable restaurant with a different approach to local culinary traditions: a lighter touch in its truffled dishes, competing with a tasty risotto with crayfish from the Nera, fettuccine with trout, or delicious grilled mushrooms.

Dal Francese, Via Riguardati 16, ✆ 0743 816 290 (*moderate*) is the ideal place for a bumper meal. Try the smoked turkey and home-made salami for *antipasto*, followed by a pasta medley of *tris al tartufo*, or *gnocchi al tartufo*; for a main course choose between trout dishes, tender grilled lamb or *braciola in agrodolce con tartufi* (chop in sweet-and-sour sauce with truffles). There's also a good wine list. *Closed Fri.*

Cascia ✉ 06043

As its name suggests, ★★**Centrale**, Piazza Garibaldi 36, ✆ 0743 76736 (*cheap*) is in a handy location, while ★★**Mini Hotel La Tavernetta**, Via Palombi, ✆/✆ 0743 71387 (*cheap*) is a family-run establishment, with eight clean comfortable rooms. It also has a very good restaurant, serving well-cooked local dishes based on wild mushrooms, salamis, trout and lamb. *Closed Tues.*

Scheggino ✉ 06040

Quiet Scheggino has one hotel, the charming little ★★**Del Ponte**, Via Borgo 15, ✆ 075 61131 (*moderate*), right on the Nera River, with 12 rooms and, in the restaurant, delicious meals based on Scheggino's two specialities: crayfish and truffles. *Closed Mon.*

Ferentillo ✉ 05034

On the SS209 south of Ferentillo, near Montefranco, ★★★**Fontegaia**, ✆ 0744 388 621, ✆ 0744 388 623 (*moderate*) is the hotel with most pretensions in the Valnerina; its rooms are very comfortable, there's a playground for children, and beautiful gardens for dining *al fresco*; the restaurant is a favourite for locals going out for a special occasion, if a bit heavy-handed with cream sauces.

Arrone ✉ 05031

Near Arrone on the SS209, ★★**Rossi**, ✆ 0744 788 372, ✆ 0744 788 305 (*cheap*) has 16 modern rooms, and one of the best restaurants in the area (*moderate*), with excellent *crostini*, spaghetti with truffles, and grills, served in a pretty garden. *Closed Fri.* On the Polino road out of Arrone, keep your eyes peeled for the **Rema** (*cheap*), a little trattoria with outdoor picnic tables, serving Umbrian fare with a flair; try the *ciriole* (home-made spaghetti) with mushrooms and grilled lamb. *Closed Mon.*

Terni ✉ 05100

Central ★★★★**Valentino**, Via Plinio il Giovane 3, ✆ 0744 402 550, ✆ 0744 403 335 (*expensive*) has comfortable modern rooms and one of the city's classiest restaurants, the **Fontanello**, featuring fresh ingredients in tasty and imaginative dishes. Near the *superstrada* exit the contemporary ★★★★**Garden**, Via Bramante 6, ✆ 0744 300 041, ✆ 0744 300 414 (*expensive*) is Terni's prettiest hotel, with comfortable rooms, plant-filled balconies and a pool. A short distance from the station, ★★★**Hotel de Paris**, Viale Stazione 52, ✆ 0744 58040, ✆ 0744 58047 (*moderate*) is nondescript but convenient. Up at Lake Piediluco, the pick of the crop is posh ★★★**Casalago**, ✆ 0744 368 421, ✆ 0744 368 425 (*moderate*), a largish hotel overlooking the water.

Tacitus, Piazza Tacito, ✆ 0744 425147 (*moderate*), in the main piazza, serves good local cooking. *Closed Mon.* For more adventurous dining try **Gulliver**, Via Sant'Alò

10, ℂ 0744 425 225 (*moderate*), owned by four locals determined to wake Terni out of its stultifying provincialism with dishes as daring as sturgeon stuffed with saffron and courgettes, and spinach with quails' eggs in a fondue sauce. *Closed Wed.*

Narni ✉ 05035

Most of the hotels are down by the river and the station, at Narni Scalo. The finest is ★★★★**Dei Priori**, Vicolo del Comune 4, ℂ 0744 726 843, ＠ 0744 726 844 (*moderate*), in a medieval palace, with very comfortable rooms and a high-quality restaurant, **La Loggia** ℂ 0744 722 744 (*moderate*) that predates the hotel. It has long been on the maps of visiting gourmets, with an amazing variety of country fare and local specialities. *Closed Mon.* For something with a touch of the Arabian Nights, try the ★★★**Minareto**, Via Cappuccini Nuovi 32, ℂ 0744 726 343, ＠ 0744 726 284 (*moderate*), on the outskirts, with eight pretty rooms and a garden, near a tiny lake.

Todi and Orvieto

Two of Umbria's best-known hill towns are easily accessible from Rome; Orvieto especially, with its stupendous cathedral and wine, is a popular destination for day-trippers. Todi is a bit further and a bit more sombre, more mysteriously Umbrian, a good foil to Orvieto. For a memorable dose of beauty and culture take in both towns and the lovely scenery in between, with a stop at Baschi for an amazing meal at one of the jewels in Italy's gastronomic crown.

Getting Around

Todi is linked by **bus** with Terni, Perugia and Rome, and by the FCU's little choochoo **trains** with Perugia and Terni. Trains arrive at the Stazione Ponte Rio, ℂ 075 894 2092. Orvieto is on the main railway line between Florence and Rome, and is also linked by bus with Terni. In both towns municipal buses make the trip up the hill; in Orvieto there is also a **funicular** from the station to the top of the town. Unfortunately only one bus a day runs between Todi and Orvieto, passing through the lovely scenery above the Tiber Valley.

Todi: the World's Most Liveable Town

Despite a name that suggests an Italian *Wind in the Willows*, Todi is a serious-minded place, perched atop its high and lonely hill, with more affinity to eagles than amphibians; it was the former who showed the ancient Umbrians where to plant the city they called *Tuter*, high atop what is now the Rocca. Later the Etruscans built their city lower down, around the Piazza del Popolo, and, according to legend, one day they went nasty, slaughtering their Umbrian neighbours and making the rest slaves. In Todi's plump and prosperous Middle Ages the eagle struck again, this time swooping down on Amelia and Terni (symbolized by the two eaglets on Todi's coat of arms); yet at the same time it produced one of Italy's great uncanonized saints, Jacopone dei Benedetti (1228–1306), the master of the *Laudesi*—medieval Franciscan poets—who, like St Francis, sang songs of praise to cheer the people. Jacopone, before becoming 'Christ's clown', was a wealthy lawyer, married to a noble lady. Like any true Italian he loved to see her dressed up to the nines and, although she gently protested, she let him have his way. Then came the day, at a public festival, when the platform she stood on collapsed; as she lay there, Jacopone ripped aside her garments to examine her injuries, only to discover that under her silks she wore a rough hair shirt. She died, and he became a convert—but such an eccentric one that the Franciscans at first refused him admission. In the end, however, he found his niche with the Spirituals, the most unworldly branch of the order, living in a monastery at Collazzone, near Perugia, where he is believed to have composed the famous Latin *Stabat Mater Dolorosa* and the *Stabat Mater Speciosa*.

Modern Todi is a sophisticated little place, famous for its carpentry and woodworking. In the past few years it has, believe it or not, consistently been voted the world's most livable town by the University of Kentucky, an accolade which has brought American tycoons rushing to buy up its villas. In April Todi hosts one of Italy's major antique fairs, and in August and September the *Mostra Nazionale dell'Artigianato*, a national crafts fair.

Tourist Information

Piazza Umberto I 6, ✆ 075 894 2686, or ✆ 075 894 3395, ✉ 075 894 2406.

Tempio della Consolazione

The best way to approach Todi is from the southwest where the road, winding its way to the clouds, passes by way of one of the most perfect of Renaissance churches, the ivory-coloured Tempio della Consolazione, designed by Cola da Caprorola in 1508, and completed 99 years later. Its serene purity of form, geometrically harmonious lines and lovely proportions are the hallmarks of Bramante, who may well have had a hand in the design. The Tempio's lonely setting lends it a special charm, best viewed from Todi's citadel. The white classical interior, in the symmetrical form of a Greek cross, contains Baroque statues of the apostles.

Piazza del Popolo

Todi's streets all converge on its magnificent Piazza del Popolo, the centre of civic life since the days of the Etruscans. The piazza is a medieval pageant in grey stone; sternest of them all, the **Palazzo dei Priori** (1293–1337) has square battlements with a chunky tower, while the **Palazzo del Popolo** (1213, with the swallowtail crenellations) and its adjacent **Palazzo del Capitano** (1290) manage to drum up more charm, with a grand Gothic stairway and attractive mullioned windows. Up on the fourth floor there's a small **Museo Etrusco-Romano** and **Pinacoteca** that you can take in if it rains, and an impressive Gothic hall with frescoes (*open 10.30–1 and 2–4.30; till 6 in the summer; closed Mon; adm*).

On the far side of the piazza the squarish **Duomo** is enthroned atop a distinguished flight of steps. Begun in the 12th century, the façade has a fine rose window and delicately decorated portal, while the interior is embellished with good Gothic capitals and a Gothic arcade with a 14th-century altarpiece; parishioners who turned around to gossip during Mass were confronted by a not-too-terrifying 16th-century vision of the *Last Judgement*, painted by Farraù da Faenza. Before leaving the piazza, be sure to take a look from its belvedere.

San Fortunato and the Rocca

Todi's medieval lanes invite aimless roaming, but if you're pressed for time head straight for the Franciscan church of **San Fortunato**, built in 1292 (take Via Mazzini), located in a prominent position atop a broad stairway. A bronze statue of Jacopone stands near the foot of the steps; his locally revered tomb is in San Fortunato's crypt. The church's unfinished façade has three recessed Romanesque portals, the central one especially lovely with its carvings of acanthus leaves and human figures. The airy interior contains Todi's greatest work of art, a fresco by Masolino of the *Madonna and Child*. Above San Fortunato, at the top of the town, the **Rocca** is Todi's ruined 14th-century citadel, public park and magnificent belvedere, offering an unforgettable view of the valley of the Tiber and the Tempio della Consolazione.

Todi ✉ *06059*   ***Where to Stay and Eating Out***

The loveliest hotel is the ★★★★★**San Valentino**, Frazione Fiore, ✆/🖷 075 894 4103 (*very expensive*), just outside town on the Perugia road, a gracious villa with just 12 rooms, each beautifully furnished (mostly with antiques), a tennis court and pool. ★★★★**Bramante**, Via Orvietana 48, ✆/🖷 075 894 8074 (*expensive*) is a 13th-century convent, just outside town, in a lovely setting. ★★★**Villa Luisa**, Via A. Cortesi 147, ✆ 075 894 8571, 🖷 075 894 8472 (*moderate*) is a pleasant place near the centre, with a garden and parking. There are no cheap hotels, but try the *agriturismo* places on the periphery: **L'Arco**, at Cardigliano, ✆ 075 894 7534; **Poponi**, Via delle Piagge 26, ✆ 075 894 8233; or **Castello di Porchiano**, at Porchiano, ✆ 075 885 3127.

In Todi, the home-made fat spaghetti is called *ombricelli*, served by preference *alla boscaiola* (with tomatoes, piquant black olives and hot peppers); the wine to look for, dating back to the days of the Roman Republic, is the dry white *Grechetto di Todi*.

The **Umbria**, Via S. Bonaventura 13, ✆ 075 894 2390 (*expensive*), under the stone arches just off the Piazza del Popolo, serves fine Umbrian cuisine with an enchanting Umbrian view. Meals begin with a delicious selection of *antipasti*, followed perhaps by *spaghetti alla tudertina* and succulent grilled *secondi*, ranging from trout to boar. *Closed Tues.* **Lucaroni**, Viale Cortesi 57, ✆ 075 894 2694 (*expensive*) offers more sophisticated dishes, such as a delicious risotto with pigeon, black truffles and port, and linguine with crab—a refreshing change after so many Umbrian meat dishes. *Closed Tues.* **Jacopone**, Piazza Jacopone, ✆ 075 894 2366 (*moderate*) serves traditional Umbrian dishes in an attractive dining room. *Closed Mon.* Tucked away down a narrow alley off the main piazza, the **Italia**, Via del Monte 27, ✆ 075 894 2643 (*moderate*) is an unpretentious welcoming trattoria, with cheerful red tablecloths. Specialities include *capriccio*, an oven-baked pasta dish. *Closed Mon.*

Orvieto

Orvieto owes much of its success to an ancient volcano. First it created the city's magnificent pedestal—a 1073ft sheer crag of tufa, resembling a mesa in the American southwest. The same volcano then enriched the hillsides below with a special mixture of minerals that are part of the alchemy in Orvieto's famous white wine. Although new buildings crowd the base of the mesa, the medieval town on top—crowned by its stupendous cathedral—looks much the same as it has for the last 500 years. The scaffolding you see around the cliffs, however, is part of a recent effort to shore it up; human progress isn't as much of a threat to the old centre as are such natural forces as erosion and landslides.

Attracted by Orvieto's incomparable defensive position, the Etruscans settled it early and named it *Volsinii*. It was one of the 12 cities of their confederation, and one that fought frequently with the Roman upstarts until those same upstarts laid it waste in 280 BC. The Etruscans departed in a huff and founded a new *Volsinii* on the shores of Lake Bolsena, leaving behind their old city (*Urbs Vetus*, hence 'Orvieto'). Like Viterbo, Orvieto in the Middle Ages was an important stronghold of the Papal States—especially important for popes who could take refuge here when their polls were down in Rome.

Tourist Information

Piazza Duomo 24, © 0763 341 772, ✉ 0763 344 433; *tn2677@krenet.it*

The Cathedral

It was during one of Orvieto's papal visitations, in the 1260s (Urban IV), that the Miracle of Bolsena occurred. A Bohemian priest named Peter, passing through on his way to Rome, was asked to celebrate Mass in the town of Bolsena. Father Peter had long been secretly sceptical about the doctrine of transubstantiation (that the Host in truth becomes the body of Christ), but during this Mass the Host itself answered his doubts by dripping blood on the altar linen. Marvelling, Peter took the linen to the Pope in Orvieto, who declared it a miracle and instituted the feast of Corpus Christi. Thomas Aquinas, also in Orvieto at the time, was instructed to compose a suitable office for the new holy day, while the Pope promised Orvieto (a bit unfair to poor Bolsena!) a magnificent new cathedral to enshrine the blood-stained relic.

The cornerstone was laid in 1290 and, though begun in the Romanesque style, its plan was transformed into Gothic by master architect Lorenzo Maitani of Siena in 1310. Subsequent master architects included such luminaries as Andrea Pisano, Orcagna and Sammicheli, but even then the mighty edifice, visible for miles around, wasn't completed until the 1600s.

The end result is one of Italy's greatest cathedrals, with a stunning, sumptuous façade resembling a giant triptych. This is Maitani's masterpiece, and why the church is called the 'Golden Lily of Cathedrals'. As you approach, you are struck first by the dazzling, technicolour hues of its mosaics, then by the elaborate prickly spires and tracery, and then by the richness and beauty of the sculptural detail. It is said that 152 sculptors worked on the cathedral, but it was Maitani himself who contributed the best work—the remarkable design and execution of the celebrated **bas-reliefs** on the lower pilasters that recount the Christian story from the Creation to the Last Judgement, a Bible in stone that captures the essence of the stories with vivid drama and detail. Maitani's *Last Judgement*, in particular, is enough to make the fresco in Todi Cathedral look as dire as a soft-touch card. Maitani also cast the four bronze figures of the Evangelists' symbols, all ready to step right off the façade, and sculpted the angels in the lunette over the central portal, who pay homage to a *Madonna* by Andrea Pisano. The great rose window is by Orcagna, and the controversial bronze doors, portraying *Works of Mercy*, are by Emilio Greco, finished in 1965.

In contrast with the soaring verticality of the façade, the sides and interior are banded with horizontal zebra stripes. Inside, in the muted light filtered through alabaster windows, the stripes merge into shadows. The lack of clutter does much to reveal the cathedral's fine proportions and height. The columns of the nave support rounded arches, and above them runs a pretty clerestory. In the nave note Gentile da Fabriano's 1426 fresco of the *Madonna*, near the baptismal font, and the 1579 *Pietà* by Ippolito Scalza, a native of Orvieto.

The greatest treasures, however, are in the chapels, especially the **Cappella della Madonna di San Brizio**, embellished with one of the finest fresco cycles of the Renaissance. The project was begun in 1447 by Fra Angelico, with the assistance of Benozzo Gozzoli. The Angelic One finished two sections—the serene *Christ in Judgement*, with the prophets, while Gozzoli contributed the hierarchies of angels. Before he could finish, however, Fra Angelico was summoned to Rome. Orvieto then commissioned Perugino to complete the work, but he never got around to it, and finally, in 1499, the city hired Luca Signorelli, who finished the vaults according to Fra Angelico's design.

The walls, however, are Signorelli's own masterpiece; his breathtaking and awesome compositions of the *Last Judgement*, the *Preaching of the Antichrist* (a very unusual subject) and the *Resurrection of the Dead* are generally acclaimed to be the forerunners of Michelangelo's *Last Judgement* in the Sistine Chapel. Yet it is hard to say that Michelangelo surpassed them; Signorelli's remarkable foreshortening skills, draughtsmanship and ability to simplify nature and architecture into their essential geometrical forms give the frescoes tremendous power. To the left of the figure of the preaching Antichrist, Signorelli has portrayed himself and Fra Angelico, both listening solemnly, as does Dante standing amid the crowd, while in the background chaos and catastrophe are busy at work. Then the world ends, a darkened sky is shot with streaks of fire, the earth shakes, and in literal detail the dead re-emerge from the earth, skeletons pulling themselves out of the ground forming new coats of flesh. Some are met by Charon, who rows them across to an overcrowded Renaissance Hell, to keep company with Signorelli's faithless mistress. Below the frescoes Signorelli painted medallions of the great poets and the pre-Socratic philosopher Empedocles, and some scenes from the *Divine Comedy*.

To the left, the **Cappella del Corporale** is frescoed with scenes of the *Miracle of Bolsena* by Ugolino of Siena (1360s) and the 1339 *Madonna dei Raccomandati* by Lippo Memmi. The magnificent silver and enamel *Reliquary of the Corporale* on the altar is by another Sienese, Ugolino di Vieri; the blood-stained linen cloth it holds is shown only on major religious holidays, and is taken around Orvieto in procession during the feast of Corpus Christi.

The Piazza del Duomo

The cathedral square is a fitting setting for the Golden Lily. On one side a row of old houses includes a couple of wine bars where you can try Orvieto's vintages and *salumeria*, while on top of the square clock tower a 14th-century figure named Maurizio strikes the hours. Opposite, in Palazzo Faina, is the beautifully renovated **Museo Claudio Faina e Civico** (*open Oct–Mar daily 10–1 and 2.30–5; April–Sept daily 10–1 and 3–7; closed Mon*), containing one of Italy's top private archaeological collections and Orvieto's excellent Etruscan collection, excavated from local tombs; the ground floor has the civic collection, with decorations from the

Belevedere temple and the 'Venus' of Cannicella; the top floor enjoys one of the best views of the cathedral. On the south side of the cathedral the **Palazzo Papale**, or Popes' Palace, begun by Boniface VIII in 1297 and finished in the 1500s, contains the **Museo dell'Opera del Duomo** (*closed for restoration until kingdom come*), with art that once filled the cathedral—statues by grand masters such as Arnolfo di Cambio and the Pisanos, and grand statues by little-known hands, especially the colossal *Apostles*. The best work is a lovely, richly coloured polyptych by Simone Martini. The adjacent Palazzo Apostolico (1304) hold the **Museo Archaeologico Nazionale** (*open daily 9–1.30 and 2.30–7, Sun 9–1; closed Mon; adm*) with another excellent collection, especially Etruscan, with two reconstructed tombs.

Smaller Churches

In contrast to its heavenly cathedral (even Pope John XXIII said that on Judgement Day the angels would bear it up to paradise), the rest of Orvieto is unpretentious and worldly, a solid, bourgeois, medieval town. On Via del Duomo stands the **Torre del Moro**, a medieval tower you can ascend and, further on, the pretty 12th-century **Palazzo del Popolo**, a tufa palace with mullioned windows and arches; the little piazza in front is the site of a colourful vegetable market. From here Via della Pace leads back to the narrow church of **San Domenico**, built in 1233, just after St Dominic's canonization—the first church ever dedicated to him. The most scholarly Dominican of them all, St Thomas Aquinas, taught here at the former monastery. Although the nave was amputated for a barracks in 1934, there's a Cardinal's tomb in the surviving transept by the great Florentine Arnolfo di Cambio (1281).

From Via del Duomo, Orvieto's main drag, Corso Cavour, continues west to the city's main square, Piazza della Repubblica. On the corner the 12th-century church of **Sant'Andrea** has an extremely unusual 12-sided campanile, pierced by mullioned windows and topped by bellicose crenellations. A 6th-century church was discovered underneath Sant'Andrea and underneath it were found an Etruscan street and buildings (*the sacristan has the key to the excavations*). Sant'Andrea basks in the memory of great events that took place within its walls: here Innocent III proclaimed the Fourth Crusade, and here, in 1281, Charles of Anjou and his glittering retinue attended the coronation of Pope Martin IV. Beyond Piazza della Repubblica lie some of Orvieto's most ancient streets, lined with tufa houses; follow them back to the northwesternmost corner of town, site of the church of **San Giovenale**, begun in 1009 and crammed full of frescoes from the 12th to the 15th centuries.

Orvieto claims one other noteworthy church, **San Lorenzo**, reached by Via Maitani from the Piazza Duomo, or on Via Scalza from Corso Cavour. Built in the 14th century, San Lorenzo shelters a cylindrical Etruscan altar under its high altar, both of which are protected by a lovely 12th-century stone canopy. Byzantine-style frescoes cover the walls, with elongated figures and staring eyes; one set depicts the life of St Lawrence, who retained his sense of humour even while being literally grilled.

Pozzo di San Patrizio

Orvieto's northeastern end (near the upper station of the funicular) is dominated by a **citadel** built in 1364 by the great papal legate, Cardinal Albornoz. Only the walls, a gate and a tower survive, encompassing a pretty little garden of parasol pines. There are lovely views from the ramparts, stretching from the shallow Paglia River all the way to the Tiber Valley. Next to the citadel lie the foundations of an **Etruscan temple** and the **Pozzo di San Patrizio** or St

Patrick's Well (*open summer daily 10–7; winter daily 10–6; adm*), designed in the 1530s by Antonio da Sangallo the Younger on the orders of the calamitous Pope Clement VII. It is a unique work of engineering, meant to supply Orvieto in times of siege; to reach the spring below, Sangallo had to dig down the equivalent of seven storeys, and to haul the water to the surface he designed two spiral stairs of 248 steps, which never cross—one for the water-carriers and their donkeys going down, another for going up. Clement, having just fled the sack of Rome, was perhaps justified in the paranoia that made him desire such a monumental drinking hole, but it was never needed. The stairs are dimly lit by windows on to the central shaft, but beware if you descend; you have to get back up again.

Down below Orvieto's northern cliffs, along the road that leads to the railway station, there are several **Etruscan tombs**, nothing special as Etruscan tombs go, but worth a look if you don't have a chance to see any of the more elaborate models. The most impressive is the 4th-century BC **Necropoli del Crocefisso** (*open daily 9–1hr before sunset*).

The Vine of Life

Orvieto Classico, Umbria's most famous wine, comes from 16 designated areas in Terni and Viterbo provinces, and consists of a careful mixture of several different grapes, with Tuscan Trebbiano and Verdello dominant. The resulting wine, either dry (Orvieto *secco*) or moderately sweet (*abboccato*), is a delicious, light straw-coloured wine; the Antinori label is one of the best, but don't neglect the others. They can be tasted and bought at *cantine* around town, except on Tuesdays, when they all close. The tourist office has a list of local vineyards which welcome visitors.

Villages around Orvieto

Between Orvieto and Todi, **Baschi** is a harmonious hill town above the Tiber Valley, near where the river widens to form the **Lago di Corbara**; the area is a popular centre for *agriturismo*, for those who dream of staying in a farmhouse amid the vineyards. **Porano**, south of Orvieto, is a pretty town with a castle, set in the rolling hills. Nearby there's a painted Etruscan tomb, the **Eskanas Tomb**; to see it, inquire at the *Comune* (town hall).

Little **Castel Giorgio**, west of Orvieto on the SS74 into Lazio, is a relatively new town, but one that has taken peculiarly well to American football, having constructed one of the finest stadiums in Europe. **Ficulle**, north of Orvieto on SS71, was the birthplace of Rome's tragic hero of the Middle Ages, Cola di Rienzo, and its castle of the Marchese Antinori produces some of Orvieto's finest wine.

Orvieto ✉ *05018*   ***Where to Stay and Eating Out***

In town there's the sumptuous ******Palazzo Piccolomini**, Piazza Ranieri 36, ✆ 0763 341 743, ✆ 0763 391 046 (*expensive*), in a medieval palace. ******Maitani**, Via Maitani 5, ✆ 0763 342 011, ✆ 0763 342 012 (*expensive*), just opposite the cathedral, has comfortable rooms and parking. A 12th-century abbey contains

★★★★La Badia, located 5km south on the road to Bagnoregio, ✆ 0763 301 959, @ 0763 305 396 (*expensive*), with great views of Orvieto. Rooms are still a bit monkish, and in the grounds there's a pool and tennis court.

The old-fashioned **★★★★Aquila Bianca**, Via Garibaldi 13, ✆ 0763 341 246, @ 0763 342 273 (*moderate*) is not particularly luxurious, but has a good central position, a wine cellar for the all-important business of tasting Orvieto, and a garage. **★★★Virgilio**, Piazza Duomo 5/6, ✆ 0763 341 882 (*moderate*) has 13 pleasant rooms, also in an excellent location. **★★★★Villa Bellago**, Strada SS448 Baschi, ✆ 0744 950 521, @ 0744 950 524 (*moderate*), about 12km outside Orvieto, on Lake Corbara near Baschi, is a lovely waterfront hotel converted from three farmhouses and set in its own grounds with a pool, and a terrace restaurant, specializing in giant *Fiorentina* steaks.

Many of Orvieto's cheaper hotels are near the train station, but **★★Duomo**, Via Maurizio 7, ✆ 0763 341 887 (*cheap*), and **★★Posta**, Via Signorelli 18, ✆ 0763 341 909 (*cheap*), both within the city walls, are basic, but clean and comfortable.

At Baschi, 13km southeast of Orvieto on Lake Corbara, you can splurge at a restaurant ranked as one of the five best in Italy: **Vissani**, on SS448, ✆ 0744 950 396 (*very expensive*). In this passionate inner sanctum of *altissima cucina*, you may taste such marvels as oysters with roast onions and thyme sauce, suckling pig, or lobster in broccoli leaves; each dish is accompanied by a specially prepared bread. A fabulous array of Italian and French cheeses and wines will help make your meal unforgettable, though so too will the bill; the restaurant is also one of the most expensive in Italy. Reserve well in advance. *Closed Wed and Sun eve.*

Il Padrino, run by Gianfranco Vissani's parents, in the same building as Vissani, ✆ 0744 950 206 (*expensive*) is rather more affordable: the pasta with seafood or asparagus is lovely, and the *secondi* are classics rarely seen (or well-prepared) in Italy, like Chateaubriand, scampi Newburg, *coq-au-vin* and sole Colbert. *Closed Wed.*

Although Orvieto sees bus loads of day-trippers from Rome, who help keep its often mediocre restaurants in business, there are still some which are worth a try. **Le Grotte del Funaro**, Via Ripa Serancia 41, ✆ 0763 343 276 (*moderate*), an elegant restaurant in a set of tufa caves, serves especially good pasta and mixed grilled meats. *Closed Mon.* **Del Pino da Checco**, Via di Piazza del Popolo 15, ✆ 0763 342 661 (*moderate*) has a lovely terrace with views over the oldest part of town, where you can also enjoy appetizing specialities like *cannelloni alla Ducale*, tagliatelle with artichokes, or *bistecca in intingolo* (beef in a savoury sauce), accompanied by Orvieto's delicious dry wines.

Sette Consoli, Piazza Sant'Angelo, ✆ 0763 343 911 (*cheap*), where you can dine outside in the summer, uses the best local ingredients (*pappardelle* with duck sauce, *gnocchi* with zucchini and mint) and has a good L50,000 *menu degustazione* with three wines. *Closed Wed.*

Lazio

On a Saturday night variety show, the television host discusses the founding of Rome with two comedians dressed up as Romulus and Remus; turning to Remus, the sillier-looking of the pair, he asks: 'What did you ever do?' Remus gets a big laugh from the audience by proudly claiming, 'Well, I founded Lazio.'

Despite being the location of the capital city, Lazio does not get much respect from the average Italian, who thinks of it as a sort of vacuum, half swamps and half poor mountain villages that need to be crossed to get to Rome. Northerners often lump it in with Campania and Calabria as part of the backward south. To an extent it is, though great changes have come in the last 60 years with land reclamation and new industry. Lazio's problem is a simple one: Rome, that most parasitic of all cities. Before there was a Rome this was probably the wealthiest and most densely populated part of non-Greek Italy, the homeland of the Etruscans as well as the rapidly civilizing nations of Sabines, Aequi, Hernici, Volscii and the Latins themselves, from whom Lazio (*Latium*) takes its name.

After the Roman triumph the Etruscan and the Italic cities shrivelled and died; those Romans who proved such good governors elsewhere caused utter ruin to their own back yard. A revival came in the Middle Ages, when Rome was only one of a score of squabbling feudal towns, but once again, when the popes restored Rome, Lazio's fortunes declined. To finance their grandiose building projects, Renaissance popes literally taxed Lazio into extinction; whole villages and large stretches of countryside were abandoned and given over to bandits, and land drained in medieval times reverted to malarial swamps. Modern Rome, at least since Mussolini's day, has begun to mend its ways; the government still considers Lazio a development area, and pumps a lot of money into it.

Not to be Missed

Many of Lazio's attractions are easily seen as day trips from Rome—Tivoli, Ostia and a garland of hill towns, all of which you'll find in a special section after Rome. Northern Lazio contains no fewer than 28 excavated **Etruscan sites**, and if these ancient charmers interest you there will be plenty of opportunities for Etruscan detours, whether you approach Rome along the SS2 (Via Cassia) from Orvieto, or the A12 and SS1 (Via Aurelia) along the coast—including the spectacular painted tombs of **Cerveteri** and **Tarquinia**. Northern Lazio also offers the fine old city of **Viterbo**, and a string of large **lakes** in a pretty landscape of jumbled hills.

In southern Lazio you'll see new land and new towns: the reclaimed Pontine Marshes, with Mussolini-founded towns like Aprilia and Latina, and others that had to be rebuilt from the bottom up after the war. Others, like **Alatri** and **Cori** wrapped in cyclopean walls, are among the oldest towns in Europe. Early monastic centres make up most of the religious sights, with **Montecassino** first among them. The coast is generally plain, with some noteworthy exceptions—the old walled port of **Gaeta**, some of the beaches around **Sperlonga** and **Terracina**, and the wetlands wilderness of the **Monte Circeo** national park.

N

10 km
5 miles

Lazio

Viterbo

Ah, Viterbo. Where else can one rest in a café on Death Square, or stroll over to the Piazza of the Fallen to pay one's respects to Our Lady of the Plague? Surrounded by grey, forbidding walls and the ghastly modern districts, the city is actually rather cute inside, full of grand churches and palaces, and medieval streets brightened with fountains and flowers. The population seems evenly divided between teenagers on scooters, as bejewelled and trendy as their counterparts in Rome, and blasé soldiers from Italy's biggest army base. Like the rest of Lazio, Viterbo has had more than its share of troubles, most of them traceable to the proximity of Rome. That geographical necessity, however, also gave Viterbo its greatest period of glory. For much of the 13th century, Viterbo, and not Rome, was the seat of the popes.

History

A small city in Etruscan and Roman times, Viterbo's modern history begins with its fortification by the Lombards in the 8th century. By 1100, it was a free *comune*, one of the few cities in this part of Italy strong and energetic enough to manage it. Viterbo was usually an enemy of Rome and, when Arnold of Brescia's revolution made Pope Eugenius III a refugee in 1145, he came here. Emperor Frederick Barbarossa soon restored the popes to Rome, but again in 1257 Martin V found Viterban hospitality gratifying when the Guelph-Ghibelline wars made Rome too hot for him. In this most confusing period of Italian history, over a dozen popes were crowned, died or at least spent time here, in short stays on their way to or from France, Tivoli—and sometimes even Rome. In 1309, when the 'Babylonian Captivity' carted the papacy off to Avignon, Viterbo could only decline, and when the popes returned, the city that had once been Rome's strongest rival found itself a mere provincial town of the Papal State.

Getting Around

Viterbo actually has three **railway** stations, all just outside the city walls. Regular FS trains to Orvieto and Florence stop at Stazione Porta Fiorentina, north of the walls on Viale Trento. Most trains for Rome leave from here too, also stopping at Stazione Porta Romana, on Viale Raniero Capocci, the big boulevard east of the walls, although lengthy maintenance work has led to irritating delays and cancellations. In addition there is a local line run by the Lazio transport authority COTRAL, which rattles along a separate route from its station next door to Porta Fiorentina, via Bagnaia, Soriano nel Cimino and Cività Castellana, to Piazzale Flaminio (Roma-Nord) station in Rome.

But at the end of the day, the fastest way to reach Viterbo from Rome is by COTRAL **buses**, leaving roughly every thirty minutes from Stazione Saxa Rubra. More buses for Tarquinia, Bolsena, Civitavecchia and other provincial towns leave from Piazza Martiri d'Ungheria, next to Piazza dei Caduti in the town centre.

Tourist Information

Piazza San Carluccio 5, ✆ 0761 304 795.

Piazza del Plebiscito

In Viterbo's centre, two not-so-fierce-looking lions, the city's ancient symbol, gaze out over the typical pair of buildings representing the often conflicting imperial and local powers: the 13th-century **Palazzo dei Priori** (or **Palazzo Comunale**, now the town hall) and its clock tower, and **Palazzo del Podestà** of the 1460s. The politicians won't mind you looking around the former and its fine Renaissance courtyard; ask to see the **Sala Regia** (*open Mon–Sat 8–2, Tues and Thurs also 3–6*), decorated with fanciful Mannerist frescoes on the history of Viterbo from Etruscan times. Across the square is the church of **Sant'Angelo**, the façade of which has for centuries incorporated a Roman sarcophagus (now replaced by a mere photograph) containing the body of a medieval lady of incomparable virtue named Galiena; accounts of her fatal charm and sad demise vary from one Viterban to another.

There are any number of directions you can take from here. Via Ascenzi, under the arch, leads to Piazza dei Caduti and the **Madonna della Peste** (*usually closed*), an octagonal Renaissance church next to the tourist office. Beyond that, by the walls, the **rocca** was built by Cardinal Albornoz in 1354 to keep watch on the Viterbans when the pope returned to Rome. This squat palace-fortress holds the small **Museo Archeologico**, containing reconstructions of Etruscan houses (not tombs, for once!) and finds from the Roman Theatre in Fèrento and Musarna (*open April–Sept Tues–Sun 9–7; Oct–Mar Tues–Sun 9–1.30; adm*). Two of Viterbo's 13th-century popes are buried in the church of **San Francesco**, near Porta Murata at the northern end of the walls. Nearby, off Piazza Verdi, the late 19th-century church of **Santa Rosa** houses the considerable remains of Viterbo's 13th-century patroness, too holy to decompose and usually on display for all to see. Santa Rosa's preaching helped the Viterbans defy a siege by the heretical Emperor Frederick II in 1243 and, to commemorate her, each year on 3 September the men of the town carry a 99ft illuminated wooden steeple called the *macchina*—which is always in danger of toppling—through the streets, surmounted by an image of Rosa. Money permitting, local artists create a new *macchina* every five years (the present one, built in 1998, is a genuine work of art).

East from Piazza del Plebiscito, Via Cavour takes you past the **Casa Poscia**, a rare 13th-century house on a stairway to the left to the **Fontana Grande**, the best of Viterbo's many fountains. Via Garibaldi leads on further east to the Roman Gate and **San Sisto**, a church in parts as old as the 9th century, with an altar made of ancient sculptural fragments. Outside the walls and across Viale Capocci, 13th-century **Santa Maria della Verità** was vandalised by 18th-century redecorators; the plaster frosting is gone now, but only fragments have survived of the Renaissance frescoes by Melozzo da Forlì. The Cappella Mazzatosta, behind an iron grille, has good frescoes of the *Marriage of the Virgin* by Renaissance artist Lorenzo da Viterbo. The adjacent cloisters have fine works from the 14th century, and the **Museo Civico** (*open Tues–Sun 9–7; in winter until 6; adm*) has an archaeological section and a picture gallery.

The Palazzo Papale

From Piazza del Plebiscito the best route of all is down Via San Lorenzo into the heart of Viterbo's oldest quarter. Three streets down and off to the left, **Santa Maria Nuova** is the best-preserved of the city's medieval churches. An ancient image of Jupiter is set into the portal, and St Thomas Aquinas once preached from the small outdoor pulpit in the corner. On the other side of Via San Lorenzo, Viterbo's old market square faces the 11th-century church of the **Gesù**, a medieval tower-fortress, one of several left in the city, and a palazzo that long ago was the town hall. To the south, trailing down from the aforementioned **Piazza della Morte**—ironically one of the lovelier squares in Viterbo—the **San Pellegrino** quarter hangs its web of alleys, arches and stairs along Via San Pellegrino with a romantic and thoroughly medieval air, though in fact few of the buildings are quite that old. The **Museo della Macchina di Santa Rosa**, Via San Pellegrino 60 (*open Sat and Sun 10–12 and 4–7; occasionally it also stays open Wed–Sun*) chronicles Viterbo's most traditional *festa*.

In the opposite direction from San Pellegrino, a bridge on Roman and Etruscan foundations—the **Ponte del Duomo**—carries over to Piazza San Lorenzo and the **Palazzo Papale**, begun in 1266. This squarish, battlemented building, very much in the style of a medieval city hall, is a finer building than the pope's present address in Rome, though admittedly much smaller. On the best part, the open Gothic loggia, you will see lions (for Viterbo) interspersed with the striped coat of arms of the French pope Clement V, who completed the building. Three popes were elected at conclaves in the palace's Great Hall.

Popes and cardinals did not always have an easy time in Viterbo. When Clement IV died—two weeks after he arrived—arguments between the French and Italian cardinals led to a two-year deadlock. Eventually the exasperated people of Viterbo tried to speed up the conclave by locking them in the palace and tearing off the roof; somehow the prelates got around this by making tents in the Great Hall. Finally the Viterbans decided to starve them out, and before long the Church was blessed with the undistinguished compromise choice of Gregory X. He had the roof fixed, but should have repaired the floor as well, since it collapsed six years later, killing his successor, John XXI. He is buried next door in the plain Romanesque **cathedral**.

Around Viterbo: Hot Mud and Tombs

West of the city, some of the Etruscans' and Romans' favourite thermal springs still do whatever it is they do that makes Italians so happy. At the ancient **Springs of Bullicame** you can stop by the roadside for a dip in a sulphurous pool, check into a hotel spa, have an aerosol inhalation to help your sinuses, and a frosting with hot mineral mud to calm your nerves.

Further west, **Tuscània** stands alone at the centre of one of the emptiest, eeriest corners of Italy, a region of low green hills where you will find Etruscan ruins, old castles and religious shrines, but no people. Tuscània was a leading Etruscan city around the 4th century BC and regained its importance for a short while in the early Middle Ages. Today the city is still recovering from a bad earthquake in 1971. Etruscan sarcophagi are on display at the **Museo Archeologico** in the former Santa Maria del Riposo convent (*open April–Sept Tues–Sun 9–7; Oct–Mar until 6; adm*). They are nothing special, but Tuscània has two unique early churches east of the town: **San Pietro** and **Santa Maria Maggiore** (*both open daily 9–1; in summer also 3–7; in winter also 2–5*), both begun in the 8th century, with additions in the 11th and 12th centuries. Besides their carved altars, pulpits and painting from the 8th–14th centuries, both have unusual sculpted façades—San Pietro's especially, with colourful Cosmati work, fragments of ancient sculpture and outlandish grotesques. Perhaps some of the churches of Rome looked like this before their Renaissance and Baroque rebuildings.

Another road west from Viterbo—this one an 8km dead end—leads to the site of **Fèrento**, a rival city that Viterbo destroyed in the Middle Ages. Little is left, really, save a very well-preserved **Teatro Romano**, where concerts are sometimes held in the summer (*open Tues–Fri and Sun 9–1, Sat 9–one hour before sunset*). East of Viterbo, the road for Orte enters the old suburb of La Quercia, passing in front of a landmark of late Renaissance architecture: **Santa Maria della Quercia**, built in the late 1470s. The distinctive 1509 façade has a carved oak tree (*quercia*) and lions, and lunettes by Andrea della Robbia over the doors.

Inside, the beautiful marble tabernacle contains a miraculous painting of the Virgin, and there is also a fine Gothic cloister; ask the custodian to let you in to the fascinating **Museo degli Ex-Voto**, filled with plaques painted over the centuries with scenes of the Madonna's miracles. **Bagnaia**, 6km east, was an old hill village expanded by wealthy Viterban bishops into a summer resort. In the 1570s Cardinal de Gambera commissioned Vignola to create **Villa Lante** (*gardens open Tues–Sun 9–one hour before sunset; guided tours every half-hour; adm*), with one of the most striking of all Renaissance complexes: two villas share a large park and classic geometric Italian garden, full of groves and statuary; water rises from a number of fountains then cascades back down decorative stairs and terraces—an impressive sight, when they feel like turning it on.

This road continues into the beech forests of the Cimino Hills, meeting **Soriano nel Cimino**, with a medieval castle and an extinct volcano, Monte Cimino, for a neighbour. South of Viterbo, if you're heading for Lake Vico (*see* below), you'll pass through the lovely town of **San Martino al Cimino**, built around a fine 13th-century French Gothic Cistercian abbey; the town itself is an unusual example of Baroque planning, full of trees and half-surrounded by a single curving lane of terraced houses.

The Monster Park at Bomarzo

Some of the same sculptors who worked on St Peter's in Rome made this shabby little nightmare, hidden away in the Lazio hills. The two works seem somehow related, opposite sides of the coin that may help in explaining the tragic, neurotic atmosphere of late 16th-century Italy. One of the Orsini, that ancient and powerful Roman family, commissioned this collection of huge, strange sculptures; he called it his *Sacro Bosco*—Sacred Wood—and in its present state it is impossible to tell whether it was the complex allegory it pretends to be, or just a joke.

The **Parco dei Mostri** (*open daily 9–one hour before sunset; adm exp*)—one of the most popular sights in Lazio—lies just outside Bomarzo, one of the most woebegone little towns in this part of Italy. The setting adds to its charm, as does the habit of the present owners of running it like an Alabama roadside attraction, complete with bars, a restaurant and a playground with a small-scale football field for the kids. Near the entrance you come upon the impressive though dilapidated Tempietto, a domed temple of unknown purpose attributed to Vignola. From there you wander the ill-kept grounds, encountering at every turn colossal monuments and eroded illegible inscriptions: a 20ft-tall screaming face, where you can walk inside the mouth, under an inscription that reads 'every thought flees', and find a small table and benches, apparently waiting for a dinner party; a life-size elephant, perhaps one of Hannibal's, crushing a terrified Roman soldier in its trunk; a giant wrestler, in the act of ripping a defeated opponent in two from the legs; and a leaning tower, just for fun. In every corner decayed Madonnas, mermaids, sphinxes, nymphs and harpies wait to spook you. All are done in a distorted, almost primitive style. It would be almost too easy to read too much into these images: a cry of pain from the degraded, humiliated Italy of the 1560s, half-pretending madness as the only way to be safe from the Spanish and the Inquisition, an exaggerated expression of the over-heated mentality of

Mannerism—or perhaps merely a symbol for the loss of mental balance that followed too many centuries of high culture and over-stimulation. Whatever, the Monster Park will make you feel like an archaeologist, discovering some peculiar lost civilization. Perhaps the Italians understand it too well; it may be the only important monument of the 16th century that neither the government nor anyone else is interested in preserving.

Viterbo ✉ *01100*   ***Where to Stay and Eating Out***

The **★★Milano**, Via San Luca 17, ✆ 0761 303 367 (*moderate*) has recently been redone with modern décor. **★★★Leon d'Oro**, Via della Cava 36, ✆ 0761 344 444 (*moderate*) is quiet and a little staid. Almost next door is **★★Roma**, Via della Cava 26, ✆ 0761 226 474 (*cheap*), with parking. The **Terme dei Papi**, Strada Bagni 12, ✆ 0761 3501, has a naturally heated outdoor pool, where swimming in January is quite fashionable (*pool open to non-residents Tues–Mon 9.30–4.30; adm L20,000 weekdays, L25,000 weekends; bring a towel*).

Restaurants here adhere to traditional Viterban dishes: slender fettuccine called *fieno* (hay), roast baby lamb, eels and fish from the lakes: *lattarini, coregone* (whitefish) or *persico* (perch). In **Il Richiastro**, Via della Marrocca 18, ✆ 0761 228 009 (*moderate*), in the courtyard and cellars of a medieval palace near Piazza Dante, you can dine on smoked trout, roast lamb, polenta and unusual home-made desserts, all fresh according to the season, prepared with pride and care, for bargain prices. *Open Thurs–Sat and Sun lunch only; closed two months in summer.* **Scaletta**, Via Marconi 45, ✆ 0761 340 003 (*moderate*) is another old favourite, with traditional cooking, and pizza in the evening. *Closed Mon.* **Tre Re**, Via Marcel Gattesco, ✆ 0761 234 619 (*cheap*), north of Piazza del Plebiscito, serves excellent dinners. *Closed Thurs.*

Three Lakes, and a Farnese Pentagon

All of the lakes of northern Lazio are volcanic craters; long ago they must have been like the famous Phlegraean Fields outside Naples. They are also the most appealing features in the Lazio landscape: not exactly off the main tourist track, but for swimming and watersports they are often more pleasant than any of the coastal beach resorts within easy reach of Rome.

Getting Around

Bracciano town is on the FS **rail** line between Rome and Viterbo, but the way to get to the lakes is by **bus**. There are frequent services from Lepanto and Agnanina termini in Rome to Bracciano and Vico, respectively, and from Viterbo to Lake Bolsena.

Lake Bolsena

This is the largest and northernmost of the three lakes. **Bolsena** town, at one end, has the medieval **Castello Mondaleschi**, with an archaeological collection (*open summer Tues–Sun 9.30–1.30 and 4–8; winter mornings only*), the 15th-century church of **Santa Cristina**, with small catacombs underneath, and narrow beaches. At the southern end, **Capodimonte** on its small promontory offers more beaches and boat excursions (*call* ✆ *0761 98213, for informa-*

tion) to the lake's two islands: the pretty rock of **Martana**, with steep granite cliffs and woods above, and **Isola Bisentina**. This was a favoured retreat of the Farnese in the 1500s, when the family was just beginning its spectacular career. They commissioned Antonio da Sangallo the Younger to build them a palace and a large domed church, **SS. Giacomo e Cristoforo**, now in decay. The island's hill also has a string of Calvary Chapels.

Towns around Lake Bolsena include **Acquapendente**, at the northern extremity of Lazio, with an ancient crypt under its cathedral, built as a copy of the Holy Sepulchre in Jerusalem, and a nature reserve on nearby Monte Rufeno; and **Montefiascone**, just south of the lake, famous for its *Est! Est! Est!* wine since a German Renaissance bishop did himself in by drinking too much of it. His tomb is in the 12th-century church **San Flaviano**. Montefiascone makes a good living from its wine, and the embroidered legend that goes with it.

Lake Vico and Caprarola

The smallest and perhaps loveliest of the lakes, Vico is ringed by rugged hills. Unspoiled marshes line some of its shore—now a wildlife reserve—and its ancient crater has a younger volcano (also extinct) poking up inside it: **Monte Venere**. Just over the hills from the lake, don't pass up a chance to see one of Italy's most arrogantly ambitious late-Renaissance palaces, the **Villa Farnese**, in Caprarola (*villa open Nov–Feb Tues–Sun 9–4; Mar–Oct until 6.30pm; adm; guided tours of the garden at 10, 11.30 and 3; May–Aug Mon–Sat also 5; adm*).

When Alessandro Farnese, member of an obscure Lazio noble family, set his sister Giulia up as mistress to Pope Alexander VI, his fortune was made; Alessandro later became Pope Paul III, a great pope who called the Council of Trent, rebuilt Rome, and kept Michelangelo busy—also a rotten pope, who oppressed his people, reinvigorated the Inquisition, and became the most successful grafter in papal history. Before long the Farnese family ruled Parma, Piacenza and most of northern Lazio. With the fantastic wealth Alessandro accumulated, his grandson, also named Alessandro, built this family headquarters. Vignola, the family architect, turned the entire town of Caprarola into a setting for the palace, ploughing a new avenue through the town as an axis that led to a grand stairway, then a set of gardens (now disappeared), and then another stairway up to the huge pentagonal villa, built over the massive foundations of an earlier, uncompleted fortress.

The palace is empty today; the Farnese lost everything in later papal intrigues, and someone, some time, probably had to sell the furniture. Nevertheless it is still an impressive place; the tour includes Vignola's elegant courtyard, a room with uncanny acoustical tricks that the guides love to demonstrate, frescoes of the *Labours of Hercules*, another with a wonderful ceiling painted with the figures of the constellations, and Vignola's decorative masterpiece— an incredible **spiral staircase** of stone columns and frescoes. The best part, however, is the 'secret garden', a park full of azaleas and rhododendrons leading up to a sculpture garden of grotesques and fantastical *telemones* that recall the Monster Park (there is a connection, as one of the Orsini of Bomarzo was Alessandro Farnese's secretary), and finally a delightful, smaller villa, the **Palazzina del Piacere**.

The hills between Lake Vico and the coast conceal no less than 12 minor Etruscan sites; all you'll see of these vanished cities, however, are the usual rock-cut tombs, some with temple-like carved façades, as at **Blera** and **Norchia**. Also at Norchia is a strange avenue stretching over 12,000 ft cut deeply into the easily worked tufa.

Lake Bracciano

This broad sheet of water is one of Rome's most popular swimming holes, and yet remains remarkably clean and beautiful. There is little of monumental interest around the lake—but a good view of it can be gained from the grim 1470s castle of the Orsini family, the **Castello Orsini-Odescalchi** (*open April–Sept Tues–Fri 10–7, Sat and Sun 9–12.30 and 3–7.30; Oct–Mar Tues–Fri 10–5, Sat and Sun 10–12 and 3–5; guided tours only; adm exp*), in the town of Bracciano. Boats run from there around the lake in summer. Trevignano and Anguillara are two pretty lakeside villages, with medieval centres and many places to eat.

Where to Stay and Eating Out

In Marta, on the south side of Lake Bolsena, **Gino al Miralago**, Lungolago Marconi 58, ✆ 0761 870 910 (*moderate*) is a lovely waterfront trattoria. *Closed Tues*. ★★★**Bella Venere**, Località Scardenato, Caprarola, ✆ 0761 612 342, ✉ 0761 612 344, on Lake Vico (*moderate*) is a gem of a small hotel with gardens, a beach, tennis courts and a large restaurant (*moderate*). *Closed Nov*. Also on Vico, ★★★**Sans Soucis sul Lago**, Via delle Nocciolette 18, ✆ 0761 612 052, Punta del Lago (*cheap*), near the road to Ronciglione, also has a beach and garden, and views over the lake.

Rieti and its Province

This comes as something of a digression, but this strip of land reaching over the Apennines to touch the borders of the Marche is also a part of Lazio. Before the Roman conquest in 290 BC it was the land of the Sabines, sometime allies but often fierce enemies of Rome. The Romans pushed their Via Salaria through here on its way to the Adriatic, generally following the route of the modern SS4 to Ascoli Piceno, and made it an important staging post.

Getting Around

Rieti is on the **rail** line between Terni and L'Aquila, but service is infrequent. There are several **buses** each day to Rome (from Stazione Tiburtina), Terni and L'Aquila.

Tourist Information

Rieti: Piazza Vittorio Emanuele II, ✆ 0746 201 146.
Terminillo: Via dei Villini 33, Pian de' Valli, ✆ 0746 261 121.

Lazio's Least-known Towns

Rieti, the capital, has a 12th-century cathedral and a small picture collection in its Museo Civico (*due to reopen in the year 2000*), and about a kilometre of well-preserved and very medieval-looking walls. The territory around it, once swamps, was drained by the Romans when they built the Marmore Falls in Terni; now it's a fertile plain with views of some of the highest peaks of the Apennines—the Gran Sasso is just over the border in Abruzzo.

There is plenty of lovely scenery and good walking country in the province, most of it in rather remote areas. South of Rieti there are the hills around the artificial lakes of **Salto** and **Turano**;

on the way to the latter you will see an impressive medieval castle, the Rocca Sinibalda. North of Rieti, **Monte Terminillo** has a modest ski resort on the slopes of its 6993ft peak; in summer the road around it makes a panoramic drive to **Leonessa**, an attractive medieval town that is one of the quietest, most out-of-the-way places in Italy. St Francis spent much time in these mountains; among the humble sanctuaries where he preached, **Greccio**, on its lovely mountaintop site west of Rieti, is said to be where the saint made the first Christmas crib; the event is celebrated with a real-life nativity scene on 24 and 26 December and 6 January.

Rieti ✉ *02100*　　　　　　　　　　　　　*Where to Stay and Eating Out*

★★★★**Quattro Stagioni**, Piazza C. Battisti 14, ✆ 0746 271 071 (*moderate*) is an elegant, comfortable hotel. Close by, **Il Grottino**, Piazza C. Battisti 4, ✆ 0746 497 683 (*moderate*) serves good, traditional meals. *Closed Tues.* A more adventurous menu draws local foodies to the family-run **Bistrot**, Piazza San Rufo 25, ✆ 0746 498 798 (*moderate*). Reserve. *Closed Sun, and Mon lunch.*

The North Coast: Tarquinia and Cerveteri

It will seem hard to believe, but this bare stretch of coast north of Rome was the richest and most heavily populated part of Etruria, including the only two sites worth visiting for those not enchanted with archaeology: the museums and necropoli at Tarquinia and Cerveteri.

Getting Around

From Lepanto terminus in Rome there are frequent **buses** to Cerveteri and Tarquinia.

Tourist Information

Tarquinia: Piazza Cavour 1, ✆ 0766 856 384 (*open Mon–Sat 8–2*).

Vulci and Tarquinia

Beginning from the Tuscan border on the coastal highway (the Roman Via Aurelia), truly dedicated Etruscophiles may wish to detour into the hills to **Vulci**, an important town in the 9th–1st centuries BC, and a renowned bronze-working centre. There are scanty ruins of the city, a small museum in modern Vulci's 13th-century **Castello dell'Abbadia**, and a large if not exciting necropolis with something like 15,000 tombs (*open Tues–Sun 9–dusk; adm*).

After the turn-off for Vulci, continuing southwards, the next Etruscan site is at the large, modern town of **Tarquinia**, of interest in its own right, with a Cosmatesque 12th-century church and a Roman aqueduct, rebuilt in the Middle Ages and still in use. In the 15th-century Palazzo Vitelleschi, many of the finest discoveries from the Etruscan city and its necropolis have been assembled for the **Museo Nazionale Tarquiniense**, on Piazza Cavour (*museum open Tues–Sun 9–7; adm; necropolis open Tues–Sun 9–one hour before sunset; adm*).

Undoubtedly the stars of the collection are the famous winged horses from the 'Altar of the Queen' temple on the acropolis: beautiful beasts, but made of clay like most Etruscan temple decorations—which explains why so few have survived. Well-carved sarcophagi are present in abundance, and Greek vases by some of the greatest 6th–5th-century BC Attic painters. The Etruscans were talented at ceramics, too, as seen by the large amount of fine *bucchero* ware: their black pottery incised or painted with the usual puzzling Etruscan images. Some of the paintings from the tombs have been relocated here for their protection, including scenes of chariot-riding and athletics—almost any subject is likely to turn up on Etruscan tomb walls.

There are not enough staff to keep all the hundreds of tombs open at Tarquinia's **necropolis**, all that remains of the city that dominated southern Etruria for centuries and enforced on Rome its early dynasty of Etruscan kings. The few you can see on any given day, however, rank among the finest products of Etruscan art. Tombs like that of 'the Lionesses', with their beautiful 'Ionic style' paintings, seem remarkably close to the art of the ancient Minoans. These paintings began to appear in the 6th century BC, and only in the tombs of the richest Etruscans; more typical of the rest is the 'Tomb of the Warrior', carved simply out of the tufa and hung with arms and trophies.

Further down the coast, on the way to Cerveteri, you'll pass the not-so-old-looking city of **Civitavecchia**, a port for Rome and the gateway for ferries to Sardinia. The big fortress overlooking the harbour was designed by Michelangelo for the popes, but there's little else to detain you. Unless, that is, you feel a sudden desire to bolt for the island of *nuraghi* and *mallorredus*, in which case repair to the offices of the Tirrenia Line or the FS ferries.

Cerveteri

Cerveteri, down the coast, was originally *Caere*, the richest if not the strongest of the Etruscan cities, and the one with the closest cultural ties to Greece. According to Herodotus it was the only non-Greek city with a sanctuary at Delphi. Cerveteri, like Tarquinia, has extensive **necropoli** (*open May–Sept Tues–Sun 9–7; Oct–April Tues–Sun 9–4; adm*), laid out in the form of a town. The site is quite large; study one of the site maps before walking too far.

The most striking section is called the Banditaccia Necropolis, where the heavy stone domes, set low to the ground, look more like bunkers than tombs. In them you see the forerunners of all the round tombs in Rome, such as the Mausolea of Augustus and Hadrian. Be sure to see the 'Tomb of the Capitals', carved from tufa to resemble the interior of an Etruscan house (the Etruscans built all their homes, public buildings and even temples out of wood, plaster and terracotta, which explains why only tombs are left).

The 'Tomb of Shields and Chairs' has unusual military decoration; another, even stranger, is covered with stone reliefs of cooking utensils and other household objects. In town, the Castello Orsini houses the **Museo Nazionale** (*open Tues–Sun 9–7; adm*), which has finds dug out from the Banditaccia, although the best pieces are now in the Villa Giulia and Vatican Museums in Rome.

Where to Stay and Eating Out

Tarquinia ✉ 01016

Après tombs, sleep at the well-run **★★San Marco**, Piazza Cavour 20, ✆ 0766 842 306 (*cheap*), or dine at **Due Orfanelle**, Vicolo Breve 4 (off Via di Porta Tarquinia), ✆ 0766 856 307 (*moderate*), on local dishes and especially good grilled meat. *Closed Tues.*

Rome

To know what Rome is, visit the little church of San Clemente, unobtrusively hidden away on the back streets behind the Colosseum. The Baroque façade conceals a 12th-century basilica with a beautiful marble choir screen 600 years older. In 1857 a cardinal from Boston discovered the original church of 313, one of the first great Christian basilicas, just underneath. And beneath *that* are two buildings and a Temple of Mithras from the time of Augustus; from it you can walk out into a Roman alley that looks exactly as it did 2000 years ago, now some 28ft below ground level. There are commemorative plaques in San Clemente, placed there by a Medici duke, a bishop of New York, and the last chairman of the Bulgarian Communist Party.

You are not going to get to the bottom of this city, whether your stay is for three days or a month. With its legions of headless statues, acres of paintings, 913 churches and megatons of artistic sediment, this metropolis of aching feet will wear down even the most resolute of travellers (and travel writers). The name Rome passed out of the plane of reality into legend some 2200 years ago, when princes as far away as China first began to hear of the faraway city and its invincible armies. At the same time the Romans were cooking up a personified goddess, the Divine Rome, and beginning the strange myth of their destiny to conquer and pacify the world, a myth that would still haunt Europe a thousand years later.

In our prosaic times, though, you may find it requires a considerable effort of the imagination to break through to the past Romes of the Caesars and popes. They exist, but first you will need to peel away the increasingly thick veneer of the 'Third Rome', the burgeoning, thoroughly up-to-date creation of post-Reunification Italy. Ancient Rome at the height of its glory had perhaps a million and a half people; today there are four million, and at any given time at least half of them will be pushing their way into the Metro train while you are trying to get off. The popes, for all their centuries of experience in spectacle and ceremony, cannot often steal the show in this new Rome, and have to share the stage with a deplorable overabundance of preposterous politicians, with *Cinecittà* and the rest of the cultural apparatus of a great nation, and of course with the tourists, who sometimes put on the best show in town. The old guard Romani, now a minority in a city swollen with new arrivals, bewail the loss of Rome's slow and easy pace, its vintage brand of *dolce vita* that once impressed other Italians, let alone foreigners. Lots of money, lots of traffic and an endless caravan of tour buses have a way of compromising even the most beautiful cities. Don't concern yourself; the present is only one snapshot from a 2600-year history, and no one has ever left Rome disappointed.

History

The beginnings are obscure enough. Historians believe the settlement of the Tiber Valley began some time about 1000 BC, when an outbreak of volcanic eruptions in the Alban Hills to the south forced the Latin tribes down into the lowlands. Beyond that there are few clues for the archaeologists to follow. But remembering that every ancient legend conceals a kernel of truth— perhaps more poetic than scientific—it would be best to follow the accounts of Virgil, the poet of the Empire, and Livy, the great 1st-century chronicler and mythographer. When Virgil wrote, in the reign of Augustus, Greek culture was an irresistible force in all the recently civilized lands of the Mediterranean. For Rome, Virgil concocted the story of Aeneas, fleeing from Troy after the Homeric sack and finding his way to Latium. Descent from the Trojans, however specious, connected Rome to the Greek world and made it seem less of an upstart.

Rome

Galleria
Nazionale
d'Arte Moderna

Museo
Nazionale
di Villa Giulia

Villa

Piazzale
Clodio

Piazza
G. Mazzini

V. D. DELLE ARTI

Stazione Roma-Viterbo

CLODIA

VIALE DEL MURO TORTO

VIA DELLA GIULIANA

VIALE ANGELICO

VIALE GIUSEPPE

VIALE MAZZINI

LUNG. DELLE ARMI

LUNG. DELLE NAVI

VIA FLAMINIA

Piazzale
Flaminio

Monte
Pincio

Pza. del
Popolo

S. Maria
Del Popolo

Villa
Medici

V.L. DI SAVOIA

CIRC. TRIONFALE

CIRCONVAL

VIALE
GIULIO

CESARE

VIA A. DORIA Trionfale

Largo
Trionfale

Piazzale
degli
Eroi

VIA CIPRO

VIA ANGELO EMO

VLE LEONE IV

VIA OTTAVIANO

VIA COLA DI RIENZO

VIA CRESCENZIO

VIA BABUINO

VIA RIPETTA

VIA DI RIPETTA

LUNG. IN AUGUSTA

LUNG. MELLINI

LUNG. MICHELANGELO

VATICANO

Piazza del
Risorgimento

Musei
Vaticani

CITTÀ DEL
VATICANO

Giardino del
Vaticano

Castel
S.Angelo

Piazza del
Risorgimento

Mausoleum of
Augustus

Ara
Pacis

Spanish
Steps

Trinità
del
Monte

V.D. DI MACELLI

V. DEL LEONE

V. DEL CONDOTTI

V. FRATTINA

V. DI MERCEDE

Piazza
Cavour

Basilica di
San Pietro

VIA AURELIA

Piazza
S. Pietro

Ospedale di
S. Spirito

LUNG. CASTELLO

Tévere

(*Tiber*)

LUNG. TOR DI NONA

VIA DEI CORONARI

Palazzo
Madama

Palazzo di
Montecitorio

Pza
Silvestro

V. DELLA SCROFA

V. DEL CORSO

Piazza
Colonna

Fontana
di Trevi

Chiesa
Nuova

Piazza
Navona

Piazza
della
Rotonda

Pantheon

Palazzo Doria
Pamphili

S. Onofrio

LUNGOTEVERE

LUNG. GIANICOLENSE

LUNG. GIULIA

V. DI RINASCIMENTO

CORSO VITTORIO EMANUELE II

Piazza
Farnese

Piazza Campo
de' Fiori

V. DEI
BARCHI

V. DEI
GIUBBONARI

VIA DEI
TEBALDI

VIA ARENULA

Piazza
Venezia

Vittoriano

Palazzo
Venezia

VIA DEL TEATRO MARCELLO

Galleria
Corsini

Palazzo
Farnese

Villa
Farnesina

Sinagoga

LUNG. CENCI

Musei
Capitolini

LUNG. FARNESINA

LUNG. R. SANZIO

Pza. S. Maria
in Trast.

Isola
Tiberina

Teatro di
Marcello

Monte
Capitolino

AURELIO

*Villa
Abamelek*

Monte Gianicolo

Piazzale
Giuseppe Garibaldi

S. Pietro in
Montorio

Pza.
G. Belli

S.Maria in
Trastevere

Pza. S.
Cosimato

S.
Crisogano

S.
Cecelia

V. DELLA LUNGARETTA

Piazza
Bocca della
Verità

VIA DEL CERCHI

VIA DEL CIRCO MASSIMO

VIA DELLE FORNACI

VIA GREGORIO VII

VIA DELLE MURA

Villa
Aurelia

VIA GARIBALDI

VIA GARIBALDI

V. NICOLA FABRIZI

VIALE GLORIOSO

V.S. FRANCESCO A RIPA

V. DEL GENOVESI

V. ANICIA

V.D.S. MICHELE

LUNG. RIPA

LUNG. AVENTINO

VIA DI S. SABINA

S. Sabina

S. Prisca

S. Alessio

Monte
Aventino

*Villa Doria
Pamphili*

*Villa Doria
Pamphili*

Piazzale
Giuseppe Garibaldi

VIA DI S. PANCRAZIO

VIA GIACINTO CARINI

VIALE DEI QUATTRO VENTI

VIALE DELLE MILIZIE

GIANICOLENSI

Ponte
Sublicio

Prioria delle Cav. di Malta

V.S. SABINA

V.S. ALESSIO

V. DI S. ANSELMO

Piazza
Albania

V. DI PIR CESTIA

VIA VITELLIA

VIA FONTEIANA

VIA A.G. BARRILI

VIA ALESSANDRO POERIO

VIALE DI TRASTÉVERE

VIA E. ROLLI

VIA PORTUENSE

Tévere

LUNGOTEVERE TESTACCIO

VIA MARMORATA

VIA N. ZABAGLIA

VIA GALVANI

VLE DI CAMPO BOARIO

Piazza
Porta S. Paolo

Piazza
Porto
S. Paolo

Porto
S. Paolo

VIALE MARCO POLO

*Monte
Testaccio*

Piramide

*Cimitero
Protestante*

Stazione
Roma-Lido
di Ostia

Stazione
Roma-Ostiense

Airport
Bus Stop

→ Stazione Trastevere
(100 metres)

N

.... Metropolitana

1 km

½ mile

As Virgil tells it, Aeneas' son Ascanius founded Alba Longa, a city that by the 800s was leader of the Latin Confederation. Livy takes up the tale with Numitor, a descendant of Ascanius and rightful king of Alba Longa, tossed off the throne by his usurping brother Amulius. In order that Numitor should have no heirs, Amulius forced Numitor's daughter Rhea Silvia into service as a Vestal Virgin. Here Rome's destiny begins, with an appearance in the Vestals' chambers of the god Mars, staying just long enough to leave Rhea Silvia pregnant with the precocious twins Romulus and Remus.

When Amulius found out he of course packed them away in a little boat, which the gods directed up the Tiber to a spot near today's Piazza Bocca della Verità. The famous she-wolf looked after the babies, until they were found by a shepherd, who brought them up. When Mars revealed to the grown twins their origin, they returned to Alba Longa to sort out Amulius, and then returned (in 753 BC, traditionally) to found the city the gods had ordained. Romulus soon found himself constrained to kill Remus, who would not believe the auguries that declared his brother should be king, and thus set the pattern for the bloody millennium of Rome's history to come. The legends portray early Rome as a glorified pirates' camp, and the historians are only too glad to agree. Finding themselves short of women, the Romans stole some from the Sabines. Not especially interested in farming or learning a trade, they adopted the hobby of subjugating their neighbours and soon polished it to an art.

Seven Kings of Rome

Romulus was the first, followed by Numa Pompilius, who laid down the forms for Rome's cults and priesthoods, its auguries and College of Vestals. Tullius Hostilius, the next, made Rome ruler of all Latium, and Ancus Martius founded the port of Ostia. The next king, Tarquinius Priscus, was an Etruscan, and probably gained his throne thanks to a conquest by one of the Etruscan city-states. Tarquin made a city of Rome, building the first real temples, the Cloaca Maxima or Great Drain, and the first Circus Maximus. His successor, Servius Tullius, restored Latin rule, inaugurated the division between patricians (the senatorial class) and plebeians, and built a great wall to keep the Etruscans out. It apparently did not work, for as next king we find the Etruscan Tarquinius Superbus (about 534 BC), another great builder. His misfortune was to have a hot-headed son like Tarquinius Sextus, who imposed himself on a noble and virtuous Roman maiden named Lucretia (cf. Shakespeare's *Rape of Lucrece*). She committed public suicide; the enraged Roman patricians, under the leadership of Lucius Junius Brutus, chased out proud Tarquin and the Etruscan dynasty forever. The republic was established before the day was out, with Brutus as first consul, or chief magistrate.

The Invincible Republic

Taking an oath never to allow another king in Rome, the patricians designed a novel form of government, a republic (*res publica*—public thing) governed by the two consuls elected by the Senate, the assembly of the patricians themselves; later innovations in the Roman constitution would include a tribune, an official with inviolable powers elected by the Plebeians to protect their interests. The two classes fought like cats and dogs at home but combined with impressive resolve in their foreign wars. Etruscans, Aequi, Hernici, Volscii, Samnites and Sabines—all powerful nations—were defeated by Rome's citizen armies. Some of Livy's best stories come from this period, such as the taking of Rome by marauding Gauls in 390, when the cackling of geese awakened the Romans and saved the citadel on the Capitoline Hill.

By 270 BC Rome had eliminated all its rivals to become master of Italy. It had taken about 200 years, and in the next 200 Roman rule would be established from Spain to Egypt. The first stage had proved more difficult. In Rome's final victory over the other Italians the city digested its rivals: whole cities and tribes simply disappeared, their peoples joining the mushrooming population of Rome. After 270 it was much the same story, but on a wider scale. In the three Punic Wars against Carthage (264–146 BC) Rome gained almost the whole of the western Mediterranean; Greece, North Africa and Asia Minor were absorbed in small bites over the next 100 years. Rome's history was now the history of the western world.

Imperial Rome

The old pirates' nest had never really changed its ways. Rome, like old Assyria, makes a fine example of that species of carnivore that can only live by continuous conquest. When the Romans took Greece they first met Culture, and it had the effect on them that puberty has on little boys. After some bizarre behaviour, evidenced in the continuous civil wars (Sulla, Marius, Pompey, Julius Caesar), the Romans began tarting up their city in the worst way, vacuuming all the gold, paintings, statues, cooks, poets and architects out of the civilized East. Beginning perhaps with Pompey, every contender for control of the now constitutionally deranged republic added some great work to the city centre: Pompey's theatre, the Julian Basilica, and something from almost every emperor up to Constantine. Julius Caesar and Augustus were perhaps Rome's greatest benefactors, initiating every sort of progressive legislation, turning dirt lanes into paved streets and erecting new forums, temples and the vast network of aqueducts. In their time Rome's population probably reached the million mark, surpassing Antioch and Alexandria as the largest city in the western world.

It was Augustus who effectively ended the Republic in 27 BC, by establishing his personal rule and reducing the old constitution to formalities. During the imperial era that followed his reign, Rome's position as administrative and judicial centre of the empire kept it growing, drawing in a new cosmopolitan population of provincials from Britain to Mesopotamia. The city became the unquestioned capital of banking and finance—and religion; Rome's policy was always to induct everyone's local god as an honorary Roman, and every important cult image and relic was abducted to the Capitoline Temple. The emperor himself was *Pontifex Maximus*, head priest of Rome, whose title derives from the early Roman veneration of bridges (*pontifex* means keeper of bridges). St Peter, of course, arrived, and was duly martyred in AD 67. His successor, Linus, became the first pope—or *pontiff*—first in the long line of hierophants who would inherit Rome's long-standing religious tradition.

For all its glitter, Rome was still the complete predator, producing nothing and consuming everything. No one with any spare *denarii* would be foolish enough to go into business with them, when the only real money was to be made from government, speculation or real estate. At times almost half the population of Roman citizens (as opposed to slaves) was on the public dole. Naturally, when things went sour they really went sour. Uncertain times made Aurelian give Rome a real defensive wall in 275. By 330 the necessity of staying near the armies at the front led the western emperors to spend most of their time at army headquarters in Milan. Rome became a bloated backwater, and after three sackings (Alaric the Goth in 410, Gaiseric the Vandal in 455 and Odoacer the Goth in 476), there was no reason to stay. The sources disagree: perhaps 100,000 inhabitants were left by the year 500, perhaps as few as 10,000.

Rome in the Shadows

Contrary to what most people think, Rome did not ever quite go down the drain in the Dark Ages. Its lowest point in prestige undoubtedly came in the 14th century, when the popes were at Avignon. The number of important churches built in the Dark Ages (most, unfortunately, baroqued later) and the mosaics that embellished them, equal in number if not in quality to those of Ravenna, testify to the city's importance. There was certainly enough to attract a few more sacks (Goths and Greeks in the 6th-century wars, Saracens from Africa in 746).

As in many other western cities, but on a larger scale, the bishops of Rome—the popes—picked up some of the pieces when civil administration disintegrated and extended their power to temporal offices. Chroniclers report fights between them and the local barons, self-proclaimed heirs of the Roman Senate, as early as 741. It must have been a fascinating place, much too big for its population though still, thanks to the popes, thinking of itself as the centre of the western world. The forum was abandoned, as were the gigantic baths, rendered useless as the aqueducts decayed. Almost all of the temples and basilicas survived, converted to Christian churches. Hadrian's massive tomb on the banks of the Tiber was converted into a fortress, the Castel Sant'Angelo, an impregnable haven for the popes in times of trouble.

The popes deserve credit for keeping Rome alive, but the tithe money trickling in from across Europe confirmed the city in its parasitical behaviour. With two outrageous forgeries, the 'Donation of Constantine' and the 'Donation of Pepin', the popes staked their claim to temporal power in Italy. Charlemagne visited the city after driving the Lombards out in 800; during a prayer vigil in St Peter's on Christmas Eve, Pope Leo III sneaked up behind the Frankish king and set an imperial crown on his head. The surprise coronation, which the outraged Charlemagne could not or would not undo, established the precedent of Holy Roman Emperors having to cross over the Alps to receive their crown from the pope; for centuries to come Rome was able to keep its hand in the political struggles of all Europe.

Arnold of Brescia and Rienzo

Not that Rome ever spoke with one voice; over the next 500 years it was only the idea of Rome, as the spiritual centre of the universal Christian community, that kept the actual city of Rome from disappearing altogether. Down to some 20–30,000 people in this era, Rome evolved a sort of stable anarchy, in which the major contenders for power were the popes and noble families. First among the latter were the Orsini and the Colonna, racketeer clans who built fortresses for themselves among the ruins and fought like gangs in 1920s Chicago. Very often outsiders would get into the game. A remarkable woman of obscure birth named Theodora took the Castel Sant'Angelo in the 880s; with the title of Senatrix she and her daughter Marozia ruled Rome for decades. Various German emperors seized the city, but were never able to hold it. In the 10th century, things got even more complicated as the Roman people began to assert themselves. Caught between the people and the barons, nine of the 24 popes in that century managed to get themselves murdered. The 1140s was a characteristic period of this convoluted history. A Jewish family, the Pierleoni, held power, and a Jewish antipope sat enthroned in St Peter's. Mighty Rome occupied itself with a series of wars against its neighbouring village of Tivoli, and usually lost. A sincere monkish reformer appeared, the Christian and democrat Arnold of Brescia; he recreated the Senate and almost succeeded in establishing Rome as a free *comune*, but in 1155 he fell into the hands of the German emperor Frederick Barbarossa, who sold him to the English pope (Adrian IV) for hanging.

Too many centuries of this made Rome uncomfortable for the popes, who frequently removed themselves to Viterbo. The final indignity came when, under French pressure, the papacy decamped entirely to Avignon in 1309. Pulling strings from a distance, the popes only made life more complicated. Into the vacuum they created stepped one of the noblest Romans of them all, later to be the subject of Wagner's first opera. Cola di Rienzo was the son of an innkeeper, but he had a good enough education to read the Latin inscriptions that lay on ruins all around him, and Livy, Cicero and Tacitus wherever he could find them. Obsessed by the idea of re-establishing Roman glory, he talked at the bewildered inhabitants until they caught the fever too. With Rienzo as Tribune of the People, the Roman Republic was reborn in 1347.

Power does corrupt, however, in Rome more than any spot on the globe, and an increasingly fat and ridiculous Rienzo was hustled out of Rome by the united nobles before the year was out. His return to power, in 1354, ended with his murder by a mob after only two months. Rome was now at its lowest ebb, with only some 15,000 people, and prosperity and influence were not to be completely restored until the reign of Pope Nicholas V after 1447.

The New Rome

The old papacy, before Avignon, had largely been a tool of the Roman nobles; periods when it was able to achieve real independence were the exception rather than the rule. In the more settled conditions of the 15th century, a new papacy emerged, richer and more sophisticated. Political power, as a guarantee of stability, was its goal, and a series of talented Renaissance popes saw their best hopes for achieving this by rebuilding Rome. By the 1500s this process was in full swing. Under Julius II (1503–13) the papal domains for the first time were run like a modern state; Julius also laid plans for the rebuilding of St Peter's, beginning the great building programme that transformed the city. New streets were laid out, especially Via Giulia and the grand avenues radiating from Piazza del Popolo; Julius' architect, Bramante, knocked down medieval Rome with such gay abandon that Raphael nicknamed him 'Ruinante'.

Over the next two centuries the work continued at a frenetic pace. Besides St Peter's, hundreds of churches were either built or rebuilt, and cardinals and noble families lined the streets with new palaces, imposing if not always beautiful. A new departure in urban design was developed in the 1580s, under Sixtus V, recreating some of the monumentality of ancient Rome. Piazzas linked by a network of straight boulevards were cleared in front of the major religious sites, each with an Egyptian obelisk. The New Rome, symbol of the Counter-Reformation and the majesty of the popes, was, however, bought at a terrible price. Besides the destruction of Bramante, buildings that had survived substantially intact for 1500 years were cannibalized for their marble; the popes wantonly destroyed more of ancient Rome than Goths or Saracens had ever managed. To pay for their programme, they taxed the economy of the Papal States out of existence. Areas of Lazio turned into wastelands as exasperated farmers simply abandoned them; the other cities of Lazio and Umbria were set back centuries in their development. The New Rome was proving as voracious a predator as the old. Worst of all, the new papacy in the 16th century instituted terror as an instrument of public policy. In the course of the previous century the last vestiges of Roman liberty had been gradually extinguished. The popes tried to extend their power by playing a game of high-stakes diplomacy between Emperor Charles V of Spain and King Francis I of France, but reaped a bitter harvest in the 1527 sack of Rome. An out-of-control imperial army occupied the city for almost a year, causing tremendous destruction, while the disastrous Pope Clement VII looked on helplessly from the Castel Sant'Angelo. Afterwards the popes were happy to become part of the Imperial-Spanish system. Political repression was fiercer than anywhere else in Italy; the Inquisition was refounded in 1542 by Paul III, and book burnings, torture of freethinkers and executions became even more common than in Spain itself.

The End of Papal Rule

By about 1610 there was no Roman foolish enough to get burned at the stake; at the same time workmen were adding the last stones to the cupola of St Peter's. It was the end of an era, but the building continued. A thick accretion of Baroque, like coral, collected over Rome. Bernini did his Piazza Navona fountain in 1650, and the Colonnade for St Peter's 15 years later. The political importance of the popes, however, disappeared with surprising finality. As Joseph Stalin was later to note, the popes had plenty of Bulls, but few army divisions, and they drifted into irrelevance in the power politics of modern Europe during the Thirty Years War.

Rome was left to enjoy a decadent but pleasant twilight. A brief interruption came when revolutionaries in 1798 again proclaimed the Roman Republic, and a French army sent the pope packing. Rome later became part of Napoleon's empire, but papal rule was restored in 1815. Another republic appeared in 1848, on the crest of that romantic year's revolutionary wave, but this time a French army besieged the city and had the pope propped back on his throne by July 1849. Garibaldi, the republic's military commander, barely escaped with his life.

For twenty years Napoleon III maintained a garrison in Rome to look after the pope, and consequently Rome became the last part of Italy to join the new Italian kingdom. After the French defeat in the war of 1870, Italian troops blew a hole in the old Aurelian wall near the Porta Pia and marched in. Pius IX, who ironically had decreed papal infallibility just the year before, locked himself in the Vatican and pouted; the popes were to be 'prisoners' until Mussolini's Concordat of 1929, by which they agreed to recognize the Italian state.

As capital of the new state, Rome underwent another building boom. New streets like Via Vittorio Veneto and Via Nazionale made circulation easier; villas and gardens disappeared under blocks of speculative building (everything around Stazione Termini, for example); long-needed projects like the Tiber embankments were built; and the new kingdom strove to impress the world with gigantic, absurd public buildings and monuments, such as the Altar of the Nation and the Finance Ministry on Via XX Settembre, as big as two Colosseums. Growth has been steady; from some 200,000 people in 1879, Rome has since increased twentyfold.

The Twentieth Century

In 1922 the city was the objective of Mussolini's 'March on Rome', when the Fascist leader used his blackshirt squads to demand, and win, complete power in the Italian government, though he himself famously made the journey into town by train, and in his best suit. Mussolini was one more figure who wanted to create a 'New Roman Empire' for Italy. For twenty years Piazza Venezia was the chosen theatre for his oratorical performances. He also had big ideas for the city itself: it was under Fascism that many of the relics of ancient Rome were first opened up as public monuments in order to remind Italians of their heritage, and Via dei Fori Imperiali was driven past the Forum, destroying some of the archaeological sites in the process. His greatest legacy was the EUR suburb, the projected site of a world exhibition for 1942, and a showcase of his preferred Fascist-classical architecture. At the end of the war it was only half built, but the Italians, not wishing to waste anything, decided to finish the project, and it now houses a few of Rome's museums and sports venues.

Since the war Rome has continued to grow fat as the capital of the often ramshackle, notoriously corrupt political system thrown up by the Italian Republic, and the headquarters of the smug *classe politica* that ran it. Rome has been accused by Lombard regionalists of drawing off wealth from the productive areas of Italy in much the same way that it once demanded to be fed by the Empire; nevertheless, Romans have joined in Italy's 'Moral Revolution' of the last few years, abusing the old-style political bosses, despite the fact that a great many in this city of civil servants themselves benefited from the system.

The city has been led by a mayor from the Green Party since 1993, and is currently in the throws of preparation for the Holy Year 2000, with over 700 public works projects. Façades are being restored, car parks added, museums refurbished and promises made for what will be one of the great tourist onslaughts of all time—officials are estimating as many as 30 million visitors over the year, most making the pilgrimage to the Vatican for the special blessing bestowed upon all who pass through the Holy Door at St Peter's, which will be opened on Christmas Day 1999 and resealed on December 31 2000. Just whether the city will get its act together in time remains to be seen.

A Little Orientation

> *There's three things I want to see in Rome:*
> *the Colosseum, St Peter's and the Acropolis.*
>
> a big-time tourist from Texas

Two Walls

Of Rome's earliest wall, built by King Servius Tullius before the republic, little remains; you can see one of the last surviving bits outside Stazione Termini. The second, built by Aurelian in 275 AD, is one of the wonders of Rome, though taken for granted. With its 19km length and 383 towers, it is one of the largest ever built in Europe—and certainly the best-preserved of antiquity. In places you can see almost perfectly preserved bastions and monumental gates.

Three Romes

Historians and Romans often think of the city in this way. Classical Rome began on the Monte Palatino, and its business and administrative centre stayed nearby, in the original Forum and the great Imperial Fora built around it. Many of the busiest parts lay to the south, where now you see only green on the tourist office's map. After Rome's fall these areas were never really rebuilt, and even substantial ruins like Trajan's Baths remain unexcavated. The Second Rome, that of the popes, had its centre in the Campus Martius, the plain west and north of the Capitoline Hill, later expanding to include the 'Leonine City' around St Peter's, and the new Baroque district around Piazza del Popolo and the Spanish Steps. The Third Rome, capital of United Italy, has expanded in all directions; the closest it has to a centre is Via del Corso.

Seven Hills

Originally they were much higher; centuries of building, rebuilding and river flooding have made the ground level in the valleys much higher, and emperors and popes shaved bits off their tops in building programmes. The **Monte Capitolino**, smallest but most important, now has Rome's City Hall, the Campidoglio, roughly on the site of ancient Rome's greatest temple, that of Jupiter Greatest and Best. The **Palatino**, adjacent to it, was originally the most fashionable district, and got entirely covered by the palaces of the emperors—the heart of the Roman Empire. The plebeian **Aventino** lies to the south of it, across the Circus Maximus. Between the Colosseum and the Stazione Termini, the **Esquilino**, the **Viminale** and the **Quirinale** stand in a row. The Quirinale was long the residence of the popes, and later of the Italian kings. Finally, there is the **Monte Celio** south of the Colosseum, now an oasis of parkland and ancient churches. Rome has other hills not included in the canonical seven: **Monte Vaticano**, from which the Vatican takes its name, **Monte Pincio**, including the Villa Borghese, and the **Gianicolo**, the long ridge above Trastevere the ancients called the Janiculum.

Fourteen Regions

Ancient Rome had neither street lights nor street signs; drunks trying to find their way home had a job on their hands. Modern Rome has plenty of both. Being Rome, of course the street signs are of marble. In the corner, you will notice a small number in Roman numerals; this refers to the *rione*, or ward. In the Middle Ages, there were 14 of these, descendants of the 14 *regii* of the ancient city; even after the fall of Rome they maintained their organization and offered protection to their people in the worst of times. You can still see the heraldic symbols of several of the *rioni* on the sides of buildings which once marked their boundaries.

Passing the Time of Day in Ancient Rome

Recreating some of the atmosphere of the old days is not hard: a score of books have been written on the subject, of which one of the best is *Daily Life in Ancient Rome* by Jerome Carcopino (available in Penguin). Roman poets such as Horace, Martial and especially Juvenal also have plenty to say about it. Life in Rome at the height of empire was an imperial pain: ridiculously high rents, high taxes, street crime, noise around the clock and neighbours from Baetica or Rhaetia with peculiar habits—but naturally everyone in the empire dreamed of someday moving there. The most significant difference between the way they lived then and our times was the sharp contrast between the quality of life in public versus private places. The average Roman citizen, usually unemployed or underemployed, could loll about magnificent baths and forums all day; only with reluctance did he drag himself home to his nasty fourth-floor flat at night.

Public Rome

The Roman *forum*, developed from the Greek *agora*, took the form of an open space surrounded by temples, basilicas and colonnades. In the centre, the original Roman Forum and the Fora of Augustus and Trajan made up a single vast complex, the public stage of Roman life. A typical Roman citizen would be there in the morning, to transact business, meet friends, watch the cosmopolitan crowd go by, or indulge in the favourite pastime of watching court proceedings in the basilica. Often they would have their own actions running; the Romans were easily the most litigious nation in all history.

Surrounding the *fora* would be the market-places, some of them imposing buildings like the Market of Trajan (in its time not unlike today's Covered Market in Istanbul).

For all their skill at plumbing, the Romans never managed to bring running water into their flats. The baths, therefore, were a daily spot on any respectable Roman's agenda. He could have stayed all day, for these great establishments were a stage for public life, and cheap and accessible even to the poorest man. Every neighbourhood had some, and counting the ones built by the emperors, they covered almost 10 per cent of Rome. The biggest ones, with bathing halls bigger than St Peter's, also included parks, museums, libraries, lunch counters and, of course *palaestrae*—athletic grounds for the Romans' favourite games. No civilization, perhaps, ever conceived a more useful way for its citizens to spend their leisure time. There were other places to pursue the classical *dolce vita*—the emperors' extensive gardens (usually open to the public), the temples, which in an irreligious age were really glorified art museums, and the taverns—one on every block, usually with upstairs and gambling in the back room. Romans were terrible gamblers; even the virtuous Augustus would regularly present his children, slaves and dinner guests with bags of *sestertii* to wager against him. Finally there were the races and games in the Colosseum or the Circus Maximus, all of them extraordinarily brutal and bloody, which occupied something on the average of 90–100 days a year. These were free, though you needed a ticket just to remind you of the imperial largesse that made it all possible. You also needed a toga, unless you were in the plebeian cheap seats, for these were among this informal city's few dress-up occasions.

Private Rome

Over 90 per cent of Romans lived in flats, in pretty but generally poorly built *insulae* up to 10 storeys in height. From the outside they looked much the same as some of the older Roman apartment blocks today, only with more imaginative façades of brick, stucco and patterned timbers. Many had balconies, and every part of these balconies and windows that received any sun would be full of climbing vines and flowers. Unfortunately most of the streets were less than 12ft across. Rich and poor Romans lived mixed together in every *regio*: the very rich in walled houses (like those at Pompeii), set perhaps next to a four-storey block with wine and oil shops, taverns and ironmongers on the ground floor, middle-class bureaucrats and clients of the rich on the first (with perhaps three or four slaves), and the very poor above them. These had the furthest to climb, and were doomed in case of fire or collapse. Both of these were constant worries. Crassus, who ruled Rome in the first Triumvirate with Caesar and Pompey, got his start as a weasling building contractor, following the fire squads.

People who lived in flats did not use them much for entertaining, or even for cooking. They had paid water-carriers, but no heating except braziers, no glass windows and little furniture. The shops that filled the ground floors of most buildings always spilled out into the narrow streets, joining the market barrows and the grammar school classes, which rented space under shop awnings or in porticoes—learning to live with distractions was a part of any Roman's education. Traffic problems were probably Rome's biggest headache after the 2nd century BC; Julius Caesar decreed an end to chariots and carriages (the rich had to get by with slave-borne litters) and banished wagons during daylight hours.

Getting There

by air

The main airport, **Leonardo da Vinci**, is usually be referred to as **Fiumicino** (✆ 06 65951). Taking a taxi from there into Rome should cost about L70,000, including airport and luggage supplements. There are two rail links from the airport to the city: to Stazioni Trastevere, Ostiense, Tuscolana and Tiburtina (*every 20mins; L7500*) and direct service to Stazione Termini, Rome's main rail station (*hourly; L15,000*).

Between 10.20pm and 7am, COTRAL buses run from outside the Arrivals hall to Stazione Ostiense, near Ⓜ Piramide (*hourly; L6000*). The train takes about 30mins from Fiumicino to Tiburtina; the bus at least 50mins. A secondary airport, **Ciampino** (✆ 06 794 941) is the base for a few passenger and charter flights. A COTRAL bus runs from here to the Anagnina stop at the southern end of the Metro A line, from where it's about 20mins to Stazione Termini (*daily 6.15am–10.20pm*).

by rail

Almost all long-distance trains arrive at and depart from the huge, chaotic but efficient **Stazione Termini**. The information and ticket windows are often terribly crowded, so allow plenty of time. There is a taxi stand in front, along with city buses to most points in Rome, and the main Metro Station is in the basement.

There are plenty of other stations: **Tiburtina** (Ⓜ Tiburtina), on the eastern edge of town, and **Ostiense** (Ⓜ Piramide), south of the Monte Aventino, serve some long-distance north–south lines. During the night (*12 midnight–5am*), Stazione Termini is shut and trains stop at the other stations. A few trains to Tuscany and Umbria start from **Ostiense** and stop at **Trastevere**, on Viale Trastevere.

The Lazio transport authority, COTRAL, also operates its own little rail network: the **Roma-Nord** line to Viterbo, from their own station on Piazzale Flaminio, north of Piazza del Popolo, and a line to **Ostia** and the Lido, from Porta San Paolo (next to the main Stazione Ostiense FS) and the Ⓜ Magliana (Line B).

by bus

COTRAL buses serve almost every town in Lazio. They leave from different locations around the edge of Rome, depending on the destination: buses heading north northwest leave from Saxa Rubra (on the Roma-Nord rail line) and Lepanto (Ⓜ Lepanto); for the south, southwest and east, buses leave from Ⓜ Anagnina, Ⓜ EUR Fermi and Ⓜ Tiburtina. For details (in Italian) about schedules and fares, call freephone, ✆ 167 431 784 (*Mon–Fri 9–1 and 2–5*). Many different companies offer long-distance bus services to and from Rome; check with the tourist office.

by road

All the *autostrade* converging on Rome run into the giant ring road, the *Grande Raccordo Anulare* or *GRA*. From there, good routes into the city are the Via Aurelia (SS1) from the west, the local SS201 *autostrada* from the airport in the southwest, and the A24 from the east. Rome is, as it has been for 2000 years, the hub of a network of ancient routes serving every direction, now transmogrified into state roads (SS) but retaining their old names and they still provide the most direct means of escaping.

Getting Around

Looking at the map, Rome seems to be made for getting around on foot. This may be so in the *centro storico* around Piazza Navona, but elsewhere it's deceptive—city blocks in the newer areas are huge, and it will always take you longer than you think to walk anywhere. The hills, the outsize scale and the traffic also make Rome a tiring place, but there is some pleasant strolling to be had in the old districts west of the Corso, around the Isola Tiberina, in old Trastevere and around the Monte Celio.

by Metro

Rome's underground system is not particularly convenient as it seems to avoid the historic parts of the city; imagine trying to dig any sort of hole in Rome, with legions of archaeologists ready to pounce. The two lines, A and B, cross at Stazione Termini and will take you to the Colosseum, around the Monte Aventino, to Piazza di Spagna, San Giovanni in Laterano, San Paolo Fuori le Mura (Outside the Walls), Piazza del Popolo, or within eight blocks of St Peter's.

Single tickets (*L1500*), also good for city buses—valid for 75mins from obliteration in the turnstile—are available from machines in Metro Stations and tobacconists, bars and kiosks.

by bus and tram

Buses are by far the best way to get around. Pick up a map of the bus routes from the **ATAC** (city bus company) booth outside Stazione Termini. Bus tickets cost L1500, and are good for travel on any ATAC city bus or tram and one metro ride—within 75mins of the first use of the ticket—which must be stamped in the machines in the back entrance of buses or trams. There are also special-price full-day tickets (which also include the Metro), as well as weekly and monthly passes available from tobacconists. Most routes run frequently, and are often crowded.

Some Useful Bus Routes

19   (tram) Piazza Risorgimento (near the Vatican)–Viale delle Milizie–Villa Borghese–Viale Regina Margherita–Porta Maggiore–San Lorenzo and Via Prenestina.

23   Musei Vaticani–Castel Sant'Angelo–Tiber banks–Porta San Paolo–S. Paolo.

30/   (tram) Villa Borghese–Viale Regina Margherita–San Lorenzo–S. Giovanni in Laterano–Colosseum–Viale Aventino–Porta San Paolo (a fun trip, taking in many sights).

36   Termini–Via Nomentana (Sant'Agnese).

46   Piazza Venezia–Corso Vittorio Emanuele–Vatican.

56   Largo Argentina–Via del Corso–Via del Tritone–Via Vittorio Veneto.

64   Termini–Via Nazionale–Corso Vittorio Emanuele–Vatican (the main bus route from the *centro storico* to the Vatican).

115   Stazione Termini–Via Nazionale–Via del Tritone–Via del Corso–Piazza Venezia–Largo Argentina–Mausoleo di Augusto (a circular minibus, weekdays 8am–9pm).

116   Via Veneto–Piazza Barberini–Via del Tritone–Piazza del Parlamento–Corso Rinascimento–Corso Vittorio Emanuele—Campo de' Fiori–Piazza Farnese–Via Giulia (a circular minibus, weekdays 8am–9pm, Sat 8am–midnight).

117   Piazza di Spagna–Via del Babuino–Piazza del Popolo–Via del Corso–Piazza Venezia–Via dei Fori Imperiali (a circular minibus).

218   S. Giovanni in Laterano–Porta San Sebastiano–Via Appia Antica–Via Ardeatina (passing the catacombs and tombs).

by taxi

Official taxis (painted yellow or white) are in plentiful supply, and easier to get at a rank in one of the main piazzas than to flag down. They are quite expensive, with sizeable surcharges for luggage, on Sundays and after 10.30 at night. Don't expect to find one when it's raining. To phone for a taxi, call ✆ 06 3570, or ✆ 06 4994; you don't pay extra for calling a cab, but expect to pay for the time it takes for it to reach you.

by car

Absolutely not recommended! Rome isn't as chaotic as Naples, but nearly so. Parking is expensive and difficult to find; many areas in the centre are closed to traffic (and the signs for them are hard to spot) and riddled with narrow, one-way streets. Rome and its cars are mortal enemies; sooner or later one or the other will have to succumb.

Tourist Information

The main office is at Via Parigi 5, ✆ 06 4889 9253, three blocks north of Stazione Termini, just behind the Terme di Diocleziano. Several other branches can be found inside **Stazione Termini**, at **Fiumicino Airport**, in front of the Colosseum, next to Castel Sant'Angelo, and on Via Nazionale next to Palazzo Esposizione. The Hotel Reservation Service, ✆ 06 699 1000 (*open daily 7am–10pm*) offers commission-free reservations at several hundred hotels in town. **Enjoy Rome**, Via Varese 39, ✆ 06 445 1843, also near Stazione Termini, is an efficient privately run English-speaking agency. Two weeklies available from newsstands, *Romac'e'* (with a short English section at the back) and *Time Out* (in Italian), are the best sources of information on what's on in Rome in the arts, culture and entertainment.

24-hour pharmacies: Piram, Via Nazionale 228, ✆ 06 488 0754; **Arenula**, Via Arenula 73, ✆ 06 6880 3278, near Largo Argentina. Lists of duty pharmacists are also posted outside all other pharmacies.

Outside banking hours money can be exchanged at **American Express**, Piazza di Spagna 38, ✆ 06 67641 (*open Mon–Fri 9–5.30, Sat 9–12.30*); **Thomas Cook**, Via della Conciliazione 23–25, ✆ 06 6830 0435 (*open Mon–Sat 8.30–6, Sun 9–1.30*); and numerous money changing shops in the centre.

Main post office: in Piazza San Silvestro, ✆ 06 6771.

Piazza Venezia

This traffic-crazed, thoroughly awful piazza may be a poor introduction to Rome, but it makes a good place to start, with the ruins of old Rome on one side and the boutiques and bureaucracies of the new city on the other. The piazza takes its name from the **Palazzo Venezia**, built for Pope Paul II in 1455, but long the Embassy of the Venetian Republic. Mussolini made it his residence, leaving a light on all night to make the Italians think he was working. His

Central Rome

VIA MERULANA

STAZIONE TERMINI

VIA MARSALA

VIA GIOVANNI

VIA MONTEBELLO

VIA INDIPENDENZA

Piazza Indipendenza

Terme di Diocleziano

VIA CERNAIA

Piazza dei Cinquecento

PRINCIPE AMEDEO

S. MARIA MAGGIORE
S. Maria Maggiore

V.C. ALBERTO

V. DI STATUTO

Monte Esquilino

VIA LABICANA

S. Clemente

VIA PIAVE

VIA CAVOUR

S. Prassede

Domus Aurea

S. DI S. GIOV. IN LATERANO

Pza. Repubblica

S. Bernardo

V. TORINO

S. URBANA

S. Pudenziana

V. G. LANZA

S. Pietro in Vincoli

VIA CLAUDIA

V. SARDEGNA

VIA XX SETTEMBRE

S. Maria della Vittoria

Largo S. Susanna

V. DL BISSOLATI

Palazzo Barberini

S. Carlino

NAPOLI D. PRETIS

Monte Viminale

VIA PANISPERNA

VIA DEI SERPENTI

Colosseo
Colosseo

Arco di Tito

SS. Giovanni e Paolo

S. Gregorio Magno

Monte Celio

VilCa

VIA BONCOMPAGNI

Palazzo Barberini

i

VIA CAVOUR

Foro di Augusto

V. DI S. GREGORIO

V. LUDOVISI

Convento dei Cappuccini

VIA BARBERINI

VIA SISTINA

VIA NAZIONALE

Largo Magnanapoli

Foro di Augusto

Arco di Costantino

VITT. VENETO

VIA DEL TRITONE

Palazzo del Quirinale

Torre delle Milizie

Carcere Mamertino

Basilica di Massenzio

Foro Romano

Monte Palatino

Piazza di Porta Capena

V. VENETO

Monte Quirinale

Foro Traiano

VIA DEI FORI IMPERIALI

Trinità del Monte

Villa Medici

Spanish Steps

V. D. MACELLI

Pza. del Quirinale

24 MAGGIO

Foro Traiano

S. Giorgio in Velabro

Arco di Costantino

Circo Massimo

S. Sabina

Fontana di Trevi

Palazzo Doria Pamphili

Piazza Venezia

Basilica di Massenzio

Tempio di Vesta

S. Maria in Cosmedin

LUNG. AVENTINO

To Piazza del Popolo

VIA BABUINO

V. B. DI LEONE

VIA DEL CORSO

Pza. Colonna

Borsa

S. Ignazio

S. Maria Sopra Minerva

Chiesa del Gesù

Palazzo Venezia

Musei Capitolini

Monte Capitolino

Tempio di Fortuna

Tempio di Vesta

V. DEL CERCHI

VIA DEL CIRCO MASSIMO

Mausoleum of Augustus

Ara Pacis

VIA RIPETTA

Palazzo di Montecitorio

Piazza della Rotonda

Pantheon

S. Eustachio

VITTORIO EMANUELE

S. Andrea della Valle

Teatro di Pompeo

Tempio di Vesta

Palazzo Massimo

Sinagoga

Teatro di Marcello

Bartolomeo

Ponte Rotto

Piazza Bocca della Verità

LUNG. RIPA

LUNG. IN AUGUSTA

LUNG. MELLINI

S. Luigi

Palazzo Madama

C. RINASCIMENTO

Piazza Navona

Sant' Agnese

Museo di Roma

Palazzo della Cancelleria

CORSO VITTORIO EMANUELE

GIUBBONARI

S. Maria d. Quercia

LUNG. CENCI

Isola Tiberina

Torre di Anguillara

V. DELLA LUNGARETTA

VIALE DI TRASTEVERE

V. D. GENOVESI

S. Cecilia

V.S. MICHELE

Tévere (Tiber)

V. DELLA SCROFA

Area Sacra Argentina

AVENTINO

LUNG. TOR DI NONA

VIA DEI CORONARI

Campo de' Fiori

Piazza Farnese

Palazzo Farnese

Palazzo Spada

VIA ARENULA

LUNG. R. SANZIO

Pza. G. Belli

Pza. S. Maria in Trast.

S. Maria in Trastevere

VS. FRANCESCO

RIPA

Pza. S. Cosimato

Piazza Cavour

LUNG. CASTELLO

VIA GIULIA

TEBALDI

LUNGOTEVERE

LUNG. FARNESINA

VIA GARIBALDI

VIA DI TRASTEVERE

Metropolitana

250 metres

250 yards

Castel S.Angelo

LUNG. GIANICOLENSE

LUNG. LUNGARA

Villa Farnesina

VIA GIACINTO CARINI

VIA COLA DI RIENZO

VIA CRESCENZIO

LUNG. SANGALLO

Galleria Corsini

S. Pietro in Montorio

VIA GARIBALDI

VIA NICOLA FABRIZI

Villa Aurelia

VIALE GLORIOSO

N

Ospedale di S. Spirito

LUNG. DELLA LUNGARA

Monte Gianicolo

Villa Abamelek

Piazzale Giuseppe Garibaldi

VIALE DELLE MURA

VIA DELLE MURA

VIA DI S. PANCRAZIO

VIA OTTAVIANO

Piazza del Risorgimento

Piazza S. Pietro

S. Onofrio

VIA DELLE FORNACI

famous balcony, from which he would declaim to the 'oceanic' crowds in the square (renamed the Forum of the Fascist Empire in those days) still holds its prominent place, a bad memory for the Italians. Nowadays the Palazzo holds a **museum** of Renaissance and Baroque decorative arts (*open Tues–Sat 9–1.30, Sun 9–1; adm exp*). The palace complex was built around the ancient church of **San Marco**, with a 9th-century mosaic in the apse. Parts of the building are as old as AD 400, and the façade is by the Renaissance architect Benedetto di Maiano.

Long ago the southern edge of this piazza had approaches up to the Monte Capitolino. The hill is still there, though it's now entirely blocked out by the **Altar of the Nation** (also known as the *Vittoriano*, the 'Wedding Cake' or the 'Typewriter'), Risorgimento Italy's own self-inflicted satire and one of the world's apotheoses of kitsch. Its size and its solid marble walls are explained by the 1880s prime minister who commissioned it; he happened to have a marble quarry in his home district of Brescia. Recounting its sculptural allegories would take pages— but of the two big bronze imperial-style *quadrigae* on top, one represents Italian Liberty and the other Italian Unity. In the centre, the modest virtues of Vittorio Emanuele II have earned him a 38ft bronze equestrian statue, perhaps the world's largest. Beneath him, Italy's Unknown Soldier sleeps peacefully with a round-the-clock guard. On the left-hand side of the monument you can see the remains of the republican Roman tomb of C. Publius Bibulus.

Monte Capitolino

Behind the *Vittoriano*, two stairways lead to the top of the hill. This is a fateful spot; in 121 BC the great reformer Tiberius Gracchus was murdered here by what today would be called a 'right-wing death squad'. Almost a millennium and a half later Cola di Rienzo was trying to escape Rome in disguise when an enraged mob recognized him by the rings on his fingers and tore him to pieces. Rienzo built the left-hand staircase, and was the first to climb it. It leads to **Santa Maria in Aracoeli**, begun in the 7th century over the temple of Juno Moneta—the ancient Roman Mint was adjacent to it. The Aracoeli, which in Rienzo's time served as a council hall for the Romans, is one of the most revered of churches; legend has it that one of the Sibyls of Tivoli prophesied the coming of Jesus and told Augustus to build a temple here to the 'first born of God'. Inside you can seek out frescoes by Pinturicchio (*San Bernardino of Siena*) and Gozzoli (*San Antonio of Padua*), and a tombstone by Donatello, near the entrance.

The second stairway takes you to the real heart of Rome, Michelangelo's **Piazza del Campidoglio**, passing a rather flattering statue of Rienzo set on a bronze pedestal. Bordering the piazza, a formidable cast of statues includes the Dioscuri, who come from Pompey's Theatre, and Marforio (in the Musei Capitolini courtyard), a river god once employed as a 'talking statue', decorated with graffiti and placards commenting on current events. The great

2nd-century AD bronze equestrian statue of the benign and philosophical emperor **Marcus Aurelius** that stood on the plinth in the middle of the piazza from the 16th century until 1981, has been fully restored and regilded and is now in the Musei Capitolini. Fortunately enough, since it was an old Roman saying that the world would end when all the gold flaked off. The Christians of old only refrained from melting him down for cash because they believed he was not Marcus Aurelius, but Constantine. A faithful copy now stands in the piazza.

The Musei Capitolini

Michelangelo's original plans may have been adapted and tinkered with by later architects, but nevertheless his plan for the Campidoglio has come out as one of the triumphs of Renaissance design. The centrepiece, the **Palazzo Senatorio**, Rome's city hall, with its distinctive stairway and bell tower, is built over the ruins of the Roman *tabularium*, the state archive. At the base of the stair note the statue of Minerva, in her aspect as the allegorical goddess Roma.

Flanking it, Michelangelo redesigned the façade of the **Palazzo dei Conservatori** (on the right), and projected the matching building across the square, the **Palazzo Nuovo**, built in the early 18th century. Together they make up the **Capitoline Museums**. Founded by Pope Clement XII in 1734, the oldest true museum in the world, the Capitolini (*open Tues–Sun 9–7; adm*) displays both the heights and depths of ancient society and culture. For the heights there are the reliefs from the triumphal arch of Marcus Aurelius—first-class work in scenes of the emperor's clemency and piety, and his triumphal receptions in Rome. Marcus always looks a little worried in these, perhaps considering his good-for-nothing son Commodus, and the empire he would inherit, sinking into corruption and excess. What was to come is well illustrated by the degenerate art of the 4th century, like the colossal bronze head, hand and foot of Constantine, parts of a colossal statue in the Basilica of Maxentius (now in the courtyard).

In between these extremes come roomfuls of statuary, including the *Capitoline She-Wolf*, the very symbol of Rome (note that the suckling twins were added to the Etruscan bronze she-wolf in the Renaissance); statues of most of the emperors, busts of Homer, Sophocles and Pythagoras; the voluptuous *Capitoline Venus*; a big baby Hercules (who may have inspired Donatello's famous *Amor* in Florence); and the *Muse Polyhymnia*, one of the most delightful statues of antiquity. Later works include lots of papal paraphernalia, a statue of Charles of Anjou by Arnolfo di Cambio and—in a small **Pinacoteca** in the Palazzo dei Conservatori— some dignified Velázquez gentlemen, looking scornfully at the other paintings, and two major works by Caravaggio, the *Fortune Teller* and *John the Baptist*. There are also some lovely 18th-century porcelains—orchestras of monkeys in powdered wigs, and such.

The best overview of the Roman Forum is to be had from behind Palazzo Senatorio. A stairway leads down from the left side to Via dei Fori Imperiali and the entrance to the Forum. On the way, beneath the church of San Giuseppe Falegnami, you can visit the **Carcere Mamertino** (*open April–Sept daily 9–12.30 and 2.30–6; Oct–Mar daily 9–12 and 2–5*), the small calaboose used by the ancient Romans for their most important prisoners—the Catiline conspirators, Vercingetorix (the Gaulish chief captured by Caesar), and finally St Peter. The southern end of the Capitol, one of the quietest corners of Rome, was the site of the temple of Jupiter Optimus Maximus (Greatest and Best), built originally by the Etruscan kings. At the time it was the largest in Italy, testimony to Rome's importance as far back as 450 BC. Along the southern edge of the hill, the cliffs you see are the somewhat reduced remains of the **Tarpeian Rock**, from which traitors and other malefactors were thrown in Rome's early days.

Along the Tiber

The early emperors did their best to import classical Greek drama to Rome, and for a while, with the poets of the Latin New Comedy, it seemed the Romans would carry on the tradition. Great theatres were built like the **Teatro di Marcello**, begun by Caesar and completed by Augustus. By the second century AD, however, theatre had already begun to degenerate into music hall, lewd performances with naked actresses and grisly murders (condemned prisoners were sometimes butchered on stage), and shows by celebrity actors probably much like some of today's unseemly spectacles. Marcellus' theatre survived into the Middle Ages, when the Orsini family converted it into their palace-fortress, the strongest after the Castel Sant'Angelo. You can still see the tall arches of the circumference surmounted by the rough medieval walls.

The streets to the west contain a mix of some of Rome's oldest houses with new buildings; the latter have replaced the old walled **ghetto**. There has been a sizeable Jewish community in Rome since the 2nd century BC; after conquering the Jews at the end of the 1st century AD, Pompey and Titus brought them to Rome as slaves. They helped finance the career of Julius Caesar, who would prove to be their greatest benefactor. For centuries they lived near this bend in the river and in Trastevere. Paul IV took time off from burning books and heretics to wall them into the tiny ghetto in 1555; at the same time he forced them to wear orange hats, attend Mass on Sunday, and limited them to the rag and old iron trades. Tearing down the ghetto walls was one of the first acts of the Italian kingdom after the entry into Rome in 1870. The exotic, eclectic main **synagogue** was built in 1904; inside, there is a small museum of the **Jewish Community** (*open Mon–Thurs 9.30–2 and 3–5, Fri 9.30–2, Sun 9.30–12; adm*).

Opposite the synagogue, the **Isola Tiberina** is joined to both sides of the river by surviving ancient bridges. In imperial times the island was sacred to Aesculapius, god of healing; a legend records how some serpents brought from the god's shrine in Greece escaped and swam to the spot, choosing the site by divine guidance. Now, as in ancient times, most of the lovely island is taken up by a hospital, the Ospedale Fatebenefratelli; in place of the Temple of Aesculapius, there is also the church of **San Bartolomeo**, most recently rebuilt in the 1690s.

The **Velabrum**, in the earliest days of Rome, was a cattle market (interestingly, in the Middle Ages, the Roman Forum itself was used for the same purpose). In this area, east of the Isola Tiberina, is **San Giorgio in Velabro**, in parts as old as the 7th century; there is a Cosmatesque altar, and early Christian fragments on the left wall. The lovely portico has been completely restored after a mafia bombing in 1993. Of the two ancient arches outside, the **Arco degli Argentari** was erected by the moneychangers in honour of Septimius Severus. The larger, the unfinished, four-sided **Janus Quadrifons**, dates from the time of Constantine.

Piazza Bocca della Verità

Tourists almost always overlook this beautiful corner along the Tiber, but here you can see two well-preserved Roman temples. Both go under false names: the round **Temple of Vesta**, used as an Armenian church in the Middle Ages, and the **Temple of Fortuna Virilis**—it now seems almost certain that they were actually dedicated to Hercules Victor and Portunus (the god of harbours) respectively. Some bits of an exotic Roman cornice are built into the brick building opposite, part of the **House of the Crescenzi**, a powerful family in the 9th century, descended from Theodora Senatrix. Look over the side of the Tiber embankment here and you can see the outlet of the **Cloaca Maxima**, the sewer begun by King Tarquin. Big enough to drive two carriages through, it is still in use today.

Just upstream, past the Ponte Palatino, a single arch decorated with dragons is all that remains of the *Pons Aemilius*. Originally built in the 2nd century BC, it collapsed twice and was last restored in 1575 by Gregory XIII, only to fall down again 20 years later. Now it is known as the 'broken bridge', or **Ponte Rotto**.

Across from the temples, the handsome medieval church with the lofty campanile is **Santa Maria in Cosmedin**, built over an altar of Hercules in the 6th century and given to Byzantine Greeks escaping from the Iconoclast emperors in the 8th. The name (like 'cosmetic') means 'decorated', but little of the original art has survived; most of what you see is from the 12th century, including some fine Cosmatesque work inside. In the portico, an ancient, ghostly image in stone built into the walls has come down in legend as the **Bocca della Verità**—the Mouth of Truth. Medieval Romans would swear oaths and close business deals here; if you tell a lie with your hand in the image's mouth he will most assuredly bite your fingers off. Try it.

The Heart of Ancient Rome

In the 1930s Mussolini built a grand boulevard between the Vittoriano and the Colosseum to ease traffic congestion and show off the ancient sites. He called it the Via del Impero, coinciding with his aspirations of returning Rome to greatness through a new empire in Africa. After Mussolini's demise the road was re-christened **Via dei Fori Imperiali**, after the Imperial Fora which it part covers. The **Imperial Fora** of Augustus, Nerva and Trajan were built to relieve congestion in the original Roman Forum. **Trajan's Forum** (*Foro di Traiano*), built with the spoils of his conquest of Dacia (modern Romania) was perhaps the grandest architectural and planning conception ever built in Rome, a broad square surrounded by colonnades, with a huge basilica flanked by two libraries and a covered market outside (the world's first shopping mall). A large part of **Trajan's Market** (*Mercati di Traiano*) still stands, with entrances on Via IV Novembre and down the stairs just to the side of Trajan's Column (*open Tues–Sun 9–one hour before sunset; adm*). Behind it, you can see Rome's own leaning tower, the 12th century **Torre delle Milizie**. All that remains of Trajan's great square is the paving and its centrepiece, the **Trajan Column** (*Colonna Traiana*). The spiralling bands of reliefs, illustrating the Dacian Wars, reach to the top, some 96ft high. They rank with the greatest works of Roman art; plaster casts are on display at eye level in the Museo della Civiltà Romana (*see* p.755). Behind the column, **Santa Maria di Loreto** is a somewhat garish High Renaissance bauble, built by Bramante and Antonio da Sangallo the Younger. The Romans liked the church so much that in the 1730s they built another one just like it next door, the **Santissimo Nome di Maria**. Scanty remains of **Caesar's Forum** (*Foro di Cesare*) and **Augustus' Forum** (*Foro di Augusto*) can be seen along the boulevard to the south.

The Roman Forum

For a place that was the centre of the Mediterranean world, there is surprisingly little to see; centuries of use as a quarry have seen to that. The word *forum* originally meant 'outside' (like the Italian *fuori*), a market-place outside the original Rome that became the centre of both government and business as the city expanded. The entrances are on Via dei Fori Imperiali at Via Cavour, and at the end of the ramp that approaches the Forum from the Colosseum side (*open April–Oct daily 9–one hour before sunset; May–Sept Mon–Sat 9–3, Sun 9–1; adm*). The **Via Sacra**, ancient Rome's most important street, runs the length of the Forum. At the end of it beneath the Capitol you will be facing the **Arch of Septimius Severus** (AD 203), with reliefs of some rather trivial victories over the Arabs and Parthians; conservative Romans of the

Central Rome 300 AD

N

VIA RECTA

VIA LATA

(CORSO VITT. EMANUELE)

(Piazza Venezia)

(Campo De' Fiori)

Martius

Campus

Capitolium

Collis

Forum

(VIA ARENULA)

Flumen Tiberis

(V. TUSCUS)

Mons Palat...

Velabrum

*before names of sights
indicates significant remains
Modern Streets and Squares
shaded in to help orientation

CAMPUS MARTIUS
1 Stadium of Domitian
2 Baths of Nero
3 *Temple of Hadrian
4 Domitian's Odeon
5 Stagnum Agrippae
6 *Pantheon
7 Baths of Agrippa
8 S[ae]pta Julia
9 Temple of Isis
10 Porticus Divorum
11 Portico of Vipsania
12 Pompey's Theatre
13 *Republican Temples
(Largo Argentina)
14 Portico of Minucia
15 Theatre of Balbus
16 Porticus Philippi
17 *Portico of Octavia
18 Circus Flaminius
19 *Temple of Apollo
20 Temple of Bellona
21 *Temple of Marcellus
22 *Temple of Hope
(S. Nicolo)
23 Forum Holitorium
24 Temple of Aesculapius
25 Warehouses

**VELABRUM AND
TIBER ISLAND**
26 *Temple of Portumnus
27 *Temple of Hercules Victor
28 Forum Boarium
29 Statio Annonae/
Altar of Heroules
30 Circus Maximus
31 Bridge of Valentinian

32 * Pons Cestius
33 * Pons Fabricius
34 * Pons Aemilius
35 Pons Probus

CAPITOL
36 * Insula (Apartment House)
37 Arx (Citadel)
38 Temple of Juno Moneta
39 Asylum - Temple of Veiovis
40 * Tabularium
41 Temple of Jupiter

FORUM
42 *Temple of Saturn
43 *Arch of Septimius Severus
44 *Curia
45 Basilica Aemilia
46 Basilica Julia
47 *Temple of the Dioscuri
48 *House of the Vestal Virgins
49 *Basilica of Maxentius
50 *Arch of Titus
51 *Temple of Venus and Rome
52 Temple of Elagabalus
53 Nero's Colossus
54 *Arch of Constantine

55 *Colosseum

PALATINE
56 *Palace of Tiberius
57 Temple of Cybele
58 *House of Augustus
59 *Stadium
60 Septizonium

CAELIAN AND QUIRINAL
61 Temple of Claudius
62 *Ludus Magnus
63 Baths of Titus
64 Baths of Trajan
65 Temple of Serapis
66 Baths of Constantine

IMPERIAL FORA
67 Temple of Trajan
68 *Trajan's Column
69 Basilica Ulpia
70 Forum of Trajan
71 *Trajan's Market
72 *Forum of Augustus
73 *Forum of Nerva -
Temple of Minerva
74 *Temple of Venus Genetrix
75 Forun of Caesar
76 Forum of Vespasian

time must have strongly resented this upstart African emperor planting his monument in such an important spot. The arch also commemorated Septimius' two sons, Geta and Caracalla; when the nasty Caracalla did his brother in, he had his name effaced from it. In front of it, the **Lapis Niger**, a mysterious stone with an underground chamber beneath it, is the legendary tomb of Romulus. The inscription down below—a threat against the profaning of this sacred spot—is one of the oldest ever found in the Latin language. The famous Golden Milestone also stood here, the 'umbilicus' of Rome and the point from which all distances in the Empire were measured. To the right is the **Curia** (the Senate House), heavily restored after centuries' use as a church (the good Baroque church behind it is **SS. Luca e Martina**, built by Pietro da Cortona in the 1660s). To the left of the arch the remains of a raised stone area were the **Rostra**, the speakers' platform under the republic, decorated with ships' prows (*rostra*) taken in a sea battle in about 320 BC. Of the great temples on the Capitol slope only a few columns remain; from left to right, the **Temple of Saturn**, which served as Rome's treasury, the **Temple of Vespasian** (three standing columns) and the **Temple of Concord**, built by Tiberius to honour the peace—so to speak—that the emperors had enforced between patricians and plebeians.

Behind the Rostra, in the open area once decorated with statues and monuments, the simple standing **column** was placed in honour of Nikephoros Phocas, Byzantine Emperor in 608—the last monument ever erected in the Forum; the Romans had to steal the column from a ruined building. Just behind it a small pool once marked the spot of one of ancient Rome's favourite legends. In 362 BC, according to Livy, an abyss suddenly opened across the Forum, and the sibyls predicted that it would not close unless the 'things that Rome held most precious' were thrown in. A consul, Marcus Curtius, took this as meaning a Roman citizen and soldier. He leapt in fully armed, horse and all, and the crack closed over him.

This section of the Forum was bordered by two imposing buildings, the **Basilica Aemilia** to the north and the **Basilica Julia** to the south, built by Caesar with the spoils of the Gallic Wars. The **Temple of Caesar** closes the east end, built by Augustus as a visual symbol of the new imperial mythology.

The adjacent **Temple of the Dioscuri** makes a good example of how temples were used in ancient times. This one was a meeting hall for men of the equestrian class (the knights, though they were really more likely to be businessmen); they had safe-deposit boxes in the basement, where the standard weights and measures of the empire were kept. Between them, the round pedestal was the foundation of the small **Temple of Vesta**, where the sacred hearth-fire was kept burning by the Vestal Virgins; ruins of their extensive apartments can be seen next door.

Two more Christian churches stand in this part of the Forum. **SS. Cosma e Damiano** was built on to the **Temple of Antoninus Pius and Faustina** in the 6th century; most of the columns survive, with a fine sculptural frieze of griffons on top. **Santa Francesca Romana** is built over a corner of Rome's largest temple, that of **Venus and Rome**. Built by Hadrian, this was a curious, double-ended shrine to the state cult; one side devoted to the Goddess Roma and the other to Venus—in the imperial mythology she was the ancestress of the Caesars.

The church entrance is outside the Forum, but the adjoining convent, inside the monumental area, houses the **Antiquarium Forense**, with Iron-Age burial urns and other paraphernalia from the Forum excavations. Between the two churches the mastodontic **Basilica of Maxentius**, finished by Constantine, remains the largest ruin of the Forum, its clumsy arches providing an illustration of the ungainly but technically sophisticated 4th century.

Near the exit the **Arch of Titus** commemorates the victories of Titus and his father Vespasian over the rebellious Jews (AD 60–80), one of the fiercest struggles Rome ever had to fight. The reliefs show the booty being carted through Rome in the triumphal parade—including the famous seven-branched golden candlestick from the holy of holies in the Temple at Jerusalem.

South of the arch a path leads up to the **Monte Palatino** (*open April–Oct daily 9–one hour before sunset; May–Sept Mon–Sat 9–3, Sun 9–1; adm*). Here, overlooking the little corner of the world that gave our language words like *senate, committee, rostrum, republic, plebiscite* and *magistrate*, you can leave democracy behind and visit the etymological birthplace of *palace*. The ruins of the imperial *Palatium* once covered the entire hill. As with the Forum, almost all the stone has been cannibalized, and there's little to see of what was once a complex half a mile long, to which a dozen of the emperors contributed.

There are good views across the Circus Maximus from just above what was once the portico from which the emperor could watch the races. Don't miss the chance to take a stroll through the gardens planted by the Farnese family over what were the imperial servants' quarters— one of the most peaceful spots in the city. The one modern building on the Palatino houses the Antiquarium, a good little collection of relics found within a stone's throw of the building.

The Colosseum

Its real name was the Flavian Amphitheatre, after the family of emperors who built it, beginning with Vespasian in AD 72; Colosseum refers to the *Colossus*, a huge gilded statue of Nero (erected by himself, of course) that stood in the square in front. There doesn't seem to be much evidence that Christians were literally thrown to lions here—there were other places for that—but what did go on was perhaps the grossest and best-organized perversity in all history. Gladiatorial contests began under the republic, designed to make Romans better soldiers by rendering them indifferent to the sight of death. Later emperors introduced new displays to relieve the monotony—men versus animals, lions versus elephants, women versus dwarfs, sea-battles (the arena could be flooded at a moment's notice), public tortures of condemned criminals, and even genuine athletics, a Greek import the Romans never much cared for. In the first hundred days of the Colosseum's opening, 5000 animals were slaughtered. The native elephant and lion of North Africa and Arabia are extinct thanks to such shenanigans.

However hideous its purpose, the Colosseum ranks with the greatest works of Roman architecture and engineering; all modern stadia have its basic plan. One surprising feature was a removable awning that covered the stands. Sailors from Cape Misenum were kept to operate it; they also manned the galleys in the mock sea-battles. Originally there were statues in every arch and a ring of bronze shields around the cornice. The concrete stands have eroded away, showing the brick structure underneath. Renaissance and Baroque popes hauled away half the travertine exterior—enough to build the Palazzo Venezia, the Palazzo Barberini, a few other palaces and bridges and part of St Peter's. Almost all of the construction work under Vespasian and Titus was performed by Jewish slaves, brought here for the purpose after the suppression of their revolt (*open Tues–Sat 9–one hour before sunset, Sun and Mon 9–2; adm*).

Just outside the Colosseum, the **Arch of Constantine** marks the end of the ancient Triumphal Way (now Via di San Gregorio) where victorious emperors and their troops would parade their captives and booty. The arch, with a coy inscription mentioning Constantine's 'divine inspiration' (the Romans weren't sure whether it was yet respectable to mention Christianity), is covered with reliefs stolen from older arches and public buildings—a sad commentary on the state of art in Constantine's day.

Domus Aurea and the Monte Esquilino

When Nero decided he needed a new palace, money was no object. Taking advantage of the great fire of AD 64 (which he apparently did *not* start), he had a huge section of Rome (temporarily renamed Neropolis) cleared to make a rural estate in the middle of town. The **Golden House** was probably the most sumptuous palace ever built in Rome, decorated in an age when Roman art was at its height, but Nero never lived to see it finished—he committed suicide during an army coup by Spanish legions. When the dust settled the new emperor Vespasian realized that this flagrant symbol of imperial decadence had to go. He demolished it, and Titus and Trajan later erected great bath complexes on its foundations; Nero's gardens and fishponds became the site of the Colosseum. In the 1500s some beautifully decorated rooms of the Domus Aurea were discovered underground, saved for use as the basement of Titus' baths. Raphael and other artists studied them closely and incorporated some of the spirit of the fresco decoration into the grand manner of the High Renaissance (our word 'grotesque', originally referring to the leering faces and floral designs of this time, comes from the finds in this 'grotto'). The rooms are at present closed for restoration, which may take years.

The **Monte Esquilino** is better known today as the *Colle Oppio*. Much of it is covered with parks; besides the Domus Aurea there are very substantial ruins of the **Terme di Traiano**, still unexcavated. On the northern slope of the hill, **San Pietro in Vincoli** takes its name from relics supposed to be the chains Peter was locked in before Nero had him crucified. They are kept over the main altar, though the real attraction of this church for non-Catholics is the famous, ill-fated **tomb of Julius II** which tortured Michelangelo for so many years. Of the original project, planned as a sort of tabernacle with 40 individual statues, the artist completed only the powerful figure of *Moses*, perhaps the closest anyone has ever come to capturing prophetic vision in stone, even if he bears a striking resemblance to Charlton Heston. All the other statues on the tomb are the work of Michelangelo's students.

San Clemente

This church, a little way to the east of the Colosseum on Via San Giovanni in Laterano, is one of the more fascinating remnants of Rome's many-layered history. One of the first substantial building projects of the Christians in Rome, the original basilica of *c.* 375 burned along with the rest of the quarter during a sacking by the Normans in 1084. It was rebuilt soon afterwards with a new Cosmatesque pavement, and the 6th-century choir screen—a rare example of sculpture from that ungifted time—saved from the original church. The 12th-century mosaic in the apse represents the *Triumph of the Cross*, and the chapel at the entrance contains a beautiful series of quattrocento frescoes by Masolino. From a vestibule, nuns sell tickets to the **Lower Church** (*open daily 9–12 and 3.30–6.30; adm*). This is the lower half of the original

San Clemente, and there are remarkable, though deteriorated, frescoes from the 900s and the 12th century. The plaque from Bulgaria, mentioned on p.715, commemorates SS. Cyril and Methodius, who went from this church to spread the Gospel among the Slavs; they translated the Bible into Old Slavonic, and invented the first Slavic alphabet (Cyrillic) to do it.

From here, steps lead down to the lowest stratum, 1st and 2nd century AD buildings divided by an alley; this includes the **Mithraeum**, the best-preserved temple of its kind after the one in Capua. The larger, neighbouring building was filled with rubble to serve as a foundation for the basilica, and the apse was later added over the Mithraeum. Father Mulhooly of Boston started excavating in the 1860s, and later excavations have revealed a Mithraic antechamber with a fine stuccoed ceiling, a Mithraic school with an early fresco, and the temple proper, a small cavern-like hall with benches for the initiates to share a ritual supper.

Mithraism was a mystery religion, full of secrets closely held by the initiates (all male, and largely soldiers) and it is difficult to say what else went on down here. Two altars were found, each with the usual image of the Persian-import god Mithras despatching a white bull, including a snake, a scorpion and a crow, and astrological symbolism. Underneath all this, there is yet a fourth building level, some foundations from the republican era. At the end of the 1st-century building you can look down into an ancient sewer or underground stream, one of a thousand entrances to the surreal sub-Roma of endless subterranean caves, buildings, rivers and lakes, mostly unexplored and unexplorable. A century ago a schoolboy fell in the water here; they found him, barely alive, in open country several kilometres from the city.

Corso Vittorio Emanuele

This street, chopped through the medieval centre in the 1880s, still hasn't quite been assimilated into its surroundings; nevertheless, this ragged, smoky traffic tunnel will come in handy when you find yourself lost in the tortuous, meandering streets of Rome's oldest quarter. Starting west from Piazza Venezia, the church of the **Gesù** (1568–84) was a landmark for a new era and the new aesthetic of cinquecento Rome. The transitional, pre-Baroque fashion was often referred to as the 'Jesuit style', and here in the Jesuits' head church architects Vignola and della Porta laid down Baroque's first law: an intimation of paradise through decorative excess. It hasn't aged well, though at the time it must have seemed to most Romans a perfect marriage of Renaissance art and a reformed, revitalized faith. St Ignatius, the Jesuits' founder, is buried in the left transept right under the altar, Spanish-style; the globe incorporated in the sculpted Trinity overhead is the biggest piece of lapis lazuli in the world.

Further west the street opens into a ghastly square called Largo Argentina. Remains of several republican-era temples, unearthed far below ground level, occupy the centre. Next comes another grand Baroque church, **Sant'Andrea della Valle**, with the city's second-tallest dome. Maderno, one of the architects of St Peter's, did most of the work. The curving façade across the street belongs to **Palazzo Massimo alle Colonne**, the masterpiece of the Renaissance architect Baldassare Peruzzi; he transplanted something of the Florentine style of monumental palaces, adding some light-hearted proto-Baroque decoration. If you can, have a look at the adjacent church of **S. Pantaleo de Parione** (*rarely open*), with its outlandish sculptural frieze of shields, trays and popes' hats piled like a rubbish heap. The Palazzo Braschi next door houses the small **Museo di Roma** (*closed almost permanently for restoration*).

One of the earliest and best of the palaces on Corso Vittorio Emanuele, the delicate **Piccola Farnesina** by Antonio da Sangallo the Younger, houses another little museum, a collection of ancient sculpture called the **Museo Barracco** (*open Tues–Sat 9–7, Sun 9–1.30; adm*). A third museum—not a well-known one—is just around the corner from Sant'Andrea: the Burcardo Theatre Museum, Via Sudario (*open by appointment, call the custodian, © 06 684 0001*) is a collection of fascinating old relics from the Roman theatrical tradition.

The biggest palace on the street, attributed to Bramante, is **Palazzo della Cancelleria**, once the seat of the papal municipal government. St Philip Neri, the gifted, irascible holy man who is patron saint of Rome, built the **Chiesa Nuova** near the eastern end of the Corso (1584). Philip was quite a character, with something of the Zen Buddhist in him. He forbade his followers any sort of philosophical speculation, but made them sing and recite poetry; two of his favourite pastimes were insulting popes and embarrassing initiates—making them walk through Rome with a foxtail sewn to the back of their coat to learn humility. As was common in those times, sincere faith and humility were eventually translated into flagrant Baroque. The Chiesa Nuova is one of the larger and fancier of the species. Its altarpiece is a *Madonna with Angels* by Rubens. Even more flagrant, outside the church you can see the curved arch-Baroque façade of the **Oratorio dei Filippini** by Borromini. The form of music called the *oratorio* takes its name from this chapel, a tribute to St Philip's role in promoting sacred music.

Campo de' Fiori

Few cities can put on such a variety of faces to beguile the visitor; depending on where you spend your time in Rome, you may come away with the impression of a city that is one great Baroque stage set, a city of grimy early 1900s palazzi and bad traffic, or a city full of nothing but ruins and parks. Around **Campo de' Fiori**, one of the spots dearest to the hearts of Romans themselves, you may think yourself in the middle of some scruffy south Italian village. Rome's market square, disorderly, cramped and chaotic, is easily the liveliest corner of the city, full of market barrows, buskers, teenage Bohemians and the folkloresque types who have lived here all their lives—the least decorous and worst-dressed crowd in Rome. During papal rule the old square was also used for executions—most notoriously the burning of Giordano Bruno in 1600. This well-travelled philosopher was the first to take Copernican astronomy to its logical extremes—an infinite universe with no centre, no room for Heaven, and nothing eternal but change. The Church had few enemies more dangerous. Italy never forgot him; the statue of Bruno in Campo de' Fiori went up only a few years after the end of papal rule.

Just east of the square, the heap of buildings around Piazzetta di Grottapinta is built over the cavea of **Teatro di Pompeo**, ancient Rome's biggest. This complex included a *curia*, the place where Julius Caesar was assassinated in 44 BC. Walk south from Campo de' Fiori and you will be thrown back from cosy medievalism into the heart of the High Renaissance with the **Palazzo Farnese**, one of the definitive works of that Olympian style. The younger Sangallo began it in 1514, and Michelangelo contributed to the façades and interiors. The building now serves as the French Embassy.

Most of the palaces that fill up this neighbourhood have one thing in common—they were made possible by someone's accession to the papacy, the biggest jackpot available to any aspiring Italian family. Built on the pennies of the faithful, they provide the most outrageous illustration of Church corruption at the dawn of the Reformation. Alessandro Farnese, who as Pope Paul III was a clever and effective pope—though perhaps the greatest nepotist ever to decorate St Peter's throne (*see* 'Caprarola', p.711)—managed to build this palace 20 years before his election, with the income from his 16 absentee bishoprics.

Palazzo Spada, just to the east along Via Capo di Ferro, was the home of a mere cardinal, but its florid stucco façade (1540) almost upstages the Farnese. Inside, the **Galleria Spada** (*open Tues–Sat 9–7, Sun 9–1; adm*) is one of Rome's great collections of 16th- and 17th-century painting. Guido Reni, Guercino and the other favourites of the age are well represented. Don't miss the courtyard, which has decoration similar to the façade, and a glass window with a view through the library to one of Rome's little Baroque treasures: the recently restored *trompe l'œil* corridor, designed by Borromini to appear four times its actual length (the statue at the end of the path is actually less than a yard in height). To the south, close to the Tiber, **Via Giulia** was laid out by Pope Julius II: a pretty thoroughfare lined with churches and palazzi from that time. Many artists (successful ones) have lived here, including Raphael.

Piazza Navona

In 1477 the area now covered by one of Rome's most beautiful piazzas was a field full of huts and vineyards, tucked inside the imposing ruins of the Stadium of Domitian. A redevelopment of the area covered the long grandstands with new houses, but the decoration had to wait for the Age of Baroque. In 1644, with the election of Innocent X, it was the Pamphili family that won the papal sweepstakes. Innocent, a great grafter and such a villainous pope that when he died no one—not even his newly wealthy relatives—would pay for a proper burial, built the ornate **Palazzo Pamphili** (now the Brazilian Embassy) and hired Borromini to complete the gaudy church of **Sant'Agnese in Agone**, begun by Carlo and Girolamo Rainaldi.

Borromini's arch-rival, Bernini, got the commission for the piazza's famous fountains; the Romans still tell stories of how the two artists carried on. Borromini started a rumour that the tall obelisk atop the central **Fontana dei Fiumi** was about to topple; when the alarmed papal commissioners arrived to confront Bernini with the news, he tied a piece of twine around it, secured the other end to a lamppost, and laughed all the way home. The fountain is Bernini's masterpiece, Baroque at its flashiest and most lovable. Among the travertine grottoes and fantastical flora and fauna under the obelisk, the four colossal figures represent the Ganges, Danube, Rio de la Plata and Nile (with the veiled head because its source was unknown). Bernini also designed the smaller **Fontana del Moro**, at the southern end. The third fountain, that of *Neptune*, was an empty basin until the nineteenth century, when the statues by Giacomo della Porta were added to make the square seem more symmetrical. Off the southern end of the piazza, at the back of Palazzo Braschi, **Pasquino** is the original Roman 'talking statue', embellished with placards and graffiti ('pasquinades') since the 1500s—one of his favourite subjects in those days was the insatiable pigginess of families like the Farnese; serious religious issues were usually too hot to touch, even for a statue.

Piazza Navona seems mildly schizoid these days, unable to become entirely part of high-fashion, tourist-itinerary Rome, yet no longer as comfortable and unpretentious as the rest of the neighbourhood. One symptom will be readily apparent should you step into any of the old cosy-looking cafés and restaurants around the piazza; they're as expensive as in any part of Rome. The best time to come to Piazza Navona is at night when the fountain is illuminated—or, if you can, for the noisy, traditional toy fair of the **Befana**, set up between just before Christmas and Epiphany. **Palazzo Altemps**, on Piazza Sant'Apollinare, now contains half of the excellent Museo Nazionale Romano (*see* p. 748). Some of the churches in the neighbourhood are worth a look, such as **Santa Maria della Pace** (*closed for restoration*), with Raphael's series of *Sibyls and Prophets* on the vaulting and a cloister by Bramante. **San Luigi dei Francesi** (*open daily 7.30–12.30 and 3.30–6.30; closed Thurs pm*), the French church in Rome, contains the great *Life of St Matthew* by Caravaggio in a chapel on the left aisle. Towards the Pantheon, **Sant'Ivo alla Sapienza** once served the English community in Rome. Borromini built them one of his most singular buildings (1660), with its dome and spiralling cupola (*open Sun 10–12*).

The Pantheon

When we consider the fate of so many other great buildings of ancient Rome we begin to understand what a slim chance it was that allowed this one to come down to us. The first Pantheon was built in 27 BC by Agrippa, Emperor Augustus' son-in-law and right-hand man, but was destroyed by fire and replaced by the present temple in 119–128 by the Emperor Hadrian, though curiously retaining Agrippa's original inscription on the pediment. Its history has been precarious ever since. In 609 the empty Pantheon was consecrated to Christianity as 'St Mary of the Martyrs'.

Becoming a church is probably what saved it, though the Byzantines hauled away the gilded bronze roof tiles soon after, and for a while in the Middle Ages the portico saw use as a fish market. The Pantheon's greatest enemy, however, was Gian Lorenzo Bernini. He not only 'improved' it with a pair of Baroque belfries over the porch (demolished in 1887), but he had Pope Urban VIII take down the bronze covering on the inside of the dome to melt down for his *baldacchino* over the altar at St Peter's. Supposedly there was enough left over to make the pope 60 cannons. (Urban was of the Barberini family, and Pasquino's comment about this act was, 'What the barbarians didn't do, the Barberini did.')

You may notice the building seems perilously unsound. There is no way a simple vertical wall can support such a heavy, shallow dome (steep domes push downwards, shallow ones outwards). Obviously the walls will tumble at any moment. That is a little joke the Roman architects are playing, for here they are showing off as shamelessly as in the Colosseum, or the aqueduct with four storeys of arches that used to run *up* to the Monte Palatino. The wall that looks so fragile is really 23ft thick and the dome on top isn't a dome at all; the real hemispherical dome lies underneath, resting easily on the walls inside. The ridges you see on the upper dome are courses of cantilevered bricks, effectively almost weightless. The real surprise, however, lies behind the enormous original bronze doors, an interior of precious marbles and finely sculpted details, the grandest and best-preserved building to have survived from the ancient world (*open Mon–Sat 9–6.30, Sun 9–1*). The movie directors who made all those Roman epics in the 1950s and '60s certainly took many of their settings from this High Imperial creation, just as architects from the early Middle Ages onwards have tried to equal it.

Brunelleschi learned enough from it to build his dome in Florence, and a visit here will show you at a glance what Michelangelo and his contemporaries were trying so hard to outdo. The coffered dome, the biggest cast concrete construction ever made before the 20th century, is the crowning audacity, even without its bronze plate. At 141ft in diameter it is probably the largest in the world (a little-known fact—but St Peter's dome is 6ft less, though much taller). Standing in the centre and looking at the clouds through the 28ft *oculus*, the hole at the top, is an odd sensation you can experience nowhere else.

Inside, the niches around the perimeter held statues of the Pantheon's 12 gods, plus those of Augustus and Hadrian; in the centre, illuminated by a direct sunbeam at midsummer noon, stood Jove. All these are gone, of course, and the interior decoration is limited to an *Annunciation*, attributed to Melozzo da Forlì, and the tombs of eminent Italians such as Raphael and kings Vittorio Emanuele II and Umberto I. The Pantheon simply stands open, with no admission charges, probably fulfilling the same purpose as in Hadrian's day—no purpose at all, save that of an unequalled monument to art and the builder's skill.

Just behind the Pantheon the big church of **Santa Maria sopra Minerva** is interesting for being one of the few medieval churches of Rome (*c*. 1280) to escape the Baroque treatment; its Gothic was preserved in restoration work in the 1840s. Two Medici popes, Leo X and Clement VII, are buried here, as is Fra Angelico. Santa Maria's Florentine connection began with the Dominican monks who designed it; they also did Florence's Santa Maria Novella. A work of Michelangelo, *Christ with the Cross*, can be seen near the high altar; the Carafa Chapel off the right aisle, where you can pay your respects to Pope Paul IV, has a series of frescoes (1489) on the *Life of St Thomas* by Filippino Lippi, his best work outside Florence.

Via del Corso

The Campus Martius, the open plain between Rome's hills and the Tiber, was the training ground for soldiers in the early days of the republic. Eventually the city swallowed it up and the old path towards the Via Flaminia became an important thoroughfare, *Via Lata* (Broad Street). Not entirely by coincidence, the popes of the 14th and 15th centuries laid out a new boulevard almost in the same place. **Via del Corso**, or simply the Corso, has been the main axis of Roman society ever since. Goethe left a fascinating account of the Carnival festivities of Rome's benignly decadent 18th century, climaxing in the horses races that gave the street its name. Much of its length is taken up by the overdone palaces of the age, such as the Palazzo Doria (1780), where the **Galleria Doria Pamphili** (*open Fri–Wed 10–5; visits to the apartments at 10.30 and 12.30; adm*), still owned by the Pamphili, has a fine painting collection—with Velazquez' *Portrait of Innocent X*, Caravaggio's *Flight into Egypt*, and works by Rubens, Titian, Brueghel and more. Guided tours of the apartments (in English by request) give an idea of the lifestyle a family expected when one of their members hit the papal jackpot.

Continuing northwards, the palaces have come down in the world somewhat, tired-looking blocks that now house banks and offices. Look on the side-streets for some hidden attractions: **Sant'Ignazio**, on Via del Seminario, is another Jesuit church with spectacular *trompe l'œil* frescoes on the ceiling; a block north, columns of the ancient **Temple of Hadrian** are incorporated into the north side of the city's tiny Stock Exchange. **Piazza Colonna** takes its name from the column of Marcus Aurelius, whose military victories are remembered in a column (just like those of Trajan); atop stands a statue of St Paul. The obelisk in adjacent Piazza di Montecitorio once marked the hours on a gigantic sundial in Emperor Augustus' garden; **Palazzo Montecitorio**, begun by Bernini, now houses the Italian Chamber of Deputies.

A little way east of Piazza Colonna is the **Fontana di Trevi**, into which you can throw your coins to guarantee your return trip to Rome. The fountain, completed in 1762, was originally planned to commemorate the restoration of Agrippa's aqueduct by Nicholas V in 1453. The source was called the 'Virgin Water' after Virgo, a young girl who had showed thirsty Roman soldiers the hidden spring. It makes a grand sight—enough to make you want to come back; not many fountains have an entire palace for a stage backdrop. The big fellow in the centre is Oceanus, drawn by horses and tritons through cascades of travertine and blue water. Across from the fountain, little **SS. Vicenzo and Anastasio** has the distinction of caring for the pickled hearts and entrails of dozen of popes; an odd custom. They're kept down in the crypt.

Further north, the Corso reaches close to the Tiber and the dilapidated and overgrown **Mausoleo di Augusto**, a cylinder of shabby brick once covered in marble and golden statues. All the Julian emperors except Nero were interred here, in the middle of what were Augustus' enormous gardens. After the centuries had despoiled the tomb of its riches the Colonna family turned the hulk into a fortress.

Further indignities were in store. Until 1823, when the pope forbade them, bullfights were popular in Rome, and a Spanish entrepreneur found the circular enclosure perfect for the *toreros*. After that the tomb was used as a circus, before Mussolini, wishing to afford the founders of Imperial Rome due respect (and perhaps intending to be buried there himself), declared it a national monument and had trees planted around it. Even so, no one quite seems to know what to do with it; it sits locked and empty.

Across the street, Augustus' **Ara Pacis** (Altar of Peace) has had a better fate. Bits and pieces of the beautiful sculpted reliefs, dug up in 1937, were joined with casts of others from museums around Europe to recreate the small building almost in its entirety. One of antiquity's noblest (and least pretentious) conceptions now sits under a glass pavilion; among the mythological reliefs, note the side facing the river, with the emperor and his family dedicating a sacrifice (*open April–Sept Tues–Sat 9–7, Sun 9–1; Oct–Mar Tues–Sat 9–4.30, Sun 9–1; adm*).

Piazza di Spagna

The shuffling crowds of tourists who congregate here at all hours of the day are not a recent phenomenon; this supremely sophisticated piazza has been a favourite with foreigners ever since it was laid out in the early 16th century. The Spaniards came first, as their embassy to the popes was established here in 1646, giving the square and the steps their name. Later, the English Romantic poets made it their headquarters in Italy; typical mementoes —locks of hair, fond remembrances, death masks—are awaiting your inspired contemplation at the Keats-Shelley Memorial House at No.26 (*open April–Sept Mon–Fri 9–1 and 3–6; Oct–Mar Mon–Fri 9–1 and 2.30–5.30; adm*). Almost every artist, writer or musician of the last century spent some time here, but today the piazza often finds itself bursting at the seams with refreshingly Philistine gawkers and wayward youth from all over the world, caught between the charms of McDonald's (the first one built in Rome) and the fancy shops around nearby Via Condotti.

All these visitors need somewhere to sit, and the popes obliged them in 1725 with the construction of the **Spanish Steps** (*Scalinata Spagnola*), an exceptionally beautiful and exceptionally Baroque ornament. The youth who loll about here are taking the place of the hopeful artists' models of the more picturesque centuries, who once crowded the steps, striking poses of antique heroes and Madonnas, waiting for some easy money. At the top of the stairs the simple but equally effective church of **Trinità dei Monti** by Carlo Maderno (early 16th century) was paid for by the King of France. At the southern end of Piazza di Spagna, a Borromini palace housed the papal office called the *Propaganda Fide*, whose job was just what the name implies. The column in front (1856) celebrates the proclamation of the Dogma of the Immaculate Conception, one of their hardest tasks. Via del Babuino, a street named after a siren on a fountain so ugly that Romans called her the 'baboon', connects Piazza di Spagna with Piazza del Popolo. Besides its very impressive antique shops, the street carries on the English connection, with All Saints' Church, a sleepy neo-pub and an English bookshop just off it.

Piazza del Popolo

If you have a choice of how you enter Rome, this is the way to do it, through the gate in the old Aurelian wall and into one of the most successful of all Roman piazzas, copied on a smaller scale all over Italy. No city has a better introduction, and the three diverging boulevards direct you with thoughtful efficiency towards your destination. Valadier, the pope's architect after the Napoleonic occupation, gave the piazza the form it has today, but the big obelisk of Pharaoh Ramses II, punctuating the view down the boulevards, arrived in the 1580s. It is 3200 years old but, like all obelisks, it looks mysteriously brand-new; Augustus brought it to Rome from Heliopolis and planted it in the Circus Maximus; it was transferred here by Pope Sixtus V. The two domed churches designed by Rainaldi, set like bookends at the entrance to the three boulevards, are from the 1670s, part of the original plan for the piazza to which Bernini and Fontana may have contributed.

Nero's ashes were interred in a mausoleum here, at the foot of the Monte Pincio. The site was planted with walnut trees and soon everyone in Rome knew that Nero's ghost haunted the grove, sending out demons—in the forms of flocks of ravens that nested there—to perform deeds of evil. In about 1100 Pope Paschal II destroyed the grove and scattered the ashes; to complete the exorcism he built a church on the site, **Santa Maria del Popolo**. Rebuilt in the 1470s, it contains some of the best painting in Rome: Caravaggio's stunning *Crucifixion of St Peter* and *Conversion of St Paul* (in the left transept), and frescoes by Pinturicchio near the altar. Raphael designed the Chigi Chapel, off the left aisle, including its mosaics.

Villa Borghese

From Piazza del Popolo a winding ramp leads up to Rome's great complex of parks. Just by coincidence this was mostly parkland in ancient times. The **Monte Pincio** once formed part of Augustus' imperial gardens, and the adjacent **Villa Medici** occupies the site of the Villa of Lucullus, the 2nd-century BC philosopher and general who conquered northern Anatolia and first brought cherries to Europe. Now the home of the French Academy, the Villa Medici was a posh jail of sorts for Galileo during his Inquisitorial trials. The Pincio, redesigned by Valadier as a lovely formal garden, offers rare views over Rome. It is separated from the **Villa Borghese** proper by the Aurelian wall and the modern sunken highway that borders it; its name, Viale del Muro Torto, means crooked wall, and refers to a section that collapsed in the 6th century and was left as it was because it was believed to be protected by St Peter.

Exploring the vast spaces of Villa Borghese, you will come across charming vales, woods and a pond (rowing boats for rent), an imitation Roman temple or two, Rococo avenues where the bewigged dandies and powdered tarts of the 1700s came to promenade, bits of ancient aqueduct and a dated **zoo** (*open daily 8–2 hours before sunset; adm*). On the northern edge of the park is a ponderous boulevard called **Viale delle Belle Arti**, where academies have been set up by foreign governments to stimulate cultural exchange. The **Galleria Nazionale d'Arte Moderna** (*open Tues–Sun 9–7; adm exp*) makes its home here in one of Rome's most inexcusable buildings (1913), but the collection includes some great works of Modigliani and the Futurists, as well as a fair sampling of 19th- and 20th-century artists from the rest of Europe.

From there, gingerly skirting the Romanian Academy, you come to the **Museo Nazionale di Villa Giulia** (*open Tues–Sun 9–7, Sun 9–2; adm exp*). If you cannot make it to Tarquinia, this is the place to get to know the Etruscans. Some of their best art has been collected here, as well as laboriously reconstructed terracotta façades to give you some idea of how an Etruscan temple looked. As usual, the compelling attraction is the Etruscans' effortless, endearing talent for portraiture: expressive faces that bridge the gap between the centuries can be seen in terracotta ex-votos (some of children), sarcophagi and even architectural decoration. Serious art is often more stylized; fine examples are the charming couple on the *Sarcophago dei Sposi* from Cerveteri, and the roof statues from the Temple of Portonaccio at Veii—these by Vulca, the only Etruscan artist whose name has survived along with his work. The museum building and its courts and gardens are attractions in themselves; Julius III had Vignola and Ammannati build this quirky Mannerist villa in 1553, and Vasari and Michelangelo may also have helped.

The fantastic trove of ancient relics and late-Renaissance and Baroque painting and sculpture—including masterpieces by Bernini and Caravaggio—at the **Museo e Galleria Borghese** (*open Tues–Sun 9–7; adm; tickets by reservation, call© 06 328 101, Mon–Fri 9.30–6*) is testimony to the legendary greed and avarice of Cardinal Scipione Borghese, nephew of Pope Paul IV. He amassed, by any means available, one of the great private collections of the 17th century and built a magnificently decorated palace on the family's property to hold it all. The display today is all the more impressive because a descendant of the Cardinal 'sold' many pieces to his brother-in-law, Napoleon Bonaparte, who put them in the Louvre.

The **Museo Borghese** (ground floor) offers an intriguing mix of great art and Roman preciosity. Often the two go hand-in-hand, as with the sensuously charged showpieces of Bernini: *Apollo and Daphne*, *The Rape of Proserpina* and especially his *David*, which the artist modestly chiselled in his own image. Canova, the hot item among sculptors in Napoleon's day, contributes a titillatingly languorous statue of Pauline Borghese (Napoleon's sister) as the *Conquering Venus*. Even the ancient world joins in the fun, with such works as the famous Hellenistic *Sleeping Hermaphrodite*. Also downstairs are several Caravaggios, including the *Madonna of the Palafrenieri*, *David with the Head of Goliath* and *St Jerome*.

No less impressive are the paintings in the **gallery** upstairs (entrance through the café in the basement), representing many of the finest 16th- and 17th-century painters: Titian's *Sacred and Profane Love*, *St Sebastian* and *Christ Scourged*, two Bernini self-portraits, Raphael's *Deposition*, Correggio's *Danae* and Rubens' *Deposition*.

Via Veneto and the Quirinale

This chain of gardens was once much bigger, but at the end of the last century many of the old villas were lost to the inevitable expansion of the city. Perhaps the greatest loss was the Villa Ludovisi, praised by many as the most beautiful of all Rome's parks. Now the choice 'Ludovisi' quarter, it has given the city one of its most famous streets, Via Veneto, the long winding boulevard of grand hotels, cafés and boutiques that stretches down from Villa Borghese to Piazza Barberini. A promenade for the smart set in the 1950s, it wears something of the forlorn air of a jilted beau now that fashion has moved on.

Pull yourself away from the passing show on the boulevard to take in the unique spectacle provided by the **Convento dei Cappuccini** at the southern end of the street, just up from Piazza Barberini (*entrance halfway up the stairs of Santa Maria della Concezione; open Fri–Wed 9–12 and 3–6; adm*). Unique, that is, outside Palermo, for, much like the Capuchin convent there, the Roman brethren have created a loving tribute to our friend Death. In the cellars 4000 dead monks team up for an unforgettable *Danse Macabre* of bones and grinning skulls, carefully arranged by serious-minded Capuchins long ago to remind us of something we know only too well.

On the other side of Piazza Barberini, up a gloomy Baroque avenue called Via delle Quattro Fontane, you'll find the **Palazzo Barberini**, one of the showier places in Rome, decorated everywhere with the bees from the family arms. Maderno, Borromini and Bernini all worked on it, with financing made possible by the election of a Barberini as Pope Urban VIII in 1623. Currently it houses the **Galleria Nazionale di Arte Antica** (*open Tues–Sun 9–7; adm*) —a misleading title, since this is a gallery devoted to Italian works of the 12th–18th centuries. Often the original decoration steals the show from the pictures: Bernini's Great Hall, for example, with a ceiling fresco by Pietro da Cortona, the *Triumph of Divine Providence*, or the ceiling in Room 7, with a fresco by Andrea Sacchi where the enthroned Virgin looking down on the round earth seems like a Baroque attempt to create a new Catholic astronomy. Works present include a Bernini self-portrait, Raphael's famous portrait of his beloved mistress *La Fornarina*, the 'baker's girl', more portraits by the Genoese artist Baciccio, lots of Caravaggios, Lippi's *Madonna* and two rather sedate pictures by El Greco. A large section of 15th-century artists not from Tuscany proves that not all the action was happening in Florence.

San Carlino (*currently closed for restoration*), on the corner of Via delle Quattro Fontane and Via Quirinale, is one of Borromini's best works—and his first one (1638), a purposely eccentric little flight of fancy built exactly the size of one of the four massive pillars that hold up the dome in St Peter's. Follow **Via Quirinale** and you'll reach the summit of that hill, covered with villas and gardens in ancient times, and abandoned in the Middle Ages. Then even the name Quirinale had been forgotten, and the Romans called the place 'Montecavallo' after the two big horses' heads projecting above the ground. During the reign of Sixtus V they were excavated to reveal monumental Roman statues of the **Dioscuri** (Castor and Pollux), probably copied from Phidias or Praxiteles.

Together with a huge basin found in the Forum, they make a centrepiece for Piazza di Quirinale. Behind it, stretching for a dreary half-kilometre along the street is the **Palazzo del Quirinale** (*open 8.30–1.30 on the second and fourth Sun of each month; adm exp*), built in 1574 to symbolize the political domination of the popes, later occupied by the kings of Italy, and now the official residence of the country's president.

Around Stazione Termini: Terme di Diocleziano and Museo Nazionale Romano

Rome's great big station takes its name from the nearby **Terme di Diocleziano**, just on the other side of Piazza dei Cinquecento. Until the popes dismantled it for building stone this was by far Rome's biggest ruin; its outer wall followed the present-day lines of Via XX Settembre, Via Volturno and Piazza dei Cinquecento, and the big semi-circular **Piazza della Repubblica**, with its mouldering, grandiose 1890s palazzi and huge fountain, occupies the site of the baths' exercise ground, or *palaestra*. All together the complex covered some 11 hectares.

Michelangelo, not on one of his better days, converted a section of the lofty, vaulted central bathhouse into the church of **Santa Maria degli Angeli**, conserving some of the building's original form, and added a broad new cloister. The cloister and adjacent building are now empty—the **Museo Nazionale Romano** (*open Tues–Sun 9–7; adm*), the greatest Italian collection of antiquities after the museum in Naples, has been relocated to two recently reno-vated *palazzi*— **Palazzo Massimo alle Terme**, right across the street, and **Palazzo Altemps**, near Piazza Navona. A block north of the baths, Piazza San Bernardo has two interesting churches: **San Bernardo**, built out of a circular library that once occupied a corner of the baths' walls, and **Santa Maria della Vittoria**, home to one of the essential works of Baroque sculp-ture, the disconcertingly erotic *St Teresa in Ecstasy* by Bernini (in a chapel off the left aisle).

The Patriarchal Basilicas: Santa Maria Maggiore

Besides St Peter's there are three Patriarchal Basilicas, ancient and revered churches under the care of the pope that have always been a part of the Roman Pilgrimage. Santa Maria Maggiore, San Paolo Fuori le Mura and San Giovanni in Laterano are all on the edges of the city, away from the polit-ical and commercial centre; by the Middle Ages they stood in open countryside, and only recently has the city grown outwards to swallow them once more.

Santa Maria Maggiore, on Monte Esquilino, was probably begun about 352, when a rich Christian saw a vision of the Virgin directing him to build a church; Pope Liberius had received the same vision at the same time, and the two supposedly found the site marked out for them by a miraculous August snowfall. The church took its current form in the 1740s, with a perfectly elegant façade by Fernando Fuga and an equally impressive rear elevation by other architects; the obelisk behind it came from the Mausoleum of Augustus. Above everything rises the tallest and fairest **campanile** in Rome, an incongruous survival from the 1380s. Inside, the most conspicuous feature is the coffered ceiling by

Giuliano da Sangallo, gilded with the first gold brought back from the New World by Columbus, a gift from King Ferdinand and Queen Isabella of Spain. In the apse there are splendid but faded mosaics from 1295 of the *Coronation of the Virgin*; others, from the 5th century, decorate the nave and the 'triumphal arch' in front of the apse. Santa Maria has a prize relic—nothing less than the genuine manger from Bethlehem, preserved in a sunken shrine in front of the altar; in front, kneeling in prayer, is a colossal, rather grotesque statue of Pope Pius IV added in the 1880s.

In 822, two decades after Charlemagne visited Rome, Pope Paschal I found the money and the talent to build works he hoped would be compared to the magnificent ruins that lay on every side. The churches he had rebuilt near Santa Maria Maggiore commemorating two sisters, early Christian martyrs of the 1st century, were not large, but they were a start, and to embellish them he imported Byzantine artists who originated a rebirth of mosaic work and painting in Rome. **Santa Pudenziana**, on Via Urbana, conserves a mosaic of *Christ and the Apostles* from the 4th century, a thoroughly classical work from the very beginnings of Christian art. At **Santa Prassede**, on Via Santa Prassede, the mosaics reveal a different world; the shadowy Rome of the not-entirely Dark Ages. The jewel of Santa Prassede is the small **San Zeno Chapel**, which Paschal intended as a mausoleum for his mother. The square vaulted chamber is entirely covered with gold-ground mosaics of Christ Pantocrator, saints and some very dignified, classical angels who look as if they never heard anything about the fall of Rome. The 9th-century mosaics around the altar are even better, if less golden.

San Giovanni in Laterano

Where is Rome's cathedral? It isn't St Peter's, and never has been. The true seat of the Bishop of Rome, and the end of a Roman Pilgrimage, is here in the shadow of the Aurelian wall, a church established by Constantine himself. The family of Plautius Lateranus, according to ancient records, had their property here confiscated after a failed coup against Nero in AD 66. It eventually became part of the imperial real estate and Constantine and his wife Fausta (whom he later executed) once kept house in the Lateran Palace. Later he donated it to Pope Miltiades as a cult centre for the Christians of Rome. Almost nothing remains of the original basilica; the sacks of the Vandals and Normans, two earthquakes and several fires have resulted in a building made up of bits and pieces from each of the last 16 centuries.

Like Santa Maria Maggiore, this church has an 18th-century exterior that is almost miraculously good, considering other Italian buildings from that age, with a west front by Alessandro Galilei (1736) that confidently and competently reuses the High Renaissance architectural vernacular. The equally fine north façade is older, done by Domenico Fontana in 1586, and incorporates the twin medieval bell tower. Entering at the west front you pass an ancient statue of Constantine, found at the baths he built on the Quirinale; the bronze doors in the central portal once graced the Senate House in the Forum.

Inside, the nave is dominated by giant statues of the Apostles (*c.* 1720), glaring down like Roman emperors of old. There is some carefree and glorious Baroque work in the side chapels—also remains of a fresco by Giotto, behind the first column on the right. Near the apse, decorated with 13th-century mosaics (of a reindeer worshipping the cross, an odd conceit probably adapted from older mosaics in Ravenna), the Papal Altar supposedly contains the heads of Peter and Paul. Below floor level is the tomb of Pope Martin V; pilgrims drop flowers and coins on him for good luck.

Rome in the later Middle Ages had evolved an architectural style entirely its own, uninterested in Gothic or reviving classicism, or, for that matter, in anything else that was going on in the rest of Italy. Sadly, almost all of it disappeared in the Renaissance and Baroque rebuildings. The towers of Santa Maria in Cosmedin and Santa Maria Maggiore are good examples of it, as well as the expressive mosaics of Pietro Cavallini and his school and the intricate, geometrical Cosmatesque pavements in this church and so many others. Perhaps the most striking survival of this lost chapter in art is the Lateran **cloister** (*open daily 9–6, until 5 in winter; adm exp*), with its pairs of spiral columns and 13th-century Cosmatesque mosaics; it completely upstages everything else in the church. All around the cloister walls, fragments from the earlier incarnations of the basilica have been assembled, a hoard of broken pretty things that includes an interesting tomb of a 13th-century bishop, which may be the work of Arnolfo di Cambio.

The Lateran's **baptistry** is no ordinary baptistry—nothing less than the first one in Christendom, converted from an older temple by Constantine; its octagonal form has been copied in other baptistries all over Italy. Inside there are unusual pairs of bronze doors on either side: one from 1196 with scenes of how the Lateran basilica appeared at that time, and the other from the Baths of Caracalla, 'singing' doors that make a low, harmonic sound when you open them slowly. Built around the baptistry are three venerable chapels with more mosaics from the early Middle Ages. The entrance to the baptistry is in Piazza San Giovanni in Laterano, behind the **Lateran Palace**, rebuilt in 1588 over the original building that had served as home for the popes from the 4th to the 14th centuries.

Across the piazza, which has the obligatory obelisk at its centre, you will see the **Scala Santa** (*open daily 6.30–12 and 3–6.30*), supposedly the stairs of Pilate's palace in Jerusalem, ascended by Christ on his way to Judgement and brought to Rome by Constantine's mother, St Helena. The more serious pilgrims ascend them on their knees. The Chapel of San Lorenzo at the top, a part of the medieval Papal Palace, contains two miraculous portraits of Jesus, painted by angels. While you're here, you have a good opportunity to explore the Aurelian Wall. The stretch of it behind the Lateran Palace probably looks much as it did originally, and the nearby **Porta Asinara** (next to Porta San Giovanni) is one of the best-preserved monumental ancient gateways.

Monte Celio

South of the Colosseum you can see nothing but trees, but on every inch of this vast tract of parkland, ancient neighbourhoods wait just a few feet beneath the surface. Modern Rome never expanded in this direction, and almost the whole of it has been preserved as open space. It's a fascinating place to walk around, if you can avoid the traffic thundering down the big boulevards towards the southern suburbs. The Monte Celio is only a small part of it, but it is one of the least known and most delightful corners of Rome. Have a picnic in the **Villa Celimontana** behind Piazza della Navicella and you may have squirrels for company.

Some of Rome's most ancient churches repose in quiet settings here, all worth a look inside if they are open: **Santo Stefano Rotondo**, the oldest circular church in Italy, was built around 470 over the ruins of a market-place of Nero's time; across the street more mosaics from the age of Paschal I (*c.* 820) can be seen in **Santa Maria in Domnica**, standing in **Piazza della Navicella**, with a fountain made in the form of an ancient Roman ship. Take the narrow road (just down hill from the church) that cuts down into the hill to **SS. Giovanni e Paolo**, built in the 4th century in the top floor of three Roman houses, which could be visited were they not closed for restoration. Down the western slope you reach **San Gregorio Magno**, begun by Pope Gregory the Great in 590. St Augustine lived here before being sent by Gregory to convert the Angles and Saxons of Britain. Adjacent to the church are several chapels with remarkable frescoes by Guido Reni, Domenichino and Pomarancio.

Circus Maximus and Terme di Caracalla (Caracalla's Baths)

Piazza Porta Capena, at the foot of the Monte Celio, has an odd decoration, an obelisk erected by Mussolini to commemorate his conquest of Ethiopia—he stole it from the Ethiopian city of Axum, although at long last it is scheduled to be returned to its rightful owner. The piazza itself is a vortex of Mussolinian pretensions; the dictator built himself a new Triumphal Way (now Via San Gregorio) along the route of the original one, to celebrate his piddling triumphs in Roman imperial style. An enormous building that was to house the Ministry of Africa to administer Mussolini's colonies found a more agreeable use after the war—as home of the United Nations Food and Agricultural Organisation (FAO). To the west, a broad green lawn is all that's left of the **Circus Maximus**. Archaeologists have estimated that as many as 300,000 Romans could squeeze in here and place their bets on the chariot races. Founded by King Tarquin and completed by Trajan, the stadium proved simply too convenient a quarry; the banked, horseshoe-shaped depression, however, still follows the line of the grandstands.

The **Terme di Caracalla** (AD 206–220), in a large park south of Porta Capena, rank with those of Diocletian as the largest and most lavish. Roughly 1000ft square, with libraries and exercise courts, the baths probably boasted more gold, marble and art than any building complex in Rome; here the Farnese family dug up such masterpieces as the *Hercules* and the *Farnese Bull*, now in the Naples Museum. In the 1700s these baths were one of the obligatory sights of the Grand Tour; their lofty, broken arches and vaults appealed to the Romantic love of ruins like no others. Much of the central building survives, with its hot and cold rooms, great hall and swimming pool, all decorated with mosaics. A large tunnel connects the baths with the area around Palazzo Venezia, a mile away; its purpose was to transport the vast amounts of wood needed to keep the baths hot. Mussolini initiated the custom (now under threat due to the frailty of the ruins) of holding summer operas here; he liked to drive his roadster through the tunnel and pop out dramatically on stage at the beginning of the festivities.

Behind the baths a stretch of the **Antonine Aqueduct** that supplied it can still be seen. On the other side, facing Via Terme di Caracalla, **SS. Nereo e Achilleo** (*open daily 10–12 and 4–6; ring for custodian*) has more mosaics from the time of Leo III (*c.* 800), a Cosmatesque floor and choir and some gruesome 16th-century frescoes of the martydoms of the saints.

The Via Appia: Rome's Catacombs

Rome's 'Queen of Roads', the path of trade and conquest to Campania, Brindisi and the East, was begun in 312 BC by Consul Appius Claudius. Like most of the consular roads outside Rome, over the centuries it became lined with cemeteries and the elaborate mausolea of the wealthy: ancient Roman practice, inherited from the Etruscans, prohibited any burials within the *pomerium*, the sacred ground of the city itself. Later the early Christians built extensive catacombs here—the word itself comes from the location, *ad catacumbas*, referring to the dip in the Via Appia near the suburban Circus of Maxentius. The Via Appia Antica (as distinguished from the modern Via Appia Nuova) makes a pleasant excursion outside the city, especially on Sundays when the road is closed to traffic all the way back to Piazza Venezia.

The road passes under the Aurelian wall at **Porta San Sebastiano**, one of the best-preserved of the old gates. It houses the **museum of the walls** (*open Tues–Sun 9–one hour before sunset; adm*), admission to which also gives you access to a well-preserved section of the 4th-century wall alongside it. Continuing along the road, after about ½km, with some ruins of tombs along the way, there is the famous church of **Domine Quo Vadis**, on the spot where Peter, fleeing from the dangers of Rome, met Christ coming the other way. 'Where goest thou, Lord?' Peter asked. 'I am going to be crucified once more,' was the reply. As the vision departed the shamed Apostle turned back, to face his own crucifixion in Rome.

Another kilometre or so takes you to the **Catacombe di San Callisto**, off on a side road to the right (*open daily 8.30–12 and 2.30–5; closed Wed and Nov; guided tours only; adm*). Here the biggest attraction is the 'Crypt of the Popes', burial places of 3rd- and 4th-century pontiffs with some well-executed frescoes and inscriptions. A word about catacombs: popular romance and modern cinema notwithstanding, these were never places of refuge from persecution, but simply burial grounds. The word 'catacombs' was only used after the 5th century; before that the Christians simply called them 'cemeteries'. The burrowing instinct is harder to explain. Few other places have ancient catacombs (Naples, Syracuse, Malta and the Greek island of Milos are among them). One of the requirements seems to be tufa, or some other stone that can be easily excavated. Even so, the work involved was tremendous, and not explainable by any reasons of necessity. Christians were still digging them after they had become a power in Rome, in Constantine's time. No one knows for certain what sort of funeral rites were celebrated in them, just as no one knows much about any of the prayers or rituals of the early Christians; we can only suspect that a Christian of the 4th century and one of the 16th would have had considerable difficulty recognizing each other as brothers in the faith.

Most catacombs began small, as private family cemeteries; over generations some grew into enormous termitaries extending for miles. Inside, most of the tombs you see will be simple *loculi*, walled-up niches with only a symbol or short inscription. Others, especially the tombs of popes or the wealthy, may have paintings of scriptural scenes, usually very poor work that reflects more on the dire state of the late Roman imagination than on the Christians.

You can detour from here another ½km west to the **Catacombe di Santa Domitilla** (*open daily 8.30–12 and 2.30–5; closed Tues and Jan; guided tours only; adm*). She was a member of a senatorial family and, interestingly, the catacombs seem to incorporate parts of earlier pagan *hypogea*, including a cemetery of the Imperial Flavian family; the paintings include an unusual *Last Supper* scene, portraying a young and beardless Jesus and Apostles in Roman dress. There is an adjacent basilica, built about the tombs of SS. Nereus and Achilleus, on Via delle Sette Chiese. Not far away is a monument to martyrs of a very different sort, the **Mausoleum of the Fosse Ardeatine**, dedicated to the three hundred and thirty-five Romans massacred by the Nazis on this spot in 1944 in retaliation for a partisan attack. Back on the Via Appia Antica, there are several catacombs near the corner of Via Appia Pignatelli, including a Jewish one; the largest are the **Catacombe di San Sebastiano** (*open daily 8.30–12 and 2.30–5; closed Thurs and Nov; guided tours only; adm*). This complex, too, began as a pagan cemetery and has intriguing paintings and incised symbols throughout. The place had some special significance for the early Christians, and it has been conjectured that Peter and Paul were originally buried here, before their removal to the basilicas in Constantine's time.

Further south, by now in fairly open country, there are the ruins of the Circus of Maxentius (*open Tues–Sun 9–one hour before sunset*), built in the early 4th century, and then the imposing, cylindrical **tomb of Cecilia Metella** (*open Tues–Sat 9–one hour before sunset, Sun and Mon 9–1*), from the time of Augustus. In the Middle Ages the Caetani family turned the tomb into a family fortress, guarding the road to the south; at other times, before and since, it was a famous rendezvous for *banditti*. The road continues, flanked by tombs and stately parasol pines, with stretches of the original paving, for 16km beyond the walls of Rome.

Monte Aventino

Every now and then, when left-wing parties walk out of negotiations, Italian newspapers may call it an 'Aventine Secession', an off-the-cuff reference to events in Rome 2500 years ago. Under the republic, the Monte Aventino was the most solidly plebeian quarter of the city. On several occasions, when legislation proposed by the senate and consuls seriously threatened the rights or interests of the people, they retired *en masse* to the Aventino and stayed there until the plan was dropped. Rome's unionists today often keep the city tied up in knots, but most are probably unaware that their ancestors had the honour of inventing the general strike.

The Aventino had another distinction in those times. In its uninhabited regions—the steep, cave-ridden slopes towards the south—Greek immigrants and returning soldiers introduced the midnight rituals of Dionysus and Bacchus. Though secret, such goings-on soon came to the attention of the senate, which rightly saw the orgies as a danger to the state and banned them in 146 BC. They must not have died out completely, however, and in the Middle Ages the Aventino had a reputation as a haunt of witches. The early Christian community also prospered here, and their churches are the oldest relics on the Aventino today.

Coming up from the Circus Maximus along Via Santa Sabina, **Santa Sabina** is a simple, rare example of a 5th-century basilica, with an atrium at its entrance like a Roman secular basilica, and an original door of cypress carved with scriptural scenes. This has been the head church of the Dominicans ever since a 13th-century pope gave it to St Dominic. Both Santa Sabina and the church of **Sant'Alessio**, down the street, have good Cosmatesque cloisters.

At the end of this street, one of the oddities only Rome can offer stands on its quiet square, oblivious of the centuries: the **Prioria delle Cavaliere di Malta**, a fancy Rococo complex designed by Giambattista Piranesi. The Knights of Malta—or more properly, the Knights Hospitallers of St John—no longer wait for the popes to unleash them against Saracen and Turk. Mostly this social club for nobles bestirs itself to assist hospitals, its original job during the Crusades. The Order's ambassadors to Italy and the Vatican still live here. You can't go inside, but the gate is the most visited in Rome for the intriguing view from the keyhole.

Elsewhere on the Aventino, **Santa Prisca** has beginnings typical of an early Roman church; its crypt, the original church, was allegedly converted from the house of the martyr Prisca, host to St Peter; the Apostle must have often presided over Mass here. **San Saba**, on Via San Saba, was founded in the 7th century by monks fleeing the Arabs in Jordan and Syria, with a 1205 rebuilding, including some Cosmatesque details, a superb mosaic floor and a crypt with 7th–11th-century frescoes.

Rome's Pyramid and Monte Testaccio

Porta San Paolo stands in one of the best-preserved sections of the Aurelian wall. The gate itself looks just as it did 1700 years ago, when it was the *Porta Ostiense*; its change of name came about because Paul passed through it on the way to his execution. Near the gate is something unique: the 92ft **Pyramid of Caius Cestius** (AD 12) may seem a strange self-tribute for a Roman, but at least Cestius, who had served in Egypt, paid for the tomb himself.

Behind it, inside the walls, the lovely **Cimitero Protestante** (*open daily 8–dusk*) is a popular point of Romantic pilgrimage. The graves of Shelley and Keats are there, recently joined by 400 British soldiers who died during the march on Rome in 1944. Just to the west is the youngest of Rome's hills, **Monte Testaccio**, made up almost entirely of pot-shards. In ancient times, wine, oil, olives, and nearly everything else was shipped in big *amphorae*; here, in what was Rome's port warehouse district, all the broken, discarded ones accumulated in one place. The hill, now grassed over, is 115ft at its highest point—there is a big cross on top—and it covers a large area. The vast cellars the Romans left beneath it are now used as workshops, wine cellars and nightclubs that make Testaccio a swinging area after dark.

San Paolo Fuori le Mura (Outside the Walls)

Paul was beheaded near the Ostia road; according to an old legend, the head bounced three times, and at each place where it hit a fountain sprung up. The Abbazia delle Tre Fontane, near EUR, occupies the site today. Later, Constantine built a basilica alongside the road as a fitting resting place for the saint. Of the five patriarchal basilicas this one has had the worst luck. Today it sits in the middle of factories, gasworks and concrete flats. Once St Paul's was the grandest of them all; 9th-century chroniclers speak of the separate walled city of 'Giovannipolis' that had grown up around it, connected to the Aurelian wall by a 1½km-long colonnade built by Pope John VIII in the 870s. The Norman sack of 1084, a few good earthquakes, and finally a catastrophic fire in 1823 wiped Giovannipolis off the map, and left us with a St Paul's that for the most part is barely more than a century old. Still, the façade of golden mosaics and sturdy Corinthian columns is pleasant to look at, and some older features survive—the 11th-century door made in Constantinople, a Gothic *baldacchino* over Paul's tomb by Arnolfo di Cambio, a beautiful 13th-century Cosmatesque cloister (almost a double of the one in the Lateran), and 5th-century mosaics over the 'Triumphal Arch' in front of the apse, the restored remains of the original mosaics from the façade, contributed by Empress Galla Placidia (*see* 'Ravenna', p.482). Art Deco is not what you would expect from those times, but Americans at least will have a hard time believing these mosaics were not done by President Roosevelt's WPA. The apse itself has some more conventional mosaics from the 13th-century Roman school, and the nave is lined with the portraits of all 263 popes. According to Roman tradition, when the remaining eight spaces are filled, the world will end.

EUR

By the late 1930s Mussolini was proud enough of his accomplishments to plan a world fair. Its theme was to be the Progress of Civilization, measured no doubt from the invention of the wheel up to the invention of the Corporate State. A vast area south of Rome was cleared and transformed into a grid of wide boulevards broken by parks and lagoons. Huge Mussolini-style pavilions were begun, and a design was accepted for an aluminium arch—forerunner of the famous one in St Louis but many times bigger—that would overspread the entire fairground. War intervening, the arch never appeared, and the Esposizione Universale di Roma never came off. After 1945 the Italians tried to make the best of it, turning EUR into a model satellite city and trade centre, on the lines of La Défense in Paris. The result will derange your senses as much as it does the average Roman's: a chilly nightmare of modernism with street names like the Boulevard of Humanism, Boulevard of Electronics and the Boulevard of Social Security.

Still, for those who can appreciate the well-landscaped macabre, EUR can be fun. Some of the older corners reveal giant fascist mosaics of heroic miners, soldiers, assembly-line workers and mothers, and at the end of the Boulevard of Civilization and Labour you can have a look at the modest masterpiece of Mussolini architecture—a small, elegantly proportioned **Palazzo della Civiltà del Lavoro**, nicknamed the Square Colosseum. Liberal, post-war Italy has rarely, if ever, been able to conceive anything with such a sure sense of design and a feeling for history.

EUR is also home to a few good museums. The **Museo della Civiltà Romana**, Piazza G. Agnelli 10 (*open Tues–Sat 9–7, Sun 9–1; adm*), a collection of antiques and exhibits including a huge scale-model of ancient Rome with every building present, is a great place to seed your imagination with visions of the old city's splendour. Others in the area include a museum of **prehistory and ethnography**, nearby in Piazza Marconi (*open Mon–Sat 9–1.30, Sun 9–1; adm*), covering civilizations before classical Rome, and a museum of the **late-Middle Ages**, on Viale Lincoln (*open Mon–Sat 9–2, Sun 9–1; adm*).

Trastevere

So often just being on the wrong side of the river encourages a city district to cultivate its differences and its eccentricities. Trastevere isn't really a Left Bank—more of a pocket-sized Brooklyn, and as in Brooklyn those differences and eccentricities often turn out to be the old habits of the whole city, preserved in an out-of-the-way corner.

The people of Trastevere are more Roman than the Romans. Indeed, they claim to be the real descendants of the Romans of old; one story traces their ancestry back to the sailors who worked the great awning at the Colosseum. Such places have a hard time surviving these days, especially when they are as trendy as Trastevere is right now. But even though such things as Trastevere's famous school of dialect poets may be mostly a memory, the quarter remains the liveliest and most entertaining in Rome. The young crowd that Trastevere attracts now provides much of the local colour, their colourful trendy clothes somehow a perfect match for the medieval alleys.

Just over Ponte Garibaldi is Piazza Sonnino, with the **Torre degli Anguillara**, an uncommon survival of the defence towers that once loomed over medieval Rome, and the 12th-century church of **San Crisogono**, with mosaics by Pietro Cavallini (master of the Roman 13th-century school) built over the remains of an earlier church. Near the bridge, the dapper statue in the top hat is Giuseppe Gioacchino Belli, one of Trastevere's 19th-century dialect poets.

Turn left on to one of the narrow streets off Viale di Trastevere and make your way to the church of **Santa Cecilia in Trastevere**, founded over the house of the 2nd-century martyr whom centuries of hagiography have turned into one of the most agreeable of saints, the inventor of the organ and patroness of music. Cecilia was disinterred in 1599, and her body was found entirely uncorrupted. Clement VIII commissioned Maderno to sculpt an exact copy from sketches made before her body dissolved into thin air; this charming work can be seen near the altar, beneath an altarpiece by Giulio Romano.

Nearby there is a *Tabernacle* by Arnolfo di Cambio similar to the one in St Paul's, and 9th-century mosaics in the apse. The church has other treasures: Renaissance tombs, including one of a 14th-century cardinal from Hertford; frescoes by the school of Pinturicchio in a chapel on the right, and a crypt built in the underlying Roman constructions, thought to be Cecilia's home (*adm*). Up in the singing gallery (*open Tues and Fri 10.30–11.30; adm*) are the remains of the original church wall decoration—a wonderful fresco of the *Last Judgement* by Cavallini.

Across Viale di Trastevere—an intrusive modern boulevard that slices the district in two—lies the heart of old Trastevere, around **Piazza Santa Maria in Trastevere** and its church. Most of this building dates from the 1140s, though the original church, begun perhaps in 222, may be the first anywhere dedicated to the Virgin Mary. The medieval building is a treasure-house of Roman mosaics, starting with the frieze with the Virgin breast-feeding Christ flanked by ten female figures on the façade, and continuing with the remarkable series from the *Life of Mary* by Cavallini in the apse, a bit of the early Renaissance 100 years ahead of schedule (*c.* 1290). Above them are earlier, more glittering mosaics from the 1140s. The piazza, and the streets around it, have been for decades one of the most popular spots in Rome for restaurants; tables are spread out wherever there's room, and there will always be a crowd in the evening.

Two Roads to St Peter's

One is broad and straight, the route of the many; the other is tortuous and narrow, and after it but few inquire. **Via della Lungara**, the route of the slothful from Trastevere, takes you past **Villa Farnesina** (*open Mon–Sat 9–1; adm*), an early 1500s palace built for the Chigi family. Inside are some of the best frescoes in Rome: the *Galatea* by Raphael and the *Cupid and Psyche Gallery*, designed by Raphael and carried out by his pupils; a prospect of the constellations and a room of false perspectives by Baldassare Peruzzi, who also designed the building; and works of Sodoma. Across the street, the **Palazzo Corsini** (*open Tues–Sat 9–7, Sun 9–1; adm*) contains an exceptional collection of 16th- and 17th-century art, including works by Caravaggio, Van Dyck, Guido Reni, Salvatore Rosa and many others—it's out of the way, but this may be the best of all Rome's many small state picture galleries.

The other road may be more difficult to find, but repays the effort with lovely gardens and views over Rome from the Gianicolo, the ancient *Janiculum*. First find Via Garibaldi, in the back streets behind Ponte Sisto, and it will carry you up to the Renaissance church of **San Pietro in Montorio**, once erroneously believed to be the spot of St Peter's upside-down crucifixion. A popular church for weddings, there are several fine paintings in the shallow chapels, including a marvellous *Flagellation* by Sebastiano del Piombo—but the real draw here is Bramante's famed **Tempietto** in the adjacent courtyard.

In so many Renaissance paintings—Perugino's *Donation of the Keys* in the Sistine Chapel or Raphael's *Betrothal of the Virgin* in Milan—the characters in the foreground take second place in interest to an ethereal, round temple centred at the perspectival vanishing point. These constructions, seemingly built not of vulgar stone but of pure intelligence and light, could stand as a symbol for the aspirations of the Renaissance. Bramante was the first actually to try to build one; his perfect little Tempietto (1502), the first building to re-use the ancient Doric order in all of its proportions, probably inspired Raphael's painting two years later.

Via Garibaldi continues up the *Janiculum* to the gushing Acqua Paola Fountain, where you should turn right along the Passeggiata del Gianicolo. The Garibaldi Monument stands at the summit, overlooking the Botanical Gardens and the rest of Rome. At the other end of the hill, going towards the Vatican, the road curves downwards, passing the Renaissance church of **Sant'Onofrio** (*open daily 9–1*), with frescoes by Peruzzi in the apse. After descending the Passeggiata del Gianicolo, cross the modern Piazza della Rovere into the Borgo district. On your right is the hospital of Santo Spirito and the church of **Santo Spirito in Sassia**. This name may ring a bell for antiquarians. 'Sassia' refers to the Saxons of England, who upon their conversion became among the most devoted servants of the Church. English princes founded this hospital in the 8th century—astounding enough when you think about it. The Angles and Saxons who settled in Rome made up almost a small village unto themselves at this bend of the Tiber, and their 'burgh' gave its name to the neighbourhood called the Borgo today.

Castel Sant'Angelo

Open daily 9–7; closed the second and fourth Tues of each month; adm.

Though intended as a resting place for a most serene emperor, this building has seen more blood, treachery and turmoil than any in Rome. Hadrian designed his own mausoleum three years before his death in 138, on an eccentric plan consisting of a huge marble cylinder surmounted by a conical hill planted with cypresses. The marble, the obelisks and the gold and bronze decorations did not survive the 5th-century sacks, but in about 590, during a plague, Pope Gregory the Great saw a vision of St Michael over the mausoleum, ostensibly announcing the end of the plague, but perhaps also mentioning discreetly that here, if anyone cared to use it, was the most valuable fortress in Europe.

There would be no papacy, perhaps, without this castle—at least not in its present form. Hadrian's cylinder is high, steep and almost solid—impregnable even after the invention of artillery. With rebellions of some sort occurring on average every two years before 1400 the popes often had recourse to this place of safety. It last saw action in the sack of 1527, when the miserable Clement VII withstood a siege of several months while his city went up in flames. The popes also used Castel Sant'Angelo as a prison; famous inmates included Giordano Bruno, Benvenuto Cellini and Beatrice Cenci (better known to the English than the Italians, thanks to Shelley's verse drama). Tosca tosses herself off the top at the end of Puccini's opera.

Inside, the recently restored spiral ramp leads up to the **Papal Apartments**, decorated as lavishly by 16th-century artists as anything in the Vatican. The **Sala Paolina** has frescoes by Perin del Vaga of events in the history of Rome, and the **Sala di Apollo** is frescoed with grotesques attempting to reproduce the wall decorations of Nero's Golden House. Above everything, a mighty statue of Michael commemorates Gregory's vision. As interesting for its structure as anything on display inside, Castel Sant'Angelo makes a great place to rest after the Vatican. The views from the roof are some of the best in Rome, and there's a café on the 4th floor. The three central arches of the **Ponte Sant'Angelo** were built by Hadrian, although the statues of angels added in 1688 steal the show; at once dubbed Bernini's Breezy Maniacs, they battle a never-ending Baroque hurricane to display the symbols of Christ's Passion.

St Peter's

Along Borgo Sant'Angelo, leading towards the Vatican, you can see the famous **covered passageway**, used by the popes since 1277 to escape to the castle when things became dangerous. The customary route, however, leads up **Via della Conciliazione**, a broad boulevard drilled by Mussolini through the tangled web of medieval streets. Critics have said it spoils the surprise, but no arrangement of streets and buildings could really prepare you for Bernini's Brobdingnagian **Piazza San Pietro**. Someone has calculated there is room for about 300,000 people in the piazza, with no crowding. Few have ever noticed Bernini's little joke on antiquity; the open space almost exactly meets the size and dimensions of the Colosseum. Bernini's **Colonnade** (1656), with 284 massive columns and statues of 140 saints, stretches around it like 'the arms of the Church embracing the world'—perhaps the biggest cliché in Christendom by now, but exactly what Bernini had in mind. Stand on either of the two dark stones at the foci of the elliptical piazza and you will see Bernini's forest of columns resolve into neat rows, a subtly impressive optical effect like the hole in the top of the Pantheon. Flanked by two lovely fountains, the work of Maderno and Fontana, the Vatican **obelisk** seems nothing special as obelisks go, but is actually one of the most fantastical relics in all Rome. This obelisk comes from Heliopolis, founded as a capital and cult centre by Akhnaton, the half-legendary Pharaoh who, according to Sigmund Freud and others, founded the first monotheistic religion, influencing Moses and all that came after. Caligula brought it over to Rome in AD 37 to decorate the now-disappeared Circus Vaticanus (later referred to as the Circus of Nero) where it would have overlooked Peter's martyrdom. In the Middle Ages it was placed to the side of the basilica, but Sixtus V moved it to where it now stands in 1586.

It may be irreverent to say so, but the original St Peter's, begun over the Apostle's tomb by Constantine in 324, may well have been a more interesting building: a richly decorated basilica full of gold and mosaics with a vast porch of marble and bronze in front and a lofty campanile, topped by the famous golden cockerel that everyone believed would some day crow to announce the end of the world. This St Peter's, where Charlemagne and Frederick II received their imperial crowns, was falling to pieces by the 1400s, conveniently in time for the popes of the Renaissance to plan a replacement. In about 1450 Nicholas V conceived an almost Neronian building programme for the Vatican, ten times as large as anything his ancestors could have contemplated. It was not until the time of Julius II, however, that Bramante was commissioned to demolish the old church and begin the new. His original plan called for a great dome over a centralized Greek cross. Michelangelo, who took over the work in 1546, basically agreed, and if he had had his way St Peter's might indeed have become the crowning achievement of Renaissance art that everyone hoped it would be.

Unfortunately over the 120 years of construction too many popes and too many artists got their hand in—Rossellino, Giuliano da Sangallo, Raphael, Antonio da Sangallo, Vignola, Ligorio, della Porta, Fontana, Bernini and Maderno all contributed something to the hotchpotch we see today. The most substantial tinkering came in the early 17th century, when a committee of cardinals decided that a Latin cross was desired, resulting in the huge extension of the nave that blocks the view of Michelangelo's dome from the piazza. Baroque architects, mistaking size and virtuosity for art, found perfect patrons in the Baroque popes, interested in the power and majesty of the papacy. Passing though Maderno's gigantic façade seems like entering a Grand

Central Station full of stone saints and angels, keeping an eye on the clocks overhead as they wait for trains to Paradise. All along the nave, markers showing the length of other proud cathedrals prove how each fails to measure up to the Biggest Church in the World. This being Rome, not even the markers are honest—Milan's cathedral is actually 63ft longer.

The best is on the right: Michelangelo's *Pietà*, now restored and kept behind glass to protect it from future madmen. Sculpted when he was only 25, it helped make Michelangelo's reputation. Its smooth and elegant figures, with the realities of death and grief sublimated on to some ethereal plane known only to saints and artists, were a turning point in religious art. From here the beautiful, unreal art of the religious Baroque was the logical next step. Michelangelo carved his name in small letters on the band around the Virgin's garment after overhearing a group of tourists from Milan who thought the *Pietà* the work of a fellow Milanese. Not much else in St Peter's really stands out. In its vast spaces scores of popes and saints are remembered in assembly-line Baroque; the paintings over most of the altars have been replaced by mosaic copies. The famous bronze statute of St Peter, its foot worn away by the touch of millions of pilgrims, is by the right front pier. Stealing the show, as he knew it would, is Bernini's great, garish **baldacchino** over the high altar, cast out of bronze looted from the Pantheon roof.

Many visitors head straight for Michelangelo's **dome** (*open May–Sept daily 8–6; Oct–April daily 8–5; adm*). To be in the middle of such a spectacular construction is worth the climb itself. You can walk out on to the roof for a view over Rome, but even more startling is the chance to look down from the interior balcony over the vast church 250ft below. In the **sacristy** (*open April–Sept daily 9–6; Oct–Mar daily 9–5; adm exp*), built in the 18th century, there are a number of treasures—those the Saracens, the imperial soldiers of 1527, and Napoleon couldn't steal. The ancient bronze cockerel from the old St Peter's is kept here, along with ancient relics, Baroque extravaganzas and a gown that belonged to Charlemagne.

Do not pass up a descent to the **Sacred Grottoes**, the foundation of the earlier St Peter's converted into a crypt. Dozens of popes are buried here, along with distinguished friends of the Church like Queen Christina of Sweden and James III, the Stuart pretender. Perhaps the greatest work of art here is the bronze tomb of Sixtus IV, a definitive Renaissance confection by Pollaiuolo, though the most visited is undoubtedly the simple monument to John XXIII.

The Musei Vaticani (Vatican Museums)

The admission (*currently L15,000*) may be the most expensive in Italy, but for that you get 10 museums in one, with the Sistine Chapel and the Raphael rooms thrown in free. Altogether almost 7km of exhibits fill the halls of the Vatican Palace, and unfortunately for you there isn't much dull museum clutter that can be passed over lightly. Seeing this infinite, exasperating hoard properly would be the work of a lifetime. On the bright side, the pope sees to it that his museum is managed more intelligently and thoughtfully than anything run by the Italian state. A choice of colour-coded itineraries, which you may follow according to the amount of time you have to spend, will get you through the labyrinth in 90 minutes, or five hours.

Near the entrance, the first big challenge is the large **Museo Egizio**—one of Europe's best Egyptian collections—and then some rooms of antiquities from the Holy Land and Syria, before the **Museo Chiaramonti**, full of Roman statuary (including famous busts of Caesar, Mark Antony and Augustus) and inscriptions. The **Museo Pio Clementino** contains some of the best-known statues of antiquity: the dramatic *Laocoön*, dug up in Nero's Golden House, and the *Apollo Belvedere*. No other ancient works recovered during the Renaissance had a greater influence on sculptors than these two. A 'room of animals' captures the more fanciful side of antiquity, and the 2nd-century 'Baroque' tendency in Roman art comes out clearly in a giant group called 'The Nile', complete with sphinxes and crocodiles—it came from a Roman temple of Isis. The bronze papal fig-leaves that protect the modesty of hundreds of nude statues are a good joke at first—it was the same spirit that put breeches on the saints in Michelangelo's *Last Judgement*, ordered by Pius IV once Michelangelo was safely dead.

The best things in the **Museo Etrusco** (*open Tues*) are Greek, a truly excellent collection of vases imported by discriminating Etruscan nobles that includes the famous picture of *Oedipus and the Sphinx*. Beyond that, there is a hall hung with beautiful high-medieval tapestries from Tournai (15th century), and the long, long **Galleria delle Carte Geografiche**, lined with carefully painted town views and maps of every corner of Italy; note the long scene of the 1566 Great Siege of Malta at the entrance. Anywhere else, with no Michelangelos to offer competition, Raphael's celebrated frescoes in the **Stanza della Segnatura** would have been the prime destination on anyone's itinerary. The *School of Athens* is too well known to require an introduction, but here is a guide to some of the figures: on Aristotle's side, Archimedes and Euclid surrounded by their disciples (Euclid, drawing plane figures on a slate, is a portrait of Bramante); off to the right, Ptolemy and Zoroaster hold the terrestrial and celestial globes. Raphael includes himself among the Aristotelians, standing between Zoroaster and the painter Sodoma. Behind Plato stand Socrates and Alcibiades, and to the left, Zeno and Epicurus. In the foreground, Pythagoras writes while Empedocles and the Arab Averroes look on. Diogenes sprawls philosophically on the steps, while isolated near the front is Heraclitus—really Michelangelo; Raphael put him in at the last minute after seeing the work in progress in the Sistine Chapel.

Across from this apotheosis of philosophy, Raphael painted a Triumph of Theology to keep the clerics happy, the *Dispute of the Holy Sacrament*. The other frescoes include the *Parnassus*, a vision of the ancient Greek and Latin poets, the *Miracle of Bolsena*, the *Expulsion of Heliodorus*, an allegory of the triumphs of the Counter-Reformation papacy, the *Meeting of Leo I and Attila* and, best of all, the solemn, spectacularly lit *Liberation of St Peter*. Nearby, there is the **Loggia** of Bramante, also with decoration designed by Raphael, though executed by other artists (*only visitable with written permission*), and the chapel of **Nicholas V**, with frescoes by Fra Angelico. The **Appartamento Borgia**, a luxurious suite built for Pope Alexander VI, have walls decorated by Pinturicchio. These run into the **Opere d'Arte Religiosa Moderna**, a game attempt by the Vatican to prove that such a thing really exists.

The Sistine Chapel (*Cappella Sistina*)

To the sophisticated Sixtus IV, building this ungainly barn of a chapel may have seemed a mistake in the first place. When the pushy, despotic Julius II sent Michelangelo up, against his will, to paint the vast ceiling, it might have turned out to be a project as hopeless as the tomb Julius had already commissioned. Michelangelo spent four years of his life (1508–12) on the Sistine Ceiling. No one can say what drove him to turn his surly patron's whim into a masterpiece: the fear of wasting those years, the challenge of an impossible task, or maybe just to spite Julius—he exasperated the pope by making him wait, and refused all demands that he hire some assistants.

Everywhere on the Sistine Ceiling you will note the austere blankness of the backgrounds. Michelangelo always eschewed stage props; one of the tenets of his art was that complex ideas

LOWER FLOOR

- Entrance
- Sala Rotonda
- Museo Pio-Clementino
- Ethnological Missionary Museum
- Gregorian Profane Museum
- Pio Christian Museum
- Pinacoteca
- Bramante's Stair
- Gabinetto dell' Apoxyomenos
- Cortile di Belvedere
- Museo Chiaramonti
- Cortile della Pigna
- Restaurant
- (Underground)
- Historical Museum
- Braccio Nuovo
- Cortile della Biblioteca
- Salone Sistina
- Galleria della Biblioteca
- Galleria Lapidaria
- Cortile de Belvedere
- Room of Aldobrandini Marriage
- Museum of Christian Art
- Borgia Apartments
- Cortile San Damaso
- Chapel of Pius V
- Sistine Chapel
- Sala Regia
- Gallery of Modern Religious Art

UPPER FLOOR

- Etruscan Museum
- Stairs (Up)
- Stairs (Down)
- Salla della Bigna
- Vase Rooms
- Galleria dei Candelabri e degli Arazzi
- Galleria delle Carte Geografiche
- Gallery of Pius V
- Stanze di Raffaello
- Loggia di Raffaello
- Sistine Chapel
- Chapel of Urban V
- Chapel of Nicholas V

1 Spiral
2 Quattro Cancelli
3 La Pigna
4 Egyptian Museum
5 Animal Room
6 Gallery of Statues
7 Mask Room
8 Gallery of Busts
9 Hall of the Muses

10 Hall of the Greek Cross
11 Museum of Pagan Antiquities
12 Rooms of Greek Originals
13 Hall of Immaculate Conception
14 Stanza del Incendio
15 Stanza della Segnatura
16 Stanza di Eliodoro
17 Sala di Costantino
18 Sala dei Chiaro Scuri

could be expressed in the portrayal of the human body alone. With sculpture, that takes time. Perhaps the inspiration that kept Michelangelo on the ceiling so long was the chance of distilling out of the Book of Genesis and his own genius an entirely new vocabulary of images, Christian and intellectual. Like most Renaissance patrons, Julius had asked for nothing more than virtuoso interior decoration. What he got was the way the Old Testament looks in the deepest recesses of the imagination.

The fascination of the Sistine Ceiling, and the equally compelling **Last Judgement** on the rear wall, done much later (1534–41), is that while we may recognize the individual figures we still have not captured their secret meanings. Hordes of tourists stare up at the heroic Adam, the mysterious *ignudi* in the corners, the Russian masseuse sibyls with their longshoremen's arms, the six-toed prophets, the strange vision of Noah's deluge. They wonder what they're looking at, a question that would take years of inspired wondering to answer. Mostly they direct their attention to the all-too-famous scene of the Creation, with perhaps the only representation of God the Father ever painted that escapes being merely ridiculous. One might suspect that the figure is really some ageing Florentine artist, and that Michelangelo only forgot to paint the brush in his hand. The restoration of the ceiling and *Last Judgement*, paid for by a Japanese television network, have accurately revealed Michelangelo's true colours— jarring, surprise colours that no interior decorator would ever choose, plenty of sea-green, with splashes of yellow and purple and dramatic shadows. No new paint was applied, only solvents to clear off the grime. Most visitors overlook the earlier frescoes on the lower walls, great works of art that would have made the Sistine Chapel famous by themselves: scenes from the *Exodus* by Botticelli, Perugino's *Donation of the Keys*, and Signorelli's *Moses Consigning his Staff to Joshua*.

More Miles in the Big Museum

There's still the **Vatican Library** to go, with its seemingly endless halls and precious manuscripts tucked neatly away in cabinets. The brightly painted rooms contain thousands of reliquaries and monstrances, medieval ivories, gold-glass medallions from the catacombs, every sort of globe, orrery and astronomical instrument. If you survive this, the next hurdle is the new and beautifully laid out **Museo Gregoriano**, with a hoard of classical statuary, mosaics and inscriptions collected by Pope Gregory XVI. Then comes a museum of **carriages** (*closed for restoration*), the **Museo Pio-Cristiano** of early-Christian art and, finally, one of the most interesting of all, though no one has time for it: the museum of **ethnology**, with wonderful art from every continent, brought home to Italy by missionaries over the centuries.

By itself the Vatican **Pinacoteca** would be by far the finest picture gallery in Rome, a representative sampling of Renaissance art from its beginnings, with some fine works of Giotto

(*Il Redentore* and the *Martyrdoms of Peter and Paul*) and contemporary Sienese painters, as well as Gentile da Fabriano, Sano di Pietro and Filippo Lippi. Don't overlook the tiny but electrically surreal masterpiece of Fra Angelico, the *Story of St Nicolas at Bari*, or the *Angelic Musicians* of Melozzo da Forlì, set next to Melozzo's famous painting of Platina being nominated by Sixtus IV to head the Vatican Library—a rare snapshot of Renaissance humanism. Venetian artists are not well represented, but there is a *Pietà* by Bellini and a *Madonna* by the fastidious Carlo Crivelli. Perhaps the best-known paintings are the *Transfiguration of Christ*, Raphael's last work, and the *St Jerome* of Da Vinci.

Vatican Practicalities

The **museums** are open Nov–Feb Mon–Sat 8.45–1.45 (last admission 12.45); the rest of the year Mon–Sat 8.45–4.45 (last admission 3.45); adm; closed Sun, except the last Sun of each month and religious holidays: open 8.45–1.45 (last admission 12.45); free. The entrance is on Viale Vaticano, to the north of Piazza San Pietro. **St Peter's** is open daily 7–7; Oct–Mar till 6; the basilica is closed when there are official ceremonies in the piazza, although visitors are allowed during mass. The dress code—no shorts, short skirts or sleeveless dresses—is strictly controlled by the papal gendarmes.

The **Vatican Information Office**, ✆ 06 6988 4466, in Piazza San Pietro (*open daily 8–7*) is very helpful, and there are Vatican post offices on the opposite side of the square and inside the Vatican Museums for distinctive postcards home. The information office arranges 2hr-long morning tours of the **Vatican Gardens**, easily Rome's most beautiful park, with a remarkable Renaissance jewel of a villa inside: the **Casino of Pius IV** (1558–62) by Pietro Ligorio and Peruzzi (*open May–Sept Mon–Sat; Oct–April once a week; L18,000 per person; reserve a few days in advance with the information office*).

Underneath the crypt of St Peter's, archaeologists in the 1940s discovered a **street of Roman tombs**, perfectly preserved with many beautiful paintings (*open Mon–Sat 9–5; adm; tours can be arranged through the Uffizio degli Scavi, just to the left of St Peter's; in the summer book early as fragile conditions permit only 15 people at a time*). The rest of the Vatican is strictly off limits, patrolled by Swiss Guards (still recruited from the three Catholic Swiss cantons).

Michelangelo also designed the **wall** that since 1929 has marked the Vatican boundaries. Behind it are things most of us will never see: several small old churches, a printing press, the headquarters of *L'Osservatore Romano* and Vatican Radio (run, of course, by the Jesuits), a motor garage, a 'Palazzo di Giustizia' and even a big shop—everything the world's smallest nation could ever need. Modern popes, in glaring contrast to their predecessors, do not take up much space. The current Papal Apartments are in a corner of the Vatican Palace overlooking Piazza San Pietro; John Paul II usually appears to say a few electrically amplified words from his window at noon on Sundays.

For tickets to the Wednesday morning **papal audience**, usually held at 11am in the piazza (*May–Sept*) or in the Nervi Auditorium (*Oct–April*), apply in advance at the Papal Prefecture—through the bronze door in the right-hand colonnade of Piazza San Pietro (*open Mon and Tues 9–1, ✆ 06 6988 3217*).

Peripheral Attractions

There are plenty of interesting things on Rome's outskirts—here is a brief review, tracing a clockwise circle around Rome from the north. Near the Tiber, the **Foro Italico** was certainly Mussolini's most blatant monument to himself: he left his mark everywhere, on a giant obelisk, in the paving stones and around the kitschy grandiose **Marble Stadium**, chiselled too deep ever to be worn away. The adjacent sports complex hosted the 1960 Olympics. Across the Tiber, on Via Salaria, **Villa Ada** once served as the hunting reserve of Vittorio Emanuele III; it's now a huge city park. The **Catacombe di Priscilla**, Via Salaria 430, are well worth the nun-led tour of the 2nd-century frescoes and the tombs of many early popes and martyrs (*open Tues–Sun 8.30–12 and 2.30–5; April–Sept til 5.30; adm*).

Via XX Settembre, the important thoroughfare coming off the Monte Quirinale, passes the Aurelian Wall at **Porta Pia**, redesigned by Michelangelo. Here it changes its name to Via Nomentana, a boulevard lined with villas which have not yet been swallowed up by creeping urbanization. A kilometre east, stop at the thoroughly charming complex of **Sant'Agnese Fuori le Mura (Outside the Walls)** (*open Mon 9–12, Tues–Sat 9–12 and 4–6, Sun 4–6*), including a 4th-century church with a beautiful early mosaic of St Agnes in the apse, and 15 ancient marble columns. Along the stairway descending to the church, early Christian reliefs and inscriptions have been arranged as in a museum; inside the church is the entrance to the small, aristocratic **catacombs** (3rd-century), absorbing parts of earlier pagan catacombs (*guided tours arranged Wed–Sun during church hours; adm*).

Around the back, through gardens where the neighbourhood children play, stands one of Rome's least known but most remarkable churches. **Santa Costanza** was built as a mausoleum for Constantia, the daughter of Emperor Constantine. In this domed, circular building—one of the finest late-Roman works—more than anywhere else, you can see the great religious turning point of the 4th century come alive; among the exquisite mosaics (regrettably not all have survived) are scenes of a grape harvest, and motifs that would be familiar to any ancient devotee of Dionysus or Bacchus. In the two side chapels are later mosaics of Christ and the Apostles.

At the end of Viale Regina Elena, tucked between Rome's university and the enormous Verano Cemetery, **San Lorenzo** is another of the seven churches on a pilgrim's itinerary. The original building, begun under Constantine, was reconstructed in the early 13th century and contains some fine work of the Cosmati family around the altar. From here you can re-enter the city through the impressive **Porta Maggiore**, built under Emperor Claudius; note how this section of the wall carries one of the ancient aqueducts on top. In the neighbourhood you can also see the **Temple of Minerva**, on Via Giolitti, a round brick ruin from the 3rd century AD, and **Santa Croce in Gerusalemme**, another of the 'Seven Churches', founded by Constantine but now thoroughly baroqued.

Almost directly under the tracks going into Stazione Termini, the **Underground Basilica**, only discovered in 1916, was not covered up by the centuries—it was built that way for a secret, possibly illegal, religious sect in the 1st century AD. Its stucco reliefs are strange; scholars can't guess anything about the cult's beliefs, but venture to call it 'neo-Pythagorian' (*contact the Soprintendenza Archeologica di Roma, Piazza Santa Maria Nova 53, ✆ 06 699 0110, for permission to visit*).

Rome isn't as exciting for big-game shoppers as Milan, though when it comes to clothing you will find all the major designers and labels well represented. There is no shortage of shops selling **antiques**, a great number of them clustered together between the Tiber and Piazza Navona; look especially off Via Monserrato, Via dei Coronari and Via dell'Anima. For **old prints**, generally inexpensive, try Casali, Piazza Rotonda 81A; Alinari, Via Alibert 16/a is a good address for artistic **black and white pictures** of old Rome. **L'Art Nouveau**, Via dei Coronari 221, offers just what its name implies. **Antiques** also show up in the celebrated Sunday morning flea market at Porta Portese, as well as anything else you can imagine, all lumped together in often surreal displays (*open just after dawn–around 12 noon*). Beware the pickpockets.

The most **fashionable shopping** is on the streets between Piazza di Spagna and the Corso. Some special items: Massoni, Largo Goldoni 48, near Via Condotti, much frequented by film stars, sells some of Rome's finest **jewellery**; for **menswear**, Testa, Via Borgognona 13, and Via Frattina 42, or Valentino Uomo, Via Condotti 13, or for **custom tailoring**, Battistoni, Via Condotti 61/a. For **women's clothes** try the outlets of the big designers in the same area: Missoni, Via del Babuino 96, Giorgio Armani, Via Condotti 77, and Via del Babuino 102, Mila Schöen, Via Condotti 51, or the Rome-based Fendi, Via Borgognona nos.8, 10, 12 and 39. For **leather**, the Gucci outlet is at Via Condotti 8, and do not miss Fausto Santini, Via Frattina 120.

Discounted designer fashion may be had at Il Discount dell'Alta Moda, Via Gesù e Maria 16/a; for **high-fashion shoes**, try Barrilà, Via Condotti 29, and Via del Babuino 33; and for **Borsalino hats**, Troncarelli, Via della Cuccagna 15, near Piazza Navona.

For a special bottle of **wine**, try Enoteca Costantini, Piazza Cavour 16, for a wide selection. If you wish to stock up on Italian **coffee**, Tazza d'Oro, Via degli Orfani 84, has special bags of the city's best, the 'Aroma di Roma'. If you need a good **book**, try the Anglo-American Book Co., Via della Vite 57, the Lion Bookshop, Via dei Greci 36, or the Economy Book Center, Via Torino 136, near Via Nazionale.

For an amazing selection of **fancy kitchen gear**, there's C.U.C.I.N.A., Via del Babuino 118/a, while for serious, **professional pans, pots and tools** head to Zucchi, Via Sant'Antonio all'Esquilino 15, near Santa Maria Maggiore. Try Image, Via della Scrofa 67, for **alternative posters, postcards and photographs**; and De Ritis, Via de' Cestari 1, for the latest **ecclesiastical fashions**, along with Madonnas, crucifixes and chalices.

Sports and Activities

Rome's main public **swimming pool** is the Piscina delle Rose, Viale America 20, in EUR, © 06 592 6717 (Ⓜ EUR Fermi) (*open June 15–Sept daily 9–7*). There is also an attractive private pool at the Centro Sportivo Italiano, Lungotevere Flaminio 55, about a half-mile north of Piazza del Popolo, © 06 323 4732 (*open in summer*). Rome's two first-division **football** clubs, AS Roma and Lazio, both play on Saturday or Sunday afternoon at the Stadio Olimpico, Via del Foro Italico (Ⓜ Linea A to Ottaviano, then bus no.32) during the season (*Sept–May*). Tickets for Lazio start at L28,000; contact Lazio Point, Via Farini 34, © 06 482 6688; or *Orbis* (*see* p.771).

For a city that has been entertaining visitors for the last 2000 years, Rome has not acquired any special flair for accommodating them. Perhaps it is just the uninterrupted flow of the curious and faithful that keeps prices higher and service and quality lower than elsewhere in Italy. From Belle Epoque palaces on Via Veneto to grimy hovels on the wrong side of Stazione Termini, there will always be somewhere for you to come home to after a hard day's sightseeing, although places with a history, a view or quiet gardens are rare. Exceptions exist, but this is probably not the place to make the big splurge. Check into some comfortable spot in the area that suits your fancy, and save your big hotel money for Venice or the Amalfi Drive. In the 1890s, when the Stazione Termini district was the choicest part of Rome, the streets around the station spawned hundreds of hotels, some quite elegant. Today much of the city's accommodation is still here. Unfortunately it has gone the way of all such 19th-century toadstool neighbourhoods: overbuilt, dingy and down-at-heel, and not at all the place to savour Rome. It's also inconvenient for most of the sights.

Rooms can be difficult to find at short notice, but the free Hotel Reservation Service, ✆ 06 699 1000, will do the looking for you. The private **Enjoy Rome** (*see* 'Tourist Information' p.728) will also make commission-free hotel bookings.

luxury

★★★★★**Hassler-Villa Medici**, Piazza Trinità dei Monti 6, ✆ 06 699 340, ✉ 06 678 9991, is one of Rome's best hotels, with a fine location at the top of the Spanish Steps and wonderful views over the city for those who book far enough in advance. Around for over a century, it has regained its position as the élite hotel of Rome, with a beautiful courtyard, deferential service and large wood-panelled rooms. ★★★★★**Excelsior**, Via V. Veneto 125, ✆ 06 47081, ✉ 06 482 6205, is also located in a choice area, though lacking the aura it had in the 1950s. The reception areas have thicker carpets, bigger chandeliers and more gilded plaster than anywhere in Italy, and most of the rooms are just as good—don't let them give you a modernized one. There are saunas, a famous bar and as much personal attention as you could ask for.

very expensive

★★★★**D'Inghilterra**, Via Bocca di Leone 14, ✆ 06 69981, ✉ 06 6992 2243, is another favourite near Piazza di Spagna. Parts of this building date from the 15th century, when it served as a prince's guest house; in its career as a hotel, since 1850, it has played host to most of the literati and artists of Europe and America. ★★★★**Forum**, Via Tor de' Conti 25, ✆ 06 679 2446, ✉ 06 678 6479, is the only fancy establishment near the ancient Forum; it's somewhat worn, but has unbeatable views from the roof terrace.

expensive

★★★★**Cardinal**, Via Giulia 62, ✆ 06 6880 2719, ✉ 06 678 6376, in the heart of the *centro storico*, is perhaps the best place to experience Renaissance Rome—in a building attributed to Bramante and completely restored, without spoiling the atmosphere. ★★★**Carriage**, Via delle Carrozze 36, ✆ 06 699 0124, ✉ 06 678 8279, almost at the foot of the Spanish Steps, is a sleepy but well-run place with air conditioning.

★★★Columbus, Via della Conciliazione 33, ✆ 06 686 5435, 📠 06 686 4874, is staid but reliable with nice rooms, some with views over St Peter's; prices are a bit high. **★★★Fontana**, Piazza di Trevi 96, ✆ 06 678 6113, 📠 06 679 0024, would be a good hotel anywhere; it is also right across the street from the Trevi Fountain—something to look at out of your window that will guarantee nice dreams.

★★★Gregoriana, Via Gregoriana 18, ✆ 06 679 4269, 📠 06 678 4258, close to the Spanish Steps but reasonably priced, is small, tasteful and gratifyingly friendly, with a devoted regular clientele—there are only 19 rooms, so book early. **★★★La Residenza**, Via Emilia 22, ✆ 06 488 0789, 📠 06 485 721, near the Via Veneto, stands out as a very pleasant base, with beautifully appointed rooms in an old town house, and some luxuries more common to the most expensive hotels.

★★★Teatro di Pompeo, Largo del Pallaro 8, ✆ 06 6830 0170, 📠 06 6880 5531, is a small hotel built on Teatro di Pompeo by Campo de' Fiori, perfect for peace and quiet. **★★★Villa Florence**, Via Nomentana 28, ✆ 06 440 3036, 📠 06 440 2709, near the Porta Pia, is a very well-run and friendly hotel in a refurbished 19th-century villa with a garden. **★★★Villa del Parco**, Via Nomentana 110, ✆ 06 4423 7773, 📠 06 4423 7572, is similar, but slightly more expensive.

moderate

★★★Hotel Sant'Anselmo, Piazza Sant'Anselmo 2, ✆ 06 578 3214, 📠 06 578 3604, up on the Monte Aventino, is a very peaceful hotel with a garden and comfortable rooms. **★★★Villa San Pio**, Via Sant'Anselmo 19, ✆ 06 574 5232, 📠 06 574 3547, run by the same management, is just as peaceful. Prices are reasonable. **★★Campo de' Fiori**, Via del Biscione 6, ✆ 06 6880 6865, 📠 06 687 6003, has small comfortable rooms and a roof terrace overlooking Campo de' Fiori.

★★Margutta, Via Laurina 34, ✆ 06 322 3674, 📠 06 320 0395, in a quiet street off Via del Babuino, has simple accommodation. **★★Sole**, Via del Biscione 76, ✆ 06 6880 6873, 📠 06 689 3787, is a large old hotel with lots of character, just off the Campo de' Fiori market. **★★Abruzzi**, Piazza della Rotonda 69, ✆ 06 679 2021, has views over the Pantheon, but none of the rooms have private bath. **★Primavera**, Via San Pantaleo 3, ✆ 06 6880 3109, 📠 06 6880 3109, is a slightly cheaper hotel just west of Piazza Navona.

cheap

★Campo Marzio, Piazza Campo Marzio 7, ✆ 06 6880 1486, is just north of the Pantheon; none of the rooms have private baths. **★Fiorella**, Via del Babuino 196, ✆ 06 361 0597, in a good location just off Piazza del Popolo, has simple rooms none with private bath. The area around Stazione Termini offers a wide choice of inexpensive hotels, ranging from plain, family-run establishments—often quite comfortable and friendly—to bizarre dives with exposed plumbing run by Sudanese and Sri Lankans for the benefit of visiting countrymen. Via Principe Amedeo is also a good place to look, particularly at no.76, a big building with a pretty courtyard that houses about eight old *pensioni*, and nos.62, 82 and 79. **★Tony**, Via Principe Amedeo 79, ✆ 06 446 6887, 📠 06 485 721, is a friendly above-average quality budget hotel. **★Katty**, Via Palestro 35, ✆ 06 444 1216, 📠 06 444 1261, is simple and clean, on a street on the east side of the station which has a number of other cheap hotels.

Eating Out

Unlike many other Italians, the Romans aren't afraid to try something new. Chinese restaurants have appeared in droves, not to mention Arab, Korean and macrobiotic places. This should not be taken as a reflection on local cooking. Rome attracts talented chefs from all over Italy, and every region is represented by a restaurant somewhere in town, giving a microcosm of Italian cuisine you'll find nowhere else.

The grand old tradition of Roman cooking has specialities as *saltimbocca* (literally 'jump in the mouth'), tender veal *scalope* cooked with ham, *stracciatella* (a soup with eggs, parmesan cheese and parsley), fried artichokes called *carciofi alla giudia* and veal *involtini*. In the less expensive places you are likely to encounter such favourites as *baccalà* (salt cod), *bucatini all'amatriciana* (in a tomato and bacon sauce) or *alla carbonara* (with egg and bacon), tripe and *gnocchi*. Unless you ask for something different, the wine will probably come from the Castelli Romani—light, fruity whites, of which the best come from Frascati and Velletri.

Though you can drop as much as L170,000 (without wine) if you follow the politicians and the TV crowd, prices somehow manage to keep close to the Italian average—Rome is much more reasonable than Milan. Watch out for tourist traps—places near a major sight with a 'tourist menu', for example. Rome also has some expensive joints that could best be described as parodies of old, famous establishments; they advertise heavily and aren't hard to smell out. Hotel restaurants, those in the de luxe class, can often be quite good but ridiculously expensive.

very expensive

Perched high above the city, **La Pergola dell'Hotel Hilton**, Via Cadlolo 4, ✆ 06 3509 2211, is currently Rome's most celebrated restaurant for *alta cucina* served in elegant surroundings with all of Rome at your feet. *Closed Sun and Mon; open for dinner only; reserve well ahead.* For fish, head to **La Rosetta**, Via della Rosetta 8, near the Pantheon, ✆ 06 686 1002, Rome's best fish-only restaurant; even if you aren't dining, step in to admire the heap of shiny fish, oysters and sea-urchins arranged on the marble slab in the hall. *Closed Sun; reserve well ahead.*

expensive

There is no better place to try *carciofi alla giudia* than right on the edge of the old ghetto at **Piperno**, Via Monte de' Cenci 9, ✆ 06 6880 6629, Rome's most famous purveyor of Roman-Jewish cooking—simple dishes on the whole, but prepared and served with refinement. *Closed Sun eve and Mon.*

Across the river, Trastevere, with its attractive piazzas and tables outside, has long been one of the most popular corners of the city for dining. Many of its restaurants specialize in fish, most notably **Alberto Ciarla**, Piazza San Cosimato 40, ✆ 06 581 8668, some way south of Santa Maria in Trastevere. The French-trained owner, proud enough to put his name on the sign, sees to it that everything is delicately and perfectly done, and graciously served: oysters, seafood ravioli and quite a few adventurous styles of *pesce crudo* (raw fish) are among the most asked for. *Dinner only;*

closed Sun. Not far away, **Sabatini**, Piazza Santa Maria in Trastevere 13, ℰ 06 581 2026, has been a Roman institution for many a year, as much for the cuisine (again, lots of seafood) as for the tables outside, which face the lovely piazza and its church. *Closed Tues in winter, Wed in summer.* Off Piazza Venezia, **Vecchia Roma**, Piazza Campitelli 18, ℰ 06 686 4604, provides good food, an imaginative seasonal menu and a lovely quiet setting with tables outdoors. *Closed Wed.*

If you find yourself anywhere around Porta San Paolo and the Testaccio district at dinnertime, don't pass up a chance to dine at the acknowledged temple of old Roman cooking, **Checchino dal 1887**, Via di Monte Testaccio 30, ℰ 06 574 6318, which has been owned by the same family for 107 years—the longest known in Rome. Both the fancy and humble sides of Roman food are well represented, with plenty of the powerful offal dishes that Romans have been eating since ancient times, and the setting is unique—on the edge of Monte Testaccio, with one of Rome's best cellars excavated underneath the hill. *Closed Sun eve and Mon.*

moderate

Dal Toscano, Via Germanico 58, ℰ 06 397 25717, is perhaps your best option in the tourist-trap Vatican area: family-run and very popular with Roman families, offering well-prepared Tuscan specialities like *pici* (rough, fresh spaghetti rolled by hand) in game sauce, and *fiorentina* steak—and home-made desserts. Reserve. *Closed Mon.* Another Tuscan place off the Via Veneto, also family-run but slightly fancier and more expensive, is **Papà Baccus**, Via Toscana 33, ℰ 06 4274 2808, which has remarkably good *prosciutto*, delicious potato ravioli and, in winter, baked fish with artichokes, along with regional soups and *fiorentina*. Reserve. *Closed Sat lunch and Sun.*

Only in Rome would you find a good French restaurant run by a Catholic lay missionary society—*sole meunière* and onion soup in the well-scrubbed and righteous atmosphere of **L'Eau Vive**, Via Monterone 85, ℰ 06 6880 1095, not far from the Pantheon. A nourishing meal at a modest price, served with serenity, will have you joining in a prayer to the Virgin before dessert; the fixed lunch menu at *L25,000* is a great bargain. *Closed Sun.* Also near the Pantheon, **Myosotis**, Vicolo della Vaccarella 3, ℰ 06 686 5554, is a great family-run restaurant with an ample menu of traditional and creative meat and fish dishes. *Closed Sun.*

The Piazza di Spagna area is not as promising for restaurants, but there are a few, of which the best, perhaps, is **Nino**, Via Borgognona 11, ℰ 06 678 6752, with a flask full of cannellini beans simmering in the window, the signpost for true, well-prepared Tuscan cuisine. *Closed Sun.* In the vicinity, a few steps from the Trevi Fountain, one safe option is **Al Presidente**, Via in Arcione 95, ℰ 06 679 7342, offering fish in all manners. **Dal Bolognese**, Piazza del Popolo 1, ℰ 06 361 11426, with tables outside on the grand piazza and a view of the Pincio, is the place to go to sample Emilian specialities—don't miss the tortellini or any other fresh pasta dish, and finish with *fruttini*, a selection of real fruit shells each filled with its own sorbet flavour. *Closed Mon.* **Paris**, Piazza San Calisto 7/a, ℰ 06 581 5378, just beyond Piazza Santa Maria in Trastevere, serves classic Roman-Jewish cuisine; particularly good is the *minestra di arzilla* (skate soup). *Closed Sun eve and Mon.* **Antico Arco**, Piazzale Aurelio 7, ℰ 06 581 5274, is well worth the climb up the Monte Gianicolo; it is a reliable, informal restaurant for no-nonsense creative Italian cuisine. Reserve. *Closed Mon.*

The quarters just outside the Aurelian wall and north and east of the Villa Borghese are more good places to look for restaurants. **Le Coppedè**, Via Taro 28/a, between Via Nomentana and Villa Ada, © 06 841 1772, is a neighbourhood restaurant totally devoted to Pugliese cuisine, which is lighter than typical Roman fare. **Semidivino**, Via Alessandria 230, © 06 4425 0795, is a classy and intimate wine bar—also good for a first-rate meal based on excellent salads, an interesting selection of cheese and pork-cured meat and comforting soups at reasonable prices. *Closed Sat lunch and Sun.*

cheap

Less expensive places are not hard to find in the *centro storico*, although chances to eat anything different from Roman cuisine are pretty low. One exception is the **Roman Lounge de l'Hotel d'Inghilterra**, Via Bocca di Leone 14, © 06 699 81500, an elegant retreat in the heart of the shopping district at the foot of the Spanish Steps, which at lunchtime offers an interesting *piatto unico* (one-dish menu) for *L35,000*; if you like their style you can return for a very expensive dinner.

The **Grappolo d'Oro**, Piazza della Cancelleria 80, © 06 686 4118, near Campo de' Fiori, offers exceptionally good value traditional Roman cooking. *Closed Sun.* **Il Collegio**, Via Pie' di Marmo 36, © 06 679 2570, not far from the Pantheon, has tables outside and a few Roman first courses along with more imaginative dishes and a good chocolate soufflé. *Closed Sat lunch and Sun.* Nearby, **Armando al Pantheon**, Salita de' Crescenzi 31, © 06 6880 3034, is an authentic Roman trattoria famous for spaghetti *cacio e pepe* (with pecorino cheese and black pepper) or *all'amatriciana*, *saltimbocca*, and a delicious ricotta tart. *Closed Sat eve and Sun.*

In Trastevere there's a small family trattoria, **Da Lucia**, Vicolo del Mattonato, © 06 580 3601, two streets north of Piazza Santa Maria, that offers local cooking in a typical setting. If you are near the Vatican, an area of forgettable tourist restaurants, venture a little way north to the **Antico Falcone**, Via Trionfale 60, © 06 3974 3385, a simple place housed in what's left of a 15th-century farmhouse, for tasty *rigatoni alla nasona* (pasta with melted cheese and tomato sauce), *melanzane* (aubergines) *alla parmigiana* and, in season, *carciofi alla giudia. Closed Tues.* An excellent budget trattoria in the centre is **Gino in Vicolo Rosini**, Vicolo Rosini 4, off Piazza del Parlamento, © 06 687 3434, near the parliament, and often crammed with civil servants and the occasional deputy. *Closed Sun.*

If the thought of a full meal sandwiched between Roman antiquities and Baroque treasures seems a bit much, consider lunch in a wine bar, which offer good selections of cured meat and cheese, soups, salads and occasional quiches and flans, and desserts (usually) made in-house. Choose from about 20 wines *in mescita* (by the glass) and hundreds by the bottle: **Trimani Winebar**, Via Cernaia 37/b, not far from Termini, © 06 446 9661 (*closed Sun*); **La Bottega del Vino di Anacleto Bleve**, Via Santa Maria del Pianto 9/11, in the Ghetto, © 06 686 5970 (*closed Sun, open for lunch only Mon, Tues and Sat, open for lunch and dinner Wed–Fri*); **Cavour 313**, Via Cavour 313, © 06 678 5496 (*closed Sun in summer, Sat eve the rest of the year*). Among the vast array of unexciting restaurants that cram the streets around Termini there are also several African places. **Africa**, Via Gaeta 46, © 06 494 1077, is an Ethiopian/Eritrean restaurant that offers spicy meals at very low prices. *Open for breakfast; closed Mon.* Also try the student area of San Lorenzo, east of the station, where there is a much better assortment of trattorias. **Tram Tram**, Via dei Reti 44, ℗ 06 446 3635, is crowded and trendy. *Closed Mon.*

pizzerias

Roman pizza is crisp and thin, although the softer, thicker Neapolitan-style pizza has recently won a fat slice of the market. Most pizzerias have tables outside and are open only for dinner, often until 2am. **Da Baffetto**, Via del Governo Vecchio 11, ℗ 06 686 1617, is a beloved institution not far from Piazza Navona, or try the large, crowded **Ivo**, Via San Francesco a Ripa 158, in Trastevere, ℗ 06 581 7082. *Closed Tues.* Or **Formula 1**, Via degli Equi 13. *Closed Sun; open eves only.* **Panattoni**, Viale Trastevere 53, ℗ 06 580 0919, is perhaps the best place to see *pizzaioli* at work. *Closed Wed.* Nearby **Dar Poeta**, Vicolo del Bologna 45, ℗ 06 588 0516, is more on the verge of Neapolitan pizza, and perhaps the only one in town with a pizza dessert, *calzone di ricotta* (filled with ricotta and chocolate) and a non-smoking room. *Closed Mon.* For strictly Neapolitan pizza, head to the pricy **Al Forno della Soffitta**, Via dei Villini 1/e, off the Via Nomentana, ℗ 06 440 4692, where they also have delicious pastry delivered daily from Naples. *Closed Sun.*

Entertainment and Nightlife

The best entertainment in Rome is often in the passing cosmopolitan spectacle of its streets; as nightlife goes, it can be a real snoozer compared with other European cities, though if you don't expect too much you'll have a good time. Like all Italians, many Romans have most of their fun with their families and a close-knit circle of friends, and teenagers will spend hours simply hanging out in or outside bars, before heading off to a club or back home. If you're determined, the back streets around the Piazza Navona or Campo de' Fiori swarm with people in the evenings, and these are the places to come to plan your night ahead, as leaflets and free tickets are always being handed out. Often these are to new places that have opened, offering a long-awaited alternative to the ultra-chic posturing in the 'in' spots of the hour. Another source is *Romac'e'* (from newsstands), with comprehensive listings and a small section in English, or the weekly *Time Out*, with listings and articles (in Italian).

Rome can be uncomfortably sticky in August, but unlike Milan, there's plenty going on. The *Estate Romana* (Roman Summer) is a three-month long festival of outdoor events, music, theatre and film (shown on outdoor screens around the city), and most museums run longer hours. Ask at the tourist office for information, check *Romac'e'*, and keep an eye out for posters. A far older Roman party is the traditional **Festa de' Noantri** in Trastevere (16–31 July), where you may well find a gust of old Roman spontaneity along with music from all across the spectrum, acrobats, dancing and stall upon stall extending down Viale Trastevere and into the quarter's piazzas.

opera, classical music, theatre and film

If you want to go to any events or concerts in Rome, try to get tickets as soon as possible to avoid disappointment. **Orbis**, Piazza Esquilino 37, ℗ 06 474 4776, is a reliable concert and theatre ticket agency (*open Mon–Sat 9.30–1 and 4–7.30*).

From November until May you can take in a performance at the **Teatro dell'Opera di Roma**, Via Firenze 72 (box office, ℗ 06 4816 0255, information, ℗ 06 481 601). Other concerts are performed at and by the **Accademia Nazionale di Santa Cecilia**, in the auditorium on Via della Conciliazione 4 (box office, ℗ 06 6880 1044, information, ℗ 06 361 1064), and by the **Accademia Filarmonica** at the **Teatro Olimpico**, Piazza Gentile da Fabriano 17 (box office, ℗ 06 323 4936, information, ℗ 06 323 4890). Medieval, Baroque, chamber and choral music are frequently performed at the **Oratorio del Gonfalone**, Via del Gonfalone 32/a, ℗ 06 687 5952.

Traditionally during the summer there has been a range of special seasons, although of late Rome has become noticeably sluggish in organizing programmes. Evening concerts are held outside in the **Teatro di Marcello**, ℗ 06 481 4800, or ℗ 06 780 4314 (*mid-June–Sept*), and concerts are performed by the Accademia di Santa Cecilia and visiting international orchestras at **Villa Giulia** (*July*). The opera moves outside in the summer—in the **Terme di Caracalla** up until a few years ago, when it was feared that the site was being damaged. Every year there is talk of a return to the glorious baths, but in the meantime the **Villa Borghese** and the **soccer stadium** serve as alternate venues.

Alternatively, you may want to do as the Romans do and head out to Umbria for the **Spoleto Festival** or the **Umbria Jazz** festival (*see* **Umbria** for both), or fight it out for a ticket to one of the big-name rock concerts at Stadio Flaminio or Palaeur (EUR's Palazzo dello Sport), neither of which win any blue ribbons.

Despite the Italian tendency to dub all foreign films, you can find films in *versione originale* at the **Alcazar**, Via Cardinal Merry del Val 14 (*Mon*); **Nuovo Sacher**, Largo Ascianghi 1 (*Mon and Tues*); **Majestic**, Via SS. Apostoli 20 (*Tues*); and **Pasquino**, on Piazza Sant'Egidio, near Santa Maria in Trastevere, ℗ 06 580 3622 (*daily*).

cafés and bars

 When you're tired of window-shopping you can rest your legs at Rome's oldest café (1760), the **Antico Caffè Greco**, Via Condotti 86, and sit where Keats and Casanova sipped their java—an institution that offers the cheapest chance for a 20-minute dose of *ancien régime* luxury in Rome. Another of the city's *grand cafés* is the **Caffè Rosati**, in Piazza del Popolo, an elegant place founded in 1922, and popular with the Roman intelligentsia, no doubt attracted by its extravagant ice-creams. Other cafés can be dignified, historic or crazily expensive—for example, the 150-year-old **Babington's Tea Rooms**, on Piazza di Spagna, for scones and tea or a full lunch in the proper Victorian atmosphere. At trendy **Sant'Eustachio**, Piazza Sant'Eustachio, near Piazza Navona, home of Rome's most famous coffee, tell them to mind the sugar.

Another kind of Roman bar is represented by the ultra-hip **Bar della Pace**, Via della Pace 3, frequented by celebrities and a place for serious posing. A more funky and friendly atmosphere can be found most evenings at **La Vineria**, Campo de' Fiori 15, a relaxed traditional wine bar/shop with tables outside.

It's not hard to find *gelato* on every corner in Rome, but hold out for the best the city has to offer, at the celebrated **Il Gelato di San Crispino**, Via della Panetteria 42, near the Trevi Fountain. Another novelty are sweets from **Il Forno del Ghetto** (*closed*

Sat), the Jewish bakery at the west end of Via del Portico d'Ottavia (note the incredible building it's in—a recycled ancient structure covered in reliefs and inscriptions).

rock, jazz and clubs

Rome has a select band of clubs with live music—*Romac'e'* will have details of current programmes at the **folk**-oriented Folkstudio, Via Frangipane 42, *©* 06 487 1063; the mainly-**rock** venues such as Big Mama, Vicolo San Francesco a Ripa 18, in Trastevere, *©* 06 581 2551; a **blues** club, Alpheus, Via del Commercio, 36/38, in Ostiense, *©* 06 574 9826; and Palladium, Piazza B. Romano 8, in Garbatella, *©* 06 511 0203, the last two well outside the usual tourist round. Also for **jazz**—which has a strong local following—there are venues like the suave Alexanderplatz, Via Ostia 9, in Prati, *©* 06 3974 2971, and the New Mississippi Jazz Club, Borgo Angelico 18/a, near San Pietro, *©* 06 6880 6348. All feature foreign as well as Italian performers.

For serious **dancing** try Alien, Via Velletri 13, near Piazza Fiume, *©* 06 841 2212, Alpheus, Via del Commercio 36, off Via Ostiense, *©* 06 574 7826, or the less juvenile (jacket required) Gilda, Via Mario de' Fiori 97, close to the Spanish Steps, *©* 06 678 4838. All are what Italians call *di tendenza*, meaning they keep up with current UK and US trends. Most indoor clubs and music venues close down completely in late July and August. This is the time, though, when **beach discos** along the coast at Ostia, Fregene and points further afield are hugely popular.

Day Trips from Rome

Getting Around

There are frequent **trains** to Ostia and Ostia Lido on the overground COTRAL line from ⓜMagliana (Line B) in Rome. The best way to get to Tivoli and Villa Adriana is by COTRAL **bus**, from Ponte Mammolo terminal. For the Castelli Romani, there are frequent COTRAL **buses** from Anagnina, at the end of Metro Line A (a 20min ride from the centre of town).

Tourist Information

Tivoli: Largo Garibaldi, *©* 0774 334 522. **Frascati**: Piazza Marconi, *©* 06 942 0331.

Ostia, the Port of Empire

According to the archaeologists, Rome's port was only founded in the 4th century BC, 400 years after Rome itself. But in the centuries of conquest Ostia grew into a major city in its own right, with a population of *c.* 100,000 and nearly 2km of *horrea* (warehouses) near the mouth of the Tiber. In the 4th century, when the flow of trade and tribute slowed, and even the grain supply from Africa was diverted to Constantinople, Ostia lost its reason for being. Malaria increased, and by AD 800 the site was abandoned. Old Father Tiber obliged future archaeologists by covering Ostia in sand and mud. Mussolini shovelled it out in the 1930s, recovering an ancient attraction that many visitors overlook. It's easy to reach by train: get off at the Ostia Antica stop (*site open daily 9–one hour before sunset; adm*).

As in Pompeii, you can walk along the streets and imagine the life in a big ancient city; the temples, frescoed houses, baths, barracks and warehouses are amazingly intact. Ostia's

Forum, with its re-erected columns of temples, is set around a little hill rather wistfully called the 'Capitol'. The small, restored **theatre** has an interesting **Mithraeum** nearby, like the one under San Clemente in Rome; there's a police station (*Caserma dei Vigili*) and the oldest **synagogue** discovered in Italy. One vast square, the 'Piazzale delle Corporazione', preserves mosaics symbolizing the various trades and businesses. On a floor mosaic in **Fortunatus' Tavern** you can see what may be the earliest known specimen of advertising: 'Fortunatus says: if you're thirsty, have a bowl of wine.' Near the ruins, spare a few minutes for the sleepy, pretty hamlet of **Ostia Antica**, also called the 'Borgo', founded as a fortress town in 830 by Pope Gregory IV; it wasn't enough to keep the Saracens out when they sacked Rome 19 years later. There is a small Renaissance church dedicated to **Sant'Aurea** (a 3rd-century Ostian martyr), and the almost startlingly elegant **castello**, erected in 1483 by Julius II (still only a cardinal), who at the time was worried about the Turks.

Tivoli and the Villa Adriana

Ancient *Tibur*, set in a cliff with a beautiful view over the Roman Campagna, became a sort of garden suburb for the senatorial class in the early days of the Empire. But a place with a view is also usually easily defensible, and by the early Middle Ages, despite all the dirty work of Goths and Huns, Tibur had changed its name to Tivoli and managed a successful transition from posh resort to feisty, independent hill town. Once, in its struggles with Rome, it even defeated its bossy neighbour in battle and captured a pope. Wealth returned in the Renaissance in the form of moneybags cardinals; one, Ippolito d'Este, son of Duke Ercole I of Ferrara, created perhaps the most fantastically worldly villa and gardens Italy has ever seen.

That is no small statement, but the **Villa d'Este** (*open Tues–Sun 9–1½ hours before sunset; adm; some days the fountains are not running—check at the Tivoli tourist office*) still has charms enough to attract hordes of day-trippers year-round. The villa itself, designed by Pietro Ligorio and decorated with Mannerist frescoes, is completely upstaged by the gardens, set on a series of terraces on the slopes. Among palms and cypresses, flowers and lawns, every turn exposes an incredible confectionery fountain: the 'Fountain of Glass' by Bernini, the 'Grotto of Diana', the 'Fountain of Dragons'—dozens, along with artificial waterfalls and pools. The cardinal's water organ and mechanical birds no longer work, but you won't regret you came.

Tivoli has a gaudy 17th-century **cathedral** and a Romanesque church, **San Silvestro**, on Via del Colle, with early medieval frescoes, which you will pass on the way to another Renaissance cardinal's fantasy, the **Villa Gregoriana** (*open daily 10–one hour before sunset; adm*). Built in a natural chasm, the shady paths and gardens are irresistible to visitors, who trip gaily down to the bottom— then realize they face quite a climb to get back to ground level. It's worth the trip, if you're up to it, for the spectacular natural waterfall on the River Aniene, and a smaller, artificial one designed by Bernini. On the edge of the abyss, you'll notice two small, remarkably well-preserved Roman temples, one circular and the other rectangular, called the **Temples of the Sibyl** and **Vesta**. There was indeed a college of sibyls in Tibur, as at Cumae near Naples, and they may possibly have kept one of these temples. Wherever, the presence of these oracular ladies, cousins to the oracle at Delphi, show the influence of Greek thought and religion in Latium from the earliest times.

Just outside the town (CAT bus no.4 from Largo Garibaldi), signs direct you to the residential neighbourhood that has grown up around **Hadrian's Villa**, the grandest palace complex ever built in Italy (*open daily 9–1½ hours before sunset; adm*). To get some idea of the scale on which a 2nd-century emperor could build, stop first at the room-sized model of the villa near the entrance. All marble and travertine, and about the same size as the monumental centre of Rome, Hadrian's dream house shows the excess that even the most intelligent and useful of emperors was capable of, and had features that would surprise even Californians—a heated beach, for example, with steam pipes under the sand.

Hadrian was an architect, whose design credits include the Pantheon; he travelled widely through the empire gathering inspiration for his villa, creating reproductions of the Canopic Temple of Alexandria, the Platonic Academy and Stoa Poikile of Athens, and others, set among huge baths, libraries, a Praetorian barracks, temples, theatres and a little palace on an island in an artificial lagoon, that may have been the emperor's private retreat. Many of the best statues in the Vatican and other museums were found here.

Even by public transport Tivoli makes an easy day-trip. To see any of the hill towns to the east and south, however, you'll need a car. Quite a few interesting little villages have managed so far to escape modern tourism: lovely **Anticoli Corrado** on its steep cliff, and **Saracinesco**, founded on a nearly inaccessible crag by Saracen raiders in the 9th century; the present towns-people are their direct descendants. Few towns can claim as glorious a past as **Subiaco**, where St Benedict retired in the late 5th century to write his *Rule* and set Christian monasticism on its way. All through the dark centuries his monasteries (originally Subiaco had twelve) provided a haven for learning and piety, and even in the 1460s the first printed books in Italy were made here by two monks from Germany.

Today the oldest buildings are in the **convent of Santa Scolastica** (*open daily 9–12.30 and 4–7*), named after Benedict's twin sister, with cloisters from the 6th and 11th centuries, and a medieval church decorated by the Cosmati. Two churches with fine late-medieval and Sienese quattrocento frescoes are all that remain of the **monastery of San Benedetto** (*open daily 9–12.30 and 3–6*), a 15-minute walk from the town. Nearby, in the gorge of the Aniene, there is a beautiful little lake with a waterfall, which may have been constructed by Nero, who had a villa at Subiaco.

South of Tivoli, **Zagarolo** is a town of Baroque churches, a medieval citadel and one thoroughly strange Baroque gate, perhaps the work of Vignola. Nearby **Palestrina**, the ancient *Praeneste* and birthplace of the 16th-century composer, has some unusual relics, in particular the **Temple of Fortuna Primigenia**, an oracle of the Latin tribes. Of the complex, rebuilt in the 1st century BC, the lower sanctuary survives, with mosaics and mysterious tablets involved in the decoding of the oracle's responses. Part of the upper sanctuary was employed as a foundation for the 17th-century Colonna-Barberini Palace, which now houses the **Museo Praeneste** (*open daily 9–one hour before sunset; adm*); here the star attraction is a beautiful mosaic with scenes of Egypt, showing the flooding of the Nile. There is a frequent COTRAL bus service from Rome to Subiaco (departures from Stazione Ponte Mammolo Metro Line B) as well as to Palestrina (from Stazione Anagnina at the end of Metro Line A).

The Castelli Romani

Before there was a Rome these towns around the Alban Hills were the strongest members of the Latin Confederation. Since being pounded into submission some 2200 years ago, their role has been reduced to that of providing the capital with wine, flowers and a place to spend summer weekends. The countryside is beautiful, even though some of the nearer 'Castelli' are being enveloped by the Roman suburbs. All these towns can be reached by COTRAL bus, from the depot at the Stazione Anagnina, on Metro Line A.

Frascati, the nearest of the Castelli and one of the most popular, was a medieval replacement for the ancient Latin city of Tusculum, destroyed in 1191. Frascati itself took some hard knocks during the Second World War, but it is still lovely, with an elegant park in the grounds of the 17th-century Villa Aldobrandini (*open Mon–Fri 9–1 and 3–6; in winter until 5*). Nearby **Grottaferrata** was built around the 11th-century abbey, founded by Sts Nilus and Bartholomew and still under the care of Greek Catholic monks; its church of Santa Maria has some medieval frescoes and some by the 17th-century artist Domenichino, as well as a fine columned campanile from the 1200s (*abbey open daily 6–12.30 and 3.30–7; in winter until dusk*). **Marino**, like Frascati, is famed for its wine; the town fountains flow with the stuff during the merry grape festival on the first Sunday of October. From here a panoramic route called Via dei Laghi passes **Lago Albano** on the way to Velletri and the south. After the lake there is a turn-off to **Rocca di Papa**, a dramatically sited town with a picturesque medieval citadel called the *Quartiere dei Bavaresi*, from the Bavarian troops of Emperor Ludwig stationed here in the 1320s. From the town you can drive up to the highest of the Alban Hills, **Monte Cavo** (3228ft), passing a spot where Hannibal camped during the Punic Wars.

From Rome the Via Appia Antica passes on the other side of Lago Albano in a dead straight line, as far as **Castel Gandolfo**, the Vatican enclave where popes take their summer holidays (although John Paul II doesn't spend much time here). After that comes the **Albano Laziale**, the ancient Alba Longa, mother city of Rome. Bits and snatches of the past abound, including a 3rd-century cistern—still in use—and the strange 'Tomb of the Horatii and Curiatii' on the road to **Ariccia**. Anyone familiar with Sir James Frazier's *The Golden Bough* (the foundation work of modern anthropology) will remember the priest of Diana who ruled the Arician Grove, the 'King of the Wood', and how as late as Roman times any man who cared to could cut some mistletoe from one of the sacred oaks, kill the king and take his place. There are still oak groves around Ariccia, and 'Diana's Mirror', the beautiful **Lake Nemi**, is still an enchanted spot, a deep blue oval surrounded by wooded hills and villas. The town of Nemi itself, a pretty place known for violets and *fragoline* (tiny strawberries), is also worth a detour.

Beyond Nemi, **Velletri** is the last of the Castelli, with a Baroque cathedral and an odd, 149ft striped tower of 1353 called the Torre del Trivio. With a car you can press on further, into the Monte Lepini and some charming old hill towns well off the beaten track. **Cori**, like Rome and so many other Latin towns, likes to trace its founding to Trojan refugees. It may well be 3000 years old; that, at least, is the date archaeologists assign to its 'cyclopean' walls, built of huge, neatly fitted polygonal stones, still visible in many places. There are also many Roman ruins, including an intact bridge and the Temple of Hercules (really of Jupiter), a small Doric building complete except for its roof.

Nearby **Ninfa** has been called the 'medieval Pompeii', a town abandoned in the 17th century because of malaria, where many of the buildings survive in an exceptionally beautiful setting, with small streams and lakes, overgrown with wildflowers and trees, and a botanical garden (*open April–first Sun of Nov, first Sat and Sun of each month; April–June also the third Sun of each month; adm exp; to be sure it's open call ☎0773 695 404*). **Norma**, built on the edges of a steep, curving cliff, seems almost like a city hanging in the air. Nearby are more cyclopean walls around the ruins of **Norba**, once capital of Rome's bitter enemies, the Volscians. It was besieged and destroyed by the legions during the Social Wars in 89 BC, never to be rebuilt.

Other possible day-trips from Rome are to the north: Viterbo and the lakes (*see* pp.706–12), and to the fascinating Etruscan necropolises at Tarquinia and Cerveteri (*see* pp.713–14).

Where to Stay and Eating Out

Ostia Antica

For lunch, try the grilled fish at **Al Monumento**, Piazza Umberto I, ✆ 06 565 0021 (*moderate*), near the castle. *Closed Mon.*

Tivoli ✉ 00019

★★★Padovano, Via Tiburtina 130, Tiburtina, ✆ 0774 530 807, ✆ 0774 531 382, is a good place to stay, and a bargain. The **Sibilla**, Via della Sibilla, ✆ 0774 335 281 (*moderate*) is famous above all else for its location, incorporating the famous 'Temple of the Sibyls' right in its building. The place lives off tourists, but the food is still good and the price is right. *Closed Mon.*

Frascati

Frascati makes a good place to eat, in restaurants like **Zarazà**, Via Regina Margherita 21, ✆ 06 942 2053 (*moderate*), with a picturesque panorama, local cooking and good Frascati wine. *Closed Mar–Nov Sun eve and Mon; the rest of the year closed Mon.*

Nemi ✉ 00040

If you have a car, the area around Nemi is a nice place to stay; try **★Al Refugio**, ✆ 06 936 8686, just outside Nemi (*cheap*), or the **★★★Culla del Lago**, Via del Lago 38, ✆ 06 936 68231 (*moderate*), in Castel Gandolfo, by Lake Albano. Outside Nemi, **Da Baffone**, Via dei Laghi Km 15, ✆ 06 963 3892 (*moderate*) does dishes with wild mushrooms, as well as good roast meats and exceptional house wine. *Closed Mon.*

Southern Lazio: Along the Coast

Getting Around

The Rome–Naples **rail** line runs parallel to the coast. For Terracina and Sabaudia, get off at Priverno; for Sperlonga, at Fondi; for Gaeta, at Formia, and take local buses. There are also regular COTRAL **buses**. Formia is the year-round port for the **Pontine Islands**, with daily departures. In the summer you can also catch a hydrofoil and ferry from Anzio or Terracina; in winter there's a ferry from Terracina (*daily 8am*) and a regular hydrofoil service from Anzio (*Sat, Sun and Mon*).

Tourist Information

Latina: Via Duca del Mare 19, ✆ 0773 695 404.
San Felice Circeo: Piazza Municipio, ✆ 0773 547 770.
Ponza: the Pro-loco, located just uphill from the port, ✆ 0771 80031, or ✆ 0771 809 866, can be useful for ferry/hydrofoil information.

The Pontine Marshes

...nowhere else has the creative power of Fascism left a deeper mark. The immense works can be summed up in the lapidary phrase of Il Duce: "You redeem the land, you found some cities."

from a 1939 Italian guidebook

You wouldn't be travelling this way 60 years ago, when the broad plain of the Pontine Marshes was the biggest no-man's-land in Italy, wracked by malaria and healthy only for the water-buffalo. Under the Romans, canals were dug to reclaim the swamps, but they became blocked up in the Dark Ages. Once again during the 13th century some of the marshes were drained, but a few centuries of papal rule had the area back to its pristine emptiness when Mussolini decided to make it one of the showpieces of his regime.

Today, except for the small corner preserved as a park and wildlife refuge, the Pontine Marshes no longer exist, and brand-new towns like Aprilia, Pomezia, Pontinia and Sabaudia sit amid miles of prosperous farms as curious monuments to the brighter side of fascism. So does **Latina**, largest of the Pontine towns and Italy's youngest provincial capital, founded in 1932, a bright and busy place built on a radial plan with plenty of trees and chunky Mussolini palazzi.

If you drive along the coast you'll pass plenty of beaches, including those of the small resort of **Anzio**, ancient *Antium*, popular with the Romans. In January 1944 the British and American forces found its beaches an ideal spot for a landing; that bloody but successful end-run forced the Germans to abandon their Gustav Line and opened the way for the liberation of Rome. Large military cemeteries surround the town.

Between Anzio and Cape Circeo the coast is almost a solid stretch of beaches and dunes. **Monte Circeo**, at the end, was an island in ancient times, one of many candidates around the Mediterranean for Homer's Isle of Circe from the *Odyssey*. **San Felice Circeo**, on its slopes, is a growing resort, offering boat trips around the big rock and its many caves.

Since 1934 much of this area has been included in the **Parco Nazionale del Circeo**, a beautiful and unspoiled expanse of watery landscape. Migratory birds of all kinds stop here twice a year, and besides a wealth of wild flowers and primeval forests you may see woodpeckers, peregrine falcons and herons—maybe even that most overdressed of sea birds, the *Cavaliere d'Italia*. Being Italy, the next compelling sight is never far; here, the Cooperativa *La Mela Cotogna*, based in Sabaudia at Largo Giulio Cesare 12, ℗ 0773 511 206, has recently been granted the permit to organize guided visits to the villa of **Emperor Domitian**, reachable by boat across the lake of Sabaudia, in the National Park.

Further down the coast the Ausonian Mountains crowd the sea at **Terracina**, once the Volscian port of *Anxur*; stop here for a look at the lovely hotchpotch of a cathedral, with a Baroque and neoclassical façade and a Moorish-looking 14th-century campanile. Inside, are remains of the Temple of Roma and Augustus and medieval mosaics in the apse and on the floor. To the east, Trajan cut a deep passage through the mountains, the 'Pisco Montano', to allow the Via Appia to continue along the coast. If you have time, take the Strada Panoramica up to the top of Monte Sant'Angelo, with the mighty stone platform of the Temple of Jupiter Anxurus, Terracina's medieval walls and wonderful views for miles along the coast.

From Terracina you can detour into the mountains: to **Fondi**, an old town that has stuck to its rectilinear Roman street plan without change; or to **Fossanova** and its 12th-century Cistercian abbey (*open summer daily 7–12.30 and 4–7.30; winter daily 3–5.30*). French monks came down in the 1130s to show the Italians how to make a proper Gothic building; the Italians weren't interested, of course, and Fossanova survives along with San Galgano in Tuscany, San Martino al Cimino near Viterbo, and a few others, as a rare example of the northern style on this side of the Alps. The church, of cathedral proportions, is a fine, sedate Burgundian Gothic work with a beautiful rose window. Not much is left inside, except the stately rows of piers and pointed arches. Fossanova was a great centre of learning in its day (St Thomas Aquinas spent time here), but after the 1400s both wealth and talent deserted it. After centuries of decadence, it was expropriated in 1873, and its treasures dispersed.

Sperlonga and Gaeta

Continuing towards Naples, **Sperlonga** is one of the most pleasant small resorts on the central Tyrrhenian coast, with a medieval quarter on its steep promontory and miles of fine beaches to either side. About 3km beyond it you may inspect the pretty sea cave called the **Grotto of Tiberius**, once fitted out as a pleasure dome for that thoroughly hedonistic emperor. Some excellent classical sculpture has been found here, including one large composition related to the *Laocoön* in the Vatican. A small museum further down the road has been built for them.

At the end of this scenic stretch of coast, **Gaeta** stands behind its medieval walls on a narrow peninsula, the grandest sight between Monte Argentario and the Bay of Naples. For a while in the early Middle Ages, this town was an important Mediterranean trading centre, a rival to Amalfi and Pisa. Its naturally defensible site made it a valued stronghold for centuries after; in 1861 it was briefly the last redoubt of the House of Bourbon, when the King of Naples and his palace guard withstood a siege from the army of the new Italy, hoping for help from France that never came. The town has a quiet medieval atmosphere, with a much rebuilt **cathedral**, a 13th-century castle and evocative, crumbling old streets and alleys around the harbour. On the hill above Gaeta you can make the difficult climb to see the rich and well-preserved tomb of a Roman general named Munatius Planctus, the founder of Lyons, France.

Nearby **Formia**, the major base for ferries to the Pontine Islands, enjoyed a blessed past as one of the gilded resorts of Imperial Rome, like Capri or Baiae. Mark Antony's men caught up with the virtuous but capitally tedious orator Cicero here, after the assassination of Caesar, and knifed him in the baths of his villa. Little of ancient Formia survived through the Dark Ages, and the little city that replaced it suffered grievously in 1944. Today Formia is entirely new, a happy and growing place that seems to have a bright future. Before Campania, the last town along the coast is **Minturno**, a medieval replacement for ancient *Minturnae*, the ruins of which, closer to the coast, include a restored theatre, bits of temples and an aqueduct.

Ponza and the Pontine Islands

An ancient volcano gave birth to the five small islands of the Pontine archipelago, and to it they owe much of their charm and eccentricities. Two are inhabited: **Ponza**, the larger and more visited, is stunningly beautiful and shaped like a crescent moon. The curve of its fishing harbour, with its oddly shaped sea rocks, arches and coves, shelters a charming pastel-tinted town and small tower.

On the other side of the island, but within walking distance, is the island's famous 'moonlit' beach, the **Chiaia di Luna**, a crescent-shaped beach beneath the steep pale cliffs. Wandering (or, far better, sailing) along its long, jagged shores, you'll discover such wonders as a volcanically created swimming pool and the glaringly white Infernal Cove, both near **Le Forna** (the only other real settlement on Ponza). Hire a boat at Ponza town or Santa Maria to visit the **Grotte di Pilato**, three grottoes connnected by tunnels dug in Republican times as part of a luxury villa, and used to store live fish for its kitchens.

The other inhabited island, tiny **Ventotene**, is a table of reddish tufa sitting on the surface of the sea; Augustus' daughter Julia found it the perfect place to build a grand villa to receive her many lovers far from the wagging tongues of Rome—although her scandalous behaviour eventually caught up with her and Ventotene became her rock of exile instead of a bower of bliss—a few bits still remain beyond the rocky beach of Cala Rossano. Later Julians found it a usefully isolated place to do their dirty work, too; Caligula's mother starved herself to death here, and Nero had his young, unwanted wife Octavia murdered in her bath; the meagre ruins of her villa stand evocative and lonely on windswept Punta Eolo.

The town of **Porto Ventotene** is piled over the old Porto Romano, carved out of tufa. There is a small museum in the Municipio (*open in the mornings*), displaying items found in Julia's villa. You can stroll around the island in less than an hour, past little fields of lentils. Here and there you will find little paths winding towards the sea, the cliffs and beaches.

The Ciociaria

If you're in a hurry to get to Naples the quickest route is the *Autostrada del Sole*, following the route of the Roman Via Casalina behind the coastal mountains. After Velletri, in the Castelli Romani, however, there are still some possible detours to delay you. This humble corner of Lazio is known as the **Ciociaria**, after the *ciocie*, or bark sandals, worn by the countrymen not so long ago when this was one of the backwaters of Italy.

Anagni, small as it is, held centre stage in European politics on several occasions during the Middle Ages. Four 14th-century popes were born here, and several others made it their summer home. Greatest among them was Boniface VIII, a nasty intriguer who had the poor timing to proclaim loudly the temporal supremacy of the popes long after anyone took the idea seriously. Captured in Anagni by the Colonna family and the forces of the King of France, Boniface received a resounding slap in the face from Sciarra Colonna that put a temporary end to papal dreams of world domination.

Parts of his palace can still be seen (*open daily 9–12.30 and 3–6; adm*), along with the stout and squarish cathedral, one of the finest in central Italy, sharing a little of the genius of the Tuscan and Puglian churches of the same period. Outside, it is 11th-century Romanesque; a rebuilding in the 1300s left it tentatively Gothic within. There is a Cosmatesque pavement and a wonderful 13th-century stone *baldacchino* over the altar. Be sure to see the crypt: its blue and gold Byzantine frescoes from the 13th century are among the best of their kind in Italy. Take some time for a walk around Anagni, a medieval time-capsule with its walls, towers and palaces, like the Casa Barnekow, that have changed little in 600 years.

Up in the mountains above Anagni, **Fiuggi** has been a popular spa for centuries; Michelangelo came here to take the waters after the strain of working on the Sistine Chapel. **Alatri**, 2400 years ago, was one of the main cities of the Hernici, an Italic tribe that differed from its neighbours by being a firm ally of Rome, a wise policy that spared Alatri the destruction that befell many of the other ancient cities of Lazio.

Consequently Alatri remains the best example we have of a pre-Roman Italian town, with almost a complete circuit of 'cyclopean' walls from about the 6th century BC. Besides these, there is another set of walls at the top of Alatri's hill marking the boundaries of the acropolis, where today the cathedral and the Bishop's Palace stand over the temples of the long-forgotten Hernici. Just outside the town there is an early Carthusian monastery, the **Certosa di Trisulti**, with buildings as old as 1210.

Along the old Via Casalina, little **Frosinone** serves as provincial capital for the Ciociaria, and the centre for all bus lines in the region. A side road from here (SS214) will take you on a delightful detour to the **Abbey of Casamari**, a little-known 13th-century French Cistercian complex with a church much like the one at Fossanova, and then to **Isola del Liri**, a pretty town with a dramatic waterfall in the middle, which hosts a blues festival each July. Further down the Via Casilina, **Aquino** is full of Roman-era ruins, including a small decorative arch.

For something really out of the way, you might venture up into the highest and least-visited corner of Lazio, the Valley of the Comino on the borders of the Abruzzo National Park. In this mountainous region there are beautiful **lakes** at Posta Fibreno and Biagio Saracinesco, and ruins of a 12th-century castle at **Vicalvi**. **Atina** is the most important town, and has been since the days of the Samnites; relics from its past are preserved in the Municipal Museum.

Montecassino

If divine guidance led St Benedict from Subiaco to found a monastery here, as the legend states, perhaps God just wasn't thinking clearly that day. Montecassino may be the most famous monastery in Italy, and it certainly owns the most dramatic site, high on a mountaintop over the Garigliano Valley, but the location has caused the honest monks nothing but trouble over the centuries. They were essential in keeping alive the traditions of letters and scholarship in the Dark Ages—all the more remarkable when you consider that Montecassino has been utterly destroyed five times.

Benedict came in 529, but the Lombards wrecked the place only 60 years later. The Saracens and the Normans repeated the scene in the 9th and 11th centuries, and an earthquake finished off what must have been one of Italy's treasures of medieval architecture in 1348. Each time the place has been rebuilt, but the reason why Montecassino attracts so much strife was demonstrated again during the Italian Campaign of 1944. The rock happens to be the most strategically important spot in central Italy, the key to either Rome or Naples, depending on which way your army is walking.

In 1944 the Germans made it the western bastion of their Gustav Line and it held up the Allied advance for four months. Enough bombs were dropped to destroy the monastery once more, without seriously disconcerting the defenders. The polyglot Allied forces of New Zealanders, Indians, Brazilians and French made unsuccessful attacks between January and May. It was the Poles who finally beat their way in, losing over 1000 men on the way up; their cemetery can be seen near the hill. The Benedictines have finished the rebuilding and, while not up to the artistic level of its predecessors, it's still a popular place to visit (*open daily 9.30–12 and 3.30–half an hour before sunset*), especially for the wonderful views.

Sperlonga ✉ 04029

Sperlonga has some nice spots around its beaches: ★★★**La Playa**, outside town in Via C. Colombo at Località Fiorelle, © 0771 549 496 (*moderate–expensive*) is modern, with pool, tennis courts and a bit of a beach, and there's also the slightly less expensive ★★★**Parkhotel Fiorelle**, © 0771 549 246 (*moderate*), very close by. There are plenty of relatively inexpensive fish restaurants by the sea; in town, try **La Bisaccia**, Via Romita 25, © 0771 54576 (*moderate*), a charming little place serving only fish and pasta dishes. *Closed Tues in winter.*

Gaeta ✉ 04024

Near Gaeta, on the coastal Via Flacca Km 23, ★★★**Summit**, © 0771 741 741 (*moderate*) is a fine modern resort hotel in a good location, if a bit large. *Open April–mid-Nov.* ★**Amyclae**, Via C. Colombo 77, © 0771 54051 (*cheap*) has doubles with balconies overlooking the sea. **Masaniello**, Piazza Commestibili 6, © 0771 462 296 (*expensive*) is perhaps Gaeta's oldest restaurant, although the succulent fish specialities are prepared in a style that's more typical of Campania than Lazio.

Formia ✉ 04023

One of the best places on the coast is ★★★★**Grande Albergo Miramare**, ©/🖥 0771 320 047 (*moderate*), on the southern edge of the town, a beautiful old villa with extensive gardens on the shore, a beach and a pool, and modernized but pleasant rooms, as well as an elegant restaurant in a little pavilion. The excellent **Zì Anna**, on Largo Paone facing the harbour, © 0771 771 063 (*moderate*) serves more seafood, classically prepared, and a surprisingly large choice of what comes out of this part of the Tyrrhenian Sea, but also memorable *primi piatti. Closed Tues.*

Pontine Islands ✉ 04027

The most picturesque place to stay on Ponza is ★★★**La Torre dei Borboni**, Via Madonna 1, © 0771 80135 (*expensive*), with a third of its rooms and apartments in an 18th-century castle with wonderful views, an excellent restaurant and a private beach. Less expensive, ★★★**Gennarino a Mare**, © 0771 80071 (*moderate*) is near Ponza's central beach, which has a good restaurant (*cheap*), with a few tables on a floating platform. *Closed Thurs out of season.* Alternatively there's **Da Luisa**, Via Chiaia di Luna, © 0771 80128 (*cheap*), or several places where you can rent a room.

A wonderful Neapolitan pastry-shop on the main drag sells delicious *sfogliatelle ricce* (warm and crisp pastry filled with a ricotta-based cream, spices and candied orange peel) and *torta caprese* (chocolate/almond cake). For a home-style meal, you can safely head to the family-run **La Lanterna**, Corso Carlo Pisacane (*cheap*).

Campania

The Italian south—the *Mezzogiorno*, the Noonday—is one of the extremities of Europe, poised in a calm sea between the Balkans and the Sahara. The contrasts within the south are greater than in the other two-thirds of Italy; from the dreamy coastline of Amalfi and Positano it is only an afternoon's drive to the grimmest deforested wastelands of the Basilicata. Some sections of the south are prosperous and forward-looking, and not too distant from their northern counterparts, while others lag astonishingly behind, despite all the efforts of the government and the *Cassa per il Mezzogiorno*. Some areas are surprising, others surprisingly empty.

In Roman times, to distinguish the *Campania* around Naples from parts further north (the present Roman *Campagna*), the southern section acquired the name of *Campania Felix*. A happy land it was, the richest and most civilized province in Italy, with a mix of Greek and Etruscan culture superimposed on the native Samnites and Ausones, not to mention the merry Oscans and their perfumed city of Capua. Campania's charm, then as now, starts with one of the most captivating stretches of coastline in Italy—the Amalfi Coast—Capri and Ischia, Sorrento, Vesuvius, the Phlegraean Fields around Pozzuoli, and the beautiful but lesser-known Cilento Coast at the southern tip of the region. Roman emperors and senators spent as much time here as business would allow, and even today it is said that the dream of every Italian is to have a villa at Capri or Sorrento overlooking the sea.

In the middle of all this, of course, sprawls Italy's third-largest city, Naples—a place that may well be either your favourite or least favourite Italian city—or both at the same time. Campania shares fully in all the complexes and problems of the Italian south as a whole. It has large new industries, ambitious planning schemes to attract still more, and substantial difficulties with pollution, poverty, soaring unemployment, corruption and crime. Though the potential certainly exists, there is a long way to go before the region can reclaim the position it had in the days of the Caesars.

Not to be Missed

Campania and the three other southern regions have almost half of Italy's coastline, though most of it is flat and not too exciting. If you are looking for classic Mediterranean scenery and a spot on the beach, the first really obvious place to send you is the spectacular **Amalfi Coast** and the **islands** around the Bay of Naples. If these long-established fleshpots are too overripe or too crowded for your tastes, press on further into the region. Try the small resorts of the **Cilento** (*see* p.852–3) or **Maratea** in the Basilicata (p.860), both well south of Naples.

Those interested in the ancient Greeks and Romans must first visit **Pompeii**, **Herculaneum**, the splendid temples at **Paestum** and then **Capua**, though the best relics from all these sites are in the great museum at Naples. From the Middle Ages, there is exotic Arab-Norman architecture in **Amalfi**, **Salerno** and **Ravello**. Inland, queer old **Benevento** is another fascinating place to visit.

Campania

A tour of less than two weeks should get you through the major sights of Campania—almost all of them are along the coast. Begin with **Naples,** and if you like it enough you can make the city a base for day trips to **Pompeii** and **Herculaneum,** the **Phlegraean Fields** or **Vesuvius,** and the **islands.** Otherwise, **Sorrento** or any of the islands can provide a more pleasant base. The **Amalfi Coast** and its towns are certainly worth two days, though you may never want to leave. **Paestum** and its Greek temples come next, and, if you're heading further south, you can continue from here along the **Cilento Coast,** or else return to Naples through inland Campania, stopping at **Benevento** to see the Arch of Trajan and the odd Egyptian relics around town, then visiting **Capua** with its unique *mithraeum* and amphitheatre and **Caserta.**

The *Feste* of Campania

In Campania any excuse will do for throwing a party, especially if it can be combined with having a day off work, and the region plays host to some of Italy's most spectacular and colourful traditional festivals or *feste*. Most of the festivities are linked to religious events and feast days, and the Madonna features prominently, often decked out garishly with bright fairy-lights and gaudy flowers and hauled through the streets atop tiny Fiats hastily covered with red velvet (with peepholes for the driver), or on platforms stoically borne by the village's fittest and strongest young men.

But many of the celebrations also have a strong pagan flavour, especially those linked to the land and the harvest, and some of the feast-day paraphernalia is unmistakably phallic (towers and obelisks are an obvious give-away).

Whatever the occasion, a village *festa* is a chance to see local traditions and ancient rites in full swing. They are jolly affairs, and outsiders are nearly always welcome. This being Campania, where eating is in itself a second religion, a visit to a *festa* will invariably involve consuming vast quantities of food, often superbly cooked in makeshift kitchens organized by the local women, and served for knock-down prices. The following are some of the best *feste* to look out for, but keep a watch for others by checking billboards in the piazzas of towns and villages.

La sagra dei gigli (Feast of the Lilies), at Nola, 27 June. The whole town commemorates the return of its 5th-century bishop St Paulinus after a long period of imprisonment in Africa. The original Nolesi welcomed him home with bunches of lilies. Today, the towns-people recall this reunion by hauling 80ft-tall wooden 'lilies' through the streets.

Festa di Sant'Anna, at Ischia, 26 July. A dazzling torchlight procession of hundreds of boats, transformed into floats, to honour the island's patron saint.

Festa dell'obelisco di paglia (Feast of the straw obelisk), at Fontanarosa, near Avellino, 14 August. A harvest thanksgiving ritual, with a giant 100ft-high spire of plaited straw, around which villagers dance and sing.

La sagra del grano (the wheat feast), at Foglianise, near Benevento, 14 August. A striking display of allegorical floats depicting famous churches and monuments, all of them made out of straw and corn-stalks.

Festa dell'Assunta (Feast of the Assumption), at Positano, 15 August. An ancient celebration in honour of the Virgin, which also recreates the landing—and the defeat—of the hated Saracens. Local townspeople dress up in costumes and stage a parade of decorated boats, before the grand finale: a dramatic firework display over the sea. In neighbouring Montepertuso there is another attractive *festa* two weeks later, the **Sagra del Fagiolo** or 'Feast of the Bean'.

Festa di San Gennaro, in Naples, 19 September. This major event commemorates Naples' patron saint, with a service held in the cathedral to witness the miracle of the liquefaction of his blood (for further details of this most Neapolitan of *festas, see* p.801). Afterwards, relieved citizens (the miracle always works) take to the streets to watch the silver statue of the saint being paraded through the streets. Needless to say, no one goes to work that day.

Festa dell'Immacolata (Feast of the Immaculate Conception), at Torre del Greco, 8 December. More than 100 local men carry a huge triumphal float, topped by the Madonna, through the streets, to commemorate the town's lucky escape from the 1861 eruption of Vesuvius.

Naples

> *The most loathsome nest of human caterpillars I was ever forced*
> *to stay in—a hell with all the devils imbecile in it.*
>
> John Ruskin

For many, Naples is the true homeland of a particular Italian fantasy, the last bastion of singing waiters and red-checked tablecloths, operatic passion and colourful poverty, balanced precariously between Love's own coastline and the menace of Vesuvius. But mention Naples or the Neapolitans to any modern, respectable north Italian, and as they gesticulate and roll their eyes to heaven you will get a first-hand lesson in the dynamics of Italy's 'Problem of the South'. Many Italians simply cannot accept that such an outlandish place can be in the same country with them, a sentiment that probably contains as much envy as contempt. Naples, the city that has given the world Enrico Caruso, Sophia Loren, pizza and syphilis (the disease appeared here in 1495, and was immediately blamed on the French garrison), may also be the first city to make social disorder into an art form.

Degradation, Italian Style

On Naples' Piazza Garibaldi you can buy a boiled pigs' organ on a stick, served with a slice of lemon, and watch eight-year-old *scugnizzi*—street children—puff on contraband Marlboros while casually tossing firecrackers into traffic. Fireworks, along with slamming doors, impromptu arias, screams, ambulance sirens and howling cats, are an essential part of the Neapolitan ambience. This anarchic symphony is harder to catch these days, unfortunately, drowned as it is under the roar of Italy's worst traffic problem. In central Naples, three-quarters of a million rude drivers chase each other around a street plan that hasn't changed much since Roman times. Meanwhile, the nation's worst air pollution keeps the hospitals full, in spite of occasional half-hearted attempts to solve the problem by only allowing drivers to take their cars out on alternate days. Every few weeks some old lady on a back alley burns to a crisp while the firemen, just down the block, gamely push illegally parked cars out of their way.

Another chronic problem is housing, enough of a nightmare even before the earthquake of 1980; on the outskirts of the city, you may see Napoletani living in stolen ship cargo containers, with windows cut in the sides, in shacks made of sheet metal and old doors, or in abandoned buses. In the city centre thousands of earthquake refugees are still camping in hotels. One bizarre side-effect of this housing shortage—found all over Italy, but particularly visible here—is the 'quivering car' phenomenon. You'll see them everywhere, especially up on Posillipo hill, cars parked nose to tail, their windows blacked out with newspaper, turned into temporary bedrooms by courting couples or even married couples who have no privacy at home. A cruel but popular prank with Neapolitan kids is to sneak up on the cars and set fire to the newspaper.

Reform has been the buzz word in recent years but the city still has to deal with the spectre of the Camorra, a loose term for the crime syndicates that keep Naples as securely strung up as any mountain village in Sicily. Crime is so well organized here that , to give one example, seagoing smugglers have formed a trade union to protect their interests against the police.

In the 18th century, when the city and its spectacular setting were a highlight of the Grand Tour, the saying was 'See Naples and die...'. Nowadays you usually can't see much of anything through the smog, and you'll probably survive if you're careful crossing streets. Don't let Naples' current degradation spoil your visit, though; you haven't seen Italy—no, you haven't seen the Mediterranean—until you have spent some time in this fascinating metropolis. The only thing subtle about Naples is its charm, and the city will probably win your heart at the same time as it is deranging your senses.

On the Other Hand...

If Naples immediately repels you, however, it means you are probably a sticky sort, and will miss all the fun. The city has an incomparable setting, and much of it is still admittedly beautiful, but its real attraction is a priceless insight into humanity, at the hands of a population of 2.2 million dangerous anarchists. The Napoletani may be numbered among the few peoples of Europe who realize they are alive, and try to enjoy it as best they can. Their history being what it is, this manifests itself in diverse ways.

The Napoletani do not stand in lines, or fill out forms, or stop for traffic signals; they will talk your ears off, run you over in their ancient Fiats, criticize the way you dress, whisper alarming propositions, give you sweets, try to pick your pockets with engaging artlessness, offer surprising kindnesses, and with a reassuring smile they will always, always give you the wrong directions. In an official capacity, they will either break the rules for you or invent new ones; in shops and restaurants, they will either charge you too much or too little. The former is much more common, though whichever it is, they will undoubtedly do it with a flourish.

If the accounts of long-ago travellers are to be believed, Naples has always been like this. Too much sunshine, and living under such a large and ill-mannered volcano, must contribute much to the effect. It would be somewhat harder to explain some of Naples' ancient distinctions. First and foremost, Naples is Italy's city of philosophers. Her greatest, Giambattista Vico, was a Neapolitan, and others, such as St Thomas Aquinas and Benedetto Croce, spent much of their time here.

Naples can also claim to be first in music. Among native composers are Gesualdo, Scarlatti and Leoncavallo, and the conservatory is claimed to be the oldest in Europe. Even today, members of the opera company at San Carlo look down on their colleagues at Milan's La Scala as a band of promising upstarts who could stand to take their jobs a little more seriously. Neapolitan popular song, expressive and intense, is an unchained Italian stereotype; the Napoletani maintain its traditions as jealously as they do their impenetrable dialect, one of the most widely spoken and robust in modern Italy.

History

Naples' rise to become the metropolis of Campania was largely the result of the lucky elimination of her rivals over the centuries. Capua, Cumae and Benevento rose and fell, and Pompeii and Herculaneum disappeared under volcanic ash, but fortune has always seemed to protect Naples from the really big disasters. As a Greek colony founded by Cumae in 750 BC, the city began with the name Neapolis (*new city*), and prospered moderately throughout the periods of Greek, Samnite and Roman rule. Belisarius, Justinian's famous general, seized the region for Byzantium in 536, after invasions of the Goths and Vandals, but a duke of Naples declared the city independent in 763, acknowledging only the authority of the pope.

The chronicles are understandably slim for this period; early medieval Naples offers us more fairy tales than facts. Many of its early legends deal with none other than the poet Virgil; somehow, folklore in the dark ages had transformed the greatest Latin poet into Master Virgil, a mighty magician who was given credit for many of the unexplainable engineering feats of the ancient Romans. Naples claimed him for its founder, and its legends told of how he built the Castel dell'Ovo, balancing it on an egg at the bottom of the harbour. Master Virgil also built a talking statue that warned the city of enemies, earthquakes or plagues, and medieval chroniclers mention the bronze horses and bronze fly he built over two of the city's gates, still to be seen in those days, and said to be magical charms on which the fortune of the city depended.

Naples lost its independence to the Normans in 1139, later passing under the rule of the Hohenstaufen emperors along with the rest of southern Italy. Charles of Anjou took over in 1266, and lopped off the head of the last Hohenstaufen, Conradin, in what is now Naples' Piazza del Mercato. Under the Angevins, Naples for the first time assumed the status and architectural embellishments of a capital. The Angevin kings of Naples, however, did little to develop their new realm, expending most of their energy in futile attempts to recapture Sicily, lost to them after the Sicilian Vespers revolution of 1282. After their line expired in 1435, with the death of Giovanni II, the kingdom fell to Alfonso V of Aragon—a fateful event, marking Spain's first foothold on the Italian mainland.

Habsburgs and Bourbons

Aragonese rule seemed promising at first, under the enlightened Alfonso. Later, though, it became clear that the Spaniards were mainly interested in milking Italy for taxes to finance further conquests. The city itself, as the seat of the viceregal court, prospered greatly; by 1600 its population of 280,000 made it perhaps the largest city on the Mediterranean. The long period of Spanish control did much to give Naples its distinct character, especially during the 17th and 18th centuries, when the city participated almost joyfully in the decadence and decay of the Spanish Empire. This period saw the construction of the scores of frilly, gloomy Baroque churches—now half-abandoned, with bushes growing out of the cornices—that add so much to the Neapolitan scene. In manners especially, the imperial Spanish influence was felt. 'Nothing', in the words of one observer, 'is cheaper here than human life.'

In 1707, during the War of the Spanish Succession, Naples passed under the rule of Archduke Charles of Austria. Prince Charles of Bourbon, however, snatched it away in 1734, and mouldering, picturesque Naples for the next 150 years made the perfect backdrop for the Rococo shenanigans of the new Bourbon kingdom. The new rulers were little improvement over the Spaniards, but immigrants from all over the south poured into the city, chasing the thousands of ducats dropped by a free-spending court. Naples became the most densely populated city in Europe (a distinction it still holds today) and crime and epidemics became widespread. Nevertheless, this was the Naples that became a major attraction for thousands of northern aesthetes doing the Grand Tour in the 18th and 19th centuries. Goethe flirted with contessas here, while the English poets were flirting with dread diseases and Lord Nelson was making eyes at Lady Hamilton. The Neapolitans are frank about it; Naples owed its prominence on the Grand Tour less to Vesuvius and the ruins of Pompeii than to good old-fashioned sex. Naples at the time was incontestably the easiest place in Europe to find some, and everyone knew it—saving Goethe and the rest the trouble of ever mentioning the subject in their travel accounts and letters home.

Garibaldi's army entered Naples in February 1861. As the new Italy's biggest basket case, the city has since received considerable assistance with its planning and social problems—though unfortunately not nearly enough to make up for the centuries of neglect. The Second World War didn't help; for four days in late September 1944, the city staged a heroic though unsuccessful revolt against the Germans. Even more damage was done by Allied bombing, not forgetting the destruction of the city's port and utilities by the retreating Nazis. While the postwar period saw considerable rebuilding, it also brought new calamities. Illegal and speculative building projects grabbed most of the already-crowded city's open space (you'll notice the almost total absence of parks), and turned the fringe areas into a nightmare of human detritus, one of the eeriest industrial wastelands of Europe.

In the political turmoil that has taken over Italy since the beginning of the nineties, with the collapse of the old parties, Naples has become one of the major bases of support for the neo-Fascists. It has, however, marked up one genuine accomplishment in the books in the last few years, though not one that will have much effect on the most serious problems—the *Centro Direzionale*, a huge modernistic development on the lines of a Neapolitan Manhattan built over the wastelands around Corso Malta, north of the Central Station. In spite of a few hiccups, most notably when the new palace of justice was mysteriously burnt to the ground (no prizes for guessing by whom), the project is currently nearing completion, its aim being to provide a new centre for the regional economy.

Bassolino, the anti-Mafia mayor who in 1994 narrowly beat Alessandra Mussolini, Benito's granddaughter and Sophia Loren's niece, is nearing the end of his second term. In his first term, the worst of the ghettos around the port went, tourist trails across Spaccanapoli were encouraged, and churches and sites long closed were reopened. Most spectacularly of all, the Piazza del Plebiscito, for a long time choked by traffic and fated to remain the city's parking lot, was emptied and cleaned up. But the excitement has fizzled out—Camorra families are still bombing each other right in the middle of town and Bassolino has lost his halo. He is now accused of addressing only the outer layer of Naples' problems rather than tackling major issues and, even worse, of anointing his successor before his term ends. At the moment there seems to be a common realization that Naples has reached a point of no return. It has either to clean itself up or perish; discussions of the city's problems in the press are often conducted in alarmingly apocalyptic tones. Leave some room for exaggeration—the Napoletani probably couldn't enjoy life properly without a permanent state of crisis.

by air

Naples' **Capodichino airport** is on the north side of the city, relatively close to the centre. It has frequent direct services to and from all major Italian destinations and to many foreign cities, including London (several flights daily). For airport information, call ✆ 081 789 6111. From 6am to midnight there is a bus service every 50 minutes (a blue bus run by Sepsa), between the airport and Piazza Municipio near the ferry harbour. For the Stazione Centrale there is the half-hourly city bus (no.14) which does not run as late. The journey takes 20–45mins, depending on the time of day. As on all city buses, tickets should be bought at a newsstand or ticket booth before boarding. Lastly, Curreri (✆ 081 801 5420) runs four daily buses (*at 9, 2, 4.30 and 7*) to Sorrento departing from the stop outside the Arrivals hall (on the right).

If you opt for a taxi, remember that on top of the fare on the meter you will officially be charged extra supplements for the airport trip and for luggage—plus, very possibly, additional unexplained 'extras' as well (*see* below). Try to agree on the fare to your destination before getting into the cab. If traffic is not too heavy—and this is a big if— the fare to the centre should not exceed L40,000.

by sea

Naples' port has more ship and hydrofoil connections than anywhere else in the Mediterranean, so you can choose to arrive by sea from—or flee to—a wide variety of places, among them the islands in the Bay of Naples, Sicily and the Aeolian Islands. Generally, ferries are cheaper than hydrofoils, but take approximately twice as long. One of the loveliest of the possible sea excursions is the night ferry to the Aeolian Islands, which arrives as the sun is rising over Vulcano.

Ferries and hydrofoils leave from three different points in Naples, but most longer-distance ferries operate from the **Stazione Marittima**, in the centre of the port near the Castel Nuovo. Consult the individual companies for timetables, otherwise look in the daily newspaper *Il Mattino*, or in *Qui Napoli.* The main companies operating from Stazione Marittima are **Tirrenia**, ✆ 081 720 1111, for Palermo and Cagliari; and **Siremar**, ✆ 081 720 1595, for the Aeolian Islands and Milazzo in Sicily. In addition, one company, **SNAV**, ✆ 081 761 23 48, operates a twice-a-day long-distance hydrofoil service from Mergellina quay to the Aeolian Islands. For more information on all boat services from Naples and hydrofoil services to the islands and ports around the bay, *see* pp.824–25 and p.838.

by rail and bus

Most visitors arrive by train at the modern **Stazione Centrale** on Piazza Garibaldi, which is also a junction for city buses and the local *Circumvesuviana* railway. Trains along the coast towards Rome or Reggio di Calabria pass through every half-hour on average. In addition, many trains also stop at **Napoli Mergellina** and **Napoli Campi Flegrei**, on the western side of the city. As well as the state FS lines, there are three **local railway lines** serving the Bay of Naples area. For more information on these regional rail lines *see* pp.812–14.

Most bus services to destinations within the province and the Campania region operate from Piazza Garibaldi, in front of the FS Stazione Centrale. An exception is the service to Salerno along the coast, which runs from Via Pisanelli, near Piazza Municipio (*see* p.814).

by road

The Naples inner ring road, the *tangenziale*, leads around the back of the city towards Pozzuoli and the Campi Flegrei. Using the *tangenziale* makes it possible to reach most of the city without going through the centre. Traffic going further south should stay on the A2 until it meets the A3, avoiding the city entirely. Once you arrive at wherever you are staying, you are categorically advised to park your car in a safe place (such as a hotel garage) and not attempt to use it anywhere within the city (*see* below).

Tourist Information

The best place to go for information about Naples itself is the well-run and friendly information booth run by the city's **Azienda Autonoma di Soggiorno** on Piazza del Gesù Nuovo, © 081 552 3328/ © 081 551 2701, in the old town (*open Mon–Sat 8.30–7.30, Sun 8.30–3.30, hols 9–2*). Their main office is in the Royal Palace, © 081 252 5711, ✉ 081 418 619.

Parco di Capodimonte

TANGENZIALE EST-OVEST DI NAPOLI

To Capodichino Airport →

VIA DON BOSCO

Museo Nazionale di Capodimonte

CORSO AMADEO DI SAVOIA

VIA TERESA D. SCALZI

VIA S. TERESA D.

Botanical Gardens

VIA FORIA

VIA ARENACCIA

Catacombe S. Gaudioso

VIA DI CRISTALLINI

VIA BELLA

VIA SANITA

VIA STELLA

CORSO G. GARIBALDI

CORSO NAVARA

Porta Gennaro

Piazzetta S. Carlo all'Arena

S. Giovanni a Carbonara

Pza. San Francesco da Paola

VIA CASANOVA

Stazione Centrale

Museo Nazionale

Piazza Cavour

VIA DI CIRILLO

VIA CARBONARA

Piazza Enrico Nicola

Porta Capuana

Pza. Principe Umberto

Pza. Museo Nazionale

S. Maria Donnaregina

Castel Capuano

Largo Madonna delle Grazie

VIA DUOMO

Girolamini

Duomo

Piazza Garibaldi

VIA DEI TRIBUNALI

CORSO ARNALDO LUCCI

Teatro Bellini

P. Miraglia

P. Bellini

1

Pza. Calenda

Porta Alba

Pza. Dante

3

VIA S. BIAGIO DEI LIBRAI

2

Palazzo Como

Pza. Nolana

Pza. Calenda

Porta Nolana

5 4

Pza. S. Pietro Colletta

VIALE LAVINAIO

Gesù Nuovo

VIA BENEDETTO CROCE

6

Piazza Nicola Amore

GARIBALDI

Montesanto

Pza. Gesù Nuovo

8 7 S. CHIARA

MEZZOCANNONE

CORSO UMBERTO I

Piazza del Mercato

Pza. Pepe

Pza. del Carmine

Porta del Carmine

VIA TOLEDO

Piazza Carità

9

V. MONTEOLIVETO

VIA G. SANFELICE

SEDILE DI PORTO

VIA NUOVA MARINA

10

VIA ARMANDO DIAZ

P. Matteotti

Pza. Giovanni Bovio

Pza. Principessa Margherita

Municipio

VIA CERVANTES

VIA MEDINA

VIA AGOSTINO DEPRETIS

VIA A. CUC DE GASPERI

Galleria Umberto I

VIA G. VERDI

Pza. Municipio

VIA A CRISTOFORO COLOMBO

Teatro Mercadante

Stazione Marittima

Molo Martello

Molo Cesario Console

Pza. Trento e Trieste

VITTORIO EMANUELE

Castelnuovo

Teatro S. Carlo

Palazzo Reale

Molo Beverello

Piazza del Plebiscito

Giardini Pubblici

VIA FERDINANDO ACTON

Molo S. Vincenzo

VIA N. SAURO

VIA PARTENHOPE

Porto San Lucia

1 S. Lorenzo Maggiore
2 S. Gregorio Armeno
3 San Severo
4 S. Giuseppe
5 S. Domenico Maggiore
6 Monastero di S. Chiara
7 Pal.Gravina
8 Pal.Penna
9 S. Anna dei Lombardi
10 Poste e Telegrafi

In summer they open offices in the Castel dell'Ovo, ℡ 081 764 5688. Information about excursions outside the city and so on is only available from the less helpful provincial tourist office **EPT**, Piazza dei Martiri 58, ℡ 081 405 311. The EPT has another office at the Stazione Centrale, ℡ 081 268 779, which may be some help in finding a hotel. Two others are to be found at the airport, ℡ 081 780 5761, and the Stazione Mergellina, ℡ 081 761 2102. The **EPT** produce good maps of the city centre and the bay itself (both free of charge). Look out for the excellent free monthly handbook, *Qui Napoli*, available at tourist offices and some hotels, which carries a great deal of useful information, timetables, listings and calendars of events. In an attempt to draw visitors into the old city, Naples has set up designated walks and keeps the points of interest along them open longer hours. Information on accompanied walks is available from the **AAST** at Piazza del Gesù Nuovo. For a fascinating trip around subterranean Naples, **Laes** (Libera Associazione Escursionisti Sottosuolo, ℡ 081 400 256), operate guided tours from Piazza Trieste e Trento (next to Piazza del Plebiscito) (*weekends at 10am*).

Getting Around

Transport around the city is a fascinating subject. Such is the state of most public transport and so impenetrable is the traffic that walking is often by far the most practical way of getting anywhere, apart from up to the heights by the *funicolari*. Orientation is a little difficult. If you arrive by sea—the only proper way to do it—you'll get a good idea of the layout. Naples' dominant landmarks, visible from almost anywhere in town, are Castel Sant'Elmo and the huge, fortress-like monastery of San Martino. They are neighbours on the steep hill that slopes down to the sea near the port, neatly dividing the city into its old and new quarters.

Modern Naples is on the western side, the busy, pleasant districts of Mergellina, Vomero and Fuorigrotta, to which middle-class Napoletani escape from the city centre at the end of each day, on their creaking old funicular railways. To the east, towards Vesuvius, lies the centre, along Via Toledo, and beyond it the oldest neighbourhoods, tall tenements jammed into a grid of narrow streets, reaching a climax in the oriental bazaar atmosphere around the Piazza del Mercato and the Piazza Garibaldi.

by bus

Given the problems involved in using cars and even taxis in Naples, visitors often find themselves left with the buses, which is small cheer, since the city has the worst bus system in Italy. Buses will be slow and usually indecently crowded. There are no schedules, no maps, and nowhere you can get accurate information; even the drivers rarely have the faintest idea what is happening. The ultimate Neapolitan experience is waiting an hour for a bus after being misinformed by line employees, and then finding out that the right bus is the one marked 'out of service'.

The confusion is compounded by the recent division of services run by the old bus company Atam under its successor ANM and other smaller companies. Most bus lines start at either Piazza Garibaldi or Piazza del Plebiscito. Some that might be useful are: **R2**, from Piazza Garibaldi to Corso Umberto and Piazza Municipio; **R3**, from Piazza Municipio to Riviera di Chiaia and Mergellina; **110/127**, from Piazza Garibaldi to Piazza Cavour and Capodimonte; **152**, from Piazza Garibaldi to Pozzuoli.

One benefit of reforms aimed at cleaning up the city's image and attracting tourists is the introduction of the new-style 'Giranapoli' ('Around Naples') bus tickets. There are two types, one lasting 90 minutes for L1500, and a day ticket for L4500. If you plan on staying in Naples for more than nine days invest in a monthly pass (L45,000), enabling you to travel on buses, the funiculars and the Metropolitana throughout the city.

The relatively new Artebus service runs through the most interesting areas of town and can be used for short hops between sights. It departs from Mergellina and must be arranged through your hotel (*Fri–Sun; free*).

by Metro and funicolare

Naples also has a sort of underground. The **Metropolitana FS**, a single line from Gianturco to Pozzuoli, is really a part of the state railway, and uses the same underground tracks as the long-distance trains. The FS runs it as anarchically as the buses, but it will be helpful for reaching the station (Piazza Garibaldi), the archaeological museum, points in Vomero and Fuorigrotta, and Solfatara. As on the buses, few people ever buy tickets.

A much more agreeable way to travel, though you can't go very far, is on the three *funicolari*, or inclined railways, up to Vomero. The longest—one of the longest in the world, in fact—is the **Funicolare Centrale**, from Via Toledo, just behind the Galleria, up to Via Cimarosa. The **Funicolare di Chiaia** also ends nearby in the same street, having started from Piazza Amedeo in Chiaia. Finally, the **Funicolare di Montesanto** travels up to Via Morghen from Montesanto Station, the start of the suburban Circumflegrea and Cumana rail lines. All three *funicolari* bring you out near the San Martino Museum and the Castel Sant'Elmo. All run daily until about 10pm.

by taxi

Neapolitan taxi drivers are uniformly dishonest, and try out any number of scams involving fixed meters, turning the meter on before you get in the car, imaginary 'surcharges' and so on. Also, the traffic is frequently so thick that relatively short journeys can take so long (and cost so much) that they're really not worth it. If you want to take a taxi to a specific destination, always try to agree on the fare in advance, whether there is a meter or not.

by car

The first thing to get straight is simply—*leave your car elsewhere*. Cars disappear in Naples with alarming frequency, and foreign number plates are especially prized. Even if you get to keep your wheels, you'll be sorry. Driving in Naples is a unique experience. Motorists studiously disregard all traffic signals and warnings, and the city has given up trying to coerce them. There are no rules, except to get there first, and fatalities are common. For scant sympathy about stolen cars, call the city police, © 081 794 1435. Check with hotels if they have secure parking (*parcheggio custodito*). If not, you might want to use the private car parks. Overnight stays can cost L20,000 and more.

Piazza del Plebiscito

After decades as a parking lot, this immense and elegant square, the centre of modern Naples, has been rescued and restored to the city. Children now come here at sundown to kick a football, under the eyes of adoring parents. The recent shows staged here by the city for the benefit of national television have even forced some northern Italians to admit Naples may not be so bad after all. The huge domed church, embracing the piazza in its curving colonnades as does St Peter's in Rome, is **San Francesco di Paola**. King Ferdinand IV, after the British restored him to power in 1815, made a vow to construct it; the great dome and classical portico were modelled after the Pantheon in Rome.

Across the square rises the equally imposing bulk of the **Palazzo Reale** (Royal Palace) (*© 081 580 8111; open Mon–Sat 9.30am–10pm, Sun and hols 9.30–8; closed Wed; adm*), begun by the Spanish viceroys in 1600, expanded by the Bourbons and finished by the kings of Italy. Umberto I, a good friend of the Neapolitans, added the eight giant figures on the façade, representing the eight houses that have ruled at Naples. It seems the 19th-century sculptors had trouble taking some of them seriously; note the preposterous figures of Charles of Anjou, whom the Neapolitans never liked, and Vittorio Emanuele II. There are Ruritanian stone sentry boxes and stone peacocks in the courtyard to recall the Bourbons, and a number of rooms inside that can be visited—the ones that escaped the bombings in the Second World War, including a suitably grand staircase, a theatre and several chambers in 18th-century style. The theatre saw the premieres of many of the works of Alessandro Scarlatti. The rear of the palace, now the home of Naples' important **Biblioteca Nazionale**, faces a pretty, little-visited garden across from the Castel Nuovo.

The Bourbons were great opera buffs, and they built Italy's largest opera house, the **San Carlo**, right next to their palace. Begun in 1737, making it older than La Scala, the theatre was sumptuously restored after a fire in 1816, during the period when Naples was the unquestioned capital of opera; so important was the theatre to the people of Naples that King Ferdinand made sure the workmen got the job done in record time—300 days. Today the San Carlo is still among the most prestigious opera houses in the world (the Neapolitans of course would place it first), and its productions are certainly among the most polished and professional, and occasionally among the most adventurous. Each season at least one lesser-known Neapolitan opera is performed. Tickets are as expensive as anywhere (up to L500,000 on an opening night). Brief tours of the theatre are possible for considerably less (*© 081 797 2111*).

Opposite the San Carlo is the grandest interior of southern Italy, the **Galleria Umberto I**. This great glass-roofed arcade, perhaps the largest in the world, was begun in 1887, nine years after the Galleria Vittorio Emanuele in Milan. The arcade is cross-shaped, with a mosaic of the zodiac on the floor at the centre, and its dome is 184ft tall; surprisingly, the Neapolitans do not seem to like it as much as they once did; even at high noon, you are likely to find its vast spaces deserted but for a few small clouds of grey-suited men arguing politics around the entrances.

Castel Nuovo

Offices open Mon–Fri 8–1, © 081 795 2003; museums Mon–Sat 9–7; adm.

The port of Naples has been protected by this odd, beautiful castle, looming over the harbour behind the Palazzo Reale and San Carlo, for some 700 years now. Charles of Anjou built it in 1279; many Napoletani still call it by the curious name of *Maschio Angioino*. Most of what you see today, however, including the eccentric, ponderous round towers, is the work of Guillermo Sagrera, the great Catalan architect who built the famous Exchange in Palma de Mallorca. Between two of these towers at the entrance, the conquering Aragonese hired the finest sculptors from all over Italy to build Alfonso's **Triumphal Arch**, a unique masterpiece of Renaissance sculpture and design inspired by the triumphal arches of the ancient Romans. The symbolism, as in the Roman arches, may be a little confusing. The figure at the top is St Michael; below him are a matched pair of sea gods, and further down, allegorical virtues and relief panels portraying Alfonso's victories and wise governance.

Inside, the castle currently houses parts of the Naples city administration and some cultural societies. If you come during office hours, someone will probably be around to show you the **Sala dei Baroni**, where the city council meets; it has a cupola with an unusual Moorish vaulting, an eight-pointed star made of interlocking arches. King Ferrante used this as his dining hall, and it takes its name from the evening when he invited a score of the kingdom's leading barons to a ball, and then arrested the lot.

There are also two museums: one, housed in the Gothic **Cappella Palatina**, next to the council hall, contains 14th- and 15th-century frescoes; the other, in the south wing, has paintings, and a good collection of silver and bronzes, from the 15th century to the present day.

Via Toledo

From the landward side of Piazza del Plebiscito and the Palace, Naples' most imposing street, Via Toledo, runs northwards past the Galleria to Piazza Carita where it becomes Via Roma. Its name commemorates its builder, Don Pedro de Toledo, the Spanish viceroy at the beginning of the 16th century, and a great benefactor of Naples. Stendhal, in 1817, rightly called this 'the most populous and gayest street in the world', and it is still the city's main business and shopping street, leading up to Capodimonte and the northern suburbs.

Don Pedro's elegant Renaissance tomb, among others, can be seen in the little church of **San Giacomo degli Spagnuoli**, now swallowed up by the 19th-century Palazzo Municipale complex, originally home to the Bourbon royal bureaucracy.

Going north along Via Toledo, any street on your left can be the entrance to the dense, crumbling, slightly sinister inner sanctum of the Neapolitan soul, the vast slum called the *Quartieri Spagnuoli*. It can be a fascinating place to walk around, in daytime at least. Lately though, thanks to battling factions of the Camorra, the *Quartieri* has achieved even more than its accustomed share of notoriety; for a while the hoods were bumping each other off at a rate of one per week. Though the *Quartieri* covers almost all the area sloping up to San Martino and Vomero, the most populous and colourful part is that immediately adjoining Via Toledo, a strict grid of narrow streets laid out by Don Pedro de Toledo and now called the *Tavoliere*, or chessboard.

To the right of Via Toledo, the confusion of Naples' half-crumbling, half-modern business centre conceals a few buildings worth a look. The **Palazzo Gravina**, on Via Monteoliveto, is a fine palace in the northern Renaissance style, built between 1513 and 1549. It now houses Naples University's Faculty of Architecture. Almost directly across the street, the church of **Monteoliveto** (*open Tues–Sat 8.30–12.30*) is a little treasure house of late-Renaissance sculpture and painting, with tombs and altars in the chapels by southern artists like Giovanni da Nola and Antonio Rosellino, as well as some frescoes by Vasari.

Spaccanapoli

This street's familiar name means 'Split-Naples', and that is exactly what it has done for the last 2600 years. On the map it changes its name with alarming frequency—Via Benedetto Croce and Via San Biagio dei Librai are two of the most prominent—but in Roman times you would have found it by asking for the *decumanus inferior*, the name for the second east–west street in any planned Roman city. No large city in all the lands conquered by Rome has maintained its ancient street plan as completely as Naples (the Greeks laid out these streets, of course, but the Romans learned their planning from them). It is easier to imagine the atmosphere of a big ancient city here than in Rome itself, or even in Pompeii. The narrow, straight streets and tall *insulae* cannot have changed much; only the forum and temples are missing. This is the heart of old Naples—and what a street it is, lined with grocery barrows and scholarly bookshops, shops that sell old violins, plaster saints, pizza, or used clothes pegs. Drama is supplied by the arch-Neapolitan characters who live here, haunting the street-corners and entertaining wan hopes of dodging the manic motorists; the colour comes from the district's laundry—down any of the long alleys of impossibly tall tenements you may see as many as a hundred full clothes-lines, swelling bravely in the breeze and hoping for a glint of southern sun. It has always been a poor neighbourhood, though even now it is not a desperate one. As always, its people live much of their life on the streets, carrying on whatever is their business from makeshift benches on the kerbs.

The Gesù Nuovo and Santa Chiara

Your introduction to this world, just off Via Toledo, is the cramped, disorderly, most characteristic of Neapolitan squares: **Piazza del Gesù Nuovo**, decorated by the gaudiest and most random of Neapolitan decorations, the **Guglia della Immacolata**. A *guglia* is a kind of Rococo obelisk, dripping with frills, saints and *putti*, of which there are three, all in this area. The unsightly, unfinished façade behind the Guglia, covered with pyramidal extrusions in dark basalt, belongs to the church of **Gesù Nuovo**. Strange as it is, the façade, originally part of a late 15th-century palace, has become one of the landmarks of Naples. The interior is typically lavish Neapolitan Baroque, gloriously overdone in acres of coloured marbles and frescoes, some by Solimena. One of his best works (dated 1725) is here, inside above the main door, depicting three angels driving the Syrian minister Eliodorus out of the Temple of Jerusalem.

Santa Chiara, just across the piazza, dates from the early 14th century, though it once had a Baroque interior as good as the Gesù; Allied bombers remodelled it to suit modern tastes in 1943, and only a few of the original Angevin tombs have survived. Don't miss the adjacent **Chiostro delle Clarisse** (*open April–Sept Mon–Sat 8.30–12.30 and 4–6.30; Oct–Mar Mon–Sat 8.30–12.30 and 4–6*), the loveliest and most peaceful spot in Naples—especially in contrast to the neighbourhood outside. So much in Naples shows the Spanish influence—like the use of the title 'Don', now largely limited to Camorra bosses—and here someone in the 1740s transplanted the Andalucian love of pictures done in painted *azulejo* tiles, turning a simple monkish cloister into a little fairyland of gaily coloured arbours, benches and columns, shaded by the only trees in the whole district.

In a vestibule off the cloister, the restorers found some earlier, highly original paintings of the Last Judgement hiding under Baroque frescoes. These were uncovered and restored, revealing an inspired 16th-century vision of the event, in a style utterly unlike the slick virtuosity of the time, with plenty of novel tortures for the damned, and angels welcoming some cute naked nuns among the elect. The **Museo dell'Opera di S. Chiara** (℗ *081 797 1256; open Thurs–Tues 9.30–1 and 3.30–5.30, Sat and Sun 9.30–1; adm*), at the rear of the cloister, houses the church treasures, marbles and an area of archaeological excavations.

The Cappella Sansevero

A few streets further down Via Benedetto Croce is tiny Piazza San Domenico, which has monuments from Naples' three most creative periods. **San Domenico Maggiore** (*under restoration*) built between 1283 and 1324, was the Dominican church in Naples. St Thomas Aquinas lived in the adjacent monastery. Later this became the favourite church of the Spanish, and it contains some interesting Renaissance funerary monuments; a better one, though, is across the piazza in the church of **Sant'Angelo a Nilo** (*open daily 8–1 and 4–7.15*)—the tomb of Cardinal Brancaccio, designed by Michelozzo, with a relief of the *Assumption of the Virgin* by Donatello (the two artists had collaborated before on the baptistry in Siena). The second of the Baroque pinnacles decorates the Piazza, the **Guglia di San Domenico**, begun after a plague in 1650. Best of all, just around the corner on Via F. de Sanctis, you can inspect Neapolitan Rococo at its very queerest in the **Sansevero Chapel** (*open Nov–June Mon–Sat 10–5; July–Oct Mon–Sat 10–6, Sun 10–1.30; adm*).

Prince Raimondo di Sangro (b. 1701), who was responsible for the final form of this, his family's private chapel, was a strange bird, a sort of aristocratic dilettante mystic. Supposedly there is a grand allegorical scheme behind the arrangement of the sculptures and frescoes he commissioned, but a work like this, only 200 years old, seems as foreign to our sensibilities and understanding as some Mayan temple. The sculptures, by little-known Neapolitan artists like Giuseppe Sammartino and Antonio Corradini, are inscrutable allegories in themselves, often executed with a breathtakingly showy virtuosity. Francesco Queirolo's *Il Disinganno* (disillusion) is an extreme case; nobody else, perhaps, has ever tried to carve a fishing-net, or the turning pages of a book, out of marble. Others, such as Sammartino's *Cristo Velato*, display a remarkable illusion of figures under transparent veils. There are a dozen or so of these large sculptural groups, all under a crazy heavenly vortex in the ceiling fresco, by Francesco Mario Russo. Down in the crypt are two complete human cardiovascular systems, removed from the bodies and preserved by Prince Raimondo in the course of his alchemical experiments.

Near San Domenico, a block south of the Spacca, is Naples' **University**, one of Europe's oldest and most distinguished. Emperor Frederick II founded it in 1224, as a 'Ghibelline' university to counter the pope's 'Guelph' university at Bologna, as well as to provide scholars and trained officials for the new state he was trying to build. It still occupies its ancient, woefully overcrowded quarters around Via Mezzocannone.

Around the Piazza del Duomo

Continuing down the Spaccanapoli (now Via San Biagio dei Librai), just around the corner on Via San Gregorio is **San Gregorio Armeno** (*chapels under restoration*), with another gaudy Baroque interior. In December, this street and others around it become Naples' famous Christmas Market, where everyone comes to buy figurines of the Holy Family, the Three Kings and all the other accessories required for their Christmas *presepi*, or manger scenes, one of the most devotedly followed of local traditions. For several weeks, hundreds of stands fill up the neighbourhood's narrow streets.

Presepi

It would not be easy to explain why the genius of Naples should have chosen Christmas cribs as a subject to elevate to an art form. After philosophy, pizza and music, it's what this city does best. Churches and private homes have always had a little competitive edge on when they begin their displays (some time in November, if not earlier).

The most extreme cases have been assembled inside the Museo Nazionale di San Martino. One is as big as a bus, and must have taken someone a lifetime; another is fitted inside an eggshell—with over a hundred figures in it. The best parts are the large, finely carved individual wooden or ceramic figures. Most represent Neapolitans of two or three centuries ago from every walk of life; with their painstakingly detailed and expressive faces, each is a genuine portrait. To have them all here in one place is like old Bourbon Naples appearing before your eyes.

Convention requires that, quite apart from the Holy Family, certain things be present in every crib. Besides the usual angels, shepherds and animals, a Roman ruin is absolutely necessary, as are several Turks in Ottoman Empire dress (which come in handy if one of the Three Kings gets lost). A band of musicians is also expected, and all the better if they too are Turks. Beggars and dwarfs earn envy for the crib-maker—there is a whole display of figures called the 'deformities'—but above all there must be tons of food everywhere there is room for it. The best cribs have the busiest cooks and the most bulging pantries, with tiny wooden roast pigs, sausages, eggs, plates of macaroni, cheeses and fancy cakes—even a pizza or two. Look out for the giant *presepe* in the Galleria Umberto at Christmas time, and watch Neapolitans throw money at it to pay for its upkeep for another year.

A little further north up Via San Gregorio is **San Lorenzo Maggiore** (late 12th century), one of Naples' finest medieval churches; Petrarch lived for a while in the adjacent monastery. In addition, recent excavations have uncovered a considerable area of Greek and Roman remains on the site. Entering via the cloister, where the base of a Roman *macellum* (market place) is being excavated, head down the stairs at the very back to see this fascinating piece of subterranean Naples.

San Paolo, across the street, isn't much to see now but, before an earthquake wrecked it in the 17th century, its façade was the portico of an ancient Roman temple to Castor and Pollux. Andrea Palladio studied it closely, and it provided inspiration for his classical villas and churches in the Veneto.

After Spaccanapoli, **Via dei Tribunali** is the busiest street of old Naples, and has been for a long time. The arcades that line the street in places, a sort of continuous covered market, are a thousand years old or more. Here, at the otherwise unremarkable **Girolamini** (*open daily 9–1*), you may see the modest tomb (at present unapproachable due to conservation) of Naples's greatest philosopher, Giambattista Vico. Northwest of the Girolamini, around Via Anticaglia, you'll find a few crooked streets, the only ones in old Naples that do not stick to the rectilinear Roman plan. These follow the outline of the **Teatro Romano**, much of which still survives, hidden under the tenements. A few arches are all that is visible from the street.

The Cathedral of San Gennaro

The wide **Via del Duomo** is a breath of fresh air in this crowded district—exactly what the city intended when they ploughed it through Old Naples after the cholera epidemic of 1884. The **Duomo** itself (*interior under restoration*) is another fine medieval building, though it is hidden behind an awful pseudo-Gothic façade pasted on in 1905. The best things are inside: the Renaissance **Cappella Minùtolo**, the tomb of Charles of Anjou and the **Cappella del Tesoro di San Gennaro**, glittering with the gold and silver of the cathedral treasure, and with frescoes by Domenichino and Lanfranco, the latter a swirling *Paradiso* in the dome (1643).

The **Basilica Santa Restituta**, a sizeable church in its own right, is tacked on to the side of the cathedral. Its columns are thought to be from the temple of Apollo that once occupied the site. Begun in 324, though often rebuilt, this is the oldest building in Naples. The ceiling frescoes are by Luca Giordano. Just off the basilica, the 5th-century **baptistry** contains a good Byzantine-style mosaic by the 14th-century artist Lello di Roma; the baptismal font itself probably comes from an ancient temple of Dionysus. From Santa Restituta's chapel you can access a collection of archaeological remains dating from the Greeks to the Middle Ages (*open daily 9–12 and 4.30–7, Sun and hols 9–12; adm*). The last and most elaborate of the *guglie*, the **Guglia San Gennaro**, designed by Cosimo Fanzago, is just outside the south transept.

If the sacristan is around, you can visit the **crypt of San Gennaro**, patron of Naples, with elaborate marble decoration from the Renaissance, and the tomb of Pope Innocent IV. Whoever is really buried here, San Gennaro (Januarius) is a rather doubtful character; most likely he is a Christian assimilation of the Roman god Janus. The saint's head is kept upstairs in the chapel named after him, along with two phials of his blood that miraculously liquefy and 'boil' three times each year—the first Sunday in May, 19 September and 16 December—so as to prove that San Gennaro is still looking out for the Napoletani. The only time the miracle has ever failed, during the Napoleonic occupation, the people of the city became enormously excited and seemed ready to revolt. At this the French commander, a true son of the Enlightenment, announced that San Gennaro had 10 minutes to come through—or else he'd shoot the Archbishop. Somehow, just in time, the miracle occurred.

On a small piazza a block north of the Duomo, **Santa Maria Donnaregina** offers more overdone Baroque, but off to the side of this 17th-century work is the smaller, original church, built in 1307 by Queen Mary of Hungary (who was none other than the wife of Charles of Anjou; her title only reflects a claim to the throne). Her elaborate tomb, and some good frescoes from the first half of the 12th century, are the sights of the church. South of the cathedral in the Via del Duomo is the **Museo Filangieri** (*© 081 203 175; open Tues–Sat 9.30–2 and 3.30–7, Sun and hols 9.30–1.30; adm*), housed in the 15th-century Palazzo Cuomo, a small collection of china, armour and curiosities. Its picture collection includes works by some of Naples' favourite artists: Luca Giordano, Mattia Preti, Ribera and others. Almost all the collection was gathered in the last forty years. Count Filangieri's original collection was much larger, but the Nazis torched it before they left in 1944.

Piazza Garibaldi

In Italian, the word for a market stand is *bancarella*. In Naples they are as much a part of everyday life as in the Middle Ages. The greatest concentration can be found in the Forcella market district, in the narrow streets east off the Via del Duomo, selling everything from stereos to light bulbs. According to the economists, at least one-third of Naples' economy is underground—outright illegal, or at the least not paying taxes or subject to any regulation.

Bootleg cassette tapes are one example; Naples is one of the world leaders in this thriving industry, and you'll have your choice of thousands of titles along these streets, though it might be a good idea to get them to play your tape before you part with any money. Hundreds of tired-looking folk sit in front of little tables selling contraband American cigarettes. This is one of the easiest means for Naples' poor to make a living, and it is all controlled by the Camorra. As in New York, whenever it rains shady characters crawl out of the woodwork selling umbrellas. You will see plenty of designer labels on the *bancarelle* —if they're real, don't ask where they came from.

Piazza Mercato, one of the nodes of the Neapolitan bazaar, has been a market square perhaps since Roman times. In the old days this was always the site of major executions, most notably that of 16-year-old Conradin, the rightful heir to the throne, by Charles of Anjou in 1268, an act that shocked all Europe. Charles ordered him buried underneath the Piazza—he couldn't be laid in consecrated ground since he had just been excommunicated for political reasons by Charles' ally the pope.

In 1647 Masaniello's Revolt started here during the festival of Our Lady of Mount Carmel; Masaniello (Tommaso Aniello), a young fisherman from Amalfi, had been chosen by his fellow conspirators to step up in the middle of the ceremonies and proclaim to the people and the viceroy that the new tax the viceroy had introduced 'no longer existed'. As the plotters had hoped, a spontaneous rising followed, and for a week Masaniello ruled Naples while the frightened viceroy locked himself up in Castel Sant'Elmo.

In Naples, unfortunately, such risings can burn out as quickly as a match; the viceroy's spies first secretly drugged Masaniello, so that he appeared drunk or mad to the people, and then in an unguarded moment they murdered him and sent his head to the viceroy. That was the end for Naples, but the incident touched off a wave of revolts across the south that took the Spaniards three years to stamp out.

The Porta Capuana

Northwest of the Piazza Garibaldi, some of Naples' shabbiest streets lead towards the Piazza Enrico de Nicola, which was once the city's main gate. The **Porta Capuana**, built in 1484, seems a smaller version of the Castel Nuovo's triumphal arch, crowded in by the same squat round towers. The **Castel Capuano**, next to it, began its life as a castle-residence for the Hohenstaufen kings. Since its construction in the 13th century it has been reshaped so many times it doesn't even look like a castle any more; for the last four centuries it has served as Naples' law courts.

If anything makes wandering into this unlikely district worthwhile, though, it is **Santa Caterina a Formiella**, facing the Porta Capuana, a church by the obscure architect Romolo Balsimelli that is one of the masterpieces of 16th-century Italian architecture. Completed in 1593, the church's bulky, squarish form was a Renaissance eccentricity, but an important stepping-stone towards the Baroque. Despite long neglect during, which its dome seemed to tilt at a more precarious angle with each year, the church has reopened to the public and further projects are under way for the conservation of its interior.

Museo Archeologico Nazionale

Open Wed–Mon 9am–10pm, Sun and hols 9–8; adm.

Back on the western side of the old city, Via Toledo, after passing Spaccanapoli and changing its name to Via Roma, continues northwards through the **Piazza Dante**, one of the most animated corners of the city; beyond this, as Via Enrico Pessina, in an area of oversized tenements and busy streets, it opens to display the crumbling palazzo containing the National Archaeological Museum.

Naples has the most important collection of Roman-era art and antiquities in the world, due partly to Vesuvius, for burying Pompeii and Herculaneum, and partly to the sharp eyes and deep pockets of the Farnese family—many of the best works here come from the collection they built up over 300 years. Unfortunately, the place is run by Neapolitans; at any given time, half of the collections will be closed for 'restorations' that never seem to happen, and what they condescend to let you see may well be the worst-exhibited and worst-labelled major museum in Europe.

On the first floor, room after room is filled with ancient sculpture. Many of the pieces on view are the best existing Roman-era copies of lost Greek statues, including some by Phidias and Praxiteles; some are masterpieces in their own right, such as the huge, dramatic ensemble called the *Farnese Bull*, the *Tyrannicides* (with other statues' heads stuck on them), and the truly heroic *Farnese Hercules* that once decorated the Baths of Caracalla. Several provocative Aphrodites compete for your attention, along with a platoon of formidable Athenas, the famous *Doryphorus* (spear-bearer), and enough Greek and Roman busts to populate a Colosseum.

Upstairs, most of the rooms are given over to finds from Pompeii. The collection of **mosaics**, mostly from Pompeii and Herculaneum, is one of the two best anywhere (the other is in Antalya, Turkey); the insight it provides into the life and thought of the ancients is priceless. There's a certain fond silliness—plenty of chickens, ducks and grinning cats, the famous *Cave Canem* (beware of the dog) mosaic from the front of a house, comic scenes from the theatre, and one wonderful panel of crocodiles and hippopotami along the Nile. Some of the mosaics are very consciously 'art': including one showing a detailed scene of the Battle of Issus, where Alexander the Great defeated the Persians, and one with a view of the Academy of Athens that includes a portrait of Plato.

Besides the mosaics, nowhere in the world will you find a larger collection of **Roman mural painting** (*see* pp.821–22), and much of it is fascinatingly modern in theme and execution. Many of the walls of Pompeiian villas were decorated with architectural fantasias that seem strangely like those of the Renaissance. Other works show an almost Baroque lack of respect for the gods—the *Wedding of Zeus and Hera*. Scholars in fact do denote a period of 'Roman Baroque', beginning about the 2nd century. From it come paintings graced by genuine winged *putti*, called *amoretti* in

Roman days. Among the most famous pictures are *The Astragal Players*—young girls shooting craps—and the beautiful *Portrait of an Unknown Woman*, a thoughtful lady holding her pen to her lips, who has become one of the best-known images from Roman art. Other attractions of the museum include large collections of jewellery, coins, fancy gladiators' armour, the famous *sezione pornografica (closed for years and unlikely to reopen in the forseeable future)*, Greek vases, decorative bronzes and a highly detailed, room-sized **scale model** of Pompeii (restored since the memorable assault on it by the authors' baby boy, back in 1980). The Egyptian collection is not a large one, but it is fun, with a dog-headed Anubis in a Roman toga, some ancient feet under glass, and a mummified crocodile.

Capodimonte

North of the museum, the neighbourhoods along Via Toledo—here called Via Santa Teresa degli Scalzi—begin to lose some of their Neapolitan intensity as they climb to the suburban heights. On the way, after changing its name again to Corso Amedeo di Savoia, the street passes an area that was full of cemeteries in Roman times. Three Christian underground burial vaults have been discovered here, with a total area of over 100,000 square metres, only part of which has been completely explored. Two may be visited: the **Catacombe di San Gennaro** (*entrance through the courtyard of the Basilica dell'Incoronata—look for the yellow signs; tours daily at 9.30, 10.15, 11.00 and 11.45; adm*) is the more interesting, with extensive early-Christian mosaics and frescoes, some as early as the 2nd century. The **Catacombe di San Gaudioso** (*tours Sun only at 9.45 and 11.45; adm*), which include the 5th-century tomb of that saint, were discovered under the church of **Santa Maria della Sanità**, on Via Sanità.

The **Parco di Capodimonte**, a well-kept and exotically tropical park, began as a hunting preserve of the Bourbons in the 18th century. Charles III built a Royal Palace here in 1738 that now houses Naples' picture gallery, the **Museo Nazionale di Capodimonte** (*open Tues–Sun 9–2; adm*). The collection is the best in the south of Italy, and especially rich in works of the late Renaissance. Some of the works you shouldn't miss: an *Annunciation* by Filippino Lippi; a Botticelli *Madonna*; the mystical portrait of the mathematician *Fra Luca Pacioli* by an unknown quattrocento artist; two wry homilies by the elder Brueghel, *The Misanthrope* and *The Blind*; works by Masaccio and Mantegna and a hilarious picture of *St Peter Martyr* by Lotto, showing that famous anti-Semitic rabble-rouser conversing nonchalantly with the Virgin Mary—with a hatchet sticking out of his head.

Five big, beautifully restored Caravaggios take up one room; others are devoted to important works by Titian. One entire wing of the museum is filled with delightfully frivolous 18th-century **porcelain figurines**; the Bourbons maintained a royal factory for making such things at Capodimonte, which is still in operation today. In another hall there are scores of 19th-century watercolour scenes of Naples and the Campanian countryside (the best of them by Giacinto Gigante). Here, for the first time, you will see the Naples that so struck the 18th-century travellers. Not much has changed, really; if only all the traffic could magically disappear, it would still be almost the same spectacular city today.

The museum's collections are mostly up on the second floor; the first, the old *piano nobile* (royal apartments), is still much the way the Bourbons left it. Persevere through the score of overdecorated chambers; the *Salotto di porcellana*, a little room entirely lined with Capodimonte porcelain, makes the whole thing worthwhile.

The Certosa di San Martino

Up on the highest point overlooking Naples, the 17th-century **Castel Sant'Elmo** (*open Tues–Sun 9–2; adm*) is an impressive enough Baroque fortification, partly built of the tufa rock on which it stands (the city now uses it to park the cars the police tow away). Next to it, hogging the best view in Naples, the Carthusians built their original, modest, monastery of **San Martino** in the early 14th century. Two centuries later, like most Carthusian branch offices, they were rolling embarrassingly in lucre; building the poshest monastery in all Italy was the only thing to do. The rebuilt **Certosa** (charterhouse) is only marginally smaller than Fort St Elmo. Built on the slope of the mountain, it is supported by a gargantuan platform, visible for miles out to sea and probably containing enough stone to construct a small pyramid.

Nobody knows exactly what is in the **Museo Nazionale di San Martino** (*open Tues–Sun 9–2; adm*), which now occupies the monastery. Intended as a museum specifically of Naples, its history, art and traditions, San Martino suffers from the same mismanagement as the Archaeological Museum; only parts are ever open, and the Grand Cloister, at the time of writing, has become a wilderness of weeds and scaffolding. Not that this should discourage you from taking the long ride up the Montesanto Funicular. The views and the architecture are marvellous, and at least they always keep open the collection of *presepi*—what the Neapolitans come here to see (*see* p.805).

Upon entering the complex, the first attraction is the **church**, another of the glories of Neapolitan Baroque, with an excess of lovely coloured inlaid marble to complement the over-abundance of painting. The work over the altar, the *Descent from the Cross*, is one of the finest of José Ribera. This tormented artist, often called *Lo Spagnuolo* in Italy, has paintings all over Naples. His popularity does not owe everything to his artistic talent; apparently he formed a little cartel with two local artists and cornered the market by hiring a gang of thugs to harry all the other painters out of town.

The cloister, the **Chiostro Grande**, even in its present state, is a masterpiece of Baroque, elegantly proportioned and gloriously original in its decoration. Also, thanks to a sculptural scheme by a pious, mad artist named Cosimo Fanzago, it is the creepiest cloister east of Seville. Fanzago (who was also one of the architects of San Martino) gives us eight figures of saints that seem more like vampires in priestly robes and mitres, a perfect background for his little enclosed garden, its wall topped with rows of gleaming marble skulls. Most of the collections are in the halls surrounding the Chiostro Grande—costume, painting, ship models and every sort of curiosity; at the corners are **belvederes** from which to look over Naples (outside the complex, a series of lovely terraced gardens offer a similar view). The *presepi* take up a few large rooms near the entrance.

West of the Piazza del Plebiscito

The hill called Pizzofalcone rises directly behind the Piazza del Plebiscito; around it was the site of Parthenope, the Greek town that antedated Neapolis and was eventually swallowed up by it (though Neapolitans still like to refer to themselves as Parthenopeans). Parthenope had a little harbour, formed by an island that is now almost completely covered by the ancient, strangely-shaped fortress of the **Castel dell'Ovo**—the one Master Virgil is said to have built balanced on an egg, hence the name. Most of it was really built by Frederick II, and expanded by the Angevins. It is closed to the public, but the Egg Castle has been the scene of many unusual events in Italian history. The island may have been part of the original Greek settlement of Parthenope. Later it contained the villa of the Roman general and philosopher Lucullus, victor over Mithridates in the Pontic Wars; Lucullus curried favour with the people by making his sumptuous gardens, and his famous library, open to the public. In the 5th century AD the villa became a home in exile for Romulus Augustulus, last of the western Roman emperors. The Goths spared him because of his youth and simple-mindedness, and pensioned him off here.

Modern Naples: the Villa Comunale

Once past the Egg Castle, a handsome sweep of coastline opens up the districts of **Chiaia** and **Mergellina**, the most pleasant parts of the new city. Here the long, pretty **Villa Comunale**, central Naples' only park, follows the shore. In it, there is an **aquarium** (*open winter Tues–Sat 9–5, Sun 9–2; summer Tues–Sat 9–6, Sun 10–6; adm*), built by the German naturalist Dr Anton Dohrn in the 1870s, and perhaps the oldest in the world. All the wide variety of sea creatures are from the Bay of Naples; depending on the time of day, you will either find them fascinating, or else overwhelmingly appetizing. When the Allied armies marched into town in 1943, the Neapolitans put on a big party for the officers. There being practically nothing decent to eat anywhere in Naples, they cleaned out the aquarium and managed an all-seafood menu. Commanding General Mark Clark is said to have got the aquarium's prize specimen, a baby manatee, though how they prepared it is not recorded.

Ask to see the murals and you will be led upstairs to see Dohrn, who was a friend and colleague of Charles Darwin, and other buddies depicted by the German artist Hans von Marees. The wall opposite has local boys frolicking naked under the orange groves. Recently restored after the 1980 earthquake, the murals are an insight into the secret life of aquariums.

Behind the park, on the Riviera di Chiaia, the **Museo Principe di Aragona Pignatelli Cortes** (*open Tues–Sat 9–2, Sun 9–2; adm*) will show you more of the same kind of decorative porcelain as at Capodimonte, along with a score of 18th- and 19th-century noble carriages, furniture and art.

If you're still not tired of little smiling figurines, you can plunge deeper into Chiaia to see the greatest collection of all at the **Museo Nazionale della Ceramica**, also known as the Duca di Martina Museum, but familiar to Neapolitans only as the **Villa Floridiana** (*open Tues–Sun, 9–2; adm*), after the tasteful 18th-century estate it occupies, with one of the loveliest gardens in Naples and one of Italy's great hoards of bric-a-brac. The museum is on Via Cimarosa, near the Funicolare di Chiaia.

Mergellina

Beginning a few streets beyond the western end of the Villa Comunale, Mergellina is one of the brightest and most popular quarters of Naples, a good place for dinner or a *passeggiata* around the busy Piazza Sannazzaro. Its centre is the **marina**, where besides small craft there are hydrofoils to Sorrento and the islands in the summer months, and excursion boats which do daily tours of the shore between the Egg Castle and Point Posillipo.

From the harbour, Mergellina rises steeply up the surrounding hills; there is a funicular up to the top (every 15 minutes). On the hillside, between the railway bridge and the tunnel that leads under the hill to Fuorigrotta, there is a Roman funerary monument that tradition has always held to be the **tomb of Virgil** (*open Tues–Sun 9–1*). The poet died in Brindisi in 19 BC on his way back from a trip to Greece. Neapolis was a city dear to him—he wrote most of the *Aeneid* here—and Virgil was brought here for burial, though ancient authors attest that the tomb was closer to the Aquarium.

Just below it lies the entrance to one of the little-known wonders of the ancient world. The **Crypta Neapolitana** (*unfortunately not due to reopen in the foreseeable future*) is a 1988ft road tunnel built during the reign of Augustus, to connect Neapolis with Pozzuoli and Baiae, the longest such work the Romans ever attempted.

Shopping

Surprisingly, no one ever thinks of Naples as one of the prime shopping destinations of Italy; this is a mistake, as there are as many pretty and unusual things to be bought here as anywhere else, and usually at lower prices. The back streets around Spaccanapoli and other old sections are still full of artisan workshops of all kinds.

The Royal Factory at Capodimonte, founded by the Bourbons, still makes what may be the most beautiful **porcelain** and **ceramic figures** in Europe, sold at the fancier shops in the city centre. Another old Neapolitan tradition is the making of **cameos** from special seashells; you'll see them everywhere, but the shops outside the Certosa di San Martino have a good selection at relatively low prices.

Via San Biagio dei Librai, the middle of the Spaccanapoli, is, as its name implies, a street of **booksellers**—but the street is also full of many more odd surprises for shoppers. Many of the **religious goods shops** have surprisingly good works in terracotta; the **Doll Hospital**, at No.81, ✆ 081 203 067, is one of the most charming shops in Naples.

All around the back streets near the Archaeological Museum, there are **antique** and **junk shops** that won't overcharge you unless you let them. The swankiest antique shops tend to be along Via Merelli, off Piazza dei Martiri. The city also has an immense twice-monthly **antiques market**, the Fiera dell'Antiquariato, held on alternate Saturday and Sunday mornings in the gardens of the Villa Comunale.

You can buy lovely **old prints** of Naples and beyond at Bowinkel, Piazza dei Martiri 24, ✆ 081 764 4344, and beautiful **candles**, including some sculpted to depict well-known Italian political and show business personalities, from the Antica Cereria, Via C. Doria 6–8, ✆ 081 549 9745. For the once-in-a-lifetime souvenir, the 150-year-old Fonderia Chiurazzi, Via Ponti Rossi 271, ✆ 081 751 2685, makes artistic **bronzes**, specializing in reproductions of works in the Museo Archeologico; if you have billions of lire to spare, they'll do them life-size, or even bigger.

For **clothes** and **shoes** the best area is again off Piazza dei Martiri, in particular along the flashy Via Chiaia. You can find its other end just to the right of the central Piazza del Plebiscito. Last of all do not miss the *bancarelle* and open **street markets** around Piazza Garibaldi. The daily catch of fish, live squid and octopus is a must, just to the right off Corso Garibaldi. Here you can also find fruit stalls that sell lemons from the Sorrentine Peninsula which are too big to cup with both hands.

very expensive

Naples does have less than its share of top-quality hotels; the Germans, inexplicably, blew up a few of them before their retreat in 1944. Two of the best are on Via Partenope, over-looking the Castel dell'Ovo, where the views over the bay more than compensate for the traffic noise below.

Visiting sheiks, kings and rock stars favour the ★★★★**Excelsior**, Via Partenope 48, ✆ 081 764 0111, ✉ 081 764 9743, Naples' finest, facing Vesuvius, with beautiful suites and a tradition of perfect service ever since 1909. You pay for space—elegant lounges, a beautiful rooftop solarium and restaurant, rooms with large beds and antique-style furniture. ★★★★**Vesuvio**, Via Partenope 45, ✆ 081 764 0044, ✉ 081 764 4483, provides the same stuff, with a lovely roof garden for dining—important since none of the rooms have good balconies.

expensive

Still on the seafront, ★★★★**Miramare**, Via N. Sauro 24, ✆ 081 764 7589, ✉ 081 764 0775, is the find in this category. The atmosphere is intimate. Some rooms are too small, but the old lift and rooftop solarium (where the restaurant will reopen) more than make up. Rooms not facing the sea are quieter. Other good bets are ★★★★**Paradiso**, Via Catullo 11, ✆ 081 761 4161, ✉ 081 761 3449, with stunning views over the bay—make sure you book a sea-facing room. For a more old-fashioned atmosphere, but further inland (near the Cumana stop Corso V. E.), try ★★★★**Parker's**, Corso Vittorio Emanuele 135, ✆ 081 761 2474, ✉ 081 663 527, which has ample charm, with plenty of polished wood, chandeliers and comfortable furniture.

moderate

Near the Stazione Centrale, ★★★**Cavour**, Piazza Garibaldi 32, ✆ 081 283 122, ✉ 081 287 488, is a well-run decent hotel in an otherwise desperate area. Book the top-floor suites for a little more than a standard room. With ample terraces and good views over Vesuvius they are a respite from the bustle below. Rooms are nicely decorated in the omnipresent Liberty style. The restaurant gets two Michelin *fourchettes*.

★★**Ausonia**, Via Caracciolo 11, ✆/✉ 081 682 278, is a clean, comfortable *pensione* with 20 rooms and nautical decoration—portholes around the numbers and nautical-theme bedspreads. The owner is kind and cheerful. Located within a *palazzo*, looking on to an interior courtyard, this is the quiet option for the Mergellina area.

cheap

There is a dearth of reasonable cheap hotels. ★★**Fontane al Mare**, Via N. Tommaseo 14, ✆ 081 764 3811, is definitely worth booking in advance, with just 21 rooms located on the last two floors of an old palazzo next to the Chiaia gardens. To take the lift, you will need to bring L100 coins! Ask for rooms without bathroom since they enjoy the great sea view and are better value. Breakfast costs extra. Another place to find cheap accommodation is Via Mezzocannone, south of Spaccanapoli. This street borders the university, and many of the most pleasant cheap lodgings in Naples can be found here—though with so many students it may be hard to find a vacancy. Naples' youth hostel is the **Ostello Mergellina**, Salita della Grotta 23, ✆ 081 761 2346, 🖂 081 761 2391, near the Mergellina Metropolitana station. IYHF cards are required.

Eating Out

Now, everyone thinks of China as a ponderous, elephantine country; Naples, on the other hand we think of as something exciting, stimulating. Perhaps the Chinese invented slow, pacific fat macaronis, not the spaghetti that moves like the waves of the sea ...

Domenico Rea

This local savant, writing in the pages of *Qui Napoli*, is carrying on one of Naples' grand old causes. Forget those old legends about Marco Polo—just imagine anyone brazen enough to say spaghetti doesn't originally come from Naples! This capital of cooking, this citadel of *Italianità*, can already claim pizza, and probably many other Italian specialities as well. Neapolitans spend as much time worrying about what's for dinner as anybody else, but like most Italians they have a perfectly healthy attitude towards the subject. Neapolitan cuisine is simple—one of the most celebrated dishes is *spaghetti alle vongole*—and even in some of the more pretentious places you will see favourites of the Neapolitan *cucina povera* sneaking onto the menu, like *pasta e fagioli*. There are very few bad or tourist restaurants, but an infinity of tiny, family-run *trattorie* or *pizzerie*; you will depart from most of them serene and satisfied.

For famous Neapolitan pizza, look for the genuine Neapolitan pizza oven, a built-in, bell-shaped affair made of stone with a broad, clean tile floor; the fire (only certain kinds of wood will do) is at the back, close to the pizza, not hidden underneath out of sight. Watch out for house wines; in cheaper places this is likely to be Gragnano from nearby Monte Faito—detestable rough stuff. On the other hand you can find some real surprises from Campania; a dry white called Greco di Tufo, and Taurasi, a distinguished red—as well as Falerno, the descendant of the ancient *Falernian* that Latin poets never tired of praising. Some restaurants are the cheapest in all Italy—as they cheat on their taxes. Others can be alarmingly expensive, especially if you order fish.

expensive

La Cantinella, Via Nazario Sauro 23, ✆ 081 464 8684, near the Castel dell'Ovo on the esplanade, is believed by many to be Naples' finest—also the place to be seen for the Parthenopeans, with a telephone on each table which they retain despite the invention of mobile telephones. Their *linguine Santa Lucia*, made with home-made pasta, octopi, squid, prawns, clams and fresh baby tomatoes, takes some beating. The risotto is also excellent. The atmosphere is smart but relaxed and the service friendly. Closer to the civic centre is **Ciro**, Via Santa Brigida 71, ✆ 081 552 4072, near the Castel Nuovo. Go ahead and order *pasta e fagioli* or any other humble pasta dish; that's what the place is famous for. They also do pizzas. On the Mergellina esplanade, **Don Salvatore**, Via Mergellina 5, ✆ 081 681 817, has been around for more than 40 years, during which time it has built up a well-deserved reputation for turning out consistently fine Neapolitan dishes, accompanied by some of the area's best wines. There are set menus; and pizza for those who want to keep the bill down. *Closed Wed.*

La Cantina di Triunfo, Riviera di Chiaia 64, ℗ 081 668 101, off the Villa Comunale approaching Piazza Sannazzaro, offers Neapolitan *cucina povera* raised to an art form—wintry chestnut or lentil soups, or in spring lighter broad bean or fresh pea soups, *polpette di baccalà*—small balls of minced salt-cod, fried or served in a fresh tomato sauce. Desserts are as good as everything else. The wine list is also exceptional, and many of the 80 grappas home-made. Reserve. *Closed Sun.* Up near the Mergellina end, **O Sole Mio**, Via Tommaso Campanella 7, ℗ 081 761 2323, is run by a fisherman's family, and you will be better advised to go straight for the seafood, in all its many forms. Try the wonderful *cassuola di pesce* (fish casserole) but tuck your napkin into your collar, Neapolitan-style, before you start! *Closed Tues.*

cheap

You can get superb pizzas at **Da Pasqualino**, Piazza Sannazzaro 78/9, ℗ 081 681 524, in Mergellina, which has outside tables. The old granny in the corner makes the superb calorie-laden *crocchette*—potato croquettes spiked with mozzarella cheese—with which the locals invariably start their meal. *Closed Tues.* In the historic centre the **Pizzeria Port'Alba**, Via Port'Alba 18, ℗ 081 459 713, founded in 1830, serves excellent pizzas for lunch and dinner. You can also get full dinners for a reasonable sum, including the house speciality, *linguine al cartoccio*—seafood pasta made into a foil parcel and baked in the oven (it is vast—go easy on the *antipasti*). You can choose either to sit inside or outside under the Port'Alba itself. **Brandi**, Salita Sant'Anna di Palazzo 1/2, ℗ 081 416 928, a pretty, lively pizzeria, claims to have invented the *margherita*, Naples' most famous pizza, with mozzarella, tomatoes and fresh basil, the 19th-century queen's favourite dish. They have two floors and a small terrace. The seafood pizza includes octopi cooked with their ink sacks intact!

Patrizia, Via Luculliano 24, cheap and homely, but occupying a million-dollar position down on the Borgo Marinara next to the Castel dell'Ovo, has barely seven tables and no menu. They serve you wine in plastic cups, the food is delicious and the prices downright ridiculous. **Trattoria Nennella**, Vico Lungo Teatro Nuovo 103–105, an amazing bargain in the *Quartieri Spagnuoli*, offers a taste of true Neapolitan food and spirit in a simple setting; while Signora Nennella plots your meal in the kitchen, her son runs the show. You are likely to be the only foreigner. *Open weekdays for lunch.*

cafés and gelaterie

 As well as the inventors of the pizza, Neapolitans are Italy's most dedicated and punctilious coffee consumers, and the city accordingly has its crop of elegant, ornate (though now often faded) 19th-century *gran caffè*, mostly not too far from the Galleria and the Piazza del Plebiscito. The best location is occupied by **Gambrinus**, Piazza Trieste e Trento, ℗ 081 417 582, overlooking the Teatro San Carlo and Piazza Plebiscito, but it's not cheap. Other fine places for a coffee can be found along the waterfront, particularly out towards Mergellina; **Ciro** is generally considered the best.

Naples also produces some great icecream and pastries. *Gelaterie* can be found all over town, but **Scimmia**, Piazza della Carità 4, just off the Via Toledo not far from Spaccanapoli, has for long been regarded as one of the city's best. **Bilancione**, Via

Posillipo, will supply both an icecream and a view. For *sfogliatelle* (wonderful flaky pastries stuffed with ricotta and candied peel), **Scaturchio**, Piazza San Domenico Maggiore, is acclaimed as the *pasticceria* in Naples.

Entertainment and Nightlife

Naples always has plenty of concerts, shows and other cultural events. The best information on programmes and times is in the newspaper, *Il Mattino*, or in the free monthly guide, *Qui Napoli*.

opera, classical music and theatre

For **opera**-lovers one of the ultimate experiences is a night at the San Carlo (box office © 081 797 2370/© 081 797 2111), but tickets are extremely hard to come by, and very pricey. Hotels may be able to get them, or you must go to the box office in person. If you manage to get a ticket, be sure to dress your best.

You may have more luck catching a **concert** at the Auditorium RAI-TV, Via Guglielmo Marconi (Fuorigrotta), © 081 725 1111; at the Conservatorio San Pietro a Maiella, Via San Pietro a Maiella, © 081 459 255; or at the Associazione Alessandro Scarlatti, Piazza dei Martiri 58, © 081 406 011, which holds concerts for **jazz**, **chamber music** and a bit of everything. Don't forget that many, often free, concerts are staged in the city's churches. **Tickets** for major events may be obtainable at the ticket offices in the Box Office, Galleria Umberto I 15–16, © 081 551 9188, and Concerteria, Via Schipa 23, © 081 761 1221.

Unless your Italian is fluent, **theatre** will probably be a frustrating experience, and if you go for one of the superbly executed dialect plays, you may not understand a word. If that doesn't put you off, the best theatres are the **Politeama**, Via Monte di Dio, © 081 764 5016; the **Cilea**, Via S. Domenico, © 081 714 3110; the **Bracco**, Via Tarsia 40, © 081 549 5904; and the **Sannazaro**, Via Chiaia 157, © 081 411 723.

clubs, bars and discos

Neapolitans are night-owls, probably thanks to their Spanish heritage, and many, especially in summer, don't even think about going out to dinner until 10pm. That doesn't leave too much time for partying, once the 2–3 hour ritual of eating is over, but there are some reasonable clubs and late-night bars (as well as some terrible ones).

The thing to remember is that some areas are best left alone after midnight, most notably the Piazza Garibaldi area near the station, and the so-called *quartiere*, the narrow side streets that run off the Via Toledo. And if the vampish hookers to be seen at every street corner after dark should take your fancy, remember to take a second look—those girls could well be boys. Naples is famous even in drag-obsessed Italy for its transvestites; some of them are positively remarkable.

A list of **clubs** can be found in *Qui Napoli*, but for a start we include La Mela, Via dei Mille 41, © 081 413 881, which has good reports from the young and beautiful crowd. The Madison Street, Via Sgambati 47, © 081 546 6566, Naples' biggest **disco**, is an institution, with different theme nights (Saturday is gay night) and an affluent young crowd. Velvet, Via Cisterna dell'Olio, in the historic centre, is an alternative disco with a rougher edge.

At the Otto Jazz Club, Piazzetta Cariati 23, ℰ 081 552 4373, you'll get **jazz** which looks for inspiration as much to the famous Neapolitan folk songs as to New Orleans. It also serves plates of pasta and light meals, and has a well-stocked bar serving 200 cocktails (their specials are beer based!). This otherwise very pleasant club is in a pretty hard area—when you leave it's best to get a taxi. *Open Thurs–Sun.*

The **bars** of Via Paladino are where it all happens (*movida*, Napoli-style). Piazza Bellini, especially in summer, is the spot where the young and trendy come to see and be seen; it is also one of the few piazzas in Naples whose **cafés** have outside tables. Try to get a table at Intra Moenia, the literary café-cum-publishing house, ℰ 081 200 720. Ferdinandstrasse, Piazza Porta Nova 8, ℰ 081 207 390, is a **gay disco-bar**, particularly crowded on Sundays.

Around the Bay

Naples' hinterlands share fully in the peculiarities and sharp contrasts of the big city. Creation left nothing half-done or poorly done; against any other part of the Italian coastline, the Campanian shore seems almost indecently blessed, possessing the kind of irresistibly distracting beauty that seduces history off the path of duty and virtue. Today, for all the troubles that come seeping out of Naples, this coast is still one of the capitals of Mediterranean languor.

In Roman days, it was nothing less than the California of the ancient world: fantastically prosperous, lined with glittering resort towns full of refugees from the Roman rat-race, as favoured by artists and poets as it was by rich patricians. Like California, though, the perfume was mixed with a little whiff of insecurity. Vesuvius would be enough, but even outside the regularly scheduled eruptions and earthquakes, the region is Vulcan's own curiosity shop. West of Naples especially, there are eternally rising and sinking landscapes, sulphurous pools, thermal springs and even a baby volcano—altogether, perhaps the most unstable corner of the broad earth's crust.

Getting Around

Naples, of course, is the hub for all transport throughout the area; buses, ferries and local commuter rail lines lead out from the city to all points (*see* p.791).

by rail

Regular FS trains aren't much help here, except for a fast trip between Naples and Salerno. Fortunately, there are the local lines, of which the most important is the refreshingly efficient **Circumvesuviana**, the best way to reach Pompei, Herculaneum and Sorrento. This line has its own ultramodern station, on Corso Garibaldi just south of the Piazza Garibaldi (ℰ 081 772 2444), but all of its trains also make a stop at the Stazione Centrale itself before proceeding east. At Centrale their station is underground, sharing space with that of the Naples Metropolitana; this can be confusing since there are no schedules posted and the ticket windows aren't marked—you need to ask someone to make sure you are heading for the right train.

The main lines run east through **Ercolano** (the stop for Herculaneum) and Torre del Greco, and then diverge near Torre Annunziata, one line heading for Sarno, out in the

The Bay of Naples

20 km

10 miles

N

farm country east of Vesuvius, and the other for Sorrento. For the excavations at Pompei take the Sorrento line to the Scavi di Pompei/Villa dei Misteri stop. Circumvesuviana trains usually run every half-hour between 5am and 10.45pm. On a *direttissima*, of which there are several daily, the Naples–Sorrento trip takes 1 hour 10 minutes—locals are considerably slower. An additional Circumvesuviana line has infrequent trains north of Vesuvius to Nola and Baia.

For the west bay, Naples' own **Metropolitana FS** goes as far as Pozzuoli-Solfatara (trains every eight minutes). The two other regional lines both have trains about every half-hour from Piazza Montesanto Station, near the Piazza Dante. The **Ferrovia Cumana** (✆ 081 551 3328) runs along the shore, through Fuorigrotta, Bagnoli, Pozzuoli and Baia to Torregáveta (trains every 10 minutes). The remarkable **Circumflegrea** (also ✆ 081 551 3328) also finishes at Torregáveta, after passing through plenty of places you probably won't want to visit (trains every 20 minutes) but usually only as far as Licola. For the stop at the archaeological site of Cumae it runs six trains daily, three in the morning and three in the afternoon. The Circumflegrea is easily the most macabre railway in the western world; the trip begins by passing a neon shrine to the Virgin Mary in the middle of the Montesanto Tunnel, and then passes through stations that are metal sheds or bombed-out ruins, with smashed and derailed cars lying alongside the tracks to give passengers something to think about. The station at Cumae is gutted and abandoned; those dodging the entrance fee can head up towards the acropolis through the thorn bushes and adder-haunted forests.

by bus

Naples city bus no.152, from Piazza Garibaldi and Via Mergellina, travels to Solfatara and Pozzuoli. There is a blue bus run by Sepsa departing Piazza Garibaldi and calling at Solfatara, Pozzuoli and Baia. From the bus stop in the centre of Baia, there are connecting buses to Cumae, Bacoli and Cape Misenum.

The Circumvesuviana makes buses unnecessary for most of the east bay. Departing from the airport there is a bus to Sorrento three times a day. The express bus from Naples to Salerno, which usually runs every half-hour, leaves from the **SITA** office on Via Pisanelli, just off the Piazza Municipio, ✆ 081 552 2176, and arrives in Salerno at the terminal at Corso Garibaldi 117, ✆ 089 226 604. SITA also runs the buses from Salerno for the Amalfi Coast, with regular departures for Sorrento (in front of the Circumvesuviana station), or stopping short at Amalfi, Ravello or other towns *en route*; they are usually so frequent that it is easy to see all the main coast towns on a day trip, hopping from one to the next. Buses are definitely the best way to do it; driving yourself can be a hair-raising experience when it's busy.

West from Naples: Pozzuoli and the Phlegraean Fields

Tourist Information

Pozzuoli: Via Campi Flegrei 9, ✆ 081 526 1481.

The very pretty coastal road leaving the city, with views of Vesuvius all through the suburb of Posillipo, passes the little island of Nisida; this was a favoured spot in ancient times, and legend has it that Brutus and Cassius planned Caesar's murder here in the villa of one of their fellow conspirators. Naples' suburbs continue through **Agnano**, a town of spas and hot springs set around a mile-wide extinct crater, and stretch as far as Pozzuoli.

Pozzuoli, Sophia Loren's home town, today is a modest little city, with only its ruins to remind it of the time when Roman Puteoli, and not Naples, was the metropolis of the bay. The amphitheatre, on Via Domiziana, near the railway station (*open daily 9–one hour before sunset; adm*) was the third-largest in the Roman world (after Rome and Capua), with 60 gates for letting the beasts in. Pozzuoli's other important ruin is a little embarrassment to the town; for centuries people here were showing off the ancient serapeum—temple to the popular Egyptian god Serapis—until some killjoy archaeologist proved the thing to be an unusually lavish *macellum*, or market. Only the foundations remain, in a park near the small harbour.

For all ancient Puteoli's size and wealth, little else remains. There is a reason, and Pozzuoli would like to introduce a new word to your vocabulary to explain it. *Bradyseism* is a rare seismic phenomenon that afflicts this town and other spots around the bay. It manifests itself in the form of 'slow' earthquakes. The level of the land fell nearly 20ft since Roman times only to begin rising in the 15th century. Most recently falling, all of Puteoli that hasn't been gently shaken to pieces over the centuries is now underwater. Roman moles and docks can still sometimes be made out beneath the surface.

Solfatara

What's troubling Pozzuoli can be seen more clearly just outside the town at Solfatara, the storm centre of what the Greeks called the **Phlegraean** (fiery) **Fields** (the *Campi Flegrei*). To the Romans, it was the *Forum Vulcani*, and a major attraction of the Campanian coast. It hasn't changed much since.

Solfatara (*open daily 8.30–one hour before sunset; adm*) is another crater of a collapsed volcano, but one that just can't be still; sulphur gas vents, bubbling mud pits and whistling superheated steam fumaroles decorate the eerie landscape. Guides are around to keep you away from the dangerous spots. Their favourite trick is to hold a smoking torch to one of the fumaroles—making a dozen others nearby go off at the same time. Solfatara is perfectly safe, even though the ground underneath feels hot and sounds strangely hollow. It is; scientists keep a close watch on the huge plug of cooled lava that underlies the whole of the area about Pozzuoli, and they say the pressure on it from below is only one third as much as it was under Vesuvius in AD 79.

We promised you a baby volcano, and you'll see it near the coast west of Pozzuoli. **Monte Nuovo** has been quiet for some time (inexplicably passing up the opportunity to celebrate its 450th birthday, on 29 September 1988). The same earthquake in 1538 that wrecked much of Pozzuoli gave birth to this little cone. It's only about 460ft tall, and an easy climb up to the crater (you can have a picnic inside it).

Capo Miseno

Baia, the next town along the coast, was nothing less than the greatest pleasure dome of classical antiquity. Anybody who was anybody in the Roman world had a villa here, with a view of the sea, beach access, and a few hundred slaves to dust the statues and clean up after the orgies. You'll find little hint of that today: Goths, malaria and earthquakes have done a thorough job of wrecking the place. Most of ancient Baiae is now underwater, a victim of the same bradyseism that afflicts Pozzuoli. In summer, a glass-bottomed boat departs from Baia harbour to see this Roman Atlantis (© *081 526 5780; Sat 12 and 4, Sun 10.30, 12 and 4; tour lasts 70mins*). On land, the extensive but humble remains of the imperial villa can be visited at the **Parco Archeologico** (*open daily 9–one hour before sunset; adm*).

At Baia, the coast curves southwards towards Bacoli and **Capo Miseno** (*Cape Misenum*), a beautiful spot that for centuries was the greatest naval base of the Roman Empire, home to 10,000 sailors (mostly Greeks and Syrians). As at Baia, foundations and bits of columns and cornices are everywhere, though nothing of any real interest has survived intact. Nearby Lake Miseno, also called the 'Dead Sea', was once a part of the base, joined to the sea by a canal.

Two other lakes, both created as a by-product of volcanic action, lie north of Capo Miseno; one, the **Lago di Fusaro**, is a large, shallow oyster farm, cut off from the sea by a sand bar near the woebegone fishing village of Torregáveta, the terminus of the Circumflegrea and Cumana railways.

The decaying Rococo palace on an island in the centre is the Casino, built in 1782 by the Bourbon kings' favourite architect, Luigi Vanvitelli. **Lago d'Averno**—Lake Avernus—may ring a bell from your school days; it's the mouth of Hell, according to the ancient Greeks, who believed any passing bird would be suffocated by the infernal fumes rising from it. Cornelius Agrippa didn't have much respect for mythology, and he turned the lake into a part of the naval base by cutting another canal.

Cumae

As the story has it, King Tarquin of Rome came here, to the most venerable and respected oracle in all the western Mediterranean, with the intention of purchasing nine prophetic books from the Cumaean Sibyl. Unwisely, he said they were too dear, whereupon the Sibyl threw three of the books into the fire and offered him the remaining six at the same price. Again he complained, and the Sibyl put three more in the flames; finally Tarquin gave up, and took the last three at the original price. It was a good bargain. The Sibylline Books guided Rome's destiny until they too were burned up in the great fire of 82 BC.

Cumae had other distinctions. As one of the first Greek foundations in Italy the city was the mother colony for Naples and many other cities of Magna Graecia. In 421 BC Cumae lost its independence to the Samnites, and declined steadily from then on; Arab raiders finally wiped the city off the map in the 9th century AD. They did a good job of it, and there is little to see at the site (*open daily 9–one hour before sunset; adm*): only the foundations of a few temples on the high **acropolis**, worth the climb for the views around Capo Miseno. One of the ruins was a famous Temple of Apollo, rebuilt by Augustus in thanks after his victory at Actium.

Just below the summit, you may visit the **cave of the Cumaean Sibyl** itself, discovered by accident in 1932. This was the setting of Aeneas' famous encounter with the Sibyl, who leads him into the underworld, described in Book 6 of Virgil's *Aeneid*. It is a place of mystery, a long series of strange, trapezoidal galleries cut out of solid rock—impressive enough, even stripped of the sumptuous decoration they must once have had (all ancient oracles were marvellously profitable). Nobody has a clear idea how old it is. By classical times, it took the form of an oracle quite like the one at Delphi. At the far end of the cave a plain alcove with two benches marks the spot where the Sibyls would inhale fumes over the sacred tripod, chew laurel leaves and go into their trance.

Nobody has made the western side of the bay a base for their holiday since the 4th century AD. If you are travelling in specially to visit the classical sites you may prefer to grab a sandwich, though there are a few good places to have a proper lunch.

Pozzuoli

On the harbour, **Del Capitano**, Via Lungomare C. Colombo 10, ✆ 081 526 2283 (*moderate*) is a good rendezvous for fish-lovers. *Closed Thurs in low season.* **Il Tempio**, Via Serapide 13, ✆ 081 866 5179 (*moderate*), overlooking the ruined temple in Pozzuoli's main square, is justly famous for its *antipasti*. Leave all the decision-making to the waiter and he will happily bring you plate after plate of mostly fish-based dishes, including octopus, fried squid, baby red mullet, clams and giant prawns, until you tell him to stop. Many people call it a day after this, and few ever get beyond the *primi*. *Closed Wed.* At **La Granzeola**, Via Cupa Fasane, ✆ 081 524 3430 (*expensive*), on the way out of Pozzuoli along the coastal road, owner-chef Carmine Russo turns fish bought directly off the local boats into a dazzling array of unusual and tasty dishes, especially with pasta. *Closed Sun.*

Baia

At **L'Altro Cucchiaro**, Via Lucullo 13, ✆ 081 868 7196 (*expensive*), you can dine on divine concoctions of seafood and pasta, as well as superb fish. The restaurant is just opposite the railway station and perfectly placed to restore your energies for a visit to the archaeological park. *Closed Sun evenings, Mon and three weeks in Aug.*

East from Naples: Mount Vesuvius and Pompeii

Tourist Information

Pompei town: Via Sacra 1, ✉ 80045, ✆ 081 850 7255, 🖂 081 863 2401, with a branch office near the Porta Marina entrance to the old Pompeii site.

Despite its fearsome reputation, and its formidable appearance looming over Naples, **Mount Vesuvius** is a midget as volcanoes go—only 4202ft. No one suspected it even was a volcano, in fact, until it surprised the people of Pompeii, Herculaneum and Stabiae on 24 August AD 79.

That titanic eruption did not include much lava, but it buried Herculaneum and Pompeii, while coating most of Italy with a thin layer of dust. Over a hundred eruptions since have destroyed various towns and villages, some more than once. But as at Mount Etna in Sicily, people just can't stay away from Vesuvius' slopes. Volcanic soil grows grapes and olives in abundance, though the novelty of it often makes the Italians exaggerate their quality. The AD 79 explosion hasn't been equalled since; it blew the top of the mountain clean off, leaving two peaks, with the main fissure in between. The lower one is called Monte Somma, or *nasone* ('big nose') by the Neapolitans; the higher, parallel peak is Vesuvius proper.

Vesuvius was last heard from in 1944. The final eruption left the lava flows you'll see on the upper slopes; it also sealed the main fissure, putting an end to the permanent plume of smoke that once was a familiar landmark. You can bet the scientists are watching Vesuvius. Despite the long hiatus, they say there is no reason to expect another eruption soon, though if it were to explode now, they warn, it would cause a catastrophe—the area around the volcano has become one of the most densely populated in all Italy. To visit the main crater (between the two peaks), take the Vesuvius bus from the Circumvesuviana stop in Ercolano; then you have a stiff half-hour climb up the ash path. Dismiss all hopes of an easy ascent to the top singing 'Funiculi, funicula' from the legendary Thomas Cook cable railway, long since defunct. The white scar up the side of the crater—left by a second funicular which was due to replace the seventies' chairlift—continues a running saga. Work halted after argument for control over it between the two communes of Torre del Greco and Ercolano. Whilst they argued, the money 'disappeared'. (*Open daily 9–one hour before sunset; adm.*)

Herculaneum

Naples' discouraging industrial sprawl spreads eastwards as far as Torre del Greco without a break. The drab suburb of **Ercolano** is a part of it, built over the mass of rock that imprisons ancient **Herculaneum**, a smaller and less famous sight than Pompeii but just as worth a visit (*open daily 9–one hour before sunset; adm*). Unlike Pompeii, an important commercial centre, Herculaneum seems to have been a wealthy resort, only about one-third the size. Also, Vesuvius destroyed them in different ways. Pompeii was buried under layers of ash, while Herculaneum, much closer to the volcano, drowned under a sea of mud. Over time the mud hardened to a soft stone, preserving the city and nearly everything in it as a sort of fossil— furniture, clothing and even some of the goods in the shops have survived.

Like Pompeii, Herculaneum was discovered by accident. In the early 1700s an Austrian officer named Prince Elbeuf had a well dug here; not too far down, the workmen struck a stone pave- ment—the stage of the city's theatre. The Bourbon government began some old-fashioned destructive excavation, but serious archaeological work only began under Mussolini. Only about eight blocks of shops and villas, some quite fashionable, have been excavated. The rest is covered not only by tens of metres of rock, but also by a dense modern neighbourhood; bringing more of Herculaneum to light is a fantastically slow and expensive operation, but new digs are still going on. At any given time, most of the buildings will be locked, but the guards wandering about have all the keys and will show you almost any of them upon request (they are not supposed to accept tips, though you will find they often seem to expect them). Many of the most interesting houses can be found along Cardo IV, the street in the centre of the excavated area.

On the corner of the Decumanus Inferior, the **House of the Wooden Partition** may be the best example we have of the façade of a Roman house: inside there is an amazingly preserved wooden screen used for separating the *tablinum*—the master's study—from the atrium. Next door, the **Trellis House** was a much more modest dwelling, with a built-in workshop; the **House of the Mosaic Atrium**, down the street, is another luxurious villa built with a mind to the sea view from the bedrooms upstairs. On the other side of the Decumanus, Cardo IV passes the **Samnite House** (so named because of its early style atrium), and further up a column with police notices painted on it stands near the **House of the Neptune**, with a lovely mythological mosaic in the atrium. Other buildings worth a visit are the **House of the Deer**, with its infamous statue of a drunken Hercules relieving himself picturesquely; the well-preserved **baths**; and the **palaestra**, or gym, with its unusual serpent fountain and rather elegant, cross-shaped swimming pool.

Beyond Ercolano, the coastal road passes through the unattractive industrial sprawl and modern housing blocks thrown up to rehouse the homeless after the earthquake in 1980. The men of **Torre del Greco** have long been famous for gathering and working coral, a business now threatened by pollution. These days, much of the coral is imported from Asia, though it is still worked locally.

The Roman Villa at Oplontis

Torre Annunziata, the next town, is another sorry place with a serious drug problem and a penchant for pasta production. The Roman villa excavated here, known as the **Villa Poppaea at Oplontis,** Via Sepolcri (*open daily 9–one hour before sunset; adm*) is well worth a detour. If you are arriving on the Circumvesuviana, exit the station, walk downhill over the cross-roads, and it's the open area on the left opposite the military zone. Two-thirds of the villa have been fully excavated, revealing an extremely opulent pad with its own private bath complex, servants' quarters, monumental reception rooms and ornamental pool. There are beautiful wall paintings, depicting rich scenes of monumental halls hung with military arms, a magnificent tripod set between a receding colonnade, bowls of figs and fresh fruit, vignettes of pastoral idylls, and a scene of Hercules with the apples of the Hesperides. The part of the villa near the road is dominated by the great atrium hall and the family quarters. Outside the latrines, partitioned for each sex, it may have been one of the slaves who left his name, scrawled in Greek, 'Remember Beryllos'.

An amphora marked with the name Poppaea has given rise to the suggestion that the villa may have belonged to the wealthy Roman family, the *gens* Poppaea, who also owned the House of Menander at Pompeii. The most infamous member of this family was Sabina Poppaea, a woman who used her charms to captivate the emperor Nero, leaving her second husband Otho—another future emperor—who was dispatched to Lusitania. Spurred on by her, Nero killed off his mother Agrippina and his first wife. Nero eventually killed Poppaea by mistake in a fit of rage in AD 65, kicking her in the abdomen while she was pregnant.

Pompeii

Herculaneum may have been better preserved, but to see an entire ancient city come to life, the only place on earth you can go is this magic time-capsule, left to us by the good graces of Mount Vesuvius. Pompeii is no mere ruin; walking down the old Roman high street, you can peek into the shops, read the graffiti on the walls, then wander off down the back streets to explore the homes of the inhabitants and appraise their taste in painting—they won't mind a bit if you do. Almost everything we know for sure concerning the daily life of the ancients was learned here, and the huge mass of artefacts and art dug up over 200 years is still helping scholars to re-evaluate the Roman world.

Though a fair-sized city by Roman standards, with a population of some 20,000, Pompeii was probably only the third or fourth city of Campania, a trading and manufacturing centre of no special distinction. Founded perhaps in the 7th century BC, the city came under the Roman sphere of influence around 200; by the fateful year of AD 79 it was still a cosmopolitan place, culturally more Greek than Roman. Vesuvius' rumblings, and the tall, sinister-looking cloud that began to form above it, gave those Pompeiians with any presence of mind a chance to leave. Only about 10 per cent of the population perished.

After the city was buried under the stones and ash of the eruption the upper floors still stuck out; these were looted, and gradually cleared by farmers, and eventually the city was forgotten altogether. Engineers found it while digging an aqueduct in 1600, and the first excavations began in 1748—a four-star attraction for northern Europeans on the Grand Tour. The early digs were far from scientific; archaeologists today sniff that they did more damage than Vesuvius. Resurrected Pompeii has had other problems: theft of artworks, a good dose of bombs in the Second World War, and most recently the earthquake of 1980. The damage from that is still being repaired, though almost all the buildings are once more open to visitors.

There are two ways to see Pompeii; spend two or three hours on the main sights, or devote the day to scrutinizing details, for a total immersion in the ancient world (the detailed guide-books sold in the stands outside will help you with this). Your ticket also entitles you to entrance to the Villa of the Mysteries (*see* p.823). This is located five minutes' walk up the Viale Villa dei Misteri, to the left on exiting the Circumvesuviana (*site open daily 9–one hour before sunset; adm*). Pompeii isn't quite a perfect time capsule; a little background will help to complete the picture. The site today is all too serene, with a small-town air. Remember that almost every building was two or three storeys high, and that most streets of a Roman town were permanent market-places.

As long as daylight lasted, Pompeii would have been crowded with improvised *bancarelle*; any wagon-driver who wished to pass would need all manner of creative cursing. At least the streets are well-paved—better than Rome itself in fact; Campania's cities, the richest in western Europe, could well afford such luxuries. All the pavements were much smoother and more even than you see them now. The purpose of the flat stones laid across the streets should not be hard to guess. They were places to cross when it rained—streets here were also drains—and the slots in them allowed wagon wheels to pass through.

The shops, open to the street in the day, would be sealed up behind shutters at night, just as they are in the old parts of Mediterranean cities today. Houses, on the other hand, turn a completely blank wall to the street; they got their light and air from skylights in the *atrium*, the roofed court around which the rooms were arranged. Later, fancier villas have a second, open court directly behind the first, designed after the Greek *peristyle*.

As in Rome, no part of town was necessarily the fashionable district; elegant villas will be found anywhere, often between two simple workmen's flats. And don't take the street names too seriously. They were bestowed by the archaeologists, often, as with the Via di Mercurio (Mercury Street), after mythological subjects depicted on the street fountains.

Roman Frescoes

 Not surprisingly, Pompeii and Herculaneum have been of prime importance in the study of Roman painting. It is impossible to know how much of this art was borrowed from the Greeks or the Etruscans, although by the time of Augustus it appears that Rome and Campania were in the vanguard. New fashions set in the palaces of the Palatine Hill were quickly copied in the villas of the Roman California. Or perhaps it was vice versa.

In Pompeii and Herculaneum four styles of painting have been defined by art historians, although as you roam the ruins you'll find that they often overlap: **Style I** (2nd century BC) was heavily influenced by Hellenistic models, especially from Alexandria: walls are divided into three sections, often by bands of stucco, with a cornice and frieze along the top and square panels (dados) on the bottom, while the middle sections are skilfully painted to resemble rich marble slabs. The predilection for deep colours, combined with the lack of windows, often makes these small rooms seem somewhat claustrophobic to us (*see* the Samnite House in Herculaneum).

Later Romans must have felt the same lack of air and space for, in about 90 BC, they moved on to the 'architectonic' **Style II**. Columns and architraves were painted around the edges of the wall, an architectural screen designed to provide an illusion of depth and space on the large central panels. At first the centres were more pseudo-marble, but landscapes and mythological scenes soon became more popular. The Villa of the Mysteries near Pompeii is a prime example; it is also one of the oldest to have portraits of real people, or at least local character types.

Vitruvius, the celebrated writer on architecture, sternly disapproved of **Style III**, which abandoned the pretence and architectural dissimulation in favour of more playful compositions in perspective. A favourite motif was patterns of foliage, fountains and candelabras, decorated with delicate, imaginative figures; these would be called 'grotesques' in the Renaissance, when Raphael and his friends rediscovered some in a Roman 'grotto' that was really a part of Nero's Golden House. The middle panels are often done in solid colours, with small scenes at the centre to resemble framed paintings. In Pompeii examples include the Houses of Lucretius Fronto and the Priest Amandus, the latter done by a remarkable artist who comes close to scientific perspective, albeit with several vanishing points.

The last fashion to hit Pompeii before Vesuvius did, **Style IV**, combines the architectural elements of Style II and the framed picture effects of Style III, but with a greater degree of elaboration and decoration. Additional small scenes are placed on the sides—landscapes, still lifes, genre scenes from everyday life and architectural *trompe l'oeil* windows done with a much more refined use of perspective (*see* the House of the Vettii). Sometimes an entire stage would be painted, with the curtain pulled aside to show a scene from a play; borders are decorated with flowers, satyrs, grotesques and frolicking Cupids (Italians call these *amoretti*). Humorous vignettes of the gods and incidents from Virgil's *Aeneid* were popular, along with images of Pompeii's divine patroness, Venus. She also inspired the subject matter of the frescoes you have to bribe the guards to see.

Around the Forum

Past the throng of hawkers and refreshment stands, the main entrance to the site takes you through the walls at the **Porta Marina**. Just inside the gate, the **Antiquarium** displays some of the artworks that haven't been spirited off to the museum in Naples, as well as some truly gruesome casts of fossilized victims of the eruption, caught in their death poses.

Two blocks beyond the Antiquarium and you're in the **forum**, orientated towards a view of Vesuvius. Unfortunately this is the worst-preserved part of town. Here you can see the tribune from which orators addressed public meetings, and the pedestals that held statues of heroes and civic benefactors, as well as the once-imposing **basilica** (the law courts), temples to Apollo and Jupiter, and, among other buildings, a public latrine and a **macellum**, or market, decorated with frescoes.

Down Mercury Street

Heading for Pompeii's old East End, there are several interesting houses along the Via di Mercurio, and the **Temple of Fortuna Augusta** on the corner of Via di Nola. The real attractions in this part of town, though, are a few lavish villas off on the side streets: the enormous **House of Pansa**; the **House of the Faun**, with the oldest-known welcome mat (set in the pavement, really); and the wonderful **House of the Vettii**, owned by a pair of wealthy brothers who were oil and wine merchants. Here are several rooms of excellent, well-preserved paintings of mythological scenes, but the guards will be whispering in your ear (if you are male) to show you the little niche off the entrance with the picture of Priapus. This over-endowed sport, in legend the son of Venus and Adonis, together with a couple of wall paintings along the lines of the Kama Sutra, has managed to make Pompeii something more than a respectable tourist trap. There are quite a few paintings of Priapus showing it off in the houses of Pompeii, besides the phallic images that adorn bakers' ovens, wine shops and almost every other establishment in town.

The Pompeiians would be terribly embarrassed, however, if they knew what you are thinking. They were a libidinous lot, like anyone else fortunate enough to live on the Campanian coast during recorded history, but the omnipresent phalluses were never meant as decoration. Almost always they are found close to the entrances, where their job was to ward off the evil eye. This use of phallic symbols against evil probably dates from the earliest times in southern Italy; the horn-shaped amulets that millions of people wear around their necks today are their direct descendants. Even so, not so long ago, women visiting Pompeii were not allowed to set eyes on the various erotic images around the site, and were obliged by the guides to wait chastely outside while their spouses or male companions went in for a peek. The nearby Via di Nola, one of Pompeii's main streets, leads to the north. It passes the **Central Baths**, a new construction that was not yet completed when Vesuvius went off, and the **House of Marcus Fronto**, with more good paintings and a reconstructed roof.

The 'New Excavations'

Beginning in 1911, the archaeologists cleared a vast area of western Pompeii, around what was probably the most important thoroughfare of the city, now the Via dell'Abbondanza. Three blocks west of the Forum, this street leads to the Via dei Teatri and the **Triangular Forum**, bordering the southern walls. Two **theatres** here are worth a visit, a large open one seating 5000, and a smaller covered one for concerts.

The big quadrangle, originally a lobby for the theatres, seems to have been converted at one point into a gladiators' barracks. This is only one of the disconcerting things you will find on the streets of Pompeii. The ruined temple in the Triangular Forum was already long ruined in AD 79, and scholars who study the art of the city find the last (fourth) period to betray a growing lack of skill and coarseness of spirit—altogether, there are plenty of clues that 1st-century Pompeii had its share of urban problems and cultural malaise.

The Via dell'Abbondanza

Next to the theatres, a small **Temple of Isis** testifies to the religious diversity of Pompeii; elsewhere around town there is graffiti satirizing that new and troublesome cult, the Christians. Three blocks north, there is a stretch of Via dell'Abbondanza that is one of the most fascinating corners of Pompeii. Among its shops are a smith's, a grocer's, a weaver's, a laundry and a typical Roman tavern with its modest walk-up brothel. The most common are those with built-in tubs facing the street—shops that sold wine, and oil for cooking and for lamps. Notices painted on the walls announce coming games at the amphitheatre, or recommend candidates for public office.

Some of the best-decorated villas in this neighbourhood are to be found along the side streets: the **House of Loreius**, the **House of Amandus**, and an odd underground chamber called the **Cryptoporticus**. Pompeii's two most impressive structures occupy a corner just within the walls: the **Palaestra**, a big colonnaded exercise yard, and the **amphitheatre**, the best-preserved in Italy, with seating for about 20,000. Tacitus records that a fight broke out here between the Pompeiians and rival supporters from Nocera in a match staged in AD 59. Nero exiled those responsible for the games and forbade further spectacles for ten years.

Not all of Pompeii's attractions are within the walls. If you have the time, it would be worth visiting the tombs around the **Via delle Tombe**. The Romans buried their dead outside their cities. The manner of burial naturally depended on wealth and status, but here you can see several of the more impressive funerary monuments to local dignitaries and their families. Finally, the famous **Villa dei Misteri**, a surburban villa located close to the same road out of Pompeii, is thought to have been used as a place of initiation in the forbidden Bacchic (or Dionysian) Mysteries, one of the cults most feared by the Roman Senate, and later by the emperors. Scenes from the myth of Dionysus and of the rituals are painted on the walls.

Modern Pompei

The town of Pompei (the modern town has one 'i'), an important pilgrimage centre, is also worth a visit, if nothing else for a look at the wonderfully overdone church, dedicated to the **Madonna di Pompei** (*open daily 6–2 and 3–6.30*). For a good view over the town and the excavations take the lift up the tower (*open daily 9–1 and 3–5; adm*). The Madonna of the church holds a special place in the affections of Neapolitan women. You'll probably see some of them, busily saying their rosaries, asking for the Madonna's intercession to help sort out their problems. If they have bare feet, this is not poverty, but devotion. Neapolitans who ask for the Madonna's help often promise to walk there barefoot from Naples (26km) if their prayers are answered.

It is only just that Pompei should play host to the **Vesuvian Museum**, on Via Colle San Bartolomeo (*open Mon–Sat 8–2; closed Sun*). This has more than enough to satisfy most basic volcano questions: prints of the volcano erupting, exhibits on the various materials produced in eruptions and much more that is explosive, if you like that kind of thing.

On leaving Pompei the road leads to the beginning of the Sorrentine Peninsula. At the foot of the peninsula lies **Castellammare di Stabia**. Roman *Stabiae* was the port of Pompeii, and the other big town destroyed by Vesuvius. Most famously it was where Pliny the Elder, who was in command of the fleet at Misenum during the AD 79 eruption, met his death as he tried to bring help to those fleeing the catastrophe. The description of the eruption and these events are recorded for posterity in his nephew's letter to Tacitus. Here, beneath a 12th-century Hohenstaufen castle, are the modern shipyards of the Italian navy. From Castellammare you can take a short ride in the cablecar up to **Monte Faito**, a broad, heavily forested mountain that may well be the last really tranquil spot on the bay—though a few hotels have already appeared—and a pleasant place for walks (*open April–Oct*).

Eating Out

If you are spending the whole day in Pompeii (which is only too easy) there is a restaurant on site just beyond the forum area through the Arch of Tiberius. The food from the self-service is nothing special, but if you wish to escape the crowds opt for the waiter service and sit out under the colonnade adjoining the ancient baths.

In modern Pompei, **Zi Caterina**, Via Roma 20, ✆ 081 850 7447 (*moderate*) has live lobsters in the tank and other noteworthy seafood dishes, and is also a good place to try Lacrima Christi wine from the nearby slopes of Vesuvius. At **Al Gamberone**, Via Piave 36, ✆ 081 863 8322 (*moderate*), close to Pompei's main church, you can feast on prawns doused in cognac and other good fish dishes. In summer you may dine outside under the lemons and oranges. *Closed Fri.*

Outside the excavations' exit, next to the amphitheatre, is **Anfiteatro**, Via Plinio 9, ✆ 081 863 1245. Here the seafood is more modest—it's one of the few places in Pompei you'll see *baccalà* (salt cod) on the menu, along with truly good *spaghetti alle vongole. Closed Fri.*

Sorrento

Getting Around

Sorrento is well connected in summer by ferries and hydrofoils which ply from the Marina Piccola to Capri, Amalfi, Positano and Naples. This is only an option during daylight hours since few crossings run later than 7.30pm. In winter only reduced services to Capri and Naples operate.

Caremar, ✆ 081 807 3077, ✉ 081 807 2479, run five ferries daily to Capri and back that take 45 minutes. **Linea Jet,** ✆ 081 878 1861, run hydrofoils to Capri eight times a day, taking 20 minutes. **Alilauro,** ✆ 081 878 1430, run 17 daily hydrofoil crossings to Capri. In addition they offer a fast alternative to the Circumvesuviana to Naples, a hydrofoil service which takes only 30 minutes. These run to both Molo Beverello near the Castel Nuovo and to the berths at Mergellina. For the return trip to Sorrento it is important to check from which station the hydrofoil is leaving. The same company operates four services daily to Positano which continue to Amalfi, as well as a daily service from Sorrento to Ischia departing at 9.30am and returning at 5.20pm.

Tourist Information

Sorrento: Via L. de Maio 35, ✉ 80067, ✆ 081 807 4033, ✉ 081 877 3397; it is a little difficult to find: from Piazza Tasso walk towards the sea into Piazza S. Antonino; the office is just off the road down to the ferry port (signposted). **Vico Equense**: Via S. Ciro 16, ✉ 80069, ✆ 081 879 8826, ✉ 081 879 9351.

After Pompei, the coastline swings outwards to meet Capri. At first, there is little intimation that you are entering one of the most beautiful corners of all Italy. The first clue comes when the coast road begins to climb into a corniche at **Vico Equense**, a pretty village that is becoming a small resort, absorbing some of the overflow from Sorrento; there is a nice beach under the cliffs at the back of the town.

Sorrento began its career as a resort in the early 19th century, when Naples began to grow too piquant for English tastes. The English, especially, have never forsaken it; Sorrento's secret is a certain perfect cosiness, comfortable like old shoes. It helps that Sorrento is a lovely, civilized old town. Not many resorts can trace their ancestry back to the Etruscans, or claim a native son like the poet Torquato Tasso. (Today, the Sorrentines are more proud of a songwriter named De Curtio, whose *Come Back to Sorrento*, according to a local brochure, ranks with *O Sole Mio* as one of the 'two most familiar songs in the world'. There's a bust of him in front of the Circumvesuviana station.)

Sorrento doesn't flagrantly chase after your money, unlike many other places in Italy, and it lacks the high-density garishness of, say, Rimini. However, if Sorrento has one big drawback, it is its lack of a decent beach—though at some of the fancier hotels you may enjoy taking a lift down to the sea. There are also several *stabilimenti*—piers jutting out into the sea, which are kitted out with loungers and beach umbrellas, for the use of which you have to pay a hire charge. There isn't much of artistic or historical interest; Sorrento was never a large town, though in the Middle Ages it was for a while an mportant trading post. The Sorrentini still recall with pride that their fleet once beat Amalfi's fleet in a sea battle (even though it was in 897). Today the population is only 15,000. It's pleasant to walk through the old streets; half the shop windows seem to be displaying *intarsia*—surprisingly fine pictures done in inlaid woods, a local craft for centuries. Look out too for the laboratories, open to the street, producing perfume and *limoncello*, the distinctive liqueur made from the lemons grown throughout the peninsula.

Around Sorrento, as far as the mountains permit, stretches one of the great garden spots of Campania, a lush plain full of vines and lemon groves. From the town, to the west you can follow the winding path to the **Bagni Regina Giovanna**, a natural sea pool where you can see the scanty ruins of the Roman **Villa di Pollio**. You can also take the short trip to **Massa Lubrense**, an uncrowded fishing village with views as far as Campanella Point, the tip of the peninsula, opposite the rugged outline of Capri. Campanella Point takes its name from the big bell that was hung here and rung to warn towns around the bay when pirates were sighted.

Sorrento ✉ *80067*   ### Where to Stay and Eating Out

Sorrento isn't the status resort it once was, but it still seems to have more four-star places than anywhere in Italy; most of them are good bargains too, compared with equivalent spots in the north.

For a plunge into a Grand Tour atmosphere, ★★★★**Grand Hotel Excelsior Vittoria**, Piazza T. Tasso 34, ✆ 081 807 1044, ✎ 081 877 1206, *exvitt@exvitt.it* (*expensive*) is the place to stay. Built at the turn of the century and owned by the same family for four generations, it's set in its own plush park complete with orange and olive groves, overlooking the sea. Wagner, Alexandre Dumas, Nietzsche, Princess Margaret, Sophia Loren and Pavarotti have all stopped by.

★★★★**Grand Hotel Ambasciatori**, Via Califano 18, ✆ 081 878 2025, ✎ 081 807 1021 (*expensive*), the best of the Manniello family chain, is away from the centre but has a palatial interior, pool, sea-bathing platform and gardens overlooking the sea. The more central ★★★★**Imperial Tramontana**, ✆ 081 878 1940, ✎ 081 807 2344, on Via Vittorio Veneto (*expensive*), set in incredible tropical gardens, has long been favoured by British travellers, as is evident from the club-like décor. It has a lift down to the private beach, and a pool.

Sorrento caters for every budget. ★★**Pensione La Tonnarella**, Via Capo 31, ✆ 081 878 1153, ✎ 081 878 2169 (*moderate*) is a real bargain: in a villa with a private beach, and a good restaurant to boot. Reserve well in advance.

In Vico Equense, the best places to stay are a little outside the town centre, notably ★★★★**Capo La Gala**, ✆ 081 801 5758, ✎ 081 879 8747 (*moderate*), on the beach at Scrajo (where there are sulphur springs)—a beautiful modern resort hotel where every room has its own private terrace overlooking the beach. There's plenty of sea, and a pool too, but full-board is usually required, especially in high season.

★★**Loreley et Londres**, Via Califano 2, ✆ 081 807 3187 (*cheap*) is a *pensione* with lovely sea views and the most romantic sunsets you'll find anywhere in town from the terrace. In summer they insist on half-board if you want one of the rooms overlooking the sea—and away from the noisy road. There is also a lift down to a private sea-bathing platform. ***Nice**, Corso Italia 257, ✆ 081 807 2530, ✆ 081 807 1154 (*cheap*), just in front of the Circumvesuviana station, is also a surprisingly good find, conveniently close to the town centre. If you have a car, a good deal is to stay up on the hill at the *azienda agrituristica* **Il Giardino di Vigliano**, Località Villazzano, Massa Lubrense, ✆ 081 533 9823 (*cheap*), a 17th-century building complete with a Saracen tower. The view of Capri from the roof terrace is breathtaking. Half-board and apartment rental are also available. They sell their own organic oil and produce.

Sorrento has every kind of restaurant, including the grand and gloriously decorated **O' Parrucchiano**, Corso Italia 67, ✆ 081 878 1321 (*very expensive–expensive*), by tradition one of Italy's best. On Piazza Tasso, **Caruso** ✆ 081 807 3156 (*very expensive–expensive*) also has a vast and inventive menu, from rich melty *crocchette ai fiori di zucca* to fresh delicate *polpetti al pomodoro*. It all comes with an extensive wine list. Try to leave room for the dessert trolley, if you can. *Closed Mon Oct–April.* If you are celebrating a special occasion, or just in the mood for a memorable experience, the place to go nowadays is **Don Alfonso**, Piazza Sant'Agata, ✆ 081 878 0026, in Sant'Agata sui Due Golfi (*very expensive–expensive*), a Michelin-starred restaurant that some food critics reckon to be the best in southern Italy. The restaurant is actually 9km outside Sorrento, but the trip is well worth it. *Closed Sun evenings Sept–May and Mon all year.*

In Sorrento, **La Lanterna**, Via S. Cesareo 23/25, ✆ 081 878 1355 (*moderate–cheap*) is right in the middle of it all, with outside tables in the alley area which are a little quieter. It has tasteful décor, friendly and efficient service and, most important, impeccable *risotto ai frutti di mare*. For one of the best deals in town, try **Da Emilia**, Via Marina Grande 62, ✆ 081 807 2720 (*moderate–cheap*), a family-run *trattoria* with tables on a terrace overlooking the sea, and an excellent-value fixed menu based on fresh local ingredients and classic Sorrento recipes. *Closed Tues.*

For a very cheap meal, or a take-away, try the **Panetteria-Pizzeria Franco**, Corso Italia 265, ✆ 081 877 2066 (*moderate–cheap*), where you sit at long wooden tables and watch your pizza prepared in front of you. A popular place with locals. For a picnic, the delicatessen **Apreda**, Via Tasso 6, ✆ 081 878 2351 (*moderate–cheap*) has a mouth-watering range of breads, hams, salami and cheeses, including the best Sorrentine *treccia* (the local variation of *mozzarella*).

Amalfi Coast

When confronted with something generally acclaimed to be the most beautiful stretch of scenery in the entire Mediterranean, the honest writer is at a loss. Few who have been there would argue the point, but describing it properly is another matter. Along this coast, where one mountain after another plunges sheer into the sea, there is a string of towns that not long ago were accessible only by boat. Today, a spectacular corniche road of 'a thousand bends' covers the route, climbing in places to a thousand feet above the sea; necessity makes it so narrow that every encounter with an oncoming vehicle is an adventure, but everyone except the driver will have the treat of a lifetime. Nature here has created an amazing vertical landscape, a mix of sharp crags and deep green forests; in doing so she inspired the Italians to add three of their most beautiful towns.

This coast has always attracted foreigners, but only relatively recently has it become a major resort area. Places like Positano have become reserves for the wealthy, and swarms of day-trippers are likely to descend at any moment. Rumour has it that the boutiques here are so fashionable that the Romans come to Positano to shop for their summer wardrobe (though you would never guess it from the baskets of frilly bikinis piled up in the street). But tourism will never spoil this area; all the engineers in Italy couldn't widen the Amalfi road, and the impossible terrain leaves no room at all for new development.

Getting Around

Buses are the only form of public transport on the Amalfi Coast. SITA services travel regularly between Sorrento and Salerno (about every 50min; see p.814).

Tourist Information

Positano: Via Saracino 4, © 089 875 067, ✆ 089 875 760. **Amalfi**: Corso Roma 19, © 089 871 107, ✆ 089 872 619. **Ravello**: Piazza Duomo, © 089 857 096, ✆ 089 857 977. **Maiori**: Corso Regina, © 089 877 452, ✆ 089 853 672. **Salerno:** Piazza V. Veneto (outside the railway station), ©/✆ 089 231 432.

Positano

To complement the vertical landscape, here is Italy's most nearly vertical town. Positano spills down from the corniche like a waterfall of pink, cream and yellow villas. The day-trippers may walk down to the sea; only the alpinists among them make it back up (fortunately, there is a regular bus service along the one main street). After the Second World War Positano became a well-known hideaway for artists and writers—many of them American, following John Steinbeck's lead—and fashion was not slow to follow. Now, even though infested with coach parties, Positano reverts to the Positanesi in the off-season, and quietens down considerably. When you get to the bottom, there is a pebbly, grey beach and the town's church, decorated with a pretty tiled dome like so many others along this coast.

If you have time, take a trip further up to **Montepertuso**, a village perched 3km above Positano, which takes its name (meaning 'hole in the mountain') from an old legend—the devil challenged the Virgin Mary to blow a hole in the mountain, saying the winner could have control of the village. The devil tried, but failed miserably, while the Virgin coolly walked through the mountainside, leaving a hole still visible today. The next town east along the drive from Positano, **Praiano**, could be Positano's little sister: with a similar beach and church, but not quite as scenic and perpendicular, and not quite as beleaguered by tourism. Her natural attractions, however, leave her ripe for creeping exploitation. After Praiano, keep an eye out for the most impressive natural feature along the drive, the steep, impenetrable **Furore Gorge**. On either side are tiny isolated villages along the shore, with beaches—if only you can find a way to get to them. Further down the road you'll notice the lift leading down to the **Grotta Smeralda** (*open April–Oct daily 9–5; Nov–Mar daily 10–6; adm*). The strange green light that is diffused throughout this sea-level cavern gives it its name. Beyond this, **Conca dei Marini** is another vertical village, with a beach and a Norman lookout tower to climb.

Positano ✉ *84017*   *Where to Stay and Eating Out*

With Positano's high-fashion status come some of the highest hotel prices in Italy. In the high season at least, most of the resort hotels along the coast will expect you to take half-board, which means having either lunch or dinner in their restaurant. Not that that's always bad—some of the better hotels have gourmet restaurants and are often extremely good value. However, there are also some equally good places elsewhere to enjoy—if you can escape! Like many of the restaurants on the *Costiera*, a good number of Positano's eateries close from November till Easter.

If you're feeling self-indulgent—and very rich—you may care to stay at what many believe to be the finest resort hotel in the country, *******San Pietro**, ℰ 089 875 455, ✆ 089 811 449 (*luxury*), 1½km outside Positano *en route* to Amalfi. The entrance is hidden behind an old chapel, part of the plan to maintain the privacy and tranquillity of its celebrity clientele. Amid the richly coloured gardens, 58 individual rooms are immaculately maintained, each with a private terrace and spectacular views. There is a private beach, tennis courts and an excursion boat. *Closed Nov–Mar.*

*******Le Sirenuse**, Via Cristoforo Colombo 30, ℰ 089 875 066, ✆ 089 811 798 (*luxury*) is the former home of a noble Neapolitan family to whom it still belongs. It became a hotel in 1951 and takes its name from the islands of the Sirens which it overlooks. Everything is done with style, from the beautifully decorated drawing room to the swimming pool with its mosaic tiles. Cool and sophisticated, it lies close to the shops and restaurant, and offers a private pool, jacuzzi and fitness area.

******Palazzo Murat**, Via dei Mulini 23, ℰ 089 875 177, ✆ 089 811 419 (*very expensive–expensive*), in the heart of Positano, is an 18th-century palazzo which once belonged to Napoleon's brother-in-law Joachim Murat, briefly King of Naples. It has plenty of old-world charm, with antiques in many rooms and a beautiful courtyard shaded by lofty palm trees, where classical concerts are sometimes staged in summer. An elegant hotel with oodles of atmosphere.

The family-run *****Casa Albertina**, Via Favolozza 4, ℰ 089 875 143, ✆ 089 811 540 (*moderate*), a few minutes from the beach, is furnished in a lovely, understated manner, the better to accentuate the views over Positano and the sea. It has a nice restaurant on the roof terrace and in the busy season its quietness can be an advantage. Half-board is compulsory during high season. *****L'Ancora**, on Via Columbo, ℰ 089 875 318, ✆ 089 811 784 (*moderate*) is a little closer to the water. Small and professionally run, it has sea views, and much-needed parking in the centre of town.

The charmingly run hotel **California**, Via Colombo 141, ☏/☏ 089 875 382 (*cheap*) is a good bargain, with 15 rooms and a lovely terrace. It is well located, slightly set back from the sea.

The restaurant **La Cambusa**, Spiaggia Grande, ☏ 089 875 432 (*expensive*), in a lovely position with a terrace looking out on to the beach, is a Positano favourite. The chef serves excellently cooked fresh fish and seafood in as many ways as you can think of, and more. A house speciality is *penne con gamberetti, rucola e pomodoro* (penne with prawns, rocket and fresh tomatoes). Across the road, **Buca Di Bacco**, Via Rampa Teglia 8, ☏ 089 875 699 (*expensive*) is another Positano institution and *the* place to stop off for a drink on the way back from the beach. The fish is always well-cooked here, and you'd be crazy to go for anything else. It also has a few rooms.

Right on Positano's beach, the centre of the action in the summer is **Chez Black**, Via Brigantino, ☏ 089 875 036 (*expensive*), a slick and sophisticated restaurant run by local entrepreneur Salvatore Russo. Good Neapolitan favourites like *spaghetti alle vongole* are done well here, and maybe a banana split with *liquore Strega* for dessert.

The pizzeria-cum-trattoria, **Lo Guarracino**, Via Positanesi d'America 12, ☏ 089 875 794 (*moderate*) is a favourite with the Positanesi, in one of Positano's most lovely spots, on a terrace perched over the sea, reached by a short walk along the cliff path towards Fornillo beach. **Da Laurito**, ☏ 089 875 022 (*moderate*), a delightful trattoria set on a small beach, is accessible by free ferry service from the jetty at Positano beach. You can have a memorable meal at the makeshift tables under a straw canopy: the speciality here are good old-fashioned recipes such as *totani con patate* (squid cooked with potatoes in a wonderful sauce of oil and garlic), washed down with white wine spiked with fresh peaches. At the end of your meal, they'll ferry you back again.

Those with a car could try **Taverna del Leone**, Via Laurito 43, ☏ 089 875 474 (*cheap*), just outside Positano heading towards Amalfi. This busy pizzeria, bustling with young Positanesi, serves tasty nosh in relaxed surroundings at very reasonable prices. For those looking for something more sophisticated, the adjoining restaurant is more formal, though equally popular. At Montepertuso, above Positano, **Il Ritrovo**, Via Monte 53, ☏ 089 811 336 (*cheap*) is a pretty trattoria, with tomatoes strung from beams and good local dishes including, a rarity in these parts, grilled meats.

Amalfi

Sometimes history seems to be kidding us. Can it be true, can this miniscule village once have had a population of 80,000? There is no room among these jagged rocks for even a fraction of that—but then we remember that in Campania anything is possible, and we read how most of the old town simply slid into the sea during a storm and earthquake in 1343. Until that moment, Amalfi was a glorious place, the first Italian city to regain its balance after the Dark Ages, the first to recreate its civic pride and its mercantile daring, showing the way to Venice, Pisa and Genoa, though she kept few of the prizes for herself.

It is only natural that the Amalfitani would try to embroider their history a bit to match such an exquisite setting. Legends tell of a nymph named Amalphi who haunted this shore and became the lover of Hercules. As for their city's founding, they'll tell you about a party of

Roman noblemen fleeing the barbarians after the fall of the Empire, who found the site a safe haven to carry on the old Roman spirit and culture.

Amalfi first appears in the 6th century; by the 9th it had achieved its independence from the dukes of Naples and become the most important trading port of southern Italy, with a large colony of merchants at Constantinople and connections with all the Muslim lands. All of this came at a time for which historical records are scarce, but Amalfi's merchant adventurers must have had as romantically exciting a time as those of Venice. Their luck turned sour in the 1130s, with one brief occupation by the Normans, and a sacking at the hands of their mortal enemies—the Pisans—after a fatal sea battle that broke Amalfi's power forever.

The disaster of 1343 ensured that Amalfi's decline would be complete, but what's left of the place today—with its 5000 or so people—is beautiful almost to excess. Over the little square around the harbour, a conspicuous inscription brags: 'Judgement Day, for the Amalfitani who go to heaven, will be a day like any other day.' The square is called **Piazza Flavio Gioia**, after Amalfi's most famous merchant adventurer (his statue looks as if he's offering you a cup of tea); he's probably another fictitious character—more Amalfitano embroidery—but they claim he invented the compass in the 12th century.

From here, an arch under the buildings leads to the centre of the town, the **Piazza del Duomo**, with a long flight of steps up to the lovely **cathedral** (9th–12th centuries). Not even in Sicily was the Arab-Norman style ever carried to such a flight of fancy as in this delicate façade, with four levels of interlaced arches in stripes of different-coloured stone (much restored a century ago). The lace-like open arches are unique in Italy, though common enough in Muslim Spain, one of the countries with which Amalfi had regular trade relations. The cathedral's greatest treasure is its set of bronze doors, with scenes from scripture. They were made in Constantinople in 1066, commissioned by the leader of the Amalfitan colony there. The interior was restored in 18th-century Baroque, with plenty of frills in inlaid coloured marble. Down in the crypt you can see the head of St Andrew, patron of the city; this relic was a part of Amalfi's share of the loot in the sack of Constantinople in 1204.

One of the oldest parts of the cathedral to survive is the **Chiostro del Paradiso** (*open daily 9–6.45; adm*), a whitewashed quadrangle of more interlaced arches (*still under restoration*). To the side of the cloister is the **Basilica del Crocifisso**, the original cathedral, where amidst the surviving frescoes many of the bits and pieces of old Amalfi that have endured its calamities have been assembled: classical sarcophagi, medieval sculptures and coats of arms. Best of all are the fragments of Cosmatesque work, brightly coloured geometric mosaics that once were parts of pulpits and pillars. Don't miss the lovely 16th-century *Madonna col Bambino* by the stairs down to the Crypt.

From the centre of Amalfi you can walk in a few minutes out to the northern edge of the city, the narrow 'Valley of the Mills', set along a streambed between steep cliffs; some of the mills that made medieval Amalfi famous for paper-making are still in operation, and there is a small **Paper Museum** (*open daily 9–1; closed Mon and Fri; adm*) in the town. You can also watch paper being made and buy paper products at **Armatruda**, Via Fiume, ℭ 089 871 315, in central Amalfi, near the museum.

Amalfi ✉ *84011*   **Where to Stay and Eating Out**

*****Santa Caterina**, ℭ 089 871 012, 🖷 089 871 351 (*very expensive*), just outside Amalfi, has perhaps the loveliest gardens of all. A converted villa, it sits on a cliff-top providing wonderful sea views from most rooms. Its staff are courteous and discreet and its atmosphere cool and elegant. One refreshing slip—family snapshots with Hillary Clinton on display in the reception.

St Francis himself is said to have founded the ****Luna**, ℭ 089 871 002, 🖷 089 871 333 (*expensive*), though the lifts and Hollywood-style pool are a little more recent. This former monastery, above the drive on Amalfi's eastern edge, was already a hotel in the waning days of the Grand Tour—Wagner stayed here while searching for his Garden of Klingsor, and they can show you the room where Ibsen wrote *A Doll's House*. Deftly modernized, it provides comfortable rooms and attentive service.

To get away from it all, your best bet is the 12th-century ****Cappuccini Convento**, Via Annunziatella 46, ℭ 089 871 877, 🖷 089 871 886 (*moderate*), built by Emperor Frederick II on a mountainside over the town, with a suitably ancient lift running down through the cliffs to the beach. The converted cells, now hotel bedrooms, are dark and unsophisticated, in keeping with the closed monastic order that once prevailed here. Set high above the tourist-infested streets, its colonnade bedecked with flowers offers the best view in Amalfi.

There is a fair collection of inexpensive hotels around the cathedral; two of the best are the tiny and elaborately furnished **Sant'Andrea**, Via Santolo Camera 1, ℭ 089 871 145 (*cheap*), with good views of the cathedral and an effusive welcome from your proprietress; and **Fontana**, Piazza Duomo 7, ℭ 089 871 530 (*cheap*), which has 16 spotless rooms offering plenty of space and a prime location at bargain prices.

Da Gemma, Via Fra Gerardo Sasso 9, ℭ 089 871 345 (*expensive*), established in 1872, is one of Amalfi's oldest restaurants, with a terrace and an excellent fish-based menu. Their *zuppa di pesce* is a wonderfully rich mixture of all sorts of different fish and seafood. Leave room for the *melanzane al cioccolato* (grilled aubergines in chocolate sauce), an unexpected but heavenly combination. *Closed Wed.* **Antico Hostaria Bacco**, Via G. B. Lama 9, Furore, ℭ 089 830 360, 🖷 089 830 352 (*expensive*), up in the hills on the road to Agerola, is a wonderful detour if you have a car. The delightful Ferraioli family serve delicious seafood *antipasti* and pasta—*ferrazzuoli* with sword fish and rocket—and, for dessert, their own *melanzane al cioccolato* (*see* above).

They also serve the local white wine—Costa d'Amalfi Furore (available for sale across the road). There are a few charming rooms (*moderate*), with views to the sea. The **Taverna degli Apostoli**, Via Sant'Anna 5, © 089 872 991 (*moderate*), almost directly under the cathedral, is cosy with a warm and informal atmosphere which when we last visited echoed with the ribald laughter of local festivities. Highly recommended. *Closed Tues.* At **Lo Smeraldino**, Piazzale dei Protontini 1, © 089 871 070 (*moderate*), at the far end of the port on the water's edge, you'll be offered the area speciality, *scialatielli ai frutti di mare*—fresh pasta with mixed seafood—and a range of good *secondi*, most notably an excellent *fritto misto*.

North of the cathedral, **Tarì**, Via P. Capuano, © 089 871 832 (*cheap*) is a pretty, welcoming trattoria with traditional checked tablecloths and service with a smile. Its cool, cavernous surroundings are a welcome respite for the hot and weary traveller. **Da Baracca**, Piazza dei Dogi, © 089 871 285 (*cheap*) is everything an Italian trattoria should be. Tables and chairs spill out on to this tranquil piazza just west of the cathedral, where diners are shielded from the midday sun by a shady awning and leafy plants. Friendly waiters proffer tasty snacks and plates of steaming pasta.

At **San Giuseppe**, Via Ruggiero II 4, © 089 872 640 (*cheap*), a family-run hostelry, the pizza is sublime—it should be: the owner is a baker. Homely bowls of pasta are also available, brought to you by a trio of portly brothers, and consumed amid the noise of television and shrieking children. *Closed Thurs.* Near the cathedral, **Da Maria**, Via Lorenzo d'Amalfi 14, © 089 871 880 (*cheap*) is a lively trattoria and pizzeria; the waiters are cheerful and helpful, and the food a cut above some of the other less expensive places.

Villages Inland: Ravello and Scala

As important as it was in its day, the Amalfitan Republic never grew very big. At its greatest extent, it could only claim a small part of this coast, including these two towns up in the mountains; like Amalfi they were once much larger and more prosperous than you see them today. **Ravello** is another beauty, a balcony overlooking the Amalfi Coast and a treasure house of exotic medieval art. As the second city of the Amalfitan Republic, medieval Ravello had a population of 30,000 (at least that's what they claim); now it provides an example of that typically Italian phenomenon—a village of 2000 with a first-rate cathedral.

Ravello's chief glories are two wonderful gardens. The **Villa Cimbrone** (*open daily 9–7; adm*) was laid out by Lord Grimthorpe, the Englishman responsible for the design of Big Ben, and has a priceless view over the Amalfi Coast. The **Villa Rùfolo** (*open daily 9–8; adm*), as fans of Wagner will be interested to know, is none other than Klingsor's magic garden. Wagner says so himself, in a note scribbled in the villa's guest book. He came here looking for the proper setting in which to imagine the worldly, Faustian enchanter of *Parsifal*, and thus his imagination was fired.

The villa itself is a remarkable 11th-century pleasure palace, a temporary abode of Charles of Anjou, various Norman kings and Adrian IV, the only English pope (1154–9), who came here when fleeing a rebellion in Rome. Even in its present, half-ruined state, it is worth a visit; inside there is a small collection of architectural fragments, including a Moorish cloister and two crumbling towers, one of which can still be climbed. The garden, with more fine views, is a semi-tropical paradise; in summer it reverberates with 'sounds and sweet airs' as the setting for various open-air concerts.

The **cathedral** is named after Ravello's patron, San Pantaleone, an obscure early martyr; they have a phial of his blood in one of the side chapels, and it 'boils' like the blood of San Gennaro in Naples whenever the saint is in the mood. Lately he hasn't been, which worries the Ravellans. The cathedral has two particular treasures: a pair of bronze doors from the 12th century, inspired by the Greek ones at Amalfi, and an exquisite pair of marble *ambones*, or pulpits, that rank among the outstanding examples of 12th–13th-century sculptural and mosaic work. Two other Ravello churches, where you can see decorative work similar to the cathedral's, are **Santa Maria a Gradello** and **San Giovanni del Toro**. From Ravello it is only a lovely 1½km walk to **Scala**, smallest and oldest of the three Amalfitan towns, with another ancient cathedral.

Between Amalfi and Ravello, before reaching the turn-off inland, the Amalfi drive passes through **Atrani**, an old village whose cathedral has another tiled dome, and yet another set of bronze doors from Constantinople. Beyond the Ravello turn, next along the way towards Salerno, come **Minori** and **Maiori**. Minori is a typical *Costiera* hill-town which, despite encroaching tourism, maintains considerable charm. Its bigger sister is somewhat less enticing, mainly due to a major flood in 1954 which washed away most of the seafront; today most of the buildings and hotels along the shore are depressingly modern. **Erchie**, a tiny hamlet on the shore far below the road, seems a lovely spot—if you can figure out a way to get down to it. Then, near the end of the drive, the real world comes back into view as the busy port of Salerno stretches before you. Here you find the tiny resort of **Cetara**, with a fine beach behind a newly constructed fishing port, and, just before Salerno, **Vietri sul Mare**, another steep and pretty town, famous throughout Italy for its beautiful *maiolica* ware. There are ceramics shops everywhere, where you can watch craftsmen hand-painting jugs, vases and tiles, and pick up souvenirs at surprisingly good prices.

Ravello ✉ *84010* **Where to Stay and Eating Out**

Ravello also has its share of dream hotels, offering no beaches, but unforgettable gardens and views down over the coast. In the shadow of Amalfi and Ravello, the two pleasant beach lidos of Minori and Maiori may seem a little dull, but they can be useful bases, especially if hotels in the better-known resorts are full.

★★★★★**Palumbo**, Via S. Giovanni del Toro 28, ✆ 089 857 244, ✆ 089 857 347, *palumbo@amalfinet.it* (*luxury*) has an incredible guest book filled with the names of the famous over the last 120 years. The entrance opens on to an elegant Arabic-style courtyard which only hints at the 12 rooms, each individually decorated with antiques. The restaurant is highly renowned, and the excellent Episcopio wine really is house wine—made on the premises. There is also a simpler *dipendenza* (a cheaper alternative) with seven rooms.

The other top establishment in Ravello is the recently renovated ★★★★★**Palazzo Sasso**, Via S. Giovanni del Toro 58, ✆ 089 818 181, 🖷 089 858 900, *info@palazzosasso.com* (*luxury*). Originally a 12th-century villa belonging to the Sasso family, it was first owned by Fra Gerardo, the founder of the Sovereign Military Order of Malta. It's here Wagner rushed back to in order to fix on paper the vision he caught in Villa Rùfolo. These days you're likely to bump into Gore Vidal having dinner in their famed Rossellini restaurant. Refreshingly, the plush décor and astonishing views come with a very friendly staff.

With the lushest gardens on the coast, ★★★**Villa Cimbrone**, Via Santa Chiara 26, ✆ 089 857 459, 🖷 089 858 072 (*very expensive*) is a very special place to stay: another elegant old villa, once the property of an English duke, set in its own parkland perched dizzyingly high on the cliffs. The 10 rooms are beautifully decorated (half with sea views) and the view from the terrace where breakfast is served is a feast all of its own. There are drawbacks, however, such as the lack of a restaurant and the 10-minute walk needed to get there (cars have to be parked further down in the village). Nonetheless, it does have a swimming pool.

★★★★**Caruso Belvedere**, Via S. Giovanni del Toro 2, ✆ 089 857 111, 🖷 089 857 372 (*expensive*) was once popular with the Bloomsbury set and with Greta Garbo (she had room 21). Behind its sun-bleached façade, this hotel encapsulates the quiet elegance of the old patrician villa it once was—even the laundry room holds a fading fresco. In the beautifully laid out gardens, there is a belvedere over the sea and mountains, and the well-tended vegetable garden and vineyard on another level provide fresh produce and the hotel's own wine for the excellent restaurant.

One of the prettiest hotels, and perhaps the most welcoming place to stay in Ravello, is the delightful ★★★★**Villa Maria**, Via Santa Chiara 2, ✆ 089 857 255, 🖷 089 857 071 (*expensive*). A light, airy charm prevails in this gracious and tastefully converted villa. The vast suite (more expensive than the normal rooms) has one of the most breathtaking terraces in Ravello and there is a beautiful eating area in the garden, sheltered by vines and graced with yet another astonishing view. The restaurant recently won an award, and is acknowledged throughout the region.

Under the same obliging ownership as the Villa Maria, and only a few minutes walk away, ★★★**Giordano**, Via Trinità 14, ✆ 089 857 255, 🖷 089 857 071 (*moderate*) is a modern hotel, with the added advantage of a heated outdoor swimming pool and solarium. Villa Maria guests have equal access to the facilities, and parking for both hotels is available here.

Along the coast in Minori, ★★★★**Villa Romana**, ✆ 089 877 237, 🖷 089 877 302 (*moderate*) is a stylish and comfortable, modern hotel, certainly the best of the hotels in the less elegant resorts of Maori and Minori. The rooftop pool is well away from crowds and car fumes, and the rooms are clean and pleasant.

For a five-star view at a third of the price in Ravello, check into ****Villa Amore, where is it?**Ⓒ/◉ 089 857 135 (*cheap*), a delightful small hotel with 12 clean simple rooms, and a lovely terrace where you can take cappuccino with the canaries. It retains a warm, homely atmosphere not common to most of the larger hotels in this area. Another gem in this price category can be found in unspoilt Scala. **Villa Giuseppina**, Ⓒ/◉ 089 857 106 (*cheap*) offers comfort and charm at affordable prices. Good food and great views from the swimming pool make this a tranquil spot to wile away those hazy days of summer. If you prefer you can stay at the older-style **Margherita** (*cheap*) which shares the facilities. Parking is easy and you can enjoy some lovely walks down to Amalfi. Just be sure to catch the bus back.

At **Cumpà Cosimo**, Via Roma 44/46, Ⓒ 089 857 156 (*moderate*), owner-cook Signora Netta Bottone is always happy to advise you on her latest concoctions and try out her school English. A holiday high-spot. At Maiori, you'll get good fresh fish at **Mammato**, Via Arsenale 6, Ⓒ 089 877 036 (*moderate*). A glass-fronted restaurant appropriately located overlooking the sea, Mammato is a popular and relaxed venue for beach bums and locals alike. *Closed Wed.*

On a side street in sleepy Minori, is the pretty and floral **Il Giardinello**, Corso V. Emanuele 17 Ⓒ 089 877 050 (*cheap*). Pass under the leafy archway, and you find yourself in an elegant restaurant, humming with appreciative diners. The menu is varied and interesting, with plenty of fish, but also pasta and the house speciality— pizza for four! Even if it's not on the agenda, one delightful reason for stopping in Vietri sul Mare is **La Locanda**, Corso Umberto 1, Ⓒ 089 761 070 (*cheap*). The food is inventive, tasty and plentiful, and served on the attractive hand-painted plates which have made the town famous. Finishing touches, rarely found in an area now consumed by tourism, make this a truly memorable experience— and if you're really good, you might even take home some pottery of your own. *Closed Mon.*

Salerno

Anywhere else in the south of Italy, a city like Salerno would be an attraction in itself; here it gets lost among the wonders of the Campanian coast—just the big town at the end of the Amalfi Drive—and few people ever stop for more than a very brief visit. Nevertheless, Salerno has its modest charms. Its setting under a backdrop of mountains is memorable. The Italian highway engineers, showing off as usual, have brought a highway to Salerno on a chain of viaducts, one lofty span after another, an unusual and pleasing ornament for the city; at night the road lights hang on the mountain slopes like strings of fairy lights on a Christmas tree.

Salerno's ancient distinction was its medical school, the oldest and finest of medieval Europe. Founded by the legendary 'Four Doctors'—an Italian, a Greek, a Jew and an Arab—the school was of the greatest importance in the transmission of Greek and Muslim science into Europe. Most of us, however, may recognize Salerno better as the site of the Allied invasion in September 1943, one of the biggest operations of the Second World War.

Salerno's port is on the outskirts of town, and the shore all through the city centre is graced with a pretty park, the Lungomare Trieste. Parallel with it, and two streets back, the Corso Vittorio Emanuele leads into the old town. Here it changes its name to Via dei Mercanti, most colourful of Salerno's old streets. The **cathedral**, a block to the north on Via del

Duomo, is set with its façade behind a courtyard, or *quadroporticos* (*currently under restoration*), with a fountain at the centre, and a detached campanile—as if it were not a church at all, but a mosque. The Corinthian columns around it come from the ancient city of Paestum, not far down the coast. The cathedral's treasures are of the same order as those of the Amalfi coast: another pair of bronze doors from Constantinople, and another beautiful pair of Cosmatesque pulpits, though a surprise comes with the overwhelming mosaic floor, 1968 square foot of marble and polychrome tiles of Byzantine inspiration. The building itself has been much restored, and many of the best original details have been preserved in the adjacent **Museo del Duomo** (*open April–Oct daily 9–7; Nov–Mar daily 9–4.30*).

From Salerno you can make an easy excursion up into the mountains to the town of **Cava de' Tirreni**. Near it, perched precariously on the slopes of the Val di Bonea, is a little-visited Benedictine monastery called **La Trinità di Cava**—rebuilt, as usual, in tiresome Baroque, but preserving a wealth of 12th–14th-century frescoes, stone-carving and Cosmati work.

Salerno ✉ *84100*   ***Where to Stay and Eating Out***

Salerno's hotels are fairly modest and utilitarian. Though the cathedral is well worth a visit, this is not a good base for a holiday. The beach is elbow-room only and covered with litter. Instead head up to Paestum where beaches are cleaner and less crowded. If you just want to stay a couple of nights, the hotels and restaurants should satisfy most explorers' needs.

****Jolly Hotel delle Palme, Lungomare Trieste 1, ✆ 089 225 222, 🖷 089 237 571 (*expensive–moderate*) is right on the seafront. *****Plaza**, Piazza Ferrovia 42, ✆ 089 224 477, 🖷 089 237 311 (*expensive–moderate*) is more than acceptable for a short stay, across from the station with comfortable modern rooms. *****Fiorenza**, Via Trento 145, ✆/🖷 089 338 800 (*expensive–moderate*) is a clean, well-run hotel, convenient for the beach.

Several cheaper hotels are around the Corso Vittorio Emanuele. Try the ****Salerno**, Via G. Vicinanza 42, ✆ 089 224 211, 🖷 089 224 432 (*cheap*)—simple but comfortable. Salerno also has a youth hostel, **Ostello per la Gioventu' Irno**, Via Luigi Guercio 112, ✆ 089 790 251, 🖷 089 252 649. *Closed daily 10.30–5; curfew 1am.*

Nicola dei Principati, Corso Garibaldi 201, ✆ 089 225 435 (*expensive*), in the old centre of Salerno, serves mainly fish, including an excellent *linguine con astice* (long pasta with lobster). At **Il Timone**, Via Generale Clark 29, ✆ 089 335 111 (*expensive*), the speciality is *tubetti alla pescatrice* (short pasta served with a delicious fish sauce). The second courses, almost all fish, are equally good. *Closed Mon.*

Vicolo della Neve, Vicolo della Neve 24, ✆ 089 225 705 (*moderate*) is one of the liveliest restaurants in town, right in the *centro storico*, an attractive place decorated with wall paintings by some of the many artists who have established it as their local. The chef turns out good Campanian favourites such as *melanzane alla parmigiana*—aubergines with mozzarella, parmesan, tomato and basil—and the classic *pasta e fagioli*. You can also order excellent pizza. *Open evenings only; closed Wed.*

At **Alla Brace**, Lungomare Trieste 11/13, ✆ 089 221 733 (*moderate*), as well as the usual fish dishes, you will be offered a host of delicious local specialities such as stuffed peppers, ravioli filled with ricotta, and a remarkable potato soufflé. There is also a wide range of home-made desserts. **Al Cenacolo**, Piazza Alfano I, ✆ 089 228 818 (*moderate*), in front of the cathedral, serves excellent seafood and is recommended by the locals.

Da Sasa, Via Diaz 42, ✆ 089 220 330 (*cheap*) is a good trattoria, with traditional home cooking and especially tasty pasta courses. For good pizza and seafood, **Pinocchio**, Lungomare Trieste 56/58, ✆ 089 229 964 (*cheap*) is also great value. Head here to dine shoulder to shoulder with Salernitani. *Closed Fri.*

The Islands of the Bay of Naples

Without a doubt, the islands in the Bay of Naples—Capri, Ischia, and to a far lesser extent Procida—are the holiday queens of the Italian islands. Despite their location, the three islands have very different geological origins. Ischia and Procida are part of an enormous submerged volcanic chain, stretching from Ventotene in the Pontine Islands down to Strómboli and the other Aeolian Islands. In not too ancient times, the two islands were connected to each other and, if the Greek geographer Strabo is to be believed, also to the Phlegraean Fields on the mainland. Phlegraean means 'fiery' in Greek, and Strabo records how, during an eruption of the now dormant volcano Epomeo on Ischia, an earthquake split Ischia–Procida from the mainland, then, in another upheaval, jolted the once-united island in twain. In this same geological cataclysm, Capri broke off from the Sorrentine Peninsula, a blow that shattered its coasts to form the island's famous cliffs.

Getting There

In summer, there are as many as six ferries and 20 hydrofoils a day from Naples to Capri, and as many to Ischia. There are also regular departures to Procida. There are frequent ferries and hydrofoils daily from Sorrento to Capri, from Pozzuoli to Procida and between Ischia and Procida. For more information on ferry services from Naples, *see* p.791 and pp.824–25. Local and longer-distance ferries and hydrofoils from Naples leave from three different points along the harbourside—**Molo Beverello** and the **Stazione Marittima**, both in the centre of the port, and **Mergellina**, further to the west. Be sure to check you know the right dock for your ticket and destination.

Capri

Getting Around

Arriving in Marina Grande, you can ascend to either Capri or Anacapri by **bus** (*daily 8am–10pm every 15 mins, 10pm–midnight every half-hour*). There is also a **funicular** that runs up to Capri town (*summer daily 6.30am–12.30am every 15 mins; Oct–April daily until 9pm*). The **chairlift** from Anacapri to Monte Solaro (12-min) runs all day (*summer 9.30–sunset; Nov–Feb 10.30–3; closed Tues*). Buses run from Capri town to Anacapri, Marina Piccola and Damecuta. There are also buses from Anacapri to the Blue Grotto, Faro and Marina Piccola. Daily **tours** of Capri by motor launch leave from Marina Grande (*June–Sept; first tour 9am*). Otherwise you can walk to most places; the beautiful trails across the island are major attractions.

Capri town: Piazza Umberto 1, ✉ 80073, ✆ 081 837 0686.
Marina Grande: at Banchina del Porto, ✆ 081 837 0634.
Anacapri: Via G. Orlandi 59/a, ✉ 80071, ✆ 089 837 1524.

Capri is pure enchantment, a delicious garden of Eden with over 800 species of flowers and plants cascading over a sheer chunk of limestone, which has been torn and eroded away into fantastic forms, most famously the incredibly blue **Grotta Azzurra**—its shimmering, iridescent blueness is caused by the reflection of light on the water in the morning.

In summer (*1 June–30 Sept*), boats for the Blue Grotto leave at 9am—when the sea is calm. The **sea excursion around the island** is a rare experience, but again possible only in good weather. Besides visiting other lovely grottoes, such as the **Grotta Bianca** and the **Grotta Verde** (the White Cave and the Green Cave), it provides breathtaking views of the cliffs and Capri's uncanny rock formations.

Flower-bedecked **Capri town** is a charming white village packed with jewellery shops and designer boutiques, and, in summer, with tourists hailing from anywhere from Berkeley to Baghdad. Capri town is the base for several walks, each more splendid than the last—aim for the famous **Faraglioni**, three towering pinnacles in the sea. From Via Tragara a stairway descends to the point and the **Porto di Tragara**, where you can take a swim. Nearby is the **Tragara terrace**, with views over monolithic **Pizzolungo** to the **Arco Naturale**, where dark pines—as everywhere else on Capri—cling to every tiny ledge they can sink their roots into.

Or head for **La Certosa** (*open daily 9–2; closed Mon*), a charming golden-hued 14th-century Carthusian charterhouse, built over one of Tiberius' villas and topped by a 17th-century Baroque tower. A few minutes away are the **Gardens of Augustus**, founded by Caesar himself. A wide variety of trees and plants grow on the fertile terraces and belvederes overlooking one of the most striking views in the world.

A narrow road (*currently closed for reinforcement work*)—Via Krupp—takes you down the cliffs in a hundred hairpin turns to the charming little port of **Marina Piccola**. There is a bus, fortunately, that makes the steep climb back up the cliffs to Capri town. A longer walk takes you to the ruins of the **Villa Jovis** (*open daily 9–one hour before sunset; adm*), Tiberius' pleasure palace, and the infamous **Salto di Tiberio**—always pointed out as the precipice from which the emperor hurled his victims.

More striking views may be had from Capri's more laid-back second town, **Anacapri**, up on the island's top shelf. There are regular buses connecting it to Marina Grande and Capri town, and a chairlift that goes up even further to the summit of **Monte Solaro**, for a fabulous view of the island and the whole of the Bay of Naples.

Capri ✉ *80073*   **Where to Stay and Eating Out**

Not surprisingly, hotel prices on Capri are well above average for the surrounding area on-shore, and rooms for the summer months are often booked up months in advance.

If money is no object, ★★★★★**Grand Hotel Quisisana**, Via Camerelle 2, ✆ 081 837 0788, ● 081 837 6080 (*very expensive*) is the place to stay in Capri town, a luxurious palace of a hotel set in its own grounds and equipped with pool, gym, tennis courts and just about everything else you could need for a smart holiday. The building was originally a sanatorium built by an Englishman, George Clark.

Outside Capri town at Punta Tragara, in a building designed by Le Corbusier, ★★★★**Punta Tragara**, Via Tragara 57, ✆ 081 837 0844, 🖃 081 837 7790 (*very expensive*) is a de luxe resort hotel, with pool, gym, restaurants and more. The architect's distinctive modern style and the predominance of strong reds, oranges and dark wood fittings come at a price, but the views from the rooms are spectacular.

★★★★**La Palma**, Via V. Emanuele, ✆ 081 837 0133, 🖃 081 837 6966 (*expensive*) is good value by Capri standards. Just above the Quisisana in Capri town, it is set in its own gardens, with lovely majolica-tiled floors in the rooms and a pleasant airy feel.The staff are charming and the whole atmosphere more comfortable than many of the more expensive hotels.

Further up on the way to Punta Tragara,★★★★**Villa Brunella**, Via Tragara 24, ✆ 081 837 0122, 🖃 081 837 0430 (*expensive*) is a pretty hotel with rooms on terraces that overlook Monte Solaro. There is a good restaurant and pool for lazing away hot afternoons. The emphasis is on villa-style accommodation and privacy, suiting those who are looking for a retreat.

Book well ahead to stay at ★★**Villa Krupp**, Viale Matteotti 12, ✆ 081 837 0362, 🖃 081 837 6489 (*moderate*), one of the loveliest and most historic, lower-priced hotels in Capri. Situated above the path up to the Gardens of Augustus, the hotel has enviable views, antique furniture and a relaxed, welcoming ambience where one can sit and compose letters all day. Trotsky stayed here and even left a samovar.

★**Stella Maris**, Via Roma 10/19, ✆ 081 837 0452, 🖃 081 837 8662 (*cheap*), close to the bus station, is a cosy family-run affair. They have been here for generations and are proud of their hospitality. ★**La Tosca**, Via D. Birago, ✆/🖃 081 837 0989 (*cheap*), still in Capri town, has tiled rooms with high ceilings. Ask for one with a view.

Capri's best restaurant has long been **La Capannina**, Via delle Botteghe 12/14, ✆ 081 837 0732 (*expensive*), set in a secluded garden in Capri town, with delicately prepared shellfish, pasta and fish, and good desserts. **I Faraglioni**, Via Camerelle 75, ✆ 081 837 0320 (*expensive*) has delectable house specialities:*crêpes al formaggio*, (paper-thin pancakes filled with cheese) and *risotto ai frutti di mare.*

Up the stairs past the cathedral and down the tunnel to the right in Capri town, **Da Gemma**, Via Madre Serafina 6, ✆ 081 837 0461, 🖃 081 837 8947 (*moderate*) is as nice in winter as in summer, a welcoming trattoria with walls decked with brass pans and ceramic plates, and superbly cooked local dishes including a fine *risotto alla pescatore*, delicious mozzarella grilled on a lemon leaf, and very good pizza.

In Anacapri, about a half-hour's walk from the Piazzetta, **Da Gelsomina la Migliara**, Via La Migliara 72, ✆ 081 837 1499 (*moderate*) offers not only home-made wine, but true home-cooked island specialities, including mushrooms collected on Monte Solaro. The risotto here is a real treat in all its forms.

Getting Around

Ischia is considerably larger than Capri, divided into six self-contained communities. **Buses** (and taxis) to the various towns on the island depart from the square next to Santa Maria di Portosalvo in Ischia Porto, near the beginning of the SS270, which circles the island. An entire circuit of the island takes about 2½hrs. **Cars** can be hired relatively cheaply here, or you may prefer to rent a *motorino* (moped).

Tourist Information

Ischia Porto: Via Iasolino, ✉ 80077, ✆ 081 991 146, near the ferry landing.

Green, mountainous and volcanic, Ischia comes in a close second to Capri in the beauty and fashion pageant, blessed with something its more famous sister totally lacks—beautiful beaches. On one—Maronti—the island's volcanic origins are more than evident. The hot mineral springs that gush all year round have attracted cure-seekers since Roman times, and are still recommended today for people suffering from rheumatism, arthritis, neuralgia and obesity. Because many of the springs are radioactive, a doctor's permission is often required before you take a soak (there are physicians on the island who specialize in prescribing such treatments, and they charge a pretty penny). The hottest spring on the island is Terme Rita, at Casamicciola, which belches from the earth at around 180°F.

Ischia Porto and adjacent **Ischia Ponte** are lively and very fashionable, the former boasting curative radioactive hotsprings, the second the storybook **Castello d'Ischia**, the fortress islet where Michelangelo's great friend the poetess Vittoria Colonna spent so many years. Also called the Castello Aragonese, the islet can be visited, with its narrow streets and 500-year-old houses; the views from the walls are superb. More wonderful views await from the summit of the extinct volcano, **Montagnone** (836ft), stretching over the Phlegraean Fields on the mainland, Ischia's little sister island Procida, and the rest of Ischia as well.

Ischia ✉ *80077* Where to Stay and Eating Out

Up a long road, just off the SS270 outside Lacco Ameno, ★★★★★**Grand Albergo Mezza Torre**, Via Mezza Torre, ✆ 081 986 111, ✆ 081 987 015 (*very expensive*) is a 60-room hotel housed in a 16th-century tower which shares the grounds of a small castle that belonged to the film director Visconti (*after much controversy now under restoration*). With a spa, tennis courts and an outdoor pool just above the beach, it cannot be beaten for good old-fashioned luxury and country-house atmosphere.

The finest hotel in Ischia Porto, ★★★★**Excelsior Belvedere**, Via Gianturco 1, ✆ 081 991 522, ✆ 081 984 100 (*expensive*) is down a side street off Corso Vittoria Colonna. It is quieter than most and guests can enjoy the fine pool and garden. Tastefully decorated with antique furniture and discreetly managed. *Closed Nov–Mar.*

★★★★**Villarosa**, Via G. Gante 13, just off Via Roma, in Ischia Porto, ✆ 081 991 316, 🖷 081 992 425 (*moderate*) is an elegant hotel screened from the outside world by a leafy forecourt. Leave behind the heat and bustle of the streets for this cool inner sanctum, tastefully furnished with a minimum of fuss and surprisingly well priced for a hotel of such finesse. Small pool, garden and thermal treatments available. *Closed Nov–Mar.*

★★★★**Punta del Sole**, Piazza Maltese, ✆ 081 989 156, 🖷 081 998 209 (*moderate*) is tucked away in a lovely flower-filled garden in the heart of Forio, a cool and restful hideaway like an oasis among the abundant bougainvillea. Leafy walks, helpful management and attractive balconies combine to make this one of the most likeable hotels on the island.

One of the least expensive places to stay in Ischia Ponte is within the Castello Aragonese itself. ★★**Il Monastero**, Castello Aragonese 39, ✆ 081 992 435 (*cheap*) has 14 clean and simple *en suite* rooms, housed in the cells where monks once slept. It's a bit of a climb, but the view is unforgettable. ★★**Bristol**, Via Fundera 72, Lacco Ameno, ✆ 081 994 566, 🖷 081 994 586 (*cheap*), with a small garden and swimming pool, is a good bet if you can't afford the plusher hotels.

For some reason, Ischia is fairly hopping with rabbits, and the locals have dreamed up endless ways of eating them, in stews, roast, or even with pasta.

Gennaro, Via Porto 66, in Ischia Porto, ✆ 081 992 917, 🖷 081 983 636 (*expensive*) serves superb giant prawns and many other delicious Ischian specialities. The food is a perfectionist's dream, carefully prepared and presented, and guaranteed to leave your tastebuds tingling.

Leaving Ischia Porto and heading out towards Casamicciola, those with transport might like to check out **Il Damiano**, Via della Vigna, on the SS270, ✆ 081 983 032 (*expensive*) which has superb views, plus beautifully cooked seafood and fish dishes—best of all the *linguine all'aragosta* (with a lobster sauce). *Open evenings only.*

Just before you reach the causeway, on the seafront in Ischia Porto, you can enjoy traditional food in unpretentious surroundings at **Da Cocò**, Piazzale Aragonese, ✆ 081 981 823 (*moderate*). Run by Salvatore di Meglio, a retired fisherman who claims to be 'in love with the sea', this relaxed eaterie comes highy recommended by the locals who cram into the noisy and friendly dining area.

Also in Ischia Porto, **Zi Nannina a Mare**, Via Cristoforo Colombo, ✆ 081 991 350 (*moderate*) is a delightful family-run *trattoria* with an outdoor terrace offering traditional, well-cooked regional specialities, based on either fish or meat.

For a delicious meal right on the harbour front in Lacco Ameno, head for **Al Delfino**, Corso A. Rizzoli 116, ✆ 081 900 252 (*moderate*). Steaming plates are carried from the kitchen across the street to the chattering clientele in the glass-fronted restaurant; try *spaghetti alle vongole*.

In the open countryside near Forio, *en route* to Santa Maria del Monte, the rustic **Cavé Gran Diavolo**, Via Bocca 56, ✆ 081 989 282 (*moderate*) serves more meat than fish, with pride of place going to Forio's famous dish, *bucatini con sugo di coniglio*—fat spaghetti served in rabbit sauce. Good local wine. *Closed Wed.*

Getting Around

There are frequent **ferry** and **hydrofoil** services from both Naples and Ischia to Procida. The harbour itself is tiny, and if you want to explore further afield, jump on one of the colourful **diesel-powered buggies** that serve as taxis. Alternatively, there is a **bus** service about every half-hour between the harbour and the other end of the island at Chiaiolella, stopping more or less at every point in between.

Tourist Information

Marina Grande: Via Roma 92, ✆ 081 810 1968, @ 081 981 904, near the ferry departure point.

Lovely, uncomplicated and tiny, Procida is in many ways the archetypal image of all that an 'Italian island' evokes in any holiday dreamer's mind, scented by groves that produce the finest lemons in Italy (the *granita* served in almost every local bar is a treat) and embellished with colourful houses as original as they are beautiful. Its main port, overlooked by the ancient village of **Corricella**, is a pastel fantasy with the undulating rhythm of a hundred arches. Steep stone stairways cascade down among the arches; from the little port they're like a hundred watchful eyes, scanning the sea for the fishermen's return.

Perched up on the promontory overhead, the **Terra Murata** (298ft, Procida's highest point) is the old walled town, where you can visit the 16th-century **Castello d'Aragona** and the church of **San Michele Arcangelo**, which, despite its exotic, almost Saracen appearance from a distance, wears a simple unadorned façade, rebuilt after the various pirates' depredations. The domes are untiled—Procida receives so little rain that tiles aren't strictly necessary, or at least worth the cost.

Beyond this minimal urban centre, Procida is an enchanting Ruritania of lemon groves and crumbling old villas, rural beauty spots, shaded walkways and narrow roads, old farmhouses and crumbling small palazzi—you can walk around it in a day, or take the bus to the south end, where **Chiaiolella**, a small fishing port, has a long stretch of sand facing the tiny wooded islet of **Vivara**, where the birds are protected these days but the rabbits are fair game. The areas around **Centane**, especially Punta Solchiaro, are especially pretty, with views over the entire east coast of the island from the belvedere.

Procida ✉ *80079*

Where to Stay and Eating Out

There are very few places to stay. However, it's an ideal spot for relaxing in the sunshine away from the crowds. There are enough ferries not to feel isolated, but your evenings will be quiet.

★★★**Crescenzo**, Via Marina Chiaiolella 33, ✆ 081 896 7255, @ 081 810 1260 (*cheap*), right on the harbour front in Chiaiolella, and a short walk to the beach, is a landmark in Procida. Its rooms are simply but pleasantly furnished, and the restaurant serves local specialities and pizza in the evening.

There are several good restaurants in the port at Marina Grande, like **La Medusa**, Via Roma 116, ✆ 081 896 7481 (*moderate*) which serves excellent seafood—the house speciality is *spaghetti ai ricci di mare* (spaghetti with sea urchins)—and good local wine literally 'on tap'. Definitely worth making the trip for.

Further along the Marina Grande, **Il Cantinone**, Via Roma 55, ✆ 081 810 1932 (*cheap*) is a low-key eaterie serving homely dishes and a very good *fritto misto di pesce*.

Campania Inland

There's more to the region than just the Bay of Naples. However, the coast and its endless attractions draw off most of the tourists, and it's a rare soul indeed who ever makes it up to old Capua, or the excellent little city of Benevento.

Getting Around

The interior of Campania makes up a rather large piece of territory—the three main towns are all provincial capitals. None are on the main **railway** lines, however, and you will have to scrutinize the schedules in Naples carefully to find your way around. For Capua take the Piedimonte Matese train from Naples to Santa Maria Capua Vetere. Trains to Caserta are rather more frequent and very convenient for the Royal Palace—the *Reggia*—which is just in front of it. **Buses** for Caserta, Capua, Avellino and Benevento leave Naples from Piazza Garibaldi, in front of the Stazione Centrale. The **CTP** (*Consorzio trasporti pubblici*), ✆ 081 700 1111, runs regular buses to Caserta (1hr) stopping at the station. From here you can also take buses to S. M. Capua Vetere.

Tourist Information

Caserta: in the Royal Palace, ✉ 81100, ✆ 0823 322 170.

Capua

This is a double city, consisting of the modern town, founded in the 9th century, and the ancient one, once the second city of Italy, but deserted in the Dark Ages and now modestly reborn as **Santa Maria Capua Vetere**. Capua can trace its founding to the Oscans, blithe folk of ancient Italy who introduced farce to the theatre, and who probably give us the word *obscene*. It is believed that the Oscan farces, banned by all decent Roman emperors, created the prototypes of the *commedia dell'arte* stock characters. All that should give you some idea of the spirit of old Capua, a city best known for beautiful women and the manufacture of perfume, and as renowned for loose morals in its day as Sybaris. Everyone but the jealous Roman historians liked to give Capua credit for defeating the great Hannibal. The Capuans had always hated those dreary dour Romans, and they eagerly took the Carthaginians' part. Hannibal's men enjoyed Capuan hospitality in the winter of 216 BC; they came out in the spring so dreamy-eyed and dissipated that they never beat the Romans again.

Of course there was hell to pay when the Romans came back, but Capua survived, and even flourished for several centuries more as the greatest city of the region. Finally, though, some even worse drudges than the Romans arrived—the Arabs, who utterly destroyed the city in about 830. The survivors refounded Capua on a new site, a little way north. At Santa Maria Capua Vetere, you can see the remains of the second-largest **amphitheatre** in Italy (*open summer daily 9–6; winter daily 9–4; adm*)—largest of all before Rome built its Colosseum. Here Spartacus began his gladiators' revolt in 73 BC. Few sections of the stands are still intact, but there is an underground network of tunnels and trap doors much like the Colosseum.

A short walk away you'll find something much more interesting—perhaps the best example of a **mithraeum** discovered anywhere in the Mediterranean (*open daily 9–4.30; closed Mon*). The cult of the god Mithras, imported from Persia by the legionaries, was for a while the most widespread of the cults that tried to fill the religious vacuum of the imperial centuries. Some scholars see in it much in common with Christianity, but the resemblance isn't readily apparent; Mithraism was an archaic, gut-level cult, with mystery initiations and bull's blood. Though it originally took hold in the army, and always remained a men-only affair, as late as the 3rd century AD it probably claimed more adherents than Christianity. The upper classes were never too impressed with it; that is why it lost out to the Christians, and why such well-executed frescoes as these are rare. The *mithraeum* is an underground hall used in the initiations and dominated by a large scene of Mithras, a typical Mediterranean solar hero, slaying a white bull with a serpent under its feet; the fresco representing the moon on the opposite wall is less well-preserved.

The new **Museo Archeologico dell'Antica Capua**, Via Roberto D'Angio (*open daily 9–7; closed Mon*) provides a convenient introduction to the site, complementing the more important Museo Campano at new Capua. Also around Santa Maria, there is a crumbling triumphal arch, and some elaborate Roman tombs, off the road to Caserta. The new Capua has all the most interesting finds from the old one at the **Museo Provinciale Campano**, Via Principi Longobardi 1/3 (*open daily 9–2; closed Mon; adm*). Just north of the town, on the slopes of Mount Tifata, a site once occupied by a temple of Diana now contains the 11th-century basilica of **Sant'Angelo in Formis**. The 12th-century frescoes here are some of the best in the south, oddly archaic figures that would seem much more at home in Constantinople than in Italy. And, more than mere artistry, there is an intense spiritual vision about these paintings—note especially the unearthly, unforgettable face of the enthroned St Michael above the portal.

North of Capua, near the border with Lazio, the last town in Campania along the Via Appia is **Sessa Aurunca**, with a Roman bridge and some other scanty ruins, as well as a 12th-century cathedral, interesting for its surviving ancient and medieval sections.

Caserta

In one shot, you can see the biggest palace in Italy, and also the most wearisome; both distinctions belong uncontestably to the **Reggia**, or Royal Palace, built here by the Bourbon King of Naples, Charles III (*Royal Apartments open Mon–Sat 9–1.30, Sun and hols 9am–9.30pm; adm*). His architect, Luigi Vanvitelli (really a Dutchman named Van Wittel) spared no expense; like the Spanish Bourbons, those of Naples were greenly jealous of Versailles, and wanted to show the big Louies back home that they, too, deserved a little respect. The Reggia, begun in 1752, has some 1200 rooms, not much compared to the 2800 of the Bourbon palace in Madrid, but larger than its Spanish cousin just the same (it's also larger than Versailles); the façade is 804ft across. Inside, as in Madrid, everything is tasteful, ornate and soberingly expensive; the only good touches from Vanvitelli's heavy hand are the elegant grand staircases. Only the **Park** (*open daily 9–one hour before sunset; adm*) makes the trip worthwhile, an amazingly long axis of pools and cascades climbing up to the famous **Diana fountain**, with a lifelike sculptural group of the goddess and her attendants catching Actaeon in the act. There is an **English garden**, the sort fashionable in the 18th century. Take a picnic.

The village of **San Leucio**, nearly 3km north of Caserta, was founded by the Bourbon kings as a paternalistic utopian experiment, and also an establishment for the manufacture of silk. Ferdinand IV, for most of his life, personally saw to every detail of its operation, even christening the children of the workers. The successor of his *Real Fabbrica* is still a centre for silk. Some 9km to the east there is the half-deserted town of **Casertavecchia**. The building of the Reggia drew most of the population down to modern Caserta, but the old town still has the 12th-century **cathedral** (*open daily 3–4*), with a great octagonal *ciborium* (a cylindrical or prismatic dome) that is one of the glories of Arab-Norman architecture.

Eating Out

Neither Capua nor Caserta makes a very attractive base, but the environs of Caserta do have some good restaurants.

Outside Casertavecchia, at the **Ritrovo dei Patriarchi**, Via Conte Landolfo 14, Località Sommana, © 0823 371 510 (*moderate*), you'll find game in abundance, including pheasant, venison, partridge and wild boar, depending on the time of year, with hearty soups and vegetable dishes. *Closed Thurs.* In the centre of Casertavecchia, **Rocca di Sant'Andrea**, Via Torre 8, © 0823 371 140 (*moderate*) offers delicious pasta dishes and a variety of *secondi*, many of which are based on meat grilled on the open fire in front of you. There is also a good selection of home-made desserts. *Closed Mon.* At **La Castellana**, Via Torre 4, © 0823 371 230 (*cheap*), near Rocca di Sant'Andrea, you can feast on wild boar or venison, when available, and an innovative selection of soup and *antipasti. Closed Thurs.* In Caserta, **La Massa**, Via Mazzini 55, © 0823 444 096 (*cheap*) is a simple, convenient place for lunch near the Reggia. *Closed Fri.*

Benevento

Getting Around

Remote Benevento is not well connected with any of Italy's main transport systems. It is on the Naples–Foggia **railway** line, but be careful about Naples–Benevento trains, as some but not all of them are operated by a private railway, and you will need to find out which—ask at the information booth in Naples' Stazione Centrale—to buy the right ticket. The private line is faster.

The most frequent public transport connections are by **bus**. The **Consorzio Trasporti Irpini**, © 081 553 4677, has regular services to Avellino (50min) and Benevento (1½hrs) from Piazza Garibaldi in Naples. In Benevento, buses to Naples and a surprising variety of other places (including one daily to Rome) leave from Piazza Pacca, on Corso Dante just west of the cathedral. There are several companies; check at the Benevento EPT for schedules.

Via Nicola Sala 31, ✉ 82100, ✆ 0824 319 911, 📠 0824 312 309, east of the city centre; information office: in Palazzo Bosco, Piazza Roma 11, ✉ 82100, ✆ 0824 319 938, *ept-bn@nigma.it*

The Duchy of Benevento

Ever since the Middle Ages, the land around Caserta and Capua has been called the *Terra del Lavoro*—cultivated land, a broad garden plain that is one of the most fertile corners of Italy. Today its lush landscapes have suffered a bit from creeping industrialism, though it's in the stretch to the south, between Caserta and Naples, where the worst modern depredations can be seen. Nowadays, the Napoletani call the towns around Afragola, Acerra and Secondigliano the 'Triangle of Death'—an industrial wasteland of shanties and power lines, ruled by the Camorra, that has Italy's worst unemployment, and some of its worst social problems.

Go east instead, up into the foothills of the Apennines towards Benevento, yet another smallish city that has often played a big role in Italian history. On an old tower in the centre of town, the city fathers have put up maps of southern Italy, showing the boundaries of the two important states of which Benevento was the capital. At first, as *Malies* or *Maloenton*, it was the leading town of the Samnites, the warlike mountain people who resisted Roman imperialism for so long. The Romans were later to make it an important stop along the Appian Way. They Latinized the name to *Maleventum*—ill wind—but after a lucky defeat of Pyrrhus of Epirus here in 275 BC, they thought it might just be a *Beneventum* after all. In AD 571 the city was captured by the bloodthirsty Lombards, becoming their southern capital. After the Lombards of the north fell to Charlemagne, the Duchy of Benevento carried on as an independent state; at its greatest extent, under relatively enlightened princes like Arechi II (*c.* 800), it ruled almost all of southern Italy. The Normans put an end to it in the 1060s.

Coming to Benevento in the winter, you're bound to think the Romans were crazy to change the name. When people in Salerno are ready to hit the beaches, you'll find the Beneventani shivering on street corners like Muscovites in their fur caps, victims of traditionally the worst weather in southern Italy. It is often claimed this makes them more serious and introspective than people on the coast—certainly coming here from Naples seems metaphorically like a trip of a thousand miles. Benevento has often been the scene of earthquakes, and the city took plenty of hard shots during the battles of 1943, but there are still enough attractions around to make a stop worthwhile.

Benevento's **cathedral** is in the lower town, the part that suffered the most in the bombings. The cathedral itself was almost a total loss; only the odd 13th-century façade remains, built of miscellaneous bits of Roman buildings—inscriptions, reliefs, friezes and pillars—arranged every which way. In the old streets behind the cathedral, you can see a dismally kept **Teatro Romano** (*open daily 9am–sunset*)—not an amphitheatre, but a place for classical drama, something rare this far north. By the time the Romans conquered them, the culture of the Samnites was almost completely Hellenized. This theatre, built under Hadrian, originally seated 20,000; it is now used for contemporary productions. All through this quarter, called the **Triggio**, you will see bits of Roman brick and medieval masonry—something ancient built into the walls of every house. There is half a Roman bridge over the River Sabato, ruins of the baths, remains of a triumphal arch and plenty of gates and stretches of the fortification walls built by the Lombards. On Via Posillipo a Baroque monument houses the **Bue Apis**, a sacred Egyptian bull sculpture found in Benevento's Temple of Isis.

Trajan's Arch

Some people claim Benevento's triumphal arch to be better than Rome's; built in AD 117, it is a serious piece of work—over 50ft of expensive Parian marble from Greece—and certainly better preserved than the ones in the capital. It marks the spot where the Appian Way entered Beneventum (now Via Traiana on the northern edge of the old town); the skilfully carved reliefs on both faces record significant events in the career of the emperor.

Trajan (AD 98–117), the conqueror of Dacia (modern-day Romania) and Mesopotamia, ranks among the greatest of the emperors, and a little commemoration would not seem out of hand; nevertheless cynics will enjoy the transparent and sometimes heavy-handed political propaganda of ornaments like this. In one of the panels, Trajan (the handsome fellow with the curly beard) is shown distributing gifts to children; in another he presides over the *institutio alimentaria*—the dole. Most of the scenes are about victories: Trajan announcing military reforms, Trajan celebrating a triumph, Jove handing Trajan one of his thunderbolts, and finally the Apotheosis, where the late emperor is received among the gods while the goddess Roma escorts Hadrian to coronation as his divinely ordained successor.

The Museo Sannio

Corso Garibaldi is Benevento's main street, just south of Trajan's Arch. Near its eastern end stands the city's oldest church, **Santa Sofia**, built in the late 8th century. It is unusual for its plan, an irregular six-pointed star, and was built for the Lombard Prince Arechi II by an architect thoroughly grounded in the mystic geometry of the early Middle Ages. The vaulting is supported by recycled Roman columns, and other columns have been hollowed out for use as holy water fonts.

The church cloister (*under restoration*) contains one of the south's more interesting provincial museums, the randomly open **Museo Sannio** (*in theory open daily 9–1; closed Mon*). *Sannio* refers to Samnium, as Benevento's province is still officially called. The 12th-century cloister has a variety of strange twisted columns under pulvins carved with even stranger scenes: monster-hunting, dancing, fantastical animals, bunnies and a camel or two. The best things in the museum are in the archaeological section. Almost all the classic vases are Campanian copies of Greek ware—the production of ceramics was the engine that drove *Campania Felix*'s economy in its glory days.

Some Samnite Curiosities

Two rooms in the museum are filled with objects from the Temple of Isis. Anyone who has read Apuleius' *The Golden Ass* will remember just how important the cult of the transcendent goddess Isis was throughout the Roman world. This Egyptian import certainly seems to have found a home in Beneventum; nowhere in Europe has so much fine Egyptian statuary been retrieved. The temple had imperial backing. One of the statues is of the founder, Emperor Domitian himself, in Egyptian dress. Other works portray priestesses, sacred boats and sphinxes, another Apis bull, and a porphyry '*cista mistica*', carved with a snake. The image of Isis is also there, formidably impressive, even without a head.

Somehow this leads naturally to Benevento's more famous piece of exotica—the witches. In the days of the Lombards, women by the hundreds would dance around a sacred walnut tree on the banks of the River Sabato ('sabbath'). Even after the official conversion to Christianity in 663, the older religion persisted, and Benevento is full of every sort of 'witch' story as a result. The best piece of modern sculpture in the Museo Sannio is a representation of the witches' dance. Of course the city has found ways to put the legend to use. In any bar in Italy, you can pick up a bottle of '*liquore Strega*' (*strega* means witch) and read on the label the proud device: 'Made next to the train station in Benevento, Italy.'

Just the other side of the Corso Garibaldi is the **Hortus Conclusus**, a small enclosed garden with installations and sculptures by a local contemporary artist. Turning west on Corso Garibaldi, the dedicatory **obelisk** from the Isis temple stands in front of the town hall. East of the museum, the Corso takes you to the **Rocca de' Rettori**, a fortress built by the popes in the 14th century, now part of the Museo Sannio; for centuries Benevento was a papal enclave surrounded by the Kingdom of Naples. Behind it there is a lovely park, the **Villa Comunale**.

Benevento ✉ *82100*   ***Where to Stay and Eating Out***

Dining in Benevento can be interesting; it's another world from the Campanian coast, with seafood replaced on the menu by rabbit, duck, lamb and veal. Samnium makes some good but little-known wines; you might ask for a bottle of stout-hearted Solopaca red.

★★★★**Gran Hotel Italiano**, Viale Principe di Napoli 137, ✆ 0824 24111, 🖷 0824 21758 (*moderate*) is located just a block from the Stazione Centrale. This is the best the city can offer—70's architecture and décor except for two amazing original prints by Piranesi. Nevertheless, the infectious enthusiasm of the owner, Sig. Italiano, the hotel's policy of providing a decent standard and a very helpful staff, all at provincial prices, makes this good value. The 20-minute walk into the historic centre is its principal drawback. It is hard to beat the ★★**Della Corte**, Piazza Piano di Corte, ✆ 0824 54819 (*cheap*), both for charm and for its location right in the heart of the historic quarter. The hotel only has seven rooms and as yet remains fairly undiscovered.

In the piazza in front of Trajan's Arch, the fun **Ristorante Teatro Gastronomico**, Via Traiano–Palazzo L. Andreotti, ✆ 0824 54605 (*moderate*) serves up a truly gastronomic menu of local specialities under a barrel vault painted with architectural backdrops lined with real balconies. In the pretty medieval area, **Nunzia**, Via Annunziata 152, ✆ 0824 29431 (*moderate*), now in its third generation, will surprise you with specialities like *cavatielli fagioli e cozze* (fresh pasta with beans and mussels). If you're too full to face the walk back to your hotel, they might even offer you a lift.

At **Pizzeria Rodolfo**, Via Meo Martini (*cheap*), you can enjoy what many consider to be the best pizza in Benevento. **Pizzeria Romana**, a stand-up *tavola calda* on the corner of Corso Dante and Corso Vittorio Emanuele, a block west of the cathedral, provides an excellent selection of very affordable delicacies for perfect picnics.

Samnium

Samnium is one of Italy's smallest provinces, but there are a few towns and villages of interest; the countryside, full of oak and walnut forests, is often reminiscent of some corner of Umbria. **Morcone**, to the north, has a memorable setting, draped on the curving slope of a hill like a Roman theatre. **Telese**, to the west on the road towards Lazio, lies near a small but pretty lake of the same name, with a popular spa establishment. The nearby ruins of the Samnite-Roman town of *Telesia* are remarkable for their perfectly octagonal walls, with gates at the cardinal points. Further north you'll find **S. Lorenzello**—famous for its ceramic ware and for being transformed into an antiques market every last weekend of the month.

Best of all, perhaps, is the town of **Sant'Agata dei Goti**, some kilometres north of the Via Appia between Benevento and Caserta, with its long line of buildings like a man-made cliff overhanging a little ravine. Sant'Agata takes its name from the Goths who founded it in the 6th century; it was badly damaged in the 1980 earthquake, and its modest monuments, the **castello** and the 12th-century **Church of Santa Menna**, are still undergoing restoration.

Southern Campania

Tourist Information

Avellino: Via Due Principati 5, ✉ 83100, ✆ 0825 74695.

Continuing this broad arc around Naples, south and east of Benevento there are few attractions, but some attractive mountain scenery in a region called **Irpinia**, consisting of most of the province of Avellino. In places, the mountains bear fine forests of oaks and chestnuts, as well as plantations of hazelnut trees; other parts are grim and bare, an introduction to the 19th-century deforestation that ruined so much of southern Italy. Irpinia was the region worst affected by the 1980 earthquake. The little provincial capital of **Avellino**, important in Norman times, has been wrecked so many times by invaders and earthquakes that little remains to be seen. In the centre, though, the 17th-century Palazzo della Dogana still retains its façade of ancient statues and its original clock tower. The main highway south from Caserta, around the back side of Vesuvius, isn't that much more promising. **Nola**, the biggest town on the route, began as another Oscan foundation. It had a famous early bishop, St Paulinus, a friend of St Augustine and also, it is claimed, the inventor of the bell (bells are *campane* in Italian, from their Campanian origin). To celebrate the anniversary of St Paulinus' return from imprisonment at the hands of the Vandals, every 27 June the people of Nola put on one of the more spectacular festivals of the south, the 'Feast of the Lilies' (*see* 'Festivals', p.786). Further south, in the hills above the city of **Nocera Inferiore**, an ancient hamlet called **Nocera Superiore** has somehow kept intact its 4th-century church, an unusual round building with a cupola that may have been converted from a pagan sanctuary.

Paestum and the Cilento

Getting Around

Paestum has a station on the main **railway** line between Naples and Reggio, but only local trains stop there. There are frequent **buses** from the Piazza Concordia in Salerno (on the shore, by the Porto

Turistico), run by several companies; some follow the coast route, while others go through Battipaglia. Some continue to resorts on the Cilento Coast.

All the Cilento towns are connected by **bus** to Salerno's Piazza Concordia; there is a bewildering list of companies, towns and schedules, but fortunately the EPT in Salerno publishes a full list of them in the front of their annual hotel book. The **railway** line only touches the Cilento Coast at two points—Ascea and Pisciotta—and, as at Paestum, not too many trains stop.

Tourist Information

Paestum: in Piazza V. Veneto, ✆ 089 231432, close by the main station, for the most complete information on transport and accommodation in Paestum and the Cilento; AAST: in the central Piazza Amendola, ✉ 84100, ✆ 089 224 744, ✆ 089 752 839; information office: Via Magna Grecia 155 (near the archaeological zone), ✆ 0828 811 016, ✆ 0828 722 322, *www.fromitaly.it/paestum* **Palinuro**: information office in Piazza Virgilio, ✆ 0974 938 144.

Paestum: A Lost City

Site open Tues–Sun 9–one hour before sunset; closed first and third Mon of every month for restoration work; museum open Tues–Sun 9–2 only; adm.

Along the coast, the route begins in a fertile plain that meets the Cilento near the ruins of **Paestum**, site of the only well-preserved Greek temples north of Sicily. And there is another important character who needs to be introduced: the anopheles mosquito, as fate would have it, gets the credit for preserving Paestum's ruins so well. By the 9th century, this once-great city was breathing its last, a victim of economic decline and Arab raiders. As its people gradually abandoned it for safer settlements in the hills, Paestum was swallowed up by the thick forests of this subtropical corner of Italy. As usual on a Mediterranean coastal plain, when the people leave the malaria mosquitoes take over. By the Middle Ages, the site of Paestum became utterly uninhabitable—it meant certain death to stay there overnight—and after a while the city's very existence was forgotten. After being hidden away, like the Mayan temples in the Mexican jungle, for almost a thousand years, the city was rediscovered in the 18th century; a crew of Charles III's road builders stumbled on the huge temples in the midst of the forest.

Originally *Poseidonia*, the city was founded in the 7th century BC by the Sybarites, on the all-important trade route up the west coast. The Romans took over in 273 BC, and Latinized the name to Paestum. Famous for its flowers, especially roses, it prospered until the end of the Roman era. Today the forests have been cleared, and the ruins of the city stand in the open on the green and quiet plain. Not only the celebrated temples have survived; much of the 5km circuit of **walls** still stands to some height, along with some of the towers and gates.

Most of Paestum's important buildings were grouped along an axis between the Porta Aurea and the Porta Giustizia, with the forum at its centre. The two grand temples (*sadly at present both wrapped up in scaffolding*) that everyone comes to see are at the southern end: the **basilica** and the **Tempio di Nettuno**, two Doric edifices in the finest classical style. The names were just guesses on the part of the early archaeologists. The 'Neptune' temple, the best preserved, was built about 450 BC. It is about 200ft long, and all of the structure survives except the roof and the internal walls. Similarities to another temple at Tarentum may suggest it was dedicated to Apollo, but Hera and Zeus are also possible contenders. The **basilica** was divided to house two cults, most probably connected with Hera, the tutelary goddess of the city. It is a century older, and a little smaller. Missing its Doric frieze and pediment, the first archaeologists did not recognize the building for a temple, hence the name Basilica.

The aesthetic may not be quite what you would expect—dimensions squat and strong rather than graceful and tall. Still, this is the classic austerity of Greek architecture at its best. If you look closely along the rows of columns, or the lines of the base, you may notice that nothing in either of them is perfectly straight. The edges bulge outwards, as they do in the Parthenon and every other Greek building; this is an architectural trick called *entasis*; it creates an optical illusion, making the lines seem straight at a distance. Greek temples like this are the most sober and serious buildings in western architecture, based on a simple system of perfect proportion. The form may seem austere and academic, but with some imagination you can picture them in their original beauty—covered in a sort of enamel made of gleaming ground marble, setting off the brilliant colours of the polychromed sculptural reliefs on the pediments and frieze. To the west, some of the streets of the city have been excavated, though very little is left to see. To the north, around the broad Forum—really a simple rectangular space in the manner of a Greek *agora*—are the remains of an amphitheatre, a round *bouleterion*, or council house, and other buildings. Still further north is the third and smallest of the surviving temples, the **Temple of Ceres**.

Paestum's **museum** holds most of the sculptural fragments and finds from the town. Some of the best reliefs are not from Paestum at all, but from the recently discovered sanctuary of Hera, a few kilometres north at the mouth of the River Sele. This temple, mentioned by many ancient writers, is said to have been founded by Jason and the Argonauts during their wanderings. From tombs excavated just outside the city come some examples of Greek fresco painting—nothing special in themselves, but they are the only ones in existence. Look out for the most famous fresco, *The Diver*, which you have probably seen reproduced innumerable times elsewhere. Even though the Greeks took painting as seriously as they did sculpture, you will not find any similar surviving examples in Greece, or anywhere else. While you are exploring Paestum, keep an eye out too for the wild flowers. More than one 19th-century traveller claimed to have found descendants of Paestum's famous roses (*bifera rosaria Paestum*) growing wild, and some may still be around.

The Cilento Coast

For many, one of the best attractions of Paestum will be the fine, long beaches that line this part of the coast. South of the ruins, the shore becomes jagged and mountainous, passing groves of pines alternating with rugged cliffs and pocket-sized beaches. Most of the villages along it have become quiet, cosy resorts that cater mostly to Italians. One is usually close to the next, and if you care to stay over, you can keep going until you find one that suits your fancy.

Agropoli comes first, then **Santa Maria di Castellabate**, **San Marco** and **Punta Licosa**, on the westernmost point of the Cilento, named after the siren, Leucosia. Legend has it that she threw herself into the sea after her failure to entice Ulysses on to the rocks. From here you can take a small boat out to an uninhabited islet, also called Licosa, where there are some unidentified ancient ruins. Further down the coast, **Acciaroli** and **Pioppi** are among the nicer resort towns of the Cilento. South of the latter, and just inland from the village of Ascea Marina, you can visit the ruins of another Greek city, **Velia**.

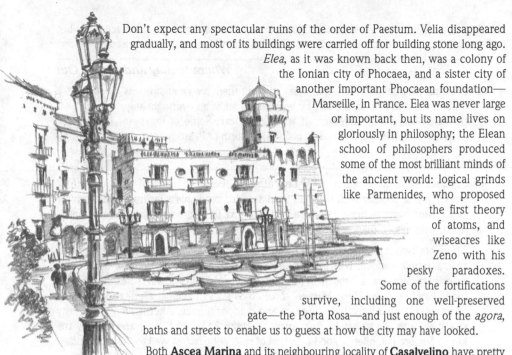

Don't expect any spectacular ruins of the order of Paestum. Velia disappeared gradually, and most of its buildings were carried off for building stone long ago. *Elea*, as it was known back then, was a colony of the Ionian city of Phocaea, and a sister city of another important Phocaean foundation—Marseille, in France. Elea was never large or important, but its name lives on gloriously in philosophy; the Elean school of philosophers produced some of the most brilliant minds of the ancient world: logical grinds like Parmenides, who proposed the first theory of atoms, and wiseacres like Zeno with his pesky paradoxes. Some of the fortifications survive, including one well-preserved gate—the Porta Rosa—and just enough of the *agora*, baths and streets to enable us to guess at how the city may have looked.

Both **Ascea Marina** and its neighbouring locality of **Casalvelino** have pretty beaches, but the best ones of all, perhaps, can be found in the rugged terrain around **Palinuro**. This town, which has a small museum of archaeological finds, takes its name from Aeneas' pilot Palinurus, who is supposedly buried here—Virgil made the whole story up for the *Aeneid*, but that hasn't stopped it from sticking fast in local legend. Beyond Palinuro, the sandy coast curves back north into the Gulf of Policastro; here two more pleasant beach villages, **Scario** and **Sapri**, mark the southern boundary of Campania.

The Inland Route: Around the Cilento

South from Salerno, the *autostrada* skirts the back edge of the Cilento on its way to Calabria. Christ may have stopped at **Eboli**, as a local saying goes, but there's no reason why you should—and that goes for **Battipaglia** and **Polla** too. The true delights of this region are subterranean: two first-rate caves on opposite slopes of the Monti Alburni. **Pertosa** (*open Tues–Sun 9–5.30; adm*), near the highway, is the easier and probably the better choice; the pot-holers (spelunkers) suspect it is connected to the other one, at **Castelcivita**, near the village of Controne, which now forms part of the National Park of Cilento, a conservation project established by local inhabitants to attract tourists to the area.

At **Teggiano** there is a 13th-century castle and cathedral, as well as a little museum. **Padula**, just off the highway, is the unlikely location of the **Certosa di San Lorenzo**, after San Martino in Naples probably the biggest and richest monastery in the south. The Certosa has been closed for over a century, but in its heyday it would have held hundreds of Carthusians, in a complex laid out in the form of a gridiron (recalling the martyrdom of St Lawrence, the same plan used in El Escorial in Spain, also dedicated to the saint). Continuously expanded and rebuilt over 400 years, the best parts are Baroque: an enormous, elegant cloister, some wonderfully garish frescoes and stucco figures in and around the chapel, and eccentric but well-executed decorative details throughout. There is a small archaeological museum.

Where to Stay and Eating Out

Most people think of Paestum as a day trip, but there are enough hotels around the site, and on the nearby beaches, to make an overnight stay possible—and very convenient if you have a car. Some of the best accommodation is at Laura beach, about 5km north of Paestum.

Paestum ✉ 84063

Set back from Laura beach, ★★★★**Le Palme**, ✆ 0828 851 025, ✆ 0828 851 507 (*moderate*) is popular with German tourists, with good sports facilities and a private beach. Just north of here, ★★**Laura**, ✆ 0828 851 068 (*moderate*) is a pretty family hotel, with helpful management, and a private beach.

There are two typical restaurants in the archaeological zone itself, both excellent, specializing in seafood: **Nettuno**, ✆ 0828 811 028 (*moderate*), under the city walls near Porta Giustizia, a family-run restaurant for over 70 years, offers freshly prepared food (*lunchtime only*); the **Museo**, ✆ 0828 811 135 (*moderate*), next door to the museum, has an informal dining room and outdoor terrace. Alternatively, for a tasty snack close to the museum, **Bar Anna**, ✆ 0828 811 196 (*moderate*), run by the kindly Signora Pia, offers a good selection of cold *antipasti*, as well as the local buffalo mozzarella in a tomato salad (*insalata alla caprese*).

Palinuro ✉ 84064

Outside Palinuro, ★★★★**King's Residence**, ✆ 0974 931 324, ✆ 0974 931 418 (*expensive*) is in a stunning setting, perched on the cliffs overlooking the *Buondormire* ('sleep well') bay. Every room comes with a terrace or balcony, and there's a pretty little private beach, with a small bar for drinks and light meals. Sleek and well run.

Just outside Palinuro, **Da Carmelo**, ✆ 0974 931 138 (*moderate*), 1km along the road towards Camerota, is a lively *trattoria* where dishes are prepared according to traditional recipes, often to the strains of Neapolitan songs belted out by a strolling minstrel with a guitar. Seafood comes highly recommended by the throng of locals. Self-catering apartments are available above the restaurant. At the two-tiered **Taverna del Porto**, in Palinuro (*cheap*), lunch is served at tables a stone's throw from the water's edge and dinner in the more formal upper level. Also near the beach, **O' Guarracino** (*cheap*) is a pretty café-cum-*trattoria* with tables under a pleasantly shady canopy.

Calabria and the Basilicata

Italy may be a country unusually blessed by fortune, but her favours are by no means evenly spread. To balance regions like the Veneto or Campania, with their manifold delights, nature has given Italy its own empty quarter, the adjacent regions of Calabria and the Basilicata. Calabria is the toe of the Italian boot, a gnarled, knobbly toe, amply endowed with corns and bunions and pointed accusingly at neighbouring Sicily. Almost all of it is ruggedly mountainous, leaving just enough room at the edges for the longest, broadest, emptiest beaches in Italy.

It can claim three natural attractions: a scenic western coast, the beautifully forested highland regions of *Aspromonte* at the toe, and the *Sila*, in the centre of the region. Most man-made attractions have been shaken to bits by the earthquakes, Calabria's eternal plague, and consequently there are plenty of ruins and ghost towns.

The Basilicata, still better known to many people under its old name of *Lucania*, takes on all-comers for the title of Italy's most obscure region. It offers plenty of lonely, wild-west landscapes and two increasingly popular destinations: the resort of Maratea and the strange city of Matera, where people used to live in caves.

Magna Graecia

It was not always this way. Starting in about 750 BC, the Greeks extensively colonized southern Italy. *Rhegium*, today's Reggio di Calabria, came first, followed in short order by Sybaris, Croton and Locris, and many others in Sicily. These towns, happily situated along the major trade route of the Mediterranean, rapidly became as cultured as those of Greece itself—and far wealthier. It was a brilliant hour, and a brief one. After a time, blessed with a lack of external enemies, the cities of 'greater Greece' took to fighting among themselves in a series of ghastly, cruel wars over the most trivial of causes, often resulting in the total destruction of a city and the massacre of its inhabitants. Weakened by their own barbarous behaviour, the Greek cities then became pawns between Rome and Carthage in the Punic Wars; the victorious Romans took a terrible vengeance on those such as Taras (Tàranto, in modern Puglia) that supported the wrong side. Roman rule meant a slow decline for the survivors, and by the 6th century the beautiful cities of Magna Graecia were abandoned to the mosquitoes.

Don't, however, come to Calabria looking for classical ruins. The great museum at Reggio gives a hint of what these cities were, but at the sites themselves almost nothing remains. Golden Sybaris has only just been found by the archaeologists, and only at Metapontum will you see so much as a few standing columns. Some may call the emptiness a monument to Greek hubris, or perhaps somehow these cities were doomed from the start. Considering Magna Graecia can be profoundly disconcerting; even in the ancient Mediterranean it is strange and rare for so many big cities to disappear so completely.

Nor has this corner of Italy been any more hospitable to civilization in the centuries since. Calabria in particular has suffered more at the hands of history than any region deserves. After the Romans and the malaria mosquito put an end to the brilliant, short-lived civilization of Magna Graecia, Calabria has endured one wrenching earthquake after another, not to mention Arab raiders and Norman bully-boys, Spaniards and Bourbons, the most vicious of

Calabria and the Basilicata

857

feudal landlords and the most backward and ignorant of monks and priests. By the 18th century all these elements had combined to effect one of the most complete social breakdowns ever seen in modern Europe. Calabria staggered into anarchy, its mountains given over to bands of cut-throats while the country people endured almost subhuman poverty and oppression. Not surprisingly, everyone who was able chose to emigrate; today there are several times as many Calabresi living in the Americas as in Calabria itself.

A New Land

While famine, disease and misgovernment were putting an end to old Calabria, natural disasters like the terrible earthquake of 1783, and the even worse one in 1908 that destroyed the city of Reggio, were erasing the last traces of it. Calabria's stage was cleared for a modest rebirth, and the opportunity for it came after the Second World War, when Mr Rockefeller's DDT made the coasts habitable for the first time in over a millennium. Within a few years a government land reform improved the lives of thousands, and the *Cassa per il Mezzogiorno's* roads and industrial projects set out to pull their economies into the 20th century.

Today, despite the many problems that remain, it's possible to see the beginnings of an entirely new Calabria. A thousand years or more ago, the Calabrians deserted their once-great port cities for wretched, though defensible, villages in the mountains. Now they are finally moving back, and everywhere around Calabria's long and fertile coasts you will see new towns and cities; some, like Locri or Metaponto, are built over the ruins of the Greek cities that are their direct ancestors. Most of this new Calabria isn't much to look at yet; the bigger towns, in fact, can be determinedly ugly (like Crotone). Calabria these days, for all its history, has an unmistakable frontier air about it. The people are simple, suspicious and a little rough. Unlike other Italians, they seem to have lots of children; they work hard, fix their own cars and tractors, and lay their concrete everywhere. So far, the changes have amounted to such a humble revolution that few people have even noticed, and the emigration rate remains enormous. But both these regions are, if anything, lands of survivors, and who is to say that they aren't now taking their first baby steps on the road to reclaiming their ancient prosperity and distinction?

Calabrian Itineraries

Most visitors only take at a look at the region if they're passing through on the way to Sicily, and have some time to spare. If so, drivers should take the old coastal road, the SS18, south through Maratea and Páola; the SS585 that connects with it branches off the A3 *Autostrada del Sole* at Lagonegro-Nord, near Maratea, and it is much more scenic a route than the *autostrada*. It takes longer, but it's a good smooth road, and actually shorter. Take as long as you like: Maratea, Práia a Mare, Vibo Valentia or Gioia Tauro make good stopovers along the way. One detour is via Cosenza into the Sila highlands—some 89km from the turn-off at Páola to San Giovanni in Fiore in the heart of the Sila. Another, shorter digression would be from Vibo Valentia, around the peninsula to Tropea and Capo Vaticano. This adds an extra 45km to the trip, through some difficult corniche roads, but it includes some of the south's best coastal scenery. Before you make the crossing over to Messina, take an hour or two for the Museum in Reggio; even if you have no particular interest in archaeology, the collection contains some of the most beautiful art you'll see in southern Italy. Similarly, travellers *en route* between Campania and Puglia can, with a few detours, take in the most interesting parts of eastern Calabria and the Basilicata, such as the cave city of Matera, the dramatic castles built by the Normans and the Emperor Frederick II, and the Greek ruins at Metapontum.

Getting Around

Two major **rail** lines pass through these regions: the Rome–Naples–Villa San Giovanni/Reggio di Calabria route along the west coast (15 trains a day), and the branch that runs from Battipaglia in Campania through Potenza and Metaponto on its way to Tàranto (6 trains a day). A third line follows the long shore of the Ionian Sea from Reggio to Tàranto. Reggio di Calabria has two railway stations: the Stazione Marittima, from which crossings are made to Messina in Sicily, and the Stazione Centrale; if you're just making a quick stop for the museum, the Marittima is closer. Rail connections to anywhere in the interior are chancy at best: a few trains go through to Cosenza, but you'll usually have to change at Páola or Sibari. There are also regular **buses** from Páola to Cosenza. At Catanzaro it's the same; coastal trains stop only at Catanzaro Lido, 9km away (though there is a regular local bus to the city centre). In Cosenza buses leave from Piazza L. Fera, at the northern end of Corso Mazzini, for Catanzaro (several daily) and points around the province, including towns in the Sila.

A pleasant way to see the Sila itself is on the old private FCL **narrow-gauge railway** that runs three trains each day between Cosenza and San Giovanni in Fiore. The FCL station in Cosenza is hard to find as it's behind the now disused FS station in the town. Near the tip of Calabria there is another attractive local rail line, around the Tropea peninsula between Pizzo and Rosarno. Matera is served only by another FCL private rail line, which runs 12 trains a day from Bari in Puglia. The station there is on Via Nazionale on the western edge of town. There is also a very slow FCL line between Potenza and Bari, via Altamura. FCL and other companies also operate daily **bus** services from Matera's Piazza Matteotti to Ferrandina, Potenza, Naples and Metaponto.

Airports in Calabria are at Lamezia-Terme (the main regional airport) on the Plain of Santa Eufemia, near the SS280 Catanzaro turn-off from the SS18, which has scheduled flights to most of the major Italian cities, and at Reggio di Calabria, just south of the city, with regular services only to Rome and Milan. Car and passenger **ferries** to Sicily leave from Villa San Giovanni—the quickest route, with the most frequent services—and Reggio di Calabria. There are three companies: FS, ✆ 0965 758 241; Caronte, ✆ 0965 756 725; and Tourist Ferry, ✆ 0965 751 413. Don't worry; the service is very frequent, and whenever you arrive you'll be directed to the ferry leaving next.

Roads aren't that bad, though you'll be skirting lakes, or crossing them, on those rare occasions when it rains. Service and petrol are never a problem anywhere on the coasts, but fill up before venturing into the mountains. Around Aspromonte—an area renowned for its bandits—it is best to avoid travelling after dark; and throughout the region women travelling alone should be prepared for some bothersome attention from men (also *see* p.xx).

The West Coast: from Maratea to Reggio di Calabria

Tourist Information

Maratea: (AAST), Piazza del Gesù 32, ✆ 0973 876 908. **Cosenza**: Via P. Rossi 70, ✆ 0984 390 595. **Vibo Valentia**: Galleria Vecchio, ✆ 0963 42008. **Villa San**

Giovanni: in the Piazza Stazione, ✆ 0965 751 160. **Reggio di Calabria**: Via Tripepi 72, near the museum, ✆ 0965 898 496/7; there are also offices at the Stazione Centrale and the airport. **Gambarie**: Piazzale Mangiaruca, ✆ 0965 743 295.

Maratea and the Coast

Just south of Campania's Cilento peninsula, a little corner of the Basilicata stretches out to touch the Tyrrhenian Sea. The scenery here differs little from the steep cliffs and green slopes of the Cilento; after Sapri, the SS18 becomes a spectacular and rugged corniche road, passing over cliffs covered with scrubby *macchia*, and soft grey beaches on hidden coves. The centre of the Basilicata's coast is **Maratea**, a pretty hill village of tiny alleys and steps, with more modern additions tucked between the cliffs by the sea far below it. Maratea has in the last few years become quite sophisticated and expensive, though the atmosphere is still pretty laid-back. Besides some of the best coastal scenery in the deep south, you can enjoy relatively uncrowded beaches and modest hotels at Acquafredda, Maratea Marina (where trains on the main Rome–Reggio rail line stop), and several other points along the coast. The town itself lies under what must be the queerest hilltop Jesus in Italy: all marble, and 66ft tall. Designed by Bruno Innocenti in 1963 at the start of Maratea's push to become a resort, from a distance it looks more like a perfume bottle with wings.

Some 10 kilometres further down the coast and you're in Calabria on a less dramatic stretch of coast, on the outskirts of another resort: **Práia a Mare**, where there is a 14th-century castle. From the beach you can rent a boat to visit the 'Blue Grotto' on the **Isola di Dino**, an un-inhabited islet just off the shore. Further south along the road is the now pretty much overdeveloped **Scalea**, and beyond it **Diamante**, a picturesque village of narrow streets, stacked on a rock above the sea. **Páola**, where the road from Cosenza meets the coast, is a larger, somewhat dishevelled resort, a fitting introduction to the towns of the 'Calabrian Riviera' to the south. Above it stands the 15th-century **Santuario di San Francesco di Pola**, dedicated to the town's most famous son, Calabria's patron saint—not the same Francis as the Saint of Assisi—and the object of pilgrimages from all over southern Italy.

Cosenza

So far, there hasn't been much reason to leave the coast. Cosenza may not be a stellar attraction, but as cities go it's the best Calabria can do. One of Calabria's chief towns throughout most of recorded history, it began as the capital of the Bruttians, the aboriginal nation from whom today's Calabrians are descended. Medieval Cosenza was a busy place: the Arabs took it twice, Norman freebooters fought over it, and at least one king of France passed through on his way to the Crusades.

The River Busento divides Cosenza neatly between the flat modern town and the old citadel on the hill. The river is famous, if only because buried somewhere beneath it is no less a personage than Alaric the Goth. Alaric—no drooling barbarian, but just another scheming Roman general with a Teutonic accent—came to Cosenza in 410, fresh from his sack of Rome and on his way to conquer Africa. He died of a fever here, and his men temporarily diverted the Busento and buried him under it, probably along with a fair share of the Roman loot. Archaeologists are still looking for it.

For all its history, Cosenza has little to show; even in Calabria, no place is more prone to earth-quakes—four big ones in the last 200 years, with added destruction by Allied bombers in

1943. The **cathedral**, a simple Gothic structure, was rebuilt under the reign of Frederick II on the ruins of the original 7th-century basilica. Inside lie buried one of Frederick's sons and Isabella of Aragon. Its best bits have been moved to the cloister of the church of **San Francesco d'Assisi**, down the hill on Via S. Francesco. The little extra effort to visit is worth it, as it contains two real treasures: a Byzantine-style relic-holder crucifix in gold and enamel, donated by Frederick himself on the occasion of the cathedral's consecration in 1222; and the shiny 13th-century Byzantine icon of the Madonna del Pilerio, believed to have saved the city from the bubonic plague of 1576 and thus made patron of Cosenza. A few blocks south of the cathedral, on Piazza XV Marzo, there is a small **Museo Civico** (*open Mon–Sat 9–1; adm*), with paintings and archaeological finds; from there you can climb up to the **castle** (*open April–Sept Mon–Sat 9–1, Thurs 9–1 and 4–6; Oct–Mar daily 9–1 only*). Originally built by the Normans, it was later modified by Frederick II, the Aragonese and the Angevins. The medieval 'reception room' has delightful capitals with floral motifs carved in pink sandstone.

The Sila

Cosenza is the best base from which to see this region, a lovely, peaceful plateau between mountains that offers an unusual experience of Alpine scenery near the southern tip of Italy. Much of the Sila is still covered with trees—beeches, oaks and pines. In summer you can find wild strawberries, and in winter—well, maybe—wolves. Some of Italy's last specimens make their stand in the Sila's wilder corners. Artificial lakes, built since the war as part of Calabria's hydroelectric schemes, add to the scenery, notably **Lake Arvo** and **Lake Cecita**, between Cosenza and the town of San Giovanni in Fiore. The Sila is the best place in Calabria for motoring or hiking, and maps and information are available from the Cosenza tourist office. Most likely you will see only the largest and prettiest section, the **Sila Grande**, in the middle, though more adventurous souls can press on to the barely accessible **Sila Greca**, to the north, or south to the **Sila Piccola**, around the little mountain resort of **Villaggio Mancuso**.

On the eastern flank of the Sila Piccola, not far from Crotone, is the interesting little town of **Santa Severina**, with a Norman castle and a cathedral with a Byzantine baptistry. Despite the name, the Sila Greca is in fact inhabited by Albanians of the Greek Orthodox faith. They came to Calabria and Sicily as refugees from the Turks in the 15th century, and today constitute one of Italy's largest ethnic minorities. Albanians can be found all over Calabria, especially here and in the north around Castrovillari; you'll know you've stumbled on one of their villages if you see a Byzantine-domed church or a statue of Skanderbeg, the Albanian national hero.

Back towards the coast south of Cosenza, and just a few kilometres from the main road up in the hills, is the town of **Nocera Terinese**, famous for only one thing—its festival every Easter, when processions of flagellants go around the town, fervently beating themselves into a bloody mess with thorn bushes, in one of the local events that is most regularly deployed to demonstrate Calabria's distance from the modern world. Further south again, the road descends to the Plain of Santa Eufemia, one of the new agricultural areas reclaimed from the mosquito. The town of **Maida**, site of one of the first French defeats during the Napoleonic Wars, gave its name to London's Maida Vale. **Pizzo** also has its Napoleonic association. The great cavalry commander, Marshal Murat, whom Bonaparte had made King of Naples, tried after Waterloo to regain his throne by beginning a new revolution in Calabria. When his boat landed here in 1815, instead of the welcome he expected, the crowd almost tore him to pieces. The Bourbons executed him a few days later in the castle, built in the 1480s by Ferdinand of Aragon.

The best part of Calabria's coast begins near Cape Vaticano. **Vibo Valentia**, a new provincial capital, has views overlooking the coast, a 12th-century castle, remains of the fortifications of the ancient Greek city of Hipponion, and a number of overwrought Baroque churches. Finds from the excavations of Hipponion are on view in the museum in the castle (*open daily 9–7; adm*). South of Vibo the main road cuts inland, but the railway and some back roads head around Cape Vaticano; this is a district of fashionable, pretty beach resorts, and difficult mountains. **Tropea** is a lovely town along the coast; next to it, on a rocky peninsula that was once an island, you can climb up to the romantically ruined Benedictine monastery of **Santa Maria dell'Isola**. The town offers some spectacular views, taking in on a clear day the island volcano of Strómboli and Sicily's northern coast.

Further south, the towns along the coast are more accessible, and some of them have grown into fair-sized holiday spots. Outside **Palmi** there is a museum and cultural complex, the **Casa di Cultura Leonida Repaci**, that, among other collections, houses the best folk museum in Calabria, and a modern art gallery with works by De Chirico and other 20th-century Italian painters (*open Mon–Wed 8–2 and 3–6, Tues, Thurs and Fri 8–2*).

Scilla, at the entrance to the Straits of Messina, marks the spot where the mythological Scylla, a daughter of Hecate changed into a dog-like sea monster, seized some of Odysseus' crewmen near the end of the *Odyssey*. In classical times Scylla meant the dangerous rocks of the Calabrian side of the straits, a counterpart to the whirlpool Charybdis towards the Sicilian shore. So many earthquakes have rearranged the topography since then that nothing remains of either. Still, the narrow straits are one of the most dramatic sights in Italy, with Messina and the Monte Peloritani visible over in Sicily, neatly balancing Reggio and the jumbled peaks of Aspromonte in Calabria.

Reggio di Calabria

The last big earthquake came in 1908, when over 100,000 people died here and in Messina across the straits. Both these cities have a remarkable will to survive, considering all the havoc earthquakes have played on them in the last 2000 years. Perhaps the setting is irresistible. Fortune has favoured them unequally in the rebuilding; though both are about the same size, Messina has made of itself a slick, almost beautiful town, while Reggio has chosen to remain swaddled in Calabrian humility. Its plain grid of dusty streets and low buildings was laid out only after the earthquake of 1783, when the destruction was even greater than in 1908 and the city had to be rebuilt from scratch.

The Allies also did a pretty thorough job of bombing Reggio in the Second World War; after all that, it's not surprising that there is little left to see of the city that began its life as Greek *Rhegium* in the 8th century BC. Some bits of Greek wall and Roman baths, and some once-grand 19th-century buildings along the waterfront promenade, are almost the only things in the city older than 1908.

Part of Reggio's shabbiness is without question due to the corrosive social effect of the local Calabrese mafia, known in dialect as the *'ndrangheta*, which continues to have a hold here stronger even than those that its wealthier partners in crime, the Sicilian Mafia and the Neapolitan Camorra, exert over their own respective backyards. The city does still have one special attraction for the visitor—its **Museo Nazionale della Magna Graecia** (*open winter Tues–Sun 9–1 and 3.30–7; summer daily 9–6; adm*), the finest collection of Greek art between Naples and Sicily.

The Warriors of Riace

The museum, directly north of the city centre on Corso Garibaldi, is a classic of Mussolini architecture built in chunky travertine. Containing a hoard as precious as anything in Greece itself, the museum would make a trip to Reggio worthwhile just for the Warriors of Riace, two bronze masterpieces that rank among the greatest productions of antiquity to have come down to us.

Found only in 1972, by divers exploring an ancient shipwreck off Riace on Calabria's Ionic coast, they are kept down in the basement in a room of their own, next to a big exhibition detailing the tremendously complex restoration job done in the seventies. These fellows, both about six-foot-seven and quite indecently virile, may perhaps have come from a temple at Delphi; no one really knows why they were being shipped to Magna Graecia. One of them has been attributed to the great sculptor Phidias.

The Warriors share the basement with a few other rare works of Greek sculpture, notably the unidentified, 5th-century BC subject called 'the Philosopher', as well as anchors and ship fittings, and amphorae that once held wine or oil—all recovered from the shipwreck, from mud well over a metre deep. The divers are convinced that the dangerous waters around Calabria may hold dozens of such treasures, so some more artefacts may have found their way to the Reggio museum by the time you arrive.

And don't neglect the rest of the museum's collections. Some of the most beautiful things in it are the terracotta **ex-voto plaques**, recovered from the temples of Magna Graecia. Most of these offerings show goddesses in the magical archaic Greek style—usually Persephone—who had influence over death—being abducted by Hades, receiving propitiatory gifts, or accepting souls into the underworld. Chickens are a recurring motif, not too surprisingly, since to the ancient Greeks a soul rises out of its burial urn the same way a chicken hatches from an egg.

Other works help complete the picture of life and art in Magna Graecia: Greek painted ceramics from Locris and from Attica, fragments of architectural decoration from various temples—some still with bits of their original paint—records of city finances on bronze tablets, and a rare early Hellenistic mosaic of a dragon, actually made in Calabria. The museum also has a collection of paintings, including two works by Antonello da Messina.

Aspromonte

All around the toe of Italy, from Palmi as far as Locri, the interior of the peninsula seems utterly impenetrable, a wall of rough peaks looming over the narrow coastal plain. In fact all of the toe is really one great round massif, called Aspromonte. The tortuous mountain roads allow few easy opportunities for climbing inland, but from the north end of Reggio a 30km route, the SS184, will take you up to **Gambarie**, with pine forests and views over the straits and Sicily.

In winter Gambarie is Calabria's unlikely ski resort, with just enough snow to get by in an average year; in summer it's a good starting-off point for walkers. Aspromonte, with its 22 summits and its Greek-speaking villages, was the haunt of the chivalrous 19th-century bandit Musolino, a sort of Calabrian Robin Hood still well remembered in these parts. His well-tended grave is in the cemetery in his birthplace, **Santo Stefano**, a little below Gambarie. Scholars who have studied the Greeks here speculate that they may be descendants of the original Greek population of Magna Graecia, holding on to their cultural identity thanks only to the barely accessible locations of their mountain villages.

On the coastal plain, snow is hardly ever seen. This is one of Italy's gardens, a panorama of lemon and orange groves. Two more exotic crops have also given some fame to the region: jasmine, which grows so well nowhere else in Italy; and bergamot, a small, hard, green orange, discovered and first cultivated only some 200 years ago. Now it is an indispensable ingredient in the making of the finest perfumes (and also the stuff used to flavour Earl Grey tea). If it is a clear day, the straits around Reggio can treat you to some of the grandest views in the south; much of the Sicilian coast is visible, and perhaps even Mount Etna will peek out from behind its usual entourage of clouds.

If you are especially lucky, you may be treated to an appearance of the famous *Fata Morgana*, the mirages of islands or many-towered cities that often appear over the straits. The name comes from the enchantress Morgan le Fay. Arthurian romance came to southern Italy with the Normans, and rooted itself deeply in these parts; old Sicilian legends have a lot to say about King Arthur. In one of the tales, Arthur sleeps and awaits his return not up in chilly England, but deep in the smoky bowels of Etna. Roger de Hauteville himself, a close relation of William the Conqueror, is said to have seen the *Fata Morgana*, and his learned men inter-preted the vision as a divine invitation to invade Sicily. Roger demurred, thinking it would be better to wait and take Sicily on his own than do it with the aid of sorcery.

Where to Stay and Eating Out

Seldom in Calabria or the Basilicata will you see a hotel older than the 1960s—a comment both on how much the regions have changed since the Second World War, and how little they had ever had to do with tourism beforehand. In the sixties there were thoughts of a tourist boom—Calabria as the new Riviera—but prob-lems with bureaucracy, bad planning and a lack of good sites for hotels has prevented this from taking off as much as had been expected. Still, if you are just passing through, there are plenty of hotels along the SS18. If you have a car the best deals are often to be found in the family-run *Aziende Agrituristiche*, where you'll taste the famed southern Italian hospitality and probably the best food in the region.

Maratea ✉ 85046

Maratea has become a mature enough resort to have some excellent accommodation. ★★★★★**Santavenere**, Via Santavenere, ✆ 0973 876 910, ✇ 0973 877 654 (*very expensive*), 1½km north of Porto di Maratea at Fiumicello-Santa Venere, is the best, a modern building, furnished with unusual elegance, in a fine setting on cliffs above the sea, with a private beach, a pool and tennis courts. Less expensive choices are many, with some of the best being a little up the coast at Acquafredda—such as ★★★★**Villa**

del Mare, ℂ 0973 878 007, ✉ 0973 878 102 (*moderate*), just off the SS18 and located up on the cliffs, with a lift down to its beach. **★★Villa degli Aranci**, Via Profiti 7, ℂ/✉ 0973 876 344 (*cheap*) is a good cheaper hotel at Maratea Fiumicello.

Za Mariuccia, Via Grotte 2, ℂ 0973 876 163 (*expensive*) is an almost perfect seafood trattoria in Maratea Porto, with tables looking out to sea, excellent *risotti*, and pasta dishes that use scampi, lobster and the very best of the fishermen's catch. *Closed Fri.* Another treasure is **Rovita**, Via Rovita 13, ℂ 0973 876 588 (*expensive*), where excellent fish is matched with equally good pastas and meat dishes, all making the most of local Basilicata produce—rocket, aubergines and so on. *Open Sept–April; closed Tues.*

Práia a Mare ✉ 87028

Here the hotels are simple places and there are plenty to choose from: **★★Calabria**, Via Roma 72, ℂ 0985 72350 (*cheap*) is near the sea and has its own stretch of beach. **Vecchio Frantoio**, on Corso da Viscigliosa (*cheap*) has a wide selection of grilled fish and seafood served with *porcini* mushrooms or rocket.

Cosenza and the Sila ✉ 87100

In Cosenza, one place to stay that's comfortable and well run is the **★★★Centrale**, Via dei Tigrai, ℂ 0984 73681 (*moderate*). The only budget hotel is also in the centre, the very inexpensive and basic **★Bruno**, Corso Mazzini 27, ℂ 0984 73889. Again in the centre, for a good meal in an informal and busy atmosphere, **Da Giocondo**, Via Piave ℂ 0984 28910 (*cheap*), will do nicely. In the old town, **L'Arco Vecchio**, Via Archi di Ciaccio (*moderate*) has a more sophisticated feel; afterwards, for a drink and some jazz, you can stroll down to **Artcafé**, on Piazza Duomo, ℂ 0984 32682. *Closed Mon.*

Elsewhere around the Sila there is very modest accommodation available at Bocchigliero and Longobucco, to the north in the Sila Greca. Around the Albanian villages, accommodation is mostly in Spezzano Albanese, including **★★★San Francesco Terme**, Loc. Bagni, ℂ 0984 953 068, ✉ 0984 953 251 (*moderate*), which caters to the spa customers; and the cheap and cheerful **★★Due Torri**, ℂ 0984 953 613, on the SS19. For *agriturismo* try the *azienda* **Piana dei Gelsi**, Loc. Pantano ℂ 0981 956 045, near Spezzano Albanese Scalo.

Vibo Valentia ✉ 89900

Accommodation here ranges from the honest and simple **★★Miramonti**, Via F. Proietti, ℂ 0963 41053 (*moderate*), to the basic **Pensione Il Terrazzino**, ℂ 0963 571 091 (*cheap*), at Bivona on the coast near the castle. The best restaurant in the area is in Vibo Marina, a locally celebrated seafood establishment called **L'Approdo**, Via Roma 22, ℂ 0963 572 640. Elaborate *frutti di mare antipasti*, grilled fish and swordfish *involtini* invite a worthwhile splurge at about L50,000.

Tropea/Cape Vaticano ✉ 88038

On one of the prettiest parts of the coast, **★★★★★Baia Paraelios**, ℂ 0963 600 300, ✉ 0963 600 074 (*expensive*) is a group of well-furnished cottages set on a terraced hill overlooking a beautiful beach. This is one of the few places along this coast where it's usually necessary to reserve some time ahead (*open May–Sept*).

For seafood, one of the best restaurants is **Vittoria**, ✆ 0963 81358, a bit out of the way by the station in Nicótera, with outdoor dining (*L40,000*). In Tropea, **Al Centro Storico**, on Via Pietro Vanea, in the centre, has a wide choice of fresh seafood, and outside tables on a little square (*L45,000*).

Reggio di Calabria ✉ 89100

Most of the hotels are clustered around the archaeological museum. The poshest is the modern ★★★★**Excelsior**, Via Vittorio Veneto 66, ✆ 0965 812 211, ✆ 0965 893 084 (*expensive*), with fully air-conditioned rooms. For a cheaper option you can try ★★**Eremo**, Via Eremo Botte 12, ✆ 0965 22433, one of the few hotels in the vicinity that has access for wheelchairs; or else the funky but friendly ★★**Diana**, Via Vitrioli 12, ✆ 0965 891 522, just off the Corso in a fascinating pre-earthquake palazzo. **Rodrigo**, Via XXIV Maggio 25, ✆ 0965 20170 (*moderate*) is one of the best places in the centre for seafood, including its speciality *ravioli Rodrigo*, stuffed with fish. *Closed Sun.* For something a bit more elegant, there's **Collina dello Scoiattolo**, on the Via Provinciale, ✆ 0965 682 255 (*moderate*), just outside town with a view of the straits, and first-class swordfish and *aragoste. Closed Wed.*

Aspromonte ✉ 89050

Gambarie has almost all of the hotels on Aspromonte, and there isn't a lot of difference between them; fortunately they all have heating. ★★★**Centrale**, Piaza Mangeruca 22, ✆ 0965 743 133, ✆ 0965 743 141 (*moderate*) will do fine; as would the only inexpensive choice, ★★**Il Ritrovo**, Via Garibaldi 15, ✆ 0965 743 021, ✆ 0965 743 264.

In summer look out for informal outdoor restaurants around Gambarie; just a few tables under the trees, and good simple cooking for next to nothing. In Sant'Alessio di Aspromonte, on the road up to Gambarie, **Nunziatina**, ✆ 0965 741 006 (*cheap*) is a local favourite and a stronghold of mountain cooking, with home-made Calabrian pastries. In summer, try **Villa Rosa** (*moderate*), on the road to Gambarie just beyond Santo Stefano—a wonderful place, with outdoor dining on a panoramic terrace, pasta with *porcini* mushrooms, and a barbecue. You must remember to ring Rosa in advance; ✆ 0965 740 500.

The Ionian Sea

Tourist Information

Locri: Via Fiume 1, ✆ 0964 29600. **Crotone**: Via Torino 148, ✆ 0962 23185. **Catanzaro**: in the Galleria Mancuso, ✆ 0961 743 901. Some of the coastal resorts open local information desks during the summer season, including **Metaponto Lido**: Viale delle Sirene, ✆ 0835 741 933.

Italy's Longest Beach

From Reggio as far as Tàranto, the coasts of Calabria and later the Basilicata are one long beach—about 500km of it, broken in only a few places by mountains or patches of industry. All along this route the pattern will be the same: sleepy new concrete settlements on the shore, within sight of their mother towns, a few kilometres further up in the mountains. In summer, you will see great rivers, like the Amendola, filled with pebbles: the terrible deforestation of Calabria in the 19th century (committed mostly by northern Europeans and corrupt Italian governments) denuded much of the interior, making its rivers raging torrents in the spring. Recent governments have worked to reforest vast tracts, especially on Aspromonte, but wherever you see bare rock on the mountains, there is land that can never be redeemed.

Many of the new villages and towns on the bottom of the toe have become little resorts—two *pensioni* and a pizzeria, on average; none is worth special mention, but you'll never have trouble finding clean water and a kilometre or so of empty (and usually trash-strewn) beach. About 3km south of **Locri** there are fragmentary ruins of the Greek city of the same name, a few bits of wall and bases of temples. Most of the art excavated from Locri has been taken to the Reggio museum and further afield (including perhaps, the famous Ludovisi throne in Rome, which has been called a fake). Enough was left behind in Locri to make the anti-quarium near the sea worth a visit (*open Tues–Sat 9–1 and 4–6, Sun 9–1*). When pirates and malaria forced the Locrians to abandon their city in the 8th century, they fled to the nearby mountains and founded **Gerace**. Though the population of its melancholy medieval centre today is only about 300, Gerace was an important centre in the Middle Ages; it has Calabria's biggest cathedral, an 11th-century Norman Romanesque work supported by columns from the ruins of Locri. The 13th-century San Francesco is the best of a few other churches that show a strong Byzantine-Norman influence in their architecture.

Roccella Iónica is an up-and-coming little town. Its hilltop setting and half-ruined castle provide one of the few breaks in the monotony of beach along the coast road. Up in the hills above Monasterace Marina, the Greek village of **Stilo** is famous for its 10th-century Byzantine church, La Cattolica, with five small domes and some medieval frescoes. Further north there is little out of the ordinary to detain you along the shore of the Gulf of Squillace as far as **Catanzaro**, the Calabrian capital. Really an overgrown mountaintop village that has straggled gradually down to the sea since the war, it is a piquant little city, the kind of place where the young men ask for a light while they give you the once-over. The city park, the Villa Trieste, has nice views, and there is a recently opened museum of carriages (*Loc. Siano north of town; open Mon–Fri 8.30–12 and 4–6; adm*), but there is little else in Catanzaro to see.

Crotone: The City of Pythagoras

Heading into the gulf of Tàranto, the ghost cities of Magna Graecia make the only distractions along a lonely coast. **Crotone**, the Greek Croton, is no ghostly ruin, but a dismal middle-sized industrial city. The old Croton was often the most powerful of the Greek cities, though it was more famous in the ancient world as the adopted home of the philosopher Pythagoras. With his scientific discoveries, mathematical mysticism and belief in the transmigration of souls, Pythagoras cast a spell over the Greek world, and particularly over Magna Graecia. He was hardly a disinterested scholar in an ivory tower; around the middle of the 6th century BC he seems to have led, or merely inspired, a mystic-aristocratic government in Croton based on his teachings. When a democratic revolution threw him out, he took refuge in Metapontum. Croton had a reputation, too, for other things: its medical school, the success of its athletes at the Olympic games, and especially its aggressive and unyielding attitude towards its neigh-bours. From all this, nothing is left but the Museo Archeologico (*open July–Sept only Tues–Sat 9–1 and 3.30–7, Sun 9–1*), with a large collection of terracotta ex votos like those at Reggio. On a promontory south of Crotone, a single standing column from a temple of Hera makes a romantic ruin on **Cape Colonne**.

Some 80km further north, from Lido Sant'Angelo, you can dip easily into the mountains at **Rossano**, one of the better-kept Calabrian hill towns. The town's particular treasure, originally in the cathedral, is a beautiful 6th-century manuscript called the *Purple Codex*, believed to be the oldest illuminated gospel anywhere, made in Syria and almost certainly brought here by eastern monks fleeing their Muslim invaders. It can now be seen in the Museo Diocesano, next to the cathedral (*to see it ask the tour guide office close by; adm*). Past Rossano, the mountains recede into the plain of **Sybaris**, named after the Greek city so renowned for luxurious decadence that even today it is echoed in the word *sybarite*.

Sybaris' misfortune was to have jealous Croton for a neighbour. Croton besieged Sybaris and took it in 510 BC. After razing the city to the ground, the Crotonites diverted the River Crati over the ruins so that it could never be rebuilt. They did such a good job, in fact, that until a few years ago modern archaeologists could not even find the site; some scholars became convinced the whole story of Sybaris was just a myth. Now that they've found it, excavations are feverishly under way, and it is hoped that the richest city of Magna Graecia may yield the archaeologists something worth the trouble it has caused them. The first finds are now on display at the **excavation site** (*open Mon–Sat 9–2 and 4–7*), but so far they consist only of items from the Roman town that was later built over the parts of old Sybaris that had not been covered by water. Sybaris stands at the mouth of the Crati, which is now a wildlife preserve for a small colony of that increasingly rare species, the Mediterranean seal.

Policoro and Metapontum

Nearing the northern boundaries of Calabria, there are castles frowning down over the sea at **Roseto** and **Rocca Imperiale** (*open summer only*), the latter built by Frederick II. The Basilicata's share of the Ionian Coast offers little change from Calabria. The new town of **Policoro** stands near the ancient city of Eraclea, and its Museo Nazionale della Siritide (*open daily 9–7; Oct–Mar 9–6; adm*) has a good collection of Greek vases and terracottas. **Metapontum** was another rich city. It based its prosperity on growing and shipping wheat; today its famous silver coins, always decorated with an ear of wheat, are especially prized by collectors. Metapontum has more ruins to show than any of the other Calabrian sites, but do not expect anything like Paestum. On the banks of the River Bradano stands the Temple of Hera that used to be called the *Tavole Palatine* by locals—the Round Table of King Arthur. Fifteen of its columns remain. The rest of the city's scanty remains, including the outlines of a horseshoe-shaped classical theatre, are a couple of kilometres' walk to the south.

Where to Stay and Eating Out

Gerace ✉ 89048

A Squella, ✆ 0964 356 086 (*cheap*), just at the entrance of the town on the Locri road, serves good pizza as well as a full menu with favourites like bean and chicory casserole and pasta with chick peas and hot peppers. *Out of season open for lunch only.*

Stilo ✉ 89900

The only hotel in Stilo, **★★San Giorgio**, Via Citarelli 8, ✆ 0965 731 153, ▣ 0965 775 047 (*cheap*) occupies a former cardinal's palace and is furnished partly in period style, with a pool and a terrace with panoramic views. *Open April–Oct.*

Catanzaro ✉ 88100

If you are passing through, there are a few simple hotels in Catanzaro: the modern and attractive ★★★**Grand Hotel**, Piazza Matteotti, ✆ 0961 701 256, ✐ 0961 741 621 (*moderate*), in the centre of town, or the cheaper but still comfortable ★★**Belvedere**, Via Italia 33, ✆ 0961 720 591 (*cheap*). Down in Catanzaro Lido, stop for dinner at **Due Romani**, on Via Murano at the coastal SS106, ✆ 0961 32097 (*moderate–cheap*), which specializes in seafood, including the best and most copious *griglia mista* we've had in Italy, at bargain prices. In the city, there is little choice and little seafood; at **La Corteccia**, Via Indipendenza 30, ✆ 0961 746 130 (*moderate–cheap*), you can eat traditional cuisine for very reasonable prices. The wine shop (with no name; *cheap*) on Vicolo San Rocchello is another, more rough-and-ready, place to sample some powerful local specialities.

Crotone ✉ 88900

Along the Ionian Coast dining is simple—perhaps a little seafood shack that is only open in the summer, or a small and cheap, but lively, pizzeria with a little terrace. There are some exceptions, such as the hotel **Da Annibale**, Via Duomo 35, ✆ 0962 795 004 (*moderate*), in Le Castella on Cape Rizzuto, not far south of Crotone, where the swordfish *involtini* is a rare treat. In Crotone, where you would least expect it, there is one very good restaurant: **Il Girrarosto**, Via Vittorio Veneto 30, ✆ 0962 22043 (*moderate*), which specializes in roast lamb and kid, but also knows what to do with swordfish and other seafood. There is a nice terrace, too.

Policoro and Metaponto ✉ 75025

Along the Basilicata's short stretch of Ionian Coast, Policoro makes the most convenient place to stop over. You'll find a number of respectable middle-range hotels, including ★★★**Callà**, Corso Pandosia 1, ✆ 0835 972 129; and ★★★**Motel Due Palme**, on the coastal road just north of Policoro at Scanzano Iónico, ✆ 0835 953 024, ✐ 0835 954 025 (*both cheap*). ★★★**Kennedy**, Viale Jonio 1, ✆/✐ 0835 741 960 (*cheap*), by the beach at Metaponto Lido, is a good bargain. In Policoro, there is a good family trattoria called **Ragno Verde**, Via Colombo 13, ✆ 0835 971 736.

The Basilicata Inland

Tourist Information

Matera: Via Viti de Marco 9, ✆ 0835 333 541. **Potenza**: Via Cavour 15, ✆ 0971 411 839, ✐ 0971 36196; and Via Alianelli 4, ✆ 0971 21812.

Matera and its Province

The interior of the Basilicata has never been one of the more welcoming regions of Italy. Divided about equally between mountains and rolling hills, the isolation of this land has usually kept it far from the major events of Italian history. The territory may be familiar if you have read Carlo Levi's *Christ Stopped at Eboli*, a novel written when the Basilicata was a national scandal, the poorest and most backward corner of all Italy. None of the famous 18th- and 19th-century travellers ever penetrated deeply into the region, and even today it is a part of the country few foreigners ever visit.

Not that they have been overlooking anything. Of all the Basilicata's towns, the only one that offers a real reason for stopping is **Matera**, a lively provincial capital of some 55,000 people that has become famous for a kind of freak-show attraction. Matera was an inhabited town since before recorded history in these parts began, and for centuries, probably millennia, its people built cave-homes and cave-churches in the easily worked tufa stone.

Until recently, the city had a certain notoriety as the most desperately poor provincial capital in Italy—and the scene of Carlo Levi's chilling book. Times are better now, but Matera has chosen to preserve rather than obliterate its terrible past by turning its poorest sections, the **Sassi**, into a sort of open-air museum—one that has made UNESCO's list of World Heritage Sites. *Sassi* are the cave neighbourhoods that line the two ravines between which Matera is built. Visitors as recently as 40 years ago reported people living in their cave-homes in almost inconceivable poverty, sharing space with pigs and chickens, their children imploring outsiders not for money, but for quinine.

Most of the buildings (and all of the caves) in the Sassi are abandoned today. You may think it somewhat macabre, visiting the scenes of past misery, but the Sassi are indeed fascinating in their own way. Don't be surprised to see a tour group of bewildered foreigners being dragged through the cave neighbourhoods' steps and winding lanes.

There are two Sassi, the wealthier *Sasso Barisano*, north of the town centre, and the poorer *Sasso Caveoso*, to the east. If you visit, before long a child or old man of the neighbourhood will come up and approach you with the offer of guide service—worth the trouble and slight expense if you have the time and find the Sassi interesting. They know where the old churches with the Byzantine frescoes are (some as old as the 9th century), and, if you can pick out enough of their southern dialect, they have plenty of stories to tell. Local guides are also probably a better option than the maps and itineraries you can pick up from the tourist office. (Alternatively, the very good Tour Service Matera on the main Piazza Vittorio Veneto 42, ✆ 0835 334 633, offers a wide range of tailor-made guided tours.)

Not all of Matera's sights are in the Sassi; there is also the 13th-century **cathedral**, a fine Romanesque building with some richly decorated side chapels; the churches of **San Francesco** and **San Giovanni Battista**, both with good façades; a 15th-century castle, the **Castello Tramontano**, above the city; an eccentric 18th-century church called the **Purgatorio**, with a leering skull over the main portal; and a first-class local archaeological museum, the **Museo Ridola** (*open daily 9–7; adm*), housed in the Baroque former convent of Santa Chiara.

The dry, austere countryside around Matera is full of tufa quarries, caves and churches. Across the Gravina ravine from the Sasso Caveoso (the one south of the cathedral), the cliffs called the **Murgia Timone** hold a number of interesting cave-churches, some with elaborate fronts, even domes, cut out of the tufa, and medieval frescoes. You'll need a map and some help from the provincial tourist office, or else a guide, to find them. Among the other places in Matera province that are worth a stop if you are passing through are **Tursi** and **Stigliano**, in the remote south of the province, two otherwise unremarkable villages both with remarkable churches. Tursi's is the sanctuary of Santa Maria D'Anglona, out in the country on the road to Policoro, a 13th-century work in an offshoot of the Pisan Romanesque style. In Stigliano, the 17th-century church of San Antonio has an odd waffle-iron façade even better than the one on the Gesù Nuovo in Naples. South of Stigliano, the wild countryside around **Aliano** offers some of the more outlandish scenery in southern Italy. Deforestation and consequent erosion have turned parts of it into a lunar landscape, exposing weirdly twisted rock formations called *calanchi*. Aliano itself is the village where Carlo Levi actually stayed during the time he describes in *Christ Stopped at Eboli*. The house in which he lived is at the bottom of the village, and now houses a museum (*open Mon–Sat 10.30–12.30 and 5–7, Sun 9.30–12.30*), dedicated to the writer and to local folklore, customs and traditional life.

Monte Vúlture and the Castles of Emperor Frederick

Western Basilicata is a province to itself, with a capital at **Potenza**, a plain, modern hilltop city regularly rattled to pieces by earthquakes. The northern end of the province, astride the important routes between Naples and Puglia, was a very busy place in the Middle Ages, full of castles and fought over by Normans, Angevins and Holy Roman Emperors. Frederick II, in particular, haunted these bleak hills; he spent three months here, just before moving on to Puglia, where he died of dysentery. His son, Manfred, and Elena of Epirus spent their honeymoon at the well-preserved castle of **Lagopésole**, halfway between Potenza and Melfi. Earlier in his reign, the great Hohenstaufen had spent some time at the castle at **Melfi**, a fortress that two centuries before had been the de Hautevilles' first Italian headquarters, where Robert Guiscard was crowned Duke of Puglia and Calabria.

The castle (*the interior still under restoration*) is well up to cinematic standards—none of Frederick's geomantical mysticism here; unlike Castel del Monte (*see* pp.886–87) this one was built strictly for defence. Little remains of the original furnishings, but there is a small archaeological museum (*open Tues–Sat 9–2, Sun 9–1; adm*). Melfi itself is a sleepy town, with little but the castle and its 11th-century cathedral to remind it of times when it often occupied the centre stage of European politics.

Looking out from Melfi's castle, the horizon to the south is dominated by the ragged, faintly menacing outline of **Monte Vúlture**, a long-extinct volcano with a forest where once it had a smoking crater. Around the back side of the mountain, the Basilicata keeps one of its few beauty spots, the little **Lakes of Monticchio**, with lovely woods and a funicular to the top of the mountain. Out east from Melfi, there is another old castle at **Venosa**, an important town in Roman times and the birthplace of the poet Horace.

Just outside the town, on the road to Puglia and near the remains of Venosa's Roman amphitheatre, you can visit what has survived of one of the most ambitious church building projects ever undertaken in the south. The Benedictine **Abbazia della Trinità**, begun in the 1050s, was never completed, but it became the resting place of four of the five famous Norman brothers: William, Drogo, Robert (Guiscard) and Humphrey de Hauteville. Their tombs are in the older, completed church, along with some very fine surviving frescoes and carved capitals; among the heaps of stones tumbled about you may notice some Hebrew inscriptions; ancient and medieval Venosa both had Jewish communities, and some Jewish catacombs have been discovered along with Christian ones on the hill east of the abbey.

Matera ✉ 75100

The place to stay in Matera is the **Sassi**, Via San Giovanni Vecchio 89, ✆ 0835 331 009, ✉ 0835 333 733 (*moderate*), right in the heart of the Sasso Barisano. A restructured 18th-century complex, each one of the 15 rooms is differently shaped to respect the original layout, and they all come with balconies overlooking the Sassi. They also have one suite with private access; and their own hostel (*cheap*). Simple but very tasteful décor and friendly and efficient service. Other good options are ★★★**Piccolo Albergo**, Via di Sariis 11, ✆ 0835 330 201; and ★★★**Italia**, Via Ridola 5, ✆ 0835 333 561 (*expensive–moderate*); some rooms in the Italia also have views over the Sassi.

Matera also has some good restaurants—**Il Castello**, Via Castello 1, ✆ 0835 333 752 (*moderate*) serves interesting *orecchiette* with mushrooms and sausage, as well as good fish and meat. *Closed Wed.* For a wide choice of simple but piquant Basilicatan dishes, and a terrace overlooking the Sassi, there is **Il Terrazzino**, Vico S. Giuseppe 7, ✆ 0835 332 503 (*moderate*), just off Piazza Vittorio Veneto. *Closed Tues.* **Trattoria Lucania**, Via Lucana 48, ✆ 0835 336 117 (*moderate*), a small restaurant offering typical regional cuisine, is very popular with the locals. *Closed Sun.*

Potenza ✉ 85100

This is the kind of place where you will share a quiet hotel with a small group of government inspectors and travelling salami salesmen. They're all on expense accounts, so there are no bargains. If you do find yourself there, try the straightforward ★★**Miramonti**, Via Caserma Lucana 30, ✆ 0971 22987/✆ 0971 411 623 (*cheap*).

Console yourself perhaps with dinner at Potenza's one exceptionally good restaurant, **Taverna Oraziana**, Via O. Flacco 2, ✆ 0971 21851 (*expensive*), where fine fresh pasta and local produce are used to recreate traditional old local recipes. *Closed Fri and Aug.* Alternatively, try the singular, employee-owned **Fuori le Mura**, Via 4 Novembre 34, ✆ 0971 25409 (*moderate*), renowned locally for its enormous choice of *antipasto* treats and good roast pork and lamb. *Closed Mon.*

Melfi ✉ 85025

★★★**Due Pini**, ✆ 0972 21031 (*cheap*), outside town at the railway station, is yet another place for travelling salesmen, convenient for an overnighter. For dining, the family-run **Vaddone**, Corso da Sant'Abruzzese, ✆ 0972 24323 (*moderate*) offers good regional cuisine washed down with local Aglianico and Vúlture wines. *Closed Sun evenings and Mon.* If you have a car, you can do much better staying in the *Azienda Agrituristica*, **Il Tratturo Regio**, Contrada del Casonetto, ✆/✉ 0972 239 295/✆/✉ 0972 24120—quite well signposted on the SS road (*cheap*).

Puglia

In many ways, this region may well be the best of Italy's south. From the forests and shining limestone cliffs of the beautiful Gargano Peninsula in the north, through the long plain of the *Tavoliere*, to the southernmost tip of Italy's heel, Puglia offers the most variety of any of the southern regions, not only physically, but in its towns and in its art: in Puglia you can see Greek remains at Tàranto, a score or so of Norman Romanesque cathedrals, Santa Claus' tomb, the end of the Appian Way, the finest Baroque city in the Mediterranean, and a town of buildings with roofs shaped like oilcans.

Ancient Puglia was home to a number of quiet, modestly cultured and prosperous nations—the Daunii around Fóggia, the Oscans, the Messapians and others. Under Roman rule it was a favoured province, Rome's gateway to the east, and one of the parts of Italy most heavily influenced by the proximity of Greek culture. In the Middle Ages, Puglia was the home of a unique culture influenced by Normans, Arabs and Greeks, fully equal in wealth and artistic talent to the cities of the north.

Not to be Missed

Puglia is a large region—and a long one, all of 405km from the northwestern corner to the tip of the Salentine Peninsula. One way of seeing the best it has to offer in little over a week would be to begin with an overnight stay at **Vieste**, on the Gargano. From there, drive south down this beautiful peninsula to **Manfredonia**, stopping on the way at **Monte Sant'Angelo** (55km). Spend a day touring the Pugliese cathedral cities or **Castel del Monte** before arriving at **Bari** (112km).

Apart from its Romanesque cathedral, Bari has little to detain you, so carry on south through Alberobello and Locorotondo to look at the *trulli* country on the way to the finest city of the south, Baroque **Lecce** (158km in one or two days; **Ostuni** makes a good stop in between). Leave a day or two for the Salentine Peninsula before cutting back west to **Tàranto**, with its superb archaeological museum.

If you have more time for Puglia, it might be difficult to choose how to spend it—the region's attractions are many and varied, and spread all over the map. The Gargano and Salentine peninsulas have the best beaches and scenery, and the most engaging towns for a stay are Lecce and Tàranto.

Puglia's greatest artistic productions are the medieval cathedrals and churches of Trani, Bari, Ruvo, Altamura, Molfetta, Bisceglie, Bitonto and Barletta, all close together in Bari province. The fascinating Castel del Monte, west of Bari, and the great castle at Lucera, are only two of the important sites associated with the reign of the 'wonder of the world', the Emperor Frederick II.

To get to know Puglia better, keep an eye open for some of the less important sights—pre-classical ruins, dolmens, relics of Greek Italy, religious centres, and especially the unique rural civilization of the *trulli* country. Puglia is not often spectacular, but the depth and meaning of its culture will come as a surprise; it is one of the regions most worth knowing.

Puglia

N

50 kms
30 miles

Adriatic Sea

Ionian Sea

Otranto
S. Cataldo
Scala
S. Cesarea Terme
Grotta
Tricase
Leuca
Calimera
Lecce
S16
Maglie
Salentine
Capo S. Maria di Leuca
I. Santa Andrea
Galatina
Nardò
Gallipoli
Copertino
Porto Cesareo
Oria
Manduria
Francavilla Fontana
Mesagne
S7
Grottaglie
S. Vito dei Normanni
Ostuni
Brindisi
Ceglie Messapico
Tàranto
Golfo di Tàranto
Martina Franca
Locorotondo
Alberobello
Mottola
Massafra
Fasano
Putignano
Castellaneta
Egnazia
Torre Canne
Castellana Grotte
Monopoli
Metaponto
Montalbano
Policoro
Rocca Imperiale
Conversano
Bitonto
Laterza
Ginosa
Bradano
Bari
Altamura
Gravina di Puglia
Matera
Aquaviva del Fonti
Ruvo di Puglia
Molfetta
Bisceglie
Trani
Andria
Corato
Castel del Monte
The Murge
L. San Giuliano
Tursi
Chiaromonte
M. Polino
Ardenblara
S534
Canosa di Puglia
Barletta
PUGLIA
Campomaggiore
Aliano
L. di Pietra di Pertusillo
Canne
Spinazzola
Cerignola
Ascoli Satriano
Venosa
Genzano di Lucania
Moliterno
M. Sirino
BASILICATA
Manfredonia
Golfo di Manfredonia
Ofanto
Bovino
Rionero in Vulture
M. Vulture
Potenza
Gargano Peninsula
M. Sant' Angelo
Vieste
L. di Varano
L. di Lesina
Candelaro
Ordona
Troia
Lucera
Foggia
San Severo
Tanagro
Golfo di Policastro
Isola di Dino
Scalea
Termoli
MOLISE
L. di Occhito
Campobasso
Benevento
Nola
Avellino
CAMPANIA
Salerno
Agropoli

875

Food and Wine in Puglia

La cucina pugliese makes use of all the natural resources at its disposal. Bari is particularly famous for fish, while Tàranto has excellent mussels, mostly from the Mare Grande—and here called *mitili*, instead of *cozze* as they are in the rest of Italy. They feature prominently on the menus of virtually all Tàranto's restaurants. In the hill towns of the interior, however, fish is a rarity and is replaced by meat—especially pork, rabbit and lamb. The 'national' dish of Puglia is *fave e cicoria*, a delicious purée of dry fava-beans served with sautéed wild chicory.

The local olive oil is dark and strong, closer to that of Greece than the lighter oils of Tuscany and Umbria; the olives too are smaller and fuller flavoured, coming from trees whose roots have to dig deep into the soil to reach water.

As in most of southern Italy, sheep make up a great part of the livestock, and the region's sheep's cheeses include the local styles of pecorino and ricotta—look out for the unusually strongly flavoured *ricotta forte*. It goes particularly well in sauces with the local pasta—*orecchiette*, 'little ears'—formed by shaping the uncooked pasta with the thumb. Another cheese speciality is *burrata*, a tear-shaped mozzarella shell filled with a heart of shredded mozzarella and cream. Puglia grows some of the best almonds in the world—used in the preparation of tasty cookies and desserts.

Pugliese wine, like the cuisine, tends to be strong and full-bodied, and has had a high reputation since Roman times. Today there are about 24 different wines produced in Puglia, including whites, reds, rosés, sparkling wines and the particularly sweet Muscat. Two that are worth looking out for are the powerful red, *Cacc'emmitte*, from Fóggia province, and the comparatively light, delicate dry white from Locorotondo.

Fóggia and its *Tavoliere*

Getting Around

Fóggia's **railway station** is on Piazza Veneto, at the end of the central Viale XXIV Maggio. It is an important junction for north–south trains—you may often have to change there—and there will usually not be a long wait for trains to Bari, Naples, Bologna or Rome. Some trains also run from Fóggia to Manfredonia.

Two separate companies operate **buses** around the province: **SITA**, ✆ 0881 773 117 (with a ticket office at Kiwi Bar opposite the station, at the corner of Viale XXIV Maggio); and **FG**, freephone ✆ 167 296 247 (with a ticket office to the left of the entrance to the station), which also operates a private railway service in northern Gargano. There are several buses a day to Manfredonia, Monte Sant'Angelo and Vieste, and also to Troia and Lucera, all departing from Piazza Veneto.

Fóggia: Via Sen. Emilio Perrone 17, ℂ 0881 723 650; quite hard to find, on the second floor of an apartment block (*open Mon–Fri 9–12.30*).

Fóggia

Fóggia, after Bari and Tàranto the third city of Puglia, was once Frederick's capital, where between campaigns he enjoyed quiet moments with his English wife, his harem, his falcons and his Muslim sorcerers. It must have been quite a place, but old Fóggia has since been obliterated by two of the usual southern plagues: earthquakes have levelled it on several occasions, and the French sacked it in 1528. Allied bombers finished off the remains, and the Fóggia you see today is a newborn—homely and awkward, but still somehow endearing. Its citizens haven't forgotten Frederick, but these days they seem more proud of **Umberto Giordano**, a composer of operas born here in 1867. The municipal theatre is named after him, and there is a big statue of him in the Piazza Giordano in the city centre, among a wonderfully eccentric set of statues of characters from his works. Giordano's big hit was *Andrea Chenier*; another of his works, with the intriguing title of *Fedora*, is claimed to be the only opera that calls for bicycles on stage. You'll be able to see one or the other during Fóggia's opera season, in the autumn.

There's a little left of old Fóggia: a charming **cathedral** divided neatly in half, like a layer cake: 12th-century Romanesque on the bottom and Baroque on top. The early medieval door on the north side was only rediscovered during the Second World War, when bombs knocked down the adjacent building. A few twisting streets to the north, on Piazza Nigri, is the **Museo Civico** (*open daily 9–1, also Mon, Tues, Thurs and Fri 5–7*), devoted to archaeological finds. The scientific section has been relocated to the **Museo Scientifico**, Via Bellavia (*open Mon–Sat 9–1, Mon and Fri also 4.30–7; adm*). The single portal with an inscription incorporated into one side of the building is the last surviving remnant of Frederick's palace. Near the museum, on Piazza Sant'Egidio, the **Chiesa della Croce** (1693–1742) is one of Puglia's more unusual churches: an elegant Baroque gate leads to a long avenue, which passes under five domed chapels that represent the stages in the passion of Christ, before arriving at the church itself.

Lucera and Troia

Why does Lucera have a cathedral from the 14th century, while almost all the other Pugliese towns built theirs back in the 12th or earlier? Well, sir, there's a story for you. In the 1230s Emperor Frederick II was hard pressed. Excommunicated by his devious rival, Pope Gregory IX, and at war with all the Guelph towns of Italy, Frederick needed some allies he could trust. At the same time, he had a problem with brigandage in some of the predominantly Muslim mountain areas of Sicily. His solution: induce 20,000 Sicilian Arabs to move to Puglia, with land grants and promises of imperial employment and favours.

The almost abandoned town of *Luceria*, once an important Roman colony, was the spot chosen, and, before anybody knew it, Frederick had conjured up an entirely Muslim metropolis 290km from Rome. The Emperor felt right at home in Lucera, and the new city became one of his favourite residences; later it would be the last stronghold of his son Manfred, in the dark days that followed Frederick's death. Charles of Anjou took the city in 1267; attempts at forced Christianization, and the introduction of settlers from Provence, caused a series of revolts among the population, which the Angevins finally settled in 1300 by butchering the lot. Little remains of Muslim Lucera, or even of the Lucera of the French; most of the Provençals could not take the summer heat, though their descendants still live in the hills to the south. Charles II began the simple, Gothic **cathedral** in 1300, directly after the massacre of the Saracens. This and the equally plain **San Francesco**, a typical barn-like Franciscan church built from recycled Roman ruins, are Lucera's monuments, as well as parts of a gate and an amphitheatre from Roman *Luceria* on the edge of town. Smaller fragments reside at the **Museo Civico** (*open Tues–Sat 9–1 and 4–7, Sun 9–1; adm*), just behind the cathedral. Frederick's **castle** (*open daily 9–1; summer also 4–7*), one of the largest ever built in Italy, was begun in 1233, the same year as the importation of the Saracens. It is still an impressive sight, with its score of towers and walls nearly a kilometre in circumference, set on a hill looking out over Lucera and the Fóggia plain. Only ruins are left of Frederick's palace inside.

South and west of Fóggia, in the foothills of the Apennines bordering the Molise and the Basilicata, you may consider a side trip to the lovely village of **Troia**, accessible by bus from Fóggia or Lucera. Its famous **cathedral** is one of the oldest and most beautiful in Puglia, and a good introduction to the glories of the Pugliese Romanesque. Troia, once the Roman town of *Aecae*, was refounded in 1017, and prospered from the start. Popes held two small church councils here in the 11th and 12th centuries; the cathedral was begun in 1093, though not finished until the time of Frederick. Much of the inspiration for the Pugliese style came from Pisa, and the Pisan trademark—blind arcades decorated with circle and diamond shapes—is in evidence here. This eclectic building has some surprises, most especially a set of Byzantine-style decorated bronze doors, similar to those in the churches of Campania, and also perhaps the most beautiful **rose window** in Italy, a small, Arab-inspired fantasy from Frederick's time; the circle is divided into 11 sections, each with a carved screen in a different geometric design. Inside, the cathedral is austere, but strangely asymmetrical, with everything on the right side just slightly out of alignment.

Two more places of interest in the pretty hills south of Fóggia are **Bovino**, a medieval-looking village with a 13th-century cathedral and some Roman remains, and **Ascoli Satriano**, where a very well-preserved triple-arched Roman bridge still spans the River Carapelle (*call ℗ 0885 796 450, for an appointment*). You can also see substantial remains of the abandoned Roman town of *Herdonia*, near **Ordona**.

Where to Stay and Eating Out

Fóggia ✉ 71100

★★★★**Cicolella**, Viale XXIV Maggio 60, ℗ 0881 688 890 (*expensive*), near the station, is the best hotel: Victorian on the outside, but remodelled within; the restaurant (*expensive*) is also one of the best in town, a good place to introduce yourself to Pugliese specialities like *orecchiette*. *Restaurant closed weekends*. The same family also operates **Pompeo** (ex Giordano), Vicolo al Piano 14, ℗ 0881 724 640 (*moderate*), which serves a wide range of local and seasonal specialities. *Closed Sun and two weeks in Aug*. And the anachronistically good and friendly **Trattoria Santa Lucia**, Via Trieste 57, ℗ 0881 770 356 (*cheap*), which has a fixed price menu (*L20,000*). *Closed Sun evenings*. Two reasonable hotels near the station are ★★★**Europa**, Via Monfalcone 52, ℗ 0881 721 057 (*moderate*), and ★**Venezia**, Via Piave 40, ℗ 0881 770 903 (*cheap*). Even San Severo has a restaurant that is worth a visit: **Le Arcate**, Piazza Cavallotti 29, ℗ 0882 226 025 (*moderate*) uses lighter variations on rustic cuisine, particularly lamb. *Closed Mon evenings*.

The Gargano Peninsula

It looks a little out of place, being the only stretch of scenic coastline between Venice and the tip of Calabria. The 'spur' of the Italian boot is, in fact, a lost chip of Yugoslavia, left behind when two geological plates separated to form the Adriatic, several million years ago. For a long time, before silt washed down by the rivers gradually joined it to the mainland, the Gargano was an island. It might as well have remained so, for the Gargano is as different from the adjacent lands in attitude as it is in its landscapes.

Getting Around

The Gargano has a little private **railway**, the *Ferrovia del Gargano*, that runs from San Severo, 30km north of Fóggia, up to Rodi Garganico and Péschici-Calenella (about six trains a day; freephone © 167 296 247, for information). Connecting **buses** will take you from Péschici to Vieste along the coast road (SP52). Buses (run by FG) are less frequent between Vieste and Manfredonia and Fóggia. There are several SITA buses a day from Manfredonia to Monte Sant'Angelo (call © 0881 773 117, for information), but seeing the Foresta Umbra and the interior of the Gargano will be hard without a **car**. The **ferryboat** service from Manfredonia calls at Vieste, Péschici, Rodi Garganico and the Tremiti Islands (*mid-June–mid-Sept daily; early-June and late-Sept 4 weekly; April–May 2 weekly*); the rest of the year, the islands are reachable only from Termoli and Manfredonia.

Manfredonia: Corso Manfredi 26, © 0884 581 998.
Vieste: Corso Fazzini 8, © 0884 707 495; and in Piazza Kennedy, © 0884 708 806.

Manfredonia

If you are coming from the north you will enter the Gargano by way of Lesina and the Gargano's lakes: the **Lago di Lesina** and the **Lago di Varano**, two large lagoons cut off from the sea by broad sand-spits. From Fóggia, the logical base for attacking the Gargano would be Manfredonia, a dusty port town with a pretty centre at the southern end of the peninsula. It is the base for ferries to the Tremiti Islands and the towns of the Gargano, as well as being a small resort in its own right. As its name implies, this town was founded by Frederick's son, Manfred, and it prospered well enough until Dragut's Turkish pirates sacked and razed it in 1620. (One of the hometown girls ended up as the favoured wife of the Sultan.) Of old Manfredonia all that is left is Manfred's **castle**, rebuilt and extended by Charles of Anjou; it now contains a small **archaeological museum** (*open daily 8.30–1.30 and 3.30–7.30; closed first and last Mon of the month; adm*). The town also has a brash 17th-century **cathedral**.

Along the Fóggia road, about 2 kilometres south of the centre of Manfredonia, you can see the ruins of **Sipontum**, (*open daily 9–12.30 and 3.30–6*) a Roman town that was finally abandoned to the malaria mosquitoes when Manfred moved the population to his healthier new city. The much more recent town of **Siponto**, next to it, is now a popular beach resort. As evidence of how important Sipontum was in the early Middle Ages, there is the impressive 11th-century church of **Santa Maria di Siponto**, close to the archaeological site, in the same style of decoration as the cathedral at Troia, only built on a square Byzantine-Greek plan. It is built over a much earlier underground, early Christian building, from around the 5th century. Another 11th-century church, very similar to Santa Maria, survives another 9km up the road to Fóggia—**San Leonardo**, an even better work, with finely sculpted portals and a small dome.

Monte Sant'Angelo

The tourists who come to the Gargano for the beaches probably never notice, but this peninsula is holy ground, and has been perhaps since the time of the ancient Daunians. Sanctuaries, ancient and modern, are scattered all over it; there are many stories of the apparitions of saints and angels, and even 25 years ago, a holy man received the stigmata at San Giovanni Rotondo.

The centre of all this, for the last thousand years at least, has been Monte Sant'Angelo, one of the most important pilgrimage towns in Italy. Before Christianity the cavern now dedicated to St Michael was the site of a dream oracle; a 5th-century bishop of Sipontum had a vision of the archangel, who left his red cloak as a token and commanded the sanctuary be converted to Christian worship. Early on, the new Monte Sant'Angelo was attracting pilgrims from all over Europe—continuing a tradition that had begun long before the site was Christianized. Among the pilgrims were the first Normans, in the 9th century. They returned home with tales of a rich and fascinatingly civilized Puglia—a place they suspected just might be a pushover for mounted, heavily armoured knights. The first Norman adventurers were not slow in taking up the challenge. All the other sites dedicated to St Michael around the coasts of Europe—including of course Mont St Michel in Normandy—are the spiritual descendants of this one, founded as the cult of St Michael spread across Christendom in the early Middle Ages.

That Monte Sant'Angelo is a special place becomes evident even before you arrive. The trip up from Manfredonia passes through an uncanny landscape: chalky cliffs dotted with caves, ancient agricultural terraces, and a strange clarity in the light and air. After much twisting and grinding of gears, you arrive at a quiet, whitewashed city, a maze of steps and tunnels.

The medieval centre of town, the **Junno**, is one of the most beautiful old quarters in southern Italy, a nonchalant harmony of colour and form that only a few coast towns in Puglia can achieve. Here you will find the **Santuario di San Michele** (*open Easter–Sept daily 7.30–7; Oct–Easter daily 7.30–12.30 and 2.30–5*), behind an eight-sided tower built by Charles of Anjou that reproduces the proportions (on one level) and much of the decoration of Frederick's Castel del Monte. The exterior of the sanctuary seems to be a normal church, with a Gothic porch and portals (mostly built in the 19th century; see if you can guess which of the two identical portals is the original 12th-century work). Above the doors is a Latin inscription: 'Terrible is this place; this is the house of God and the Gate of Heaven.'

Inside, instead of the expected church, there is a long series of steps leading down to the cavern, passing a beautiful pair of bronze doors made in Constantinople in 1076, perhaps by the same artists who did the ones at Amalfi Cathedral. In the darkness most of the scenes are difficult to make out, but Jacob's ladder and the expulsion from Eden stand out clearly. Down in the cave, it is chilly and dark; in the old days pilgrims would come down on their knees, shuffling through the puddles to kiss the image of the archangel. The grotto is laid out like a small chapel. There are plenty of bits of medieval sculptural work around, but the best is a wonderful crazy-medieval bishop's chair, from the 12th century.

The town records give us an almost endless list of celebrity pilgrims: a dozen popes, King Ferdinand of Spain, four Holy Roman Emperors, saints Bernard, Thomas Aquinas, Catherine of Siena, and so on; even St Francis, and they can show you the mark he made on the cavern wall. Behind the altar you can see the little well that made this a holy site in the first place. Long before there was a St Michael, indigenous religions of Europe had a great reverence for springs and underground streams; many scholars believe the idea of dragons began with a primeval fascination with buried streams and accompanying lines of telluric forces beneath the earth's surface; the sleepless 'eye' of the dragon is the fountain, where these forces come to the surface. In the icons of Monte Sant'Angelo, as well as in the endless souvenir figurines hawked outside the sanctuary, Michael is shown dispatching Lucifer in the form of a dragon.

There's more to see in Monte Sant'Angelo, and more oddities. Downhill from the sanctuary, next to the half-ruined church of San Pietro, stands the 12th-century so-called **tomb of Rotari** (*open mornings; if closed see custodian in San Michele*). The idea that this was the tomb of 'Rotarus', a Lombard chief, stems from a misreading of one of the inscriptions. It is now believed this was intended to be a baptistry—a very large and unusual baptistry, if so; it is hard to make out the original intention since much of it has been swallowed up into the surrounding buildings. Some of the sculpted detail is extremely odd; note the figure of a woman nursing a serpent (or dragon).

In the same Junno district, the town has opened a small museum of the folk arts and culture of the Gargano, the **Museo Tancredi** (*open April–Sept Mon 8–2, Tues–Sat 8–2 and 2.30–8, Sun 10–12.30 and 3.30–7; Oct–Mar Mon–Sat 8–2, Tues also 4–7; adm*). On the top of the town there is a romantically ruined Norman castle, rebuilt by the Aragonese kings, but left quite alone ever since.

Padre Pio

From the back of Monte Sant'Angelo a narrow road leads into the heart of the Gargano, eventually branching off to the 'Forest of Shadows' (*see* below) or **San Giovanni Rotondo**, a little town on the slopes of Monte Calvo. Here, besides the strange round temple that gives the town its name (believed, like the tomb of Rotari, to have been intended as a baptistry), there is a 16th-century monastery called **Santa Maria delle Grazie**, that for over 50 years was the home of Padre Pio de Pietralcina, a simple priest who not only received the stigmata, on his hands, feet and side, but also had the ability to appear before cardinals in Rome while his body was sleeping back in the Gargano. His burial place is in the crypt of the modern sanctuary nearby. The Church always has its suspicions about phenomena like these, but over the last 30 years veneration of Padre Pio has spread all over the world, and San Giovanni is a major pilgrimage site. After careful 'research', Vatican experts have decreed that the devil had nothing to do with Padre Pio's miraculous healing powers; the saint was beatified in May 1999.

West of San Giovanni, and, like it, an old stop on the pilgrimage route to Monte Sant'Angelo, is the town of **San Marco in Lamis**, which has similarly always been a monastic centre. The present, huge Franciscan house, with a modern interior, dates from the 16th century.

Vieste

Once past Monte Sacro, on the coast north of Monte Sant'Angelo, you are in the holiday Gargano, on an exceptionally lovely coastline of limestone cliffs, clean blue sea and good beaches decorated with old watchtowers, or stumps and columns of rock and other curious formations. Vieste, at the tip of the peninsula, is in the middle of it, a lively and beautiful white town on white cliffs, surrounded by beaches. Though managing to retain its old charm, Vieste has become one of the major resorts of the southern Adriatic. On Via Duomo, near the centre of the old town, is the **Chianca Amara**, or 'bitter stone', where, it is believed, 5000 of the town's people were beheaded by the Turks when they sacked Vieste in 1554. Nearby are the 11th-century **cathedral**, with 18th-century additions, and a **castle** built by Frederick II, with fine views over the town. Places of interest along the enchanting coast near Vieste include **San Felice** cove, with a little beach and a natural arch in the cliffs, and the **Grotta Sfondata** ('bottomless cave'), one of a few marine grottos and lagoons accessible by boat tours from Vieste. There is also a peculiar early Christian *hypogeum* (cave for burials) on the coast, at the site of a long-disappeared town called *Merinum*. On the Gargano's northern coast, **Péschici** and **Rodi Garganico** are two other pretty fishing villages that are now fast-developing resorts, and particularly crowded in August. Boats call at both of them for the Tremiti Islands and, from either village, or from Vieste itself, it is a relatively easy excursion by bus or car up the mountains to the **Foresta Umbra**, the 'forest of shadows', a thick, primeval forest of beeches, oaks and pines, similar to those that covered most of Puglia in the Middle Ages.

The Tremiti Islands

In winter, this minuscule archipelago 40km from the coast has a population of about 50. August, however, finds it crawling with most of the 100,000 holiday-makers who annually spill over from the resorts of the Gargano. The islands have the same well-scoured limestone coasts as the peninsula, though there is only one beach, on the larger island of **San Domino**.

The Tremiti Islands enter the history books only as a place of exile—Augustus' daughter and Charlemagne's troublesome Italian father-in-law were both confined here—or as a monkish retreat. From the 18th century they were used as a penal colony. The only sight, on the smaller island of **San Nicola** where ferries from the mainland disembark, is a huge, half-ruined fortress monastery begun by Benedictines in the 11th century. Local ferries run from there to San Domino, which has the only hotels. It's a beauty of an island, well forested and surrounded with wonderful coves and lagoons set in a translucent blue-green sea. If you can avoid coming in July or August, when the hordes of day-trippers sail in, the Tremitis can be a perfect spot to let your watch run down. In the summer months, be prepared to face hungry mosquitoes.

Where to Stay and Eating Out

Manfredonia ✉ 71043

****Gargano**, Viale Beccarini 2, ✆ 0884 587 621 (*moderate*) is the best hotel in town, with a sea-water pool and views from every room. Its restaurant (*expensive–moderate*) offers a range of fish dishes from soup to mixed fry. *Closed Tues and several weeks in Nov.* A more basic choice is ***Sipontum**, Via di Vittorio 229, ✆ 0884 542 916 (*cheap*). Manfredonia's restaurants are mostly around the port, and most specialize in seafood; At cool modern **Il Baracchio**, Corso Roma 38, ✆ 0884 583 874 (*moderate*), the octopus salad has to be tasted to be believed. *Closed Thurs and two weeks in July.*

San Giovanni Rotondo ✉ 71013

Built in 1998, ****Masseria Agropolis**, Località Sant'Egidio, ✆ 0882 456 599 (*expensive*) is an impressive, if a bit sterile, compound, with a large pool, cultivated fields, on-site cooking workshops and food-preparation seminars, and horse-riding.

Vieste ✉ 71019

The best beach hotels are slightly garish—a bit of Rimini on the Gargano. Less than 1km south of the town centre, ****Pizzomunno**, Lungomare Enrico Mattei, ✆ 0884 708 741, 📠 0884 707 325 (*very expensive*) is a gorgeous place with sailing, sports, a pool, a beautiful beach and a noisy disco. *Closed Nov–Mar.* Their restaurant is highly rated (*expensive*). *Open daily in season; closed Nov–Feb.* ***Pensione San Giorgio**, Via Madonna della Libertà 43, ✆ 0884 708 618 (*cheap*), in the centre, has a good restaurant for guests only. *Full-board mandatory in Aug; L100,000 per person.*

Some good hotels can be found along the coasts around Vieste—usually in lovely spots, but convenient only if you have a car. ***Gabbiano Beach**, ✆ 0884 706 376 (*cheap*), 7km north on the road to Péschici, is one of the least expensive, though it has its own beach, pool and sailing facilities. *Closed Oct–Mar.* You will find a large selection of similar hotels in Péschici and Rodi Garganico. ***Péschici**, Via San Martino 31, ✆ 0884 964 195 (*cheap*) has good views, and more facilities than most comparable hotels. *Full-board mandatory in Aug; L95,000 per person; closed in winter.*

Not all the good restaurants are in hotels; **Vecchia Vieste**, Via Mafrolla 32, ✆ 0884 707 083 (*moderate*) offers seafood and specialities like *involtini alla viestiana*. *Closed Nov–April.* Many people in Vieste think their finest restaurant is the **San Michele**, Viale XXIV Maggio 72, ✆ 0884 708 143 (*moderate*), for fish grilled or in soups. *Closed Mon in low season; winter closure depends on business, usually Nov–Feb.* For a similar price you can eat seafood or grilled meats at **Box 19**, Via Santa Maria di Merino 19, ✆ 0884 705 229 (*moderate–cheap*). *Closed Mon in low season, and*

Nov. One of Péschici's best restaurants, set up in a natural cave, is **Dragone**, Via Duomo 8, © 0884 701 212 (*expensive–moderate*), in the centre of the old town. *Closed Tues in low season, and Nov–March.*

Tremiti Islands ✉ 71100

If you want to stay over it's worth booking in advance at the eight-room ★★**Al Faro**, © 0882 463 424 (*moderate–cheap*), near the central square on San Domino. *Closed Oct–Easter.* Its restaurant is excellent value for money, serving home cooking influenced by the food traditions of the San Nicola monastery, washed down with good wines. You even get to choose your own fish out of the fridge. ★**Gabbiano**, © 0882 463 401 (*cheap*) is an alternative place to eat. Reserve.

Monte Sant'Angelo ✉ 71037

Al Grottino, Corso Vittorio Emanuele 179, © 0884 561 132, is a place where you can pay about L25,000 for a dinner worth double—roast lamb and kid, truly elegant *antipasti*, sweets and cheeses, and one memorable dish called *orecchiette in carrozza*. *Closed Mon.* A handy choice for lunch is **Garden Paradise**, Via Basilica 51, © 0884 563 904 (*cheap*), with lots of pasta dishes but no fish.

Down the Coast to Bari

If you take the main route, a little bit inland, you will be passing through the *Tavoliere*, the long, plain that stretches the length of Puglia. *Tavoliere* means a chessboard; 2000 years ago, when the Romans first sent in surveyors to apportion the land among their Punic War veterans, this flat plain—the only one south of the Po—gave the methodical rectangularity of the Roman mind a chance to express itself. They turned the plain into a grid of neatly squared roads and farms; many of their arrow-straight roads survive, and the many centuries have only succeeded in throwing a few kinks into the rest. In some parts, if not for the olive groves and vineyards, you might think you were in Iowa.

Getting Around

Two different **railways** serve this area and, unusually for Puglia, you're more likely to find a train than a bus to many destinations. All the coastal towns from Barletta to Monópoli are on the main FS east coast route. From Barletta, there is an FS branch line to the south with infrequent services to Spinazzola and Altamura. In addition, one of the **three private regional lines** that operate from Bari, the *Ferrovia Bari-Nord*, © 080 521 3577, runs a very frequent service through the inland towns such as Andria, Ruvo and Bitonto to Bari.

There are also reasonably regular **buses** along the coast road, and to inland destinations from Barletta or Bari. Unfortunately, Castel del Monte is just about the hardest place to reach in Puglia: call the guides at the castle or the tourist office in Andria for timetables for the scarce bus service.

Tourist Information

Barletta: Via Ferdinando d'Aragona 95, © 0883 331 331. **Trani**: Via Cavour 140, © 0883 588 830. **Ruvo di Puglia**: Via Vittorio Veneto 48, © 080 361 549.

Barletta's Colossus

The coastal road, though just as flat, has more to see than the inland route, passing through a string of attractive medieval port towns, each with its contribution to the Pugliese Romanesque in the shape of a grand old cathedral. **Barletta**, the first of them coming from the north, is the best introduction, and it contains a unique and astounding sight. On Corso Vittorio Emanuele, beside the church of San Sepolcro, stands the largest bronze statue from antiquity now in existence, locally known as the **Colosso**.

To come upon this 20-foot figure in the middle of a busy city street, wearing an imperial scowl and a pose of conquest, with a cross and a sphere in his hands, is like lapsing into a dream. Scholars have debated for centuries who it might be. Obviously a late Roman emperor, and the guesses have mentioned Valentinian, Heraclius and Marcian; the last is most probable, and especially intriguing, since the triumphal column of Marcian (a rather useless emperor with no real successes to commemorate) still stands in Istanbul, and the statue of the emperor that once stood on top of it was probably carried away by the Venetians after the sack of Constantinople in 1204. A ship full of booty from that sack foundered off Barletta's coast, and the Colosso washed up on a nearby beach; the superstitious citizens let it stay there for decades before they got up enough nerve to bring it into the city. The figure is surpassingly strange, a monument to the onset of the Dark Ages; the costume the emperor wears is only a pale memory of the dress of Marcus Aurelius or Hadrian, with a pair of barbaric-looking leather boots instead of imperial buskins.

San Sepolcro, finished in the 13th century, is interesting in its own right. Above the plain French Gothic vaulting, there is an octagonal dome, recalling the Holy Sepulchre in Jerusalem. Corso Garibaldi leads from here into the heart of old Barletta and the 12th-century **cathedral**. Look on the left-hand wall, between the façade and the campanile, and you will see a cornice supported by thirteen strange figures. If you have a good eye, you may make out the letters on them that make an acrostic of Richardus Rex I—Richard the Lionheart, who contributed to the embellishment of the cathedral on his way to the Crusades.

Nearby is the 13th-century church of **Sant'Andrea**, with another fine façade, the main portal of which, from 1240, was the work of the Dalmatian sculptor, Simon di Ragusa. The Third Crusade was launched from Barletta's often-rebuilt **Castello** (*open Tues–Sun 9–1 and 3–6; adm*), in a great council of Frederick and his knights. Apart from a collection of antiques, coins and armour, the castle houses the **Pinacoteca Giuseppe de Nittis**, which has in its collection the only surviving statue of Frederick II—a little the worse for wear, poor fellow—as well as a large collection of works by the local painter Giuseppe de Nittis (1846–84). The admission ticket to the castle will also get you into the **Cantina della Disfida**, in Via Cialdini, where, in 1503, thirteen Italian knights got fed up with disrespect from their French allies and challenged their thirteen best men to a tourney. The Italians all won. The 'Disfida (challenge) di Barletta', something every Italian schoolboy hears about, gets re-enacted in one of Puglia's largest pageants on the second weekend in September.

Trani

The next town along the coast, Trani is a sun- and sea-washed old port that still has a large and prosperous fishing fleet. It was an important merchant town in the early Middle Ages—it once fought a war with Venice, and its merchant captains created perhaps the first code of laws of the sea since ancient times. Trani's famous **cathedral** (*open daily 8.30–12 and 3–6*) stands in an open piazza on the edge of the sea, another excellent work of the Pugliese Romanesque, and a monument to the age of the Crusades. At the centre of the façade is another pair of 12th-century bronze doors, very much like the ones in so many other cities of the south. These are special, though, since the artist who did them and several others in the town is a native: Barisano of Trani.

Inside, the most remarkable things are underground. This cathedral is really three buildings stacked on the same site; the lower church, **Santa Maria della Scala**, is the earlier, Byzantine cathedral, and below that is the **crypt of San Leucio**, an unusual early Christian church or catacomb with solid marble columns and bits of medieval frescoes. Some of Trani's other notable buildings are the **Ognissanti** (*usually closed*), a typical church of the 12th-century Knights Templar; the **Palazzo Caccetta**, a rare (for southern Italy) example of late Gothic architecture from the 1450s; and two small churches that were once synagogues, **Santa Maria Scolanova** and **Sant'Anna**, converted after the Spaniards expelled Trani's long-established Jewish community in the 16th century.

From Trani, **Bisceglie** is the next town, with another good Romanesque cathedral. Then comes **Molfetta**, with a cathedral like Trani's on the harbour's edge, the **Duomo Vecchio**. This may be the most peculiar of them all: its plan, subtly asymmetrical like that of Troia, has a wide nave covered by three domes, the central one being elliptical. The west front is almost blank, while the back side has elaborate carved decoration, and a door that leads into the apse. Molfetta also has another cathedral, the Baroque **Duomo Nuovo**, from 1785.

Castel del Monte

Open Oct–Mar daily 9–1; April–Sept daily 9–7; adm; official guides offer very good tours in Italian and English (donations appreciated).

In Enna, the 'navel of Sicily', Emperor Frederick built a mysterious, octagonal tower at the highest point in town. In Puglia, this most esoteric Emperor erected one of the most puzzling palaces of all time. It, too, is a perfect octagon and, if you have been travelling through the

region with us, you will have noticed that nearly every town has at least one eight-sided tower, bastion or campanile, and that often enough Frederick was originally behind them. Castel di Santa Maria del Monte, to give it its original title, was begun by Frederick in the 1240s on a high hill overlooking the Pugliese *Tavoliere*, south of the town of Andria. At each of the eight corners of Castel del Monte is a slender tower, also octagonal.

The building, though 79ft tall, has only two storeys; each has eight rooms, almost all interconnected, and each facing the octagonal courtyard. The historians sometimes try to explain the castle as one of Frederick's hunting lodges. This won't do; the rooms each have only one relatively small window, and in spite of the wealth of sculpted stone the castle once had, it would have seemed more like a prison than a forest retreat—and in fact the Emperor's grandsons, the heirs of his son Manfred, were later imprisoned here for thirty years. Neither is it a fortification: there are no ramparts, no slits for archers, and not even a defensible gate. Some writers have suggested that Frederick had an artistic monument in mind. The entrance to the castle, the so-called 'triumphal arch', is a work unique for the 13th century, an elegant classical portal that prefigures the Renaissance. Inside, every room was decorated with columns, friezes and reliefs in Greek marble, porphyry and other precious stones. Almost all of these have disappeared, vandalized by the noblemen who owned the castle over the last five centuries. Only the delicately carved double windows survive, one to each room.

At Castel del Monte, however, it is the things you can't see that are the most interesting. This is nothing less than the Great Pyramid of Italy, and the secrets Frederick built into it have for centuries attracted the attention of cranks and serious scholars alike. Whole books have been written about the measurements and proportions of the castle, finding endless repetitions of the Golden Section, its square and cubic roots, relations to the movements of the planets and the stars, the angles and proportions of the five-pointed star, and so on. The relation of the castle to the ancient surveying of the Pugliese plain is a fascinating possibility. Frederick's tower in Enna has been found to be the centre of an enormous rectilinear network of alignments, uniting scores of ancient temples, towers and cities in straight lines that run the length and breadth of the island. The tower is believed to be built on the site of some forgotten holy place; the alignments and the vast 'geometrical temple' they form probably predate even the Greeks. No one has yet suggested that Castel del Monte replaced any ancient site, but the particular care of Puglia's ancient surveyors, and the arrangement of the region's holy places, sanctuaries and Frederick's castles, suggest that something strange may be hidden here.

Around the *Tavoliere*

The nearest town to Castel del Monte is **Andria**, a large and thriving centre. Another of the cities associated with Frederick, Andria has an inscription from the Emperor on its St Andrea's Gate, honouring it for its loyalty. Two of Frederick's wives, Yolande of Jerusalem and Isabella of England, daughter of King John, are buried in the crypt of Andria's cathedral.

Back towards the northwest, on the banks of the River Ofanto between Barletta and Canosa di Puglia (SS93), you can visit the site of the Battle of Cannae; here, in 216 BC, Hannibal trapped and annihilated four Roman legions in one of the most famous battles of history. Military strategists still study the Carthaginians' brilliant ambush. At the time, Hannibal and his elephants had already been in Italy for two years. Cannae was the opportunity they were waiting for, and historians are puzzled why he didn't immediately follow it up with a march on Rome. The chance was missed; Hannibal spent another eight years campaigning fruitlessly in Italy, while the Romans were out conquering Spain and North Africa. Cannae also taught the Romans to be careful, and it could be said that Hannibal's great victory meant the defeat not of Rome, but of Carthage.

In Roman times **Canosa di Puglia** was one of the most important towns in the region; the reminders of its former status include three large tombs, excavated in 1843, and a collection of archaeological relics in the **Museo Civico**, Via Varrone 57 (*open Tues–Sun 8–2*). The town isn't much today, but its otherwise undistinguished five-domed cathedral has in its courtyard the **tomb of Bohemund**, a striking marble chapel with a small cupola (octagonal, of course) that holds the remains of the doughty Crusader. Bohemund was the son of Robert Guiscard, renowned for valour and chivalry, who seized the main chance when the First Crusade was being preached, and ended up Prince of Antioch. The most remarkable feature of his tomb is the pair of bronze doors, signed by an artist named Roger of Melfi. The one on the left, inscribed with geometrical arabesques, is a single slab of bronze. Inside the cathedral, you may notice the early medieval bishop's chair, resting on two weary-looking stone elephants.

Four Towns, Four More Cathedrals

In this corner of Bari province, there are altogether eight noteworthy cathedrals on a narrow strip of land only some 64km long. They are the only real monuments—nothing has been built ambitiously and well around here since the 14th century—and they stand as the best evidence of Puglia's greatest period of culture and prosperity. One of the best cathedrals in Puglia is at **Ruvo di Puglia**, an ancient settlement that was famous in classical times for pottery—reproducing Greek urns at a lower price, above all between the 5th and the 3rd centuries BC, when the trade was at its most flourishing.

A large collection of locally made urns, and some Greek imports too, can be seen at the **Museo Jatta** in Piazza Bovio (*open Mon–Sat 8.30–1.30, Fri and Sat also 2.30–7.30; adm*). The **cathedral** is a tall, almost Gothic work, with a richly decorated façade and a fine rose window. The arches along the sides of the building are decorated with figures of pagan gods, copied from surviving pieces of ancient Ruvo's pottery.

Bitonto, the centre of olive oil production in Puglia, has a similar cathedral; here the best features of the exterior are the side galleries and the carvings of fantastical animals and scriptural scenes over the three front portals. Inside, there is a famous pulpit of 1226 displaying a fierce-looking eagle; on one side a curious, primitive relief shows Emperor Frederick, Isabella of England and their family.

Puglia's southern borders make up a distinct region, a slightly elevated jumble of plain and rolling hills called **Le Murge**. Here the most important town, nowadays thriving on its well-known bread, shipped all over Italy, is **Altamura**, founded by Frederick on the site of an abandoned ancient city. For centuries Altamura was a town of some distinction, even having its own university. Its rather advanced outlook led Altamura to support the French, and the short-lived Parthenopean Republic, during the Napoleonic Wars. As a result the Army of the Holy Faith, a mob led by a cardinal and egged on by monks, sacked and burned the city in 1799.

The university never recovered, but Altamura still has a beautiful **cathedral**, begun by Frederick in 1232; heavy damage from an earthquake in 1316 accounts for the departures from the Pugliese norm. The building retains its exceptional rose window and portal, but the twin towers above were added during the Renaissance. For some reason, in the course of doing so, they turned the cathedral backwards—the old portal and rose window were carefully taken apart, and placed where the apse used to be. The recently re-opened **Museo Archeologico**, Via Santeramo 88 (*open Mon–Sat 8.30–1.30 and 2.30–7.30, Sun also 8.30–1.30*) houses one of Italy's most interesting collections, with first-rate finds related to the people of the Murge from prehistoric times to the Middle Ages.

Gravina in Puglia, on the road towards Potenza, has the fourth cathedral, but it is only a dull 15th-century replacement for the Norman original. Gravina does have other charms. The town is set above a steep ravine, lined with caves where the inhabitants took refuge from pirates and barbarians during the Dark Ages.

One of the town's churches, **San Michele delle Grotte** (*contact the Cooperativa Benedetto XIII, inside the cathedral, for free tours in English of San Michele and other cave-churches*) is a cave too, with a heap of human bones believed to be those of victims of 8th-century Arab pirates. Other churches show somewhat eccentric versions of Renaissance styles, notably the **Madonna delle Grazie**, near the railway station. On Piazza Santomasi there is a **museum** (*open Mon–Sat 9–1 and 4–7, Sun 9–1*), with a full-size reconstruction of another cave church, and fragments of Byzantine frescoes.

Where to Stay and Eating Out

Hotels are surprisingly sparse in Bari province, but it does better for restaurants; every town has at least one place to eat worth staying for.

Barletta ✉ 70051

If you insist on staying in Barletta, ★★★★**Artù**, Piazza Castello 67, ✆ 0883 332 121 (*moderate*), between the castle and the cathedral, will do. The **Antica Cucina**, ✆ 0883 521 718 (*expensive*) has light, tasty fish dishes and good desserts. *Closed Sun evenings, Mon and July.*

Trani ✉ 70059

★★★★**Royal**, Via De Robertis 29, ✆ 0883 588 777 (*moderate*) has quiet rooms, all renovated in the original Liberty décor. The **Padri Bernabiti**, on Piazza Tiepolo, ✆ 0883 481 180, offer basic, clean rooms with great views (*doubles L40,000; reception closed 1–5; curfew 1am; book ahead*). The best-value place for fish and shellfish is **La Nicchia**, Corso Imbriani 22, ✆ 0883 482 020 (*cheap*). *Closed Thurs.* **Torrente Antico**, Via Fresco 3, ✆ 0883 487 911 (*expensive*) serves local produce, both fish and meat, in interesting ways, and the best local wines. *Closed Sun eve, Mon and July.* There are cute places in the harbour, but they tend to be touristy and overpriced.

Molfetta ✉ 70056

The ★★★**Molfetta Garden**, Via Provinciale per Terlizzi, ✆ 080 334 1722 (*moderate–cheap*) is a good-value, modern hotel with tennis courts. **Bufi**, Via Vittorio Emanuele 15, ✆ 080 397 1597 (*expensive*), with a spectacular wine-cellar, presents old and in many cases near-forgotten recipes in innovative ways. *Closed Mon and last two weeks in Jan.* Another adventurous but cheaper restaurant is the **Bistrot**, Via Dante 33, ✆ 080 397 5812 (*moderate*), where the specialities include the chef's *gamberi* and *spaghetti Forza 4*. *Closed Wed and two central weeks of Aug.*

Andria

The excellent, though overpriced, **La Fenice**, Via Firenze 35, ✆ 0883 550 260 (*expensive*) has a choice of three tempting *menu degustazione*: fish, meat and traditional dishes. *Closed Mon.*

Gravina in Puglia

At the panoramic restaurant, **Madonna della Stella**, Via Madonna della Stella, ✆ 080 325 6383 (*moderate*) everything is strictly local. *Closed Tues and Feb.* The more eclectic **Osteria**, Piazza Pellicciari 4, ✆ 080 326 1872 (*cheap*) has a Pugliese/Emilian mix of delicious specialities like *cavatelli ai legumi* and pumpkin or walnut ravioli. *Closed Sun evenings, Mon and last two weeks of Aug.*

Bari

Somehow Bari should be a more interesting place. The second city of the *Mezzogiorno* is a bustling town full of sailors and fishermen, and also boasts a university and a long heritage of cultural distinction. Bari nonetheless will be a disappointment if you come here expecting Mediterranean charm and medieval romance. If, on the other hand, you'd like to see a southern city that has come close to catching up with the rest of Italy economically, Bari will be just the place. Its newer districts, jammed with noisy traffic, exhibit a thoroughly northern glitter, and the good burghers who stroll down the Corso Cavour for their evening *passeggiata* are among the most overdressed in Italy. Be warned, though—and you probably will be, time and again—that the city has one of the highest street crime rates in the country.

Getting Around

by air

Bari's **airport**, about 9km west of the city at Palese, has connections to Rome, Milan, Turin, Pisa and some other destinations. There is a special airport bus from the central train station (L5000).

by sea

For anyone in Italy discovering a sudden desire to bolt, there are regular **ferries** from Bari to Corfu, mainland Greece (Igoumenitsa and Patras), Albania, Croatia and Turkey. All ferries leave from the Stazione Marittima on the Molo San Vito, which is connected with the main FS train station by bus no.20. **Car ferry** services to Greece are operated by the Ventouris line, Lo Russo, Via Piccinni 33, ✆ 080 521 2840 (*June–Sept daily; the rest of the year three times a week*); and Superfast, ✆ 080 528 2828, whose ferries are faster but slightly more expensive. **Adriatica**, Via Liside 4, ✆ 080 553 1555, or Stazione Marittima, ✆ 080 523 5825, runs ferries to Dubrovnik (Fri and Sun) and to Montenegro (Tues, Fri and Sat). CTS, Via Fornari 7, ✆ 080 521 3244, is a helpful travel agent.

by rail

Bari is an important junction on the main FS east coast line, and there is also a busy branch line from Bari to Tàranto. There are also three **private regional railways** that run from the city. The *Ferrovia Sud-Est* (FSE), ✆ 080 546 2111, runs from Bari's central FS station (on Piazza Aldo Moro) to Lecce, Tàranto (in competition with the FS) and towns in the *trulli* country. Nearby is the *Ferrovia Bari-Nord* station, ✆ 080 521 3577, with frequent trains to Andria and the towns *en route*; while *Ferrovie Calabro-Lucane* (FCL), ✆ 080 572 5111, on Corso Italia, goes to Altamura and to Matera in the Basilicata.

by bus

There are scheduled long-distance bus services from Bari to Rome, Naples and other major Italian cities, most of which also leave from Piazza Aldo Moro, although bus services to coastal towns north of Bari operate from Piazza Eroi del Mare (on the east side of the port). **SITA** buses (Largo Sorrentino behind the FS train station) connect Bari with inland and southern towns, while the **private rail lines' bus services** (FCL and FSE) leave respectively from stations on Corso Italia and Largo Ciaia.

Tourist Information

Piazza Aldo Moro 32/a, © 080 524 2244, to the right of the FS station (*open Mon–Sat 8.30–1*). **Stop Over**, Via Nicolei 47, © 080 523 2716 (*open Mon–Fri 9.30–1 and 4.30–8*) is perhaps more useful. There are also two branch offices: outside the FS train station, and at the Stazione Marittima (*open in summer daily 9.30–8*).

The Town That Stole Santa Claus

Bari can trace its history back to before the Romans, but it began to make a name for itself only in the 10th century. As an important trading city, and seat of a nominally independent Byzantine governor, Bari was sometimes a rival of Venice, though more often its ally. Robert Guiscard and his Normans, who took the city in 1071, favoured Bari and helped it become the leading town of Puglia. Sixteen years later, in 1087, a fleet of Barese merchants in Antioch got word that some of their Venetian counterparts were planning a little raid on Myra, on what is now the southern coast of Turkey. Their intention was to pinch the mortal remains of St Nicholas, Myra's 4th-century bishop, canonized for his generosity and good deeds. Relic-stealing was a cultural imperative for medieval Italians, and the Barese sneaked in by night and beat the Venetians to their prey, something that did not happen often in those days.

The Greek Christians of Myra were disgusted by the whole affair, but the Baresi had them outmatched, and so St Nicholas went west (his sarcophagus was too heavy to move, and so you can still see it today in the museum at Antalya, Turkey). On 7 May the Baresi celebrate their cleverness with a historical procession in traditional dress from the Castello Svevo to the Basilica di San Nicola across Corso Vittorio Emanuele and Molo Sant'Antonio. At the six o'clock mass the following day, the name of the *peschereccio* (fishing boat) that will have the honour of carrying the effigy of the saint to sea and leading the procession of boats in the harbour is drawn. Usually around 9pm an ancient icon of the saint is held up to receive the homage of the crowds on shore, recreating the scene of Nicholas' arrival 900 years ago. Other boats usually hire out space for those who'd like to go along and follow the procession.

To provide a fitting home for such an important saint, Bari began almost immediately to construct the **Basilica di San Nicola**, at the centre of the old town. Unfortunately, here the original ambition overreached the ability of succeeding generations to finish the job. The two big towers remain unfinished, and much of the decorative scheme was abandoned, giving the church a dowdy, barn-like appearance. Still, this is the first of the great Pugliese churches, the place where the style was first translated from Norman French to southern Italian. Inside, the only surprise is the tomb of Bona Sforza, Queen of Poland and Duchess of Bari. The daughter of a 16th-century Duke of Milan, she inherited Bari on her mother's side and as a teenager was packed off to marry Sigismund, one of Poland's greatest kings. She survived him and had a brief but memorable career as a dowager queen before retiring to sunny Puglia in her last years. Near the main altar, note the wonderful 11th-century bishop's throne, one of the greatest works of medieval sculpture in Puglia; its legs, carved into the figures of men groaning as if they were supporting some unbearable burden, must have been a good joke on any fat bishop of Bari over the centuries.

Down in the crypt you can pay your respects to St Nicholas. There will nearly always be somebody down there praying: Nicholas' tomb is one of the south's most popular places of pilgrimage. Most of the visitors today are local, but an Orthodox chapel has been added to accommodate pilgrims from Greece and Russia. The church is also home to a centre for ecumenical studies, as the Baresi try to make amends after nine centuries. One of Nicholas' tricks is to exude gallons of a brownish liquid the faithful call manna, to which all sorts of miracles are attributed; half the families in this part of Puglia have a phial of it for good luck.

Around Old Bari

The **cathedral** (*open daily 8.30–1 and 5–7*) is south of San Nicola, and difficult to distinguish although it was begun almost a century later. The plan is the same, as is the general feeling of austerity broken by small areas of richly detailed carving around some of the doors and windows. Unlike San Nicola, the cathedral still has its original beam ceiling, interrupted only by an octagonal cupola, and much more suited to its Romanesque plainness. Two unusual features are the stone *baldacchino* over the main altar, and the *trullo*, the large round building adjacent to the north wall that once served as the baptistry. Old Bari, as we have said, is a bit drab for a medieval historic centre. There is a reason for this, in that Bari has had more than its share of trouble. The Normans levelled it once after a revolt; more recently, a plague in the 1650s wiped out nearly the entire population, and the port area was heavily bombed in the Second World War. As a result, some parts of old Bari have the air of a new town. The labyrinthine old street plan survives—it's famous, in fact, for being one of the easiest places in all Italy to get lost. There will be no trouble, however, finding the **castle** (*open Tues–Sat 9–1 and 3.30–7, Sun 9–1; adm*), just across the Piazza Odegitria from the cathedral. The Normans began it, Frederick II completed it, and later centuries added the polygonal bastions to deflect cannonballs. Inside, some sculpted reliefs and windows survive from Frederick's time, along with bits of sculpture and architectural fragments from all over Puglia. Excavations on the castle grounds have revealed parts of the centre of Roman Bari, directly underneath.

Modern Bari

On your way up towards the railway station you will cross the Corso Vittorio Emanuele—site of both the city hall and Bari's famous fish market, and also the boundary between the old city and the new. When Bari's fortunes began to revive, at the beginning of the 19th century, Joachim Murat's Napoleonic government laid out this broad rectilinear extension to the city. It has the plan of an old Greek or Roman town, only with wider streets, and it fits Bari well; many of the streets have an open view to the sea.

Via Sparano di Bari and Corso Cavour are the choicest shopping streets. Bari's two museums are in the new town. The **Pinacoteca Provinciale** (*open Mon–Sat 9.30–1 and 4–7, Sun 9.30–1; adm*) is in the Palazzo della Provincia on Lungomare Nazario Sauro, and has a good selection of south Italian art—few Neapolitans are represented, though there is a genuine Neapolitan *presepio* (crib). Look out for the impressive works made by members of the Vivarini family. The **Museo Archeologico** (*closed for restoration*) occupies a corner of Bari University's sprawling, crowded palace on the Piazza Umberto I. As is usual in southern museums, the star exhibits are classical ceramics: painted vases from Attica, including one very beautiful figure of the Birth of Helen from Leda's egg, and also several Pugliese copies, some of which are as good as the best of the Greeks. Much of the rest of the collection is devoted to the pre-Greek Neolithic cultures of Puglia.

Bari ✉ *70100*   ***Where to Stay and Eating Out***

Bari makes the most convenient base for seeing the whole region, but it is a major business centre, and full of bad hotels at outrageous prices. It is also famous for fish and, like all the smaller towns around it, still sends its own fishing fleet out each morning.

★★★★**Villa Romanazzi Carducci**, Via Capruzzi 326, © 080 542 7400 (*expensive*) has comfortable rooms facing a rather spartan garden, and is not a total rip-off. ★★★**Grand Hotel Moderno**, Via Crisanzio 60, © 080 521 3313 (*moderate*), and ★★★**Costa**, Via Crisanzio 12, © 080 521 9015 (*moderate*) are unremarkable but pleasant hotels at half the price.★★**Giulia** (*cheap*), in the same building as the Costa, is one of the best budget options.

The more adventurous should try the highly rated **Murat de l'Hotel Palace**, Via Lombardi 13, © 080 521 6551 (*expensive*), a restaurant totally devoted to some of the most daring innovative Italian cuisine. *Closed Sun and Aug.* **Deco' del Kursaal Santa**

Lucia, Largo Adua 5, ✆ 080 524 6070 (*expensive–moderate*) is a more traditional, classier place near Molo San Nicola. *Closed Mon and Aug.* A few steps down the road, at no.19, **Taverna Verde**, ✆ 080 554 0870 (*cheap*) is a popular place for fish and beer. *Closed Sun, last two weeks of Aug, and 24 Dec–6 Jan.* Arguably the best trattoria in town, **Terranima**, Via Putignani 213, ✆ 080 521 9725 (*moderate*) has a daily menu featuring few but very solid dishes served in a pretty ambiance. *Closed Sun and Aug.* The informal **Al Pescatore**, Via Federico II di Svevia 8 (*moderate*) serves excellent grilled fish. *Closed Sun.* **Da Tommaso**, ✆ 080 530 0038 (*cheap*), out of town at Palese Marina, is also good for seafood. *Closed Mon.* **Enzo e Ciro**, Via Imbriani 79, ✆ 080 554 1535 (*cheap*) serve good pizzas. *Closed Sun in summer.*

The *Trulli* Country

Southwest of Bari is a small but especially attractive region of little towns set amid an extraordinary, unique man-made landscape, given its character by one of the oldest forms of building in Italy still in regular use—the strange, whitewashed dome-roofed houses known as *trulli.*

The Love of *Trulli*

 It takes you by surprise. Turning a corner of the road or passing the crest of one of the low hills of the Murge, all at once you meet a kind of landscape you have never seen before. Low stone walls neatly partition the countryside, around acres of vines propped up on arbours, covering the ground like low flat roofs. The houses are the strange part: smooth whitewashed structures in a bewildering variety of shapes and forms, each crowned with one or more tall conical stone roofs. These are the *trulli*, and when there are enough of them in one place, they make a picture that might be at home in Africa, or in a fairy tale, but certainly nowhere else in Italy.

The *trulli* are still built these days; the dome is easier to raise than it looks, and the form is adaptable to everything from tool sheds to petrol stations. It is anybody's guess as to their origins; some scholars have mentioned the Saracens, others (less probably) the Mycenaean Greeks. None of the *trulli* you see today are more than a century or two old. They are exotically beautiful, but if the form has any other advantage, it would be that the domes give warmer air a chance to rise, making the houses cooler in the broiling Pugliese summers. Beyond that one modest tangible contribution, there is no real reason for building *trulli*—only that they are an inseparable part of the lives of the people who live in this part of Puglia. There is no special name for the area around Alberobello where most of the *trulli* are concentrated; people simply call it the '*trulli* district'.

Trulli are built of limestone, with thick, whitewashed walls and only a few tiny windows. The domes are limestone too, a single row of narrow slates wound in a gradually decreasing spiral up to the top. Most have some sort of decoration at the point, and a few of the older ones are embellished with some traditional but obscure symbols. The precious rain waters that fall on the roof are collected through an ingenious system of slanted "waterways" in an underground cistern, usually located at the centre of the main room. *Trulli* seem only to come in one size; when a *trullo*-dweller needs more room, he simply has another unit added on. In this way, some of the fancier *trullo* palaces come to resemble small castles—Loire châteaux built for hobbits. Grandest of all is the one on Piazza Sacramento in Alberobello, the only specimen with a second floor; they call it the *Sovrano*, or Supreme *Trullo*.

Getting Around

One of the best ways to see the area is on the Ferrovia Sud-Est rail line between Bari and Tàranto or Lecce, which stops at most of the *trulli* country towns such as Alberobello, Locorotondo and Martina Franca. At Martina Franca the Lecce and Tàranto lines divide. The FSE also operates **bus** services to the area from Tàranto and Bari.

Tourist Information

Ostuni: on Corso Mazzini , ✆ 0831 301 268, in the old town in the summer; and at Via Dottor V. Continelli 47, ✆ 0831 303 775, in the new town the rest of the year.
Fasano: Piazza Ciaia 10, ✆ 080 441 3086.
Martina Franca: Piazza Roma 35, ✆ 080 480 5702.

Alberobello, Locorotondo and Ostuni

The **Valle d'Itria**, between the towns of Putignano and Martina Franca, is the best place for *trullo*-hunting. **Alberobello**, a delightful village that is the *trullo* capital, has over a thousand of them (and perhaps as many craft shops) in two neighbourhoods called the Rione Monti and the Ala Piccola. Even the church of **Sant'Antonio** is based on the *trullo* design. There are plenty more out in the countryside, especially around nearby **Locorotondo**, a town on a hill with views all around the Itria Valley. Locorotondo itself is a gleaming white town topped not with *trulli*, but tidy rows of distinctive gables. The street plan, from which the town takes its name, is neatly circular, built around an ancient well dedicated to St George.

The towns and villages in this district must be counted among the most beautiful in southern Italy. In each of them, white arches and steps climb the hillsides, sometimes punctuated by *trulli* and topped with surprisingly grand Baroque churches. You can spend as much time exploring these little towns as you care to. **Ostuni**, one of the best, has an ornate 16th-century cathedral and a handful of other Renaissance and Baroque confections standing out among its white streets—including even a Neapolitan-style *guglia* (spire). The **Chiesa delle Monacelle** (*open daily 9–1 and 4.30–7.30; longer hours in summer; adm*) is home to Delia, the archaeological highlight of Ostuni, a well-preserved skeleton of a pregnant young woman found in a crouched position, her skull decorated with coloured beads and stones before burial during what must have been a mystic, religious ceremony. The church also hosts a permanent display on prehistoric agriculture in southern Italy. The evening *passeggiata* in Ostuni goes on until well past midnight, and souvenir shops, restaurants and pizzerias stay open late. Ostuni also has the advantage of being near the sea, at the centre of the long strip of very modest but peaceful beach resorts that line the coast between Monópoli and Brindisi.

Martina Franca is the highest town in Puglia, with a garland of Baroque monuments, including the old ducal palace and a cathedral at the top, which towers over the city like a castle. It has a nobler but less cheerful air than Ostuni, and for 10 days between July and August it becomes an important point on the cultural map when it hosts the **Valle d'Itria Festival**, ✆ 0831 480 5100, an international music festival that attracts major opera, classical and jazz performers from around the world (*information on tickets from the tourist office*).

Caves, *Laure* and a Dolmen

Nor are the attractions of this area limited to *trulli* and white towns. The people around the **Grotte di Castellana** never tire of bragging that their famous grotto is the most beautiful in Italy. They may be right: the deepest section of the grotto tour, called the *Caverna Bianca*, is a glistening wonderland hung with thousands of bright glassy stalactites (*open April–Sept daily 8.30–12 and 2.30–6; Oct–Mar daily 9–12 and 2–5; in Aug also tours at 9pm; tours hourly (c. 1hr 45min); adm very exp*). Like much of Puglia, this region is what the geologists would call karst topography: built mostly of easily dissolving limestone, the territory is laced with every sort of cave, accompanied by such phenomena as streams and rivers that disappear into the ground, only to pop back up to the surface a few miles away.

In the Middle Ages the more inviting of the caves filled up with Greek Basilian monks. Here, following their burrowing instinct just as they did in Asia Minor and elsewhere, the Greek hermits turned literally dozens of caves into hidden sanctuaries and chapels. The best are around Tàranto, but there are a couple—**Grotta di San Biagio** and **Grotta di San Giovanni**—outside the town of **San Vito dei Normanni**, and some more along the ravines near the town of **Fasano**, where they are called *laure*.

Also near Fasano, just off the Ostuni road at the village of Montalbano, you can visit what may be the most impressive **dolmen** in the south. Puglia's earliest cultures were not often great builders, but they could be counted among the most sophisticated of all the Mediterranean Neolithic peoples. Much of their geometric pottery, which you can see scattered among Puglia's museums, is distinctively beautiful. This dolmen, a chamber formed by one huge slab of rock propped horizontally over two others, has acquired the odd local nickname of *Tavola di Re Artù*, or Table of the Knights—the Round Table of King Arthur. Along the coast north of Fasano are the scanty ruins of the Messapian-Roman town of **Egnazia**. The site is worth a brief visit, if only to admire the stupendous polychromatic mosaics with geometrical patterns and wild beasts, currently housed in the small museum, which also contains some Messapian artefacts, pottery and architectural fragments (*open July–Sept daily 8.30–1.30 and 2.30–dusk; Oct–June closed Sun afternoons; adm*).

All across this area there are dozens of privately owned *trulli* whose owners rent them out to visitors as part of the local Agriturismo programme. You can get more information from tourist offices.

Alberobello ✉ 70011

*******Hotel dei Trulli**, Via Cadore 32, ✆ 080 432 3555 (*expensive*) is a group of *trulli* cottages set in a garden and beautifully furnished, each with its own patio. There is also a pool, and a fair restaurant.

There is also another of Puglia's finest 'creative' restaurants, **Il Poeta Contadino** ('The Peasant Poet'), Via Indipendenza 21, ✆ 080 432 1917 (*very expensive*)—the food and wine are among the best you'll find; the atmosphere is soothing and sophisticated. *Closed Sun evenings, and Mon Sept–Jan.* The **Trullo d'Oro**, Via Cavallotti 27, ✆ 080 432 1820 (*expensive–moderate*) has fancier cuisine: try the *spiedini* Pugliese style. *Closed Mon, and 6 Jan–1st week of Feb.* **Cucina dei Trulli**, Via Ferdinando IV 31, ✆ 080 432 1511 (*cheap*) is a family-run restaurant which has been in business for over a century as part of the budget hotel Lanzillotta, and has excellent home cooking. *Closed Tues in winter.*

Locorotondo ✉ 70010

****Al Casale**, Via Gorizia 41, 080 431 1377 (*cheap*) is a good bargain choice not far from the centre. For dinner a bottle of Locorotondo wine is mandatory: a pale, dry white made by the local cooperative, much more delicate than most of the strong wines of Puglia. They'll be glad to slip you a bottle with the stuffed peppers or *coniglio al forno* at **Casa Mia**, a fine establishment on Via Cisternino, ✆ 080 431 1218 (*cheap*). *Closed Tues.* At the small, intimate **Centro Storico**, Via Eroi di Dogali 6, ✆ 080 431 5473 (*moderate*), the owner's love of food is obvious in the care taken with the cooking and presentation. *Closed Wed in winter.*

Castellana Grotte

Near Castellana Grotte, there's the friendly **Taverna degli Artisti**, Via Matarrese 23, ✆ 080 496 8234 (*cheap*), where you might try the *cannelloni* or the lamb *torcini*. *Closed Sun.* If you don't mind spending a bit more, **Fontanina**, on the Alberobello road outside town, ✆ 080 496 8010 (*moderate*) is another welcoming restaurant that serves generous portions of traditional food. *Closed Mon.*

Ostuni ✉ 72017

****Tre Torri**, Via Vittorio Emanuele 298, ✆ 0831 331 114 (*cheap*) is fine for a short stay. Along the shoreline at Rosa Marina (on the SS379 north of Ostuni), ******Rosa Marina**, ✆ 0831 350 411 (*expensive*), with its sharp modern design, is also a comfortable place, with a pool and a private beach.

Savelletri di Fasano ✉ 72010

The recently opened *******Masseria San Domenico**, on the *strada litoranea*, ✆ 080 482 7990 (*very expensive–expensive*), not far from Egnazia, is one of the most relaxing and luxurious hotels in Puglia. The renovated buildings of an old manor house set amid the olive groves look out on to a beautiful swimming pool (filled with filtered sea water) in the shape of a natural lake.

Martina Franca ✉ 74015

★★★**Dell'Erba**, Via dei Cedri 1, ✆ 080 430 1055 (*moderate*) has a garden, pool and child-minding facilities, as well as an excellent restaurant.

Tàranto

According to legend, Tàranto was founded by Taras, a son of Poseidon who came riding into the harbour on the back of a dolphin. According to the historians, however, it was only a band of Spartans, shipped here in 708 BC to found a colony. They chose a good spot: probably the best harbour in Italy, and the only good one at all on the Ionian Sea. Not surprisingly, their new town of Taras did well. Until the Romans cut it down to size, Taras was the metropolis of Magna Graecia, a town feared in war but more renowned in philosophy. Taras, now Tàranto, is still an interesting place, with an exotic old quarter, a good museum, and excellent seafood. Nevertheless, the best part of the story is all in the past.

History: Rotten Shellfish, Sheep With Overcoats

With its harbour, and with the help of a little Spartan know-how on the battlefield, Taras had hardly any trouble acquiring both wealth and political power. By the 4th century BC, the population had reached 300,000. In its palmiest days, Taras' prosperity depended on an unusual variety of luxury goods. Its oysters were a highly prized delicacy as far away as Rome. Another shellfish, the murex, provided the purple dye—really a deep scarlet—used for the robes of Roman emperors and every other style-conscious ruler across the Mediterranean. This imperial purple, the most expensive stuff of the ancient world, was obtained by allowing masses of the murex to rot in the sun; an enormous heap of the shells, with perhaps the mollusc who coloured Caesar's cloak somewhere near the bottom, was mentioned by travellers only a century ago. For a similarly high price, the Tarantines would have been happy to provide you with the cloth, too. Their sheep were known for the softest and best wool available, and the Tarantine shepherds actually put coats on their flocks to keep it nice.

If contemporary historians are to be believed, Taras managed to avoid most of the terrible inter-city conflicts of Magna Graecia simply by being much larger and more powerful than its neighbours. And it was spared civil troubles by a sound constitution, with a mix of aristocratic and democratic elements. Pythagoras spent part of his life in Taras, an exile from his native Croton, and he helped to set a philosophic tone for the city's affairs. The height of Taras' glory was perhaps the long period of rule under a Pythagorean mathematician and philosopher named Archytas (*c.* 400 BC), a paragon of wisdom and virtue in the ancient world. Plato himself came to visit Archytas, though he never mentions Taras in his writings.

When Taras and Rome went to war in 282 BC, they did so as equals. Taras called in Pyrrhus of Epirus as an ally, but after 10 years of inconclusive Pyrrhic victories, the Romans gained the upper hand and put an end to Taras' independence. Rome graciously refrained from razing the city to the ground after Taras helped Hannibal in the Second Punic War; just the same, the Tarantines felt the iron grip of the victors, and their city quickly dwindled both in wealth and importance. Of all the Greek cities of the south, Taras, along with Reggio, proved to be the best survivor. Throughout the Dark Ages the city never quite disappeared, and by the time of the Crusades it was an important port once more.

The modern city, italianized to Tàranto, substantially industrialized and a major base for the Italian navy, has known little of philosophers or well-dressed sheep, but still manages to send its fame around the world in other ways. The city gave its name to the *tarantula* but, before you change your travel plans, there really are no large hairy poisonous spiders in Puglia, just a few innocent little brown ones. Their bite isn't much, but some notoriety still clings to them, thanks to the religious pathology of the southern Italian. Throughout antiquity and the Middle Ages various cults of dancing were current around the Mediterranean. Everything from the worship of Dionysus to the medieval Dance of Death touched this region, and when the Catholic church began to frown on such carrying on, the urge took strange forms. People bitten by spiders became convinced they would die, and that their only salvation was to dance the venom out of their system—dance until they dropped, in fact. Sometimes they would dance for four days or more, while musicians played for them, and their friends sought to discover the magic colour—the 'colour' of that particular spider—that would calm the stricken dancer. *Tarantism*, as 19th-century psychologists came to call it, is rarely seen anywhere in the south these days, and for that matter neither is the *tarantella*, a popular style of music that took its name from this bit of folklore, and was in vogue a century ago.

Getting Around

There are two **railway** lines, but both use the central station at the far western end of town—between the old town and the steel mills—on Piazzale Duca d'Aosta. Regular FS trains leave for Lecce, Brindisi, Bari and further north, as well as for the horrible endless trip around the Ionian Sea to Reggio Calabria. On one or another of the FS lines you can get to Massafra, Castellaneta, Grottaglie or Manduria. FSE local trains, which operate from one side of the station, will take you to Locorotondo, Martina Franca and Alberobello (✆ 099 470 4463). The FSE also operates a large proportion of the province's **bus** services (✆ 099 477 4627): several a day for Alberobello, Bari or Lecce leave from Piazza Castello; their buses for Ostuni and Manduria leave from Via Di Palma. SITA buses to Matera also leave from Piazza Castello, and there are daily buses to Naples run by the Miccolis company from the train station. Buses to Metaponto leave from Piazza Castello.

Tourist Information

Tàranto: Corso Umberto I 113, ✆ 099 453 2392.
Massafra: Via Vittorio Veneto 15 (*open Mon–Fri 9–12 and 4–7*).

The Città Vecchia

Perhaps unique among cities, Tàranto has two 'seas' all to itself. Its harbour consists of two large lagoons, the **Mare Grande** and the **Mare Piccolo**. The city is on a narrow strip of land between them, broken into three pieces by a pair of narrow channels. Today, the westernmost section, around the railway station, is almost entirely filled up with Italy's biggest steel plant, begun as the showpiece project of the *Cassa per il Mezzogiorno* in the early fifties. This gargantuan complex provides an unexpected and memorable sight if you enter the city by night. Directly below the station along the Via Duca d'Aosta, a bridge takes you over to the old town, a nearly rectangular island that is only four blocks wide, but still does its best to make you lose your way. The ancient Tarantines, lacking any sort of hill, made the island their acropolis—though in those days it was still attached to the mainland. Most of the temples were here, along with a famous gold-plated bronze statue of Zeus that was the second largest piece of sculpture in the world, surpassed only by the Colossus of Rhodes. Today all that remains of ancient Taras are some columns from a **Temple of Poseidon** which have been re-erected in the main square next to Tàranto's **castello**—built in the 1480s by King Ferdinand of Spain and currently owned by the navy. From the square a swinging bridge connects the old town with the new. The Mare Piccolo, besides being an enormous oyster and mussel farm for the fishermen of Tàranto, is also the home of one of Italy's two main naval bases. If you come by very early in the morning when the bridge is open, you may see big warships waiting their turn with little fishing boats to squeeze their way through the narrow channel.

Follow the fishermen home, at the crack of dawn, and you'll end up in the **fish market** on Via Cariati, near the docks at the opposite end of the Città Vecchia. In sometimes slick and up-to-date Italy this is one of the places where you can most truly believe you are in the Mediterranean: a wet and mildly grubby quay awash with the sounds and smells of the sea, where tired fishermen appear before sunrise to have coffee, sort out the catch and bang the life out of octopuses on the stones. Of course there are plenty of cats around; true 'aristocats' they are, the descendants of the first cats of Europe. Ancient historians record how the ancient Tarantines imported them from Egypt.

From the fish market pick your way a short distance across the Città Vecchia to the **cathedral**, built and rebuilt in a hotchpotch of styles, beginning in the 11th century. Most of the last, florid Baroque remodelling has been cleared away, except a curious coffered ceiling, with two golden statues suspended from it. Roman columns and capitals support the arches, and there is a good medieval baptismal font under a *baldacchino*. Some bits of mosaic survive on the floor; mosaics in the Byzantine manner were important in all Puglia's medieval churches. Tàranto's cathedral is dedicated to St Cataldus, a Munster Irishman who did good works here on his way to the Crusades; you can see his tomb down in the crypt. The rest of the Città Vecchia's back streets hold few surprises. The area was down at heel and half forgotten for a long time but, with Tàranto's new-found prosperity, the city is putting a good deal of money into restoring old palaces and other monuments, and it is already beginning to make a difference.

The Museo Nazionale

> *Piazza Archita (entrance Corso Umberto I 41), just two streets west of the swinging bridge; open Tues–Sat 8.30–1.30 and 2.30–7.30, Sun and Mon 8.30–1.30; cheaper adm while under restoration.*

As in Bari, crossing over from the sleepy old town into the hyperactive new centre is a startling contrast. Tàranto has nothing to envy Bari these days; its new town is surprisingly bright, busy and sprawling, with as many grey-suited businessmen as blue-clad sailors. There aren't many modern sights here, but the best of Magna Graecia is on display at the Museo. With building activity going full-blast around Tàranto, new discoveries are being made all the time; already the collection rivals those of Reggio and Naples. There are some fine pieces of sculpture from temples and funeral sites, including the well-preserved 6th-century BC tomb of an athlete, a head of Aphrodite and several other works attributed to the school of Praxiteles, and also a wonderful bronze of the god Poseidon, in the angular, half-oriental Archaic style.

The museum also has what is believed to be the largest collection of Greek terracotta figures in the world. They are fascinating, in their thousands, the middle-class *objets d'art* of antiquity. The older ones are more consciously religious images of Dionysus, Demeter or Persephone, that served the same purpose as the crucifix on the wall of a modern Italian family. Later examples give every evidence of creeping secularism: ladies at their *toilette*, grotesque theatre masks, comic dancers and mythological figures. A few are copies of famous monuments: one figurine reproduces a statue of Nike, or Victory, erected in Taras after one of Pyrrhus' defeats of the Romans—and later moved to the Roman forum after the war went the other way.

Among the fragments from Taras' buildings there is an entire wall of leering Medusas, protection against the evil eye—as much a preoccupation among the ancient Greeks as it is with southern Italians today. Besides a large collection of delicate jewellery and coins, many minted with the city's own symbol of Taras riding his dolphin, there is also an important selection of Greek ceramics, including fine examples of the earlier, less-common black figure-work. In one room a rare evocation of Magna Graecia at play is provided on vases by scenes of Athene and contending athletes, near a case full of such odd finds as javelin points and a genuine ancient discus. The museum has been under restoration for several years, and about half of the rooms are closed indefinitely. However, the current display includes most of the highlights of the collection, with one big exception: the stunning floor mosaics dug out of Roman houses in the area, which have been transferred to the museum at Egnazia.

Towns Around Tàranto

Grottaglie, just 15 minutes by train to the east of the city, is the ceramics capital of southeast Italy. The town's potters continue to produce plates, vases and pots in enormous quantities, and attract throngs of visitors on summer weekends, eager to buy their traditional, and sometimes more modern, styles. Further along the road and rail line towards Brindisi is **Francavilla Fontana**, which takes its title of 'free town' from a favour granted by King Ferdinand IV. The town conserves several 14th–18th-century palaces, including a small one belonging to the 18th-century Bourbon kings, as a reminder of its days as a feudal stronghold. Nearby **Oria** has a history much the same. Frederick II built a strong castle here (1227–33; *open daily spring/summer 9–12 and 4–6; the rest of the year daily 4–6, weekends also 9–12; adm; free guided visits in English*), with three tall round towers, which now resembles a toy fortress; the city has assembled a collection of antiquities and bric-à-brac inside. In the Middle Ages Oria had an important Jewish community; the ghetto and its buildings are still intact, one of few in Italy which has survived.

Oria is believed to have been the capital of the ancient Messapians, a quietly civilized people who suffered many indignities at the hands of the Greek colonists, and finally succumbed to the allure of classical culture. **Céglie Messápico**, south of Ostuni, was another of their cities, and it is here you can see the Messapians' most noteworthy surviving monuments. The *specchie* are tall conical stepped towers; they get their name intriguingly from the Latin *speculum* (mirror), but no one has the faintest idea what they are or what purpose they served. One is in Ceglie itself, and the other two out in the country. The most impressive, the 36ft **Specchia Miano**, is 7km down the road from Ceglie to Francavilla—turn right up the road to *Masseria Bottari* farm and walk through the field on the right.

Manduria was another Messapian city, mentioned in the histories as fighting continuous wars with Taras. Ruins of its fortifications can still be seen—three concentric circuits, of which the outermost is three miles around—along with caves, necropoli and a famous well mentioned in Pliny's *Natural History*. To find the well, turn right in front of the church of the Cappuccini, on Via Sant'Antonio. The new city has an interesting cathedral, with a beautifully carved Renaissance rose window and portals.

Massafra

West of Tàranto, a very short distance back toward Le Murge and Matera, you can visit one of the most unusual cities in Puglia. Massafra, even more than Matera, was a city of troglodytes and monks. A steep ravine, the **Gravina di San Marco**, cuts the city in two. The ravine and surrounding valleys are lined with caves, and many of these were expanded into cave-chapels, or *laure*, by Greek monks in the early Middle Ages.

Between the caves and the old church crypts, it has been estimated that there are over a hundred medieval frescoes in, around and under Massafra—some of considerable artistic merit. One of the best is a beautiful Byzantine Virgin called *La Vergine della Scala*, in Santa Maria della Scala, reached from Via del Santuario in the old town of Massafra by a long naïf-Baroque set of stairs. The Madonna is shown receiving the homage of two kneeling deer. Adjacent to the sanctuary, some more—this time 13th-century—paintings can be seen in the **Cripta della Bona Nova**. At the bottom of the ravine is the **Farmacia del Mago Greguro**, a rather neglected complex of caves, believed to have once been used by the monks to store and prepare medicinal herbs.

The local tourist office provides a free guided tour (tips welcome) to both Santa Maria della Scala and the Farmacia, as well as other less famous cave-churches in town (such as the crypts of Sant'Antonio and San Leonardo), which you will need to join since the sites are not marked and custodians do not stick around to open the gate. (*Reserve a couple of days ahead by calling © 099 880 4695; in summer tours usually start at 10 and 5.*)

Other cave-churches and frescoes can be seen at **Mottola**, **Palagianello** and **Ginosa**, built like Massafra over a ravine full of caves. **Laterza**, perched on a 650ft-deep gorge near the border with the Basilicata, has about 180 caves and *laure*, of which some 30 can be visited (*contact the Pro Loco, Via Galilei 3, for information*). **Castellaneta** also has a ravine, the steepest and wildest of them all, and some cave-churches, but this town cares more to be known as the birthplace, in 1895, of Rudolph Valentino. There's a monument to him in the main square, with a life-size ceramic statue of the old matinée idol dressed as the Sheik of Arabia; local fans are about to turn the actor's house into a museum.

Tàranto ✉ 74100   ***Where to Stay and Eating Out***

Most of the better hotels are inconveniently located on the far eastern edge of town. One well-run spot in the centre is the ★★★**Plaza**, Via d'Aquino 46, facing Piazza Archita, © 099 459 0775 (*moderate*). Most of the rooms have a balcony over the square. The real bargains are in the old town, in the picturesque environs of the fish market. ★★**Sorrentino**, Piazza Fontana 7, © 099 470 7456 (*cheap*) is clean and shipshape. West of the city, at **Castellaneta Marina**, the ★★★★**Golf Hotel**, Località Riva dei Tessali, © 099 843 9251 (*expensive*) is a resort complex of cottages in a grove near the links—not much of a course, really, but a full 18 holes, and a genuine novelty in these parts.

The fish market in Tàranto is naturally the place to go for dinner; you can leave a place like **Posillipo a Mare**, Via Cariati 38, ✆ 099 411 519, with a bill of L25,000 or less. *Closed Fri.* For something a little more elegant, there's **Al Gambero**, just across the channel at Vico del Ponte 4, ✆ 099 471 1190 (*moderate*), which has earned a high reputation with its creative dishes involving nearly all the marine delicacies in the Ionian Sea. *Closed Mon and Nov.* At the sophisticated **Le Vecchie Cantine**, Via Girasoli 23, ✆ 099 777 2589 (*expensive–moderate*), the menu changes daily, but is always focused on fish. *Open eve only, closed Wed in winter, and Jan.*

All of these places feature the local speciality: mussels, or *cozze* (also called *mitili*). Another good seafood restaurant offering such things as roast squid and *tubettini alle cozze* is **Da Mimmo**, Via Giovinazzi 18, ✆ 099 459 3733 (*cheap*). *Closed Wed and two weeks in Aug.* There are many good cheap places in the new city: the **Ristorante-Pizzeria Mario**, Via Acclaio 68, ✆ 099 26008, besides good pizza, has seafood dinners for under L20,000; even better is the **Ristorante Basile**, Via Pitagora 76, ✆ 099 452 6240 (*cheap*), across from the main park. *Closed Sat.*

Outside Tàranto at Céglie Messápico, there's one of the finest restaurants in Puglia, **Al Fornello da Ricci**, Contrada Montevicoli, ✆ 0831 377 104 (*expensive*), an absolute must for foodies interested in Pugliese cuisine. *Closed Mon evenings, Tues, three weeks in Sept and 10 days in Feb.*

The Salentine Peninsula

It has lovely Lecce and dowdy Brindisi, some flat but unusual countryside, the sun-bleached and sea-washed old towns of Gallipoli and Otranto, lots of caves and Neolithic remains. Its coastline, while not as ruggedly beautiful as that of the Gargano, does have its charms, not least of which is that it is relatively uncrowded. Not many tourists, even Italians, make their way to this distant Land's End. If you are beachcombing or backpacking, and can resist the temptation of the ferries to Greece, this might be a good place to spend a lazy week or so.

Getting Around

by air

Brindisi's Casale **airport** is 4km north of the city and has regular flights to Rome, Milan and Verona. There is a frequent bus service between the airport and the main FS rail station in the city centre.

by sea

Brindisi is the most important Italian port for **ferries** to Greece, and has daily connections almost year round to Corfu, Patras and Igoumenitsa, with several a day in the busy summer season. All ferries leave from the Stazione Marittima, in the centre of the port. The EPT office has up-to-date information on schedules and prices. In summer that's not much help—book a passage before you get to Brindisi if you plan to travel in July and August. If you do need to buy a boat ticket here, avoid the ticket touts; even the enormous number of agencies in Brindisi offering ferry tickets are notoriously unreliable. Buy tickets from the boat companies themselves or an approved agent. The two most established **ferry companies** are Adriatica, Stazione Marittima, ✆ 0831

523 825, and Hellenic Mediterranean, Corso Garibaldi 8, ✆ 0831 528 531; while the most reliable **travel agents** are UTAC Viaggi, Via Santa Lucia 11, ✆ 0831 560 780, and Grecian Travel, Corso Garibaldi 65, near the harbour, ✆ 0831 597 884. Ferries also operate between the little port of Otranto and Corfu and Igoumenitsa (*June–Sept*). They are faster than many of the Brindisi boats, but more expensive.

by rail

Lecce is a terminus for long sleeper runs across Italy to Rome and Milan. All of these trains also pass through Brindisi, and both towns have very frequent trains heading for Bari or Tàranto. In addition, there is always the tired but game FSE, which has services from Lecce to Otranto, Gallipoli and Nardò, as well as some to Bari and Tàranto via Manduria (Lecce FSE information, ✆ 0832 668 233).

by bus

In **Brindisi**, buses to all provincial towns and nearby cities leave from the Viale Porta Pia; Marozzi, ✆ 0831 521 684, and Miccolis, ✆ 0831 560 678, operate bus services to Rome and Naples respectively, with several daily departures from Lungomare Regina Margherita, near the tourist office. In **Lecce**, most buses to towns in the Salentine, run by STP, ✆ 0832 302 873, leave from Via Adua near the old western walls; while FSE, Via Torre del Parco, near Porta Napoli, ✆ 0832 347 634, connects Lecce with Tàranto, from where you can reach other destinations in the region.

Tourist Information

Brindisi: Piazza Dionisio, off Lungomare Regina Margherita, ✆ 0831 523 072. **Lecce**: Via Vittorio Emanuele II 24, ✆ 0832 248 092. **Otranto**: Via Pantaleone 12, ✆ 0836 801 436, in the new town. **Santa Cesarea Terme**: Via Roma 209, ✆ 0836 944 043.

Brindisi

The word *brindisi* in Italian means a toast. It's just a coincidence; the name comes from the original Greek colony of *Brentesion*, and it isn't likely that anyone has ever proposed a toast to this grey and dusty port. Brindisi today is what it was in Roman times: the gangplank to the boat for Greece. On the Lungomare Regina Margherita, to the right of the port, a small piazza at the top of a formal stairway holds a magnificent **Roman column**, once topped by the statue of an emperor, that marked the end of the Appian Way.

For six centuries all of Rome's trade with the East, all its legions heading toward new conquests, and all its trains of triumphant or beaten emperors and generals passed through *Brundisium*. From the 11th century on, the city reassumed its old role when it became one of the most important Crusader ports. A memory of this survives too; if you enter the city from the north or west you will pass the **Tancredi Fountain**, an Arab-inspired work built by the Norman chief Tancred. Here the Christian knights watered their horses a last time before setting out for the Holy Land.

As a city where people have always been more concerned with coming and going than settling down, Brindisi has not saved up a great store of monuments and art. Travel agents and shipping offices are more in evidence than anything else. But, if you're staying, there are a few things to look at. Alongside the 12th-century **cathedral**, rebuilt in warmed-over Baroque, there is a small exotic-looking portico with striped pointed arches; this is all that remains of the **Temple**, headquarters church of the Knights Templar, and closely related to The Temple in London. Nearby, a small collection of ancient Pugliese relics has been assembled at the **Museo Archeologico** (*open daily 9–1; April–Sept Mon–Fri also 3–6.30; Oct–March Tues and Thurs 3–6.30*). Down Via San Giovanni, a few blocks south, another curious souvenir of the Templars has survived, the round church of **San Giovanni al Sepolcro**, built in the late 11th century, with fanciful carvings of dancers and lions on the portal. Back on the waterfront, on Viale Regina Margherita, there is a small local ferry that runs across the harbour to the 164ft-high **monument to Italian sailors**, erected by Mussolini in 1933. A lift goes up to the top, from where there are good views of the comings and goings of the port.

Santa Maria del Casale

The greatest of Brindisi's attractions, however, lies just north of the city, near the sports complex on the way to the airport (bus no.4 from the main train station will drop you not too far, by request). Santa Maria del Casale (*to visit ring the bell at the gate*) is a church unlike any other in Italy; built in the 1320s, in an austere, almost modern economy of vertical lines and arches, the façade is done in two shades of sandstone, not striped as in so many other Italian churches, but shaped into a variety of simple, exquisite patterns. The interior, a simple, barn-like space, is painted with equally noteworthy frescoes in the Byzantine manner. The wall over the entrance is covered with a remarkable visionary **Last Judgement** by an artist named Rinaldo of Tàranto, full of brightly coloured angels and apostles, saints and sinners; a river of fire washes the damned into the inferno, while above the fish of the sea disgorge their human prey to be judged. Many of the other frescoes, in the nave and transepts, have become badly faded, though they are still of interest.

Brindisi ✉ *72100*   ***Where to Stay and Eating Out***

Brindisi's hotel-keepers, accustomed to folks staying one night on their way to Greece, have not been inspired to exert themselves, and there are no outstanding places. ★★★★**Internazionale**, Lungomare Regina Margherita 26, ✆ 0831 523 473 (*moderate*) is the best, and very convenient for the ferry docks. This is a well-kept older hotel with grandmotherly furnishings, and maybe you'll get one of the rooms with a marble fireplace.

★★★**Barsotti**, Via Cavour 1, ✆ 0831 560 877 (*moderate*) is a plain but acceptable place, near the train station. The central ★★**Europa**, Piazza Cairoli 5, ✆ 0831 528 546 (*cheap*) is a reasonable quality hotel on one of the two main squares between the train station and the ferry terminal.

La Lanterna, Via G. Tarantina 14, ✆ 0831 564 026 (*expensive–moderate*), behind the Appian Way column, is the city's most elegant restaurant, which manages to mix traditional and newly invented ways of cooking and presenting meat, seafood and pasta. *Closed Sun and three weeks in Aug.*

For something simpler, but still good, try **Trattoria Pantagruele**, Via Salita di Ripalta 1–3, ✆ 0831 560 605 (*moderate*); save room for the delicious home-made desserts. *Closed weekends in July and Aug, Sun evenings and Mon the rest of the year, and two* *weeks in Aug.* Otherwise, there are any number of pizzerias and trattorias along the Corso Umberto and Corso Garibaldi where you can find something cheap, filling and quick. At Carovigno, about 18 miles north of Brindisi, there's an interesting, traditional restaurant called **Giàsotto l'Arco**, Corso Vittorio Emanuele 71, © 0831 996 286 (*moderate*). Reserve the table on the private balcony if you can. *Closed Mon and Jan.*

Lecce

Unfortunately for the traveller, you will have to come a long way, to the furthest corner of Puglia and the last city in this book, to find the most beautiful town in southern Italy. Lecce is worth the trip. Its history, and its tastes, have given it a fate and a look different from any other Italian town. First and foremost, Lecce is a Baroque city—not the chilly, pompous Baroque of Rome, but a sunny, almost frivolous style Lecce created on its own.

Lecce started as a Messapian town, and flourished as the Roman *Lupiae*, but really only came into its own during the Middle Ages, as the centre of a semi-independent county comprising most of the Salentine Peninsula. Lecce enjoyed royal favour under the Spaniards in the 16th century; with its location near the front lines of the continual wars between Habsburg and Turk, Lecce often found itself the centre of attention even though it was not a port. During the Spanish centuries, while every other southern city except the royal seat of Naples was in serious decline, the 'Athens of Puglia' was enjoying a golden age, attaining distinction in literature and the arts. Lecce also found the wealth virtually to rebuild itself, and took the form we see today with the construction of dozens of palaces, churches and public buildings in the city's own distinctive style.

Even though Lecce was doing well under the Spaniards and Bourbons, it was hardly enjoying the privilege of being ruled by them. On the contrary, Lecce's resistance to the new order manifested itself in four serious revolts. First, in 1648, came a popular revolution coinciding with Masaniello's revolt in Naples and, like it, bloodily repressed by Spanish troops. A second rebellion, in 1734, almost succeeded; the rebels were tricked into submitting by the Bourbons, who offered them reforms that were later withdrawn. In the wake of the French revolution, another revolt occurred, and the last came in 1848; the Leccesi worked hard for the unification of Italy, and contributed to the fight both men and ideas.

Piazza Sant'Oronzo

A Baroque city, of course, was conceived as a sort of theatre set, its squares as stages on which these decorous gentlemen could promenade. An odd chance has given Lecce's main piazza something even better—a genuine arena right in the middle. In 1901, much to the surprise of the Leccese, workmen digging the basement for a new bank building discovered a **Roman amphitheatre**, with seats for some 20,000, directly under the city centre. In the thirties the half that lay under the piazza was excavated; occasionally the city uses it for concerts and shows. Only the lower half of the grandstands has survived; the stones of the top levels were probably carted away for other buildings long ago, allowing the rest to become gradually buried and forgotten.

In Brindisi, by the column that marked the end of the Appian Way, you may have noticed the pedestal of a vanished second column. Lightning toppled it in 1528, and the Brindisians let it lie until 1661, when the city of Lecce bought it and moved it here, attaching a copper statue of

Lecce

SS. Nicolò
e Cataldo

VIA S. NICOLA
VIALE D. STUDENTI

Obelisk
Porta di Napoli
VIA PRINC. DI SAVOLA
University
VIA ADUA
VIA TARANTO
VIA G. PALMIERI
VIA L. PRATO
VIA UMBERTO I
Palazzo del Governo
Giardino
Pubblico
VIALE S. FRANCESCO
Santa
Croce
VIALE A. COSTA
Gesù
VIALE 25 LUGLIO
Town Hall
Piazza
S. Oronzo
Sedile
VIA SALV. TRINCHESE
Castle
Roman
amphitheatre
Santa
Irene
V. RUBICHI
VIA VITT. EMANUELE
V. AUGUSTO IMPER.
Post Office
VIALE CAVALLOTTI
Seminary
VIA G. LIBERTINI
Piazza del
Duomo
Cathedral
Santa
Chiara
Piazza
Vit. Eman.
Santa
Maria
della
Grazia
VIALE G. MARCONI
Piazzetta
S. Lucia
Porta
Rudiae
Archbishops'
Palace
V. D'ARAGONA
V. PALADINI
Roman
Theatre
San Matteo
Rosario
VIA A. DIAZ
VIA D. PERRONI
Porta
San Biagio
VIALE FRANC.
VIALE OTRANTO
Carmine
VIA B. CAIROLI
VIALE GALLIPOLI
VIA LOMBARDIA
VIA DON BOSCO
Accademia
Belle Arti
VIALE ORONZO QUARTA
Bus Station
VIALE DUCE D'ABRUZZI
Museo Sigismundo
Castromediano
Piazza
Argento
Train
Station

N

300 metres
300 yards

their patron, Sant'Oronzo (Orontius), the first bishop of Lecce, and supposedly a martyr during the persecutions of Nero. What appears to be a small pavilion in the middle of the square over-looking the amphitheatre is the **Sedile**, an elegant early masterpiece of the Leccese style (1596) that was once the town hall. The lovely portico, now glassed in, serves as the tourist office.

Santa Croce and San Matteo

North of Piazza Sant'Oronzo, the most outrageous Baroque of all awaits along Via Umberto I. **Santa Croce** was begun in 1549, but not completed until 1680, giving Lecce's Baroque berserkers a chance at the façade. The lower half of it is original, done mainly in a sober Renaissance style. The portal, however, and every thing above it, is a fond fancy of Giuseppe Zimbalo and his colleague Cesare Penna. Among the florid icing decoration the rose window stands out, made of concentric choirs of tiny angels. Look carefully at the figures on the corbels supporting the second level: among the various cartoon monsters can be made out Romulus' and Remus' she-wolf, a few dragons, a Turk, an African and a German. Always have a look inside Lecce's churches if they are open; Santa Croce's interior is one of the best, with striking altars in the transept chapels by Penna and Antonio Zimbalo, although the best piece is the high altar of coloured marble which belonged to the church of San Nicola e Cataldo. Giuseppe Zimbalo also designed the **Palazzo del Governo** next door, originally a monastery.

Behind Santa Croce, Lecce's **Giardini Pubblici,** sadly sporting more concrete walks than trees or flowerbeds, and the nearby **castle** built by Emperor Charles V, mark old Lecce's eastern edge. The castle (*currently under restoration*) will be used to host exhibitions, conferences and cultural events. For an interesting walk through the old town, start from Piazza Sant'Oronzo down Via Augusto Imperatore (Augustus was in Lecce when he got the news of Julius Caesar's assassination). This street passes another Baroque church, the recently restored **Santa Chiara**, and a Salesian convent with a skull and crossbones over the portal—the ultimate Spanish touch. Even better, in a small garden opposite the church there is the most preposterous statue of Vittorio Emanuele in all Italy, surpassing even the bronze colossus on the Altar of the Nation in Rome. This Vittorio is smaller, but the contrast between his ponderous moustaches and jaunty stance leaves him looking half-pirate, half-leader of the firemen's band.

The next Baroque church is **San Matteo** (1700), architecturally the most adventurous of the lot, with an elliptical nave and a complex façade that is convex on the lower level and concave above. Continue straight down Via Perroni, and you will come to one of Lecce's fine Baroque town gates, the **Porta San Biagio**. To prove that this city's curiosities are not all Baroque, there is the neoclassical **war memorial**, across Piazza Roma near the gate, and off to its right a block of mansions, built around the turn of the century, in a style that imitates the Alhambra in Spain, complete with pointed arches, minarets and Koranic inscriptions.

Piazza del Duomo

Leaving Piazza Sant'Oronzo by Via Vittorio Emanuele you pass the church of **Sant'Irene**, a relatively modest Baroque church of the 1720s, with a statue of the saint above the main portal. If you're not careful you may entirely miss the little alley off to the left that leads to the **Piazza del Duomo**, one of the finest Baroque architectural groups anywhere, all recently restored. It was the plan of the designers to keep this square cut off from the life of the city, making it a sort of tranquil stone park; the alley off Via Vittorio Emanuele is the only entrance.

The **cathedral** (1659–70) is one of the finest works of Giuseppe Zimbalo. To make the building stand out in the L-shaped medieval piazza, Zimbalo gave it two façades: one on the west front and a second, more gloriously ornate one, facing the open end of the piazza. The angular, unusually tall campanile (223ft), with its simple lines and baby obelisks, echoes the Herreran style of imperial Spain. Unfortunately, the bell tower has been declared unsafe, and the exceptional views over the city and most of the Salentine Peninsula may be a thing of the past. Adjoining the cathedral are the complementary façades of the **Palazzo Vescovile** and the **Seminario**, the latter the work of Giuseppe Cino, a pupil of Zimbalo.

Behind the cathedral, in the back streets off Via Paladini, there is a small but well-preserved **Teatro Romano** (*at the time of writing it is being put back into shape to open as a summer concert venue*). In the opposite direction Via Libertini passes several good churches, including the unique **Rosario** (1691–1728), also known as **San Giovanni Battista**, the last and most unusual work of Giuseppe Zimbalo. Just beyond it the street leaves the city through the **Porta**

Rudiae, the most elaborate of the city's gates, bearing yet another statue of Sant'Oronzo. Leading away to the right from here, Via Adua follows the northwestern face of this diamond-shaped city, passing the remains of the walls Charles V rebuilt to keep out Turkish corsairs; further up, you don't need to read Latin to recognize another relic of Charles' in the **triumphal arch**, erected in 1548. Most destructive and least modest of monarchs, Charles erected monuments like this around the Mediterranean, usually after unsuccessful revolts, to remind the people who was boss. This one, featuring crowned screaming eagles and a huge Spanish coat-of-arms, is a grim reminder of the militaristic, almost totalitarian government with which the Habsburgs tried to conquer Europe.

In a little park in front of the arch there is an attractive monument to the less grisly, though thoroughly useless King Ferdinand I, called the **Obelisk**. From here Via San Nicola leads off to the city cemetery, behind an elegant 19th-century neoclassical gate; go through the real entrance of the cemetery—a much plainer gate to the left—and at the end of the straight path, to the right, stands the church of **Santi Nicola e Cataldo** (*open daily 9–12; also June–Aug Mon–Sat 5–7; earlier afternoon hours the rest of the year; donations welcome*). The façade is typical Baroque, but if you look carefully you will notice that the portal and rose window are much older. Behind the 18th-century front hides one of the best Pugliese Romanesque churches, and one of the only medieval monuments to survive in Lecce. The nave and the dome are unusually lofty, and the carvings on the portal and elsewhere are especially good. A tiny door to the right of the apse leads to the two cloisters; on the way back, note the stations of the Via Crucis set in the open space before the church.

The Museo Sigismondo Castromediano

Viale Gallipoli, at the southern end of the old town, not far from the railway station; open Mon–Fri 9–1.30 and 2.30–7.30, Sun 9–1.30; closed Sat.

The founder of this collection, now Lecce's city museum, was a duke, and also a famous local patriot who fought against the Bourbons and earned long spells in the Neapolitan dungeons. His prison memoirs shocked Europe in the 1850s, and moved William Gladstone to a few rousing anti-Bourbon speeches. Duke Sigismondo would be happy if he could see his little collection, now housed in one of the most modern museums in Italy—a corkscrew-shaped ramp through its middle makes it accessible to wheelchair users. The most prized works are several Pugliese and Greek vases, found all over the Salentine Peninsula, though there is also a good collection of medieval art and architectural fragments, and a small picture gallery.

Leccese Baroque

One critic has called Baroque the 'most expensive style of architecture ever invented'. Considering all the hours of skilled labour it took to carve all those curlicues and rosettes, this may well be true. Lecce, like southern Sicily, some parts of Spain, and Malta—all places where southern Baroque styles were well developed—was fortunate to have an inexhaustible supply of a perfect stone. *Pietra di Lecce* is a kind of sandstone of a warm golden hue, possessing the additional virtues of being extremely easy to carve and becoming hard as granite after a few years. Almost all of Lecce is built of it, giving the city the appearance of one great, delicately crafted architectural ensemble.

The artists and architects who made Lecce's Baroque were almost all local talent, most notably Antonio and Giuseppe Zimbalo, who between them designed many of Lecce's finest buildings in the mid 16th century, and carried the style to its wildest extremes. Leccese Baroque does not involve any new forms or structural innovations. The difference is in the decoration, with an emphasis on vertical lines and planes of rusticated stonework, broken by patches of the most intricate and fanciful stone-carving Baroque ever knew. These churches and palaces, along with the hundreds of complementary little details that adorn almost every street—fountains, gates, balconies and monuments—combine to form an elegant and refined cityscape that paradoxically seems all gravity and restraint. Leccese Baroque owes more than a little to Spanish influences, and the city itself still has an air of Spanish reserve about it. As a king of Spain once described a similar Baroque city—Valetta, in Malta—Lecce is a 'town built for gentlemen'.

Lecce ✉ 73100   *Where to Stay and Eating Out*

Expensive, and tastefully renovated in 1997, ★★★★**Patria Palace**, in Piazzetta Riccardi, ✆ 0832 245 111 (*expensive*) has many rooms with a view of Santa Croce. ★★★**Risorgimento**, Via Augusto Imperatore 19, ✆ 0832 242 125 (*moderate*), in the centre, is an attractive, older hotel. The ★★★**Grand Hotel**, Viale Oronzo Quarta 28, ✆ 0832 309 405, near the station (*cheap*) offers faded elegance.

Although Lecce is an inland city, many of its restaurants have always specialized in fish. **Barbablu**, Via Umberto I 7, ✆ 0832 241 183 (*expensive*) is the trendiest place in Lecce, serving traditional dishes prepared with an innovative flair. *Closed Sun evenings, Mon, several weeks in June and Nov.* One popular place, a little way out of the centre, is **Gino e Gianni**, Via Adriatica, ✆ 0832 399 210 (*moderate*), with a long list of traditional local seafood dishes. *Closed Wed and two weeks in Aug.* For excellent home cooking, try the friendly and reliable **Trattoria Casareccia**, Via Colonnello Archimede Costadura 19, ✆ 0832 245 178 (*cheap*). *Closed Sun evenings and Mon.*

The Tip of the Salentine

Italy's furthest southeastern corner is one of the quieter parts of the country. It has a low, rocky coastline, rather like the Gargano but without the mountains, a number of towns in the Leccese Baroque style, and a lonely beach or two. One of its most noticeable features—and this is true for all of the Salentine Peninsula—is the eccentricity of the rural architecture. There are a few ancient *trulli*, low-domed houses of unknown age. Around them there are little houses with flat roofs curled up at the corners, some recent artistic do-it-yourself experiments in cinder-block and many tiny pink Baroque palaces, sitting like jewel-boxes in a prairie landscape of olive trees, tobacco and wildflowers, even in December.

Flying Saints and Land's End

The towns here show an almost African austerity, excepting perhaps **Nardò**, decorated with a lovely square, Piazza Salandra, in which there is a *guglia* (spire) as frilly as those in Naples. Nardò's much rebuilt 11th-century cathedral retains some medieval frescoes. Near the town walls, on Via Giuseppe Galliano, is a strange, unexplained circular temple called the *Osanna*, built in 1603. Among the other interesting towns and villages around Lecce are **Acaia**, with a romantically ruined Aragonese castle; **Galatina**, with a wonderful set of Renaissance frescoes in the 1392 church of **Santa Caterina**; and **Calimera**, one of the centres of Puglia's Greek community—oddly enough the town's name means 'good morning' in Greek. Very few people anywhere in Puglia actually still speak Greek, though their thick dialect has led many writers into thinking so; the Greeks left are more likely to be descendants of 16th-century refugees from Albania than of the ancient Greek colonists.

Nearby **Copertino** was the home of the original flying monk in the early 17th century. St Joseph of Copertino, a carpenter's son born in a stable, was a simple fellow, if his many biographers are to be believed, but he got himself canonized for his nearly effortless talent for levitating. Thousands saw him do it, including the pope's emissaries, a king of Poland and a Protestant German duke, who immediately converted. Joseph's heart is buried under the altar of the little church named after him. Copertino also has a large Angevin castle.

On the Ionian Coast, **Porto Césareo** is a peculiar little resort, facing two islets inhabited entirely by rabbits. The larger, **Gallipoli,** like its namesake on the Hellespont, was once thought of highly by somebody; the name comes from the Greek *kalli poli,* or 'beautiful city'. The old quarter still has a Greek air about it, with whitewashed houses scoured by the sea air and fishermen folding their nets in the little port. The oldest part, once an island, is now bound to the mainland and dominated by a huge castle with squat rounded bastions, parts of which date back to the Byzantines. There is a Baroque cathedral that would look right at home in Lecce, and a Baroque nymphaion, a trough-like fountain decorated with caryatids and badly faded mythological reliefs. Gallipoli has the best sort of museum, on Via De Pace © 0833 264 224 (*open April–Sept daily 9–1 and 5–7; Oct–Mar daily 9–1 and 4–6*)—nothing pretentious, nothing even labelled, but good fun, in a big atrium lined with dusty bookshelves and full of cutlasses, whalebones, cannonballs, coins, amphorae and even a crocodile skeleton.

The Salentine's southern tip, not surprisingly, is called Land's End—*Finibus Terrae*. The spot is marked by **Santa Maria di Leuca**, built over the ruins of a temple of Minerva that must have been a familiar landmark to all ancient mariners. The church's altar stone fulfilled the same purpose in the original temple. As in the Land's Ends of Celtic Europe, this corner of the Salentine has quite a few standing stones and dolmens, left from the days of the Messapians or perhaps even earlier. The most important Neolithic monument is called the *Centopietre*— 'hundred stones'—near the village of **Patù**, a small temple of two aisles divided by columns, with flat stone slabs for a roof. Coming back up the Adriatic side towards Otranto, the coast is lined with caves, many showing evidence of Stone-Age habitation or later religious uses. The **Grotta Zinzulusa**, hung with stalactites, may be the one worth visiting. Just to the north is a thermal spa, **Santa Cesarea Terme**, built around a charming neo-Moorish bath-house.

Otranto

Readers of Gothic novels might choose to leave Otranto out of their itineraries, but there's no reason to be afraid. Horace Walpole, when he was writing his *Castle of Otranto*, knew nothing about the place; he merely picked the name off a map. There really is a **castle**, built by the Aragonese in the 1490s, which in Walpole's times was probably already largely in ruins. The structure has recently been thoroughly restored and is now used as a meeting point for cultural events (*open daily 8–1; also mid-June–mid-Sept 5pm–midnight*). Otranto today (stress on the first syllable, as for most Pugliese towns), is probably most familiar as a better option than Brindisi for ferries to Greece. Although originally a Messapian settlement, the city first entered the Mediterranean consciousness as Greek *Hydruntion*, conquered and probably resettled by Taras, and its proud citizens still refer to themselves as *Idruntini*. It rivalled Brindisi as Rome's window on the east, and reappeared in the 11th century as one of the leading Crusader ports. Otranto's finest hour came in 1480, during Naples' wars with the Turks and their Venetian allies; according to a delicately embroidered legend, Turkish pirates sacked the city, killing some 12,000 or so, and massacred the 800 survivors when they refused, to a man, to forsake Christianity. The place hasn't been the same since; only recently, and thanks to the ferry business, is Otranto beginning to regain some of the importance it had in the Middle Ages.

If you're not bound for Greece, the best reason for visiting is the **cathedral**, begun in the 11th century by the Normans, and the only one in the south to have conserved an entire medieval **mosaic pavement**. The vigorous, primitive early medieval figures are the work of a priest named Pantaleone, from about 1165. Three great trees stand at the centre of his composition, supporting small encircled images that encompass all creation: scriptural scenes, animals, heroes, symbols of the months and seasons, Alexander the Great, and even King Arthur.

Where to Stay and Eating Out

Gallipoli ✉ 73014

Most of the available accommodation is along the outlying beaches. There are some fine modern resort hotels at Baia Verde, on the Via Litoranea to S. Maria di Leuca: ★★★★**Costa Brada**, ✆ 0833 202 551 (*expensive*), and ★★★**Le Sirenuse**, ✆ 0833 202 536 (*moderate*) are both typical white Mediterranean palaces, and both have good restaurants. The coastal areas are well supplied with places to eat: at **Il Capriccio**, Viale Bovio 14, ✆ 0833 261 545 (*expensive*) you can choose from a great variety of seafood dishes, as well as trying the local speciality, *orecchiette alla gallipolina*. *Closed Mon and Nov.*

Otranto ✉ 73028

Try the 10-room ★★★**Albania**, Via S. Francesco di Paola 10, ✆ 0836 801 183 (*cheap*); or, nearer the beaches, ★★★**Miramare**, Viale Lungomare 55, ✆ 0836 801 024 (*cheap*). The inland towns all have only basic accommodation.

Otranto's best restaurant is **Da Sergio**, Corso Garibaldi 9, ✆ 0836 801408 (*moderate*), even though the Sergio of the title prides himself on having a local clientele and is inclined to be patronizing to foreigners. His father is a fisherman, and the restaurant has particularly good fish. *Closed Wed, Jan and Feb.*

Acroterion: decorative protrusion on the rooftop of an Etruscan, Greek or Roman temple. At the corners of the roof they are called *antefixes*.

Ambones: twin pulpits in some southern churches (singular: *ambo*), often elaborately decorated.

Atrium: entrance court of a Roman house or early church.

Badia: *abbazia*, an abbey or abbey church.

Baldacchino: baldachin, a columned stone canopy above the altar of a church.

Basilica: a rectangular building usually divided into three aisles by rows of columns. In Rome this was the common form for law courts and other public buildings, and Roman Christians adapted it for their early churches.

Borgo: from the Saxon *burh* of San Spirito in Rome: a suburb.

Bucchero ware: black, delicately thin Etruscan ceramics, usually incised or painted.

Calvary chapels: a series of outdoor chapels, usually on a hillside, that commemorate the stages of the Passion of Christ.

Campanile: a bell-tower.

Campanilismo: local patriotism; the Italians' own word for their historic tendency to be more faithful to their home towns than to the abstract idea of 'Italy'.

Camposanto: a cemetery.

Cardo: transverse street of a Roman *castrum*-shaped city.

Carroccio: a wagon carrying the banners of a medieval city and an altar; it served as the rallying point in battles.

Cartoon: the preliminary sketch for a fresco or tapestry.

Caryatid: supporting pillar or column carved into a standing female form; male versions are called *telamones*.

Castrum: a Roman military camp, always neatly rectangular, with straight streets and gates at the cardinal points. Later the Romans founded or refounded cities in this form, hundreds of which survive today (Lucca, Aosta, Florence, Pavia, Como, Brescia, Ascoli Piceno, Ancona are clear examples).

Cavea: the semicircle of seats in a classical theatre.

Cenacolo: fresco of the Last Supper, often on the wall of a monastery refectory.

Ciborium: a tabernacle; the word is often used for large freestanding tabernacles, or in the sense of a *baldacchino* (q.v.).

Comune: commune, or commonwealth, referring to the governments of the free cities of the Middle Ages. Today it denotes any local government, from the Comune di Roma down to the smallest village.

Condottiere: the leader of a band of mercenaries in late medieval and Renaissance times.

Confraternity: a religious lay brotherhood, often serving as a neighbourhood mutual-aid and burial society, or following some specific charitable work (Michelangelo, for example, belonged to one that cared for condemned prisoners in Rome).

Cosmati work: (or *Cosmatesque*): referring to a distinctive style of inlaid marble or enamel chips used in architectural decoration (pavements, pulpits, paschal candlesticks, etc.) in medieval southern Italy. The Cosmati family of Rome were its greatest practitioners.

Cupola: a dome.

Cyclopean walls: fortifications built of enormous, irregularly polygonal blocks, as in the pre-Roman cities of Latium.

Decumanus: street of a Roman *castrum*-shaped city parallel to the longer axis, the central, main avenue called the Decumanus Major.

Duomo: cathedral.

Architectural, Artistic & Historical Terms

Forum: the central square of a Roman town, with its most important temples and public buildings. The word means 'outside', as the original Roman Forum was outside the first city walls.

Fresco: wall painting, the most important Italian medium of art since Etruscan times. It isn't easy; first the artist draws the *sinopia* (q.v.) on the wall. This is covered with plaster, but only a little at a time, as the paint must be on the plaster before it dries. Leonardo da Vinci's endless attempts to find clever short-cuts ensured that little of his work would survive.

Ghibellines: (see *Guelphs*). One of the two great medieval parties, supporters of the Holy Roman Emperors.

Gonfalon: the banner of a medieval free city; the *gonfaloniere*, or flag bearer, was often the most important public official.

Grotesques: carved or painted faces used in Etruscan and later Roman decoration; Raphael and other artists rediscovered them in the 'grotto' of Nero's Golden House in Rome.

Guelphs: (see *Ghibellines*). The other great political faction of medieval Italy, supporters of the Pope.

Hypogeum: underground burial cavern, usually of pre-Christian religions.

Intarsia: work in inlaid wood or marble.

Laura: a Greek cave-chapel or monastic cell of southern Puglia, often with frescoes.

Lozenge: the diamond shape—like stripes, one of the trademarks of Pisan architecture.

Narthex: the enclosed porch of a church.

Naumachia: mock naval battles, like those staged in the Colosseum.

Opus reticulatum: Roman masonry consisting of diamond-shaped blocks.

Palazzo: not just a palace, but any large, important building (though the word comes from the Imperial *palatium* on Rome's Palatine Hill).

Palio: a banner, and the horse race in which city neighbourhoods contend for it in their annual festivals. The most famous is at Siena.

Pantocrator: Christ 'ruler of all', a common subject for apse paintings and mosaics in areas influenced by Byzantine art.

Pietra dura: rich inlay work using semi-precious stones, perfected in post-Renaissance Florence.

Pieve: a parish church, especially in the north.

Predella: smaller paintings on panels below the main subject of a painted altarpiece.

Presepio: a Christmas crib.

Pulvin: stone, often trapezoidal, that supports or replaces the capital of a column; decoratively carved examples can be seen in many medieval southern cloisters.

Putti: flocks of plaster cherubs with rosy cheeks and bums that infested much of Italy in the Baroque era.

Quadriga: chariot pulled by four horses.

Quattrocento: the 1400s—the Italian way of referring to centuries (*quattrocento, cinquecento*, etc.).

Sinopia: the layout of a *fresco* (q.v.) etched by the artist on the wall before the plaster is applied. Often these are works of art in their own right.

Stigmata: a miraculous simulation of the bleeding wounds of Christ, appearing in holy men like St Francis in the 12th century, and Padre Pio of Puglia in our own time.

Telamon: see *Caryatid.*

Thermae: Roman baths.

Tondo: round relief, painting or terracotta.

Transenna: marble screen separating the altar area from the rest of an early Christian church.

Travertine: hard, light-coloured stone, sometimes flecked or pitted with black, sometimes perfect. The most widely used material in ancient and modern Rome.

Triclinium: the main hall of a Roman house, used for dining and entertaining.

Triptych: a painting, especially an altarpiece, in three sections.

Trompe l'œil: art that uses perspective effects to deceive the eye—for example, to create the illusion of depth on a flat surface, or to make columns and arches painted on a wall seem real.

Tympanum: the semicircular space, often bearing a painting or relief, above the portal of a church.

General and Travel

Barzini, Luigi, *The Italians* (Hamish Hamilton, 1964). A perhaps too clever account of the Italians by an Italian journalist living in London, but one of the classics.

Douglas, Norman, *Old Calabria* (Century, 1983). Reprint of a rascally travel classic.

Goethe, J. W., *Italian Journey* (Penguin Classics, 1982). An excellent example of a genius turned to mush by Italy; brilliant insights and big, big mistakes.

Haycraft, John, *Italian Labyrinth* (Penguin, 1987). One of the latest attempts to unravel the Italian mess.

Hutton, Edward, *Florence, Assisi, and Umbria Revisited*; *Venice and Venetia*; *Siena and Southern Tuscany*; *Naples and Campania Revisited* and *Rome* (Hollis & Carter).

Keates, Jonathan, *Italian Journeys* (Picador, 1991). An argument for re-examining the neglected charms of northern Italy.

McCarthy, Mary, *The Stones of Florence* and *Venice Observed* (Penguin, 1986). Brilliant evocations of Italy's two great art cities, with an understanding that makes many other works on the subject seem sluggish and pedantic; don't visit them without it.

Morris, James, *Venice* (Faber & Faber, 1960). Another classic account of 'the world's most beautiful city'.

Morton, H. V., *A Traveller in Rome* and *A Traveller in Southern Italy* (Methuen, 1957, 1969). Among the most readable and delightful accounts of the region in print. Morton is a sincere scholar, and a true gentleman. Also a good friend to cats.

Newby, Eric, *Love and War in the Apennines* (Picador, 1983). Newby's account of his war days, when Italian villagers hid him from the Nazis.

Nichols, Peter, *Italia, Italia* (Macmillan, 1973). An account of modern Italy by an old Italy hand.

History

Acton, Harold, *The Bourbons of Naples* (Methuen, 1956).

Burckhardt, Jacob, *The Civilization of the Renaissance in Italy* (Harper & Row, 1975). The classic on the subject (first published 1860), the mark agaist which scholars still level their poison arrows of revisionism.

Carcopino, Jérome, *Daily Life in Ancient Rome* (Penguin, 1981). A thorough and lively account of Rome at the height of Empire—guaranteed to evoke empathy from modern city dwellers.

Ginsborg, Paul, A *History of Contemporary Italy: Society and Politics 1943–1988* (Penguin, 1990). A good modern account of events up to the fall of Rome.

Hale, J. R. (ed.), *A Concise Encyclopaedia of the Italian Renaissance* (Thames and Hudson, 1981). An excellent reference guide, with many concise, well-written essays.

Hibbert, Christopher, *Benito Mussolini*; *Rise and Fall of the House of Medici* and *Rome* (Penguin, 1965, 1979, 1985).

Joll, James, *Gramsci* (Fontana, 1977). A look at the father of modern Italian communism, someone we all should get to know better.

Masson, Georgina, *Frederick II of Hohenstaufen* (London, 1957).

Morris, Jan, *The Venetian Empire* (Faber & Faber, 1980). A fascinating account of the Serenissima's glory days.

Further Reading

Norwich, John Julius, *The Normans in the South* (Thames and Hudson, 1967).

Origo, Iris, *The Merchant of Prato* (Penguin, 1963). Everyday life in medieval Tuscany with the father of modern accounting, Francesco di Marco Datini.

Procacci, Giuliano, *History of the Italian People* (Penguin, 1973). An in-depth view from the year 1000 to the present—also an introduction to the wit and subtlety of the best Italian scholarship.

Rand, Edward Kennard, *Founders of the Middle Ages* (Dover reprint, New York), a little-known but incandescently brilliant work that can explain Jerome, Augustine, Boethius and other intellectual currents of the decaying classical world.

Art and Literature

Boccaccio, Giovanni, *The Decameron* (Penguin, 1972). The ever-young classic by one of the fathers of Italian literature. Its irreverent worldliness still provides a salutary antidote to whatever dubious ideas persist in your mental baggage.

Calvino, Italo, *Invisible Cities* and *If Upon a Winter's Night a Traveller* (Picador). Provocative fantasies that could only have been written by an Italian. Something even better is his recent compilation of Italian folktales, a little bit Brothers Grimm and a little bit Fellini.

Cellini, *Autobiography of Benvenuto Cellini* (Penguin, trans. by George Bull). Fun reading by a swashbuckling braggart and world-class liar.

Clark, Kenneth, *Leonardo da Vinci* (Penguin).

Dante Alighieri, *The Divine Comedy* (plenty of equally good translations). Few poems have ever had such a mythical significance for a nation. Anyone serious about understanding Italy and the Italian world view will need more than a passing acquaintance with Dante.

Gadda, Carlo Emilio, *That Awful Mess on Via Merulana* (Quartet Books, 1980). Italy during the Fascist era.

Gilbert and Linscott, *Complete Poems and Selected Letters of Michelangelo* (Princeton Press, 1984).

Henig, Martin (ed.), *A Handbook of Roman Art* (Phaidon, 1983). Essays on all aspects of ancient Roman art.

Lawrence, D. H., *Etruscan Places* (Olive Press).

Levi, Carlo, *Christ Stopped at Eboli* (Penguin, 1982). Disturbing post-war realism.

Levy, Michael, *Early Renaissance* (Penguin, 1967) and *High Renaissance* (Penguin, 1975). Old-fashioned accounts of the period, with a breathless reverence for the 1500s—but still full of intriguing interpretations.

Murray, Linda, *The High Renaissance* and *The Late Renaissance and Mannerism* (Thames and Hudson, 1977). Excellent introduction to the period; also Peter and Linda Murray, *The Art of the Renaissance* (Thames and Hudson, 1963).

Pavese, Cesare, *The Moon and the Bonfire* (Quartet, 1979). Post-war classic.

Petrarch, Francesco, *Canzoniere and Other Works* (Oxford, 1985). The most famous poems by the 'First Modern Man'.

Vasari, Giorgio, *Lives of the Artists* (Penguin, 1985). Readable, anecdotal accounts of the Renaissance greats by the father of art history, also the first professional Philistine.

Wittkower, Rudolf, *Art and Architecture in Italy 1600–1750* (Pelican, 1986). The Bible on Baroque, erudite and full of wit.

The fathers of modern Italian were Dante, Manzoni, and television. Each did their part in creating a national language from an infinity of regional and local dialects; the Florentine Dante, the first 'immortal' to write in the vernacular, did much to put the Tuscan dialect in the foreground of Italian literature. Manzoni's revolutionary novel, *I Promessi Sposi* (*The Betrothed*), heightened national consciousness by using an everyday language all could understand in the 19th century. Television in the last few decades is performing an even more spectacular linguistic unification; although the majority of Italians still speak a dialect at home, school, and work, their TV idols insist on proper Italian.

Perhaps because they are so busy learning their own beautiful but grammatically complex language, Italians are not especially apt at learning others. English lessons, however, have been the rage for years, and at most hotels and restaurants there will be someone who speaks some English. In small towns and out of the way places, finding an Anglophone may prove more difficult. The words and phrases below should help you out in most situations, but the ideal way to come to Italy is with some Italian under your belt.

Pronunciation

Italian words are pronounced phonetically. Every vowel and consonant (except 'h') is sounded. Consonants are the same as in English, except the 'c' which, when followed by an 'e' or 'i', is pronounced like the English 'ch' (*cinque* thus becomes 'cheenquay'). Italian 'g' is also soft before 'i' or 'e' as in *gira*, pronounced 'jee-ra'. 'H' is never sounded; 'z' is pronounced like 'ts'. The consonants 'sc' before the vowels 'i' or 'e' become like the English 'sh' as in 'sci', pronounced 'shee'; 'ch' is pronouced like a 'k' as in Chianti, kee-an-tee; 'gn' as 'ny' in English (*bagno*, pronounced 'ban-yo'; while 'gli' is pronounced like the middle of the word 'million' (Castiglione, pronounced 'Ca-steely-oh-nay'). Vowel pronunciation is: 'a' as in English father; 'e' when unstressed is pronounced like 'a' in 'fate' as in *mele*, when stressed can be the same or like the 'e' in 'pet' (*bello*); 'i' is like the 'i' in 'machine'; 'o' like 'e', has two sounds, 'o' as in 'hope' when unstressed (*tacchino*), and usually 'o' as in 'rock' when stressed (*morte*); 'u' is pronounced like the 'u' in 'June'. The accent usually (but not always!) falls on the penultimate syllable. Also note that, in the big northern cities, the informal way of addressing someone as you, *tu*, is widely used; the more formal *lei* or *voi* is commonly used in provincial districts.

Time

What time is it?	*Che ore sono?*	today	*oggi*
day/week	*giorno/settimana*	tomorrow	*domani*
month	*mese*	soon	*fra poco*
morning/afternoon	*mattina/pomeriggio*	later	*dopo/più tardi*
evening	*sera*	It is too early	*È troppo presto*
yesterday	*ieri*	It is too late	*È troppo tardi*

Days

Monday	*lunedì*	Friday	*venerdì*
Tuesday	*martedì*	Saturday	*sabato*
Wednesday	*mercoledì*	Sunday	*domenica*
Thursday	*giovedì*		

Language

Numbers

one	*uno/una*	forty	*quaranta*
two/three/four	*due/tre/quattro*	fifty	*cinquanta*
five/six/seven	*cinque/sei/sette*	sixty	*sessanta*
eight/nine/ten	*otto/nove/dieci*	seventy	*settanta*
eleven/twelve	*undici/dodici*	eighty	*ottanta*
thirteen/fourteen	*tredici/quattordici*	ninety	*novanta*
fifteen/sixteen	*quindici/sedici*	hundred	*cento*
seventeen/eighteen	*diciassette/diciotto*	one hundred & one	*centouno*
nineteen	*diciannove*	two hundred	*duecento*
twenty	*venti*	one thousand	*mille*
twenty-one	*ventuno*	two thousand	*duemila*
thirty	*trenta*	million	*milione*

Useful Words and Phrases

yes/no/maybe	*si/no/forse*	Good night	*Buonanotte*
I don't know	*Non lo so*	Goodbye	*Arrivederla* (formal),
I don't understand	*Non capisco*		*arrivederci/ciao*
…(Italian)	*…(italiano)*		(informal)
Does someone here	*C'è qualcuno qui*	What do you call this	*Come si chiama questo*
…speak English?	*…che parla inglese?*	…in Italian?	*…in italiano?*
Speak slowly	*Parla lentamente*	What?/Who?/Where?	*Che?/Chi?/Dove?*
Could you assist me?	*Potrebbe aiutarmi?*	When?/Why?	*Quando?/Perché?*
Help!	*Aiuto!*	How?	*Come?*
Please	*Per favore*	How much?	*Quanto?*
Thank you (v. much)	*(Molte) grazie*	I am lost	*Mi sono smarrito*
You're welcome	*Prego*	I am hungry/thirsty	*Ho fame/sete*
It doesn't matter	*Non importa*	sleepy	*Ho sonno*
All right	*Va bene*	I am sorry	*Mi dispiace*
Excuse me	*Mi scusi*	I am tired	*Sono stanco*
Be careful!	*Attenzione!*	I am ill	*Mi sento male*
Nothing	*Niente*	Leave me alone	*Lasciami in pace*
It is urgent!	*È urgente!*	good	*buono;bravo*
How are you?	*Come sta?*	bad	*male;cattivo*
Well, and you?	*Bene, e lei?*	hot/cold	*caldo/freddo*
What is your name?	*Come si chiama?*	slow/fast	*lento/rapido*
Hello	*Salve/ciao* (both informal)	up/down	*su/giù*
Good morning	*Buongiorno* (formal hello)	big/small	*grande/piccolo*
Good afternoon/	*Buonasera*	here/there	*qui/lì*
evening (also formal hello)			

Transport

airport	*aeroporto*	platform	*binario*
bus stop	*fermata*	taxi	*tassì*
bus/coach	*autobus/pullman*	ticket	*biglietto*
railway station	*stazione ferroviaria*	customs	*dogana*
train	*treno*	seat (reserved)	*posto (prenotato)*

Shopping, Service, Sightseeing

I would like...	*Vorrei...*	money	*soldi*
Where is/are...	*Dov'è/ Dove sono...*	newspaper (foreign)	*giornale (straniero)*
How much is it?	*Quanto costa questo?*	pharmacy	*farmacia*
open	*aperto*	police station	*commissariato*
closed	*chiuso*	policeman	*poliziotto*
cheap	*a buon prezzo*	post office	*ufficio postale*
expensive	*caro*	sea	*mare*
bank	*banca*	shop	*negozio*
beach	*spiaggia*	room	*camera*
bed	*letto*	tobacco shop	*tabaccaio*
church	*chiesa*	WC	*toilette/ bagno*
entrance/exit	*entrata/uscita*	men	*Signori/ Uomini*
hospital	*ospedale*	women	*Signore/ Donne*

Useful Hotel Vocabulary

I'd like a double room please	*Vorrei una camera doppia, per favore*
I'd like a single room please	*Vorrei una camera singola, per favore*
with bath, without bath	*con bagno, senza bagno*
for two nights	*per due notti*
We are leaving tomorrow morning	*Partiamo domani mattina*
Is there a room with a balcony?	*C'è una camera con balcone?*
There isn't (aren't) any hot water, soap, light, toilet paper, towels	*Manca/Mancano acqua calda, sapone, luce, carta igienica, asciugamani*
May I pay by credit card?	*Posso pagare con carta di credito?*
May I see another room please?	*Per favore potrei vedere un' altra camera?*
Is breakfast included?	*E compresa la prima colazione?*
How do I get to the town centre?	*Come posso raggiungere il centro città?*

Driving

near/far	*vicino/lontano*	garage	*garage*
left/right	*sinistra/destra*	This doesn't work	*Questo non funziona*
straight ahead	*sempre diritto*	mechanic	*meccanico*
forward/backwards	*avanti/indietro*	map/town plan	*carta/ pianta*
north/south	*nord/sud*	Where is the road to...?	*Dov'è la strada per...?*
east	*est/ oriente*	breakdown	*guasto/panne*
west	*ovest/ occidente*	driving licence	*patente di guida*
round the corner	*dietro l'angolo*	driver	*guidatore*
crossroads	*bivio*	speed	*velocità*
street/road	*strada/via*	danger	*pericolo*
square	*piazza*	parking	*parcheggio*
car hire	*noleggio macchina*	no parking	*sosta vietata*
motorbike	*motocicletta*	narrow	*stretto*
scooter	*Vespa*	bridge	*ponte*
bicycle	*bicicletta*	toll	*pedaggio*
petrol/diesel	*benzina/ gasolio*	slow down	*rallentare*

Travel Directions

I want to go to...	*Desidero andare a...*
How can I get to...?	*Come posso andare a...?*
Do you stop at...?	*Ferma a...?*
Where is...?	*Dov'è...?*
How far is it to...?	*Quanto siamo lontani da...?*
What is the name of this station?	*Come si chiama questa stazione?*
When does the next ... leave?	*Quando parte il prossimo...?*
From where does it leave?	*Da dove parte?*
How long does the trip take...?	*Quanto tempo dura il viaggio?*
How much is the fare?	*Quant'è il biglietto?*
Have a good trip	*Buon viaggio!*

Italian Menu Vocabulary

Antipasti (Hors d'œuvres)

These before-meal treats can include almost anything; among the most common are:

antipasto misto	mixed antipasto
bruschetta	garlic toast (sometimes with tomatoes)
carciofi (sott'olio)	artichokes (in oil)
frutti di mare	seafood
funghi (trifolati)	mushrooms (with anchovies, garlic, and lemon)
gamberi ai fagioli	prawns (shrimps) with white beans
mozzarella (in carrozza)	cow or buffalo cheese (fried with bread in batter)
prosciutto (con melone)	raw ham (with melon)
salsicce	sausages

Minestre (Soups) and Pasta

These dishes are the principal typical first courses (*primi*) served throughout Italy.

agnolotti	ravioli with meat
cacciucco	spiced fish soup
cappelletti	small ravioli, often in broth
crespelle	crêpes
frittata	omelette
gnocchi	potato dumplings
orecchiette	ear-shaped pasta, often served with turnip greens
panzerotti	ravioli filled with mozzarella, anchovies, and egg
pappardelle alla lepre	pasta with hare sauce
pasta e fagioli	soup with beans, bacon, and tomatoes
pastina in brodo	tiny pasta in broth
risotto (alla milanese)	Italian rice (with stock, saffron and wine)
spaghetti all'amatriciana	with spicy pork and chilli sauce
spaghetti alla carbonara	with bacon, eggs, and black pepper
spaghetti al sugo/ragù	with meat sauce
spaghetti alle vongole	with clam sauce
stracciatella	broth with eggs and cheese

Formaggio (Cheese)

Bel Paese	a soft white cow's cheese
cacio/ caciocavallo	pale yellow, often sharp cheese
fontina	rich cow's milk cheese
groviera	mild cheese (gruyère)
gorgonzola	soft blue cheese
Parmigiano	Parmesan cheese
pecorino	sharp sheep's cheese
provolone	sharp, tangy cheese; *dolce* is less strong
stracchino	soft white cheese

Carne (Meat)

abbacchio	milk-fed lamb
agnello	lamb
animelle	sweetbreads
anatra	duck
arista	pork loin
arrosto misto	mixed roast meats
bocconcini	veal mixed with ham and cheese and fried
bollito misto	stew of boiled meats
braciola	chop
brasato di manzo	braised beef with vegetables
bresaola	dried raw meat (similar to ham)
carne di castrato/ suino	mutton/pork
carpaccio	thin slices of raw beef served with piquant sauce
cassoeula	winter stew with pork and cabbage
cervello	brains
...al burro nero	...in black butter sauce
cervo	venison
cinghiale	boar
coniglio	rabbit
cotoletta	veal cutlet
...alla milanese	...fried in breadcrumbs
...alla bolognese	...with ham and cheese
fagiano	pheasant
faraona	guinea fowl
...alla creta	...in earthenware pot
fegato	liver (usually of veal)
...alla veneziana	...with filling
lombo di maiale	pork loin
lumache	snails

maiale (al latte)	pork (cooked in milk)
manzo	beef
osso buco	braised veal knuckle with herbs
pancetta	rolled pork
pernice	partridge
petto di pollo	boned chicken breast
...sorpresa	...stuffed and deep fried
piccione	pigeon
pizzaiola	beef steak with tomato and oregano sauce
pollo	chicken
...alla cacciatora	...with tomatoes and mushrooms
...alla diavola	...grilled
...alla marengo)	...fried with tomatoes, garlic and wine
polpette	meatballs
quaglie	quails
rane	frogs
rognoni	kidneys
saltimbocca	veal scallop with *prosciutto*, sage, wine and butter
scaloppine	thin slices of veal sautéed in butter
spezzatino	pieces of beef or veal, usually stewed
spiedino	meat on a skewer or stick
stufato	beef braised in white wine with vegetables
tacchino	turkey
vitello	veal

Pesce (Fish)

aciughe or Alici	anchovies	nasello	hake
anguilla	eel	orata	bream
aragosta	lobster	ostriche	oysters
aringa	herring	pesce spada	swordfish
baccalà	dried salt cod	polipi/ polpi	octopus
bonito	small tuna	pesce azzurro	various types of small fish
branzino	sea bass	pesce di San Pietro	John Dory
calamari	squid	rombo	turbot
cappe sante	scallops	sarde	sardines
cefalo	grey mullet	sgombro	mackerel
cozze	mussels	sogliola	sole
dorato	gilt head	squadro	monkfish
fritto misto	mixed fried delicacies	stoccafisso	wind-dried cod
gamberetto	shrimp	tonno	tuna
gamberi (di fiume)	prawns (crayfish)	triglia	red mullet (rouget)
granchio	crab	trota	trout
insalata di mare	seafood salad	trota salmonata	salmon trout
lampreda	lamprey	vongole	small clams
merluzzo	cod	zuppa di pesce	mixed fish in sauce/stew

Contorni (Side Dishes, Vegetables)

asparagi	asparagus	melanzane	aubergine/eggplant
carciofi (alla giudia)	artichokes (deep fried)	patate (fritte)	potatoes (fried)
cavolfiore	cauliflower	peperoni	sweet peppers
cavolo	cabbage	peperonata	stewed peppers, onions, etc.
ceci	chickpeas	piselli (al prosciutto)	peas (with ham)
cetriolo	cucumber	pomodoro (i)	tomato(es)
cipolla	onion	porri	leeks
fagioli	white beans	radice	radish
fagiolini	French (green) beans	rapa	turnip
fave	broad beans	sedano	celery
finocchio	fennel	spinaci	spinach
funghi (porcini)	mushrooms (boletus)	verdure	greens
insalata (mista, verde)	salad (mixed, green)	zucca	pumpkin
lattuga	lettuce	zucchini	courgettes
lenticchie	lentils		

Bevande (Beverages)

acqua minerale	mineral water	latte	milk
con/ senza gas	with/without fizz	limonata	lemon soda
aranciata	orange soda	succo di frutta	fruit juice
birra (alla spina)	beer (draught)	tè	tea
caffè (freddo)	coffee (iced)	vino	wine
cioccolata	chocolate	rosso, bianco, rosato	red, white, rosé
(con panna)	(with cream)		

Dolci (Desserts)

amaretti	macaroons	semifreddo	refrigerated cake
coppa gelato	assorted ice-cream	sorbetto	sorbet/sherbet
crema caramella	caramel-topped custard	spumone	a soft ice-cream
crostata	fruit flan	tiramisù	sponge fingers, coffee,
gelato	icecream		Mascarpone, chocolate
(produzione propria)	(home-made)	torrone	nougat
granita	flavoured water ice,	torta	cake, tart
	(usually lemon or coffee)	zabaglione	whipped eggs and
panettone	sponge cake with		Marsala wine, served hot
	candied fruit and raisins	zuppa inglese	trifle

Frutta (Fruit, Nuts)

albicocche	apricots	melagrana	pomegranate
ananas	pineapple	mele	apples
arance	oranges	melone	melon
banane	bananas	more	blackberries
ciliege	cherries	nocciole	hazelnuts
cocomero	watermelon	noci	walnuts
datteri	dates	pera	pear
fichi	figs	pesca	peach
fragole (con panna)	strawberries (with cream)	pesca noce	nectarine
frutta di stagione	fruit in season	pinoli	pine nuts
lamponi	raspberries	pompelmo	grapefruit
macedonia di frutta	fruit salad	prugna/ susina	prune/plum
mandarino	tangerine	uva	grapes
mandorle	almonds		

Cooking Terms, Miscellaneous

aceto (balsamico)	vinegar (balsamic)	miele	honey
affumicato	smoked	olio	oil
aglio	garlic	pane (tostato)	bread (toasted)
bicchiere	glass	panini	sandwiches
burro	butter	panna	cream
conto	bill	pepe	pepper
costoletta/ cotoletta	chop	peperoncini	hot chilli peppers
coltello	knife	ripieno	stuffed
cucchiaio	spoon	rosmarino	rosemary
forchetta	fork	sale	salt
forno	oven	salsa	sauce
fritto	fried	salvia	sage
ghiaccio	ice	tazza	cup
griglia	grill	tavola	table
in bianco	without tomato	tovagliolo	napkin
limone	lemon	tramezzini	finger sandwiches
marmellata	jam	uovo	egg
menta	mint	zucchero	sugar

CADOGAN

'Humorous, informed...
irresistible'

Tuscany
Umbria & the Marches

Italian Riviera

Lombardy, Milan &
the **Italian Lakes**

the Italy series

Italy

Florence, Siena, Pisa, Lucca

Rome

Rome, Padua & Assisi *NEW*

Rome, Venice & Florence

Venice

**Bay of Naples &
Southern Italy**

The Italian Riviera *NEW*

**Lombardy, Milan &
the Italian Lakes**

Rome & the Heart of Italy *NEW*

Sicily

**Tuscany, Umbria &
the Marches**

Venetia & the Dolomites

covering more than you can possibly imagine

Note: Page numbers in *italics* indicate maps

Index

caves *see under* Grotta
Cavour (town) 96
Cavour, Count Camillo 56–7, 96, 121
Cecilia, St 755
Cecina 640
Cedegolo 261
Céglie Messápico 901, 903
Celano 539, 540
Celesti, Andrea 271
Celestine V, Pope (Pietro Morrone) 536–7, 541
Celle Ligure 142
Cellini, Benvenuto 65, 75, 569, 571
Cencenighe 391
Cèneda *see* Vittorio Veneto
Cento 479
Ceppo Morelli 224
Ceres 98
Ceresole Reale 99
Ceriale 140, 143
Cernobbio 241, 244
Cerreto d'Esi 509
Cerro al Volturno 546
Certosa di Galluzzo 596
Certosa di Pavia 64, 204–5, 206
Certosa di Pisa 624
Certosa di San Lorenzo 853–4
Ceruti, Giacomo Antonio 264, 267
Cerveno 261
Cerveteri 62, 704, 713, 714, 746
Cervia-Milano Marittima 492
Cervino *see* Matterhorn
Cervo 131, 138–9
Cesana 96
Cesari, Pompeo 538
Cesena 473–4, 493
Cesenatico 492
Cetara 834
Cevedale 249
Challant family 101, 102
Challant-St-Victor 101
Chambave 102
Chamois 102
Champoluc 101, 103
Chardin, Jean Baptiste 573
Charlemagne, Emperor 50, 120, 263, 720
Charles V, Emperor 54, 69, 177, 393, 458–9, 463, 722, 909
Charles VIII, King of France 53, 177
Charles of Anjou 52, 802
Château-Cambrésis, Treaty of 605
Châtillon 102
Chavez, Georges 225
Chécrouit-Val Veny 109–10
Cherasco 121
Chiaia di Luna 780
Chiaioella 843
Chianciano Terme 646, 648, 649
Chianti (region) 597
Chiara, Santa *see* Clare, St
Chiaravalle della Colomba (abbey) 443
Chiávari 157, 160–1, 164
Chiavenna 247
Chienti valley 516–17
Chieri 120
Chiesa in Valmalenco 248, 250
Chieti 61, 526, 528, 530

Chioggia 53, 146, 293, 337–8
Chiomonte 95
Chiusa/Klausen 411
Chiusi 62, 646, 648, 649, 660, 661
Chiusi della Verna 653–4
Christians (early) 49, 62–3, 751–2, 804, 823
Christmas *see* presepi
Cicero, Marcus Tullius 46, 779
Cilea, Francesco 77
Cilento (town) 784
Cilento Coast 6, 784, 785, 851, 852–4
Cimabue 464, 558, 565, 573, 584, 587, 620, 674–5, 677
Cima da Conegliano 187, 298, 317, 320, 322, 323, 378
Cima Grappa 356
Cimarosa, Domenico 77
Cimbergo 261
Cime Bianche 102
cinema 59, 68, 74, 492, 496, 692
  see also film festivals
Cino, Giuseppe 908
Cinque Terre 131, 157, 165–6, 168–9
Cinque Torri 410
Ciociaria 780–81
Ciompi revolt 556
Circeo National Park 704, 778
Circumvesuviana 812
Cisano 282
Cispadane Republic 452
Città di Castello 660, 679–80, 682, 683
Città della Pieve 660, 661–2
Civate 243
Cividale del Friuli 63, 288, 415, 420, 432, 433–5
Cividate Camuno 260
Civitanova Marche 513, 516
Civitavecchia 706, 714
Civitella del Tronto 532
Civitoli, Matteo 609
Clare, St 658, 674, 675, 676–7
Classe *see* Ravenna
Claviere 94, 96
Clement VII, Pope (Giulio de' Medici) 393, 557–8, 570, 701, 722, 743, 757
Clemer, Hans 124
Cles (town) 383, 394, 402
Cles, Bernardo 394, 395, 398, 402
Clitunno 660, 683, 685, 688
Clusane 258–60, 262
Clusone 256, 257
Cocullo 24, 543
Codroipo 416, 419
Codussi (Coducci), Mauro 65, 297, 312, 319, 320, 322
Cogne (town) 99, 107–11
  see also Val di Cogne
Cogoleto 142
Cogorno 161
Cola dell'Amatrice 519, 520, 537
Cola di Rienzo *see* Rienzo
Coldirodi 135
Cólico 238, 247
Collabo/Klobenstein 406
Collazzone 696
Colle del Gran Bernardo 107
Colle Isarco/Gossensass 412

Colle di Joux 101
Colle della Maddalena 126
Colleoni, Bartolomeo 251, 254, 256, 322
Colle Santa Lucia 383, 386, 391
Colle di Val d'Elsa 640
Colline Metallifere 643–4
Collio (Brescia) 268
Collio (Gorizia) 416, 431
Collodi 20, 603
Colombaro 258
Colombetti 224
Colonna family 720, 744, 780
Colonna, Vittoria 841
Colorno 440, 444
Col Visentin 380
Comacchio 475, 481
Comacina 241, 244
Comeglians 436
Comelico 387, 390
commedia dell'arte 23, 69–70, 257, 844
Commodus, Emperor 48, 731
Como (town) 63, 174, 237–41, 243
  see also Lake Como
Compiano 450
comuni 50–52, 176–7, 721
Conca dei Marini 829
Concordat 58, 722
Conegliano 288, 375, 377, 378, 379
Cónero Riviera 500, 509, 512
confetti 541
Constance, Treaty of 176
Constantine, Emperor 49, 175, 738, 749–50, 754
Constantinople *see* Byzantium
Controne 853
Copertino 911
Corelli, Arcangelo 77
Corfinio 540, 545
Cori 62, 704, 776
Cormòns 431–2
Cornaro, Caterina 294, 353–4
Cornello dei Tasso 257
Corniglia 166
Corno Grande 526, 533, 534
Corradini, Antonio 799
Correggio (town) 452
Correggio, Antonio Allegri 65, 445, 447, 449, 452, 746
Corricella 843
Corridonia 516
Cortina d'Ampezzo 288, 386, 388–90, 410, 424
Cortona 5, 650–51, 653, 655, 656
Corvara in Badia 408, 409
Cosenza 858, 859, 860–61, 865
Cosmati work 64
  Amalfi Coast 64, 832, 837
  Pisa 620
  Rome 64, 750, 753, 754
  Subiaco 775
  Tuscània 708
Cossa, Francesco del 187, 475, 477
Costa, Lorenzo 475
Costiera dei Cèch 248
Costigliole d'Asti 120, 122
Cottius 95
Courmayeur 82, 100, 107, 109–11

Norchia 711
Norcia 663, 690–91, 693–4
Norma 776
Normans 51, 53, 63, 524, 847, 864, 871, 880, 912
Notaresco 526
Novacella 383, 411
Novalesa 95
Nova Levante/Welschnofen 408, 409, 411
Novara 63, 66, 112, 113–14, 116
Novate Mezzola 247
Nove 356, 357
Novellara 452
Numana 510, 512, 513
Nus 102
Octavian see Augustus
Oderzo 377–8, 379
Odoacer 49, 202, 720
Olmi, Ermanno 74
Omegna 222–4
Oneglia see Imperia
Oneta 69, 257
opera 13, 14, 20, 25, 66, 77–8
    Bologna 469
    Florence 78, 560, 594
    Fóggia 77, 877
    Genoa 157
    Macerata 516
    Martina Franca 896
    Milan 184, 199
    Modena 457
    Naples 78, 788, 796, 811
    Parma 444–5, 448, 451
    Pésaro 502
    Reggio Emilia 452
    Rome 78, 751, 771–2
    Spoleto 24, 683, 685, 688–90
    Torre del Lago Puccini 614
    Trieste 429
    Turin 93
    Venice 77, 78, 316, 332
    Verona 13, 368, 372, 374
    see also composers' names
Opi 543
Oplontis see Torre Annunziata
Orbetello 628–9
Orcagna, Andrea 64, 559, 569, 584, 587, 622, 698–9
Ordona 878
Oria 901
Ormea 127
Orobie Alps 256–7
Oropa 115, 116
Orrido di Sant'Anna 231
Orsini family 693, 709, 711, 712, 720, 732
Orta San Giulio 24, 222–6
Orte 660
Ortisei/Sankt Ulrich in Gröden 408–9, 410
Ortles 249
Ortona 526, 528
Ortonovo 168
Orvieto 64, 65, 660, 690, 695, 697–702
Oscans 784, 844, 850, 874
Ósimo 514
Ospedaletti 135
Ossaia 661
Osteno 236

Ostia 62, 718, 726, 773–4, 777
Ostrogoths 49, 482, 488
Ostuni 874, 895–6, 897, 899
Otranto 63, 903, 904, 911–12
Otto I (the Great), Emperor 50, 282
Ötzi 405
Oulx 95
Ovid 541, 542
Ovindoli 540
Pacentro 542
Pacher, Michael 406, 412
Paderno Ponchielli 211
Padova see Padua
Padua 24, 48, 66, 288, 297, 342–8, 343, 424
    Basilica di Sant'Antonio 63, 342, 345–6
Padula 853
Paeligni 524
Paestum 6, 45, 62, 837, 850–52, 854
Paganini 449
Pagani, Vincenzo 504
Palagianello 902
Palanfre 126
Palazzolo sul Oglio 258
Paleoveneti 348
Pale di San Martino 382, 398–9
Palestrina (town) 775
Palestrina, Giovanni Pierluigi da 77, 228, 775
Palinuro 851, 853, 854
palios 23, 35
    Alba (donkeys) 121
    Asti 119, 122
    Emilia-Romagna 472–3, 479
    Gubbio 680
    Legnano 24
    Siena 24, 472–3, 632
Palizzi, Filippo 529
Palladio, Andrea 54, 65, 288, 297, 324–5, 355, 359–61, 432, 433, 800
    villas 341, 350, 352, 353, 355, 357, 362–3
Pallanza 227, 230–31, 232
Pallavicini family 443, 444
Pallavicino, Oberto 443
Palmanova 420
Palmaria see Isola Palmaria
Palma Vecchio 298, 321, 361
Palmi 862, 863
Pamphili family 741, 743
Páola 858, 859
Paolo Veneziano 273, 297, 316, 338, 426
papacy 50–58, 72, 719–23
    Anagni 780
    Avignon 52, 706, 720, 721
    Viterbo 706–8, 721
    see also Papal States; Vatican City
Papal States 52, 53, 445, 458, 503, 685, 721
Parco del Delta del Po 481
Parco Minitalia 20, 256
Parco dei Mostri (Monster Park) see Bomarzo
Parco Naturale Adamello-Brenta 400, 401
Parco Naturale di Campo dei Fiori 234
Parco Naturale dell'Circeo see Circeo National Park
Parco Naturale Paneveggio-Pale di San Martino 382, 397, 399

Parco Naturale di Sassi 456
Parco Natura Viva 282
Parco Nazionale dell'Abruzzo see Abruzzo National Park
Parco Nazionale del Cilento see National Park of Cilento
Parco Nazionale del Gran Paradiso see Gran Paradiso National Park
Parco Nazionale delle Incisioni Rupestri Preistoriche see National Park of Prehistoric Engravings
Parco Nazionale dello Stelvio see Stelvio National Park
Parco del Po 351
Parma 63, 64, 440, 441, 444–51, 446–47
Parmigianino (Francesco Mazzola) 65, 443, 445, 447, 449
Parthenope 805–6
Paschal I, Pope 749, 750
Pasolini, Pier Paolo 74
Passignano sul Trasimeno 660–61
Passo Campo Carlo Magno 402
Passo di Cereda 399
Passo del Diavolo 543
Passo di Falzarego 410
Passo di Gardena 409
Passo di Giau 391
Passo del Grostè 401
Passo del Lupo 456
Passo del Maniva 268
Passo Mendola 402
Passo Monte Moro 225
Passo Pordoi 410
Passo della Presolana 257
Passo del Prete Morto 548
Passo di Sella 409
Passo del Sempione see Simplon Pass
Passo di Stelvio 250
Passo di Tonale 261
Patù 911
Paul, St 754
Paul III, Pope (Alessandro Farnese) 663, 664, 711, 722, 740
Paul IV, Pope 528, 732, 743
Paulus Diaconus 433
Pavarotti, Luciano 454, 457
Pavese, Cesare 76
Pavia 49, 50, 54, 174, 177, 202–6
    San Michele 63, 203–4
    see also Certosa di Pavia
Pavullo 455
Pazzi conspiracy 566
Pedaso 513
Pedemonte 116
Pegli 61, 142
Peio 402
Pella 222
Pellegrino di San Daniele 419
Pellico, Silvio 127
Pellizzano 402
Pelmo 387, 408
Penna in Teverina 693
Penna, Cesare 907, 908
Penne 525, 526, 527
Pentapolis 502
Pepin (the Short), King 292, 372
Pergolesi, Giovanni Battista 77